ScottForesman
LITERATURE
AND INTEGRATED STUDIES

Middle School: Grade Six

Middle School: Grade Seven

Middle School: Grade Eight

Forms in Literature

World Literature

American Literature

English Literature

The cover features a detail of Dante Gabriel Rossetti's *The Beloved,* which also appears on this page. Rossetti (1828–1882), who achieved equal fame as a painter and a poet, is known for the sensuousness and exoticism of his works in both areas. *Tate Gallery, London*

ScottForesman
LITERATURE
AND INTEGRATED STUDIES

English Literature

Senior Consultants

Alan C. Purves
State University of New York at Albany

Carol Booth Olson
University of California, Irvine

Carlos E. Cortés
University of California, Riverside (Emeritus)

ScottForesman
A Division of HarperCollins*Publishers*

Editorial Offices: Glenview, Illinois
Regional Offices: San Jose, California • Tucker, Georgia
Glenview, Illinois • Oakland, New Jersey • Dallas, Texas

Visit ScottForesman's Home Page at http://www.scottforesman.com

Acknowledgments

Texts

8 Reuse of abridgment of *Beowulf: The Oldest English Epic,* translated by Charles W. Kennedy from pages 3-101. Reprinted by permission. **35** From *Grendel,* by John Gardner. Copyright © 1971 by John Gardner. Reprinted by permission of Alfred A. Knopf Inc. **47–48** "The Prologue" and "The Pardoner's Prologue and Tale" from *The Canterbury Tales* by Geoffrey Chaucer, translated by Nevill Coghill (Penguin Classics 1951, Fourth revised edition, 1977). Copyright © 1951, 1958, 1960, 1975, 1977 by Nevill Coghill. Reproduced by permission of Penguin Books Ltd. **61** From *Sir Gawain And The Green Knight,* translated by M. R. Ridley. Reprinted by permission of Reed Consumer Books. **88** From *A Distant Mirror* by Barbara W. Tuchman. Copyright © 1978 by Barbara W. Tuchman. Reprinted by permission of Random House, Inc. **92** From *The Once and Future King* by T.H. White. Reprinted by permission. **192** From *Ancient Egyptian Literature, Three Volumes,* by Miriam Lichtheim, pp. 125-126. Copyright © 1973-1980 by The Regents of the University of California. Reprinted by permission of The University of California Press. **193** "Aeschylus" from *The Eumenides,* translated by Richmond Lattimore. Copyright © 1953 by The University of Chicago. Reprinted by permission. **194** From *Crime And Punishment* by Feodor Dostoevski. Reprinted by permission. **211** "Summer is Gone" from *A Book Of Ireland,* edited by Frank O'Connor. Reprinted by permission. **212** "Fern Hill" by Dylan Thomas from *The Poems Of Dylan Thomas.* Copyright 1952 by The Trustees for the Copyrights of Dylan Thomas. Reprinted by permission of New Directions Publishing Corporation and David Higham Associates Limited. **219** "Lineage" from *Crow* by Ted Hughes. Reprinted by permission. **239** From "David's Story" and "The Bubble Boy" by Carol Ann with Kent Demaret in *People Weekly,* October 29, 1984 and November 5, 1984. Copyright © 1984 by Time, Inc. Reprinted by permission. **241** From *Six Degrees* Of Separation by John Guare. Copyright © 1990 by John Guare. Reprinted by permission of Vintage Books, a Division of Random House Inc. **244** Lyrics only of "We Are The World" by Michael Jackson and Lionel Richie. Reprinted by permission. **280** "Postcard from Paradise" by Chris Williamson. Copyright ©1993 by Bird Ankles Music (BMI). Reprinted by permission of Chris Williamson. **369** Excerpts from *Fame In The 20th Century* by Clive James. Reprinted by permission. **389** Excerpt from A Room of One's Own by Virginia Woolf. Reprinted by permission. **394** Lyrics only of "London Pride" by Noel Coward. Reprinted by permission. **394** "October 10, 1940" from *This Is London* by Edward R. Murrow. Reprinted by permission. **434** Abridgment of "The Power Of Dreams" by George Howe Colt in *Life,* September 1995. Reprinted by permission. **507** From "The Monster's Human Nature" by Stephen Jay Gould in *Natural History,* July 1994. Copyright © 1994 by the American Museum of Natural History. Reprinted by permission.

continued on page 1017

ISBN: 0-673-29450-1

Copyright © 1997
Scott, Foresman and Company, Glenview, Illinois
All Rights Reserved. Printed in the United States of America.

1.800.554.4411
http://www.scottforesman.com

1 2 3 4 5 6 7 8 9 10 DR 03 02 01 00 99 98 97 96

Senior Consultants

Alan C. Purves
Professor of Education and Humanities, State University of New York at Albany; Director of the Center for Writing and Literacy. Dr. Purves developed the concept and philosophy of the literature lessons for the series, consulted with editors, reviewed tables of contents and lesson manuscript, wrote the Assessment Handbooks, and oversaw the development and writing of the series testing strand.

Carol Booth Olson
Director, California Writing Project, Department of Education, University of California, Irvine. Dr. Olson conceptualized and developed the integrated writing strand of the program, consulted with editors, led a team of teachers in creating literature-based Writing Workshops, and reviewed final manuscript.

Carlos E. Cortés
Professor Emeritus, History, University of California, Riverside. Dr. Cortés designed and developed the multicultural strand embedded in each unit of the series and consulted with grade-level editors to implement the concepts.

Series Consultants

Visual and Media Literacy/Speaking and Listening/Critical Thinking
Harold M. Foster. Professor of English Education and Secondary Education, The University of Akron, Akron. Dr. Foster developed and wrote the Beyond Print features for all levels of the series.

ESL and LEP Strategies
James Cummins. Professor, Modern Language Centre and Curriculum Department, Ontario Institute for Studies in Education, Toronto.

Lily Wong Fillmore. Professor, Graduate School of Education, University of California at Berkeley.

Drs. Cummins and Fillmore advised on the needs of ESL and LEP students, helped develop the Building English Proficiency model for the program, and reviewed strategies and manuscript for this strand of the program.

Fine Arts/Humanities
Neil Anstead. Coordinator of the Humanitas Program, Cleveland Humanities Magnet School, Reseda, California. Mr. Anstead consulted on the fine art used in the program.

Reviewers and Contributors

Pupil and Teacher Edition
Jay Amberg, Glenbrook South High School, Glenview, Illinois **Edison Barber,** St. Anne Community High School, St. Anne, Illinois **Lois Barliant,** Albert G. Lane Technical High School, Chicago, Illinois **James Beasley,** Plant City Senior High School, Plant City, Florida **Linda Belpedio,** Oak Park/River Forest High School, Oak Park, Illinois **Richard Bruns,** Burges High School, El Paso, Texas **Kay Parks Bushman,** Ottawa High School, Ottawa, Kansas **Jesús Cardona,** John F. Kennedy High School, San Antonio, Texas **Marlene Carter,** Dorsey High School, Los Angeles, California **Patrick Cates,** Lubbock High School, Lubbock, Texas **Timothy Dohrer,** New Trier Township High School, Winnetka, Illinois **Margaret Doria,** Our Lady of Perpetual Help High School, Brooklyn, New York **Lucila Dypiangco,** Bell Senior High School, Bell, California **Judith Edminster,** Plant City High School, Plant City, Florida **Mary Alice Fite,** Columbus School for Girls, Columbus, Ohio **Montserrat Fontes,** Marshall High School, Los Angeles, California **Diane Fragos,** Turkey Creek Middle School, Plant City, Florida **Joan Greenwood,** Thornton Township High School, Harvey, Illinois **William Irvin,** Pittsfield Public Schools, Pittsfield, Massachusetts **Carleton Jordan,** Montclair High School, Montclair, New Jersey **Mark Kautz,** Chapel Hill High School, Chapel Hill, North Carolina **Elaine Kay,** Bartow High School, Bartow, Florida **Roslyn Kettering,** West Lafayette Junior/Senior High School, West Lafayette, Indiana **Kristina Kostopoulos,** Lincoln Park High School, Chicago, Illinois **Julia Lloyd,** Harwood Junior High School, Bedford, Texas **John Lord,** Ocean Township High School, Oakhurst, New Jersey **Dolores Mathews,** Bloomingdale High School, Valrico, Florida **Jim McCallum,** Milford High School, Milford, Massachusetts **Monette Mehalko,** Plant City Senior High School, Plant City, Florida **Lucia Podraza,** DuSable High School, Chicago, Illinois **Frank Pool,** Anderson High School, Austin, Texas **Alice Price,** Latin School, Chicago, Illinois **Anna J. Roseboro,** The Bishop's School, La Jolla, California **Peter Sebastian,** Granite Hills High School, El Cajon, California **Rob Slater,** East Forsyth High School, Winston Salem, North Carolina **Catherine Small,** Nicolet High School, Glendale, Wisconsin **Dennis Symkowiak,** Mundelein High School, Mundelein, Illinois **Rosetta Tetteh,** Senn High School, Chicago, Illinois **Pamela Vetters,** Harlandale High School, San Antonio, Texas **Polly Walwark,** Oak Park High School, Oak Park, Illinois **Karen Wrobleski,** San Diego High School, San Diego, California **Dru Zimmerman,** Chapel Hill High School, Chapel Hill, North Carolina

Contents

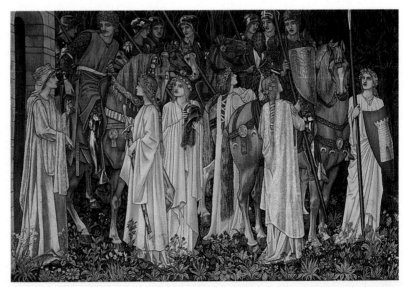

Part 2: Codes of Honor

Unit 2 The Elizabethan Era
The Lure of Ambition

Unit 3 The Seventeenth Century

Part 1: The Meaning of Life

Part 2: The Fall from Grace

Unit 4 The Age of Reason

Part 1: A Focus on Society

Part 2: Other People's Lives

Unit 5 The Romantic Era

Part 1: Visions and Dreams

Part 2: The Outsider

Part 3: Exceeding Human Limits

Unit 6 The Victorians

Part 1: The Struggle to Understand

Part 2: Hope and Despair

Unit 7 The Early Twentieth Century

Part 1: Upward Mobility

Part 2: War and Aftermath

Part 3: The Search for Identity

Unit 8 The Later Twentieth Century
Part 1: The Passing of Empire

Part 2: The Slant View

Glossaries, Handbooks, and Indexes

Genre Overview

Short Stories

Novel Excerpts

Tales, Romances, and Narratives

Poetry

Feature Overview

Visual Overviews

Interdisciplinary Studies

Language Histories

Writing Workshops

Beyond Print

Themes in English Literature

Model for Active Reading

Good readers read actively. They become involved in what they read, relating the characters and situations to people and events in their own lives. They question, clarify, predict, and in other ways think about the story or article they are reading. These three students agreed to let us in on their thoughts as they read "The Lumber-Room." You might have different ideas and questions than they did about this story. However, their ways of responding will give you ideas for how you can get actively engaged as you read literature.

DEAN TSILIKAS I'm seventeen years old, and basically I'm interested in politics. Maybe I'll start out in law and then go into politics. What kinds of books are part of my library? I like mysteries a lot. And I also like to read magazines.

ANDRIA LOPEZ When I grow up, I'm looking to a career in international business and foreign languages. I'm really into foreign languages. I'm seventeen years old. I do a lot of reading. I'll read anything that anyone recommends to me. I love all kinds of poetry.

LEAH VAUGHN I'm seventeen. I want to be a criminal psychologist when I grow up. I like to read mysteries—that's all I've ever liked to read, ever since I was a little girl. Now that I'm in high school, I have a lot of schoolwork to do, and I don't read as much as I'd like to.

Six Reading Strategies

Following are some of the techniques that good readers use often without being aware of them.

Question Ask questions that arise as you read.

Example: Why doesn't the author ever tell us the aunt's name?

Predict Make reasoned guesses, based on what's happened so far, about what might happen next.

Example: I think Nicholas is going to be in real trouble once the aunt gets out of the rain-water tank.

Clarify Clear up confusion and answer questions.

Example: This woman is not really Nicholas's aunt—she only pretends to be.

Summarize Review some of the main ideas or events.

Example: Nicholas is delighted with the things he finds in the lumber-room. They fill him with a sense of awe and wonder.

Evaluate Reason from common sense, established guidelines, and evidence to arrive at sound opinions and valid conclusions.

Example: The aunt doesn't seem to like children very much. She even seems to take pleasure in punishing them.

Connect Compare the text with something in your own experience, with another text, or with ideas within the text.

Example: I've known some people who are like the aunt in this story—people who seem to find no joy in living and who don't want others to be happy, either.

One of the elements that add to the eeriness and surrealism of P. J. Crook's paintings is her habit of extending the painting onto the frame, as in *Terrible Twins* (1989). Do you agree, as some people claim, that it is the duty of adults to provide limits for children? Might it then be the duty of children to test those limits?

The LUMBER-ROOM

SAKI (H. H. MUNRO)

The children were to be driven, as a special treat, to the sands at Jagborough. Nicholas was not to be of the party; he was in disgrace. Only that morning, he had refused to eat his wholesome bread-and-milk on the seemingly frivolous ground that there was a frog in it. Older and wiser and better people had told him that there could not possibly be a frog in his bread-and-milk and that he was not to talk nonsense; he continued, nevertheless, to talk what seemed the veriest nonsense, and described with much detail the coloration and markings of the alleged frog. The dramatic part of the incident was that there really was a frog in Nicholas's basin of bread-and-milk; he had put it there himself, so he felt entitled to know something about it. The sin of taking a frog from the garden and putting it into a bowl of wholesome bread-and-milk was enlarged on at great length, but the fact that stood out clearest in the whole affair, as it presented itself to the mind of Nicholas, was that the older, wiser, and better people had been proved to be profoundly in error in matters about which they had expressed the utmost assurance.

"You said there couldn't possibly be a frog in my bread-and-milk; there *was* a frog in my bread-and-milk," he repeated, with the insistence of a skilled tactician who does not intend to shift from favorable ground.

So his boy-cousin and girl-cousin and his quite uninteresting younger brother were to be taken to Jagborough sands that afternoon and he was to stay at home. His cousins' aunt, who insisted,

---

DEAN It says that Nicholas is "in disgrace." That seems pretty harsh, if all he did was put a frog in his bowl. (evaluate)

LEAH I think that Nicholas is trying to prove that the adults are wrong—that's why he put the frog in his bowl. (clarify)

ANDRIA So far, the attitude of the story seems to be very anti-adult. Maybe the adults won't turn out to be as smart as they think they are. (predict)

DEAN Nicholas's age isn't given, but I think he must be about seven or eight, maybe nine years old. Do you agree? (question)

ANDRIA I agree that he's young—and he also seems very intelligent. (evaluate)

by an unwarranted stretch of imagination, in styling herself his aunt also, had hastily invented the Jagborough expedition in order to impress on Nicholas the delights that he had justly forfeited by his disgraceful conduct at the breakfast-table. It was her habit, whenever one of the children fell from grace, to improvise something of a festival nature from which the offender would be rigorously debarred; if all the children sinned collectively they were suddenly informed of a circus in a neighboring town, a circus of unrivalled merit and uncounted elephants, to which, but for their depravity, they would have been taken that very day.

A few decent tears were looked for on the part of Nicholas when the moment for the departure of the expedition arrived. As a matter of fact, however, all the crying was done by his girl-cousin, who scraped her knee rather painfully against the step of the carriage as she was scrambling in.

"How she did howl," said Nicholas cheerfully, as the party drove off without any of the elation of high spirits that should have characterized it.

"She'll soon get over that," said the *soi-disant*[1] aunt; "it will be a glorious afternoon for racing about over those beautiful sands. How they will enjoy themselves!"

"Bobby won't enjoy himself much, and he won't race much either," said Nicholas with a grim chuckle; "his boots are hurting him. They're too tight."

"Why didn't he tell me they were hurting?" asked the aunt with some asperity.

"He told you twice, but you weren't listening. You often don't listen when we tell you important things."

"You are not to go into the gooseberry garden," said the aunt, changing the subject.

"Why not?" demanded Nicholas.

"Because you are in disgrace," said the aunt loftily.

Nicholas did not admit the flawlessness of the reasoning; he felt perfectly capable of being in disgrace and in a gooseberry garden at the same moment. His face took on an expression of considerable obstinacy. It was clear to his aunt that he was determined to get into the gooseberry garden, "only," as she remarked to herself, "because I have told him he is not to."

Now the gooseberry garden had two doors by which it might be entered, and once a small person like Nicholas could slip in there he could effectually disappear from view amid the masking growth of artichokes, raspberry canes, and fruit bushes. The aunt had many other things to do that afternoon, but she spent an hour or

---

1. **soi-disant** (swa dē zän), *adj.* calling oneself thus; self-styled; so-called.

DEAN Who exactly is this woman? In the story, she's referred to as "his cousins' aunt." Does that imply that she's not Nicholas's aunt also? (question)

ANDRIA It seems like the aunt does this often—she punishes the children by telling them where she would have taken them if they hadn't been so bad. (summarize)

DEAN The aunt is so mean—she reminds me of the wicked stepmother from Cinderella. (connect)

LEAH They're going to Jagborough in a carriage. This story must take place a long time ago. (evaluate)

LEAH The footnote says that *soi-disant* means "self-styled, so-called." So she's not his aunt after all—she just pretends that she is. (clarify)

DEAN Nicholas is expected to cry when the children leave for Jagborough. But he doesn't—instead, he seems to be in a good mood. That doesn't seem normal to me—most young children would cry, complain, throw a tantrum. (connect)

LEAH The aunt doesn't seem like a very caring person—she doesn't pay attention to the children's needs, like when Nicholas's cousin tells her that his boots are too tight. She seems small and petty—she's "a woman of few ideas." (evaluate)

two in trivial gardening operations among flower beds and shrubberies, whence she could keep a watchful eye on the two doors that led to the forbidden paradise. She was a woman of few ideas, with immense powers of concentration.

Nicholas made one or two sorties into the front garden, wriggling his way with obvious stealth of purpose towards one or other of the doors, but never able for a moment to evade the aunt's watchful eye. As a matter of fact, he had no intention of trying to get into the gooseberry garden, but it was extremely convenient for him that his aunt should believe that he had; it was a belief that would keep her on self-imposed sentry-duty for the greater part of the afternoon. Having thoroughly confirmed and fortified her suspicions, Nicholas slipped back into the house and rapidly put into execution a plan of action that had long germinated in his brain. By standing on a chair in the library one could reach a shelf on which reposed a fat, important-looking key. The key was as important as it looked; it was the instrument which kept the mysteries of the lumber[2]-room secure from unauthorized intrusion, which opened a way only for aunts and such-like privileged persons. Nicholas had not had much experience of the art of fitting keys into keyholes and turning locks, but for some days past he had practised with the key of the schoolroom door; he did not believe in trusting too much to luck and accident. The key turned stiffly in the lock, but it turned. The door opened, and Nicholas was in an unknown land, compared with which the gooseberry garden was a stale delight, a mere material pleasure.

Often and often Nicholas had pictured to himself what the lumber-room might be like, that region that was so carefully sealed from youthful eyes and concerning which no questions were ever answered. It came up to his expectations. In the first place it was large and dimly lit, one high window opening on to the forbidden garden being its only source of illumination. In the second place it was a storehouse of unimagined treasures. The aunt-by-assertion was one of those people who think that things spoil by use and consign them to dust and damp by way of preserving them. Such parts of the house as Nicholas knew best were rather bare and cheerless, but here there were wonderful things for the eye to feast on. First and foremost there was a piece of framed tapestry that was evidently meant to be a fire-screen. To Nicholas it was a living, breathing story; he sat down on a roll of Indian hangings, glowing in wonderful colors beneath a layer of dust, and took in all the details of the tapestry picture. A man, dressed in the hunting costume of

---
2. **lumber,** old furniture and other household items no longer being used; useless bric-a-brac.

DEAN   Even if she isn't really his aunt, I still think Nicholas's attitude toward her is not normal for a young child. He does seem twisted. He seems to like to toy with his aunt. (evaluate)

ANDRIA   I don't think he's twisted. He's a tough little kid. He's playing her game—it's like a war between them. (evaluate)

LEAH   It's almost like the aunt is a child too. She's toying with Nicholas also, but Nicholas is wise to his aunt's little tricks—she does things like this all the time. (evaluate)

ANDRIA   What Nicholas does here shows that he's more intelligent than most kids his age. Look at the way he manipulates his aunt and carries out his plan for getting into the lumber-room. (connect)

LEAH   Yes, Nicholas does seem really intelligent. He's already worked out a plan in his mind, practiced opening a lock with a key, etc. (evaluate)

DEAN   The lumber-room seems to be a symbol of the forbidden—at least what's forbidden to the young. (connect)

ANDRIA   Nicholas really appreciates the lumber-room, but his aunt doesn't. She has such a narrow-minded outlook—she thinks that things are spoiled by using them. (summarize)

some remote period, had just transfixed a stag with an arrow; it could not have been a difficult shot because the stag was only one or two paces away from him; in the thickly growing vegetation that the picture suggested it would not have been difficult to creep up to a feeding stag, and the two spotted dogs that were springing forward to join in the chase had evidently been trained to keep to heel till the arrow was discharged. That part of the picture was simple, if interesting, but did the huntsman see, what Nicholas saw, that four galloping wolves were coming in his direction through the wood? There might be more than four of them hidden behind the trees, and in any case would the man and his dogs be able to cope with the four wolves if they made an attack? The man had only two arrows left in his quiver, and he might miss with one or both of them; all one knew about his skill in shooting was that he could hit a large stag at a ridiculously short range. Nicholas sat for many golden minutes revolving the possibilities of the scene; he was inclined to think that there were more than four wolves and that the man and his dogs were in a tight corner.

But there were other objects of delight and interest claiming his instant attention: there were quaint twisted candlesticks in the shape of snakes, and a teapot fashioned like a china duck, out of whose open beak the tea was supposed to come. How dull and shapeless the nursery teapot seemed in comparison! And there was a carved sandal-wood box packed tight with aromatic cotton-wool, and between the layers of cotton-wool were little brass figures, hump-necked bulls, and peacocks and goblins, delightful to see and to handle. Less promising in appearance was a large square book with plain black covers; Nicholas peeped into it, and, behold, it was full of colored pictures of birds. And such birds! In the garden, and in the lanes when he went for a walk, Nicholas came across a few birds, of which the largest were an occasional magpie or wood-pigeon; here were herons and bustards, kites, toucans, tiger-bitterns, brush turkeys, ibises, golden pheasants, a whole portrait gallery of undreamed-of creatures. And as he was admiring the coloring of the mandarin duck and assigning a life-history to it, the voice of his aunt in shrill vociferation of his name came from the gooseberry garden without. She had grown suspicious at his long disappearance, and had leapt to the conclusion that he had climbed over the wall behind the sheltering screen of the lilac bushes; she was now engaged in energetic and rather hopeless search for him among the artichokes and raspberry canes.

"Nicholas, Nicholas!" she screamed, "you are to come out of this at once. It's no use trying to hide there; I can see you all the time."

It was probably the first time for twenty years that any one had smiled in that lumber-room.

DEAN This whole thing about the tapestry—is it a symbol of Nicholas's fight against the adults? (question)

ANDRIA I think so. Nicholas has the role of the huntsman, and the wolves are the adults. (clarify, connect)

DEAN So if Nicholas is the huntsman, he's just trying to do his own thing, but the wolves—his aunt and the other adults—are trying to stop him from doing what he wants to do. (connect)

LEAH What do you think might happen? (question)

DEAN The outcome could be that the huntsman could escape and the wolves could feed on the stag. And maybe Nicholas will outwit the adults. (predict)

DEAN This room helps me understand why Nicholas has so much anger toward his aunt. His aunt has kept him away from all these beautiful things. Why should she hide this room from him? It's like she doesn't want him to enjoy his life. (clarify, evaluate)

ANDRIA Going back to the tapestry—I think the stag stands for bad things Nicholas does. He does bad things to distract people. The wolves could feast on the stag, paying no attention to the huntsman. In the same way, Nicholas distracts his aunt by making her think he will try to get into the gooseberry garden. (evaluate)

LEAH It's like the aunt is playing games with Nicholas. (evaluate)

Presently the angry repetitions of Nicholas's name gave way to a shriek, and a cry for somebody to come quickly. Nicholas shut the book, restored it carefully to its place in a corner, and shook some dust from a neighboring pile of newspapers over it. Then he crept from the room, locked the door, and replaced the key exactly where he had found it. His aunt was still calling his name when he sauntered into the front garden.

"Who's calling?" he asked.

"Me," came the answer from the other side of the wall; "didn't you hear me? I've been looking for you in the gooseberry garden, and I've slipped into the rain-water tank. Luckily there's no water in it, but the sides are slippery and I can't get out. Fetch the little ladder from under the cherry tree—"

"I was told I wasn't to go into the gooseberry garden," said Nicholas promptly.

"I told you not to, and now I tell you that you may," came the voice from the rain-water tank, rather impatiently.

"Your voice doesn't sound like aunt's," objected Nicholas; "you may be the Evil One tempting me to be disobedient. Aunt often tells me that the Evil One tempts me and that I always yield. This time I'm not going to yield."

"Don't talk nonsense," said the prisoner in the tank; "go and fetch the ladder."

"Will there be strawberry jam for tea?" asked Nicholas innocently.

"Certainly there will be," said the aunt, privately resolving that Nicholas should have none of it.

"Now I know that you are the Evil One and not aunt," shouted Nicholas gleefully; "when we asked aunt for strawberry jam yesterday she said there wasn't any. I know there are four jars of it in the store cupboard, because I looked, and of course you know it's there, but *she* doesn't, because she said there wasn't any. Oh, Devil, you *have* sold yourself!"

There was an unusual sense of luxury in being able to talk to an aunt as though one was talking to the Evil One, but Nicholas knew, with childish discernment, that such luxuries were not to be over-indulged in. He walked noisily away, and it was a kitchenmaid, in search of parsley, who eventually rescued the aunt from the rain-water tank.

Tea that evening was partaken of in a fearsome silence. The tide had been at its highest when the children had arrived at Jagborough Cove, so there had been no sands to play on—a circumstance that the aunt had overlooked in the haste of organizing her punitive expedition. The tightness of Bobby's boots had had disastrous effect on his temper the whole of the afternoon, and

DEAN I wonder what has happened to the aunt? She must be in some kind of trouble—she seems to need Nicholas's help. (question, predict)

DEAN The aunt is in dire need of help, all right. And what does Nicholas do? He plays games with her. (clarify)

ANDRIA I don't think she's about to die! The aunt is a person who thinks way too much of herself. It's Nicholas's job to let her know this. (evaluate)

LEAH It's like Nicholas is saying: "Look, I tricked her." (clarify)

ANDRIA I don't think the aunt's detention in the rain-water tank is unmerited. If I'd been insulted like that, I would have done the same thing. She deserves it. (evaluate)

LEAH Nicholas seems to really like to provoke his aunt. In that way he seems like a typical little kid. (connect)

DEAN Even if she does deserve it, I don't think it's normal for a child of Nicholas's age to want revenge, to want to teach his aunt a lesson. (evaluate)

DEAN It seems like the aunt now fears Nicholas, because of what happened with the rain-water tank. (evaluate)

ANDRIA I don't think the aunt is scared of him—I think she now realizes how intelligent he is. I bet she won't play these childish games with Nicholas anymore. She knows he's beyond all that. (evaluate, predict)

altogether the children could not have been said to have enjoyed themselves. The aunt maintained the frozen muteness of one who has suffered undignified and unmerited detention in a rain-water tank for thirty-five minutes. As for Nicholas, he, too, was silent, in the absorption of one who has much to think about; it was just possible, he considered, that the huntsman would escape with his hounds while the wolves feasted on the stricken stag.

DEAN The tapestry seems to be a symbol of how Nicholas views the struggle between the adults and the children. (connect)

LEAH I think the tapestry is used to show us that Nicholas is the living, breathing story. (connect)

Discussion After Reading

General Comments

DEAN The whole story seems to be about what is going on in Nicholas's mind—what he sees and feels. The narrator favors Nicholas and is on his side. (summarize)

ANDRIA The narrator doesn't give the aunt much credit, so I wouldn't want to know what she thinks anyway. The way the narrator focuses on Nicholas makes the reader think he is smarter than the aunt. The whole story seems to downplay the role of adults and their intelligence. (evaluate)

DEAN It's true that it's the children versus the adults. But I still think that Nicholas's satirical or cynical view of his aunt just doesn't seem right for a child this young. (evaluate)

LEAH Well, we did agree that Nicholas seems a lot smarter and more advanced than other kids his age. (clarify)

ANDRIA If *lumber* means "useless bric-a-brac," I think they misnamed the room, because there's a lot of good stuff in there. (evaluate)

LEAH Well, the stuff is useless to the aunt. It's her useless stuff. (clarify)

DEAN To Nicholas, the room is beautiful. He's submerged in a world filled with things he's never seen before. (clarify)

ANDRIA Once Nicholas is in the lumber-room, that's where he finds his identity. (evaluate)

LEAH I agree. That's where you learn who Nicholas is. The other stuff is just superficial. Once he's in the lumber-room, he acts like other little kids. It's his aunt who forces him to be conniving. She makes him act more grown-up than he should. (evaluate)

Is it sometimes difficult for you to talk about literature once you've read it? Take some cues from active readers, who reflect and respond in a variety of ways. After reading "The Lumber-Room," these three students reveal their personal reactions (Shaping Your Response) and literary responses (Analyzing the Story), along with the connections they have made to their own experiences (Extending the Ideas). These are the types of questions you will find in this book.

Shaping Your Response

At the beginning of the story, Nicholas is "in disgrace." Do you think that he is really a wicked, sinful boy? Explain.

DEAN　When I think of Nicholas, I have a picture in my mind of a wicked little kid, with horns sticking out of his head like the devil, just smiling at his aunt.

LEAH　I don't think he's evil—that's too strong a word.

DEAN　I agree. But you can't tell me Nicholas is a normal child.

ANDRIA　I would not say that all children are as intelligent as Nicholas, who's able to plan ahead and manipulate others. When he's in the lumber room, looking at bird pictures in the book, you see that he's just as interesting and amazing as these birds. He's not an evil, wicked child—he's a good kid. It's just that his aunt never takes the time to open up his "book covers" and see who he is.

Analyzing the Story

How would you characterize the tone of this story? How does the tone contribute to the overall effect?

DEAN　I think the tone is satirical.

ANDRIA　I agree. The adults are being satirized. So many of the words that are used are directed against adults.

LEAH　I agree that the tone is sarcastic and cynical throughout most of the story. But I think the tone changes when Nicholas is in the lumber-room. He's happier because he's focusing on the wonderful things that are locked up inside this room.

DEAN　In the lumber-room, Nicholas has stepped into a world where there's no longer an aunt to deal with or worry about. That's why the tone changes.

Extending Your Ideas

Nicholas seems to be fascinated by what is forbidden. Suggest other stories or real-life situations in which characters have similar fascinations.

DEAN　The depiction of the lumber-room as a forbidden paradise reminds me of the story of Adam and Eve, from the Bible.

LEAH　The gooseberry garden in this story reminds me of *The Secret Garden.*

DEAN　Kids in general are fascinated by the forbidden. When I was a little kid, if someone told me not to do something, of course I did it. I assume that a fascination with the forbidden is part of every child's life.

MEDIEVAL LITERATURE

Getting Even

Codes of Honor

HISTORICAL OVERVIEW

Like most lands with long histories, the island of Britain underwent a series of invasions and occupations. The mild climate and fertile soil of the southern part was inviting to outsiders. The long, irregular coastline provided safe anchorage for invading fleets. Each successive invasion brought bloodshed and sorrow, but each also brought a new people with their own culture. Typically, new waves of immigrants came from the east and south, and the displaced refugees fled to the west and north, into what would become Wales, Ireland, and Scotland. But always some remained to blend with the newcomers and form a new culture that was a product of all its parts. Thus, through conflict and combination these different peoples created a nation.

2 CELTS

The Celts spread throughout Europe before reaching the British Isles. They built walled farms and hut villages and grew crops, using bronze and then iron tools. Separate tribes, each with its own king, warred with each other, erecting timber and stone fortresses and riding to battle in two-wheeled chariots. Their priests—called *druids*—conducted sacrifices in forest shrines.

INVASIONS

1 EARLY INHABITANTS

Cave dwellers lived on the island in prehistoric times. Invaders from what is now Spain and Portugal overcame their fragile culture, creating a society sophisticated enough to erect Stonehenge, the circle of huge upright stones on Salisbury Plain.

6 NORMANS

In a decisive battle at Hastings, William, Duke of Normandy (now northwest France) defeated the other claimants to the disputed English monarchy. During a lengthy struggle called the Norman Conquest, most of the Anglo-Saxon nobility was wiped out. William redistributed their lands and established a system of land ownership called *feudalism*.

3 ROMANS

Already dominating the Mediterranean world, Roman armies made Britain a part of the Roman Empire. The province of Britain was prosperous, with over 100 administrative centers. Straight, well-made Roman roads connected walled cities containing meeting halls, law courts, temples, amphitheaters, and public baths, as well as elaborate sanitation systems.

AND OCCUPATIONS

5 VIKINGS

Crossing the North Sea from Denmark and Norway, at first only a few boats came seeking to plunder coastal monasteries and towns. These early raids gave way to regular attacks, then to entire armies commanded by kings. They established the Danelaw, covering most of central Britain, where Danish law was in force.

4 ANGLO-SAXONS

Germanic tribes from the European mainland, including Angles, Saxons, and Jutes, began their invasions. Vigorous warriors and skilled seamen, they settled their own people on the conquered land, which came to be known—after the Angles—as England. Their tribal society was ruled by warrior kings who led their men into battle, the kind of society celebrated in the epic poem *Beowulf.*

Key Dates

about 600 B.C.
The Celtic invasion begins.

55 B.C.
Romans begin to establish a province.

407
Romans start to withdraw.

449
The Anglo-Saxon invasion begins.

about 725
Beowulf *is written down.*

787
The Viking invasion begins.

1066
William the Conqueror wins the Battle of Hastings in the Norman Conquest.

3

Part One

Getting Even

It's a theme that's almost as popular in human history as love or success: What do you do about people who have done something to you, and what do you do to them in return? Sometimes the answer is humorous, but more often it's serious—even bloody.

 Multicultural Connection **Choice** is often influenced by the cultural values of the society in which we live. The so-called heroic values that emphasize bravery and loyalty to family or clan can sometimes cause people to act in certain ways; on the other hand, they can sometimes restrict the actions that people perform. In the following selections, to what extent do the cultural values of individuals either cause or restrict the choices they make?

Literature

Interdisciplinary Study **Faces of Evil**

Writing Workshop **Expository Writing**

Beyond Print **Technology**

Reading an Epic Poem

The Germanic tribes who invaded Britain in the fifth century had a long literary tradition, carried on chiefly by wandering story tellers or musicians called *scops* who composed and recited or sang poems about past heroes and their brave deeds. These epic poems served warrior cultures by boosting tribal pride and teaching a code of values. The Anglo-Saxons (a term that came to refer to all the Germanic invaders of Britain, including Angles, Saxons, and Jutes) carried this oral tradition with them when they sailed westward to the place we now call England.

Understand Anglo-Saxon verse. Simple, direct, and relatively flexible, Anglo-Saxon verse is well fitted to oral composition and recitation. Here are a few lines from *Beowulf*. Written in the original Anglo-Saxon or Old English, it looks very different from the English we know. Nor does it sound like twentieth-century English.

The break in the middle of each line is called a *caesura* (si zhur′é); thus each line of verse divides into two half-lines. Each half-line contains two stressed syllables, making four strong beats to each line.

Alliteration, the repetition of initial sounds, is used, usually in the stressed syllables. Anglo-Saxon poetry is seldom rhymed.

The flexibility of the Anglo-Saxon language was a help to the scop, who at times must have composed his poetry on the spot. For example, if the first stressed syllable in a line started with an *h* sound, the scop could continue *on hranrade* ("on the whale-road"); if the line began with an *s* sound, he could use *on seglrade* ("on the sail-road"). To say "warrior," he could choose among *beorn, freca,* and *wiga,* which all mean the same but have different sounds and different connotations.

Alliterating words are in red.

Fyrst forð ġewāt;
bāt under beorge.
on stefn stigon,—
sund wið sande;

flota wæs on ȳðum,
Beornas ġearwe
strēmas wundon,

— Half line

— Caesura

A literal translation is: "Time forth went; floater was on waves, / boat under cliff. Warriors eager / on prow climbed; streams eddied, / sea against sand."

Another characteristic of Anglo-Saxon poetry is its use of metaphorical compounds, called **kennings:** for example, "whale-road" and "sail-road" both mean "sea." "Peace-weaver" for woman and "candle of heaven" for the sun are further examples of these descriptive comparisons that add beauty and a certain mystery to Anglo-Saxon poetry.

Examine the sentence structure. The version of *Beowulf* that follows has been translated from the Old English, but the translator has conveyed the quality of the poetry as well as the actions. Read the lines as you would prose lines, looking for the subject and the verb. Recognize also that many phrases are repetitions of what has just been said, added for greater emphasis.

Be aware of the nature of the epic hero. The heroic actions described in epic poetry—perilous journeys, battles with monsters, and so on—may be familiar to you; however, concepts of heroes differ from culture to culture. As you read *Beowulf,* look for clues that tell what this hero is like. Winning always matters, but the epic focus is more on *how* the hero fights. Read to learn what strategies Beowulf uses and how he responds to challenges.

Understand the purpose of the speeches. Characters in epics rarely make casual conversation. Instead, they communicate through formal speeches, boasting of their own accomplishments, challenging hostile rivals, advising each other about how to act, and philosophizing about human destiny.

Notice parallelisms. The epic of *Beowulf* begins with the story of King Scyld, who does not play any part in what follows, but who is mentioned because his story parallels or is similar to the story of Beowulf. (Scyld does not appear in this excerpt.) This comparison of people and events from earlier times is meant to add to the stature of the hero; he is thus seen as part of a long heroic tradition. Characters further this comparison by recalling their own and each other's family histories and past deeds of glory.

Look for symbolic descriptions. The *Beowulf* poet does not spend much time describing the appearance of people and places, but when he does, it is for a specific purpose. He dwells upon the beauty of Hrothgar's mead-hall because it represents certain ideals: order, security, human closeness. Much description occurs in the form of **epithets**—descriptive phrases that often occur in a series and refer in different ways to the same person. For example, King Hrothgar is referred to as "Prince of the Danes, protector of Scyldings, Lord of nations, and leader of men."

Appreciate the pageantry. Ceremony plays an important part in Anglo-Saxon life. When Beowulf arrives in Hrothgar's kingdom, Hrothgar throws a banquet for him, complete with formal speeches and lavish gifts. Such ceremony figures heavily in the rest of the poem. King Hrothgar delivers a speech and formally presents the hero with gifts, which the poet lists in detail. The oratory and the rewards define what the poet considers the most important values in life: honor, loyalty, and perseverance.

Before Reading

from Beowulf

The **Beowulf** Poet

The identity of the person who wrote *Beowulf* is a mystery. Some think the poet was a **scop,** or singing poet, associated with an Anglo-Saxon court. Scops composed their poetry extemporaneously, recounting past history and present events and preserving a record of people's achievements. Although the poem is based in part on traditional Germanic tales and has many pagan elements, the author seems to have been acquainted with the Bible and with Christianity, to which the Anglo-Saxons began to convert in the 500s. The poem was first written down sometime between A.D. 650 and 850.

Building Background

Imagine the Scene In the large wooden meeting-hall, the king and his thanes, or knights, gather, along with their wives, children, and servants. It is the end of the day—a time for feasting and for listening to tales of heroes. As the sounds of the day give way to nighttime sounds, and the fearsome darkness closes in, they huddle more closely together before a ruddy fire, drawn by the warmth, by the sounds of the scop strumming his lyre, and by the desire to hear a good story. "Tell us," someone says eagerly, "about Grendel and about how Beowulf killed that gruesome monster."

Literary Focus

Alliteration The repetition of sounds, usually consonants, at the beginnings of words or accented syllables is called **alliteration** (ə lit ə rā′shən). Note the repeated sounds in these lines:

> Grim and greedy the gruesome monster,
>
> Fierce and furious, launched attack, . . .

In Anglo-Saxon verse, alliteration is used for emphasis and to provide a kind of verbal music. Alliteration also makes words and phrases easier to remember, and since a scop recited his poems from memory, a device that made lines easier to remember would have been welcome.

Writer's Notebook

Unlock Your Word-Hoard The hero, Beowulf, after being asked who he is and where he comes from and why, unlocks "his word-hoard"; that is, he begins to tell about himself. What makes Beowulf a hero— his own claims, other people's claims, or his own deeds? Before starting to read, write down in your notebook all the qualities you think a hero should have. As you read, check to see which ones Beowulf possesses.

◄ The saga of Sigurd the Dragon-Slayer
is depicted in a group of carvings that
grace the entrance to a Norwegian
church built in the 1100s. In this detail
from one of the carvings, Sigurd is
shown slaying the fearsome dragon
Fáfnir. What does the style of this
wood carving suggest to you about
the artistic skills of these people?
About what they consider important?

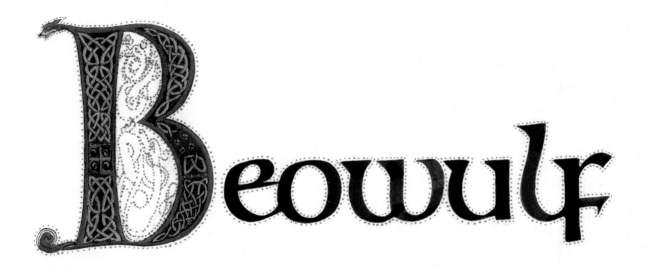

Beowulf

To Hrothgar was granted glory in war,
Success in battle; retainers bold
Obeyed him gladly; his band increased
To a mighty host. Then his mind was moved
5 To have men fashion a high-built hall,
A mightier mead-hall than man had known,
Wherein to portion to old and young
All goodly treasure that God had given,
Save only the folk-land, and lives of men.
10 His word was published to many a people
Far and wide o'er the ways of earth
To rear a folk-stead richly adorned;

Beowulf (bā′ō wulf).
1 Hrothgar (hrōth′gar), king of the Danes.

6 mead (mēd), *n.* an alcoholic drink made from fermented honey and water.

9 folk-land, common land owned by the community. Germanic tribal law reserved this land for grazing.
11 o'er, over.

The task was speeded, the time soon came
That the famous mead-hall was finished and done.
15 To distant nations its name was known,
The Hall of the Hart; and the king kept well
His pledge and promise to deal out gifts,
Rings at the banquet. The great hall rose
High and horn-gabled, holding its place. . . .
20   Then an evil spirit who dwelt in the darkness
Endured it ill that he heard each day
The din of revelry ring through the hall,
The sound of the harp, and the scop's sweet song.
A skillful bard sang the ancient story
25 Of man's creation; how the Maker wrought
The shining earth with its circling waters;
In splendor established the sun and moon
As lights to illumine the land of men;
Fairly adorning the fields of earth
30 With leaves and branches; creating life
In every creature that breathes and moves.
So the lordly warriors lived in gladness,
At ease and happy, till a fiend from hell
Began a series of savage crimes.
35 They called him Grendel, a demon grim
Haunting the fen-lands, holding the moors,
Ranging the wastes, where the wretched wight
Made his lair with the monster kin;
He bore the curse of the seed of Cain
40 Whereby God punished the grievous guilt
Of Abel's murder. Nor ever had Cain
Cause to boast of that deed of blood;
God banished him far from the fields of men;
Of his blood was begotten an evil brood,
45 Marauding monsters and menacing trolls,
Goblins and giants who battled with God
A long time. Grimly He gave them reward!
      Then at the nightfall the fiend drew near
Where the timbered mead-hall towered on high,
50 To spy how the Danes fared after the feast.
Within the wine-hall he found the warriors
Fast in slumber, forgetting grief,
Forgetting the woe of the world of men.
Grim and greedy the gruesome monster,
55 Fierce and furious, launched attack,
Slew thirty spearmen asleep in the hall,
Sped away gloating, gripping the spoil,

16 Hall of the Hart, Hrothgar's mead-hall, or meeting hall. The hart or male deer was a symbol of Germanic kingship.
19 horn-gabled, perhaps with roof ornaments carved to resemble a stag's, or deer's, antlers.
22 revelry, (rev′əl rē) *n.* noisy partying.
23 scop's sweet song. The scop (skop) was the tribe's storyteller, chanting his tales to the sound of a harp.
25 wrought, (rôt), *adj.* made. *Wrought* is an archaic past tense of the verb *work*.

35 Grendel (gren′dl).

39 seed of Cain. In the Bible, Cain murders his brother Abel and is driven into the wilderness by God (Genesis 4:8–14). According to later legend his offspring included a variety of monsters.

45 maraud (mə rôd′), *v.* go about in search of plunder.

■ What impression do you get of Grendel throughout this selection—that he is an animal behaving as an animal behaves or that he is a rational creature planning to murder humans and eat them?

Dragging the dead men home to his den.
Then in the dawn with the coming of daybreak
60 The war-might of Grendel was widely known.
Mirth was stilled by the sound of weeping;
The wail of the mourner awoke with day.
And the peerless hero, the honored prince,
Weighted down with woe and heavy of heart,
65 Sat sorely grieving for slaughtered thanes,
As they traced the track of the cursed monster.
From that day onward the deadly feud
Was a long-enduring and loathsome strife.
      Not longer was it than one night later
70 The fiend returning renewed attack
With heart firm-fixed in the hateful war,
Feeling no rue for the grievous wrong.
'Twas easy thereafter to mark the men
Who sought their slumber elsewhere afar,
75 Found beds in the bowers, since Grendel's hate
Was so baldly blazoned in baleful signs.
He held himself at a safer distance
Who escaped the clutch of the demon's claw.
So Grendel raided and ravaged the realm,
80 One against all, in an evil war
Till the best of buildings was empty and still.
'Twas a weary while! Twelve winters' time
The lord of the Scyldings had suffered woe,
Sore affliction and deep distress.
85 And the malice of Grendel, in mournful lays,
Was widely sung by the sons of men. . . .

The Coming of Beowulf

Then tales of the terrible deeds of Grendel
Reached Hygelac's thane in his home with the Geats;
Of living strong men he was the strongest,
90 Fearless and gallant and great of heart.
He gave command for a goodly vessel
Fitted and furnished; he fain would sail
Over the swan-road to seek the king
Who suffered so sorely for need of men.
95 And his bold retainers found little to blame
In his daring venture, dear though he was;
They viewed the omens, and urged him on.
Brave was the band he had gathered about him,
Fourteen stalwarts seasoned and bold,
100 Seeking the shore where the ship lay waiting. . . .

63 peerless (pir′lis), *adj.* without equal; matchless.
63 honored prince, Hrothgar.
65 thanes, warriors. A thane ranked between an earl (a nobleman) and an ordinary freeman.

72 rue (rü), *n.* regret.
73 'twas, it was.

83 lord of the Scyldings, Hrothgar. His grandfather, Scyld (shild), was founder of the Danish line of kings, the Scyldingas.
88 Hygelac's thane . . . Geats, Beowulf. Hygelac (hī′jə lak) was king of the Geats (yā′əts), a people who lived in south-western Sweden. Hygelac actually lived and was famous for his unusual height. He died in battle in A.D. 521.
90 gallant (gal′ənt), *adj.* noble in spirit or in conduct.

■ Anglo-Saxon poetry often makes use of a poetic device known as **kenning.** The writer uses a compound word that names something in a metaphorical way. For example, line 93 refers to the "swan-road." What sort of "road" would swans travel on?

99 stalwart (stôl′wərt), *n.* strong, brave, and steadfast person.

Beowulf's Welcome at Hrothgar's Court

Wulfgar saluted his lord and friend:
"Men from afar have fared to our land
Over ocean's margin—men of the Geats,
Their leader called Beowulf—seeking a boon,
105 The holding of parley, my prince, with thee.
O gracious Hrothgar, refuse not the favor!
In their splendid war-gear they merit well
The esteem of earls; he's a stalwart leader
Who led this troop to the land of the Danes."
110   Hrothgar spoke, the lord of the Scyldings:
"Their leader I knew when he still was a lad.
His father was Ecgtheow; Hrethel the Geat
Gave him in wedlock his only daughter.
Now is their son come, keen for adventure,
115 Finding his way to a faithful friend.
Sea-faring men who have voyaged to Geatland
With gifts of treasure as token of peace,
Say that his hand-grip has thirty men's strength.
God, in His mercy, has sent him to save us—
120 So springs my hope—from Grendel's assaults.
For his gallant courage I'll load him with gifts!
Make haste now, marshal the men to the hall,
And give them welcome to Danish ground."
          Then to the door went the well-known warrior,
125 Spoke from the threshold welcoming words:
"The Danish leader, my lord, declares
That he knows your kinship; right welcome you come,
You stout sea-rovers, to Danish soil.
Enter now, in your shining armor
130 And vizored helmets, to Hrothgar's hall.
But leave your shields and the shafts of slaughter
To wait the issue and weighing of words."
          Then the bold one rose with his band around him,
A splendid massing of mighty thanes;
135 A few stood guard as the Geat gave bidding
Over the weapons stacked by the wall.
They followed in haste on the heels of their leader
Under Heorot's roof. Full ready and bold
The helmeted warrior strode to the hearth;

101 **Wulfgar** (wulf′gar), Hrothgar's herald, an official who carries messages.

105 **parley** (pär′lē), *n.* conference.

108 esteem (e stēm′), *n.* high regard.

112 **Ecgtheow** (edj′thā ō), Beowulf's father.
112 **Hrethel** (hreth′l), Beowulf's mother's father.

■ Many lines in Beowulf are devoted to tracing kinship, or family relationships. What does this tell you about the society of these people?

138 **Heorot** (hā′ə rot), Hrothgar's mead-hall, the "Hall of the Hart."

140 Beowulf spoke; his byrny glittered,
His war-net woven by cunning of smith:
"Hail! King Hrothgar! I am Hygelac's thane,
Hygelac's kinsman. Many a deed
Of honor and daring I've done in my youth.

145 This business of Grendel was brought to my ears
On my native soil. The sea-farers say
This best of buildings, this boasted hall,
Stands dark and deserted when sun is set,
When darkening shadows gather with dusk.

150 The best of my people, <u>prudent</u> and brave,
Urged me, King Hrothgar, to seek you out;
They had in remembrance my courage and might.
Many had seen me come safe from the conflict,
Bloody from battle; five foes I bound

155 Of the giant kindred, and crushed their clan.
Hard-driven in danger and darkness of night
I slew the nicors that swam the sea,
Avenged the woe they had caused the Weders,
And ended their evil—they needed the lesson!

160 And now with Grendel, the fearful fiend,
Single-handed I'll settle the strife!
Prince of the Danes, protector of Scyldings,
Lord of nations, and leader of men,
I beg one favor—refuse me not,

165 Since I come thus faring from far-off lands—
That I may alone with my loyal earls,
With this hardy company, cleanse Hart-Hall.
I have heard that the demon in proud disdain
Spurns all weapons; and I too scorn—

170 May Hygelac's heart have joy of the deed—
To bear my sword, or sheltering shield,
Or yellow buckler, to battle the fiend.
With hand-grip only I'll grapple with Grendel;
Foe against foe I'll fight to the death,

175 And the one who is taken must trust to God's grace! . . .
If death shall call me, he'll carry away
My gory flesh to his fen-retreat
To gorge at leisure and gulp me down,
Soiling the marshes with stains of blood.

180 There'll be little need longer to care for my body!
If the battle slays me, to Hygelac send
This best of corselets that covers my breast . . .
Finest of byrnies. Fate goes as Fate must!"

140 **byrny,** shirt of chain mail.
150 **prudent** (prüd′nt), *adj.*
sensible; discreet.
157 **nicor** (nik′ər), *n.* a water
demon, animal in shape.
158 **Weders** (vā′dərz),
Beowulf's people, the Swedes.

■ Notice that the poet often
uses a series of descriptive
names (called **epithets**) to
refer to the same person, as
in lines 162–163. What do
you learn about Hrothgar in
these lines?

■ The Beowulf poet is fond
of **understatement,** a statement that expresses a fact less
emphatically than it should.
What makes line 180 an
example of understatement?

This iron warrior's helmet, with its
cap covered by richly decorated
bronze sheets, dates from
Sweden of the 600s. What does
the helmet's construction suggest
about the dangers faced by the
warrior who wore it? What does
the helmet's rich ornamentation
suggest about the warrior's status
in his society?

Then in the beer-hall were benches made ready
185 For the Geatish heroes. Noble of heart,
Proud and stalwart, they sat them down
And a beer-thane served them; bore in his hands
The patterned ale-cup, pouring the mead,
While the scop's sweet singing was heard in the hall.
190 There was joy of heroes, a host at ease,
A welcome meeting of Weder and Dane.

Unferth Taunts Beowulf

Then out spoke Unferth, Ecglaf's son,
Who sat at the feet of the Scylding lord,
Picking a quarrel—for Beowulf's quest,
195 His bold sea-voyaging, irked him sore;
He bore it ill that any man other
In all the earth should ever achieve
More fame under heaven than he himself:
"Are you the Beowulf that strove with Breca
200 In a swimming match in the open sea,
Both of you wantonly tempting the waves,
Risking your lives on the lonely deep
For a silly boast? No man could dissuade you,
Nor friend nor foe, from the foolhardy venture
205 Of ocean-swimming; with outstretched arms
You clasped the sea-stream, measured her streets,
With plowing shoulders parted the waves.
The sea-flood boiled with its wintry surges,
Seven nights you toiled in the tossing sea;
210 His strength was the greater, his swimming the stronger! . . .
Therefore, I ween, worse fate shall befall,
Stout as you are in the struggle of war,
In deeds of battle, if you dare to abide
Encounter with Grendel at coming of night."
215   Beowulf spoke, the son of Ecgtheow:
"My good friend Unferth, addled with beer
Much have you made of the deeds of Breca!
I count it true that I had more courage,
More strength in swimming than any other man.
220 In our youth we boasted—we were both of us boys—
We would risk our lives in the raging sea.
And we made it good! We gripped in our hands
Naked swords, as we swam in the waves,

192 Unferth (un′fèrth), **Ecglaf's** (edj′lafs) **son.** Unferth's name can be interpreted as "Peacebreaker."

199 Breca (brek′ə), a friend of Beowulf's youth.

203 dissuade (di swād′), *v.* persuade not to do something.

■ Unferth's role is a common one in epic poetry, that of the king's rude retainer who mocks the hero. What questions does this episode raise in your mind?

Guarding us well from the whales' assault.
225 In the breaking seas he could not outstrip me,
Nor would I leave him. For five nights long
Side by side we strove in the waters
Till racing combers wrenched us apart,
Freezing squalls, and the falling night,
230 And a bitter north wind's icy blast.
Rough were the waves; the wrath of the sea-fish
Was fiercely roused, but my firm-linked byrny,
The gold-adorned corselet that covered my breast,
Gave firm defense from the clutching foe.
235 Down to the bottom a savage sea-beast
Fiercely dragged me and held me fast
In a deadly grip; none the less it was granted me
To pierce the monster with point of steel.
Death swept it away with the swing of my sword.
240   "The grisly sea-beasts again and again
Beset me sore; but I served them home
With my faithful blade as was well-befitting. . . .
Fate often delivers an undoomed earl
If his spirit be gallant! And so I was granted
245 To slay with the sword-edge nine of the nicors.
I have never heard tell of more terrible strife
Under dome of heaven in darkness of night,
Nor of man harder pressed on the paths of ocean.
But I freed my life from the grip of the foe
250 Though spent with the struggle. The billows bore me,
The swirling currents and surging seas,
To the land of the Finns. And little I've heard
Of any such valiant adventures from you!" . . .

Beowulf Slays Grendel

In the hall as of old were brave words spoken,
255 There was noise of revel; happy the host
Till the son of Healfdene would go to his rest.
He knew that the monster would meet in the hall
Relentless struggle when light of the sun
Was dusky with gloom of the gathering night,
260 And shadow-shapes crept in the covering dark,
Dim under heaven. The host arose.
Hrothgar graciously greeted his guest,
Gave rule of the wine-hall, and wished him well,
Praised the warrior in parting words:
265 "Never to any man, early or late,
Since first I could brandish buckler and sword,

228 combers, waves.

231 wrath, (rath), *n.* great anger.

252 Finns, probably the Lapps, inhabitants of Finmarken, around the North Cape in the northern extremity of Norway and above the Arctic Circle.

256 Healfdene (hā′alf den ə), Hrothgar's father.

266 brandish (bran′dish), *v.* wave threateningly; flourish.

284 ere, (er), *conj.* before.
303 ravager (rav′ij ər), *n.*
destroyer.

Have I trusted this ale-hall save only to you!
Be mindful of glory, show forth your strength,
Keep watch against foe! No wish of your heart
270 Shall go unfulfilled if you live through the fight."
     Then Hrothgar withdrew with his host of retainers,
The prince of the Scyldings, seeking his queen,
The bed of his consort. The King of Glory
Had stablished a hall-watch, a guard against Grendel,
275 Dutifully serving the Danish lord,
The land defending from loathsome fiend.
The Geatish hero put all his hope
In his fearless might and the mercy of God!
He stripped from his shoulders the byrny of steel,
280 Doffed helmet from head; into hand of thane
Gave inlaid iron, the best of blades;
Bade him keep well the weapons of war.
Beowulf uttered a gallant boast,
The stalwart Geat, ere he sought his bed:
285 "I count myself nowise weaker in war
Or grapple of battle than Grendel himself.
Therefore I scorn to slay him with sword,
Deal deadly wound, as I well might do!
Nothing he knows of a noble fighting,
290 Of thrusting and hewing and hacking of shield,
Fierce as he is in the fury of war.
In the shades of darkness we'll spurn the sword
If he dares without weapon to do or to die.
And God in His wisdom shall glory assign,
295 The ruling Lord, as He deems it right."
Then the bold in battle bowed down to his rest,
Cheek pressed pillow; the peerless thanes
Were stretched in slumber around their lord. . . .
But the hero watched awaiting the foe,
300 Abiding in anger the issue of war.
     From the stretching moors, from the misty hollows,
Grendel came creeping, accursed of God,
A murderous ravager minded to snare
Spoil of heroes in high-built hall.
305 Under clouded heavens he held his way
Till there rose before him the high-roofed house,
Wine-hall of warriors gleaming with gold.
Nor was it the first of his fierce assaults
On the home of Hrothgar; but never before
310 Had he found worse fate or hardier hall-thanes!
Storming the building he burst the portal,

Though fastened of iron, with fiendish strength;
Forced open the entrance in savage fury
And rushed in rage o'er the shining floor.
315 A baleful glare from his eyes was gleaming
Most like to a flame. He found in the hall
Many a warrior sealed in slumber,
A host of kinsmen. His heart rejoiced;
The savage monster was minded to sever
320 Lives from bodies ere break of day,
To feast his fill of the flesh of men.
But he was not fated to glut his greed
With more of mankind when the night was ended!
    The hardy kinsman of Hygelac waited
325 To see how the monster would make his attack
The demon delayed not, but quickly clutched
A sleeping thane in his swift assault,
Tore him in pieces, bit through the bones,
Gulped the blood, and gobbled the flesh,
330 Greedily gorged on the lifeless corpse,
The hands and the feet. Then the fiend
        stepped nearer,
Sprang on the Sea-Geat lying outstretched,
Clasping him close with his monstrous claw.
But Beowulf grappled and gripped him hard,
335 Struggled up on his elbow; the shepherd of sins
Soon found that never before had he felt
In any man other in all the earth
A mightier hand-grip; his mood was humbled,
His courage fled; but he found no escape!

■ One unlucky thane is torn to pieces before Beowulf grapples with Grendel. Is this because of carelessness on Beowulf's part? If not, what might be the poet's intention here?

The Oseberg ship was a magnificent Viking vessel built in the 800s. It served as a royal barge before becoming the ship grave of a Norwegian queen. Before burial, the ship was loaded with elegant furniture, clothing, and other items that the queen would need in her royal afterlife. What does this Viking burial custom suggest about the Vikings' concept of life after death? ▼

340 He was fain to be gone; he would flee to the darkness,
The fellowship of devils. Far different his fate
From that which befell him in former days!
The hardy hero, Hygelac's kinsman,
Remembered the boast he had made at the banquet;
345 He sprang to his feet, clutched Grendel fast,
Though fingers were cracking, the fiend pulling free.
The earl pressed after; the monster was minded
To win his freedom and flee to the fens.
He knew that his fingers were fast in the grip
350 Of a savage foe. Sorry the venture,
The raid that the ravager made on the hall.
           There was din in Heorot. For all the Danes,
The city-dwellers, the stalwart Scyldings,
That was a bitter spilling of beer!
355 The walls resounded, the fight was fierce,
Savage the strife as the warriors struggled.
The wonder was that the lofty wine-hall
Withstood the struggle, nor crashed to earth,
The house so fair; it was firmly fastened
360 Within and without with iron bands
Cunningly smithied; though men have said
That many a mead-bench gleaming with gold
Sprang from its sill as the warriors strove.
The Scylding wise men had never weened
365 That any ravage could wreck the building,
Firmly fashioned and finished with bone,
Or any cunning compass its fall,
Till the time when the swelter and surge of fire
Should swallow it up in a swirl of flame.
370   Continuous tumult filled the hall;
A terror fell on the Danish folk
As they heard through the wall the horrible wailing,
The groans of Grendel, the foe of God
Howling his hideous hymn of pain,
375 The hell-thane shrieking in sore defeat.
He was fast in the grip of the man who was greatest
Of mortal men in the strength of his might,
Who would never rest while the wretch was living,
Counting his life-days a menace to man.
380   Many an earl of Beowulf brandished
His ancient iron to guard his lord,
To shelter safely the peerless prince.
They had no knowledge, those daring thanes,
When they drew their weapons to hack and hew,

364 ween (wēn), *v.* suppose;
believe.

367 compass (kum′pəs), *v.*
plot; scheme.

369 swirl of flame, one of a
number of references in the
poem to the later burning of
Heorot.

385 To thrust to the heart, that the sharpest sword,
The choicest iron in all the world,
Could work no harm to the hideous foe.
On every sword he had laid a spell,
On every blade; but a bitter death
390 Was to be his fate; far was the journey
The monster made to the home of fiends.
    Then he who had wrought such wrong to men,
With grim delight as he warred with God,
Soon found that his strength was feeble and failing
395 In the crushing hold of Hygelac's thane.
Each loathed the other while life should last!
There Grendel suffered a grievous hurt,
A wound in the shoulder, gaping and wide;
Sinews snapped and bone-joints broke,
400 And Beowulf gained the glory of battle.
Grendel, fated, fled to the fens,
To his joyless dwelling, sick unto death.
He knew in his heart that his hours were numbered,
His days at an end. For all the Danes
405 Their wish was fulfilled in the fall of Grendel.
The stranger from far, the stalwart and strong,
Had purged of evil the hall of Hrothgar,
And cleansed of crime; the heart of the hero
Joyed in the deed his daring had done.
410 The lord of the Geats made good to the East-Danes
The boast he had uttered; he ended their ill,
And all the sorrow they suffered long
And needs must suffer—a foul offense.
The token was clear when the bold in battle
415 Laid down the shoulder and dripping claw—
Grendel's arm—in the gabled hall!

The Joy of the Danes

When morning came, as they tell the tale,
Many a warrior hastened to hall,
Folk-leaders faring from far and near
420 Over wide-running ways, to gaze at the wonder,
The trail of the demon. Nor seemed his death
A matter of sorrow to any man
Who viewed the tracks of the vanquished monster
As he slunk weary-hearted away from the hall,
425 Doomed and defeated and marking his flight
With bloody prints to the nicors' pool.
The crimson currents bubbled and heaved

Earlier (in lines 168–173 and again in lines 285–293), Beowulf has declared that he will use no weapons to fight Grendel. How does that **choice** contribute to his success and to his status as a hero among his people?

397 grievous (grē′vəs), *adj.* causing great pain or suffering; severe.

In eddying reaches reddened with gore;
The surges boiled with the fiery blood.
430 But the monster had sunk from the sight of men.
In that fenny covert the cursed fiend
Not long thereafter laid down his life,
His heathen spirit; and hell received him.
    Then all the comrades, the old and young,
435 The brave of heart, in a blithesome band
Came riding their horses home from the mere.
Beowulf's <u>prowess</u> was praised in song;
And many men stated that south or north,
Over all the world, or between the seas,
440 Or under the heaven, no hero was greater,
More worthy of rule. But no whit they slighted
The gracious Hrothgar, their good old king. . . .
    Then spoke Hrothgar; hasting to hall
He stood at the steps, stared up at the roof
445 High and gold-gleaming; saw Grendel's hand:
"Thanks be to God for this glorious sight!
I have suffered much evil, much outrage from Grendel,
But the God of glory works wonder on wonder.
I had no hope of a haven from sorrow
450 While this best of houses stood badged with blood,
A woe far-reaching for all the wise
Who weened that they never could hold the hall
Against the assaults of devils and demons.
But now with God's help this hero has compassed
455 A deed our cunning could no way contrive.
Surely that woman may say with truth,
Who bore this son, if she still be living,
Our ancient God showed favor and grace
On her bringing-forth! O best of men,
460 I will keep you, Beowulf, close to my heart
In firm affection; as son to father
Hold fast henceforth to this foster-kinship.
You shall know not want of treasure or wealth
Or goodly gift that your wish may crave,
465 While I have power. For poorer deeds
I have granted guerdon, and graced with honor
Weaker warriors, feebler in fight.
You have done such deeds that your fame shall flourish
Through all the ages! God grant you still
470 All goodly grace as He gave before."
    Beowulf spoke, the son of Ecgtheow:
"By the favor of God we won the fight,

431 covert (kuv′ərt), *n.* hiding place.

435 blithesome (blĩᴛʜ′səm), *adj.* happy and cheerful.

437 prowess (prou′is), *n.* bravery; daring.

■ What happens to Grendel's hand?

466 guerdon (gėrd′n), *n.* reward.

Did the deed of valor, and boldly dared
The might of the monster. I would you could see
475 The fiend himself lying dead before you!
I thought to grip him in stubborn grasp
And bind him down on the bed of death,
There to lie straining in struggle for life,
While I gripped him fast lest he vanish away.
480 But I might not hold him or hinder his going
For God did not grant it, my fingers failed.
Too savage the strain of his fiendish strength!
To save his life he left shoulder and claw,
The arm of the monster, to mark his track. . . ."
485   Then slower of speech was the son of Ecglaf,
More wary of boasting of warlike deeds,
While the nobles gazed at the grisly claw,
The fiend's hand fastened by hero's might
On the lofty roof. Most like to steel
490 Were the hardened nails, the heathen's hand-spurs,
Horrible, monstrous; and many men said
No tempered sword, no excellent iron,
Could have harmed the monster or hacked away
The demon's battle-claw dripping with blood.
495 In joyful haste was Heorot decked
And a willing host of women and men
Gaily dressed and adorned the guest-hall.
Splendid hangings with sheen of gold
Shone on the walls, a glorious sight
500 To eyes that delight to behold such wonders.
The shining building was wholly shattered
Though braced and fastened with iron bands;
Hinges were riven; the roof alone
Remained unharmed when the horrid monster,
505 Foul with evil, slunk off in flight,
Hopeless of life. It is hard to flee
The touch of death, let him try who will;
Necessity urges the sons of men,
The dwellers on earth, to their destined place
510 Where the body, bound in its narrow bed,
After the feasting is fast in slumber.

This ferocious human mask is just one of the many intricate carvings that decorate a wooden cart found aboard the Oseberg ship (see pages 16–17). What might the mask suggest about the Viking view of human nature?

After Reading

Making Connections

Shaping Your Response

1. Does Grendel get what he deserves? Does he deserve what he gets?

2. How heroic is Beowulf? Give him a heroism rating from 0% to 100%. Then explain your rating.

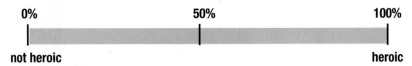

0%	50%	100%
not heroic		heroic

Analyzing the Epic Poem

3. Beowulf insists upon fighting Grendel without weapons. How does the way in which he fights the monster contribute to his success and increase his stature as a hero?

4. How does the poet build suspense throughout this episode?

5. Grendel has some traits that make him seem human, but in most respects he seems superhuman. What characteristics mark him as such?

Extending the Ideas

6. Throughout *Beowulf* there is emphasis on family heritage and on the importance of one's loyalties to a leader. Do the ancient Danes seem to be more concerned with these matters than other cultures you're familiar with—or less so?

7. Even today stories are told about monsters such as Big Foot and the Loch Ness monster that some people think might be real. What is it about monsters that is appealing? Do you find this appeal odd at the end of the 1900s? Why or why not?

Literary Focus: Alliteration

The repetition of sounds at the beginning of words or accented syllables is called **alliteration.** Which words alliterate in lines 87–90? in lines 150–155? Find some other alliterative passages in *Beowulf* and read them aloud. Do these passages make the lines more rhythmical? Do they make the meaning clearer?

Vocabulary Study

Match each lettered definition to the appropriate vocabulary word. You will not use all the definitions.

1. compass
2. dissuade
3. esteem
4. gallant

a. persuade not to do something
b. noisy partying
c. severe
d. great anger

5.	grievous	**e.**	high regard
6.	peerless	**f.**	bravery
7.	prowess	**g.**	search for plunder
8.	prudent	**h.**	without equal
9.	revelry	**i.**	scheme
10.	wrath	**j.**	noble in spirit
		k.	sensible

Expressing Your Ideas

Writing Choices

Writer's Notebook Update Does Beowulf live up to the heroic qualities you recorded in your notebook before reading the selection? Make a list of the heroic traits Beowulf demonstrates and write a paragraph or two about his heroism. First define heroism and then describe Beowulf's different heroic characteristics. Support your ideas with examples from the poem.

A Night to Forget Imagine that you are a thane or a member of a thane's family in Hrothgar's court on a night when Grendel attacks. Write a **letter** to a friend or relative in another country about what happens. You might start by describing the mead-hall during the evening meal; next tell how you feel as you prepare for sleep. Then tell of Grendel's awful attack. How do you escape?

Reconstructing Grendel You're the person in charge of special effects for a filming of this first part of *Beowulf*. The poet is not very specific about what Grendel looks like, however. Write a **description** of the monster, taking into account where he lives, how he acts, and what descriptive details the poet does provide, to aid your crew in creating the creature. Don't forget to include colors and textures.

Other Options

Sutton Who? In 1939 archaeologists excavated a large burial mound on an English estate called Sutton Hoo. Here, in the hull of what had once been an eighty-five foot wooden ship, they uncovered the richest hoard of Anglo-Saxon objects ever found. No trace of a body was found, but the coins, silver, jewels, and other articles indicate that Anglo-Saxon culture was far more advanced than had previously been imagined. Do some **research** on this fabulous find at Sutton Hoo and **report** to the class.

Listen! Composers of music for films are skilled at creating mood. Find some **recorded music** that seems to suit at least part of the section of *Beowulf* that you have just read and play it for the class—perhaps as background music for an oral reading.

Before Reading

Folk Ballads

Balladeers

Most early ballads were composed by anonymous musicians or entertainers. As generations of ballad singers passed their songs on, they added or dropped verses and changed details, such as names of people and places. Sometimes details were changed to please certain audiences and sometimes because a singer forgot or garbled some of the words. In the 1700s, hundreds of immigrants from the British Isles to America brought their ballads with them to Virginia, North Carolina, and the Appalachian Mountain region. They made further changes. For example, in the version of "Edward" included here, a hawk and a horse are mentioned. In an American version they have been changed to a grey mare and a coon dog. In the Scottish "Lord Randal," he bequeathes hell and fire to his love. In one American version, he leaves a rope to hang her. In effect, then, anyone who sings (and alters) a ballad is a composer.

Building Background

Nobleman Poisoned! In many ways, folk ballads served as the tabloid newspapers of their day. Ballad content is usually sensational, frequently criminal, often romantic, and occasionally supernatural. Drownings, poisonings, hangings, and hauntings are standard ballad fare, and "Lord Randal" and "Edward" are both about murders. Outlaws such as Robin Hood and unhappy—often tragic—love affairs figure prominently. Comic ballads, although few in number, usually deal with domestic disagreements.

Literary Focus

Repetition Words, sounds, phrases, or whole lines are often repeated throughout a ballad. This **repetition** is used for melodic effect, to provide emphasis, to unify parts of the ballad, or to build suspense. For example, the first three lines of each stanza of "Lord Randal" are similar. The mother's question changes from "O where ha' you been?" in line 1 to "And wha met you there?" in line 5. This **incremental repetition,** the repetition of lines that contain some small additions or increments, is used to advance the story and build to a climax. The repetition of lines at the end of each stanza is called a **refrain.** Use a chart such as the following to help you analyze the repetition in these three ballads.

Ballad	Words and Phrases	Lines and Refrains
Lord Randal		
Edward		
Get Up and Bar the Door		

Writer's Notebook

Heard Any Good Stories? What makes a good topic for a ballad? Almost anything, provided there's a good story involved. Think of sensational stories you have read or heard about. Jot down a few ideas for ballads in your notebook.

Lord Randal

"O where ha' you been, Lord Randal my son?
And where ha' you been, my handsome young man?"
"I ha' been at the greenwood; Mother, make my bed soon,
For I'm wearied wi' hunting and fain wad lie down."

5　"And wha met you there, Lord Randal my son?
And wha met you there, my handsome young man?"
"O I met wi' my true-love; Mother, make my bed soon,
For I'm wearied wi' hunting and fain wad lie down."

"And what did she give you, Lord Randal my son?
10　And what did she give you, my handsome young man?"
"Eels fried in a pan; Mother, make my bed soon,
For I'm wearied wi' hunting and fain wad lie down."

"And wha gat your leavins, Lord Randal my son?
And wha gat your leavins, my handsome young man?"
15　"My hawks and my hounds; Mother, make my bed soon,
For I'm wearied wi' hunting and fain wad lie down."

"And what becam of them, Lord Randal my son?
And what becam of them, my handsome young man?"
"They stretched their legs out and died; Mother, make my bed soon,
20　For I'm wearied wi' hunting and fain wad lie down."

"O I fear you are poisoned, Lord Randal my son,
I fear you are poisoned, my handsome young man."
"O yes, I am poisoned; Mother, make my bed soon,
For I'm sick at the heart and fain wad lie down."

25　"What d'ye leave to your mother, Lord Randal my son?
What d'ye leave to your mother, my handsome young man?"
"Four and twenty milk kye; Mother, make my bed soon,
For I'm sick at the heart and fain wad lie down."

"What d'ye leave to your sister, Lord Randal my son?
30　What d'ye leave to your sister, my handsome young man?"
"My gold and my silver; Mother, make my bed soon,
For I'm sick at the heart and fain wad lie down."

"What d'ye leave to your brother, Lord Randal my son?
What d'ye leave to your brother, my handsome young man?"

---

1 ha', have.

4 wearied . . . down, wearied with hunting, and gladly would lie down. *Down* is pronounced in the Scottish manner (dŭn) to rhyme with *soon*.
5 wha, who.

11 eels . . . pan, a method of poisoning that appears in many old ballads.

13 wha . . . leavins, who ate the food you didn't eat?

17 becam, became.

27 kye, cows.

35 "My houses and my lands; Mother, make my bed soon,
For I'm sick at the heart and fain wad lie down."

"What d'ye leave to your true-love, Lord Randal my son?
What d'ye leave to your true-love, my handsome young man?"
"I leave her hell and fire; Mother, make my bed soon,
40 For I'm sick at the heart and fain wad lie down."

Edward

"Why dois your brand sae drap wi bluid,
            Edward, Edward,
Why dois your brand sae drap wi bluid,
And why sae sad gang yee O?"
5 "O I hae killed my hauke sae guid,
            Mither, mither,
O I hae killed my hauke sae guid,
And I had nae mair bot hee O."

"Your haukis bluid was nevir sae reid,
10   Edward, Edward,
Your haukis bluid was nevir sae reid,
My deir son I tell thee O."
"O I hae killed my reid-roan steid,
            Mither, mither,
15 O I hae killed my reid-roan steid,
That erst was sae fair and frie O."

"Your steid was auld, and ye hae gat mair,
            Edward, Edward,
Your steid was auld, and ye hae gat mair,
20 Sum other dule ye drie O."
"Oh I hae killed my fadir deir,
            Mither, mither,
O I hae killed my fadir deir,
Alas, and wae is mee O!"

25 "And whatten penance wul ye drie for that,
            Edward, Edward,
And whatten penance wul ye drie for that?
My deir son, now tell me O."

During the medieval period, the hunt was an important and beloved pastime of the nobility. In this idyllic scene, serfs are shown grooming their lord's hunting dogs. How do the peace and tranquillity of this scene contrast with the events described in these three folk ballads? ➤

1 **dois . . . bluid,** does your sword so drip with blood.
4 **gang yee,** go you.
5 **hae . . . guid,** have killed my hawk so good.

6 **Mither,** Mother.

8 **nae . . . hee,** no more but him.
9 **haukis . . . reid,** hawk's blood was never so red.

12 **deir,** dear.
13 **reid-roan steid,** red-roan horse. "Red-roan" means a red coat mottled with white or grey.
16 **erst . . . frie,** once was so fair and free.
17 **auld,** old.
17 **mair,** more.

20 **sum . . . drie,** some other sorrow you suffer.
21 **fadir,** father.

24 **wae,** woe. "Woe is me" is a traditional expression for "I am greatly troubled or saddened."
25 **whatten penance,** what kind of penance. A penance is any act done to show that one is sorry for wrongdoing.

"Ile set my feit in yonder boat,
            Mither, mither,
Ile set my feit in yonder boat,
And Ile fare ovir the sea O."
30

"And what wul ye doe wi your towirs and your ha,
            Edward, Edward,
35 And what wul ye doe wi your towirs and your ha,
That were sae fair to see O?"
"Ile let thame stand tul they doun fa,
            Mither, mither,
Ile let thame stand tul they doun fa,
40 For here nevir mair maun I bee O."

"And what wul ye leive to your bairns and your wife,
            Edward, Edward,
And what wul ye leive to your bairns and your wife,
Whan ye gang ovir the sea O?"
45 "The warldis room, late them beg thrae life,
            Mither, mither,
The warldis room, late them beg thrae life,
For thame nevir mair wul I see O."

"And what wul ye leive to your ain mither deir,
            Edward, Edward,
50
And what wul ye leive to your ain mither deir?
My deir son, now tell me O."
"The curse of hell frae me sall ye beir,
            Mither, mither,
55 The curse of hell frae me sall ye beir,
Sic counseils ye gave to me O." ✦

Get Up and Bar the Door

It fell about the Martinmas time,
And a gay time it was then,
When our goodwife got puddings to make,
And she's boild them in the pan.

5 The wind sae cauld blew south and north,
And blew into the floor;
Quoth our goodman to our goodwife,
"Gae out and bar the door."

1 Martinmas time, Martinmas is a church festival that falls on November 11 and honors St. Martin.
3 puddings, sausages.
5 cauld, cold.
8 gae, go
8 bar the door, that is, set the wooden bar across the door so that it cannot blow open or be opened by anyone from outside.

"My hand is in my hussyfskap,
10 Goodman, as ye may see;
An it shoud nae be barrd this hundred year,
It's no be barrd for me."

They made a paction tween them twa,
They made it firm and sure,
15 That the first word whaeer shoud speak,
Shoud rise and bar the door.

Then by there came two gentlemen,
At twelve o clock at night,
And they could neither see house nor hall,
20 Nor coal nor candlelight.

"Now whether is this a rich man's house,
Or whether is it a poor?"
But neer a word wad ane o them speak,
For barring of the door.

25 And first they ate the white puddings,
And then they ate the black;
Tho muckle thought the goodwife to hersel,
Yet neer a word she spake.

Then said the one unto the other,
30 "Here, man, tak ye my knife;
Do ye tak aff the auld man's beard,
And I'll kiss the goodwife."

"But there's nae water in the house,
And what shall we do than?"
35 "What ails ye at the pudding-broo,
That boils into the pan?"

O up then started our goodman,
An angry man was he:
"Will ye kiss my wife before my een,
40 And scad me wi pudding-bree?"

Then up and started our goodwife,
Gied three skips on the floor:
"Goodman, you've spoken the foremost word,
Get up and bar the door." ✎

---

9 hussyfskap (hus′if skap), *n*. housewife's work.
11 an . . . nae, if it should not.
12 no . . . for, not going to be barred by.
13 paction . . . twa, pact, or agreement, between the two of them.
15 whaeer, whoever.

23 neer . . . ane, never a word would any (either the goodwife or the goodman).

25 they, that is, the "two gentlemen."

27 tho muckle, though much.
28 spake, spoke.

31 aff, off.

35 ails . . . pudding-broo, why can't you use the hot broth in which the sausages are cooking.

39 een, eyes.
40 scad, scald.

42 gied, gave.

After Reading

Making Connections

Shaping Your Response

1. These ballads are fairly typical of the tragic and comic ballads of the British Isles. Which of these three ballads appeals to you most? Why?

Analyzing the Folk Ballads

2. The story in a ballad can be told through narration or through **dialogue.** In which ballad is the story told mainly through narration? Compare the effect with that of the ballads told through dialogue.

3. The legacies or "testaments" that Lord Randal leaves to various people are another element that appears in many folk ballads. Explain how each legacy seems appropriate to the person Lord Randal leaves it to.

4. The listener is not told what "counseils," or advice, Edward's mother gave him. What do you think it might have been, based on information in the ballad?

5. What is **ironic** about the situation and the ending in "Get Up and Bar the Door"?

Extending the Ideas

6. If Edward appeared today in a court of law, what do you think his defense might be? What are his chances at being judged guilty or not guilty?

7. Does the kind of argument the goodwife and goodman get into in "Get Up and Bar the Door" have any counterpart in today's culture? Explain.

Literary Focus: Repetition

Repetition is a literary technique in which words, lines, phrases, and sounds are repeated. Repetition of lines that contain some small additions or increments is called **incremental repetition;** repetition of whole lines at the end of stanzas is called **refrain.** Point out several examples of the use of repetition in "Get Up and Bar the Door" or "Edward." What is the chief effect of the repetition in each ballad? To provide emphasis? unity? suspense?

Expressing Your Ideas

Writing Choices

Writer's Notebook Update Choose one of the story ideas you jotted down and think about how the story could be developed. List the major characters, actions, secrets to be revealed, and so on.

I Write the Songs Try writing a **ballad** of from three to five stanzas based on a comic or a tragic story. Follow the style of one of the ballads you have just read. Before you start, it may help you to list some words, phrases, and lines that you want to repeat for various effects.

Inquiring Minds Want to Know If a tabloid newspaper story could be a ballad, why can't a ballad be a **newspaper story?** Take another look at "Lord Randal" and decide why he was poisoned by his true-love. Was he unfaithful? Was she? Was there another reason? Write the story in newspaper style, using your imagination to fill in names, places, and so on. Explain the reason for this crime and how you, as a reporter, found out the truth.

Other Options

Class Balladeer Find a book or a recording of old ballads and **perform** or **play** some of them for the class. There are hundreds of these old songs available; in addition to those imported from England and other countries, many were created by balladeers in the Appalachian mountains, on the western frontier, and in other parts of the country.

Instrumental Instruction In this painting by the Italian painter Simone Martini (1284–1344), the musicians are playing a double flute and a mandola, a larger variety of a mandolin. Find some drawings or paintings of other early musical instruments and show them as part of a **talk on early instruments.** You may not be able to bring any early instruments to class, but you might bring modern instruments and demonstrate how they differ.

Getting Even

Faces of Evil

Multicultural Connection

Every culture in the world seems to have some concept of the opposing forces of good and evil. In many cultures, however, good and evil exist in the same beings. The Hindu goddess, Kali, for example, is both creator and destroyer. Which of the beings on these pages seem to combine good and evil?

EVIL

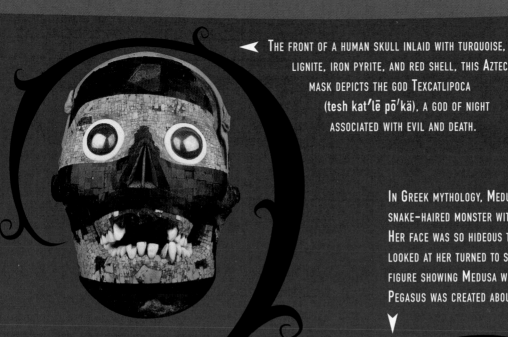

The front of a human skull inlaid with turquoise, lignite, iron pyrite, and red shell, this Aztec mask depicts the god Texcatlipoca (tesh kat′lē pō′kä), a god of night associated with evil and death.

In Greek mythology, Medusa was a snake-haired monster with protruding fangs. Her face was so hideous that anyone who looked at her turned to stone. This clay figure showing Medusa with the winged horse Pegasus was created about 620–610 B.C.

With staring eyes and protruding fangs, this Indonesian mask depicts a witch, Rangda, and is used in the performance of the dance dramas of the island of Bali.

FROM EAST

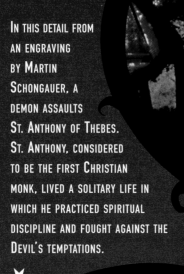

This detail in stained glass is from one of twenty-eight windows located in a late 15th-century Fairford church in southwest England. The devil's head shown here is a detail from windows that depict The Day of Judgment, when sinners will be judged and cast into Hell.

In this detail from an engraving by Martin Schongauer, a demon assaults St. Anthony of Thebes. St. Anthony, considered to be the first Christian monk, lived a solitary life in which he practiced spiritual discipline and fought against the Devil's temptations.

Evil takes many faces in contemporary movies, but some of the faces have proved popular enough to appear in sequel after sequel. Freddie Krueger haunted the dreams of teenagers in the *Nightmare on Elm Street* films, while Jason (wearing his trademark hockey mask) murdered right and left in the *Friday the 13th* movies. Darth Vader, having chosen "the dark side," represented evil in the *Star Wars* trilogy.

T O   W E S T

John Gardner
from GRENDEL

What if the story of Beowulf were told from the point of view of the monster Grendel?

I touch the door with my fingertips and it bursts, for all its fire-forged bands—it jumps away like a terrified deer—and I plunge into the silent, hearth-lit hall with a laugh that I wouldn't much care to wake up to myself. I trample the planks that a moment before protected the hall like a hand raised in horror to a terrified mouth (sheer poetry, ah!) and the broken hinges rattle like swords down the timbered walls. The Geats are stones, and whether it's because they're numb with terror or stiff from too much mead, I cannot tell. I am swollen with excitement, bloodlust and joy and a strange fear that mingle in my chest like the twisting rage of a bone-fire. I step onto the brightly shining floor and angrily advance on them. They're all asleep, the whole company! I can hardly believe my luck and my wild heart laughs, but I let out no sound. Swiftly, softly, I will move from bed to bed and destroy them all, swallow every last man. I am blazing, half-crazy with joy. For pure, mad prank, I snatch a cloth from the nearest table and tie it around my neck to make a napkin. I delay no longer.

I seize up a sleeping man, tear at him hungrily, bite through his bone-locks and suck hot, slippery blood. He goes down in huge morsels, head, chest, hips, legs, even the hands and feet. My face and arms are wet, matted. The napkin is sopping. The dark floor steams, I move on at once and I reach for another one (whispering, whispering, chewing the universe down to words), and I seize a wrist. A shock goes through me. Mistake!

It's a trick! His eyes are open, were open all the time, cold-bloodedly watching to see how I work. The eyes nail me now as his hand nails down my arm. I jump back without thinking (whispering wildly: *jump back without thinking*). Now he's out of his bed, his hand still closed like a dragon's jaws on mine. Nowhere on middle-earth, I realize, have I encountered a grip like his. My whole arm's on fire, incredible, searing pain—it's as if his crushing fingers are charged like fangs with poison. I scream, facing him, grotesquely shaking hands—dear long-lost brother, kinsman-thane—and the timbered hall screams back at me. I feel the bones go, ground from their sockets, and I scream again. I am suddenly awake. The long pale dream, my history, falls away. The meadhall is alive, great cavernous belly, gold-adorned, bloodstained, howling back at me, lit by the flickering fire in the stranger's eyes. He has wings. Is it possible? And yet it's true: out of his shoulders come terrible fiery wings. I jerk my head, trying to drive out illusion. The world is what it is and always was. That's our hope, our chance. Yet even in times of catastrophe we people it with tricks. Grendel, Grendel, hold fast to what is true!

Suddenly, darkness. My sanity has won. He's only a man; I can escape him. I plan. I feel the plan moving inside me like thaw-time waters rising between cliffs. When I'm ready, I give a ferocious kick—but something's wrong: I am spinning—*Wa!*—falling through bottomless space—*Wa!*—snatching at the huge twisted roots of an oak…a blinding flash of fire…no, darkness. I concentrate. I have fallen! Slipped on blood. He viciously twists my arm behind my back. By accident, it comes to me, I have given him a greater advantage. I could laugh. *Woe, woe!*

And now something worse. He's whispering—spilling words like showers of sleet, his mouth three inches from my ear. I will not listen. I continue whispering. As long as I whisper myself I need not hear. His syllables lick at me, chilly fire. His syllables lick at me, chilly fire. His syllables lick at me, chilly fire. His syllables lick . . .

Responding

1. What details in the story change with this shift of point of view? Does Grendel seem to recognize how much a monster he appears to humans? How does he react to the humans' attitude?

2. Which of the faces on pages 32-34 seems to you most truly evil? Why?

Writing Workshop

Heroes Old and New

Assignment How has the concept of the hero changed since the time when *Beowulf* was written? Write an essay in which you answer this question.

WRITER'S BLUEPRINT

Product	An interpretive essay
Purpose	To explore the concept of the hero
Audience	People who have read *Beowulf*
Specs	To write a successful, essay you should:

❑ Choose a modern fictional hero from books, movies, or television, or a real-life hero from recent history, to compare and contrast with Beowulf.

❑ Begin your essay in a dramatic manner that shows the two heroes in action and identifies your purpose for writing.

❑ Go on to compare and contrast your heroes in terms of <u>three</u> of the aspects of comparison listed below, using a clear comparison-contrast organization. Include specific examples of both heroes' words and actions to support your comparisons and contrasts, including quotations from literature where appropriate.

Aspects of comparison: —the worlds in which the heroes exist—the obstacles they must overcome—the resources, physical and mental, that they must rely on to overcome these obstacles—the weaknesses that make them vulnerable to their enemies—the qualities of character that make them heroes—other aspects of your own choosing

❑ Conclude by answering the question: How has the concept of the hero changed since the time when *Beowulf* was written?

❑ Write focused paragraphs that each keep to one main idea.

❑ Follow the rules of grammar, usage, spelling, and mechanics, including correct pronoun reference.

The instructions that follow are designed to lead you to a successful essay.

Brainstorm to find fictional heroes to pair with Beowulf. Working with a group, make a list of modern characters that your group sees as heroic. Try to include a wide variety of characters from books, movies, and television. Then choose the person you'll be comparing and contrasting with Beowulf.

Diagram ideas for comparison. Draw a Venn diagram like the one that follows. Label each circle with the heroes' names. Then make notes about them based on the aspects of comparison listed in the Blueprint. Where the circles intersect, write about what the two heroes have in common. In the outer part of the two circles, write what is unique to Beowulf and to your modern hero.

> **OR . . .**
> Instead of fictional heroes, use real people from recent history or someone you know personally whom you see as heroic. Consider moral courage and leadership as well as physical bravery.

> **LITERARY SOURCE**
> Grim and greedy the gruesome monster,
> Fierce and furious, launched attack,
> Slew thirty spearmen asleep in the hall,
> Sped away gloating, gripping his spoil,
> Dragging the dead men home to his den.
> *from* Beowulf
> (*lines 54–58*)

Beowulf
1. lives in ancient times
2. has a super-natural **enemy—** Grendel
3. relies on brute strength

and so on . . .

1. both have enemies
2. both are courageous, willing to act

and so on . . .

Indiana Jones
1. lives in modern times
2. has mortal enemies
3. is cunning

and so on . . .

Choose the three best aspects for comparison from your Venn diagram—the aspects that best illustrate the similarities and differences between your two heroes. These are the aspects you'll use to compare and contrast them. Note specific examples of each aspect you chose. Look for specific things your heroes and their friends and foes do and say to illustrate each aspect.

Plan your essay. On the next page are two methods for organizing a comparison–contrast essay. Choose the method you feel more comfortable with. Use the information you gathered in prewriting to help you make notes on each bulleted point.

OR . . .
Use your own method for planning, whatever works for you. Just make sure it addresses the points in the Writer's Blueprint.

Method 1	Method 2
Introduction • Beowulf in action • The modern hero in action • My purpose for writing	**Introduction** • Beowulf in action • The modern hero in action • My purpose for writing

Body: Discuss one at a time
• Beowulf   Heroic aspect 1 . . .
        Examples . . .
        Heroic aspect 2 . . .
        Examples . . .
        Heroic aspect 3 . . .
        Examples . . .
• Modern Hero   Heroic aspect 1 . . .
        Examples . . .
        Heroic aspect 2 . . .
        Examples . . .
        Heroic aspect 3
        Examples . . .
	Body: Compare/contrast as you go
	• Aspect 1
	        Beowulf . . . .Examples . . .
	        Modern hero . . .Examples . . .
	
	• Aspect 2
	        Beowulf . . .Examples . . .
	        Modern hero . . .Examples . . .
	
	• Aspect 3
	        Beowulf . . . .Examples . . .
	        Modern hero . . .Examples . . .

Conclusion • How the concept of the hero has (has not) changed since Beowulf was written)	**Conclusion** • How the concept of the hero has (has not) changed since Beowulf was written

Ask a partner to look over your plan before you draft. Use these questions as a guide.

✔ Do I have enough specific examples of my heroes' words and actions to illustrate each aspect?

✔ Am I following the Specs in the Writer's Blueprint?

Use your partner's comments to help you revise your plan.

STEP **2** DRAFTING

Refer to your plan as you draft. Here are some drafting tips you might use.

• You don't have to draft the introductory paragraph first. Some writers prefer to write the body first, and then write the introduction and conclusion.

• When you draft the body, use words like these to help make your comparisons and contrasts:

Comparison: both, and, like, same, similar, in the same way, alike
Contrast: while, unlike, on the other hand, different, but, yet, instead

3 REVISING

Ask a partner for comments on your draft before you revise it.

✔ Have I followed the Specs in the Writer's Blueprint?

✔ Have I begun in a dramatic way and made my purpose clear?

✔ Have I used specific examples for my three aspects of comparison?

Revising Strategy

Keeping to the Main Idea

An essay is usually more convincing when each paragraph is focused on a single idea. If a paragraph mixes up two main ideas—especially if the writer hasn't planned this—the result can be confusing.

In the Student Model the paragraph as first drafted mixes up two main ideas (resources and worlds). Based on a partner's comment, the writer revised the paragraph so that it now deals with resources only.

> **COMPUTER TIP**
> As you revise, **boldface the main idea** of each paragraph. Then you can easily glance back to the main idea to make sure each sentence focuses on it. Remove this bold-face when you make your final copy.

Is this about worlds or resources? Beowulf and Indiana Jones used the resources they had to get out of sticky situations. ~~They also existed in different worlds.~~ For example, Beowulf relied on his strength when he attacked Grendel to defend the innocent. Indiana Jones relied on his intelligence to find a way out of a sealed chamber full of poisonous snakes. ~~On the other hand, Beowulf existed in an ancient world while Indiana Jones lived in the early 1900s.~~

STUDENT MODEL

4 EDITING

Ask a partner to review your revised draft before you edit. When you edit, look for errors in grammar, usage, spelling, and mechanics. Look especially for unclear pronoun references.

Editing Strategy

Clarifying Pronoun References

Pronouns like *he, she, they,* and *it* can be confusing if you fail to make clear which person, object, or idea the pronoun refers to.

FOR REFERENCE
For more help on pronoun reference, see the Language and Grammar Handbook at the back of this text.

Reference unclear	When the enemy faced the hero on the bridge *he* shook with terror.

Somebody shook, but was it the hero or the enemy? Here are two ways to clear up the problem.

Substitute a noun	When the enemy faced the hero on the bridge, *the enemy* shook with terror.
Change the word order	The enemy shook with terror as he faced the hero on the bridge.

Search your draft for these kinds of problems with pronouns.

STEP 5 PRESENTING

Try these ideas as you read your essay aloud:

- If you chose a hero from a television show or movie, show videotaped clips of her or him in action.

- Make a poster to illustrate the similarities and differences between your two heroes and use it as a graphic aid as you present.

STEP 6 LOOKING BACK

Self-evaluate. Rate your paper on each item in the Writer's Blueprint, from 6 (superior) to 1 (inadequate).

Reflect. Write your thoughts on these questions.

✔ Do all heroes make good role models for your own life? Explain.

✔ Review the ratings you gave yourself, and describe what you might do the next time you write to improve any rating that was less than superior.

For Your Working Portfolio Add your interpretive essay and your reflection responses to your working portfolio.

Beyond Print

Glossary of Technology Terms

As you use computers and other technologies, you need to understand certain terms. Here are some common technology terms.

Application A particular computer program or piece of software.

Bulletin Board Service (BBS) An individual or company that allows users to connect to their server to download or upload information.

CD ROM Compact Disc Read Only Memory; this is used to store information, such as text, sounds, pictures, and movies.

Database An organized collection of information.

Desktop The area on a computer screen that contains icons, menus, and windows.

Directory A particular area in the computer or storage that contains all applications and files.

Download To copy a file from a server or network.

Home Page The first screen that appears when you access a server on the World Wide Web; it can contain text, graphics, and sound.

Internet A series of computer servers connected together across the country and world, allowing a user who is connected to the Internet to access any information stored on those servers.

Menu A pull-down list of items at the top of the computer screen.

Multimedia Any combination of media types, including text, sound, pictures, and video.

Network Two or more computers connected together.

Server A computer that operates a network.

Upload To copy a file onto a server or network.

Activity

Create a glossary of your own with other Technology Terms. Keep this in your notebook and add to it as you come across new terms.

MEDIEVAL

HISTORICAL OVERVIEW

Under the system called feudalism, the king owned all lands and distributed them to his vassals (tenants) according to merit or favoritism. Every citizen's life was rigidly prescribed from birth to death. The class you were born into was where you stayed, for the most part, and it determined to a large degree how you lived.

Although there were actually more classes than shown here, and each class had its own divisions, these were the main groups of people. The monarch—the king (England hadn't had any queens yet)—was, of course, in a class by himself.

Serf

The laborers of the lowest class were dependent upon their lords and tied to their lands, not allowed to leave or change jobs without permission. They worked the fields, raised the cattle, wove the cloth, and did all of the thousands of jobs that maintain life.

Merchant

The merchant class was new, born of increasing trade. This class held the most promise for improving one's life, for as the class grew, it became more powerful—eventually developing the guild, an early form of trade union, as a means of controlling products.

CLASSES

Cleric

Knight

Noble

Key Dates

1096
The First Crusade begins.

1167
Oxford University is founded.

1170
Thomas à Becket is murdered.

1215
King John signs the Magna Carta.

1339
The Hundred Years War starts between France and England.

1348
Black Death appears in England.

1386
Chaucer begins writing The Canterbury Tales.

1476
Caxton establishes the first printing press in England.

Medieval learning was maintained by the men and women of the Church. Churches and monasteries were often small, self-sufficient cities. As they acquired lands and property, some of the clergy became powerful, clashing at times with the nobility or even the king.

The mounted warrior became the chief symbol of the code of chivalry (see page 88). Fighting was both a way of life and a way up the social ladder. Knighthood was developed partly to provide troops for the Crusades, expeditions to recover the Holy Lands from the Turks.

Landholders ran the country's day-to-day political and social life. Often wealthy and powerful, owning many houses and great tracts of land, they lived lavishly and struggled among themselves or with the king.

Part Two

Codes of Honor

Honor means different things to different people. It is a sense of what is right or proper; it is nobility of mind; it is integrity; it is respect or high regard. Some people live their lives trying to get around it; some die trying to uphold it.

 Multicultural Focus Membership in a **group** involves the collective development of codes, rules for behavior that individuals are expected to follow. In this period of history, such group codes included loyalty, bravery, honesty, courtesy—and the honor to uphold these values even when no one else was watching. In what respects do the characters in these selections follow or depart from their codes of honor?

Before Reading

from The Canterbury Tales by Geoffrey Chaucer

translated by Nevill Coghill

Geoffrey Chaucer
1342?–1400

Throughout most of his life Geoffrey Chaucer (jef′rē chô′sər) was connected in some way with members of the royal family. In 1359 he was sent to France to fight in the Hundred Years' War. Chaucer was taken prisoner but was ransomed in the following year; King Edward III himself contributed toward his ransom. Some years later, he began undertaking diplomatic missions to France, Spain, and Italy for the king. In his later life as a customs official, he and his wife, Philippa Roet, who also had court connections, lived in free lodgings above Aldgate in London. There he liked to retire "as an hermyte," he says, after his working day was done. He lost or gave up his job in 1386 and probably began writing *The Canterbury Tales* soon thereafter.

Building Background

A Very Special Journey It's a fine spring morning. The air is soft, the birds are singing, and the earth is beginning to send forth green shoots. It's a perfect time to set out on a journey—say, to the cathedral at Canterbury, the shrine of the martyr Saint Thomas à Becket, murdered in 1170 for resisting the policies of King Henry II. Visiting a holy place was a popular pastime in the Middle Ages, not only for religious reasons, but because it was an adventure. And the journey there and back, known as a **pilgrimage,** is an ideal setting for presenting a varied group of travelers who tell stories to entertain each other. Thus, *The Canterbury Tales* is an ingenious concoction of character sketches, conversations, and stories—all set within the frame, or larger narrative, of this pilgrimage, undertaken by twenty-nine pilgrims (and Chaucer) who meet each other at the Tabard Inn in Southwark, across the Thames River from London. Representing a cross section of the population of England in the 1300s, Chaucer's pilgrims—also called *palmers*—range in rank from a knight to a poor plowman, and the tales they tell range from sermons to off-color jokes. Chaucer planned to include 120 stories, two told by each pilgrim each way on the journey, but he managed only twenty-four, some of these incomplete, before his death.

Literary Focus

Irony The contrast between what appears to be and what really is, is called **irony.** Different types of irony include *verbal, dramatic,* and *situational,* in which something occurs contrary to what is expected or intended. Irony can be bitter or humorous, and in the hands of a master storyteller it is highly effective. Look for instances of irony in *The Pardoner's Prologue* and *Tale.*

Writer's Notebook

A Modern Pilgrimage How would you update the idea of a group of travelers telling their stories to each other during a journey? What kinds of people might take a modern pilgrimage? Where would they go and for what purpose? How would they travel? In your notebook, jot down some answers to these questions.

The Canterbury Tales

Geoffrey Chaucer

In the General Prologue to all the tales, Chaucer briefly introduces each pilgrim, who then tells a bit about himself or herself before relating a tale. The lines below are the opening of the General Prologue in Chaucer's English and in modern English.

THE PROLOGUE

Whan that Aprille with hise shoures sote
The droghte of March hath perced to
   the rote,
And bathed every veyne in swich licour
Of which vertu engendred is the flour;
5 Whan Zephirus eek with his sweete breeth
Inspired hath in every holt and heeth
The tendre croppes, and the yonge sonne
Hath in the Ram his halfe cours yronne,
And smale fowles maken melodye
10 That slepen al the night with open iye
(So priketh hem Nature in hir corages):
Thanne longen folk to goon on pilgrimages,
And palmeres for to seken straunge strondes,
To ferne halwes, couthe in sondry londes;
15 And specially from every shires ende
Of Engelond to Caunterbury they wende,
The holy blisful martir for to seeke,
That hem hath holpen whan that they were seke.
      Bifel that in that seson on a day,
20 In Southwerk at the Tabard as I lay
Redy to wenden on my pilgrimage
To Caunterbury with ful devout corage,
At nyght was come into that hostelrye
Wel nine and twenty in a companye
25 Of sondry folk, by aventure yfalle
In felawship, and pilgrimes were they alle
That toward Caunterbury wolden ryde.

THE PROLOGUE

When in April the sweet showers fall
And pierce the drought of March to the root,
   and all
The veins are bathed in liquor of such power
As brings about the engendering of the flower,
5 When also Zephyrus with his sweet breath
Exhales an air in every grove and heath
Upon the tender shoots, and the young sun
His half-course in the sign of the *Ram* has run,
And the small fowl are making melody
10 That sleep away the night with open eye
(So nature pricks them and their heart engages)
Then people long to go on pilgrimages
And palmers long to seek the stranger strands
Of far-off saints, hallowed in sundry lands,
15 And specially, from every shire's end
Of England, down to Canterbury they wend
To seek the holy blissful martyr, quick
To give his help to them when they were sick.
      It happened in that season that one day
20 In Southwark, at *The Tabard*, as I lay
Ready to go on pilgrimage and start
For Canterbury, most devout at heart,
At night there came into that hostelry
Some nine and twenty in a company
25 Of sundry folk happening then to fall
In fellowship, and they were pilgrims all
That towards Canterbury meant to ride.

◄ In this illustration from a manuscript of the 1400s, characters from *The Canterbury Tales* are shown on their pilgrimage to the shrine of St. Thomas à Becket. If you were to make a pilgrimage for religious or other reasons, where would you go? Why?

THE PARDONER'S PROLOGUE

"My lords," he said, "in churches where I preach
I cultivate a haughty kind of speech
And ring it out as roundly as a bell;
I've got it all by heart, the tale I tell.
5 I have a text, it always is the same
And always has been, since I learnt the game,
Old as the hills and fresher than the grass,
Radix malorum est cupiditas.
　　　　"But first I make pronouncement whence I come,
10 Show them my bulls in detail and in sum,
And flaunt the papal seal for their inspection
As warrant for my bodily protection,
That none may have the impudence to irk
Or hinder me in Christ's most holy work.
15 Then I tell stories, as occasion calls,
Showing forth bulls from popes and cardinals,
From patriarchs and bishops; as I do,
I speak some words in Latin—just a few—
To put a saffron tinge upon my preaching
20 And stir devotion with a spice of teaching.
Then I bring all my long glass bottles out
Cram-full of bones and ragged bits of clout,
Relics they are, at least for such are known.
Then, cased in metal, I've a shoulder-bone,
25 Belonging to a sheep, a holy Jew's.
'Good men,' I say, 'take heed, for here is news.
Take but this bone and dip it in a well;
If cow or calf, if sheep or ox should swell
From eating snakes or that a snake has stung,
30 Take water from that well and wash its tongue,
And it will then recover. Furthermore,
Where there is pox or scab or other sore,
All animals that water at that well
Are cured at once. Take note of what I tell.
35 If the good man—the owner of the stock—
Goes once a week, before the crow of cock,
Fasting, and takes a draught of water too,
Why then, according to that holy Jew,
He'll find his cattle multiply and sell.

8 Radix . . . cupiditas. "Avarice (greed for wealth) is the root of all evil." *[Latin]*
10 bull, formal announcement or official decree from the pope.

19 saffron (saf′rən), *n.* an orange-yellow spice used to color and flavor certain dishes, such as rice.
22 clout, cloth.

25 sheep . . . Jew's, that is, he is claiming that the sheep's bone belonged to some biblical patriarch, such as Abraham, Isaac, or Jacob.

32 pox, any disease, such as chicken pox or small pox, characterized by skin eruptions.

■ Why does the Pardoner carry these relics around with him?

40 "'And it's a cure for jealousy as well;
For though a man be given to jealous wrath,
Use but this water when you make his broth,
And never again will he mistrust his wife,
Though he knew all about her sinful life,
45 Though two or three clergy had enjoyed her love.
        "'Now look; I have a mitten here, a glove.
Whoever wears this mitten on his hand
Will multiply his grain. He sows his land
And up will come abundant wheat or oats,
50 Providing that he offers pence or groats.
        "'Good men and women, here's a word of warning;
If there is anyone in church this morning
Guilty of sin, so far beyond expression
Horrible, that he dare not make confession,
55 Or any woman, whether young or old,
That's cuckolded her husband, be she told
That such as she shall have no power or grace
To offer to my relics in this place.
But those who can acquit themselves of blame
60 Can all come up and offer in God's name,
And I will shrive them by the authority
Committed in this papal bull to me.'
        "That trick's been worth a hundred marks a year
Since I became a Pardoner, never fear.
65 Then, priestlike in my pulpit, with a frown,
I stand, and when the yokels have sat down,
I preach, as you have heard me say before,
And tell a hundred lying mockeries more.
I take great pains, and stretching out my neck
70 To east and west I crane about and peck
Just like a pigeon sitting on a barn.
My hands and tongue together spin the yarn
And all my antics are a joy to see.
The curse of avarice and cupidity
75 Is all my sermon, for it frees the pelf.
Out come the pence, and specially for myself,
For my exclusive purpose is to win
And not at all to castigate their sin.
Once dead what matter how their souls may fare?
80 They can go blackberrying, for all I care!
        "Believe me, many a sermon or devotive
Exordium issues from an evil motive.
Some to give pleasure by their flattery
And gain promotion through hypocrisy,

50 pence or groats. *Pence* is the plural of *penny;* a groat is an old English coin worth four pence.

56 cuckold (kuk′əld), *v.* be unfaithful to.

61 shrive (shrīv), *v.* hear the confession of and grant forgivness to.
63 a hundred marks. A mark was a coin of much higher denomination than a groat. In other words, the Pardoner has been making good money from "that trick."
66 yokel (yō′kəl), *n.* a country person. It is often meant as an insult, as the Pardoner means it here.

74 avarice (av′ər is), *n.*
. . . cupidity (kyū pid′ə tē), *n.* Avarice is greed for wealth; cupidity is the eager desire to possess something.
75 pelf, money.
78 castigate (kas′tə gāt), *v.* punish in order to correct.

82 exordium (eg zôr′dē əm), *n.* introductory part of a speech.

85 Some out of vanity, some out of hate;
   Or when I dare not otherwise debate
   I'll put my discourse into such a shape,
   My tongue will be a dagger; no escape
   For him from slandering falsehood shall there be
90 If he has hurt my brethren or me.
   For though I never mention him by name
   The congregation guesses all the same
   From certain hints that everybody knows,
   And so I take revenge upon our foes
95 And spit my venom forth, while I profess
   Holy and true—or seeming holiness.
            "But let me briefly make my purpose plain;
   I preach for nothing but for greed of gain
   And use the same old text, as bold as brass,
100 *Radix malorum est cupiditas.*
   And thus I preach against the very vice
   I make my living out of—avarice.
   And yet however guilty of that sin
   Myself, with others I have power to win
105 Them from it, I can bring them to repent;
   But that is not my principal intent.
   Covetousness is both the root and stuff
   Of all I preach. That ought to be enough.
            "Well, then I give examples thick and fast
110 From bygone times, old stories from the past.
   A yokel mind loves stories from of old,
   Being the kind it can repeat and hold.
   What! Do you think, as long as I can preach
   And get their silver for the things I teach,
115 That I will live in poverty, from choice?
   That's not the counsel of my inner voice!
   No! Let me preach and beg from kirk to kirk
   And never do an honest job of work,
   No, nor make baskets, like St. Paul, to gain
120 A livelihood. I do not preach in vain.
   There's no apostle I would counterfeit;
   I mean to have money, wool and cheese and wheat
   Though it were given me by the poorest lad
   Or poorest village widow, though she had
125 A string of starving children, all agape.
   No, let me drink the liquor of the grape
   And keep a jolly wench in every town!
            "But listen, gentlemen; to bring things down
   To a conclusion, would you like a tale?

90 brethren (breᴛʜ′rən), *n. pl.* the fellow members of a church.

107 covetousness (kuv′ə təs-nis), *n.* desire for things that belong to others.

117 kirk, church.

119 make baskets . . . St. Paul, a reference to St. Paul the Hermit, not the Apostle Paul.

125 agape (ə gāp′), *adj.* open-mouthed with wonder or surprise.

130 Now as I've drunk a draught of corn-ripe ale,
By God it stands to reason I can strike
On some good story that you all will like.
For though I am a wholly vicious man
Don't think I can't tell moral tales. I can!
135 Here's one I often preach when out for winning;
Now please be quiet. Here is the beginning."

THE PARDONER'S TALE *Drunks*

. . . It's of three rioters I have to tell
Who, long before the morning service bell,
Were sitting in a tavern for a drink.
And as they sat, they heard the hand-bell clink
5 Before a coffin going to the grave;
One of them called the little tavern-knave
And said "Go and find out at once—look spry!—
Whose corpse is in that coffin passing by;
And see you get the name correctly too."
10 "Sir," said the boy, "no need, I promise you;
Two hours before you came here I was told.
He was a friend of yours in days of old,
And suddenly, last night, the man was slain,
Upon his bench, face up, dead drunk again.
15 There came a privy thief, they call him Death,
Who kills us all round here, and in a breath
He speared him through the heart, he never stirred.
And then Death went his way without a word.
He's killed a thousand in the present plague,
20 And, sir, it doesn't do to be too vague
If you should meet him; you had best be wary.
Be on your guard with such an adversary,
Be primed to meet him everywhere you go,
That's what my mother said. It's all I know."
25 The publican joined in with, "By St. Mary,
What the child says is right; you'd best be wary,
This very year he killed, in a large village
A mile away, man, woman, serf at tillage,
Page in the household, children—all there were.
30 Yes, I imagine that he lives round there.
It's well to be prepared in these alarms,
He might do you dishonor." "Huh, God's arms!"
The rioter, said, "Is he so fierce to meet?
I'll search for him, by Jesus, street by street.
35 God's blessed bones! I'll register a vow!
Here, chaps! The three of us together now,

■ The Pardoner admits to being "a wholly vicious man." What do you think of this confession?

6 knave (nāv), *n.* servant.
15 privy (priv′ē), *adj.* secret; hidden.
22 adversary (ad′vər ser′ē), *n.* opponent; enemy.
25 publican (pub′lə kən), *n.* tavern keeper.
28 tillage (til′ij), *n.* cultivation of land.

This pilgrim's badge from the 1300s shows Thomas à Becket riding in triumph as Archbishop of Canterbury. Pilgrims wore badges like this around their necks or pinned to their hats. What kind of souvenirs do pilgrims obtain today? ▼

Preach about Good Sell indulgence

Hold up your hands, like me, and we'll be brothers
In this affair, and each defend the others,
And we will kill this traitor Death, I say!
40 Away with him as he has made away
With all our friends. God's dignity! Tonight!"
      They made their bargain, swore with appetite,
These three, to live and die for one another
As brother-born might swear to his born brother.
45 And up they started in their drunken rage
And made towards this village which the page
And publican had spoken of before.
Many and grisly were the oaths they swore,
Tearing Christ's blessed body to a shred;
50 "If we can only catch him, Death is dead!"
      When they had gone not fully half a mile,
Just as they were about to cross a stile,
They came upon a very poor old man
Who humbly greeted them and thus began,
55 "God look to you, my lords, and give you quiet!"
To which the proudest of these men of riot
Gave back the answer, "What, old fool? Give place!
Why are you all wrapped up except your face?
Why live so long? Isn't it time to die?"
60   The old, old fellow looked him in the eye
And said, "Because I never yet have found,
Though I have walked to India, searching round
Village and city on my pilgrimage,
One who would change his youth to have my age.
65 And so my age is mine and must be still
Upon me, for such time as God may will.
      "Not even Death, alas, will take my life;
So, like a wretched prisoner at strife
Within himself, I walk alone and wait
70 About the earth, which is my mother's gate,
Knock-knocking with my staff from night to noon
And crying, 'Mother, open to me soon!
Look at me, Mother, won't you let me in?
See how I wither, flesh and blood and skin!
75 Alas! When will these bones be laid to rest?
Mother, I would exchange—for that were best—
The wardrobe in my chamber, standing there
So long, for yours! Aye, for a shirt of hair
To wrap me in!' She has refused her grace,
80 Whence comes the pallor of my withered face.
      "But it dishonored you when you began

🐾 What is the nature of the **group** that the three rioters form at this point? Do you think they will be able to keep their group intact long enough to fulfill their purpose?

■ Why do you suppose the rioters treat the old man the way they do?

70 mother's gate, the grave, the entrance to "mother earth."

78 shirt of hair, rough shirt made of horsehair, worn to make the wearer suffer as a penance.

To speak so roughly, sir, to an old man,
Unless he had injured you in word or deed.
It says in holy writ, as you may read,
85 'Thou shalt rise up before the hoary head
And honor it.' And therefore be it said
'Do no more harm to an old man than you,
Being now young, would have another do
When you are old'—if you should live till then.
90 And so may God be with you, gentlemen,
For I must go whither I have to go."

  "By God," the gambler said, "you shan't do so,
You don't get off so easy, by St. John!
I heard you mention, just a moment gone,
95 A certain traitor Death who singles out
And kills the fine young fellows hereabout.
And you're his spy, by God! You wait a bit.
Say where he is or you shall pay for it,
By God and by the Holy Sacrament!
100 I say you've joined together by consent
To kill us younger folk, you thieving swine!"

  "Well, sirs," he said, "if it be your design
To find out Death, turn up this crooked way
Towards that grove, I left him there today
105 Under a tree, and there you'll find him waiting.
He isn't one to hide for all your prating.
You see that oak? He won't be far to find.
And God protect you that redeemed mankind,
Aye, and amend you!" Thus that ancient man.
110   At once the three young rioters began
To run, and reached the tree, and there they found
A pile of golden florins on the ground,
New-coined, eight bushels of them as they thought.
No longer was it Death those fellows sought,
115 For they were all so thrilled to see the sight,
The florins were so beautiful and bright,
That down they sat beside the precious pile.
The wickedest spoke first after a while.
"Brothers," he said, "you listen to what I say.
120 I'm pretty sharp although I joke away.
It's clear that Fortune has bestowed this treasure
To let us live in jollity and pleasure.
Light come, light go! We'll spend it as we ought.
God's precious dignity! Who would have thought
125 This morning was to be our lucky day?

  "If one could only get that gold away,

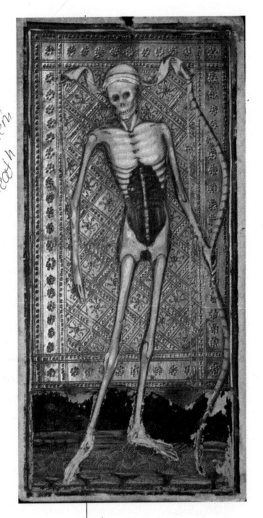

▲ This tarot card, part of a deck of playing cards from the 1400s, shows Death as a skeleton grasping an archer's bow in one hand and an arrow in the other. How is this representation of Death similar to the way Death is portrayed in *The Pardoner's Tale?* How is it different?

104 grove (grōv), *n.* group of trees.
112 florin, coin originally issued in Florence, Italy; various coins of the same name were later used in other European countries.

The Pardoner's Tale **53**

Back to my house, or else to yours, perhaps—
For as you know, the gold is ours, chaps—
We'd all be at the top of fortune, hey?
130 But certainly it can't be done by day.
People would call us robbers—a strong gang,
So our own property would make us hang.
No, we must bring this treasure back by night
Some prudent way, and keep it out of sight.
135 And so as a solution I propose
We draw for lots and see the way it goes;
The one who draws the longest, lucky man,
Shall run to town as quickly as he can
To fetch us bread and wine—but keep things dark—
140 While two remain in hiding here to mark
Our heap of treasure. If there's no delay,
When night comes down we'll carry it away,
All three of us, wherever we have planned."
        He gathered lots and hid them in his hand
145 Bidding them draw for where the luck should fall.
It fell upon the youngest of them all,
And off he ran at once towards the town.
        As soon as he had gone the first sat down
And thus began a parley with the other:
150 "You know that you can trust me as a brother;
Now let me tell you where your profit lies;
You know our friend has gone to get supplies
And here's a lot of gold that is to be
Divided equally amongst us three.
155 Nevertheless, if I could shape things thus
So that we shared it out—the two of us—
Wouldn't you take it as a friendly act?"
        "But how?" the other said. "He knows the fact
That all the gold was left with me and you;
160 What can we tell him? What are we to do?"
        "Is it a bargain," said the first, "or no?
For I can tell you in a word or so
What's to be done to bring the thing about."
"Trust me," the other said, "you needn't doubt
165 My word. I won't betray you, I'll be true."
        "Well," said his friend, "you see that we are two,
And two are twice as powerful as one.
Now look; when he comes back, get up in fun
To have a wrestle; then, as you attack,
170 I'll up and put my dagger through his back
While you and he are struggling, as in game;

134 **prudent** (prüd′nt), *adj.*
sensible; discreet.

This shield from the late 1400s was not intended for combat but for display at a tournament. The image of Death reflects the knight's willingness to die in battle to honor his lady. Why might images of death have been so widespread in medieval art?

Then draw your dagger too and do the same.
Then all this money will be ours to spend,
Divided equally of course, dear friend.
175 Then we can gratify our lusts and fill
The day with dicing at our own sweet will."
Thus these two miscreants agreed to slay
The third and youngest, as you heard me say.

   The youngest, as he ran towards the town,
180 Kept turning over, rolling up and down
Within his heart the beauty of those bright
New florins, saying, "Lord, to think I might
Have all that treasure to myself alone!
Could there be anyone beneath the throne
185 Of God so happy as I then should be?"

   And so the Fiend, our common enemy,
Was given power to put it in his thought
That there was always poison to be bought,
And that with poison he could kill his friends.
190 To men in such a state the Devil sends
Thoughts of this kind, and has a full permission
To lure them on to sorrow and perdition;
For this young man was utterly content
To kill them both and never to repent.

195   And on he ran, he had no thought to tarry,
Came to the town, found an apothecary
And said, "Sell me some poison if you will,
I have a lot of rats I want to kill
And there's a polecat too about my yard
200 That takes my chickens and it hits me hard;
But I'll get even, as is only right,
With vermin that destroy a man by night."

   The chemist answered, "I've a preparation
Which you shall have, and by my soul's salvation
205 If any living creature eat or drink
A mouthful, ere he has the time to think,
Though he took less than makes a grain of wheat,
You'll see him fall down dying at your feet;
Yes, die he must, and in so short a while
210 You'd hardly have the time to walk a mile,
The poison is so strong, you understand."

   This cursed fellow grabbed into his hand
The box of poison and away he ran
Into a neighbouring street, and found a man
215 Who lent him three large bottles. He withdrew
And deftly poured the poison into two.

177 miscreant (mis′krē ənt),
n. wicked person; villain.

186 Fiend, Satan; the devil.

■ Who do you think is going
to come out on top of
this situation?

192 perdition (pər dish′ ən),
n. damnation.

196 apothecary (ə poth′ə-
ker′ē), *n.* pharmacist.

202 vermin (vėr′mən), *n. pl.
or sing.* small animals, such as
roaches and mice, that are
troublesome or destructive.

He kept the third one clean, as well he might,
For his own drink, meaning to work all night
Stacking the gold and carrying it away.
220 And when this rioter, this devil's clay,
Had filled his bottles up with wine, all three,
Back to rejoin his comrades sauntered he.
       Why make a sermon of it? Why waste breath?
Exactly in the way they'd planned his death
225 They fell on him and slew him, two to one.
Then said the first of them when this was done,
"Now for a drink. Sit down and let's be merry,
For later on there'll be the corpse to bury."
And, as it happened, reaching for a sup,
230 He took a bottle full of poison up
And drank; and his companion, nothing loth,
Drank from it also, and they perished both.
       There is in Avicenna's long relation
Concerning poison and its operation,
235 Trust me, no ghastlier section to transcend
What these two wretches suffered at their end.
Thus these two murderers received their due,
So did the treacherous young poisoner too.

       "'O cursed sin! O blackguardly excess!
240 O treacherous homicide! O wickedness!
O gluttony that lusted on and diced!
O blasphemy that took the name of Christ
With habit-hardened oaths that pride began!
Alas, how comes it that a mortal man,
245 That thou, to thy Creator, Him that wrought thee,
That paid His precious blood for thee and bought thee,
Art so unnatural and false within?
       "'Dearly beloved, God forgive your sin
And keep you from the vice of avarice!
250 My holy pardon frees you all of this,
Provided that you make the right approaches,
That is with sterling, rings, or silver brooches.
Bow down your heads under this holy bull!
Come on, you women, offer up your wool!
255 I'll write your name into my ledger; so!
Into the bliss of Heaven you shall go.
For I'll absolve you by my holy power,
You that make offering, clean as at the hour
When you were born. . . .' That, sirs, is how I preach.
260 And Jesu Christ, soul's healer, aye, the leech
Of every soul, grant pardon and relieve you

233 Avicenna's long relation.
Avicenna was an eleventh-
century Arab physician who
wrote a reference book (the
"long relation") on poison.
242 blasphemy (blas′fə mē),
n. abuse of or contempt for
God.
257 absolve (ab solv′), *v.*
free a person from guilt or
punishment for sin.
260 leech, here, doctor. In
earlier times physicians used
leeches to draw blood from
patients as a method of
treating diseases.

Of sin, for that is best, I won't deceive you.
　　　　"One thing I should have mentioned in my tale,
Dear people. I've some relics in my bale

265 And pardons too, as full and fine, I hope,
As any in England, given me by the Pope.
If there be one among you that is willing
To have my <u>absolution</u> for a shilling
Devoutly given, come! and do not harden

270 Your hearts but kneel in humbleness for pardon;
Or else, receive my pardon as we go.
You can renew it every town or so
Always provided that you still renew
Each time, and in good money, what is due.

275 It is an honor to you to have found
A pardoner with his credentials sound
Who can absolve you as you ply the spur
In any accident that may occur.
For instance—we are all at Fortune's beck—

280 Your horse may throw you down and break your neck.
What a security it is to all
To have me here among you and at call
With pardon for the lowly and the great
When soul leaves body for the future state!

285 And I advise our Host here to begin,
The most enveloped of you all in sin.
Come forward, Host, you shall be the first to pay,
And kiss my holy relics right away.
Only a groat. Come on, unbuckle your purse!"

290 　　　　"No, no," said he, "not I, and may the curse
Of Christ descend upon me if I do!
You'll have me kissing your old breeches too
And swear they were the relic of a saint. . . ."
　　　　The Pardoner said nothing, not a word;

295 He was so angry that he couldn't speak.
"Well," said our Host, "if you're for showing <u>pique</u>,
I'll joke no more, not with an angry man."
　　　　The worthy Knight immediately began,
Seeing the fun was getting rather rough,

300 And said, "No more, we've all had quite enough.
Now, Master Pardoner, perk up, look cheerly!
And you, Sir Host, whom I esteem so dearly,
I beg of you to kiss the Pardoner.
　　　　"Come, Pardoner, draw nearer, my dear sir.

305 Let's laugh again and keep the ball in play."
They kissed, and we continued on our way.

264 bale, bundle.

268 absolution (ab′sə-lü′shən), *n.* a declaration that frees a person from guilt or punishment for sin.

285 Host, the keeper of the Tabard Inn, where the pilgrims gather before setting out. The Host proposes the story-telling and accompanies the pilgrims to judge which tale is best.

296 pique (pēk), *n.* anger; wounded pride.

298 Knight, another one of the pilgrims.

After Reading

Making Connections

Shaping Your Response

1. In one word or phrase, describe the Pardoner.

2. The Pardoner admits to being a "wholly vicious man" (line 133) and yet he preaches moral tales designed to show that avarice is a vice. Do you think he represents typical human behavior? Explain.

Analyzing the Narrative Poem

3. The three rioters set out to find "this traitor Death." Instead, they find the old man, who directs them to the tree where they find the money. Who do you think the old man is?

4. After relating his tale, the Pardoner tries to sell the pilgrims his pardon and offers his relics for kissing. How likely is it that the pilgrims will buy his indulgences?

5. In your opinion, does *The Pardoner's Tale* illustrate the **theme** of his Latin text, "Radix malorum est cupiditas"? Explain.

Extending the Ideas

6. Chaucer wrote *The Pardoner's Tale* in the 1300s. Relate some examples you have heard from the 1990s of people like the three rioters who cause their own downfalls or deaths.

Literary Focus: Irony

Irony lies in the contrast between what appears to be and what really is. In situational irony, something occurs contrary to what the characters expect or intend. Explain the irony in these situations from *The Pardoner's Tale:*

1. The tavern keeper tells the rioters, "you'd best be wary" of Death, but they swear that when they catch him, "Death is dead!"

2. The "very poor old man" claims that Death won't take his life.

3. The three rioters look for Death under a tree in a nearby grove. When they find money instead, they forget about looking for Death.

4. After his tale, the Pardoner tells the other pilgrims that it is "an honor" for them to have found him.

Vocabulary Study

An analogy is a relationship. An analogy can be expressed this way:

TREE : GROVE :: house : village (Read: "Tree is to grove as house is to village.")

Word analogy tests require you to determine the relationship between a pair of words and then to choose another pair of words with the same relationship. In this example, you would first determine that a tree is found in a grove and then look for another pair of words in which something (house) is found in something else (village). Word analogies may reflect relationships such as antonyms (love : enmity); synonyms (abject : miserable); cause-effect (gunshot : injury); or person-place (teacher : classroom).

Study the relationship of each of the following pairs of words in capital letters; then choose another pair that has the same relationship.

1. AVARICE : GREED ::
   a. vice : wickedness   **b.** church : tavern
   c. minister : sermon   **d.** spring : fall

2. PUBLICAN : TAVERN ::
   a. rage : anger   **b.** death : life
   c. preacher : pulpit   **d.** writer : poet

3. ADVERSARY : FRIEND ::
   a. fish : water   **b.** heat : cold
   c. wheat : grain   **d.** wing : bird

4. SIN : ABSOLUTION ::
   a. rainstorm : flooding   **b.** fever : medicine
   c. imagination : fancy   **d.** sadness : tears

5. INSULT : PIQUE ::
   a. dislike : hate   **b.** twilight : night
   c. velvet : cloth   **d.** praise : pleasure

Expressing Your Ideas

Writing Choices

Writer's Notebook Update Choose some of the people you have listed who are representative of society today and who might go on a modern-day pilgrimage. Write character descriptions of two or three of them.

The Homeville Tales Use the notes you wrote in your notebook and plan a **television series** in which the travelers and their tales would be updated. Describe the cast of characters and the place where they meet to share their stories.

Other Options

In the Flesh? Create an **illustration** for *The Pardoner's Prologue* or *Tale* in any medium that you wish. Your work might be on paper, modeled in clay, or created from cloth or canvas. Or, you might choose to mime or to act out the story using simple costumes and props.

Heaven for Sale In order to increase business, the Pardoner has hired you as his publicity agent. Create a **poster** that will advertise what the Pardoner has to offer and that will increase sales of indulgences. Remember that an effective picture and a good, snappy headline may be more effective than a lot of words.

Before Reading

from Sir Gawain and the Green Knight

The Gawain–poet
late 1300s

Who is the author? We don't know. Although four of his works, including *Sir Gawain* (gä′wän) *and the Green Knight,* survive in a single manuscript, we don't even know the author's name. What was he like? There at least we can make some guesses. He wrote in a provincial dialect which suggests he lived in the West Midlands, northwest of London. He entertained his aristocratic audience with descriptions of the grandeur of English castles and the fierceness of the English countryside. He knew details of castle life and courtly behavior. He believed in the search for knightly perfection.

Building Background

The Medieval Romance In the medieval period the term *romance* had little to do with romantic love; it meant instead a long narrative in verse or prose telling of the adventures of a hero. These stories usually include knights, ladies in distress, kings, villains—and often a touch of the supernatural. Central to the medieval romance is the **code of chivalry,** the rules and customs connected with knighthood. Originally *chivalry* (from the French word *chevalier,* meaning "knight" or "horseman") referred to the training of knights for warfare. The concept broadened to include qualities of courtly behavior: bravery, honor, courtesy, generosity, respect for women, protection of the weak, and fairness to enemies. The materials for the medieval romance in English are mainly drawn from the stories of King Arthur and the knights of the Round Table at Camelot, where Arthur held his court (see also pages 88–93), as is *Sir Gawain and the Green Knight*.

Literary Focus

Foreshadowing Many authors make a point of dropping hints to their readers, suggestions about what's to come later in the action. This technique, called **foreshadowing,** creates suspense and encourages the reader to guess about future events and the outcome of the story. Sometimes a single word, sometimes a description, sometimes a character's action—or lack of action—will be just the hint that starts the reader guessing. As you read this romance, look for hints about what Gawain will face.

Writer's Notebook

Knight in Shining Armor When you hear the phrase "knight in shining armor," you might imagine a handsome, heroic figure charging into battle. Yet the medieval code of chivalry extended far beyond strength and bravery. Create a diagram in which you list in one circle qualities that you imagine a medieval knight would possess. In the other circle, list the traits you think a modern "knight" should possess. What traits do they share? List them where the circles overlap.

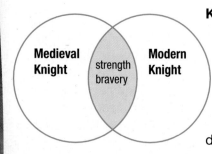

SIR GAWAIN AND THE GREEN KNIGHT

translated by
M.R. RIDLEY

Part 1

King Arthur lay at Camelot at Christmas, with many of his lords, great knights, all the noble brotherhood of the Round Table, and they kept high revel with carefree merrymaking. There were many tourneys, with gallant jousting of knights, and after the jousting they rode to the court for song

Legends of King Arthur and his Knights of the Round Table have inspired writers, poets, and artists for centuries. This painting entitled *Sir Galahad* by George Frederick Watts (1817–1904) shows an interpretation from the 1800s. What elements of knighthood are idealized here? ➤

and dance; the festival went on full fifteen days, with all the banqueting and jollity that could be devised.

On New Year's Day there was a great banquet, with double portions, for the whole company. First, Mass was sung in the chapel, with loud chanting of the priests and the rest, and they celebrated the octave of Christmas.[1] When the service came to an end, the King came into the great hall with his knights, and some hurried forward with the New Year's gifts held high above their heads, and there was a busy contest for them; those that won a prize were glad, but even the ladies who won nothing laughed at their failure. So they made merry till it was time for dinner, and then they washed and went to their appointed seats, the noblest, as was right, at the high table. In the center of the dais[2] sat the Queen, Guenevere,[3] with her clear gray eyes, loveliest of ladies, splendidly gowned.

But Arthur would not sit down to eat till all the rest were served. He was so glad in his youth, and boyish in his eagerness, and his young blood ran high and his mind was restless, so that he never could be idle or sit still for long. But there was something else that kept him from his seat, a custom that his high heart had devised, that on a great festival such as this he would eat no meat till he had heard some strange tale of adventure, of the deeds of princes, or feats of arms, some great wonder which he might listen to and believe; or it might be that some strange knight would come, and ask him to name one of his own true knights to joust[4] with him, each staking his life on his skill, and granting the other such advantage as fortune should bring him.

So the tables were set with the choicest fare, and the trumpets sounded a fresh fanfare as a sign that the feast might begin. But the notes had hardly died away when there swung in at the hall door a fearsome warrior, the tallest of all on earth. From the neck to the waist he was so thick-set and squarely built, and he was so long in flank and limb, that one might have thought he was half a

giant; but he was in fact a man, as mighty as any horse could bear in saddle, but yet shapely in his mightiness, burly in back and breast, but slender in the waist and with clean-run limbs. They were all amazed at his color, for they saw that he was bright green all over. His clothes were green, too. He wore a plain close-fitting coat of green, and over that a gay green mantle, lined with close-trimmed white fur. The hood of the mantle was the same, green outside and lined with white fur, and he had thrown it back off his hair so that it lay on his shoulders. His legs were clothed in long green hose, close-fitting, so that you could see the play of the muscles under them. He rode a huge green horse; his mane and his tail, green as the rest of him, were curled and combed and plaited with thread-of-gold and adorned with emeralds.

They all looked at him in wonder, as he sat there on his great horse, flashing and bright as the lightning; and they thought that if it came to fighting there could be no man in the world who could withstand him, so mighty a warrior he seemed. But he wore no armor, no helmet, nor hauberk, nor gorget;[5] he carried no shield, nor lance, nor sword. In one hand he held a bunch of holly, the tree that stays greenest of all when the leaves fall from others in autumn. But in the other hand he grasped his one weapon, and a terrible enough weapon it was, a prodigious[6] battle-ax, with a spike sticking out beyond the head.

The Green Knight rode up the hall, right to the dais, fearless of danger. He greeted no one as he rode, but looked straight before him over

---

1. **the octave of Christmas.** The observance of major feasts like Christmas occupied a full week, concluding on the eighth day.
2. **dais** (dā′is), *n.* a raised platform at one end of a hall for a throne or seats of honor.
3. **Guenevere** (gwen′ə vir).
4. **joust** (joust), *v.* fight on horseback with spear-like lances.
5. **hauberk** (hô′bərk), *n.* . . . **gorget** (gôr′jit), *n.* A hauberk was a flexible coat of armor made of small loops of chain linked together. A gorget was a piece of armor for the throat.
6. **prodigious** (prə dij′əs), *adj.* huge.

their heads, and the first words he spoke were: "Where is the ruler of this company? It is he that I want to see and to have plain speech with him." And with that he let his eyes rove over the company, and scanned each man to see who might seem to be a knight of renown.

Long they gazed at him, astonished what this marvel might mean, the Green Knight on the green horse, greener than grass, both gleaming more like a piece of jewelry, green enamel on gold, than like flesh and blood. They all scanned him, to see what it was that stood there, and walked round him, wondering what his purpose was. They had seen many marvels, but never before such a marvel as this, and they thought he must be some phantom from the land of Faërie.[7] And all were amazed at his words, and some were afraid to answer, and some waited in courtesy for the King to make reply. So they sat still as stones, and there was heavy silence through the great hall, as though they were all asleep.

There was Arthur's adventure for him, plain before his eyes. He stood before the dais, fearless, and gave the stranger a ready salutation. "You are welcome, sir, to this place. I am the master of this house, and my name is Arthur. Light down from your horse, I pray you, and stay and eat with us, and after that let us know what your will is."

But the Green Knight answered him: "Not so; so God help me, who sits throned above the skies, it was none of my errand to wait any while in this dwelling. But your renown, my lord, is spread wide about the world, and the warriors that live in your castle are held to be the best, the stoutest to ride out in their steel-gear, bravest and worthiest of all men on earth, valiant to contend with in all fair contests, and here, I have heard it

THEY HAD SEEN MANY MARVELS, BUT NEVER BEFORE SUCH A MARVEL AS THIS. . . .

told, all the true ways of courtesy are known. It is that which has drawn me hither today. You may be sure by this branch which I bear in my hand that I come in peace, seeking no danger. For if I had made my journey with battle in my thoughts, I have a hauberk at home, and a helmet, a shield and a sharp spear, bright-shining, and other weapons too, and I can wield them. But since I look for no war, I wear the softer clothes of a traveler. If you are bold as all men tell, you will grant me freely the sport that I ask for."

Arthur said, "Sir knight, even if it is just a combat that you crave, we can find a man to fight you."

"No," said he. "I am telling you the truth, it is no fight that I am seeking. All who are sitting around the hall are no more than beardless children, and if I were buckled in my armor, and riding my war charger, there is no man here who could match his feeble might against mine in combat. All I ask in this court is just a Christmas game, seeing that it is the time of Noel and New Year, and here are many young warriors. If there is any man in this hall who counts himself bold enough, hot in blood and rash in brain, stoutly to change stroke for stroke with me, I will give him, as a free gift, this battle-ax. It is heavy enough, and he can wield it as he pleases. I shall abide the first blow, unarmed as I am now. If any man is bold enough to test what I say, let him come swiftly to me and grasp this weapon—I quit-claim[8] it forever, and he can keep it for his own—and I shall stand up to his stroke, steady on the floor of this hall. But you must proclaim my right to have a free blow at him in return, though I will grant him the respite

---

7. **Faërie** (fā′ėr ē), fairyland.
8. **quit-claim,** give up claim to.

of a year and a day. Now let us see quickly, dares any man speak?"

SUMMARIZE: What Christmas challenge does the Green Knight offer to the court?

They had been astonished at first, when he rode into the hall, but they were stiller than ever now, both high and low. The Green Knight turned in his saddle, and his angry eyes roved savagely over the rows of sitting men, and he bent his bristling eyebrows, that flashed green as he moved, and he waved his beard as he sat and waited for someone to rise. And when no one answered his challenge he coughed scornfully, and gave himself a great stretch with an air of insulting them, and started to speak.

"Well," said he, "is this Arthur's house, of which the renown runs through so many kingdoms? What has happened to your conceit and your boasted conquests, the fierceness of your wrath and your high words? All the revels and the renown of the famous Round Table are overturned with one word of one man, for you are all cowering for fear, and no one has lifted a finger." And he threw back his head, and laughed loud in their faces. The King felt the insult, and shame made the blood rush to his fair forehead and cheek, as the tempest of his anger rose, and he felt the anger also of his knights rising all round him. And he moved boldly forward, and stood by the Green Knight's stirrup, and spoke.

"Sir, by heaven, what you ask is foolishness. If it is folly that you seek, it is folly you shall rightly find. There is not a man in this hall that is afraid of your big words. Give me your battle-ax, for God's sake, and I will grant you myself the boon[9] you have asked for." He gave him his hand, and the knight got proudly down from the saddle to the floor. Arthur took the ax in his hand, and grasped the helve,[10] and swung it this way and that, trying the weight to see what the feel of it would be when he struck. The stout warrior stood there before him, towering head and shoulders above any man in the hall. He stood grimly stroking his beard, and not a muscle in his stern face moved as he drew down his coat, no more daunted or dismayed for the stroke that was coming than if someone on the seat beside him had offered him a goblet of wine.

Then Gawain, from where he sat by the Queen's side, leaned forward and spoke to the King. "I pray you, my lord, in plain words, let this combat be mine. Bid me rise from my seat and stand by you, so that without discourtesy to my liege[11] lady the Queen I can leave her side; and I will give you my counsel before all this noble company. In truth it is not seemly, when such a challenge is thrown out in your hall, that you yourself should be so eager to take it up, when there are sitting all round you so many of your knights. There are none in the world firmer of will, or stauncher fighters on a stricken field. I may be the weakest of all of them, and the feeblest of wit; there is nothing about me to praise except that you are my uncle, and all the virtue that is in me is the blood I share with you. But since this business is so foolish, and beneath your dignity as King, and since I have made my request first, grant it to me. Whether I have spoken fittingly or not, I leave to this company to decide. Let them speak their minds freely."

QUESTION: What questions do you have about the way Gawain describes himself and his behavior to this point?

So the knights whispered together, and they were all of one mind, that the crowned King should be relieved of the challenge, and Gawain given the game.

Then the King commanded Gawain to rise from his place; and he rose quickly, and came

---

9. boon (bün), *n.* favor.
10. **helv** (helv), *n.* handle.
11. liege (lēj), *adj.* honorable; having a right to respect and service.

and knelt before the King, and grasped the great ax. And the king let him take it, and lifted up his hand and gave him the blessing of God, and cheerfully bade him be hardy both of heart and hand. "Take care, cousin,"[12] he said, "over your blow; and if you direct it aright I am well sure that you will stand up to the blow that he will deal you later."

Gawain went to the Green Knight with the battle-ax in hand, and the Knight waited for him, calm and undismayed, and spoke to Gawain. "Before we go forward with this business, let us say over again our covenant.[13] First, I ask you, sir, tell me truly your name."

"I am called Gawain," he said, "I that am to deal you this buffet,[14] whatever happens later; and a year from today I will come, and no man else with me, and you shall deal me another blow in return, with what weapon you will."

And the Green Knight answered. "Sir Gawain, so may I thrive as I am wondrously eager that you shall let drive at me. By God, sir, I am glad that it is from your hand that I am to get what I asked for here; and you have rehearsed exactly, point by point, all the covenant that I sought of the King, except this—Promise me, on your honor, that at the year's end you yourself will come and seek me out wherever you think I may be found, and take from me the wages for whatever you deal me today before this noble company."

"Where am I to look for you?" said Gawain. "Where do you live? By God who made me, I know nothing of your dwelling, nor from what king's court you come, nor your name. Tell me truly your name, and where you live, and I will use all the skill I have to win my way thither; and

> THE FAIR HEAD FELL FROM THE NECK AND ROLLED AMOUNG THE FEASTERS, WHO PUSHED IT AWAY WITH THEIR FEET.

that I swear on my troth[15] as a true knight."

"That is enough for New Year," said the Green Knight; "I need no more. If, when you have done me the courtesy of your blow, I tell you my house and my home and my own name, you will know all about me and be able to keep tryst.[16] And if I do not speak, you will be all the better off, for you can stay in your own land, and seek no further. But enough words! Take your grim tool in your hand, and let us see what kind of a man you are with the ax!"

"Gladly, sir knight," said Gawain, and ran his finger along the edge of the ax.

The Green Knight at once took up his stand, with his head a little bent, and his long hair thrown forward over the crown of his head, so that the naked flesh of his neck showed ready for the stroke. Gawain gripped his ax, and put his left foot forward to get his balance; then he hove up the ax above his head and brought it down swiftly and surely on the bare flesh, so that the sharp steel shore clean through the flesh and the bones and clove his neck in two, and the bright blade drove on and bit into the ground. The fair head fell from the neck and rolled among the feasters, who pushed it away with their feet. The blood spurted from the body and shone bright on the green mantle. The Green Knight did not fall nor even stagger, but

---

12. **cousin.** This term was loosely used to express close kinship.
13. **covenant** (kuv′ə nent), *n.* solemn agreement.
14. **buffet** (buf′it), *n.* blow; strike.
15. **troth** (trôth), *n.* faithfulness; loyalty.
16. **tryst** (trist), *n.* appointed meeting.

strode firmly forward among the knights, and laid hold of his fair head and lifted it up. Then he turned to his horse, gathered the reins, put his foot in the stirrup-iron and swung himself into the saddle. He held his head by the hair, in his hand, and settled himself in his seat as calmly as though nothing had happened to him, though he sat there headless; and he turned himself about, his gruesome bleeding trunk, and many were in dread of him before he had ended what he had to say.

For he held the head in his hand, and turned it so that it faced full at the guests on the high table. And the eyelids lifted, and the eyes gazed at them wide open; and the lips moved, and the head spoke.

"Sir Gawain, be prompt to come as you have promised and seek faithfully till you find me, as you have sworn now in this hall in the hearing of these knights. Make your way to the Green Chapel, I charge you, to receive such a blow as you have just dealt—well you deserve it—to be promptly paid on the morning of next New Year's Day. For men know me as the Knight of the Green Chapel. Seek therefore to find me and fail not, but come, or be called recreant[17] for ever."

With that he gave a roar, and wheeled his horse, and flung out at the hall door with his head in his hand; and the sparks flashed from the flints beneath his horse's hooves. To what land he went no man knew, any more than they had known whence he had come to them. The King and Gawain laughed together at the strangeness of the adventure, but all men there kept it in their hearts for a marvel.

Now take good heed, Sir Gawain, that you do not shrink, but go through to the end with this perilous venture that you have taken upon you.

A year later, after a feast in his honor, Sir Gawain sets off to keep his promise to the Green Knight. After journeying through grim landscapes and fighting dragons, ogres, and wild beasts, Gawain arrives, half dead with the cold and the sleet, at a shimmering castle. There he is warmly welcomed by the lord of the castle. Following days filled with Christmas feasting, games, and music, the lord of the castle plans three days of hunting in the forests and fields, but urges Gawain to rest in the castle in preparation for his upcoming challenge. The lord also offers a bargain to Gawain: "Whatever game I kill in the forest, it shall be yours, and whatever good fortune you come by here, give me that in exchange, whether it is of trifles or of something better." They agree to exchange their winnings at the end of each day.

On the first day the lord and his men hunt and kill many swift deer. In the meantime, Gawain, approached in his bed by the queen, reluctantly accepts a single kiss from her. At day's end the king gives Gawain his kill; in return Gawain kisses the king. At the end of the second day, the king returns with a huge boar for Gawain, who, having had a second visit from the queen, kisses the king twice.

Part 2

Gawain lay and slept quietly and sound all night, but the lord, who was full of his hunting, was up and about with the dawn. After they had heard Mass they ate a hasty breakfast, and the lord asked for his horse and went out to meet his knights, who were ready for him, dressed and mounted before the gates of the hall. It was a glorious morning; the hoarfrost sparkled bright on the ground, and the sun rose fiery red against the cloudrack, and his bright rays cut through the mists overhead. The huntsmen uncoupled by the side of a coppice,[18] and the rocks in the wood rang to the notes of the horns. Some of the hounds picked up the scent of the fox where he was lying, and they dashed this way and that across it as they were trained. One of them gave

---

17. recreant (rek′rē ənt), *n.* coward.
18. coppice (kop′is), *n.* a thicket of small trees.

tongue on it, the huntsman called to him, and all the rest made after him, panting in full cry on a high scent. The fox ran before them, and soon they made him break covert, and as soon as they saw him they bayed furiously. He twisted and turned through many a rough patch of undergrowth, and doubled back, and often waited in the bottom of a hedge to listen. So the cunning fox led them, the lord and his men, all round and about, over hill and dale, till noon.

Meantime Gawain at home slept soundly through the cold morning within the fair curtains. But the lady could not sleep for she was still set in her heart on making love to him. She came in and closed the door behind her. Then she threw open a window, and called to Gawain and mocked him gaily.

"Gawain, Gawain, how can you sleep so sound on so bright a morning?"

Gawain was deep sunk in sleep, but at this he woke and heard her.

He had been deep in gloomy dreams, and muttering as he dreamed, like a man troubled with a throng of dreary thoughts, how that day he had to meet his destiny at the Green Chapel, when he encountered the Green Knight, and had to stand up to his stroke and make no resistance. But when that gracious lady came in he came to his waking senses, and swam up out of his dreams, and made haste to answer her greeting. The lady came to him, laughing sweetly, and bent over him and softly kissed him, and he welcomed her with good cheer. And when he saw her so lovely and so gaily arrayed, with her flawless beauty and her sweet color, joy welled up and warmed his heart. And they smiled gently at each other, and fell into gay talk, and all was joy and happiness and delight between them. It would have been a perilous[19] time for both of them, if Mary[20] had not taken thought for her knight. For that noble princess urged him so, and pressed him so hard to confess himself her lover, that at last he must needs either accept her love or bluntly refuse her. And he was troubled for his courtesy, for fear that he should behave like a churl, but more afraid of a wound to his honor, if he behaved badly to his host, the lord of the castle. And that at any rate, he said to himself, should not happen. So he laughed a little, though kindly, and put aside all the fond loving words that sprang to her lips.

And she said, "You are to blame, Gawain, if you have no love for the woman that holds you so near her heart, of all women on earth most sorely stricken, unless it is that you already have a lover that pleases you better, and you plighted your troth to her so surely that you will not break faith—and that is what I am coming to believe. Tell me the truth now, for God's sake, and do not hide it, nor make any pretense."

With a kindly smile, said Gawain, "By St. John I have no lover, nor will have one now."

"That," said she, "hurts more than anything else you could say. But I have my answer, and it wounds. Give me one kiss, and I will leave you. There is nothing left for me but sorrow, for I love you dearly." She stooped with a sigh and gave him a sweet kiss, and then she stood up, and said as she stood by him, "Now, my dear, as I go away, do at least this for me; give me some gift, if it is only your glove, that I can have something to remind me of you and lessen my grief."

"I wish I had here," said Gawain, "for your sake, the most precious thing I have in the world. You have deserved ten times over a richer gift of thanks than any I could offer. But to give you a love gift would avail but little, and it is not fitting for your honor to have a glove as a keepsake of Gawain."

"Well," said the lovely lady, "Gawain, noblest of knights, even if I can have nothing of yours, you shall have something of mine." And she held out to him a rich ring of the red gold, with a bright jewel blazing on it that flashed as bright as the sunrays. It was worth a king's ransom, but Gawain refused it.

---

19. **perilous** (per'ə ləs), *adj.* dangerous.
20. **Mary,** the mother of Jesus, here thought of as Gawain's guardian saint.

She said, "If you refuse my ring, because it seems too rich, and you will not be so beholden to me, then I will give you my girdle, which is a cheaper gift." And she took hold of a belt that was fastened round her waist, clasped over her tunic under the bright mantle. It was fashioned of green silk, and trimmed with gold, embroidered only round the edges and adorned with pendants. That she offered to him, and besought him to take it, unworthy gift though it was. But he said that he would accept nothing, neither gold nor keepsake.

"Now are you refusing this silk," said she, "Because it seems so cheap a gift? It seems so, I know, a small thing and of little value. But if a man knew the powers that are knit into its fabric, he might hold it at a higher rate. Any man that is girt with this green girdle, when it is close clasped around him, there is no man under heaven that can cut him down, and he cannot be slain by any skill upon earth."

Then Gawain thought about it again, and it came into his head that this was the very thing for the peril that lay before him, when he came to the chapel to meet his doom, and that if he could escape death he would owe much to the charmed girdle. So he was more patient with her as she pressed it on him, and let her speak on. She offered it to him again, and prayed him earnestly to take it, and in the end he consented, and she gave it him eagerly. But she besought him for her sake never to reveal it, but to keep it loyally hidden from her lord. And he promised her that no man should ever know of it, but themselves only. And he thanked her many times and deeply from the bottom of his heart. And she kissed him the third time. Then she took her leave and left him there.

CLARIFY: What gift does Gawain accept from the queen? What special powers does she claim it possesses?

Let us leave him there at his ease, with love all about him, and go back to the lord who was still out in the country at the head of his hunt. By now he had killed the fox that he had hunted all day. As he jumped a hedge to get a view of the rascal, and heard the pack that sped after him, he had seen the fox making his way through a tangled thicket, and all the pack in full cry at his heels. He watched him and waited carefully and drew his bright sword and aimed at him. The fox swerved from the steel, and would have drawn back, but a hound was on him before he could recover, and there right before the horse's hooves they all fell on him and worried[21] him.

The lord dismounted in haste and grasped the fox, snatching him quickly from the hounds' mouths, and held him high over his head and hollaed at the top of his voice, while the hounds bayed fiercely round him. The huntsmen hurried to his call, and then they skinned the fox, and then turned homeward, for it was near nightfall, blowing great blasts on the horns as they rode. At length the lord got down at his own castle, and found there a fire burning brightly on the hearth, and Gawain beside it.

He met his host in the middle of the hall, and greeted him merrily, and said to him courteously, "Tonight I will be the first to make good our covenant, that we made with so happy an outcome, and sealed it with the draught of wine." Then he embraced the lord and give him three kisses, as loving and eager as he could make them.

"By God!" said the lord, "you are doing well at your new trade, if you made a cheap bargain."

"No matter for the bargain," said Gawain at once, "so long as I have paid you in full what I owed you."

"Marry," said the other, "mine are poor winnings to set beside yours, for I have hunted all day and I have nothing to show for it but this miserable fox skin—the devil take it!—and that is a poor exchange for the precious things that

---

21. **worry** (wèr′ē), *v.* seize with the teeth.

◄ 🐾 A knight and a lady are shown in a garden in this painting from the 1400s. What **group** codes or rules for behavior do they seem to you to be obeying—or breaking?

you have pressed on me, three such warm and loving kisses."

"None the less," said Gawain, "I thank you."

And the lord told him all the tale of the hunt as they stood there. And he appointed one of his men to set Gawain on his way, and bring him over the hills, so that he should have no trouble with his road, and guide him through woodland and brake by the shortest track. Gawain thanked him for his kindness, and then he took his leave of the noble ladies. Then they brought him with lights to his room, and left him to go content to bed. Perhaps he slept less soundly than before, for he had much on his mind for the morrow to keep him awake.

Let him lie there peacefully, for now he is near the goal that he has been seeking. If you will listen, I will tell you how they fared.

Part 3

And New Year's Day drew near, and the night passed, and day drove hard on the heels of the dark. And all the wild weather in the world seemed to be about the castle. There were clouds above that sent their cold breath down to the ground, and there was bitter cold from the north, torturing all ill-clad men. And the snow shivered down bitingly, and pinched all the wild creatures. And the whistling wind swooped down from the heavens and in the dales drove the snow into great drifts.

Sir Gawain and the Green Knight **69**

Sir Gawain listened as he lay in his bed, and for all that he kept his eyes shut it was little he slept. And as each cock crew he knew that his hour was coming nearer. Swiftly he got up, before the dawn, by the dim light of a lamp that gleamed in his room, and he called to his servant, who answered him straightaway, and bade him bring his mail shirt and saddle his horse. The servant rose and brought Gawain his clothes, and dressed him in his full armor. Gawain put this armor on, as gleaming a warrior as any between Britain and the far land of Greece, and he thanked his man, and told him to bring his horse.

And while he put on the glorious clothes—his coat, with the badge clearly worked on velvet, trimmed and set about with precious stones, with embroidered seams, and lined inside with fur—yet he did not leave off the love lace, the lady's gift. That, you may be sure, Gawain for his own sake did not forget. When he had belted on his sword round his hips, then he wound twice round his waist, swiftly and close, the green silken girdle, fit for a fair knight and shining out against the splendid scarlet of the cloth. But it was not for its richness that he wore it, or for pride in its pendants that glittered with the gleam of polished gold, but to save his life, when he had to stand in the face of danger, and, by his covenant, not stir a weapon in his own defense. And now the brave knight was ready to go out to his fate.

There was Gringolet[22] ready waiting for him, his great war-charger. So Gawain rode his way with the one squire who was to guide him on his road to the dolorous[23] place where he was to abide the grim onslaught. They passed by banks where all the boughs were bare, and the icy cold seemed to cling to the cliffs under which they rode. The clouds rode high, but there was ill weather under them. The mist drizzled on the moor and was heavier on the tops of the hills, so that each had a cap and a cloak of mist about it.

The streams swirled and broke about their banks, and foamed white as they came down in spate.[24] It was a hard wandering way they had to find when it lay through woods, till it came to the hour of dawn. Then they were high on a hill, and the white snow lay all round them. And his squire bade Gawain halt.

"Now I have brought you hither, my lord, and you are not far from the place which you have asked for and sought so earnestly. But now I shall tell you the truth, since each day that I have known you the more I have grown to love you; if you would do as I advise, you would fare the better. The place that you press forward to is held full perilous. In that waste land there dwells a man as evil as any on earth. He is stalwart, and grim, and a lover of blows, and mightier than any man on middle-earth, huger than Hector of Troy[25] or any four knights of Arthur's house. And this is what he does at the Green Chapel. There is never a man passes that way, however proud of his prowess in arms, but he smites him down and kills him. He is a violent man, and he knows no mercy in his heart, and I tell you the truth, if once you come there, no matter if you had twenty lives, you are a dead man, if the knight has his will with you. He has dwelt here a long time, and fought many combats, and there is no guard against his grim blows.

"Therefore, for God's sake, sir, leave the man well alone, and go some other way and ride to another country, where Christ may be your speed. And I will turn home again, and I promise you besides that I will keep our secret truly, and never let drop a word that you flinched from meeting any man."

"All the thanks of my heart," said Gawain, slowly, "and good luck to you, who wish me well.

---

22. **Gringolet** (gring′gə let).
23. dolorous (dol′ər əs), *adj.* sorrowful.
24. spate (spāt), *n.* a sudden flood.
25. **middle-earth . . . Hector of Troy.** Middle-earth is an archaic term for the world. Hector was the greatest warrior in the ancient Trojan War.

I am sure that you would truly keep my secret; but however close you kept it, if I now turned aside, and made haste to flee in the way you tell me to, then I should be a coward knight, and there could be no excuse."

Then he spurred Gringolet, and picked up the track, and made his way along the bank by the side of a shaw,[26] and rode along the rough bank right down to the dale. He reined in Gringolet and halted, and turned on this side and that, looking for the chapel.

IN THAT WASTE LAND THERE DWELLS A MAN AS EVIL AS ANY ON EARTH.

He saw nothing like it anywhere, and he thought this strange. Then a little way away over the field he saw a small mound, a smooth swelling knoll, by the waterside where a cascade fell down, and the water of the brook bubbled in the basin as though it were boiling. Gawain gave Gringolet his head and came to the mound, and got down quietly and fastened the reins to the rough bough of a lime tree. Then he walked over to the mound, and strode all round it, wondering what it was. There was a hole in one end, and one on each side, and it was all overgrown with patches of grass; whether it was only an old cave or just a split in a rock, he could not make out.

"Well!" said he, "is this the Green Chapel? This is the kind of place where the devil might say matins[27] at midnight! It is a desolate place, and this chapel, if it is the chapel, is evil looking, all overgrown. It is the right place for the knight in green to perform his devotions after the devil's fashion. I am beginning to think in my heart that it is the fiend that has appointed me this tryst, to destroy me here. It is an unchancy chapel, bad luck to it, the least hallowed church that ever I came into!"

With helm on head and lance in hand he came up to the mound, and then he heard, from a rock high up on a hill beyond the brook, a wondrous loud noise. Hark! it re-echoed on the cliff with the sound of a scythe being whetted on a grindstone. Hark! it whirred and rasped, like water at a mill; it rushed and rang, fearful to hear. Then said Gawain, "By God, this device, I think, is meant to greet me and to sound the challenge for me as I come. God's will be done. To say 'Woe is me!' does not help in the least. And though I may have to give up my life, no mere noise is going to scare me."

Then Gawain called aloud, "Who is master here, to keep tryst with me? For now am I, Sir Gawain, walking here and ready. If any man wants aught[28] of me, let him come hither quickly, now or never, to work his will."

"Stay," said a voice from the bank above his head, "and swiftly you shall have all that I once promised you."

Yet the speaker went on for a while with the noise of his whetting before he would come down. Then he made his way down by the side of a crag, and came hurtling out of a crack in the rock with a grim weapon, a new Danish ax, with a massive blade on it, curving by the haft, whetted with a whetstone, and four foot long, measured by the thong that gleamed bright on the haft. There was the Green Knight, appareled as before, the same in his face and his limbs, his locks and his beard, except that this time he strode firmly on his feet, setting the haft to the ground beside him as he walked. And when he came to the water, not wanting to wade

---

26. **shaw,** a small wood or grove.
27. **matins** (mat′nz), morning prayers.
28. **aught** (ôt), *pron.* anything.

it, he used his ax as a jumping pole and leaped over, and came striding lissomely[29] forward, fierce and fell,[30] over the broad stretch of snow that lay all around.

Sir Gawain bent his head no farther than he must for courtesy, and greeted him. The other said, "Sir knight, now men may know that you are one who keeps tryst. Gawain, so God guard me, I tell you you are very welcome to my dwelling, and you have timed your travelings as a true man should. You know the covenants that we made between us. Twelve months ago today you took what chance gave you and I was to give you prompt quittance this New Year's Day. Here we are in this valley by our two selves, and there are no men to part us, however tight we lock swaying in combat. Take your helm off your head, and take your wages, making no more resistance than I made then, when you whipped my head off at one blow."

"Nay," said Gawain, "by the Lord God who gave me life, I shall have no grudge against you, not a grain, for any harm that may fall to me. But keep yourself to the one stroke, and I will stand still, and give you free leave to strike as you will." So he leaned his head down and bared his neck, showing the white skin, making as though he did not care, and giving no sign of fear.

Then the Green Knight got himself quickly ready, took firm hold of his grim tool to smite Gawain, and gathered every ounce of strength in his body together as he rose to the stroke, and drove at him as mightily as though he had a mind to destroy him. And if it had fallen as hard and as true as he seemed to intend, the doughtiest[31] warrior alive would have been dead of the blow. But Gawain glanced sideways at the blade as it came swooping down to strike him to the earth, and he could not help his shoulders shrinking a little from the keen steel. And the Green Knight with a turn of his wrist swerved the blade aside, and then he told Gawain what he thought of him.

"You cannot be Gawain, that is held so good a knight, who never, they say, quailed for any host of men on hill or on dale. And now you flinched like a coward before you felt even a scratch. That is not what I have ever heard of Gawain. I did not flinch nor flee when you aimed your blow at me, and I made no evasions in Arthur's hall. My head fell at my feet, but did I flinch? Not I. And now you quail before any harm comes to you. So I deserve to be called a better knight than you are."

Said Gawain, "I shrank once, but I will not again, even if my head falls on the stones, though I cannot, like you, put it back again on my shoulders if it does! Get ready again, and come to the point. Deal me my doom, and do it out of hand. I will stand up to your stroke, and start away no more till your ax has struck me, and I pledge my troth to that."

"Have at you then," said the other, and hove up the ax, and looked at him as fiercely as though he were mad with anger, and aimed a mighty blow at him; but just as the blade came down he held back before it could wound him. Gawain awaited the stroke steadfastly, and flinched this time not the least, but stood still as a stone or the stump of a tree that is anchored with a hundred roots round a rock in the ground.

Then merrily spoke the Green Knight: "Hm! Now that you have got your courage back, it is time to hit you in earnest. Throw back the hood that Arthur gave you, and see whether your neck can stand the blow that is coming."

To which Gawain, now full of wrath, replied in anger, "Drive on, fierce knight; you are too long over your threats. I wonder that you are not scared by your own fierceness."

"Faith," said the Green Knight, "if you are so furious, I will not delay, nor be slow in letting you have what you have come for. Ready!" Then he took his stance for the stroke, and set his lips and

---

29. lissomely (lis′əm lē), *adv.* limberly; supplely.
30. fell (fel), *adj.* fierce; savage.
31. doughtiest (dou′tē əst), *adj.* bravest.

knit his brows. It was no wonder that Gawain, with no hope of rescue, little liked the look of him.

He lifted the ax lightly and let it deftly down just by the bare neck. And though he swung at him hard he did him no more hurt than to graze him on one side, so that the very tip of the blade just broke the skin, and the bright blood spurted over his shoulders to the ground. And when Gawain saw the blood red on the snow, he leapt forward more than a spear length, and seized his helm and set it on his head, and gave a twitch with his shoulders to bring his shield round in front of him, and flashed out his bright sword, and spoke fiercely—Never since his mother bore him had he been so gay, now that his trial was over.

"Stop your blows, sir, and deal me no more. I have endured one stroke in this place without making any return; but if you deal me another, be very sure that I will pay it back forthwith, and give you blow for blow again. There is only the one blow due to fall to me here—those were the terms of the covenant made between us in Arthur's hall—so now, good sir, hold your hand."

The Green Knight held off and rested on his ax, the haft on the ground and his arms on the blade, and he watched Gawain standing there, bold and fearless, full armed again, and with never a thought of flinching. And he was glad to see it, and he spoke cheerfully to him in a great voice, so that his words rang clear like bells.

"Good knight, be not so wrathful. No man has here misused you unmannerly, or treated you otherwise than as the covenant allowed, which we made at the King's court. I promised you a stroke, and you have had it and you can count yourself well paid. That blow is full quittance[32] of all that you owe me. Had I wished, I could perhaps have dealt you a buffet more harshly, and done you injury. But, as it was, first I threatened you with a feint, and gave you no wound. That was for the agreement we made the first night at my castle, and for the next day, when you kept troth loyally, and gave me back, like a true man, your gains for the day. And the second feint was for the next day after, when again you had my dear lady's kisses and gave me them again. For those two days I aimed the two strokes at you that were no more than feints and did you no scathe. A true man pays his debts and then need fear no danger. But the third time you failed in your trust, and for that you had to take your third blow and the wound.

"For it is my own green girdle that you are wearing, and it was my own wife that gave it you. I know all about your kisses, and the love-making of my wife, and how you bore yourself, for it was I myself that brought it about. I sent her to make trial of you, and surely I think that you are the most faultless knight that ever trod upon earth. As a pearl for price by the side of a white pea, so, by God's truth, is Gawain beside other gay knights. But just over the girdle, sir, you failed a little, and came short in your loyalty; yet that was not for any intrigue nor for love-making, but just that you loved your life, and I do not blame you for it."

Gawain stood in thought a long while, so overcome with grief that he groaned in his heart, and all the blood in his body seemed to rush to his face as he winced for shame at what the Green Knight said. And the first words that he said were, "Curse upon cowardice and covetousness both; there is evil power in them to destroy a man's virtue." Then he laid his hand to the knot of the girdle, and loosed it, and threw it savagely from him to the Green Knight, and said, "Lo, there is my broken faith, curse on it. I was afraid of your blow, so cowardice taught me to make terms with covetousness, and forget my true nature, the generosity and loyalty that belong to true knights. Now I have shown myself false, I that ever was afraid of any treachery or untruth, and hated them. I make my confession to you, sir knight, between the two of us. I have behaved very ill. Let me now do what I can to gain your good will; and afterwards I will show that I have learned my lesson."

---

32. **quittance** (kwit′ns) *n.* release from debt or obligation.

This illuminated (highly decorated) capital letter from the manuscript of a romance of the 1300s shows Sir Gawain. What does his costume suggest to you about the job of a knight?

The Green Knight laughed, and said to him friendlily, "Such harm as I took, I count it wholly cured. You have made such free confession that all your faults are cleansed, and besides you have done your penance at the edge of my blade. I hold you purged of all your offenses and as clean as if you had never failed in virtue since the day you were born. And I give you the gold-hemmed girdle that is green as my gown. Sir Gawain, you will be able to think back on this day's contest when you ride out among great princes. It will be a noble token of the meeting of two chivalrous knights at the Green Chapel. And now, this very New Year's Day, you shall come back with me to my castle, and we will finish off happily the rest of the revel[33] that we left." He pressed him to come, and said, "We must put you on good terms again with my wife, who behaved as your enemy."

"Nay," said Gawain, and took hold of his helm and lifted it from his head, and thanked the Green Knight. "I have stayed too long already. All happiness be yours, and may the great God grant it you, he that brings honor to men. Commend me to your fair and gracious lady, and to that other also, those two whom I honor, who with their devices so cunningly beguiled[34] me. But it is no marvel if a fool goes astray in his wits, and through the wiles of women comes to sorrow.

"But for your girdle—and may God reward you for your kindness—that I will wear with the best will in the world, not for the sake of the splendid gold, nor the silk, nor the pendants that hang from it, nor its costliness, nor the lovely work in it, nor for the honor that I shall get when I am seen wearing it, but as a memorial of my sin. I shall look at it often when I ride out proudly, and I shall feel remorse in my heart for the fault and frailty of the erring flesh, which is so ready to catch the infection and the stain of ill-doing. So when pride stirs in my heart for my prowess in arms, one glance at the love lace will humble me. But there is one thing I would ask you. Will you tell me your true name that you are called by? Then I will ask no more."

"I will tell you truly," said the other. "Bercilak de Haut-desert[35] I am called in my own land. And it is the might of Morgan la Fay[36] that has brought all this about. She dwells in my house, and she knows all the cunning of magical lore and the crafty ways of it, and has learned the mysteries of Merlin,[37] for once she had dealings in love with that great wizard, who knows all your knights at home. And so Morgan the goddess is her name, and there is never a man so high and proud but she can humble and tame him.

"It was she who sent me to your splendid halls, to make trial of your pride, and to see

---

33. **revel** (rev′əl) v. noisy good time.
34. **beguile** (bi gīl′) v. entertain; amuse.
35. **Bercilak de Haut-desert** (bėr′sə läk də ō′dā ser).
36. **Morgan la Fay,** "Morgan the Fairy," King Arthur's half-sister, a witch who continually plots against him.
37. **Merlin,** a wizard, Arthur's teacher and counselor.

whether there was truth in the report that runs through the world of the great renown of the Round Table. She sent this marvel to steal your wits away from you, and she hoped to have daunted Guenevere and brought her to death with dismay at that same strange figure that stood like a phantom before the high table, and spoke from the head that he held in his hand. She is that ancient lady whom you saw at my castle, and she is your own aunt, Arthur's half-sister, daughter of that Duchess of Tintagel on whom Uther[38] later begat Arthur, that now is King. So now I ask you, sir knight, come back to my halls and meet your aunt again, and by my faith I wish you as well as any man on earth for your true loyalty."

But Gawain still said no, and could not be persuaded. So they embraced and kissed and commended each other to the Prince of Paradise, and parted there in the snow. Gawain mounted and rode off, hasting to the King's castle, and the knight in the bright green went his own way.

And Gawain on Gringolet, with his life given back to him, rode through many wild ways, sometimes with a roof over his head at night, and sometimes sleeping under the stars. He had many adventures by the way, and won many victories. The wound in his neck was healed, and he wore the shining girdle about it, slantwise like a baldric[39] to his other side, and fastened under his left arm in a knot, the token of his fault, to remind him of the stain of it. So he came to the court, sound and whole. And great joy rose in the castle when the great King knew that the good Sir Gawain was come, and rejoiced over it. And the King kissed the knight, and the Queen too, and then many a true knight thronged round him to greet him and ask him how he had fared. He told them all the wonders, all the hardships he had, the adventure at the chapel, and the way the Green Knight dealt with him, the love of the lady, and at last the love lace. And he bared his neck and

showed them the wound that he took at the knight's hand as punishment for his failure in troth. When he came to the telling of this part he was tormented, and groaned for grief and sorrow, and the blood rushed to his cheeks with the shame of what he had to confess.

"See, my lord," said Sir Gawain, and laid his hand on the girdle, "this is the band that is sign of my fault, my disgrace, the mark of the cowardice and the covetousness that I yielded to, the token of my broken troth. And I must needs wear it as long as I live. For no man can hide his scar, nor rid himself of it; when once it is fastened upon him it will never depart."

> 🌿 Predict: Why will Gawain always wear the green belt? How will the brotherhood of the Round Table demonstrate their group solidarity with Gawain?

The King comforted the knight, and all the court laughed kindly, and agreed, to cheer him, that all the lords and ladies of the Round Table, everyone of the brotherhood, should wear a slanting baldric of bright green, just like Gawain's. So that became a part of the glory of the Round Table, and ever after a man that wore it was honored. So the ancient books of romance tell us.

And may He that wore the crown of thorns bring us to His bliss.

---

38. **Tintagel** (tin taj′əl) . . . **Uther.** Tintagel is an area in Cornwall, in southwest England, associated in legend with Arthur's birth. Uther Pendragon was Arthur's Father.
39. baldric (bôl′drik), *n.* a belt hung from one shoulder to the opposite side of the body, to support the wearer's sword.

After Reading

Making Connections

Shaping Your Response

1. In your opinion, does the fact that the Green Knight uses magic make him more or less a challenge? Does it make Gawain more or less a hero?

Analyzing the Romance

2. Why is it appropriate that the Green Knight's challenge is taken up by Sir Gawain instead of by King Arthur himself?

3. Point out elements of magic or the supernatural that appear throughout this legend. Why do you suppose they are included?

4. How does the author illustrate examples of the code of chivalry and courtly love? Use examples from the text in your answer.

5. Why does Gawain throw away the green girdle? Why does he retrieve it?

Extending the Ideas

6. 🐾 What does the behavior of the members of King Arthur's court reveal about how these people as a **group** regard insults to honor? Compare their reactions with the reactions of people today who are insulted or mocked.

7. It is important for Gawain to keep his part of the bargain with the Green Knight, yet he has very good reasons to want to break his promise. What circumstances would cause you to break—or keep—a promise you had made?

Literary Focus: Foreshadowing

The warning of the squire who guides Sir Gawain, the appearance of the Green Chapel, the strange sound Gawain hears: each is a different kind of **foreshadowing** of Gawain's second meeting with the Green Knight. What does each hint about what might happen at that meeting? What other examples of foreshadowing can you find?

Vocabulary Study

Many of the words in *Sir Gawain and the Green Knight* are archaic, or at least they are not used very much today. Match each numbered definition with its lettered word. You will not use all the words.

1. brave
2. favor
3. sudden flood
4. sorrowful
5. huge

a. hauberk
b. prodigious
c. boon
d. liege
e. spate

f. recreant
g. dolorous
h. lissomely
i. doughtiest
j. baldric

Expressing Your Ideas

Writing Choices

Writer's Notebook Update Look again at the qualities you listed for a modern "knight in shining armor." Select a characteristic that you consider to be important and write a paragraph explaining why that trait is desirable for a modern knight.

How Perfect Can You Get? Sir Gawain has often been called the perfect knight. The challenges he faces at the hands of the Green Knight test his character greatly, yet he comes through. Write a one-page **character sketch** of Sir Gawain in which you describe how he changes or matures as a result of his experiences.

Destroyers of Virtue "Curse upon cowardice and covetousness both; there is evil power in them to destroy a man's virtue," says Gawain after he learns from the Green Knight the truth about his ordeal. Write an **essay** in which you agree or disagree with Gawain's claim. Support your position with specific examples from other literary sources or with anecdotes from real life.

Well-Versed Choose one of the exploits of Sir Gawain and turn it into a **poem, song lyric,** or **rap.** Perform your work for the class.

Other Options

What's Important to Me The medieval knight, proud of his heritage, his skill, and his devotion to duty, displayed his personal heraldic shield, a colorful coat of arms. This carefully constructed design immediately indicated to any observer those elements of his life that were most important to him. Design a **coat of arms** for Sir Gawain or for yourself. Your coat of arms should reflect family background, personal character, interests, and accomplishments.

True Then, True Now You are a television journalist working on a magazine show. (Think of *Sixty Minutes*.) Create an **interview** with Sir Gawain (or any one of the other characters). Ask about what the character did and why he or she did it. You might want to confront one character with what another character says. (For example: "Morgan la Fay, Bercilak de Haut-desert claims that you can humble and tame any man, no matter how high and proud. Why would you want to do that?") If possible, videotape your segment to screen in class.

Before Reading

The Day of Destiny from Morte Darthur

by Sir Thomas Malory

Sir Thomas Malory
1400?–1471

We are not sure of the exact identity of the author of the *Morte Darthur* ("The Death of Arthur"). The most likely candidate is Sir Thomas Malory of Newbold Revell, a knight from Warwickshire who led a very different life from the chivalrous and gallant knights of the story. Malory served in Parliament briefly and may have fought in France. In 1450 he seems to have become involved in a feud with another noble. Such feuds were common in England at the time. Malory and his men rustled cattle, kidnapped prisoners, and raided churches. He was arrested in 1451. Malory seems to have made powerful enemies, who kept him in jail off and on for years awaiting trial, though he was eventually released. Later in life Malory was again jailed, probably for siding against the Yorkist faction in the Wars of the Roses. While in Newgate Jail, Malory gathered the tales of Arthur and retold them in *Morte Darthur,* the most complete single version of the legends of King Arthur and his court. Malory may have died in jail.

Building Background

History or Legend? According to Gerald of Wales, a writer who was alive at the time, on a cool morn in 1190 four monks, carrying pickaxes and shovels, stole away to the burial ground at Glastonbury Abbey, a Christian monastery in the southwest of England. There, under the cover of mist, they began to dig. Several feet down, metal clinked on stone. The monks soon uncovered a grave marker and a cross with the words: "Here lies buried the renowned King Arthur in the Isle of Avalon." A few feet farther down, they unearthed a huge oak log, inside of which was a large skeleton with a smashed skull and a smaller skeleton with wisps of golden hair—the remains of the legendary King Arthur and Queen Guinevere! Fact or fiction? Truth or hoax? History or legend? That there was a historical figure behind the legend of Arthur is generally accepted. But through many centuries the imaginations of storytellers in many nations have transformed history into something very different from fact.

In *Morte Darthur,* when Arthur's illegitimate son Mordred discovers the secret love affair between Guinevere and Sir Lancelot, he brings about a crisis that leads to war between him and King Arthur. In this selection, the war is coming to its end.

Literary Focus

Protagonist/Antagonist The **protagonist,** the main or lead character, is always the character most central to the action of a story. Often the protagonist possesses heroic qualities. In contrast to the protagonist is the **antagonist,** the character who opposes or is in conflict with the main character. As you read, observe the techniques the author uses to signal the reader who is the protagonist here.

Writer's Notebook

Leading the Way King Arthur, the leader of his country, is renowned for establishing order in a lawless land and for defending what is right and just. Do these same principles hold true for leaders throughout history? Make a list of characteristics you expect any leader in any nation must have in order to be effective.

THE DAY of DESTINY

SIR THOMAS MALORY

And quickly King Arthur moved himself with his army along the coastline westward, toward Salisbury. And there was a day assigned betwixt King Arthur and Sir Mordred, that they should meet upon a field beside Salisbury and not far from the coast. And this day was assigned as Monday after Trinity Sunday,[1] whereof King Arthur was passing glad that he might be <u>avenged</u>[2] upon Sir Mordred.

Then Sir Mordred stirred up a crowd of people around London, for those from Kent, Sussex and Surrey, Essex, Suffolk, and Norfolk stayed for the most part with Sir Mordred. And many a full noble knight drew unto him and also to the King; but they that loved Sir Lancelot drew unto Sir Mordred.

So upon Trinity Sunday at night King Arthur dreamed a wonderful dream, and in his dream it seemed that he saw upon a platform a chair, and the chair was fixed to a wheel,[3] and there upon sat King Arthur in richest cloth of gold that might be made. And the King dreamed there was under him, far below him, a hideous deep black water, and therein were all kinds of serpents and dragons and wild beasts foul and horrible. And suddenly the King dreamed that the wheel turned up side down, and he fell among the serpents, and every beast took him by a limb. And the King cried out as he lay in his bed,

"Help! help!"

And then knights, squires, and yeomen[4] awaked the King, and then he was so amazed that he knew not where he was. And so he remained awake until it was nearly day, and then he fell into a slumber again, neither sleeping nor completely awake.

Then it seemed to the King that there came Sir Gawain unto him with a number of fair ladies with him. So when King Arthur saw him he said,

---

1. **Trinity Sunday,** the eighth Sunday after Easter.
2. avenge (ə venj′), *v.* revenge.
3. **wheel.** The wheel of fortune, symbolizing the rapid changes of human destiny, was a favorite medieval image.
4. **squires . . . yeomen.** A squire (skwīr) was a personal attendant to a knight; a yeoman (yō′mən) was a member of the king's bodyguard.

"Welcome, my sister's son. I thought you had died! And now I see thee alive, great is my debt to Almighty Jesus. Ah, fair nephew, who be these ladies that come hither with you?"

"Sir," said Sir Gawain, "all these be fair ladies for whom I have fought for, when I was a living man. And all these are those that I did battle for in righteous quarrels, and God hath given them that aid for their earnest prayers; and because I did battle for them for their rights, they brought me hither unto you. Thus hath God given me leave for to warn you of your death: for if ye fight tomorrow with Sir Mordred, as ye both have agreed, doubt ye not ye shall be slain,[5] and the greatest part of your people on both sides. And for the great concern and good that Almighty Jesus has had for you, and for pity of you and many other good men that shall be slain, God hath sent me to you of His special grace to give you warning that in no way ye do battle tomorrow, but instead that ye make a treaty for a month and a day. And request this urgently, so that tomorrow you can delay. For within a month shall come Sir Lancelot with all his noble knights, and rescue you loyally, and slay Sir Mordred and all that ever will stay with him."

> **PREDICT: What visions come to King Arthur in his dreams? What do they fore-shadow might happen?**

Then Sir Gawain and all the ladies vanished, and at once the King called upon his knights, squires, and yeomen, and charged them quickly to fetch his noble lords and wise bishops unto him. And when they were come the King told them of his vision; that Sir Gawain had told him and warned him that if he fought on the morn, he should be slain.

◄ This illustration from the 1400s shows King Arthur and his son Mordred battling each other at Camlan. What does their style of fighting suggest about what kind of people they were?

Then the King commanded Sir Lucan the Butler and his brother Sir Bedivere the Bold, with two bishops with them, and charged them in any way to make a treaty for a month and a day with Sir Mordred:

"And spare not, offer him lands and goods as much as ye think reasonable."

So then they departed and came to Sir Mordred where he had a grim host of a hundred thousand, and there they entreated[6] Sir Mordred a long time. And at the last Sir Mordred agreed for to take over Cornwall and Kent during King Arthur's lifetime; and after that all England, after the days of King Arthur.

Then were they agreed that King Arthur and Sir Mordred should meet betwixt both their hosts, and each of them should bring fourteen persons. And so they came with this word unto Arthur. Then he said,

"I am glad that this is done"; and so he went into the field.

And when King Arthur departed he warned all his host that if they saw any sword drawn, "look ye come on fiercely and slay that traitor, Sir Mordred, for I in no way trust him." In like manner Sir Mordred warned his host that "and ye see any manner of sword drawn, look that ye come on fiercely and so slay all that before you stand, for in no way will I trust in this treaty." And in the same way said Sir Mordred unto his host: "for I know well my father will be avenged upon me."

And so they met as they had arranged, and were agreed and accorded thoroughly. And wine was fetched, and they drank together. Just then came an adder out of a little heath-bush, and it stung a knight in the foot. And so when the knight felt himself so stung, he looked down and saw the adder; and at once he drew his sword to slay the adder, and thought of no other harm. And when the host on both sides saw

---

5. slay (slā), v. **slew, slain, slaying.** kill with violence.
6. entreat (en trēt′), v. beg.

that sword drawn, then they blew trumpets and horns, and shouted grimly, and so both hosts attacked each other. And King Arthur mounted his horse and said, "Alas, this unhappy day!" and so rode to his men, and Sir Mordred in like wise.

And never since was there seen a more grievous battle in no Christian land, for there was only slashing and riding, thrusting and striking, and many a grim word was there spoken of one to the other, and many a deadly stroke. But ever King Arthur rode through the battle against Sir Mordred many times and acted full nobly, as a noble king should do, and at all times he never hesitated. And Sir Mordred did his utmost that day and put himself in great peril.

And thus they fought all the day long, and never ceased 'till the noble knights were fallen on the cold earth. And yet they fought still 'till it was near night, and by then was there a hundred thousand lay dead upon the earth. Then was King Arthur wild with wrath beyond measure, when he saw his people so slain because of him.

And so he looked about himself and could see no more of all his host and of good knights left no more alive but two knights: Sir Lucan the Butler and his brother, Sir Bedivere; and yet they were very badly wounded.

"Jesus have mercy!" said the King, "where are all my noble knights gone? Alas, that ever I should see this grievous day! For now," said King Arthur, "I am come to mine end. But would to God," said he, "that I knew now where were that traitor Sir Mordred that hath caused all this mischief."

Then King Arthur looked about and was aware where stood Sir Mordred leaning upon his sword among a great heap of dead men.

"Now give me my spear," said King Arthur unto Sir Lucan, "for yonder I have seen the traitor that all this woe hath wrought."[7]

"Sir, let him be," said Sir Lucan, "for he brings misfortune. And if ye pass this unfortunate day ye shall be right well revenged. And, good lord, remember ye of your night's dream and what the

spirit of Sir Gawain told you last night, and God of His great goodness hath preserved you hitherto. And for God's sake, my lord, leave this battle, for, blessed be God, ye have won the field; for yet be here three alive, and with Sir Mordred is not one alive. And therefore if ye leave now, this wicked day of destiny is past!"

"Now come death, come life," said the King, "now I see him yonder alone, he shall never escape my hands! For at a better advantage shall I never have him."

"God speed you well!" said Sir Bedivere.

Then the King took his spear in both his hands, and ran towards Sir Mordred, crying out and saying,

"Traitor, now is thy death-day come!"

And when Sir Mordred saw King Arthur he ran towards him with his sword drawn in his hands, and there King Arthur struck Sir Mordred under the shield, with a thrust of his spear, through and beyond the body more than a foot. And when Sir Mordred felt that he had his death's wound he thrust himself with the might that he had up to the hand guard of King Arthur's spear, and then he smote[8] his father, King Arthur, with his sword holding it in both his hands, upon the side of the head, so that the sword pierced the helmet and the outer membrane of the brain. And with that Sir Mordred dashed down stark dead to the earth.

And noble King Arthur fell in a swoon[9] to the earth, and there he swooned several times, and Sir Lucan and Sir Bedivere several times lifted him up. And so weakly betwixt them they led him to a little chapel not far from the sea, and when the King was there, he thought himself reasonably eased.

Then heard they people cry in the field.

"Now go thou, Sir Lucan," said the King,

---

7. wrought (rôt), v. ARCHAIC. a past tense and a past participle of **work.**
8. smite (smīt), v. **smote, smit ten** or **smote, smiting.** hit; give a hard blow to.
9. swoon (swün), n., v. faint.

"and help me to learn what means that noise in the field."

So Sir Lucan departed, though he was grievously wounded in many places; and as he rode he saw and noticed by the moonlight how the plunderers and robbers were come into the field to plunder[10] and to rob many a full noble knight of brooches and bracelets and of many a good ring and many a rich jewel. And those that were not yet dead, there they slew them for their armor and their gold.

When Sir Lucan understood this he came to the King as soon as he might, and told him all which he had heard and seen.

"Therefore by my advice," said Sir Lucan, "it is best that we bring you to some town."

"I would that it were so," said the King, "but I may not stand, my head fails so. . . . Ah, Sir Lancelot!" said King Arthur, "this day have I missed thee! And alas, that ever I was against thee! For now I have my death, whereof Sir Gawain warned me in my dream."

Then Sir Lucan took up the King on one side and Sir Bedivere the other side, and in the lifting up the King swooned, and in the lifting Sir Lucan fell in a swoon, and part of his guts fell out of his body, and with that the noble knight's heart burst. And when the King awoke he beheld Sir Lucan, how he lay foaming at the mouth and part of his guts lay at his feet.

"Alas," said the King, "this is to me a very sad sight, to see this noble duke die so for my sake, for he would have helped me that had more need of help than I! Alas, that he would not complain for himself, for his heart was so set to help me. Now Jesu have mercy upon his soul!"

Then Sir Bedivere wept for the death of his brother.

"Now leave this mourning and this weeping, gentle knight," said the King, "for all this will not help me. For know thou well, if I might live myself, the death of Sir Lucan would grieve me evermore. But my time passeth on fast," said

the King. "Therefore," said King Arthur unto Sir Bedivere, "take thou here Excalibur,[11] my good sword, and go with it to the yonder water side; and when thou comest there, I charge thee throw my sword in that water, and come again and tell me what thou seest there."

"My lord," said Sir Bedivere, "your commandment shall be done, and lightly bring you word again."

So Sir Bedivere departed. And on the way he beheld that noble sword, and the pommel and the haft[12] was all precious stones. And then he said to himself, "If I throw this rich sword in the water, of this shall never come good, but harm and loss." And then Sir Bedivere hid Excalibur under a tree, and so as soon as he might he came again unto the King and said he had been at the water and had thrown the sword into the water.

"What saw thou there?" said the King.

"Sir," he said, "I saw nothing but waves and wind."

"That is untruly said by thee," said the King. "And therefore go thou lightly again, and do my commandment; as thou art to me beloved and dear, spare not, but throw it in."

Then Sir Bedivere returned again and took the sword in his hand; and yet he thought it a sin and shame to throw away that noble sword. And so again he hid the sword and returned again and told the King that he had been at the water and done his commandment.

"What sawest thou there?" said the King.

"Sir," he said, "I saw nothing but lapping waters and darkening waves."

"Ah, traitor unto me and untrue," said King Arthur, "now hast thou betrayed me twice! Who

---

10. plunder (plun′dər), v. steal by force, especially during war.

11. **Excalibur** (ek skal′ə bər), the sword that Arthur had received as a young man from the Lady of the Lake and that he must return at the time of his death. It served as his symbol of kingship.

12. **pommel . . . haft.** A pommel is a rounded knob on the haft, which is the handle of a sword.

In *The Last Sleep of Arthur in Avalon,* painted by Sir Edward Burne-Jones between 1881 and 1898, the dying King is cared for by a queen and her ladies. What is the mood of the painting? How does the artist create that mood? ➤

would believe that thou hast been to me so beloved and dear, and also named so noble a knight, that thou would betray me for the wealth of this sword? But now go again lightly; for thy long tarrying putteth me in great jeopardy of my life, for I am growing cold. And if thou do not now as I bid thee, if ever I may see thee, I shall slay thee by mine own hands, for thou wouldst for my rich sword see me dead."

Then Sir Bedivere departed and went to the sword and lightly took it up, and so he went unto the water side. And there he bound the belt about the hilt, and threw the sword as far into the water as he might. And there came an arm and an hand above the water, and took it and seized it, and shook it thrice and brandished,[13] and then vanished with the sword into the water.

So Sir Bedivere came again to the King and told him what he saw.

"Alas," said the King, "help me hence, for I dread me I have tarried[14] over long."

Then Sir Bedivere took the King upon his back and so went with him to the water side. And when they were there, even close by the bank floated a little barge with many fair ladies on it, and among them all was a queen, and all of them had black hoods. And all of them wept and shrieked when they saw King Arthur.

"Now put me into that barge," said the King.

And so he did softly, and there received him three ladies with great mourning. And so they set him down, and in one of their laps King Arthur laid his head. And then the queen said,

---

13. brandish (bran′dish), *v.* wave or shake threateningly.
14. tarry (tar′ē), *v.* delay.

"Ah, my dear brother! Why have ye tarried so long from me? Alas, this wound on your head hath caught overmuch cold!"

And then they rowed away from the land, and Sir Bedivere beheld all those ladies go away from him. Then Sir Bedivere cried out and said,

"Ah, my lord Arthur, what shall become of me, now ye go from me and leave me here alone among mine enemies?"

"Comfort thyself," said the King, "and do as well as thou mayest, for in me is no trust for to trust in. For I must go into the vale of Avilion[15] to heal me of my grievous wound. And if thou hear never more of me, pray for my soul!"

But ever the queen and ladies wept and shrieked, that it was pitiful to hear. As soon as Sir Bedivere had lost sight of the barge he wept and wailed, and so entered the forest and traveled all night.

CLARIFY: How is King Arthur transported to his resting place?

And in the morning he was aware, betwixt two wan woods, of a chapel and a hermitage. Then was Sir Bedivere fearful, and thither he went, and when he came into the chapel he saw where lay a hermit groveling[16] on all fours, close there by a tomb was new dug. When the hermit saw Sir Bedivere he knew him well, for he was but little before Bishop of Canterbury that Sir Mordred put to flight.

"Sir," said Sir Bedivere, "what man is there here buried that ye pray so earnestly for?"

"Fair son," said the hermit, "I know not truly but only guess. But this same night, at midnight, there came a number of ladies and brought here a dead corpse and prayed me to bury him. And here they offered a hundred candles, and they gave me a thousand coins."

"Alas!" said Sir Bedivere, "that was my lord King Arthur, which lieth here buried in this chapel."

Then Sir Bedivere swooned, and when he awoke he prayed the hermit that he might stay with him still, there to live with fasting and prayers:

"For from hence will I never go," said Sir Bedivere, "by my will, but all days of my life stay here to pray for my lord Arthur."

"Sir, ye are welcome to me," said the hermit, "for I know you better than you think that I do: for ye are Sir Bedivere the Bold, and the full noble Duke Sir Lucan the Butler was your brother."

Then Sir Bedivere told the hermit all as ye have heard before, and so he remained with the hermit that was before the Bishop of Canterbury. And there Sir Bedivere put upon himself poor clothes, and served the hermit full lowly in fasting and in prayers.

Thus of Arthur I find no more written in books that have been written, nothing more of the very certainty of his brave death I never read . . .

Yet some men say in many parts of England that King Arthur is not dead, but had by the will of Our Lord Jesu gone into another place; and men say that he shall come again, and he shall win the Holy Cross. Yet I will not say that it shall be so, but rather would I say: here in this world he changed his life. And many men say that there is written upon the tomb this:

HIC IACET ARTHURUS,
REX QUONDAM REXQUE FUTURUS.

Here Lies Arthur,
King Once and King That Will Be.

---

15. **Avilion** (ə vil′yən), often called **Avalon** (av′ə lon), a legendary island, an earthly paradise, the final resting place of King Arthur.
16. grovel (gruv′əl), v. crawl humbly on the ground.

After Reading

Making Connections

1. If you were Sir Bedivere, do you think you would react the same way he does about the sword Excalibur?

2. Why do you think Arthur insists on fighting Mordred man-to-man?

3. What do the plunderers Sir Lucan sees on the battlefield suggest to you about England's future after Arthur's death?

4. In your opinion, how realistic are Malory's descriptions of battle scenes?

5. On the night before he is scheduled to go into battle Arthur has two dreams. What do these dreams seem to **foreshadow?**

6. What is **ironic** about the episode with the adder?

7. What elements of magic or the supernatural do you find in this legend?

8. According to Malory, people have continued to believe for centuries that King Arthur did not die, but that he is waiting to return to rule again. Why might people be attracted to such a belief?

9. The tales of Authur and his court have continued to intrigue writers and readers for centuries. Modern authors such as John Steinbeck, Mary Stewart, and Marion Zimmer Bradley have all penned their versions of the legend, and dozens of movies have dealt with characters and events of Arthur's court. Why do you think this story still holds such fascination?

Literary Focus: Protagonist/Antagonist

How is it made clear that King Arthur is the **protagonist** and that Mordred is the **antagonist?** Draw a chart like the following. Under each character's name list descriptive phrases from the text that help to establish the character's role. Then do the same thing for Gawain as the protagonist and the Green Knight as the antagonist.

Protagonist	Antagonist
King Arthur	Mordred
Sir Gawain	Green Knight

avenge
brandish
entreat
grovel
plunder
slay
smite
swoon
tarry
wrought

Vocabulary Study

Malory uses strong verbs in his telling of the events surrounding the final battle between Arthur's and Mordred's forces. Among the most descriptive verbs Malory uses are forms of those in the list. Copy the words and write out their definitions (use the Glossary or the footnotes with the selection). Then use at least five of the words in a paragraph about a fight between a protagonist and antagonist such as King Arthur and Mordred.

Expressing Your Ideas

Writing Choices

Writer's Notebook Update Written on Arthur's tomb are these now famous words: "Here Lies Arthur, King Once and King That Will Be." Assume that King Arthur has indeed returned. List some of the challenges he would face.

A Different Angle You are Sir Bedivere, the only survivor of this fierce battle. Write a **narrative** of Arthur's last day from your own, first-person point of view; that is, use the pronoun "I." Include your account of Arthur's combat with Mordred, your reasons for hiding Excalibur, and your feelings and actions after Arthur departs in the barge. Be sure not to include information you couldn't know without someone's telling you.

A Tale of a Vale Arthur tells Bedivere that the queen and her ladies are taking him "into the vale of Avilion" where he will be healed. What do you think this miraculous land is? Is it an afterlife, or a special, magical spot here on earth? What else can it do, besides heal grievous wounds? Use your imagination to write a **description** of Avilion and its wonders.

Other Options

The Round Table Revisited Form a group with other classmates to create some new knights and new adventures. Work together to create a **skit** in which your knights return to King Arthur's court to share the stories of their conquests.

More Court News You have met only a few of the exciting characters of King Arthur's court; there are many more in the various legends, including Galahad, Guinevere, Lancelot, Merlin, Morgan la Fay, Percival, and Tristram. Research one of these characters and prepare a **picture essay** (a combination of pictures and captions) in the form of a bulletin board, a scrapbook, or a file in a multimedia computer program.

Hanging Around Lining the walls of medieval castles were tapestries, large woven panels picturing historic events, mythical characters, and other compositions. Create a design for a **wall hanging** that pictures one of the adventures you have read about. If possible, cover a wall with white paper or butcher paper and make your design full-sized.

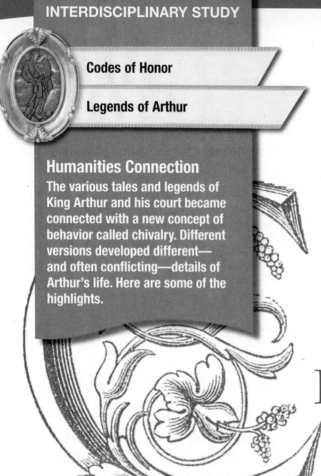

Codes of Honor

Legends of Arthur

Humanities Connection

The various tales and legends of King Arthur and his court became connected with a new concept of behavior called chivalry. Different versions developed different— and often conflicting—details of Arthur's life. Here are some of the highlights.

CHIVALRY

by Barbara Tuchman

Chivalry was a moral system governing the whole of noble life. It developed at the same time as the great crusades of the 12th century as a code intended to fuse the religious and martial spirits and somehow bring the fighting man into accord with Christian theory. A moral gloss was needed that would allow the Church to tolerate the warriors in good conscience and the warriors to pursue their own values in spiritual comfort. A code evolved that put the knight's sword arm in the service of justice, right, piety, the Church, the widow, the orphan, and the oppressed.

Chivalry developed its own principles. Prowess, that combination of courage, strength, and skill, was the prime essential.

Honor and loyalty were the ideals, and so-called courtly love the presiding genius. Courtly love required its disciple to be in a chronically amorous condition, and largesse was the necessary accompaniment.

Prowess was not mere talk, for the function of physical violence required real stamina. To fight on horseback or foot wearing 55 pounds of plate armor, to give and receive blows with sword or battle-ax that could cleave a skull or slice off a limb at a stroke, to spend half of life in the saddle through all weathers and for days at a time, was not a weakling's work.

Loyalty, meaning the pledged word, was chivalry's fulcrum. The extreme emphasis given to it derived from the time when a pledge between lord and vassal was the only form of government. A knight who broke his oath was charged with "treason" for betraying the order of knighthood. The concept of loyalty did not preclude treachery or the most egregious trickery as long as no knightly oath was broken.

Chivalry was regarded as a universal order of all Christian knights, a trans-national class moved by a single ideal, much as Marxism later regarded all workers of the world. It was a military guild in which all knights were theoretically brothers.

Sir Lancelot hands down his shield to a lady as a mark of chivalry.

THE REGAL KING ARTHUR IS PORTRAYED IN THIS DETAIL FROM A FRENCH TAPESTRY, ABOUT 1385.

In the performance of his function, the knight must be prepared, as John of Salisbury wrote, "to shed your blood for your brethren— and, if needs must, to lay down your life."

Fighting filled the noble's need of something to do, a way to exert himself. It was his substitute for work. His leisure time was spent chiefly in hunting, otherwise in games of chess, backgammon, and dice, in songs, dances, pageants, and other entertainments. Long winter evenings were occupied listening to the recital of interminable verse epics. The sword offered the workless noble an activity with a purpose, one that could bring him honor, status, and, if he was lucky, gain. If no real conflict was at hand, he sought tournaments, the most exciting, expensive, ruinous, and delightful activity of the noble class.

Tournaments started without rules or lists as an agreed-upon clash of opposing units. Though justified as training exercises, the impulse was the love of fighting.

If tournaments were an acting-out of chivalry, courtly love was its dreamland. Courtly love was understood by its contemporaries to be love for its own sake, romantic love, true love, physical love, unassociated with property or family, and consequently focused on another man's wife, since only such an illicit liaison could have no other aim but love alone.

As its justification, courtly love was considered to ennoble a man, to improve him in every way. It would make him concerned to show an example of goodness, to do his utmost to preserve honor, never letting dishonor touch himself or the lady he loved.

If the fiction of chivalry molded outward behavior to some extent, it did not, any more than other models that man has made for himself, transform human nature. Yet, if the code was but a veneer over violence, greed, and sensuality, it was nevertheless an ideal, as Christianity was an ideal, toward which man's reach, as usual, exceeded his grasp.

Beautiful Guinevere is surrounded
by her ladies-in-waiting.

ARTHUR AND

Merlin, the bearded magician,
leads Arthur down the path
to his kingship.

HIS COURT

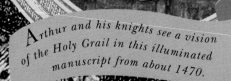

Arthur and his knights see a vision of the Holy Grail in this illuminated manuscript from about 1470.

IN DANTE GABRIEL ROSSETTI'S ILLUSTRATION, GUINEVERE WRINGS HER HANDS, AND LANCELOT GRABS HIS SWORD AFTER THE TWO LOVERS ARE DISCOVERED TOGETHER IN THE QUEEN'S CHAMBER.

Arthur and his court were presented dramatically in the stage musical Camelot. In the movie version, Arthur, Guinevere, and Lancelot wear costumes inspired by designs of the Middle Ages.

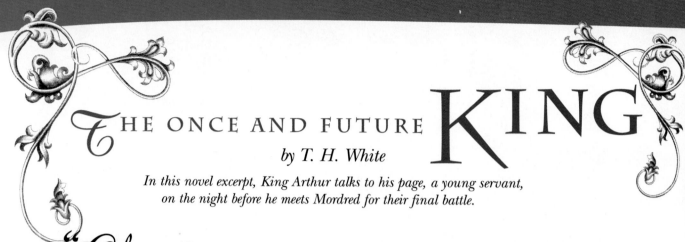

THE ONCE AND FUTURE KING

by T. H. White

*In this novel excerpt, King Arthur talks to his page, a young servant,
on the night before he meets Mordred for their final battle.*

"Oh page?"

"My lord?"

"What is your name?"

"Tom, my lord," [the boy] said politely.

"Where do you live?"

"Near Warwick, my lord. At a place called Newbold Revell. It is a pretty one."

"How old are you?"

"I shall be thirteen in November, my lord."

"Tell me, Tom, what do you intend to do tomorrow?"

"I shall fight, sir. I have a good bow."

"And you will kill people with this bow?"

"Yes, my lord. A great many, I hope."

"Suppose they were to kill you?"

"Then I should be dead, my lord."

"I see."

"Shall I take the letter now?"

"No, Tom. Sit down and try to listen. Could you understand if I asked you not to fight tomorrow?"

"I should want to fight," [Tom] said stoutly.

"Everybody wants to fight, Tom, but nobody knows why. Suppose I were to ask you not to fight, as a special favor to the King? Would you do that?"

"I should do what I was told."

"Listen, then. I am a very old man, Tom, and you are young. When you are old, you will be able to tell what I have told tonight, and I want you to do that. Do you understand this want?"

"Yes, sir. I think so."

ARTHUR IS TAKEN TO THE ISLAND OF AVALON TO HEAL HIS WOUND.

"Put it like this. There was a king once, called King Arthur. That is me. When he came to the throne of England, he found that all the kings and barons were fighting against each other like madmen, and, as they could afford to fight in expensive suits of armor, there was practically nothing which could stop them from doing what they pleased. They did a lot of bad things, because they lived by force. Now this king had an idea, and the idea was that force ought to be used, if it were used at all, on behalf of justice, not on its own account. Follow this, young boy. He thought that if he could get his barons fighting for truth, and to help weak people, and to redress wrongs, then their fighting might not be such a bad thing as once it used to be. So he gathered together all the true and kindly people that he knew, and he dressed them in armor, and he made them knights, and taught them his idea, and set them down, at a Round Table. There were a hundred and fifty of them in the happy days, and King Arthur loved his Table with all his heart. He was prouder of it than he was of his own dear wife, and for many years his new knights went about killing ogres, and rescuing damsels, and saving poor prisoners, and trying to set the world to rights. That was the King's idea."

"I think it was a good idea, my lord."

"It was, and it was not. God knows."

"What happened to the King in the end?"

"For some reason, things went wrong. The Table split into factions, a bitter war began, and all were killed."

The boy interrupted confidently.

"No," he said, "not all. The King won. We shall win."

"Everybody was killed," he repeated, "except a certain page. I know what I am talking about."

"My lord?"

"This page was called young Tom of Newbold Revell near Warwick, and the old

King Arthur accuses his son Mordred of being a traitor and vows to kill him.

King sent him off before the battle, upon pain of dire disgrace. You see, the King wanted there to be somebody left, who would remember their famous idea. He wanted badly that Tom should go back to Newbold Revell, where he could grow into a man and live his life in Warwickshire peace—and he wanted him to tell everybody who would listen about this ancient idea, which both of them had once thought good. Do you think you could do that, Thomas, to please the King?"

The child said, with the pure eyes of absolute truth: "I would do anything for King Arthur."

Responding

1. How do you think King Arthur might have adapted the code of chivalry so that his people could live more at peace with each other?

2. What elements of the code seem to be most responsible for the downfall of the Round Table?

3. In your opinion, what elements of chivalry are still alive today? What elements should we try to revive?

Language History

The Language of Court and Chapel

 There were many tourneys with gallant jousting of knights, and after the jousting they rode to the court for song and dance . . . .

When you read this passage at the beginning of *Sir Gawain and the Green Knight*, you encounter a number of words that entered the English language during the Middle Ages: *tourneys, gallant, jousting, dance*. What kind of social world do these words reflect?

In 1066, French-speaking Normans conquered England. The Norman Conquest had major long-term consequences for the English language. For the next three and a half centuries, English was substantially altered and expanded by contact with the French spoken by the invaders. For the first two centuries (1066–1250), the infusion of French words was relatively slight. Words adopted from the French during this period reflect the outlook of the ruling class (*noble, dame, chivalry, servant, messenger*) or religious concerns (*sermon, communion, confession, clergy, convent*).

By 1250, when ties between England and Normandy had loosened and English nationalism was making itself felt, many more French words began to be assimilated into English—particularly words associated with government, law, and business, such as *crown, state, reign, authority, tax, judge, pardon*. Also notable are the number of words from social and cultural life (*dance, recreation, poet, tragedy, story, music, art*) and food and clothing (*beef, bacon, olive, gown, boot, robe*).

During these same centuries, the dialect of Old English spoken by the people of the East Midlands, the area that included London, was becoming looked upon as the standard form of the language, as "the King's English." Around 1370 Geoffrey Chaucer wrote in this dialect, giving it literary status. Both modern English and American English are directly descended from this East Midlands dialect.

Writing Workshop

Is Chivalry Dead?

Assignment You have read about the code of honor known as chivalry, a value system that some people believed in and strove for during medieval times. Write an essay in which you discuss to what extent chivalry exists in today's society.

WRITER'S BLUEPRINT

Product   An essay of opinion

Purpose   To convince readers of your opinions on chivalry, past and present

Audience   People who have only a vague idea of what chivalry is about

Specs   As the writer of a successful essay, you should:

❑ Discuss chivalry as it was seen in medieval times. Focus on three of the following aspects: self-control, courtesy, loyalty, truthfulness, honor, keeping promises, courage, generosity.

❑ Discuss to what extent you think chivalry exists in today's society. Base your discussion on the three aspects you chose above. Support your opinions by citing events you have witnessed in your life and learned of through newspapers, radio, and TV.

❑ End by giving your conclusions about what has happened to the concept of chivalry since medieval times, based on your discussion. Define your terms clearly throughout.

❑ Follow the rules of grammar, usage, spelling, and mechanics. Pay special attention to subject-verb agreement.

STEP  PREWRITING

Brainstorm aspects of chivalry in medieval times. Working with a group, discuss the literature and interdisciplinary materials. Organize your notes in a chart like the one on the next page.

LITERARY SOURCE
"Thus the fair lady tested him, and tempted him to wrong, whatever else she wished of him. But he kept her at a distance so skillfully that he failed in neither courtesy nor honor, . . ."

from *Sir Gawain and the Green Knight*

Aspects of medieval chivalry	Notes
Self-Control	It's an ideal you strive for, especially knights. You keep the object of temptation at a distance at all times. (Gawain)
Courtesy	Especially with a man toward a woman. It's a skill, an art. (Gawain)

Discuss aspects of chivalry in modern times. Make notes on your discussion and organize them in a chart like the one above.

Plan your essay. The three-part plan that follows is closely based on the Writer's Blueprint. If you decide to use it, make notes about each bulleted point.

OR . . .
Do it your way. Create your own writing plan. Just be sure it deals with the points in the Writer's Blueprint.

Part One (chivalry in medieval times)
• A general statement about my three aspects
• Discussion of aspect #1
and so on . . .

Part Two (chivalry in modern times)
• A general statement about my three aspects
• Opinions about aspect #1
• Facts to support #1 opinions
and so on . . .

Part Three (conclusions about chivalry in modern times)
• My conclusions based on Part 2
• A closing statement

STEP 2 DRAFTING

Before you draft, review the Blueprint and your writing plan.

As you draft, think about your point of view. If you'd like to write from an unusual point of view, try one of these ideas:

• Write as if you were someone from medieval times who's been taken by a time machine into the present.

• Write as if you're someone from the present who's traveled back in time, and you're explaining things to people from medieval times.

But if you choose an unusual point of view, don't forget that you still need to write in the form of an essay.

3 REVISING

Ask a partner for comments on your draft before you revise it.

✔ Did I support my opinions with facts?

✔ Have I clearly defined my terms?

Revising Strategy

Clarifying Abstract Terms

Abstract terms like *self-control, courtesy,* and *loyalty* mean different things to different people. Be sure to give your readers an idea of what they mean to you. If you don't, they may be left with questions like these.

Unclear   Maintaining self-control is beneficial. (*What do you mean by self-control?*)

Better   Self-control, the ability to stay calm in times of stress, is beneficial. (*Beneficial? How?*)

Clear   Self-control, the ability to stay calm in times of stress, helps you to make rational decisions.

Look through your draft and circle any abstract terms that still need clarifying. One way to clarify abstract terms is by adding concrete examples, as in the student model that follows. The last two sentences were added during revising.

> A man who was chivalrous in medieval times was loyal to his king and his country. He would give up his life, if necessary, in order to protect the lives and honor of those around him. Such loyalty was apparent in "Day of Destiny." Sir Gawain's loyalty to the throne was apparent when he chose to combat the stranger who appeared in search of a duel.

to clarify "loyal"

STUDENT MODEL

Ask a partner to review your revised draft before you edit. As you edit, watch for errors in grammar, usage, spelling, and mechanics. Pay special attention to errors in subject-verb agreement.

Editing Strategy

Making Subjects and Verbs Agree

When you edit your sentences, keep these two simple rules in mind:

- A singular subject takes a singular verb. (A *knight* always *treats* a woman with courtesy.)

- A plural subject takes a plural verb. (*Knights* never *treat* women with disrespect.)

Be especially careful about sentences where several other words come between the subject and verb:

A list of important aspects appears in the final paragraph. (The verb, *appears,* must agree with the subject, *list,* not the nearer word *aspects.*)

The opinions expressed in this essay are entirely my own. (The subject is *opinions,* not *essay.*)

Notice how this writer edited to correct errors in subject-verb agreement.

FOR REFERENCE
You'll find more rules for subject-verb agreement in the Language and Grammar Handbook at the back of this book.

COMPUTER TIP
If you use a spell-checker, remember that it won't catch mistakes like writing *your* when you mean *you're.* Always proofread carefully for spelling.

○   Honor to one's country, family, and friends ~~are~~ *is* lacking in modern

American society. An example of how modern day society lacks honor

○   among its members ~~are~~ *is* the actions of politicians. Politicians often

express the view on socio-economic issues that will get them the most

○   votes.

STUDENT MODEL

STEP 5 PRESENTING

Here are three ideas for presenting and enhancing your paper.

- Have a point-counterpoint reading/discussion. Work with a partner whose opinions are significantly different from yours. Read your papers to the class or a small group and discuss the opposing points of view.

- Conduct a poll of your classmates, asking if they agree or disagree that chivalry still exists in today's world. Add a statistical table to your paper reporting your findings, and discuss the results.

- Include a cover page with writing and drawings that have a medieval look.

STEP 6 LOOKING BACK

Self-evaluate. What grade would *you* give your essay? Look back at the Writer's Blueprint and evaluate yourself on each point, from 6 (superior) down to 1 (inadequate).

Reflect. Think about what you have learned from writing this essay as you write answers to these questions.

✔ What insights have you gained into your own code of honor by writing this paper?

✔ Compare your rough draft with your finished copy. Jot down comments about the kinds of changes you made. What do they tell you about your strengths and weaknesses as a writer?

For Your Working Portfolio Add your essay and reflection responses to your working portfolio.

Beyond Print

The Middle Ages in the Movies

Knights, ladies, castles, wizards, tournaments—all these are standard elements in films that use the Middle Ages as a background. Some of these films are basically fantasies that employ medieval settings. Other films attempt to create the authentic look and feel of the historical Middle Ages. Many films mix history and romance. But whether a film primarily aims at fantasy or fact, it must feel right; that is, it must meet the audience's expectations about what the Middle Ages were like—and, of course, provide a satisfying spectacle. In trying to create a vivid impression of a remote time such as the Middle Ages, movie makers concentrate on the following areas.

Dialogue What the actors are given to say is critically important in establishing a period feeling. In a film about the Middle Ages, the dialogue has to avoid two dangers: (1) language so authentically "medieval" that it sounds stilted; or (2) language so modern that it sounds out-of-place. The first problem occurs when the characters use too many *thee's* and *thou's* and archaic words like *prithee* and *forsooth*. The second problem can result from overuse of highly contemporary speech, such as slang, or simply speech that makes romantic medieval characters sound too "everyday." If, as happens in one film, King Richard the Lionheart's queen complains to him, "War, war! That's all you think about, Dick Plantagenet!" the audience may think she sounds a bit too much like a bored housewife in a sitcom complaining about her husband's addiction to football.

Spectacle Whether a film presents medieval reality or fantasy, spectacle is a vital element. The quality of battle scenes—whether they emphasize the picturesque aspects of war or its butchery—is important. So are the special effects often used in medieval fantasies to produce images of fire-breathing dragons or Arthur's enchanted sword rising from the lake.

Set Design The basic set for most films about the Middle Ages is a castle. Some films try to glamorize these damp and drafty fortresses, while others make a more serious attempt to convey how uncomfortable living in them must have been.

Costume In general, filmmakers probably do a better job with period costume than with other areas of historical research. Medieval clothing, from the richly embroidered gowns of courtiers to peasants' muddy rags, is convincingly recreated. The knight in armor is the most familiar image of the Middle Ages, and filmmakers have generally taken care to depict vividly these warriors clanking about in their steel suits.

Music Period music is frequently employed in films to help create historical atmosphere. However, when the period is the Middle Ages this is less likely to be true, since most modern audiences would probably find the sound of authentic medieval melodies and instruments very strange. What's most important with music is that it contribute to creating the proper mood, whether the mood is heroic or romantic or eerie.

Activity Options

1. Collect examples of dialogue from films dealing with the Middle Ages that you feel show either a successful or a disastrous attempt to give a contemporary feel to this historical period.

2. With other students, look at a videotape of a film dealing with some medieval subject—for example, King Arthur, Robin Hood, or the Crusades—and discuss how the filmmakers have dealt with the issues of dialogue, spectacle, set design, costume, and music. What impression of the Middle Ages does the film create—gritty or glamorous?

3. Create a collage that collects historical portraits of famous medieval figures, such as Richard the Lionheart and Eleanor of Aquitaine, with images of the actors that have played them.

This poster advertised Warner Brothers' 1938 classic *The Adventures of Robin Hood*. What version of the Middle Ages—history or romance—does this poster convey? ➤

Multicultural Connections

Choice

Part One: Getting Even In *Beowulf,* the monster Grendel gets even with humans by killing and eating them, but the hero Beowulf takes the ultimate revenge on Grendel. In the folk ballads "Lord Randal" and "Edward," revenge seems implicit in the motives for the murders, but it is explicit in the curses that the speakers leave. "In Get Up and Bar the Door," the goodman and goodwife almost bring mischief on themselves through stubbornly trying to get even with each other.

■ How do the groups these characters belong to determine the choices they make in to deal how with their enemies?

Groups

Part Two: Codes of Honor In "The Pardoner's Tale" the three rioters swear to be brothers, but they violate their code when they kill each other off trying to keep all the gold. Sir Gawain is true to his code when he accepts the Green Knight's challenge, when he submits himself a year later, and when he gives the lord the lady's kisses, but he violates it by not reporting the green girdle. Because neither Arthur nor Mordred trusts the other to keep their agreement, a simple misunderstanding in killing a snake leads to the battle in which almost all are killed. Sir Bedivere almost violates his code when he lies to Arthur about disposing of Excalibur.

■ Discuss how the choices made by the rioters, Gawain, and Bedivere to stray from their group values bring negative results to all of them.

Activities

1. Create a graphic organizer to display different kinds of groups to be found in your community or in the country. Consider this question: How many groups might an average person belong to at the same time? during his or her lifetime?

2. Discuss when it may be desirable for teenagers to break out of various groups they belong to and when it is more desirable not to.

3. Share the most difficult choice you have had to make. What were the pressures on you to choose one way or the other? What determined your final choice?

Independent and Group Projects

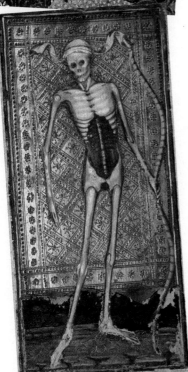

Oral Presentation

Put Yourself in the Picture How would you have fit in medieval English society? To which of the classes of people shown on pages 42–43 would you have wanted to belong? Would you have had to work for a living? What would you have done when you weren't working? Describe your life as a medieval person and tell about yourself in a five-minute presentation—in costume if you wish.

Media

Not Easy Being Green We're never told how Gawain's foe became green—was he born that way, or did something colorful happen to him? For that matter, we know little enough about many of the characters in this unit. With a group, develop a talk show with one person playing a host or hostess and others representing various characters. Plan in advance what questions to ask and what answers to give. You might also want to plan some amusing chitchat among all the participants.

Art

Package Tours! Create a travel brochure designed to appeal to medieval travelers who wish to make the pilgrimage to Canterbury or any other places mentioned in this unit. You may want to include a map, a list of possible places to stay or stop for a meal along the way, and a description of sights to see. You might do some research about travel in the Middle Ages to find out what travelers' options were. (Hint: They were few.) Include advertising, illustrations, and a price list as well.

Research

Digging Up the Past There are many ancient—and mysterious— monuments in Britain, dating from medieval times and from long before. Research one of these sites, such as Tintagel Castle, Stonehenge, the stones at Avebury, the Cerne Giant at Cerne Abbas, or the White Horse of Uffington. (See your teacher for some other interesting research topics.) After you have done the appropriate research give a multimedia presentation on the historic place of your choice.

The Elizabethan Era

The Lure of Ambition
Pages 106–206

THEMES IN ENGLISH LITERATURE

Nature: Garden or Wilderness?
Theme Portfolio, pages 207–219

HISTORICAL OVERVIEW

The Renaissance was marked by the rebirth of humanity's belief in its potential. "Men can do all things if they will," exulted the Italian architect LeonBattista Alberti, who made good his boast by mastering a dozen fields, from poetry to engineering. Two notable examples of this Renaissance ideal of multifaceted achieve- ment—Queen Elizabeth I of England (1553–1603) and the Italian artist Leonardo da Vinci (1452–1519)—appear on these pages, surrounded by objects reflecting the range of their interests. In addition to being a skillful ruler, Elizabeth was a poet, linguist, musician, and scholar. Leonardo was a painter, inventor, architect, engineer, and scientist. Both these individuals reflect the creative energy of the Renaissance and its delight in new discoveries.

NEW PERSPECTIVES
for humanity

Key Dates

1455
Gutenberg prints Bible using moveable type.

1492
Columbus reaches the Western Hemisphere.

1505
Da Vinci paints Mona Lisa.

1517
Martin Luther posts his 95 Theses attacking abuses in the Church.

1543
Copernicus publishes his theory that the sun, not the earth, is the center of the solar system.

1558
Elizabeth I becomes queen of England.

1599
The Globe Theater is built.

1609
Galileo builds his telescope.

The Lure of Ambition

Who doesn't desire to be best-loved, to be well-known, to be powerful? Ambition, the desire to distinguish oneself in some way, has led many people to great achievements in all areas of human endeavor. It has led others to ruthless, immoral, and sometimes deadly acts.

Multicultural Connection **Individuality** may arise either from accepting or rejecting different cultural norms or group standards. Yet selfish actions that lead to success and power today may still bring about loss or even destruction tomorrow. People in positions of leadership remain responsible to the groups to which they belong; in a sense they may be *more* responsible than others. To what degree does Macbeth's rejection of cultural norms contribute to his downfall?

Before Reading

Sonnets 18, 29, 71, 116, and 130

by William Shakespeare

William Shakespeare
1564 –1616

Born to a prosperous glove maker at Stratford-on-Avon, William Shakespeare attended grammar school only until age 14. By age 18 he was married to 26-year-old Anne Hathaway, and by age 21 he was the father of three children: Susanna, and the twins Judith and Hamnet. While his family stayed behind in Stratford, Shakespeare journeyed to London. There he lived for much of the next 25 years, acting and writing over 200 poems and over 40 plays.

(For more about Shakespeare, see page 117.)

Building Backround

A Conventional Love Isolated from his family, Shakespeare wrote poems of praise, love, and despair. Many of these are addressed to a young man or to a "dark lady." Were they real people with whom he had real love affairs? Perhaps. But during the Elizabethan era writers often wrote to fulfill a **literary convention**—a device that becomes an accepted element through habitual use. One of the conventions of the day was for a poet to choose a fancy name (usually inspired by Greek or Roman mythology) for an imaginary woman and then complain to her—in elaborate verse—that she didn't love the poet enough.

Literary Focus

Shakespearean Sonnet The Shakespearean sonnet, adapted from an Italian form, follows tight literary conventions:

The sonnet is 14 lines long.

Each line follows the rhythmic meter of iambic pentameter. (See the Glossary of Literary Terms.)

The rhyme scheme is *a b a b c d c d e f e f g g*.

The ideas are divided into four sections: three parts of four lines each (quatrains) plus a final part of two lines (couplet). The quatrains may present three statements or examples, while the couplet usually comments on the preceding lines or provides a conclusion or application.

Some sonnets also reflect their Italian origins by having the ideas divided into eight lines of statement (octave) and six lines of conclusion (sestet).

As you read the sonnets, notice how Shakespeare divides his ideas.

Writer's Notebook

What Do Poets Write About? Two common **themes** you will see developed in this sampling of Shakespeare's sonnets are the immortalization of love and beauty and the inevitable decay that comes with time. List some other general themes, applicable to all men and women, that you think are appropriate for short poems.

Sonnet 18

Shall I compare thee to a summer's day?
Thou art more lovely and more temperate.
Rough winds do shake the darling buds of May,
And summer's lease hath all too short a date.
5 Sometimes too hot the eye of heaven shines,
And often is his gold complexion dimmed;
And every fair from fair sometimes declines,
By chance or nature's changing course untrimmed.
But thy eternal summer shall not fade
10 Nor lose possession of that fair thou owest;
Nor shall Death brag thou wanderest in his shade,
When in eternal lines to time thou growest.
　　　So long as men can breathe or eyes can see,
　　　So long lives this, and this gives life to thee.

Sonnet 29

When, in disgrace with Fortune and men's eyes,
I all alone beweep my outcast state,
And trouble deaf heaven with my bootless cries,
And look upon myself and curse my fate,
5 Wishing me like to one more rich in hope,
Featured like him, like him with friends possessed,
Desiring this man's art and that man's scope,
With what I most enjoy contented least;
Yet in these thoughts myself almost despising,
10 Haply I think on thee, and then my state,
Like to the lark at break of day arising
From sullen earth, sings hymns at heaven's gate;
　　　For thy sweet love remembered such wealth brings
　　　That then I scorn to change my state with kings.

Sonnet 71

No longer mourn for me when I am dead
Than you shall hear the surly sullen bell
Give warning to the world that I am fled
From this vile world, with vilest worms to dwell.
5 Nay, if you read this line, remember not
The hand that writ it; for I love you so
That I in your sweet thoughts would be forgot

2 temperate (tem′pər it), *adj.* moderate.

8 untrimmed, reduced; deprived of beauty.
10 fair thou owest, beauty you possess.

3 bootless (büt′lis), *adj.*

9 despise (di spīz′), *v.* scorn.

2 sullen (sul′ən), *adj.* gloomy.
2 bell. The bell was rung after someone had died so that those who heard it might pray for the departed soul.

◄ Nicholas Hilliard painted this miniature portrait, known as *A Young Man Among Roses,* around 1588. What do the young man's pose and his surroundings seem to suggest about his outlook on life? Can you imagine the young man's writing or reciting a sonnet to his love? Why or why not?

If thinking on me then should make you woe.
O, if, I say, you look upon this verse

10 When I perhaps compounded am with clay,
Do not so much as my poor name rehearse,
But let your love even with my life decay,
     Lest the wise world should look into your moan
     And mock you with me after I am gone.

Sonnet 116

Let me not to the marriage of true minds
Admit impediments. Love is not love
Which alters when it alteration finds,
Or bends with the remover to remove.

5 Oh no! It is an ever-fixèd mark,
That looks on tempests and is never shaken;
It is the star to every wandering bark,
Whose worth's unknown although his height be taken.
Love's not Time's fool, though rosy lips and cheeks

10 Within his bending sickle's compass come;
Love alters not with his brief hours and weeks,
But bears it out even to the edge of doom.
     If this be error and upon me proved,
     I never writ, nor no man ever loved.

Sonnet 130

My mistress' eyes are nothing like the sun;
Coral is far more red than her lips' red;
If snow be white, why then her breasts are dun;
If hairs be wires, black wires grow on her head.

5 I have seen roses damasked, red and white,
But no such roses see I in her cheeks;
And in some perfumes is there more delight
Than in the breath that from my mistress reeks.
I love to hear her speak, yet well I know

10 That music hath a far more pleasing sound.
I grant I never saw a goddess go;
My mistress, when she walks, treads on the ground.
     And yet, by heaven, I think my love as rare
     As any she belied with false compare.

2 impediment (im ped′ə-
mənt), *n.* obstruction.
4 or bends . . . remove, or
changes when the loved one is
unfaithful.
7 bark, ship.

10 within . . . come, Time is
often represented as an old
man carrying a sickle, a
curved blade used for cutting
down tall grasses or, metaphorically, human souls.
Youth ("rosy lips and
cheeks") also comes within
his range ("compass").

3 dun, dull gray.

5 damasked, variegated;
multicolored.

11 go, walk.
14 any she, any woman.
14 belie (bi lī′), *v.* misrepre-
sent.

After Reading

Making Connections

1. Like most Elizabethan sonneteers, Shakespeare uses **imagery** drawn from nature and common experience. Which image in these sonnets can you picture most clearly?

2. Some readers feel that Shakespeare, in Sonnet 18, is paying greater tribute to **poetic convention** than to his love. What do you think?

3. According to the speaker in Sonnet 18, his beloved's "eternal summer shall not fade." How is this possible?

4. Point out the contrast in Sonnet 29 that carries the meaning of the poem.

5. Sonnet 71 contains many words and phrases that suggest the unpleasantness of death. In your opinion, what, if anything, seems to lift it out of the grave?

6. How is **metaphor** used in Sonnet 116 to demonstrate how firm and steady love should be?

7. 🐾 Sonnet 130 seems to celebrate **individuality.** How does the speaker first upset your expectations about the beauty of the beloved and then fulfill your expectations about the beloved?

8. Which sonnets contain elements of **hyperbole,** or exaggeration? Point them out and explain what effect they have on the poems.

9. So popular have sonnets been that poets have continued writing them well into the 1900s. Why do you suppose poets choose an art form like the sonnet to express themselves?

10. How do the ideas expressed about fame and beauty in Shakespeare's sonnets compare with ideas about fame and beauty that people hold today?

Literary Focus: Shakespearean Sonnet

A Shakespearean **sonnet** is a fourteen-line poem in iambic pentameter. In each sonnet, statements or examples are presented, and then a conclusion is reached. For each of Shakespeare's sonnets, show where the conclusion begins. (What word or words does the poet use to signal that a new idea is coming?) Write a one-sentence summary of each sonnet to show how the statements and conclusions work together to present one main idea.

Vocabulary Study

Match each example with the appropriate vocabulary word. You will not use all the words.

belie
bootless
despise
impediment
temperate
sullen

1. "Why no—all those things you heard about me are lies. I swear I've never even looked at another woman!"

2. "Sure, I believe in getting involved in a relationship, but not *too* involved."

3. "Oh, I guess I'm just feeling miserable because I never seem to be able to talk to people without making a fool of myself."

4. "I hate him, that's all. I just can't stand to be in the same room with him."

5. "Yes, I'd like to go out with you, but you know my parents are very strict about my dating anyone."

Expressing Your Ideas

Writing Choices

Writer's Notebook Update Look back at the poetic themes you listed. Can you add to that list? Select a theme you like and jot down some ideas about statements and conclusions you could use to express it and about images that would help get the idea across.

The Poet in You Try your hand at writing a **sonnet.** Use this check list to make sure that you follow the conventions of the sonnet.

☐ 14 lines

☐ Rhythmic scheme

☐ Rhyme scheme

☐ Idea change after line 8 or line 12

Dear Will . . . Imagine that William Shakespeare has dedicated one of his sonnets to you. Write him a **personal letter** acknowledging receipt of the poem, expressing your opinion of the quality of the writing, and explaining your feelings at having this poem dedicated to you.

Other Options

Shakespeare in Art In his sonnets Shakespeare creates a word picture of his emotions. Select one of these poems and find a painting or a photograph that expresses similar emotions. If you prefer, create an **artwork** of your own. Be prepared to explain your choice of artwork to the class.

Shakespeare Rocks! Shakespeare's words have been set to music time and time again, from classical opera to modern jazz. Try your hand at adapting any of his sonnets into a contemporary **rock lyric.** You may use the entire poem or just a phrase or two to base your lyric on. If you can, set your lyric to music and perform your rock song for the class.

Reading a Shakespearean Play

The words may look old-fashioned. The sentences may seem awkward. Don't worry. There are a lot of things you can do to make reading Shakespearean drama easier. Here are some guidelines you can follow.

Read the scene summary. Because Shakespeare based many of his plays on old, familiar stories, his audiences often knew the plot lines of the play before they attended a performance. If you read the summary of each scene (in a colored box immediately after the scene heading) before you read the scene, you'll know what to expect.

Read the scene straight through. Try to get the sense of an entire passage by reading each scene straight through, without stopping to struggle with difficult words or sentences. Once you understand the action of the entire scene, you can go back and concentrate on the details.

Use the marginal notes. In the margins you will find definitions of unfamiliar words. When a passage is quite difficult, you will find an entire phrase or sentence rewritten in language you can understand.

Now reread the scene summary. Does it make sense? Through your own reading, do you see each event described in the summary? If so, you're ready to move on. If not, find a partner and reread the scene together.

Think about the characters. Concentrate on the major **characters.** Listen to what they say to others and to themselves. (That may mean that you'll need to reread a long speech.) Listen to what other characters say about them. Watch how other characters relate to them. Look for alliances between characters. Look for

conflicts. Try to figure out what makes each character tick! What motivates him? What troubles her? It may even help to visualize each character's physical appearance.

Understand the stage conventions. Shakespearean theater had its own conventional way of doing things. Watch for a character to speak in an **aside,** which means that the audience can hear his or her thoughts, but that the other characters on stage cannot. At other times, a character alone on stage will deliver a **soliloquy,** a speech that gives voice to his or her inmost thoughts and feelings.

Rearrange inverted sentences. In common usage speakers most often place the subject of a sentence before the verb. Many of Shakespeare's sentences, however, are inverted; for example, Lady Macbeth's doctor says, "More needs she the divine than the physician." When you encounter such passages, simply rearrange the word order to place the subject first. Rearranged, this sentence would read: "She needs the divine [priest] more than the physician."

Interpret metaphors. Many important ideas in the play are developed through **metaphor.** Ask yourself what comparison is suggested and how this comparison affects the overall meaning of the passage. For example, when King Duncan greets Macbeth, whom he has just rewarded with a new title, he says, "I have begun to plant thee, and will labor / To make thee full of growing." Here he uses *plant* and *growing* metaphorically to tell Macbeth that other honors will be forthcoming.

Read passages aloud. You are, after all, reading a script meant to be performed by actors. Try reading speeches aloud and visualizing the action as it unfolds. You'll soon discover that most of the play is in verse. Don't let this throw you. Read for the sense, using the punctuation as an aid to understanding the sentence structure.

Understand the plot structure. The structure of any narrative may be visualized as in this diagram. The introduction or **background** (also called *exposition*) is what the viewer or reader needs to know about the characters and their situation at the beginning. The **conflict** is what sets the events of the story in motion. What the main character does to battle the conflict and achieve the goal constitutes the **rising action** (also called the *complication*); in this part also the conflict may be renewed or new conflicts introduced. The **climax** is the turning point (also called the *crisis*), at which the main character takes the decisive action that will bring about

the conclusion. The climax is often also the most exciting point of the story. The **falling action** is attended by a lessening of tension. The outcome or conclusion is the **resolution** (also called *denouement*) of the conflict and the events that occur thereafter. In a Shakespearean play, generally act 1 will contain the exposition and conflict; act 2 the rising action; act 3 the climax; act 4 the falling action; and act 5 the resolution.

Do the literary focus activities. These brief writing and plotting exercises after each act will help you understand the development of the **plot.** You will see that events do not happen in isolation. Rather, one event leads to the next, which leads to the next, and so on. Look for these chains of causes and effects. You'll then begin to understand what events happen and why they happen.

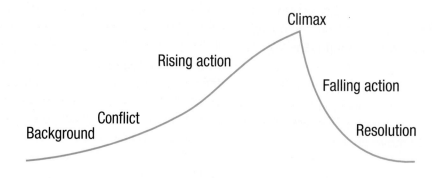

Climax

Rising action

Falling action

Conflict

Background

Resolution

Before Reading

Macbeth

by William Shakespeare

During the time that Shakespeare lived in London, he wrote poetry and plays, acted, and helped to manage the theater. He became a full shareholder in his acting company (the Lord Chamberlain's Men, later the King's Men), and he was part owner of the Globe Theater (see pages 146–147) and later of Blackfriars Theater. Shakespeare made frequent visits back to Stratford, where he bought one of the finest houses in town. He returned home in 1610 to be with his wife until his death six years later. Although some of Shakespeare's plays were published during his lifetime, not until after his death was an effort made to collect them in a single volume. The *First Folio,* the first edition of Shakespeare's collected plays, appeared in 1623.

Building Background

That Scottish Play It's August 7, 1606, and the first production of Shakespeare's *Macbeth* has begun. King James of England, entertaining the visiting King Christian IV of Denmark, delights in the opening scene with the three weird sisters, for he believes that witches have cast spells on his own life. He hails the appearance of the noble Banquo, for he has traced his lineage back to this Scottish nobleman. He appreciates the dark, foreboding mood Shakespeare has created. Only after the play is over does King James learn that the black mood has extended to the play itself: Hal Berridge, the boy actor playing Lady Macbeth, has died backstage. From that first performance and from a series of other mishaps, disasters, and deaths associated with the play, *Macbeth* has come to be considered a tragedy so unlucky that some actors and directors never call it by name. They simply call it "that play" or "that Scottish play."

Literary Focus

Plot Structure The **plot,** a series of related events that make up a story, is the organizational pattern for a narrative work. The structure of a five-act Shakespearean play can be described as a rising and falling of the fortunes of the main character, as is shown in the diagram on page 116. In act 1, the background, sometimes called *exposition,* tells the viewers or readers what they need to know about the characters, setting, and so on—particularly what has happened previously to bring the characters to this situation. Watch for ways in which Shakespeare transmits such information through action and dialogue.

Writer's Notebook

What Makes a Tragedy? In 1598 John Florio, Shakespeare's contemporary, defined tragedy: "A tragedy or mournful play being a lofty kind of poetry and representing personages of great state and matter of much trouble, a great broil or stir; it beginneth prosperously and endeth unfortunately. . . ." Make a list of people you know or have read about whose lives began prosperously and ended unfortunately.

MACBETH

WILLIAM SHAKESPEARE

CHARACTERS

DUNCAN, *King of Scotland*
MALCOLM ⎫
DONALBAIN ⎭ *his sons*

MACBETH, *Thane of Glamis, later of Cawdor, later King of Scotland*
LADY MACBETH

BANQUO, *a thane of Scotland*
FLEANCE, *his son*
MACDUFF, *Thane of Fife*
LADY MACDUFF
SON *of Macduff and Lady Macduff*

LENNOX ⎫
ROSS |
MENTEITH ⎬ *thanes and noblemen*
ANGUS | *of Scotland*
CAITHNESS ⎭

SIWARD, *Earl of Northumberland*
YOUNG SIWARD, *his son*

SEYTON, *an officer attending Macbeth*
Another LORD
ENGLISH DOCTOR
SCOTTISH DOCTOR
GENTLEWOMAN *attending Lady Macbeth*
CAPTAIN *serving Duncan*
PORTER
OLD MAN
Three MURDERERS *of Banquo*
FIRST MURDERER *at Macduff's castle*
MESSENGER *to Lady Macbeth*
MESSENGER *to Lady Macduff*
SERVANT *to Macbeth*
SERVANT *to Lady Macbeth*
Three WITCHES *or* WEIRD SISTERS
HECATE, *leader of the Witches*
Three APPARITIONS

Lords, Gentlemen, Officers, Soldiers, Murderers, and Attendants

This poster, created by Edmund Dulac for a 1911 staging of *Macbeth,* shows Macbeth with the three Witches who foretell his future. What is the mood of this illustration? How does the artist create that mood? ➤

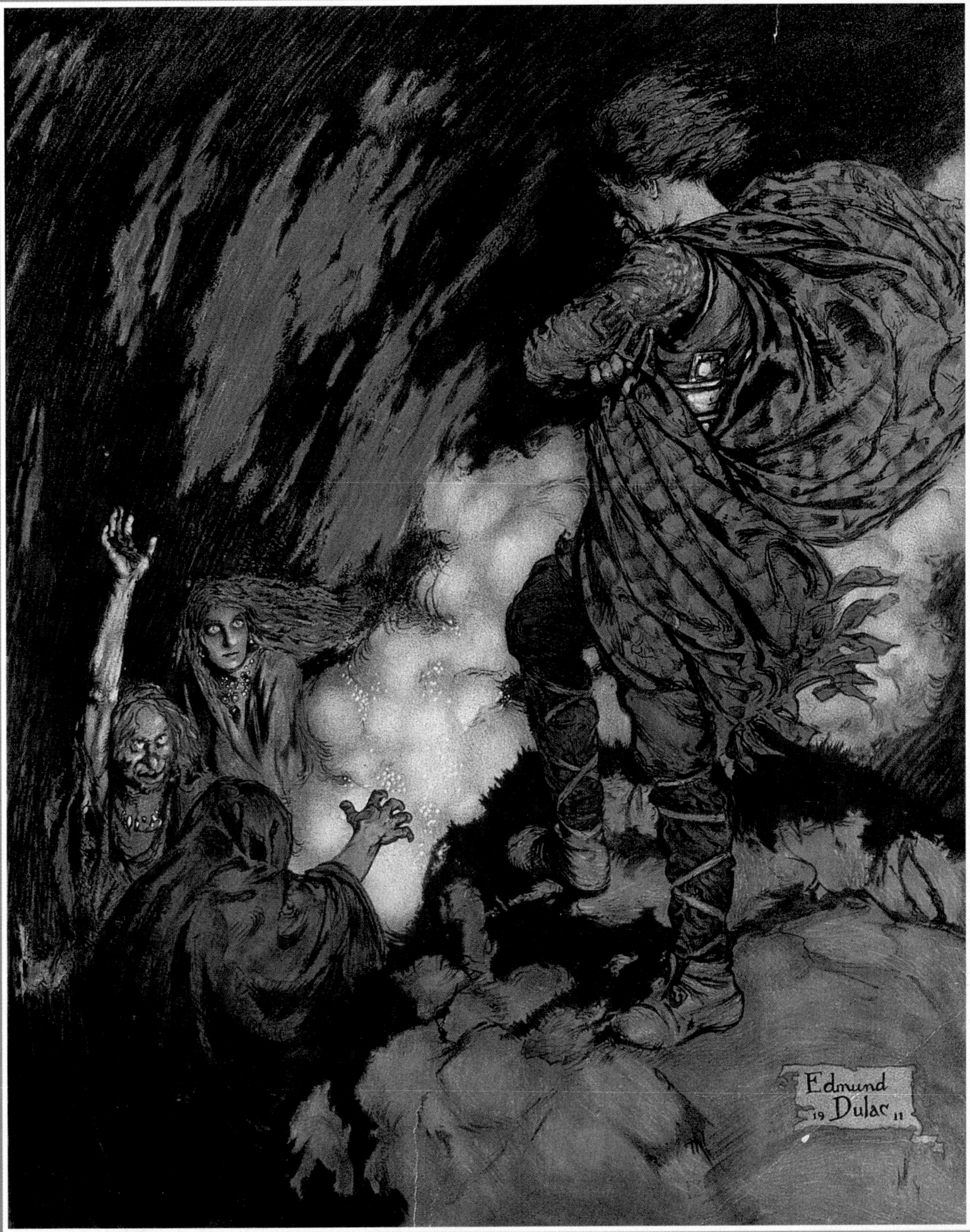
Edmund
19 Dulac 11

Act One

SCENE 1

Summary *Three Witches agree to meet Macbeth on a lonely wasteland later that day.*

A wasteland somewhere in Scotland. Thunder and lightning. Enter three WITCHES.

FIRST WITCH. When shall we three meet again?
  In thunder, lightning, or in rain?
SECOND WITCH. When the hurlyburly's done,
  When the battle's lost and won.
5 **THIRD WITCH.** That will be ere the set of sun.
FIRST WITCH. Where the place?
SECOND WITCH.   Upon the heath.
THIRD WITCH. There to meet with Macbeth.
FIRST WITCH. I come, Grimalkin!
10 **SECOND WITCH.** Paddock calls.
THIRD WITCH. Anon.
ALL. Fair is foul, and foul is fair,
  Hover through the fog and filthy air.

9 Graymalkin, a gray cat.
10 Paddock, a toad.
11 anon (ə non′), *adv.* soon.

SCENE 2

Summary *King Duncan learns from the Captain of his army that his chief rival Macdonwald has been killed by the brave Macbeth. Ross, a nobleman, tells him that Macbeth has also defeated a traitor, the Thane of Cawdor. Duncan orders Cawdor executed and names Macbeth the new Thane of Cawdor.*

A camp near Forres, north of Edinburgh. Battle noises sound offstage. Enter DUNCAN, MALCOLM, DONALBAIN, LENOX, *with* ATTENDANTS, *meeting a bleeding* CAPTAIN.

DUNCAN. What bloody man is that? He can report,
  As seemeth by his plight, of the revolt
  The newest state.
MALCOLM.   This is the sergeant
  Who like a good and hardy soldier fought
5 'Gainst my captivity. Hail, brave friend!
  Say to the King the knowledge of the broil
  As thou didst leave it.
CAPTAIN.   Doubtful it stood,
  As two spent swimmers that do cling together
  And choke their art. The merciless Macdonwald—
10 Worthy to be a rebel, for to that
  The multiplying villainies of nature

thane, a Scottish nobleman, just below an earl.

9 choke their art, hinder each other's ability to swim.

Do swarm upon him—from the Western Isles
Of kerns and gallowglasses is supplied;
And Fortune, on his damnèd quarrel smiling
15 Showed like a rebel's whore. But all's too weak;
For brave Macbeth—well he deserves that name—
Disdaining Fortune, with his brandished steel,
Which smoked with bloody execution,
Like valor's minion carved out his passage
20 Till he faced the slave,
Which ne'er shook hands nor bade farewell to him
Till he unseamed him from the nave to th' chops,
And fixed his head upon our battlements.
DUNCAN. O valiant cousin, worthy gentleman!
25 **CAPTAIN.** As whence the sun 'gins his reflection
Shipwrecking storms and direful thunders break,
So from that spring whence comfort seemed to come
Discomfort swells. Mark, King of Scotland, mark.
No sooner justice had, with valor armed,
30 Compelled these skipping kerns to trust their heels
But the Norweyan lord, surveying vantage,
With furbished arms and new supplies of men,
Began a fresh assault.
DUNCAN. Dismayed not this our captains, Macbeth and Banquo?
35 **CAPTAIN.** Yes, as sparrows eagles, or the hare the lion.
If I say say sooth, I must report they were
As cannons overcharged with double cracks,
So they doubly redoubled strokes upon the foe.
Except they meant to bathe in reeking wounds
40 Or memorize another Golgotha,
I cannot tell.
But I am faint. My gashes cry for help.
DUNCAN. So well thy words become thee as thy wounds;
They smack of honor both. Go get him surgeons.
(*Exit* CAPTAIN, *attended. Enter* ROSS *and* ANGUS.)
45 Who comes here?
MALCOLM.　　　　The worthy Thane of Ross.
LENNOX. What a haste looks through his eyes!
So should he look that seems to speak things strange.
ROSS. God save the King!
DUNCAN. Whence cam'st thou, worthy thane?
50 **ROSS.** From Fife, great King,
Where the Norweyan banners flout the sky
And fan our people cold.
Norway himself, with terrible numbers,
Assisted by that most disloyal traitor,

12 the western isles, Ireland and the Hebrides.
13 kerns and gallowglasses, Irish foot soldiers.
14–15 Fortune . . . whore. Fortune at first smiled upon him then deserted him.

■ According to the captain, what kind of a soldier and leader is Macbeth?

17 disdain (dis dān′), *v.* scorn.
17 brandish (bran′dish), *v.* wave threateningly.
19 minion (min′yən), *n.* favorite; darling.
20 slave, Macdonwald.
22 unseamed him . . . chaps, split him from navel to jaws.
24 cousin, Duncan and Macbeth are first cousins, but the term is often used to describe other family relationships.
31 Norweyan, Norwegian.

36 sooth, (süth), *n.* truth.

40 memorize . . . Golgotha, make the area as memorable for bloodshed as the place where Jesus was crucified.

51 flout, (flout), *v.* treat with scorn or contempt.
53 Norway himself, the king of Norway.

55   The Thane of Cawdor, began a dismal conflict,
Till that Bellona's bridegroom, lapped in proof,
Confronted him with self-comparisons,
Point against point, rebellious arm 'gainst arm,
Curbing his lavish spirit; and to conclude,
60   The victory fell on us.

DUNCAN.   Great happiness!

ROSS. That now
Sweno, the Norways' king, craves composition;
Nor would we deign him burial of his men
Till he disbursèd at Saint Colme's Inch
65   Ten thousand dollars to our general use.

DUNCAN. No more that Thane of Cawdor shall deceive
Our bosom interest. Go pronounce his present death,
And with his former title greet Macbeth.

ROSS. I'll see it done.

70   DUNCAN. What he hath lost noble Macbeth hath won.

SCENE 3

Summary *Macbeth and Banquo meet the three Witches. They call Macbeth Thane of Glamis, Thane of Cawdor, and king hereafter. They tell Banquo that his descendants will be kings. After the Witches vanish, one of their prophecies is confirmed when two noblemen tell Macbeth he has been named Thane of Cawdor.*

Thunder. Enter the three WITCHES.

FIRST WITCH. Where hast thou been, sister?

SECOND WITCH. Killing swine.

THIRD WITCH. Sister, where thou?

FIRST WITCH. A sailor's wife had chestnuts in her lap,
5   And munched, and munched, and munched. "Give me," quoth I.
"Aroint thee, witch!" the rump-fed runnion cries.
Her husband's to Aleppo gone, master o' the *Tiger*;
But in a sieve I'll thither sail,
And like a rat without a tail
10   I'll do, I'll do, and I'll do.

SECOND WITCH. I'll give thee a wind.

FIRST WITCH. Thou'rt kind.

THIRD WITCH. And I another.

FIRST WITCH. I myself have all the other,
15   And the very ports they blow,
All the quarters that they know
I' the shipman's card.
I'll drain him dry as hay.
Sleep shall neither night nor day

56–57 Bellona's bridegroom . . . self-comparisons. Macbeth, dressed in armor, matched him with equal strength. Bellona (bə lō′nə) was the Roman goddess of war.

62 composition, a peace treaty.

64 disburse (dis pėrs′), *v.* pay out.

64 Saint Colme's Inch, an island off the coast of Scotland.

67 bosom interest, intimate trust.

6 aroint (ə roint′) **thee,** get out of here.

6 runnion (ron′yən), *n.* mangy creature.

7 Aleppo, city in NW Syria, famous as a trading center.

9 without a tail. It was believed that witches could change themselves into animals, but could be detected by some deformity.

17 shipman's card, compass card or chart.

20   Hang upon his penthouse lid.
  He shall live a man forbid.
  Weary sev'nnights nine times nine
  Shall he dwindle, peak, and pine.
  Though his bark cannot be lost,
25   Yet it shall be tempest tossed.
  Look what I have.

SECOND WITCH. Show me, show me.

FIRST WITCH. Here I have a pilot's thumb,
  Wrecked as homeward he did come.
  (A drum sounds offstage.)

30 **THIRD WITCH.** A drum, a drum!
   Macbeth doth come.

ALL *(dancing).* The Weird Sisters, hand in hand,
  Posters of the sea and land,
  Thus do go about, about,
35   Thrice to thine, and thrice to mine,
  And thrice again, to make up nine.
  Peace! The charm's wound up.
  (Enter MACBETH *and* BANQUO.*)*

MACBETH. So foul and fair a day I have not seen.

BANQUO. How far is 't called to Forres? What are these,
40   So withered and so wild in their attire,
  That look not like th' inhabitants o' th' earth
  And yet are on 't? Live you? Or are you aught
  That man may question? You seem to understand me
  By each at once her chappy finger laying
45   Upon her skinny lips. You should be women,
  And yet your beards forbid me to interpret
  That you are so.

MACBETH.   Speak, if you can. What are you?

FIRST WITCH. All hail, Macbeth! Hail to thee, Thane of Glamis!

SECOND WITCH. All hail, Macbeth! Hail to thee, Thane of Cawdor!

50 **THIRD WITCH.** All hail, Macbeth, that shalt be king hereafter!

BANQUO. Good sir, why do you start and seem to fear
  Things that do sound so fair? I' the name of truth,
  Are ye fantastical or that indeed
  Which outwardly ye show? My noble partner
55   You greet with present grace and great prediction
  Of noble having and of royal hope,
  That he seems rapt withal. To me you speak not.
  If you can look into the seeds of time
  And say which grain will grow and which will not,
60   Speak then to me, who neither beg nor fear
  Your favors nor your hate.

20 penthouse lid, eyelid.
21 forbid, accursed.
22 sev'nnights, seven-nights; weeks.

■ What kind of power do the witches seem to have?

▲ Illustration by Charles Ricketts from *The Tragedie of Macbeth,* reproduced in the players' Shakespeare, after the Folio of 1623 (Ernest Benn, 1923). How do you predict the presence of the witches will affect the development of the plot?

48 Glamis (glämz).

57 rapt withal, completely absorbed by it.

FIRST WITCH. Hail!

SECOND WITCH. Hail!

THIRD WITCH. Hail!

65 **FIRST WITCH.** Lesser than Macbeth, and greater.

SECOND WITCH. Not so happy, yet much happier.

THIRD WITCH. Thou shalt get kings, though thou be none.
So all hail, Macbeth and Banquo!

FIRST WITCH. Banquo and Macbeth, all hail!

70 **MACBETH.** Stay, you imperfect speakers, tell me more!
By Sinel's death I know I am Thane of Glamis,
But how of Cawdor? The Thane of Cawdor lives
A prosperous gentleman; and to be king
Stands not within the prospect of belief,

75 No more than to be Cawdor. Say from whence
You owe this strange intelligence, or why
Upon this blasted heath you stop our way
With such prophetic greeting? Speak, I charge you.
(The WITCHES *vanish*.)

BANQUO. The earth hath bubbles, as the water has,

80 And these are of them. Whither are they vanished?

MACBETH. Into the air; and what seemed corporal melted,
As breath into the wind. Would they had stayed!

BANQUO. Were such things here as we do speak about?
Or have we eaten on the insane root

85 That takes the reason prisoner?

MACBETH. Your children shall be kings.

BANQUO.   You shall be king.

MACBETH. And Thane of Cawdor too. Went it not so?

BANQUO. To th' selfsame tune and words. Who's here?
(*Enter* ROSS *and* ANGUS.)

ROSS. The King hath happily received, Macbeth,

90 The news of thy success; and when he reads
Thy personal venture in the rebels' fight,
His wonder and his praises do contend
Which should be thine or his. Silenced with that,
In viewing o'er the rest o' the selfsame day

95 He finds thee in the stout Norweyan ranks,
Nothing afeard of what thyself didst make,
Strange images of death. As thick as tale
Came post with post, and every one did bear
Thy praises in his kingdom's great defense,

100 And poured them down before him.

ANGUS.   We are sent
To give thee from our royal master thanks,
Only to herald thee into his sight,

---

67 **get,** beget; father.

71 **Sinel,** Macbeth's father. Macbeth had inherited the title.

84 **insane root,** a root that causes hallucinations or insanity.

92 **contend,** (kən tend′), *v.* fight; struggle.
93 **silenced,** speechless with admiration.

96–97 **nothing . . . death.** Macbeth killed, but did not fear death for himself.
98 **post with post,** one messenger after another.

Not pay thee.

ROSS. And, for an earnest of a greater honor,
105   He bade me, from him, call thee Thane of Cawdor;
    In which addition, hail, most worthy thane.
    For it is thine.

BANQUO.   What, can the devil speak true?

MACBETH. The Thane of Cawdor lives. Why do you dress me
    In borrowed robes?

ANGUS.   Who was the thane lives yet,
110   But under heavy judgment bears that life
    Which he deserves to lose. Whether he was combined
    With those of Norway, or did line the rebel
    With hidden help and vantage, or that with both
    He labored in his country's wrack, I know not;
115   But treasons capital, confessed and proved,
    Have overthrown him.

MACBETH (aside).   Glamis, and Thane of Cawdor!
    The greatest is behind. (To ROSS and ANGUS.) Thanks for your pains.
    (Aside to BANQUO.) Do you not hope your children shall be kings
    When those that gave the Thane of Cawdor to me
120   Promised no less to them?

BANQUO (to MACBETH).   That, trusted home,
    Might yet enkindle you unto the crown,
    Besides the Thane of Cawdor. But 'tis strange;
    And oftentimes to win us to our harm
    The instruments of darkness tell us truths,
125   Win us with honest trifles, to betray 's
    In deepest consequence.
    Cousins, a word, I pray you.

(He converses apart with ROSS and ANGUS.)

MACBETH (aside). Two truths are told,
    As happy prologues to the swelling act
130   Of the imperial theme. I thank you, gentlemen.
    (Aside.) This supernatural soliciting
    Cannot be ill, cannot be good. If ill,
    Why hath it given me earnest of success
    Commencing in a truth? I am Thane of Cawdor.
135   If good, why do I yield to that suggestion
    Whose horrid image doth unfix my hair
    And make my seated heart knock at my ribs,
    Against the use of nature? Present fears
    Are less than horrible imaginings.
140   My thought, whose murder yet is but fantastical,
    Shakes so my single state of man

104 **earnest,** promise.

112 **line,** support.

117 **behind,** to come.

120–121 That . . . crown.
Complete belief in the witches may arouse in you the ambition to become king.

■ Compare Macbeth's reaction to the witches' prophecies with Banquo's reaction. What do you think Macbeth might be willing to do in order to see the witches' prophecy fulfilled?

131 **soliciting** (sə lis′it ing), n. temptation.

That function is smothered in <u>surmise</u>,
And nothing is but what is not.

BANQUO. Look how our partner's rapt.

145 **MACBETH** (*aside*). If chance will have me king, why, chance may
    crown me
Without my stir.

BANQUO.   New honors come upon him,
Like our strange garments, cleave not to their mold
But with the aid of use.

MACBETH (*aside*).   Come what come may,
Time and the hour runs through the roughest day.

150 **BANQUO.** Worthy Macbeth, we stay upon your leisure.

MACBETH. Give me your favor. My dull brain was wrought
With things forgotten. Kind gentlemen, your pains
Are registered where every day I turn
The leaf to read them. Let us toward the King.

155 (*Aside to* BANQUO.) Think upon what hath chanced,
    and at more time,
The interim having weighed it, let us speak
Our free hearts each to other.

BANQUO (*to* MACBETH). Very gladly.

MACBETH (*to* BANQUO). Till then, enough. Come, friends.

SCENE 4

Summary *The king thanks Macbeth and Banquo for their brave fighting. He names his son Malcolm as his successor. Macbeth, his ambition growing, realizes that Malcolm is an obstacle to fulfilling the witches' prophecy that he will be king. He begins to plan to murder King Duncan.*

Trumpets sound offstage. Enter DUNCAN, LENNOX, MALCOLM, DONALBAIN, *and* ATTENDANTS.

DUNCAN. Is execution done on Cawdor? Are not
Those in commission yet returned?

MALCOLM.   My liege,
They are not yet come back. But I have spoke
With one that saw him die, who did report

5 That very frankly he confessed his treasons,
Implored Your Highness' pardon, and set forth
A deep repentance. Nothing in his life
Became him like the leaving it. He died
As one that had been studied in his death

10 To throw away the dearest thing he owed
As 'twere a careless trifle.

DUNCAN.   There's no art
To find the mind's construction in the face.

Margin notes:

142 surmise (sər mīz′), *n.* guesswork.

140–143 My thought . . . is not. My thought, in which the murder is still only a fantasy, so disturbs me that all power of action is smothered by imagination, and only unreal imaginings seem real to me.

147 strange garments, new clothes.

150 we stay . . . leisure, we stand ready to serve when you call.

153–154 where . . . read them, in my mind and heart.

11–12 There's no art . . . face. There is no way of judging a person's thoughts from his or her appearance.

He was a gentleman on whom I built
An absolute trust.

(*Enter* MACBETH, BANQUO, ROSS, *and* ANGUS.)

                         O worthiest cousin!

15 The sin of my ingratitude even now
Was heavy on me. Thou art so far before
That swiftest wing of recompense is slow
To overtake thee. Would thou hadst less deserved,
That the proportion both of thanks and payment
20 Might have been mine! Only I have left to say,
More is thy due than more than all can pay.

MACBETH. The service and the loyalty I owe,
In doing it, pays itself. Your Highness' part
Is to receive our duties; and our duties
25 Are to your throne and state children and servants,
Which do but what they should by doing everything
Safe toward your love and honor.

DUNCAN.   Welcome hither!
I have begun to plant thee, and will labor
To make thee full of growing. Noble Banquo,
30 That hast no less deserved, nor must be known
No less to have done so, let me infold thee
And hold thee to my heart.

BANQUO.   There if I grow,
The harvest is your own.

DUNCAN.   My plenteous joys,
Wanton in fullness, seek to hide themselves
35 In drops of sorrow. Sons, kinsmen, thanes,
And you whose places are the nearest, know
We will establish our estate upon
Our eldest, Malcolm, and whom we name hereafter
The Prince of Cumberland; which honor must
40 Not unaccompanied invest him only,
But signs of nobleness, like stars, shall shine
On all deservers. From hence to Inverness,
And bind us further to you.

MACBETH. The rest is labor which is not used for you.
45 I'll be myself the harbinger and make joyful
The hearing of my wife with your approach;
So humbly take my leave.

DUNCAN.   My worthy Cawdor!

MACBETH (*aside*). The Prince of Cumberland! This is a step
On which I must fall down or else o'erleap,
50 For in my way it lies. Stars, hide your fires;
Let not light see my black and deep desires.

17 recompense (rek′əm-
pens), *n.* reward.

37 establish . . . upon, name
as heir to the throne.

42 Inverness, the location of
Macbeth's castle, Dunsinane.
44 the rest . . . you. Resting is
work for me, when I am
doing nothing to help you.
45 harbinger (här′bən jər),
n. forerunner.

■ What are Macbeth's
"black and deep desires"?
What stands in his way?

◄ The acclaimed actress Ellen Terry (1847–1928) is shown in her role as Lady Macbeth in this 1889 painting by John Singer Sargent. If you were casting a contemporary production of *Macbeth,* what actress would you choose to play the role of Lady Macbeth? Explain your choice.

The eye wink at the hand; yet let that be
Which the eye fears, when it is done, to see.   *(Exit.)*
DUNCAN. True, worthy Banquo. He is full so valiant,
55   And in his <u>commendations</u> I am fed;
It is a banquet to me. Let's after him,
Whose care is gone before to bid us welcome.
It is a peerless kinsman.   *(Trumpets sound.)*

55 commendation (kom′ən-
dā′shən), *n.* praise.

SCENE 5

Summary *When she reads Macbeth's letter about the witches' prophecies, Lady Macbeth begins to plot also—especially when she learns that Duncan will spend the night as their guest. When Macbeth returns, she encourages him to commit the murder soon.*

Macbeth's castle at Inverness. Enter LADY MACBETH *reading a letter.*

LADY MACBETH *(reads).* "They met me in the day of success; and I have
learned by the perfect'st report they have more in them than mortal knowledge. When I burnt in desire to question them further,
they made themselves air, into which they vanished. Whiles I stood
rapt in the wonder of it came missives from the King, who all-
hailed me 'Thane of Cawdor,' by which title, before these Weird
Sisters saluted me, and referred me to the coming on of time with
'Hail, king that shalt be!' This have I thought good to deliver thee,
my dearest partner of greatness, that thou mightst not lose the
dues of rejoicing by being ignorant of what greatness is promised
thee. Lay it to thy heart, and farewell."
    Glamis thou art, and Cawdor, and shalt be
What thou art promised. Yet do I fear thy nature;
It is too full o' the milk of human kindness
To catch the nearest way. Thou wouldst be great,
Art not without ambition, but without
The illness should attend it. What thou wouldst highly,
That wouldst thou holily; wouldst not play false,
And yet wouldst wrongly win. Thou'dst have, great Glamis,
That which cries "Thus thou must do," if thou have it,
And that which rather thou dost fear to do
Than wishest should be undone. Hie thee hither,
That I may pour my spirits in thine ear
And chastise with the valor of my tongue
All that impedes thee from the golden round
Which fate and metaphysical aid doth seem
To have thee crowned withal.   *(Enter a* MESSENGER.*)*
                       What is your tidings?

MESSENGER. The King comes here tonight.

LADY MACBETH.   Thou'rt mad to say it!
Is not thy master with him, who, were't so,
Would have informed for preparation?

MESSENGER. So please you, it is true. Our thane is coming.
One of my fellows had the speed of him,
Who, almost dead for breath, had scarcely more
Than would make up his message.

LADY MACBETH.   Give him tending;
He brings great news.   *(Exit* MESSENGER.*)*
                The raven himself is hoarse
That croaks the fatal entrance of Duncan
Under my battlements. Come, you spirits
That tend on mortal thoughts, unsex me here
And fill me from the crown to the toe top-full
Of direst cruelty! Make thick my blood;

5 **missive** (mis′iv), *n.*
message.

■ What does this letter
reveal about the relationship
between Macbeth and Lady
Macbeth?

17 **illness . . . it,** the
unscrupulousness you need
to achieve that ambition.

25 **golden round,** the crown.
26 **metaphysical,** supernatural.

32 **had the speed of him,**
outdistanced him.

35 **raven.** Long believed to
be a bird of ill omen, the
raven was said to foretell
death by its croaking.
38 **mortal thoughts,**
murderous thoughts.

Stop up th' access and passage to remorse,
That no compunctious visitings of nature
Shake my fell purpose, nor keep peace between
Th' effect and it! Come to my woman's breasts
45 And take my milk for gall, you murdering ministers,
Wherever in your sightless substances
You wait on nature's mischief! Come, thick night,
And pall thee in the dunnest smoke of hell,
That my keen knife see not the wound it makes,
50 Nor heaven peep through the blanket of the dark
To cry "Hold, hold!"   (*Enter* MACBETH.)
                    Great Glamis! Worthy Cawdor!
Greater than both by the all-hail hereafter!
Thy letters have transported me beyond
This ignorant present, and I feel now
55 The future in the instant.

MACBETH.   My dearest love,
Duncan comes here tonight.

LADY MACBETH.   And when goes hence?

MACBETH. Tomorrow, as he purposes.

LADY MACBETH.   O, never
Shall sun that morrow see!
Your face, my thane, is as a book where men
60 May read strange matters. To beguile the time,
Look like the time; bear welcome in your eye,
Your hand, your tongue. Look like th' innocent flower,
But be the serpent under 't. He that's coming
Must be provided for; and you shall put
65 This night's great business into my dispatch,
Which shall to all our nights and days to come
Give solely sovereign sway and masterdom.

MACBETH. We will speak further.

LADY MACBETH.   Only look up clear.
To alter favor ever is to fear.
70 Leave all the rest to me.

SCENE 6

Summary *Duncan and his sons arrive at Macbeth's castle and are welcomed by Lady Macbeth.*

Outside Macbeth's castle. Music sounds offstage. Enter DUNCAN, MALCOLM, DONALBAIN, BANQUO, LENNOX, MACDUFF, ROSS, ANGUS, *and* ATTENDANTS *carrying torches.*

DUNCAN. This castle hath a pleasant seat. The air
Nimbly and sweetly recommends itself

42 compunctious . . . nature, natural feelings of compassion.
43–44 keep peace . . . and it, come between my intention and my carrying out of it.

48 pall (pôl), *v.* wrap.
48 dunnest, darkest; murkiest.

60 beguile (bi gīl′), *v.* deceive.
60–61 To beguile . . . time, to deceive people, act as they expect you to act.

69 to alter . . . fear, to change facial expression shows fear.

Unto our gentle senses.

BANQUO.   This guest of summer,
The temple-haunting martlet, does approve
5   By his loved mansionry that the heaven's breath
Smells wooingly here. No jutty, frieze,
Buttress, nor coign of vantage but this bird
Hath made his pendent bed and procreant cradle.
Where they most breed and haunt, I have observed
10 The air is delicate.   (*Enter* LADY MACBETH.)

DUNCAN.   See, see, our honored hostess!
The love that follows us sometimes is our trouble,
Which still we thank as love. Herein I teach you
How you shall bid God 'ild us for your pains,
And thank us for your trouble.

LADY MACBETH.   All our service
15 In every point twice done, and then done double,
Were poor and single business to contend
Against those honors deep and broad wherewith
Your Majesty loads our house. For those of old,
And the late dignities heaped up to them,
20 We rest your hermits.

DUNCAN.   Where's the Thane of Cawdor?
We coursed him at the heels, and had a purpose
To be his purveyor; but he rides well,
And his great love, sharp as his spur, hath holp him
To his home before us. Fair and noble hostess,
25 We are your guest tonight.

LADY MACBETH.   Your servants ever
Have theirs, themselves, and what is theirs in compt
To make their audit at Your Highness' pleasure,
Still to return your own.

DUNCAN.   Give me your hand.
Conduct me to mine host. We love him highly,
30 And shall continue our graces towards him.
By your leave, hostess.

SCENE 7

Summary *Macbeth decides he cannot murder Duncan, but Lady Macbeth convinces him once more. They plan to drug Duncan's servants and to murder him in his sleep.*

Outside a dining hall in MACBETH'S *castle. Music sounds offstage. Attendants with torches and servants with dishes of food cross the stage and exit.*

MACBETH. If it were done when 'tis done, then 'twere well
It were done quickly. If th' assassination

---

4 martlet . . . does approve, swallow demonstrates.
6–8 no jutty . . . procreant cradle. The swallow has built a nest in every architectural space available.

13 God 'ild, literally "God yield," used in returning thanks.

20 We rest your hermits. Like religious hermits, we will pray for you.
22 purveyor (pər vā′ ər), *n.* forerunner.

25–28 Your servants . . . own. Since we are your servants, all that we have is ready to be delivered to you.

Could trammel up the consequence, and catch
With his surcease success—that but this blow
5   Might be the be-all and the end-all!—here,
But here, upon this bank and shoal of time,
We'd jump the life to come. But in these cases
We still have judgment here, that we but teach
Bloody instructions, which, being taught, return
10   To plague th' inventor. This evenhanded justice
Commends th' ingredience of our poisoned chalice
To our own lips. He's here in double trust:
First, as I am his kinsman and his subject,
Strong both against the deed; then, as his host,
15   Who should against his murderer shut the door,
Not bear the knife myself. Besides, this Duncan
Hath borne his faculties so meek, hath been
So clear in his great office, that his virtues
Will plead like angels, trumpet-tongued, against
20   The deep damnation of his taking-off;
And Pity, like a naked newborn babe
Striding the blast, or heaven's cherubin, horsed
Upon the sightless couriers of the air,
Shall blow the horrid deed in every eye,
25   That tears shall drown the wind. I have no spur
To prick the sides of my intent, but only
Vaulting ambition, which o'erleaps itself
And falls on th' other—   (*Enter* LADY MACBETH.)
How now, what news?
30 **LADY MACBETH.** He has almost supped. Why have you left the chamber?
MACBETH. Hath he asked for me?
LADY MACBETH.   Know you not he has?
MACBETH. We will proceed no further in this business.
He hath honored me of late, and I have bought
Golden opinions from all sorts of people,
35   Which would be worn now in their newest gloss,
Not cast aside so soon.
LADY MACBETH.   Was the hope drunk
Wherein you dressed yourself? Hath it slept since?
And wakes it now, to look so green and pale
At what it did so freely? From this time
40   Such I account thy love. Art thou afeard
To be the same in thine own act and valor
As thou art in desire? Wouldst thou have that
Which thou esteem'st the ornament of life,
And live a coward in thine own esteem,
45   Letting "I dare not" wait upon "I would,"

4 **surcease** (sər sēs′), *n.* death.

7 **jump,** risk.

17 **faculties,** royal powers.

20 **taking-off,** murder.

22 **striding the blast,** riding the wind.
23 **couriers of the air,** winds.

25–28 **I have . . . th' other.** I have nothing to stimulate me to accomplishing my purpose but ambition, which is apt to become too great.

43 **ornament of life,** the crown.

Like the poor cat i' the adage?

MACBETH.   Prithee, peace!
  I dare do all that may become a man;
  Who dares do more is none.

LADY MACBETH.   What beast was't, then,
  That made you break this enterprise to me?
50 When you durst do it, then you were a man;
  And, to be more than what you were, you would
  Be so much more the man. Nor time nor place
  Did then adhere, and yet you would make both.
  They have made themselves, and that their fitness now
55 Does unmake you. I have given suck, and know
  How tender 'tis to love the babe that milks me;
  I would, while it was smiling in my face,
  Have plucked my nipple from his boneless gums
  And dashed the brains out, had I so sworn as you
60 Have done to this.

MACBETH.   If we should fail?

LADY MACBETH.   We fail?
  But screw your courage to the sticking place
  And we'll not fail. When Duncan is asleep—
  Whereto the rather shall his day's hard journey
  Soundly invite him—his two chamberlains
65 Will I with wine and wassail so convince
  That memory, the warder of the brain,
  Shall be a fume, and the receipt of reason
  A limbeck only. When in swinish sleep
  Their drenchèd natures lies as in a death,
70 What cannot you and I perform upon
  Th' unguarded Duncan? What not put upon
  His spongy officers, who shall bear the guilt
  Of our great quell?

MACBETH.   Bring forth men-children only!
  For thy undaunted mettle should compose
75 Nothing but males. Will it not be received,
  When we have marked with blood those sleepy two
  Of his own chamber and used their very daggers,
  That they have done 't?

LADY MACBETH.   Who dares receive it other,
  As we shall make our griefs and clamor roar
80 Upon his death?

MACBETH.   I am settled, and bend up
  Each corporal agent to this terrible feat.
  Away, and mock the time with fairest show.
  False face must hide what the false heart doth know.

[handwritten annotations:]
— not a question
— she will drug them to make them sleep
— They will blame the guards for his murder
Macbeth is admiring his wife's courage and manliness
→ He is ready to kill Duncan

[margin notes:]
46 cat . . . adage. The adage, or proverb, is "The cat would eat fish, but would not wet her feet."

52–53 nor time . . . adhere, there was no suitable time or place to commit the murder.

66–68 memory . . . only, memory and reason both will disappear, like the vapor of the alcohol they drink.

72 spongy, drunken.
73 quell, murder.

74 mettle (met′l), *n.* courage.

■ What does Lady Macbeth reveal about herself in this scene?

80–81 bend up . . . feat, direct all my bodily powers to executing the murder.

After Reading

Making Connections

Shaping Your Response

1. Which character do you believe is the stronger, Macbeth or Lady Macbeth? Why do you think so?

Analyzing the Play

2. Why do you think Macbeth and Banquo react in the ways they do to the prophecies of the witches and to their fulfillment?

3. An **aside** is a dramatic convention in which a character voices his or her thoughts so that the audience—but not the other characters—can hear. What is foreshadowed by Macbeth's aside in scene 3, lines 128–143?

4. A **soliloquy** is a dramatic convention in which a character voices his or her thoughts while alone on stage. What does Macbeth's soliloquy in scene 7, lines 1–28 reveal about his state of mind?

Extending the Ideas

5. Macbeth and Lady Macbeth seem to be very ambitious. How far can ambition lead a person into asserting his or her **individuality** over that of others? How far is too far?

Literary Focus: Plot Structure

In act 1, Shakespeare establishes the setting and the mood, introduces the characters and presents the conflicts that will drive the **plot.**

1. Write the names of the characters you feel will be key in the plot.

2. In one sentence describe the situation and identify the conflicts.

3. List the steps Macbeth and Lady Macbeth plan to follow in the assassination of King Duncan.

Vocabulary Study

Select the word that fits the meaning of each sentence.

1. King Duncan (disdains, contends) the Thane of Cawdor because he is a traitor.

2. Duncan gives Macbeth Cawdor's title as a (surmise, recompense) for his brave fighting.

3. The Scottish army will not allow the Norwegian king to bury his men until he (disburses, flouts) money to them.

4. Macbeth wants to be the (harbinger, minion) of the news of the witches' predictions.

5. Macbeth praises Lady Macbeth for her (commendation, mettle) in wanting to proceed with the murder of Duncan.

Act Two

SCENE 1

Summary *Macbeth seeks to gain the loyalty of Banquo. As he waits for Lady Macbeth's signal that all is in order for the murder of Duncan, a vision of a dagger appears before him.*

Courtyard of MACBETH'S *castle. Enter* BANQUO *and* FLEANCE, *carrying a torch.*

BANQUO. How goes the night, boy?

FLEANCE. The moon is down, I have not heard the clock.

BANQUO. And she goes down at twelve.

FLEANCE.   I take 't, 'tis later, sir.

BANQUO. Hold, take my sword.   *(He gives him his sword.)*
        There's husbandry in heaven;
5   Their candles are all out. Take thee that too.
        (He gives him his belt and dagger.)
        A heavy summons lies like lead upon me,
        And yet I would not sleep. Merciful powers,
        Restrain in me the cursèd thoughts that nature
        Gives way to in repose.
        (Enter MACBETH *and a* SERVANT *with a torch.)*
10   Give me my sword. Who's there?   *(He takes the sword.)*

MACBETH. A friend.

BANQUO. What, sir, not yet at rest? The King's abed.
        He hath been in unusual pleasure,
        And sent forth great largess to your offices.
15   This diamond he greets your wife withal,
        By the name of most kind hostess, and shut up
        In measureless content.   *(He gives a diamond.)*

MACBETH.   Being unprepared,
        Our will became the servant to defect,
        Which else should free have wrought.

20 **BANQUO.** All's well.
        I dreamt last night of the three Weird Sisters.
        To you they have showed some truth.

MACBETH.   I think not of them.
        Yet, when we can entreat an hour to serve,
        We would spend it in some words upon that business,
25   If you would grant the time.

BANQUO.   At your kind'st leisure.

MACBETH. If you shall cleave to my consent when 'tis,
        It shall make honor for you.

BANQUO.   So I lose none
        In seeking to augment it, but still keep
        My bosom franchised and allegiance clear,

---

4 **husbandry,** economy.

■ At this point, what questions might you ask Banquo about his "cursèd thoughts"?

14 **great largess . . . offices,** many gifts of money to be distributed among your servants.
16–17 **shut up . . . content,** has ended his day greatly contented.
17–19 **being unprepared . . . wrought.** The unexpectedness of Duncan's visit has prevented us from entertaining him as we would have liked.

26 **if you . . . when 'tis,** if you ally yourself with me when the time comes.

28 **augment** (ôg ment′), *v.* increase.

30   I shall be counseled.

MACBETH.   Good repose the while!

BANQUO. Thanks, sir. The like to you.

(*Exit* BANQUO *with* FLEANCE.)

MACBETH (*to* SERVANT). Go bid thy mistress, when my drink is ready,
    She strike upon the bell. Get thee to bed.   (*Exit* SERVANT.)
    Is this a dagger which I see before me,

35   The handle toward my hand? Come, let me clutch thee.
    I have thee not, and yet I see thee still.
    Art thou not, fatal vision, sensible
    To feeling as to sight? Or art thou but
    A dagger of the mind, a false creation,

40   Proceeding from the heat-oppressèd brain?
    I see thee yet, in form as palpable
    As this which now I draw.   (*He draws a dagger.*)
    Thou marshall'st me the way that I was going,
    And such an instrument I was to use.

45   Mine eyes are made the fools o' th' other senses,
    Or else worth all the rest. I see thee still,
    And on thy blade and dudgeon gouts of blood,
    Which was not so before. There's no such thing.
    It is the bloody business which informs

50   Thus to mine eyes. Now o'er the one half world
    Nature seems dead, and wicked dreams abuse
    The curtained sleep. Witchcraft celebrates
    Pale Hecate's offerings, and withered Murder,
    Alarumed by his sentinel, the wolf,

55   Whose howl's his watch, thus with his stealthy pace,
    With Tarquin's ravishing strides, towards his design
    Moves like a ghost. Thou sure and firm-set earth,
    Hear not my steps which way they walk, for fear
    Thy very stones prate of my whereabouts

60   And take the present horror from the time
    Which now suits with it. Whiles I threat, he lives;
    Words to the heat of deeds too cold breath gives.   (*A bell rings.*)
    I go, and it is done. The bell invites me.
    Hear it not, Duncan, for it is a knell

65   That summons thee to heaven or to hell.

SCENE 2

Summary *Macbeth murders Duncan, but, in his confused state, fails to leave the daggers behind to incriminate Duncan's servants. Lady Macbeth returns the daggers to the bedchamber.*

A room in the castle. Enter LADY MACBETH.

27–30 So I . . . counseled. As long as I do not lose my honor in trying to increase it, and keep myself free and my loyalty to Duncan unstained, I will listen to you.

41 palpable (pal′pə bəl), *adj.* definite.
43 thou marshal'st me, you lead me.

47 dudgeon (duj′ən), *n.* handle.
49 inform, appear.

53 Hecate (hek′ə tē), goddess of witchcraft.

56 Tarquin (tär′kwən), one of the tyrannical kings of early Rome, who raped the chaste Lucrece.
59 prate, talk foolishly.

◄ This illustration by Charles Ricketts is from *The Tragedie of Macbeth*, published in 1923. How does the dagger in Lady Macbeth's hand symbolize the guilt that she and her husband share? How do their differing poses illustrate their distinct reactions to the king's murder?

LADY MACBETH. That which hath made them drunk hath
    made me bold;
  What hath quenched them hath given me fire. Hark! Peace!
  It was the owl that shrieked, the fatal bellman,
  Which gives the stern'st good-night. He is about it.
5   The doors are open; and the surfeited grooms
  Do mock their charge with snores. I have drugged their possets,
  That death and nature do contend about them
  Whether they live or die.
MACBETH (*offstage*).   Who's there? What, ho!
LADY MACBETH. Alack, I am afraid they have awaked,
10   And 'tis not done. Th' attempt and not the deed
  Confounds us. Hark! I laid their daggers ready;
  He could not miss 'em. Had he not resembled
  My father as he slept, I had done 't.

Duncan looked like her father so she couldn't kill him herself

3 owl . . . bellman. The screech of an owl was often interpreted as an omen of death.
6 posset, drink made of hot milk curdled with wine or ale.

Macbeth—Act Two, Scene 2   **137**

(Enter MACBETH *carrying bloody daggers.)*
　　My husband!
15　MACBETH. I have done the deed. Didst thou not hear a noise?
　　LADY MACBETH. I heard the owl scream and the crickets cry.
　　　Did not you speak?
　　MACBETH. When?
　　LADY MACBETH. Now.
20　MACBETH. As I descended?
　　LADY MACBETH. Ay.
　　MACBETH. Hark! Who lies i' the second chamber?
　　LADY MACBETH. Donalbain.
　　MACBETH *(looking at his hands).* This is a sorry sight.
25　LADY MACBETH. A foolish thought, to say a sorry sight.
　　MACBETH. There's one did laugh in 's sleep, and one cried
　　　　"Murder!"
　　　That they did wake each other. I stood and heard them.
　　　But they did say their prayers, and addressed them
　　　Again to sleep.
　　LADY MACBETH.　　There are two lodged together.

29 **two,** Malcolm and Donalbain.

30　MACBETH. One cried "God bless us!" and "Amen!" the other,
　　　As they had seen me with these hangman's hands.
　　　List'ning their fear, I could not say "Amen"
　　　When they did say "God bless us!"
　　LADY MACBETH. Consider it not so deeply.

31 **hangman's hands.** In Elizabethan England, the hangman also had to "draw"—remove the entrails from—some of his victims.

35　MACBETH. But wherefore could not I pronounce "Amen"?
　　　I had most need of blessing, and "Amen"
　　　Stuck in my throat.
　　LADY MACBETH.　　　These deeds must not be thought
　　　After these ways; so, it will make us mad.
　　MACBETH. Methought I heard a voice cry "Sleep no more!
40　　Macbeth does murder sleep," the innocent sleep,
　　　Sleep that knits up the raveled sleave of care,
　　　The death of each day's life, sore labor's bath,
　　　Balm of hurt minds, great nature's second course,
　　　Chief nourisher in life's feast—

41 **raveled sleave,** tangled thread.

　　LADY MACBETH.　　　　　What do you mean?
45　MACBETH. Still it cried "Sleep no more!" to all the house;
　　　"Glamis hath murdered sleep, and therefore Cawdor
　　　Shall sleep no more; Macbeth shall sleep no more."
　　LADY MACBETH. Who was it that thus cried? Why, worthy thane,
　　　You do unbend your noble strength to think
50　　So brainsickly of things. Go get some water
　　　And wash this filthy witness from your hand.
　　　Why did you bring these daggers from the place?
　　　They must lie there. Go, carry them and smear

The sleepy grooms with blood.

MACBETH.   I'll go no more.
55   I am afraid to think what I have done;
  Look on 't again I dare not.

LADY MACBETH.   Infirm of purpose!
  Give me the daggers. The sleeping and the dead
  Are but as pictures. 'Tis the eye of childhood
  That fears a painted devil. If he do bleed,
60   I'll gild the faces of the grooms withal,
  For it must seem their guilt.
(She takes the daggers and exits. Knocking sounds offstage.)

MACBETH.   Whence is that knocking?
  How is 't with me, when every noise appalls me?
  What hands are here? Ha! They pluck out mine eyes.
  Will all great Neptune's ocean wash this blood
65   Clean from my hand? No, this my hand will rather
  The multitudinous seas incarnadine,
  Making the green one red.
(Enter LADY MACBETH.*)*

LADY MACBETH. My hands are of your color, but I shame
  To wear a heart so white. *(Knock.)* I hear a knocking
70   At the south entry. Retire we to our chamber.
  A little water clears us of this deed.
  How easy is it, then! Your constancy
  Hath left you unattended. *(Knock.)* Hark! More knocking.
  Get on your nightgown, lest occasion call us
75   And show us to be watchers. Be not lost
  So poorly in your thoughts.

MACBETH. To know my deed, 'twere best not know myself. *(Knock.)*
  Wake Duncan with thy knocking! I would thou couldst.

SCENE 3

Summary *A drunken porter opens the castle gate for Macduff and Lennox. Macduff discovers Duncan's body and awakens the household. Macbeth kills Duncan's servants in a fury—he says—over their having murdered the king. Duncan's sons, Malcolm and Donalbain, now fearing for their own lives, flee the country.*

The courtyard. Knocking sounds offstage. Enter a PORTER.

PORTER. Here's a knocking indeed! If a man were porter of hell gate,
  he should have old turning the key. *(Knock.)* Knock, knock, knock!
  Who's there, i' the name of Beelzebub? Here's a farmer that
  hanged himself on th' expectation of plenty. Come in time! Have
5   napkins enough about you; here you'll sweat for 't. *(Knock.)*
  Knock, knock! Who's there, in th' other devil's name? Faith, here's

56 infirm (in fèrm′), *adj.* weak.

60–61 I'll gild . . . guilt. I'll paint the servants' faces with Duncan's blood to indicate their guilt.

66 incarnadine, redden.
67 making . . . red, staining the green sea blood red.

72–73 Your constancy . . . unattended. You look disturbed and uneasy.
75 watchers, awake.
77 To know . . . myself. It is better to be lost in my thoughts than to be aware of what I have done.

■ Who is the porter pretending to be as he talks to the farmer, the equivocator, and the tailor?

2 old, plenty of.
3 Beelzebub (bē el′zə bub), a Devil.
4 on the expectation of plenty, because he tried illegally to earn an excess profit on his crops.
5 napkins enough, handkerchiefs to wipe off the sweat caused by the heat of Hell.

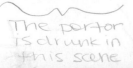
The portor
is drunk in
this scene

an equivocator, that could swear in both the scales against either scale, who committed treason enough for God's sake, yet could not equivocate to heaven. O, come in, equivocator. *(Knock.)* Knock,

10 knock, knock! Who's there? Faith, here's an English tailor come hither for stealing out of a French hose. Come in, tailor. Here you may roast your goose. *(Knock.)* Knock, knock! Never at quiet! What are you? But this place is too cold for hell. I'll devil-porter it no further. I had thought to have let in some of all professions

15 that go the primrose way to th' everlasting bonfire. *(Knock.)* Anon, anon! *(He opens the gate.)* I pray you, remember the porter.
   (Enter MACDUFF *and* LENNOX.)

MACDUFF. Was it so late, friend, ere you went to bed,
   That you do lie so late?

PORTER. Faith, sir, we were carousing till the second cock; and drink,
20   sir, is a great provoker of three things.

MACDUFF. What three things does drink especially provoke?

PORTER. Marry, sir, nose-painting, sleep, and urine. Lechery, sir, it provokes and unprovokes: it provokes the desire but it takes away the performance. Therefore much drink may be said to be an equivo-

25   cator with lechery: it makes him and it mars him; it sets him on and it takes him off; it persuades him and disheartens him, makes him stand to and not stand to; in conclusion, equivocates him in a sleep and, giving him the lie, leaves him.

MACDUFF. I believe drink gave thee the lie last night.

30 **PORTER.** That it did, sir, i' the very throat on me. But I requited him for his lie, and, I think, being too strong for him, though he took up my legs sometimes, yet I made a shift to cast him.

MACDUFF. Is thy master stirring?   *(Enter* MACBETH.)
   Our knocking has awaked him. Here he comes.   *(Exit* PORTER.)

35 **LENNOX.** Good morrow, noble sir.

MACBETH.   Good morrow, both.

MACDUFF. Is the King stirring, worthy thane?

MACBETH.   Not yet.

MACDUFF. He did command me to call timely on him.
   I have almost slipped the hour.

MACBETH.   I'll bring you to him.

MACDUFF. I know this is a joyful trouble to you,
40   But yet 'tis one.

MACBETH. The labor we delight in physics pain.
   This is the door.

MACDUFF.   I'll make so bold to call,
   For 'tis my limited service.   *(Exit* MACDUFF.)

LENNOX. Goes the King hence today?

45 **MACBETH.** He does; he did appoint so.

LENNOX. The night has been unruly. Where we lay,

7 equivocator (i kwiv′ ə kāt/ər), *n.* person who uses expressions with double meaning in order to mislead.

11 stealing . . . hose. Tailors were often accused of stealing cloth. Since French hose (breeches) at this period were short and tight, it would take a clever tailor to cut them smaller so as to steal the excess cloth.

12 goose, a pressing iron used by a tailor.

15 primrose . . . bonfire, path of pleasure leading to everlasting damnation in Hell.

19 second cock, about 3:00 in the morning.

30 requite (ri kwīt′), *v.* repay.

37 timely, early.

41 physics pain, relieves that labor of its troublesome (painful) aspect.

43 limited, appointed.

Our chimneys were blown down, and, as they say,
Lamentings heard i' th' air, strange screams of death,
And prophesying with accents terrible
50 Of dire combustion and confused events
New hatched to the woeful time. The obscure bird
Clamored the livelong night. Some say the earth
Was feverous and did shake.

MACBETH.   'Twas a rough night.
LENNOX. My young remembrance cannot parallel
55 A fellow to it.   (*Enter* MACDUFF.)
MACDUFF.   O, horror, horror, horror!
Tongue nor heart cannot conceive nor name thee!
MACBETH AND LENNOX. What's the matter?
MACDUFF. Confusion now hath made his masterpiece!
Most sacrilegious murder hath broke ope
60 The Lord's anointed temple and stole thence
The life o' the building!
MACBETH. What is 't you say? The life?
LENNOX. Mean you His Majesty?
MACDUFF. Approach the chamber and destroy your sight
65 With a new Gorgon. Do not bid me speak;
See, and then speak yourselves.   (*Exit* MACBETH *and* LENNOX.)
                                        Awake, awake!
Ring the alarum bell. Murder and treason!
Banquo and Donalbain, Malcolm, awake!
Shake off this downy sleep, death's counterfeit,
70 And look on death itself! Up, up, and see
The great doom's image! Malcolm, Banquo,
As from your graves rise up and walk like sprites
To countenance this horror! Ring the bell.   (*Bell rings.*)
(*Enter* LADY MACBETH.)

LADY MACBETH. What's the business,
75 That such a hideous trumpet calls to parley
The sleepers of the house? Speak, speak!
MACDUFF. O gentle lady,
'Tis not for you to hear what I can speak.
The repetition in a woman's ear
80 Would murder as it fell.   (*Enter* BANQUO.)
                              O Banquo, Banquo,
Our royal master's murdered!
LADY MACBETH.   Woe, alas!
What, in our house?
BANQUO.   Too cruel anywhere.
Dear Duff, I prithee, contradict thyself
And say it is not so.

■ Visualize the unruly night Lennox describes. What state of the times is suggested by these events?

51 **obscure bird,** owl.

55 **A fellow to it,** an equal to it.

60 **Lord's . . . temple,** an allusion to the idea that a king is God's representative. The metaphorical temple is the king's body.

65 **Gorgon,** a horrible monster of Greek legend. Whoever looked at her was turned to stone. (See the picture of Medusa on page 33.)

71 **great doom's image,** sight as awful as Judgment Day.

(*Enter* MACBETH, LENNOX, *and* ROSS.)

85 **MACBETH.** Had I but died an hour before this chance
  I had lived a blessèd time; for from this instant
  There's nothing serious in mortality.
  All is but toys. Renown and grace is dead;
  The wine of life is drawn, and the mere lees
90   Is left this vault to brag of.

(*Enter* MALCOLM *and* DONALBAIN.)

DONALBAIN. What is amiss?

MACBETH.   You are, and do not know 't.
  The spring, the head, the fountain of your blood
  Is stopped, the very source of it is stopped.

MACDUFF. Your royal father's murdered.

MALCOLM.   O, by whom?

95 **LENNOX.** Those of his chamber, as it seemed, had done 't.
  Their hands and faces were all badged with blood;
  So were their daggers, which unwiped we found
  Upon their pillows. They stared and were distracted;
  No man's life was to be trusted with them.

100 **MACBETH.** O, yet I do repent me of my fury,
  That I did kill them.

MACDUFF.   Wherefore did you so?

MACBETH. Who can be wise, amazed, temp'rate and furious,
  Loyal and neutral, in a moment? No man.
  Th' expedition of my violent love
105   Outran the pauser, reason. Here lay Duncan,
  His silver skin laced with his golden blood,
  And his gashed stabs looked like a breach in nature
  For ruin's wasteful entrance; there the murderers,
  Steeped in the colors of their trade, their daggers
110   Unmannerly breeched with gore. Who could refrain
  That had a heart to love, and in that heart
  Courage to make 's love known?

LADY MACBETH (*fainting*).   Help me hence, ho!

MACDUFF. Look to the lady.

MALCOLM (*aside to* DONALBAIN). Why do we hold our tongues,
115   That most may claim this argument for ours?

DONALBAIN (*aside to* MALCOLM). What should be spoken here,
   where our fate,
  Hid in an auger hole, may rush and seize us?
  Let's away. Our tears are not yet brewed.

MALCOLM (*aside to* DONALBAIN). Nor our strong sorrow upon the
   foot of motion.

120 **BANQUO.** Look to the lady. (LADY MACBETH *is helped out.*)
  And when we have our naked frailties hid,

87 mortality, human life.

89–90 The wine of life . . . brag of. Duncan is dead, and those men who are left behind cannot compare to him.

■ What reasons does Macbeth give for murdering the servants?

104 expedition (ek′spə-dish′ən), *n.* haste.

[handwritten: Duncan is the natural King]

115 that most . . . ours, we who are most concerned with this death.

117 augur (ô′gər) **hole,** obscure hiding place.

121 our . . . hid, gotten dressed.

That suffer in exposure, let us meet
And question this most bloody piece of work
To know it further. Fears and scruples shake us.
125   In the great hand of God I stand, and thence
Against the undivulged pretense I fight
Of treasonous malice.

MACDUFF.   And so do I.

ALL.   So all.

MACBETH. Let's briefly put on manly readiness
And meet i' the hall together.

ALL.   Well contented.

(Exit all but MALCOLM *and* DONALBAIN.*)*

130 **MALCOLM.** What will you do? Let's not consort with them.
To show an unfelt sorrow is an office
Which the false man does easy. I'll to England.

DONALBAIN. To Ireland, I. Our separated fortune
Shall keep us both the safer. Where we are,
135   There's daggers in men's smiles; the nea'er in blood,
The nearer bloody.

MALCOLM.   This murderous shaft that's shot
Hath not yet lighted, and our safest way
Is to avoid the aim. Therefore to horse,
And let us not be dainty of leave-taking,
140   But shift away. There's warrant in that theft
Which steals itself when there's no mercy left.

SCENE 4

> **Summary** *Macduff tells Ross that Malcolm and Donalbain are suspected of murdering their father and that Macbeth has been named king.*

Outside MACBETH'S *castle. Enter* ROSS *with an* OLD MAN.

OLD MAN. Threescore and ten I can remember well,
Within the volume of which time I have seen
Hours dreadful and things strange, but this sore night
Hath trifled former knowings.

ROSS.   Ha, good father,
5   Thou seest the heavens, as troubled with man's act,
Threatens his bloody stage. By th' clock 'tis day,
And yet dark night strangles the traveling lamp.
Is 't night's predominance or the day's shame
That darkness does the face of earth entomb
10   When living light should kiss it?

OLD MAN.   'Tis unnatural,
Even like the deed that's done. On Tuesday last
A falcon, towering in her pride of place,

124 scruple (skrü′pəl), *n.* doubt.
126–127 against . . . malice. I will fight against the unknown purpose which prompted this act of treason.
128 put . . . readiness, get dressed.

■ Why do Malcolm and Donalbain decide to flee?

135–136 the nea'er . . . bloody, the closer in kinship to Duncan, the greater the chance of being murdered.
139 dainty of, ceremonious about.
140–141 there's warrant . . . left, we are justified in stealing away in these merciless times.

7 traveling lamp, the sun.

Was by a mousing owl hawked at and killed.

ROSS. And Duncan's horses—a thing most strange and certain—

15   Beauteous and swift, the minions of their race,
Turned wild in nature, broke their stalls, flung out,
Contending 'gainst obedience, as they would
Make war with mankind.

OLD MAN.   'Tis said they eat each other.

ROSS. They did so, to th' amazement of mine eyes

20   That looked upon 't.   (*Enter* MACDUFF.)
                              Here comes the good Macduff.
How goes the world, sir, now?

MACDUFF.   Why, see you not?

ROSS. Is 't known who did this more than bloody deed?

MACDUFF. Those that Macbeth hath slain.

ROSS.   Alas the day,
What good could they pretend?

MACDUFF.   They were suborned.

25   Malcolm and Donalbain, the King's two sons,
Are stol'n away and fled, which puts upon them
Suspicion of the deed.

ROSS.   'Gainst nature still!
Thriftless ambition, that will ravin up
Thine own life's means! Then 'tis most like

30   The sovereignty will fall upon Macbeth.

MACDUFF. He is already named and gone to Scone
To be invested.

ROSS.   Where is Duncan's body?

MACDUFF. Carried to Colmekill,
The sacred storehouse of his predecessors

35   And guardian of their bones.

ROSS.   Will you to Scone?

MACDUFF. No, cousin, I'll to Fife.

ROSS.   Well, I will thither.

MACDUFF. Well, may you see things well done there. Adieu,
Lest our old robes sit easier than our new!

ROSS. Farewell, father.

40   **OLD MAN.** God's benison go with you, and with those
That would make good of bad, and friends of foes!

■ Visualize the unusual and unnatural events described by Ross and the old man. What might these events **foreshadow**?

24 what . . . pretend, what profit could they have been seeking?
24 suborn (sə bôrn′), *v.* hire or bribe.

28 ravin up, devour.
29 own life's means, parent.

31 Scone, the place where Scottish kings were crowned.
32 invest, (in vest′), *v.* install in office with a ceremony.
33 Colmekill, Iona Island, off the west coast of Scotland.

40 benison (ben′ə zən), *n.* blessing.

After Reading

Making Connections

1. Based on what you have seen of their characters and actions, do you think Macbeth and Lady Macbeth will make a good king and queen? Explain.

2. Explain how Macbeth's and Lady Macbeth's states of mind after the murder are expressed through their speeches and actions.

3. The drunken porter's speeches are an example of **comic relief**. Why do you think Shakespeare might have placed this scene immediately after the murder scene?

4. Explain how Macduff, Banquo, Malcolm, and Donalbain each react to Duncan's murder in a way that reflects his personal position.

5. How important an issue do you think gender is in physical strength? in mental strength? in moral strength? Have your opinions on the strengths of Macbeth and Lady Macbeth changed since act 1?

Literary Focus: Plot Structure

"What's done is done," says Lady Macbeth in act 3. In the second act of a Shakespearean play, the protagonist usually takes an action that cannot be reversed or undone. In this act Macbeth murders Duncan. Use a plot diagram like the one shown on page 116 to chart the rising action of the plot. Write the events that occur on the night of the murder and the characters who cause them to happen.

Vocabulary Study

Select the word that is most nearly similar in meaning to the numbered word.

1. augment   **a.** decrease   **b.** motivate

                       c. move   **d.** increase

2. suborn   **a.** bribe   **b.** cover

                       c. obey   **d.** raise

3. requite   **a.** repeat   **b.** pay back

                       c. honor   **d.** set up

4. palpable   **a.** capable   **b.** deadly

                       c. honest   **d.** definite

5. scruple   **a.** doubt   **b.** sum of money

                       c. vague thought   **d.** escape

The Globe Theater

The flag has just been raised high above the roof of the Globe theater. The play is ready to begin. London Bridge is crowded with men on horseback riding to the theater. Others come by boat along the Thames River. They come for afternoon performances only, because there are no artificial lights. As they stream into this many-sided, three-story structure, which looks like a large Elizabethan town house, the men separate according to class. The groundlings (apprentices and the lower class) mingle about in the large open yard area. A rowdy bunch, they shove and push. The middle class folks wend their way to the galleries. The noblemen strut up to the special seats in boxes or on the stage. Vendors wander through the crowd hawking food and drink. The mood is festive, carnival-like. It is a man's afternoon out. There are no women in the audience, just as there are no women on stage.

The first Globe theater, completed in 1599, burned to the ground in 1613. The second Globe, which was built immediately afterward, stood until 1644. From a few surviving maps, carpenters' contracts, and verbal descriptions, we can put together the following picture of the Globe. The main acting area, the Platform, extended well into the yard so that the spectators almost surrounded the actors. At the back was the Study, a curtained room used for interior scenes. In the floor of the Platform were several trap doors. Imagine smoke, fog, and apparitions, or ghosts, rising and falling! Macbeth's witches would appear and vanish via these trap doors. The main stage entrances, on either side of the Platform, were large permanent doors.

On the second level was another curtained room, the Chamber, typically used for domestic scenes. In front of this was a narrow balcony called the Tarras (ter′is). Often the Tarras and the Platform would be used together with the Tarras representing a hill, the wall of a town, or

a gallery from which observers watched the action below. On the third level was a narrow musicians' gallery. Above it were the Huts which housed a pulley system for lowering objects supposed to appear from midair. Sound effects such as thunder or battle alarums (sounds of fighting) also came from the Huts.

There was very little scenery in a Shakespearean play. A desk, a bed, or a chair suggested the setting. Notice how often Shakespeare announces a change of scene with a trumpet or a few lines of dialogue. Costumes were usually not historically accurate. Instead, actors would be dressed in typical Elizabethan clothing. There were no actresses; all women's parts were played by boys.

Around the world Shakespearean-type theaters have been designed with permanent open stages meant to capture the style of the original. A full-size replica of the Globe, part of a Shakespearean complex, opened in 1996 close to the original site in London.

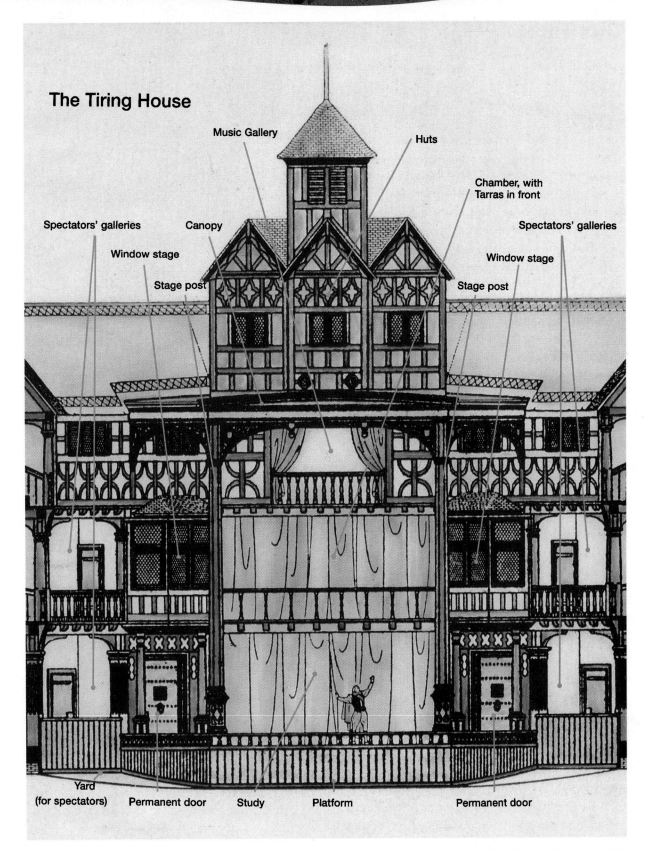

The Tiring House

Music Gallery

Huts

Chamber, with Tarras in front

Spectators' galleries

Canopy

Spectators' galleries

Window stage

Window stage

Stage post

Stage post

Yard
(for spectators)

Permanent door

Study

Platform

Permanent door

Act Three

SCENE 1

Summary *Because the Witches have promised that the descendants of Banquo will be kings, Macbeth hires Murderers to kill Banquo and his son, Fleance.*

MACBETH'S *castle. Enter* BANQUO.

BANQUO. Thou hast it now—King, Cawdor, Glamis, all
As the weird women promised, and I fear

He suspects Macbeth—Thou played'st most foully for 't. Yet it was said
It should not stand in thy posterity,

5   But that myself should be the root and father
Of many kings. If there come truth from them—
As upon thee, Macbeth, their speeches shine—
Why, by the <u>verities</u> on thee made good,   **8 verity** (ver′ə tē), *n.* truth.
May they not be my oracles as well

10   And set me up in hope? But hush, no more.
(*Music sounds offstage. Enter* MACBETH *as king,* LADY MACBETH, LENNOX,
ROSS, LORDS, *and* ATTENDANTS.)
MACBETH. Here's our chief guest.
LADY MACBETH.   If he had been forgotten,
It had been as a gap in our great feast
And all-thing unbecoming.   **13 all-thing,** in every way.
MACBETH. Tonight we hold a solemn supper, sir,

15   And I'll request your presence.
BANQUO.   Let Your Highness
Command upon me, to the which my duties   ■ Macbeth wants to know
Are with a most indissoluble tie   about Banquo's plans. What
Forever knit.   do you think he will do with
MACBETH. Ride you this afternoon?   this information?

20 **BANQUO.** Ay, my good lord.
MACBETH. We should have else desired your good advice,
Which still hath been both grave and prosperous,   **22 which . . . prosperous,**
In this day's council; but we'll take tomorrow.   which always has been
Is 't far you ride?   thoughtful and fruitful.

25 **BANQUO.** As far, my lord, as will fill up the time
Twixt this and supper. Go not my horse the better,
I must become a borrower of the night
For a dark hour or twain.
MACBETH. Fail not our feast.

30 **BANQUO.** My lord, I will not.
MACBETH. We hear our bloody cousins are bestowed
In England and in Ireland, not confessing   **33 parricide** (par′ə sīd), *n.*
Their cruel parricide, filling their hearers   crime of killing a father.

In this Charles Ricketts illustration from *The Tragedie of Macbeth* (1923), a servant brings in the two Murderers whom Macbeth persuades to kill Banquo and his son, Fleance. The Second Murderer claims, "I am reckless what I do to spite the world!" What sort of events can bring people to the condition where they don't care what happens to them?

With strange invention. But of that tomorrow,
35 When therewithal we shall have cause of state
Craving us jointly. Hie you to horse. Adieu,
Till you return at night. Goes Fleance with you?
BANQUO. Ay, my good lord. Our time does call upon 's.
MACBETH. I wish your horses swift and sure of foot,
40 And so I do commend you to their backs.
Farewell. (*Exit* BANQUO.)
Let every man be master of his time
Till seven at night. To make society

35–36 cause . . . jointly, affairs of state demanding the attention of both of us.

The sweeter welcome, we will keep ourself
45   Till suppertime alone. While then, God be with you!
     (*Exit all but* MACBETH *and a* SERVANT.)
        Sirrah, a word with you. Attend those men
        Our pleasure?
     SERVANT. They are, my lord, without the palace gate.
     MACBETH. Bring them before us.   (*Exit* SERVANT.)
                              To be thus is nothing,
50   But to be safely thus. Our fears in Banquo
     Stick deep, and in his royalty of nature
     Reigns that which would be feared. 'Tis much he dares;
     And to that dauntless temper of his mind
     He hath a wisdom that doth guide his valor
55   To act in safety. There is none but he
     Whose being I do fear; and under him
     My genius is rebuked, as it is said
     Mark Antony's was by Caesar. He chid the sisters
     When first they put the name of king upon me,
60   And bade them speak to him. Then, prophetlike,
     They hailed him father to a line of kings.
     Upon my head they placed a fruitless crown
     And put a barren scepter in my grip,
     Thence to be wrenched with an unlineal hand,
65   No son of mine succeeding. If 't be so,
     For Banquo's issue have I filed my mind;
     For them the gracious Duncan have I murdered,
     Put rancors in the vessel of my peace
     Only for them, and mine eternal jewel
70   Given to the common enemy of man
     To make them kings, the seeds of Banquo kings.
     Rather than so, come fate into the list,
     And champion me to th' utterance! Who's there?
     (*Enter* SERVANT *and two* MURDERERS.)
        Now go to the door, and stay there till we call.   (*Exit* SERVANT.)
75   Was it not yesterday we spoke together?
     MURDERERS. It was, so please Your Highness.
     MACBETH.   Well then, now
        Have you considered of my speeches? Know
        That it was he in the times past which held you
        So under fortune, which you thought had been
80   Our innocent self. This I made good to you
        In our last conference, passed in probation with you
        How you were borne in hand, how crossed, the instruments,
        Who wrought with them, and all things else that might
        To half a soul and to a notion crazed

[handwritten margin note, lines 50–54:] He wants to be sure he will remain King

46 Sirrah (sir′ə), ordinary form of address used in speaking to children and servants.

53 dauntless (dônt′lis), *adj.* brave.

55–58 There is none . . . Caesar. Macbeth's ambition is silently condemned by Banquo's loyalty. Mark Antony feared Octavius Caesar as a political, not personal, enemy, and this is how Macbeth regards Banquo. **58 chid** (chid), past tense of *chide* (chīd), *v.* scold.

66 filed, defiled; made impure.

68 rancor, (rang′kər), *n.* ill will; hatred.
69–70 mine eternal . . . man, given my soul to the Devil.

72 list, battlefield.

73 champion . . . utterance, fight me to the death.

To become King would seem to be about the greatest achievement of **individuality** that anyone could hope for. Why is Macbeth still dissatisfied?

81 passed in probation, gave detailed proof.
82 borne in hand, deceived.

84 notion crazed, half-wit.

85   Say, "Thus did Banquo."

FIRST MURDERER.   You made it known to us.

MACBETH. I did so, and went further, which is now
    Our point of second meeting. Do you find
    Your patience so predominant in your nature
    That you can let this go? Are you so gospeled

90   To pray for this good man and for his issue,
    Whose heavy hand hath bowed you to the grave
    And beggared yours forever?

FIRST MURDERER.   We are men, my liege.

MACBETH. Ay, in the catalogue ye go for men,
    As hounds and greyhounds, mongrels, spaniels, curs,

95   Shoughs, water-rugs, and demi-wolves are clept
    All by the name of dogs. The valued file
    Distinguishes the swift, the slow, the subtle,
    The housekeeper, the hunter, every one
    According to the gift which bounteous nature

100   Hath in him closed, whereby he does receive
    Particular addition from the bill
    That writes them all alike; and so of men.
    Now, if you have a station in the file,
    Not i' the worst rank of manhood, say 't,

105   And I will put that business in your bosoms
    Whose execution takes your enemy off,
    Grapples you to the heart and love of us,
    Who wear our health but sickly in his life,
    Which in his death were perfect.

SECOND MURDERER.   I am one, my liege,

110   Whom the vile blows and buffets of the world
    Hath so incensed that I am reckless what
    I do to spite the world!

FIRST MURDERER.   And I another,
    So weary with disasters, tugged with fortune,
    That I would set my life on any chance

115   To mend it or be rid on 't.

MACBETH.   Both of you
    Know Banquo was your enemy.

MURDERERS.   True, my lord.

MACBETH. So is he mine, and in such bloody distance
    That every minute of his being thrusts
    Against my near'st of life. And though I could

120   With barefaced power sweep him from my sight
    And bid my will avouch it, yet I must not,
    For certain friends that are both his and mine,
    Whose loves I may not drop, but wail his fall

89 **gospeled,** religious.

95 **shoughs . . . clept,** shaggy dogs, water dogs, and half-wolves are called.
96 **valued file,** list according to worth.

101–102 **particular . . . alike,** specific qualifications along with the general characteristics.

■ Why do you think Macbeth feels it necessary to convince the Murderers that Banquo is their enemy, instead of simply hiring them to kill him?

113 **tugged with,** pulled about by.

117 **in such bloody distance,** with such hostility.
118–119 **thrusts . . . life,** threatens my very existence.
121 **bid . . . avouch it,** take responsibility for it.
123 **but . . . fall,** I must pretend to weep for his death.

[handwritten annotation: he cannot take responsibility / he has to pretend to be upset]

Who I myself struck down. And thence it is
125   That I to your assistance do make love,
       Masking the business from the common eye
       For sundry weighty reasons.
SECOND MURDERER.   We shall, my lord,
       Perform what you command us.
FIRST MURDERER.   Though our lives—
MACBETH. Your spirits shine through you. Within this hour at most
130   I will advise you where to plant yourselves,
       Acquaint you with the perfect spy o' the time,
       The moment on 't, for 't must be done tonight,
       And something from the palace; always thought
       That I require a clearness. And with him—
135   To leave no rubs nor botches in the work—
       Fleance his son, that keeps him company,
       Whose absence is no less material to me
       Than is his father's, must embrace the fate
       Of that dark hour. Resolve yourselves apart;
140   I'll come to you anon.
MURDERERS. We are resolved, my lord.
MACBETH. I'll call upon you straight. Abide within.   (*Exit* MURDERERS.)
       It is concluded. Banquo, thy soul's flight,
       If it find heaven, must find it out tonight.

SCENE 2

> **Summary** *Lady Macbeth scolds Macbeth for brooding about Duncan's murder. Macbeth hints to Lady Macbeth about his plan to murder Banquo and Fleance.*

Another room in the castle. Enter LADY MACBETH *and a* SERVANT.
LADY MACBETH. Is Banquo gone from court?
SERVANT. Ay, madam, but returns again tonight.
LADY MACBETH. Say to the King I would attend his leisure
       For a few words.
5 **SERVANT.** Madam, I will.
LADY MACBETH. Naught's had, all's spent,
       Where our desire is got without content.
       'Tis safer to be that which we destroy
       Than by destruction dwell in doubtful joy.   (*Enter* MACBETH.)
10   How now, my lord? Why do you keep alone,
       Of sorriest fancies your companions making,
       Using those thoughts which should indeed have died
       With them they think on? Things without all remedy
       Should be without regard. What's done is done.

Margin notes:

■ What reasons does Macbeth give for not killing Macduff himself? How wise do you think his action is?

133 **something from,** some distance from.
134 **clearness,** freedom from suspicion.

139 **resolve yourselves,** make up your minds.

(handwritten note:) They have what they want but are still not happy

(handwritten note:) worry

13–14 **Things . . . regard.** You shouldn't worry about things you can't change.

Sleep being disrupted represents the guilt he feels

→ they both feel this way but only he admits it

15 **MACBETH.** We have scorched the snake, not killed it.
She'll close and be herself, whilst our poor malice
Remains in danger of her former tooth.
But let the frame of things disjoint, both the worlds suffer,
Ere we will eat our meal in fear and sleep
20 In the affliction of these terrible dreams
That shake us nightly. Better be with the dead,
Whom we, to gain our peace, have sent to peace,
Than on the torture of the mind to lie
In restless ecstasy. Duncan is in his grave;
25 After life's fitful fever he sleeps well.
Treason has done his worst; nor steel, nor poison,
Malice domestic, foreign levy, nothing
Can touch him further.
LADY MACBETH. Come on,
30 Gentle my lord, sleek o'er your rugged looks.
Be bright and jovial among your guests tonight.
MACBETH. So shall I, love, and so, I pray, be you.
Let your remembrance apply to Banquo;
Present him eminence, both with eye and tongue—
35 Unsafe the while, that we
Must lave our honors in these flattering streams
And make our faces vizards to hearts,
Disguising what they are.
LADY MACBETH. You must leave this.
MACBETH. O, full of scorpions is my mind, dear wife!
40 Thou know'st that Banquo and his Fleance lives.
LADY MACBETH. But in them nature's copy's not eterne.
MACBETH. There's comfort yet; they are assailable.
Then be thou jocund. Ere the bat hath flown
His cloistered flight, ere to black Hecate's summons
45 The shard-borne beetle with his drowsy hums
Hath rung night's yawning peal, there shall be done
A deed of dreadful note.
LADY MACBETH. What's to be done?
MACBETH. Be innocent of the knowledge, dearest chuck,
Till thou applaud the deed. Come, seeling night,
50 Scarf up the tender eye of pitiful day,
And with thy bloody and invisible hand
Cancel and tear to pieces that great bond
Which keeps me pale! Light thickens,
And the crow makes wing to th' rooky wood;
55 Good things of day begin to droop and drowse,
Whiles night's black agents to their preys do rouse.
Thou marvel'st at my words, but hold thee still.

it's better to be dead then to live in what they have done

nothing can bother Duncan now that he is dead, they show the advantages of being dead

she doesn't know yet about his plan to kill Banquo

Macbeth is now taking over and trying to show his manhood to Lady Macbeth

15 scorched, cut.

18 let the frame . . . suffer, if the universe breaks apart, earth and heaven will perish.

■ What evidence is there that Macbeth's deeds are beginning to trouble his conscience?

24 restless ecstasy, suffering.

27 malice . . . levy, civil war, foreign invasion.

31 jovial (jō′vē əl), *adj.* cheerful.

34 present him eminence, show him special favor.
37 vizard (viz′ərd), *n.* mask.
35–38 unsafe the while . . . what they are. We are unsafe as long as we must flatter and appear to be what we are not.

41 But . . . eterne. They will not live forever.
43 jocund (jok′ənd) *adj.* cheerful; merry.

49 seeling, blinding. To *seel* is a technical term used in falconry for sewing up the eyelids of a young hawk to make him used to the hood.
50 scarf up, blindfold.

Things bad begun make strong themselves by ill.
So, prithee, go with me.

SCENE 3

Summary *Banquo is killed by the Murderers, but Fleance escapes.*

A park near MACBETH'S *castle. Enter three* MURDERERS.

FIRST MURDERER. But who did bid thee join with us?

THIRD MURDERER.   Macbeth.

SECOND MURDERER (*to the* FIRST MURDERER). He needs not our
    mistrust, since he delivers
Our offices and what we have to do
To the direction just.

FIRST MURDERER.   Then stand with us.

5   The west yet glimmers with some streaks of day.
Now spurs the lated traveler pace
To gain the timely inn, and near approaches
The subject of our watch.

THIRD MURDERER. Hark, I hear horses.

10 **BANQUO** (*offstage*). Give us a light there, ho!

SECOND MURDERER. Then 'tis he. The rest
That are within the note of expectation
Already are i' the court.

FIRST MURDERER. His horses go about.

15 **THIRD MURDERER.** Almost a mile; but he does usually—
So all men do—from hence to th' palace gate
Make it their walk.

(*Enter* BANQUO *and* FLEANCE, *with a torch.*)

SECOND MURDERER. A light, a light!

THIRD MURDERER. 'Tis he.

20 **FIRST MURDERER.** Stand to 't.

BANQUO. It will be rain tonight.

FIRST MURDERER. Let it come down! (*They attack* BANQUO.)

BANQUO. O, treachery! Fly, good Fleance, fly, fly, fly!
Thou mayst revenge. O slave! (*He dies.* FLEANCE *escapes.*)

25 **THIRD MURDERER.** Who did strike out the light?

FIRST MURDERER.   Was 't not the way?

THIRD MURDERER. There's but one down; the son is fled.

SECOND MURDERER. We have lost best half of our affair.

FIRST MURDERER. Well, let's away and say how much is done.

SCENE 4

Summary *At a banquet Macbeth praises the absent Banquo, but then he is terrified by the appearance of the ghost of Banquo which only he can see. Because of Macbeth's odd behavior, Lady Macbeth dismisses the guests. Macbeth vows to return to the witches for more information.*

A hall in the castle. There is a banquet prepared. Enter MACBETH, LADY MAC-BETH, ROSS, LENNOX, LORDS *and* ATTENDANTS.

MACBETH. You know your own degrees; sit down. At first
    And last, the hearty welcome.   *(They sit.)*
LORDS.   Thanks to Your Majesty.
MACBETH. Ourself will mingle with society
    And play the humble host.
5   Our hostess keeps her state, but in best time,
    We will require her welcome.

In *The Three Witches,* painted by Henry Fuseli in 1783, the heads of the three evil hags from *Macbeth* are shown in profile, overlapping each other. Compare this painting with the Dulac poster on page 119. How are the two artists' conceptions of the witches similar? How are they different?

1 degrees, rank. Guests at state banquets were seated according to social or political rank.

5 keeps her state, remains seated on her throne.

LADY MACBETH. Prounounce it for me, sir, to all our friends,
For my heart speaks they are welcome.

(FIRST MURDERER *appears at the door.*)

MACBETH. See, they encounter thee with their hearts' thanks.
10   Both sides are even. Here I'll sit i' the midst.   *(He sits.)*
Be large in mirth; anon we'll drink a measure.
The table round.   *(He goes to the* MURDERER.)
        There's blood upon thy face.

FIRST MURDERER. 'Tis Banquo's, then.

MACBETH. 'Tis better thee without than he within.
15   Is he dispatched?

FIRST MURDERER. My lord, his throat is cut. That I did for him.

MACBETH. Thou art the best o' the cutthroats.
Yet he's good that did the like for Fleance;
If thou didst it, thou art the nonpareil.

20 **FIRST MURDERER.** Most royal sir, Fleance is scaped.

MACBETH. Then comes my fit again. I had else been perfect,
Whole as the marble, founded as the rock,
As broad and general as the casing air.
But now I am cabined, cribbed, confined, bound in
25   To saucy doubts and fears. But Banquo's safe? ~dead

FIRST MURDERER. Ay, my good lord. Safe in a ditch he bides,
With twenty trenchèd gashes on his head,
The least a death to nature. —nature is always described as disrupted

MACBETH.   Thanks for that.
There the grown serpent lies; the worm that's fled
30   Hath nature that in time will venom breed,
No teeth for th' present. Get thee gone. Tomorrow
We'll hear ourselves again.   *(Exit* FIRST MURDERER.)

LADY MACBETH.   My royal lord,
You do not give the cheer. The feast is sold
That is not often vouched, while 'tis a-making,
35   'Tis given with welcome. To feed were best at home;
From thence, the sauce to meat is ceremony;
Meeting were bare without it.

(The GHOST OF BANQUO *appears and sits in* MACBETH'S *place.*)

where macbeth would be sitting if Duncan was still alive

MACBETH.   Sweet remembrancer!
Now, good digestion wait on appetite,
And health on both!

LENNOX.   May 't please Your Highness sit?

40 **MACBETH.** Here had we now our country's honor roofed
Were the graced person of our Banquo present,
Who may I rather challenge for unkindness
Than pity for mischance.

ROSS.   His absence, sir,

■ Why do you think
Macbeth doesn't sit on his
throne during the banquet?

14 'Tis better . . . within.
The blood is better on you
than in him.

19 nonpareil (non′pə rel′),
n. one without equal.

23 casing, enveloping.

32 hear ourselves, talk it over.

**33–37 The feast is . . . without
it.** Unless a host keeps his
guests assured of their welcome, the meal is like one
bought at an inn, and one
might as well dine at home.
When one is away from
home, ceremony should
accompany the meal.
40 here had . . . roofed, we
would have all our country's
most honored men here.
**42–43 who may I . . .
mischance,** who is, I hope,
absent because he has
chosen not to attend rather
than because he has been
prevented from coming by
some misfortune.

Lays blame upon his promise. Please 't Your Highness
45   To grace us with your royal company?
MACBETH (*seeing his place occupied*). The table's full.
LENNOX.   Here is a place
      reserved, sir.
MACBETH. Where?
LENNOX. Here, my good lord. What is 't that moves Your Highness?
MACBETH. Which of you have done this?
LORDS.   What, my good lord?
50 **MACBETH.** Thou canst not say I did it. Never shake
      Thy gory locks at me.
ROSS. Gentlemen, rise. His Highness is not well.
(*They start to get up from the table.*)
LADY MACBETH. Sit, worthy friends. My lord is often thus,
      And hath been from his youth. Pray you, keep seat.
55   The fit is momentary; upon a thought
      He will again be well. If much you note him
      You shall offend him and extend his passion.
      Feed, and regard him not.   (*She confers apart with* MACBETH.)
                          Are you a man?
MACBETH. Ay, and a bold one, that dare look on that
60   Which might appall the devil.
LADY MACBETH.   O, proper stuff!
      This is the very painting of your fear.
      This is the air-drawn dagger which, you said,
      Led you to Duncan. O, these flaws and starts,
      Impostors to true fear, would well become
65   A woman's story at a winter's fire,
      Authorized by her grandam. Shame itself!
      Why do you make such faces? When all's done,
      You look but on a stool.
MACBETH.   Prithee, see there!
      Behold, look! Lo, how say you?
70   Why, what care I? If thou canst nod, speak too.
      If charnel houses and our graves must send
      Those that we bury back, our monuments
      Shall be the maws of kites.   (*The* GHOST *disappears.*)
LADY MACBETH. What, quite unmanned in folly?
75 **MACBETH.** If I stand here, I saw him.
LADY MACBETH.   Fie, for shame!
MACBETH. Blood hath been shed ere now, i' th' olden time,
      Ere humane statute purged the gentle weal;
      Ay, and since, too, murders have been performed
      Too terrible for the ear. The time has been
80   That, when the brains were out, the man would die,

55 **upon a thought,** in a moment.

57 **extend his passion,** prolong his fit.

61 **painting,** representation.

64 **imposters to,** imitations of.

■ Who can see the ghost of Banquo and who cannot?

71–73 **If charnel . . . kites.** If morgues and graves cannot keep our bodies buried, our burial place should be the stomachs of birds of prey.

77 **ere . . . weal,** before laws allowed us to protect society from violent persons.

Macbeth—Act Three, Scene 4   **157**

And there an end; but now they rise again
With twenty mortal murders on their crowns,
And push us from our stools. This is more strange
Than such a murder is.

LADY MACBETH.   My worthy lord,
85   Your noble friends do lack you.

MACBETH.   I do forget.
Do not muse at me, my most worthy friends;
I have a strange infirmity, which is nothing
To those that know me. Come, love and health to all!
Then I'll sit down. Give me some wine. Fill full.

(He is given wine. The GHOST *reappears.)*
90   I drink to the general joy o' th' whole table,
And to our dear friend Banquo, whom we miss.
Would he were here! To all, and him, we thirst,
And all to all.

LORDS.   Our duties and the pledge.   *(They drink.)*

MACBETH (*seeing* GHOST). Avaunt, and quit my sight! Let the earth
          hide thee!
95   Thy bones are marrowless, thy blood is cold;
Thou hast no speculation in those eyes
Which thou dost glare with!

LADY MACBETH.   Think of this, good peers,
But as a thing of custom. 'Tis no other;
Only it spoils the pleasure of the time.

100 **MACBETH.** What man dare, I dare.
Approach thou like the rugged Russian bear,
The armed rhinoceros, or th' Hyrcan tiger;
Take any shape but that, and my firm nerves
Shall never tremble. Or be alive again
105   And dare me to the desert with thy sword.
If trembling I inhabit then, protest me
The baby of a girl. Hence, horrible shadow!
Unreal mockery, hence! (*Exit* GHOST.) Why, so; being gone,
I am a man again. Pray you, sit still.
110 **LADY MACBETH.** You have displaced the mirth, broke the good meeting
With most admired disorder.

MACBETH.   Can such things be,
And overcome us like a summer's cloud,
Without our special wonder? You make me strange
Even to the disposition that I owe,
115   When now I think you can behold such sights
And keep the natural ruby of your cheeks
When mine is blanched with fear.

ROSS.   What sights, my lord?

he spoils the party

82 **mortal . . . crowns,** deadly wounds on their heads.

86 **muse,** wonder.

92 **thirst,** wish to drink.

94 **avaunt** (ə vônt′), *interj.* begone; go away.

96 **speculation,** power to see.

98 **thing of custom,** customary (usual) thing.

102 **Hyrcan,** of Hyrcania, in ancient times a region near the Caspian Sea.

106–107 **If trembling . . . girl.** If I still tremble, call me a girl's doll.

111 **admired,** wondered at.

113–114 **You make . . . owe.** You make me wonder at my own nature.

LADY MACBETH. I pray you, speak not. He grows worse and worse;
　　Question enrages him. At once, good night.
120　　Stand not upon the order of your going,
　　But go at once.
LENNOX.　　　　　Good night, and better health
　　Attend His Majesty!
LADY MACBETH.　　　A kind good night to all!
(*Exit* LORDS *and* ATTENDANTS.)
MACBETH. It will have blood, they say; blood will have blood.
　　Stones have been known to move, and trees to speak:
125　　Augurs and understood relations have
　　By maggotpies and choughs and rooks brought forth
　　The secret'st man of blood. What is the night?
LADY MACBETH. Almost at odds with morning, which is which.
MACBETH. How sayst thou, that Macduff denies his person
130　　At our great bidding?
LADY MACBETH.　　　Did you send to him, sir?
MACBETH. I hear it by the way; but I will send.
　　There's not a one of them but in his house
　　I keep a servant fee'd. I will tomorrow—
　　And betimes I will—to the Weird Sisters. *— witches*
135　　More shall they speak, for now I am bent to know
　　By the worst means the worst. For mine own good
　　All causes shall give way. I am in blood
　　Stepped in so far that, should I wade no more,
　　Returning were as tedious as go o'er.
140　　Strange things I have in head, that will to hand,
　　Which must be acted ere they may be scanned.
LADY MACBETH. You lack the season of all natures, sleep.
MACBETH. Come, we'll to sleep. My strange and self-abuse
　　Is the initiate fear that wants hard use.
145　　We are yet but young in deed.

SCENE 5

Summary *Hecate reprimands the Witches for dealing with Macbeth without her permission.*

A wilderness. Thunder. Enter the three WITCHES, *meeting* HECATE.
FIRST WITCH. Why, how now, Hecate? You look angerly.
HECATE. Have I not reason, beldams as you are?
　　Saucy and overbold, how did you dare
　　To trade and traffic with Macbeth
5　　In riddles and affairs of death,
　　And I, the mistress of your charms,
　　The close contriver of all harms,

120 stand not . . . going, don't take the time to leave in order of rank.
125–127 Augurs . . . blood. Through talking birds (magpies, crows, and rooks), omens correctly interpreted have led to the discovery of the most secretive of murderers.

133 fee'd, paid (a fee) to spy.
133–134 I will . . . sisters. I will go very early to the witches.

141 which . . . scanned, which must be done before they can be discussed.
143–144 My strange . . . use. My peculiar actions arise from the fact that I am inexperienced at crime.

2 beldam (bel′dəm), *n.* old hag.

7 contriver, planner; schemer.

Was never called to bear my part
Or show the glory of our art?

10 And, which is worse, all you have done
Hath been but for a wayward son,
Spiteful and wrathful, who, as others do,
Loves for his own ends, not for you.
But make amends now. Get you gone,
15 And at the pit of Acheron
Meet me i' the morning. Thither he
Will come to know his destiny.
Your vessels and your spells provide,
Your charms and everything beside.
20 I am for th' air. This night I'll spend
Unto a dismal and a fatal end.
Great business must be wrought ere noon.
Upon the corner of the moon
There hangs a vaporous drop profound;
25 I'll catch it ere it comes to ground,
And that, distilled by magic sleights,
Shall raise such artificial sprites
As by the strength of their illusion
Shall draw him on to his confusion.
30 He shall spurn fate, scorn death, and bear
His hopes 'bove wisdom, grace, and fear.
And you all know, security
Is mortals' chiefest enemy.
(Music offstage and a song: "Come away, come away," *etc.)*
Hark! I am called. My little spirit, see,
35 Sits in a foggy cloud and stays for me.   *(Exit.)*
FIRST WITCH. Come, let's make haste. She'll soon be back again.

SCENE 6

Summary *Lennox says he is suspicious of Macbeth. He learns that Macduff has gone to England to meet Malcolm and to seek the help of the English king against Macbeth.*

MACBETH'S *castle. Enter* LENNOX *and another* LORD.
LENNOX. My former speeches have but hit your thoughts,
Which can interpret farther. Only I say
Things have been strangely borne. The gracious Duncan
Was pitied of Macbeth; marry, he was dead.
5 And the right valiant Banquo walked too late,
Whom you may say, if 't please you, Fleance killed,
For Fleance fled. Men must not walk too late.
Who cannot want the thought how monstrous

[handwritten margin note: Lennox does not believe this is what really happened]

11 **wayward** (wā′wərd), *adj.* disobedient; willful.

14 **amends** (ə mendz′), *n.* compensation.
15 **Acheron** (ak′ə ron′), a river in Hell.

26 **sleight** (slīt), *n.* trick.

29 **confusion,** destruction.

32 **security,** overconfidence.

1–2 **My former . . . farther.** My earlier speeches have only given you ideas, from which you can draw your own conclusions.
3 **borne,** conducted; carried out.

It was for Malcolm and for Donalbain

10 To kill their gracious father? Damnèd fact!
How it did grieve Macbeth! Did he not straight
In pious rage the two delinquents tear
That were the slaves of drink and thralls of sleep?
Was not that nobly done? Ay, and wisely too;

15 For 'twould have angered any heart alive
To hear the men deny 't. So that I say
He has borne all things well; and I do think
That had he Duncan's sons under his key—
As, an 't please heaven, he shall not—they should find

20 What 'twere to kill a father. So should Fleance.
But peace! For from broad words, and 'cause he failed
His presence at the tyrant's feast, I hear
Macduff lives in disgrace. Sir, can you tell
Where he bestows himself?

LORD.   The son of Duncan,

25 From whom this tyrant holds the due of birth,
Lives in the English court, and is received
Of the most pious Edward with such grace
That the <u>malevolence</u> of fortune nothing
Takes from his high respect. Thither Macduff

30 Is gone to pray the holy king, upon his aid,
To wake Northumberland and warlike Siward,
That by the help of these—with Him above
To ratify the work—we may again
Give to our tables meat, sleep to our nights,

35 Free from our feasts and banquets bloody knives,
Do faithful homage, and receive free honors—
All which we pine for now. And this report
Hath so exasperate the King that he
Prepares for some attempt of war.

40 **LENNOX.** Sent he to Macduff?

LORD. He did; and with an absolute "Sir, not I,"
The cloudy messenger turns me his back
And hums, as who should say, "You'll rue the time
That clogs me with this answer."

LENNOX.   And that well might

45 Advise him to a caution, t' hold what distance
His wisdom can provide. Some holy angel
Fly to the court of England and unfold
His message ere he come, that a swift blessing
May soon return to this our suffering country

50 Under a hand accursed!

LORD: I'll send my prayers with him.

[handwritten note:] If they were in front of Macbeth they would be killed like the guards

[handwritten note:] he feels that Macduff is the next victim

13. thrall (thrôl), *n.* slave.

■ Do you think Lennox is speaking sincerely here, or with **irony**?

21 from broad words, because he spoke frankly.

27 Edward, Edward the Confessor, King of England 1042–1066.
28 malevolence (mə lev′ə-ləns), *n.* ill will.

■ What seems to be the general mood in Scotland? Do people have reason to feel this way?

42 cloudy, displeased.
43 rue, regret.
44 clogs, obstructs.

45 advise him . . . provide, warn him (Macduff) to keep what safe distance he can (from Macbeth).

Macbeth—Act Three, Scene 6   **161**

After Reading

Making Connections

1. At this point, what advice would you give to Macbeth and Lady Macbeth?

2. Why do you think Macbeth fears Banquo as he does?

3. How does Macbeth manipulate the two murderers into agreeing to kill Banquo?

4. Why do you think Macbeth doesn't tell Lady Macbeth about the plans he has made to have Banquo and Fleance murdered?

5. How well do you think Lady Macbeth manages to cover up for Macbeth's odd behavior at the banquet?

6. Trace the **irony** in Lennox's speech to the Lord in scene 6. What special meaning does it give his speech?

7. Macbeth talks about giving his soul to the common enemy of man, the Devil. He knows his actions so far are wrong, yet he persists. What causes people to take actions they know are clearly evil?

Literary Focus: Plot Structure

Act 3 is considered the **climax** of the play. Macbeth and Lady Macbeth have achieved their greatest desire—Macbeth is king. However, the escape of Fleance changes their fortune; it is the **turning point** or **dramatic reversal** of the plot. List other events in this act that that might reverse the fortunes of Macbeth and Lady Macbeth. Place them on a chart such as the one on page 116.

Vocabulary Study

Select the word that is most nearly *opposite* in meaning to the numbered word.

1. dauntless   **a.** brave   **b.** bright   **c.** fearful   **d.** feeble

2. jovial   **a.** clever   **b.** greedy   **c.** sincere   **d.** unhappy

3. malevolence   **a.** good will   **b.** untruthfulness   **c.** ill will   **d.** mystery

4. verity   **a.** seriousness   **b.** truth   **c.** falsehood   **d.** profit

5. chide   **a.** lower   **b.** praise   **c.** raise   **d.** separate

Act Four

SCENE 1

Summary *Macbeth visits the witches again and asks them to prophesy his future. They show him three visions: an armed head, a bloody child, and a child wearing a crown and carrying a tree. They also show a line of eight kings followed by the ghost of Banquo, indicating that Banquo's descendants will rule. Later, learning that Macduff has gone to England, Macbeth plans the murders of Macduff's wife and children.*

A cave. In the middle, a large cooking pot. Thunder. Enter the three WITCHES.

FIRST WITCH. Thrice the brinded cat hath mewed.

SECOND WITCH. Thrice, and once the hedgepig whined.

THIRD WITCH. Harpier cries. 'Tis time, 'tis time!

FIRST WITCH. Round about the cauldron go;

5   In the poisoned entrails throw.
   Toad, that under cold stone
   Days and nights has thirty-one
   Sweltered venom, sleeping got,
   Boil thou first i' the charmèd pot.

10 **ALL** *(dancing round the cauldron).* Double, double, toil and trouble;
   Fire burn, and cauldron bubble.

SECOND WITCH. Fillet of a fenny snake,
   In the cauldron boil and bake;
   Eye of newt and toe of frog,

15   Wool of bat and tongue of dog,
   Adder's fork and blindworm's sting,
   Lizard's leg and owlet's wing,
   For a charm of powerful trouble,
   Like a hell-broth boil and bubble.

20 **ALL.** Double, double, toil and trouble;
   Fire burn, and cauldron bubble.

THIRD WITCH. Scale of dragon, tooth of wolf,
   Witches' mummy, maw and gulf
   Of the ravined salt-sea shark,

25   Root of hemlock digged i' the dark,
   Liver of blaspheming Jew,
   Gall of goat, and slips of yew
   Slivered in the moon's eclipse,
   Nose of Turk and Tartar's lips,

30   Finger of birth-strangled babe
   Ditch-delivered by a drab,
   Make the gruel thick and slab.
   Add thereto a tiger's chaudron
   For th' ingredients of our cauldron.

1 brinded, brindled; spotted or streaked.
2 hedge pig, hedge hog.
3 Harpier, the Third Witch's familiar spirit.
4 cauldron (kôl′drən), *n.* large kettle.
5 entrails (en′trālz), *n. pl.* intestines.

12 fillet . . . snake, slice of a snake from a fen, or swamp.

17 owlet, a small owl.

23 maw and gulf, stomach and throat.
24 ravined (rav′ənd), *adj.* ravenous; very hungry.

27 yew, evergreen tree, thought to be poisonous.

31 drab, whore.
32 slab, slimy.
33 chaudron (chô′drən), *n.* intestines.

35 **ALL.** Double, double, toil and trouble;
　　　Fire burn, and cauldron bubble.
　　SECOND WITCH. Cool it with a baboon's blood,
　　　Then the charm is firm and good.　　(*Enter* HECATE.)
　　HECATE. O, well done! I commend your pains,
40　　And everyone shall share in' the gains.
　　　And now about the cauldron sing
　　　Like elves and fairies in a ring,
　　　Enchanting all that you put in.
　　(*Music and a song: "Black spirits," etc. Exit* HECATE.)
　　SECOND WITCH. By the pricking of my thumbs,
45　　Something wicked this way comes.
　　　　　Open, locks,
　　　　　Whoever knocks!　　(*Enter* MACBETH.)
　　MACBETH. How now, you secret, black, and midnight hags?
　　　What is 't you do?
　　ALL.　　　　　　　A deed without a name.
50 **MACBETH.** I conjure you, by that which you profess,
　　　Howe'er you come to know it, answer me.
　　　Though you untie the winds and let them fight
　　　Against the churches, though the yeasty waves
　　　Confound and swallow navigation up,
55　　Though bladed corn be lodged and trees blown down,
　　　Though castles topple on their warders' heads,
　　　Though palaces and pyramids do slope
　　　Their heads to their foundations, though the treasure
　　　Of nature's germens tumble all together,
60　　Even till destruction sicken, answer me
　　　To what I ask you.
　　FIRST WITCH.　　　　　Speak.
　　SECOND WITCH.　　　　　　　Demand.
　　THIRD WITCH.　　　　　　　　　We'll answer.
　　FIRST WITCH. Say if thou'dst rather hear it from our mouths
　　　Or from our masters?
　　MACBETH.　　　　　　　Call 'em. Let me see 'em.
　　FIRST WITCH. Pour in sow's blood, that hath eaten
65　　Her nine farrow; grease that's sweaten
　　　From the murderer's gibbet throw
　　　Into the flame.
　　ALL.　　　　　　Come high or low.
　　　Thyself and office deftly show!
　　(*Thunder. The* FIRST APPARITION, *a soldier's head, appears.*)
　　MACBETH. Tell me, thou unknown power—
　　FIRST WITCH.　　　　　　　　　He knows thy thought.
70　　Hear his speech, but say thou naught.

50 conjure (kən jùr′), *v.* request earnestly; entreat

53 yeasty, foamy.

55 though . . . lodged, though grain, still green, may be beaten down.
56 warder, guard or watchman.
59 nature's germens, the seeds by which nature's cycles operate.
60 sicken, is in excess.

65 farrow (far′ō), piglets; baby pigs.
66 gibbet (jib′it), gallows used for hanging.

apparition (ap ə rish′ən), *n.* ghost; phantom.

70 naught (nôt), *n.* nothing.

▲ *Macbeth, Banquo, and the Witches* by George Cattermole is a watercolor of the 1800s. How does the style of this picture suggest the mystery and horror of the apparition scene?

FIRST APPARITION. Macbeth! Macbeth! Macbeth! Beware Macduff,
  Beware the Thane of Fife. Dismiss me. Enough.   (*It disappears.*)
MACBETH. Whate'er thou art, for thy good caution, thanks;
  Thou hast harped my fear aright. But one word more—

74 **harped,** guessed.

75 **FIRST WITCH.** He will not be commanded. Here's another,
  More potent than the first.
  (*Thunder. The* SECOND APPARITION, *a bloody child.*)
SECOND APPARITION. Macbeth! Macbeth! Macbeth!
MACBETH. Had I three ears, I'd hear thee.
SECOND APPARITION. Be bloody, bold, and resolute; laugh to scorn
80 The power of man, for none of woman born
  Shall harm Macbeth.   (*It disappears.*)
MACBETH. Then live, Macduff; what need I fear of thee?
  But yet I'll make assurance double sure,
  And take a bond of fate. Thou shalt not live,

84 **take . . . fate,** make sure that fate's promise is fulfilled.

85 That I may tell pale-hearted fear it lies,
  And sleep in spite of thunder.
  (*Thunder. The* THIRD APPARITION, *a child crowned, with a tree in his hand.*)
                  What is this
  That rises like the issue of a king
  And wears upon his baby brow the round
  And top of sovereignty?

88–89 **round and top,** crown.

ALL.   Listen, but speak not to 't.
90 **THIRD APPARITION.** Be lion-mettled, proud, and take no care
  Who chafes, who frets, or where conspirers are.
  Macbeth shall never vanquished be until *→the woods move*
  Great Birnam Wood to high Dunsinane Hill *to the hill*
  Shall come against him.   (*It disappears.*)

93 **Dunsinane,** (dun′sə nān′).

MACBETH.   That will never be.
95 Who can impress the forest, bid the tree
  Unfix his earthbound root? Sweet bodements, good!
  Rebellious dead, rise never till the wood
  Of Birnam rise, and our high-placed Macbeth
  Shall live the lease of nature, pay his breath

95 **impress,** force to serve as soldiers.
96 **bodement** (bōd′mənt), *n.* prophecy.

100 To time and mortal custom. Yet my heart
  Throbs to know one thing. Tell me, if your art
  Can tell so much: shall Banquo's issue ever
  Reign in this kingdom?

99–100 **pay his breath . . . custom,** die a natural death.

ALL.   Seek to know no more.
MACBETH. I will be satisfied. Deny me this,
105 And an eternal curse fall on you! Let me know.
  (*The cauldron sinks out of sight. Music sounds offstage.*)
  Why sinks that cauldron? And what noise is this?
FIRST WITCH. Show!
SECOND WITCH. Show!

THIRD WITCH. Show!

110 **ALL.** Show his eyes, and grieve his heart;
Come like shadows, so depart!

(*A show of eight* KINGS, *the last carrying a magic mirror. They are followed by*
BANQUO'S GHOST.)

MACBETH. Thou art too like the spirit of Banquo. Down!
Thy crown does sear mine eyeballs. And thy hair,
Thou other gold-bound brow, is like the first.

115 A third is like the former. Filthy hags,
Why do you show me this? A fourth? Start, eyes!
What, will the line stretch out to th' crack of doom?
Another yet? A seventh? I'll see no more.
And yet the eighth appears, who bears a glass

120 Which shows me many more; and some I see
That twofold balls and treble scepters carry.
Horrible sight! Now I see 'tis true,
For the blood-boltered Banquo smiles upon me
And points at them for his.   (*The apparitions disappear.*)
What, is this so?

125 **FIRST WITCH.** Ay, sir, all this is so. But why
Stands Macbeth thus amazedly?
Come, sisters, cheer we up his sprites
And show the best of our delights.
I'll charm the air to give a sound,

130 While you perform your antic round,
That this great king may kindly say
Our duties did his welcome pay.

(*Music. The* WITCHES *dance; then they disappear.*)

MACBETH. Where are they? Gone? Let this pernicious hour
Stand aye accursèd in the calendar!

135 Come in, without there!   (*Enter* LENNOX.)

LENNOX.   What's Your Grace's will?

MACBETH. Saw you the Weird Sisters?

LENNOX.   No, my lord.

MACBETH. Came they not by you?

LENNOX.   No, indeed, my lord.

MACBETH. Infected be the air whereon they ride,
And damned all those that trust them! I did hear

140 The galloping of horse. Who was 't came by?

LENNOX. 'Tis two or three, my lord, that bring you word
Macduff is fled to England.

MACBETH.   Fled to England!

LENNOX. Ay, my good lord.

MACBETH (*aside*). Time, thou anticipat'st my dread exploits.

145 The flighty purpose never is o'ertook

119 **glass,** a magic mirror
showing the future.
121 **twofold . . . scepters.**
The balls and scepters
symbolize the sovereignty
of England and Scotland,
and the kingdoms of
England, Scotland, and
Ireland which were united
for the first time under
James I, eighth of the Stuart
kings.
123, **blood-boltered,** having
hair matted with blood.
127, **sprites,** spirits.
130 **antic round,** grotesque
dance in a circle.
133 **pernicious,** (pər-
nish′əs), *adj.* fatal; deadly.
134 **aye,** (ā), *adv.* forever.

■ Summarize the prophe-
cies that the apparitions
have brought Macbeth.

Macbeth says he will kill Macduff's wife and children

Unless the deed go with it. From this moment
The very firstlings of my heart shall be
The firstlings of my hand. And even now,
To crown my thoughts with acts, be it thought and done:
150   The castle of Macduff I will surprise,
Seize upon Fife, give to th' edge o' the sword
His wife, his babes, and all unfortunate souls
That trace him in his line. No boasting like a fool;
This deed I'll do before this purpose cool.
155   But no more sights! Where are these gentlemen?
Come, bring me where they are.

SCENE 2

Summary *Ross tells Lady Macduff that her husband has fled the country.*
Murderers hired by Macbeth kill Lady Macduff and her children.

MACDUFF'S *castle at Fife. Enter* LADY MACDUFF, *her* SON, *and* ROSS.
LADY MACDUFF. What had he done to make him fly the land?
ROSS. You must have patience, madam.
LADY MACDUFF.   He had none.
His flight was madness. When our actions do not,
Our fears do make us traitors.
ROSS.   You know not
5   Whether it was his wisdom or his fear.
LADY MACDUFF. Wisdom? To leave his wife, to leave his babes,
His mansion, and his titles in a place
From whence himself does fly? He loves us not,
He wants the natural touch; for the poor wren,
10   The most diminutive of birds, will fight,
Her young ones in her nest, against the owl.
All is the fear and nothing is the love,
As little is the wisdom, where the flight
So runs against all reason.
ROSS.   My dearest coz,
15   I pray you, school yourself. But, for your husband,
He is noble, wise, judicious, and best knows
The fits o' the season. I dare not speak much further,
But cruel are the times when we are traitors
And do not know ourselves, when we hold rumor
20   From what we fear, yet know not what we fear,
But float upon a wild and violent sea
Each way and none. I take my leave of you;
Shall not be long but I'll be here again.
Things at the worst will cease, or else climb upward
25   To what they were before. My pretty cousin,

145–148 The flighty . . . hand. One must act at once if one is to accomplish one's purpose. From now on I shall put my thoughts into immediate action.

■ What message has Ross apparently brought to Lady Macduff?

7 titles, possessions.

9 he wants. . . . touch, he lacks natural human affection.
10 diminutive (də min′yə-tiv), *adj.* very small.

14 coz, cousin.
15 school, control.
16 judicious (jü dish′ əs), *adj.* sensible; showing good judgment.
17 fits . . . season, violence of the times.
18–19 are traitors . . . ourselves, are accused of treason without thinking of ourselves as traitors.
19–20 hold rumor. . . . fear, believe rumors that grow out of fears.

Blessing upon you!

LADY MACDUFF. Fathered he is, and yet he's fatherless.

ROSS. I am so much a fool, should I stay longer
It would be my disgrace and your discomfort.

30   I take my leave at once.   (*Exit* ROSS.)

LADY MACDUFF. Sirrah, your father's dead;
And what will you do now? How will you live?

SON. As birds do, Mother.

LADY MACDUFF.   What, with worms and flies?

SON. With what I get, I mean; and so do they.

35 **LADY MACDUFF.** Poor bird! Thou'dst never fear
The net nor lime, the pitfall nor the gin.

SON. Why should I, Mother? Poor birds they are not set for.
My father is not dead, for all your saying.

LADY MACDUFF. Yes, he is dead. How wilt thou do for a father?

40 **SON.** Nay, how will you do for a husband?

LADY MACDUFF. Why, I can buy me twenty at any market.

SON. Then you'll buy 'em to sell again.

LADY MACDUFF. Thou speak'st with all thy wit,
And yet, i' faith, with wit enough for thee.

45 **SON.** Was my father a traitor, Mother?

LADY MACDUFF. Ay, that he was.

SON. What is a traitor?

LADY MACDUFF. Why, one that swears and lies.

SON. And be all traitors that do so?

50 **LADY MACDUFF.** Every one that does so is a traitor,
And must be hanged.

SON. And must they all be hanged that swear and lie?

LADY MACDUFF. Every one.

SON. Who must hang them?

55 **LADY MACDUFF.** Why, the honest men.

SON. Then the liars and swearers, are fools, for there are liars and
swearers enough to beat the honest men and hang them up.

LADY MACDUFF. Now, God help thee, poor monkey!
But how wilt thou do for a father?

60 **SON.** If he were dead, you'd weep for him; if you would not, it were a
good sign that I should quickly have a new father.

LADY MACDUFF. Poor prattler, how thou talk'st!

(*Enter a* MESSENGER.)

MESSENGER. Bless you, fair dame! I am not to you known,
Though in your state of honor I am perfect.

65   I doubt some danger does approach you nearly.
If you will take a homely man's advice,
Be not found here. Hence with your little ones!
To fright you thus, methinks, I am too savage;

36 lime, birdlime, a sticky substance used to catch birds.
36 gin, trap.

48 swears and lies, swears allegiance and then breaks his oath.

62 prattler, (prat′lər) *n.* babbler; foolish talker.
64 in your . . . perfect, I know of your honorable rank.
65 doubt, suspect.

To do worse to you were fell cruelty,
70 Which is too nigh your person. Heaven preserve you!
I dare abide no longer.   (*Exit* MESSENGER.)

LADY MACDUFF.   Whither should I fly?
I have done no harm. But I remember now
I am in this earthly world, where to do harm
Is often <u>laudable</u>, to do good sometimes
75 Accounted dangerous folly. Why then, alas,
Do I put up that womanly defense
To say I have done no harm?   (*Enter* MURDERERS.)
                              What are these faces?

FIRST MURDERER. Where is your husband?

LADY MACDUFF. I hope in no place so unsanctified
80 Where such as thou mayst find him.

FIRST MURDERER.   He's a traitor.

SON. Thou liest, thou shag-haired villain!

FIRST MURDERER.   What, you egg?
(*He stabs him.*) Young fry of treachery!

SON.   He has killed me, Mother.
    Run away, I pray you!   (*He dies.*)
(*Exit* LADY MACDUFF *crying* "Murder!" *followed by the* MURDERERS *with the*
SON'S *body.*)

SCENE 3

Summary *Malcolm tests Macduff's loyalty. Convinced that Macduff is not allied to Macbeth, Malcolm invites him to join with the forces that will attempt to overthrow Macbeth. They learn from Ross that Lady Macduff and the children have been murdered, and Macduff and Malcolm prepare to return to Scotland.*

The palace of the King of England. Enter MALCOLM *and* MACDUFF.

MALCOLM. Let us seek out some desolate shade, and there
    Weep our sad bosoms empty.

MACDUFF.   Let us rather
    Hold fast the mortal sword, and like good men
    Bestride our downfall'n birthdom. Each new morn
5 New widows howl, new orphans cry, new sorrows
    Strike heaven on the face, that it resounds
    As if it felt with Scotland and yelled out
    Like syllable of dolor.

MALCOLM.   What I believe, I'll wail;
    What know, believe; and what I can redress,
10 As I shall find the time to friend, I will.
    What you have spoke it may be so, perchance.
    This tyrant, whose sole name blisters our tongues,

---

74 laudable (lô′də bəl), *adj.*
praiseworthy.

At this point
Macbeth has
killed five

■ In his meeting with
Malcolm what attitude
toward his country is
Macduff trying to convey?

4 bestride. . . . birthdom,
defend our fallen
fatherland.

8 dolor, (dōlor), *n.* grief.
9 redress, (ri dres′) *v.* set
right; remedy.
10 to friend, suitable.

Was once thought honest. You have loved him well;
He hath not touched you yet. I am young; but something
15 You may deserve of him through me, and wisdom
To offer up a weak, poor, innocent lamb
T' appease an angry god.
MACDUFF. I am not treacherous.
MALCOLM. But Macbeth is.
20 A good and virtuous nature may recoil
In an imperial charge. But I shall crave your pardon.
That which you are my thoughts cannot transpose;
Angels are bright still, though the brightest fell.
Though all things foul would wear the brows of grace,
25 Yet grace must still look so.
MACDUFF. I have lost my hopes.
MALCOLM. Perchance even there where I did find my doubts.
Why in that rawness left you wife and child,
Those precious motives, those strong knots of love,
Without leave-taking? I pray you,
30 Let not my jealousies be your dishonors,
But mine own safeties. You may be rightly just,
Whatever I shall think.
MACDUFF. Bleed, bleed, poor country!
Great tyranny, lay thou thy basis sure,
For goodness dare not check thee; wear thou thy wrongs,
35 The title is affeered! Fare thee well, lord.
I would not be the villain that thou think'st
For the whole space that's in the tyrant's grasp,
And the rich East to boot.
MALCOLM. Be not offended.
I speak not as in absolute fear of you.
40 I think our country sinks beneath the yoke;
It weeps, it bleeds, and each new day a gash
Is added to her wounds. I think withal
There would be hands uplifted in my right;
And here from gracious England have I offer
45 Of goodly thousands. But, for all this,
When I shall tread upon the tyrant's head,
Or wear it on my sword, yet my poor country
Shall have more vices than it had before,
More suffer, and more sundry ways than ever,
50 By him that shall succeed.
MACDUFF. What should he be?
MALCOLM. It is myself I mean, in whom I know
All the particulars of vice so grafted
That, when they shall be opened, black Macbeth

14–15 but something . . . me, but you may win favor from Macbeth by betraying me.

20–21 recoil. . . . charge, reverse itself through loyalty to the king.
22 transpose, change.
23 brightest fell, Satan, once the "brightest" angel in Heaven, warred with God and was defeated by him.

27 rawness, haste.

30–31 let not . . . safeties, I am suspicious not to dishonor you but because I wish to assure my own safety.

35 The title . . . affeered. Your (tyranny's) title is confirmed.
44 England, the king of England.

Murderers creep up on Lady Macduff and her son in this illustration by Charles Ricketts (1923). How does this picture convey the mood of the scene? ▼

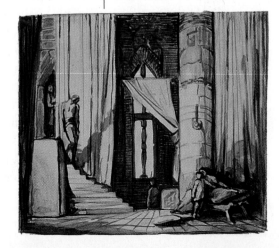

Will seem as pure as snow, and the poor state
55 Esteem him as a lamb, being compared
With my confineless harms.

MACDUFF. Not in the legions
Of horrid hell can come a devil more damned
In evils to top Macbeth.

MALCOLM. I grant him bloody,
Luxurious, avaricious, false, deceitful,
60 Sudden, malicious, smacking of every sin
That has a name. But there's no bottom, none,
In my voluptuousness. Your wives, your daughters,
Your matrons, and your maids could not fill up
The cistern of my lust, and my desire
65 All continent impediments would o'erbear
That did oppose my will. Better Macbeth
Than such an one to reign.

MACDUFF. Boundless intemperance
In nature is a tyranny; it hath been
Th' untimely emptying of the happy throne
70 And fall of many kings. But fear not yet
To take upon you what is yours. You may
Convey your pleasures in a spacious plenty,
And yet seem cold; the time you may so hoodwink.
We have willing dames enough. There cannot be
75 That vulture in you to devour so many
As will to greatness dedicate themselves,
Finding it so inclined.

MALCOLM. With this there grows
In my most ill-composed affection such
A stanchless avarice that, were I king,
80 I should cut off the nobles for their lands,
Desire his jewels and this other's house,
And my more-having would be as a sauce
To make me hunger more, that I should forge
Quarrels unjust against the good and loyal,
85 Destroying them for wealth.

MACDUFF. This avarice
Sticks deeper, grows with more pernicious root
Than summer-seeming lust, and it hath been
The sword of our slain kings. Yet do not fear;
Scotland hath foisons to fill up your will
90 Of your mere own. All these are portable,
With other graces weighed.

MALCOLM. But I have none. The king-becoming graces,
As justice, verity, temperance, stableness,

56 confineless harms, unlimited evil.
59 luxurious (lug zhùr′ē əs), *adj.* lustful.
59 avaricious (av′ə rish′əs), *adj.* greedy for money.
60 sudden, violent.
61–62 but . . . voluptuousness (və lup′chü əs nis), but I need my senses pleased far more than Macbeth does.
64 cistern (sis′tərn), *n.* reservoir for holding water.

Summarize the charges that Malcolm levels against himself. Is the kind of **individuality** he is expressing here truly worse than Macbeth's?

72 convey (kən vā′), *v.* obtain secretly.
73 the time . . . hoodwink, the age you may thus deceive.

78 ill-composed affection, evil disposition.
79 stanchless avarice, excessive greed.

87 summer-seeming, short-lived.
89 foisons (foi′zənz), *n.* resources; plenty.
90–91 All these . . . weighed. These weaknesses are bearable, considering your other virtues.

Bounty, perseverance, mercy, lowliness,

95 Devotion, patience, courage, fortitude,
   I have no relish of them, but abound
   In the division of each several crime,
   Acting it many ways. Nay, had I power, I should
   Pour the sweet milk of concord into hell,

100 Uproar the universal peace, confound
   All unity on earth.

MACDUFF.   O Scotland, Scotland!

MALCOLM. If such a one be fit to govern, speak.
   I am as I have spoken.

MACDUFF.   Fit to govern?
   No, not to live. O nation miserable,

105 With an untitled tyrant bloody-sceptered,
   When shalt thou see thy wholesome days again,
   Since that the truest issue of thy throne
   By his own interdiction stands accurst
   And does blaspheme his breed? Thy royal father

110 Was a most sainted king; the queen that bore thee,
   Oft'ner upon her knees than on her feet,
   Died every day she lived. Fare thee well.
   These evils thou repeat'st upon thyself
   Hath banished me from Scotland. O my breast,

115 Thy hope ends here!

MALCOLM.   Macduff, this noble passion,
   Child of integrity, hath from my soul
   Wiped the black scruples, reconciled my thoughts
   To thy good truth and honor. Devilish Macbeth
   By many of these trains hath sought to win me

120 Into his power, and modest wisdom plucks me
   From overcredulous haste. But God above
   Deal between thee and me! For even now
   I put myself to thy direction and
   Unspeak mine own detraction, here abjure

125 The taints and blames I laid upon myself
   For strangers to my nature. I am yet
   Unknown to woman, never was forsworn,
   Scarcely have coveted what was mine own,
   At no time broke my faith, would not betray

130 The devil to his fellow, and delight
   No less in truth than life. My first false speaking
   Was this upon myself. What I am truly
   Is thine and my poor country's to command—
   Whither indeed, before thy here-approach,

135 Old Siward with ten thousand warlike men,

99 concord (kon′kôrd), *n.*
agreement.

108 interdiction (in′tər-dik′shən), *n.* decree.
109 blaspheme his breed,
slander his parentage.

112 died . . . lived, prepared
for death by daily prayers
and self-sacrifice.

117 black scruples,
suspicions of Macduff's
treachery.
119 trains, plots.

124 abjure (ab jür′), *v.*
take back.

Already at a point, was setting forth.
Now we'll together; and the chance of goodness
Be like our warranted quarrel! Why are you silent?

MACDUFF. Such welcome and unwelcome things at once
140 'Tis hard to reconcile. (*Enter a* DOCTOR.)

MALCOLM. Well, more anon. Comes the King forth, I pray you?

DOCTOR. Ay, sir. There are a crew of wretched souls
That stay his cure. Their malady convinces
The great essay of art; but at his touch—
145 Such sanctity hath heaven given his hand—
They presently amend.

MALCOLM.   I thank you, Doctor. (*Exit* DOCTOR.)

MACDUFF. What's the disease he means?

MALCOLM.   'Tis called the evil.
A most miraculous work in this good king,
Which often, since my here-remain in England,
150 I have seen him do. How he solicits heaven
Himself best knows; but strangely-visited people,
All swoll'n and ulcerous, pitiful to the eye,
The mere despair of surgery, he cures,
Hanging a golden stamp about their necks
155 Put on with holy prayers; and 'tis spoken,
To the succeeding royalty he leaves
The healing benediction. With this strange virtue
He hath a heavenly gift of prophecy,
And sundry blessings hang about his throne
160 That speak him full of grace. (*Enter* ROSS.)

MACDUFF.   See who comes here.

MALCOLM. My countryman, but yet I know him not.

MACDUFF. My ever-gentle cousin, welcome hither.

MALCOLM. I know him now. Good God betimes remove
The means that makes us strangers!

ROSS.   Sir, amen.

165 **MACDUFF.** Stands Scotland where it did?

ROSS.   Alas, poor country,
Almost afraid to know itself. It cannot
Be called our mother, but our grave; where nothing
But who knows nothing is once seen to smile;
Where sighs and groans and shrieks that rend the air
170 Are made, not marked; where violent sorrow seems
A modern ecstasy. The dead man's knell
Is there scarce asked for who, and good men's lives
Expire before the flowers in their caps,
Dying or ere they sicken.

MACDUFF.   O, relation

---

136 at a point, prepared.
137–138 and the chance . . . quarrel, and may our chance of success be as strong as the justness of our cause.
143 stay his cure, wait for him to cure them.
143–144 convinces . . . art, defies cure by any medical skill.

147 the evil, scrofula, a disease characterized by swelling of the lymphatic glands. It was called "the king's evil" because of a belief that it could be healed by the touch of a king.
150 solicit (sə lis′it), *v.* appeal to.

167–168 nothing . . . smile, no one except a person who knows nothing ever smiles.
171 modern ecstasy, common feeling.
171 dead man's knell (nel), the sound of a bell rung for a person who has died.

175   Too nice, and yet too true!

MALCOLM.   What's the newest grief?

ROSS. That of an hour's age doth hiss the speaker;
    Each minute teems a new one.

MACDUFF.   How does my wife?

ROSS. Why, well.

MACDUFF.   And all my children?

ROSS.   Well too.

MACDUFF. The tyrant has not battered at their peace?

180 **ROSS.** No, they were well at peace when I did leave 'em.

MACDUFF. Be not a niggard of your speech. How goes 't?

ROSS. When I came hither to transport the tidings
    Which I have heavily borne, there ran a rumor
    Of many worthy fellows that were out,

185   Which was to my belief witnessed the rather
    For that I saw the tyrant's power afoot.
    Now is the time of help. (*To* MALCOLM.) Your eye in Scotland
    Would create soldiers, make our women fight,
    To doff their dire distresses.

MALCOLM.   Be 't their comfort

190   We are coming thither. Gracious England hath
    Lent us good Siward and ten thousand men;
    An older and a better soldier none
    That Christendom gives out.

ROSS.   Would I could answer
    This comfort with the like! But I have words

195   That would be howled out in the desert air,
    Where hearing should not latch them.

MACDUFF.   What concern they?
    The general cause? Or is it a fee-grief
    Due to some single breast?

ROSS.   No mind that's honest
    But in it shares some woe, though the main part

200   Pertains to you alone.

MACDUFF.   If it be mine,
    Keep it not from me; quickly let me have it.

ROSS. Let not your ears despise my tongue forever,
    Which shall possess them with the heaviest sound
    That ever yet they heard.

MACDUFF.   Hum! I guess at it.

205 **ROSS.** Your castle is surprised, your wife and babes
    Savagely slaughtered. To relate the manner
    Were, on the quarry of these murdered deer,
    To add the death of you.

MALCOLM.   Merciful heaven!

174–175 relation too nice, report too exact.

176 doth hiss the speaker, causes the speaker to be hissed because his news is already out of date.
177 teems, brings forth.

■ Why do you think Ross doesn't tell Macduff immediately what has happened to his family?

184 out, in arms; prepared for war.

196 latch, catch the sound of.

197 fee-grief, personal sorrow.

207 quarry, heap of dead bodies.

What, man, ne'er pull your hat upon your brows;
210   Give sorrow words. The grief that does not speak
Whispers the o'erfraught heart and bids it break.

MACDUFF. My children too?

ROSS.   Wife, children, servants, all
That could be found.

MACDUFF.   And I must be from thence!
My wife killed too?

ROSS.   I have said.

MALCOLM.   Be comforted.
215   Let's make us medicines of our great revenge
To cure this deadly grief.

MACDUFF. He has no children. All my pretty ones?
Did you say all? O hell-kite! All?
What, all my pretty chickens and their dam
220   At one fell swoop?

MALCOLM. Dispute it like a man.

MACDUFF. I shall do so;
But I must also feel it as a man.
I cannot but remember such things were,
225   That were most precious to me. Did heaven look on
And would not take their part? Sinful Macduff,
They were all struck for thee! Naught that I am,
Not for their own demerits, but for mine,
Fell slaughter on their souls. Heaven rest them now!

230 **MALCOLM.** Be this the whetstone of your sword. Let grief
Convert to anger; blunt not the heart, enrage it.

MACDUFF. O, I could play the woman with mine eyes
And braggart with my tongue! But, gentle heavens,
Cut short all intermission. Front to front
235   Bring thou this fiend of Scotland and myself;
Within my sword's length set him. If he scape,
Heaven forgive him too!

MALCOLM.   This tune goes manly.
Come, go we to the King. Our power is ready;
Our lack is nothing but our leave. Macbeth
240   Is ripe for shaking, and the powers above
Put on their instruments. Receive what cheer you may.
The night is long that never finds the day.

228 demerit (dē mer′it), *n.*
fault or defect.
230 whetstone (hwet′stōn′),
n. stone for sharpening
knives or tools.

239 Our lack . . . leave. We
only need the King's permission to depart.

After Reading

Making Connections

Shaping Your
Response

1. How much influence do you think the witches have on Macbeth's decisions? Assign a number of stars—from ★ for *Little* to ★★★★★ for *A Great Deal*—to their influence. Explain your rating.

Analyzing the Play

2. Why does Macbeth decide to murder Macduff's family?

3. What is the cause and what is the effect of Malcolm's accusing himself of so many vices when Macduff comes to see him?

4. In your opinion, does Shakespeare's portrait of Macduff bearing his grief at the news of the murder of his wife and children seem realistic?

Extending the Ideas

5. What kinds of prophecies do some people in our time seek and follow?

Literary Focus: Plot Structure

By now Macbeth has murdered King Duncan and his servants, Banquo, and Macduff's wife and children. What is his motive— or justification—for each murder? Can you see a pattern emerging from these murders? What can you predict about Macbeth's future?

Vocabulary Study

An analogy is a relationship. Word analogies may reflect relationships such as antonyms, synonyms, object to action, quality to object, and so on. Study the relationship of each of the following pairs of words in capital letters; then choose another pair that has the same relationship.

1. LAUDABLE : COMMENDABLE ::
  a. sensible : lively   **b.** intelligent : dumb
  c. careful : cautious   **d.** impatient : angry

2. DIMINUTIVE : ATOM ::
  a. rainfall : rainbow   **b.** fast: meteor
  c. overshoe : foot   **d.** anxiety : worry

3. CAULDRON : BOIL ::
  a. oven : roast   **b.** potato : slice
  c. pull : wagon   **d.** toast : butter

4. ABJURE : EXPRESS ::
  a. calm : tranquil   **b.** agile : clumsy
  c. greedy : cruel   **d.** unpleasant : unkind

5. CISTERN : WATER ::
  a. hay : loft   **b.** bucket : handle
  c. mountain : snow   **d.** vase : flowers

Act Five

SCENE 1

Summary *Walking and talking in her sleep, Lady Macbeth reveals to a Doctor and a Gentlewoman the crimes she and Macbeth have committed.*

MACBETH'S *castle. Enter a* DOCTOR OF PHYSIC *and a* WAITING-GENTLEWOMAN.

DOCTOR. I have two nights watched with you, but can perceive no truth in your report. When was it she last walked?

GENTLEWOMAN. Since His Majesty went into the field, I have seen her rise from her bed, throw her nightgown upon her, unlock her
5 closet, take forth paper, fold it, write upon 't, read it, afterwards seal it, and again return to bed; yet all this while in a most fast sleep.

DOCTOR. A great perturbation in nature, to receive at once the bene- fit of sleep and do the effects of watching! In this slumbery agita-
10 tion, besides her walking and other actual performances, what, at any time, have you heard her say?

GENTLEWOMAN. That, sir, which I will not report after her.

DOCTOR. You may to me, and 'tis most meet you should.

GENTLEWOMAN. Neither to you nor anyone, having no witness to con-
15 firm my speech. (*Enter* LADY MACBETH, *with a candle.*) Lo, you, here she comes! This is her very guise, and, upon my life, fast sleep. Observe her. Stand close.   (*They stand aside.*)

DOCTOR. How came she by that light?

GENTLEWOMAN. Why, it stood by her. She has light by her continually.
20 'Tis her command.

DOCTOR. You see her eyes are open.

GENTLEWOMAN. Ay, but their sense are shut.

DOCTOR. What is it she does now? Look how she rubs her hands.

GENTLEWOMAN. It is an accustomed action with her to seem thus wash-
25 ing her hands. I have known her continue in this a quarter of an hour.

LADY MACBETH. Yet here's a spot.

DOCTOR. Hark, she speaks. I will set down what comes from her, to sat- isfy my remembrance the more strongly.   (*He writes.*)
30 **LADY MACBETH.** Out, damned spot! Out, I say! One—two—why then 'tis time to do 't. Hell is murky. Fie, my lord, fie, a soldier, and afeard? What need we fear who knows it, when none can call our power to account? Yet who would have thought the old man to have had so much blood in him?
35 **DOCTOR.** Do you mark that?

LADY MACBETH. The Thane of Fife had a wife. Where is she now? What, will these hands ne'er be clean? No more o' that, my lord, no more o' that; you mar all with this starting.

8 **perterbation** (pėr′tər-bā′shən), *n.* disturbance.

13 **meet,** suitable.

16 **guise** (gīz), *n.* appearance.

■ The contrasts between darkness and light have been emphasized through- out the play. Why do you think Lady Macbeth must have light by her at all times?

MR MARSTON AS MACDUFF.

London Published by J. REDINGTON, 73 Hoxton Street, Formerly called 208 Hoxton Old Town.

This hand-colored engraving from the early 1800s shows the actor M. Marston costumed for his role of Macduff in a contemporary revival of *Macbeth*. What does the pose the artist has chosen to capture suggest about he acting styles of the period?

DOCTOR. Go to, go to. You have known what you should not.

40 **GENTLEWOMAN.** She has spoke what she should not, I am sure of that. Heaven knows what she has known.

LADY MACBETH. Here's the smell of the blood still. All the perfumes of Arabia will not sweeten this little hand. O, o, o!

DOCTOR. What a sigh is there! The heart is sorely charged.

45 **GENTLEWOMAN.** I would not have such a heart in my bosom for the dignity of the whole body.

DOCTOR. Well, well, well.

GENTLEWOMAN. Pray God it be, sir.

DOCTOR. This disease is beyond my practice. Yet I have known those
50 which have walked in their sleep who have died holily in their beds.
LADY MACBETH. Wash your hands, put on your nightgown; look not
   so pale! I tell you yet again, Banquo's buried. He cannot come out
   on 's grave.
DOCTOR. Even so?
55 **LADY MACBETH.** To bed, to bed! There's knocking at the gate. Come,
   come, come, come, give me your hand. What's done cannot be
   undone. To bed, to bed, to bed!   (*Exit* LADY MACBETH.)
DOCTOR. Will she go now to bed?
GENTLEWOMAN. Directly.
60 **DOCTOR.** Foul whisperings are abroad. Unnatural deeds
   Do breed unnatural troubles. Infected minds
   To their deaf pillows will discharge their secrets.
   More needs she the divine than the physician.
   God, God forgive us all! Look after her;
65 Remove from her the means of all annoyance,
   And still keep eyes upon her. So, good night.
   My mind she has mated, and amazed my sight.
   I think, but dare not speak
GENTLEWOMAN.   Good night, good Doctor.

63 **More needs . . .
physician.** She needs a priest
more than a doctor.
65 **annoyance,** injury to herself.
67 **mated,** confused.

SCENE 2

Summary *The Scottish leaders agree to march toward Birnam Wood to join
Malcolm and Macduff's forces.*

The countryside near Dunsinane. Drums sound and banners wave. Enter
MENTEITH, CAITHNESS, ANGUS, LENNOX, *and* SOLDIERS.
MENTEITH. The English power is near, led on by Malcolm,
   His uncle Siward, and the good Macduff.
   Revenges burn in them, for their dear causes
   Would to the bleeding and the grim alarm
5 Excite the mortified man.
ANGUS.   Near Birnam Wood
   Shall we well meet them; that way are they coming.
CAITHNESS. Who knows if Donalbain be with his brother?
LENNOX. For certain, sir, he is not. I have a file
   Of all the gentry. There is Siward's son,
10 And many unrough youths that even now
   Protest their first of manhood.
MENTEITH.   What does the tyrant?
CAITHNESS. Great Dunsinane he strongly fortifies.
   Some say he's mad, others that lesser hate him
   Do call it valiant fury; but for certain
15 He cannot buckle his distempered cause

3–5 **their dear causes . . .
man,** their deeply felt causes
would arouse a dead man to
bloody battle.

10 **unrough,** beardless.
11 **protest . . . manhood,**
call themselves men for the
first time.

14 **valiant** (val'yənt), *adj.*
courageous.

Within the belt of rule.

ANGUS.   Now does he feel
His secret murders sticking on his hands;
Now minutely revolts upbraid his faith-breach.
Those he commands move only in command,
20   Nothing in love. Now does he feel his title
Hang loose about him, like a giant's robe
Upon a dwarfish thief.

MENTEITH.   Who then shall blame
His pestered senses to recoil and start,
When all that is within him does condemn
25   Itself for being there?

CAITHNESS.   Well, march we on
To give obedience where 'tis truly owed.
Meet we the med'cine of the sickly weal,
And with him pour we in our country's purge
Each drop of us.

LENNOX.   Or so much as it needs
30   To dew the sovereign flower and drown the weeds.
Make we our march towards Birnam.

SCENE 3

Summary *Macbeth hears reports from the Doctor about Lady Macbeth's illness and from a Servant about the advancing armies. Still he relies on the prophecies of the Witches.*

MACBETH'S *castle. Enter* MACBETH, DOCTOR, *and* ATTENDANTS.

MACBETH. Bring me no more reports. Let them fly all!
Till Birnam Wood remove to Dunsinane,
I cannot taint with fear. What's the boy Malcolm? —Big deal
Was he not born of woman? The spirits that know
5   All mortal consequences have pronounced me thus:
"Fear not, Macbeth. No man that's born of woman
Shall e'er have power upon thee." Then fly, false thanes,
And mingle with the English epicures!
The mind I sway by and the heart I bear
10   Shall never sag with doubt nor shake with fear.   (*Enter* SERVANT.)
The devil damn thee black, thou cream-faced loon!
Where gott'st thou that goose look?

SERVANT. There is ten thousand—

MACBETH.   Geese, villain?

SERVANT.   Soldiers, sir.

MACBETH. Go prick thy face and over-red thy fear,
15   Thou lily-livered boy. What soldiers, patch?
Death of thy soul! Those linen cheeks of thine

[handwritten: macbeth thinks he is invincible]

15–16 **He cannot . . . rule.** He cannot control the situation.
18 **upbraid** (up brād′), *v.* find fault with.
18 **now . . . faith-breach,** every minute, those who revolt against him blame his faithlessness.

27–29 **Meet we . . . us.** We go to meet Malcolm, who will heal the sickness of our country, and to offer our lives in the curing process.

1 **them,** the thanes.

3 **taint** (tānt), *v.* become infected.

8 **epicure** (ep′ə kyùr), *n.* lover of luxury.
9 **I sway by,** I am directed by.

14 **prick thy face . . . fear,** go prick or pinch your pale cheeks to bring some color into them.
15 **patch,** fool.

Are counselors to fear. What soldiers, whey-face?

SERVANT. The English force, so please you.

MACBETH. Take thy face hence. (*Exit* SERVANT.) Seyton! I am
    sick at heart
20 When I behold—Seyton, I say!—This push
    Will cheer me ever, or disseat me now.
    I have lived long enough. My way of life
    Is fall'n into the sere, the yellow leaf.
    And that which should accompany old age,
25 As honor, love, obedience, troops of friends,
    I must not look to have, but in their stead
    Curses, not loud but deep, mouth-honor, breath
    Which the poor heart would fain deny and dare not.
    Seyton!   (*Enter* SEYTON.)

30 **SEYTON.** What's your gracious pleasure?

MACBETH.   What news more?

SEYTON. All is confirmed, my lord, which was reported.

MACBETH. I'll fight till from my bones my flesh be hacked.
    Give me my armor.

SEYTON. 'Tis not needed yet.

35 **MACBETH.** I'll put it on.
    Send out more horses. Skirr the country round.
    Hang those that talk of fear. Give me mine armor.
    How does your patient, Doctor?

DOCTOR. Not so sick, my lord,
40 As she is troubled with thick-coming fancies
    That keep her from her rest.

MACBETH.   Cure her of that.
    Canst thou not minister to a mind diseased,
    Pluck from the memory a rooted sorrow,
    Raze out the written troubles of the brain,
45 And with some sweet oblivious antidote
    Cleanse the stuffed bosom of that perilous stuff
    Which weighs upon the heart?

DOCTOR.   Therein the patient
    Must minister to himself.

MACBETH. Throw physic to the dogs! I'll none of it.
50 Come put mine armor on. Give me my staff.
    (ATTENDANTS *arm him.*)
    Seyton, send out. Doctor, the thanes fly from me—
    Come, sir, dispatch—If thou couldst, Doctor, cast
    The water of my land, find her disease,
    And purge it to a sound and pristine health,
55 I would applaud thee to the very echo,
    That should applaud again—Pull 't off, I say—

20 push, attack.

■ Summarize Macbeth's "I
have lived long enough"
speech. Compare Macbeth's
life to that of Duncan, the
first person Macbeth killed.

36 skirr (skėr), *v.* scour.

45 oblivious (ə bliv′ē əs),
adj. unmindful; forgetful.

51 send out, send out more
scouts.
52–53 cast . . . land, diagnose
my country's illness.
54 pristine (pris′tēn′), *adj.*
original.
56 pull 't off, referring to
some part of his armor.

What rhubarb, senna, or what purgative drug
Would scour these English hence? Hear'st thou of them?
DOCTOR. Ay, my good lord. Your royal preparation
60 Makes us hear something.
MACBETH.   Bring it after me.
I will not be afraid of death and bane,
Till Birnam Forest come to Dunsinane.   (*Exit all but the* DOCTOR.)
DOCTOR. Were I from Dunsinane away and clear,
Profit again should hardly draw me here.

SCENE 4

Summary *The Scottish and English forces come together at Birnam Wood. In order to conceal their numbers, each man cuts a branch from a tree and carries it before him.*

Drums sound and banners wave. Enter MALCOLM, SIWARD, MACDUFF, SIWARD'S SON, MENTEITH, CAITHNESS, ANGUS, LENNOX, ROSS, *and* SOLDIERS, *marching.*
MALCOLM. Cousins, I hope the days are near at hand
That chambers will be safe.
MENTEITH.   We doubt it nothing.
SIWARD. What wood is this before us?
MENTEITH.   The wood of Birnam.
MALCOLM. Let every soldier hew him down a bough
5 And bear 't before him. Thereby shall we shadow
The numbers of our host and make discovery
Err in report of us.
SOLDIERS.   It shall be done.
SIWARD. We learn no other but the confident tyrant
Keeps still in Dunsinane and will endure
10 Our setting down before 't.
MALCOLM.   'Tis his main hope;
For where there is advantage to be given,
Both more and less have given him the revolt,
And none serve with him but constrainèd things
Whose hearts are absent too.
MACDUFF.   Let our just censures
15 Attend the true event, and put we on
Industrious soldiership.
SIWARD.   The time approaches
That will with due decision make us know
What we shall say we have and what we owe.
Thoughts speculative their unsure hopes relate,
20 But certain issue strokes must arbitrate—
Towards which advance the war.

57 **purgative** (pėr′gə tiv), *adj.* causing the bowels to empty.
60 **it,** the armor.
61 **bane** (bān), *n.* destruction.

6 **discovery,** Macbeth's scouts.

10 **setting down before 't,** laying siege to it (the castle at Dunsinane).

12 **both more and less,** both nobles and common people.

14–15 **let . . . event,** let our judgment await the actual outcome of the battle.
19–21 **Thoughts . . . war.** We are now speculating on the basis of our hopes; only after the battle will we know the real outcome.
20 **arbitrate** (är′bə trāt), *v.* decide a dispute.

SCENE 5

Summary *Macbeth learns that Lady Macbeth has died. Hearing next that Birnam Wood is moving toward Dunsinane, Macbeth suspects the Witches have deceived him. He decides to fight actively.*

Outside MACBETH'S *castle. Enter* MACBETH, SEYTON, *and* SOLDIERS, *with drums and banners.*

MACBETH. Hang out our banners on the outward walls.
The cry is still, "They come!" Our castle's strength
Will laugh a siege to scorn. Here let them lie
Till famine and the ague eat them up.

5 Were they not forced with those that should be ours,
We might have met them dareful, beard to beard,
And beat them backward home.   *(Crying is heard offstage.)*
                              What is that noise?

SEYTON. It is the cry of women, my good lord.   *(He goes to the door.)*

MACBETH. I have almost forgot the taste of fears.

10 The time has been my senses would have cooled
To hear a night-shriek, and my fell of hair
Would at a dismal treatise rouse and stir
As life were in 't. I have supped full with horrors;
Direness, familiar to my slaughterous thoughts,

15 Cannot once start me.   *(SEYTON returns.)*
                              Wherefore was that cry?

SEYTON. The Queen, my lord, is dead.

MACBETH. She should have died hereafter;
There would have been a time for such a word.
Tomorrow, and tomorrow, and tomorrow

20 Creeps in this petty pace from day to day
To the last syllable of recorded time,
And all our yesterdays have lighted fools
The way to dusty death. Out, out, brief candle!
Life's but a walking shadow, a poor player

25 That struts and frets his hour upon the stage
And then is heard no more. It is a tale
Told by an idiot, full of sound and fury,
Signifying nothing.   *(Enter a* MESSENGER.*)*
Thou com'st to use thy tongue; thy story quickly.

30 **MESSENGER.** Gracious my lord,
I should report that which I say I saw,
But know not how to do 't.

MACBETH.   Well, say, sir.

MESSENGER. As I did stand my watch upon the hill,
I looked toward Birnam, and anon, methought,

35 The wood began to move.

---

4 ague (ā′gyü), *n.* fever.
5 forced, reinforced.

12 dismal treatise (trē′tis), tragic account.

What implications does such a philosophy have for any person's feelings of **individuality**?

Macduff, holding Macbeth's head, kneels before the new King of Scotland in this Charles Ricketts illustration from *The Tragedie of Macbeth* (1923). Do you think Macbeth deserves his fate? Why or why not? ➤

MACBETH. Liar and slave!

MESSENGER. Let me endure your wrath if 't be not so.
Within this three mile may you see it coming;
I say, a moving grove.

MACBETH. If thou speak'st false,
Upon the next tree shall thou hang alive
40 Till famine cling thee. If thy speech be sooth,
I care not if thou dost for me as much.
I pull in resolution, and begin
To doubt th' equivocation of the fiend
That lies like truth. "Fear not, till Birnam Wood
45 Do come to Dunsinane," and now a wood
Comes toward Dunsinane. Arm, arm, and out!
If this which he avouches does appear,
There is nor flying hence nor tarrying here.
I 'gin to be aweary of the sun,
50 And wish th' estate o' the world were now undone.
Ring the alarum bell! Blow wind, come wrack,
At least we'll die with harness on our back.

40 cling, shrivel up.

42 I pull in resolution, I weaken in confidence.
43 doubt the equivocation (i kwiv′ə kā′shən), fear the deception.

47 avouch (ə vouch′), *v.* affirm.

SCENE 6

Summary *The army prepares for battle.*

Near the castle. Drums sound and banners wave. Enter MALCOLM, SIWARD, MAC-
DUFF, *and their army, with tree branches.*

MALCOLM. Now near enough. Your leafy screens throw down,
And show like those you are. You, worthy uncle,
Shall with my cousin, your right noble son,
Lead our first battle. Worthy Macduff and we
5 Shall take upon 's what else remains to do,
According to our order.

SIWARD. Fare you well.
Do we but find the tyrant's power tonight,
Let us be beaten, if we cannot fight.

MACDUFF. Make all our trumpets speak! Give them all breath,
10 Those clamorous harbingers of blood and death.

2 uncle, Siward.

10 clamorous (klam′ər əs), *adj.* noisy.

SCENE 7

Summary *Young Siward attacks Macbeth, and Macbeth kills Young Siward.*

Another part of the field. Enter MACBETH.

MACBETH. They have tied me to a stake. I cannot fly,
But bearlike I must fight the course. What's he
That was not born of woman? Such a one
Am I to fear, or none. (*Enter* YOUNG SIWARD.)

1–2 They have . . . course. In bearbaiting, a popular sport in Shakespeare's time, a bear was tied to a stake and forced to fight rounds with dogs set upon it in relays.

5 **YOUNG SIWARD.** What is thy name?

MACBETH. Thou'lt be afraid to hear it.

YOUNG SIWARD. No, though thou call'st thyself a hotter name
   Than any is in hell.

MACBETH.   My name's Macbeth.

YOUNG SIWARD. The devil himself could not pronounce a title
10   More hateful to mine ear.

MACBETH.   No, nor more fearful.

YOUNG SIWARD. Thou liest, abhorrèd tyrant! With my sword
   I'll prove the lie thou speak'st.   (*They fight, and* MACBETH *kills*
   YOUNG SIWARD.)

MACBETH.   Thou was born of woman.
   But swords I smile at, weapons laugh to scorn,
   Brandished by man that's of a woman born.   (*Exit.*)
(*Sounds of battle offstage. Enter* MACDUFF.)

15 **MACDUFF.** That way the noise is. Tyrant, show thy face!
   If thou be'st slain, and with no stroke of mine,
   My wife and children's ghosts will haunt me still.
   I cannot strike at wretched kerns, whose arms
   Are hired to bear their staves. Either thou, Macbeth,
20   Or else my sword with an unbattered edge
   I sheathe again undeeded. There thou shouldst be;
   By this great clatter one of greatest note
   Seems bruited. Let me find him, Fortune,
   And more I beg not.
(MACDUFF *exits. Sounds of battle offstage. Enter* MALCOLM *and* SIWARD.)

25 **SIWARD.** This way, my lord. The castle's gently rendered:
   The tyrant's people on both sides do fight,
   The noble thanes do bravely in the war,
   The day almost itself professes yours,
   And little is to do.

MALCOLM.   We have met with foes
30   That strike beside us.

SIWARD.   Enter, sir, the castle.

SCENE 8

Summary *Macbeth fights and is killed by Macduff. Malcolm is hailed as king of Scotland. He vows to right the wrongs created by Macbeth and Lady Macbeth.*

Another part of the field. Enter MACBETH.

MACBETH. Why should I play the Roman fool and die
   On mine own sword? Whiles I see lives, the gashes
   Do better upon them.   (*Enter* MACDUFF.)

MACDUFF.   Turn, hellhound, turn!

23 **bruit** (brüt), *v.* announce by a great noise.

25 **rendered,** surrendered.

30 **strike beside us,** join us and fight on our side.

1–2 **Why . . . sword?** Why should I kill myself, as the Romans did? (The Romans considered suicide more honorable than capture.)
2 **lives,** living persons.

MACBETH. Of all men else I have avoided thee.
5   But get thee back! My soul is too much charged
With blood of thine already.
MACDUFF.   I have no words;
My voice is in my sword, thou bloodier villain
Than terms can give thee out!   *(They fight.)*
MACBETH.   Thou losest labor.
As easy mayst thou the intrenchant air
10   With thy keen sword impress as make me bleed.
Let fall thy blade on vulnerable crests;
I bear a charmèd life, which must not yield
To one of woman born.
MACDUFF.   Despair thy charm,
And let the angel whom thou still hast served
15   Tell thee, Macduff was from his mother's womb
Untimely ripped.
MACBETH. Accursèd be that tongue that tells me so,
For it hath cowed my better part of man!
And be these juggling fiends no more believed
20   That palter with us in a double sense,
That keep the word of promise to our ear
And break it to our hope. I'll not fight with thee.
MACDUFF. Then yield thee, coward,
And live to be the show and gaze o' the time!
25   We'll have thee, as our rarer monsters are,
Painted upon a pole, and underwrit,
"Here may you see the tyrant."
MACBETH.   I will not yield
To kiss the ground before young Malcolm's feet
And to be baited with the rabble's curse.
30   Though Birnam Wood be come to Dunsinane,
And thou opposed, being of no woman born,
Yet I wll try the last. Before my body
I throw my warlike shield. Lay on, Macduff,
And damned be him that first cries, "Hold, enough!"
(They fight and exit. Enter, with drums sounding and banners waving,
MALCOLM, SIWARD, ROSS, THANES, *and* SOLDIERS.*)*
35 **MALCOLM.** I would the friends we miss were safe arrived.
SIWARD. Some must go off; and yet, by these I see
So great a day as this is cheaply bought.
MALCOLM. Macduff is missing, and your noble son.
ROSS. Your son, my lord, has paid a soldier's debt.
40   He only lived but till he was a man,
The which no sooner had his prowess confirmed
In the unshrinking station where he fought,

6 blood of thine, that is, Macduff's wife and children.

9 intrenchant (in tren′- chənt), *adj.* invulnerable; incapable of being hurt.

15–16 from his mother's . . . ripped, born in a Caesarean operation.

18 cow (kou), *v.* frighten.

20 palter (pôl′tər), *v.* trifle deceitfully; play tricks.

26. painted . . . pole, your picture painted on a board which will be displayed from a pole.

36 go off, die.

But like a man he died.

SIWARD.   Then he is dead?

ROSS. Ay, and brought off the field. Your cause of sorrow
45   Must not be measured by his worth, for then
      It hath no end.

SIWARD.   Had he his hurts before?

ROSS. Ay, on the front.

SIWARD.   Why then, God's soldier be he!
      Had I as many sons as I have hairs
      I would not wish them to a fairer death.
50   And so, his knell is knolled.

MALCOLM.   He's worth more sorrow,
      And that I'll spend for him.

SIWARD.   He's worth no more.
      They say he parted well and paid his score,
      And so, God be with him! Here comes newer comfort.

(Enter MACDUFF, *with* MACBETH'S *head.)*

MACDUFF. Hail, King! For so thou art. Behold where stands
55   Th' usurper's cursèd head. The time is free.
      I see thee compassed with thy kingdom's pearl,
      That speak my salutation in their minds,
      Whose voices I desire aloud with mine.
      Hail, King of Scotland!

60 **ALL.** Hail, King of Scotland!   *(Music sounds offstage.)*

MALCOLM. We shall not spend a large expense of time
      Before we reckon with your several loves
      And make us even with you. My thanes and kinsmen,
      Henceforth be earls, the first that ever Scotland
65   In such an honor named. What's more to do
      Which would be planted newly with the time,
      As calling home our exiled friends abroad
      That fled the snares of watchful tyranny,
      Producing forth the cruel ministers
70   Of this dead butcher and his fiendlike queen—
      Who, as 'tis thought, by self and violent hands
      Took off her life—this, and what needful else
      That calls upon us, by the grace of Grace
      We will perform in measure, time, and place.
75   So, thanks to all at once and to each one,
      Whom we invite to see us crowned at Scone.

56 compassed . . . pearl,
surrounded by the nobles
of your kingdom.

62 reckon (rek′ən),
v. settle accounts.

After Reading

Making Connections

1. List five words to describe Lady Macbeth's behavior. Do you think Shakespeare gives a convincing portrayal of her mental illness?

2. On a scale of 1 to 10, how responsible do you think Macbeth is for his own downfall? On the same scale, how responsible is Lady Macbeth for Macbeth's downfall? Be prepared to explain your answers.

1   10

Not responsible   Responsible

Analyzing the Play

3. Even though he hears about an advancing army, why does Macbeth still feel that he is safe?

4. To *equivocate* is to use expressions of double meaning in order to mislead. Explain whether or not the witches have equivocated.

5. How well do both Macbeth and Lady Macbeth seem to understand themselves, their strengths, and their limitations?

6. In literature, characters are frequently used as **foils;** that is, the traits of one point up by contrast the traits of another. What traits of Macbeth are pointed up by contrast with Duncan? with Young Siward? with Malcolm? How does Lady Macduff serve as a foil for Lady Macbeth?

7. Why is it particularly appropriate that Macduff is the one who finally kills Macbeth?

Extending the Ideas

8. Does the execution of a murderer make up for his or her crime? How? For whom?

9. 👆 Why do you think people turn to an outside or supernatural force for help in living their lives? Does depending on another force heighten or lessen one's own **individuality?**

Literary Focus: Plot Structure

Write down the three prophecies the Witches make in act 1. Each of these prophecies causes Macbeth to take some action that advances the plot. Trace the cause-effect actions that result from each prophecy. Do the same for act 4.

Vocabulary Study

In each of the following sentences, select the word in parentheses that best fits the meaning of the sentence.

1. Macbeth is often so absorbed in his thoughts of murder that he is

(oblivious, pristine) to the words and actions of those around him.

2. With a tyrant in charge, there is no one who can (upbraid, arbitrate) with him to help ease the awful conditions.

3. Macbeth believes he need not fear death and (bane, epicure) until Birnam Wood comes to Dunsinane.

4. When the messenger (avouches, bruits) that Birnam Wood is moving toward Dunsinane, Macbeth knows the end is near.

5. When Macbeth decides to leave his castle to fight, he once again becomes the (clamorous, valiant) warrior.

Expressing Your Ideas

Writing Choices

Writer's Notebook Update Review the definition of *tragedy* on page 117. Generally, the downfall of the main character in a tragedy is brought about through a tragic flaw in the character's personality or through a tragic error. Review the list of unfortunate people in your notebook. Were the forces that brought about their downfalls tragic flaws or tragic errors?

It's Fate After All The word *weird* comes from an Anglo-Saxon word meaning "fate." One interpretation of the three "weird sisters" is that they represent the beings who determine fate: the Past, the Present, and the Future. Write an **analysis** of the predictions of the witches, discussing to what extent you believe Macbeth is guided or controlled by them.

Dear Diary You are one of the invited guests at Macbeth's banquet. After you are dismissed by Lady Macbeth, you decide to record everything in your diary for future reference. Write a **diary entry** in which you describe your host and hostess and the events of the evening. You may wish to include your own theories about what was happening. Remember, *you* couldn't see Banquo's ghost.

Other Options

The Old Song and Dance The scenes with the three witches and Hecate offer the contrast of song and dance to the seriousness of the tragedy. Join with other classmates to choose appropriate music and to **choreograph** one or more of the witches' scenes. Add costumes and props, if you wish, and perform your dance for your class.

Block the Scene The banquet in act 3, scene 4 requires very careful positioning and moving of characters because of the many activities going on simultaneously. Work in a small group to block out this scene on paper, indicating where the various characters should be positioned and where they should move. Once you have developed your **stage directions,** assign parts and stage the scene.

Advertise *Macbeth* The illustration on page 119 is from a poster used to advertise a production of Macbeth in 1911. You have been selected to promote your school's production of *Macbeth*. Create a **poster** emphasizing an important theme, character, or event in the play. You might include an appropriate quote. Display your poster in the classroom.

The Lure of Ambition

The Burden of Guilt

Humanities Connection

Human beings have always had difficulty in dealing with the burden of guilt. The following selections suggest different dimensions of this problem.

BLO

from the Book of the Dead

I have not done crimes against people,
I have not mistreated cattle, . . .
I have not blasphemed a god,
I have not robbed the poor.
I have not done what the god abhors,
I have not maligned a servant to his master.
I have not caused pain,
I have not caused tears.
I have not killed.
I have not ordered to kill,
I have not made anyone suffer.
I have not damaged the offerings in the temples, . . .
I have not added to the weight of the balance,
I have not falsified the plummet of the scales.
I have not taken milk from the mouth of children,
I have not deprived cattle of their pasture.
I have not snared birds in the reeds of the gods,
I have not caught fish in their ponds.
I have not held back water in its season,
I have not dammed a flowing stream, . . .
I am pure, I am pure, I am pure, I am pure! . . .

In this excerpt from the ancient Egyptian Book of the Dead, *people are advised what to say at their final judgment before the god Osiris.*

On the right in the scene below from the Book of the Dead, *the heart of the deceased is being weighed by the jackal-headed god Anubis against a feather. Below the scale is a monster, Ammet – part-crocodile, part-lion, and part hippopotamus – that devours the hearts of the wicked.*

O D Y

Before the start of the Trojan War, the Greek King Agamemnon (ag′ə mem′non) sacrifices his daughter Iphigenia (if′ə jə nī′ə) to the gods to obtain favorable winds for his warships, as shown in this ancient vase painting.

After the war, Queen Clytemnestra (klī′tem-nes′trə) and her lover Aegisthus (ē jis′thŭs) murder Agamemnon on his return and take his throne. Her son Orestes (ô res′tēs) later murders Clytemnestra and Aegisthus in retribution for his father's death. In these speeches, the Furies, goddesses of vengeance, threaten what they will do to punish Orestes for his deed.

So. Here the man has left a clear trail behind; keep on, keep on, as the unspeaking accuser tells us, by whose sense, like hounds after a bleeding fawn, we trail our quarry by the splash and drip of blood. And now my lungs are blown with abundant and with wearisome work, mankilling. My range has been the entire extent of land, and, flown unwinged across the open water, I am here, and give way to no ship in my pursuit. Our man has gone to cover somewhere in this place. The welcome smell of human blood has told me so.

Look again, look again,
search everywhere, let
not the matricide
steal away and escape…

You must give back for her blood from the living man
red blood of your body to suck, and from your own
I could feed, with bitter-swallowed drench,
turn your strength limp while yet you live and
    drag you down
where you must pay for the pain of the murdered mother,
and watch the rest of the mortals stained with violence
against god or guest

or hurt parents who were close and dear,
each with the pain upon him that his crime deserves…
You are consecrate to me and fattened for my feast,
and you shall feed me while you live, not cut down first
at the altar. Hear the spell I sing to bind you in.

Come then, link we our choral. Ours
to show forth the power
and terror of our music, declare
our rights of office, how we conspire
to steer men's lives.
We hold we are straight and just. If a man
can spread his hands and show they are clean,
no wrath of ours shall lurk for him.
Unscathed he walks through his life time.
But one like this man before us, with stained
hidden hands, and the guilt upon him,
shall find us beside him, as witnesses
of the truth, and we show clear in the end
to avenge the blood of the murdered.

H A N D S

BLOODY HANDS

from *Crime and Punishment*
by Feodor Dostoevski

All at once, in one flash, he recollected everything. For the first moment he thought he was going mad. A dreadful chill came over him; but the chill was from the fever that had begun long before in his sleep. Now he was suddenly taken with violent shivering, so that his teeth chattered and all his limbs were shaking. He opened the door and began listening; everything in the house was asleep. With amazement he gazed at himself and everything in the room around him, wondering how he could have come in the night be fore without fastening the door, and have flung himself on the sofa without undressing, without even taking his hat off. It had fallen off and was lying on the floor near his pillow.

"If anyone had come in, what would he have thought? That I'm drunk but . . ."

He rushed to the window. There was light enough, and he began hurriedly looking himself all over from head to foot, all his clothes; were there not traces? But there was no doing it like that; shivering with cold, he began taking off everything and looking over again. He turned everything over to the last threads and rags, and mistrusting himself, went through his search three times. But there seemed to be nothing, no trace, except in one place, where some thick drops of congealed blood were clinging to the frayed edge of his trousers. He picked up a big claspknife and cut off the grayed threads. There seemed to be nothing more.

Suddenly he remembered that the purse and the things he had taken out of the old woman's box were still in his pockets! He had not thought till then of taking them out and hiding them! He had not even thought of them while he was examining his clothes! What next? Instantly he rushed to take them out, and fling them on the table. When he had pulled out everything, and turned the pocket inside out to be sure there was nothing left, he carried the whole heap to the corner. The paper had come off the bottom of the wall and hung there in tatters. He began stuffing all the things into the hole under the paper: "They're in! All out of sight, and the purse too!" he thought gleefully, getting up and gazing blankly at the hole which bulged out more than ever. Suddenly he shuddered all over with horror; "My God!" he whispered in despair: "what's the matter with me? Is that hidden? Is that the way to hide things?" He had not reckoned on having trinkets to hide. He had only thought of money, and so had not prepared a hiding–place. "But now, now, what am I glad of?" he thought. "Is that hiding things? My reason's deserting me—simply!" He sat down on the sofa in exhaustion and was at once shaken by another unbearable fit of shivering.

Mechanically he drew from a chair beside him his old student's winter coat, which was still warm though almost in rags, covered himself up with it and once more sank into drowsiness and delirium. He lost consciousness.

Not more than five minutes had passed when he jumped up a second time, . . . and with painful concentration he fell to gazing about him again, at the floor and everywhere, trying to make sure he had not forgotten anything. The conviction, that all his faculties, even memory, and the simplest power of reflection were failing him, began to be an insufferable torture.

"Surely it isn't beginning already! Surely it isn't my punishment coming upon me? It is!"

The frayed rags he had cut off his trousers were actually lying on the floor in the middle of the room, where any one coming in would see them!

"What is the matter with me!" he cried again, like one distraught.

Then a strange idea entered his head; that, perhaps, all his clothes were covered with blood, that, perhaps, there were a great many stains, but that he did not see them, did not notice them because his perceptions were failing, were going to pieces . . . his reason was clouded. . . .

During World War II over six million Jews and other people died or were murdered in Nazi concentration camps. After the war, Adolph Eichmann was captured in Argentina, where he had fled, and was brought to Israel to stand trial for his part in the killings. He was convicted in December, 1961, and was hanged the next year. Here is part of his statement.

from the trial of   Adolph Eichmann

It is difficult to say what constitutes guilt, and I must make the distinction between guilt from the legal point of view and from the human aspect. . .

[The] guilt must be borne by those who were responsible for political decisions: when there is no responsibility there can be no guilt or blame. . .

The head of state ordered the deportations, and the part I played in them emanated from the master at the top. . . I had to obey. . .

Ethically I condemn myself and try to argue with myself. I wish to say, in conclusion, that I have regret and condemnation for the extermination of the Jewish people which was ordered by the German rulers, but I myself could not have done anything to prevent it. I was a tool in the hands of the strong and the powerful and in the hands of fate itself. . .

I do not consider myself guilty from the legal point of view. I was only receiving orders and carrying out orders. . . .

Responding

1. How did these societies differ in values from ours today?

2. Which of the acts considered sinful by the ancient Egyptians would still be unacceptable behavior now?

3. Do you believe that a person is responsible for his or her own actions even if that person has been told or ordered by others to perform those actions?

Lady Macbeth in Therapy

Interview with Diane Bray

Most of Diane Bray's clients are adults and older adolescents experiencing emotional distress. They are anxious or depressed, having relationship problems, addiction problems or difficulties as a result of emotional trauma or abuse. In private practice in Connecticut, Ms. Bray is a Certified Psychiatric Clinical Nurse Specialist and has been doing therapy for twenty-three years.

"Many factors influence our thoughts, feelings, behavior, and the choices we make in life. My goal as Lady Macbeth's therapist would be to help her become aware of these factors and how they've affected her behavior. I would want to know about her childhood and the kind of parenting she received. Sometimes in current relationships, we act out previous conflicts we've had with those closest to us, especially our parents. I would want to know about her relationship with her husband. How do they handle conflict and intimacy issues and how does she really feel about him? Is he really as soft-hearted as she thinks? He ends up killing Duncan, and later she has more trouble with the remorse than Macbeth.

"Culture and society also influence our roles and behavior. I wonder what it was like to be a female at the time of the play. Was a woman's only means of self-expression through her husband? How angry is Lady Macbeth about her limited opportunities?

"The development of Lady Macbeth's conscience is another important issue. I don't typically see people who have committed major crimes. Many people feel rage, but most find healthy ways to deal with their anger. Their conscience and control over their impulses keep them from acting out the rage. At first glance, Lady Macbeth looks cold–blooded as she and Macbeth plot the murder. But even in that scene in act 1, she wants to remove her remorse so she can carry out the deed. After the murder, she warns her husband not to think of it or it will make him mad. She is the voice of conscience and the predictor of what actually happens to her. Macbeth himself is responsible for the act, but doesn't seem to feel remorse and, in fact, goes into battle and orders additional murders.

"The goals of treatment are self knowledge, self acceptance, and being able to take responsibility for behavior and its consequences. Most treatment is done on an outpatient basis. However, Lady Macbeth, so out of touch with reality and unable to care for herself, would be put in a psychiatric hospital. She would get medication and therapy and would continue treatment after she left the hospital."

Responding
1. Why do you think Lady Macbeth commits suicide?

2. In your opinion, should a person be allowed to plead not guilty to a crime by reason of insanity? You might want to express your opinions in "Lady Macbeth on Trial," the Writing Workshop that begins on page 198.

Language History

The Language of the Elizabethans

 When we landed we founde fewe people, for the Lorde of that place was gone with divers Canoas above 400 miles of, upon a journey towardes the heade of Orenoque to trade for gold, and to buy women of the Canibals . . . .

Sir Walter Raleigh, *The Discoverie of Guiana* (1596)

By the time of Shakespeare, about half the population of London knew how to read, and that number continued to increase. Writers went on spelling words according to their own tastes or their dialectal backgrounds, however; the word *fellow,* for example, was spelled variously as *fallow, felowe, felow,* and *fallowe.*

The growth of the printing press increased the necessity for uniformity in language, and numerous "how-to" books on spelling and usage were printed during the late 1500s. On the one hand, preoccupation with a uniform language grew out of a strong sense of national identity. On the other hand, experimentation with new vocabulary and new means of expression grew out of the adventurous spirit of the Elizabethans.

The language grew to accommodate the new discoveries being made in scholarship and science. Experts estimate that more than ten thousand words were added to English during the last part of the 1500s. Words were borrowed or adapted from Latin and Greek *(antipathy, catastrophe, external, halo, anachronism, emphasis, strenuous);* French *(bigot, alloy, detail);* Italian *(balcony, cameo, stanza);* and Spanish and Portuguese *(alligator, negro, potato, tobacco, cannibal).*

Shakespeare himself was a notorious coiner and borrower of words. Many words originated by Shakespeare are still in common use today—for example, *monumental, lonely, hurry, castigate, assassination, majestic, excellent, fretful,* and *obscene.* As an originator of phrases, Shakespeare is preeminent. To him we are indebted for such phrases as *disgraceful conduct, flesh and blood, cold comfort, a foregone conclusion, the sound and the fury,* and *vanish into thin air.* Through his contributions not only to literature but also to English vocabulary and everyday speech, Shakespeare continues to speak to us across the centuries.

Writing Workshop

Lady Macbeth on Trial

Assignment Do you think Lady Macbeth was as guilty of Duncan's murder as Macbeth? Write an essay in which you argue to what extent you think Lady Macbeth is guilty of the crime. See the Writer's Blueprint for details.

WRITER'S BLUEPRINT

Product   A persuasive essay

Purpose   To convince readers of your views on the degree to which Lady Macbeth is responsible for the murder of Duncan

Audience   People who have read or seen *Macbeth*

Specs   To write an effective essay, you should:

❏ Summarize the events leading to Duncan's murder in order to create a context for your argument.

❏ Give your opinion about the degree of Lady Macbeth's guilt and cite ample evidence from the text to support it, including direct quotations where appropriate.

❏ Address opposing points of view and refute them with logical reasons.

❏ Present clear cause-and-effect relationships throughout.

❏ Close by saying what you think should happen to Lady Macbeth as a result of her part in the murder, and why.

❏ Follow the rules of grammar, usage, spelling, and mechanics. Take special care to avoid comma splices.

---

1 PREWRITING

Chart the events that led to the murder. Review the play and make an evidence chart like the one below. List any evidence—actions, words— that relate to Lady Macbeth's involvement in the crime. For each piece of evidence, list a source: the act and scene where you found it. Include quotes where appropriate. Also, decide what this evidence shows about Lady Macbeth's part in the crime. (You might also want to reread "Lady Macbeth in Therapy" on page 196.)

Pieces of Evidence	Sources	What Evidence Shows
In his letter about the witches, Macbeth calls her "partner" and appeals to her ambition.	"My dearest partner of greatness . . . what greatness is promised thee." (act 1, scene 5)	

Tally the evidence. Put a plus sign next to the pieces of evidence that point to Lady Macbeth's guilt and a minus sign next to those that indicate she is either not guilty or is being persuaded to participate in the crime by Macbeth.

Quickwrite your conclusions. Look over your chart and spend a few minutes writing about what the evidence seems to show. Is Lady Macbeth:

- as guilty as Macbeth?

- less guilty but still responsible for the crime?

- not guilty by reason of insanity?

- an innocent victim of circumstances beyond her control?

Make your decision and circle the pieces of evidence from your chart that support it. Look back at the play if you feel you need more evidence.

Consider opposing points of view. Now look over the pieces of evidence from your chart that do <u>not</u> support your decision. What arguments could someone make to support a position different from yours? What logical reasons could you offer to refute them? Quickwrite for a few minutes about opposing points of view.

OR. . .
Get together with a partner who's taking an opposing point of view and discuss your positions. Take notes on your partner's position and ask questions.

Plan your essay. Reread the Writer's Blueprint. Then use your prewriting notes to help you create an outline like the one shown. As you plan, make sure you're presenting a sound argument based on solid evidence. See the Revising Strategy in Step 3 of this lesson.

- **Introduction**

  Events leading to the murder

- **Body–Part One**

  Your opinion on the degree of Lady Macbeth's guilt
  Piece of evidence + source
  Piece of evidence + source
  and so on . . .

(Note: present your pieces of evidence in time order, carrying the reader through the play from start to finish, or present them in order of strength, from weakest to strongest.)

- **Body–Part Two**

  An opposing point of view
  Reasons to support it
  Reasons to refute it
  Another opposing point of view
  and so on . . .

- **Conclusion**

  What should happen to Lady Macbeth
  Reasons why

Ask a partner to comment on your plan before you begin drafting. Use your partner's responses to help you revise your plan.

✔ Have I gathered strong evidence to support my opinion?

✔ Have I followed the Specs in the Writer's Blueprint?

OR . . .
Do Body–Part Two <u>before</u> Body–Part One. Refute opposing points of view before offering yours as the logical alternative.

STEP  **DRAFTING**

Before you draft, gather together your prewriting materials and review the Writer's Blueprint.

As you draft, use your writing plan. These drafting tips may help:

- Begin with a quote from the play that strongly supports your opinion, and return to it later on when you state your opinion.

- Devote a paragraph to each of your three or four strongest pieces of evidence. Try to weave the other pieces of evidence into these paragraphs where they belong.

3 REVISING

Ask a partner for comments on your draft before you revise it.

✔ Have I clearly stated and supported my views on Lady Macbeth's guilt or innocence?

✔ Have I refuted opposing points of view?

✔ Have I presented strong cause-effect connections?

> **COMPUTER TIP**
> As you revise, save each version of your essay with a slightly different name, for example, MacbVer1, MacbVer2, and so on. This way you can always return to a previous version if you need to.

Revising Strategy

Connecting Cause to Effect

Test the strength of your arguments by asking yourself whether you have presented clear connections between causes and effects. The connection might be clear in your mind, but that's not enough. It's your responsibility to make it as clear to your readers as it is to you.

Weak Connection	After the witches spoke to Macbeth, he did the murder. *(Just because event #1 occurred a little while before event #2 doesn't mean that #1 caused #2.)*
Strong Connection	While speaking to Macbeth, the witches appealed to his latent ambition, and this appeal helped push him to commit the murder. *(Now we see how the witches helped cause the murder.)*

Notice how the writer has strengthened cause-effect connections in the student model on the next page.

Some people might think that Macbeth was innocent and it
But Macbeth knew what he was doing. While thinking about killing
was all Lady Macbeth's fault. ~~Macbeth said~~ "We still have judgement
Duncan he said,
                     ^
here, that we but teach bloody instructions, which, being taught,

return to plague th' inventor" (act 1, scene 7).

STUDENT MODEL

STEP 4 EDITING

Ask a partner to review your revised draft before you edit. When you edit, look for errors in grammar, usage, spelling, and mechanics. Be sure to look for comma splices.

Editing Strategy

Correcting Comma Splices

Thinking about complex topics may lead you to write separate sentences as if they were one long sentence, spliced together with commas. For example:

Comma Splice	Macbeth knew what he was doing, he was aware of the terrible act he was about to commit well before he did it.
Corrected	Macbeth knew what he was doing. He was aware of the terrible act he was about to commit well before he did it.

As you edit, be on the lookout for comma splices. Correct them by separating the individual sentences.

FOR REFERENCE. . .
More tips on correcting comma splices can be found in the Language and Grammar Handbook at the back of this book.

5 PRESENTING

To present your essay, consider these ideas.

- Find classmates whose points of view differ from yours. Read your essays to a jury of classmates, who will then confer and vote to select the most convincing argument.

- Illustrate your essay with drawings of Lady Macbeth that show her thinking thoughts or speaking words that exemplify your feelings about her.

6 LOOKING BACK

Self-evaluate. Evaluate your essay on each item in the Writer's Blueprint, giving yourself a score for each one from 6 (superior) down to 1 (inadequate).

Reflect. What did you learn from writing this essay? Write your thoughts in response to these questions:

✔ After arguing in favor of your point of view, what do you think of yourself as a persuasive thinker? Do you think you might someday be good at, say, writing ads or practicing law?

✔ What are your overall feelings about Lady Macbeth? Does she show strengths of character? If so, what do you think about how she uses those strengths?

For Your Working Portfolio Add your essay and your reflections to your working portfolio.

Beyond Print

Performing Shakespeare

One way to get familiar with any play is to act it out. This will help you get a better sense of what the words mean, who the people are, and what they're doing and feeling. Here are some tips on performing *Macbeth* in your classroom.

Select Scenes. Get familiar with the characters and the story. Then single out key scenes you might perform. In small groups, read and discuss these scenes. Take your time. Try to understand as much as possible. When passages are difficult, refer to the notes and talk them over.

Rehearse. Read through your scenes and learn the language. Then read through again and try to act the character. Next block out scenes, which means getting up and moving about. Decide where to make entrances and exits. Plan who will stand where and what actions are needed. Finally, have a dress rehearsal—at least one run-through with no stops.

Reading the Poetry. When you watch movies or listen to recordings of Shakespearean plays, you may notice the actors using a heightened style, a kind of delivery that emphasizes the poetry of the language. Don't worry about it. Read to get the meaning across and to express the emotions.

Perform the Scenes. Perform the various scenes in the order they come in the play. You might introduce scenes with brief descriptions of what took place before.

Afterwards. Discuss the play. What did you learn by performing it—about your character? about the themes? about the difficulties of putting on this play? Watch a movie version of *Macbeth* and compare your interpretations with those of the movie.

Activitiy Options

1. Polish your scenes and put them on for other classes.

2. Write a brief description of what you did to prepare the play for performance and what you learned from your experience.

Multicultural Connections

Individuality

The Lure of Ambition Uncontrolled ambition has been the downfall of many a man and woman throughout history. It is ambition that spurs Macbeth and Lady Macbeth to commit the first murder, that of King Duncan, and it is ambition that causes Macbeth to kill others to maintain his position.

In a sense, ambition is a desire to express one's individuality to the greatest degree possible. It is the desire to break out of the group and its rules for behavior. But it is the group that acknowledges an individual and keeps him or her special, and that means that the individual still has responsibilities to the group.

Macbeth wants the glory of kingship, but he shirks the responsibilities of leading his people in a sensible and dignified way and of assuring their personal safety—one of the bases for founding a society in the first place. His is, in a sense, individuality run amok.

■ How do you think Macbeth might have realized his ambition to express his individuality and yet not have crossed that line that alienates him from his society?

Activities

1. Watch a videotape of a production of *Macbeth.* Discuss how the actor playing the protagonist manages, through voice and body movements, to get across the motivations that cause him to commit so many murders.

2. Stage a number of scenes from *Macbeth*. You can work with your books or with scripts so that you don't have to memorize all the lines, but you should rehearse enough to be able to speak the lines with some facility. See Performing Shakespeare on page 204.

3. Although there was very little costuming in Shakespeare's day, modern productions of his plays often include elaborate costumes. Design costumes for Macbeth, Lady Macbeth, and their guests to wear in the banquet scene in act 3. Since all the guests are noblemen themselves, and since a tartan was a common pattern for Scotsmen to wear (see the illustration on page 179), how will you show Macbeth's individuality and his position as king?

Independent and Group Projects

Media

A (Wo)man for All Seasons Someone who does a great variety of things is often described as a Renaissance man. Who in today's world might be described as a Renaissance man or woman? Make a list of the characteristics of your ideal Renaissance person. You might consider your grandmother, your social studies teacher, your science laboratory partner. Use a scrapbook or a multimedia computer program to assemble a personal profile of this person as a Renaissance man or woman.

Oral Presentation

Support for the Arts Throughout the history of England and many other nations as well, writers, musicians, and artists have been encouraged to pursue their talents through pensions or grants from their governments. Since 1965 in the United States, creativity has been encouraged by the National Endowment for the Arts. With a partner, research the National Endowment for the Arts and prepare a debate on whether grants from the organization should continue.

Panel Discussion

Violence Today Today's American society has been called the most violent in all of history, perhaps because of the violence presented in the movies and on television. Watch a television show known for its violence. Record the number of violent acts. Join classmates who have watched similar programs and have a panel discussion on the impact of violence in the media. Are your chosen programs more or less violent than *Macbeth*?

Research

Researching the Elizabethan Era Select one of the following topics or choose a topic of your own on which to do independent research. Then write a report of your findings.

- Elizabethan attitudes toward ghosts and witchcraft
- Adult and child acting companies
- Public and private theaters
- Critical theories on Macbeth's or Lady Macbeth's character
- The role of women in Shakespeare's day

Nature

*Garden
or Wilderness?*

THEMES *in*
ENGLISH
LITERATURE

Nature~

We are all undeniably a part of nature, but how people feel about nature takes many forms. Some look upon nature as benevolent, a teacher, a parent, a healer, the source of all that is good in life. Some think that nature is neutral, in itself neither helpful nor harmful to humankind. And some look upon nature as an enemy, set to destroy individuals—who are, after all, comparatively helpless in its power. How you feel about nature may influence whether you prefer it wild and natural, as in wilderness, or tamed, as in a garden.

NATURE NEVER DECEIVES US; IT IS ALWAYS WE WHO DECEIVE OURSELVES.

Jean Jacques Rousseau (1762)

Love of Nature

There is a pleasure in the pathless woods,
There is a rapture[1] on the lonely shore,
There is society, where none intrudes,
By the deep Sea, and music in its roar:
I love not Man the less, but Nature more,
From these our interviews, in which I steal
From all I may be, or have been before,
To mingle with the universe, and feel
What I can ne'er express, yet cannot all conceal.

Lord Byron (1812)

---

1. **rapture** (rap′chər), *n.* strong feeling of delight or joy.

Thomas Gainsborough, Mr. and Mrs.
Robert Andrews *(1748)*

Rural Leisure

Oh friendly to the best pursuits of man,

Friendly to thought, to virtue, and to peace,

Domestic life in rural leisure passed!

Few know thy value, and few taste thy sweets,

Though many boast thy favors, and affect

To understand and choose thee for their own.

But foolish man foregoes his proper bliss,

Even as his first progenitor,[1] and quits,

Though placed in paradise (for earth has still

Some traces of her youthful beauty left)

Substantial happiness for transient joy.

Scenes formed for contemplation, and to nurse

The growing seeds of wisdom; that suggest,

By every pleasing image they present,

Reflections such as meliorate[2] the heart,

Compose the passions, and exalt the mind . . . .

William Cowper (1785)

1. **progenitor** (prō jen′ə tər), *n.* ancestor.
2. **meliorate** (mē′lyə rāt′), *v.* improve.

Summer Is Gone

My tidings for you: the stag bells,
Winter snows, summer is gone.

Wind high and cold, low the sun,
Short his course, sea running high.

Deep-red the bracken, its shape all gone—
The wild-goose has raised his wonted cry.

Cold has caught the wings of birds;
Season of ice—these are my tidings.

Anonymous (800s)

NATURE, TO BE

COMMANDED,

MUST BE OBEYED.

Francis Bacon (1620)

"Blow, winds..."

Blow, winds, and crack your cheeks! Rage, blow!

You cataracts and hurricanoes,[1] spout

Till you have drenched our steeples, drowned the cocks![2]

You sulfurous and thought-executing fires,[3]

Vaunt-couriers[4] of oak-cleaving thunderbolts,

Singe my white head! And thou, all-shaking thunder,

Strike flat the thick rotundity[5] o' the world!

Crack nature's molds, all germens[6] spill at once

That makes ingrateful man! . . .

I tax not you, you elements, with unkindness;

I never gave you kingdom, called you children.

You owe me no subscription.[7] Then let fall

Your horrible pleasure. Here I stand your slave,

A poor, infirm, weak, and despised old man.

John Martin's painting The Bard *(1817) illustrates Thomas Gray's poem in which a Welsh poet delivers a bitter prophesy to Edward I as the British king and his army invade Wales.*

William Shakespeare (1605)

---

1. **cataract** (kat′ə rakt′). . . **hurricano** (hėr′ə kā′nō), waterfall and waterspout.
2. **cocks,** weathervanes.

3. **thought-executing fires,** lightning, acting with the quickness of thought.
4. **vaunt-courier,** forerunner.
5. **rotundity** (rō tun′də tē), *n.* roundness.

6. **germen** (jėr′mən), *n.* seed.
7. **subscription,** allegiance.

Religion and Poetry in Nature

from *Intimations of Immortality* ...

There was a time when meadow, grove, and stream,
The earth, and every common sight,
    To me did seem
    Appareled[1] in celestial[2] light,
The glory and the freshness of a dream.
 It is not now as it hath been of yore;
   Turn wheresoe'er I may,
     By night or day,
The things which I have seen I now can see no more.

    The Rainbow comes and goes,
    And lovely is the Rose,
    The Moon doth with delight
Look round her when the heavens are bare;
    Waters on a starry night
    Are beautiful and fair;
   The sunshine is a glorious birth;
   But yet I know, where'er I go,
That there hath passed away a glory from the earth.

William Wordsworth (1807)

. . . I DO NOT REMEMBER TO HAVE GONE
TEN PACES WITHOUT AN EXCLAMATION
THAT THERE WAS NO RESTRAINING: NOT A
PRECIPICE,[1] NOT A TORRENT, NOT A CLIFF,
BUT IS PREGNANT WITH RELIGION AND
POETRY. THERE ARE CERTAIN SCENES THAT
WOULD AWE AN ATHEIST INTO BELIEF
WITHOUT THE HELP OF OTHER ARGUMENT.

Thomas Gray (1739)

from **FERN HILL**

Now as I was young and easy under the apple boughs
About the lilting house and happy as the grass was green,
   The night above the dingle[1] starry,
    Time let me hail and climb
   Golden in the heydays of his eyes,
And honored among wagons I was prince of the apple towns
And once below a time I lordly had the trees and leaves
    Trail with daisies and barley
   Down the rivers of the windfall light.

And as I was green and carefree, famous among the barns
About the happy yard and singing as the farm was home,
   In the sun that is young once only,
    Time let me play and be
   Golden in the mercy of his means,
And green and golden I was huntsman and herdsman, the
       calves
Sang to my horn, the foxes on the hills barked clear and cold,
    And the sabbath[2] rang slowly
   In the pebbles of the holy streams. . . .

Dylan Thomas (1946)

---

1. **appareled** (ə par′əld), *adj.* dressed.
2. **celestial** (sə les′chəl), *adj.* heavenly.

1. **precipice** (pres′ə pis), *n.* cliff or steep mountainside.

1. **dingle** (ding′gəl), *n.* a small, deep, shady valley.
2. **sabbath** (sab′əth), *n.* day of worship.

O Glorious Nature!

[Theocles] turned away his eyes from me, musing awhile by himself; and soon afterwards, stretching out his hand, as pointing to the objects round him, he began:

"Ye fields and woods, my refuge from the toilsome world of business, receive me in your quiet sanctuaries[1] and favor my retreat and thoughtful solitude. Ye verdant[2] plains, how gladly I salute ye! Hail all ye blissful mansions! known seats! delightful prospects![3] majestic beauties of this earth, and all ye rural powers and graces! Blessed be ye chaste abodes[4] of happiest mortals, who here in peaceful innocence enjoy a life unenvied, though divine; whilst with its blessed tranquillity it affords a happy leisure and retreat for man, who, made for contemplation, and to search his own and other natures, may here best meditate the cause of things, and, placed amidst the various scenes of Nature, may nearer view her works.

"O glorious nature! supremely fair and sovereignly[5] good! all-loving and all-lovely, all-divine! whose looks are so becoming and of such infinite grace; whose study brings such wisdom, and whose contemplation such delight; whose every single work affords an ampler scene, and is a nobler spectacle than all which ever art presented! O mighty Nature! wise substitute of Providence![6] impowered creatress! Or thou impowering Deity, supreme creator! Thee I invoke and thee alone adore. To thee this solitude, this place, these rural meditations are sacred; whilst thus inspired with harmony of thought, though unconfined by words, and in loose numbers,[7] I sing of Nature's order in created beings, and celebrate the beauties which resolve in thee, the source and principle of all beauty and perfection . . . ."

This image of St. James Park in London is from a history of gardens published in 1887.

Here he stopped short, and starting as out of a dream: "Now, Philocles," said he, "inform me, how have I appeared to you in my fit? Seemed it a sensible kind of madness, like those transports which are permitted to our poets? or was it downright raving?"

Anthony Ashley Cooper, Third Earl of Shaftesbury (1709)

---

1. **sanctuary** (sangk′chŭ er′ē), *n.* place of refuge or protection.
2. **verdant** (vėrd′nt), *adj.* green.
3. **prospect** (pros′pekt), *n.* view; scene.
4. **chaste** (chāst) **abode** (ə bōd′), simple, plain home.
5. **sovereignly** (sov′rən lē), *adv.* powerfully.
6. **Providence** (prov′ə dəns), *n.* God.
7. **in loose numbers,** unconfined by strict poetic meter.

PICTURESQUE PRINCIPLES

Edward returned to them with fresh admiration of the surrounding country; in his walk to the village, he had seen many parts of the valley to advantage; and the village itself, in a much higher situation[1] than the cottage, afforded a general view of the whole, which had exceedingly pleased him. This was a subject which ensured Marianne's attention, and she was beginning to describe her own admiration of these scenes, and to question him more minutely on the objects that had particularly struck him, when Edward interrupted her by saying, "You must not inquire too far, Marianne—remember I have no knowledge in the picturesque,[2] and I shall offend you by my ignorance and want of taste if we come to particulars. I shall call hills steep, which ought to be bold; surfaces strange and uncouth,[3] which ought to be irregular and rugged; and distant objects out of sight, which ought only to be indistinct through the soft medium of a hazy atmosphere. You must be satisfied with such admiration as I can honestly give. I call it a very fine country—the hills are steep, the woods seem full of fine timber, and the valley looks comfortable and snug—with rich meadows and several neat farm houses scattered here and there. It exactly answers my idea of a fine country, because it unites beauty with utility—and I dare say it is a picturesque one too, because you admire it; I can easily believe it to be full of rocks and promontories,[4] gray moss and brush wood, but these are all lost on me. I know nothing of the picturesque."

"I am afraid it is but too true," said Marianne; "but why should you boast of it?"

"I suspect," said Elinor, "that to avoid one kind of affectation,[5] Edward here falls into another. Because he believes many people pretend to more admiration of the beauties of nature than they really feel, and is disgusted with such pretensions,[6] he affects greater indifference and less discrimination in viewing them himself than he possesses. He is fastidious[7] and will have an affectation of his own."

"It is very true," said Marianne, "that admiration of landscape scenery is become a mere jargon.[8] Every body pretends to feel and tries to describe with the taste and elegance of him who first defined what picturesque beauty was. I detest jargon of every kind, and sometimes I have kept my feelings to myself, because I could find no language to describe them in but what was worn and hackneyed[9] out of all sense and meaning."

"I am convinced," said Edward, "that you really feel all the delight in a fine prospect which you profess[10] to feel. But, in return, your sister must allow me to feel no more than I profess. I like a fine prospect, but not on picturesque principles. I do not like crooked, twisted, blasted trees. I admire them much more if they are tall, straight and flourishing. I do not like ruined, tattered cottages. I am not fond of nettles, or thistles, or heath blossoms. I have more pleasure in a snug farm-house than a watchtower—and a troop of tidy, happy villagers please me better than the finest banditti[11] in the world."

Jane Austen (1811)

---

1. **situation** (sich′ū ā′shən), *n.* location; place.
2. **picturesque** (pik′chə resk′), *adj.* quaint or interesting enough to be used as the subject of a picture.
3. **uncouth** (un kŭth′), *adj.* crude.
4. **promontory** (prom′ən tôr′ē), *n.* high point of land.
5. **affectation** (af′ek tā′shən), *n.* pretense; unnatural behavior to impress others.
6. **pretension** (pri ten′shən), *n.* showy display.
7. **fastidious** (fa stid′ē əs), *adj.* hard to please; dainty in taste.
8. **jargon** (jär′gən), *n.* language of a special group or profession.
9. **hackneyed** (hak′nēd), *adj.* used too often; commonplace.
10. **profess** (prə fes′), *v.* claim.
11. **banditti** (băn dē′tē), bandits. *[Italian]*

Thomas Tyndale, A Cottage Garden

Anthony Green, The Flower
Arranger *(1982)*

*This tapestry depicts
a formal garden
from the late 1600s.*

215

Thames River at Twilight

. . . The day was ending in a serenity[1] of still and exquisite brilliance. The water shone pacifically;[2] the sky, without a speck, was a benign[3] immensity of unstained light; the very mist on the Essex marshes was like a gauzy and radiant fabric, hung from the wooded rises inland, and draping the low shores in diaphanous[4] folds. Only the gloom to the west, brooding over the upper reaches, became more somber[5] every minute, as if angered by the approach of the sun.

And at last, in its curved and imperceptible[6] fall, the sun sank low, and from glowing white changed to a dull red without rays and without heat, as if about to go out suddenly, stricken to death by the touch of that gloom brooding over a crowd of men.

Forthwith a change came over the waters, and the serenity became less brilliant but more profound.[7] The old river in its broad reach rested unruffled at the decline of day, after ages of good service done to the race that peopled its banks, spread out in the tranquil[8] dignity of a waterway leading to the uttermost ends of the earth. We looked at the venerable[9] stream not in the vivid flush of a short day that comes and departs forever, but in the august[10] light of abiding memories. And indeed nothing is easier for a man who has, as the phrase goes, "followed the sea" with reverance and affection, than to evoke the great spirit of the past upon the lower reaches of the Thames. The tidal current runs to and fro in its unceasing service, crowded with memories of men and ships it had borne to the rest of home or to the battles of the sea. It had known and served all the men of whom the nation is proud, from Sir Francis Drake to Sir John Franklin, knights all, titled and untitled—the great knights-errant of the sea . . . . Hunters for gold or pursuers of fame, they all had gone out on that stream, bearing the sword, and often the torch, messengers of the might within the land, bearers of a spark from the sacred fire. What greatness had not floated on the ebb of that river into the mystery of an unknown earth! . . . The dreams of men, the seed of commonwealths, the germs of empires . . .

Joseph Conrad (1902)

IT IS THE PRESERVATION OF THE SPECIES, NOT OF INDIVIDUALS, WHICH APPEARS TO BE THE DESIGN OF DEITY THROUGHOUT THE WHOLE OF NATURE.

Mary Wollstonecraft (1796)

---

1. **serenity** (sə ren′ə tē), *n.* peace and quiet; calmness.
2. **pacifically** (pə sif′ik lē), *adv.* peacefully.
3. **benign** (bi nīn′), *adj.* kindly in feeling.
4. **diaphanous** (dī af′ə nəs), *adj.* transparent.

5. **somber** (som′bər), *adj.* dark; gloomy.
6. **imperceptible** (im′pər sep′tə bəl), *adj.* gradual; very slight.
7. **profound** (prə found′), *adj.* very deep.
8. **tranquil** (trang′kwəl), *adj.* calm; peaceful.

9. **venerable** (ven′ər ə bəl), *adj.* deserving respect because of age or importance.
10. **august** (ô gust′), *adj.* majestic; inspiring admiration.

from THE WANDERER

J. M. W. Turner, Fishermen upon a Lee Shore *(about 1805)*

A wise man must fathom how frightening it will be
When all the riches of the world stand waste,
As now in diverse[1] places in this middle-earth
Old walls stand, tugged at by the winds
And hung with hoar-frost, buildings in decay.
The wine-halls crumble, heartbroken lords
Lie dead, all the proud followers
Have fallen by the wall . . . .
Thus the Creator laid this world waste
Until the ancient works of the giants were deserted,
Hushed without the hubbub of milling inhabitants.
Then he who contemplates these noble ruins,
And who deeply ponders this dark life,
Wise in his mind, will often remember
The countless slaughters of the past and speak these words:
Where has the horse gone? Where the man? Where the giver of gold?
Where is the feasting-place? And where the pleasures of the hall?
I mourn the gleaming cup, the warrior in his corselet,[2]
The glory of the prince. How time has passed away,
Darkened under the shadow of night even as if it had never been . . . .
Storms crash against these rocky slopes;
Falling sleet and snow fetter[3] the world;
Winter howls, then darkness draws on,
The night-shadow casts gloom and brings
Fierce hailstorms from the north to frighten men.
Nothing is ever easy in the kingdom of earth,
The world beneath the heavens is in the hands of fate.
Worldly possessions are ephemeral,[4] friends pass away,
Here man is transient[5] and kinsman transient,
The whole world becomes a wilderness.

Anonymous (900s?)

---

1. **diverse** (də vėrs′), *adj.* different; varied.
2. **corselet** (kôrs′lit), *n.* armor for the upper part of the body.

3. **fetter** (fet′ər), *v.* bind; restrain.
4. **ephemeral** (i fem′ər əl), *adj.* lasting for only a very short time.

5. **transient** (tran′shənt), *adj.* passing soon.

World's End

In H. G. Wells's classic science fiction novel, The Time Machine, *the Traveler has invented a machine that takes him back or forward in time. Here he decides to travel as far into the future as he can.*

"I cannot convey the sense of abominable[1] desolation that hung over the world. The red eastern sky, the northward blackness, the salt Dead Sea, the stony beach crawling with these foul, slow-stirring monsters, the uniform poisonous-looking green of the lichenous[2] plants, the thin air that hurt one's lungs; all contributed to an appalling effect. I moved on a hundred years, and there was the same red sun—a little larger, a little duller—the same dying sea, the same chill air, and the same crowd of earthly crustacea[3] creeping in and out among the green weed and the red rocks. And in the westward sky I saw a curved pale line like a vast new moon.

"So I traveled, stopping ever and again, in great strides of a thousand years or more, drawn on by the mystery of the earth's fate, watching with a strange fascination the sun grow larger and duller in the westward sky, and the life of the old earth ebb away. At last, more than thirty million years hence, the huge red-hot dome of the sun had come to obscure nearly a tenth part of the darkling[4] heavens. Then I stopped once more, for the crawling multitude of crabs had disappeared, and the red beach, save for its livid green liverworts[5] and lichens, seemed lifeless. And now it was flecked with white. A bitter cold assailed[6] me. Rare white flakes ever and again came eddying[7] down. To the north-eastward, the glare of snow lay under the starlight of the sable sky, and I could see an undulating[8] crest of hillocks pinkish-white. There were fringes of ice along the sea margin, with drifting masses further out; but the main expanse of that salt ocean, all bloody under the eternal sunset, was still unfrozen.

"I looked about me to see if any traces of animal-life remained. A certain indefinable apprehension still kept me in the saddle of the machine. But I saw nothing moving, in earth or sky or sea. The green slime on the rocks alone testified that life was not extinct. A shallow sandbank had appeared in the sea and the water had receded from the beach. I fancied I saw some black object flopping about on this bank, but it became motionless as I looked at it, and I judged that my eye had been deceived, and that the black object was merely a rock. The stars in the sky were intensely bright and seemed to me to twinkle very little.

"Suddenly I noticed that the circular westward outline of the sun had changed; that a concavity,[9] a bay, had appeared in the curve. I saw this grow larger. For a minute perhaps I stared aghast[10] at this blackness that was creeping over the day, and then I realised that an eclipse was beginning. Either the moon or the planet Mercury was passing across the sun's disk. Naturally, at first I took it to be the moon, but there is much to incline me to believe that what I really saw was the transit of an inner planet passing very near to the earth.

"The darkness grew apace; a cold wind began to blow in freshening gusts from the east, and the showering white flakes in the air increased in number. From the edge of the sea came a ripple and whisper. Beyond these lifeless sounds the world was silent. Silent? It would be hard to convey the stillness of it. All the sounds of man, the bleating of sheep, the cries of birds, the hum of insects, the stir that makes the background of our lives—all that was over. As the darkness thickened, the

---

1. **abominable** (ə bom′ə nə bəl), *adj.* disgusting; hateful.
2. **lichenous** (lī′kə nəs), *adj.* of lichens, combinations of fungus and alga.
3. **crustacea** (krus′tā′shə), *n.* class of shellfish including crabs, lobsters, and shrimp.
4. **darkling** (därk′ling), *adj.* dark; dim.
5. **liverwort** (liv′ər wèrt′), *n.* plant related to and resembling moss.
6. **assail** (ə sāl′), *v.* attack.
7. **eddy** (ed′ē), *v.* move in a whirling motion.
8. **undulating** (un′jə lā ting), *adj.* waving.
9. **concavity** (kon kav′ə tē), *n.* hollow; curving in.
10. **aghast** (ə gast′), *adj.* struck with surprise or horror.

eddying flakes grew more abundant, dancing before my eyes; and the cold of the air more intense. At last, one by one, swiftly, one after the other, the white peaks of the distant hills vanished into blackness. The breeze rose to a moaning wind. I saw the black central shadow of the eclipse sweeping towards me. In another moment the pale stars alone were visible. All else was rayless obscurity. The sky was absolutely black.

"A horror of this great darkness came on me. The cold, that smote[11] to my marrow,[12] and the pain I felt in breathing overcame me. I shivered, and a deadly nausea seized me. Then like a red-hot bow in the sky appeared the edge of the sun. I got off the machine to recover myself. I felt giddy and incapable of facing the return journey. As I stood sick and confused I saw again the moving thing upon the shoal—there was no mistake now that it was a moving thing—against the red water of the sea. It was a round thing, the size of a football perhaps, or, it may be, bigger, and tentacles trailed down from it; it seemed black against the weltering[13] blood-red water, and it was hopping fitfully about. Then I felt I was fainting . . . ."

H. G. Wells (1895)

LINEAGE

In the beginning was Scream
Who begat Blood
Who begat Eye
Who begat Fear
Who begat Wing
Who begat Bone
Who begat Granite
Who begat Violet
Who begat Guitar
Who begat Sweat
Who begat Adam
Who begat Mary
Who begat God
Who begat Nothing
Who begat Never
Never, Never, Never

Who begat Crow

Screaming for Blood
Grubs, crusts
Anything
Trembling featherless elbows in the nest's filth.

Ted Hughes (1970)

RESPONDING

1. Do you agree more with people who see nature as a healer, as neutral, or as a destroyer? Explain your reasons.

2. Have you ever learned anything from nature? Explain the lesson and the circumstances.

3. A large number of "doomsday" books and movies have depicted life in a much-changed society after civilization as we know it has been destroyed—often in a nuclear war. Do you think it is possible for people to destroy nature? Why or why not?

4. Do you prefer neat, tidy gardens or "irregular and rugged" wilderness? Describe your favorite outdoor view.

11. **smite** (smīt), *v.* give a hard blow to.
12. **marrow** (mar′ō), *n.* inmost part.
13. **weltering** (wel′tər ing), *adj.* rolling or tumbling about.

UNIT **3**

The Seventeenth Century

The Meaning of Life
Part One, pages 222–249

The Fall from Grace
Part Two, pages 250–289

221

The Vanity

HISTORICAL OVERVIEW

The writers in this section—Donne, Herrick, and Marvel—show a strong awareness of the changes produced by time. Their accounts of youth and its pleasures are haunted by mortality. The artists of the 1600s shared this feeling and produced many paintings that symbolically expressed their sense of the vanity of earthly things. One of these, *The Knight's Dream,* by the Spanish artist Antonio de Pereda (1608–1678), shows a young nobleman fallen asleep in his chair. On the table appear the contents of his dream, the symbols of his foolish ambitions—wealth, military glory, love, the arts, scholarship. The end of all things human is symbolized by the two skulls. An angel carries a banner with a Latin inscription grimly evoking death: "Eternally he stings, swiftly he flies and kills."

of Earthly Things

Within the scroll: ÆTERNE PVNGIT CITO VOLAT ET OCCIDIT

Key Dates

1603
Elizabeth I dies and James I becomes king.

1611
Authorized Version, or King James Bible, is issued.

1617
Ben Jonson made Poet Laureate by James I.

1618
Sir Walter Raleigh is executed.

1642
Civil War begins between Royalists and Puritans.

1649
King Charles I is beheaded and the Puritan Commonwealth is established.

1660
Monarchy is restored under Charles II.

Part One

The Meaning of Life

"Who am I? Why am I here? Where am I going?" Such questions have been asked since the beginnings of human consciousness. For answers, some people turn to religion, seeking meaning not in life now, but in life after death. Others deny that there is a life after death, seeking meaning in the here and now. Most of the British writers of the 1600s probably believed in a Christian God (worshipped according to either the Catholic or Protestant faiths). But most of them also followed the literary conventions of the day, protesting their spiritual love and physical desire in highly formalized verse forms.

Multicultural Focus As you read the literature in Part One, reflect on how this search for truth and the meaning of life is influenced by the different writers' differing viewpoints, or **perspectives.**

Before Reading

John Donne
1572–1631

During a time when Catholics were often persecuted in England, John Donne's religion prevented him from receiving a university degree, and his brother was imprisoned for protecting a Catholic priest. Donne studied law and became secretary to the politically influential Sir Thomas Egerton. When Donne secretly married Egerton's niece, her father had him imprisoned, Egerton dismissed him, and he was unable to find suitable work for many years. Donne renounced the Catholic faith and, at the urging of King James, became an Anglican (Church of England) priest. In 1621 Donne was made Dean of St. Paul's Cathedral in London, where he became a celebrated preacher.

Building Background

His Life and Work John Donne's writing parallels his life. Before he married Anne More he had several love affairs, and his early poetry reflects a cynical view about women. Poet John Dryden wrote that Donne "perplexes the minds of the fair sex with nice speculations of philosophy, when he should engage their hearts, and entertain them with the softnesses of love." After he married Anne, Donne composed ardent love poems for her. When he became a priest he wrote religious poetry and prose. He even wrote attacks on Catholics, despite his early upbringing, perhaps to gain the favor of the king.

Literary Focus

Metaphor and Conceit A figure of speech that shows a comparison between two basically unlike things that have something in common is called a **metaphor.** The comparison may be stated or implied. For example, "Scarlet and yellow kites were bright patches on a quilt of dark clouds" compares kites to patches and clouds to a quilt. A **conceit** is an elaborate and surprising metaphor comparing two very dissimilar things. It has been described as stretching a metaphor to the breaking point. As you read these works by Donne, look for the metaphors and the conceits.

Writer's Notebook

Finding the Right Words In the 1600s and 1700s, it was customary to write elaborate poetry or letters to convey one's feelings. Today we might search for a greeting card to express our thoughts, satisfied to let an anonymous writer or artist convey our thanks or affections. In your notebook jot down several occasions for which a personal note or a greeting card might be appropriate. (You might glance at the greeting card racks in a local store to get ideas for unusual occasions.)

Song

John Donne

Go and catch a falling star,
    Get with child a mandrake root,[1]
Tell me where all past years are,
    Or who cleft the devil's foot;
5 Teach me to hear mermaids singing,
Or to keep off envy's stinging,
    And find
    What wind
Serves to advance an honest mind.

10 If thou beest born to strange sights,
    Things invisible to see,
Ride ten thousand days and nights,
    Till age snow white hairs on thee;
Thou, when thou returnest, will tell me
15 All strange wonders that befell thee,
    And swear
    Nowhere
Lives a woman true, and fair.

If thou findest one, let me know;
20   Such a pilgrimage were sweet.
Yet do not; I would not go,
    Though at next door we might meet.
Though she were true when you met her,
And last till you write your letter,
25   Yet she
    Will be
False, ere I come, to two or three.

A mandrake *(Solanaceae mandragora)* is shown in this woodcut from *Commentaries on the Six Books of Dioscorides* by Dierandrea Mattiolo (Prague, 1563). Mandrakes were known to have medicinal properties and were thought by some to be magical as well. What other plants do you know of that are considered magical by some people?

---

1. **get . . . mandrake root.** Mandrake (man′drāk) is an herb with a forked root that supposedly resembles a human figure. Recognizing this resemblance as well as the impossibility of a plant's reproducing as humans do, Donne includes this in his catalogue of fantastic achievements.

A Valediction: Forbidding Mourning

John Donne

As virtuous men pass mildly away,
    And whisper to their souls to go,
Whilst some of their sad friends do say,
    The breath goes now, and some say, no;

5 So let us melt, and make no noise,
    No tear-floods, nor sigh-tempests move,
'Twere profanation of our joys
    To tell the laity our love.

Moving of the earth brings harms and
    fears,
10   Men reckon what it did and meant,
But trepidation of the spheres,
    Though greater far, is innocent.[1]

Dull sublunary[2] lovers' love
    (Whose soul is sense)[3] cannot admit
15 Absence, because it doth remove
    Those things which elemented[4] it.

But we, by a love, so much refined
    That our selves know not what it is,
Inter-assurèd of the mind,
20   Care less, eyes, lips, and hands to miss.

Our two souls therefore, which are one,
    Though I must go, endure not yet
A breach,[5] but an expansion,
    Like gold to airy thinness beat.

25 If they be two, they are two so
    As stiff twin compasses[6] are two;
Thy soul the fixed foot, makes no show
    To move, but doth, if the other do.

And though it in the center sit,
30   Yet when the other far doth roam,
It leans, and hearkens after it,
    And grows erect, as that comes home.

Such wilt thou be to me, who must
    Like the other foot, obliquely run;
35 Thy firmness makes my circle just,
    And makes me end where I begun.

---

valediction (val/ə dik/shən), *n.* a bidding farewell.
Donne wrote this poem to his wife before he left on
an extended trip to France.

1. **trepidation . . . innocent.** Movements of the heavenly
   spheres, though greater than those of an earthquake, provoke no fears in nor danger to humans.
2. **sublunary** (sub lŭ/nər ē), *adj.* beneath the moon;
   that is, earthly and subject to change.
3. **whose soul is sense,** that is, loves that are confined to
   physical perceptions.
4. **element** (el/ə ment/), *v.* compose; make up.
5. breach (brēch), *n.* break or gap.
6. **compasses.** The image is of the instrument used for
   drawing a circle. One branch or leg of the compass
   is held steady, while the other leg is rotated to draw
   the circle. Anne is the "fixed foot."

Meditation 17

John Donne

Now this bell, tolling softly for another, says to me, Thou must die.

Perchance he for whom this bell tolls[1] may be so ill as that he knows not it tolls for him; and perchance I may think myself so much better than I am, as that they who are about me and see my state, may have caused it to toll for me, and I know not that. The church is catholic, universal; so are all her actions; all that she does belongs to all. When she baptizes a child, that action concerns me, for that child is thereby connected to that head which is my head too, and ingrafted into that body whereof I am a member.[2] And when she buries a man, that action concerns me. All mankind is of one author and is one volume; when one man dies, one chapter is not torn out of the book, but translated into a better language, and every chapter must be so translated. God employs several translators; some pieces are translated by age, some by sickness, some by war, some by justice; but God's hand is in every translation and his hand shall bind up all our scattered leaves again for that library where every book shall lie open to one another. As therefore the bell that rings to a sermon calls not upon the preacher only, but upon the congregation to come, so this bell calls us all; but how much more me, who am brought so near the door by this sickness.

---

1. toll (tōl), *v.* ring.
2. **When she baptizes . . . member.** The church, referred to as "she," is the head of all, as well as a body made up of its members.

There was a contention as far as a suit[3] (in which both piety[4] and dignity, religion and estimation,[5] were mingled) which of the religious orders should ring to prayers first in the morning; and it was determined that they should ring first that rose earliest. If we understand aright the dignity of this bell that tolls for our evening prayer, we would be glad to make it ours by rising early, in that application, that it might be ours as well as his whose indeed it is. The bell doth toll for him that thinks it doth; and though it intermit[6] again, yet from that minute that that occasion wrought upon him, he is united to God. Who casts not up his eye to the sun when it rises? But who takes off his eye from a comet when that breaks out? Who bends not his ear to any bell which upon any occasion rings? But who can remove it from that bell which is passing a piece of himself out of this world? No man is an island, entire of itself; every man is a piece of the continent, a part of the main. If a clod be washed away by the sea, Europe is the less, as well as if a promontory[7] were, as well as if a manor of thy friend's or of thine own were. Any man's death diminishes me, because I am involved in mankind; and therefore never send to know for whom the bell tolls; it tolls for thee.

Neither can we call this a begging of misery or a borrowing of misery, as though we were not miserable enough of ourselves, but must fetch in more from the next house, in taking upon us the misery of our neighbors. Truly it were an excusable covetousness[8] if we did; for affliction[9] is a treasure, and scarce any man hath enough of it. No man hath affliction enough that is not matured and ripened by it, and made fit for God by that affliction. If a man carry treasure in bullion, or in a wedge of gold, and have none coined into current monies, his treasure will not defray him as he travels. Tribulation[10] is treasure in the nature of it, but it is not current money in the use of it, except we get nearer and nearer our home, heaven, by it. Another man may be sick too, and sick to death, and this affliction may lie in his bowels, as gold in a mine, and be of no use to him; but this bell, that tells me of his affliction, digs out and applies that gold to me, if by this consideration of another's danger, I take mine own into contemplation, and so secure myself by making my recourse[11] to my God, who is our only security.

---

3. **contention . . . suit,** a controversy that went as far as a lawsuit.
4. **piety** (pī′ə tē), *n.* reverence for God.
5. **estimation** (es′tə mā′shən), *n.* self-esteem.
6. **intermit** (in′tər mit′), *v.* break off.
7. promontory (prom′ən tôr′ē), *n.* a high point of land extending from the coast into the water.
8. **covetousness** (kuv′ə təs nis), *n.* desire for things that belong to others.
9. affliction (ə flik′shən), *n.* pain; misery.
10. **tribulation** (trib′yə lā′shən), *n.* great trouble.
11. recourse (rē′kôrs), *n.* appeal for help or protection.

Metaphor - man is a chapter
all mankind is one book
library - heaven

◄ *Cathedral in Winter* was painted by Ernst Ferdinand Oehme in 1821. What mood does the artist create in this painting? How does he create that mood?

After Reading

Making Connections

Shaping Your
Response

1. Do you agree with Donne, in "Song," that all women are untrue? What about men?

2. If someone wrote a love poem to you, how would you react to being compared to a compass foot?

Analyzing the
Selections

3. The speaker issues seven commands in the first stanza of "Song." What do they have in common?

4. What seems to be the speaker's state of mind in "Song," and what do you **infer** might account for it?

5. Compare the speaker and his love in "A Valediction: Forbidding Mourning" with the "dull sublunary lovers" of stanza 4 by listing descriptions that you imagine would apply to either couple.

6. For what general reasons might a bell be tolled? According to "Meditation 17," which reason is most important? Why?

Extending the Ideas

7. In "Meditation 17," Donne writes that "any man's death diminishes me because I am involved in mankind." Would most people today be likely to agree with this **perspective?** Explain.

Literary Focus: Metaphor and Conceit

A **metaphor** compares two basically unlike things that have something in common. A **conceit** is also a metaphor but a more elaborate one. In "A Valediction: Forbidding Mourning," Donne compares his and Anne's souls to twin compasses (really the two legs of one compass). Which soul is compared to the "fixed foot," and why does this comparison seem appropriate? Would you classify this as a conceit? Why or why not? In "Meditation 17," Donne compares man to a chapter in a book and to a piece of the continent. (He probably meant *man* to include all people, women as well.) Choose one of these metaphors and explain the similarity between a person and the thing to which he or she is compared.

Vocabulary Study

On your paper, write the listed word that fits each description (you will not use all the listed words). Then assign numbers to some of the letters, following the pattern in parentheses after the description. Finally put those letters in numerical order 1–12 to get the answer to the last description.

affliction
breach
piety
promontory
recourse
toll

1. A fee or a charge or the sound of a bell. (• 10 • •)

2. If you practice this, then you may escape hell. (9 • 7 • •)

3. A quarrel, a breakthrough, or often, a gap. (• • 11   4 • 6)

4. This prominent feature is found on a map. (1 • • • • • 12 • 8 •)

5. When you need protection, you ask for the same. (• 3   5 • • 2 • •)

To honor his monarch, what John Donne became.
(1 2 3 4 5 6 7 8 / 9 10 11 12)

Expressing Your Ideas

Writing Choices

Writer's Notebook Update Look again at your list of occasions for sending a greeting card. Jot down a few words or phrases for each occasion that seem appropriate for expressing the emotions that occasion brings out.

Pick a Card . . . Any Card Design a **greeting card** to someone you admire, love, or want to thank. Use some of the words and phrases you listed in your notebook to describe your feelings toward that person or your wishes upon a certain occasion. Write in rhymed verse if you wish. Illustrate your greeting card with an original drawing or with magazine art or photographs.

Taking a Toll Suppose you accept that "the bell tolls for thee." Does this change the way you behave (*ought* it to?), or do you put this thought aside and live life as usual? Write a response to Donne's statement in the form of a guest **editorial** for your school or community newspaper. To prove your point, include a personal anecdote or one that you have read about that illustrates how what happens to some people affects others.

Other Options

Up Close and Personal Choose a historic figure from the 1500s or the 1600s such as one of the following and portray that person in a one-man or one-woman show of no more than ten minutes: Mary Queen of Scots, Sir Walter Raleigh, the Earl of Essex, Christopher Marlowe, Queen Elizabeth I, King Charles I. After doing some research, write a **monologue** in the first person that helps to explain the person to a modern audience. Then, portray your chosen person as you read your sketch to your audience.

Words and Music Donne's poem is entitled "Song," and the word suggests music. Find and play a **musical setting** that these words can be sung to, or else write a melody or some chords that can be played on a guitar or a synthesizer while the poem is being recited. Make a recording of your best performance to share with other classes.

Before Reading

To the Virgins, to Make Much of Time
Upon Julia's Clothes by Robert Herrick

Delight in Disorder by Robert Herrick
To His Coy Mistress by Andrew Marvell

Robert Herrick
1591–1674

Herrick spent nearly thirty years of his life as a country parson. When the Puritans came to power in 1647, he was expelled from his ministry for his loyalty to the Royalist cause. Following the literary convention of the day, Herrick addressed many of his poems to imaginary mistresses.

Andrew Marvell
1621–1678

Born in Yorkshire, Andrew Marvell received a degree at Cambridge. In 1659, Marvell was elected a member of Parliament. He wrote both poetry and prose; the latter, often critical of royal power and therefore dangerous, was published anonymously.

Building Background

Revolution, Plague, and Fire These are turbulent times. The stubbornness of King Charles I leads to civil war between the Royalists and the Parliamentary party. In 1649, Charles is executed, his head chopped off. Puritan leader Oliver Cromwell assumes power. In 1660 Charles II reclaims the throne of his father, but England suffers further turmoil with an outbreak of the plague in 1665 and the Great Fire of London in 1666. Among the types of literature new to England during the Renaissance is **carpe diem** (kär⁄pe dē⁄em) poetry. *Carpe diem* is Latin for "seize (take advantage of) the day," and this poetry emphasizes that life is brief and that youth must pursue the pleasures of the present. The theme is popular, for disease or politics could quickly shorten one's life, if one lives past childhood to begin with. Obviously, it is necessary to "seize the day" at an early age.

Literary Focus

Hyperbole Writers sometimes use an extravagant statement or a figure of speech involving great exaggeration called **hyperbole** (hī pėr⁄ bə lē). "My love stretches to the farthest reaches of the universe," or "If I fail this test, I'll die" are both examples of hyperbole. Often used for emphasis or to demonstrate sincerity, hyperbole sometimes is used to create humor.

Writer's Notebook

Some experts estimate that during the later years of the 1500s, more than ten thousand words were added to the English language, partly through the importation of foreign terms. Shakespeare both borrowed and coined many words still in use today. Herrick didn't make up the word *liquefaction* (line 3 in "Upon Julia's Clothes"), but he used it in an unusual way. Find the word in an unabridged dictionary or in the *Oxford English Dictionary* and study the entry. As you read through these poems and others to come, keep a list of words in your notebook that you find particularly colorful or useful.

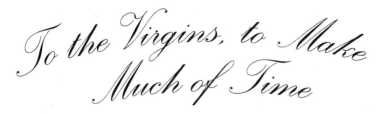

To the Virgins, to Make Much of Time

ROBERT HERRICK

Gather ye rosebuds while ye may,
    Old time is still a-flying;
And this same flower that smiles today,
    Tomorrow will be dying.

5 The glorious lamp of heaven, the sun,
    The higher he's a-getting,
The sooner will his race be run,
    And nearer he's to setting.

That age is best which is the first,
10   When youth and blood are warmer,
But being spent, the worse, and worst
    Times still succeed the former.

Then be not coy, but use your time,
    And while ye may, go marry;
15 For having lost but once your prime,
    You may forever tarry.

16 tarry (tar′ē), *v.* remain; stay.

Upon Julia's Clothes

ROBERT HERRICK

Whenas in silks my Julia goes,
Then, then, methinks, how sweetly flows
That liquefaction of her clothes.

Next, when I cast mine eyes and see
5 That brave vibration each way free,
O, how that glittering taketh me!

5 brave, bright; splendid.

Delight in Disorder

ROBERT HERRICK

A sweet disorder in the dress
Kindles in clothes a wantonness.
A lawn about the shoulders thrown
Into a fine distraction;
5 An erring lace, which here and there
Enthralls the crimson stomacher;
A cuff neglectful, and thereby
Ribbons to flow confusèdly;
A winning wave, deserving note,
10 In the tempestuous petticoat;
A careless shoestring, in whose tie
I see a wild civility—
Do more bewitch me than when art
Is too precise in every part.

To His Coy Mistress

ANDREW MARVELL

Had we but world enough, and time,
This coyness, Lady, were no crime.
We would sit down, and think which way
To walk, and pass our long love's day.
5 Thou by the Indian Ganges' side
Shouldst rubies find; I by the tide
Of Humber would complain. I would
Love you ten years before the Flood,
And you should, if you please, refuse
10 Till the Conversion of the Jews.
My vegetable love should grow
Vaster than empires and more slow;
An hundred years should go to praise
Thine eyes, and on thy forehead gaze;

2 **wantonness** (wonʹtən nis), *n.* lack of restraint.
3 **lawn,** linen scarf.

5 **erring** (ėrʹing), *adj.* wandering; straying.
6 **enthrall** (en thrôlʹ), *v.* hold captive.
6 **stomacher,** an ornamental covering for the stomach and bodice.

13 **bewitch** (bi wichʹ), *v.* charm; fascinate.

7 **Humber,** the river that flows through Marvell's home town of Hull.
7 **complain,** that is, sing sad love songs.
8 **flood,** the biblical flood.
10 **conversion of the Jews.** It was a popular belief among Christians that Jews would convert to Christianity just before the end of the world.
11 **vegetable,** growing as slowly as vegetation.

15 Two hundred to adore each breast,
    But thirty thousand to the rest;
    An age at least to every part,
    And the last age should show your heart.
    For, Lady, you deserve this state;
20 Nor would I love at lower rate.

    But at my back I always hear
    Time's wingèd chariot hurrying near;
    And yonder all before us lie
    Deserts of vast eternity.
25 Thy beauty shall no more be found,
    Nor, in thy marble vault, shall sound
    My echoing song; then worms shall try
    That long-preserved virginity,
    And your quaint honor turn to dust,
30 And into ashes all my lust.
    The grave's a fine and private place,
    But none, I think, do there embrace.

    Now therefore, while the youthful hue
    Sits on thy skin like morning dew,
35 And while thy willing soul transpires
    At every pore with instant fires,
    Now let us sport us while we may,
    And now, like amorous birds of prey,
    Rather at once our time devour
40 Than languish in his slow-chapped power.
    Let us roll all our strength and all
    Our sweetness up into one ball,
    And tear our pleasures with rough strife
    Thorough the iron gates of life;
45 Thus, though we cannot make our sun
    Stand still, yet we will make him run.

19 **state,** dignity.

27 **try,** test.

29 **quaint,** fastidious; out-of-fashion.

35 transpire (tran spīr′), *v.* breathe out.

40 languish (lang′guish), *v.* become weak or worn out.
40 **slow-chapped,** slow-jawed.

44 **thorough,** through.

After Reading

Shaping Your Response

1. Is the advice in "To the Virgins, to Make Much of Time" the kind of advice you would be likely to take, or not? Explain.

2. How would a person sympathetic to women's rights be likely to respond to "To His Coy Mistress"?

Analyzing the Poems

3. One reader has commented that the speaker in "Upon Julia's Clothes" seems to be "hooked" in line 6, much as a fish on a line. What justification can you find in the poem for this interpretation?

4. Which poems here are examples of **carpe diem** poems? What makes them so?

5. If stanza 1 of "To His Coy Mistress" speaks of an ideal world and stanza 2 brings us back to reality, what does stanza 3 do? Fill in a chart like the following as a help in answering.

To His Coy Mistress	
Stanza 1	In an ideal world, I would . . .
Stanza 2	But in the real world . . .
Stanza 3	Therefore . . .

Extending the Ideas

6. If you were writing the copy for a newspaper ad for clothing, how would you describe the kind of clothes and style the speaker in "Delight in Disorder" seems to prefer?

7. From what **perspective** do most *carpe diem* poems seem to be written? How would these poems be likely to differ if they were written from the perspective of a young woman? a much older man? a parent? a twentieth-century person?

Literary Focus: Hyperbole

A figure of speech or a statement involving great exaggeration is called **hyperbole.** Hyperbole is often used to heighten emotional effect. What is exaggerated in the first stanza of "To His Coy Mistress"? Why might the speaker use hyperbole here?

Vocabulary Study

Write the word from the list that best completes the meaning of each sentence (and maintains the rhythm). You will not use all the words.

bewitch
enthralls
erring
languish
transpire
wantonness

1. Though she ____ a crowd with wit,

2. Her ____ ways we must admit.

3. Her beauty does ____, it's true;

4. Her ____ is charming too;

5. But one could ____ ere she's through!

Expressing Your Ideas _____

Writing Choices

Writer's Notebook Update Try using the word *liquefaction* in a sentence of your own and continue to add unusual or interesting words to your notebook.

To Her Eager Lover Suppose you are the "coy mistress" that the speaker addresses in Marvell's poem. (Or, you might be a "coy mister.") Write a **reply** to the speaker. Do you buy his "seize the day" argument, or not? If you wish, write your reply in verse, using Marvell's poem as a model.

Seize the What? Is *carpe diem* a sensible motto for today's world? Write a brief **essay** exploring the advantages and disadvantages of living for the now. You might include examples of people who have lived both ways. Conclude by telling how you would prefer to live and why.

Other Options

Style Guide In England of the 1600s, dress varied according to one's social class or religious leanings. Research the styles of clothing worn by women, men, royalty, commoners, and Puritans and present your findings to the class in the form of an **illustrated talk.** You might display photocopies, colored drawings, or fashion dolls, or else you might use a multimedia computer program that allows you to include text, illustrations, and sound effects.

Time and Time Again Design and present an illustrated **timeline** that helps clarify the turbulent social and political events in England from the death of Elizabeth I in 1603 to the restoration of the monarchy in 1660. Do some additional research to find out what other people and events you might add. (See Up Close and Personal on page 231 for a partial list of people of the period.)

Musical Notes Work with a partner to prepare a series of short presentations on composers through the ages. Henry Purcell (1659–1695) wrote over 600 musical works, including anthems, works for royal occasions, and one opera, *Dido and Aeneas.* Find a short account of his life and recordings of some of his work and prepare and give a **musical lecture** on this famous English composer.

The Meaning of Life

No Man is an Island

Science Connection

No man...nor woman, nor child...is an island. David proved that physical isolation from the world does not have to mean a life of solitude and loneliness. Although he lived his short twelve years in a plastic bubble and never felt the direct touch of a hand, David was strongly connected to his family and friends.

THE BUBBLE BOY
by Carol Ann with Kent Demaret

In September 1971 a Texas baby, identified only as David, was born in Houston with a rare disorder: severe combined immunodeficiency (SCID). This left him with no defense against germs and bacteria. Because his older brother, also named David, had died of the same affliction a year before at seven months, doctors decided from the moment of the new boy's birth to isolate him in a sterile plastic bubble.

Their hope was that, in time, David might develop his own immune system or that a cure would be found for SCID, a condition that affects 200 U.S. babies annually. In the following . . . David's mother, Carol Ann (the family withholds its surname), tells of raising her son in his sterile world. . . .

Love but don't touch. That was the rule for the dozen years of David Phillip's life. He spent 12 years in plastic bubbles, isolated from germs or bacteria. Isolated, too, from any human touch or kiss. But never isolated from love, and he knew that. . . . We wanted David to live as normally as possible, to marvel at whatever part of the world he could reach but never to consider himself a curiosity. . . .

David . . . was born at 7 A.M. on September 21, 1971, but not before extraordinary precautions had been taken for his birth . . . When the doctor lifted my tiny, just-born son in his double-gloved hands, . . . he was placed in a plastic isolator bubble. . . . It was three days before I got to see David. When I got to the door of his room I was overwhelmed by the apparatus. I guess I was expecting something smaller, like the bassinet-size isolators used for premature babies. Instead there was the isolator bubble for David, and another for his supplies. Large, floppy black gloves were attached to the sides of the bubbles. Hoses were pumping in filtered air and there was the hum of the motors. I never forgot that moment, and in later years it helped me in dealing with visitors to our home who were startled at the sight of David's equipment. The first two months of his life were spent in the hospital, and the fact that we got to take him home at all was a wonderful surprise. His life-support systems seemed so formidable and there were always so many people hovering over him that realistically we didn't think he would ever leave the hospital. . .

ALONE

Five-year-old David can only be an observer from his plastic bubble at Texas Children's Hospital. David's family and the medical staff hoped that David would either develop a normal immune system as he matured or that a cure would be discovered for his deadly disease.

Interdisciplinary Study **239**

In the first glorious days David spent at home . . . I really began to feel the excitement of caring for David by myself. He slept on ultrasoft sheepskin, and I could cradle him with the gloves at feeding time and sometimes I kissed him through the plastic. If I held him long enough I could feel the warmth of his skin, and I was certain that he could feel mine. I liked to position him so he could feel my heartbeat; I had read someplace that that was important to a newborn. Often he would nap in my arms as I held him with the gloves. . .

In spite of his isolation David seemed to go through all the normal stages other children did. There was a period when he got very sassy with me and . . . he . . . also went through a tantrum stage. Outbursts were understandable because it bothered him that he had so little control over his life. Someone would have to turn on the TV set for him, or change the channel or turn off the light. He was independent minded and later improvised ways to help himself. Reaching into the gloves on the side of the bubble, he would manipulate a stick about five feet long to turn lights on and off and open and shut doors. . .

There was no one dramatic moment when David learned that he had an immune deficiency. I'm sure it was more of an evolving understanding for him, with much of the awareness coming during his frequent stays in the hospital. He was told, however, that his older brother had died of the same disorder.

All his life he . . . tried to keep us from being gloomy. . . I remember thinking I couldn't live without him, that if he died, I would too. But I didn't feel that way at the end. I think he did something to me. I don't know what. In some ways I could never understand my little boy—his courage, and how he took it all so gracefully all those years. If he had the courage to die as he did, how could I not have the courage to go on living?

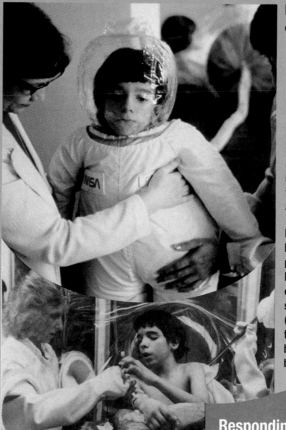

REACHING

OUT

David was able to spend an occasional hour outside in his NASA–designed space suit. Because his time outdoors was so limited, David noticed and appreciated things that most people miss or take for granted. One day, after looking at leaves, David commented, "Mom, did you notice that they are one color on one side and another color on the other side?"

David spent most of his life in the hospital, encased in plastic bubbles to protect him from bacteria and viruses. David was one of about two hundred children who are born every year with severe combined immunodeficiency (SCID). Since doctors are now able to treat the disease successfully with bone marrow transplants, David's bubble is a thing of the past.

Responding

1. A baby can be warm, well–fed, and rested, but without sufficient touching cannot thrive. Since David could not be touched directly, what kind of nurturing did he receive from his parents and the hospital personnel that insured his normal psychological development?

2. You saw how David was able to cope with his disability and stay connected to family and friends. How would you manage in David's situation? What would you do to keep linked to loved ones?

Humanities Connection

John Donne's famous words in "Meditation 17" have resounded down through the years and, if possible, mean more today than ever before. In literature, in music, in art, in world events and in our daily lives, the message comes to us over and over—we are responsible for each other.

CASE STUDIES FROM *ONE TO ONE*

by George L. Beiswinger

The following case studies are from the files of the Big Brother/ Big Sister organization. This organization pairs children in need of guidance with adult volunteers from the community.

KATHY wanted to expose Anita (9 years old) to an environment that was quite different from the only one she had known. Kathy showed Anita how to wash and style her hair and care for her skin. Together, they worked on a new dress for Anita. Kathy chose the pattern, and Anita selected the material—possibly the first meaningful decision that she had ever made. After several months, and hours of practicing good table manners at Kathy's, the pair went to a nice restaurant. Anita wore her new dress.

Anita is beginning to understand that she need not accept what fate hands her. She has choices, and she is learning that desired goals can be attained through planning and self-discipline.

COMING TOGETHER

FRED never learned to assume responsibilities that he was quite capable of handling. Instead, he had developed a whining, complaining personality, often using his handicap as an excuse for lack of accomplishment.

His mother referred him to Big Brothers / Big Sisters. He was matched with Robert, who was disabled as a result of infantile paralysis and had to wear leg braces. Needless to say, Robert gave Fred little sympathy, and the latter quickly learned not to expect any. Instead, Robert focused attention on the many things that Fred could do. Fred learned responsibility and concern for others when he and Robert participated in fund-raising campaigns for the BB/BS agency, as well as for another social-service organization.

BOB attempted to build Mike's self-esteem by pointing out his good attributes. Mike lived in a neighborhood where there were many Hispanics, from whom he had picked up a fair knowledge of Spanish. Bob, too, spoke Spanish, and he sought to capitalize on this coincidence by helping Mike improve this skill through further study. They even visited a Spanish art exhibit. Mike was also encouraged to participate in organized sports. His pride knew no bounds when he won a bowling trophy. Mike learned to ice-skate at a local sports arena. These physical activities provided an excellent, socially acceptable outlet for his former, negatively-channeled aggression, and his new language skills gave a wondrous boost to his self-esteem. These gains were reflected in his relations with others. His grades improved. As he once helped, Bob now hopes to obtain scholarship aid for Mike.

Interdisciplinary Study   **241**

FROM SIX DEGREES OF SEPARATION
by John Guare

I read somewhere that everybody on this planet is separated by only six other people. Six degrees of separation. Between us and everybody else on this planet. The president of the United States. A gondolier in Venice. Fill in the names. I find that A] tremendously comforting that we're so close and B] like Chinese water torture that we're so close. Because you have to find the right six people to make the connection. It's not just big names. It's anyone. A native in a rain forest. A Tierra del Fuegan. An Eskimo. I am bound to everyone on this planet by a trail of six people. It's a profound thought. . . . How every person is a new door, opening up into other worlds. Six degrees of separation between me and everyone else on this planet. But to find the right six people. . . .

In 1948, three years after the end of the second world war, East and West Berlin established separate governments. East Germany built a concrete and barbed wire wall in 1961 dividing the city and making it almost impossible for citizens to travel between the two sections. Many who tried were shot. The wall was finally opened in 1989 after massive protests by East Germans demanding more freedom.

S E P A R

FROM THE TASK
by William Cowper

'Twere well, says one sage erudite, profound,
Terribly arched and aquiline his nose,
And overbuilt with most impending brows,
'Twere well could you permit the world to live
As the world pleases. What's the world to you?
Much. I was born of woman, and drew milk
As sweet as charity from human breasts.
I think, articulate, I laugh and weep
And exercise all functions of a man.
How then should I and any man that lives
Be strangers to each other? Pierce my vein,
Take of the crimson stream meandering there,
And catechise it well. Apply your glass,
Search it, and prove now if it be not blood
Congenial with thine own. And if it be,
What edge of subtlety canst thou suppose
Keen enough, wise and skilful as thou art,
To cut the link of brotherhood, by which
One common Maker bound me to the kind. . . .

FROM MENDING WALL
by Robert Frost

Before I built a wall I'd ask to know
What I was walling in or walling out,
And to whom I was like to give offense.
Something there is that doesn't love a wall,
That wants it down. . . .

A T I O N

WORDS AND MUSIC BY MICHAEL JACKSON
AND LIONEL RICHIE

There comes a time when we heed a certain call
When the world must come together as one
There are people dying
And it's time to lend a hand to life
The greatest gift of all

> We can't go on pretending day by day
> That someone, somewhere will soon make a change
> We are all a part of God's great big family
> And the truth, you know,
> Love is all we need

CHORUS:
We are the world, we are the children
We are the ones who make a brighter day
So let's start giving
There's a choice we're making
We're saving our own lives
It's true and we'll make a better day
Just you and me

Send them your heart so they'll know that someone cares
And their lives will be stronger and free
As God has shown us by turning stones to bread
So we all must lend a helping hand

(REPEAT CHORUS)

> When you're down and out, there seems no hope at all
> But if you just believe there's no way we can fall
> Let us realize that a change can only come
> When we stand together as one

WE ARE THE WORLD

Responding

1. What do you have to offer another person to help him or her cope with the world?

2. Think of a person—any person. What other people connect you?

3. "There's a choice we're making," go to the words of the song, "We're saving our own lives." In what sense is this true?

Writing Workshop

Making the Abstract Concrete

Assignment You've read writing in which the authors deal with big, abstract ideas, such as brotherhood and the nature of time, in remarkably specific, down-to-earth ways. Now see how well you can do the same thing.

WRITER'S BLUEPRINT

Product A collage, summary, and speech

Purpose To illustrate an abstract idea

Audience An assembly of your classmates

Specs As the creator of a successful collage and speech, you should:

❑ Choose an abstract idea drawn from the literature, such as brotherhood, living fully in the moment, true love, or time and change.

❑ Assemble a collage of fifteen or more images and quotations that illustrate your topic. For example, to illustrate brotherhood, you might use a photo of a family picnic and the John Donne quote "No man is an island." Look for images in magazines and newspapers, or sketch them yourself. For quotations, consider sources such as poems, song lyrics, bumper stickers, ads, and journal entries.

❑ Write a summary in which you list the five most significant elements in your collage and briefly give your thoughts on how each element illustrates your topic.

❑ Make note cards from your summary for a speech about your topic, using your collage as a graphic aid.

❑ Begin your speech by introducing your topic and collage. Then deal with each of the five most significant elements in turn. Conclude by summarizing your thoughts on the topic.

❑ Follow the rules of grammar, usage, mechanics, and spelling. Take special care not to confuse adjectives and adverbs.

Review the literature. In a small group, look back at the selections for the abstract ideas the writers deal with and the images they use to bring those ideas to life. Use a chart like the one shown. When you finish, look your chart over and select the topic you'll be using.

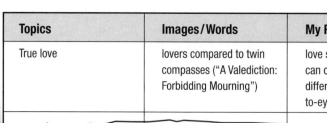

Topics	Images/Words	My Reactions
True love	lovers compared to twin compasses ("A Valediction: Forbidding Mourning")	love so strong that you can overcome differences and see eye-to-eye

Create your collage. Follow these steps:

- Gather your materials. Make sketches of your own. Find pictures from magazines and newspapers. Look for song lyrics, bumper stickers, lines of poetry, single words—whatever works for you. Use your chart as a guide.

- Do a rough diagram of where you plan to place each element.

- Assemble the elements on paper, poster board, a cardboard box, or whatever medium seems to work best for you.

Rate the elements in your collage. Look back at what you've created and choose the five elements you think are most significant. Then rank those five in order of significance, from least (1) to most (5).

Plan your written summary by making a chart for your five chosen elements like the one you made in "Review the literature." This will serve as your writing plan.

STEP **2** DRAFTING

Before you draft your summary, be sure you have your writing plan and collage laid out in front of you.

As you draft, follow your writing plan, moving from the least significant element to the most significant. For your most significant element, be sure to tell why it's most significant. You might draft your summary as a numbered list or as a series of paragraphs, with one paragraph per element.

3 REVISING

Ask a partner to comment on your draft before you revise it. Use this checklist as a guide.

✔ Have I chosen an abstract idea as my topic?

✔ Have I summarized the significance of five elements from my collage?

✔ Do all the elements relate clearly to the topic?

Revising Strategy

Making Your Intentions Clear

In writing, knowing what you want to say is only half the battle. The other half is putting your thoughts down so they're as clear to the reader as they are to you. For example, you may have a crystal-clear picture of exactly how the elements in your collage illustrate your topic, but you still have to communicate this vision. You have to make your intentions clear.

In the student model below, the writer hasn't quite made it clear, in her initial draft, exactly what an image of a starry night sky has to do with her topic: Time. Notice how she's revised to make her intentions clearer.

3. Image of a starry night sky: Time slips away. Stars are like memories.

We forget far more of our past than we remember. So many moments are
, *like the stretches of empty space between the stars.*
lost to us forever. Time is loss as well as opportunity. . . .

STUDENT MODEL

4 EDITING

Ask a partner to review your revised draft before you edit. When you edit, look for errors in grammar, usage, spelling, and mechanics. Look over each sentence to make sure you have not confused adjectives and adverbs.

Editing Strategy

FOR REFERENCE
See the Language and Grammar Handbook for more information about adjectives and adverbs.

Using Adjectives and Adverbs Correctly

Good, real, and *strong* are adjectives that modify nouns or pronouns, not verbs. *Well*, *really*, and *strongly* are adverbs. Use them to modify verbs, adjectives, or other adverbs.

Don't write: I think this image works *real good*.
Write: I think this image works *really well*.
Don't write: I feel *strong* about this image.
Write: I feel *strongly* about this image.

Take care to avoid confusing adjectives and adverbs in your writing.

STEP 5 PRESENTING

Prepare a speech based on your collage and summary. Make note cards for each of your five elements, based on what you wrote in your summary. See the Beyond Print article that follows this lesson for information on delivering a speech.

STEP 6 LOOKING BACK

Self-evaluate. Look back at the Writer's Blueprint and give your paper a score for each item, from 6 (superior) to 1 (inadequate).

Reflect. Respond to these questions in writing.

✔ In this assignment you worked in three different modes: visual, written, and spoken. Which one did you like best? Why?

✔ Did finding concrete images to illustrate an abstract concept make that concept more meaningful to you? Why or why not?

For Your Working Portfolio Add your collage, note cards, and reflection responses to your working portfolio.

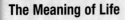
Beyond Print

Talking to an Audience

Speaking before an audience worries many people, but it needn't; after all, you talk to other people every day. Here are some pointers on how to make your audience pay attention to what you have to say.

Rehearse. You're not making a fool of yourself. Successful speakers do rehearse—by themselves, out loud, and perhaps several times over. Not only do you become more familiar with your material, but you can also try out different gestures and vocal emphasis.

Get organized. If you spend the first minute or so in front of an audience shuffling your notes, they may suspect that you aren't quite ready to talk to them. Get everything in order before you walk to the front. This includes any visuals you may use.

Maintain good posture. Good posture actually helps you project your voice better. Stand on both feet so that you are in balance when you want to gesture or move. If there is a desk or podium for your notes, you may grasp it—lightly—but don't lean your weight on it.

Make eye contact. Talk *to* your audience. Pick one person and direct a sentence or two right at her or him; then pick another, and so on.

Speak loudly and clearly. You don't have to shout, but your speech is worthless if your audience can't hear you. Speak in a normal voice, but try to project your voice to the back wall of the room.

Avoid meaningless vocalisms. Some people fill every pause with "Ummm" or "Uhhh" or other noises. You may not be able to avoid these altogether, but try. Silence is better.

Make simple, meaningful gestures. You may have seen speakers waving their arms all over the place. While making some gestures is preferable to standing stock still, keep them simple and natural.

Activity Option

Use these pointers when you deliver the speech you wrote in the Writing Workshop, "Making the Abstract Concrete."

HISTORICAL OVERVIEW

Milton's *Paradise Lost* and the King James Bible present visions of struggle between good and evil that reflect the passionate religious strife of the 1600s. England was pulled apart as a result of a three-sided struggle between the Anglicans (the established Protestant Church of England), the Catholics who wanted to end Anglicanism, and the Puritans who felt England needed further religious reform. Civil war erupted between Anglican supporters of King Charles and Puritan Parliamentary forces led by Oliver Cromwell. The king was defeated, tried for treason, and beheaded. England became a Puritan Commonwealth under Parliament's rule.

The illustration on the right shows an image of Satan by French artist Gustave Doré against depictions of heaven (top), the Garden of Eden (center), and Hell (bottom).

THE FALL

FROM GRACE

Part Two

The Fall from Grace

Since the beginnings of civilization, people have looked to the past with envy and regret for a "golden age" of simplicity and perfection, when everyone enjoyed God's grace, the favor and love of God. The stories of how people lost that favor and love—how they fell from grace—are many and varied.

 Multicultural Connection **Communication** involves cultural uses of language that come down to us over time as well as new forms of language that are constantly evolving as cultures change over time. The language of Milton and the King James Bible has influenced for hundreds of years the way people communicate (and the way they think about religion). How do the styles of the following selections contribute to the meanings they communicate?

Before Reading

On His Having Arrived at the Age of Twenty-three

On His Blindness

from **Paradise Lost** by John Milton

John Milton
1608–1674

John Milton's father, a London notary, provided him with the best of educations: St. Paul's School, Christ College at Cambridge, six years of private study at his country house, and a year's tour of Europe. Returning home, Milton tutored and wrote poetry (he had mastered Greek, Latin, and Hebrew, as well as a number of modern European languages). A Puritan, he served as a secretary in the Commonwealth, the government declared after Charles I was executed for treason. He became totally blind in 1652. At the end of the Puritan regime, Milton was considered an enemy of the government; he was heavily fined and lost most of his property. At that time he began to write *Paradise Lost*.

Building Background

A Dream Come True For most of his lifetime, John Milton dreamed of writing an epic poem better than all others. His notebooks list the ninety-nine topics he considered; among them, Samson, King Arthur, and Macbeth. In 1660, ousted from government service, Milton finally began his grand poem, choosing as its setting the entire universe and as its theme mankind's fall from grace as told in the biblical story of the temptation of Adam and Eve. With his three teenage daughters serving as his secretaries, Milton dictated for hours each day. Finally in 1665, he completed the twelve books of what is still regarded as the finest epic poem in the English language.

Literary Focus

Symbol A **symbol** is something concrete, such as an object or an action, that signifies something abstract, such as an idea. The same object can symbolize different things to different people: a lily might symbolize beauty to one person but death to another. To determine whether an author is using a symbol, ask the following questions:

- Is a particular object or action stressed or repeated?

- Does a character think about something abstract whenever that object or action is mentioned? Do you, as a reader, do so?

Writer's Notebook

From Concrete to Abstract These objects are often used symbolically: sun, skull, lion, rose, flag, champagne bottle, diamond ring, black cat, light bulb, dark clouds. What abstract idea does each concrete **symbol** convey to you? Create a chart like the following and jot down a few words in response to each word or phrase. Compare your interpretations with those of your classmates. Continue the chart with symbols you find as you read the following selections.

Symbol	Abstract Idea	Symbol	Abstract Idea
sun	warmth, understanding	skull	death

On His Having Arrived at the Age of Twenty-Three

John Milton

How soon hath Time, the subtle thief of youth,
Stolen on his wing my three and twentieth year!
My hasting days fly on with full career,
But my late spring no bud or blossom showeth.
5 Perhaps my semblance might deceive the truth,
That I to manhood am arrived so near,
And inward ripeness doth much less appear,
That some more timely-happy spirits endueth.
Yet be it less more, or soon or slow,
10 It shall be still in strictest measure even
To that same lot, however mean or high,
Toward which Time leads me, and the will of Heaven;
All is, if I have grace to use it so,
As ever in my great Task-Master's eye.

3 **with full career,** at full speed.
5 **semblance** (sem′bləns), *n.* youthful appearance.

8 **endue** (en dü′), *v.* provide.

10 **even,** adequate; that is, his "inward ripeness," or inner readiness, will be up to whatever destiny Time and Heaven are leading him to.

On His Blindness

John Milton

When I consider how my light is spent,
Ere half my days, in this dark world and wide,
And that one talent which is death to hide
Lodged with me useless, though my soul more bent
5 To serve therewith my Maker, and present
My true account, lest He, returning, chide;
"Doth God exact day-labor, light denied!"
I fondly ask. But Patience, to prevent
That murmur, soon replies: "God doth not need
10 Either man's work or His own gifts; who best
Bear His mild yoke, they serve Him best. His state
Is kingly—thousands at His bidding speed
And post o'er land and ocean without rest;
They also serve who only stand and wait."

3 **talent,** the gift of writing. This is an allusion to Jesus's parable of the "unprofitable servant," condemned for burying his one talent, or coin, instead of investing it. (Matthew 25:15–30)
8 **fondly,** foolishly.

PARADISE LOST

John Milton

*Opening with the **invocation,** or call for poetic inspiration, and the posing of
the question he will answer in the poem, Milton begins his epic **in medias res,**
or "in the middle of things." The archangel Satan and "his horrid crew," having waged war against God in Heaven, have been plunged down into Hell
where they roll in the "fiery gulf."*

Of man's first disobedience, and the fruit
Of that forbidden tree, whose mortal taste
Brought death into the world, and all our woe,
With loss of Eden, till one greater Man
5 Restore us, and regain the blissful seat,
Sing, heavenly Muse—that on the secret top
Of Oreb, or of Sinai, didst inspire
That shepherd who first taught the chosen seed
In the beginning how the heavens and earth
10 Rose out of Chaos; or if Sion hill
Delight thee more, and Siloa's brook that flowed
Fast by the oracle of God, I thence
Invoke thy aid to my adventurous song,
That with no middle flight intends to soar

6 Muse, In Greek myth nine
Muses each watched over a
different field of art or science and inspired its artists.
Urania (yù rā′nē ə) was the
muse of astronomy.
7–8 Oreb (ôr′eb) **. . . Sinai**
(sī′nī) **. . . chosen seed.** Oreb
and Sinai are two names for
the peak in the Sinai peninsula of Egypt where Moses
received the word of God to
bring to the the Jewish people (the "chosen seed").
10 Chaos (kā′os), the infinite space in which formless
matter was thought to have
existed before God created
the heavens and earth.
10–11 Sion (sī′ən) **hill
. . . Siloa's** (sī lō′əz) **brook,**
places near the temple in
Jerusalem.

15 Above the Aonian mount, while it pursues
   Things unattempted yet in prose or rhyme.
   And chiefly Thou, O Spirit, that dost prefer
   Before all temples the upright heart and pure,
   Instruct me, for Thou knowest; Thou from the first
20 Wast present, and, with mighty wings outspread,
   Dove-like satest brooding on the vast abyss
   And madest it pregnant: what in me is dark,
   Illumine; what is low, raise and support—
   That to the height of this great argument
25 I may assert eternal providence,
   And justify the way of God to men.
        Say first, for Heaven hides nothing from thy view,
   Nor the deep tract of Hell, say first what cause
   Moved our grand parents in that happy state,
30 Favored of Heaven so highly, to fall off
   From their Creator, and transgress His will
   For one restraint, lords of the world besides?
   Who first seduced them to that foul revolt?
   The infernal serpent—he it was whose guile,
35 Stirred up with envy and revenge, deceived
   The mother of mankind, what time his pride
   Had cast him out from Heaven, with all his host
   Of rebel angels, by whose aid aspiring
   To set himself in glory above his peers,
40 He trusted to have equalled the Most High,
   If he opposed; and with ambitious aim
   Against the throne and monarchy of God
   Raised impious war in Heaven and battle proud
   With vain attempt. Him the Almighty Power
45 Hurled headlong flaming from the ethereal sky
   With hideous ruin and combustion down
   To bottomless perdition, there to dwell
   In adamantine chains and penal fire,
   Who durst defy the Omnipotent to arms.
50   Nine times the space that measures day and night
   To mortal men, he with his horrid crew
   Lay vanquished, rolling in the fiery gulf
   Confounded though immortal. But his doom
   Reserved him to more wrath; for now the thought
55 Both of lost happiness and lasting pain
   Torments him; round he throws his baleful eyes,
   That witnessed huge affliction and dismay
   Mixed with obdúrate pride and steadfast hate.
   At once as far as Angels' ken he views

15 Aonian (ā ō′nē ən)
mount, a Greek mountain,
the home of the Muses.
Milton intends to write a
Christian epic greater than
earlier non-Christian Greek
and Latin poetry.

■ What is the **epic question**
that Milton poses?

29 grand parents, Adam and
Eve.
31 transgress (trans gres′), v.
sin against.
32 restraint (ri strānt′), n.
limit; restriction.
34 guile (gīl), n. deceit.

■ What kind of behavior do
you expect from someone
motivated by envy and
revenge? by pride and hate?

48 adamantine (ad′ə-
man′tēn), adj. immovable.
52 vanquish (vang′kwish), v.
defeat.
53 confounded (kən-
found′id), adj. overthrown.
56 baleful (bāl′fəl), adj.
destructive.
58 obdurate (ob′dər it), adj.
unrepentant.
59 ken (ken), n. range of
vision.

*Angel Michael Binding the
Dragon* by William Blake shows
one interpretation of the war in
Heaven that resulted in the
expulsion of Satan and his rebel
angels from Heaven. How does
this interpretation compare with
Milton's version? ➤

60 The dismal situation waste and wild:
A dungeon horrible, on all sides round
As one great furnace flamed, yet from those flames
No light, but rather darkness visible
Served only to discover sights of woe,
65 Regions of sorrow, doleful shades, where peace
And rest can never dwell, hope never comes
That comes to all; but torture without end
Still urges, and a fiery deluge, fed
With ever-burning sulphur unconsumed:
70 Such place eternal justice had prepared
For those rebellious, here their prison ordained
In utter darkness, and their portion set
As far removed from God and light of Heaven
As from the center thrice to the utmost pole.
75 O how unlike the place from whence they fell!
There the companions of his fall, overwhelmed
With floods and whirlwinds of tempestuous fire,
He soon discerns, and weltering by his side
One next himself in power, and next in crime,
80 Long after know in Palestine, and named
Beelzebub. To whom the arch-enemy,
And thence in Heaven called Satan, with bold words
Breaking the horrid silence thus began. . . .

Addressing Beelzebub, Satan boldly declares that, although he has been thrown into Hell, he will continue to fight God with all his might.

"All is not lost; the unconquerable will,
85 And study of revenge, immortal hate,
And courage never to submit or yield—
And what is else not to be overcome?
That glory never shall His wrath or might
Extort from me. To bow and sue for grace
90 With suppliant knee, and deify His power—
Who from the terror of this arm so late
Doubted His empire—that were low indeed,
That were an ignominy and shame beneath
This downfall; since by fate the strength of gods
95 And this empyreal substance cannot fail,
Since through experience of this great event,
In arms not worse, in foresight much advanced,
We may with more successful hope resolve
To wage by force or guile eternal war. . . ."

67 to all. The greatest torment of Hell was the absence of hope of salvation.
68 deluge (del′yüj), *n.* downpour; a heavy fall, as of rain.

■ Summarize Milton's idea of Hell.

77 tempestuous (tem pes′-chü əs), *adj.* stormy; violent.
78 weltering (wel′tər ing), *adj.* tossing.
80 Palestine (pal′ə stīn), the Holy Land, now divided chiefly between Israel and the Palestinians.
81 Beelzebub (bē el′zə bub), Satan's chief associate.

85 study of, search for.

91 who, I (Satan) who.
92 doubted, feared.
93 ignominy (ig′nə min′ē), *n.* disgrace.
95 this empyreal (em pir′ē-əl) **substance cannot fail.** The fallen angels are still heavenly, and therefore immortal; they cannot die ("fail").

100 "Fallen cherub, to be weak is miserable,
Doing or suffering: but of this be sure,
To do aught good never will be our task,
But ever to do ill our sole delight,
As being the contrary to His high will
105 Whom we resist. If then His providence
Out of our evil seek to bring forth good,
Our labor must be to pervert that end,
And out of good still to find means of evil. . . .
Seest thou yon dreary plain, forlorn and wild,
110 The seat of desolation, void of light,
Save what the glimmering of these livid flames
Casts pale and dreadful? Thither let us tend
From off the tossing of these fiery waves,
There rest, if any rest can harbor there,
115 And reassembling our afflicted powers,
Consult how we may hence forth most offend
Our enemy, our own loss how repair,
How overcome this dire calamity,
What reinforcement we may gain from hope;
120 If not, what resolution from despair. . . ."
        Forthwith upright he rears from off the pool
His mighty stature; on each hand the flames
Driven backward slope their pointing spires, and rolled
In billows, leave in the midst a horrid vale.
125 Then with expanded wings he steers his flight
Aloft, incumbent on the dusky air
That felt unusual weight, till on dry land
He lights, if it were land that ever burned
With solid, as the lake with liquid fire;
130 And such appeared in hue; as when the force
Of subterranean wind transports a hill
Torn from Pelorus, or the shattered side
Of thundering Etna, whose combustible
And fuelled entrails thence conceiving fire,
135 Sublimed with mineral fury, aid the winds,
And leave a singéd bottom all involved
With stench and smoke: such resting found the sole
Of unblest feet. Him followed his next mate,
Both glorying to have scaped the Stygian flood
140 As gods, and by their own recovered strength,
Not by the sufferance of supernal power.

100 cherub (cher′əb), *n.* one of the second highest order of angels.
102 aught (ôt), *pron.* anything.

110 desolation (des′ə-lā′shən), *n.* sad loneliness.

115 afflicted (ə flikt′id), *adj.* cast out.

118 dire (dīr), *adj.* dreadful.

■ What does Satan tell Beelzebub about the work the fallen angels must do?

126 incumbent (in-kum′bənt), *adj.* pressing down.

132 Pelorus (pə lōr′əs), northeastern Sicily.
133 Etna (et′nə), the volcano of Mount Etna in Sicily.

139 Stygian (stij′ē ən) **flood,** waters of the river Styx (stiks) in Hell.

"Is this the region, this the soil, the clime,"
Said then the lost archangel, "this the seat
That we must change for Heaven, this mournful gloom
145 For that celestial light? Be it so, since He
Who now is sovereign can dispose and bid
What shall be right. Farthest from Him is best,
Whom reason hath equalled, force hath made supreme
Above His equals. Farewell, happy fields,
150 Where joy for ever dwells: hail, horrors! hail,
Infernal world! and thou, profoundest Hell,
Receive thy new possessor: one who brings
A mind not to be changed by place or time.
The mind is its own place, and in itself
155 Can make a heaven of Hell, a hell of Heaven.
What matter where, if I be still the same,
And what I should be, all but less than He
Whom thunder hath made greater? Here at least
We shall be free; the Almighty hath not built
160 Here for His envy, will not drive us hence:
Here we may reign secure, and in my choice
To reign is worth ambition, though in Hell.
Better to reign in Hell than serve in Heaven.
But wherefore let we then our faithful friends,
165 The associates and co-partners of our loss,
Lie thus astonished on the oblivious pool,
And call them not to share with us their part
In this unhappy mansion, or once more
With rallied arms to try what may be yet
170 Regained in Heaven, or what more lost in Hell?"
         So Satan spake, and him Beelzebub
Thus answered: "Leader of those armies bright,
Which but the Omnipotent none could have foiled,
If once they hear that voice, their liveliest pledge
175 Of hope in fears and dangers, heard so oft
In worst extremes, and on the perilous edge
Of battle when it raged, in all assaults
Their surest signal, they will soon resume
New courage and revive, though now they lie
180 Grovelling and prostrate on yon lake of fire,
As we erewhile, astounded and amazed—
No wonder, fallen such a pernicious height!"
         He scarce had ceased when the superior fiend
Was moving toward the shore; his ponderous shield,
185 Ethereal temper, massy, large, and round,
Behind him cast; the broad circumference

145 **celestial** (sə les′chəl),
adj. heavenly.

159 **Almighty** (ôl mī′tē),
God, also called Creator.

166 **oblivious** (ə bliv′ē əs)
pool, lake of forgetfulness.

173 **Omnipotent** (om nip′ə-
tənt), *n.* all-powerful one;
God.
176 **perilous** (per′ə ləs), *adj.*
dangerous.

182 **pernicious** (pər nish′əs),
adj. causing great harm or
damage.

■ Describe Satan's armor.

Hung on his shoulders like the moon, whose orb
Through optic glass the Tuscan artist views
At evening from the top of Fesole,
190 Or in Valdarno, to descry new lands,
Rivers or mountains in her spotty globe.
His spear, to equal which the tallest pine
Hewn on Norwegian hills, to be the mast
Of some great ammiral, were but a wand,
195 He walked with to support uneasy steps
Over the burning marl, not like those steps
On heaven's azure; and the torrid clime
Smote on him sore besides, vaulted with fire.
Nathless he so endured, till on the beach
200 Of that inflamèd sea, he stood and called
His legions, angel forms, who lay entranced,
Thick as autumnal leaves that strew the brooks
In Vallombrosa, where the Etrurian shades
High over-arched embower; or scattered sedge
205 Afloat, when with fierce winds Orion armed
Hath vexed the Red Sea coast, whose waves overthrew
Busiris and his Memphian chivalry,
While with a perfidious hatred they pursued
The sojourners of Goshen, who beheld
210 From the safe shore their floating carcasses
And broken chariot wheels—so thick bestrewn,
Abject and lost, lay these, covering the flood,
Under amazement of their hideous change.
He called so loud that all the hollow deeps
215 Of Hell resounded: "Princes, Potentates,
Warriors, the flower of Heaven, once yours, now lost,
If such astonishment as this can seize
Eternal Spirits; or have ye chosen this place
After the toil of battle to repose
220 Your wearied virtue, for the case you find
To slumber here, as in the vales of Heaven?
Or in this abject posture have ye sworn
To adore the Conqueror, who now beholds
Cherub and seraph rolling in the flood
225 With scattered arms and ensigns, till anon
His swift pursuers from Heaven gates discern
The advantage, and descending tread us down
Thus drooping, or with linkèd thunderbolts
Transfix us to the bottom of this gulf?
230 Awake, arise, or be for ever fallen!"...

188–190 through optic glass . . . Fesole (fē′sōl) **. . . Valdarno** (val där′nō). Through the telescope the astronomer Galileo uses on the hills and in the valleys near Florence, Italy.
194 ammiral, admiral's flagship.
196 marl (märl), *n.* earth.
199 nathless (nāth′ les), *adv.* nevertheless.

203 Vallombrosa (val′əm brō′-sə) **. . . Etrurian** (ē trür′ē ən) **shades,** a valley near Florence in the Etruscan area of Italy.
205 Orion (ô rī′ən), the constellation of the hunter, visible in autumn, the time of harsh storms.
206 Red Sea, an arm of the Indian Ocean between Africa and the Arabian peninsula.
207–209 Busiris (bū sī′rəs) **. . . Gosen** (gō′shən). Busiris is the name Milton gives to the pharaoh of Egypt who enslaved the Israelites. At the time, the Israelites lived in Goshen, a part of Egypt. When Moses led them out of slavery, the pharaoh pursued them with his army (the "Memphian chivalry"). The Egyptians were drowned when the Red Sea closed over them after God had parted it for the Israelites.

■ While Satan and Beelzebub are making plans, where are the other fallen angels?

212 abject (ab′jekt), adj. miserable.
224 seraph (ser′əf), *n.* one of the highest order of angels.

... Above them all the archangel: but his face
Deep scars of thunder had intrenched, and care
Sat on his faded cheek, but under brows
Of dauntless courage, and considerate pride
235 Waiting revenge. Cruel his eye, but cast
Signs of remorse and passion, to behold
The fellows of his crime, the followers rather
(Far other once beheld in bliss), condemned
For ever now to have their lot in pain—
240 Millions of spirits for his fault amerced
Of Heaven, and from eternal splendors flung
For his revolt—yet faithful how they stood,
Their glory withered; as, when heaven's fire
Hath scathed the forest oaks or mountain pines,
245 With singed top their stately growth, though bare,
Stands on the blasted heath. He now prepared
To speak; whereat their doubled ranks they bend
From wing to wing, and half enclose him round
With all his peers: attention held them mute.
250 Thrice he assayed, and thrice, in spite of scorn,
Tears, such as angels weep, burst forth: at last
Words interwove with sighs found out their way:
          "O myriads of immortal spirits! O powers
Matchless, but with the Almighty!—and that strife
255 Was not inglorious, though the event was dire,
As this place testifies, and this dire change,
Hateful to utter. But what power of mind,
Foreseeing or presaging, from the depth
Of knowledge past or present, could have feared
260 How such united force of gods, how such
As stood like these, could ever know repulse?
For who can yet believe, though after loss,
That all these puissant legions, whose exile
Hath emptied Heaven, shall fail to re-ascend,
265 Self-raised, and re-possess their native seat?
For me, be witness all the host of Heaven,
If counsels different, or danger shunned
By me have lost our hopes. But He who reigns
Monarch in Heaven till then as one secure
270 Sat on His throne, upheld by old repute,
Consent or custom, and His regal state

240–241 amerced (ə mėrst′) **... Heaven,** exiled from Heaven.

250 assay (ə sā′), *v.* attempt.

■ With what emotions do you think Satan delivers his speech to his angel comrades?

258 presage (pri sāj′), *v.* predict.
263 puissant (pwis′nt), *adj.* powerful.

This picture of the fallen angels appeared in the first illustrated edition of *Paradise Lost,* published in London in 1688. What qualities of Satan seem to be emphasized here? of hell? ➤

Put forth at full, but still His strength concealed—
Which tempted our attempt, and wrought our fall.
Henceforth His might we know, and know our own,
275 So as not either to provoke, or dread
New war provoked. Our better part remains,
To work in close design, by fraud or guile,
What force effected not; that He no less
At length from us may find, who overcomes
280 By force hath overcome but half his foe.
Space may produce new worlds; whereof so rife
There went a fame in Heaven that He ere long
Intended to create, and therein plant
A generation whom his choice regard
285 Should favor equal to the sons of Heaven.
Thither, if but to pry, shall be perhaps
Our first eruption—thither, or elsewhere;
For this infernal pit shall never hold
Celestial spirits in bondage, nor the abyss
290 Long under darkness cover. But these thoughts
Full counsel must mature. Peace is despaired;
For who can think submission? War, then, war
Open or understood, must be resolved."

281 **rife** (rīf), *adj.* widespread.
282 **fame,** rumor.

■ Against what rumored creation of God does Satan intend to wage his war?

☙ Given the character of Satan as Milton has presented him, what are the chances of meaningful **communication** ever occurring between the forces of evil and the forces of good?

Book 1 ends with the building of the palace of Pandemonium (that is, "All Demons") and with preparations for a council of war. The story of Satan's meeting with Adam and Eve in the Garden of Eden follows. Satan tempts Eve, who in turn persuades Adam to eat the forbidden fruit of the Tree of Knowledge. For this disobedience, Adam and Eve are driven from Paradise out into the world. The twelfth and last book of the poem closes with the pair standing hand in hand upon the threshold of the world. Paradise, "so late their happy home," lies behind them. Sadly and penitently they face the future, their punishment softened only by the promise of the ultimate redemption of man by Christ.

After Reading

Making Connections

Shaping Your Response

1. Jot down two words that describe Milton as a young man and two words that describe him as an older man. Do you think he has changed? In what way?

2. Explain how "On His Having Arrived . . ." makes use of the **sonnet** structure. How do the last six lines relate to the first eight lines?

Analyzing the Poems

3. In "On His Blindness" what do you think the speaker means by asking, "Doth God exact day-labor, light denied?"

4. How would you interpret Patience's answer, "They also serve who only stand and wait"? How does that thought console the speaker?

5. Describe Satan, pointing out the methods of **characterization** Milton uses to create this picture.

6. Explain how you think pride has brought Satan to his current position and how it influences the plans he is making.

7. In light of his recent defeat by God, evaluate Satan's intent to wage a different kind of war from now on.

8. 🗣 How might Milton's blindness and political exile have influenced his **communication** of ideas and attitudes in *Paradise Lost*?

Extending the Ideas

9. Compare Milton's vision of Satan and Hell with other images you are familiar with from literature or movies.

Literary Focus: Symbol

Beginning with lines 22–23 (". . . what in me is dark, / Illumine . . .") and throughout *Paradise Lost,* Milton emphasizes the **symbols** of darkness and light. Find at least three other examples of the darkness / light symbolism. In each example, what do you think darkness and light stand for?

Vocabulary Study

Select the word that is most nearly similar in meaning to the numbered word.

1. guile
   a. association
   b. deceit
   c. guilt
   d. leadership

2. dire
   a. dreadful
   b. made visible
   c. spoken
   d. without end

3. vanquish
   a. change
   b. disappear
   c. diminish
   d. defeat

4. transgress
  a. ask about
  b. give up
  c. give back
  d. sin against

5. baleful
  a. destructive
  b. fortunate
  c. mysterious
  d. stubborn

6. desolation
  a. comfort
  b. meanness
  c. sad loneliness
  d. place to live

7. tempestuous
  a. cold
  b. mischievous
  c. soft
  d. stormy

8. restraint
  a. new attempt
  b. limit; restriction
  c. question
  d. freedom

9. abject
  a. descriptive
  b. incomplete
  c. miserable
  d. sufficient

10. deluge
  a. downpour
  b. misunderstanding
  c. great hope
  d. specialty

Expressing Your Ideas

Writing Choices

Writer's Notebook Update Select one of the symbols you identified earlier and write a few lines in which you develop that symbol by describing a concept or idea that you want your reader to understand better. If you wish, write the lines in poetic form.

Sin at Work Satan's sin of pride is one of the traditional "seven deadly sins"; the others are envy, anger, lust, avarice, gluttony, and sloth. Do a little research on the seven deadly sins. Then select one of the other sins and write a **short story** showing that sin at work.

So This Is Hell What's your idea of what Hell might be like? Write a one-page **description** of that infamous place where people are said to go after death and of the people that go there. (You might want to study the visions of Hell in the Interdisciplinary Study on pages 276–280 before you begin writing.)

Other Options

On My Having Arrived . . . Inspired by Milton's poem "On His Having Arrived at the Age of Twenty-three," create a **collage** that illustrates your current state in life and your attitude toward life as you arrive at the age of—whatever you are. You can use drawings, pictures cut from magazines or newspapers, and even words and phrases in your collage.

Worth a Thousand Words? Select one of the scenes from *Paradise Lost* and create a **work of art** that depicts the emotions and tensions of the scene. You might choose to do a painting or a sculpture, for example, or an abstract piece that makes use of line and color. Add an appropriate quote from Milton as a caption.

Before Reading

from Genesis
The Twenty-third Psalm

The King James Bible

As the Hampton Court Conference of 1604 draws to a close, those assembled propose that they honor King James for his peacemaking work among the hostile religious factions of Great Britain. They authorize a new translation of the Bible. And so fifty-four scholars and students of divinity, divided into six teams, begin their research. Working at Westminster, at Cambridge, and at Oxford, the teams read earlier English translations, and they read in the original languages, Hebrew, Aramaic, and Greek. They write with an eye to simplifying the language. Each team then submits its work to a review team who hear each verse read aloud. The final judgment is on the sound and the flow of the words. In 1611, eight years after it was began, the Authorized Version of the Bible, known as the King James Bible, is published. In the introduction to this work, the translators explain that from many good Bibles they have created "one principal good one."

Building Background

The Bible is not one book but a collection of many books including many different types of literature. Christians divide the Bible into two sections—the Old Testament, containing the laws, history, and literature of the Jews, and the New Testament. Jews do not include the New Testament in their Bibles. The first book in the Bible is called *Genesis* (jen′ə sis), from Greek, "be born," and most of it is devoted to the history of the tribal ancestors of the Jews, the patriarchs Abraham, Isaac, and Jacob. In order to set this history in the widest possible context, the first chapters of Genesis give an account of the creation of the world and of the parents of the human race, Adam and Eve. Other books in what Christians call the Old Testament include sermons and visions of Jewish prophets and miscellaneous psalms, proverbs, moral tales, and love songs. Despite the many types of literature included in the Bible, the subject of all these works is basically the same—the divine order of human events, the ways in which God operates in the lives of people on Earth.

Literary Focus

Style   The way a writer uses language to convey his or her ideas is called **style**. Style involves an author's choice of words and the arrangement of those words into sentences and paragraphs. An author's style may be simple or elaborate, elegant or folksy, conversational or formal. As you read, look especially for these elements of style:

- concrete terms and images
- straightforward phrases and sentences
- repetition and parallel structure

Writer's Notebook

The Garden of Eden   Most cultures of the world have some counterpart of the Garden of Eden, the perfect land in which God originally placed the first human beings, Adam and Eve. Jot down a few descriptive words and phrases that come to your mind when you think of the Garden of Eden.

Genesis

The King James Bible

This large (21 feet by 15 feet, 3 inches) tapestry showing Adam and Eve being driven from the Garden of Eden was woven in Brussels, Belgium, in the 1500s. What do details in the tapestry—including the border—suggest about what they are leaving behind? about what they have to look foward to?

Chapter 1

In the beginning God created the heaven and the earth. And the earth was without form and void; and darkness was upon the face of the deep. And the Spirit of God moved upon the face of the waters. And God said, "Let there be light": and there was light. And God saw the light, that it was good: and God divided the light from the darkness. And God called the light Day, and the darkness he called Night. And the evening and the morning were the first day.

And God said, "Let there be a firmament[1] in the midst of the waters, and let it divide the waters from the waters." And God made the firmament, and divided the waters which were under the firmament from the waters which were above the firmament: and it was so. And God called the firmament Heaven. And the evening and the morning were the second day.

And God said, "Let the waters under the heaven be gathered together unto one place, and let the dry land appear": and it was so. And God called the dry land Earth; and the gathering together of the waters called he Seas: and God saw that it was good.

And God said, "Let the earth bring forth grass, the herb yielding seed, and the fruit tree yielding fruit after his kind, whose seed is in itself, upon the earth": and it was so. And the earth brought forth grass, and herb yielding seed after his kind, and the tree yielding fruit, whose seed was in itself, after his kind: and God saw that it was good. And the evening and the morning were the third day.

And God said, "Let there be lights in the firmament of the heaven to divide the day from the night; and let them be for signs, and for seasons, and for days, and years: And let them be for lights in the firmament of the heaven to give light upon the earth": and it was so. And God made two great lights; the greater light to rule the day, and the lesser light to rule the night: he made the stars also. And God set them in the firmament of the heaven to give light upon the earth, and to rule over the day and over the night, and to divide the light from the darkness: and God saw that it was good. And the evening and the morning were the fourth day.

And God said, "Let the waters bring forth abundantly the moving creature that hath life, and fowl that may fly above the earth in the open firmament of heaven." And God created great whales, and every living creature that moveth, which the waters brought forth abundantly, after their kind, and every winged fowl after his kind: and God saw that it was good. And God blessed them, saying, "Be fruitful, and multiply, and fill the waters in the seas, and let fowl multiply in the earth." And the evening and the morning were the fifth day.

And God said, "Let the earth bring forth the living creature after his kind, cattle, and creeping thing, and beast of the earth after his kind": and it was so. And God made the beast of the earth after his kind, and cattle after their kind, and every thing that creepeth upon the earth after his kind: and God saw that it was good.

And God said, "Let us make man in our image, after our likeness: and let them have dominion[2] over the fish of the sea, and over the fowl of the air, and over the cattle, and over all the earth, and over every creeping thing that creepeth upon the earth." So God created man in his own image, in the image of God created he him; male and female created he them. And God blessed them, and God said unto them, "Be fruitful, and multiply, and replenish[3] the earth, and subdue[4] it: and have dominion over the fish of the sea, and over the fowl of the air, and over every living thing that moveth upon the earth."

And God said, "Behold, I have given you every herb bearing seed, which is upon the face of all

---

1. **firmament** (fėr′mə mənt), *n.* sky.
2. **dominion** (də min′yən), *n.* control.
3. replenish (ri plen′ish), *v.* refill.
4. subdue (səb dü′), *v.* conquer.

the earth, and every tree, in which is the fruit of a tree yielding seed; to you it shall be for meat. And to every beast of the earth, and to every fowl of the air, and to every thing that creepeth upon the earth, wherein there is life, I have given every green herb for meat": and it was so.

And God saw every thing that he had made, and behold, it was very good. And the evening and the morning were the sixth day.

Chapter 2

Thus the heavens and the earth were finished, and all the host of them. And on the seventh day God ended his work which he had made; and he rested on the seventh day from all his work which he had made. And God blessed the seventh day, and sanctified[5] it: because that in it he had rested from all his work which God created and made.

These are the generations of the heavens and of the earth when they were created, in the day that the Lord God made the earth, and the Heavens, and every plant of the field before it was in the earth, and every herb of the field before it grew: for the Lord God had not caused it to rain upon the earth, and there was not a man to till the ground. But there went up a mist from the earth, and watered the whole face of the ground. And the Lord God formed man of the dust of the ground, and breathed into his nostrils the breath of life; and man became a living soul.

And the Lord God planted a garden eastward in Eden; and there he put the man whom he had formed. And out of the ground made the Lord God to grow every tree that is pleasant to the sight, and good for food; the tree of life also in the midst of the garden, and the tree of knowledge of good and evil. . . .

And the Lord God took the man, and put him into the garden of Eden to dress it and to keep it. And the Lord God commanded the man, saying, "Of every tree of the garden thou mayest freely eat: But of the tree of knowledge of good and evil, thou shalt not eat of it: for in the day that thou eatest thereof thou shalt surely die."

And the Lord God said, "It is not good that the man should be alone; I will make him a help meet for him." And out of the ground the Lord God formed every beast of the field, and every fowl of the air, and to every beast of the field; but for Adam there was not found a help meet for him.

And the Lord God caused a deep sleep to fall upon Adam, and he slept: and he took one of his ribs, and closed up the flesh instead thereof; and the rib, which the Lord God had taken from man, made he a woman, and brought her unto the man.

And Adam said, "This is now bone of my bones, and flesh of my flesh; and she shall be called Woman, because she was taken out of Man."

Therefore shall a man leave his father and his mother, and shall cleave unto his wife: and they shall be one flesh. And they were both naked, the man and his wife, and were not ashamed.

Chapter 3

Now the serpent was more subtle than any beast of the field which the Lord God had made. And he said unto the woman, "Yea, hath God said, 'Ye shall not eat of every tree of the garden'?"

And the woman said unto the serpent, "We may eat of the fruit of the trees of the garden: but of the fruit of the tree which is in the midst of the garden, God hath said, 'Ye shall not eat of it, neither shall ye touch it, lest ye die.' "

And the serpent said unto the woman, "Ye shall not surely die: for God doth know that in the day ye eat thereof, then your eyes shall be opened, and ye shall be as gods, knowing good and evil."

EVALUATE: Is the serpent using his ability to communicate in order to trick Adam and Eve?

---

5. **sanctify** (sangk′tə fī), *v.* make holy.

And when the woman saw that the tree was good for food, and that it was pleasant to the eyes, and a tree to be desired to make one wise, she took of the fruit thereof, and did eat, and gave also unto her husband with her; and he did eat. And the eyes of them both were opened, and they knew that they were naked; and they sewed fig leaves together, and made themselves aprons.

And they heard the voice of the Lord God walking in the garden in the cool of the day: and Adam and his wife hid themselves from the presence of the Lord God amongst the trees of the garden.

And the Lord God called unto Adam, and said unto him, "Where art thou?"

And he said, "I heard thy voice in the garden, and I was afraid, because I was naked; and I hid myself."

And he said, "Who told thee that thou wast naked? Hast thou eaten of the tree, whereof I commanded thee that thou shouldest not eat?"

And the man said, "The woman whom thou gavest to be with me, she gave me of the tree, and I did eat."

And the Lord God said unto the woman, "What is this that thou hast done?" And the woman said, "The serpent beguiled[6] me, and I did eat."

And the Lord God said unto the serpent, "Because thou hast done this, thou art cursed above all cattle, and above every beast of the field, upon thy belly shalt thou go, and dust shalt thou eat all the days of thy life: and I will put enmity[7] between thee and the woman, and between thy seed and her seed; it shall bruise thy head, and thou shalt bruise his heel."

Unto the woman he said, "I will greatly multiply thy sorrow and thy conception; in sorrow thou shalt bring forth children; and thy desire shall be to thy husband, and he shall rule over thee."

And to Adam he said, "Because thou hast hearkened unto the voice of thy wife, and hast eaten of the tree, of which I commanded thee, saying, 'Thou shalt not eat of it': cursed is the ground for thy sake; in sorrow shalt thou eat of it all the days of thy life; thorns also and thistles shall it bring forth to thee; and thou shalt eat the herb of the field, in the sweat of thy face shalt thou eat bread, till thou return unto the ground; for out of it wast thou taken; for dust thou art, and unto dust shalt thou return."

And Adam called his wife's name Eve; because she was the mother of all living. Unto Adam also and to his wife did the Lord God make coats of skins, and clothed them.

And the Lord God said, "Behold, the man is become as one of us, to know good and evil: and now, lest he put forth his hand, and take also of the tree of life, and eat, and live for ever": therefore the Lord God sent him forth from the garden of Eden, to till the ground from whence he was taken. So he drove out the man; and he placed at the east of the garden of Eden Cherubim,[8] and a flaming sword which turned every way, to keep the way of the tree of life.

---

6. beguile (bi gīl′), v. trick.
7. enmity (en′mə tē), n. hatred.
8. cherubim (cher′ə bim), n. angels.

The Twenty-third Psalm

There have been many translations of the Bible. Judge the achievement of the King James version by comparing it with some other translations. Here are four versions of the Twenty-third Psalm (säm), a sacred song or poem—the King James translation, one published before it, and two versions published later.

The Great Bible (1539)

The Lord is my shepherd; therefore can I lack nothing. He shall feed me in a green pasture, and lead me forth beside the waters of comfort. He shall convert my soul, and bring me forth in the paths of righteousness for his name's sake. Yea, though I walk through the valley of the shadow of death, I will fear no evil, for thou art with me. Thy rod and thy staff comfort me. Thou shalt prepare a table before me against them that trouble me; thou has anointed my head with oil, and my cup shall be full. But thy loving-kindness and mercy shall follow me all the days of my life and I will dwell in the house of the Lord forever.

The King James Bible (1611)

The Lord is my shepherd; I shall not want.
He maketh me to lie down in green pastures:
   he leadeth me beside the still waters.
He restoreth my soul: he leadeth me in the
5   paths of righteousness for his name's sake.
Yea, though I walk through the valley of the
   shadow of death, I will fear no evil: for thou
   art with me; thy rod and thy staff they
   comfort me.
10 Thou preparest a table before me in the
   presence of mine enemies: thou anointest
   my head with oil; my cup runneth over.
Surely goodness and mercy shall follow me all
   the days of my life: and I will dwell in the
15   house of the Lord forever.

The Bay Psalm Book (1640)

The Lord to me a shepherd is,
    want therefore shall not I.
He in the folds of tender grass,
    doth cause me down to lie:
5 To waters calm me gently leads,
    restore my soul doth he:
He doth in paths of righteousness
    for his name's sake lead me.
Yea though in valley of death's shade
10   I walk, none ill I'll fear:
Because thou art with me, thy rod
    and staff my comfort are.
For me a table thou hast spread,
    in presence of my foes:
15 Thou dost anoint my head with oil,
    my cup it overflows.
Goodness and mercy surely shall
    all my days follow me:
And in the Lord's house I shall dwell
20   so long as days shall be.

These two paintings of Shepherds with their flocks are from medieval illuminated manuscripts. Why do you think such a common image was used by the writer of the Twenty-third Psalm as a metaphor for God?

The New English Bible (1970)

The Lord is my shepherd; I shall want nothing.
    He makes me lie down in green pastures,
and leads me beside the waters of peace;
    he renews life within me,
5 and for his name's sake guides me in the right path.
Even though I walk through a valley dark as death
I fear no evil, for thou art with me,
thy staff and thy crook are my comfort.

Thou spreadest a table for me in the sight of
10 my enemies;
    thou hast richly bathed my head with oil,
    and my cup runs over.
Goodness and love unfailing, these will
follow me
15   all the days of my life,
    and I shall dwell in the house of the Lord
    my whole life long.

After Reading

Making Connections

Shaping Your
Response

1. Do you feel sympathy for Adam and Eve in the story? Why or why not?

2. Which version of the Twenty-third Psalm do you prefer? Why?

Analyzing the
Selections

3. What do you think God means by saying that the lights in the firmament can be "for signs, and for seasons, and for days, and years."?

4. Why do you suppose God gives man dominion over all of the animals on earth?

5. How and why does the behavior of Adam and Eve change after they have eaten the forbidden fruit?

6. Do the particular punishments God inflicts upon Eve, Adam, and the serpent seem appropriate? Explain.

Extending the Ideas

7. All cultures of the world **communicate** from generation to generation their versions of how the world—along with its people and animals—was created. Share with the class some stories you have heard.

Literary Focus: Style

Style is not what is said, but *how* it is said. The authors of the King James Bible use a style that is simple and straightforward, yet elegant and dignified. Review the first three chapters of Genesis, noting the following elements of style. Find and write down other examples of these style elements.

Style Element	Example	Further Examples
Use of *and* to begin sentences	"And God said . . . ."	
Use of repetition	". . . and God saw that it was good."	
Use of parallel structure	". . . the greater light to rule the day, and the lesser light to rule the night."	

Vocabulary Study

Select the letter of the situation that best demonstrates the meaning of the numbered word.

1. enmity
   a. a teenager getting ready for her first date
   b. a politician addressing the voters
   c. a soldier confronting the opposition on the battlefield

2. replenish
   a. a stock boy putting merchandise on empty shelves
   b. a farmer harvesting his fields
   c. a zookeeper cleaning animal cages

3. beguile
   a. a beggar with his hand out
   b. a guide leading a tour group
   c. a salesman selling worthless land

4. sanctify
   a. a scholar studying in a quiet place
   b. a minister blessing a marriage
   c. a teacher approving a theme topic

5. subdue
   a. a debtor paying a bill
   b. an army gaining control over new territory
   c. an employee giving a suggestion to the boss

Expressing Your Ideas

Writing Choices

Writer's Notebook Update How does your list of descriptive words about the Garden of Eden compare with the picture created in Genesis? What words can you add to your list? Using some of the words on your list, write your own paragraph describing the Garden of Eden.

Advise Adam and Eve At the end of Genesis, Chapter 3, Adam and Eve have been banished by God from the Garden of Eden. They are ready to enter the world. Write a **letter of advice** to Adam and Eve, telling them what they should expect and how they can best survive in this new, unfamiliar world.

Illuminate the Text During the Middle Ages monks copied out texts by hand, often adding fanciful capital letters (see pages 46 and 79) and illustrations of daily life or of their notions of biblical times (see pages 56, 74, and 272–273). Create your own **illuminated manuscript** by copying out your favorite version of the Twenty-third Psalm—perhaps on poster-sized cardboard. Add whatever capital letters and illustrations you please, and perhaps some fancy borders or curlicues.

Other Option

Stage a Children's Play Choose another story from the Bible. (Your teacher may be able to suggest some possiblilites.) Working with a small group, write a dramatic version of this story suitable for presentation to young children. If possible, stage your **play** for a grade school class.

The Fall From Grace

Heaven, Hell, and Paradise

Humanities Connection

The existence of other worlds than ours has always occupied the human imagination. Some of these imaginings were of heavenly realms of light and joy; others were of infernal regions of darkness and horror. The following pages offer some glimpses of heaven, hell, and paradise.

The Peach-Blossom Fountain

T'ao Ch'ien, translated by Herbert Giles

Towards the close of the fourth century A.D., a certain fisherman of Wu-ling, who had followed up one of the river branches without taking note whither he was going, came suddenly upon a grove of peach trees[1] in full bloom, extending some distance on each bank, with not a tree of any other kind in sight. The beauty of the scene and the exquisite perfume of the flowers filled the heart of the fisherman with surprise, as he proceeded onwards, anxious to reach the limit of this lovely grove. He found that the peach trees ended where the water began, at the foot of a hill; and there he espied what seemed to be a cave with light issuing from it. So he made fast his boat, and crept in through a narrow entrance, which shortly ushered him into a new world of level country, of fine houses, of rich fields, of fine pools, and of luxuriance of mulberry and bamboo. Highways of traffic ran north and south;

sounds of crowing cocks and barking dogs were heard around; the dress of the people who passed along or were at work in the fields was of a strange cut; while young and old alike appeared to be contented and happy.

One of the inhabitants, catching sight of the fisherman, was greatly astonished; but, after learning whence he came, insisted on carrying him home, and killed a chicken and placed some wine before him. Before long, all the people of the place had turned out to see the visitor, and they informed him that their ancestors had sought refuge here, with their wives and families, from the troublous times of the house of Ch'in[2] adding that they had thus become finally cut off from the rest of the human race. They then enquired about the politics of the day, ignorant of the establishment of the Han dynasty[3] and of course of the

---

1. **peach trees**, symbols of immortality in Chinese tradition.
2. **Ch'in**, or **Qin** (chin), short-lived dynasty that ruled China at the end of the third century B.C.
3. **Han dynasty**, one of the greatest Chinese dynasties, ruling from 202 B.C. to A.D. 220; successors of the Qin.

The Earthly Paradise

Sir John Mandeville (1300s)

Of Paradise I cannot speak properly, for I have not been there; and that I regret. But I shall tell you as much as I have heard from wise men . . . . The Earthly Paradise, so men say, is the highest land on earth; it is so high it touches the sphere of the moon. For it is so high that Noah's flood could not reach it, though it covered all the rest of the earth. Paradise is encircled by a wall; but no man can say what the wall is made of. It is grown all over with moss and bushes so that no stone can be seen, nor anything else a wall might be made of. The wall of Paradise stretches from the south to the north; there is no way into it open because of ever burning fire, which is the flaming sword that God set up before the entrance so that no man should enter.

  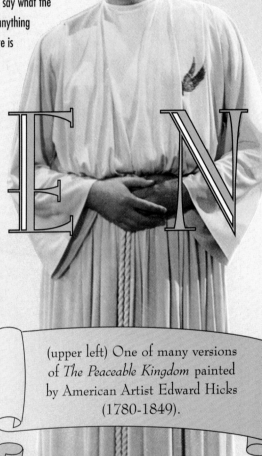

AVEN

later dynasties which had succeeded it. And when the fisherman told them the story, they grieved over the vicissitudes of human affairs.

Each in turn invited the fisherman to his home and entertained him hospitably, until at length the latter prepared to take his leave. "It will not be worth while to talk about what you have seen to the outside world," said the people of the place to the fisherman, as he bade them farewell and returned to his boat, making mental notes of his route as he proceeded on his homeward voyage.

When he reached home, he at once went and reported what he had seen to the Governor of the district, and the Governor sent off men with him to seek, by the aid of the fisherman's notes, to discover this unknown region. But he was never able to find it again. Subsequently, another desperate attempt was made by a famous adventurer to pierce the mystery; but he also failed, and died soon afterwards of chagrin, from which time forth no further attempts were made.

(upper left) One of many versions of *The Peaceable Kingdom* painted by American Artist Edward Hicks (1780-1849).

Jack Benny plays an angel with the unpleasant assignment of signaling the end of the world in the 1945 movie *The Horn Blows at Midnight.*

HELL

FROM THE INFERNO

DANTE ALIGHIERI (1312)

I AM THE WAY INTO THE CITY OF WOE.
I AM THE WAY TO A FORSAKEN PEOPLE.
I AM THE WAY INTO ETERNAL SORROW.

SACRED JUSTICE MOVED MY ARCHITECT.
I WAS RAISED HERE BY DIVINE OMNIPOTENCE.
PRIMORDIAL LOVE AND ULTIMATE INTELLECT.

ONLY THOSE ELEMENTS TIME CANNOT WEAR
WERE MADE BEFORE ME, AND BEYOND TIME I STAND.
ABANDON ALL HOPE YE WHO ENTER HERE.

Wax figures from the 1600s of the Blessed
(right) and Damned (left).

YE WHO ENTER HERE

Three versions of Hell: (above) the Gate of Hell from illustrations for Dante's *Inferno* by William Blake; (below) *The Triumph of Death* by Pieter Bruegel the Elder; (right) a cartoon by Gary Larson.

Postcard from Paradise

by Cris Williamson

A dream of how things might have changed if Columbus had jumped ship on the island of Guanahani, chosen the Arawak people as his own, and burned all existing maps to the new world.

This is a Postcard from Paradise. . .a Postcard from Paradise. . .
This is a Postcard from Paradise

I had a dream. . . it was 1492. . .
In the name of the King and Queen
Columbus sailed the ocean blue
And when he saw a light from the deck of the Little Girl
He spoke into the night, "This is a brand new world!"
With the next day's dawning, he could not believe his eyes;
His crew was up and yawning, and he said,
   "Boys, this is Paradise!"
     "And I am going over. . .
     And I am going it alone;
     Tell them Christopher Columbus
     Is never, ever coming home."

Chorus:
    This is a Postcard from Paradise
    This place is so damn nice!
    Hello, Ferdinand! Hello Isabel!
    I'm lying in the sand, and I never felt so well;
    There is no gold here, no silver in the mine;
    It's never cold here, and the weather suits me fine!
    This is a Postcard from Paradise. . .
       a Postcard from Paradise. . .
    This is a Postcard from Paradise.

And in my dream, Colon became the Dove . . .
Folding his sea-blue wings into the open arms of love;
Coming through the seas that rolled, breaking silver on the shore
Where the sunlight shines like gold,
Columbus changed forever more.
Good-by, Columbus . . .
The map is burning in your hand;
And not one among us knows the way to the Promised Land.
    La Querencia . . .
    I swear by the Holy Sea! (See?)
    These are my new friends. . . this is my new home,
    Island Guanahani.
And the caravels turned around,
Sailing back to the King and Queen,
And Paradise was never found . . .
In my dream . . .oh, what a dream!

[Repeat chorus]

Responding

1. Describe other versions of either Heaven or Hell that you have heard about.

2. If Heaven were to contain any elements of earthly pleasure, which would you choose for yourself as an everlasting reward?

3. If Hell were to contain any elements of earthly torment, which do you imagine they might be?

Language History

The Language of the King James Bible

 And the Lord God formed man of the dust of the ground, and breathed into his nostrils the breath of life; and man became a living soul.

Genesis 2:7

This eloquent passage, taken from the book of Genesis in the King James Bible, illustrates why that work has been called "the noblest monument of English prose." The sheer brilliance of its language makes the King James version deserving of that epithet. In contrast to the ornamental style characteristic of some prose in the early 1600s, the King James version preserves the old language and plain style of the earlier English versions of the Bible. Its extensive use of concrete terms and images, its straightforward phrases and sentences, its balance and parallelism in many passages—all make for a dignified simplicity most compatible with religious feeling and ritual.

The profound impact of the King James Bible can be seen in the work of a multitude of writers and speakers, who—generation after generation—have been deeply influenced by the plain, yet poetic, language and style of the King James version. Abraham Lincoln, for example, used the language of the King James Bible in this sentence from a famous speech about slavery: "A house divided against itself cannot stand." Many phrases and expressions commonly used in everyday speech also have their origins in the King James Bible—for example, *the salt of the earth; a sign of the times; the apple of my eye; a thorn in the flesh; all is vanity;* and *to everything there is a season*. Still widely read and quoted nearly four hundred years after its first printing, the King James Bible has had a unique influence not only on religious thought but on English language and literature as well.

Writing Workshop

A Landscape of Symbols

Assignment In *Paradise Lost*, Milton uses vivid imagery to describe the landscape to which Satan has been banished, a landscape meant to symbolize Satan's character. Write an essay in which you interpret the landscape of Hell as symbolic of Satan's character.

WRITER'S BLUEPRINT

Product   An interpretive essay

Purpose   To analyze symbols in literature

Audience   People who have read *Paradise Lost*

Specs   As the writer of a successful essay, you should:

❏ Begin in a dramatic way to engage the reader.

❏ Present your conclusions about the symbolic relationships between landscape and character. Back up these conclusions with evidence from the poem, including direct quotations.

❏ End by drawing your separate conclusions together into a paragraph that restates them with a fresh emphasis.

❏ Include any visuals—sketches, diagrams, maps—that will liven up or clarify your conclusions.

❏ Use parallel structure for emphasis and clarity.

❏ Follow the rules of grammar, usage, spelling, and mechanics. Pay special attention to forms of adjectives and adverbs.

Interpret a familiar landscape. Practice interpreting a familiar landscape before you work with Milton's. Visualize a room that's familiar to you, your own or someone's close to you. Make a list of objects in the room that say something important about the person who lives there.

Create a sketch. To help you visualize Milton's landscape, use colored pencils or markers to sketch the landscape described in the poem. On the back of your landscape, explain at least two ways you have represented the symbolic relationship between Satan and his landscape.

Chart the symbolic relationships in *Paradise Lost.* With a partner, search Milton's poem for quotations that show relationships between aspects of Satan's character and the landscape of Hell.

Character Elements (Satan)	Landscape Elements (Hell)
inability to see truth and goodness	"As one great furnace flamed, yet from those flames/No light, but rather darkness visible. . . ." (lines 62–63)

Plan your essay. Organize your ideas in a plan similar to the one that follows.

Introduction
- Dramatic quote or strong statement (to engage the reader)

Body
- First conclusion (an element from the landscape and how it symbolizes an aspect of Satan's character)
  Evidence from poem
- Second conclusion
  Evidence from poem
  and so on . . .

Conclusion
- Summary of conclusions from body
- Fresh emphasis on Satan and landscape of Hell

Visuals
- Sketches or other graphics to include

OR . . .
Before you make your sketch, do research to see how various artists have illustrated *Paradise Lost* since Milton's time. See the interdisciplinary study on Heaven and Hell beginning on page 278.

LITERARY SOURCE

"A dungeon horrible, on all sides round
As one great furnace flamed, yet from those flames
No light, but rather darkness visible. . . ."
from *Paradise Lost* by John Milton

OR . . .
Organize the body of your essay in a different way. First present evidence from the poem to support your conclusions, and then state the conclusions themselves.

Ask a partner to review your plan.

✔ Have I come up with strong conclusions, supported by evidence from the poem, to show the relationship between landscape and character?

✔ Are my conclusions restated at the end of my paper in a fresh and emphatic way?

✔ Am I following the Specs in the Writer's Blueprint?

Use your partner's comments to help you revise your plan.

STEP 2 DRAFTING

Before you write, review the Writer's Blueprint, your character and landscape chart, visual representations, and writing plan.

As you draft, don't spend time correcting mistakes in spelling and punctuation. Concentrate on getting your ideas on the page. Consider these suggestions.

• Instead of writing your essay in your own voice, consider writing it from the point of view of an eyewitness visiting Milton's version of Hell, or as Satan himself. If you write as Satan, be sure to have him interpret the landscape from a point of view that is favorable to himself.

• Use parallel structure to emphasize and clarify the points you make. (See the Revising Strategy in Step 3 of this lesson.)

STEP 3 REVISING

COMPUTER TIP
Save the revised version of your essay in a new file with a new name. This allows you to compare the two versions, or even incorporate something from the first draft back into the revised version.

Ask a partner for comments on your draft before you revise it.

✔ Have I concentrated on the relationship between Satan and the landscape of Hell?

✔ Have I supported my conclusions with examples from the poem?

✔ Have I used parallel structure for emphasis and clarity?

Revising Strategy

Using Parallel Structure

Sentences with parallel structure use the same grammatical form to express similar ideas of equal importance. Parallel structure creates balance and rhythm within paragraphs and within individual sentences. It is essential when you list items in a series. Read these two sentences aloud to hear how much smoother the revised, parallel version is.

Not Parallel: Milton believed that the Christian religion was a matter involving God, the Bible, and to include the individual human being. (two nouns and a phrase)

Parallel: Milton believed that the Christian religion was a matter involving God, the Bible, and the individual human being. (three nouns)

When you revise, read your draft aloud to yourself. When a sentence sounds awkward, check it with the idea of parallel structure in mind. See the student model that follows.

> Satan must be in control at all times. His thirst for power can only be quenched in a setting where his power is able to grow *contradiction* without challenge, complication, or ~~is ever contradicted in any way~~.
>
> He must realize his goal "To set himself in glory among his peers." (line 39). In order to succeed at this he must be in control of a place "as far removed from God and light of Heaven / As from the center thrice to the utmost pole." (lines 73–74)

STUDENT MODEL

STEP 4 EDITING

Ask a partner to review your revised draft before you edit. As you edit, look for errors in grammar, usage, spelling, and mechanics. Look especially for problems with forms of adjectives and adverbs.

Editing Strategy

FOR REFERENCE
Look for more information about forms of adjectives and adverbs in the Language and Grammar Handbook at the back of this text.

Using Adjectives and Adverbs Correctly

When you edit, take care to see that you've formed the comparative and superlative forms of adjectives and adverbs correctly. Most of the time, use -er or -est: holier, quicker, yellowest, soonest.

For some longer words, use *more* or *most* instead: more corrupt, most carelessly.

Never use *more* and -er or *most* and -est together. Write *more dangerous,* not *more dangerouser.* Write *latest,* not *most latest.*

STEP 5 PRESENTING

- Have a read around. In a small group, pass your essays around until everyone has read each one. Use your essays as the basis for a round-table discussion on the subject of symbols in literature.

- If another class has read and written about *Paradise Lost*, exchange papers with them. Get together and compare ideas.

STEP 6 LOOKING BACK

Self-evaluate. What grade would *you* give your essay? Look back at the Writer's Blueprint and give yourself a score for each item, from 6 (superior) to 1 (inadequate).

Reflect. Think about what you've learned while writing this essay.

✔ Write a note to your teacher describing how you developed your essay. What prewriting and planning activities helped you most? Attach this note to your essay when you hand it in.

✔ Look at the various drafts of your paper. What are three major improvements you made in the final version?

For Your Working Portfolio Add your essay and your reflection responses to your working portfolio.

The Fall from Grace

Technology

Beyond Print

Basic Word Processing

Some people don't take full advantage of word processing, possibly because they're not yet familiar enough with it. Here are some pointers on using this powerful tool to create your documents.

Compose at the keyboard. Many people still use pen and paper to write and then retype it. However, as your keyboarding skills improve you should be able to eliminate using a pen and compose your entire document using only the word processor.

Don't worry about mistakes. Since editing text is so simple on the computer, let yourself go and *just write!* You can always go back and fix your mistakes later.

Learn the capabilities. Every time you use your word processor, try a different tool or function. Learn to perform a spelling check or grammar check, center headings, insert page numbers, create footnotes or endnotes, create charts or graphs.

Use the available tools. But don't use them blindly. The spelling checker is a marvelous help; however, don't forget that it only checks spelling, not usage. Always proofread your documents.

Save your documents. Power outages and system errors can cause the computer to lose hours worth of writing, so get into the habit of saving often. A good rule of thumb is to save after every paragraph.

Limit the number of fonts. Generally, more than three fonts in the same document become confusing to read. Serif fonts like Times, Bookman, or Palatino are easier to read in the body of a document, while sans-serif fonts like Helvetica make nice headings and titles. Use special font styles like outline, shadow, bold, and italic sparingly.

<u>Fonts</u>
Times
Bookman
Palatino
Helvetica

<u>Styles</u>
outline
shadow
bold
italic

Activity Options

1. Start by brainstorming essay ideas on the screen. Print out this list.

2. Open a new document and create an outline. Print it out.

3. Compose your essay on screen, using the outline as a guide.

Multicultural Connections

Perspectives

Part One: The Meaning of Life The relative shortness and difficulty of life in the 1600s undoubtedly contributed toward the unique perspective of *carpe diem* ("seize the day") literature, a perspective that John Donne, Robert Herrick, Andrew Marvell, and hundreds of other writers have communicated over the centuries. The same short-ness and difficulty may lead to other perspectives as well, such as Donne's declaration that "no man is an island," that we are all a part of each other and responsible for each other.

■ Which of the selections in this part do you feel does the best job of communicating a particular perspective?

Communication

Part Two: The Fall from Grace The religious faith of Christianity is in itself a unique perspective, but it is one that has been susceptible to various interpretations at various times, depending on how its tenets have been communicated, by whom and to whom. Although both *Paradise Lost* and the King James Bible are landmarks in Christian lit-erature, both were the products of a particular time and place, and both reflect the perspectives of their creators.

■ When a writer undertakes to communicate a particular perspective, or to create a narrative that dramatizes that perspective, how much individuality do you think that writer can—or should be allowed to—put into his or her work?

Activities

1. Find examples of *carpe diem* writings from other periods of history, for example in song lyrics of the 1900s (such as "You'd Better Stop and Smell the Roses" or "It's Today" from the musical *Mame*).

2. Research creation stories from some other religions. Each group member can research a different religion and then give a brief oral summary to the group or to the whole class.

3. Develop a skit that illustrates the concept that no man is an island. Your skit should run about 10 minutes. You can use any place and any time in history as a setting. Rehearse and present it in reader's theater format—with scripts in hand—to the class.

Independent and Group Projects

Music

Perform a Poem Hundreds of seventeenth-century poems have been set to music by composers of their day or by later composers. Find and listen to a recording of a musical setting for one or two poems, or compose music for one of the poems in this unit and perform the song for the class. Your composition can be in a modern or traditional idiom.

Media

Defining the Age What is your general impression of the seventeenth century, its people, and its literature? Do some further research on the political or social history of the era or on a seventeenth century author and his writing. Use a multimedia computer program or a video camera to prepare a documentary that explains your subject to a new audience of your classmates. Use any kinds of graphics, music, and sound effects you think appropriate.

Panel Discussion

What Is Sin? Milton and other writers of the period often pondered the nature of sin and evil. Topics such as the widespread presence of evil in the world, possible reasons for sin, and the notion that humans are becoming more and more evil are troubling ones. Although there may be no definitive explanations, you might at least come close to demonstrating what evil is or what it does. Organize a panel discussion in your class. If possible, include people from a variety of cultures. Make certain that there are guidelines to assure that everyone's beliefs will be heard respectfully.

Art

Rebus Verse Seventeenth century writers loved word play and elaborate conceits. A rebus is a game in which pictures substitute for syllables, words, or phrases. For example, a rebus for the first line of Donne's "Song" might be: Go and [picture of a catcher's mitt] a falling [picture of a star]. Devise a rebus for the rest of "Song" or for another poem of your choosing and display it on a bulletin board.

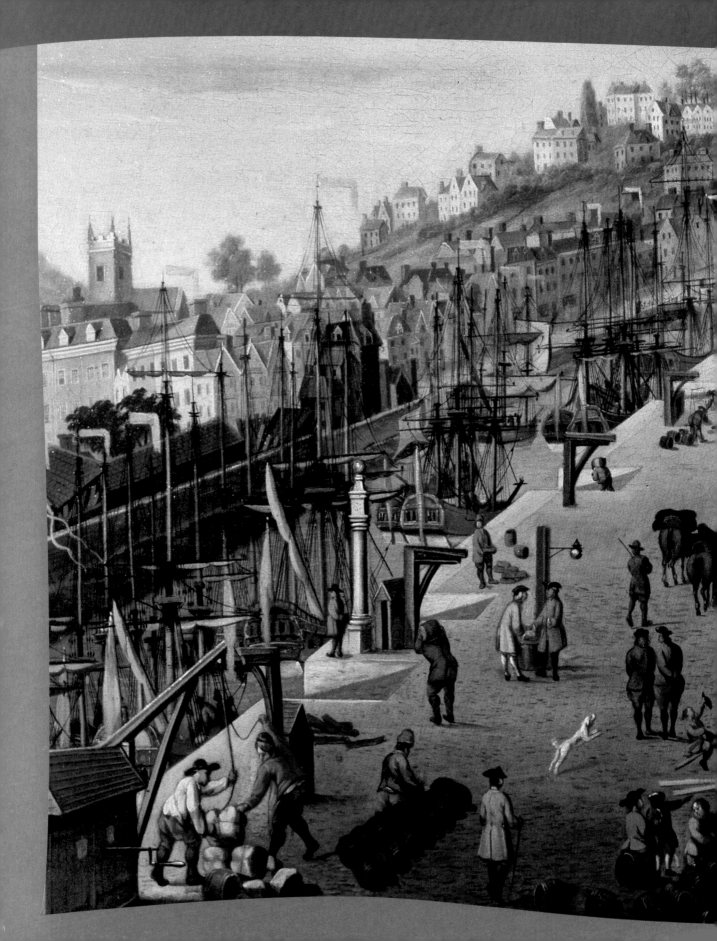

The Age of Reason

A Focus on Society

Other People's Lives

THEMES IN ENGLISH LITERATURE

London

THE PEOPLE

HISTORICAL OVERVIEW

In England, and particularly in London, the huge inequality in the distribution of wealth created shocking contrasts. In the streets the silks and brocades and powdered wigs, the gilded coaches and sedan chairs of the rich moved against a background of rags, filth, stench, and crime. Men and women of fashion went to plays at Drury Lane Theatre or sipped wine and watched fireworks at Vauxhall Gardens, while thousands of men, women, and children lived in dire poverty. For most English people the uncertainty of life was grim. As Samuel Johnson, who had risen from the life of an impoverished hack-writer to that of a celebrated man of letters, knew from experience, "He that sees before him to his third dinner, has a long prospect." In a climate of gross injustice like this, satire flourished.

ON THE STREETS

In this illustration, the broad range of English society is represented by different types of people that might have been observed in the London streets of the 1700s.

Key Dates

1652
The first coffeehouse opens in London.

1660
The monarchy is restored under Charles II.

1660
The theaters reopen.

1662
The Royal Society is founded to encourage scientific research.

1665
The plague kills 70,000 in London.

1666
The Great Fire of London occurs.

1688
The Glorious Revolution creates a limited monarchy.

1710
St. Paul's Cathedral is completed.

1755
Johnson's Dictionary is published.

Part One

A Focus on Society

In an age when scientists, astronomers, and navigators were using their newly developed instruments to focus on the microscopic world or on the heavens, writers were using their intelligence and their wit to focus on the society in which they lived. What they saw sometimes moved them to anger or righteous indignation. Sometimes it moved them to laughter.

 Multicultural Connection **Interactions** refer to encounters between people of diverse cultural backgrounds. The results may be varied: confusion, conflict, attempts to shut out or welcome in. Sometimes when people see things they don't like in other people they try to change those things; sometimes they simply scorn them. What different cultural notions do people in the following selections bring to their various encounters?

Before Reading

A Modest Proposal

by Jonathan Swift

Jonathan Swift
1667–1745

Swift summed up his own life: "Perhaps I may allow, the Dean / Had too much satire in his veins / And seemed determined not to starve it, / Because no age could more deserve it." He was born in Dublin, Ireland. After receiving a degree at Trinity College, he served for some years as secretary to Sir William Temple, a writer and diplomat. Ordained an Anglican priest, in 1713 he was made Dean of St. Patrick's Cathedral in Dublin, a great disappointment to him, for he had been hoping to receive a church in England. He was known as England's greatest prose satirist, although much of his work was published anonymously. His most famous work, *Gulliver's Travels,* was published in 1726 and became a best seller.

Building Background

The Evils of Tyranny In Swift's time, Ireland was ruled by England, and absentee English landlords collected all the revenues while making few improvements to the land. According to Swift, Ireland was "a bare face of nature, without houses or plantations; filthy cabins, miserable, tattered, half-starved creatures, scarce in human shape; one insolent, ignorant, oppressive squire [chief landowner in a district] to be found in twenty miles riding; a parish church to be found only in a summer day's journey; a bog of fifteen miles round; every meadow a slough [swamp], and every hill a mixture of rock, heath, and marsh. . . . There is not an acre of land in Ireland turned to half its advantage, yet it is better improved than the people; and all these evils are effects of English tyranny." In "A Modest Proposal," Swift pretends to be a "projector," an expert planner, who has a scheme to solve Ireland's problems.

Literary Focus

Satire Gentle or bitter, **satire** is the use of irony, sarcasm, or wit to expose a human weakness or social evil, usually with the purpose of inspiring reform. The title of Swift's essay is an example of *irony* since, as you will see, his proposal is not modest at all. *Sarcasm* is the use of language to hurt or ridicule; for example, Swift says he doesn't want to hear of any other solutions until there is "at least some glimpse of hope that there will ever be some hearty and sincere attempt to put them in practice." *Wit* is the power to express cleverly ideas that are unusual, striking, or amusing. As you read "A Modest Proposal," look for unusual ideas and examples of irony and sarcasm, and then decide whether Swift's satire is effective.

Writer's Notebook

Skewering with the Pen Swift was kind to people in trouble or in need, but he scorned those who were boring, stupid, lazy, or corrupt. Although he felt that no times deserved satire more than the age in which he lived, would he alter that view if he could observe today's society? What types of people or political situations today are ripe for satire? Jot down some ideas in your notebook.

A Modest PROPOSAL

FOR PREVENTING THE CHILDREN OF POOR PEOPLE IN IRELAND FROM BEING A BURDEN TO THEIR PARENTS OR COUNTRY, AND FOR MAKING THEM BENEFICIAL TO THE PUBLIC

Jonathan Swift

It is a melancholy object to those who walk through this great town,[1] or travel in the country, when they see the streets, the roads, and cabin doors crowded with beggars of the female sex, followed by three, four, or six children, all in rags, and importuning[2] every passenger for an alms. These mothers, instead of being able to work for their honest livelihood, are forced to employ all their time in strolling to beg sustenance[3] for their helpless infants—who, as they grow up, either turn thieves for want of work, or leave their dear native country in flight for the Pretender[4] in Spain, or sell themselves to the Barbados.[5]

I think it is agreed by all parties that this prodigious number of children in the arms, or on the backs, or at the heels of their mothers, and frequently of their fathers, is, in the present deplorable state of the kingdom, a very great additional grievance; and therefore whoever could find out a fair, cheap, and easy method of making these children sound and useful members of the commonwealth would deserve so well of the public as to have his statue set up for a preserver of the nation.

But my intention is very far from being confined to provide only for the children of professed beggars: it is of a much greater extent and shall take in the whole number of infants at a certain age who are born of parents in effect as little able to support them as those who demand our charity in the streets.

As to my own part, having turned my thoughts for many years upon this important subject and maturely weighed the several schemes of other projectors, I have always found them grossly mistaken in their computation. It is true, a child just dropped from its dam may be supported by her milk for a solar year

---

1. **this great town,** Dublin, Ireland.
2. **importune** (im′pôr tün′), *v.* ask urgently; beg.
3. **sustenance** (sus′tə nəns), *n.* support; means of living.
4. **the Pretender,** James Stuart (1688–1766), son of King James II and "pretender," or claimant, to the throne. He was Catholic, and Ireland was loyal to him.
5. **sell . . . Barbados.** Many poverty-stricken Irish "sold" themselves to work for a specified number of years in the West Indies or other British possessions in exchange for boat fare across the Atlantic.

with little other nourishment: at most, not above the value of two shillings, which the mother may certainly get, or the value in scraps, by her lawful occupation of begging; and it is exactly at one year old that I propose to provide for them in such a manner, as, instead of being a charge upon their parents or the parish, or wanting food and raiment[6] for the rest of their lives, they shall, on the contrary, contribute to the feeding, and partly to the clothing, of many thousands.

There is likewise another great advantage in my scheme: that it will prevent those voluntary abortions and that horrid practice of women murdering their bastard children, alas!, too fre-quent among us, sacrificing the poor innocent babes, I doubt more to avoid the expense than the shame, which would move tears and pity in the most savage and inhuman breast.

The number of souls in this kingdom being usually reckoned one million and a half, of these I calculate there may be about two hundred thousand couple whose wives are breeders; from which number I subtract thirty thousand couple who are able to maintain their own children (although I apprehend there cannot be so many, under the present distresses of the kingdom); but this being granted, there will remain

6. raiment (rā′mənt), n. clothing.

▲ In *The Vagrants* (1868), Frederick Walker depicts the harsh reality of poverty, as experienced by a family of wanderers. How does Swift use his satiric skills to express his own concern about poverty and injustice? Give at least one example.

an hundred and seventy thousand breeders. I again subtract fifty thousand for those women who miscarry, or whose children die by accident or disease within the year. There only remain a hundred and twenty thousand children of poor parents annually born. The question therefore is: How this number shall be reared and provided for? which, as I have already said, under the present situation of affairs, is utterly impossible by all the methods hitherto proposed. For we can neither employ them in handicraft or agriculture; we neither build houses (I mean in the country) nor cultivate land: they can very seldom pick up a livelihood by stealing until they arrive at six years old, except where they are of towardly[7] parts; although I confess they learn the rudiments[8] much earlier; during which time they can, however, be properly looked upon only as probationers; as I have been informed by a principal gentleman in the county of Cavan, who protested to me that he never knew above one or two instances under the age of six, even in a part of the kingdom so renowned for the quickest proficiency in that art.

I am assured by our merchants that a boy or a girl before twelve years old is no saleable commodity; and even when they come to this age they will not yield above three pounds or three pounds and half-a-crown at most, on the exchange; which cannot turn to account either to the parents or kingdom, the charge of nutriment and rags having been at least four times that value.

I shall now, therefore, humbly propose my own thoughts, which I hope will not be liable to the least objection.

I have been assured by a very knowing American of my acquaintance in London that a young healthy child, well nursed, is, at a year old, a most delicious, nourishing, and wholesome food, whether stewed, roasted, baked, or

> ... A YOUNG HEALTHY CHILD, WELL NURSED, IS, AT A YEAR OLD, A MOST DELICIOUS, NOURISHING, AND WHOLESOME FOOD ....

boiled; and I make no doubt that it will equally serve in a fricassee or a ragout.[9]

I do therefore humbly offer it to public consideration, that of the hundred and twenty thousand children already computed, twenty thousand may be reserved for breed, whereof only one-fourth part to be males; which is more than we allow to sheep, black cattle, or swine; and my reason is that these children are seldom the fruits of marriage, a circumstance not much regarded by our savages; therefore one male will be sufficient to serve four females. That the remaining hundred thousand may, at a year old, be offered in sale to the persons of quality and fortune through the kingdom—always advising the mother to let them suck plentifully in the last month, so as to render them plump and fat for a good table. A child will make two dishes at an entertainment for friends; and when the family dines alone, the fore or hind quarter will make a reasonable dish, and, seasoned with a little pepper or salt, will be very good boiled on the fourth day, especially in winter.

I have reckoned upon a medium that a child just born will weigh twelve pounds, and in a solar year, if tolerably nursed, increases to twenty-eight pounds.

QUESTION: At what point during this essay did you, the reader, begin to question just what Swift was getting at? What questions come to mind?

I grant this food will be somewhat dear, and therefore very proper for landlords, who, as

---

7. **towardly** (tôrd′lē), *adj.* promising; ready to learn.
8. **rudiment** (rü′də mənt), *n.* basic understanding.
9. **ragout** (ra gü′), *n.* a highly seasoned meat stew.

they have already devoured most of the parents, seem to have the best title to the children.

Infants' flesh will be in season throughout the year, but more plentifully in March, and a little before and after: for we are told by a grave author, an eminent French physician,[10] that fish being a prolific diet, there are more children born in Roman Catholic countries about nine months after Lent than at any other season; therefore, reckoning a year after Lent, the markets will be more glutted than usual, because the number of popish infants is at least three to one in this kingdom; and therefore it will have one other collateral[11] advantage, by lessening the number of papists among us.

I have already computed the charge of nursing a beggar's child (in which list I reckon all cottagers, laborers, and four-fifths of the farmers) to be about two shillings per annum, rags included; and I believe no gentleman would repine[12] to give ten shillings for the carcass of a good fat child, which, as I have said, will make four dishes of excellent nutritive meat when he has only some particular friends or his own family to dine with him. Thus the squire will learn to be a good landlord and grow popular among his tenants; the mother will have eight shillings net profit and be fit for work till she produces another child.

Those who are more thrifty (as I must confess the times require) may flay the carcass—the skin of which, artificially[13] dressed, will make admirable gloves for ladies and summer-boots for fine gentlemen.

As to our city of Dublin, shambles[14] may be appointed for this purpose in the most convenient parts of it, and butchers we may be assured will not be wanting; although I rather recommend buying the children alive and dressing them hot from the knife, as we do roasting pigs.

A very worthy person, a true lover of his country, and whose virtues I highly esteem, was lately pleased, in discoursing on this matter, to offer a refinement upon my scheme. He said that many gentlemen of this kingdom, having of late destroyed their deer, he conceived that the want of venison might be well supplied by the bodies of young lads and maidens, not exceeding fourteen years of age, nor under twelve; so great a number of both sexes in every country being now ready to starve for want of work and service; and these to be disposed of by their parents, if alive, or otherwise by their nearest relations. But with due deference to so excellent a friend and so deserving a patriot, I cannot be altogether in his sentiments; for as to the males, my American acquaintance assured me from frequent experience, that their flesh was generally tough and lean, like that of our schoolboys, by continual exercise, and their taste disagreeable; and to fatten them would not answer the charge. Then as to the females, it would, I think, with humble submission, be a loss to the public, because they soon would become breeders themselves; and besides, it is not improbable that some scrupulous people might be apt to censure such a practice (although indeed very unjustly) as a little bordering upon cruelty; which, I confess, has always been with me the strongest objection against any project, how well soever intended.

But in order to justify my friend, he confessed that this expedient was put into his head by the famous Psalmanazar,[15] a native of the island Formosa, who came from thence to London above twenty years ago, and in conversation told my friend that in his country, when any young

---

10. **grave author . . . physician,** Francois Rabelais (1495?–1553), who was not a "grave" (serious) author but a satirical one.
11. **collateral** (kə lat′ər əl), *adj.* secondary; indirect.
12. **repine** (ri pīn′), *v.* fret; complain.
13. **artificially** (är′tə fish′əl ē), *adv.* artfully; skillfully.
14. **shambles,** slaughterhouses.
15. **Psalmanazar,** a Frenchman who passed himself off in England as a Formosan and wrote a fictitious "true" account of Formosa in which he described cannibalism.

person happened to be put to death, the executioner sold the carcass to persons of quality as a prime dainty; and that in his time the body of a plump girl of fifteen, who was crucified for an attempt to poison the emperor, was sold to his Imperial Majesty's prime minister of state and other great mandarins[16] of the court, in joints from the gibbet,[17] at four hundred crowns. Neither indeed can I deny that if the same use were made of several plump young girls in this town who, without one single groat to their fortunes, cannot stir abroad without a chair, and appear at playhouse and assemblies in foreign fineries which they will never pay for, the kingdom would not be the worse.

Some persons of a desponding spirit are in great concern about that vast number of poor people who are aged, diseased, or maimed; and I have been desired to employ my thoughts what course may be taken to ease the nation of so grievous an encumbrance. But I am not in the least pain upon that matter, because it is very well known that they are every day dying and rotting, by cold and famine, and filth and vermin, as fast as can be reasonably expected. And as to the younger laborers, they are now in almost as hopeful a condition: they cannot get work, and consequently pine away for want of nourishment to a degree that if at any time they are accidentally hired to common labor, they have not strength to perform it; and thus the country and themselves are happily delivered from the evils to come.

I have too long digressed and therefore shall return to my subject. I think the advantages by the proposal which I have made are obvious and many, as well as of the highest importance.

For first, as I have already observed, it would greatly lessen the number of papists with whom we are yearly overrun, being the principal breeders of the nation, as well as our most dangerous enemies; and who stay at home on purpose with a design to deliver the kingdom to the Pretender, hoping to take their advantage by the absence of so many good Protestants, who have chosen rather to leave their country than stay at home and pay tithes against their conscience to an idolatrous Episcopal curate.[18]

Secondly, the poorer tenants will have something valuable of their own, which by law may be made liable to distress,[19] and help to pay their landlord's rent; their corn and cattle being already seized, and money a thing unknown.

> CLARIFY: What seem to be the interactions between the poor people and the rest of society, especially the landlords?

Thirdly, whereas the maintenance of an hundred thousand children, from two years old and upwards, cannot be computed at less than ten shillings a piece per annum, the nation's stock will be thereby increased fifty thousand pounds per annum—besides the profit of a new dish introduced to the tables of all gentlemen of fortune in the kingdom who have any refinement in taste. And the money will circulate among ourselves, the goods being entirely of our own growth and manufacture.

Fourthly, the constant breeders, besides the gain of eight shillings sterling per annum by the sale of their children, will be rid of the charge of maintaining them after the first year.

Fifthly, this food would likewise bring great custom to taverns, where the vintners[20] will certainly be so prudent as to procure the best

---

16. **mandarin** (man′dər ən), *n.* a powerful or influential person.
17. gibbet (jib′it), *n.* gallows, a structure for hanging criminals.
18. **Protestants . . . curate.** Swift is here attacking dissenting Protestants who have left Ireland and avoided paying tithes on the grounds that Anglican Church practices were "idolatrous."
19. **distress,** distraint, the legal seizure of property for payment of debts.
20. vintner (vint′nər), *n.* wine merchant.

receipts[21] for dressing it to perfection and, consequently, have their houses frequented by all the fine gentlemen, who justly value themselves upon their knowledge in good eating: and a skilful cook, who understands how to oblige his guests, will contrive to make it as expensive as they please.

I CAN THINK OF NO ONE OBJECTION THAT WILL POSSIBLY BE RAISED AGAINST THIS PROPOSAL. . . .

Sixthly, this would be great inducement to marriage, which all wise nations have either encouraged by rewards or enforced by laws and penalties. It would increase the care and tenderness of mothers towards their children, when they were sure of a settlement for life to the poor babes, provided in some sort by the public, to their annual profit instead of expense. We should soon see an honest emulation[22] among the married women, which of them could bring the fattest child to the market. Men would become as fond of their wives during the time of their pregnancy as they are now of their mares in foal, their cows in calf, or sows when they are ready to farrow; nor offer to beat or kick them (as is too frequent a practice) for fear of a miscarriage.

Many other advantages might be enumerated. For instance, the addition of some thousand carcasses in our exportation of barrelled beef; the propagation[23] of swine's flesh, and improvement in the art of making good bacon, so much wanted among us by the great destruction of pigs, too frequent at our tables—which are no way comparable in taste or magnificence to a well-grown, fat yearling child, which, roasted whole, will make a considerable figure at a Lord Mayor's feast, or any other public entertainment. But this and many others I omit, being studious of brevity.

Supposing that one thousand families in this city would be constant customers for infants' flesh, besides others who might have it at merry meetings, particularly weddings and christenings, I compute that Dublin would take off annually about twenty thousand carcasses; and the rest of the kingdom (where probably they will be sold somewhat cheaper) the remaining eighty thousand.

I can think of no one objection that will possibly be raised against this proposal, unless it should be urged, that the number of people will be thereby much lessened in the kingdom. This I freely own, and it was indeed one principal design in offering it to the world. I desire the reader will observe that I calculate my remedy for this one individual kingdom of Ireland, and for no other that ever was, is, or, I think, ever can be upon earth. Therefore let no man talk to me of other expedients:[24] of taxing our absentees at five shillings a pound; of using neither clothes nor household furniture except what is of our own growth and manufacture; of utterly rejecting the materials and instruments that promote foreign luxury; of curing the expensiveness of pride, vanity, idleness, and gaming in our women; of introducing a vein of parsimony,[25] prudence, and temperance; of learning to love our country, wherein we differ even from Laplanders, and the inhabitants of Topinamboo;[26] of quitting our animosities[27] and factions, nor act any longer like the Jews, who were murdering one another at the very moment their city was taken;[28] of

---

21. **vintners . . . receipts,** that is, wine merchants will be sure to find the best recipes.
22. **emulation** (em′yə lā′shən), *n.* rivalry.
23. **propagation** (prop′ə gā′shən), *n.* breeding and raising.
24. **expedient** (ek spē′dē ənt), *n.* means of bringing about a desired result.
25. **parsimony** (pär′sə mō′nē), *n.* stinginess.
26. **Topinamboo,** an area of Brazil.
27. **animosity** (an′ə mos′ə tē), *n.* dislike; ill will.
28. **city was taken.** While the Roman Emperor Titus was besieging Jerusalem, which he destroyed in A.D. 70, groups of fanatics within the city were fighting each other.

being a little cautious not to sell our country and consciences for nothing; of teaching landlords to have at least one degree of mercy towards their tenants; lastly, of putting a spirit of honesty, industry, and skill into our shopkeepers, who, if a resolution could now be taken to buy only our native goods, would immediately unite to cheat and exact upon us in the price, the measure, and the goodness, nor could ever yet be brought to make one fair proposal of just dealing, though often and earnestly invited to it.

EVALUATE: What can you conclude about these "other expedients"? Are they sensible or not?

Therefore, I repeat, let no man talk to me of these and the like expedients till he has at least some glimpse of hope that there will ever be some hearty and sincere attempt to put them in practice.

But as to myself, having been wearied out for many years with offering vain, idle, visionary thoughts, and at length utterly despairing of success, I fortunately fell upon this proposal, which, as it is wholly new, so it hath something solid and real, of no expense and little trouble, full in our own power, and whereby we can incur no danger in disobliging England. For this kind of commodity will not bear exportation, the flesh being of too tender a consistence to admit a long continuance in salt, although perhaps I could name a country which would be glad to eat up our whole nation without it.[29]

After all, I am not so violently bent upon my own opinion as to reject any offer proposed by wise men which shall be found equally innocent, cheap, easy, and effectual. But before something of that kind shall be advanced in contradiction to my scheme, and offering a better, I desire the author or authors will be pleased maturely to consider two points. First, as things now stand, how they will be able to find food and raiment for a hundred thousand useless mouths and backs? And, secondly, there being a round million of creatures in human figure throughout this kingdom whose whole subsistence, put into a common stock, would leave them in debt two millions of pounds sterling—adding those who are beggars by profession to the bulk of farmers, cottagers, and laborers, with the wives and children who are beggars in effect—I desire those politicians who dislike my overture,[30] and may perhaps be so bold as to attempt an answer, that they will first ask the parents of these mortals whether they would not at this day think it a great happiness to have been sold for food at a year old, in the manner I prescribe, and thereby have avoided such a perpetual scene of misfortunes as they have since gone through by the oppression of landlords, the impossibility of paying rent without money or trade, the want of common sustenance, with neither house nor clothes to cover them from the inclemencies of weather, and the most inevitable prospect of entailing the like, or greater miseries, upon their breed for ever.

I profess, in the sincerity of my heart, that I have not the least personal interest in endeavouring to promote this necessary work, having no other motive than the public good of my country, by advancing our trade, providing for infants, relieving the poor, and giving some pleasure to the rich. I have no children by which I can propose to get a single penny; the youngest being nine years old, and my wife past child-bearing.

---

29. **a country . . . without it.** Another way of saying that the English are devouring or swallowing the Irish.
30. **overture** (ō′vər chər), *n.* proposal or offer.

After Reading

Making Connections

Shaping Your Response

1. If you had not been told that this essay is a **satire,** at what point would you have realized it for yourself?

2. Do you find this essay shocking? Assign it a 1–12 rating on the shock meter.

Shock Meter

Analyzing the Essay

3. Paragraph 4 refers to "a child just dropped from its dam," and the essay contains other examples of terms usually applied only to animals. Why do you suppose the narrator uses such language?

4. In what ways, according to the narrator, are the Irish responsible for their own circumstances?

5. If the narrator truly believes that his other expedients aren't worth talking about, why do you think he includes them?

6. If Swift's intention is to inspire reform, what kind of reform is he suggesting?

7. Of the people living during Swift's time, who do you think would have been most annoyed by this essay? most approving?

Extending the Ideas

8. Many of the problems Swift mentions still exist in the world today. Are the reasons for these problems the same kinds of **interactions** as described here? Are there additional reasons? Discuss.

Literary Focus: Satire

Satirical writing, whether for television, films, or print, is usually aimed at reforming some human weakness or some evil of society. Irony, sarcasm, and wit are all part of the technique of **satire.**

1. Swift says that he is "wearied out . . . with offering vain, idle, visionary thoughts" and so "fell upon this proposal." What is ironic about this?

2. "Landlords," Swift says, "who, as they have already devoured most of the parents, seem to have the best title to the children." What makes this an example of sarcasm?

3. Find a passage that you think best illustrates Swift's wit.

Vocabulary Study

On your paper, write the letter of the word or phrase that best completes each of the following sentences.

1. *Raiment* is most likely to be kept in a ____.
   a. kitchen   **b.** living room   **c.** closet   **d.** dining room

2. *Ragout* would probably be found in a ____.
   a. kitchen   **b.** porch   **c.** field   **d.** church

3. People who practice *parsimony* would probably ____.
   a. refuse to give to the poor   **b.** exercise daily
   c. eat only vegetables   **d.** refuse to wear leather or fur

4. Someone headed for a *gibbet* has probably ____.
   a. had too much to eat   **b.** been visiting a zoo
   c. been suffering from overwork   **d.** been convicted of a crime

5. *Vintners* are in the business of selling ____.
   a. cheese   **b.** wine   **c.** cloth   **d.** medicine

Expressing Your Ideas

Writing Choices

Writer's Notebook Update Now that you've read "A Modest Proposal," think about some of the possible modern targets for satire that you jotted down in your notebook. Write a paragraph or so about one of the topics.

Not So Modest? Reread the full title on page 296. Then write an **essay** in which you explain why this title is meant to be taken ironically. Suggest some reasons why Swift might have used irony instead of making straightforward statements.

Music, Manners, and Malls Newspaper columnists often satirize some aspect of popular culture, and the fads and tastes of young people are frequently ripe areas for satire. Write a **satirical column** dealing with a current interest among your friends or acquaintances that could be published in a school paper or magazine.

Other Options

"In My Opinion . . . " Some people have objected to including Swift's essay in a textbook on the grounds that it is about "eating babies" and is generally unsuitable for

high school readers. Do you agree that some topics are "unsuitable" for reading in school? If so, what might they be? Work with a partner to stage a call-in **radio talk show,** in which one person (either caller or talk-show host) objects to the essay and the other defends it.

Art as Social Commentary William Hogarth (1697–1764) was an English painter and engraver whose works often satirized English life. What does he seem to be satirizing in this caricature of British judges titled "The Bench"? Think of an issue that you feel strongly about and create a **satirical drawing** to represent your point of view.

Before Reading

The Education of Women

by Daniel Defoe

Daniel Defoe
1661?–1731

A candle merchant's son, born in London, Daniel Defoe attended Morton's Academy for Dissenters (Protestants who were not members of the Anglican Church). Never one to live a retiring life, he took part in an armed rebellion against King James II led by the Duke of Monmouth. He engaged in various commercial ventures that were mostly unsuccessful. He was imprisoned once for bankruptcy and a second time for writing a pamphlet attacking the government's religious policies. Later he was employed as a secret agent. He wrote hundreds of pamphlets and books, many anonymously or under a pseudonym. Defoe is considered one of the pioneers of the English novel and is best known for *Robinson Crusoe* (1719), *Moll Flanders* (1722), and *A Journal of the Plague Year* (1722).

Building Background

Should Women Be Educated? In 1698 when Defoe published this essay (which was included in a miscellany of schemes to improve social conditions) the number of educated women in England had changed little since medieval times, when only a few girls were taught in nunneries. Since most of the powerful people in society thought women were inferior to men and should not be educated beyond their expected roles as wife and mother, even upper-class women received little formal learning. Many middle- and lower-class parents were fearful that too much learning made girls dissatisfied with their lives and less attractive to men; their daughters usually received no education at all until the establishment by Parliament of charity schools. When girls of any social class were taught to read, they were discouraged from reading fiction. Clergymen in particular warned that novels were not instructive and were likely to corrupt the morals of young women.

Literary Focus

Theme An underlying meaning of a literary work is a **theme.** A theme may be implied, or it may be directly stated. One of Swift's themes in "A Modest Proposal," for example, is that English tyranny over Ireland has caused great misery. Themes in nonfiction are clarified by supporting examples, the author's stated point of view, and word choice. When Swift writes that there is no need to worry about "aged, diseased, or maimed" poor because they are dying every day of famine and filth, he is supporting his theme with a powerful satirical example, but he never states his point of view directly. To discover how Defoe supports his theme, consider the examples he uses to develop his topic, which is stated in the title of the essay.

Writer's Notebook

Reform Schools? In your notebook, jot down some current problems in American education. Consider school financing, student achievement, books, supplies and equipment, curriculum, or health and safety issues.

The Education of Women

Daniel Defoe

I have often thought of it as one of the most barbarous customs in the world, considering us as a civilized and a Christian country, that we deny the advantages of learning to women. We reproach the sex every day with folly[1] and impertinence, while I am confident, had they the advantages of education equal to us, they would be guilty of less than ourselves.

One would wonder, indeed, how it should happen that women are conversible[2] at all, since they are only beholding to natural parts[3] for all their knowledge. Their youth is spent to teach them to stitch and sew or make baubles. They are taught to read, indeed, and perhaps to write their names or so, and that is the height of a woman's education. And I would but ask any who slight the sex for their understanding, what is a man (a gentleman, I mean) good for that is taught no more?

I need not give instances or examine the character of a gentleman with a good estate and of a good family and with tolerable parts, and examine what figure he makes for want of education.

---

1. folly (fol′ē), *n.* a being foolish; lack of sense.
2. **that women are conversable,** that women can hold a conversation.
3. **beholding . . . parts,** dependent upon natural abilities.

▲ When Winslow Homer painted this watercolor, *Blackboard,* in 1877, educational opportunities for women had expanded from the time of Defoe, but women still did not have equal access to education. Do you think that women and men today have equal educational opportunities? Why or why not?

The soul is placed in the body like a rough diamond and must be polished, or the luster of it will never appear; and 'tis manifest[4] that as the rational soul distinguishes us from brutes, so education carries on the distinction and makes some less brutish than others. This is too evident to need any demonstration. But why then should women be denied the benefit of instruction? If knowledge and understanding had been useless additions to the sex, God Almighty would never have given them capacities, for He made nothing needless. Besides, I would ask such what they can see in ignorance that they should think it a necessary ornament to a woman? or how much worse is a wise woman than a fool? or what has the woman done to forfeit the privilege of being taught? Does she plague us with her pride and impertinence? Why did we not let her learn, that she might have had more wit? Shall we upbraid[5] women with folly, when 'tis only the error of this inhuman custom that hindered them being made wiser?

The capacities of women are supposed to be greater and their quicker than those of the men; and what they might be capable of being plain from some instances of such who this ag... being given room in the world, the men... injustic... and mocks us if we denied women the advantages of education for fear they should vie[6] with the men in their improvements.

To remove this... a woman... might have had... an equal... cation in a... I propose the draft of... that purpose.

Wherefore the academy I... differ but little from public... such ladies as were willing to... should have all the advantages of learning suitable to their genius.[8] But since some severities of discipline more than ordinary would be absolutely necessary to preserve the reputation of the house, that persons of quality and fortune might not be

afraid to venture their children thither, I shall venture to make a small scheme by way of essay.[9]

The house I would have built in a form by itself, as well as in a place by itself. The building should be of three plain fronts, without any jettings or bearing-work,[10] that the eye might at a glance see from one coign[11] to the other; the gardens walled in the same triangular figure, with a large moat, and but one entrance. When thus every part of the situation was contrived as well as might be for discovery, and to render intriguing dangerous, I would have no guards, no eyes, no spies set over the ladies, but shall expect them to be tried by the principles of honor and strict virtue. . . .

CLARIFY: Why does Defoe think the academy would need a moat?

In this house, the persons who enter should be taught all sorts of breeding suitable both to their genius and quality, and in particular, music and dancing, which it would be cruelty to bar the sex of, because they are their darlings; but besides this, they should be taught languages, as particularly French and Italian; and I would venture the injury of giving a woman more tongues than one. They should, as a particular study, be taught all the graces of speech and all the necessary air of conversation, which our common education is so defective in that I need not expose it. They should be brought to read books, and especially history; and so to read as to make them

---

4. **manifest** (man′ə fest), *adj.* plain; clear.
5. **upbraid** (up brād′), *v.* find fault with; blame.
6. **vie** (vī), *v.* compete.
7. **public schools,** schools that prepared boys for the universities.
8. **their genius,** their special abilities.
9. **essay** (es′ā), *n.* trial.
10. **without any jettings or bearing-work.** Jettings are parts jutting out from a perpendicular wall; bearing-works are supports for these parts.
11. **coign** (koin), *n.* a stone-reinforced corner.

understand the world and be able to know and judge of things when they hear of them.

To such whose genius would lead them to it, I would deny no sort of learning; but the chief thing, in general, is to cultivate the understandings of the sex, that they may be capable of all sorts of conversation; that, their parts and judgments being improved, they may be as profitable in their conversation as they are pleasant.

. . . . You rarely see them lumpish and heavy when they are children, as boys will often be.

Women, in my observation, have little or no difference in them, but as they are or are not distinguished by education. Tempers, indeed, may in some degree influence them, but the main distinguishing part is their breeding.

The whole sex are generally quick and sharp. I believe I may be allowed to say generally so, for you rarely see them lumpish and heavy when they are children, as boys will often be. If a woman be well bred, and taught the proper management of her natural wit, she proves generally very sensible and retentive;[12] and without partiality, a woman of sense and manners is the finest and most delicate part of God's creation, the glory of her Maker, and the great instance of His singular regard to man, His darling creature, to whom He gave the best gift either God could bestow or man receive. And 'tis the sordidest piece of folly and ingratitude in the world to withhold from the sex the due luster which the advantage of education gives to the natural beauty of their minds.

A woman well bred and well taught, furnished with the additional accomplishments of knowledge and behavior, is a creature without comparison; her society is the emblem of sublimer enjoyments; her person is angelic and her conversation heavenly; she is all softness and sweetness, peace, love, wit, and delight. She is every way suitable to the sublimest wish, and the man that has such a one to his portion has nothing to do but rejoice in her and be thankful.

On the other hand, suppose her to be the very same woman, and rob her of the benefit of education, and it follows thus:

If her temper be good, want of education makes her soft and easy. Her wit, for want of teaching, makes her impertinent[13] and talkative. Her knowledge, for want of judgment and experience, makes her fanciful and whimsical.[14] If her temper be bad, want of breeding makes her worse, and she grows haughty, insolent,[15] and loud. If she be passionate, want of manners makes her termagant[16] and a scold, which is much at one with lunatic. If she be proud, want of discretion (which still is breeding) makes her conceited, fantastic, and ridiculous. And from these she degenerates to be turbulent, clangorous,[17] noisy, nasty, and the devil.

Me thinks mankind for their own sakes—since, say what we will of the women, we all think fit at one time or other to be concerned with them—should take some care to breed them up to be suitable and serviceable, if they expected no such thing as delight from them. Bless us! what care do we take to breed up a good horse

---

12. **retentive** (ri ten′tiv), *adj.* able to remember easily.
13. impertinent (im pèrt′n ənt), *adj.* rudely bold.
14. **whimsical** (hwim′zə kəl), *adj.* having many odd notions or fancies.
15. **insolent** (in′sə lənt), *adj.* insulting.
16. **termagant** (tèr′mə gənt), *adj.* violent and quarrelsome.
17. **clangorous** (klang′ər əs), *adj.* with a loud, harsh, ringing sound.

and to break him well! and what a value do we put upon him when it is done, and all because he should be fit for our use! and why not a woman? Since all her ornaments and beauty without suitable behavior is a cheat in nature, like the false tradesman who puts the best of his goods uppermost, that the buyer may think the rest are of the same goodness.

That Almighty First Cause which made us all is certainly the fountain of excellence, as it is of being, and by an invisible influence could have diffused equal qualities and perfections to all the creatures it has made, as the sun does its light, without the least ebb or diminution to Himself, and has given indeed to every individual sufficient to the figure His providence had designed him in the world.

I believe it might be defended if I should say that I do suppose God has given to all mankind equal gifts and capacities in that He has given them all souls equally capable, and that the whole difference in mankind proceeds either from accidental difference in the make of their bodies or from the foolish difference of education. . . . and this is manifested by comparing it with the difference between one man or woman and another.

And herein it is that I take upon me to make such a bold assertion that all the world are mistaken in their practice about women; for I cannot think that God Almighty ever made them so delicate, so glorious creatures, and furnished them with such charms, so agreeable and so delightful to mankind, with souls capable of the same accomplishments with men, and all to be only stewards of our houses, cooks, and slaves.

*N*ot that I am for exalting the female government in the least; but, in short, I would have men take women for companions, and educate them to be fit for it. A woman of sense and breeding will scorn as much to encroach[18] upon the prerogative[19] of the man as a man of sense will scorn to oppress the weakness of the woman. But if the women's souls were refined and improved by teaching, that word would be lost; to say the *weakness of the sex* as to judgment would be nonsense, for ignorance and folly would be no more found among women than men. I remember a passage which I heard from a very fine woman. She had wit and capacity enough, an extraordinary shape and face, and a great fortune, but had been cloistered up all her time, and, for fear of being stolen, had not had the liberty of being taught the common necessary knowledge of women's affairs; and when she came to converse in the world, her natural wit made her so sensible of the want of education that she gave this short reflection on herself: "I am ashamed to talk with my very maids," says she, "for I don't know when they do right or wrong. I had more need go to school than be married."

SUMMARIZE: Summarize Defoe's reasons for proposing that women be educated.

I need not enlarge on the loss the defect of education is to the sex, nor argue the benefit of the contrary practice; 'tis a thing will be more easily granted than remedied. This chapter is but an essay at the thing, and I refer the practice to those happy days, if ever they shall be, when men shall be wise enough to mend it.

---

18. **encroach** (en krōch′), *v.* tresspass; intrude.
19. **prerogative** (pri rog′ə tiv), *n.* right or privilege that nobody else has.

After Reading

Making Connections

Shaping Your
Response

1. In your opinion, is this essay persuasive? Do you think it would have changed anyone's mind at the time it was written?

Analyzing the Essay

2. Defoe says that "the soul is placed in the body like a rough diamond and must be polished, or the luster of it will never appear." What does this **simile** have to do with education?

3. Why does Defoe seem to think it necessary to provide directions for building an academy for women?

4. 👣 Educating women would certainly change the **interactions** between men and women. Summarize the advantages to both men and women that Defoe claims would follow from providing an education for women.

5. Defoe says he is not "for exalting the female government" and that "A woman of sense and breeding will scorn . . . to encroach upon the prerogative of the man . . . ." What does he mean, and why do you think he includes such remarks?

Extending the Ideas

6. Have all the problems with women's education that Defoe criticizes been eliminated in the United States today? in the world? Explain.

Literary Focus: Theme

Theme, either directly stated or implied, is an underlying meaning of a work. Where does Defoe state his theme? What techniques does he use to support this theme? What do you think is his most effective argument? his least effective argument?

Vocabulary Study

On your paper, write the word from the list that best completes the meaning of each sentence. You will not use all the words.

**essay
folly
impertinent
manifest
prerogative
vie**

1. In the past, men often claimed the ____ of education.

2. Some individuals, however, thought it was ____ to deny education to women.

3. Defoe and others believed that lack of learning made women ____.

4. According to Defoe, it was ____ that denying education to women was an inhuman custom.

5. He wondered whether men feared that an educated woman would ____ with men.

Expressing Your Ideas

Writing Choices

Writer's Notebook Update Look back at the list of current problems in education that you wrote in your notebook. Choose one of these and in a sentence or two state your position on this problem.

"In My Opinion . . ." Put yourself in the place of a man or woman of 1698 reading Defoe's essay. With which parts of it would you agree? With which would you disagree? Organize your thoughts and express them in a **letter to the editor** of a newspaper. (*The Review, The Tatler,* and *The Spectator* were weekly or bimonthly newspapers popular in the early 1700s.) Support your points with examples and write to convince other newspaper readers to share your opinions.

Be Reasonable! Both Swift and Defoe, as well as Alexander Pope, the author who comes next, were writing in a period (late 1600s to mid-1700s) that has come to be known as the Age of Reason. This period was characterized by a belief in reason rather than sensory experience or religious faith as the answer to life's problems. Pope wrote two lines that help to clarify this belief:

  Know then thyself, presume not God to scan;
  The proper study of mankind is Man.

Can you find any flaws in this belief? Examine this idea in an **essay.**

Other Options

Pressing the Issue Women's education is not a high priority in many parts of the world, and in fact, it is actively opposed in some countries. With a partner, research some of the reasons for lack of women's education and the efforts by international organizations such as UNESCO to raise literacy rates, and give an **oral report** to the class. Include visuals if possible.

A Better Job? Some people feel that men and women should be educated primarily for the work force; others feel that such an emphasis goes against the basic purpose of education: to develop the individual for any situation in life—moral, spiritual, and economic. With a partner, consider these ideas, develop an argument for each side, and present your **debate** to the class.

The Look of Learning Defoe has some rather particular ideas about how a school for women should be constructed. What does your ideal learning place look like? Draw a **picture** or **diagram** of a place that you feel would provide the best learning environment possible. Label or write captions for parts of your diagram that are not immediately apparent. (For example, would you put computers in every room, all together in a technology center—or not include them at all? For that matter, are there even rooms?) Display your picture in the classroom.

Before Reading

from The Rape of the Lock
from An Essay on Criticism by Alexander Pope

Alexander Pope
1688–1744

Stricken with tuberculosis of the spine at an early age, Alexander Pope was crippled and in almost constant pain for most of his life. A Catholic in an age of violent anti-Catholicism, his religion prevented him from receiving a university education, holding public office, or voting, and he was educated chiefly at home. His *Essay on Criticism*, written when he was twenty-three, first made him famous. He earned a large income from his poetry, translations of the *Iliad* and the *Odyssey* (two ancient Greek epic poems), and other writings. In 1718 he moved with his mother to Twickenham, now a suburb of London. Here he devoted much time to landscape gardening and to entertaining friends. He later became known as the "wasp of Twickenham" because of his stinging satire.

Building Background

The Social Whirl "The Rape of the Lock" (here the word *rape* means simply "theft") is a poem written in the style of a serious epic poem but it is called a **mock-epic** because of its subject matter. On the surface, Pope's poem is about a quarrel between two families. Yet it contains much social criticism, as noted by biographer Maynard Mack: "Pope represents the absurdities of the fashionable world with affection, and with an eye to the delicate beauties that its best graces unfold. We recognize too the shrewdness of his perception that the contemporary counterpart of the epic hero in his own society—in prestige, influence, authority, and tribute exacted—is the beautiful, marriageable, well-dowered young woman: the profitable 'match.'"

In this society, where the death of a husband or a lap dog is equally serious and where the theft of a lock of hair is sufficient cause for war, values must be out of order.

Literary Focus

Heroic Couplet/Epigram A **heroic couplet** is a pair of rhymed lines that contain a complete thought. The lines are written in iambic pentameter (see the Glossary of Literary Terms), a meter that is often used for serious epics having to do with heroes, and thus the couplet is called "heroic." Heroic verse is now used more for satire or mock-epics, since few people write serious epic poems today.

An **epigram** is a short, witty verse, usually of two or four lines, that often ends with a twist. This heroic couplet by Pope is also an epigram:

Hope springs eternal in the human breast;
Man never is, but always to be blessed.

Writer's Notebook

Rhyming Pairs How would you go about writing rhymed verse? Would you start by making a list of rhyming words or think of the rhymes as you wrote? Choose a general topic (friendship, school, work) and jot down some rhyming words of one or two syllables that you could use to write about that topic.

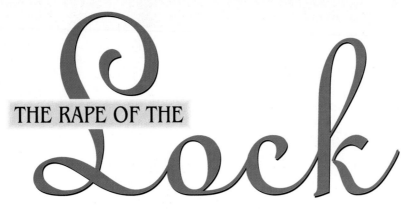

THE RAPE OF THE Lock

An Heroic-Comical Poem

Alexander Pope

Pope wrote this poem at the request of a friend who asked him to make peace between both sides in a quarrel that had arisen when Lord Petre (the Baron in the poem) snipped off a lock of hair from the head of Arabella Fermor (Belinda in the poem). To show how trivial was the basis of the quarrel, Pope exaggerated it still further, puffing it up to epic importance in this "heroic-comical" form. Pope apparently succeeded in healing the breach between the families involved, but the real-life hero and heroine never married. Lord Petre married a younger and richer heiress and died of smallpox within a year. Arabella Fermor married another gentleman, and they had six children.

Canto 1

What dire offence from amorous causes springs,
What mighty contests rise from trivial things,
I sing—this verse to Caryll, Muse! is due;
This, even Belinda may vouchsafe to view.
5 Slight is the subject, but not so the praise,
If she inspire, and he approve my lays.
  Say what strange motive, Goddess! could compel
A well-bred Lord to assault a gentle Belle?
O say what stranger cause, yet unexplored,
10 Could make a gentle Belle reject a Lord?
In tasks so bold, can little men engage,
And in soft bosoms dwells such mighty rage?
  Sol through white curtains shot a timorous ray,
And oped those eyes that must eclipse the day.
15 Now lapdogs give themselves the rousing shake,
And sleepless lovers, just at twelve, awake.
Thrice rung the bell, the slipper knocked the ground,
And the pressed watch returned a silver sound.
Belinda still her downy pillow pressed,
20 Her guardian Sylph prolonged the balmy rest.
'Twas he had summoned to her silent bed

3 Caryll, John Caryll, who suggested that Pope write the poem to heal the breach between the two families.
18 pressed watch. When the stem is pressed on this type of watch, it chimes the nearest hour or quarter hour.
20 sylph (silf), *n.* one of the spirits which, according to an old belief, inhabit the air. This one is named Ariel.

The three illustrations with this poem were created by Aubrey Beardsley for an edition of *The Rape of the Lock* published in 1896. In this illustration, entitled "The Toilet," what does Belinda's elaborate grooming ritual suggest about the value she places on her appearance? ➤

The morning dream that hovered over her head.
A youth more glittering than a birth-night beau
(That even in slumber caused her cheek to glow)
25 Seemed to her ear his winning lips to lay,
And thus in whispers said, or seemed to say . . . .
"Hear and believe! thy own importance know,
Nor bound thy narrow views to things below.
Some secret truths, from learnèd pride concealed,
30 To maids alone and children are revealed. . . ."

Ariel explains that "unnumbered spirits" fly around Belinda and that sylphs can take whatever shape and sex they wish.

"A Sylph am I, who thy protection claim,
A watchful sprite, and Ariel is my name.
Late, as I ranged the crystal wilds of air,
In the clear mirror of thy ruling star
35 I saw, alas! some dread event impend,
Ere to the main this morning sun descend.
But heaven reveals not what, or how, or where:
Warned by the Sylph, oh pious maid, beware!
This to disclose is all thy guardian can:
40 Beware of all, but most beware of man!"
He said; when Shock, who thought she slept too long,
Leaped up, and waked his mistress with his tongue.
'Twas then, Belinda, if report say true,
Thy eyes first opened on a billet-doux;
45 Wounds, charms and ardors were no sooner read,
But all the vision vanished from thy head.
And now, unveiled, the toilet stands displayed,
Each silver vase in mystic order laid.
First, robed in white, the nymph intent adores,
50 With head uncovered, the cosmetic powers.
A heavenly image in the glass appears,
To that she bends, to that her eyes she rears;
The inferior priestess, at her altar's side,
Trembling, begins the sacred rites of pride.
55 Unnumbered treasures ope at once, and here
The various offerings of the world appear;
From each she nicely culls with curious toil,
And decks the goddess with the glittering spoil.
This casket India's glowing gems unlocks,
60 And all Arabia breathes from yonder box.
The tortoise here and elephant unite,
Transformed to combs, the speckled and the white.

■ What is Belinda dreaming about?

23 birth-night beau, a gentleman dressed in fine clothes for the sovereign's birthday.

■ Prophetic dreams are part of the epic tradition. What might Ariel's warning foreshadow?

41 Shock, Belinda's dog.

44 billet-doux (bil′ē dü′), *n.* love letter. *[French]*

47 toilet, dressing table.

■ What impression do you get of Belinda from the contents of her dressing table?

53 inferior priestess, Belinda's maid Betty.

57 cull (kul), *v.* pick out; select.
59 casket, here, a small box.
60 Arabia, source of perfumes.

Here files of pins extend their shining rows,
Puffs, powder, patches, bibles, billet-doux.
65 Now awful beauty puts on all its arms;
The fair each moment rises in her charms,
Repairs her smiles, awakens every grace,
And calls forth all the wonders of her face;
Sees by degrees a purer blush arise,
70 And keener lightnings quicken in her eyes.
The busy Sylphs surround their darling care;
These set the head, and those divide the hair,
Some fold the sleeve, whilst others plait the gown;
And Betty's praised for labors not her own.

Canto 2

75 Not with more glories, in the ethereal plain,
The sun first rises over the purpled main,
Than issuing forth, the rival of his beams
Launched on the bosom of the silver Thames.
Fair nymphs and well-dressed youths around her shone,
80 But every eye was fixed on her alone. . . .
        This nymph, to the destruction of mankind,
Nourished two locks, which graceful hung behind
In equal curls, and well conspired to deck
With shining ringlets the smooth ivory neck.
85 Love in these labyrinths his slaves detains,
And mighty hearts are held in slender chains.
With hairy springes we the birds betray,
Slight lines of hair surprise the finny prey,
Fair tresses man's imperial race ensnare,
90 And beauty draws us with a single hair.
        The adventurous Baron the bright locks admired,
He saw, he wished, and to the prize aspired.
Resolved to win, he meditates the way,
By force to ravish, or by fraud betray;
95 For when success a lover's toil attends,
Few ask, if fraud or force attained his ends. . . .

64 patches, tiny pieces of black silk pasted on the face to show off fine skin.
65 awful, awe-inspiring.

75 ethereal plain, the sky.

78 launched . . . Thames. Belinda now sets forth on a Thames River boat on her way to Hampton Court, one of the royal palaces.

85 labyrinth (lab'ə rinth'), *n.* maze.
87 springe (sprinj), *n.* snare to catch birds.

The Baron has collected various items such as a glove and love letters from former lovers, but he now seeks to possess something of Belinda's. Ariel, aware of the threat to Belinda, summons his fellow sylphs and sends them to their various stations about Belinda to guard her every precious possession.

"This day, black omens threat the brightest fair
That ever deserved a watchful spirit's care;
Some dire disaster, or by force, or sleight,
100 But what, or where, the fates have wrapped in night—
Whether the nymph shall break Diana's law,
Or some frail China jar receive a flaw,
Or stain her honor, or her new brocade,
Forget her prayers, or miss a masquerade,
105 Or lose her heart, or necklace, at a ball;
Or whether Heaven has doomed that Shock must fall.
Haste then, ye spirits! to your charge repair:
The fluttering fan be Zephyretta's care;
The drops to thee, Brillante, we consign;
110 And, Momentilla, let the watch be thine;
Do thou, Crispissa, tend her favourite lock;
Ariel himself shall be the guard of Shock.
    "To fifty chosen Sylphs, of special note,
We trust the important charge, the petticoat:
115 Oft have we known that sevenfold fence to fail,
Though stiff with hoops, and armed with ribs of whale.
Form a strong line about the silver bound,
And guard the wide circumference around.
    "Whatever spirit, careless of his charge,
120 His post neglects, or leaves the fair at large,
Shall feel sharp vengeance soon overtake his sins,
Be stopped in vials, or transfixed with pins;
Or plunged in lakes of bitter washes lie,
Or wedged whole ages in a bodkin's eye:
125 Gums and pomatums shall his flight restrain,
While clogged he beats his silken wings in vain;
Or alum styptics with contracting power
Shrink his thin essence like a rivelled flower.
Or, as Ixion fixed, the wretch shall feel
130 The giddy motion of the whirling mill,
In fumes of burning chocolate shall glow,
And tremble at the sea that froths below!"
    He spoke; the spirits from the sails descend;
Some, orb in orb, around the nymph extend,
135 Some thrid the mazy ringlets of her hair,

■ Are the "dire" disasters that might happen of equal importance?

101 Diana's law, chastity. Diana was the Roman goddess of the moon and protector of women.

109 drops, dangling earrings.

122 vial (vī′əl), *n.* small bottle for holding medicines or the like.
124 bodkin, a large needle.
125 pomatums, perfumed ointments for the hair.
128 rivelled (riv′ld) *adj.* wrinkled or shrivelled.
129 Ixion. In Greek myth, he was fastened to an endlessly revolving wheel in Hades as punishment for making love to Juno, queen of the gods.

135 thrid (thrid), *v.* past-tense of *thread,* pass through.

Some hang upon the pendants of her ear;
With beating hearts the dire event they wait,
Anxious and trembling for the birth of fate.

Canto 3

Close by those meads, for ever crowned with flowers,
140 Where Thames with pride surveys his rising towers,
There stands a structure of majestic frame,
Which from the neighboring Hampton takes its name.
Here Britain's statesmen oft the fall foredoom
Of foreign tyrants, and of nymphs at home;
145 Here thou, great Anna! whom three realms obey,
Dost sometimes counsel take—and sometimes tea.
    Hither the heroes and the nymphs resort,
To taste awhile the pleasures of a court;
In various talk the instructive hours they passed,
150 Who gave the ball, or paid the visit last.
One speaks the glory of the British queen;
And one describes a charming Indian screen;
A third interprets motions, looks, and eyes;
At every word a reputation dies.
155 Snuff, or the fan, supply each pause of chat,
With singing, laughing, ogling, and all that. . . .

Belinda joins the pleasure-seekers at Hampton Court and wins at a card game called ombre over the Baron, who covets her locks of hair. As the game ends and they all have refreshments (including coffee, a new rage in London), the Baron seizes his opportunity.

Coffee (which makes the politician wise,
And see through all things with his half-shut eyes)
Sent up in vapors to the Baron's brain
160 New stratagems, the radiant lock to gain.
Ah cease, rash youth! desist ere 'tis too late,
Fear the just gods, and think of Scylla's fate!
Changed to a bird, and sent to flit in air,
She dearly pays for Nisus' injured hair!
165   But when to mischief mortals bend their will,
How soon they find fit instruments of ill!
Just then, Clarissa drew with tempting grace
A two-edged weapon from her shining case;
So ladies in romance assist their knight,
170 Present the spear, and arm him for the fight.
He takes the gift with reverence, and extends
The little engine on his fingers' ends;

▲ "The Barge," an Aubrey Beardsley illustration dating from 1896, shows Belinda on the vessel that transports her to Hampton Court. Notice that the barge is as richly ornamented as its passengers. How might you react if you were to encounter the scene depicted in this illustration? What makes these people seem somewhat ridiculous to the modern observer?

145 Anna, Queen Anne, who reigned 1702–1714.
162 Scylla's fate. In Greek legend, Scylla (sil′ə), daughter of Nisus, was changed into a bird because she cut off a golden hair (and the source of his power) from her father's head and offered it to her lover.
168 two-edged weapon, scissors.

The Rape of the Lock   **319**

This just behind Belinda's neck he spread,
As over the fragrant steams she bends her head.
175　Swift to the lock a thousand sprites repair,
A thousand wings, by turns, block back the hair,
And thrice they twitched the diamond in her ear;
Thrice she looked back, and thrice the foe drew near.
Just in that instant, anxious Ariel sought
180　The close recesses of the virgin's thought;
As, on the nosegay in her breast reclined,
He watched the ideas rising in her mind,
Sudden he viewed, in spite of all her art,
An earthly lover lurking at her heart.
185　Amazed, confused, he found his power expired,
Resigned to fate, and with a sigh retired.
　　　The peer now spreads the glittering forfex wide,
To enclose the lock; now joins it, to divide.
Even then, before the fatal engine closed,
190　A wretched Sylph too fondly interposed;
Fate urged the shears, and cut the Sylph in twain
(But airy substance soon unites again),
The meeting points the sacred hair dissever
From the fair head, for ever and for ever!
195　　　Then flashed the living lightning from her eyes,
And screams of horror rend the affrighted skies.
Not louder shrieks to pitying heaven are cast,
When husbands or when lapdogs breathe their last;
Or when rich China vessels, fallen from high,
200　In glittering dust and painted fragments lie!
　　　"Let wreaths of triumph now my temples twine,"
(The victor cried) "the glorious prize is mine!
While fish in streams, or birds delight in air,
Or in a coach and six the British fair,
205　As long as Atalantis shall be read,
Or the small pillow grace a lady's bed,
While visits shall be paid on solemn days,
When numerous wax-lights in bright order blaze,
While nymphs take treats, or assignations give,
210　So long my honor, name, and praise shall live!"
　　　What time would spare, from steel receives its date,
And monuments, like men, submit to fate!
Steel could labor of the gods destroy,
And strike to dust the imperial towers of Troy;
215　Steel could the works of mortal pride confound,
And hew triumphal arches to the ground.

181 nosegay (nōz′gā′), *n.* bunch of flowers.

■ Why can't Ariel protect Belinda?

187 forfex, scissors.

193 dissever (di sev′ər), *v.* separate.

205 Atalantis, a popular book of court scandal and gossip.

209 assignation (as′ig-nā′shən), *n.* a secret meeting of lovers.

214 Troy, city in the northwest part of ancient Asia Minor (now Turkey), site of the legendary Trojan War.

What wonder then, fair nymph! thy hairs should feel
The conquering force of unresisted steel?

Canto 4

Belinda, furious, delivers an indignant speech.

. . ."For ever cursed be this detested day,
220 Which snatched my best, my favourite curl away!
Happy! ah ten times happy had I been,
If Hampton Court these eyes had never seen!
Yet am not I the first mistaken maid,
By love of courts, to numerous ills betrayed.
225 Oh had I rather unadmired remained
In some lone isle, or distant northern land;
Where the gilt chariot never marks the way,
Where none learn ombre; none ever taste bohea!
There kept my charms concealed from mortal eye,
230 Like roses that in deserts bloom and die.
What moved my mind with youthful lords to roam?
O had I stayed, and said my prayers at home!
'Twas this, the morning omens seemed to tell;
Thrice from my trembling hand the patch box fell;
235 The tottering china shook without a wind;
Nay, Poll sat mute, and Shock was most unkind!
A Sylph too warned me of the threats of fate,
In mystic visions, now believed too late!
See the poor remnants of these slighted hairs!
240 My hands shall rend what even thy rapine spares:
These, in two sable ringlets taught to break,
Once gave new beauties to the snowy neck;
The sister lock now sits uncouth, alone,
And in its fellow's fate foresees its own;
245 Uncurled it hangs, the fatal shears demands;
And tempts once more thy sacrilegious hands.
Oh hadst thou, cruel! been content to seize
Hairs less in sight, or any hairs but these!"

Canto 5

She said: the pitying audience melt in tears,
250 But fate and Jove had stopped the Baron's ears.
In vain Thalestris with reproach assails,
For who can move when fair Belinda fails?
Not half so fixed the Trojan could remain,
While Anna begged and Dido raged in vain.

228 bohea (bō hā′), *n.* an expensive tea.

■ What does Belinda wish she had done to prevent her favorite curl from being snatched?

240 rend (rend), *v.* tear apart.
240 rapine (rap′ən), *n.* robbery by force; plunder.

251 Thalestis (thal es′trəs), Belinda's friend, named for a queen of the Amazons and thus fiercely militant.
254 Anna . . . vain. In the *Aeneid,* Anna was unable to persuade Aeneas to remain faithful to her sister Dido. The comparison is to Thalestris, friend of Belinda, whose reproaches to the Baron are also in vain.

255 Then grave Clarissa graceful waved her fan;
Silence ensued, and thus the nymph began.
     "Say, why are beauties praised and honored most,
The wise man's passion, and the vain man's toast?
Why decked with all that land and sea afford,
260 Why angels called, and angel-like adored?
Why round our coaches crowd the white-gloved beaux,
Why bows the side-box from its inmost rows?
How vain are all these glories, all our pains,
Unless good sense preserve what beauty gains:
265 That men may say, when we the front-box grace,
'Behold the first in virtue, as in face!'
Oh! if to dance all night, and dress all day,
Charmed the smallpox, or chased old age away,
Who would not scorn what housewife's cares produce,
270 Or who would learn one earthly thing of use?
To patch, nay ogle, might become a saint,
Nor could it sure be such a sin to paint.
But since, alas! frail beauty must decay,
Curled or uncurled, since locks will turn to grey;
275 Since painted or not painted, all shall fade,
And she who scorns a man, must die a maid;
What then remains, but well our power to use,
And keep good humor still whatever we lose?
And trust me, dear! good humor can prevail,
280 When airs, and flights, and screams, and scolding fail.
Beauties in vain their pretty eyes may roll;
Charms strike the sight, but merit wins the soul."
     So spoke the dame, but no applause ensued;
Belinda frowned, Thalestris called her prude.
285 "To arms, to arms!" the fierce virago cries,
And swift as lightning to the combat flies.
All side in parties, and begin the attack;
Fans clap, silks rustle, and tough whalebones crack;
Heroes' and heroines' shouts confusedly rise,
290 And bass and treble voices strike the skies.
No common weapons in their hands are found;
Like gods they fight, nor dread a mortal wound. . . .

271 ogle (ō′gəl), *v.* look at with desire.

■ What generalization can you make about the **interactions** between the men and women of high society featured in this poem?

285 virago (və rā′gō), *n.* strong vigorous woman; here, Thalestris.

■ What are Belinda's weapons?

297 endue (en dū′), *v.* furnish; supply.
301 gnome (nōm), *n.* spirit inhabiting the earth.
306 bodkin, here, an ornamental hairpin.
323–324 Othello . . . handkerchief. In Shakespeare's play *Othello*, the title character becomes enraged at his wife Desdemona when she cannot show him a prized handkerchief which he thinks she has given to a lover.

Belinda attacks the Baron, but they are both deprived of the precious lock as it rises into the skies, there to become changed into a heavenly body and thus immortalized.

    See, fierce Belinda on the Baron flies,
With more than usual lightning in her eyes;
295 Nor feared the chief the unequal fight to try,
Who sought no more than on his foe to die.
But this bold lord, with manly strength endued,
She with one finger and a thumb subdued:
Just where the breath of life his nostrils drew,
300 A charge of snuff the wily virgin threw;
The Gnomes direct, in every atom just,
The pungent grains of titillating dust.
Sudden, with starting tears each eye overflows,
And the high dome re-echoes to his nose.
305   "Now meet thy fate," incensed Belinda cried,
And drew a deadly bodkin from her side.
(The same, his ancient personage to deck,
Her great great grandsire wore about his neck
In three seal rings; which after, melted down,
310 Formed a vast buckle for his widow's gown:
Her infant grandame's whistle next it grew,
The bells she jingled, and the whistle blew;
Then in a bodkin graced her mother's hairs,
Which long she wore, and now Belinda wears.)
315   "Boast not my fall" (he cried) "insulting foe!
Thou by some other shalt be laid as low.
Nor think, to die dejects my lofty mind;
All that I dread is leaving you behind!
Rather than so, ah let me still survive,
320 And burn in Cupid's flames—but burn alive."
    "Restore the lock!" she cries; and all around
"Restore the lock!" the vaulted roofs rebound.
Not fierce Othello in so loud a strain
Roared for the handkerchief that caused his pain.
325 But see how oft ambitious aims are crossed,
And chiefs contend till all the prize is lost!
The lock, obtained with guilt, and kept with pain,
In every place is sought, but sought in vain:
With such a prize no mortal must be blest,
330 So Heaven decrees! with Heaven who can contest?
    Some thought it mounted to the lunar sphere,
Since all things lost on earth are treasured there.
There heroes' wits are kept in ponderous vases,

▲ In "The Rape of the Lock" (Aubrey Beardsley, 1896), the Baron, scissors in hand, is poised to commit the dastardly deed. What kind of social world does this illustration reflect?

The Rape of the Lock   **323**

And beaus' in snuffboxes and tweezer cases.
335 There broken vows, and deathbed alms are found,
And lovers' hearts with ends of ribbon bound;
The courtier's promises, and sick man's prayers,
The smiles of harlots, and the tears of heirs,
Cages for gnats, and chains to yoke a flea,
340 Dried butterflies, and tomes of casuistry.
        But trust the Muse—she saw it upward rise,
Though marked by none but quick, poetic eyes:
(So Rome's great founder to the heavens withdrew,
To Proculus alone confessed in view.)
345 A sudden star, it shot through liquid air,
And drew behind a radiant trail of hair.
Not Berenice's locks first rose so bright,
The heavens bespangling with dishevelled light.
The Sylphs behold it kindling as it flies,
350 And pleased pursue its progress through the skies.
        This the beau monde shall from the Mall survey,
And hail with music its propitious ray.
This, the blessed lover shall for Venus take,
And send up vows from Rosamonda's lake.
355 This Partridge soon shall view in cloudless skies,
When next he looks through Galileo's eyes;
And hence the egregious wizard shall foredoom
The fate of Louis, and the fall of Rome.
        Then cease, bright nymph! to mourn thy ravished hair
360 Which adds new glory to the shining sphere!
Not all the tresses that fair head can boast
Shall draw such envy as the lock you lost.
For, after all the murders of your eye,
When, after millions slain, yourself shall die;
365 When those fair suns shall set, as set they must,
And all those tresses shall be laid in dust;
This lock, the Muse shall consecrate to fame,
And 'midst the stars inscribe Belinda's name!

340 tomes of casuistry, books containing overly subtle reasoning about ethical issues.
343–344 Rome's great founder . . . view, Romulus, who supposedly ascended to heaven, witnessed only by a Roman senator named Proculus.
347 Berenice's locks. According to legend, Berenice offered her hair to Venus for the safe return of her husband from war. The hair was transformed into a heavenly constellation.
351 beau monde . . . Mall, fashionable society will see the transformed lock of hair from the promenade in St. James's Park.
354 Rosamonda's lake, in St. James's Park.
355–358 Partridge . . . Rome. John Partridge (1644–1715) was an astrologer who annually predicted the downfall of the King of France and the Pope. "Galileo's eyes" is a reference to the telescope.
357 egregious (i grē′jəs), *adj.* extraordinarily bad.
359 ravished (rav′isht), *adj.* stolen.

■ Does this poem have a happy ending? Why or why not?

An Essay on Criticism

Alexander Pope

Pope's couplets and epigrams are often quoted. Here is a sample.

1. 'Tis with our judgments as our watches; none
   Go just alike, yet each believes his own.
2. Let such teach others who themselves excel,
   And censure freely who have written well.
3. Music resembles poetry; in each
   Are nameless graces which no methods teach.
4. Of all the causes which conspire to blind
   Man's erring judgment, and misguide the mind,
   What the weak head with strongest bias rules,
   Is pride, the never-failing vice of fools.
5. Trust not yourself: but your defects to know,
   Make use of every friend—and every foe.
6. A little learning is a dangerous thing;
   Drink deep, or taste not the Pierian spring.[1]
   There shallow draughts intoxicate the brain,
   And drinking largely sobers us again.
7. 'Tis not a lip, or eye, we beauty call,
   But the joint force and full result of all.
8. True wit is Nature to advantage dressed,
   What oft was thought, but ne'er so well expressed.
9. As shades more sweetly recommend the light,
   So modest plainness sets off sprightly wit.
10. Words are like leaves; and where they most abound,
    Much fruit of sense beneath is rarely found.
11. True ease in writing comes from art, not chance,
    As those move easiest who have learned to dance.
12. Be not the first by whom the new are tried,
    Nor yet the last to lay the old aside.
13. Some praise at morning what they blame at night,
    But always think the last opinion right.
14. We think our fathers fools, so wise we grow;
    Our wiser sons, no doubt, will think us so.
15. Good nature and good sense must ever join;
    To err is human, to forgive divine.

---

1. **Pierian** (pī ir′ē ən) **spring,** that is, inspiration; from
   Pieria, where the Greek Muses were born.

After Reading

Making Connections

Shaping Your Response

1. Write three words that you think describe "The Rape of the Lock." List all the words you and your classmates come up with and tally their frequency. Finally, create one or more word webs to show how your class feels about the poem.

2. Arabella Fermor and Lord Petre were apparently amused and flattered at being the subjects of this poem. How would you have reacted at reading such a treatment of your own experiences? Explain.

Analyzing the Poems

3. Line 53 refers to a priestess and an altar and line 54 refers to sacred rites. Are these references appropriate? Explain.

4. Epics often contain references to classical mythology. Explain how such references contribute to the **mock-epic** nature of this poem.

5. What do you think is the purpose of Clarissa's speech in canto 5 (lines 257-282)?

6. How does "The Rape of the Lock" fit the definition of **satire** (see page 295)? In your opinion, is it a successful satire?

Extending the Ideas

7. Has the "warfare" between the sexes changed since Pope's time, or are the **interactions** about the same today as they were then? Discuss.

8. Which of the quotations from "An Essay on Criticism" do you think has the most to communicate to today's world? Why?

Literary Focus: Heroic Couplet/Epigram

In a **heroic couplet,** a pair of rhymed lines written in iambic pentameter, the second line may complete the thought of the first, restate it, expand it, or contrast it. What does the second line do in this example?

> Beauties in vain their pretty eyes may roll;
> Charms strike the sight, but merit wins the soul.

An **epigram,** a short witty verse, usually ends with a wry twist. What clever turn of thought is contained in this epigram?

> Trust not yourself; but your defects to know,
> Make use of every friend—and every foe.

Expressing Your Ideas

Writing Choices

Writer's Notebook Update Try your hand at writing a heroic couplet (or an epigram). Use some of the ideas and rhyming words you jotted down.

Know Any Good Satirists? Who are some modern satirists? Research three or four columnists, radio commentators, or comedians on television. What are their topics? Write a **profile,** such as might appear in a popular magazine, of one or more of them. Describe their usual subject matter and their satirical techniques. End by telling which satirist you prefer and why.

How Far Is Too Far? How far should a comedian or talk-show host go in satirizing public figures or ethnic, religious, or social groups? Some people feel that satirists go too far and should respect some limits, while others feel that our freedom of speech means "anything goes." In a **letter to the editor** of your local newspaper, examine the difference, if any, between satire and spite, remembering the purpose of satire.

"Dah-h-h-ling—!" Imagine a meeting between Belinda and a young society woman of today. (If you don't know any society women, think of a character from a TV show.) What might they have to say to each other? Would they be friends or would they end up having a "cat fight"? Write the **dialogue** of their meeting. You might work with some classmates to read it aloud.

Other Options

Picture This Editorial cartoons are almost always satirical. Look through at least five issues of a daily paper, including a Sunday paper, to see what topics are currently the focus of the cartoons on the editorial page. ("Our Glorious Leaders" in the Interdisciplinary Study on pages 328–329 shows some examples of editorial cartoons.) Then try your hand at creating an **editorial cartoon**.

On a More Serious Note It's possible that Belinda might have settled down enough to attend a performance of one of George Frederick Handel's works. Handel (1685–1759) was born in Germany but settled permanently in England, where he wrote oratorios (including the well-known *Messiah),* operas, choral works, and works for orchestra. With one or more partners, prepare an **illustrated report** on Handel. Take turns describing his life and work, and supply some brief examples of his music.

"Begin the Attack" Physical conflict is a subject that is endlessly explored in various media from ballet to movie fight sequences. Plan the **choreography** of the fight between Belinda and the Baron. You could stage it as an elaborate dance of the 1700s or as a modern brawl. Include some of the other characters if you wish. Use sensible precautions; you know that even the most violent movie fight is carefully planned and thoroughly rehearsed so that no one gets injured.

Satirical Thrusts

A Focus on Society

Popular Culture Connection

No one in the public eye seems to be immune from being the subject of someone's satirical view. U.S. Presidents and the British Royal Family have been particulary vulnerable, as shown by these political cartoons and puppet caricatures.

Satirical Thrusts

Reprinted Courtesy of The Boston Globe

Lyndon Johnson

"We are not going to send American boys 9,000 or 10,000 miles away to do what Asian boys ought to be doing for themselves."
—Lyndon Johnson (1964 campaign)

Bill Clinton

Ronald Reagan & George Bush

Jimmy Carter

Queen Elizabeth & Prince Charles

The Spitting Image, a 1986 weekly show from Britain, entertained television audiences with approximately 400 rubbery puppets and satirical wit. The program broke all television rules and delivered heartless skits from the Royal family to the Pope and the President of the United States.

Richard Nixon

"I am not a crook . . . anymore."

Responding

1. Do you agree that anyone at anytime in any circumstances ought to be fair game for a satirist?

2. What, in general, seems to be the message of most political satire?

Career Connection

Satire is alive and well and living in many places, one of them being your daily newspaper. Here a political cartoonist talks about his job.

HOPING FOR A VISCERAL REACTION

Interview with Jack Higgins

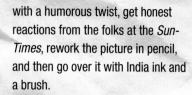

One of only a few political cartoonists for major newspapers who prefer to use local rather than national or international politics as inspiration, Jack Higgins works for the *Chicago Sun-Times*. Two early interests of his—drawing and politics—merged in his college years to become his career.

"I've been drawing since about two-and-a-half. Through high school, I was largely self-taught from how-to books. In college, my major was economics, but I took anatomy and other art courses, and these took me to a higher skill level. With a teacher critiquing me, I could immediately see my mistakes.

"My interest in politics also came at a young age. On election day when I was a boy, the politicians gave us kids palm cards to pass out to voters. These were cards that could be hidden in the palm of the hand and listed who to vote for. No one was supposed to campaign within a hundred feet of the polling place, but kids passing out these little cards weren't noticed. Afterwards, the politicians took us out for ice cream. To me, politics was a sport.

"I started thinking about political cartooning in college when I saw Paul Szep's work for the *Boston Globe*. I liked his methods and meatiness, his directness, his wit and vinegar. He was doing cartoons on local politics in Boston. I thought, 'Chicago is a lot like Boston!' I realized that art came in handy for cartooning. I liked being able to study the

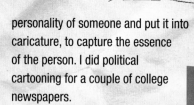

personality of someone and put it into caricature, to capture the essence of the person. I did political cartooning for a couple of college newspapers.

"My creative method is to get up at 4:00 A.M. My mind is clear then. I start reading newspapers and taking notes. If I get angry about something, I write it down. Then I write down everything I can think of about what makes me angriest that day. From that, I develop a pencil sketch—usually

with a humorous twist, get honest reactions from the folks at the *Sun-Times*, rework the picture in pencil, and then go over it with India ink and a brush.

"Although political cartoons are called satire, I don't like to use that term. Putting labels on takes the fun out. My art comes from deeply within me. I don't over analyze it. And I hope for a visceral reaction to my work from readers. The language of the cartoonist is very different from that of the writer, who analyzes an issue and fashions a logical argument. We cartoonists give you about ten seconds to let the picture sink in, and then we hope it will stay in the back of your mind to shape your thoughts."

1. Discuss the ways in which your reaction as a viewer to a cartoon is different from your reaction as a reader to an essay or article.

2. Do you agree that labeling cartoons as satire takes the fun out of it? Why or why not?

3. Which of the issues in today's news gives you a visceral (gut) reaction?

Writing Workshop

My Modest Proposal

Assignment Using Jonathan Swift's "A Modest Proposal" as a model, offer your own satirical solution to one of society's problems.

WRITER'S BLUEPRINT

Product	A satirical essay
Purpose	To provoke change through ridicule
Audience	Readers of a magazine of current events
Specs	As the writer of an effective essay, you should:

❏ Imagine that you're writing for a magazine that publishes articles about current events. Focus on a controversial issue, a problem that people are divided on, such as what to do about homelessness, government inefficiency, smoking, litter, teen pregnancy, or illiteracy.

❏ Introduce the problem and your concerns in a serious, reasonable tone. Then propose your unrealistic, exaggerated solution, which will be the opposite of your true position on the issue. Present this solution step by step in this same reasonable tone, using some of the satirical techniques that Swift employs in "A Modest Proposal."

❏ Mention realistic alternatives to your solution and dismiss them in this same reasonable tone.

❏ Conclude by summing up how the world will be a better place after your solution is adopted.

❏ Make smooth transitions between ideas.

❏ Follow the rules of grammar, usage, spelling, and mechanics. Avoid careless spelling mistakes.

STEP **1** PREWRITING

Analyze the literature. Look back at Swift's "A Modest Proposal" and list quotes from the text that show Swift's use of each of these satirical techniques: sarcasm, exaggeration, flattering the reader, appealing to

OR . . .
Working in a group, take turns reading "A Modest Proposal" aloud. Let group members identify satirical techniques as they hear them.

LITERARY SOURCE
"A child will make two dishes at an entertainment for friends; and when the family dines alone, the fore or hind quarter will make a reasonable dish. . . ."
    from "A Modest Proposal" by Jonathan Swift

OR . . .
Plan a series of visuals to go along with your writing. Make rough sketches of situations that illustrate your modest proposal in action.

logic and reason, creating an aura of objectivity, appealing to emotions, dehumanizing the subject. Then look for these techniques in other sources, such as the TV show *Saturday Night Live,* the writings of Woody Allen and Dave Barry, or articles in *Mad Magazine.*

Choose an issue to satirize. Select a controversial issue that will be familiar to your readers and about which you know enough to write convincingly.

Make a writing plan. Look over the examples that follow. Then complete a plan like this one for your own modest proposal.

Problem: the divisive controversy over smoking

My true position: that smoking should be banned

The unrealistic solution I will propose: (See the Literary Source.)

—Everyone will be forced to take up smoking.

—All laws regulating smoking will be struck down . . .

How this solution will be brought about:

—The U.S. Congress will pass a law stating that . . .

—Cigarettes will be made available to kids in candy machines and . . .

My reasons:

—Since this is a democratic society, we should all be equally at risk.

—People will smoke anyway, so why not . . .

Opposing positions—my responses:

—Smoking is hazardous to your health—true, but people smoke anyway, so why not . . .

How the world will be a better place:

—Since everyone will be smoking, there will be less conflict . . .
and so on . . .

STEP **2** DRAFTING

As you draft, keep these suggestions in mind:

• Keep your notes on satirical techniques at hand and look for places to use them.

- Don't make the mistake of telling your audience that you're not serious. The fun of reading satire is joining with the author in momentarily imagining that these outrageous ideas are reasonable.

- Connect one idea to the next, using smooth transitions. For more information, see the Revising Strategy in Step 3 of this lesson.

REVISING

Ask a partner for comments on your draft before you revise it. Pay special attention to making smooth transitions.

Revising Strategy

Making Smooth Transitions

Your satire will be full of different ideas. When you connect these ideas with smooth transitions, your readers will feel comfortable because they'll know where you're taking them. Notice how the writer of the student model added transitions to connect ideas.

> There is only one option left at this point, *That is, we should* to enforce smoking everywhere and in everyone's lives. Of course nonsmokers are not used to the horrid smell and bitter taste that smokers have grown to love. *On the other hand,* It is not that difficult to get used to. If nonsmokers just gave in and tried it there would be no more controversy. Society would be in perfect harmony.

STUDENT MODEL

STEP 4 EDITING

Ask a partner to review your revised draft before you edit. When you edit, look for errors in grammar, usage, spelling, and mechanics. Pay special attention to catching careless spelling mistakes.

Editing Strategy

Avoiding Careless Spelling Mistakes

Many simple words are misspelled because they're so familiar that we tend to overlook them. To catch careless misspellings, proofread your draft several times for different kinds of errors. Set aside one time just for spelling. Here are some commonly misspelled words to watch for:

friend	finally	something	usually
probably	really	themselves	because
favorite	especially	different	except

STEP 5 PRESENTING

Here are some ideas for presenting your modest proposal.

- With other members of your class, publish a satirical magazine complete with essays, cartoons, and an appealing cover.

- Collaborate with a small group to adapt your satirical essay into a sketch to be performed as part of a comedy revue.

STEP 6 LOOKING BACK

Self-evaluate. Look back at the Writer's Blueprint and give yourself a score on each point, from 6 (superior) to 1 (inadequate).

Reflect. Write your responses to these questions.

✔ In general, which do you think is the more effective way to make a controversial point: satire or straightforward criticism? Why?

✔ Compare your rough draft with your finished copy. Did you follow the Revising Strategy (using transitional phrases to connect ideas) and Editing Strategy (avoiding careless spelling mistakes)?

For Your Working Portfolio Add your satirical essay and your reflection responses to your working portfolio.

Beyond Print

Analyzing Political Cartoons

All cartoons may use the same tools—including satire—to make a point, but political cartoons (also called editorial cartoons) may have more of a point, or a sharper one. Review the cartoons in Satirical Thrusts on pages 328–329. Consider these questions.

What is the central issue? What is it about in general? Poverty? Gun control? War in a foreign country? Look for labels on people or places, or look for familiar (if exaggerated) faces to help identify the issue.

How does the art comment on the issue? Political cartoon art is often exaggerated. Faces are distorted to look sly or stupid or evil. Look at what is included besides people. Unusual clothing may be symbolic; other symbols may be evident as well. The characters' physical relationships to each other and the actions they are performing are usually important.

What does a caption contribute? Political cartoons often include simple but punchy captions. These are not always straightforward but may be heavily ironic or sarcastic. Study how the caption works together with the art.

What is the cartoonist's viewpoint? Whatever the central issue is, does the cartoonist seem finally to be in favor of it or against it? Does the cartoonist seem to wish that the subjects of the cartoon were behaving differently? that you, the viewer, would do something in response?

Is it convincing? Finally, you be the judge. Is the cartoon funny and right on target? Does it work for you? Remember, you don't have to agree with all the political beliefs of a satirist in order to appreciate a satire; likewise, you can enjoy a cartoon and appreciate its effectiveness even if it doesn't make you want to change the world accordingly.

Activity Option

Work in a small group to collect and study a number of cartoons from around the country on the same theme or central issue. How many different viewpoints can you identify? How do the different cartoonists use their art to express their different viewpoints?

A Kaleidoscope

HISTORICAL OVERVIEW

The Age of Reason delighted in examining human character—in general and in particular individuals. Many of the writers of the period, including Samuel Pepys, Samuel Johnson, and James Boswell, produced a great variety of vivid and insightful descriptions of themselves and others in diaries, journals, letters, autobiographies, biographies, and other writings. One reason for this was the belief that literature, by presenting examples of human behavior—both good and bad—should serve the function of improving people's morals. Another reason was the growing influence of a middle-class audience for literature, who wanted to read about people like themselves. But the main reason, most likely, was simply the perennial fascination exerted by human personality.

I sighed as a lover; I obeyed as a son.

1725 ~ Edward Gibbon, on his father's refusal to let him marry. *Memoirs of My Own Life*

He had some wit, . . . but it was of that sort which is rather happy than permanent. Once a week he might say a good thing.

1762 ~ Oliver Goldsmith, *The Life of Richard Nash*

I give my self sometimes admirable advice, but I am incapable of taking it.

1725 ~ Lady Mary Wortley Montagu, letter

EDWARD GIBBON

OLIVER GOLDSMITH

MARY WORTLEY

# of Characters

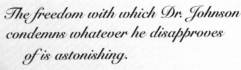

The freedom with which Dr. Johnson condemns whatever he disapproves of is astonishing.

1778 ~ Fanny Burney, diary entry

He hated all whom he was required to obey. . . . He felt not so much the love of liberty as repugnance to authority.

1779 ~ Samuel Johnson, Life of Milton

Miss Blachford is agreeable enough. I do not want people to be very agreeable, as it saves me the trouble of liking them a good deal.

1798 ~ Jane Austen, letter

FANNY BURNEY

SAMUEL JOHNSON

JANE AUSTEN

Key Dates

1652
First coffeehouse opens in London.

1660
The monarchy is restored under Charles II.

1660
The theaters reopen.

1662
The Royal Society is founded to encourage scientific research.

1665
The plague kills 70,000 in London.

1666
The Great Fire of London occurs.

1688
The Glorious Revolution creates a limited monarchy.

1710
St. Paul's Cathedral is completed.

1730
Hogarth completes his satirical graphic series The Rake's Progress.

1755
Johnson's Dictionary *is published.*

Part 2

Other People's Lives

Is any pastime more widely enjoyed than minding other people's business? From watching our next-door neighbors through a window to reading a magazine article about a movie actor's divorce to watching television dramatizations of the sexy or tragic events in some celebrity's life story, we are fascinated by other people. Perhaps it is in part because we hope sometime, somehow to be able to tell about ourselves.

🐾 **Multicultural Connection** **Communication** plays an integral role when groups and persons of different backgrounds come into contact with each other, observe each other, attempt to talk with each other, or write about their perceptions of each other. Each of the following selections is in a different genre, or form. How are they similar in their attempts to communicate understandings about people's lives? How do they differ?

Before Reading

from The Diary

by Samuel Pepys

Samuel Pepys
1633–1703

Educated at St. Paul's School, London, and Magdalene College, Cambridge, Samuel Pepys (pēps) spent much of his lifetime as a civil servant, working for many years as an official in the Admiralty, the government agency that runs the British navy. In 1673 he was promoted to Secretary to the Admiralty and that same year became a member of Parliament. He left public service in 1689. The remaining years of his life Pepys devoted to amassing and cataloguing a 3,000-volume library, which he donated to his college. In literary circles Pepys is remembered for his fresh and spontaneous diaries in which he recorded his life from age 26 to age 36.

Building Background

Through Great Events—and Small Each evening Samuel Pepys took out his leather notebook and his pen and dashed down his impressions of the day. His mind worked quickly, and, because he used a special shorthand, his thoughts often tumbled together. He re-created the burned dinner his wife prepared, the headache he had because he drank too much wine, his wife's flirting with the dance instructor. He described his new silk suit with the gold buttons, his attempts to learn the multiplication tables, the crowd at a cock fight. He presented the silly sermon he heard at church, the first time he saw a woman acting on stage, the contracts he wrote as a member of the Navy Board. He depicted the Lord Chancellor snoring during Privy Council meetings, the King in his elegant velvet robes on coronation day, the Great Plague of 1665 striking at the houses of friends. Through great events—and small—for ten years (1660–1669) Pepys recorded the details of his life in London. A century and a half later, in 1819, a young scholar at Magdalene College labored over the six leather-bound diaries of Pepys, deciphering the chicken-scratch shorthand. Early editions of the diaries suppressed material considered unsuitable or scandalous. Not until the 1970s were Pepys's complete diaries published.

Literary Focus

Imagery The use of details that appeal to the senses (that is, call for a sensory response) is called **imagery**. Sensory images often help a reader experience an action or a scene by creating mental pictures. Which of your senses would you expect to be stimulated by reading an account of a great fire devastating a city?

Writer's Notebook

"Dear Diary . . ." Everyone enjoys talking about his or her life, but few are able to maintain the discipline necessary to record the events of their lives day after day for an extended period. Have you ever tried to keep a diary? Did you succeed? Why or why not? Write a brief account of your diary-keeping experience, or else write a diary entry for your most memorable day of this week.

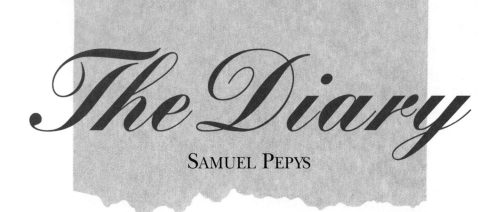

The Diary

SAMUEL PEPYS

The portion of Pepys's diary included here deals largely with the Great Fire of London, which started on September 2, 1666, and raged out of control for almost a week. Before it was extinguished, it had destroyed two-thirds of London. More than 13,000 houses were burned, plus other buildings, including 87 churches and St. Paul's Cathedral. Miraculously, fewer than ten people seem to have died in the fire, but tens of thousands were homeless, camping out in makeshift tents in the fields adjacent to London. It is difficult to comprehend what the burning of London meant in its day. Pepys helps us to realize some of this through his vivid eyewitness descriptions. One thing, however, he does not tell us, for he did not know it: never again was London paralyzed by the plague, perhaps because the fire destroyed the rats that carried the plague as well as the old buildings that harbored them.

SEPTEMBER 2, 1666 (Lord's day). Some of our maids sitting up late last night to get things ready against our feast today, Jane [Pepys's maid] called us up about three in the morning, to tell us of a great fire they saw in the City.[1] So I rose and slipped on my nightgown, and went to her window; and thought it to be on the backside of Mark Lane at the farthest; but, being unused to such fires as followed, I thought it far enough off; and so went to bed again, and to sleep. About seven rose again to dress myself, and there looked out at the window, and saw the fire not so much as it was, and further off. So to my closet[2] to set things to rights, after yesterday's cleaning. By and by Jane comes and tells me that she hears that above 300 houses have been burned down tonight by the fire we saw, and that it is now burning down all Fish Street, by London Bridge. So I made myself ready presently, and walked to the Tower;[3] and there got up upon one of the high places, Sir J.

Robinson's little son going up with me; and there I did see the houses at that end of the bridge all on fire, and an infinite[4] great fire on this and the other side the end of the bridge; which, among other people, did trouble me for poor little Michell and our Sarah on the bridge.[5] So down with my heart full of trouble, to the Lieutenant of the Tower, who tells me that it begun this morning in the King's baker's house in Pudding Lane, and that it hath burned St. Magnus's Church and most part of Fish Street already. So I down to the waterside, and there

---

1. **the City,** the area within the medieval walls of London; the business district.
2. **closet,** study.
3. **Tower,** the Tower of London, a medieval fort on the Thames River.
4. **infinite** (in′fə nit), *adj.* endless.
5. **on the bridge.** In Pepys's time, London Bridge was covered with houses and shops.

▲ This painting, *The Great Fire of London, Showing Ludgate and Old St. Paul's,* was done by an unknown British artist in the late 1600s. Do you think the artist succeeds in depicting what Pepys refers to as the "extraordinary vehemence" of the fire? Explain your answer.

got a boat,[6] and through bridge and there saw a lamentable[7] fire. Poor Michell's house, as far as the Old Swan, already burned that way, and the fire running further, that, in a very little time, it got as far as the Steelyard, while I was there. Everybody endeavoring to remove their goods, and flinging into the river, or bringing them into lighters[8] that lay off; poor people staying in their houses as long as till the very fire touched them, and then running into boats, or clambering[9] from one pair of stairs, by the waterside, to another. And, among other things, the poor pigeons, I perceive, were loath[10] to leave their houses, but hovered about the windows and balconies, till some of them burned their wings, and fell down.

Having stayed, and in an hour's time seen the fire rage every way; and nobody, to my sight, endeavoring to quench[11] it, but to remove their goods, and leave all to the fire, and having seen it get as far as the Steelyard, and the wind mighty high, and driving it into the city: and everything, after so long a drought,[12] proving combustible,[13] even the very stones of churches; and, among other things, the poor steeple by which pretty Mrs.—— lives, and whereof my old schoolfellow Elborough is parson, taken fire in the very top, and there burned till it fell down; I to Whitehall,[14] with a gentleman with me who desired to go off from the Tower, to see the fire, in my boat; to Whitehall, and there up to the King's closet in the Chapel, where people come about me, and I did give them an account dismayed them all, and word was carried into the King. So I was called for, and did tell the King and Duke of York what I saw; and, that unless his Majesty did command houses to be pulled down, nothing could stop the fire. They seemed much troubled, and the King commanded me to go to my Lord Mayor[15] from him, and command him to spare no houses, but to pull down before the fire every way. The Duke of York bid me tell him, that if he would have any more soldiers, he shall; and so did my Lord Arlington afterwards, as a great secret. Here meeting with Captain Cocke, I in his coach, which he lent me, and Creed with me to Paul's;[16] and there walked along Watling Street, as well as I could, every creature coming away loaden with goods to save, and here and there, sick people carried away in beds. Extraordinary good goods carried in carts and on backs. At last met my Lord Mayor in Canning Street, like a man spent, with a handkerchief about his neck. To the King's message, he cried like a fainting woman, "Lord! what can I do? I am spent; people will not obey me. I have been pulling down houses; but the fire overtakes us faster than we can do it." That he needed no more soldiers; and that, for himself, he must go and refresh himself, having been up all night. So he left me, and I him, and walked home, seeing people all almost distracted, and no manner of means used to quench the fire. The houses, too, so very thick thereabouts, and full of matter for burning, as pitch and tar, in Thames Street; and warehouses of oil, and wines, and brandy, and other things. Here I saw Mr. Isaake Houblon, that handsome man, prettily dressed and dirty at his door at Dowgate, receiving some of his brothers' things, whose houses were on fire; and, as he says, have been removed twice already; and he doubts (as it soon proved) that they must be, in a little time, removed from his house also, which was a sad consideration. And to see the churches all filling with goods by people who themselves should have been quietly there at this time.

---

6. **boat.** Small boats rowed by "watermen" were a common form of transportation in the city.
7. **lamentable** (lam′ən tə bəl), *adj.* sorrowful.
8. **lighter,** small, flat-bottomed boat.
9. **clamber** (klam′bər), *v.* climb awkwardly or with difficulty.
10. **loath** (lōth), *adj.* reluctant.
11. **quench** (kwench), *v.* drown out; put out.
12. **drought** (drout), *n.* period of dry weather.
13. **combustible** (kəm bus′tə bəl), *adj.* easily burned.
14. **Whitehall,** the king's residence and offices in London.
15. **Lord Mayor,** of London.
16. **Paul's,** St. Paul's Cathedral. Pepys travels back toward the fire, to one of the largest churches in London, which the fire is soon to destroy.

John Keeling's fire engine is shown in this illustration. Fire-fighting equipment such as this lacked efficient pumps and flexible hose. Do you think that a fire on the scale of the Great Fire of London could occur today in a city equipped with modern fire-fighting equipment? Why or why not?

By this time, it was about twelve o'clock; and so home, and there find my guests, which was Mr. Wood and his wife Barbary Shelden, and also Mr. Moone; she mighty fine, and her husband, for aught I see, a likely man. But Mr. Moone's design and mine, which was to look over my closet, and please him with the sight thereof, which he hath long desired, was wholly disappointed; for we were in great trouble and disturbance at this fire, not knowing what to think of it. However, we had an extraordinary dinner, and as merry as at this time we could be.

While at dinner, Mrs. Batelier come to enquire after Mr. Woolfe and Stanes (who, it seems, are related to them) whose houses in Fish Street are all burned, and they in a sad condition. She would not stay in the fright.

As soon as dined, I and Moone away, and walked through the City, the streets full of nothing but people and horses and carts loaden with goods, ready to run over one another, and removing goods from one burned house to another. They now removing out of Canning Street, which received goods in the morning, into Lombard Street, and further; and among others, I now saw my little goldsmith Stokes receiving some friend's goods, whose house itself was burned the day after. We parted at Paul's; he home, and I to Paul's Wharf, where I had appointed a boat to attend me, and took in Mr. Carcasse and his brother, whom I met in the street, and carried them below and above bridge too and again to see the fire, which was now got further, both below and above, and no likelihood of stopping it. Met with the King and Duke of York in their barge, and with them to Queenhithe, and there called Sir Richard Browne to them. Their order was only to pull down houses apace,[17] and so below bridge at the waterside; but little was or could be done, the fire coming upon them so fast. Good hopes there was of stopping it at the Three Cranes above, and at Buttulph's Wharf below bridge, if care be used; but the wind carries it into the city, so as we know not, by the waterside, what it do there. River full of lighters and boats taking in goods, and good goods swimming in the water; and only I observed that hardly one lighter or boat in three that had the goods of a house in, but there was a pair of virginals[18] in it. Having seen as much as I could now, I away to Whitehall by appointment, and there walked to St. James's Park; and there met my wife, and Creed, and Wood, and his wife, and walked to my boat; and there upon the water again, and to the fire up and down, it still increasing, and the wind great. So near the fire as we could for smoke; and all over the Thames, with one's face in the wind, you were almost burned with a shower of fire-drops. This is very true; so as houses were burned by these drops and flakes of fire, three or four, nay, five or six houses, one from another. When we could endure no more upon the water, we to a little ale house on the Bankside,

---

17. **apace** (ə pās′), *adv.* quickly; fast.
18. **virginal,** small legless piano.

over against the Three Cranes, and there stayed till it was dark almost and saw the fire grow; and, as it grew darker, appeared more and more; and in corners and upon steeples, and between churches and houses, as far as we could see up the hill of the city, in a most horrid, malicious,[19] bloody flame, not like the fine flame of an ordinary fire. Barbary and her husband away before us. We stayed till, it being darkish, we saw the fire as only one entire arch of fire from this to the other side the bridge, and in a bow up the hill for an arch of above a mile long; it made me weep to see it. The churches, houses, and all on fire, and flaming at once; and a horrid noise the flames made, and the cracking of houses at their ruin. So home with a sad heart, and there find everybody discoursing[20] and lamenting the fire; and poor Tom Hater come with some few of his goods saved out of his house, which was burned upon Fish Street Hill. I invited him to lie at my house, and did receive his goods; but was deceived in his lying there, the news coming every moment of the growth of the fire; so as we were forced to begin to pack up our own goods, and prepare for their removal; and did by moonshine, it being brave, dry, and moonshine and warm weather, carry much of my goods into the garden; and Mr. Hater and I did remove my money and iron chests into my cellar, as thinking that the safest place. And got my bags of gold into my office, ready to carry away, and my chief papers of accounts also there, and my tallies into a box by themselves. So great was our fear, as Sir W. Batten hath carts come out of the country to fetch away his goods this night. We did put Mr. Hater, poor man! to bed a little; but he got but very little rest, so much noise being in my house, taking down of goods.

> 🐾 **EVALUATE: How important a role does communication play in fighting the fire and in evacuating the city?**

SEPTEMBER 3. About four o'clock in the morning, my Lady Batten sent me a cart to carry away all my money and plate and best things to Sir W. Rider's at Bednall Green; which I did, riding myself in my nightgown in the cart; and, Lord! to see how the streets and the highways are crowded with people, running and riding and getting of carts at any rate to fetch away things. I find Sir W. Rider tired with being called up all night and receiving things from several friends. His house full of goods, and much of Sir W. Batten and Sir W. Penn's. I am eased at my heart to have my treasure so well secured. Then home with much ado to find a way. Nor any sleep all this night to me nor my poor wife. But then, and all this day, she and I and all my people[21] laboring to get away the rest of our things, and did get Mr. Tooker to get me a lighter to take them in, and we did carry them (myself some) over Tower Hill, which was by this time full of people's goods, bringing their goods thither. And down to the lighter, which lay at the next quay[22] above the Towerdock. And here was my neighbor's wife, Mrs.——, with her pretty child and some few of her things, which I did willingly give way to be saved with mine. But there was no passing with anything through the postern,[23] the crowd was so great. At night, lay down a little upon a quilt of W. Hewer in the office (all my own things being packed up or gone); and after me, my poor wife did the like—we having fed upon the remains of yesterday's dinner, having no fire nor dishes, nor any opportunity of dressing anything.

SEPTEMBER 4. Up by break of day to get away the remainder of my things, which I did by a lighter at the Iron Gate; and my hands so few,

---

19. malicious (mə lish′əs), *adj.* evil.
20. **discourse** (dis kôrs′), *v.* talk.
21. **my people,** Pepys's servants.
22. **quay** (kē), *n.* landing place for ships.
23. **postern** (pō′stərn), *n.* a small door or gate.

that it was the afternoon before we could get them all away.

Sir W. Penn and I to Tower Street, and there met the fire burning three or four doors beyond Mr. Howells; whose goods, poor man (his trays and dishes, shovels etc., were flung all along Tower Street in the kennels,[24] and people working therewith from one end to the other), the fire coming on in that narrow street, on both sides, with infinite fury. Sir W. Batten, not knowing how to remove his wine, did dig a pit in the garden and laid it in there; and I took the opportunity of laying all the papers of my office that I could not otherwise dispose of. And in the evening Sir W. Penn and I did dig another and put our wine in it, and I my Parmesan cheese as well as my wine and some other things.

. . . the whole heaven on fire

This night Mrs. Turner, who poor woman, was removing her goods all this day—good goods, into the garden, and knew not how to dispose of them—and her husband supped with my wife and I at night in the office, upon a shoulder of mutton from the cook's, without any napkin or anything, in a sad manner but were merry. Only, now and then walking into the garden and saw how horridly the sky looks, all on a fire in the night, was enough to put us out of our wits; and indeed it was extremely dreadful, for it looks just as if it was at us, and the whole heaven on fire. I after supper walked in the dark down to Tower Street, and there saw it all on fire at the Trinity house on that side and the Dolphin Tavern on this side, which was very near us—and the fire with extraordinary vehemence.[25] Now begins the practice of blowing up of houses in Tower Street, those next the Tower, which at first did frighten people more than anything; but it stopped the fire where it was done—it bring-

ing down the houses to the ground in the same places they stood, and then it was easy to quench what little fire was in it, though it kindled nothing almost. W. Hewer this day went to see how his mother did, and comes late home, but telling us how he hath been forced to remove her to Islington, her house in Pye Corner being burned. So that it is got so far that way and all the Old Bailey, and was running down to Fleet Street. And Paul's is burned, and all Cheapside. I wrote to my father this night; but the posthouse being burned, the letter could not go.

SEPTEMBER 5. I lay down in the office again upon W. Hewer's quilt, being mighty weary, and sore in my feet with going till I was hardly able to stand. About two in the morning my wife calls me up, and tells me of new cries of "Fire!"—it being come to Barking Church, which is the bottom of our land. I up; and finding it so, resolved presently to take her away, and did, and took my gold (which was about £2350). W. Hewer, and Jane down by Proundy's boat to Woolwich; but, Lord! what a sad sight it was by moonlight, to see the whole city almost on fire, that you might see it plain at Woolwich, as if you were by it. There, when I come, I find the gates[26] shut, but no guard kept at all; which troubled me, because of discourse now begun, that there is plot in it,[27] and that the French had done it. I got the gates open, and to Mr. Shelden's, where I locked up my gold, and charged my wife and W. Hewer never to leave the room without one of them in it, night or day. So back again, by the way seeing my goods well in the lighters at Deptford, and watched well by people. Home,

---

24. **kennel,** ditch down the center of the road for water and garbage.
25. **vehemence** (vē′ə məns), *n.* forcefulness; violence.
26. **gates,** to the dockyard.
27. **that there is plot in it,** that is, that the fire has been deliberately set.

and whereas I expected to have seen our house on fire, it being now about seven o'clock, it was not. But to the fire, and there find greater hopes than I expected; for my confidence of finding our office on fire was such, that I durst not ask anybody how it was with us, till I come and saw it not burned. But, going to the fire, I find, by the blowing up of houses, and the great help given by the workmen out of the King's yards, sent up by Sir W. Penn, there is a good stop given to it, as well as at Mark Lane end as ours; it having only burned the dial of Barking Church, and part of the porch, and was there quenched. I up to the top of Barking steeple, and there saw the saddest sight of desolation[28] that I ever saw; everywhere great fires, oil-cellars, and brimstone, and other things burning. I became afeard to stay there long, and therefore down again as fast as I could, the fire being spread as far as I could see it; and to Sir W. Penn's, and there eat a piece of cold meat, having eaten nothing since Sunday, but the remains of Sunday's dinner. Here I met with Mr. Young and Whistler; and having removed all my things, and received good hopes that the fire at our end is stopped, they and I walked into the town, and find Fenchurch Street, Gracious Street, and Lombard Street all in dust. The Exchange[29] a sad sight, nothing standing there, of all the statues or pillars, but Sir Thomas Gresham's picture in the corner. Walked into Moorfields, our feet ready to burn, walking through the town among the hot coals, and find that full of people, and poor wretches carrying their goods there, and everybody keeping his goods together by themselves; and a great blessing it is to them that it is fair weather for them to keep abroad night and day; drank there, and paid twopence for a plain penny loaf. Thence homeward, having passed through Cheapside, and Newgate Market, all burned; and seen Anthony Joyce's house in fire; and took up, which I keep by me, a piece of glass of Mercer's Chapel in the street, where much more was, so melted and buckled with the heat of the fire like parchment. I also did see a poor cat taken out of a hole in a chimney, joining to the wall of the Exchange, with the hair all burned off the body, and yet alive. So home at night, and find there good hopes of saving our office; but great endeavors of watching all night, and having men ready; and so we lodged them in the office, and had drink and bread and cheese for them. And I lay down and slept a good night about midnight; though, when I rose, I heard that there had been a great alarm of French and Dutch[30] being risen, which proved nothing. But it is a strange thing to see how long this time did look since Sunday, having been always full of variety of actions, and little sleep, that it looked like a week or more, and I had forgot almost the day of the week.

SEPTEMBER 6. Up about five o'clock, and there met Mr. Gawden at the gate of the office (I intending to go out, as I used every now and then to do, to see how the fire is) to call our men to Bishopsgate, where no fire had yet been near, and there is now one broke out—which did give great grounds to people, and to me too, to think that there is some kind of plot in this (on which many by this time have been taken, and it hath been dangerous for any stranger to walk in the streets); but I went with the men and we did put it out in a little time, so that that was well again. It was pretty to see how hard the women did work in the kennels sweeping of water; but then they would scold for drink and be as drunk as devils. I saw good butts of sugar broke open in the street, and people go and take handfuls out and put into beer and drink it. And now all being pretty well, I took boat and over to Southwark, and took boat on the other side the bridge and so to Westminster, thinking to

---

28. **desolation** (des′ə lā′shən), *n.* ruin; destruction.
29. **the Exchange,** a large building in which merchants met to discuss business.
30. **French and Dutch,** England's enemies at the time.

shift myself,[31] being all in dirt from top to bottom. But could not there find any place to buy a shirt or pair of gloves, Westminster Hall being full of people's goods—those in Westminster having removed all their goods, and the Exchequer money put into vessels to carry to Nonsuch.[32] But to the Swan, and there was trimmed. And then to Whitehall, but saw nobody, and so home. A sad sight to see how the River looks—no houses nor church near it to the Temple—where it stopped. At home did go with Sir W. Batten and our neighbor Knightly (who, with one more, was the only man of any fashion left in all the neighborhood hereabouts, they all removing their goods and leaving their houses to the mercy of the fire) to Sir R. Ford's, and there dined, in an earthen platter a fried breast of mutton, a great many of us. But very merry; and indeed as good a meal, though as ugly a one, as ever I had in my life. Thence down to Deptford, and there with great satisfaction landed all my goods at Sir G. Carteret's, safe, and nothing missed I could see, or hurt. This being done to my great content, I home; and to Sir W. Batten's, and there with Sir R. Ford, Mr. Knightly, and one Withers, a professed lying rogue, supped well; and mighty merry and our fears over. From them to the office and there slept, with the office full of laborers, who talked and slept and walked all night long there. But strange it was to see Clothworkers Hall on fire these three days and nights in one body of Flame—it being the cellar, full of Oil.

SEPTEMBER 7. Up by five o'clock and, blessed be God, find all well, and by water to Paul's Wharf. Walked thence and saw all the town burned, and a miserable sight of Paul's church, with all the roofs fallen and the body of the choir fallen into St. Faith's[33]—Paul's school also—Ludgate—Fleet Street—my father's house, and the church, and a good part of the Temple the like. So to Creeds lodging near the New Exchange, and there find him laid down upon a bed—the house all unfurnished, there being fears of the fire's coming to them. There borrowed a shirt of him—and washed. To Sir W. Coventry at St. James's, who lay without Curtains, having removed all his goods—as the King at Whitehall and everybody had done and was doing. He hopes we shall have no public distractions upon this fire, which is what everybody fears—because of the talk of the French having a hand in it. And it is a proper time for discontents—but all men's minds are full of care to protect themselves and save their goods. The militia is in arms everywhere.

SUMMARIZE: What are the possible theories about the origin of the fire?

This day our merchants first met at Gresham College, which by proclamation is to be their Exchange. Strange to hear what is bid for houses all up and down here—a friend of Sir W. Riders having £150 for what he used to let for £40/per annum. Much dispute where the Custom House shall be; thereby the growth of the City again to be foreseen. My Lord Treasurer, they say, and others, would have it at the other end of the town. I home late to Sir W. Penn, who did give me a bed—but without curtains or hangings, all being down. So here I went the first time into a naked bed, only my drawers on—and did sleep pretty well; but still, both sleeping and waking, had a fear of fire in my heart, that I took little rest.

---

31. **shift myself,** change clothes.
32. **Nonsuch,** a royal palace in Surrey, a district south of London.
33. **St. Faith's,** a chapel under St. Paul's Cathedral.

After Reading

Making Connections

Shaping Your Response

1. Which episodes about the fire stand out most clearly in your mind? Why?

Analyzing the Diary

2. From this excerpt, what can you tell about Pepys's everyday home life in normal times?

3. During the fire how does Pepys conduct himself as a public official? as a husband? as a friend?

4. What can you tell about Pepys's reputation in the community by the way he is treated by the nobility and by his friends?

5. Make a list of the items Pepys chooses to save from his home. What does each item contribute toward a **characterization** of the man?

6. 👆 Pepys used a private shorthand to write his diaries for himself and was not concerned with **communication** to a reading public. How might he have written differently if he had known that you would be reading his intimate thoughts hundreds of years later?

Extending the Ideas

7. Pepys describes the people waiting too long to leave their homes that eventually burn down around them. You may have seen or read examples of similar behavior in media accounts of floods and hurricanes. What is it about human nature that causes people to react in this way?

8. Pepys says that "the militia is in arms everywhere." In times of disaster why are armed forces often involved?

Literary Focus: Imagery

Imagery may appeal to the sense of sight, hearing, taste, smell, or touch. Effective imagery often appeals to more than one sense at a time. Which of your senses were most aroused by Pepys's descriptive language? Chart some of the words or phrases that helped to stimulate those senses.

Sense	Examples
sight	
hearing	
taste	
smell	
touch	

Vocabulary Study

For each numbered word write the letter of its synonym. You will not use all the synonyms. Then use each of the numbered words in a sentence that shows you understand the meaning of the word.

1. combustible   **a.** sorrowful
2. infinite   **b.** easily burned
3. lamentable   **c.** full of joy
4. loath   **d.** endless
5. malicious   **e.** reluctant
        f. evil

Expressing Your Ideas

Writing Choices

Writer's Notebook Update Keep a personal diary for at least one week. Try to follow Pepys's example of recording not only your personal thoughts but also observations of the people and events around you. Don't worry about grammar and sentence structure. You might even want to use your own form of shorthand.

Tell It as It Was Write a **descriptive narrative** of an exciting or dangerous event in your life. (If your life hasn't been especially exciting or dangerous, write about a fictional event.) Write in the first person and look for ways to characterize yourself as one who's part of the action. Look for fresh, crisp verbs and adjectives to convey the spirit and emotion of the event.

London Burns! You are a newspaper reporter for an early version of *The Times* of London presenting the essential facts of the fire to the public. Write a brief **news story** for one of the six days, concentrating on *who, what, when, where,* and, if you wish, *why* and *how.*

Other Options

A Human Story In Pepys's account, the fire becomes a backdrop for a tale of human interest. Often human-interest tales can be captured in the looks exchanged between mother and child or in the wrinkles of an old face. Find a magazine photograph—or snap a picture yourself—that portrays human interest. Display the photograph and **tell the human story** it suggests with a small group or the class as your audience.

My Book This calligraphic sketch is one of many Samuel Pepys had created to decorate the title pages of his magnificent collection of books. Design a **personal bookplate** for your private book collection. Include designs that are meaningful—perhaps symbolic—in your own life.

From Pepys's calligraphical collection.

Before Reading

Dignity and Uses of Biography
from the Dictionary of the English Language
Letter to Chesterfield by Samuel Johnson

Samuel Johnson
1709–1784

Samuel Johnson was an unattractive figure: blind in one eye, half-deaf, misshapen by disease, and sloppy in dress and personal habits. He spent only one year at Pembroke College, Oxford, before leaving for lack of funds. After an unsuccessful attempt at teaching, Johnson went to London, where he began a long period of writing for magazines, eventually founding two periodicals, *The Rambler* and *The Idler.* The three major projects of his life, any one of which could be considered a life's work, were the *Dictionary of the English Language* (1755), a complete edition of Shakespeare (1765), and the ten-volume *Lives of the English Poets* (1781), a combination of biography and literary criticism.

Building Background

"Done by an Oxford Hand" Discouraged by the lack of a university degree and by the kinds of writing he was forced to do to earn his meager existence, Samuel Johnson seized upon the offer by bookseller Robert Dodsley to create a new dictionary of the English language. Guaranteed a fee of £1,575 Johnson rented a house, hired six clerks, and organized a dictionary workshop on the top floor. Using his own books and those borrowed from friends, Johnson read biography, drama, essays, history, poetry, and science. As he read, he underlined the words to be defined (40,000 in all) and marked passages to be quoted (116,000 quotations). The clerks copied the material on slips of paper which were pasted into 80 large notebooks. Johnson then wrote the definitions and the word origins. The process continued for nine years, being completed shortly after Johnson was awarded an honorary Master of Arts degree from Oxford. That he could include that degree on the title page was so important to Johnson! An Oxford man, however, was heard to say, "It is in truth doing ourselves more honor than him to have such a work done by an Oxford hand."

Literary Focus

Denotation / Connotation The dictionary meaning of a word is its **denotation.** The emotional associations that surround a word are the word's **connotation.** Denotations are constant; they are the same for everyone. Connotations vary from person to person based on individual attitudes and experiences. Copy the following words and write a denotion and a connotation for each of them: *school, winter, job, family, gun.* As you read Johnson's dictionary entries, look for examples of connotation in his definitions.

Writer's Notebook

That's Not Fair! Have you ever felt that you were the victim of unfairness—at home, at school, or among your friends? Write down two or three examples. If you can't think of personal examples, jot down examples of unfair acts you have observed being done to others.

Dignity and Uses of BIOGRAPHY

SAMUEL JOHNSON

All joy or sorrow for the happiness or calamities of others is produced by an act of the imagination that realizes the event, however fictitious, or approximates it, however remote, by placing us for a time in the condition of him whose fortune we contemplate. So that we feel, while the deception lasts, whatever motions would be excited by the same good or evil happening to ourselves.

Our passions are therefore more strongly moved in proportion as we can more readily adopt the pains or pleasure proposed to our minds by recognizing them at once our own or considering them as naturally incident to[1] our state of life. It is not easy for the most artful writer to give us an interest in happiness or misery which we think ourselves never likely to feel and with which we have never yet been made acquainted. Histories of the downfall of kingdoms and revolutions of empires are read with great tranquillity.[2] The imperial tragedy pleases common auditors only by its pomp of ornament and grandeur of ideas; and the man whose faculties have been engrossed by business, and whose heart never fluttered but at the rise or fall of stocks, wonders how the attention can be seized or the affection agitated by a tale of love.

Those parallel circumstances and kindred[3] images to which we readily conform our minds are, above all other writings, to be found in narratives of the lives of particular persons; and therefore no species of writing seems more worthy of cultivation than biography, since none can be more delightful or more useful, none can more certainly enchain the heart by irresistible interest, or more widely diffuse[4] instruction to every diversity of condition.

CLARIFY: How does Johnson suggest that we can experience another's joy or sorrow?

The general and rapid narratives of history, which involve a thousand fortunes in the business of a day and complicate innumerable incidents in one great transaction, afford few lessons applicable to private life, which derives its comforts and its wretchedness from the right or wrong management of things which nothing but their frequency makes considerable—"Parva si non fiunt quotidie,"[5] says Pliny—and which can have no place in those relations which never descend below the consultation of senates, the motions of armies, and the schemes of conspirators.

I have often thought that there has rarely passed a life of which a judicious[6] and faithful narrative would not be useful. For not only every man has, in the mighty mass of the world, great numbers in the same condition with himself, to whom his mistakes and miscarriages, escapes and expedients,[7] would be of immedi-

---

1. **incident to,** belonging to.
2. tranquillity (trang kwil′ə tē), *n.* peacefulness.
3. **kindred** (kin′drid), *adj.* similar.
4. **diffuse** (di fyüz′), *v.* spread.
5. **Parva . . . quotidie,** small things are important because they happen daily. *[Latin]*
6. judicious (jü dish′əs), *adj.* wise.
7. expedient (ek spē′dē ənt), *n.* method of bringing about desired results.

ate and apparent use, but there is such an uniformity in the state of man, considered apart
from adventitious[8] and separable decorations
and disguises, that there is scarce any possibility
of good or ill but is common to human kind. A
great part of the time of those who are placed at
the greatest distance by fortune or by temper
must unavoidably pass in the same manner, and
though, when the claims of nature are satisfied,
caprice[9] and vanity and accident begin to produce discriminations[10] and peculiarities, yet the
eye is not very heedful or quick which cannot
discover the same causes still terminating their
influence in the same effects, though sometimes accelerated, sometimes retarded, or perplexed by multiplied combinations. We are all
prompted by the same motives, all deceived by
the same fallacies,[11] all animated by hope,
obstructed by danger, entangled by desire, and
seduced by pleasure.

**CLARIFY: Does Johnson believe people
are more alike or more different?**

It is frequently objected to relations of particular lives that they are not distinguished by
any striking or wonderful vicissitudes.[12] The
scholar who passed his life among his books, the
merchant who conducted only his own affairs,
the priest whose sphere of action was not
extended beyond that of his duty, are considered as no proper objects of public regard, however they might have excelled in their several
stations, whatever might have been their learning, integrity, and piety. But this notion arises
from false measures of excellence and dignity,
and must be eradicated[13] by considering that in
the esteem of uncorrupted reason what is of
most use is of most value.

It is, indeed, not improper to take honest
advantages of prejudice and to gain attention
by a celebrated name; but the business of the
biographer is often to pass slightly over those

performances and incidents which produce vulgar greatness, to lead the thoughts into domestic privacies, and display the minute details of
daily life where exterior appendages[14] are cast
aside and men excel each other only by prudence[15] and by virtue. The account of Thuanus[16]
is, with great propriety,[17] said by its author to
have been written that it might lay open to pos-

8. **adventitious** (ad′ven tish′əs), *adj.* accidental.
9. **caprice** (ke prēs′), *n.* whim.
10. **discrimination** (dis krim′ə nā′shən), *n.* distinction.
11. **fallacy** (fal′ə sē), *n.* false idea.
12. **vicissitude** (və sis′ə tüd), *n.* change in fortune.
13. **eradicate** (i rad′ə kāt), *v.* erase.
14. **appendage** (ə pen′dij), *n.* addition.
15. **prudence** (prüd′ns), *n.* wisdom.
16. **Thuanus**. Each of the proper names found in the
    remainder of this essay refers to a biographer or to
    the subject of a biography.
17. propriety (prə prī′ə tē), *n.* proper behavior.

This biographical painting, by an unknown artist, showing scenes from the life and death of Sir Henry Unton (1557?–1596). According to Johnson, what is the purpose of biography? How is that purpose similar to what the artist tries to accomplish in this painting?

terity the private and familiar character of that man, *cujus ingenium et candorum ex ipsius scriptis sunt olim semper miraturi* ("whose candor and genius will to the end of time be by his writings preserved in admiration").

There are many invisible circumstances which, whether we read as inquirers after natural or moral knowledge, whether we intend to enlarge our science or increase our virtue, are more important than public occurrences. Thus Sallust, the great master of nature, has not forgot in his account of Cataline to remark that his walk was now quick and again slow, as an indication of a mind revolving something with violent commotion. Thus the story of Melanchthon affords

a striking lecture on the value of time by informing us that when he made an appointment he expected not only the hour but the minute to be fixed, that the day might not run out in the idleness of suspense. And all the plans and enterprises of De Wit are now of less importance to the world than that part of his personal character which represents him as careful of his health and negligent[18] of his life.

But biography has often been allotted to writers who seem very little acquainted with the nature of their task or very negligent about the performance. They rarely afford any other

---

18. **negligent** (neg′lə jənt), *adj.* careless.

account than might be collected from public papers, but imagine themselves writing a life when they exhibit a chronological series of actions or preferments,[19] and so little regard the manners or behavior of their heroes, that more knowledge may be gained of a man's real character by a short conversation with one of his servants than from a formal and studied narrative begun with his pedigree and ended with his funeral.

If now and then they condescend[20] to inform the world of particular facts, they are not always so happy as to select the most important. I know not well what advantage posterity[21] can receive from the only circumstance by which Tickell has distinguished Addison from the rest of mankind, the irregularity of his pulse. Nor can I think myself overpaid for the time spent in reading the life of Malherbe by being enabled to relate, after the learned biographer, that Malherbe had two predominant opinions; one that the looseness of a single woman might destroy all her boast of ancient descent, the other that the French beggars made use very improperly and barbarously of the phrase *noble gentleman*, because either word included the sense of both.

There are, indeed, some natural reasons why these narratives are often written by such as were not likely to give much instruction or delight, and why most accounts of particular persons are barren and useless. If a life be delayed till interest and envy are at an end, we may hope for impartiality[22] but must expect little intelligence. For the incidents which give excellence to biography are of a volatile[23] and evanescent[24] kind, such as soon escape the memory and are rarely transmitted by tradition. We know how few can portray a living

PREDICT: If Johnson were writing a biography, what kinds of details would he be likely to include about his subject?

acquaintance except by his most prominent and observable particularities and the grosser features of his mind; and it may be easily imagined how much of this little knowledge may be lost in imparting it, and how soon a succession of copies will lose all resemblance of the original.

If the biographer writes from personal knowledge and makes haste to gratify the public curiosity, there is danger lest his interest, his fear, his gratitude, or his tenderness overpower his fidelity and tempt him to conceal if not to invent. There are many who think it an act of piety to hide the faults or failings of their friends, even when they can no longer suffer by their detection. We therefore see whole ranks of characters adorned with uniform panegyric,[25] and not to be known from one another but by extrinsic[26] and casual circumstances. "Let me remember," says Hale, "when I find myself inclined to pity a criminal, that there is likewise a pity due to the country." If we owe regard to the memory of the dead, there is yet more respect to be paid to knowledge, to virtue, and to truth.

---

19. **preferment** (pri fėr′mənt), *n.* promotion.
20. **condescend** (kon′di send′), *v.* lower oneself.
21. **posterity** (po ster′ə tē), *n.* generations of the future.
22. **impartiality** (im′pär shē al′ə tē), *n.* fairness.
23. **volatile** (vol′ə təl), *adj.* changing rapidly.
24. **evanescent** (ev′ə nes′nt), *adj.* soon passing away.
25. **panegyric** (pan′ə jir′ik), *n.* extravagant praise.
26. **extrinsic** (ek strin′sik), *adj.* external.

Dictionary of the English Language

SAMUEL JOHNSON

Johnson's reputation as a scholar and writer was established in 1755 with the publication of his Dictionary. Selling for ninety shillings and filling two large volumes, the Dictionary was the most comprehensive English lexicon ever published. In Italy and France similar dictionaries, prepared under the direction of national academies, represented the work of forty or more men. Johnson prepared his single-handedly, with the help of six clerks. The following entries are selected either for their comprehensiveness or for the personal touches they show.

alliga′tor. The crocodile. This name is chiefly used for the crocodile of America, between which, and that of Africa, naturalists have laid down this difference, that one moves the upper, and the other the lower jaw; but this is now known to be chimerical,[1] the lower jaw being equally moved by both.

bu′lly. (Skinner derives this word from *burly,* as a corruption in the pronunciation; which is very probably right; or from *bulky,* or *bulleyed;* which are less probable. May it not come from *bull,* the pope's letter, implying the insolence[2] of those who came invested with authority from the papal court?) A noisy, blustering, quarrelling fellow: it is generally taken for a man that has only the appearance of courage.

bu′tterfly. A beautiful insect, so named because it first appears at the beginning of the season for butter.

chi′cken. (3) A term for a young girl.

chiru′rgeon. One that cures ailments, not by internal medicines, but outward applications. It is now generally pronounced, and by many written, *surgeon.*

cough. A convulsion[3] of the lungs, vellicated by some sharp seriosity.[4] It is pronounced *coff.*

to cu′rtail. (*curto,* Latin. It was anciently written *curtal,* which perhaps is more proper; but dogs that had their tails cut, being called *curtal* dogs, the word was vulgarly conceived to mean originally *to cut the tail,* and was in time written according to that notion.) (1) To cut off; to cut short; to shorten.

dedica′tion. (2) A servile address to a patron.

den. (1) A cavern or hollow running horizontally, or with a small obliquity,[5] under ground; distinct from a hole, which runs down perpendicularly.

dull. (8) Not exhilarating; not delightful; as, *to make dictionaries is* dull *work.*

e′ssay. (2) A loose sally[6] of the mind; an irregular indigested piece; not a regular and orderly composition.

exci′se. A hateful tax levied upon commodities,[7] and adjudged not by the common judges of property, but wretches hired by those to whom excise is paid.

fa′vorite. (2) One chosen as a companion by his superior; a mean wretch whose whole business is by any means to please.

fun. (A low cant[8] word.) Sport; high merriment; frolicksome delight.

ga′mbler. (A cant word, I suppose, for *game,*

---

1. **chimerical** (kə mer′ə kəl), *adj.* imaginary.
2. insolence (in′sə ləns), *n.* bold rudeness.
3. **convulsion** (kən vul′shən), *n.* spasm.
4. **vellicated . . . serosity,** with many fluids moving around.
5. **obliquity** (ə blik′wə tē), *n.* inclination.
6. **sally,** outburst.
7. **commodity** (kə mod′ə tē), *n.* anything bought and sold.
8. **cant** (kant), *adj.* slang; jargon.

or *gamester*.) A knave[9] whose practice it is to invite the unwary[10] to game and cheat them.

to gi′ggle. To laugh idly; to titter; to grin with merry levity. It is retained in Scotland.

goat. A ruminant[11] animal that seems a middle species between deer and sheep.

gra′vy. The serous juice that runs from flesh not much dried by the fire.

to hiss. To utter a noise like that of a serpent and some other animals. It is remarkable, that this word cannot be pronounced without making the noise which it signifies.

itch. (1) A cutaneous disease[12] extremely contagious, which overspreads the body with small pustules filled with a thin serum, and raised as microscopes have discovered by a small animal. It is cured by sulphur.

lexico′grapher. A writer of dictionaries; a harmless drudge, that busies himself in tracing the original, and detailing the signification of words.

lunch, lu′ncheon. As much food as one's hand can hold.

ne′twork. Any thing reticulated or decussated,[13] at equal distances, with interstices[14] between the intersections.

oats. A grain, which in England is generally given to horses, but in Scotland supports the people.

pa′rasite. One that frequents rich tables, and earns his welcome by flattery.

pa′stern. (1) The knee of a horse.

pa′tron. (1) One who countenances,[15] supports, or protects. Commonly a wretch who supports with insolence, and is paid with flattery.

pe′nsion. An allowance made to any one without an equivalent. In England it is generally understood to mean pay given to a state hireling for treason to his country.

pe′nsioner. (2) A slave of state hired by a stipend to obey his master.

sa′tire. A poem in which wickedness or folly is censured.[16] Proper *satire* is distinguished, by the generality of the reflections, from a *lampoon* which is aimed against a particular person; but they are too frequently confounded.[17]

shre′wmouse. A mouse of which the bite is generally supposed venomous, and to which vulgar tradition assigns such malignity,[18] that she is said to lame the foot over which she runs. I am informed that all these reports are calumnious,[19] and that her feet and teeth are equally harmless with those of any other little mouse. Our ancestors however looked on her with such terror, that they are supposed to have given her name to a scolding woman, whom for her venom they call a *shrew*.

so′nnet. (1) A short poem consisting of fourteen lines, of which the rhymes are adjusted by a particular rule. It is not very suitable to the English language, and has not been used by any man of eminence since Milton.

To′ry. (A cant term, derived, I suppose, from an Irish word signifying a savage.) One who adheres to the ancient constitution of the state, and the apostolical hierarchy[20] of the Church of England, opposed to a Whig.[21]

Whig. (2) The name of a faction.

wi′tticism. A mean attempt at wit.

to worm. (2) To deprive a dog of something, nobody knows what, under his tongue, which is said to prevent him, nobody knows why, from running mad.

---

9. **knave** (nāv), *n.* rogue.
10. **unwary,** careless.
11. **ruminant** (rü′mə nənt), *adj.* cud chewing.
12. **cutaneous disease,** disease of the skin.
13. **reticulated** (ri tik′yə lā tid) **or decussated** (di kus′ā tid), *adjs.* intricately woven or crossed.
14. **interstice** (in tėr′stis), *n., pl.* **-stices** (-stə sēz), a narrow opening.
15. **countenance** (koun′tə nəns), *v.* encourage.
16. **censure** (sen′shər), *v.* criticize.
17. **confound** (kon found′), *v.* confuse.
18. **malignity** (mə lig′nə tē), *n.* ill will.
19. **calumnious** (kə lum′nē əs), *adj.* slanderous.
20. **apostolical** (ap′ə stol′ə kəl) **hierarchy** (hī′ə rär′kē), organization by rank within the church.
21. **opposed to a Whig.** Whigs were the political party supporting Parliamentary control of government. Tories, like Johnson, were royalists favoring the monarchy.

Letter to Chesterfield

SAMUEL JOHNSON

In 1746, when Johnson first proposed the idea of compiling a dictionary, he discussed the project with Lord Chesterfield, who expressed interest, and, in the custom of literary patronage, gave Johnson a gift of 10 pounds. Later Chesterfield apparently approved the plan for the dictionary and promised Johnson continued financial support. That support never materialized. When the Dictionary *finally appeared in 1755, Chesterfield expressed the desire to be regarded as its patron. Johnson wrote him this letter in response.*

To the Right Honorable
the Earl of Chesterfield
February 7, 1755.
My Lord,

I have lately been informed by the proprietor of *The World*,[1] that two papers, in which my *Dictionary* is recommended to the public, were written by your Lordship. To be so distinguished is an honor which, being very little accustomed to favors from the great, I know not well how to receive, or in what terms to acknowledge.

When, upon some slight encouragement, I first visited your Lordship, I was overpowered, like the rest of mankind, by the enchantment of your address; and could not forbear to wish that I might boast myself *"Le vainqueur du vainqueur de la terre,"*[2] that I might obtain that regard for which I saw the world contending; but I found my attendance so little encouraged, that neither pride nor modesty would suffer me to continue it. When I had once addressed your Lordship in public, I had exhausted all the art of pleasing which a retired and uncourtly scholar can possess. I had done all that I could; and no man is well pleased to have his all neglected, be it ever so little.

Seven years, my Lord, have now passed, since I waited in your outward rooms, or was repulsed[3] from your door; during which time I have been pushing on my work through difficulties, of which it is useless to complain, and have brought it, at last, to the verge of publication, without one act of assistance, one word of encouragement, or one smile of favor. Such treatment I did not expect, for I never had a patron before.

The shepherd in Virgil grew at last acquainted with Love, and found him a native of the rocks.[4]

Is not a patron, my Lord, one who looks with unconcern on a man struggling for life in the water, and, when he has reached ground, encumbers[5] him with help? The notice which you have been pleased to take of my labors, had it been early, had been kind; but it has been delayed till I am indifferent,[6] and cannot enjoy it; till I am solitary, and cannot impart it; till I am known, and do not want it. I hope it is no very cynical asperity[7] not to confess obligations where no benefit has been received, or to be unwilling that the public should consider me as owing that to a patron, which Providence has enabled me to do for myself.

Having carried on my work thus far with so little obligation to any favorer of learning, I shall not be disappointed though I should conclude it, if less be possible, with less; for I have been long wakened from that dream of hope, in which I once boasted myself with so much exultation.

My Lord,
Your Lordship's most humble,
Most obedient servant,

Sam. Johnson

---

1. ***The World,*** a newspaper run by a friend of Johnson's.
2. ***"Le vainqueur . . . de la terre,"*** "The conqueror of the conqueror of the world." *[French]*
3. **repulse** (ri puls′), *v.* drive away.
4. **The shepherd . . . rocks.** Johnson is referring to a passage in the *Eclogues,* a collection of pastoral poems by the Latin poet Virgil (70–19 B.C.), that speaks of the cruelty of love.
5. **encumber** (en kum′bər), *v.* burden.
6. **indifferent** (in dif′ər ənt), *adj.* not interested.
7. **asperity** (a sper′ə tē), *n.* harshness.

After Reading

Making Connections

Shaping Your Response

1. What do you think of Johnson's choices of vocabulary in his dictionary definitions?

2. If you were Lord Chesterfield, how would you respond to Johnson's letter?

Analyzing the Selections

3. Some of the words in Johnson's *Dictionary* have the same meanings today as they did in Johnson's time; the meanings of other words have changed considerably. Find examples of each. What reasons can you give for changes in a word's meaning over time?

4. Find examples of Johnson's revealing his own personality through his definitions and discuss what each example shows. Why do you suppose Johnson writes so personally in a reference work?

5. 🐾 A **communication** between members of different social classes often reflects the writer's sense of status. Why do you suppose Johnson uses polite expressions like "My lord" and "Most obedient servant" in a letter written basically to convey his anger?

6. Do you agree with the values that Johnson finds in the literary form of biography in his essay "Dignity and Uses of Biography"? Explain.

Extending the Ideas

7. In your opinion, should a biographer tell all the truth—good and bad—about his or her subject?

Literary Focus: Connotation / Denotation

Copy these words from Johnson's *Dictionary* and write his denotation and connotation for each of them: *favorite, lexicographer, oats, patron, pension.* Then write a denotation and a connotation that you know for each of these words: *beauty, taxes, home, yellow, car.* Compare your responses with those of your classmates.

Vocabulary Study

Answer the following questions, giving reasons for your answers.

1. If the biographer treated his subject with *impartiality,* would he be critical, fair, full of praise, or telling only half the story?

2. If a biography were *calumnious,* what advice might you give to the biographer?

3. Are the leather binding and elaborate lettering on Johnson's *Dictionary* better examples of *judicious* or *extrinsic* features?

4. If a clerk copying quotations displayed *negligent* work habits, would Johnson praise him, scold him, or send him to a doctor?

5. If Johnson found a *fallacy* in a dictionary manuscript, would he correct it, pronounce it, or answer it?

6. If the clerks experienced a period of *tranquillity,* were they fighting, eating, relaxing, or copying?

7. In addressing Lord Chesterfield with respect, was Johnson behaving with *insolence* or *propriety?*

8. Would Johnson have been justified in treating Chesterfield with greater *asperity?* Explain.

9. Which is the better example of an *expedient*—borrowing books from friends or his not getting money from Chesterfield?

10. In which does Johnson *censure* the most—his essay, letter, or dictionary entries?

Expressing Your Ideas

Writing Choices

Writer's Notebook Update Look back at the instances of unfairness listed in your notebook. Select one of those unfair acts and write a few sentences describing the situation.

Defining Slang Select ten slang or colloquial expressions you and your friends use and prepare personalized definitions for them. Work with other members of your class to compile a **dictionary of teenage expressions.**

Johnson Right or Wrong Select one of the following quotations from Johnson and write a brief **essay,** with supporting examples, in which you agree or disagree with his viewpoint.

- "Every man wishes to be wise, and they who cannot be wise are almost always cunning."

- "No man ever yet became great by imitation."

- "It is better to suffer wrong than to do it, and happier to be sometimes cheated than not to trust."

Other Options

Find Celebrity Details Select a celebrity currently being featured in magazines and tabloids. Collect pictures and clippings to make a **bulletin board display** of the biographical information revealed about this personality. Categorize your display into important and non-important details, pointing out those items which might be made up or exaggerated.

Chart the Famous Work with a group of classmates to survey a general biographical reference source. Before you begin, make a list of professions, such as Theater, Business, Art, Music, and Science. Tally the number of famous people that belong to each profession. Then construct a graph or chart that graphically compares the number of famous people in the professions you have chosen. In your display or presentation to the class, what generalizations can you make about why the numbers compare as they do?

Before Reading

from The Life of Samuel Johnson, LL.D.

by James Boswell

James Boswell
1740–1795

Son of a distinguished Scottish judge and educated at the universities of Glasgow, Edinburgh, and Utrecht (in Holland), Boswell practiced law in Scotland and later in England. He spent most of his literary career chronicling the life of Samuel Johnson, first in *Journal of a Tour to the Hebrides* (1785), an account of a trip he and Johnson took to the western isles of Scotland, and later in his masterpiece of biography, *The Life of Samuel Johnson, LL.D.* (1791). Boswell, a member of the Literary Club, which met weekly for conversation at The Turk's Head Tavern, recorded Johnson's conversations and activities. Although Boswell himself was witty and charming, he is most remembered for his accurate reports of the brilliant witticisms of Johnson.

Building Background

The Perfect Biography "I am absolutely certain," wrote Boswell, "that my mode of biography, which gives not only a history of Johnson's visible progress through the world, and of his publications, but a view of his mind, in his letters and conversations, is the most perfect that can be conceived, and will be more of a Life than any work that has ever yet appeared." How had Boswell collected the material for this perfect biography? In the twenty-one years of his friendship with Samuel Johnson, Boswell kept a very detailed journal, often recording Johnson's conversations word for word as he spoke. Following Johnson's death, Boswell conducted extensive interviews with many of Johnson's contemporaries. He prepared questionnaires for Johnson's closest friends. He acquired letters written by Johnson and to Johnson. He ran "half over London" to verify a date or confirm a piece of information. Then Boswell selected those anecdotes which were most characteristic of the Johnson he knew and admired and transformed them into vivid, lifelike scenes.

Literary Focus

Characterization The techniques an author uses to develop the personality of a character, fictional or real, are called **characterization.** An author can describe any or all of the following in presenting each character:

- physical appearance
- personality traits
- thoughts and feelings
- speech and behavior
- interactions with other characters

As you read his characterization of Johnson, notice which techniques Boswell uses most often.

Writer's Notebook

Just the Facts? You are about to read portions of the biography of a famous literary figure. Make a list of the kinds of information you would expect to learn about the subject of any biography.

The Life of Samuel Johnson, LL.D.

James Boswell

On London

Talking of a London life, he said, "The happiness of London is not to be conceived but by those who have been in it. I will venture to say, there is more learning and science within the circumference of ten miles from where we now sit, than in all the rest of the kingdom."

BOSWELL. "The only disadvantage is the great distance at which people live from one another."

JOHNSON. "Yes, Sir; but that is occasioned by the largeness of it, which is the cause of all the other advantages."

BOSWELL. "Sometimes I have been in the humor of wishing to retire to a desert."

JOHNSON. "Sir, you have desert enough in Scotland."

I suggested a doubt, that if I were to reside in London, the exquisite zest with which I relished it in occasional visits might go off, and I might grow tired of it.

JOHNSON. "Why, Sir, you find no man, at all intellectual, who is willing to leave London. No, Sir, when a man is tired of London, he is tired of life; for there is in London all that life can afford."

On Eating

At supper, this night he talked of good eating with uncommon satisfaction. "Some people (said he) have a foolish way of not minding, or pretending not to mind, what they eat. For my part, I mind my belly very studiously, and very carefully; for I look upon it that he who does not mind his belly will hardly mind anything else."

He now appeared to me *Jean Bull philosophe,*[1] and he was, for the moment, not only serious but vehement.[2] Yet I have heard him, upon other occasions, talk with great contempt of people who were anxious to gratify their palates; and the 206th number of his *Rambler* is a masterly essay against gulosity.[3] His practice, indeed, I must acknowledge, may be considered as casting the balance of his different opinions upon this subject, for I never knew any man who relished good eating more than he did. When at table, he was totally absorbed in the business of the moment; his looks seemed riveted to his plate; nor would he, unless when in very high company, say one word, or even pay the least attention to what was said by others, till he had satisfied his appetite, which was so fierce, and indulged with such intenseness, that while in the act of eating, the veins of his forehead swelled, and generally a strong perspiration was visible. To those whose sensations were delicate, this could not but be disgusting; and it was doubtless not very suitable to the character of a philosopher, who should be distinguished by self-command. But it must be owned that Johnson, though he could be rigidly *abstemious,*[4] was not a *temperate* man either in eating or drinking. He could refrain, but he could not use moderately. He told me that he had fasted two

---

1. *Jean Bull philosophe,* John Bull the philosopher. *[French]* John Bull is the personification of the British nation, the typical Englishman.
2. vehement (vē′ə mənt), *adj.* forceful.
3. gulosity (gyŭ los′i tē), *n.* excessive appetite.
4. abstemious (ab stē′mē əs), *adj.* moderate.

The Life of Samuel Johnson　**361**

James Boswell (left) and Samuel Johnson (right) are shown dining in London in this cartoon entitled "A Chop House." In what ways does the cartoonist's depiction of Johnson's eating habits agree with Boswell's description of those habits? Why do you think Boswell is shown in this pose?

days without inconvenience, and that he had never been hungry but once. They who beheld with wonder how much he ate upon all occasions when his dinner was to his taste could not easily conceive what he must have meant by hunger, and not only was he remarkable for the extraordinary quantity which he ate, but he was, or affected to be, a man of very nice discernment[5] in the science of cookery. He used to descant[6] critically on the dishes which had been at table where he had dined or supped, and to recollect minutely what he had liked.

He about the same time was so much displeased with the performances of a nobleman's French cook, that he exclaimed with vehemence, "I'd throw such a rascal into the river"; and he then proceeded to alarm a lady at whose house he was to sup, by the following manifesto[7] of his skill: "I, Madam, who live at a variety of good tables, am a much better judge of cookery, than any person who has a very tolerable cook, but lives much at home; for his palate is gradually adapted to the taste of his cook; whereas,

Madam, in trying by a wider range, I can more exquisitely judge."

When invited to dine, even with an intimate friend, he was not pleased if something better than a plain dinner was not prepared for him. I have heard him say on such an occasion, "This was a good dinner enough, to be sure: but it was not a dinner to *ask* a man to."

On the other hand, he was wont to express, with great glee, his satisfaction when he had been entertained quite to his mind. One day when he had dined with his neighbor and landlord, in Boltcourt, Mr. Allen, the printer, whose old housekeeper had studied his taste in everything, he pronounced this eulogy:[8] "Sir, we could not have had a better dinner, had there been a *Synod*[9] *of Cooks*."

---

5. **discernment** (də zėrn′mənt), *n.* judgment.
6. **descant** (des kant′), *v.* talk at great length.
7. **manifesto** (man′ə fes′tō), *n.* public declaration.
8. **eulogy** (yŭ′lə jē), *n.* speech of praise.
9. **synod** (sin′əd), *n.* convention.

On the Dictionary

That he was fully aware of the arduous[10] nature of the undertaking, he acknowledges; and shows himself perfectly sensible of it in the conclusion of this "Plan"; but he had a noble consciousness of his own abilities, which enabled him to go on with undaunted spirit.

Dr. Adams found him one day busy at his Dictionary, when the following dialogue ensued.

ADAMS. "This is a great work, Sir. How are you to get all the etymologies?"[11]

JOHNSON. "Why, Sir, here is a shelf with Junius, and Skinner,[12] and others; and there is a Welsh gentleman who has published a collection of Welsh proverbs, who will help me with the Welsh."

ADAMS. "But, Sir, how can you do this in three years?"

JOHNSON. "Sir, I have no doubt that I can do it in three years."

ADAMS. "But the French Academy,[13] which consists of forty members, took forty years to compile their Dictionary."

JOHNSON. "Sir, thus it is. This is the proportion. Let me see; forty times forty is sixteen hundred. As three to sixteen hundred, so is the proportion of an Englishman to a Frenchman."

With so much ease and pleasantry could he talk of that prodigious[14] labor which he had undertaken to execute.

On Books and Reading

JOHNSON. "Sir, I love the acquaintance of young people; because, in the first place, I don't like to think myself growing old. In the next place, young acquaintances must last longest, if they do last; and then, Sir, young men have more virtue than old men; they have more generous sentiments in every respect. I love the young dogs of this age: they have more wit and humor and knowledge of life than we had; but then the dogs are not so good scholars. Sir, in my early years I read very hard. It is a sad reflection, but a true one, that I knew almost as much at eighteen as I do now. My judgment, to be sure, was not so good; but I had all the facts. I remember very well, when I was at Oxford, an old gentleman said to me, 'Young man, ply your book diligently now, and acquire a stock of knowledge; for when years come upon you, you will find that poring upon books will be but an irksome task.'"

JOHNSON. "Idleness is a disease which must be combated; but I would not advise a rigid adherence to a particular plan of study. I myself have never persisted in any plan for two days together. A man ought to read just as inclination leads him: for what he reads as a task will do him little good. A young man should read five hours in a day, and so may acquire a great deal of knowledge."

On Pity

JOHNSON. "Pity is not natural to man. Children are always cruel. Savages are cruel. Pity is acquired and improved by the cultivation of reason. We may have uneasy sensations for seeing a creature in distress, without pity; for we have not pity unless we wish to relieve them. When I am on my way to dine with a friend, and finding it late, have bid the coachman make haste, if I happen to attend when he whips his horses, I may feel unpleasantly that the animals are put to pain, but I do not wish him to desist. No, sir, I wish him to drive on."

---

10. arduous (är′jü əs), *adj*. difficult.
11. etymology (et′ə mol′ə jē), *n*. word origin.
12. **Junius . . . Skinner.** Their books were sources for many of Johnson's etymologies for the Germanic languages.
13. **French Academy,** a society of men and women of letters whose purpose is to uphold correct usage of the French language.
14. **prodigious** (prə dij′əs), *adj*. vast.

Talking of our feeling for the distresses of others:

JOHNSON. "Why, Sir, there is much noise made about it, but it is greatly exaggerated. No, Sir, we have a certain degree of feeling to prompt us to do good; more than that, Providence does not intend. It would be misery to no purpose."

BOSWELL. "But suppose now, Sir, that one of your intimate friends were apprehended for an offense for which he might be hanged."

JOHNSON. "I should do what I could to bail him, and give him any other assistance; but if he were once fairly hanged, I should not suffer."

BOSWELL. "Would you eat your dinner that day, Sir?"

JOHNSON. "Yes, Sir; and eat it as if he were eating it with me. Why, there's Baretti[15] who is to be tried for his life tomorrow, friends have risen up for him on every side; yet if he should be hanged, none of them will eat a slice of plum pudding the less. Sir, that sympathetic feeling goes a very little way in depressing the mind."

The Social Order

I described to him an impudent[16] fellow from Scotland, who affected to be a savage, and railed at all established systems.

JOHNSON. "There is nothing surprising in this, Sir. He wants to make himself conspicuous. He would tumble in a hogsty, as long as you looked at him and called to him to come out. But let him alone, never mind him, and he'll soon give it over."

I added that the same person maintained that there was no distinction between virtue and vice.

JOHNSON. "Why, Sir, if the fellow does not think as he speaks, he is lying; and I see not what honor he can propose to himself from having the character of a liar. But if he does really think that there is no distinction between virtue and vice, why, Sir, when he leaves our houses let us count our spoons."

He again insisted on the duty of maintaining subordination of rank.

JOHNSON. "Sir, I would no more deprive a nobleman of his respect, than of his money. I consider myself as acting a part in the great system of society, and I do to others as I would have them to do to me. I would behave to a nobleman as I should expect he would behave to me, were I a nobleman and he Sam Johnson. Sir, there is one Mrs. Macaulay in this town, a great republican. One day when I was at her house, I put on a very grave countenance,[17] and said to her, 'Madam, I am now become a convert to your way of thinking. I am convinced that all mankind are upon an equal footing; and to give you an unquestionable proof, Madam, that I am in earnest, here is a very sensible, civil, well-behaved fellow-citizen, your footman; I desire that he may be allowed to sit down and dine with us.' I thus, Sir, showed her the absurdity of the leveling doctrine. She has never liked me since. Sir, your levelers wish to level *down* as far as themselves; but they cannot bear leveling *up* to themselves. They would all have some people under them; why not then have some people above them?"

On Slavery

After supper I accompanied him to his apartment, and at my request he dictated to me an argument in favor of the negro who was then claiming his liberty, in an action in the Court of Session in Scotland. He had always been very zealous[18] against slavery in every form, in which I with all deference[19] thought that he discovered "a zeal without knowledge." Upon one occasion, when in company with some very grave

---

15. **Baretti,** Johnson's friend who was tried and acquitted for murder.
16. impudent (im′pyə dənt), *adj.* very rude.
17. **countenance** (koun′tə nəns), *n.* expression.
18. zealous (zel′əs), *adj.* enthusiastic.
19. **deference** (def′ər əns), *n.* respect.

men at Oxford, his toast was, "Here's to the next insurrection of the negroes in the West Indies."

His violent prejudice against our West Indian and American settlers appeared whenever there was an opportunity. Towards the conclusion of his "Taxation no Tyranny," he says "how is it that we hear the loudest yelps for liberty among the drivers of negroes?"

On Johnson's Character

His figure was large and well-formed, and his countenance of the cast of an ancient statue; yet his appearance was rendered strange and somewhat uncouth, by convulsive cramps, by the scars of that distemper which it was once imagined the royal touch could cure,[20] and by a slovenly[21] mode of dress. He had the use only of one eye; yet so much does mind govern, and even supply the deficiency of organs, that his visual perceptions, as far as they extended, were uncommonly quick and accurate. So morbid was his temperament, that he never knew the natural joy of a free and vigorous use of his limbs; when he walked, it was like the struggling gait of one in fetters;[22] when he rode, he had no command or direction of his horse, but was carried as if in a balloon. That with his constitution and habits of life he should have lived seventy-five years, is a proof that an inherent *vivida vis*,[23] is a powerful preservative of the human frame.

He was prone to superstition, but not to credulity.[24] Though his imagination might incline him to a belief of the marvelous and the mysterious, his vigorous reason examined the evidence with jealousy. He was a sincere and zealous Christian, of high Church-of-England and monarchical principles, which he would not tamely suffer to be questioned; and had, perhaps, at an early period, narrowed his mind somewhat too much, both as to religion and politics. His being impressed with the danger of extreme latitude[25] in either, though he was of a very independent spirit, occasioned his appearing somewhat unfavorable to the prevalence of that noble freedom of sentiment which is the best possession of man. Nor can it be denied, that he had many prejudices; which, however, frequently suggested many of his pointed sayings, that rather show a playfulness of fancy than any settled malignity. He was steady and inflexible in maintaining the obligations of religion and morality; both from a regard for the order of society, and from a veneration[26] for the Great Source of all order: correct, nay stern in his taste; hard to please, and easily offended; impetuous[27] and irritable in his temper, but of a most humane and benevolent heart, which showed itself not only in a most liberal charity, as far as his circumstances would allow, but in a thousand instances of active benevolence.

He was afflicted with a bodily disease, which made him often restless and fretful; and with a constitutional melancholy, the clouds of which darkened the brightness of his fancy, and gave a gloomy cast to his whole course of thinking: we, therefore, ought not to wonder at his sallies of impatience and passion at any time; especially when provoked by obtrusive ignorance, or presuming petulance;[28] and allowance must be made for his uttering hasty and satirical sallies even against his best friends. And, surely, when it is considered, that "amidst sickness and sorrow," he exerted his faculties in so many works for the benefit of mankind and particularly that he achieved the great and admirable Dictionary of our language, we must be astonished at his resolution.

---

20. **distemper . . . cure.** Johnson had scrofula which, it was believed, could be cured by the touch of a monarch. Although he was taken to Queen Anne as a young child, he was not cured.
21. **slovenly** (sluv′ən lē), *adj.* untidy.
22. **fetter** (fet′ər), *n.* chain or shackle for the feet.
23. *vivida vis,* life force. *[Latin]*
24. **credulity** (krə dü′lə tē), *n.* a too great readiness to believe.
25. **latitude** (lat′ə tüd), *n.* freedom.
26. **veneration** (ven′ə rā′shən), *n.* respect.
27. **impetuous** (im pech′ū əs), *adj.* impulsive.
28. **petulance** (pech′ə ləns), *n.* bad temper.

The solemn text, "of him to whom much is given, much will be required," seems to have been ever present to his mind, in a rigorous sense, and to have made him dissatisfied with his labors and acts of goodness, however comparatively great; so that the unavoidable consciousness of his superiority was, in that respect, a cause of disquiet. He suffered so much from this, and from the gloom which perpetually haunted him, and made solitude frightful, that it may be said of him, "If in this life only he had hope, he was of all men most miserable."

He loved praise, when it was brought to him; but was too proud to seek for it. He was somewhat susceptible of flattery. As he was general and unconfined in his studies, he cannot be considered as master of any one particular science; but he had accumulated a vast and various collection of learning and knowledge, which was so arranged in his mind, as to be ever in readiness to be brought forth. But his superiority over other learned men consisted chiefly in what may be called the art of thinking, the art of using his mind; a certain continual power of seizing the useful substance of all that he knew, and exhibiting it in a clear and forcible manner; so that knowledge, which we often see to be no better than lumber in men of dull understanding, was, in him true, evident, and actual wisdom.

His moral precepts[29] are practical; for they are drawn from an intimate acquaintance with human nature. His maxims carry conviction; for they are founded on the basis of common sense, and a very attentive and minute survey of real life. His mind was so full of imagery, that he might have been perpetually a poet; yet it is remarkable, that, however rich his prose is in this respect, his poetical pieces, in general, have not much of that splendor, but are rather distinguished by strong sentiment, and acute observation, conveyed in harmonious and energetic verse, particularly in heroic couplets. Though usually grave, and even awful in his deportment, he possessed uncommon and peculiar powers of wit and humor; he fre-quently indulged himself in colloquial pleasantry; and the heartiest merriment was often enjoyed in his company; with this great advantage, that, as it was entirely free from any poisonous tincture[30] of vice or impiety, it was salutary[31] to those who shared in it.

He had accustomed himself to such accuracy in his common conversation, that he at all times expressed his thoughts with great force, and an elegant choice of language, the effect of which was aided by his having a loud voice, and a slow deliberate utterance. In him were united a most logical head with a most fertile imagination, which gave him an extraordinary advantage in arguing: for he could reason close or wide, as he saw best for the moment. Exulting in his intellectual strength and dexterity, he could, when he pleased, be the greatest sophist[32] that ever contended in the lists of declamation; and, from a spirit of contradiction, and a delight in showing his powers, he would often maintain the wrong side with equal warmth and ingenuity: so that, when there was an audience, his real opinions could seldom be gathered from his talk; though, when he was in company with a single friend, he would discuss a subject with genuine fairness; but he was too conscientious to make error permanent and pernicious,[33] by deliberately writing it; and, in all his numerous works, he earnestly inculcated[34] what appeared to him to be the truth; his piety being constant, and the ruling principle of all his conduct.

Such was Samuel Johnson, a man whose talents, acquirements, and virtues were so extraordinary, that the more his character is considered the more he will be regarded by the present age, and by posterity, with admiration and reverence.

---

29. **precept** (prē′sept), *n.* principle.
30. **tincture** (tingk′chər), *n.* trace; tinge.
31. salutary (sal′yə ter/ē), *adj.* beneficial.
32. **sophist** (sof′ist), *n.* clever but misleading speaker.
33. pernicious (pər nish′əs), *adj.* harmful.
34. **inculcate** (in kul′kāt), *v.* teach by repetition.

After Reading

Making Connections

Shaping Your
Response

1. List the personal qualities you think a biographer should have.

2. If ★ is *Okay* and ★★★★★ is *Excellent,* how many stars do you think Johnson would have given Boswell's biography?

3. Would you enjoy meeting and talking with Samuel Johnson? Why or why not?

Analyzing the
Biography

4. What role does Boswell play in his biography of Johnson? Why might he act this way?

5. Why do you think Boswell sometimes reports Johnson's conversations as if they were part of a play?

6. List some of the negative characteristics of Boswell's Johnson. In your opinion, why might Boswell choose to reveal so many negative characteristics?

7. What do you think is the overall impression Boswell wants to give about Johnson?

Extending the Ideas

8. In your opinion, what is a proper balance between the public's "right to know" and an individual's right to privacy; that is, how much of a person's private life should be revealed by a biographer?

9. 👣 How might the **communication** of the facts of a person's life be affected by differences in group identities between a biographer and a subject?

Literary Focus: Characterization

Jot down ten characteristics of Samuel Johnson that stand out in Boswell's characterization. Then place each of the characteristics on a chart like the one below, under as many heads as you think are appropriate. Are the characteristics evenly divided among the techniques, or does your list suggest that Boswell favors one particular kind of characterization?

Techniques of Characterization	Characteristics Recalled
Physical appearance	
Personality traits	
Thoughts and feelings	
Speech and behavior	
Interactions with other characters	

The Life of Samuel Johnson   367

Vocabulary Study

abstemeous
arduous
impetuous
impudent
pernicious
salutary
slovenly
vehement
zealous

Select five of the adjectives listed and write a description of a verbal argument between two rivals. Be sure that each sentence demonstrates your understanding of the word's meaning. Use your Glossary, if necessary.

Expressing Your Ideas

Writing Choices

Writer's Notebook Update Go back to your list of biographical information and place a check mark by each kind of information that you learned about Johnson. Did Boswell provide you with the information you expected to get? Make a list of the topics Boswell covered that you hadn't anticipated.

A Modern Boswell You have observed your friends and family members for many years. Who better, then, to write a **biographical sketch** of one of them than you? Recall a special incident that reveals an important aspect of your family member's personality. Following Boswell's example, you might retell the incident in dialogue, with characters' names added.

About Me Write—not the entire history of your life thus far—but one **autobiographical anecdote** that will reveal an important quality of your character. Review the techniques of characterization listed in the Literary Focus and try to use at least three of those techniques in your characterization of yourself.

Other Options

Advertise Boswell's Book Boswell's *The Life of Samuel Johnson, LL.D.* had to compete with several other biographies issued soon after Johnson's death. Create a **poster** for a bookseller's window to advertise Boswell's book. What about Boswell's portrait of Johnson can you emphasize to create interest in this particular biography?

The Time of Your Life Construct a **time line** of your life, including not only milestone events (maybe moving to a new town or getting your driver's license) but also small but memorable incidents (maybe the first holiday you can remember or your first bicycle). Illustrate your time line with your own drawings, family snapshots, and found objects such as ticket stubs, postcards, and letters.

"Let Me Ask You . . ." In the Writing Workshop that follows, you will have a chance to write a biography of someone you know. With your teacher's help, plan and conduct an **interview** of the subject of your biography. Be sure to have a list of questions before you talk to your subject. Listen carefully (see page 380) and be sure to record your subject's words accurately.

History Connection

How did people become celebrities in the past? In the following article, critic Clive James provides a brief account of how the star system operated historically.

A Short History of Fame

by Clive James

There was always fame. As long as there have been human beings, there has always been fame. It's a human weakness.

No other kind of living creature knows anything about fame, not even the peacock, who certainly craves attention but lacks the brain to know why. In every human group of any size, someone becomes famous, and it's a fair bet this has always been true. . . . When people lived in caves, every cave had someone famous in it. But that was as far as his, or her, fame went. There was no way of transmitting it except to write on the cave wall. By the time the cave dwellers found out how to do that, they were already on their way out of the cave, living in bigger and bigger groups that needed kings and queens whose importance had to be drummed into their own people and any other people they might conquer. It could be done by unsophisticated means, such as shouting the monarch's name in unison over and over so that it echoed in the surrounding hills. Or it could be done by sophisticated means: by song, by story, by some form of elementary graven image.

These elementary graven images grew less elementary as time went by. Showcases for them grew more elaborate. The famous person could order a showcase in advance of his own death and so transmit his fame through time. Pit, tumulus, mastaba: there was a steady line of progress in such devices

which reached a peak—if the word is not too appropriate—in the pyramid. But as a means of transmitting the Pharaoh's fame the pyramid had one conspicuous drawback. People had to come and see it. They could see it from some distance because it was tall and—for the brief time between the occupant's interment and the arrival of the first thieves—clad in high-quality brick veneer. But it could not be sent to them. Out of sight, out of mind. Yet the pyramid also had a conspicuous virtue: relative permanence. Thus we still remember the name of Cheops, although only the Egyptologists among us know precisely what Cheops did that, say, Rameses II didn't. To the rest of us, Cheops is the man who built the big pointed building. We might guess, correctly, that he got to do that only because he ruled the known world, which at that time extended about a month's chariot ride each side of the Nile. We have only the vaguest idea of what he looked like because portraits at the time were so stylized that one Pharaoh looked pretty much like another: big hat, little beard, things to hold, one foot in front of the other.

A certain amount of time having gone by, Alexander the Great achieved fame for conquering as much of the world as he could reach. His fame was transmitted by several means. His body was embalmed and kept on show in Alexandria, a practice repeated recently with the corpses of Lenin in Moscow and Mao Tse-tung in Peking, and with the same limitations, largely to do with air conditioning. . . . After Alexander the pace picked up, although it remained a requirement for world fame that it was hard to get without conquering the world first. Julius Caesar was even better at that than Alexander. Caesar also had the advantage that he built roads, got home more often and was therefore easier to sculpt . . . . Coins, busts, bas-reliefs and cameos of Julius Caesar all looked at least roughly like the man himself. He also added a promising new device to the range of means by which fame could be transmitted. He wrote his memoirs. . . . Unfortunately they were mainly about battles . . . The commentaries would have served him better for containing some of the self-justification that modern politicians go in for. Caesar had a lot to justify: he owned gladiators, for example, until he was forced to sell them. . . .

The Dark Ages were a dark age for fame, too. Attila the Hun was another world conqueror in the old sense, but all he did was tear things down. He never put anything up, not even a statue to himself. Few eyewitnesses survived to say what he looked like. Outside his group of low-life associates, he had no ambitions to be remembered for anything except the usual Hunnish activities—pillage, raping and pyromania. He burned records rather than kept them, so the picture of his personality was never filled out even to the extent that later ages might speculate about it. Consequently he is just a name, without really being famous at all. Genghis Khan is almost in the same case. He was an Eastern Attila with the same attitude problem. Once again the globetrotting psychopath's chief monument was a long trail of smoking ruins. . . .

Conquering the world with a paintbrush and a chisel instead of the sword and the cross, Michelangelo was the man who spelled the Italian Renaissance to the civilized world, which had grown to be almost as big as the old classical world had been before the barbarians got loose. Michelangelo was keenly interested in his own glory. He thought big: king-sized sculptures, frescoes with a Cinerama spread, a whole ceiling laid out like a curved split screen.

He regarded himself as a cut above all those other hacks. Unfortunately he left us no reliable self-portrait beyond a flayed skin in the Last Judgment. Though a distinguished poet, he also neglected to write his memoirs, leaving the job principally to Vasari, who was a better writer than painter, though not by much. The consequence once again was lasting fame but little image control, allowing later generations complete latitude to concoct their own version of the greatest graphic artist of all time. . . . The emphasis on the judicious husbandry of national resources [by Queen Elizabeth I of England] extended to the control of her own publicity. Prominent playwrights of the period were not encouraged to include any character too closely resembling her in their five-act blank-verse outpourings. The portrait as a means of transmitting fame had always been hampered by how long it took to paint one. With Queen Elizabeth it took even longer because so many finely detailed jewels had to be included. She could write—if she had never been Queen she would still count among the accomplished minor poets of the period—but what she wrote was not for publication. Though word-of-mouth had it that she could be quite merry at court when the Earl of Essex was in town, the impression of the Great Queen that went down to the ages was of a woman hampered by a severe nature. . . . The great ruler thought fame unruly, and kept it on a short leash.

But it was bursting to get loose as more books and periodicals were published. In the next couple of centuries, rulers of various degrees of absoluteness acquired the habit of glorifying themselves by building whole cities— Peter the Great's Petersburg was merely the most conspicuous example—but what really spread their fame was movable type, moving by the million pieces every hour of the day. It could make you famous whether your blood was blue or not. By the early, romantic, unruly nineteenth century, the young poet John Keats wasn't just dreaming of being a great poet, he was dreaming of fame itself. The young poet Byron got what Keats dreamed of. He published a long poem, *Childe Harold's Pilgrimage,* that all the young ladies loved. He woke up to find that he had become famous overnight. From then on, all the young ladies loved him, and not just in Britain but on a European scale. He was written up week by week. The periodicals were making a difference.

Napoleon conquered Europe with the sword instead of the pen. But he realized that fame was a weapon too. He was written about constantly. His portraits took almost as long to turn out as Queen Elizabeth's, because the dedication to simple dress that he started off with gave way to a taste for the sumptuosity that impressed the populace. The huge painting of his coronation as Emperor took so long to complete that he had started rewriting European history all over again before it was finished. But engravings could be quickly turned out for the periodicals and they fixed the essentials of his appearance for all time. . . Images were growing more complex as time went on—still simple, but more like life. Napoleon would have approved. He wanted to be famous, and he wanted his fame to last after death. He was still giving interviews in his final exile.

Only forty years after Napoleon died, Abraham Lincoln was President of the United States. Lincoln didn't especially want to be famous, but by now there was no choice. America's political importance was growing and no politically powerful figure could any longer get out of being famous. If Lincoln was impatient about posing for his portrait, and too busy to meet all but the quickest sketch artists, there was a new device that could capture his image in a matter of minutes. With the advent of photography, fame started to accelerate. Here was a way for a face to be everywhere in almost no time. And it didn't have to hang on the wall, it could just appear in the periodical that came out every week—or, another new idea, in the newspaper that came out every day. When Lincoln spoke at Gettysburg, hardly anybody was there to hear it. Perhaps it was a good thing. He had a high, not very satisfactory voice, its timbre nothing like as sonorous as his syntax. With no means of transmitting the sound, the speech drifted away on the wind. But when the words appeared in the paper, it was almost like being there, and probably better. It had happened only yesterday. When Lincoln was assassinated, publications all over the country had the news by telegraph, and all over the world not long after. The press was speeding things up. It needed the news.

Catherine the Great

Responding

1. How do the types of people who became famous in the past differ from today's celebrities?

2. Are the rewards of fame worth its drawbacks? Why or why not?

Fine Art Connection

As Clive James observes, artists have long served to fix the the the way the world pictures famous people. On these pages are four such celebrity portraits.

LOUISE ELISABETH VIGÉE-LEBRUN
Marie Antoinette (1780s)

One of the few women who made a successful career as an artist before modern times, Vigée-Lebrun was both court painter and confidante of the Queen of France, Marie Antoinette.

ANTOINE JEAN GROS
Napoleon at Arcole (1796)

Gros made his reputation by contributing historical paintings that helped to embody vividly the legend of Napoleon Bonaparte.

Seeing

MATHEW BRADY

Abraham Lincoln (1862)

Employing the new medium of
photography, Brady recorded the terrible
burden of leadership during
the Civil War in a series of portraits of
President Abraham Lincoln.

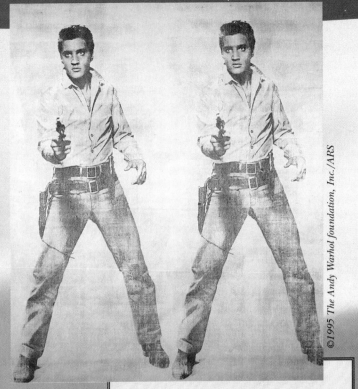

ANDY WARHOL

Elvis (1963)

One of the best known figures in the pop art
style of painting, Warhol frequently created works
that were multiple images of familar
American icons, such as
Marilyn Monroe and Elvis Presley.

Stars

*"In the future,
everyone will be world-famous
for fifteen minutes."*
—Andy Warhol

Responding

1. What one word would you use to sum up the impression created by each of these portraits?

2. If you were famous, which of these four artists would you choose to paint your portrait? Explain your answer.

Language History

Greater Simplicity and Precision

 They have exacted from all their members a close, naked, natural way of speaking . . . .

Thomas Sprat,
The History of the Royal Society of London (1667)

During the late 1600s, the English people reacted against ornamental prose and unregulated spontaneity of expression, calling instead for an ordered, rational language. The Royal Society, founded by a group of learned men and scientists, demanded of its members "a close, naked, natural way of speaking, positive expressions, clear senses, a native easiness, bringing all things as near the Mathematical plainness as they can, and preferring the language of Artizans, Countrymen, and Merchants, before that of Wits or Scholars."

Those caught in the surge toward a simpler and more precise language—among them Swift, Johnson, and Lord Chesterfield—tended to disparage what they called "cant" or "low speech." These arbiters of language realized that the English language was in a muddle: words still had widely variant meanings, spellings, and pronunciations, and the general instability of the language was a barrier to clear communication.

The urge to introduce order into the language is evident in hundreds of projects undertaken during the course of the eighteenth century. Johnson's ponderous two-volume *Dictionary,* great achievement though it was, offered only a partial solution to the problems of standardizing the language, and before the century ended there were many other attempts.

While the neoclassicism of the 1700s did much to tone down the bizarre and freakish aspects of speech of the 1600s, it did not, in spite of its insistence on rules and rigidity, stamp out the rich variety of the English language. Although both Johnson and Swift objected to the use of such words as *humbug, prig, doodle, bamboozle, fib, bully, fop, banter, stingy, fun,* and *prude,* those words continued in use then as they do today, evidence of the fact that people—not grammar books or dictionaries—make and perpetuate language.

Writing Workshop

Someone You Should Know

Assignment In this part of the unit you read biographical writings. Now write a biographical sketch about someone you know.

WRITER'S BLUEPRINT

Product	A biographical sketch
Purpose	To bring a person to life on paper
Audience	Newspaper readers in your community
Specs	To write a successful paper, you should:

- ❑ Imagine that you are writing a biographical sketch for a feature in a local newspaper entitled "Someone You Should Know." Focus on someone in your community who interests you and whom you can observe and interview in person.

- ❑ Begin by showing your subject in action, doing something characteristic and interesting (to hook the reader), then by giving a few basic facts about him or her (to orient the reader).

- ❑ Go on to discuss three of the following elements of your subject's life: personality, likes and dislikes, occupation, interests, background. Include quotations from an interview.

- ❑ Conclude with your personal reactions to your subject.

- ❑ Write smoothly. Take care to avoid a succession of choppy sentences.

- ❑ Follow the rules of grammar, usage, spelling, and mechanics. Take care to punctuate quotations correctly.

STEP **1** PREWRITING

Brainstorm a list of possible subjects for a biographical sketch. You might consider family members or neighbors. Also, think about all the people you know through various activities, including school, sports, part-time jobs—even your doctor or hairstylist. Then choose one person from your list to be your subject. Remember that this should be some-one you can observe and interview in person and who is willing to participate.

Gather background information about your subject. Make a list of people who know your subject—friends, co-workers, family members, former teachers, etc. Talk with two or three of these people about your subject, and take careful notes. Consider questions like: *What do you most admire about ____? What is the most interesting fact you know about ____? Can you think of an anecdote that would give an insight into ____'s personality?*

Make a web of interesting elements. Now that you know a little more about your subject, select three of these elements to focus on: personality, likes and dislikes, occupation, interests, background. Create a web similar to the one shown in which you list details you already know about each element.

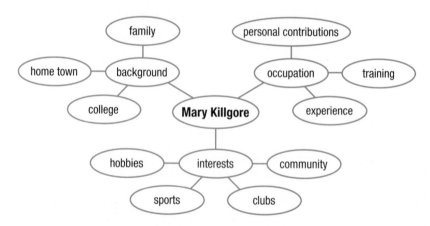

Interview your subject. Contact your subject and arrange a time and place to conduct an interview. Come prepared with questions that focus on the three elements you've selected. Think of asking these three kinds of questions:

- **General** questions: *What sorts of things do you do in your spare time?*

- **Specific** questions about details connected with the general questions: *Why did you take up skydiving?*

- **Follow-up** questions to expand on the information in the specific questions: *You say skydiving has made you a more careful person. What do you mean by "careful"?*

During the interview, listen carefully. For ideas on effective listening, see the Beyond Print article on page 380.

OR . . .
If you have access to a tape recorder and your subject feels comfortable about it, tape the interview. Later on, listen to it and take your notes then.

Try a quickdraw. Sketch your subject in action, doing something characteristic. Insert dialogue bubbles with appropriate quotes. At the bottom, write a few of your personal reactions to your subject.

Plan your biographical sketch. Look back at the information you've gathered on your subject and organize your notes into a plan like the one shown here.

Introduction
My subject doing something characteristic
Basic facts about him or her

Body
First element of my subject's life
    Quotations from interview
Second element
    Quotations from interview
Third element
    Quotations from interview

Conclusion
My personal reactions to my subject

STEP 2 DRAFTING

Before you draft, look over your prewriting materials and reread the Writer's Blueprint.

As you draft, concentrate on putting your ideas on paper. Worry about spelling and punctuation mistakes in the revising and editing stages. Here are some drafting tips.

- For the body, begin each section with a topic sentence that clearly identifies the element you are describing. (See the Literary Source for an example.)

- For the conclusion, review your interview notes to find a quote that you feel characterizes your subject better than any other, and use it as a basis for your closing comments.

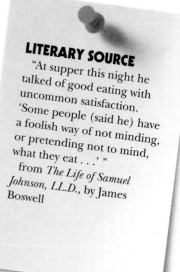

LITERARY SOURCE
"At supper this night he talked of good eating with uncommon satisfaction. 'Some people (said he) have a foolish way of not minding, or pretending not to mind, what they eat . . .'"
from *The Life of Samuel Johnson, LL.D.,* by James Boswell

STEP 3 REVISING

Ask a partner to comment on your draft before you revise it. Use the checklist on the next page as a guide.

✔ Did I focus on three elements of the subject's life?

✔ Did I include details from an interview with the person?

✔ Does my writing flow smoothly?

Revising Strategy

Avoiding Choppy Writing

Sometimes writers deliberately string together choppy sentences for dramatic effect:

> Lightning struck. Trees fell. The windows broke. The roof caved in.

More often, though, short, choppy sentences strung together call attention to themselves without the writer wanting them to:

> Mary Killgore went to college during the Sixties. She attended the University of Oregon. Mary majored in economics. She had a minor in Asian history. Mary went twelve months out of the year. She got her bachelor's degree in three years.

Effective writing moves along so smoothly that the reader often doesn't notice when one sentence ends and another begins:

> Mary Killgore attended the University of Oregon during the Sixties. She majored in economics with a minor in Asian history. By going twelve months out of the year, she got her bachelor's degree in three years.

When you revise, keep an eye out for successions of short sentences strung together, especially if they have the same structure. You might find that by combining some of them, you clarify meaning as well as make the writing flow, as in the student model below.

C. J. definitely has a full calendar. School is his top priority. *but*
His job is also a high priority. Sports *and* are important. Leisure *are* is also
important. *to* A well-balanced life ~~is necessary~~. "I guess if I had to
choose, the job would be the first thing to go," he noted. "I need the
income to go toward future college expenses, though," he said.

STUDENT MODEL

4 EDITING

Ask a partner to review your revised draft before you edit. Look over each paragraph to make sure you are punctuating quotations correctly.

Editing Strategy

Punctuating Quotations Correctly

Enclose words taken directly from a printed source or speech in quotation marks: Mary said, "I had a happy childhood."

More than one quote can appear in the same paragraph as long as the speaker hasn't changed:

> Mary said, "My mother thinks I was a naughty child." She thought a moment and then smiled slyly. "But I wouldn't call it naughty. I'd call it mischievous," she winked.

FOR REFERENCE
More information on punctuating quotations appears in the Language and Grammar Handbook at the back of this text.

STEP 5 PRESENTING

- Create a "wall of fame" at your local library, using the biographical sketches from your class along with photographs of your subjects.

- Make a copy of your biographical sketch for the person featured in it.

STEP 6 LOOKING BACK

Self-evaluate. Look back at the Writer's Blueprint and give yourself a score for each item, from 6 (superior) to 1 (inadequate).

Reflect. Write answers to these questions.

✔ How closely did the interview with your subject follow your planned questions? What unexpected turns did it take?

✔ If you were to interview and write a biographical sketch of a famous person, who would you choose and why?

For Your Working Portfolio Add your biographical sketch and reflection responses to your working portfolio.

Beyond Print

Interviewing

Effective listening requires practice and discipline. When interviewing one or more subjects, you want to be sure that you are listening effectively so that you don't waste their time or yours. Here are some pointers.

Pay attention. Make as much eye contact as is comfortable for you both. Watch your subject's facial expressions and body language also.

Think as you listen. You should be working with a list of questions you prepared in advance, but that doesn't mean you should follow your list slavishly. Listen to be sure that your subject is actually answering the question you asked, but be prepared to follow your subject off on little bypaths if they seem interesting and possibly relevant to your project.

Give the speaker feedback. Look and sound interested in what the speaker is saying. It's good to give verbal responses such as "Oh, that's interesting," or "I didn't know that" as long as they are natural to you. Ask your subject for more details when you think they might be useful.

Take notes. Some interviewers like to use a tape recorder—with permission, of course—to be sure they have an accurate record of their subject's words. You can conduct an effective interview with a pen and notebook, however. Don't try to record the interview word for word. Just write down key words or particularly useful phrases as you hear them; then try to summarize the answer to each question. It may help to give your subject an oral summary so that you can both check your accuracy. After the interview, write up your notes as soon as possible. That way, it will be easier to remember what your notes mean.

Follow up. It should go without saying that you have been friendly and courteous throughout the interview and have thanked your subject sincerely for his or her time. It is a nice idea to send your subject a copy of the interview after have written it up.

Activity Option

Interview one or more subjects in the preparation of your biography, Someone You Should Know, pages 373–377.

Multicultural Connections

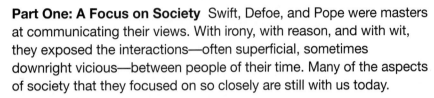

Interactions

Part One: A Focus on Society Swift, Defoe, and Pope were masters at communicating their views. With irony, with reason, and with wit, they exposed the interactions—often superficial, sometimes downright vicious—between people of their time. Many of the aspects of society that they focused on so closely are still with us today.

■ People have written satire for years, yet little, apparently, has changed. If it seems certain that writing is not going to change society, why bother? Why should writers continue to expose social ills even when the people responsible for them don't pay attention?

Communication

Part Two: Other People's Lives Communication plays an integral role when groups and persons of different backgrounds come into contact and interact with each other. Pepys, Johnson, and Boswell all devoted their considerable energies to communicating their understandings about people's lives and interactions.

■ What do you think is the single most important piece of information you can get from learning about another person's life?

Activities

1. Collect several weeks' worth of tabloid newspapers and magazines that feature celebrities. Survey who's in the news and for what reasons. Devise some sort of graphic organizer to summarize your findings. What conclusions can you come to about who becomes a celebrity and why?

2. What's funny? Browse library shelves for jokebooks or ask adults of your acquaintance to tell you their favorite jokes. Collect jokes (in good taste) from at least two different cultures—more, if possible. Compare them in terms of subject matter, type of humor, and so on. You may come away with more questions than conclusions. Ask the questions.

3. Prepare a dialogue between at least two people demonstrating how communication—or the lack of it—affects their interaction.

Independent and Group Projects

Drama

"They Call Me the Wasp of Twickenham" Prepare an "autobiographical" sketch of one of the authors in this unit. Include his comments on a piece of his writing (or someone else's writing), details from a period of his life, and perhaps some of his personal idiosyncrasies. Present your sketch to the class in the form of a dramatic monologue in which you play the role of the author.

Research

Read the Book, See the Movie The first novels were written during the 1700s. Notable were *Pamela* by Samuel Richardson (1740), *Joseph Andrews* by Henry Fielding (1742), and *Tristram Shandy* by Laurence Sterne (1760), but perhaps the most popular was Fielding's *Tom Jones* (1749). Read enough of the book to get a feel for the style and the period details. Then view the modern movie version, noting especially the picture of eighteenth-century life it presents. Write a review in which you concentrate on how well the movie portrays life in an earlier time.

Art

Costume Models Costume in the 1700s was elaborate, colorful, and decorative, and the men's outfits were sometimes as fancy as the women's. Find some books on costume history and dress at least two dolls with period costumes. If you're better with paints or colored pencils than you are with needle and thread, prepare costume plates instead. If the information is available, label your models with the year and the name of the person depicted.

Media

The Eighteenth-century Scene Create a magazine that reflects the daily life of England in the 1700s. After doing a little research, you might include news stories, feature stories, fashions, sports, music commentary, illustrations, and advertisements. If you are working with a group, give each member a separate assignment, such as research, writing, cover design, or layout. If possible, use your school's desktop publishing facilities to print an issue of your magazine for circulation to your classmates.

LONDON

THEMES *in* ENGLISH LITERATURE

London

~ capital city of England and hub of the British Empire ~ is both loved and hated, enthusiastically embraced and viciously denounced. In this section you will experience what various writers and artists have expressed about their experiences in what was once the largest city in the world.

LONDON,

THOU ART

THE FLOWER

OF CITIES ALL.

William Dunbar (1500s)

A DESCRIPTION OF LONDON

Houses, churches, mixed together,
Streets unpleasant in all weather;
Prisons, palaces contiguous,[1]
Gates, a bridge, the Thames irriguous.[2]

5 Gaudy things enough to tempt ye,
Showy outsides, insides empty;
Bubbles, trades, mechanic arts,
Coaches, wheelbarrows and carts.

Warrants, bailiffs,[3] bills unpaid,
10 Lords of laundresses afraid;
Rogues that nightly rob and shoot men,
Hangmen, aldermen and footmen.

Lawyers, poets, priests, physicians,
Noble, simple, all conditions:
15 Worth beneath a threadbare cover,
Villainy bedaubed all over.

Women black, red, fair and gray,
Prudes and such as never pray,
Handsome, ugly, noisy, still,
20 Some that will not, some that will.

Many a beau[4] without a shilling,[5]
Many a widow not unwilling;
Many a bargain, if you strike it:
This is London! How d'ye like it?

John Bancks (1738)

---

1. **contiguous** (kən tig′yŭ əs), *adj.* adjoining; near.
2. **irriguous** (i rig′yŭ əs), *adj.* watery.
3. **bailiff** (bā′lif), officer of the court.
4. **beau** (bō), *n.* young man courting a woman. *[French]*
5. **shilling,** coin equal to twelve pennies.

FOG EVERYWHERE

Implacable[1] November weather. As much mud in the streets, as if the waters had but newly retired from the face of the earth, and it would not be wonderful to meet a Megalosaurus,[2] forty feet long or so, waddling like an elephantine[3] lizard up Holborn Hill. Smoke lowering down from chimney-pots, making a soft black drizzle, with flakes of soot in it as big as full-grown snowflakes—gone into mourning, one might imagine, for the death of the sun. Dogs, undistinguishable in mire. Horses, scarcely better; splashed to their very blinkers.[4] Foot passengers, jostling one another's umbrellas, in a general infection of ill-temper, and losing their foot-hold at street-corners, where tens of thousands of other foot passengers have been slipping and sliding since the day broke (if this day ever broke), adding new deposits to the crust upon crust of mud, sticking at those points tenaciously[5] to the pavement, and accumulating at compound interest.

Fog everywhere. Fog up the river, where it flows among green aits and meadows; fog down the river, where it rolls defiled among the tiers of shipping, and the waterside pollutions of a great (and dirty) city. Fog on the Essex marshes, fog on the Kentish heights. Fog creeping into the cabooses of collier-brigs;[6] fog lying out on the yards, and hovering in the rigging of great ships; fog drooping on the gunwales[7] of barges and small boats. Fog in the eyes and throats of ancient Greenwich pensioners,[8] wheezing by the firesides of their wards; fog in the stem and bowl of the afternoon pipe of the wrathful skipper, down in his close cabin; fog cruelly pinching the toes and fingers of his shivering little 'prentice[9] boy on deck. Chance people on the bridges peeping over the parapets[10] into a nether sky of fog, with fog all round them, as if they were up in a balloon, and hanging in the misty clouds.

Charles Dickens (1853)

---

1. **implacable** (im plā′kə bəl), *adj.* unyielding.
2. **Megalosaurus** (meg′ə lō sôr′əs), *n.* a large dinosaur.
3. **elephantine** (el′ə fan′tēn), *adj.* elephant-like.

4. **blinkers,** leather flaps to keep a horse from seeing sideways.
5. **tenaciously** (ti nā′shəs lē), *adv.* stubbornly.
6. **collier-brigs,** coal barges.
7. **gunwale** (gun′l), *n.* the upper edge of

the side of a ship.
8. **pensioners,** retired people.
9. **'prentice,** apprentice, a young person learning a trade.
10. **parapet** (par′ə pet), *n.* a low wall or barrier

WESTMINSTER BRIDGE

Earth has not anything to show more fair:
Dull would he be of soul who could pass by
A sight so touching in its majesty:
This City now doth, like a garment, wear
5 The beauty of the morning; silent, bare,
Ships, towers, domes, theaters, and temples lie
Open unto the fields, and to the sky;
All bright and glittering in the smokeless air.
Never did sun more beautifully steep
10 In his first splendor, valley, rock, or hill;
Ne'er saw I, never felt, a calm so deep!
The river glideth at his own sweet will:
Dear God! the very houses seem asleep;
And all that mighty heart is lying still!

William Wordsworth (1807)

Coffee Houses

In London there are a great number of coffee-
houses, most of which, to tell the truth, are
not over clean or well furnished, owing to the
quantity of people who resort to these places
and because of the smoke, which would
quickly destroy good furniture. Englishmen are
great drinkers. In these coffee-houses you can
partake of chocolate, tea, or coffee, and of all
sorts of liquors, served hot; also in many places
you can have wine, punch, or ale. . . . What
attracts enormously in these coffee-houses are
the gazettes[1] and other public papers. All
Englishmen are great newsmongers.[2] Workmen
habitually begin the day by going to coffee-
rooms in order to read the latest news. I have
often seen shoeblacks and other persons of that
class club together to purchase a farthing[3]
paper. . . . Some coffee-houses are a resort for
learned scholars and for wits; others are the
resort of dandies or of politicians, or again of
professional newsmongers.

Ferdinand de Saussure (1700s)

1. **gazette** (gə zet′), *n.* newspaper.
2. **newsmonger** (nūz′mung′gər), *n.* person who spreads news or gossip.

3. **farthing** (fär′thing), *n.* a former British coin equal to a fourth of a British penny.

John Henry Henshall, Behind the Bar *(1882)*

Gustave Doré, Wentworth Street, Whitechapel *(1872)*

William Powell Frith, The Railway Station *(1862)*

LONDON,

that great cesspool[1] into

which all the loungers

of the Empire are

irresistibly drained.

Sir Arthur Conan Doyle (1887)

1. **cesspool** (sis′pül′), *n.* sewer.

Saturday Night in London

In London the masses can be seen on a scale and in conditions not to be seen anywhere else in the world.

I have been told, for example, that on Saturday nights half a million working men and women and their children spread like the ocean all over town, clustering particularly in certain districts, and celebrate their sabbath[1] all night long until five o'clock in the morning, in other words guzzle and drink like beasts to make up for a whole week. They bring with them their weekly savings, all that was earned by hard work and with many a curse. Great jets of gas burn in meat and food shops, brightly lighting up the streets. It is as if a grand reception were being held for those white negroes. Crowds throng the open taverns and the streets. There they eat and drink. The beer houses are decorated like palaces. Everyone is drunk, but drunk joylessly, gloomily and heavily, and everyone is somehow strangely silent. Only curses and bloody brawls occasionally break that suspicious and oppressively sad silence. . . . Everyone is in a hurry to drink himself into insensibility. . . .wives in no way lag behind their husbands and all get drunk together, while children crawl and run about among them.

One such night—it was getting on for two o'clock in the morning—I lost my

London

I wander through each chartered[1] street,
Near where the chartered Thames does flow.
And mark in every face I meet
Marks of weakness, marks of woe.

In every cry of every Man,
In every Infant's cry of fear,
In every voice: in every ban,[2]
The mind-forged manacles[3] I hear
How the Chimney-sweepers cry
Every blackening Church appalls,[4]
And the hapless Soldier's sigh,
Runs in blood down Palace walls.

But most through midnight streets I hear
How the youthful Harlots curse
Blasts the new-born Infant's tear
And blights with plagues the Marriage hearse.

William Blake (1794)

---

1. **chartered,** given by written authority. Blake is making a bitter pun on freedom and limitations.
2. **ban,** prohibition.

3. **manacle** (man′ə kəl), *n.* handcuff.
4. **appall** (ə pôl′), *v.* fill with dismay; terrify.

1. **sabbath** (sab′əth), *n.* day of worship.

way and for a long time trudged the streets in the midst of a vast crowd of gloomy people, asking my way almost by gestures, because I do not know a word of English. I found my way, but the impression of what I had seen tormented me for three days afterwards. The populace[2] is much the same anywhere, but there all was so vast, so vivid that you almost physically felt things which up till then you had only imagined. In London you no longer see the populace. Instead, you see a loss of sensibility, systematic, resigned and encouraged. . . . what we have here is a repudiation[3] of our social formula, an obstinate[4] and unconscious repudiation; an instinctive repudiation at any cost, in order to achieve salvation, a horrified and disgusted repudiation of the rest of us. Those millions of people, abandoned and driven away from the feast of humanity, push and crush each other in the underground darkness into which they have been cast by their elder brethren, they grope around seeking a door at which to knock and look for an exit lest they be smothered to death in that dark cellar. This is the last desperate attempt to huddle together and form one's own heap, one's own mass and to repudiate everything, the very image of man if need be, only to be oneself, only not to be with us. . . .

Feodor Dostoevski (1863)

In people's eyes,

in the swing, tramp, and trudge; in the

bellow and uproar; the carriages,

motor cars, omnibuses,[1] vans, sandwich

men[2] shuffling and swinging; brass

bands; barrel organs; in the triumph

and the jingle and the strange high

singing of some airplane overhead was

what she loved; life; London; this

moment in June.

Virginia Woolf (1925)

Walking in London

London life was very favorable for such a break. There is no town in the world which is more adapted for training one away from people and training one into solitude than London. The manner of life, the distances, the climate, the very multitude of the population in which personality vanishes, all this together with the absence of Continental diversions[1] conduces[2] to the same effect. One who knows how to live alone has nothing to fear from the tedium of London. The life here, like the air here, is bad for

---

2. populace (pop′yə lis), *n.* the common people.
3. repudiation (ri pyū′dē ā′shən), *n.* rejection.
4. obstinate (ob′stə nit), *adj.* stubborn.

1. omnibuses, public busses.
2. sandwich men, men wearing advertising boards front and back.

1. diversion (də vėr′zhən), *n.* entertainment.
2. conduce (kən dūs′), *v.* contribute.

the weak, for the frail, for one who seeks a prop outside himself, for one who seeks welcome, sympathy, attention; the moral lungs here must be as strong as the physical lungs, whose task it is to separate oxygen from the smoky fog. The masses are saved by battling for their daily bread, the commercial classes by their absorption in heaping up wealth, and all by the bustle of business; but nervous and romantic temperaments, fond of living among people, fond of intellectual sloth and of idly luxuriating in emotion, are bored to death here and fall into despair.

Wandering lonely about London, through its stony lanes and stifling passages, sometimes not seeing a step before me for the thick, opaline[3] fog, and colliding with shadows running—I lived through a great deal.

Alexander Herzen (1968)

C. R. W. Nevinson's Amongst the Nerves of the World *(about 1930) depicts London's newspaper district, Fleet Street, with St. Paul's Cathedral in the distance.*

PRELUDE 1

The winter evening settles down
With smell of steaks in passageways.
Six o'clock.
The burnt-out ends of smoky days.
5 And now a gusty shower wraps
The grimy scraps
Of withered leaves about your feet
And newspapers from vacant lots;
The showers beat
10 On broken blinds and chimney-pots,
And at the corner of the street
A lonely cab-horse steams and stamps.
And then the lighting of the lamps.

T. S. Eliot (1917)

---

3. **opaline** (ō′pə līn), *adj.* like an opal, with a peculiar play of colors.

André Derain, St. Paul's from the Thames *(1906)*

St. Paul's stands amid the smoke after a German bombing raid in 1940.

391

DULL LONDON

It begins the moment you set foot ashore, the moment you step off the boat's gangway. The heart suddenly, yet vaguely, sinks. It is no lurch of fear. Quite the contrary. It is as if the life-urge failed, and the heart dimly sank. You trail past the benevolent policeman and the inoffensive passport officials, through the fussy and somehow foolish customs—we don't *really* think it matters if somebody smuggles in two pairs of false-silk stockings—and we get into the poky but inoffensive train, with poky but utterly inoffensive people, and we have a cup of inoffensive tea from a nice inoffensive boy, and we run through small, poky but nice and inoffensive country, till we are landed in the big but unexciting station of Victoria, when an inoffensive porter puts us into an inoffensive taxi and we are driven through the crowded yet strangely dull streets of London to the cosy yet strangely poky and dull place where we are going to stay. And the first half-hour in London, after some years abroad, is really a plunge of misery. The strange, the gray and uncanny,[1] almost deathly sense of *dullness* is overwhelming. Of course, you get over it after a while, and admit that you exaggerated. You get into the rhythm of London again, and you tell yourself that it is *not* dull. And yet you are haunted, all the time, sleeping or waking, with the uncanny feeling: It is dull! It is all dull! This life here is one vast complex of dullness! I am dull! I am being dull! My spirit is being dulled! My life is dulling down to London dullness. . . .

Now to feel like this about one's native land is terrible. I am sure I am an exceptional, or at least an exaggerated case. Yet it seems to me most of my fellow-countrymen have the pinched, slightly pathetic look in their faces, the vague, wondering realization: It is dull! It is always essentially dull! My life is dull!

Of course, England is the easiest country in the world, easy, easy and nice. Everybody is nice, and everybody is easy. The English people on the whole are surely the *nicest* people in the world, and everybody makes everything so easy for everybody else, that there is almost nothing to resist at all. But this very easiness and this very niceness become at last a nightmare. It is as if the whole air were impregnated with chloroform or some other pervasive[2] anaesthetic, that makes everything easy and nice, and takes the edge off everything, whether nice or nasty. As you inhale the drug of easiness and niceness, your vitality begins to sink. Perhaps not your physical vitality, but something else: the vivid flame of your individual life. England can afford to be so free and individual because no individual flame of life is sharp and vivid. It is just mildly warm and safe. You couldn't burn your fingers at it. Nice, safe, easy: the whole ideal. And yet under all the easiness is a gnawing uneasiness, as in a drug-taker.

D. H. Lawrence (1932)

1. **uncanny** (un kan′ē), *adj.* strange and mysterious.

2. **pervasive** (pər vā′siv), *adj.* spreading throughout.

Entertainments

I will now try to describe what a ball was like in Victorian and Edwardian days. Your hostess and her daughter stood at the head of the staircase, each of these ladies holding a fan and a bouquet. The guests struggled up the stairs, as there was invariably a crush. No ball or entertainment was considered a success unless there were far more guests present than the ball-and-supper-rooms could accommodate with comfort. Your name, or names as the case might be, were announced, and after shaking hands with your hostess you drifted away to the ballroom, the young ladies in search of their partners and the mamas, dowagers, and chaperons proceeding to seat themselves on small gilt chairs along the wall. The daughters, unless they were dancing,

stood by their side. The young girls who were not fortunate in finding partners were rather cruelly termed "wallflowers." I do not think that there are any "wallflowers" nowadays!

If you were seen dancing more than once with the same young man, the latter ran the risk of being questioned as to what were "his intentions," and I wonder how many budding romances came to nought owing to these very searching and rather tactless questions.

The following day, visiting-cards had to be left on one's hostess of the party, ball, or dinner of the preceding evening. I believe the leaving of visiting-cards has gone out of fashion, and a little note of "thank you," often accompanied by a few carefully chosen flowers, has taken their place.

Princess Marie Louise (1946)

All That Life Can Afford

I suggested a doubt, that if I were to reside in London, the exquisite zest with which I relished it in occasional visits might go off, and I might grow tired of it. JOHNSON. "Why, Sir, you find no man, at all intellectual, who is willing to leave London. No, Sir, when a man is tired of London, he is tired of life; for there is in London all that life can afford."

James Boswell (1791)

"This is London . . ."

After the Fall of France in June 1940, Germany prepared to invade England. In an attempt to destroy British defenses, the Germans began an intensive air assault against England in August 1940. Early in September the focus of the German air raids shifted to the British capital, London. A 32-year-old American newsman, Edward R. Murrow (1908-1965), became famous for his radio broadcasts from London during the Battle of Britain. The following is an excerpt from his broadcast for October 10, 1940.

This is London, ten minutes before five in the morning. Tonight's raid has been widespread. London is again the main target. Bombs have been reported from more than fifty districts. Raiders have been over Wales in the west, the Midlands, Liverpool, the southwest, and northeast. So far as London is concerned, the outskirts appear to have suffered the heaviest pounding. The attack has decreased in intensity since the moon faded from the sky.

All the fires were quickly brought under control. That's a common phrase in the morning communiqués.[1] I've seen how it's done; spent a night with the London fire brigade. For three hours after the night attack got going, I shivered in a sandbag crow's-nest atop a tall building near the Thames. It was one of the many fire-observation posts. There was an old gun barrel mounted above a round table marked off like a compass. A stick of incendiaries[2] bounced off rooftops about three miles away. The observer took a sight on a point where the first one fell, swung his gun sight along the line of bombs, and took another reading at the end of the line of fire. Then he picked up his telephone and shouted above the half gale that was blowing up there, "Stick of incendiaries—between 190 and 220—about three miles away." Five minutes later a German bomber came boring down the river. We could see his exhaust trail like a pale ribbon stretched straight across the sky. Half a mile downstream there were two eruptions and then a third, close together. The first two looked like some giant had thrown a huge basket of flaming golden oranges high in the air. The third was just a balloon of fire enclosed in black smoke above the housetops. The observer didn't bother with his gun sight and indicator for that one. Just reached for his night glasses, took one quick look, picked up his telephone, and said, "Two high explosives and one oil bomb," and named the street where they had fallen. . . .

There was peace and quiet inside for twenty minutes. Then a shower of incendiaries came down far in the distance. They didn't fall in a line. It looked like flashes from an electric train on a wet night, only the engineer was drunk and driving his train in circles through the streets. One sight at the middle of the flashes and our observer reported laconically, "Breadbasket at 90—covers a couple of miles." Half an hour later a string of fire bombs fell right beside the Thames. Their white glare was reflected in the black, lazy water near the banks and faded out in midstream where the moon cut a golden swathe broken only by the arches of famous bridges.

We could see little men shoveling those fire bombs into the river. One burned for a few minutes like a beacon right in the middle of a bridge. Finally those white flames all went out. No one bothers about the white light, it's only when it turns yellow that a real fire has started.

I must have seen well over a hundred fire bombs come down and only three small fires were started. The incendiaries aren't so bad if there is someone there to deal with them, but those oil bombs present more difficulties.

As I watched those white fires flame up and die down, watched the yellow blazes grow dull and disappear, I thought, what a puny effort is this to burn a great city.

Edward R. Murrow (1940)

---

1. **communiqué** (kə myü′nə kā), *n.* official bulletin or statement. *[French]*

2. **incendiary** (in sen′dē er′ē), *n.* shell or bomb containing chemical agents that cause fire.

London Pride

There's a little city flower—every spring unfailing
Growing in the crevices by some London railing
Though it has a Latin name, in town and country-side
We in England call it London Pride.

London Pride has been handed down to us.
London Pride is a flower that's free.
London Pride means our own dear town to us,
And our pride it forever will be.

Woa Liza see the coster[1] barrows,
Vegetable marrows and the fruit piled high.
Woa Liza little London sparrows,
Covent Garden Market[2] where the costers cry.
Cockney[3] feet mark the beat of history.
Every street pins a memory down.
Nothing ever can quite replace
The grace of London Town.

In our city darkened now—street and squares and crescent
We can feel our living past in our shadowed present
Ghosts beside our starlit Thames who lived and loved and died
Keep throughout the ages London Pride.

London Pride has been handed down to us.
London Pride is a flower that's free.
London Pride means our own dear town to us,
And our pride it forever will be.

Gray city stubbornly implanted,
Taken so for granted for a thousand years.
Stay city smokily enchanted,
Cradle of our memories and hopes and fears.
Every Blitz[4] your resistance toughening
From the Ritz to the Anchor and Crown,[5]
Nothing ever could override
The Pride of London Town.

Noel Coward (1941)

THE LAST CIVILIZED METROPOLIS IN THE WORLD.

John Canaday (1972)

RESPONDING

1. Summarize the sorts of reasons people have for loving London or for hating it. Do these reasons seem persuasive to you? Explain.
2. Do the details that make people respond positively or negatively seem to change over the years; that is, if you loved London then are you likely to hate it now (or vice versa)?
3. Which detail or description of London appeals to you the most? the least? Why?
4. Make a generalization about what happens when different artists look at the same monument or building (such as St. Paul's Cathedral on page 391) at different times over the years.
5. From the differing treatments of Londoners on page 387, what can you infer about the attitude of the artist in each case toward the particular group of people he portrays?

---

1. **coster,** street vendor.
2. **Covent Garden Market,** a large street market in the middle of London.
3. **cockney** (cok′nē), *n.* nickname for an inhabitant of the eastern section of London who speaks a particular dialect of English.
4. **blitz** (blits), *n.* Nazi bombing attack during World War II.
5. **Ritz . . . Crown,** that is, from the fine hotels to the corner taverns.

The Romantic Era

Visions and Dreams

The Outsider

Exceeding Human Limits

A Cultural

HISTORICAL OVERVIEW

In the later 1700s and early 1800s, there was a movement away from the culture of the Age of Reason, which emphasized the value of rationalism and focused on contemporary society for artistic subject matter. In both literature and the visual arts, the new Romantic spirit was particularly evident in writers' and artists' choices of subject matter. The following are cultural trends that were characteristic of the Romantic Era:

- a reverance for nature in its grander aspects, such as mountain landscapes;
- a celebration of childhood;
- an interest in folklore;
- an fascination with antiquity, particularly the Middle Ages;
- a curiosity about dreams, visions, and madness;
- a focus on individual experience, particularly that of the artist.

Thomas Rowlandson's drawing Doctor Syntax Sketching After Nature *(1812) satirizes the Romantic Era's pursuit of picturesque nature.*

The popularity of collections of fairy tales such as those by the Grimm brothers in Germany sparked a widespread interest in folklore (a word coined in 1846).

Revolution

In the poems and pictures of his book Songs of Innocence (1789), William Blake created images of childhood as paradise.

The Romantic Era's fascination with the Middle Ages was reflected in the popularity of Gothic novels such as Horace Walpole's The Castle of Otranto. *Set in a medieval castle complete with underground passages, trap doors, dark stairways, and mysterious rooms, Walpole's novel began the fashion for strange tales full of weird landscapes, haunted ruins, sinister noblemen, and innocent heroines.*

CASTLE OF OTRANTO. CH XXXVIII.
Theodore, conducting Isabella to the Cavern, to protect her from the fury of Manfred.

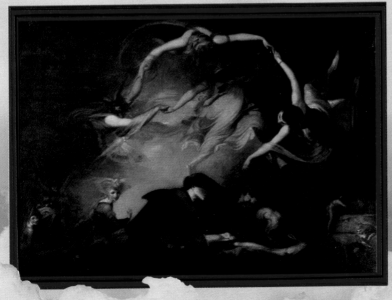

Henry Fuseli's painting The Shepherd's Dream (1793), with its vision of fairies circling above the sleeping shepherd, suggests the Romantic interest in visionary experiences.

Key Dates

1755
A massive earthquake in Lisbon undercuts belief in rational world order.

1764
The Castle of Otranto *starts fashion for Gothic novels.*

1785
Percy's collection of English and Scottish ballads published.

1798
Wordsworth and Coleridge's Lyrical Ballads *published.*

1799
Rosetta stone found in Egypt.

1812
Publication begins of Grimms' collection of German folktales.

1816
Elgin marbles removed from the Parthenon are purchased by the British Museum.

Part One

Visions and Dreams

Not all of life can be measured scientifically and considered logically. There are people who place greater trust in dreams, visions, and other heightened states of emotion.

 Multicultural Connection One focus of the Romantic Era was on the **individuality** of the "common" men and women who made up most of the work force, and who, the poets felt, achieved dignity through their work. Some Romantic poets achieved their own individuality, however, above or beyond the cultural norms of the rest of society.

Before Reading

The Tyger
A New Jerusalem

by William Blake

William Blake
1757–1827

William Blake was born in London and lived most of his life in a working class section of the city. Trained as an engraver, Blake supported himself as an illustrator throughout his life (See page 407.) As a child of four, Blake had his first mystical experience when he reported that he saw God's face. By the time he was eight, he related that he had seen angels in a field, the prophet Ezekiel, and a tree filled with angels. By the time of his marriage, Blake had become so consumed in mystical belief that his wife is said to have remarked: "I have very little of Mr. Blake's company. He is always in Paradise."

The Lamb
from Auguries of Innocence

Building Background

A New Vision In his best-known works William Blake avoided the classical allusions and formal language that characterized the work of earlier poets. Instead he developed a childlike simplicity, lyricism, and visual immediacy that place him firmly with the group of Romantic poets, although his poetry is more visionary than that of most later Romantics. Largely unappreciated during his lifetime, he lived in poverty, his life driven by mystical experiences and a search for truth. Between 1783 and 1794 Blake wrote, illustrated, and printed his most famous lyric poems in *Songs of Innocence* and *Songs of Innocence and Experience: Shewing* [showing] *the Two Contrary States of the Human Soul.* He prepared his own illustrative engravings for these poems, and either he or his wife Catherine tinted each illustration by hand.

Literary Focus

Analogy An **analogy** is a comparison made between two situations, people, or ideas that are somewhat alike but unlike in most respects. Sometimes the comparison simply places two like things side by side and the reader must make the connection, as is often true of Blake. Sometimes a new, unfamiliar, or complex object or idea is explained through comparison to a familiar or simpler one. Look for the analogy or comparison as you read Blake's poetry, particularly "The Lamb."

Writer's Notebook

Look Around You Blake's poetry is characterized by strong **imagery,** which he achieves through careful choice of words. Look up from your reading at the scene around you—at the room you're in or outdoors through a window—and jot down some words and phrases that describe the scene. Try to choose words that call up specific and strong images. For example, not *door* but *golden oak door;* not *sound of an airplane* but *distant rumble of a 747.*

The Tyger

WILLIAM BLAKE

Tyger! Tyger! burning bright
In the forests of the night,
who & made you? What immortal[1] hand or eye
Could frame thy fearful symmetry?[2]

5 In what distant deeps or skies
Burned the fire of thine eyes?
On what wings dare he aspire?[3]
What the hand dare seize the fire?

And what shoulder, & what art,
10 Could twist the sinews[4] of thy heart?
And when thy heart began to beat,
What dread Hand? & what dread feet?

What the hammer? what the chain?
In what furnace was thy brain?
15 What the anvil? what dread grasp
Dare its deadly terrors clasp?

When the stars threw down their spears
And watered heaven with their tears,
Did he smile his work to see?
20 Did he who made the Lamb make thee?

Tyger! Tyger! burning bright
In the forests of the night,
What immortal hand or eye
Dare frame thy fearful symmetry?

---

1. immortal (i môr′tl), *adj.* living forever.
2. symmetry (sim′ə trē), *n.* pleasing proportions between the parts of a whole; harmony.
3. aspire (ə spīr′), *v.* rise high.
4. **sinew** (sin′yü), *n.* tendon; also, strength; energy.

This hand-colored engraving, entitled *Tiger,* was created by the British artist Edward J. Detmold (1883–1957). In what ways does the artist's depiction of the tiger agree with the image Blake creates in "The Tyger"? ➤

The Lamb

WILLIAM BLAKE

Little Lamb, who made thee?
  Dost thou know who made thee?
Gave thee life & bid thee feed
By the stream & o'er the mead;[1]
5 Gave thee clothing of delight,
Softest clothing wooly bright;
Gave thee such a tender voice,
Making all the vales[2] rejoice!
  Little Lamb who made thee?
10 Dost thou know who made thee?

Little Lamb, I'll tell thee,
Little Lamb, I'll tell thee!

He is callèd by thy name,
For he calls himself a Lamb:[3]
15 He is meek & he is mild;
He became a little child.
I a child & thou a lamb,
We are callèd by his name.
  Little Lamb, God bless thee!
20 Little Lamb, God bless thee!

---

1. **mead** (mēd), *n.* meadow.
2. **vale** (vāl), *n.* valley.
3. **Lamb,** symbol of Jesus Christ as Redeemer: "Behold the Lamb of God, which taketh away the sin of the world." (John 1:29)

A New Jerusalem

WILLIAM BLAKE

And did those feet in ancient time[1]
Walk upon England's mountains green?
And was the holy Lamb of God
On England's pleasant pastures seen?

5 And did the Countenance Divine
Shine forth upon our clouded hills?
And was Jerusalem builded here,
Among these dark Satanic Mills?[2]

Bring me my Bow of burning gold!
10 Bring me my Arrows of desire!

Bring me my Spear! O clouds, unfold!
Bring me my Chariot of fire!

I will not cease from Mental Fight,
Nor shall My Sword sleep in my hand,
15 Till we have built Jerusalem
In England's green & pleasant Land.

---

1. **feet . . . time,** an allusion to legends that during the part of Jesus' life not described in the Bible, he traveled to many lands, including the British Isles.
2. **Satanic Mills,** mills of the mind, not industrial mills.

Auguries of Innocence

WILLIAM BLAKE

To see a World in a Grain of Sand
And a Heaven in a Wild Flower,
Hold Infinity in the palm of your hand
And Eternity in an hour.

5   A Robin Red breast in a Cage
Puts all Heaven in a Rage.
A dove house filled with doves & Pigeons
Shudders Hell through all its regions.
A dog starved at his Master's Gate
10 Predicts the ruin of the State.
A Horse misused upon the Road
Calls to Heaven for Human blood.
Each outcry of the hunted Hare
A fiber from the Brain does tear.
15 A Skylark wounded in the wing,
A Cherubim[1] does cease to sing.
The Game Cock clipped & armed for fight[2]
Does the Rising Sun affright.
Every Wolf's & Lion's howl
20 Raises from Hell a Human Soul.
The wild deer, wandering here & there,
Keeps the Human Soul from Care.
The Lamb misused breeds Public strife
And yet forgives the Butcher's Knife.
25 The Bat that flits at close of Eve
Has left the Brain that won't Believe.
The Owl that calls upon the Night
Speaks the Unbeliever's fright.
He who shall hurt the little Wren
30 Shall never be beloved by Men.
He who the Ox to wrath[3] has moved
Shall never be by Woman loved.
The wanton Boy that kills the Fly
Shall feel the Spider's enmity.[4]

35 He who torments the Chafer's[5] sprite
Weaves a Bower[6] in endless Night.
The Caterpillar on the Leaf
Repeats to thee thy Mother's grief.
Kill not the Moth nor Butterfly,
40 For the Last Judgment draweth nigh.
He who shall train the Horse to War
Shall never pass the Polar Bar.
The Beggar's Dog & Widow's Cat,
Feed them & thou wilt grow fat.
45 The Gnat that sings his Summer's song
Poison gets from Slander's tongue.
The poison of the Snake & Newt[7]
Is the sweat of Envy's Foot.
The Poison of the Honey Bee
50 Is the Artist's Jealousy.
The Prince's Robes & Beggar's Rags
Are Toadstools on the Miser's Bags.
A truth that's told with bad intent
Beats all the Lies you can invent.
55 It is right it should be so;
Man was made for Joy & Woe;
And when this we rightly know
Through the World we safely go. . . .

---

augury (ô′gyər ē), *n.* sign; omen.
1. **cherubim** (cher′ə bim), *n.* plural of *cherub,* one of the second highest order of angels.
2. **game cock . . . for fight,** in the sport of cockfighting, the natural spurs on the legs of specially bred roosters are often trimmed so that metal spurs can be fastened on.
3. **wrath** (rath), *n.* great anger.
4. **enmity** (en′mə tē), *n.* hostility; hatred.
5. **chafer** (chā′fər), *n.* beetle.
6. bower (bou′ər), *n.* shelter.
7. **newt** (nüt), *n.* salamander.

After Reading

Making Connections

1. Judging from his poetry only, what one word or phrase would you use to describe William Blake?

2. Blake also wrote (in "The Marriage of Heaven and Hell"), "The roaring of lions, the howling of wolves . . . are portions of eternity, too great for the eye of man." How does this help explain Blake's attitude toward the creature in "The Tyger"?

3. "The Lamb" is from *Songs of Innocence,* in which the poems recapture the happiness of childhood. "The Tyger" is from *Songs of Experience,* in which the poems are in part about social evils and reveal Blake's attempt to reconcile evil and good. He believed that the innocence of childhood must be balanced by the wisdom gained through experience, however painful and disenchanting. What qualities of the lamb and the tiger are emphasized in these matched poems?

4. The **connotation** of a word is what is suggested in addition to the literal meaning. What connotation does the word *Jerusalem* seem to have to Blake? to his readers?

5. Summarize one **theme** of "Auguries of Innocence."

6. 👁 Comment on the **individuality** of Blake—the person and the poet—based on what you have read of his poetry and what you have read about his life.

7. What art form do you think Blake would choose to express his visions if he were living today—movies, multimedia, computer graphics, or what?

Literary Focus: Analogy

An **analogy** is a comparison made between two people, situations, or ideas that are somewhat alike but unlike in most respects. The analogy in "The Lamb" is between the innocent lamb with a "tender voice" and Jesus as the Lamb of God, also "meek and mild," who according to Christian belief came to earth as the son of God. The analogy deals in part with the mystery of creation. What does it mean for Jesus to be called by the names of the child and the lamb? What does it mean for the child and the lamb to be called by the same names as Jesus? What analogy can you find in "The New Jerusalem"?

Vocabulary Study

Write the letter of the word that is not related in meaning to the other words in the set.

aspire
bower
immortal
mead
symmetry

1. **a.** mead   **b.** field   **c.** hillside   **d.** pasture

2. **a.** shelter   **b.** bower   **c.** refuge   **d.** tombstone

3. **a.** wicked   **b.** sinful   **c.** immortal   **d.** evil

4. **a.** concert   **b.** symmetry   **c.** opera   **d.** play

5. **a.** aspire   **b.** rise   **c.** ascend   **d.** hunt

Expressing Your Ideas

Writing Choices

Writer's Notebook Update Look over the words or phrases you jotted down to describe a scene, and write a descriptive paragraph of that scene using some of those words. You might use spatial order in your paragraph.

Digging Deep Choose one of Blake's poems, and in an **essay** describe how he has used one or more of the following literary techniques and discuss their effect on the poem: alliteration, repetition, metaphor, symbol, imagery, connotation.

Dear Mr. Blake Blake once wrote in a letter: "What is Grand is necessarily obscure to Weak men. That which can be made Explicit [clear] to the Idiot is not worthy my care." Suppose he had written this in a letter to you. Write a **letter** to Blake agreeing or disagreeing with his views.

Other Options

What Happened When Create an illustrated **time line** showing major events of the industrial revolution in England and America during Blake's lifetime (1757–1827). Include inventions and technical advances.

I Want! This is a metal engraving that William Blake created as an illustration for *The Gates of Paradise* (1793). Create a **visual expressing aspiration,** or ambition, and your views toward it. Your visual could be a piece of sculpture in paper, clay, or metal; it could be a collage; it could be computer art or animation. Even if you think that Blake's image of a stepladder to the moon is a bit of an exaggeration, you need not be limited by anything except your imagination.

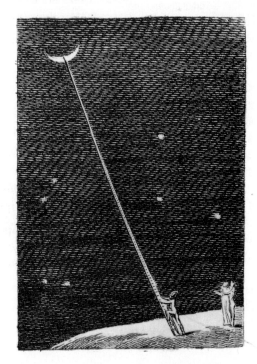

Before Reading

Tintern Abbey
My Heart Leaps Up
The World Is Too Much with Us by William Wordsworth

William Wordsworth
1770–1850

During the summer of 1790 Wordsworth went on a walking tour of Switzerland and France and returned to England fired with enthusiasm for the French Revolution. After his graduation from Cambridge, he returned to France, where he fell in love with Annette Vallon. They had a daughter, but lack of funds forced his return to England, and declaration of war between Britain and France in 1793 prevented his return to France. He later saw Vallon and helped support their daughter, however. In 1802 he married a childhood friend, Mary Hutchinson, and they had five children, two of whom died at an early age. Wordsworth was not universally liked (poet John Keats thought him an egotist). However, Wordsworth achieved national recognition and great public respect before his death.

Building Background

Devising the Plan The beginning of Wordsworth's friendship with poet Samuel Taylor Coleridge in 1795 led to two revolutionary ideas about poetry. In 1798 they published *Lyrical Ballads.* The book was at first not well received by critics or other poets. In a preface to an expanded edition in 1800 Wordsworth stated that "all good poetry is the spontaneous overflow of powerful feelings" and that poetry must be in the language "really used by men"; that is, in simple, direct language. Both ideas were revolutionary in that they helped to free poetry from earlier rigid ideas about suitable subject matter and language.

Literary Focus

Blank Verse Blank verse is unrhymed and written in iambic pentameter—which, of all the various rhythms, is closest to the natural rhythms of English speech. (See the Glossary of Literary Terms.) The heroic couplets of Alexander Pope (see page 313) are also in iambic pentameter; the difference is that they rhyme and blank verse does not. As you read "Tintern Abbey," consider whether Wordsworth's poetic lines actually do sound like natural English speech.

Writer's Notebook

Dorothy's Journals The journals of Wordsworth's sister Dorothy contain vivid descriptions of landscape, walking, and weather:

"1st March [1798] . . . . The shapes of the mist, slowly moving along, exquisitely beautiful; passing over the sheep they almost seemed to have more of life than those quiet creatures. The unseen birds singing in the mist."

Try keeping a journal for several days of your walking and the weather and the landscape you travel through daily.

Lines Composed a Few Miles Above Tintern Abbey

On Revisiting the Banks of the Wye During a Tour. July 13, 1798

William Wordsworth

Wordsworth wrote this poem during a walking tour with his sister Dorothy along the River Wye. The beautiful ruin of Tintern Abbey, once a monastery, is located in a deep valley at the river's edge. Wordsworth later wrote that "no poem of mine was composed under circumstances more pleasant for me to remember than this."

Five years have passed; five summers, with
    the length
Of five long winters! and again I hear
These waters, rolling from their
    mountain-springs
With a soft inland murmur. Once again
5 Do I behold these steep and lofty cliffs,
That on a wild secluded scene impress
Thoughts of more deep seclusion;
    and connect
The landscape with the quiet of the sky.
The day is come when I again repose
10 Here, under this dark sycamore, and view
These plots of cottage-ground, these
    orchard-tufts,
Which at this season, with their
    unripe fruits,
Are clad[1] in one green hue, and lose
    themselves
'Mid groves and copses.[2] Once again I see
15 These hedge-rows, hardly hedge-rows,
    little lines
Of sportive wood run wild: these
    pastoral farms,
Green to the very door; and wreaths
    of smoke
Sent up, in silence, from among the trees!
With some uncertain notice, as might seem

20 Of vagrant[3] dwellers in the houseless woods,
Or of some Hermit's cave, where by his fire
The Hermit sits alone.
          These beauteous forms,
Through a long absence, have not been
    to me
As is a landscape to a blind man's eye:
25 But oft, in lonely rooms, and 'mid the din
Of towns and cities, I have owed to them
In hours of weariness, sensations sweet,
Felt in the blood, and felt along the heart;
And passing even into my purer mind,
30 With tranquil restoration:—feelings too
Of unremembered pleasure: such, perhaps,
As have no slight or trivial influence
On that best portion of a good man's life,
His little, nameless, unremembered acts
35 Of kindness and of love. Nor less, I trust,
To them I may have owed another gift,
Of aspect more sublime;[4] that blessed mood
In which the burthen[5] of the mystery,
In which the heavy and the weary weight

---

1. clad (klad), *adj.* clothed.
2. copse (kops), *n.* thicket of small bushes or shrubs.
3. vagrant (vā′grənt), *adj.* wandering.
4. **sublime** (sə blīm′), *adj.* noble; grand; exalted.
5. **burthen** (bėr′ᴛнən), *n.* burden.

40 Of all this unintelligible world,
    Is lightened—that serene and blessed
        mood,
    In which the affections gently lead us on,
    Until, the breath of this corporeal[6] frame
    And even the motion of our human blood
45 Almost suspended, we are laid asleep
    In body, and become a living soul:
    While with an eye made quiet by the power
    Of harmony, and the deep power of joy,
    We see into the life of things.
                            If this
50 Be but a vain belief, yet, oh! how oft—
    In darkness and amid the many shapes
    Of joyless daylight; when the fretful stir
    Unprofitable, and the fever of the world,
    Have hung upon the beatings of my heart—
55 How oft, in spirit, have I turned to thee,
    O sylvan[7] Wye! thou wanderer through
            the woods,
    How often has my spirit turned to thee!

    And now, with gleams of half-
            extinguished thought,
    With many recognitions dim and faint,
60 And somewhat of a sad perplexity,[8]
    The picture of the mind revives again:
    While here I stand, not only with the sense
    Of present pleasure, but with pleasing
            thoughts
    That in this moment there is life and food
65 For future years. And so I dare to hope,
    Though changed, no doubt, from what I
            was when first
    I came among these hills; when like a roe[9]
    I bounded o'er the mountains, by the sides
    Of the deep rivers, and the lonely streams,
70 Wherever nature led: more like a man
    Flying from something that he dreads
            than one
    Who sought the thing he loved. For
            nature then
    (The coarser pleasures of my boyish days,
    And their glad animal movements all
            gone by)

75 To me was all in all. I cannot paint
    What then I was. The sounding cataract[10]
    Haunted me like a passion: the tall rock,
    The mountain, and the deep and
            gloomy wood,
    Their colors and their forms, were
            then to me
80 An appetite; a feeling and a love,
    That had no need of a remoter charm,
    By thought supplied, nor any interest
    Unborrowed from the eye. That time
            is past,
    And all its aching joys are now no more,
85 And all its dizzy raptures. Not for this
    Faint I, nor mourn nor murmur; other gifts
    Have followed; for such loss, I would believe,
    Abundant recompense.[11] For I have learned
    To look on nature, not as in the hour
90 Of thoughtless youth; but hearing
            oftentimes
    The still, sad music of humanity,
    Nor harsh nor grating, though of ample
            power
    To chasten[12] and subdue. And I have felt
    A presence that disturbs me with the joy
95 Of elevated thoughts; a sense sublime
    Of something far more deeply interfused,[13]
    Whose dwelling is the light of setting suns,
    And the round ocean and the living air,
    And the blue sky, and in the mind of man:
100 A motion and a spirit, that impels
    All thinking things, all objects of all thought,

---

6. corporeal (kôr pôr′ē əl), *adj.* of or for the body.
7. sylvan (sil′vən), *adj.* of or flowing through woods.
8. perplexity (pər plek′sə tē), *n.* confusion.
9. roe (rō), *n.* a small deer.
10. cataract (kat′ə rakt′), *n.* waterfall.
11. **recompense** (rek′əm pens), *n.* payment; reward.
12. chasten (chā′sn), *v.* discipline.
13. interfuse (in′tər fyüz′), *v.* blend; mix.

Tintern Abby, a 1931 poster created by Freda Lingstrom, advertised a package tour of the Wye Valley. Does the scene depicted in this poster make you want to visit the Wye Valley? Why or why not? ➤

GREAT WESTERN RAILWAY

TINTERN ABBEY
IN THE WYE VALLEY — ENGLAND

And rolls through all things. Therefore am
    I still
A lover of the meadows and the woods,
And mountains; and of all that we behold
105 From this green earth; of all the mighty
    world
Of eye, and ear—both what they
    half create,
And what perceive; well pleased to
    recognize
In nature and the language of the sense
The anchor of my purest thoughts,
    the nurse,
110 The guide, the guardian of my heart,
    and soul
Of all my moral being.
                Nor perchance,
If I were not thus taught, should I
    the more
Suffer my genial spirits[14] to decay:
For thou art with me here upon the banks
115 Of this fair river; thou my dearest Friend,[15]
My dear, dear Friend; and in thy voice
    I catch
The language of my former heart, and read
My former pleasures in the shooting lights
Of thy wild eyes. Oh! yet a little while
120 May I behold in thee what I was once,
My dear, dear Sister! and this prayer
    I make,
Knowing that Nature never did betray
The heart that loved her; 'tis her privilege,
Through all the years of this our life,
    to lead
125 From joy to joy: for she can so inform[16]
The mind that is within us, so impress
With quietness and beauty, and so feed
With lofty thoughts, that neither
    evil tongues,
Rash judgments, nor the sneers of
    selfish men,
130 Nor greetings where no kindness is, nor all
The dreary intercourse of daily life,
Shall e'er prevail against us, or disturb

Our cheerful faith, that all which we
    behold
Is full of blessings. Therefore let the moon
135 Shine on thee in thy solitary walk;
And let the misty mountain-winds be free
To blow against thee: and, in after years,
When these wild ecstasies shall be matured
Into a sober pleasure; when thy mind
140 Shall be a mansion for all lovely forms,
Thy memory be as a dwelling-place
For all sweet sounds and harmonies; oh!
    then,
If solitude, or fear, or pain, or grief,
Should be thy portion, with what healing
    thoughts
145 Of tender joy wilt thou remember me,
And these my exhortations![17] Nor,
    perchance—
If I should be where I no more can hear
Thy voice, nor catch from thy wild eyes
    these gleams
Of past existence—wilt thou then forget
150 That on the banks of this delightful stream
We stood together; and that I, so long
A worshipper of Nature, hither[18] came
Unwearied in that service: rather say
With warmer love—oh! with far deeper
    zeal[19]
155 Of holier love. Nor wilt thou then forget,
That after many wanderings, many years
Of absence, these steep woods and
    lofty cliffs,
And this green pastoral landscape, were
    to me
More dear, both for themselves and for
    thy sake!

---

14. **genial spirits,** powers native to the poet.
15. **my dearest Friend,** Dorothy, Wordsworth's sister.
16. **inform,** inspire.
17. exhortation (eg′zôr tā′shən), *n.* strong urging to do something.
18. **hither** (hiŦH′ər), *adv.* here.
19. **zeal** (zēl), *n.* eager desire.

My Heart Leaps Up

William Wordsworth

My heart leaps up when I behold
    A rainbow in the sky:
So was it when my life began;
So is it now I am a man;
5 So be it when I shall grow old,
    Or let me die!
The Child is father of the Man;
And I could wish my days to be
Bound each to each by natural piety.[1]

---

1. **piety** (pī′ə tē), *n.* godliness; devotion to God.

The World Is Too Much with Us

William Wordsworth

The world is too much with us; late and soon,
Getting and spending, we lay waste our powers:
Little we see in Nature that is ours;
We have given our hearts away, a sordid boon![1]
5 This Sea that bares her bosom to the moon,
The winds that will be howling at all hours,
And are up-gathered now like sleeping flowers;
For this, for everything, we are out of tune;
It moves us not. Great God! I'd rather be
10 A Pagan suckled in a creed outworn;
So might I, standing on this pleasant lea,
Have glimpses that would make me less forlorn;
Have sight of Proteus rising from the sea;
Or hear old Triton[2] blow his wreathèd horn.

---

1. **boon** (būn), *n.* benefit.
2. **Proteus** (prō′tē əs) . . . **Triton** (trīt′n), sea gods in
   classical Greek mythology.

After Reading

Making Connections

Shaping Your Response

1. The poster that accompanies "Tintern Abbey" dates from 1931. Why do you think people might still be interested in this place 130 years or more after Wordsworth published his poem?

Analyzing the Poems

2. What does Wordsworth seem to have gained from nature?

3. Discuss some of the **themes** you find in "Tintern Abbey."

4. "My Heart Leaps Up" is generally considered a summary of Wordsworth's philosophy. In your opinion, how does line 7 fit in with this philosophy?

Extending the Ideas

5. Do the ideas in "The World Is Too Much with Us" apply to modern life? Explain.

6. 👣 Most of Wordsworth's poetry is about himself—a common enough idea today but an idea unheard of in its time. What are the advantages and disadvantages of art focusing on the **individual** in this way?

Literary Focus: Blank Verse

Blank verse is unrhymed iambic pentameter. Of all the regular English verse forms it is the most fluid and comes closest to the natural rhythms of English speech, yet it is readily altered for passages of passion and grandeur. Look again at the beginning of "Tintern Abbey." Note that Wordsworth has varied the basic blank verse pattern. The end of line 2, for example, should be read as one unit with line 3 and the beginning of line 4. This avoids a sing-song effect.

1. Read aloud lines 9–14, paying attention to the punctuation and not stopping at the ends of lines.

2. A pause—called a **caesura** (si zhùr′ə)—can also affect the blank verse pattern. What line contains such a pause?

3. Read lines 22–24. How is the blank verse pattern altered here?

Vocabulary Study

Decide whether or not the statement made about each italicized word is correct. Write *Correct* or *Incorrect* on your paper.

1. A *copse* could be found in the ocean.

2. A *sylvan* retreat will probably have mosquitoes.

3. A *vagrant* teenager is likely to be on the honor roll.

4. "May I have a drink of water?" is an *exhortation*.

5. A *cataract* is sure to be damp.

6. A book with long, involved sentences and many hard words may add to a person's feeling of *perplexity.*

7. Green is the result of yellow and blue being *interfused*.

8. If joy is mixed with sorrow, it is *corporeal*.

9. A woman buying a heavy coat will find herself *clad* for cold weather.

10. A policeman is likely to stop and *chasten* a speeding driver.

Expressing Your Ideas

Writing Choices

Writer's Notebook Update If you are keeping a journal of your wanderings and weather, take a few minutes to review what you have written. Then beside each entry, tell how you felt or what you thought at those times. Read part of your journal to the class.

Keep it Brief A lyric poem such as "My Heart Leaps Up" is usually short, expresses some emotion, and is highly personal. Try writing a **lyric poem** based on an entry from your journal or on some other topic you have been thinking about.

Don't Miss It! The illustration of Tintern Abbey on page 411 is a travel poster issued by the Great Western Railway, and William and Dorothy Wordsworth were in effect playing tourists when they visited Tintern Abbey in 1798. What sort of publicity would draw tourists to such a place? Write a **travel brochure** for Tintern Abbey. It may help first to locate the River Wye on a map of England. (It winds back and forth across the border between England and Wales on its way to the Bristol Channel.) The beautiful ruin of Tintern Abbey is located in a deep valley at the river's edge. Review the poem for other details you might use. If you wish, add some graphics such as a map and a picture of the abbey.

Other Options

William and William What do you think Wordsworth and Blake might say to each other if they had a chance to meet? Each one expressed strong opinions about art and society; from what you've read of their work, do you think they would agree or disagree? Work with a partner to plan a **dialogue** in which William Blake and William Wordsworth meet and discuss their own—and each other's—work. Present your dialogue for the class.

Beauteous Forms The "beauteous forms" of the landscape around Tintern Abbey inspired Wordsworth to "see into the life of things" and to write his poem. Find a painting, photograph, or other graphic that expresses how you feel about nature. Find out some background about the work, if possible, and about the artist. Give a five-minute **art talk** in which you show and tell about your chosen work and explain your reaction to it.

Before Reading

Kubla Khan

by Samuel Taylor Coleridge

Samuel Taylor Coleridge
1772–1834

Samuel Taylor Coleridge was a poet, critic, philosopher, theologian, lecturer, and journalist. He was also a great talker. "Charles, did you ever hear me preach?" he once asked essayist Charles Lamb. "I never heard you do anything else," his friend replied. Born in Devonshire, Coleridge was a precocious child. He attended school in London and college at Cambridge. His stimulating association with Wordsworth led to his writing "Kubla Khan." Coleridge struggled most of his life against an opium addiction. This, an unhappy marriage, and a quarrel with Wordsworth in 1810, which was never completely resolved, contributed to his physical and mental decline, and he died at 61 in London.

Building Background

Images on a Stream Coleridge himself described how "Kubla Khan" came to be written: In the summer of 1797 he was staying in a farmhouse in Exmoor, between Porlock and Linton. After taking a prescription drug (opium) for an illness, he fell asleep while reading about the Chinese emperor Kublai Khan (1216?–1294). "The author continued for about three hours in a profound sleep, at least of the external senses, during which time he has the most vivid confidence that he could not have composed less than from two to three hundred lines; if that indeed can be called composition in which all the images rose up before him as *things* . . . . On awaking he appeared to himself to have a distinct recollection of the whole, and taking his pen, ink, and paper, instantly and eagerly wrote down the lines that are here preserved. At this moment he was unfortunately called out by a person on business from Porlock, and detained by him above an hour, and on his return to his room, found, to his no small surprise and mortification, that though he still retained some vague and dim recollection of the general purport of the vision, yet, with the exception of some eight or ten scattered lines and images, all the rest had passed away like the images on the surface of a stream . . . ."

Literary Focus

Rhythm/Meter In speech or writing in general, the arrangement of stressed and unstressed syllables is called **rhythm;** in poetry the pattern is called **meter.** A **foot** is a group of syllables, usually consisting of one accented syllable and one or more unaccented syllables. Lines of poetry can be **scanned,** or divided into feet, by indicating the stressed and unstressed syllables. The result is called **scansion.** (See the Glossary of Literary Terms.) As you read "Kubla Khan," notice the varying meters Coleridge uses and the overall effect of their combination.

Writer's Notebook

How vividly do you dream? For two or three nights, try writing down what you remember of your dreams. Do this as soon as possible after you awake; dreams have a way of fading quickly from memory.

KUBLA KHAN

SAMUEL TAYLOR COLERIDGE

In Xanadu[1] did Kubla Khan
A stately pleasure-dome decree:
Where Alph, the sacred river, ran
Through caverns measureless to man
5 Down to a sunless sea.
So twice five miles of fertile ground
With walls and towers were girdled round:
And there were gardens bright with sinuous rills,[2]
Where blossomed many an incense-bearing tree;
10 And here were forests ancient as the hills,
Enfolding sunny spots of greenery.

But oh! that deep romantic chasm[3] which slanted
Down the green hill athwart[4] a cedarn cover!
A savage place! as holy and enchanted
15 As e'er beneath a waning moon was haunted
By woman wailing for her demon-lover!
And from this chasm, with ceaseless turmoil seething,
As if this earth in fast thick pants were breathing,

---

1. **Xanadu** (zan′ə dū), an altered form of Xamdu, mentioned by Samuel Purchas as a residence of Kubla Khan. *Purchas's Pilgimage* is the book Coleridge was reading when he fell asleep.
2. **sinuous** (sin′yŭ əs) **rills,** winding streams.
3. **chasm** (kaz′əm), *n.* deep opening; gap.
4. **athwart** (ə thwôrt′), *adv.* crosswise.

A mighty fountain momently was forced:
20 Amid whose swift half-intermitted burst
Huge fragments vaulted like rebounding[5] hail,
Or chaffy grain beneath the thresher's flail:[6]
And 'mid these dancing rocks at once and ever
It flung up momently the sacred river.
25 Five miles meandering with a mazy[7] motion
Through wood and dale the sacred river ran,
Then reached the caverns measureless to man,
And sank in tumult to a lifeless ocean:
And 'mid this tumult Kubla heard from far
30 Ancestral voices prophesying war!
     The shadow of the dome of pleasure
     Floated midway on the waves;
     Where was heard the mingled measure
     From the fountain and the caves.
35 It was a miracle of rare device,
A sunny pleasure-dome with caves of ice!
     A damsel with a dulcimer[8]
     In a vision once I saw:
     It was an Abyssinian[9] maid,
40   And on her dulcimer she played,
     Singing of Mount Abora.
     Could I revive within me
     Her symphony and song,
     To such a deep delight 'twould win me,
45 That with music loud and long,
I would build that dome in air,
That sunny dome! those caves of ice!
And all who heard should see them there,
And all should cry, Beware! Beware!
50 His[10] flashing eyes, his floating hair!
Weave a circle round him thrice,
And close your eyes with holy dread,
For he on honey-dew hath fed,
And drunk the milk of Paradise.

Royal Lovers on a Terrace is a miniature portrait that was painted by Bal Chand in about 1633. What elements of the painting help to create its mood of tenderness and tranquillity? ➤

---

5. **rebounding** (ri bound′ing), *adj.* bouncing back.
6. **flail** (flāl), *n.* instrument for threshing—separating—grain by hand.
7. **mazy** (mā′zē), *adj.* like a maze, a network of paths.
8. **damsel** (dam′zəl) . . . **dulcimer** (dul′sə mər), a young girl with a stringed musical instrument.
9. **Abyssinian** (ab′ə sin′ē ən), from what is now Ethiopia, a country in East Africa.
10. **his,** the speaker's.

عمل بالحند

After Reading

Making Connections

1. In their poems for *Lyrical Ballads,* Wordsworth set out to give "the charm of novelty to things of every day," while Coleridge set out to give "the interest of novelty by the modifying colors of imagination" by writing about more unusual and supernatural subjects. How well do you think he did? Give "Kubla Khan" a rating on the Novelty Meter. Be prepared to explain your rating.

Novel

10
9
8
7
6
5
4
3
2
1
0

Common

2. Find examples of Coleridge's use of **imagery** in this poem. To what senses do these images appeal, for the most part?

3. Trace the chain of causes and effects that the maid has upon the speaker and that the speaker expects to have upon others.

4. 🖉 Summarize the elements in the poem—including the story of its creation (see page 416)—that express the poet's **individuality.** Discuss how possible it may be for anyone to be totally caught up in his or her personal vision and yet retain a measure of group identity.

5. The speaker plans to create "music loud and long" such that hearers will not only be able to see the pleasure dome but will think that the speaker is having a holy vision. Why do you think people ascribe such great power to music? Can you relate some personal experiences that illustrate this power?

Literary Focus: Rhythm / Meter

Rhythm is the arrangement of stressed and unstressed syllables in speech or writing—called **meter** in poetry. A **foot** is a group of accented and unaccented syllables. An **iambic foot** has one unaccented syllable followed by an accented syllable (⌣ ′), as in the word *until*. Another kind of foot is the **trochaic,** with one accented syllable followed by an unaccented syllable (′ ⌣), as in the word *happen*. A three-foot line is called **trimeter;** a four-foot line is called **tetrameter;** a five-foot line is called **pentameter.** Choose five running lines of "Kubla Khan" and analyze the meter, demonstrating how Coleridge has combined different kinds of feet and different line lengths.

Expressing Your Ideas

Writing Choices

Writer's Notebook Update If you have managed to record a few dream images, recast some of them into lines of poetry. You can use rhyme and meter, as Coleridge did, or let them flow in free verse.

Xanadu to You Coleridge modified the name *Xanadu* from one he had found in a travel book, probably intending it to sound exotic and foreign. Invent a name for a faraway land that might be used in a fantasy game or a television show. Then write a brief **travelogue,** mentioning some of the sights to be found there (perhaps some of the sounds, smells, and tastes as well). Are there supernatural elements in your land? Describe them.

In Short Here is a whimsical attempt to reduce "Kubla Khan" to just a few lines.

> Sleepy Samuel has a dream:
> Gardens, ice, and river mazy.
> There he spies a singing maid,
> And she really drives him crazy—
> Makes his eyes flash and his hair float.
> Some maid.
> Some poet.

Choose another selection from this book and write a brief **humorous summary** of it, using rhythm and rhyme.

Other Options

Decree a Pleasure Dome Create an illustration, an **illustrated map,** or a scene in miniature depicting the various images mentioned in "Kubla Khan." For example, you would probably include the pleasure dome, the River Alph, the caves of ice, and the "damsel with a dulcimer."

Mime a Rime Working with a small group, locate and read Coleridge's "The Rime of the Ancient Mariner." Choose a scene and draw up plans for a **video.** Consider whether to include music or sound effects; whether to use actual people, puppets, or animation; and whether you want a realistic or a fantastic depiction of the poem. If time and equipment allow, complete your plans and film the scene.

Exotic Means "Foreign" If you could choose to dream about any unusual place in the world, where would it be? Choose a country that interests you and do a little research on it. Then give a brief **oral description** of your chosen place, emphasizing its beauty or other interesting features. If possible, display some pictures to illustrate your talk.

Before Reading

La Belle Dame Sans Merci
Ode to a Nightingale by John Keats

John Keats
1795–1821

John Keats wrote of himself and fellow poet Lord Byron: "There is this great difference between us: he describes what he sees—I describe what I imagine. Mine is the hardest task. . . ." His parents died when he was still young, and despite Keats's care, his brother Tom died of tuberculosis, a disease that would claim Keats as well. An intense and hopeless love affair with Fanny Brawne was anguish for the passionate young man who desired marriage but found himself thwarted by financial difficulties and worsening health. After a desperate flight to Italy to find a healthy climate, he died at age twenty-five and was buried in Rome under the epitaph he wrote for himself: "Here lies one whose name was writ in water."

Building Background

A Friend's Remembrance After the death of his brother Tom, Keats spent nearly a year with a friend, Charles Armitage Brown, who described the circumstances surrounding the writing of one of his poems as follows: "In the spring a nightingale had built her nest near my house. Keats felt a tranquil and continual joy in her song; one morning he took his chair from the breakfast table to the grass plot under a plum tree, where he sat for two or three hours. When he came into the house, I perceived he had some scraps of paper in his hand, and these he was quietly thrusting behind the books. On inquiry, I found those scraps, four or five in number; the writing was not well legible, and it was difficult to arrange the stanzas. With his assistance I succeeded, and this was his 'Ode to a Nightingale.'" The first and last stanzas constitute a frame for the succession of dreamlike thoughts.

Literary Focus

Onomatopoeia The use of words whose sound imitates the sound of the thing spoken of is called **onomatopoeia** (on′ə mat′ə pē′ə). The words *hiss, purr, boom,* and *gurgle* are all onomatopoetic words. Onomatopoeia creates images of sound and adds to the feeling or mood of a work. In line 50 of "Ode to a Nightingale," Keats writes of "The murmurous haunt of flies on summer eves." His use of *murmurous* and the repetition of the *m* sound in *summer* effectively create the drowsy sound and feeling of a warm evening out-of-doors, and the repeated *z* sound in *flies* and *eves* suggest the buzzing sound that insects make. Look for other instances of onomatopoeia in Keats's poems.

Writer's Notebook

What's that Sound? Stop reading for a few minutes and listen to the sounds around you. Then jot down some onomatopoetic words that seem to imitate those sounds. Some words such as *purr* are also called **echoic,** because they seem to echo or imitate a sound and are derived from that sound. For example, find the word *boom* in a dictionary and read the derivation.

La Belle Dame Sans Merci

JOHN KEATS

*Translated from the French, the title means "the beautiful lady without pity."
The poem is probably based on the centuries-old ballad "True Thomas," which
tells how a man was enchanted by the Queen of Elfland and lured to her
home, where he had to serve her for seven years. Keats takes up that story after
the seven years are over, the spell has been broken, and the knight, now
journeying home, meets a curious passerby.*

O, what can ail thee, knight-at-arms,
    Alone and palely loitering?
The sedge has withered from the lake,
    And no birds sing.

5 O, what can ail thee, knight-at-arms,
    So haggard and so woe-begone?
The squirrel's granary is full,
    And the harvest's done.

I see a lily on thy brow,
10   With anguish moist and fever dew;
And on thy cheeks a fading rose
    Fast withereth too.

I met a lady in the meads,
    Full beautiful—a faery's child,
15 Her hair was long, her foot was light,
    And her eyes were wild.

I made a garland for her head,
    And bracelets too, and fragrant zone;[1]
She looked at me as she did love,
20   And made sweet moan.

---

1. **zone,** belt.

The inspiration for La Belle Dame Sans Merci, painted in 1926 by Frank Cadogan Cowper, was Keats's poem of the same title. What attitude does the beautiful lady seem to have toward the knight who lies at her feet?

I set her on my pacing steed,[2]
    And nothing else saw all day long;
For sidelong would she bend, and sing
    A faery's song.

25 She found me roots of relish sweet,
    And honey wild, and manna dew,
And sure in language strange she said—
    "I love thee true."

She took me to her elfin grot,[3]
30   And there she wept and sighed full sore.
And there I shut her wild wild eyes
    With kisses four.

And there she lullèd me asleep
    And there I dreamed—Ah! woe betide![4]
35 The latest dream I ever dreamed
    On the cold hill side.

I saw pale kings and princes too,
    Pale warriors, death-pale were they all;
They cried—"La Belle Dame sans Merci
40   Hath thee in thrall!"[5]

I saw their starved lips in the gloam,[6]
    With horrid warning gapèd wide,
And I awoke and found me here,
    On the cold hill's side.

45 And this is why I sojourn[7] here
    Alone and palely loitering,
Though the sedge has withered from the lake,
    And no birds sing.

---

2. steed, horse.
3. grot (grot), *n.* grotto; a cave or cavern. *[Archaic]*
4. **betide** (bi tīd′), *v.* happen [to me].
5. thrall (thrôl), *n.* bondage; condition of being under
   some power or influence.
6. gloam (glōm), *n.* gloaming; twilight.
7. **sojourn** (sō′jėrn′), *v.* stay for a time.

Ode to a Nightingale

JOHN KEATS

My heart aches, and a drowsy numbness pains
    My sense, as though of hemlock[1] I had drunk,
Or emptied some dull opiate to the drains
    One minute past, and Lethe-wards[2] had sunk:
5 'Tis not through envy of thy happy lot,
    But being too happy in thine happiness—
        That thou, light-wingèd Dryad[3] of the trees,
        In some melodious plot
Of beechen green, and shadows numberless,
10   Singest of summer in full-throated ease.

O, for a draught[4] of vintage![5] that hath been
    Cooled a long age in the deep-delved earth,
Tasting of Flora[6] and the country green,
    Dance, and Provençal[7] song, and sunburnt mirth!
15 O for a beaker full of the warm South,

---

1. hemlock (hem′lok), *n.* a poison.
2. **Lethe-wards,** towards Lethe (lē′thē), river of forgetfulness in Hades, the underworld home of the dead.
3. **dryad** (drī′əd), *n.* a tree nymph; in classical mythology, a nymph is one of the lesser goddesses of nature.
4. **draught** (draft), *n.* drink.
5. **vintage** (vin′tij), *n.* wine of fine quality.
6. **Flora** (flôr′ə), in Roman myths, the goddess of flowers and vegetation.
7. **Provençal** (prō′vən säl′) **song.** Provence, in southern
France, was famous during the Middle Ages for its
songs about love and chivalry.

Full of the true, the blushful Hippocrene,[8]
    With beaded bubbles winking at the brim,
        And purple-stainèd mouth;
    That I might drink, and leave the world unseen,
20   And with thee fade away into the forest dim:

Fade far away, dissolve, and quite forget
    What thou among the leaves hast never known,
The weariness, the fever, and the fret
    Here, where men sit and hear each other groan;
25 Where palsy shakes a few, sad, last grey hairs,
    Where youth grows pale, and spectre-thin, and dies;
        Where but to think is to be full of sorrow
          And leaden-eyed despairs,
    Where Beauty cannot keep her lustrous eyes,
30   Or new Love pine at them beyond tomorrow.

Away! away! for I will fly to thee,
    Not charioted by Bacchus[9] and his pards,
But on the viewless[10] wings of Poesy,[11]
    Though the dull brain perplexes and retards:
35 Already with thee! tender is the night,
    And haply the Queen-Moon is on her throne,
        Clustered around by all her starry Fays;[12]
          But here there is no light,
    Save what from heaven is with the breezes blown
40   Through verdurous[13] glooms and winding mossy ways.

I cannot see what flowers are at my feet,
    Nor what soft incense hangs upon the boughs,
But, in embalmèd darkness, guess each sweet
    Wherewith the seasonable month endows
45 The grass, the thicket, and the fruit-tree wild;
    White hawthorn, and the pastoral eglantine;
        Fast fading violets covered up in leaves;
          And mid-May's eldest child,

---

8. **Hippocrene** (hip′ə krēn′), a fountain in Greece,
regarded as a source of poetic inspiration.
9. **Bacchus** (bak′əs), god of wine, often represented in
a carriage drawn by leopards (pards).
10. **viewless**, invisible.
11. **poesy** (pō′ə sē), n. poetry. [Archaic]
12. **fay** (fā), n. fairy.
13. **verdurous** (vėr′jər əs), adj. green and fresh.

The coming musk-rose, fully of dewy wine,
50   The murmurous haunt of flies on summer eves.

Darkling[14] I listen; and, for many a time
    I have been half in love with easeful Death,
Called him soft names in many a musèd rhyme,
    To take into the air my quiet breath;
55 Now more than ever seems it rich to die,
    To cease upon the midnight with no pain,
        While thou art pouring forth thy soul abroad
           In such an ecstasy!
    Still wouldst thou sing, and I have ears in vain—
60   To thy high requiem[15] become a sod.

Thou wast not born for death, immortal Bird!
    No hungry generations tread thee down;
The voice I hear this passing night was heard
    In ancient days by emperor and clown:
65 Perhaps the self-same song that found a path
    Through the sad heart of Ruth, when, sick for home,
        She stood in tears amid the alien corn;[16]
           The same that oft-times hath
    Charmed magic casements,[17] opening on the foam
70   Of perilous seas, in faery lands forlorn.[18]

Forlorn! the very word is like a bell
    To toll me back from thee to my sole self!
Adieu! the fancy[19] cannot cheat so well
    As she is famed to do, deceiving elf.
75 Adieu! adieu! thy plaintive[20] anthem fades
    Past the near meadows, over the still stream,
        Up the hill-side; and now 'tis buried deep
           In the next valley-glades:
    Was it a vision, or a waking dream?
80   Fled is that music—Do I wake or sleep?

---

14. darkling (därk′ling), *adv.* in the dark.
15. requiem (rek′wē əm), *n.* musical service or hymn for the dead.
16. **Ruth . . . corn.** According to the Bible story, Ruth left her homeland to go with Naomi, her mother-in-law, to Judah, a country foreign to her, where she worked in the corn (wheat) fields. (Ruth 2:1–23).
17. casement (kās′mənt), *n.* window.
18. forlorn (fôr lôrn′), *adj.* abandoned; desolate.
19. **fancy,** imagination.
20. plaintive (plān′tiv), *adj.* mournful.

After Reading

Making Connections

Shaping Your Response

1. If Keats were living today, how do you think he would be making a living?

Analyzing the Poems

2. What emotions does the nightingale's song arouse in the speaker? What is it about the song that seems to cause these emotions?

3. What is the **mood** of "La Belle Dame Sans Merci," and how does the setting contribute to that mood?

4. To what senses does the **imagery** in "La Belle Dame Sans Merci" mainly appeal?

5. One of Keats's basic ideas was that beauty is permanent and changeless. Where is this idea made clear in "To a Nightingale"?

6. ☜ Compare the speakers in these two poems in terms of the degree of **individuality** each has gained or lost.

Extending the Ideas

7. American author F. Scott Fitzgerald titled one of his novels *Tender Is the Night* (from line 35 of "Ode to a Nightingale"). What other phrases from the poem would make good book titles?

8. What kind of writing is being done about nature today?

Literary Focus: Onomatopoeia

Onomatopoeia refers to the use of words, like *murmur,* whose sound imitates the sound of the thing spoken of. In what way is the word *forlorn* "like a bell" tolling in lines 71–72 of "Ode to a Nightingale"? Find other examples in this poem of words or phrases you consider onomatopoetic.

Vocabulary Study

Some words are used frequently in discussing certain subjects. For example, *garlic* is a word you would expect to find in a cookbook. Match each lettered vocabulary word with the title of the book in which you would be most likely to find the word.

1. *The Abandoned Cottage*   a. verdurous
2. *The Fortunate Gardener*   b. casement
3. *The Case of the Poisoned Peach* c. grot
4. *The Carpenter's Guide*   d. requiem
5. *Making Money at the Racetrack*   e. hemlock
6. *Exploring Caverns and Caves*   f. thrall

7. *Church Music Through the Ages*   g. darkling
8. *Slavery in Egypt During the Pharaohs* h. forlorn
9. *Stories to Tell After Midnight*   i. steed
10. *A Song at Twilight*   j. gloam

Expressing Your Ideas

Writing Choices

Writer's Notebook Update Write some phrases using the onomatopoetic or echoic words you wrote in your notebook. Use as many of those words as you can.

Analyzing Imagery In an **essay** analyze Keats's use of imagery in "Ode to a Nightingale." Start by stating the purpose of the paper. Then analyze the images stanza by stanza. How does Keats achieve his visual and auditory effects? In your conclusion, tell to what degree an understanding of the imagery is essential to comprehending the meaning of the whole poem.

Rap What aspects of nature might be appropriate for a rap poem? Tornadoes? Earthquakes? Sunsets? Spring growth? Summer heat? Write a **rap poem** about some aspect of nature.

Other Options

Perform "Romantically" In a small group, prepare a **performance** by reading several short poems by any of the authors in this part, accompanied by suitable background music by a composer of the Romantic period. Research recordings of Franz Liszt or Frederic Chopin to find suitable pieces. Practice reading aloud before your presentation.

What Else Happened? Not just their work, but their lives as well place these poets within the Romantic tradition. Find biographical material on more aspects of any writer's life than are given in this part. Then present an **oral report** to the class.

The Romantic Poet in You Much of the writing of the Romantic poets consisted of describing their emotional reactions to scenes of nature. Take a portable tape recorder with you into a park or some other natural area. As you walk about, let your thoughts fly free, and describe what you see and your reactions to it in a kind of **stream-of-consciousness monologue.** As you listen to your tape later, you may or may not decide to edit out certain sections before sharing your monologue with a small group of classmates.

Visions and Dreams

Visionary Experiences

Multicultural Connection

From the beginning, human beings have sought to understand dreams and visions. What did these experiences mean? Could they be a guide for life? On the following pages are accounts of how several cultures sought strength and wisdom in visionary experiences.

A World of Dreamers

The following fable about the Chinese philosopher Chuang Tzu suggests that our dreams may be as real—or unreal—as our waking expereiences.

Chuang Tzu and the Butterfly

translated by **Burton Watson**

Once Chuang Tzu dreamt he was a butterfly, a butterfly flitting and fluttering around, happy with himself and doing as he pleased. He didn't know he was Chuang Tzu. Suddenly he woke up and there he was, solid and unmistakable Chuang Tzu. But he didn't know if he was Chuang Tzu who had dreamt he was a butterly, or a butterfly dreaming he was Chuang Tzu. Between Chuang Tzu and a butterfly there must be *some* distinction! This is called the Transformation of Things . . . .

A delicate butterfly appears in this detail of a painting by Ch'en Hung-shou (1598–1652).

The Delphic Oracle

The Greeks sought wisdom by consulting oracles, visionaries who were associated with various sanctuaries throughout the Greek world. The most celebrated of these sites was Delphi, which was located on the lower slopes of Mount Parnassus in central Greece. The Greeks believed the spot to be the navel of the world, saying that their supreme god Zeus had released two eagles, one from the east and one from the west, and flying toward each other they had met there. The site was originally sacred to the earth-goddess Gaea (je′ə).

The Greeks told the story of a monstrous serpent, Python, who guarded the spot. The god Apollo came to Delphi, slew Python, and established his oracle there. Apollo was called *Pythian* in memory of this deed. The priestess of Apollo at Delphi was called the *Pythia* or the *Pythoness*. The Delphic oracle was consulted on a variety of questions, both private and public.

Those who wished to consult the oracle first performed the rite of purification and sacrificed to Apollo. Precedence among pilgrims was generally determined by lot, although occasionally granted as a privilege. A male priest, the sole attendant of the Pythia, related the questions and interpreted the answer. The priestess, seated on the sacred tripod, delivered the god's word while in a frenzied state. How this condition was induced is not completely clear. Excavation at Delphi has shown as improbable the theory that the priestess inhaled vapors issuing from a hole in the earth. Such practices as chewing laurel leaves and drinking the water from the Castalian spring which flowed near the sanctuary may have assisted, but the major cause was probably the priestess's own complete faith in the power of the god to speak through her. The influence of Delphi, felt throughout the entire Mediterranean world for several centuries, began to decline from the fourth century B.C. onward. The sanctuary was finally closed by the Christian emperor Theodosius in A.D. 390.

This vase painting shows a petitioner standing before the priestess of Delphi, who is seated on her tripod and holding a branch of laurel sacred to her patron, the god Apollo.

A shaman, or "medicine man," among the Crow, a Plains Indian people, is shown performing a healing ritual in this painting by George Catlin (1796–1872). Dreams and other visionary experiences were an important part of such shamanistic practices.

The Plains Indian Power Vision

The experience of the universe as mysterious and powerful is basic to the psychology of all human religion. The human awareness that in this mystery and power is the source of birth and sterility, strength and blight, food and want, life and death, has led all peoples to try to engage the more-than-human, the supernatural, to their benefit through religious practice. In American Indian cultures the supernatural was the object of a great deal of activity. The effort was not to organize a consistent body of beliefs, but rather through liturgy and ordeal to come to some direct experience of the supernatural, and from this experience to obtain guidance for life and protection from danger.

Among the small, semi-nomadic groups which formed the nations of the Great Plains, the emphasis was on ordeal and vision. The individual males sought visions which would enable them to be successful hunters and warriors. The ordeal involved isolation from the tribe, prolonged fasting, and sometimes self-inflicted injury to encourage visions when they did not come. The visions took a variety of forms but had a standard outline. The supernatural would manifest itself as a being combining animal and human natures. The hunter would accompany this being and when they arrived at its dwelling, which might be deep in the forest or above the clouds or under the sea, he would receive the "spirit power" which he sought, usually consisting of a song to be used when power was needed and some sort of fetish or talisman, the hunter's "medicine," which the being would give him or which he must find or make, and which involved a special ritual for its proper use. However, the procedure involved in gaining the power vision need not be so strenuous. A vision might even arrive unsought, coming as a dream in sleep, or accompanying a fever.

Responding

1. In the three cultures represented here—ancient China, ancient Greece, and Plains Indians—do dreams and visions seem to have been considered more or less significant than waking experience?

2. Do you think dreams are a useful guide to life decisions? Why or why not?

The Power of Dreams

by George Howe Colt

Dreams have tantalized humans since our earliest ancestors first curled up for a nap. Four thousand years before the birth of Freud, Egyptian priests were trying to interpret dreams. Aristotle believed that dreams are an early warning system for illness, and recent studies suggest he may have been right. Dreams have been credited with the creation of Mont St. Michel, the discovery of the structure of the benzene molecule, fixing Jack Nicklaus's golf swing, Lyndon Johnson's decision not to run for reelection in 1968, many of the routes mapped out by Harriet Tubman for the Underground Railroad, and enough novels, poems and paintings to fill the libraries and museums of a small civilization. There is something about the ephemeral nature of dreams that makes us insist they must have meaning—if we could just decipher what it is.

Each night, of course, hundreds of people dream what seems to be the Great American Novel but, on waking, find it to be gibberish. And studies of prophetic dreams are inconclusive. When it came out in court that O. J. Simpson had dreamed of killing his wife shortly before she was murdered, dream psychologist Gayle Delaney was asked if Simpson's dream was an indication of guilt. "We really don't have anything research-wise about whether dreams can predict future behavior," she says. "And lots of people dream of killing people when they have absolutely no intention of doing it." Which doesn't mean such dreams shouldn't be strip-mined for meaning. "Doing therapy without dream interpretation," Delaney says, "is like doing orthopedics without X-rays."

Dreams are so intimate, so fantastic, that many dreamers are not surprised—and perhaps are even secretly pleased—that dreams have proved so elusive to science. Over the years, people have believed dreams were caused by the weather, stars, God, the devil, indigestion, slamming doors, pickles and abusive parents. The physiological study of dreams didn't really take off until 1952,  when a graduate student at the University of Chicago attached electrodes to his son and discovered REM sleep, the period characterized by rapid eye movement under eyelids. By waking sleepers up, the researcher was able to pinpoint, for the first time, exactly when a sleeping person was dreaming.

Here is some of what we have learned since then: We all dream, even if we don't remember our dreams. Our most fertile dreaming occurs in REM sleep. We enter REM about 90 minutes after nodding off, and it occurs more frequently and for longer periods as sleep progresses. We also dream sporadically during non-REM sleep, although in a less elaborate form. We spend two of every 24 hours dreaming, adding up to more than five years of our lives.

Here is something we don't know: Why dreaming is so much more bizarre and magical than waking. In 1988, Harvard neurophysiologist J. Allan Hobson shocked the dream world by announcing that he might have the answer. The chemistry of sleep, he said, is very different from the chemistry of the awake brain. "There are three neuromodulators in the brain stem," he explains. "They determine mood and memory, cognition and emotion. But they change during sleep. In REM sleep, your brain is being bathed in a totally different chemical bath." Dreams were not the "royal road to the unconscious," as Freud had it, but neurological misfirings, as random as the ramblings of an Alzheimer's patient. Says Hobson, "Under the adverse working conditions of REM sleep, the brain is making the best of a bad job."

If Hobson is right, Freud's psychoanalytic theory of dreams is as dated as the flat-earth theory—which explains why distressed analysands have been storming into therapists' offices wanting to know whether the dreams they'd spent years and fortunes recounting were meaningless chemical detritus; outraged dream workers called Hobson a spoilsport. But Hobson, who keeps a dream journal and loves discussing dreams with patients, has clarified his position: "We're not saying dreams have no meaning. We're saying dreams have meaning and they have nonsense. The problem is deciding which is which. In many instances the meaning of dreams is so clear they hardly need interpretation. The real question arises over the idea that images in dreams are symbols. When people interpret that stuff as if it were meaningful, and then sell those interpretations, it's quackery."

To many dreamers, such studies merely confirm what they have known all along— dreams are critical to good mental health. Even if we don't interpret them, even if we don't remember them, many experts agree that the unexamined dream is worth having. Dreaming is therapeutic. Precisely because of their bizarre and unfettered visual vocabulary, dreams make connections more broadly than we're able to when awake and may be able to solve problems our self-conscious conscious minds can't.

Fine Art Connection
The dark side of visionary experience is well represented by Henry Fuseli's famous painting, *The Nightmare* (1790–91).

THE DARK SIDE

Responding

1. What three words would you choose to describe the mood of this painting?

2. How does the mood of this painting compare to Fuseli's *The Shepherd's Dream* on page 399?

Language History

The Language of the Romantic Era

It is an ancient Mariner,
    And he stoppeth one of three.
"By thy long gray beard and glittering eye,
    Now wherefore stopp'st thou me? . . ."

He holds him with his skinny hand;
    "There was a ship," quoth he.
"Hold off! unhand me, graybeard loon!"
    Eftsoons his hand dropt he.

During the Romantic Era, many archaic words and obsolete verb forms were reintroduced into the language, partly as a result of the Romanticists' interest in the Middle Ages. In "The Rime of the Ancient Mariner" (1798), Samuel Taylor Coleridge uses *thy* and *thou* for *your* and *you*, *quoth* for *said* and *eftsoons* for *immediately*; he uses the old verb forms *stoppeth*, *stopp'st*, and *dropt*; and he uses inverted sentence structure (in lines 4 and 8). These words, not only old but odd, were scarcely likely to be adopted in conversation, but they served to acquaint readers with the language of England's past. In their search for color the Romanticists also included slang and dialect terms, and although these forms were sparsely used in comparison with their use in literature today, they began to find acceptance in writing.

The years of the Romantic Movement are notable for the beginnings of really serious attempts to set up a standard of pronunciation. In 1773 William Kendrick published the first dictionary that indicated vowel sounds, and he was quickly copied by both English and American lexicographers. Because many lexicographers felt that words should be pronounced as they are spelled, there was a tendency to reestablish older pronunciations.

The Romantic writers were largely concerned with bringing naturalness and simplicity back into the language. Some of them felt that borrowed or foreign words should be eliminated because they corrupted the mother tongue. This discrimination against foreign words was not widespread, for English had become quite stabilized by this time.

Writing Workshop

A Place of One's Own

Assignment Romantic poets are enchanted by the beauty and power of nature. Write an article in which you describe a place in nature and its effect on you.

WRITER'S BLUEPRINT

Product	A travel article
Purpose	To re-create a scene from nature that is special to you
Audience	Readers of a travel magazine
Specs	As the writer of a successful article, you should:

❑ Imagine that you have been commissioned by a travel magazine to write an article for a regular feature entitled "Our Favorite Places." Choose a place in nature that you know well and that appeals to you: a well-known place of great beauty, such as the Grand Canyon, or a more ordinary location that nevertheless appeals greatly to you.

❑ Begin by introducing your place. Where is it? How can it be reached?

❑ Go on to describe this place so clearly and so vividly that readers can imagine themselves in it. Use at least three of the senses (sight, sound, smell, taste, touch) in your description. Use the first-person ("I") point of view to describe how this place makes you feel and why.

❑ Use a clear spatial organization to guide your readers through the scene, from one element to another. Since you're guiding your readers along, you may want to address them directly, as "you," from time to time.

❑ Follow the rules of grammar, usage, spelling, and mechanics.

1 PREWRITING

Revisit the literature. Jot down a list of places described in the poems. For each place on your list, jot down key descriptive words and phrases from the poem—words and phrases that you feel helped bring the place to life. Think of this as making a collection of vivid imagery, which may give you ideas for your own writing later on in this lesson.

Brainstorm a list of places in nature that give you strong feelings, such as peace, sadness, happiness, fear. Then brainstorm descriptive words and phrases about the places on your list. Choose the place that brought forth the most vivid images.

> **OR . . .**
> If you can, pay a visit to your place and gather firsthand observations.

Make a web of vivid imagery to describe your natural scene. Include words that appeal to as many of the senses as you can, and any comparisons that occur to you, as in this example:

Try a quickwrite. Write for five minutes about the details in your web and about how the place makes you feel. Write quickly. The point of a quickwrite is to record your thoughts as they come to mind. Look back at the results and decide whether you need to do some more thinking and add more details to your web. You may even decide to choose another place instead.

> **OR . . .**
> Draw a picture of the scene and label it with sensory details.

Talk a partner through your scene, using spatial organization, describing each element in order as you look around or move through the space, element by element. Here are some methods of spatial organization you might use.

- Near to far: "You enter the canyon through a narrow path between two tall pines. Immediately in front of you is a. . . ."

- Far to near: "In the distance is the roaring falls itself, which empties into a turbulent pool, which in turn empties into a narrow steam flowing toward you. . . ."

- Left to right: "At your left is a canyon wall, which winds right towards the falls. . . ."

- Right to left: "Immediately on your right hand is a pine forest whose needles crunch underfoot as you make your way out of it, to the left, where a twisting path leads into the canyon. . . ."

- Low to high: "A cushiony bed of pine needles crunches underfoot. Looking up, you discover. . . ."

- High to low: "The sky itself seems to flow into the canyon, as if sucked in by the sky-blue falls, which at its apex trembles as if in fear of falling over the edge, then tumbles dizzily downwards. . . ."

Choose one of these methods, or some other method of your choice, to lay out the elements of your scene. Think of it as taking your readers by the hand and leading them along. Remember, this is a guided tour, and the guide is you.

Formulate a plan. Look back at your prewriting materials as you make your writing plan. Here is one way to organize your notes.

- Introduction: where place is and how we can reach it

- First element of the scene (based on the method of spatial organization you've chosen)
  Sensory details
  Feelings

- Second element of the scene
  Sensory details
  Feelings

  and so on . . .

2 DRAFTING

Before you write, look back at your prewriting notes and writing plan. Then reread the Writer's Blueprint.

As you draft, concentrate on getting the ideas in your plan down on paper. Here are some tips to get you started.

- Start your article by explaining how you discovered this special place.

- Begin with a vivid sensory description that instantly transports the reader to your place.

- Begin by approaching the place, on foot or by some other mode of transportation, and describing what you see and hear as you approach. Similarly, you might end your article by describing how things look as you depart.

- Write a lead sentence that opens your introduction in an intriguing way: "A thick curtain of leaves blocked my view. As I lifted my hands to part it, something low to the ground made rustling noises on the other side, and I hesitated. Did I really want to intrude on this hidden, private world?"

3 REVISING

Ask a partner to comment on your draft before you revise it. Use this checklist as a guide.

✔ Have I explained how this place makes me feel?

✔ Have I appealed to at least three senses in the description?

✔ Did I use vivid imagery?

✔ Did I guide the reader through my place using spatial organization?

Revising Strategy

Using Spatial Order Terms

Once you've chosen a method of spatial organization, it's important to use words and phrases that will help readers follow your organization. Spatial order words, like those listed below, provide information about spatial relationships that will guide readers along.

Distance	Direction	Position
beyond	to the right	in front of
in the distance	to the left	in back of
close by	ahead	above
near	up	below
far	down	behind

In the student model, notice how the writer has added spatial order words to guide the reader from near to far.

○   My favorite trail is the pond trail. It starts out by meandering
        Beyond the stream
along a small stream. It travels through a forest of maple and oak.

○   You can hear the wind blowing softly through the leaves and smell
        Once through the forest,
the damp spring earth. The stream empties into a large pond covered

○   with waterlilies.

STUDENT MODEL

STEP 4 EDITING

Ask a partner to review your revised draft before you edit. When you edit, look for errors in grammar, usage, spelling, and mechanics. Watch for spelling errors caused by getting letters in the wrong order.

Editing Strategy

Getting Letters in the Right Order

Some words are misspelled because they have combinations of letters that are easy to write in the wrong order, like these:

li<u>ce</u>nse	remod<u>el</u>	grateful	p<u>oe</u>try	b<u>ui</u>lding	en<u>em</u>y
ju<u>dg</u>ed	bea<u>ut</u>iful	thi<u>rt</u>een	ton<u>gu</u>e	th<u>ou</u>sand	n<u>ei</u>ghbor
p<u>er</u>form	sol<u>di</u>er	pi<u>ec</u>es	thr<u>ough</u>	unus<u>ua</u>l	pr<u>ef</u>er

When you edit your writing, pay special attention to words like these.

> ○ My cares are simply forgotten as soon as I enter the
>
> *preserve.*
> ~~perserve.~~ I also feel excitement when I catch a glimpse of a deer or
>
> *grateful*
> ○ rabbit darting across the trail. Mostly, I feel ~~greatful~~ for the serene
>
> *beauty*
> ~~baeuty~~ of this place.

STUDENT MODEL

STEP 5 PRESENTING

- Suggest to the editors of your school paper that they run a column called "Our Favorite Places," and include several of these articles.

- Include a picture or a map of your favorite place with your article.

STEP 6 LOOKING BACK

Self-evaluate. Look back at the Writer's Blueprint and give yourself a score for each item, from 6 (superior) to 1 (inadequate).

Reflect. Write answers to these questions.

✔ How was writing a descriptive article different from other forms of writing, such as research reports or analytical essays? How was it similar?

✔ How has this article changed your view of your special place?

For Your Working Portfolio Add your travel article and reflection responses to your working portfolio.

Beyond Print

Reading a Painting

Many Romantic poems are paintings with words. Think of the lines in Wordsworth's "Tintern Abbey" or Keats's "Ode to a Nightingale" that are devoted to description. The Romantics thought of nature as so much more than just trees and flowers: it was a metaphor for the unlimited spirit of mankind; it was a way to experience the perfection of God. This painting, *Hadleigh Castle* by John Constable (1776–1837), is typical of the Romantic era. As you look at it more closely, here are some questions to ask yourself by way of "reading" what the artist is trying to say.

Subject Matter What is shown in the picture? Where is the castle mentioned by the title? Are there humans or animals? What other aspects of nature are depicted? Of all these—architecture, humans, animals, and aspects of nature—which receives the most emphasis?

Composition Look closely at the shapes and at their arrangement in space. Which are stronger, vertical or horizontal elements? What major shape draws your eye? What balances that shape? Are there lines or other arrangements of shapes that cause your eye to follow a particular path through the painting?

Colors What colors are used, and how do they influence the mood of the painting? What do you think you are intended to feel? Where is the darkest part? Why there? Where does the painting lighten up? Why there?

Context Interpret the general meaning. How does a ruined castle fit in with the Romantics' fascination with things of the past? (Would you know these are castle ruins if you weren't told?) From what you know about the Romantics, why do you suppose Constable includes the thick, ominous clouds; the rough sea; the shore with its windswept shrubs? Why does he include the cows and men and dog at all? How about the boats? How do all these elements—and the overall mood—fit into Romantic ideas?

A Critical View What do you think the painter was trying to accomplish? How well did he accomplish it? Do you like or dislike the painting? Why?

Activity Options

1. Using the criteria suggested and your own answers to the questions, explain to someone unfamiliar with this painting how it works and how it achieves its effects.

2. Write a Romantic poem based on this painting, using the poems in this part as models. You might call your poem "Ode to Hadleigh Castle." How can you make use of the various elements, including the men and animals? How can you transmit the mood? As an alternative, make up a story about this painting, giving the characters names and explaining what they are doing and why.

A SOCIAL REVOLUTION

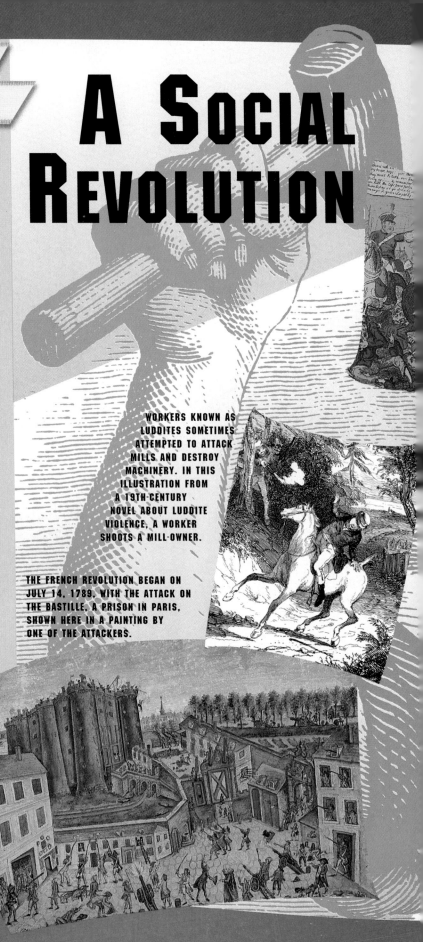

HISTORICAL OVERVIEW

The Age of Reason saw evil as basic to human nature; the Romantics saw humanity as naturally good, but corrupted by economic conditions, organized religion, education, and government. The Industrial Revolution began in England in the mid-1700s and soon transformed the English economy, bringing fortunes to a few factory-owners and misery to thousands of workers who were displaced by new machines or toiled long hours for small wages and lived in hideous slums. For a time, the French Revolution expressed the political and social idealism of the Romantics, but the Reign of Terror and Napoleon's rise to power brought disillusionment. However, the example of the French sparked nationalist revolutions in many places, including Haiti, South America, and Greece.

WORKERS KNOWN AS LUDDITES SOMETIMES ATTEMPTED TO ATTACK MILLS AND DESTROY MACHINERY. IN THIS ILLUSTRATION FROM A 19TH-CENTURY NOVEL ABOUT LUDDITE VIOLENCE, A WORKER SHOOTS A MILL-OWNER.

THE FRENCH REVOLUTION BEGAN ON JULY 14, 1789, WITH THE ATTACK ON THE BASTILLE, A PRISON IN PARIS, SHOWN HERE IN A PAINTING BY ONE OF THE ATTACKERS.

IN THE ENGLISH MANUFACTURING CITY OF MANCHESTER ON AUGUST 16, 1819, MOUNTED TROOPS CHARGED A CROWD OF 60,000 WORKING-CLASS MEN, WOMEN, AND CHILDREN PETITIONING FOR ECONOMIC AND POLITICAL REFORMS. THE SO-CALLED "PETERLOO MASSACRE" RESULTED IN 11 DEAD AND HUNDREDS INJURED.

IN 1832 THE BRITISH PARLIAMENT PASSED A REFORM BILL THAT INCREASED THE ELECTORATE BY FIFTY PERCENT. THIS CARTOON, IN SUPPORT OF THE MEASURE, SHOWS POLITICAL CORRUPTION BEING GROUND UP AND A TRIUMPHANT BRITANNIA EMERGING.

AFTER DECADES OF AGITATION, BRITISH ABOLITIONISTS (WHOSE MEDALLION BY JOSIAH WEDGEWOOD APPEARS HERE) WERE SUCCESSFUL IN OUTLAWING THE SLAVE TRADE IN 1807.

INSPIRED BY THE EXAMPLE OF THE FRENCH REVOLUTION, SLAVES ON HAITI REBELLED IN 1791. IN 1804 HAITI BECAME THE FIRST INDEPENDENT BLACK NATION IN THE WESTERN HEMISPHERE.

Key Dates

1789
The French Revolution begins.

1791
Slaves on Haiti rebel against the French.

1793
The Reign of Terror begins in France.

1807
England abolishes the slave trade.

1811
Luddites begin destroying machinery.

1804
Napoleon becomes emperor.

1819
The Peterloo Massacre occurs.

1821
Greeks begin their struggle for independence.

Part Two

The Outsider

People find themselves in the position of an outsider for a variety of reasons, but it may be their own choice to stand apart, to assert their individuality. When people who rebel find important social causes to fight for, they can sometimes make a considerable difference in the lives of those around them.

 Multicultural Focus **Change** creates challenges by introducing new dimensions to cultural situations. People respond both by clinging to existing cultural patterns and by changing those traditions to fit new situations. In this way, new cultures are created or old ones are modified, both by deliberate acts of people and by the simple fact that change is bound to occur. In the following selections, who are the rebels, what cultural situations do they face, and what changes do they hope to bring about?

Before Reading

A Man's a Man for A' That
A Red, Red Rose
Auld Lang Syne by Robert Burns

Robert Burns
1759–1796

Robert Burns was born into poverty on a small farm in Scotland. His early years were spent as a plowboy. Although his formal schooling lasted no longer than two years, he read widely. Burns was considered a wild fellow: he drank heavily and he fathered several children by at least four different women. In 1786 the publication of *Poems, Chiefly in the Scottish Dialect* made him an overnight success, but polite society regarded him only as a rustic novelty. In 1787 he joined with James Johnson to begin the task of preserving the songs of his nation in *The Scots Musical Museum*. Before his early death at age 37, he had compiled and composed over 300 songs for this collection and for George Thomson's *Select Collection of Scottish Airs*.

Building Background

The "Untutored Ploughman" Although they were very poor, Robert Burns's father gave him books so that he could read the great English writers. His mother taught him Scottish songs and legends. But Burns claimed that his inspiration to be a poet came at age fifteen from a pretty girl who worked and sang alongside him in the fields. When she told him that one of the songs she was singing had been written by a nobleman's son, the "untutored ploughman" (as he later called himself) determined to compose a better song. Always fascinated with the sounds and the rhythms of the Scots language, Burns recreated the lilt of the language in this first poem, "Handsome Nell." As he continued to write, the poems he composed became intermingled with the songs his mother had sung. Thus, Burns became the poet of the Scottish people, the spokesman for the Scottish community, writing in their earthy, folksy language about everyday country life. In his collection of songs some are wholly Burns's own; some are traditional folk airs; most are his improvisations from fragments of songs from many nameless Scottish singers.

Literary Focus

Dialect A variety of language used in a particular region or by a particular social class is a **dialect.** Dialect is distinguished from standard language by vocabulary, pronunciation, and grammatical form. In the poetry of Robert Burns you will read the dialect of Scottish English. His poems are generally left as original instead of translated like Chaucer because Burns achieved fame as a dialect poet.

Writer's Notebook

My Love Is Like . . . Probably the most popular subject of poets is love: true love, unrequited love, lost love. Often a poet uses the technique of **simile,** a comparison using *like* or *as,* to relate his or her lover or situation to an object. Burns compares his love to a red, red rose and to a sweet melody. Jot down five or six other ways a lover might complete the sentence: "My love is like . . . ."

A Man's a Man for A' That

Robert Burns

Is there, for honest poverty,
That[1] hings[2] his head, and a' that;
The coward-slave, we pass him by,
We dare be poor for a' that!
5 For a' that, and a' that,
Our toils obscure, and a' that,
The rank is but the guinea's stamp,[3]
The man's the gowd[4] for a' that.

What though on hamely[5] fare we dine,
10 Wear hoddin-grey,[6] and a' that;
Gie[7] fools their silks, and knaves their
      wine,
A man's a man for a' that.
For a' that, and a' that,
Their tinsel[8] show, and a' that;
15 The honest man, tho' e'er sae poor,
Is king o' men for a' that.

Ye see yon birkie, ca'd[9] a lord,
Wha struts, and stares, and a' that;
Tho' hundreds worship at his word,
20 He's but a coof[10] for a' that.
For a' that, and a' that,
His ribband, star,[11] and a' that,
The man of independent mind,
He looks and laughs at a' that.

25 A prince can mak a belted[12] knight,
A marquis, duke, and a' that;
But an honest man's aboon[13] his might,
Guid faith, he mauna fa'[14] that!
For a' that, and a' that,

30 Their dignities, and a' that,
The pith[15] o' sense, and pride o' worth,
Are higher rank than a' that.

Then let us pray that come it may,
As come it will for a' that,
35 That sense and worth, o'er a' the earth,
Shall bear the gree,[16] and a' that.
For a' that, and a' that,
It's coming yet, for a' that,
That man to man, the warld o'er,
40 Shall brothers be for a' that.

---

a', all.
1. **that,** one that; a person who.
2. **hings,** hangs.
3. **guinea's stamp,** stamped, bas-relief impression on a gold coin.
4. **gowd,** gold.
5. **hamely,** homely; simple.
6. **hoddin-grey,** coarse grey wool.
7. **gie,** give.
8. **tinsel** (tin′səl), *adj.* showy but not worth much.
9. **birkie . . . ca'd,** fellow . . . called.
10. **coof,** fool.
11. **ribband . . . star,** decorations of the order of knight-hood.
12. **belted,** decorated; distinguished.
13. **aboon,** above.
14. **mauna fa',** must not claim.
15. **pith** (pith), *n.* essential part.
16. **bear the gree,** claim the first place.

This 1908 oil painting by British artist Sir George Clausen (1852–1944) is entitled *The Boy and the Man.* Like so many of Clausen's works, this one depicts farm workers in the English countryside—strong, heroic figures doing the backbreaking work that was essential to an agricultural way of life. Do you think the artist might agree with the ideas Burns expresses in his poem "A Man's a Man for A' That"? Why or why not?

A Red, Red Rose

Robert Burns

O my luve's[1] like a red, red rose,
That's newly sprung in June;
O my luve's like the melodie
That's sweetly played in tune.

5 As fair art thou, my bonie[2] lass,
So deep in luve am I;
And I will luve thee still, my dear,
Till a' the seas gang[3] dry.

Till a' the seas gang dry, my dear,
10 And the rocks melt wi' the sun;
And I will luve thee still, my dear,
While the sands o' life shall run.

And fare thee weel,[4] my only luve!
And fare thee weel a while!
15 And I will come again, my luve,
Tho' it were ten thousand mile!

---

1. **luve,** love
2. **bonie,** bonnie; pretty.
3. **gang,** go.
4. **weel,** well.

Auld Lang Syne

Robert Burns

Should auld acquaintance be forgot,
And never brought to min'?
Should auld acquaintance be forgot,
And auld lang syne?
    CHORUS:
5   For auld lang syne, my dear,
    For auld lang syne,
    We'll tak a cup o' kindness yet
    For auld lang syne.

And surely ye'll be your pint-stowp,[1]
10 And surely I'll be mine!
And we'll tak a cup o' kindness yet
For auld lang syne.

We twa[2] hae run about the braes,[3]
And pu'd the gowans[4] fine;
15 But we've wandered monie a weary fit[5]
Sin'[6] auld lang syne.

We twa hae paidled i' burn[7]
From mornin' sun till dine;[8]
But seas between us braid[9] hae roared
20 Sin' auld lang syne.

And there's a hand, my trusty fiere,[10]
And gie's a hand o' thine;
And we'll tak a right guid-willie waught[11]
For auld lang syne.

---

auld lang syne, old long ago; the good old days.
1. **ye'll . . . pint-stowp,** you'll pay for your pint of drink.
2. **twa,** two.
3. **braes,** hillsides.
4. **pu'd the gowans,** pulled the daisies.
5. **monie . . . fit,** many a weary footstep.
6. **sin',** since.
7. **paidled i' burn,** paddled in the brook.
8. **dine,** noon.
9. **braid,** broad.
10. **fiere,** friend.
11. **right . . . waught,** hearty goodwill toast.

After Reading

Making Connections

Shaping Your
Response

1. Imagine Robert Burns doing an oral reading of his poetry. With what emotions do you imagine Burns might have read each of these three poems?

Analyzing the Poems

2. In "A Man's a Man for A' That" why do you think Burns calls poverty "honest"?

3. What distinctions does Burns draw between the working man and the nobleman?

4. 👆 In this poem, inspired by the French Revolution, what **change** does Burns pray will be in the future for humankind?

5. Do you imagine the "bonie lass" in "A Red, Red Rose" is a new love or someone the speaker has loved for a while? What lines from the poem justify your response?

6. In "Auld Lang Syne" what might the speaker be suggesting about the longevity of friendships established when people are young?

7. What do the **images** Burns uses in his poetry suggest about his life?

Extending the Ideas

8. Do Burns's ideas about poverty, rank, dignity, and so on, have any application today? Do people still make these distinctions?

9. Why might an author choose to write in a dialect instead of a standard language, no matter what the language is?

Literary Focus: Dialect

Burns's poetry demon-
strates differences
between the Scottish
dialect and standard
British English. Not only
is American English dif-
ferent in many ways from
the English spoken in Great
Britain, but also within America there
are many regional dialects. Jot down the
name you would give to these common items:
a carbonated soft drink, a sweet pastry, a long seat for more than one person, a person who acts in a stupid manner, a place to live. Com-
pare your responses with those of your classmates. (Perhaps you can come up with other things that have different dialectal names.) If your responses are different, can you explain those differences based on region of the country?

Vocabulary Study

The notes have helped you to translate Robert Burns's Scottish English. Now try your hand at translating the following lines taken from Burns's poem "And I'll Kiss Thee Yet." You'll need to concentrate on the underlined words. (See also the notes to the folk ballads on pages 25–29.)

> When in my arms, <u>wi' a'</u> thy charms,
> I clasp my countless treasure, O,
> I seek <u>nae mair o'</u> Heav'n to share
> Than <u>sic</u> a moment's pleasure, O!
>
> 5 And by thy <u>een sae bonie</u> blue
> I swear I'm thine for ever, O!
> And on thy lips I seal my vow,
> And break it shall I never, O!

Expressing Your Ideas

Writing Choices

Writer's Notebook Update Complete the following **similes,** comparisons introduced by *like* or *as.* Share your favorite similes with your classmates.

> Happiness is like. . . .
> Trust is like. . . .
> Peace is like. . . .
> Friendship is like. . . .
> School spirit is like. . . .

Capture a Holiday Spirit Burns's "Auld Lang Syne" is traditionally sung on New Year's Eve because people feel it captures the spirit of friendship and remembering the good old days. Select a favorite holiday and try to capture the spirit of that day in a short **descriptive paragraph.** Put your description together with paragraphs by your classmates to compile a Book of Holidays.

Brothers Be? Write a **letter** to Robert Burns in which you discuss for him the status of his 200-year-old prediction in "A Man's a Man for A' That":

> "It's coming yet, for a' that,
> That man to man, the warld o'er,
> Shall brothers be for a' that."

Other Option

That Was Then; This Is Now Think about a good friend from your childhood who has moved to another town. You haven't seen your friend for several years now, but you still remember the good times you used to share. Assemble a **collection of photographs and drawings** that will bring your friend up to date and let him or her know how you've changed and how you've stayed the same. Entitle your collection "That Was Then; This Is Now." After comparing your collection with your classmates, send it to your friend.

Before Reading

from A Vindication of the Rights of Woman

by Mary Wollstonecraft

Mary Wollstonecraft
1759–1797

Daughter of an abusive, alcoholic father and a submissive mother, from her early years on Mary Wollstonecraft was very conscious of the oppression of women. After working as a companion to an old woman and running a small school, she went to London to begin writing, an occupation traditionally reserved for men. Neglected and abandoned by an American writer whose child she bore, Mary Wollstonecraft attempted suicide twice. Later she found brief happiness when she married the social philosopher William Godwin. At age 38 Mary Wollstonecraft died of blood poisoning, just ten days after the birth of their daughter, Mary Godwin, the future author of *Frankenstein*.

Building Background

"I wish them to be taught to think" Mary Wollstonecraft arrived at her deep convictions about women's rights from the circumstances of her own life. She observed the women around her being abused and belittled by men. She saw women lacking self-respect and self-confidence. As a teenager Mary Wollstonecraft frequently intervened when her father assaulted her mother, often taking the blows herself. She watched the mother of her best friend sewing into the early morning hours in an endless struggle to earn a living for her family. As a young, single mother Mary faced criticism and prejudice. She helped her sister escape from the husband she was sure had driven her insane. She saw her best friend, already ill when she married, die shortly after childbirth. Mary believed that without an adequate education, which was denied to all but the wealthy, women would continue to be disadvantaged and oppressed. She knew women needed to be "taught to think."

Literary Focus

Allusion An **allusion** is a brief reference to a person, event, place, or work of art. An allusion, which may refer to myth, literature, history, religion, or any aspect of ancient or modern culture, can be a simple mention of a name or a brief quotation from a work. If you recognize an allusion, it should remind you of an idea that the author only wants to hint at in his or her work. Look for the allusions Wollstonecraft makes.

Writer's Notebook

Women's Rights? In 1792 Mary Wollstonecraft was one of the first spokeswomen for the rights of women. What do you imagine was the position of women during her time, not only in England but also in the United States? What rights did they have? What rights given to men did they not have? List some descriptions of life for women before—and even into—the twentieth century.

A VINDICATION OF
THE RIGHTS OF WOMAN

Mary Wollstonecraft

CHAPTER 2

To account for, and excuse the tyranny of man, many <u>ingenious</u>[1] arguments have been brought forward to prove, that the two sexes, in the acquirement of virtue, ought to aim at attaining a very different character: or, to speak explicitly, women are not allowed to have sufficient strength of mind to acquire what really deserves the name of virtue. Yet it should seem, allowing them to have souls, that there is but one way appointed by providence[2] to lead *mankind* to either virtue or happiness.

If then women are not a swarm of ephemeron[3] triflers, why should they be kept in ignorance under the <u>specious</u>[4] name of innocence? Men complain, and with reason, of the follies and caprices of our sex, when they do not keenly satirize our headstrong passions and grovelling vices. Behold, I should answer, the natural effect of ignorance! The mind will ever be unstable that has only prejudices to rest on, and the current will run with destructive fury when there are no barriers to break its force. Women are told from their infancy, and taught by the example of their mothers, that a little knowledge of human weakness, justly termed cunning, softness of temper, *outward* obedience, and a scrupulous attention to a puerile kind of propriety,[5] will obtain for them the protection of man; and should they be beautiful, every thing else is needless, for at least twenty years of their lives. . . .

SUMMARIZE: What are the lessons that Wollstonecraft sees young girls being taught?

The most perfect education, in my opinion is, such an exercise of the understanding as is best calculated to strengthen the body and form the heart. Or, in other words, to enable the individual to attain such habits of virtue as will render it independent. In fact, it is a farce to call any being virtuous whose virtues do not result from the exercise of its own reason. This was Rousseau's opinion respecting men.[6] I extend it to women, and confidently assert, that they have

---

vindication (vin′də kā′shən), *n.* defense; justification.
1. ingenious (in jē′nyəs), *adj.* cleverly planned.
2. **providence** (prov′ə dəns), *n.* God's care and help.
3. **ephemeron** (i fem′ər ən), *adj.* short-lived.
4. specious (spē′shəs), *adj.* apparently good, but not really so.
5. **propriety** (prə prī′ə tē), *n.* proper behavior.
6. **Rousseau's opinion . . . men.** Jean Jacques Rousseau (1712–1778) argued that an individual's natural goodness is distorted by the false values of civilization.

A Vindication of the Rights of Woman   **457**

been drawn out of their sphere by false refinement, and not by an endeavour to acquire masculine qualities. Still the regal homage which they receive is so intoxicating, that till the manners of the times are changed, and formed on more reasonable principles, it may be impossible to convince them, that the illegitimate power, which they obtain by degrading themselves, is a curse, and that they must return to nature and equality, if they wish to secure the placid satisfaction that unsophisticated affections impart. But for this epoch we must wait—wait, perhaps, till kings and nobles, enlightened by reason, and, preferring the real dignity of man to childish state, throw off their gaudy hereditary trappings; and if then women do not resign the arbitrary power of beauty, they will prove that they have *less* mind than man. . . .

Many are the causes that, in the present corrupt state of society, contribute to enslave women by cramping their understandings and sharpening their senses. One, perhaps, that silently does more mischief than all the rest, is their disregard of order.

To do every thing in an orderly manner, is a most important precept,[7] which women, who, generally speaking, receive only a disorderly kind of education, seldom attend to with that degree of exactness that men, who from their infancy are broken into method, observe. This negligent kind of guesswork, for what other epithet[8] can be used to point out the random exertions of a sort of instinctive common sense, never brought to the test of reason? prevents their generalizing matters of fact, so they do to-day what they did yesterday, merely because they did it yesterday. . . .

CLARIFY: Explain what Wollstonecraft means by a "disorderly kind of education."

Women are, therefore, to be considered either as moral beings, or so weak that they must be entirely subjected to the superior faculties of men.

Let us examine this question. Rousseau declares, that a woman should never, for a moment feel herself independent, that she should be governed by fear to exercise her *natural* cunning, and made a coquettish[9] slave in order to render her a more alluring object of desire, a *sweeter* companion to man, whenever he chooses to relax himself. He carries the arguments, which he pretends to draw from the indications of nature, still further, and insinuates[10] that truth and fortitude, the corner stones of all human virtue, shall be cultivated with certain restrictions, because with respect to the female character, obedience is the grand lesson which ought to be impressed with unrelenting rigor.

What nonsense! when will a great man arise with sufficient strength of mind to puff away the fumes which pride and sensuality have thus spread over the subject! If women are by nature inferior to men, their virtues must be the same in quality, if not in degree, or virtue is a relative idea; consequently, their conduct should be founded on the same principles and have the same aim.

Connected with man as daughters, wives, and mothers, their moral character may be estimated by their manner of fulfilling those simple duties; but the end, the grand end of their exertions should be to unfold their own faculties, and acquire the dignity of conscious virtue. They may try to render their road pleasant; but ought never to forget, in common with man, that life yields not the felicity[11] which can satisfy an immortal soul. I do not mean to insinuate, that either sex should be so lost, in abstract reflections or distant views, as to forget the affections and duties that lie before them, and

---

7. **precept** (prē′sept), *n.* rule of action or behavior.
8. epithet (ep′ə thet), *n.* descriptive expression.
9. **coquettish** (kō ket′ish), *adj.* like a flirt.
10. **insinuate** (in sin′yü āt), *v.* hint.
11. **felicity** (fə lis′ə tē), *n.* happiness.

are in truth, the means appointed to produce the fruit of life; on the contrary, I would warmly recommend them, even while I assert, that they afford most satisfaction when they are considered in their true subordinate light.

CHAPTER 9

. . . But what have women to do in society? I may be asked, but to loiter with easy grace; surely you would not condemn them to suckle fools and chronicle small beer![12] No. Women might certainly study the art of healing, and be physicians as well as nurses.

How much more respectable is the woman who earns her bread by fulfilling any duty, than the most accomplished beauty!—beauty did I say?—so sensible am I of the beauty of moral loveliness, or the harmonious propriety that attunes the passions of a well-regulated mind, that I blush at making the comparison; yet I sigh to think how few women aim at attaining this respectability by withdrawing from the giddy whirl of pleasure, or the indolent[13] calm that stupefies the good sort of women it sucks in.

Proud of their weakness, however, they must always be protected, guarded from care, and all the rough toils that dignify the mind. If this be the fiat[14] of fate, if they will make themselves insignificant and contemptible,[15] sweetly to waste "life away," let them not expect to be valued when their beauty fades, for it is the fate of the fairest flowers to be admired and pulled to pieces by the careless hand that plucked them. In how many ways do I wish, from the purest benevolence, to impress this truth on my sex; yet I fear that they will not listen to a truth that dear bought experience has brought home to many an agitated bosom, nor willingly resign the privileges of rank and sex for the privileges of humanity, to which those have no claim who do not discharge its duties.

CLARIFY: What does Wollstonecraft believe will happen to women who rely solely on their beauty?

Those writers are particularly useful, in my opinion, who make man feel for man, independent of the station he fills, or the drapery of factitious[16] sentiments. I then would fain convince reasonable men of the importance of some of my remarks, and prevail on them to weigh dispassionately the whole tenor of my observations. I appeal to their understandings; and, as a fellow-creature, claim, in the name of my sex, some interest in their hearts. I entreat them to assist to emancipate their companion, to make her a *help meet*[17] for them!

Would men but generously snap our chains, and be content with rational fellowship instead of slavish obedience, they would find us more observant daughters, more affectionate sisters, more faithful wives, more reasonable mothers—in a word, better citizens. We should then love them with true affection, because we should learn to respect ourselves; and the peace of mind of a worthy man would not be interrupted by the idle vanity of his wife, nor the babes sent to nestle in a strange bosom, having never found a home in their mother's.[18]

---

12. **to suckle . . . beer,** to breastfeed babies and keep track of trivial matters. In Shakespeare's *Othello* (act two, scene 1, line 160) Iago gives Desdemona this description of how a woman should spend her life.
13. **indolent** (in′dl ənt), *adj.* lazy.
14. **fiat** (fī′ət), *n.* command.
15. **contemptible** (kən temp′tə bəl), *adj.* worthless; deserving scorn.
16. **factitious** (fak tish′əs), *adj.* artificial.
17. ***help meet,*** companion or helper. In the Bible (Genesis, chapter 2), God creates Eve to be a help meet (suitable) for Adam.
18. **sent to nestle . . . mother's,** given to a nurse to be cared for.

A Vindication of the Rights of Woman **459**

After Reading

Making Connections

Shaping Your
Response

1. What color would you use to describe the emotions of Mary Wollstonecraft as revealed through her essay? Explain your choice.

Analyzing the Essay

2. Why do you think Wollstonecraft feels the education of young girls is inadequate? Do you agree with her?

3. What attitudes does Wollstonecraft display towards men? towards other women? Why do you think she feels this way?

4. 👁 Wollstonecraft believes that educated women will be "more observant daughters, more affectionate sisters, more faithful wives, more reasonable mothers, . . . better citizens." Discuss how education could bring about the **change** Wollstonecraft describes.

Extending the Ideas

5. Wollstonecraft praises writers who "make man feel for man." What do you think she means? What authors have you read who have created such a feeling in you?

6. Compare the **theme** of Wollstonecraft's essay with that of Daniel Defoe's "The Education of Women" (see page 306). How are Defoe and Wollstonecraft alike and how are they different in the literary tools they use to get their themes across?

7. Is Wollstonecraft's prescription for a perfect education—"to strengthen the body and form the heart"—still valid today? Would you add any other goals for today's students and teachers?

Literary Focus: Allusion

In this selection Mary Wollstonecraft uses **allusion,** references to historical or literary writings, persons, events, or places. Locate the three allusions in the text. What do you think was Wollstonecraft's purpose in selecting each allusion?

Vocabulary Study

**epithet
factitious
indolent
ingenious
specious**

Many vocabulary words are misunderstood because they look like or sound like other words. Confusing one word for another can often lead to misinterpretation. In each of the following sentences, select the correct word. Use your Glossary or a dictionary, if necessary.

1. Mary Wollstonecraft believes that her plea for equality for women is not (indolent, insolent), but sensible for both men and women.

2. Wollstonecraft admits that some of the arguments used to prove the inferiority of women are (ingenious, ingenuous).

3. In arguing for the education of women, Wollstonecraft challenges what she considers to be the (spacious, specious) arguments of men.

4. Wollstonecraft wants to help women understand the difference between the (factitious, fictitious) and the real feelings of men.

5. An (epitaph, epithet) on Mary Wollstonecraft's tombstone might well include mention of her most famous work, *A Vindication of the Rights of Woman.*

Expressing Your Ideas

Writing Choices

Writer's Notebook Update Which of the conditions you listed in your notebook do you think has improved the most for women? Write a paragraph or so in which you discuss what the improvements have been, why you believe they occurred, and whether more improvements are necessary.

Schools Today The artist who created this cartoon seems to feel that education today is male-centered. Do you agree? Are girls today short-changed by American schools? From your personal experience in an American high school write an **editorial** for your school newspaper responding to the cartoon shown here.

Playing It Fair You are an employer who believes in equal-opportunity employment. Write a one-page equal opportunity **policy statement** to be given to all prospective employees. You may wish to consider such issues as gender, race, religion, age, appearance, marital status.

Other Options

Speak Your Mind! There is an international conference on the status of women in the world. You can be any woman from any country, or you can be yourself. Prepare a **speech** which you will present to the conference addressing what you feel is the single most critical issue in women's rights today. After your class has listened to all of the speeches, discuss which issue is most important.

Train Up a Child "Train up a child in the way he should go," says the Bible, "and when he is old, he will not depart from it." (Proverbs 22:6). Prepare a **lesson** on an aspect of women's rights that would be suitable for a class of fourth graders. Remember that you will be teaching both girls and boys. Include teaching aids such as dolls, toys, and photographs.

Darkow. Reprinted with special permission of North America Syndicate.

Before Reading

She Walks in Beauty
When We Two Parted

by George Gordon, Lord Byron

**George Gordon,
Lord Byron**
1788–1824

At the age of ten, George Gordon inherited a fortune and became Lord Byron, the title which gave him a seat in the House of Lords. He lived an eccentric life. While on a tour of Europe, he swam the Hellespont (a strait in Turkey), lived with bandits, visited a sultan's harem, and wrote *Childe Harold's Pilgrimage.* After only one year of marriage, his wife took their young daughter and returned to her father. Rumors of madness, abandonment, and scandalous sexuality forced him to leave England, never to return. For a time he lived with Percy and Mary Shelley in Italy. Always a champion of liberty, Byron raised an army and contributed large sums of money to the Greek fight for independence from Turkey. He died of a fever in Greece, at the age of thirty-six.

Building Background

"Let us have wine and women, mirth and laughter,
Sermons and soda-water the day after."

This rhyming couplet, from his famous mock epic poem. *Don Juan,* might well have served as a motto for the life—and the poetry—of the intense young poet, Lord Byron. His earliest love affair with Mary Duff, a cousin, when both were only seven, is celebrated in one of his first love poems, "When I Roved a Young Highlander." Enchanted by the beauty of his many lovely cousins, intrigued by the mystery of young ladies of aristocratic birth, Byron recorded his passions, his obsessions, his loves, and his regrets in lyric after lyric. Among the many subjects of his poetry were the "Maid of Athens," whom he met on his European tour; Caroline Lamb, who frequently dressed as a footman in order to get closer to Byron; his half sister Augusta, with whom he had more than one steamy affair; the young Claire Clairmont, stepdaughter of philosopher William Godwin; and Teresa Guioccioli, perhaps his last and greatest love. Indeed, it is difficult to separate the life and the poetry of the Byron once described by Caroline Lamb as "mad, bad, and dangerous to know."

Literary Focus

Diction The writer's choice of words and phrases is called **diction.** This choice may involve a range of words from formal to informal or from old-fashioned—even archaic—to modern and slangy. Sometimes a poet will make use of what are known as poetic contractions; for example, Byron uses *o'er* for *over*. This choice of words, involving both denotation and connotation, is meant to have a certain effect on a reader. As you read Byron's poems, think about what effect Byron's diction actually has on you.

Writer's Notebook

Taking Leave What sort of thoughts might you have and what sort of emotions might you feel if you had to go away from someone to whom you felt very close? Jot some impressions of your possible thoughts and emotions. Would you share them with the other person?

She Walks in Beauty

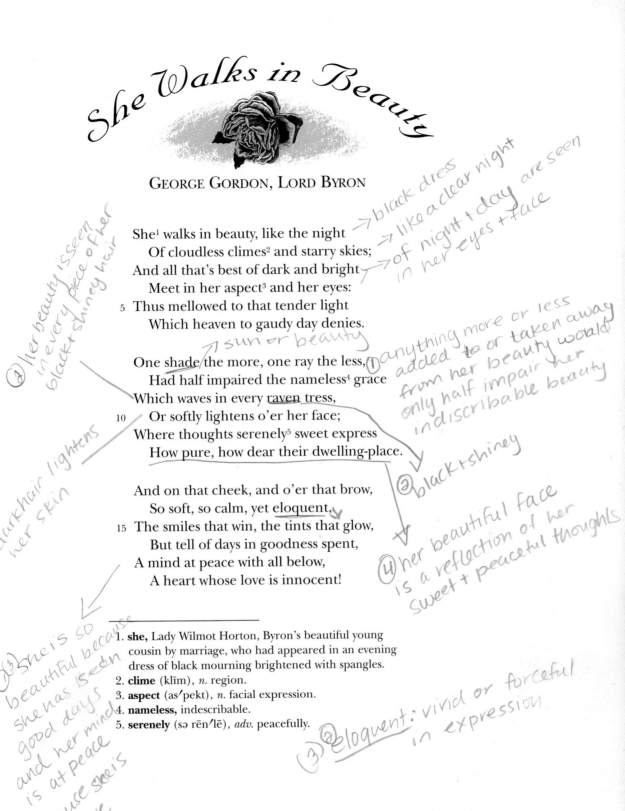

GEORGE GORDON, LORD BYRON

She[1] walks in beauty, like the night
   Of cloudless climes[2] and starry skies;
And all that's best of dark and bright
   Meet in her aspect[3] and her eyes:
5 Thus mellowed to that tender light
   Which heaven to gaudy day denies.

One shade the more, one ray the less,
   Had half impaired the nameless[4] grace
Which waves in every raven tress,
10   Or softly lightens o'er her face;
Where thoughts serenely[5] sweet express
   How pure, how dear their dwelling-place.

And on that cheek, and o'er that brow,
   So soft, so calm, yet eloquent,
15 The smiles that win, the tints that glow,
   But tell of days in goodness spent,
A mind at peace with all below,
   A heart whose love is innocent!

Handwritten annotations:

black dress
like a clear night
of night + day are seen in her eyes + face

① her beauty is seen in every piece of her black + shiney hair

sun or beauty

① anything more or less added to or taken away from her beauty would only half impair her indiscribable beauty

③ dark hair lightens her skin

② black + shiney

④ her beautiful face is a reflection of her sweet + peaceful thoughts

⑤ she is so beautiful because she has seen good days and her mind is at peace because she is in love

---

1. **she,** Lady Wilmot Horton, Byron's beautiful young cousin by marriage, who had appeared in an evening dress of black mourning brightened with spangles.
2. **clime** (klīm), *n.* region.
3. **aspect** (as′pekt), *n.* facial expression.
4. **nameless,** indescribable.
5. **serenely** (sə rēn′lē), *adv.* peacefully.

⑥ eloquent: vivid or forceful in expression

When We Two Parted

GEORGE GORDON, LORD BYRON

When we two parted
   In silence and tears,
Half broken-hearted
   To sever for years,
5 Pale grew thy cheek and cold,
   Colder thy kiss;
Truly that hour foretold
   Sorrow to this.

The dew of the morning
10   Sunk chill on my brow—
It felt like the warning
   Of what I feel now.
Thy vows are all broken,
   And light is thy fame;
15 I hear thy name spoken,
   And share in its shame.

They name thee before me,
   A knell to mine ear;
A shudder comes o'er me—
20   Why wert thou so dear?
They know not I knew thee,
   Who knew thee too well—
Long, long shall I rue thee,
   Too deeply to tell.

25 In secret we met—
   In silence I grieve,
That thy heart could forget,
   Thy spirit deceive.
If I should meet thee
30   After long years,
How should I greet thee?—
   With silence and tears.

In *Broken Vows,* an 1856 painting by Philip Hermogenes Calderon, a betrayed woman suffers in silence, while those who are the cause of her sorrow commune happily on the other side of the wall. Have you ever been betrayed by someone you loved and trusted? What feelings did you experience when you learned of the betrayal? Explain how the artist's choice of details and composition help to tell the story. ➤

18 **knell** (nel), *n.* mournful sound.

20 **wert,** were.

23 **rue** (rü), *v.* regret.

After Reading

Making Connections

Shaping Your
Response

1. Do you think the speaker in these two poems is describing real emotions or just being "poetic"? Explain your answer.

Analyzing the Poems

2. In "She Walks in Beauty" what do you think the speaker gains by describing his beauty in starlight rather than in daylight?

3. What seems to be the speaker's physical ideal?

4. What spiritual ideals are apparently present in the woman?

5. Which aspects of beauty—the physical or the spiritual—do you think the speaker emphasizes more?

6. In "When We Two Parted" what **foreshadowings** and warnings does the speaker seem to have about the future of the relationship?

7. Imagine some circumstances that might have brought about the **change** in their relationship that the speaker is so unhappy about.

Extending the Ideas

8. In what ways might one or both of these poems suggest that the author was in opposition to the traditional reserve of English society?

9. In your opinion, to what extent does Byron's picture of ideal physical and spiritual beauty correspond with modern definitions of ideal beauty?

Literary Focus: Diction

The writer's **diction,** or choice of words and phrases, influences a reader's reaction to the writer's work. List words and phrases from these two poems that are different from the words and phrases you use normally. After each word or phrase write the way you would say it. Finally, write a sentence or two describing Byron's overall diction and your reaction to it.

Expressing Your Ideas

Writing Choices

Writer's Notebook Update Writers of fiction and drama know that diction can be a powerful tool of **characterization.** First write a description of a distinctive diction that you're familiar with; for example: "teenager raised in Texas" or "immigrant from Vietnam, to whom English is a second language." Then rewrite your thoughts about leaving in this character's voice, controlling his or her diction through your choice of words and sentence structures.

Inside and Out Write a **description**—in either poetry or prose—of a person who has made a strong impression on you. Include not only a physical description but also a description of the person's inner character or spiritual qualities. Do the person's physical qualities reveal anything about his or her character and personality?

Meeting / Parting The lovers in "When We Two Parted" separate in "silence and tears." Think about a close relationship you have had with someone or imagine fictional characters in a relationship. Write a **poem** in which you describe your meeting and/or your parting. Begin and end your poem with strong words (like *silence* and *tears*) so that you capture your mood for the reader.

Other Options

That's My Ideal Select pictures from a variety of popular magazines and catalogues to put together a **bulletin board display** of what you believe to be the ideals of beauty in America today. You might add quotations about beauty or paragraphs from articles about cosmetics, health, and so on.

Westminster Abbey Although Lord Byron is regarded as one of the greatest English poets, he was denied burial in Poets' Corner of Westminster Abbey in London. Research this famous resting place of England's renowned writers and present your findings in an **oral report.** If possible, illustrate your report with pictures of Westminster Abbey and of the people who are buried there.

Mixing Art and Politics Although Byron lived a notorious life, he died a hero to the Greeks in whose cause he fought (see the Interdisciplinary Study beginning on page 475). Do you believe writers and other artists ought to involve themselves with politics or other causes, such as poverty or the environment— or should they be content to be good artists? Work with a partner to plan and present a **debate** on this question. You might want to use as examples artists (such as movie stars) from our time who have been particularly vocal on behalf of one cause or another.

Before Reading

Ode to the West Wind
Ozymandias

by Percy Bysshe Shelley

Percy Bysshe Shelley
1792–1822

Son of a conservative country squire, Percy Shelley was expelled after only a year at Oxford for collaborating on a pamphlet called *The Necessity of Atheism*. At nineteen he married sixteen-year-old Harriet Westbrook. Two years later he left England with a new love, Mary Godwin, daughter of philosopher William Godwin and writer Mary Wollstonecraft. Harriet was left behind with one child and another on the way. Following Harriet's suicide, Percy and Mary married and settled in Italy. Here the eccentric and passionate Shelley wrote many lyric poems and his masterpiece, *Prometheus Unbound*. In 1822, when he was nearing his thirtieth birthday, Shelley drowned when his boat was caught in a violent storm.

Building Background

"Be thou me, impetuous one" A true Romantic, Percy Bysshe Shelley often drew his inspirations from nature just as his poetic idol, William Wordsworth, did. Of the motivation for his "Ode to the West Wind," Shelley wrote: "This poem was conceived and chiefly written in a wood that skirts the Arno, near Florence [Italy], and on a day when that tempestuous wind, whose temperature is at once mild and animating, was collecting the vapors which pour down the autumnal rains. They began, as I foresaw, at sunset with a violent tempest of hail and rain, attended by the magnificent thunder and lightning peculiar to the Cisalpine regions." In calling upon the "impetuous" wind to be his guide, Shelley asks that his poetry may strike a spark of hope among mankind.

Literary Focus

Apostrophe A figure of speech in which an absent person, an inanimate object, or an abstract concept is directly addressed is called **apostrophe.** Following are examples of each kind. What apostrophe can you find in Shelley's poetry?

Kind	Example	Source
absent person	"Here thou, great Anna!. . ."	Pope's "The Rape of the Lock" (page 319, line 145)
inanimate object	"O sylvan Wye! thou wanderer through the woods. . ."	Wordsworth's "Tintern Abbey" (page 410, line 56)
abstract concept	"Time, thou anticipat'st my dread exploits. . ."	Shakespeare's *Macbeth,* act four, scene 1 (page 167, line 144)

Writer's Notebook

My Private Place When you want to be alone—to think, to dream, to talk to yourself—where do you go? Jot down five or more adjectives that describe a place where you go to be alone with your thoughts.

ODE TO THE WEST WIND

PERCY BYSSHE SHELLEY

1

O wild West Wind, thou breath of Autumn's being,
Thou, from whose unseen presence the leaves dead
Are driven, like ghosts from an enchanter fleeing,

Yellow, and black, and pale, and hectic red,
5 Pestilence[1]-stricken multitudes: O thou,
Who chariotest to their dark wintry bed

The wingèd seeds, where they lie cold and low,
Each like a corpse within its grave, until
Thine azure sister of the Spring shall blow

10 Her clarion[2] o'er the dreaming earth, and fill
(Driving sweet buds like flocks to feed in air)
With living hues and odors plain and hill;

Wild Spirit, which art moving everywhere;
Destroyer and preserver; hear, oh, hear!

2

15 Thou on whose stream, mid the steep sky's commotion,
Loose clouds like earth's decaying leaves are shed,
Shook from the tangled boughs of Heaven and Ocean,

Angels of rain and lightning: there are spread
On the blue surface of thine airy surge,
20 Like the bright hair uplifted from the head

Of some fierce Maenad,[3] even from the dim verge
Of the horizon to the zenith's height,
The locks of the approaching storm. Thou dirge[4]

---

1. **pestilence** (pes′tl əns), *n.* epidemic disease.
2. **clarion** (klar′ē ən), *n.* trumpet call.
3. **maenad** (mē′nad), a priestess of Dionysus, Greek god of wine, who was worshipped with savage rites.
4. **dirge** (dèrj), *n.* funeral song.

Of the dying year, to which this closing night
25 Will be the dome of a vast sepulcher,[5]
Vaulted with all thy congregated might

Of vapors, from whose solid atmosphere
Black rain, and fire, and hail will burst: oh hear!

——
3
——

Thou who didst waken from his summer dreams
30 The blue Mediterranean, where he lay,
Lulled by the coil of his crystàlline streams,

Beside a pumice isle in Baiae's bay,[6]
And saw in sleep old palaces and towers
Quivering within the wave's intenser day,

35 All overgrown with azure moss and flowers
So sweet, the sense faints picturing them! Thou
For whose path the Atlantic's level powers

Cleave themselves into chasms,[7] while far below
The sea-blooms and the oozy woods which wear
40 The sapless foliage of the ocean, know

Thy voice, and suddenly grow gray with fear,
And tremble and despoil[8] themselves: oh, hear!

——
4
——

If I were a dead leaf thou mightest bear;
If I were a swift cloud to fly with thee;
45 A wave to pant beneath thy power, and share

The impulse of thy strength, only less free
Than thou, O uncontrollable! If even
I were as in my boyhood, and could be

The comrade of thy wanderings over Heaven,
50 As then, when to outstrip the skyey speed
Scarce seemed a vision—I would ne'er have striven

As thus with thee in prayer in my sore need.
Oh, lift me as a wave, a leaf, a cloud!
I fall upon the thorns of life! I bleed!

55 A heavy weight of hours has chained and bowed
One too like thee—tameless, and swift, and proud.

—
5
—

Make me thy lyre, even as the forest is:
What if my leaves are falling like its own!
The tumult[9] of thy mighty harmonies

60 Will take from both a deep, autumnal tone,
Sweet though in sadness. Be thou, Spirit fierce,
My spirit! Be thou me, impetuous[10] one!

Drive my dead thoughts over the universe
Like withered leaves to quicken a new birth;
65 And, by the incantation[11] of this verse,

Scatter, as from an unextinguished hearth
Ashes and sparks, my words among mankind!
Be through my lips to unawakened earth

The trumpet of a prophecy! O Wind,
70 If Winter comes, can Spring be far behind?

---

5. sepulcher (sep′əl kər), *n.* tomb.
6. **Baiae's** (bä′yäz) **bay.** Baiae, on the Bay of Naples in
   Italy, was a famous Roman seaside resort.
7. **the Atlantic's . . . into chasms,** the calm waters of the
   Atlantic Ocean stirred up into huge waves, with deep
   valleys between them.
8. **despoil** (di spoil′), *v.* undress.
9. tumult (tü′mult), *n.* commotion.
10. impetuous (im pech′ü əs), *adj.* rash; hasty.
11. incantation (in′kan tā′shən), *n.* magic spell.

·OZYMANDIAS·

PERCY BYSSHE SHELLEY

I met a traveler from an antique land
Who said: Two vast and trunkless legs of stone
Stand in the desert . . . Near them, on the sand,
Half sunk, a shattered visage lies, whose frown,
5 And wrinkled lip, and sneer of cold command,
Tell that its sculptor well those passions read
Which yet survive, stamped on these lifeless things,
The hand that mocked them, and the heart that fed;
And on the pedestal these words appear:
10 "My name is Ozymandias, king of kings:
Look on my works, ye Mighty, and despair!"
Nothing beside remains. Round the decay
Of that colossal wreck, boundless and bare
The lone and level sands stretch far away.

Ozymandias (oz/i man′dē əs), more commonly known as Ramses II, was an Egyptian pharaoh who ruled about 1200 B.C. He had an evil reputation for persecuting the Israelites, making him a likely subject for Shelley, an opponent of tyranny.

8 **The hand . . . fed,** that is, the passions carved in the stone have outlived the hand that sculpted ("mocked") them and the pharaoh's heart that created them.

The Questioner of the Sphinx was painted in 1863 by American artist Elihu Vedder (1836–1923). Perhaps the "questioner" thinks that over the ages, the sphinx has accumulated extraordinary wisdom. Imagine that an ancient Egyptian sphinx were able to answer a question you posed to it. What would the question be? ➤

After Reading

Making Connections

Shaping Your Response

1. Which image of the wind stands out most in your mind?

Analyzing the Poems

2. Why do you think the speaker calls the wind both "destroyer and preserver" and also "thou dirge of the dying year"?

3. In what sense might the West Wind be a spirit "moving everywhere"?

4. In the fourth stanza the speaker draws a comparison between himself and the West Wind. How are they alike? In what ways are they different?

5. Why does the speaker call on the West Wind for assistance?

6. In the final stanza the speaker moves from wanting to be a sweet "lyre" to wanting to be a strong "trumpet." What do you think this change might indicate about the speaker's attitude toward himself? What shift in **tone** do you sense?

7. What do you think the "frown, / And wrinkled lip" and the "sneer of cold command" might indicate about either the sculptor's or the speaker's attitude toward Ozymandias? toward tyranny in general?

8. Given the description of the present condition of the statue and landscape, what **irony** is there in the inscription on the pedestal?

Extending the Ideas

9. How do lines 47–52 of "Ode to the West Wind" echo Wordsworth's pictures of childhood, as expressed in "Tintern Abbey" (see page 409)?

10. 🐾 In "Ozymandias" what commentary, if any, might Shelley be making on **change** that comes with time?

Literary Focus: Apostrophe

Shelley uses **apostrophe,** or direct address, in several different phrases as he speaks to the West Wind. List as many phrases as you can find.

1. Why do you think Shelley uses apostrophe?

2. What does he gain in thought or feeling by addressing the Wind as a powerful being?

Vocabulary Study

Decide whether the second word in each pair is a synonym or antonym of the italicized vocabulary word. On your paper, write *S* for synonym or *A* for antonym.

1. *dirge*—ditty
2. *pestilence*—disease
3. *sepulcher*—cradle
4. *tumult*—commotion
5. *impetuous*—cautious

Expressing Your Ideas

Writing Choices

Writer's Notebook Update Using the adjectives you listed to describe your quiet place, write a brief description of that place, telling why it is a source of comfort for you.

I Am a . . . Shelley compares himself to the West Wind, "tameless, and swift, and proud." In what element of nature can you find a similarity to yourself? Write a **poem** in which you compare yourself to the stars or the rain or the dawn or a river or some other element of nature. You can use Shelley's "Ode" as a model, or you might write instead in a freer verse form of your own

Immortal Architecture Shelley quotes the inscription on the pedestal of Ozymandias's statue. Select a physical structure—a statue, a monument, a prominent building, a bridge, a church—and write an **inscription** for it in which you express the statement this structure seems to be making to the world. Ozymandias was a person, but you might write as if the bridge or other structure you choose has a personality and can speak. Would it be conscious of or concerned about immortality?

Other Options

The Best and Happiest Shelley defined poetry as "the record of the best and happiest moments of the happiest and best minds." What form of personal expression would you choose to record a "best and happiest moment"? Music? Dance? Ceramics? Photography? Poetry? Select your favorite medium of artistic expression and record one of your **happiest moments.**

Shelley's Mysterious Death The death of Shelley is surrounded by mystery. Although the standard explanation is that he drowned in a violent storm, many believe he was the victim of a brutal murder. Research the various theories of Shelley's death and with a classmate present an **oral report** for your class.

R. I. P. Percy Bysshe Of all of the famous Romantic poets, Percy Bysshe Shelley had the shortest life: he died before his thirtieth birthday. Research the important facts of his life and death and **design a monument** for him. Monuments from the 1800s were often elaborate, and might include a short epitaph, a portrait bust, tools of a person's occupation, and/or symbols of fame, importance, or everlasting life.

The Outsider

Rebels with Causes

Multicultural Connection

Some years ago a popular movie was entitled "Rebel Without a Cause." All the people you will read about here were rebels, in that their actions were often unpopular or put them in jeopardy. But they all had causes that they considered important enough to work for, to fight for, to dedicate their lives to.

REBELS WITH CAUSES

> **"I** hold it, that a little rebellion, now and then is a good thing, and as necessary in the political world as storms in the physical."
>
> *Thomas Jefferson, letter to James Madison*
> *January 30, 1787*

Simón Bolívar

Simón Bolívar

Revolutionary Leader

Simón Bolívar (1783 – 1830) enjoyed a life of wealth and privilege as a member of one of Venezuela's oldest and most prosperous families. He married young and was settling into the life of a wealthy land-owner, when his beloved wife died suddenly and tragically. The young Bolívar left Venezuela and traveled to Europe where he pursued the life of a playboy, but true happiness eluded him. The emptiness of his personal life, along with the tumultuous political events then occurring in Europe, inspired Bolívar to work to liberate his homeland from Spanish rule. Back in Venezuela, Bolívar joined the struggle for independence and became one of South America's most important revolutionary leaders. Bolívar and his forces eventually liberated Venezuela, Colombia, Bolivia, Ecuador, and Peru. Although the struggle to oust the Spaniards lasted nearly fifteen years, Bolívar never wavered in his dedication to his cause. He is remembered and revered as "El Libertador" (The Liberator) of South America.

> *Bolívar traveled to Europe where he pursued a life of a playboy but true happiness eluded him*

WOMEN PIONEERS

Emmeline Pankhurst

Equal Voting Rights Pioneer

Emmeline Pankhurst (1858 – 1928) dedicated her life to the cause of winning equal voting rights for British women. Her career as an activist began after her marriage to the radical Dr. Richard Pankhurst; together, the Pankhursts worked for a variety of social and political causes. In 1889, they established the Women's Franchise League to advance the cause of women's suffrage. After her husband's death, Pankhurst and her daughters Christabel and Sylvia continued to work, forming the Women's Social and Political Union in 1903. Pankhurst and her followers were activists: they staged rallies, demonstrations, and parades; lobbied Parliament; heckled the opposition; and finally resorted to acts of vandalism in order to make their voices heard. Many women, including Pankhurst and her daughter Christabel, were imprisoned because of their activities in support of full voting rights for women. The hunger strikes that Pankhurst waged in prison severely damaged her health, and she died in 1928, the same year that British women finally won equal voting rights.

Lucretia Mott

Women's Rights Convention

During her long and productive life, Lucretia Mott (1793 – 1880) dedicated herself to the abolition of slavery as well as the advancement of women's rights. Mott became a Quaker minister at the age of twenty-eight, following a series of family misfortunes, including the death of her young son. She helped to establish two anti-slavery organizations and gave impassioned speeches about the cause, despite the physical dangers abolitionists faced from hostile pro-slavery forces. At the World Anti-Slavery Convention in London in 1840, Mott was outraged when the male delegates would not allow her and the other female delegates to be seated. Along with Elizabeth Cady Stanton, whom she had met at the London gathering, Mott and Stanton organized the Women's Rights Convention that met in Seneca Falls, New York, in 1848. At this convention, the women's rights movement in the United States was formally launched. Until the end of her life, Mott continued to labor in the service of her causes. When slavery was finally abolished, she began to work on behalf of black voting rights.

Fusaye Ichikawa

Women's Rights Activist

∽∾∿∾∽

She founded the New Women's Association to fight for women's right to make political speeches– this in a time when women were not even allowed to listen to political speeches

∽∾∿∾∽

Fusaye Ichikawa (1893 – 1981) began her adult life as a village schoolteacher. She went on to become the first female reporter for the newspaper *Nagoya Shimbun*, then a stockbroker's clerk, and finally a trade union worker. Between 1918 and 1920 she founded the New Women's Association to fight for women's right to make political speeches— this in a time when women were not even allowed to listen to political speeches or to attend political meetings. During the 1920s she directed the Women's Committee for the International Labour Organization. In 1924 Ichikawa was co-founder of the women's Suffrage League, and in 1945 she founded the League of Women Voters. Elected to the Upper House of Councillors in the Diet of 1952, the first woman member of the legislative branch of the Japanese government, she served there until 1970. All her life she remained in the forefront of the struggle for women's political rights, leading campaigns against licensed prostitution and corruption in elections, opposing pay raises for politicians, and donating part of her salary to women's causes.

Margaret Sanger

Planned Parenthood Pioneer

∽∾∿∾∽

Many of these women, unable to adequately care for the children they already had, begged Sanger to tell them how to avoid becoming pregnant again

∽∾∿∾∽

As a student nurse in the early 1900s, Margaret Sanger (1883 – 1966) often helped to deliver the babies of poor women. Many of these women, unable to adequately care for the children they already had, begged Sanger to tell them how to avoid becoming pregnant again. When Sanger tried to share this information in a newspaper column, she was stopped from doing so by "obscenity laws" then in effect. Wanting to help these women "whose miseries were as vast as the sky," Sanger went to Europe—where attitudes about birth control were more enlightened—to find more information. Sanger's attempts to publish this information in the United States resulted in her being arrested for violating obscenity laws. The charges were dropped, but the laws remained on the books. In her struggle to legalize the distribution of birth control information, she opened this country's first birth control clinic in New York City in 1916. In 1953, Sanger was named the first president of the International Planned Parenthood Federation.

Florence Nightingale

Founder of Modern Nursing

Nightingale wasted no time getting the filthy hospital cleaned up

As a young woman, Florence Nightingale (1820 – 1910) deeply resented the restrictions placed on her by her parents and the upper-class British society into which she was born. At the age of twenty-four, she began to study nursing on her own. Nightingale enrolled in a nursing school and later became the superintendent of a London hospital. In 1854, Nightingale was asked to sail to the Crimea to oversee the care of British soldiers who had been wounded in the Crimean War. Appalled by the conditions she found at the military hospital, Nightingale wasted no time in getting the filthy hospital cleaned up and demanding from British Army officials the supplies that were so sorely needed. A later visit to the front lines of the war nearly killed Nightingale, who contracted Crimean fever there. She never fully regained her health, but she continued to work tirelessly on behalf of her causes. When she died at the age of ninety, she had already secured her place in history as the founder of modern nursing.

REBELS WITH CAUSES

Toussaint L'Ouverture

"The Black Napoleon"

Toussaint remained steadfast in his devotion to the cause of freedom

Toussaint L'Ouverture (1743 – 1803) was born into slavery in the French colony of Saint Domingue, now known as Haiti. After spending nearly fifty years as a slave, L'Ouverture became a leader of the slave rebellion that broke out in 1791. A brilliant military strategist, L'Ouverture commanded the black army that not only forced France to proclaim the freedom of the slaves, but also ousted the British and Spanish soldiers who had invaded the colony. The military leaders whom L'Ouverture defeated, as well as L'Ouverture himself, attributed much of his success to the extraordinary discipline he instilled in his soldiers. Saint Domingue remained under French control, however, and Napoleon Bonaparte sent a huge fleet to restore slavery. L'Ouverture —who came to be known as "The Black Napoleon"— then led a revolution whose goal it was to liberate Saint Domingue. Despite his failing health, L'Ouverture remained steadfast in his devotion to the cause of freedom. He died in a French prison less than a year before Saint Domingue became the independent nation of Haiti.

Lord Byron

Rebel Poet

Although best known as one of the most popular and influential of the English Romantic poets, George Gordon, Lord Byron (1788 – 1824), also involved himself in controversial social and political issues. The rebellious tone and spirit that often characterized his poetry were also reflected in Byron's own adventurous and unconventional life. Byron decided in 1823 to join the Greek struggle for liberation from Turkish rule. He set sail in July 1823, in a ship he had loaded with arms, ammunition, medical supplies, and cash, ending up at Missolonghi, capital of the Greek provisional government that represented the main group of rebels, where he advised the Greek military leaders on strategic planning, formed an artillery unit, commanded six hundred infantrymen—and helped to finance the whole operation. Despite the tremendous energy Byron devoted to the cause, his health was failing, and he died in Missolonghi on April 19, 1824.

Chavez, right, and supporters

Cesar Chavez

Labor Rights Organizer

Cesar Chavez (1927–1993) grew up on a farm in Yuma, Arizona. When he was ten, his family lost their land and took to the road as migrant farm workers. Wages were low and the conditions were harsh, but the Chavezes were determined to survive. As a teenager, Chavez quit school and began following the crops in California. After serving in World War II, he rejoined the ranks of migrant farm workers. As Chavez became involved with a group called the Community Service Organization (CSO), he developed strong political and organizational skills. He also became convinced that farm workers needed a union. In 1962 he founded the National Farm Workers Association which merged with another farm workers union and became the United Farm Workers of America (UFW) in 1973. During the 1960s and '70s, Chavez organized strikes and nationwide boycotts to force growers to bargain with the union. In his long career as a labor union organizer and leader, Chavez never wavered from his policy of nonviolence.

Responding

1. In your opinion, what do all these people have in common? What are their differences?

2. Who are the rebels working and fighting today? What are their causes?

3. What cause do you consider important enough to dedicate yourself to?

Career Connection

In most careers the employees work efficiently, serving the business interests of the employer. A union organizer, however, does not work smoothly or quietly to serve companies. Tanya Wallace brings strong opinions and energy to her work on behalf of other workers.

A PASSION FOR JUSTICE

Interview with

Tanya Wallace

In college, Ms. Wallace wanted a career in which she could help and empower people

Growing up in Chicago, Tanya Wallace knew about the benefits unions brought to workers: both of her parents were active in their unions. In college, Ms. Wallace wanted a career in which she could help and empower people. She "really had a passion about injustices in our society." But majoring in criminal justice, she had no thought of working for a union. In her senior year, a representative from the AFL-CIO Organizing Institute in California visited her campus to recruit organizers. After talking with the institute's recruiter, she realized that in a career as a union organizer, she could turn her passion for justice into action.

After completing four months of training with the Organizing Institute, Ms. Wallace became a union organizer for the Union of Needle Trades Industrial and Textile Employees (UNITE!), a member union of the AFL-CIO. Ms. Wallace now lives in the Atlanta area. Most of her work is in the South. She discusses her job as an organizer:

"Usually I get called in by dissatisfied workers. They don't like what's going on at their company. If a company doesn't have a union, it operates according to rules in an employee handbook, and in fine print, the handbook says the company reserves the right to change the rules as it sees fit. Such open-endedness can lead to uneven and unfair application of the regulations. When a union is established, management and labor discuss and agree upon the rules, which are put in a contract that's signed by and binding for both parties.

"The first thing I do when I get a call to organize a union is to go and meet the workers who asked for help. I talk with them and find out about the company and their problems. I start to identify the leaders and to enhance their skills. Then we make up a list of names and addresses of everyone in the work force and have what is called a blitz. This is a weekend to kick off the campaign, and we try to see every single person and talk to them before the company tries to scare them. Even though it's illegal, sometimes management will threaten employees, in both subtle and blatant ways, who show an interest in a union.

"Some workers have been fired for helping to organize, but they have all said to me, 'I knew what I was getting into, and I'd do it again.' My union has gotten all of those employees their jobs back with full back pay! People, including some in white-collar jobs, are getting tired of being stepped on, and they are thinking of the kind of work environment they want to leave their children. Too

much money is being funneled into the pockets of a greedy few in big business, at the expense of the workers. Unions give people a chance for their slice of the American pie and to be treated with dignity and respect."

Responding

1. What do you think is important when choosing a career?

2. The title of this Interdisciplinary Study is "Rebels with Causes." How do you think Tanya Wallace fits that description?

Writing Workshop

Changing the World

Assignment A saturation research paper is a unique kind of research report that uses both fictional and nonfictional techniques to report factual information in a vivid, dramatic manner. Write a saturation research paper about a special kind of outsider: a social reformer. Focus on an event from this person's life as seen through this person's eyes.

WRITER'S BLUEPRINT

Product   A saturation research paper
Purpose   To dramatize a significant event in the life of a social reformer
Audience   People interested in social reform
Specs   As the writer of a successful paper, you should:

❏ Saturate yourself in your topic. Use every reliable source you can find, including museum exhibits, interviews with experts, videos, diaries, history books, biographies and autobiographies, magazine and newspaper articles, and online sources.

❏ Use first-person ("I") point of view to narrate your event, as if you actually were this person living these moments in time. (You might include a third-person introduction to set the stage for your first-person account.)

❏ Begin by setting the scene, using vivid imagery, including sights, sounds, and smells, to give your reader a "you are there" feeling right from the start.

❏ Go on to narrate your event in present tense, as if it were happening now, using first-person narration and dialogue. Along the way, be sure you make it clear who your character is, what his or her goals are, and why this event is significant.

❏ Use subordination to help signal how ideas are related.

❏ Follow the rules of punctuation, spelling, grammar, and mechanics. Make sure the facts you present are drawn from reliable sources that you have documented in a Works Cited list.

Choose a topic. In a group, brainstorm potential topics. Use anything you've read or seen about social reformers, including the literature in this part. Each topic should consist of (1) a reformer and (2) an event in that person's life. On your own, review the list and choose the topic that you find most interesting. Here are sample topic ideas from the literature and from the Interdisciplinary Study on pages 475–480.

—Toussaint L'Ouverture fighting against French control of Haiti
—Lucretia Mott at the Seneca Falls Women's Rights Convention in 1848
—César Chávez leading a farm workers' strike
—Mary Wollstonecraft publishing her book on women's rights

Put your event into perspective. Make a time line that notes historical events that influenced your topic event or were influenced by it. Use your time line to help guide your research.

Organize your research questions. Begin by writing down everything you already know about your topic. Then make a list of questions you want to answer. Number the questions and use them to guide your research. The sample questions below are based on the publication of Mary Wollstonecraft's book advocating equal rights for women.

1. Who finally published her book?

2. What problems did she run into trying to find a publisher?

3. What inspired her to write the book?

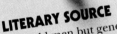

LITERARY SOURCE
"Would men but generously snap our chains, and be content with rational fellowship instead of slavish obedience, they would find us more observant daughters, more affectionate sisters, more faithful wives, more reasonable mothers—in a word, better citizens."
from *A Vindication of the Rights of Woman* by Mary Wollstonecraft

Brainstorm research sources for gathering information in your school and community. Consider sources such as libraries, historical societies, museums, and the Internet.

Carry out your research, using your questions as a guide. Be prepared to add new questions as you learn more.

Consult **primary sources,** such as news accounts, letters, photos, and eyewitness accounts, as well as **secondary sources,** such as biographies, historical fiction, and history books.

Record each source you consult on a numbered **source card** in the order you find it. Then, as you take notes from various sources, mark each **note card** with the numbers of both the source of the information and the question it addresses.

Source Card

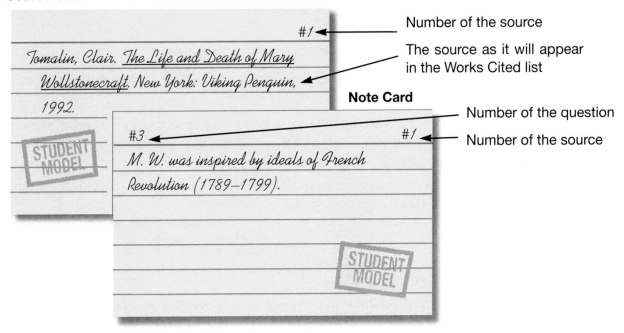

Tomalin, Clair. *The Life and Death of Mary Wollstonecraft.* New York: Viking Penguin, 1992.

STUDENT MODEL

Number of the source

The source as it will appear in the Works Cited list

Note Card

#3

M. W. was inspired by ideals of French Revolution (1789–1799).

#1

STUDENT MODEL

Number of the question

Number of the source

As you research, look for answers to your questions.

Try a quickwrite. Write for five minutes in the voice of the person you chose. Describe the event as if you were actually living through it. If you find you can't describe the event because you don't have enough information, go back and gather more facts.

Plan the report. Organize your notes into a plan like the one shown here.

Setting the scene	Narrating the event
Vivid images —sights —sounds —smells —movements	What happened first —vivid images —my thoughts and feelings —possible lines of dialogue
My reactions —thoughts —feelings	What happened next —vivid images —my thoughts and feelings —possible lines of dialogue
	and so on . . .

OR . . .
Conduct an interview in which the reformer (you) tells a reporter (a partner) what is happening, your feelings about the event, and why the event is significant. Make notes on the results and use them as you plan.

2 DRAFTING

Start drafting. Here are some drafting tips.

- Close your eyes and visualize yourself taking part in the event as it unfolds around you.

- Include excerpts from fictitious conversations your subject might have had with others as a way of giving dramatic life to your factual information about the event.

- Use subordinating clauses to show how ideas are related. See the Revising Strategy that follows.

3 REVISING

Ask a partner to comment on your draft before you revise it. Use this checklist as a guide.

✔ Is it clear to you whom I'm writing as and what event I'm portraying?

✔ Have I made this person's goals clear to you?

✔ Have I included a Works Cited list?

✔ Could I use subordination to help emphasize relationships between ideas?

Revising Strategy

Using Subordination

Many of the statements you make in your writing will be related to each other in special ways. You can emphasize these relationships through subordination—that is, by linking these statements with conjunctions such as *although, because, if, when,* and *while,* or relative pronouns such as *who, which,* and *that.* Notice how the writer of the student model on the next page revised this passage in order to emphasize relationships.

My book will finally be published this year. ^*Although* It may be considered controversial by many, I hope people will read it with an open mind. ~~Society must~~ *If society is to* move forward, ~~To do so~~ it must change its views toward women. People ^*who* cling to old prejudices, ~~These people~~ must become enlightened.

STEP 4 EDITING

Ask a partner to review your revised draft before you edit. When you edit, look for errors in grammar, usage, spelling, and mechanics. Be careful to use the correct form for a Works Cited list.

Editing Strategy

Citing Works in Correct Form

A research paper includes a list called *Works Cited* to tell the reader what sources you used in your research.

- List all the sources you actually consulted, in alphabetical order.

- Give page numbers for magazine articles, but not for books.

- Indent the second and subsequent lines of each entry.

The correct form changes slightly for different types of sources, as shown in the following student model.

Behrman, Cynthia. "Mary Wollstonecraft." <u>World Book Encyclopedia,</u> 1988 ed.

Janes, R. M. "On the Reception of Mary Wollstonecraft's 'A Vindication of the Rights of Women.'" <u>Journal of Historical Ideas,</u> Volume 39, pp. 293–302.

Tomalin, Claire. <u>The Life and Death of Mary Wollstonecraft</u>. New York: Viking Penguin, 1992.

Consider these ideas for presenting your paper:

- Turn it into a dramatic monologue delivered by the subject himself or herself.

- Illustrate it with headlines and pictures from current periodicals that relate to the social issue your subject addressed.

Self-evaluate. What grade would *you* give your paper? Look back at the Writer's Blueprint and evaluate yourself on each point, from 6 (superior) to 1 (inadequate).

Reflect. Think about what you've learned from writing this paper as you write answers to these questions.

✔ How do you, personally, feel about your subject's cause and his or her methods?

✔ What was the most helpful source you consulted? Why?

✔ What sorts of things did you have to think about in order to *become* your character and write in his or her voice?

For Your Working Portfolio Add your paper and reflection responses to your working portfolio.

Beyond Print

Electronic Research

Using today's technology can make researching quick and enjoyable. A **database** is any collection of information or data. A **self-contained database** is accessed through a computer terminal. The information is stored electronically, often on a CD-ROM.

- **Electronic Card Catalogs** Many libraries have transferred their traditional card catalog systems to computer systems. Printers connected to the system allow you to print out the information.

- **Electronic Reference Materials** An entire encyclopedia may be contained on an individual CD-ROM. There are also dictionaries, thesauruses, atlases, almanacs, and other references.

- **Periodical Databases** Some databases list magazine and newspaper articles, and may provide abstracts or entire articles.

An **on-line database** is located outside your immediate area; it is accessed through a telephone line and modem.

- **Library Memberships and Networks** Libraries often purchase on-line memberships to a variety of research services. You can search on-line for resources at other libraries. Often, these resources can be sent to you as an inter-library loan.

- **Individual Memberships** For a fee, members can access on-line encyclopedias, magazines, reviews, interviews, and subject-specific databases. They can also post questions and receive answers.

- **The Internet** The Internet is a world-wide series of computers hooked together through telephone lines. It is accessed via modem through institutions or consumer on-line services.

Activity Options

1. Ask your school or local librarian for a tour of the library's electronic research resources. Keep lists of resources in your notebook.

2. Generate a list of keywords on a topic. Then try using these keywords on several different databases to search your topic.

A Scientific

HISTORICAL OVERVIEW

The Romantic Era saw technological and scientific developments that shaped the modern world. A series of inventions in weaving technology and steam power made possible England's rapid development into the world's dominant industrial nation. Science was also developing rapidly in this period. The conquest of the air began with hot-air balloon ascents in France. Pioneering work in electricity by scientists such as Michael Faraday would make possible the development of electric power half a century later. Naturalist Charles Darwin began research that would revolutionize the view of the development of life on earth. Contemplating scientific and technological change, the Romantic writers were both fascinated and fearful.

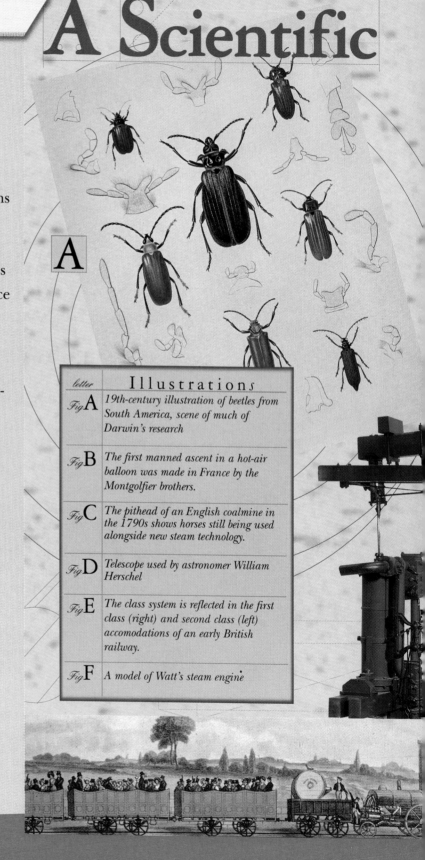

letter	Illustrations
Fig A	19th-century illustration of beetles from South America, scene of much of Darwin's research
Fig B	The first manned ascent in a hot-air balloon was made in France by the Montgolfier brothers.
Fig C	The pithead of an English coalmine in the 1790s shows horses still being used alongside new steam technology.
Fig D	Telescope used by astronomer William Herschel
Fig E	The class system is reflected in the first class (right) and second class (left) accomodations of an early British railway.
Fig F	A model of Watt's steam engine

Revolution

Key Dates

1769
Arkwright builds first textile factories.

1776
Watt invents a new type of steam engine.

1781
Herschel discovers the planet Uranus.

1783
First balloon ascension by Montgolfier brothers.

1796
Jenner begins vaccinating against smallpox.

1800
Volta builds forerunner of electric battery.

1821
Faraday demonstrates principle of electric generator.

1829
Stephenson wins prize with his locomotive.

1831
Darwin starts voyage of the Beagle.

1833
Babbage conceives forerunner of computer.

489

Part Three

Exceeding Human Limits

A theme that was central to Romanticism was the desire to test and break through human limits—and the fear of the possible consequences of such an attempt. One of those limits is the borderline between life and death. People's fascination with creating life and conquering death was age-old during the Romantic era and remains very much with us today.

☸ Multicultural Connection The cultural values of the society in which a person lives influence to a very large degree any **choice** that person makes. What is important to the society at large becomes important to individuals in society. When a person chooses to break out of those social boundaries, however, that person may find a greater degree of freedom—or may find that choice has become more limited than before.

Before Reading

from Frankenstein

by Mary Shelley

Mary Shelley
1797–1851

Mary Shelley was only eighteen when she began writing *Frankenstein.* As the daugher of feminist Mary Wollstonecraft and the radical writer William Godwin, and as the wife of poet Percy Bysshe Shelley, she lived at the center of the Romantic Revolution. Mary Godwin first met Percy Shelley in 1812. They ran away to the Continent, leaving behind Shelley's wife Harriet and two children. Two years later, following Harriet's suicide, they married. By age twenty-four, Mary Shelley was a widow who had lost three of her four children and who struggled to support herself.

Building Background

Imagine the Scene Percy and Mary Shelley and the moody, brilliant young poet Lord Byron are on holiday together in Switzerland. Rainy weather forces them to remain indoors for days on end, and along with John William Polidori, Byron's physician, the group passes the time reading ghost stories. One night, Lord Byron proposes that they each try to write a ghost story. All four initially welcome the task, but only Mary Shelley perseveres, searching in vain for a story idea until one night when, after a long discussion of Erasmus Darwin's experiments to animate lifeless matter, she has a vivid dream. In her own words: "When I placed my head on my pillow I did not sleep, nor could I be said to think. My imagination, unbidden, possessed and guided me . . . I saw—with shut eyes but acute mental vision—I saw the pale student of unhallowed arts kneeling beside the thing he had put together." The next day she begins to write down what eventually becomes the novel *Frankenstein*.

Literary Focus

Mood The atmosphere or overall emotional content is the **mood** of a work. *Frankenstein* is considered a *gothic novel,* or novel of terror. Gothic novels became extremely popular in the 1700s, and the form has survived to this day in the novels of authors such as Stephen King and Thomas Tryon. As you read *Frankenstein,* consider how the author creates a mood of suspense and dread. What role does language play in establishing this mood?

Writer's Notebook

Frankly, Who's Frankenstein? Many people who have never read Mary Shelley's novel know a lot about Frankenstein's monster— through movies, comic books, cartoons, or even music videos. Write down your impressions of the creature based on how you've seen him portrayed in popular culture. Later you may want to compare your description with that of Mary Shelley's.

Frankenstein

Mary Shelley

PART 1

Victor Frankenstein has left his home in Geneva, Switzerland, to study natural science at the University of Ingolstadt, Germany. There, Frankenstein astounds his professors by his mastery of chemistry and research procedures and his passion to probe "the deepest mysteries of creation." Eventually Frankenstein plans to return home to his family and fiancée, Elizabeth, but now his experiments take over his life. In this part, Frankenstein tells his story to Robert Walton, an explorer who has helped him. Victor Frankenstein is speaking.

One of the phenomena which had peculiarly attracted my attention was the structure of the human frame, and, indeed, any animal endued[1] with life. Whence, I often asked myself, did the principle of life proceed? It was a bold question, and one which has ever been considered as a mystery; yet with how many things are we upon the brink of becoming acquainted, if cowardice or carelessness did not restrain our inquiries. I revolved these circumstances in my mind, and determined thenceforth to apply myself more particularly to those branches of natural philosophy which relate to physiology. Unless I had been animated by an almost supernatural enthusiasm, my application to this study would have been irksome, and almost intoler-

---

1. **endued** (en düd′), *adj.* provided with a quality or power.

able. To examine the causes of life, we must first have recourse to death. I became acquainted with the science of anatomy: but this was not sufficient; I must also observe the natural decay and corruption of the human body. In my education my father had taken the greatest precautions that my mind should be impressed with no supernatural horrors. I do not ever remember to have trembled at a tale of superstition, or to have feared the apparition of a spirit. Darkness had no effect upon my fancy; and a churchyard was to me merely the receptacle of bodies deprived of life, which, from being the seat of beauty and strength, had become food for the worm. Now I was led to examine the cause and progress of this decay, and forced to spend days and nights in vaults and charnel houses.[2] My attention was fixed upon every object the most insupportable to the delicacy of the human feelings. I saw how the fine form of man was degraded and wasted; I beheld the corruption of death succeed to the blooming cheek of life; I saw how the worm inherited the wonders of the eye and brain. I paused, examining and analyzing all the minutiae[3] of causation, as exemplified in the change from life to death, and death to life, until from the midst of this darkness a sudden light broke in upon me—a light so brilliant and wondrous, yet so simple, that while I became dizzy with the immensity of the prospect which it illustrated, I was surprised that among so many men of genius who had directed their inquiries towards the same science, that I alone should be reserved to discover so astonishing a secret.

Remember, I am not recording the vision of a madman. The sun does not more certainly shine in the heavens, than that which I now affirm is true. Some miracle might have produced it, yet the stages of the discovery were distinct and probable. After days and nights of incredible labor and fatigue, I succeeded in discovering the cause of generation and life; nay, more, I became myself capable of bestowing animation upon lifeless matter.

The astonishment which I had at first experienced on this discovery soon gave place to delight and rapture. After so much time spent in painful labor, to arrive at once at the summit of my desires was the most gratifying consummation of my toils. But this discovery was so great and overwhelming that all the steps by which I had been progressively led to it were obliterated, and I beheld only the result. What had been the study and desire of the wisest men since the creation of the world was now within my grasp. Not that, like a magic scene, it all opened upon me at once: the information I had obtained was of a nature rather to direct my endeavors so soon as I should point them towards the object already accomplished. . . .

I see by your eagerness, and the wonder and hope which your eyes express, my friend, that you expect to be informed of the secret with which I am acquainted; that cannot be: listen patiently until the end of my story, and you will easily perceive why I am reserved upon that subject. I will not lead you on, unguarded and ardent[4] as I then was, to your destruction and infallible misery. Learn from me, if not by my precepts, at least by my example, how dangerous is the acquirement of knowledge, and how much happier that man is who believes his native town to be the world, than he who aspires to become greater than his nature will allow.

CLARIFY: Why do you think Victor Frankenstein doesn't tell his listener, Robert Walton, the secret of life?

When I found so astonishing a power placed within my hands, I hesitated a long time con-

---

2. **charnel house,** place where dead bodies or bones are laid.
3. **minutiae** (mi nü′shē ē), *n. pl.* very small matters; trifling details.
4. **ardent** (är′nt), *adj.* very enthusiastic; eager.

cerning the manner in which I should employ it. Although I possessed the capacity of bestowing animation, yet to prepare a frame for the reception of it, with all its intricacies of fibers, muscles, and veins, still remained a work of inconceivable difficulty and labor. I doubted at first whether I should attempt the creation of a being like myself, or one of simpler organization; but my imagination was too much exalted by my first success to permit me to doubt of my ability to give life to an animal as complex and wonderful as man. The materials at present within my command hardly appeared adequate to so arduous[5] an undertaking; but I doubted not that I should ultimately succeed. I prepared myself for a multitude of reverses; my operations might be incessantly baffled, and at last my work be imperfect: yet, when I considered the improvement which every day takes place in science and mechanics, I was encouraged to hope my present attempts would at least lay the foundations of future success. Nor could I consider the magnitude and complexity of my plan as any argument of its impracticability. It was with these feelings that I began the creation of a human being. As the minuteness of the parts formed a great hindrance to my speed, I resolved, contrary to my first intention, to make the being of a gigantic stature; that is to say, about eight feet in height, and proportionably large. After having formed this determination, and having spent some months in successfully collecting and arranging my materials, I began.

No one can conceive the variety of feelings which bore me onwards, like a hurricane, in the first enthusiasm of success. Life and death appeared to me ideal bounds, which I should first break through, and pour a torrent of light into our dark world. A new species would bless me as its creator and source; many happy and excellent natures would owe their being to me. No father could claim the gratitude of his child so completely as I should deserve theirs. Pursuing these reflections, I thought that if I could bestow animation upon lifeless matter, I might in process of time (although I now found it impossible) renew life where death had apparently devoted the body to corruption.

These thoughts supported my spirits, while I pursued my undertaking with unremitting ardor. My cheek had grown pale with study, and my person had become emaciated[6] with confinement. Sometimes, on the very brink of certainty, I failed; yet still I clung to the hope which the next day or the next hour might realize. One secret which I alone possessed was the hope to which I had dedicated myself; and the moon gazed on my midnight labors, while, with unrelaxed and breathless eagerness, I pursued nature to her hidden places. Who shall conceive the horrors of my secret toil, as I dabbled among the unhallowed damps of the grave, or tortured the living animal to animate the lifeless clay? My limbs now tremble and my eyes swim with the remembrance; but then a resistless, and almost frantic, impulse urged me forward; I seemed to have lost all soul or sensation but for this one pursuit. It was indeed but a passing trance that only made me feel with renewed acuteness so soon as, the unnatural stimulus ceasing to operate, I had returned to my old habits. I collected bones from charnel houses; and disturbed, with profane fingers, the tremendous secrets of the human frame. In a solitary chamber, or rather cell, at the top of the house, and separated from all the other apartments by a gallery and staircase, I kept my workshop of filthy creation: my eyeballs were starting from their sockets in attending to the details of my employment. The dissecting room and the slaughter-house furnished many of my materials; and often did my human nature turn with loathing from my occupation, whilst, still urged on by an eagerness which perpetually increased, I brought my work near to a conclusion.

---

5. **arduous** (är′jü əs), *adj.* hard to do; requiring much effort.
6. **emaciated** (i mā′shē āt əd), *adj.* unnaturally thin.

...I saw the dull yellow eye of the creature open....

The summer months passed while I was thus engaged, heart and soul, in one pursuit. It was a most beautiful season; never did the fields bestow a more plentiful harvest, or the vines yield a more luxuriant vintage: but my eyes were insensible to the charms of nature. And the same feelings which made me neglect the scenes around me caused me also to forget those friends who were so many miles absent, and whom I had not seen for so long a time. I knew my silence disquieted them; and I well remembered the words of my father: "I know that while you are pleased with yourself, you will think of us with affection, and we shall hear regularly from you. You must pardon me if I regard any interruption in your correspondence as a proof that your other duties are equally neglected."

I knew well, therefore, what would be my father's feelings; but I could not tear my thoughts from my employment, loathsome in itself, but which had taken an irresistible hold of my imagination. I wished, as it were, to procrastinate[7] all that related to my feelings of affection until the great object, which swallowed up every habit of my nature, should be completed.

I then thought that my father would be unjust if he ascribed my neglect to vice, or faultiness on my part; but I am now convinced that he was justified in conceiving that I should not be altogether free from blame. A human being in perfection ought always to preserve a calm and peaceful mind, and never to allow passion or a transitory[8] desire to disturb his tranquillity. I do not think that the pursuit of knowledge is an exception to this rule. If the study to which you apply yourself has a tendency to weaken your affections, and to destroy your taste for those simple pleasures in which no alloy can possibly mix, then that study is certainly unlawful, that is to say, not befitting the human mind. If this rule were always observed; if no man allowed any pursuit whatsoever to interfere with the tranquillity of his domestic affections, Greece had not been enslaved; Caesar would have spared his country; America would have been discovered more gradually; and the empires of Mexico and Peru had not been destroyed.

But I forget that I am moralizing in the most interesting part of my tale; and your looks remind me to proceed.

My father made no reproach in his letters, and only took notice of my silence by inquiring into my occupations more particularly than before. Winter, spring, and summer passed away during my labors; but I did not watch the blossom or the expanding leaves—sights which before always yielded me supreme delight—so deeply was I engrossed in my occupation. The leaves of that year had withered before my work drew near to a close; and now every day showed me more plainly how well I had succeeded. But my enthusiasm was checked by my anxiety, and I appeared rather like one doomed by slavery to toil in the mines, or any other unwholesome trade, than an artist occupied by his favorite employment. Every night I was oppressed by a slow fever, and I became nervous to a most painful degree; the fall of a leaf startled me, and I shunned my fellow creatures as if I had been guilty of a crime. Sometimes I grew alarmed at the wreck I perceived that I had become; the energy of my purpose alone sustained me: my labors would soon end, and I believed that exercise and amusement would then drive away incipient[9] disease; and I promised myself both of these when my creation should be complete.

It was on a dreary night of November that I beheld the accomplishment of my toils. With an

---

7. **procrastinate** (prō kras′tə nāt), *v.* put things off until later; delay.
8. **transitory** (tran′sə tôr′ē), *adj.* passing soon or quickly.
9. **incipient** (in sip′ē ənt), *adj.* just beginning; in an early stage.

anxiety that almost amounted to agony, I collected the instruments of life around me, that I might infuse a spark of being into the lifeless thing that lay at my feet. It was already one in the morning; the rain pattered dismally against the panes, and my candle was nearly burnt out, when, by the glimmer of the half-extinguished light, I saw the dull yellow eye of the creature open; it breathed hard, and a convulsive motion agitated its limbs.

How can I describe my emotions at this catastrophe, or how delineate[10] the wretch whom with such infinite pains and care I had endeavored to form? His limbs were in proportion, and I had selected his features as beautiful. Beautiful!—Great God! His yellow skin scarcely covered the work of muscles and arteries beneath; his hair was of a lustrous black, and flowing; his teeth of a pearly whiteness; but these luxuriances only formed a more horrid contrast with his watery eyes, that seemed almost of the same color as the dun white sockets in which they were set, his shriveled complexion and straight black lips.

> **CONNECT: How does the description of the creature compare with the description you wrote in your Writer's Notebook?**

The different accidents of life are not so changeable as the feelings of human nature. I had worked hard for nearly two years, for the sole purpose of infusing life into an inanimate body. For this I had deprived myself of rest and health. I had desired it with an ardor that far exceeded moderation; but now that I had finished, the beauty of the dream vanished, and breathless horror and disgust filled my heart. Unable to endure the aspect of the being I had created, I rushed out of the room, and continued a long time traversing my bedchamber, unable to compose my mind to sleep. At length lassitude[11] succeeded to the tumult I had before endured; and I threw myself on the bed in my clothes, endeavoring to seek a few moments of forgetfulness. But it was in vain: I slept, indeed, but I was disturbed by the wildest dreams. I thought I saw Elizabeth, in the bloom of health, walking in the streets of Ingolstadt. Delighted and surprised, I embraced her; but as I imprinted the first kiss on her lips, they became livid with the hue of death; her features appeared to change, and I thought that I held the corpse of my dead mother in my arms; a shroud enveloped her form, and I saw the grave-worms crawling in the folds of the flannel. I started from my sleep with horror; a cold dew covered my forehead, my teeth chattered, and every limb became convulsed: when, by the dim and yellow light of the moon, as it forced its way through the window shutters, I beheld the wretch—the miserable monster whom I had created. He held up the curtain of the bed; and his eyes, if eyes they may be called, were fixed on me. His jaws opened, and he muttered some inarticulate sounds, while a grin wrinkled his cheeks. He might have spoken, but I did not hear; one hand was stretched out, seemingly to detain me, but I escaped, and rushed down stairs. I took refuge in the courtyard belonging to the house which I inhabited; where I remained during the rest of the night, walking up and down in the greatest agitation, listening attentively, catching and fearing each sound as if it were to announce the approach of the demoniacal corpse to which I had so miserably given life.

Oh! no mortal could support the horror of that countenance.[12] A mummy again endued with animation could not be so hideous as that wretch. I had gazed on him while unfinished; he was ugly then; but when those muscles and joints were rendered capable of motion, it became a thing such as even Dante[13] could not have conceived.

---

10. **delineate** (di lin′ē āt), v. describe in words; portray.
11. **lassitude** (las′ə tüd), n. lack of energy; weariness.
12. **countenance** (koun′tə nəns), n. face; features.
13. **Dante** (1265–1321), Italian poet, author of the *Inferno,* about a journey into Hell.

I passed the night wretchedly. Sometimes my pulse beat so quickly and hardly that I felt the palpitation[14] of every artery; at others, I nearly sank to the ground through languor and extreme weakness. Mingled with this horror, I felt the bitterness of disappointment; dreams that had been my food and pleasant rest for so long a space were now become a hell to me; and the change was so rapid, the overthrow so complete!

Morning, dismal and wet, at length dawned, and discovered to my sleepless and aching eyes the church of Ingolstadt, its white steeple and clock, which indicated the sixth hour. The porter opened the gates of the court, which had that night been my asylum, and I issued into the streets, pacing them with quick steps, as if I sought to avoid the wretch whom I feared every turning of the street would present to my view. I did not dare return to the apartment which I inhabited, but felt impelled to hurry on, although drenched by the rain which poured from a black and comfortless sky. . . .

PART 2

When Frankenstein finally returns to his rooms the creature has disappeared. He is greatly relieved and makes no attempt to search for him. After being away six years, Frankenstein receives news of the murder of his youngest brother, William, by an unknown strangler. Frankenstein intuitively realizes that the murderer is his own creation. In a terrible injustice, a former servant is executed for the crime. Crushed by feelings of guilt and despair, Frankenstein suffers a nervous collapse and impulsively wanders alone in the Alps. Finally he climbs Montanvert Mountain. Victor Frankenstein is speaking.

It was nearly noon when I arrived at the top of the ascent. For some time I sat upon the rock that overlooks the sea of ice. A mist covered both that and the surrounding mountains. Presently a breeze dissipated[15] the cloud, and I descended upon the glacier. The surface is very uneven, rising like the waves of a troubled sea, descending low, and interspersed by rifts that sink deep. The field of ice is almost a league in width, but I spent nearly two hours in crossing it. The opposite mountain is a bare perpendicular rock. From the side where I now stood Montanvert was exactly opposite, at the distance of a league; and above it rose Mont Blanc, in awful majesty. I remained in a recess of the rock, gazing on this wonderful and stupendous scene. The sea, or rather the vast river of ice, wound among its dependent mountains, whose aerial summits hung over its recesses. Their icy and glittering peaks shone in the sunlight over the clouds. My heart, which was before sorrowful, now swelled with something like joy; I exclaimed—"Wandering spirits, if indeed ye wander, and do not rest in your narrow beds, allow me this faint happiness, or take me, as your companion, away from the joys of life."

As I said this, I suddenly beheld the figure of a man, at some distance, advancing towards me with superhuman speed. He bounded over the crevices in the ice, among which I had walked with caution; his stature, also, as he approached, seemed to exceed that of man. I was troubled: a mist came over my eyes, and I felt a faintness seize me; but I was quickly restored by the cold gale of the mountains. I perceived, as the shape came nearer (sight tremendous and abhorred!) that it was the wretch whom I had created. I trembled with rage and horror, resolving to wait his approach, and then close with him in mortal combat. He approached; his countenance bespoke bitter anguish, combined with disdain and malignity, while its unearthly ugliness rendered it almost too horrible for human eyes. But I scarcely observed this; rage and hatred had at first deprived me of utterance, and I recovered only

---

14. **palpitation** (pal′pə tā′shən), *n.* rapid beating; throb.
15. dissipate (dis′ə pāt), *v.* spread in different directions; scatter.

▲ This still from the famous 1931 movie verson of *Frankenstein* shows one film maker's conception of Frankenstein's monster, played here by Boris Karloff. Compare this portrayal of the monster with the description Shelley gives in *Frankenstein*. How are the two similar? How are they different?

to overwhelm him with words expressive of furious detestation and contempt.

"Devil," I exclaimed, "do you dare approach me? and do not you fear the fierce vengeance of my arm wreaked on your miserable head? Begone, vile insect! or rather, stay, that I may trample you to dust! and, oh! that I could, with the extinction of your miserable existence, restore those victims whom you have so diabolically murdered!"

"I expected this reception," said the demon. "All men hate the wretched; how, then, must I be hated, who am miserable beyond all living

Frankenstein   **499**

Wretched devil! you reproach me with your creation . . . .

things! Yet you, my creator, detest and spurn me, thy creature, to whom thou art bound by ties only dissoluble[16] by the annihilation of one of us. You purpose to kill me. How dare you sport thus with life? Do your duty towards me, and I will do mine towards you and the rest of mankind. If you will comply with my conditions, I will leave them and you at peace; but if you refuse, I will glut the maw of death, until it be satiated[17] with the blood of your remaining friends."

"Abhorred monster! fiend that thou art! the tortures of hell are too mild a vengeance for thy crimes. Wretched devil! you reproach me with your creation; come on, then, that I may extinguish the spark which I so negligently bestowed."

My rage was without bounds; I sprang on him, impelled by all the feelings which can arm one being against the existence of another.

He easily eluded me, and said—

"Be calm! I entreat you to hear me, before you give vent to your hatred on my devoted head. Have I not suffered enough that you seek to increase my misery? Life, although it may only be an accumulation of anguish, is dear to me, and I will defend it. Remember, thou hast made me more powerful than thyself; my height is superior to thine; my joints more supple. But I will not be tempted to set myself in opposition to thee. I am thy creature, and I will be even mild and docile to my natural lord and king, if thou wilt also perform thy part, the which thou owest me. Oh, Frankenstein, be not equitable to every other, and trample upon me alone, to whom thy justice, and even thy clemency[18] and affection, is most due. Remember, that I am thy creature; I ought to be thy Adam; but I am rather the fallen angel, whom thou drivest from joy for no misdeed. Everywhere I see bliss, from which I alone am irrevocably excluded. I was

benevolent and good; misery made me a fiend. Make me happy, and I shall again be virtuous."

"Begone! I will not hear you. There can be no community between you and me; we are enemies. Begone, or let us try our strength in a fight, in which one must fall."

"How can I move thee? Will no entreaties cause thee to turn a favorable eye upon thy creature, who implores thy goodness and compassion? Believe me, Frankenstein: I was benevolent; my soul glowed with love and humanity: but am I not alone, miserably alone? You, my creator, abhor me; what hope can I gather from your fellow creatures, who owe me nothing? they spurn and hate me. The desert mountains and dreary glaciers are my refuge. I have wandered here many days; the caves of ice, which I only do not fear, are a dwelling to me, and the only one which man does not grudge. These bleak skies I hail, for they are kinder to me than your fellow-beings. If the multitude of mankind knew of my existence, they would do as you do, and arm themselves for my destruction. Shall I not then hate them who abhor me? I will keep no terms with my enemies. I am miserable, and they shall share my wretchedness. Yet it is in your power to recompense me, and deliver them from an evil which it only remains for you to make so great that not only you and your family, but thousands of others, shall be swallowed up in the whirlwinds of its rage. Let your compassion be moved, and do not disdain me. Listen to my tale: when you have heard that, abandon or commiserate[19] me, as you shall judge that I deserve. But hear me. The guilty are allowed, by human laws, bloody as they are, to speak in their own defense before

---

16. **dissoluble** (di sol′yə bəl), *adj.* capable of being dissolved.
17. **satiate** (sā′shē āt), *v.* satisfy fully.
18. **clemency** (klem′ən sē), *n.* mercy or leniency.
19. **commiserate** (kə miz′ə rāt), *v.* pity; sympathize with.

they are condemned. Listen to me, Frankenstein. You accuse me of murder; and yet you would, with a satisfied conscience, destroy your own creature. Oh, praise the eternal justice of man! Yet I ask you not to spare me: listen to me; and then, if you can, and if you will, destroy the work of your hands."

SUMMARIZE: What does the creature seem to think Victor Frankenstein owes him, as his creator?

"Why do you call to my remembrance," I rejoined, "circumstances, of which I shudder to reflect, that I have been the miserable origin and author? Cursed be the day, abhorred devil, in which you first saw light! Cursed (although I curse myself) be the hands that formed you! You have made me wretched beyond expression. You have left me no power to consider whether I am just to you or not. Begone! relieve me from the sight of your detested form."

"Thus I relieve thee, my creator," he said, and placed his hated hands before my eyes, which I flung from me with violence; "thus I take from thee a sight which you abhor. Still thou canst listen to me, and grant me thy compassion. By the virtues that I once possessed, I demand this from you. Hear my tale; it is long and strange, and the temperature of this place is not fitting to your fine sensations; come to the hut upon the mountain. The sun is yet high in the heavens; before it descends to hide itself behind yon snowy precipices, and illuminate another world, you will have heard my story, and can decide. On you it rests whether I quit for ever the neighborhood of man, and lead a harmless life, or become the scourge of your fellow-creatures, and the author of your own speedy ruin."

As he said this, he led the way across the ice: I followed. My heart was full, and I did not answer him; but, as I proceeded, I weighed the various arguments that he had used, and deter-mined at least to listen to his tale. I was partly urged by curiosity, and compassion confirmed my resolution. I had hitherto supposed him to be the murderer of my brother, and I eagerly sought a confirmation or denial of this opinion.

For the first time, also, I felt what the duties of a creator towards his creature were, and that I ought to render him happy before I complained of his wickedness. These motives urged me to comply with his demand. We crossed the ice, therefore, and ascended the opposite rock. The air was cold, and the rain again began to descend: we entered the hut, the fiend with an air of exultation, I with a heavy heart and depressed spirits. But I consented to listen; and, seating myself by the fire which my odious[20] companion had lighted, he thus began his tale.

PART 3

The creature describes his attempts to become part of the human family, studying in secret the ways of family life and reading books to develop his feelings and intellect. As a result, the creature comes to real-ize his similarity to humanity and yet his complete alienation and loneliness, which awakens in him stirrings of envy, resentment, and rebellion. The creature demands that Frankenstein create a female for him as a companion.

Frankenstein finds a lonely cottage on one of the Orkney Islands, off Scotland, to fulfill his promise. But he can scarcely bring himself to enter his laboratory for days at a time. Fearful that a female creation may be even more "malignant" than her mate, he destroys his work. The creature sees the act and tells Frankenstein angrily, ". . . I go; but remember, I shall be with you on your wed-ding-night."

The monster keeps his deadly promise and mur-ders Elizabeth. Frankenstein's father perishes in grief. Frankenstein himself sets out in pursuit of his creation—a quest that takes him, finally, to the

---

20. **odious** (ō′dē əs), *adj.* hateful; offensive.

I entered the cabin where lay the remains of my ill-fated and admirable friend. Over him hung a form which I cannot find words to describe; gigantic in stature, yet uncouth and distorted in its proportions. As he hung over the coffin his face was concealed by long locks of ragged hair; but one vast hand was extended, in color and apparent texture like that of a mummy. When he heard the sound of my approach he ceased to utter exclamations of grief and horror and sprung towards the window. Never did I behold a vision so horrible as his face, of such loathsome yet appalling hideousness. I shut my eyes involuntarily and endeavored to recollect what were my duties with regard to this destroyer. I called on him to stay.

He paused, looking on me with wonder; and, again turning towards the lifeless form of his creator, he seemed to forget my presence, and every feature and gesture seemed instigated by the wildest rage of some uncontrollable passion.

"That is also my victim!" he exclaimed: "in his murder my crimes are consummated; the miserable series of my being is wound to its close! Oh, Frankenstein! generous and self-devoted being! what does it avail that I now ask thee to pardon me? I, who irretrievably destroyed thee by destroying all thou lovedst. Alas! he is cold, he cannot answer me."

His voice seemed suffocated; and my first impulses, which had suggested to me the duty of obeying the dying request of my friend, in destroying his enemy, were now suspended by a mixture of curiosity and compassion. I approached this tremendous being; I dared not again raise my eyes to his face, there was something so scaring and unearthly in his ugliness. I attempted to speak, but the words died away on my lips. The monster continued to utter wild and incoherent[21] self-reproaches. At length I gathered resolution to address him in a pause of the tempest of his passion: "Your repentance," I said, "is now superfluous.[22] If you had listened to the voice of conscience, and heeded the stings of remorse, before you had urged your diabolical vengeance to this extremity, Frankenstein would yet have lived."

"And do you dream?" said the demon; "do you think that I was then dead to agony and remorse? . . . But when I discovered that he, the author at once of my existence and of its unspeakable torments, dared to hope for happiness; that while he accumulated wretchedness and despair upon me he sought his own enjoyment in feelings and passions from the indulgence of which I was for ever barred, then impotent envy and bitter indignation filled me with an insatiable[23] thirst for vengeance. I recollected my threat and resolved that it should be accomplished. . . . And now it is ended; there is my last victim!"

I was at first touched by the expressions of his misery; yet, when I called to mind what Frankenstein had said of his powers of eloquence and persuasion, and when I again cast my eyes on the lifeless form of my friend, indignation was rekindled within me. "Wretch!" I said, "it is well that you come here to whine over the desolation that you have made. You throw a torch into a pile of buildings; and when they are consumed you sit among the ruins and lament the fall. Hypocritical fiend! if he whom you mourn still lived, still would he be the object, again would he become the prey, of your accursed vengeance. It is not pity that you feel; you lament only because the victim of your malignity is withdrawn from your power."

---

21. **incoherent** (in′kō hir′ənt), *adj.* having no logical connection of ideas; confused.
22. **superfluous** (sù pėr′flü əs), *adj.* needless; unnecessary.
23. **insatiable** (in sā′shə bəl), *adj.* extremely greedy; not able to be satisfied.

CLARIFY: What is Robert Walton's initial response to the creature? Why do you suppose he changes his mind?

"Oh, it is not thus—not thus," interrupted the being; "yet such must be the impression conveyed to you by what appears to be the purport[24] of my actions. Yet I seek not a fellow-feeling in my misery. No sympathy may I ever find. When I first sought it, it was the love of virtue, the feelings of happiness and affection with which my whole being overflowed, that I wished to be participated. . . . But now crime has degraded me beneath the meanest animal. No guilt, no mischief, no malignity, no misery, can be found comparable to mine. When I run over the frightful catalogue of my sins, I cannot believe that I am the same creature whose thoughts were once filled with sublime and transcendent[25] visions of the beauty and the majesty of goodness. But it is even so; the fallen angel becomes a malignant devil. Yet even that enemy of God and man had friends and associates in his desolation; I am alone.

"You, who call Frankenstein your friend, seem to have a knowledge of my crimes and his misfortunes. But in the detail which he gave you of them he could not sum up the hours and months of misery which I endured, wasting in impotent passions. For while I destroyed his hopes, I did not satisfy my own desires. They

---

24. **purport** (pėr′pôrt), *n.* meaning; main idea.
25. **transcendent** (tran sen′dənt), *adj.* going beyond ordinary limits; superior; extraordinary.

In *Arctic Shipwreck,* an 1824 painting by Caspar David Friedrich, elements of nature unleash their fury, a ship sinks, and people become the victims of powerful natural forces. Victor Frankenstein himself perishes on a ship in the Arctic, in the midst of a barren, forbidding landscape. In *Frankenstein,* who are the victims? Who are the victimizers? Do some characters fill both roles? ▼

were for ever ardent and craving; still I desired love and fellowship, and I was still spurned. Was there no injustice in this? Am I to be thought the only criminal when all human kind sinned against me? . . . I, the miserable and the abandoned, am an abortion, to be spurned at, and kicked, and trampled on. Even now my blood boils at the recollection of this injustice.

"But it is true I am a wretch. I have murdered the lovely and the helpless; I have strangled the innocent as they slept, and grasped to death his throat who never injured me or any other living thing. I have devoted my creator, the select specimen of all that is worthy of love and admiration among men, to misery; I have pursued him even to that irremediable[26] ruin. There he lies, white and cold in death. You hate me; but your abhorrence cannot equal that with which I regard myself. I look on the hands which executed the deed; I think on the heart in which the imagination of it was conceived, and long for the moment when these hands will meet my eyes, when that imagination will haunt my thoughts no more.

"Fear not that I shall be the instrument of future mischief. My work is nearly complete. . . . I shall quit your vessel on the ice-raft which brought me thither, and shall seek the most northern extremity of the globe; I shall collect my funeral pile and consume to ashes this miserable frame, that its remains may afford no light to any curious and unhallowed wretch who would create such another as I have been. I shall die. I shall no longer feel the agonies which now consume me, or be the prey of feelings unsatisfied, yet unquenched. He is dead who called me into being; and when I shall be no more the very remembrance of us both will speedily vanish. I shall no longer see the sun or stars, or feel the winds play on my cheeks. Light, feeling, and sense will pass away; and in this condition must I find my happiness. Some years ago, when the images which this world affords first opened upon me, when I felt the cheering warmth of summer, and heard the rustling of the leaves and the warbling of the birds, and these were all to me, I should have wept to die; now it is my only consolation. Polluted by crimes, and torn by the bitterest remorse, where can I find rest but in death?

"Farewell! I leave you, and in you the last of human kind whom these eyes will ever behold. Farewell, Frankenstein! If thou wert yet alive, and yet cherished a desire of revenge against me, it would be better satiated in my life than in my destruction. . . .

"But soon," he cried, with sad and solemn enthusiasm, "I shall die, and what I now feel be no longer felt. Soon these burning miseries will be extinct. I shall ascend my funeral pile triumphantly, and exult in the agony of the torturing flames. The light of that conflagration[27] will fade away; my ashes will be swept into the sea by the winds. My spirit will sleep in peace; or if it thinks, it will not surely think thus. Farewell."

He sprung from the cabin-window, as he said this, upon the ice-raft which lay close to the vessel. He was soon borne away by the waves and lost in darkness and distance.

---

26. **irremediable** (ir′i mē′dē ə bəl), *adj.* that cannot be corrected or remedied; incurable.
27. **conflagration** (kon′flə grā′shən), *n.* a great and destructive fire.

After Reading

Making Connections

Shaping Your Response **1.** In your opinion, does this story still have the power to frighten readers? Explain.

2. For which character do you have more sympathy—Victor Frankenstein or his creature? Why?

Analyzing the Novel Excerpt **3.** Compare Frankenstein's reaction to his creation as he is working on it to his reaction after it has come to life.

4. Do you believe the creature's explanation that he was once "benevolent and good" but is now changed? Explain.

5. 👁 Frankenstein declares that "there can be no community between you and me; we are enemies." What, in your opinion, makes them enemies? Why can't they make the **choice** to be otherwise?

6. The monster challenges Frankenstein, "Do your duty towards me, and I will do mine towards you . . . ." What do you think should be the duties of a creator toward a creation? of a creation toward a creator?

7. What do you think is the major **theme** of the story?

Extending the Ideas **8.** Does *Frankenstein* remind you of any popular movies or stories of today? What do they have in common? How are horror stories and movies today different from Mary Shelley's tale?

9. Why do you think this story is still popular after so many years?

Literary Focus: Mood

The atmosphere or feeling of a written work is its **mood.** The mood of a selection may be romantic, sad, eerie, lighthearted, dreamlike—the possibilities cover the range of emotions. Authors create mood through the setting, characters, actions, and descriptive details. Gothic novels, like *Frankenstein,* try to create a mood of horror.

1. What details, descriptions, and events help create a mood of horror in this selection?

2. Jot down a list of at least a dozen words or phrases Mary Shelley uses that enhance the mood of this story.

Vocabulary Study

Which word does not belong? Write the letter of the word that is not related in meaning to the other words in the set.

1. **a.** beginning   **b.** early   **c.** incipient   **d.** ridiculous

2. **a.** sympathize   **b.** pity   **c.** scorn   **d.** commiserate

clemency	3.	**a.** leniency	**b.** disturbance	**c.** mercy	**d.** clemency
commiserate	4.	**a.** needless	**b.** superfluous	**c.** unnatural	**d.** unnecessary
delineate	5.	**a.** transitory	**b.** eternal	**c.** long lived	**d.** constant
dissipate	6.	**a.** vitality	**b.** lassitude	**c.** enthusiasm	**d.** energy
incipient	7.	**a.** delineate	**b.** portray	**c.** betray	**d.** describe
lassitude	8.	**a.** odious	**b.** offensive	**c.** peculiar	**d.** hateful
odious	9.	**a.** approve	**b.** procrastinate	**c.** delay	**d.** put off
procrastinate	10.	**a.** spread	**b.** concentrate	**c.** dissipate	**d.** scatter
superfluous					
transitory					

Expressing Your Ideas

Writing Choices

Writer's Notebook Update Put your impressions of Frankenstein's creature into a double-column format. In the second column write words and phrases from Mary Shelley that either confirm your impressions or contradict them.

Modern Terrors Have monsters lost their power to scare, or have real modern terrors such as nuclear weaponry or AIDS diverted most of the public's fears toward themselves and away from fictional creatures? Write a brief **essay** in which you explore this question, citing specific public events or fictional creations.

Invent a Monster Character Mary Shelley invented the story of Frankenstein's monster to entertain friends during a rainy summer. If you were going to invent a character for a tale of terror, what would it be like? Write a **descriptive paragraph** that establishes your character and tells what special powers he or she has. (You might want to use this character in writing My Own Monster; see the Writer's Workshop on page 513.)

Other Options

For or Against? A **debate** is a formal way to argue for and against a particular statement, called a *proposition*. With a partner, consider one of the moral questions that arise in *Frankenstein,* and develop an argument for each side. Then present your debate to the class. Here are some possible propositions:

- Victor Frankenstein has no right to act as a creator.

- A creator has certain responsiblities toward his or her creation.

- Modern scientific experimentation is like a Frankenstein's monster.

Creating Life, Conquering Death The news media today present countless stories about people who are pushing, if not exceeding, the human limits of life and death—for example, keeping alive prematurely born babies or freezing people after death in hopes of reviving them at a later date. Locate one or more of these stories and share it with the class. (See also the Interdisciplinary Study on page 507.) If you find several stories on similar topics, you might combine them in an **oral report.**

Exceeding Human Limits

Creating Life

Science Connection
In the following article, scientist Stephen Jay Gould argues that Hollywood has consistently misinterpreted the theme of Mary Shelley's novel.

The Monster's Human Nature

Stephen Jay Gould

Hollywood knows only one theme in making monster movies, from the archetypal *Frankenstein* of 1931 to [the recent] megahit, *Jurassic Park*. Human technology must not go beyond an intended order decreed by God or set by nature's laws. No matter how benevolent the purposes of the transgressor, such cosmic arrogance can only lead to killer tomatoes, very large rabbits with sharp teeth, giant ants in the Los Angeles sewers, or even larger blobs that swallow entire cities. Yet these films often use far more subtle books as their sources and, in so doing, distort the originals beyond all thematic recognition.

The trend began in 1931 with *Frankenstein,* Hollywood's first great monster "talkie" (although Boris Karloff only grunted, while Colin Clive, as Henry Frankenstein, emoted). Hollywood decreed its chosen theme by the most "up-front" of all conceivable strategies. The film begins with a prologue (even before the titles roll), featuring a well-dressed man standing on stage before a curtain, to issue both a warning about potential fright and to announce the film's deeper theme as the story of "a man of science who sought to create a man after his own image without reckoning upon God."

This 1831 illustration shows a terror-struck Victor Frankenstein fleeing from his creation.

In the movie, Dr. Waldman, Henry's old medical school professor, speaks of his pupil's "insane ambition to create life," a diagnosis supported by Frankenstein's own feverish words of enthusiasm: "I created it. I made it with my own hands from the bodies I took from graves, from the gallows, from anywhere."

The best of a carload of sequels, *The Bride of Frankenstein* (1935) makes the favored theme even more explicit in a prologue featuring Mary Wollstonecraft Shelley (who wrote *Frankenstein* when she was only nineteen years old and published the story two years later in 1818). In conversation with her husband, Percy, and their buddy Lord Byron, she states: "My purpose was to write a moral lesson of the punishment that befell a mortal man who dared to emulate God."

Shelley's *Frankenstein* is a rich book of many themes, but I can find little therein to support the Hollywood reading. The text is neither a diatribe on the dangers of technology nor a warning about overextended ambition against a natural order. We find no passages about disobeying God—an unlikely subject for Mary Shelley and her free-thinking friends (Percy had been expelled from Oxford in 1811 for publishing a defense of atheism). Victor Frankenstein (I do not know why Hollywood changed him to Henry) is guilty of a great moral failing, as we shall see later, but his crime is not technological transgression against a natural or divine order.

We can find a few passages about the awesome power of science, but these words are not negative. Professor Waldman, a sympathetic character in the book, states, for example:

They [scientists] penetrate into the recesses of nature, and show how she works in her hiding places. They ascend into the heavens; they have discovered how the blood circulates, and the nature of the air we breathe. They have acquired new and almost unlimited powers.

We do learn that ardor without compassion or moral consideration can lead to trouble, but Shelley applies this argument to any endeavor, not especially to scientific discovery (her examples are, in fact, all political). Victor Frankenstein says:

A human being in perfection ought always to preserve a calm and peaceful mind, and never to allow passion or a transitory desire to disturb his tranquillity. I do not think that the pursuit of knowledge is an exception to this rule. If the study to which you apply yourself has a tendency to weaken your affections . . . then that study is certainly unlawful, that is to say, not befitting the human mind. If this rule were always observed . . . Greece had not been enslaved; Caesar would have spared his country; America would have been discovered more gradually; and the empires of Mexico and Peru had not been destroyed.

Victor's own motivations are entirely idealistic: "I thought, that if I could bestow animation upon lifeless matter, I might in process of time (although I now found it impossible) renew life where death had apparently devoted the body to corruption." Finally, as Victor expires in the Arctic, he makes his most forceful statement on the dangers of scientific ambition, but he only berates himself and his own failures, while stating that others might well succeed. Victor says his dying words to the ship's captain who found him on the polar ice:

Farewell, Walton! Seek happiness in tranquillity, and avoid ambition, even if it be only the apparently innocent one of distinguishing yourself in science and discoveries. Yet why do I say this? I have myself been blasted in these hopes, yet another may succeed.

In this scene from the 1935 film **The Bride of Frankenstein,** *Elsa Lanchester as Mary Shelley is shown telling her horror story to her husband and Lord Byron.*

. . . But Karloff's *Frankenstein* contains an even more serious and equally prominent distortion of a theme that I regard as the primary lesson of Mary Shelley's book—another lamentable example of Hollywood's sense that the American public cannot tolerate even the slightest exercise in intellectual complexity. Why is the monster evil? Shelley provides a nuanced and subtle answer that, to me, sets the central theme of her book. But Hollywood opted for a simplistic solution, so precisely opposite to Shelley's intent that the movie can no longer claim to be telling a moral fable (despite the protestations of the man in front of the curtain, or of Mary Shelley herself in the sequel) and becomes instead, as I suppose the maker intended all along, a pure horror film. . . .

The monster is evil because Henry unwittingly makes him of evil stuff. Later in the film, Henry expresses his puzzlement at the monster's nasty temperament, for he made his creature of the best materials. But Waldman, finally realizing the source of the monster's behavior, tells Henry: "The brain that was stolen from my laboratory was a criminal brain." Henry then counters with one of the cinema's greatest double takes, and finally manages a feeble retort, "Oh well, after all, it's only a piece of dead tissue." "Only evil will come from it," Waldman replies, "you have created a monster and it will destroy you" —true enough, at least until the next sequel. . . .

Karloff's intrinsically evil monster stands condemned by the same biological determinism that has so tragically and falsely restricted the lives of millions who committed no transgression besides membership in a despised race, sex, or social class. . . . Shelley's monster is not evil by inherent constitution. He is born unformed, carrying the predispositions of human nature, but without the specific manifestations that can only be set by upbringing and education. . . . [It is] the cruel rejection of his natural fellow [that] drives him to fury and revenge. (Even as a murderer, the monster remains fastidious and purposive. Victor Frankenstein is the source of his anger, and he only kills the friends and lovers whose deaths will bring Victor the most grief; he does not, like Godzilla or the Blob, rampage through cities.) . . . He becomes evil, of course, because humans reject him so violently and so unjustly. His resulting loneliness becomes unbearable. . . .

But why is the monster so rejected if his feelings incline towards benevolence, and his acts to evident goodness? Shelley tells us that all humans reject and even loathe the monster for a visceral reason of literal superficiality: his truly terrifying ugliness — a reason heartrending in its deep injustice and profound in its biological accuracy and philosophical insight about the meaning of human nature. . . . Frankenstein's creature becomes a monster because he is cruelly ensnared by one of the deepest predispositions of our biological inheritance — our aversion toward seriously malformed individuals. . . .

Frankenstein's monster was a good man in an appallingly ugly body. His countrymen could have been educated to accept him, but the person responsible for that instruction — his creator, Victor Frankenstein — ran away from his foremost duty, and abandoned his creature at first sight. Victor's sin does not lie in misuse of technology or hubris in emulating God; we cannot find these themes in Mary Shelley's account. Victor failed because he followed a predisposition in human nature — visceral disgust at the monster's appearance — and did not undertake the duty of any creator or parent: to teach his own charge and to educate others in acceptance. . . .

Responding

1. Does Mary Shelley's *Frankenstein* present a positive view of science? of scientists? Explain.

2. Do you agree that "Hollywood knows only one theme in making monster movies"? Why or why not?

Multicultural Connection

Mary Shelley's *Frankenstein* is a famous example of a theme—the fashioning of a human being—that has been explored throughout the cultures of the world in a wide variety of artistic and literary forms.

◄

The full title of Mary Shelley's novel is Frankenstein, or the Modern Prometheus. *According to Greek mythology, Prometheus creates human beings by fashioning them out of clay. Prometheus attempts to aid his creatures by stealing fire from heaven, for which he is punished by the gods. In this detail from a Roman carving, Prometheus is shown animating a human being he has just shaped from clay.*

Creators &

◄

This statue depicts Coatlicue (kō at′lə kü ē), *"the lady of the serpent skirt," a fearsome Aztec deity who is the mother of the gods. Associated equally with life and death, she both creates human beings and devours corpses.*

►

A synthetic human made from flesh, not machinery, is an android. One movie that features androids is Blade Runner. *Technically, Victor Frankenstein's creature is an android.*

According to Chinese mythology, human beings were created from clay by Nu Kwa, a goddess who was half serpent and half woman. She is shown on the right in a rubbing from a Han dynasty stone carving.

Tiki is the creator god of the Maori people of New Zealand. Like Prometheus, he uses clay to make the first human beings.

In Jewish legends of the 1500s, the Golem, a mute creature formed from clay, is given life by a rabbi. In some versions the Golem becomes uncontrollable, forcing the rabbi to destroy his creation. ➤

Creatures

Responding

1. What characteristics are shared by two or more of these creators?

2. Why is Victor Frankenstein a "modern Prometheus"? How does Frankenstein's behavior to his creature differ from that of Prometheus?

Popular Culture Connection

Mary Shelley's novel and the many movies based on it have helped create the image of the scientist in modern popular culture. The cover illustration from this 1938 British science fiction magazine shows a scientist engaged, like Victor Frankenstein, in bringing a creature to life.

Responding

Do you think that the attitude of the general public toward science and technology today is basically positive? Why or why not?

Writing Workshop

My Own Monster

Assignment Using Mary Shelley's *Frankenstein* as a model, narrate a scene for your own horror story featuring a synthetic life form.

WRITER'S BLUEPRINT

Product   A scene for a horror story

Purpose   To explore the theme of exceeding human limits

Audience   People who enjoy suspense

Specs   As the writer of a successful scene, you should:

❑ Decide on a point of view—first person ("I") or third person ("He," "She," "It")—and stay with it when you write.

❑ Narrate your scene in a sequence of events with a clear beginning, middle, and end.

❑ Focus on a synthetic life form.

❑ Use dialogue that helps reveal your characters' thoughts and feelings.

❑ Convey a strong mood, such as suspense or triumph, through specific sights and sounds.

❑ Follow the rules of grammar, usage, spelling, and mechanics. Punctuate dialogue correctly.

OR . . .
Rent a video of a favorite horror movie and view it critically. Take notes on the characters, action, and settings. Study how the filmmakers convey mood through lighting, music, color, and camera angles.

STEP 1 PREWRITING

Research favorite horror stories. With a small group, think of the literature you've read and the movies and TV shows you've seen that tell stories like the one you're about to write.

• What are your favorite horror stories?

• What are some favorite scenes, creatures, characters, and settings from these stories? What makes them so memorable?

Brainstorm creature characteristics. To help you develop a unique creature, first reread the description of Frankenstein's monster on page 497. See if you can draw the monster, based on Shelley's vivid descriptive language. Then discuss other possible characteristics for a synthetic life form and arrange them in a web like the one shown.

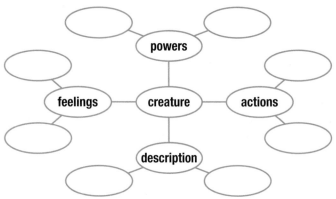

LITERARY SOURCE
"Beautiful—Great God! His yellow skin scarcely covered the work of muscles and arteries beneath; his hair was of a lustrous black, and flowing; his teeth of a pearly whiteness . . . ."
from *Frankenstein* by Mary Shelley

Try a quickwrite. For five or ten minutes, write about your scene. How will it start? How will it end? What will happen in-between? Jot down whatever comes to mind about the plot, characters, and setting.

Plan the scene. Use an organizer like the one shown to plot out your scene from start to finish.

OR . . .
If you're good at drawing, you might make a storyboard instead of an organizer. Draw a picture on a separate piece of paper to represent each event and make notes on the back about action, dialogue, and mood.

Events	Possible Dialogue	Mood	Sights and Sounds to Convey Mood
1. We open in the lab with scientist and assistant as they discover elixir of life.	Scientist: "We shall be gods now, Jamie!" Jamie: "Gods? I wonder."	suspenseful, ominous	—monster's glistening skin —bubbling of greenish liquid —scientist's pounding pulse —clock ticking —dark shadows
2.			

 **DRAFTING**

As you write, keep these tips in mind:

- Begin with dialogue. Have one character ask another character a question that gets things rolling.

- Use a frame-and-flashback structure. Begin in the present as the main character introduces the scene. Write the rest of the scene in past tense as a flashback, and return to the present for a closing comment from the main character.

COMPUTER TIP
If you use frame-and-flashback structure, you might put the present-tense parts of the scene in italics.

STEP 3 REVISING

Make a drawing of your life form and set it aside. When you exchange papers, in the next step, draw each other's "monsters," based on the writer's text. When you return papers and drawings, compare your partner's drawing with your own to see whether your description is vivid enough to help the reader "get the picture."

Ask a partner to look over your draft and comment before you revise.

✔ Have I written a scene for a horror story featuring a synthetic life form of my own design?

✔ Have I narrated the scene from a consistent point of view throughout?

✔ What kind of mood have I created? What are some sights and sounds I could add to strengthen this mood?

Revising Strategy

LITERARY SOURCE
"I started from my sleep with horror; a *cold dew* covered my forehead, my *teeth chattered*, and every limb became convulsed: when, by the *dim and yellow light of the moon*, as it forced its way through the window shutters, I beheld the wretch— the *miserable monster* whom I had created."
from *Frankenstein* by Mary Shelley

Strengthening Mood

Mood is important in horror fiction. Notice the details that contribute to the mood of dread and repulsion in the Literary Source at the right. Notice similar details in the second sentence below.

weak mood	I looked carefully around the unfamiliar room for signs that the creature might be there or perhaps somewhere nearby.
strong mood	As my pulse pounded, my terrified eyes peered into the strange room's gloomy shadows for signs of the lurking creature.

Look for ways to strengthen the mood when you revise your scene.

Ask a partner to review your revised draft before you edit it. When you edit, watch for errors in grammar, usage, spelling, and mechanics. Pay special attention to problems with verb tense.

Editing Strategy

FOR REFERENCE
For more on consistent verb tense, see the Language and Grammar Handbook at the back of this text.

Maintaining Consistent Verb Tense

Shifting verb tenses to go into and out of a flashback is fine, but you don't want to confuse readers by shifting tenses without good reason. Why has the writer of the passage below, who's narrating his scene in past tense, made the revising change?

I threw my arms in the air and roared with joy.

"We've done it, Jamie!" I cried.

"Yes!" he ~~answers~~ *answered* back, "We have."

STUDENT MODEL

Notice how the writer of the draft below, who's narrated her scene in present tense, fixed mistakes with inconsistent verb tense.

The people here don't know that I'm the cause of all this.

There are children here. A little boy holds a teddy bear that ~~was~~ *is*

missing one eye. A girl holds the hem of her dress and swings it up

and down. Some people came here prepared with extra food and

changes of clothing. Others simply ran like rabbits down a hole.

"Just think of them up there," ~~said~~ *says* a man. "Running around

on our sidewalks, in our buildings."

5 PRESENTING

Here are suggestions for presenting your narrative:

- Read your story to family members and friends in a suitably suspenseful atmosphere, with dark shadows and tense music in the background.

- With your final copy, consider including sketches of characters, floor plans of rooms, maps of settings—whatever you think might make your story more vivid and inviting.

6 LOOKING BACK

Self-evaluate. How would *you* rate your narrative? Look back at the Writer's Blueprint and evaluate it on each point, from 6 (superior) to 1 (inadequate).

Reflect. Look back at your scene as if someone else had written it and write answers to these questions:

✔ What does the scene tell me about the author's attitude toward exceeding human limits?

✔ On a scale of 1 (dull) to 10 (terrifying), how suspenseful and horrifying was this scene?

✔ Would I like to read more horror stories by this writer? Why?

For Your Working Portfolio Add your finished product and reflection responses to your working portfolio.

Beyond Print

Looking at Horror Movies

You may or may not find Mary Shelley's original *Frankenstein* a novel of horror today, but almost all of the movies and television programs that have been based on it have emphasized elements of horror. Although Hollywood may be the world's movie capital, England, Germany, France, and other countries have turned out notable horror movies as well. Here are some of the techniques that filmmakers of all countries have found effective.

- **Setting** A spooky setting, such as a drafty castle, an abandoned house, a graveyard at night, always adds a horrific effect. What is the setting in this photograph from the 1931 movie *Frankenstein*?

- **Composition** The closeness of people and objects to the camera lens and their arrangement within the picture frame can create emotional impact. A typical composition might show a monster looming over a helpless victim, but here Igor (an assistant of Dr. Frankenstein's) is shown menacing the creature.

- **Movement** A slow, methodical movement—such as when a killer stalks a victim—helps to build suspense. A lightning fast movement— such as when a killer suddenly strikes—helps create shock.

- **Editing** Film editing is the process of cutting images apart and re-arranging them with other images. In one scene, for example, you may see a monster attacking, then a closeup of the screaming victim, then the monster's teeth and claws, then the torch the victim has dropped, and so on.

- **Sound** Screams are to be expected in horror films, as well as some non-human noises for the monster to make. Violent music often serves as a background for violent actions, but sometimes dead silence can create an unbearable suspense.

- **Lighting** Darkness and shadows are horrific in themselves, which is why so many scenes take place by moonlight, or with the light of candles or a torch, as is shown here. Note the shadows cast on the stone walls by the flickering torch.

- **Makeup** Horror movies are renowned for their creative use of lifelike makeup—and now latex masks and body parts—to create frightening creatures. The famous monster makeup worn by Boris Karloff in *Frankenstein* took hours to apply.

- **Special FX** *FX* stands for "effects." Today, technological effects such as morphing (a technique that blends one person or object into another) and computer animation have raised the art to a high level.

Activity Options

1. What is happening in this frame from the movie *Frankenstein?* What do you think will happen next? Draw one frame that shows what might have happened immediately before this composition and another frame that shows what might happen next.

2. Plan a scene for a horror movie based on your writing in My Own Monster (pages 513–517). You might create a storyboard version of the scene you wrote to show setting, camera angles, lighting—and, of course, character makeup. What special effects would heighten the effect of horror in your movie scene?

❦ Multicultural Connections

Individuality

Part One: Visions and Dreams Blake, Wordsworth, Coleridge, and Keats, all writers of great individuality, changed the artistic life of England and pointed out further necessary changes.

■ Do you think it's more important for people to work toward realizing their own individuality, their own visions and dreams, or to make the choice to work for change to benefit others?

Change

Part Two: The Outsider The choice to assert your individuality can also make you an outsider; the efforts of Burns, Wollstonecraft, Byron, and Shelley to change the lives of their fellow humans, however, made them part of the greater community.

■ Choose the single most important change that should be made in your culture. Is it important enough for you to work actively for it?

Choice

Part Three: Exceeding Human Limits A person can choose to live among human beings or apart, to work with them or separately, as does Shelley's Victor Frankenstein.

■ Which human limit do you think is the most important one not to exceed? What changes would our culture experience if that limit were broken? What would its effect be on individuality?

Activities

1. Construct a sociogram for your group, in which each person is represented by a circle with a name, and the circles are connected by lines to show relationships. Extend your sociogram to show friends, classmates, and family members.

2. Who are the people working for change in our culture and in other cultures? How successful have they been so far? Create a prize, such as the Nobel Peace Prize, and award it.

3. Compile a bulletin board of newspaper and magazine articles on various human limits—such as genetic engineering—that are currently being tested, if not broken. Keep it up to date.

Independent and Group Projects

Media

Create a Mini-Biography Choose one of the writers in this unit and create a ten-minute audio or video biography, focusing on the life or career of that person or on the lasting impact of his or her work. You will have to do some research to find additional images and, perhaps, writing or quotations. Include music, sound effects, and graphics as appropriate.

Debate

Escape or Reform? The Romantic period was characterized in part by a love of nature, idealization of rural life, and appreciation for wild scenery, untouched by human attempts at "improvement." Were these sentiments an attempt to escape the smoke-filled skies of expanding industrial towns and the wretched poverty of their inhabitants? Or were Romantic writers hoping to stimulate reform? Organize two teams to debate the question of how much influence a writer can hope to have. Team members may have to do some further research on writers and their causes.

Research

On the Go You are organizing a "Romantic Highlights Tour" of England. Prepare a brochure, complete with map, of your destinations. What places will you visit? Will you include a few descriptive paragraphs of each place? Will your tour include hikes? cycling? climbing? lectures? cozy inns or camping out? Will you include in your brochure photos of places or people?

Oral Report

A Novel Experience Two notable English novelists during the Romantic Era were Jane Austen and Sir Walter Scott. With your teacher's help, choose a novel by either of these writers, read it, and review it for the class. As an alternative, watch a videotape of a movie that has been made from one of their novels and review it, concentrating on what you understand to be the Romantic elements of the stories they tell.

The Victorians

The Struggle to Understand

Hope and Despair

THEMES IN ENGLISH LITERATURE

Rule, Britannia!

HISTORICAL OVERVIEW

The Victorian era climaxed England's rise to economic and military supremacy. The first modern, industrialized nation, England ruled the largest empire in history—at its greatest extent more than a quarter of the globe. However, England was also suffering the effects of great economic, social, and cultural changes. Rapid industrialization, huge population growth, and movement to cities in search of jobs left thousands of people living in hideous urban slums. Agitation for reform raised fears of class warfare. New scientific thought, particularly Darwin's *Origin of Species,* challenged the religious faith of many. Nevertheless there was a prevailing belief that change would bring improvement, and thus developed the Victorian faith in progress. The individuals profiled on these pages are among those who shaped the era.

Tireless opponent of the slave trade and discoverer of Victoria Falls, Scottish missionary David Livingstone spent much of his life in Africa. A combination of philanthropy and exploration, his career typified the restless urge of the Victorians to travel to unknown corners of the world.

David Livingstone 1813-1873

Builder of bridges, tunnels, railways, and steamships, Brunel was one of the great engineers responsible for shaping modern Britain. He is best remembered for the *Great Eastern,* which for 40 years remained the largest ship afloat and was used to lay the first successful transatlantic cable.

Isambard Kingdom Brunel 1806-1859

There were many successful female writers in mid-Victorian England, but there existed a general assumption that they wrote "women's novels." When Mary Ann Evans published her fiction under the name "George Eliot," she was asserting her intention to rival the greatest novelists of the day.

George Eliot 1819-1880

Eminent Victorians

Charles Darwin 1809-1882

When his *Origin of Species* appeared in 1859, Darwin's vision of an immensely ancient earth in which life had not been created according to a divine plan but had simply evolved as a result of "the survival of the fittest" shook the mid-Victorian world to its foundations.

Queen Victoria 1819-1901

On June 20, 1837, 18-year-old Victoria became queen of England. That night she wrote in her diary, "I am very young and . . . inexperienced, but I am sure, that very few have more real good will and more desire to do what is fit and right than I have." During a 63-year reign, she proved herself worthy.

Key Dates

1836
Darwin concludes scientific voyage on the Beagle.

1837
Victoria is crowned queen.

1851
The Great Exhibition opens.

1855
Livingstone discovers Victoria Falls.

1854
The Crimean War begins.

1858
Brunel's Great Eastern *is launched.*

1859
Origin of Species is published.

1876
Queen Victoria is named Empress of India.

Part One

The Struggle to Understand

The Victorian age was one of strong contrasts. Depending on your focus (and sometimes your control of power), you might describe the nation as proof of the blessing of "the Ordering and Creating God" (Charles Kingsley) or as a split nation, with rich and poor "formed by a different breeding . . . [and] not governed by the same laws" (Benjamin Disraeli).

Multicultural Connection The Industrial Revolution brought about many **changes,** both economic and social. Typically, people responded either by embracing those changes or by rejecting them with anger or despair. How do the characters in the following selections struggle to understand and to respond to the changes that are occurring in their culture?

Literature

Before Reading

The Lady of Shalott

Ulysses

Lyric 106 from In Memoriam

Crossing the Bar

by Alfred, Lord Tennyson

Alfred, Lord Tennyson
1809–1892

Alfred Tennyson's closest friend at Cambridge University was Arthur Henry Hallam, and it was he who urged Tennyson to publish his first volume, *Poems, Chiefly Lyrical* in 1830. When Hallam died suddenly on a trip to Vienna, Tennyson was devastated. In the months following Hallam's death, Tennyson crafted "Ulysses" and some of the lyrics that were to become *In Memoriam, A. H. H.* This volume brought enormous critical and public success and profits that enabled Tennyson to marry Emily Sellwood, to whom he had long been engaged. Many more volumes of poetry were to follow. Tennyson became poet laureate of England in 1850, meaning that he was officially recognized for his work, and Queen Victoria made him a nobleman in 1884, thus entitling him to be called, like Byron, a lord.

Building Background

A Source of Inspiration Camelot and the legendary King Arthur are a constant source of inspiration for writers, musicians, movie makers, and artists, and Tennyson was no exception. His interest in Arthur began in his childhood, and "The Lady of Shalott" was his first poem based on the Arthurian legends. Shalott is the same place as Astolat, where, according to Malory's *Morte Darthur,* Lancelot (see page 88 and 90–91) meets a lady known as the Fair Maid of Astolat. Tennyson frequently had disagreements with artists hired to depict his Arthurian scenes. According to biographer Robert Barnard Martin, after an illustrated edition of his poems was published, he confronted artist Holman Hunt, demanding to know why "the Lady of Shalott in the illustration had 'her hair wildly tossed about as if by a tornado.' Hunt mildly explained that he wanted to convey the idea of the catastrophe that had overtaken her, but Tennyson insisted, 'I didn't say her hair was blown about like that.'" Tennyson later wrote *Idylls of the King,* twelve connected poems based on Arthurian legend.

Literary Focus

Rhyme Rhyme is the exact repetition of sounds in at least the final accented syllable of two or more words. If the rhyme occurs at the ends of lines, it is called **end rhyme.** If the rhyme occurs within the line, it called **internal rhyme.** A **rhyme scheme** is any pattern of rhyme in a stanza or poem. The scheme of the first stanza of "The Lady of Shalott," for example, is *aaaabcccb.* The first rhyme and all the words rhyming with it are labeled *a;* the second rhyme is labeled *b;* the third rhyme is labeled *c;* and so on.

Writer's Notebook

Victoria and Victorias Because of Queen Victoria's long and influential reign, a number of places and things were named for her: an open carriage for two; a genus of water lilies; a lake and a waterfall in Africa; an island in the Arctic; a region in Antarctica; a mountain in New Guinea; and the Victoria Cross, awarded to British soldiers and sailors for extreme valor. Jot down some American places or things named for people. Are any of them named for women?

ALFRED, LORD TENNYSON

▲ *Mariana,* painted in 1871 by Sir John Everett Millais (1829–1896), was inspired by a Tennyson poem of the same title. What elements of the painting give it a romantic, medieval quality? What might the woman's pose suggest about her state of mind?

PART 1

On either side the river lie
Long fields of barley and of rye,
That clothe the wold[1] and meet the sky;
And through the field the road runs by
5   To many-towered Camelot;[2]
And up and down the people go,
Gazing where the lilies blow
Round an island there below,
    The island of Shalott.

10 Willows whiten, aspens quiver,
Little breezes dusk and shiver
Through the wave that runs for ever
By the island in the river
    Flowing down to Camelot.
15 Four gray walls, and four gray towers,
Overlook a space of flowers,
And the silent isle embowers[3]
    The Lady of Shalott.

By the margin, willow-veiled
20 Slide the heavy barges trailed
By slow horses; and unhailed
The shallop[4] flitteth silken-sailed
    Skimming down to Camelot:
But who hath seen her wave her hand?
25 Or at the casement[5] seen her stand?
Or is she known in all the land,
    The Lady of Shalott?

---

1. **wold** (wōld), *n.* high, rolling country, bare of woods.
2. **Camelot,** the place of King Arthur's court.
3. **embower** (em bou′ər), *v.* enclose in a shelter of leafy branches.
4. **shallop** (shal′əp), *n.* a small boat with a sail or oars.
5. **casement** (kās′mənt), *n.* window that opens on hinges.

Only reapers, reaping early
In among the bearded barley,
30 Hear a song that echoes cheerly
From the river winding clearly,
    Down to towered Camelot:
And by the moon the reaper weary,
Piling sheaves in uplands airy,
35 Listening, whispers "'Tis the fairy
    Lady of Shalott."

PART 2

There she weaves by night and day
A magic web with colors gay.
She has heard a whisper say,
40 A curse is on her if she stay
    To look down to Camelot.
She knows not what the curse may be,
And so she weaveth steadily,
And little other care hath she,
45   The Lady of Shalott.

And moving through a mirror clear
That hangs before her all the year,
Shadows of the world appear,
There she sees the highway near
50   Winding down to Camelot:
There the river eddy whirls,
And there the surly village churls,[6]
And the red cloaks of market girls,
    Pass onward from Shalott.

55 Sometimes a troop of damsels[7] glad,
An abbot on an ambling pad,[8]
Sometimes a curly shepherd lad,
Or long-haired page in crimson clad,
    Goes by to towered Camelot;
60 And sometimes through the mirror blue
The knights come riding two and two:
She hath no loyal knight and true,
    The Lady of Shalott.

But in her web she still delights
65 To weave the mirror's magic sights,
For often through the silent nights

A funeral, with plumes and lights
    And music, went to Camelot:
Or when the moon was overhead,
70 Came two young lovers lately wed;
"I am half sick of shadows," said
    The Lady of Shalott.

PART 3

A bow-shot from her bower eaves,
He rode between the barley sheaves,
75 The sun came dazzling through the leaves,
And flamed upon the brazen[9] greaves
    Of bold Sir Lancelot.
A red-cross knight for ever kneeled
To a lady in his shield,
80 That sparkled on the yellow field,
    Beside remote Shalott.

The gemmy bridle glittered free,
Like to some branch of stars we see
Hung in the golden Galaxy.[10]
85 The bridle bells rang merrily
    As he rode down to Camelot:
And from his blazoned baldric[11] slung
A mighty silver bugle hung,
And as he rode his armor rung,
90   Beside remote Shalott.

All in the blue unclouded weather
Thick-jewelled shone the saddle leather,
The helmet and the helmet feather
Burned like one burning flame together,
95   As he rode down to Camelot.
As often through the purple night,
Below the starry clusters bright,

6. **churl** (chèrl), *n.* a freeman of the lowest rank.
7. **damsel** (dam′zəl), *n.* a young girl.
8. **pad,** a slow riding horse.
9. **brazen** (brā′zn) **greave** (grēv), brass armor for the leg below the knee.
10. **Galaxy,** the Milky Way.
11. **blazoned baldric** (bôl′drik), an ornamental (emblazoned) belt hung from one shoulder to the opposite side to support the wearer's bugle or sword.

The Lady of Shalott   **529**

Some bearded meteor, trailing light,
    Moves over still Shalott.

100 His broad clear brow in sunlight glowed;
On burnished hooves his war horse trode;[12]
From underneath his helmet flowed
His coal-black curls as on he rode,
    As he rode down to Camelot.
105 From the bank and from the river
He flashed into the crystal mirror,
"Tirra lirra," by the river
    Sang Sir Lancelot.

She left the web, she left the loom,
110 She made three paces through the room,
She saw the water lily bloom,
She saw the helmet and the plume,
    She looked down to Camelot.
Out flew the web and floated wide;
115 The mirror cracked from side to side;
"The curse is come upon me," cried
    The Lady of Shalott.

Part 4

In the stormy east wind straining,
The pale yellow woods were waning,
120 The broad stream in his banks
       complaining.
Heavily the low sky raining
    Over towered Camelot;
Down she came and found a boat
Beneath a willow left afloat,
125 And round about the prow she wrote
    The Lady of Shalott.

And down the river's dim expanse
Like some bold seer in a trance,
Seeing all his own mischance—
130 With a glassy countenance
    Did she look to Camelot.
And at the closing of the day
She loosed the chain, and down she lay;
The broad stream bore her far away,
135   The Lady of Shalott.

Lying, robed in snowy white
That loosely flew to left and right—
The leaves upon her falling light—
Through the noises of the night
140   She floated down to Camelot:
And as the boathead wound along
The willowy hills and fields among,
They heard her singing her last song,
    The Lady of Shalott.

145 Heard a carol, mournful, holy,
Chanted loudly, chanted lowly,
Till her blood was frozen slowly,
And her eyes were darkened wholly,
    Turned to towered Camelot.
150 For ere she reached upon the tide
The first house by the water-side,
Singing in her song she died,
    The Lady of Shalott.

Under tower and balcony,
155 By garden wall and gallery,
A gleaming shape she floated by,
Dead-pale between the houses high,
    Silent into Camelot.
Out upon the wharfs they came,
160 Knight and burgher,[13] lord and dame,
And round the prow they read her name,
    The Lady of Shalott.

Who is this? and what is here?
And in the lighted palace near
165 Died the sound of royal cheer;
And they crossed themselves for fear,
    All the knights at Camelot:
But Lancelot mused a little space;
He said, "She has a lovely face;
170 God in his mercy lend her grace,
    The Lady of Shalott."

---

12. **trode** (trōd), *v.* an archaic past tense of *tread*, step.
13. **burgher** (bėr′gər), *n.* citizen.

ULYSSES

ALFRED, LORD TENNYSON

In the legendary Trojan War, the Greeks besieged Troy for ten years to win back the beautiful queen Helen. After their victory the warrior king Ulysses (yü-lis′ēz), *a victim of hostile gods, wandered for ten more years, sailing unknown seas, battling with monsters, and even journeying to the land of the dead, before he reached his island home of Ithaca. There, he had to kill a band of rivals who wished to seize his wife Penelope* (pə nel′ə pē) *and his lands. Homer's* Odyssey *comes to an end there, but Tennyson concludes that after such adventures Ulysses could not rest content at home.*

It little profits that an idle king,
By this still hearth, among these barren crags,
Matched with an agèd wife, I mete and dole
Unequal laws unto a savage race,
5   That hoard, and sleep, and feed, and know not me.
I cannot rest from travel: I will drink
Life to the lees: all times I have enjoyed
Greatly, have suffered greatly, both with those
That loved me, and alone; on shore, and when
10   Through scudding drifts the rainy Hyades
Vexed the dim sea: I am become a name;
For always roaming with a hungry heart
Much have I seen and known; cities of men
And manners, climates, councils, governments,
15   Myself not least, but honored of them all;
And drunk delight of battle with my peers,
Far on the ringing plains of windy Troy.
I am part of all that I have met;
Yet all experience is an arch wherethrough
20   Gleams that untraveled world whose margin fades
Forever and forever when I move.
How dull it is to pause, to make an end,
To rust unburnished, not to shine in use!
As though to breathe were life! Life piled on life
25   Were all too little, and of one to me
Little remains: but every hour is saved
From the eternal silence, something more,

3 mete and dole, distribute and give in small portions.

7 lees (lēz), *n. pl.* dregs; the least desirable part.

10 Hyades (hī′ə dēz′), cluster of stars in the constellation Taurus, supposed by the ancients to be a sign of rain when they rose with the sun.

27 eternal silence, death.

A bringer of new things; and vile it were
For some three suns to store and hoard myself,
30 And this gray spirit yearning in desire
To follow knowledge like a sinking star,
Beyond the utmost bound of human thought.
This is my son, mine own Telemachus,
To whom I leave the scepter and the isle—
35 Well-loved of me, discerning to fulfill
This labor, by slow prudence to make mild
A rugged people, and through soft degrees
Subdue them to the useful and the good.
Most blameless is he, centered in the sphere
40 Of common duties, decent not to fail
In offices of tenderness, and pay
Meet adoration to my household gods,
When I am gone. He works his work, I mine.
There lies the port; the vessel puffs her sail:
45 There gloom the dark, broad seas. My mariners,
Souls that have toiled, and wrought, and thought with me—
That ever with a frolic welcome took
The thunder and the sunshine, and opposed
Free hearts, free foreheads—you and I are old;
50 Old age hath yet his honor and his toil;
Death closes all: but something ere the end,
Some work of noble note, may yet be done,
Not unbecoming men that strove with gods.
The lights begin to twinkle from the rocks:
55 The long day wanes: the slow moon climbs: the deep
Moans round with many voices. Come, my friends,
'Tis not too late to seek a newer world.
Push off, and sitting well in order smite
The sounding furrows; for my purpose holds
60 To sail beyond the sunset, and the baths
Of all the western stars, until I die.
It may be that the gulfs will wash us down:
It may be we shall touch the Happy Isles,
And see the great Achilles, whom we knew.
65 Though much is taken, much abides; and though
We are not now that strength which in old days
Moved earth and heaven; that which we are, we are;
One equal temper of heroic hearts,
Made weak by time and fate, but strong in will
70 To strive, to seek, to find, and not to yield.

33 Telemachus (tə lem′ə kəs).

42 meet (mēt), *adj.* fitting. *[Archaic]*

46 wrought (rôt), *v.* worked. *[Archaic]*

49 you, Ulysses' companions. **60–61 baths . . . stars.** In ancient belief, the stars literally plunge into the sea at the edge of the earth. **63 Happy Isles,** a paradise for dead heroes like Achilles (ə kil′ēz), who fought beside Ulysses at Troy.

In *The King* by Max Beckmann, the hooded, mysterious-looking woman standing behind the king seems to have his ear, while the young woman kneeling and embracing him seems to have his heart. The hooded woman's left hand is raised in a gesture that suggests she is at odds with the other woman. Like Ulysses, the king seems to feel the pull of two opposing forces. Which one do you think might ultimately triumph? Why? ➤

LYRIC 106

ALFRED, LORD TENNYSON

Ring out, wild bells, to the wild sky,
    The flying cloud, the frosty light:
    The year is dying in the night;
Ring out, wild bells, and let him die.

5 Ring out the old, ring in the new,
    Ring, happy bells, across the snow:
    The year is going, let him go;
Ring out the false, ring in the true.

Ring out the grief that saps the mind,
10   For those that here we see no more;
    Ring out the feud of rich and poor,
Ring in redress to all mankind.

Ring out a slowly dying cause,
    And ancient forms of party strife;
15   Ring in the nobler modes of life,
With sweeter manners, purer laws.

Ring out the want, the care, the sin,
    The faithless coldness of the times;
    Ring out, ring out my mournful rhymes,
20 But ring the fuller minstrel in.

Ring out false pride in place and blood,
    The civic slander and the spite;
    Ring in the love of truth and right,
Ring in the common love of good.

12 redress (re dres′), *n.* a setting right; relief.

14 strife (strīf), *n.* a quarreling; fighting.

20 minstrel (min′strel), *n.* musician, singer, or poet.

25 Ring out old shapes of foul disease;
    Ring out the narrowing lust of gold;
    Ring out the thousand wars of old,
 Ring in the thousand years of peace.

    Ring in the valiant man and free,
30   The larger heart, the kindlier hand;
    Ring out the darkness of the land,
 Ring in the Christ that is to be.

29 valiant (val′yənt), *adj.* brave; courageous.

CROSSING THE BAR

ALFRED, LORD TENNYSON

Sunset and evening star,
    And one clear call for me!
 And may there be no moaning of the bar,
    When I put out to sea,

5 But such a tide as moving seems asleep,
    Too full for sound and foam,
 When that which drew from out the boundless deep
    Turns again home.

 Twilight and evening bell,
10   And after that the dark!
 And may there be no sadness of farewell,
    When I embark;

 For though from out our bourne of Time and Place
    The flood may bear me far,
15 I hope to see my Pilot face to face
    When I have crossed the bar.

bar, sandbar; an underwater ridge of sand across a harbor.

13 bourne (bôrn), *n.* boundary; limit.
15 Pilot. The word has the double meaning of one who steers a ship in or out of a harbor, and God.

After Reading

Making Connections

Shaping Your Response

1. What do you think kills the Lady of Shalott? Is she responsible for her own death?

2. In your opinion, why do people write poetry about old age and death?

Analyzing the Poems

3. Explain how the **setting,** both the place and the season, contributes to the **mood** of "The Lady of Shalott."

4. How do lines 22 and 23 in "Ulysses" help to explain his decision?

5. Explain how the structure and **repetition** in Lyric 106 reflect the topic of bells.

6. What is the extended **metaphor** in "Crossing the Bar"?

7. Compare and contrast the **rhythms** and **style** (including mood, imagery, and repetition) of Tennyson's poems.

Extending the Ideas

8. If you were to make your own list of hopes for the future, what things would be different from the speaker's hopes for **changes** to come in Lyric 106?

9. In your opinion, what is it about the Arthurian legends that continues to fascinate writers and movie makers even today?

Literary Focus: Rhyme

Rhyme is the exact repetition of sounds in at least the final accented syllables of two or more words. **Rhyme scheme** is any pattern of rhyme in a stanza or poem. Chart the rhyme scheme in the first three stanzas of "Lyric 106." Does the poem have **end rhyme** or **internal rhyme**?

More About the Author

Poet Laureate To the ancient Greeks, laurel was a symbol of distinction and was used to form a crown of honor for poets and heroes. In England's Middle Ages, the title *poet laureate* was applied to any eminent poet. The office became official when Charles II appointed John Dryden poet laureate in 1670. The duties of poet laureate have included producing verses on birthdays and court occasions, but William Wordsworth accepted the laureateship on the condition that he would not necessarily have to do so, and the office became an honorary one. Tennyson, who followed Wordsworth into the office, did much to elevate the office in the eyes of his fellow poets.

Expressing Your Ideas

Writing Choices

Writer's Notebook Update Can you imagine an automobile, flower, lake, or product named for you? Suppose that you are forty years older than you are now and have become famous. Describe the things and places that bear your name.

What Happens Next? Novelists and poets often write sequels to classic or traditional stories, as Tennyson did in "Ulysses." Sometimes a sequel deals with the fortunes of a minor character in the original work. Write a **dialogue** between Ulysses' wife Penelope or his son Telemachus and Ulysses when he announces that he is leaving again. Or, you might write a dialogue between Ulysses and his companions prior to their setting out on the proposed voyage.

Righting Old Wrongs In Lyric 106, Tennyson mentions a number of wrongs, such as "the feud of rich and poor," that he wants to see ended with the old year. Review the poem, choose three of these wrongs, and write an **editorial** in which you demonstrate whether there is or is not still evidence of them in the U. S. today.

Other Options

A Far Country Fictitious places such as Camelot, Xanadu, or Shalott seem more appealing sometimes than actual places. In a small group, create a **fictitious place** that you would find appealing. Choose among the following:

- Name and map the country and its geography.
- Using graphics, outline the type of government and the economy.
- Describe the characteristics and beliefs of the people, using illustrations when possible.
- Identify the chief leisure-time interests of the inhabitants.
- Create an illustrated history of the country.

Show-and-Tell Research the personal life and career of any Victorian artist, such as those whose works illustrate the early Victorian writers in this part, and give an **illustrated oral report** to the class. Show examples of your chosen artist's work and discuss especially elements of his or her artisitc style.

"So Long, It's Been Good to Know You" Folk songs, cowboy songs, blues, rock lyrics, and much country and western music deal with the theme of restlessness and moving on. Compile your own **musical show** by playing some songs for the class that could depict Ulysses' urge to leave home again—and his wife's possible reactions.

Before Reading

Sonnet 43 by Elizabeth Barrett Browning
Porphyria's Lover by Robert Browning
My Last Duchess by Robert Browning

Elizabeth Barrett Browning
1806–1861

Elizabeth Barrett published her first collection of verse at twenty, but illness made her a recluse. In 1846 she married Robert Browning. *Sonnets from the Portuguese,* in which Sonnet 43 appeared, chronicles her love for him.

Robert Browning
1812–1889

Robert Browning decided early to become a poet and worked at his craft diligently. In 1855 he published a collection of dramatic monologues titled *Men and Women* and in 1868–9 published *The Ring and the Book,* a lengthy poem about an obscure Roman murder.

Building Background

Love and Letters One of the world's most famous courtships began with the letters between two poets, Elizabeth Barrett and Robert Browning. At age thirty-nine Elizabeth was the better known of the two. She had referred to his collection, *Bells and Pomegranates,* in her *Poems* (1844). An admirer of her work for several years, Robert began his first letter (January 10, 1845) with the words "I love your verses with all my heart, dear Miss Barrett." Then, as if carried away by his feelings, after several lines he wrote: "I do, as I say, love these verses with all my heart—and I love you too." Elizabeth, then an invalid, replied the next day, though with somewhat more reserve. Eventually they wrote each other 574 letters, including one that she asked him to burn. They did not meet in person until May 20, 1845, when Robert visited her. Despite some misgivings, Elizabeth eventually came to love Robert too. Because her father had forbidden any of his children to marry, Elizabeth and Robert were wed secretly in St. Marylebone Church in London on September 12, 1846, with two witnesses only—his cousin and her maid. The couple fled to Italy, and Mr. Barrett refused to see the Brownings or their son (born in 1849) ever again.

Literary Focus

Dramatic Monologue A **dramatic monologue** is a poem in which a fictional character speaking in the first person reveals details of dramatic situation, characterization, and setting. A silent listener or audience is often, but not always, assumed to be present. Since the speaker's thoughts are subjective—and frequently self-serving—readers must watch for hints as to the true situation. As you read Robert Browning's two poems, both dramatic monologues, be ready to make some inferences about the speakers and the events described.

Writer's Notebook

Characterize a Person Think of a person you know well and jot down some adjectives that describe that person. Think of words that describe physical characteristics or actions as well as words that describe the person's character and personality.

Sonnet 43

Elizabeth Barrett Browning

How do I love thee? Let me count the ways.
I love thee to the depth and breadth and height
My soul can reach, when feeling out of sight
For the ends of Being and ideal Grace.
5 I love thee to the level of everyday's
Most quiet need, by sun and candlelight.
I love thee freely, as men strive for Right;
I love thee purely, as they turn from Praise.
I love thee with the passion put to use
10 In my old griefs, and with my childhood's faith,
I love thee with a love I seemed to lose
With my lost saints—I love thee with the breadth,
Smiles, tears, of all my life!—and, if God choose,
I shall but love thee better after death.

Porphyria's Lover

Robert Browning

The rain set early in tonight,
    The sullen wind was soon awake,
It tore the elm-tops down for spite,
    And did its worst to vex the lake:
5   I listened with heart fit to break
When glided in Porphyria; straight
    She shut the cold out and the storm,
And kneeled and made the cheerless grate
    Blaze up, and all the cottage warm;
10   Which done, she rose, and from her form
Withdrew the dripping cloak and shawl,
    And laid her soiled gloves by, untied
Her hat and let the damp hair fall,
    And, last, she sat down by my side
15   And called me. When no voice replied,

Porphyria (por fir′ē ə).

4 vex (veks), *v.* disturb; agitate.

She put my arm about her waist,
    And made her smooth white shoulder bare,
And all her yellow hair displaced,
    And stooping, made my cheek lie there,
20   And spread, o'er all, her yellow hair,
Murmuring how she loved me—she
    Too weak, for all her heart's endeavor,
To set its struggling passion free
    From pride, and vainer ties dissever,
25   And give herself to me forever.
But passion sometimes would prevail,
    Nor could tonight's gay feast restrain
A sudden thought of one so pale
    For love of her, and all in vain:
30   So, she was come through wind and rain.
Be sure I looked up at her eyes
    Happy and proud; at last I knew
Porphyria worshiped me: surprise
    Made my heart swell, and still it grew
35   While I debated what to do.
That moment she was mine, mine, fair,
    Perfectly pure and good: I found
A thing to do, and all her hair
    In one long yellow string I wound
40   Three times her little throat around,
And strangled her. No pain felt she;
    I am quite sure she felt no pain.
As a shut bud that holds a bee,
    I warily oped her lids: again
45   Laughed the blue eyes without a stain.
And I untightened next the tress
    About her neck; her cheek once more
Blushed bright beneath my burning kiss:
    I propped her head up as before,
50   Only, this time my shoulder bore
Her head, which droops upon it still:
    The smiling rosy little head,
So glad it has its utmost will,
    That all it scorned at once is fled,
55   And I, its love, am gained instead!
Porphyria's love: she guessed not how
    Her darling one wish would be heard.
And thus we sit together now,
    And all night long we have not stirred,
60   And yet God has not said a word!

24 dissever (di sev′ər), *v.* separate.

46 tress (tres), *n.* lock, curl, or braid of hair.
53 utmost (ut′mōst), *adj.* greatest; highest.

In *The Kiss,* a 1908 oil painting by Viennese artist Gustav Klimt (1862–1918), the two lovers have skin that appears lushly sensual. What elements of the painting contrast with the lovers' skin, making it appear even more sensual? ➤

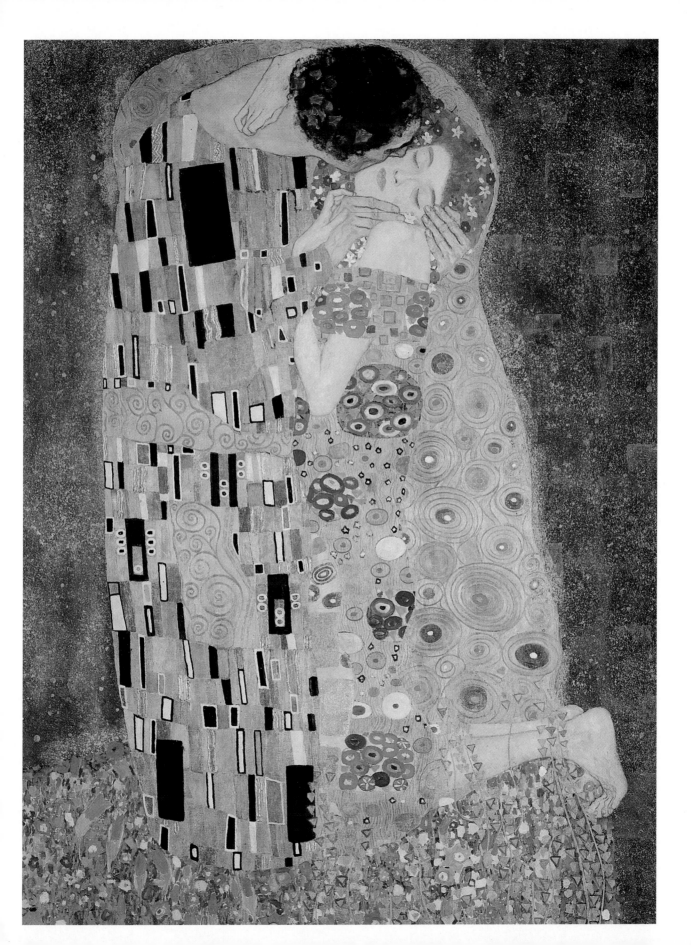

My Last Duchess

Robert Browning

The place is the city of Ferrara in northern Italy. The time is the 1500s. The speaker is the Duke of Ferrara, who is negotiating for a marriage with a count's daughter.

That's my last duchess painted on the wall,
Looking as if she were alive. I call
That piece a wonder, now: Frà Pandolf's hands
Worked busily a day, and there she stands.
5 Will 't please you sit and look at her? I said
"Frà Pandolf" by design, for never read
Strangers like you that pictured countenance,
The depth and passion of its earnest glance,
But to myself they turned (since none puts by
10 The curtain I have drawn for you, but I)
And seemed as they would ask me, if they durst,
How such a glance came there; so, not the first
Are you to turn and ask thus. Sir, 'twas not
Her husband's presence only, called that spot
15 Of joy into the Duchess' cheek: perhaps
Frà Pandolf chanced to say, "Her mantle laps
Over my lady's wrist too much," or "Paint
Must never hope to reproduce the faint
Half-flush that dies along her throat": such stuff
20 Was courtesy, she thought, and cause enough
For calling up that spot of joy. She had
A heart—how shall I say?—too soon made glad,
Too easily impressed; she liked whate'er
She looked on, and her looks went everywhere.
25 Sir, 'twas all one! My favor at her breast,
The dropping of the daylight in the West,
The bough of cherries some officious fool
Broke in the orchard for her, the white mule
She rode with round the terrace—all and each
30 Would draw from her alike the approving speech,
Or blush, at least. She thanked men—good! but thanked
Somehow—I know not how—as if she ranked
My gift of a nine-hundred-years-old name
With anybody's gift. Who'd stoop to blame

3 Frà Pandolf, the painter, a monk.

11 durst (dėrst), *v.* a past tense of *dare. [Archaic]*

16 mantle (man′tl), *n.* cloak.

27 officious (ə fish′əs), *adj.* meddlesome.

35 This sort of trifling? Even had you skill
    In speech—which I have not—to make your will
    Quite clear to such an one, and say, "Just this
    Or that in you disgusts me; here you miss,
    Or there exceed the mark"—and if she let
40 Herself be lessoned so, nor plainly set
    Her wits to yours, forsooth, and made excuse—
    E'en then would be some stooping; and I choose
    Never to stoop. Oh sir, she smiled, no doubt,
    Whene'er I passed her; but who passed without
45 Much the same smile? This grew; I gave commands;
    Then all smiles stopped together. There she stands
    As if alive. Will 't please you rise? We'll meet
    The company below, then. I repeat,
    The Count your master's known munificence
50 Is ample warrant that no just pretense
    Of mine for dowry will be disallowed;
    Though his fair daughter's self, as I avowed
    At starting, is my object. Nay, we'll go
    Together down, sir. Notice Neptune, though,
55 Taming a sea-horse, thought a rarity,
    Which Claus of Innsbruck cast in bronze for me!

41 forsooth (fôr sü̇th′), *adv.* in truth; indeed. *[Archaic]*

49 munificence (myü̇ nif′ə-səns), *n.* very great generosity.
50 pretense (prē′tens), *n.* claim.
51 dowry (dou′rē), *n.* money or property that a woman brings to the man she marries.
52 avow (ə vou′), *v.* declare openly; admit.
54 Neptune, the Roman god of the sea.
56 Claus of Innsbruck, a fictitious sculptor.

After Reading

Making Connections

Shaping Your Response

1. How would you respond if Sonnet 43 had been written for you?

2. If you had to defend Porphyria's lover in a court of law, what would your defense be?

Analyzing the Poems

3. In Sonnet 43, what details imply a former life, and what do they add to the feelings expressed?

4. In your opinion, which lines in "Porphyria's Lover" contain the **climax** or emotional peak of the poem?

5. What can you **infer** about the Duke's feelings for his wife and for Frà Pandolf in "My Last Duchess" and the reasons for those feelings?

6. What sort of "commands" (line 45) do you infer the Duke gave?

Extending the Ideas

7. Suppose that the story of "My Last Duchess" is expanded and about to be made into a film, and you are in charge of setting up a casting call. List the characters' names, their descriptions (some of which you will have to make up), and then suggest suitable actors for the roles.

8. 👁 Which of the speakers in these three poems do you think would be most resistant to **changes** in society or in his or her personal circumstances and which of the speakers would be most accepting? Explain your choices.

Literary Focus: Dramatic Monologue

In a **dramatic monologue** a fictional character reveals a dramatic situation and, often, details of characterization and setting. If a listener is present within the dramatic situation, he or she is silent. Since the speaker may not be entirely objective, readers must usually make inferences about a situation and about the speaker's true feelings.

1. Describe the setting of "Porphyria's Lover."

2. How does the speaker try to justify his murder to himself? Is there an audience or a listener?

3. When the Duke in "My Last Duchess" insists that he is primarily interested in the Count's "fair daughter's self" (line 52), what inference can you draw?

4. What sort of report do you think the listener, the Count's envoy or representative, will deliver to the Count?

Expressing Your Ideas

Writing Choices

Writer's Notebook Update Review the adjectives you jotted down to describe someone you know. Then write a brief description of that person in the form of a poem, using rhyme if you can. Here is an example:

> Blue-eyed, curly-haired, not too proud;
> Anxious, careful, but somewhat loud.

My Husband the Duke Write a **dramatic monologue** from the young Duchess's point of view. Make the setting the room where she is having her portrait painted. The listener could then be Fra Pandolf. The dramatic situation might begin when footsteps are heard. You might consider beginning with this answer to a question from Fra Pandolf: "That's my husband, passing in the hall. . . ."

How He Does It Write an **essay** in which you analyze how Browning employs the technique of dramatic monologue in "My Last Duchess." First define the term. Then describe how the words of the Duke create a sense of place and time, a specific listener, and a dramatic situation. Last, analyze the discrepancy between what the Duke says and what you infer about him and what you infer about what actually happened before these negotiations for a new wife.

Other Options

Thus We Sit Together Now Prepare an **oral reading** of either of Browning's dramatic monologues printed here. For greatest effectiveness, think of them not just as poems to be recited but as scripts to be acted. Consider details of voice, gesture, and facial expression. Rehearse until you are satisfied you're communicating the character and the ideas, and perform your reading for the class.

Looking As If They Were Alive Bring to class a number of library books that have color reproductions of portraits from the past. Divide into small groups and examine some of these pictures together. What can you tell about the subjects from their facial expressions, posture, dress, and pictured possessions? What can you tell about the painters' eras from their subjects and styles of painting? (See also Looking at a Portrait on page 851.) Make each group member responsible for a brief **illustrated report** of the group's conclusions.

How Do I Love Thee? Imagine that someone has just asked you a question like the one that prompts Sonnet 43 (except that you can substitute another emotion if you wish). Create an **artwork,** such as a painting, collage, or paper sculpture, that expresses the extent of your emotion or else "counts the ways," as Elizabeth Barrett Browning does.

Before Reading

A Mad Tea-Party from Alice's Adventures in Wonderland

by Lewis Carroll

Lewis Carroll (Charles Lutwidge Dodgson)
1832–1898

Charles Lutwidge Dodgson was a college lecturer in mathematics and also wrote works on mathematics and logic, booklets of games and puzzles, some light poetry, and a variety of witty pamphlets. He is best known, however, for *Alice's Adventures in Wonderland* (1865), *Through the Looking-Glass* (1872), and *The Hunting of the Snark* (1876), all of which he published under the pen name Lewis Carroll. Though a serious academic, there was in him a vein of childlike playfulness. He once wrote to a friend, a young girl: "I had just time to look into the kitchen and saw your birthday feast getting ready, a nice dish of crusts, bones, pills, cotton-bobbins, and rhubarb and magnesia. 'Now,' I thought, 'she will be happy!'"

Building Background

The Adventures Begin Alice's adventures in Wonderland grow out of Dodgson's affection for a little girl, Alice Liddell, daughter of the Dean of Christ Church. On July 4, 1862, Dodgson and a friend take the three Liddell girls, Alice among them, boating on the Thames. As they row along, Dodgson begins to tell extemporaneous stories of Alice's adventures underground—how Alice dreams that she chases a White Rabbit down a rabbit hole to a world filled with such characters as the Cheshire Cat, the Mad Hatter, the March Hare, the Duchess, the King and Queen of Hearts, and the Mock Turtle. Among Alice's adventures are her discovery that eating from one side of a curious mushroom will make her shrink, and eating from the other side will make her grow. At the end of the day, Alice Liddell asks him to write out the adventures for her. He does, and the book has been enjoyed by young and old alike ever since. Before "A Mad Tea-Party" begins, Alice has just come in sight of the the March Hare's house, which has chimneys shaped like ears and a roof thatched with fur.

Literary Focus

Pun A **pun** is a humorous use of a word that can have different meanings, or of two or more words with the same or nearly the same sound but different meanings. A pun is also called a play on words. The old riddle, "What has four wheels and flies?" uses a pun based on two definitions of *fly,* one meaning "housefly" and the other meaning "to move through the air." Since the answer to the riddle is "a garbage truck," one can see how puns also came to be known as the lowest form of humor. As you read, look for Carroll's clever use of puns.

Writer's Notebook

A World of Dreams Carroll once wrote: "We often dream without the least suspicion of unreality: 'sleep hath its own world,' and it is often as lifelike as the other." Much of "A Mad Tea-Party" is like a dream. In your notebook, jot down some unreal characters and situations one might meet in a dream but not in real life.

▲ The Mad Hatter, the Dormouse, and the March Hare have tea with Alice in *Dreamchild*, a film about the real-life Alice Liddell, for whom Charles Dodgson created *Alice's Adventures in Wonderland*. Does this scene match his description of the mad tea party? Why or why not?

A MAD TEA-PARTY

LEWIS CARROLL

There was a table set out under a tree in front of the house, and the March Hare and the Hatter were having tea at it: a Dormouse[1] was sitting between them, fast asleep, and the other two were using it as a cushion, resting their elbows on it, and talking over

---

1. **dormouse,** not a mouse but a kind of rodent that resembles a squirrel.

THE HATTER'S REMARK SEEMED TO HER TO HAVE NO SORT OF MEANING IN IT, AND YET IT WAS CERTAINLY ENGLISH.

its head. "Very uncomfortable for the Dormouse," thought Alice; "only, as it's asleep, I suppose it doesn't mind."

The table was a large one, but the three were all crowded together at one corner of it. "No room! No room!" they cried out when they saw Alice coming. "There's *plenty* of room!" said Alice indignantly, and she sat down in a large armchair at one end of the table.

"Have some wine," the March Hare said in an encouraging tone.

Alice looked all round the table, but there was nothing on it but tea. "I don't see any wine," she remarked.

"There isn't any," said the March Hare.

"Then it wasn't very civil of you to offer it," said Alice angrily.

"It wasn't very civil of you to sit down without being invited," said the March Hare.

"I didn't know it was *your* table," said Alice; "it's laid for a great many more than three."

"Your hair wants cutting," said the Hatter. He had been looking at Alice for some time with great curiosity, and this was his first speech.

"You should learn not to make personal remarks," Alice said with some severity: "it's very rude."

The Hatter opened his eyes very wide on hearing this; but all he *said* was, "Why is a raven like a writing-desk?"

"Come, we shall have some fun now!" thought Alice. "I'm glad they've begun asking riddles—I believe I can guess that," she added aloud.

"Do you mean that you think you can find out the answer to it?" said the March Hare.

"Exactly so," said Alice.

"Then you should say what you mean," the March Hare went on.

"I do," Alice hastily replied; "at least—at least I mean what I say—that's the same thing, you know."

"Not the same thing a bit!" said the Hatter. "Why, you might just as well say that 'I see what I eat' is the same thing as 'I eat what I see'!"

"You might just as well say," added the March Hare, "that 'I like what I get' is the same thing as 'I get what I like'!"

"You might just as well say," added the Dormouse, who seemed to be talking in his sleep, "that 'I breathe when I sleep' is the same thing as 'I sleep when I breathe'!"

"It *is* the same thing with you," said the Hatter, and here the conversation dropped, and the party sat silent for a minute, while Alice thought over all she could remember about ravens and writing-desks, which wasn't much.

The Hatter was the first to break the silence. "What day of the month is it?" he said, turning to Alice: he had taken his watch out of his pocket, and was looking at it uneasily, shaking it every now and then, and holding it to his ear.

Alice considered a little, and said, "The fourth."

"Two days wrong!" sighed the Hatter. "I told you butter wouldn't suit the works!" he added, looking angrily at the March Hare.

"It was the *best* butter," the March Hare meekly replied.

"Yes, but some crumbs must have got in as well," the Hatter grumbled: "you shouldn't have put it in with the bread-knife."

The March Hare took the watch and looked at it gloomily: then he dipped it into his cup of tea, and looked at it again: but he could think of nothing better to say than his first remark, "It was the *best* butter, you know."

Alice had been looking over his shoulder with some curiosity. "What a funny watch!" she remarked. "It tells the day of the month, and doesn't tell what o'clock it is!"

"Why should it?" muttered the Hatter. "Does *your* watch tell you what year it is?"

"Of course not," Alice replied very readily: "but that's because it stays the same year for such a long time together."

"Which is just the case with *mine*," said the Hatter.

Alice felt dreadfully puzzled. The Hatter's remark seemed to her to have no sort of meaning in it, and yet it was certainly English. "I don't quite understand you," she said as politely as she could.

"The Dormouse is asleep again," said the Hatter, and he poured a little hot tea on to its nose.

The Dormouse shook its head impatiently, and said, without opening its eyes, "Of course, of course: just what I was going to remark myself."

"Have you guessed the riddle yet?" the Hatter said, turning to Alice again.

"No, I give it up," Alice replied: "what's the answer?"

"I haven't the slightest idea," said the Hatter. "Nor I," said the March Hare.

Alice sighed wearily. "I think you might do something better with the time," she said, "than wasting it in asking riddles that have no answers."[2]

"If you knew Time as well as I do," said the Hatter, "you wouldn't talk about wasting *it*. It's *him*."

"I don't know what you mean," said Alice.

"Of course you don't!" the Hatter said, tossing his head contemptuously. "I dare say you never even spoke to Time!"

"Perhaps not," Alice cautiously replied: "but I know I have to beat time when I learn music."

"Ah! that accounts for it," said the Hatter. "He won't stand beating. Now, if you only kept on good terms with him, he'd do almost anything you liked with the clock. For instance, suppose it were nine o'clock in the morning, just

time to begin lessons: you'd only have to whisper a hint to Time, and round goes the clock in a twinkling! Half-past one, time for dinner!"

("I only wish it was," the March Hare said to itself in a whisper.)

"That would be grand, certainly," said Alice thoughtfully: "but then—I shouldn't be hungry for it, you know."

"Not at first, perhaps," said the Hatter: "but you could keep it to half-past one as long as you liked."

"Is that the way *you* manage?" Alice asked.

The Hatter shook his head mournfully. "Not I!" he replied. "We quarreled last March—just before *he* went mad, you know—" (pointing with his teaspoon at the March Hare) "—it was at the great concert given by the Queen of Hearts, and I had to sing

> *'Twinkle, twinkle, little bat!*
> *How I wonder what you're at!'*

You know the song, perhaps?"

"I've heard something like it," said Alice.

"It goes on, you know," the Hatter continued, "in this way—

> *'Up above the world you fly,*
> *Like a teatray in the sky.*
> *Twinkle, twinkle—'"*

Here the Dormouse shook itself, and began singing in its sleep, "*Twinkle, twinkle, twinkle, twinkle—*"and went on so long that they had to pinch it to make it stop.

"Well, I'd hardly finished the first verse," said the Hatter, "when the Queen bawled out, 'He's murdering the time! Off with his head!'"

"How dreadfully savage!" exclaimed Alice.

"And ever since that," the Hatter went on in a mournful tone, "he won't do a thing I ask! It's always six o'clock now."

---

2. **no answers.** Carroll later supplied this answer: "Because it can produce a few notes, though they are very flat; and it is never put with the wrong end in front." Among other popular suggestions is this one: Because they both stand on legs, and should be made to shut up.

A bright idea came into Alice's head. "Is that the reason so many tea-things are put out here?" she asked.

"Yes, that's it," said the Hatter with a sigh: "it's always tea-time, and we've no time to wash the things between whiles."

"Then you keep moving round, I suppose?" said Alice.

"Exactly so," said the Hatter: "as the things get used up."

"But when you come to the beginning again?" Alice ventured to ask.

"Suppose we change the subject," the March Hare interrupted, yawning. "I'm getting tired of this. I vote the young lady tells us a story."

"I'm afraid I don't know one," said Alice, rather alarmed at the proposal.

"Then the Dormouse shall!" they both cried. "Wake up, Dormouse!" And they pinched it on both sides at once.

The Dormouse slowly opened his eyes. "I wasn't asleep," he said in a hoarse, feeble voice: "I heard every word you fellows were saying."

"Tell us a story!" said the March Hare.

"Yes, please do!" pleaded Alice.

"And be quick about it," added the Hatter, "or you'll be asleep again before it's done."

"Once upon a time there were three little sisters," the Dormouse began in a great hurry; "and their names were Elsie, Lacie, and Tillie;[3] and they lived at the bottom of a well—"

"What did they live on?" said Alice, who always took a great interest in questions of eating and drinking.

"They lived on treacle,"[4] said the Dormouse, after thinking a minute or two.

"They couldn't have done that, you know," Alice gently remarked: "they'd have been ill."

"So they were," said the Dormouse; "*very* ill."

Alice tried a little to fancy to herself what such an extraordinary way of living would be like, but it puzzled her too much, so she went on: "But why did they live at the bottom of a well?"

"Take some more tea," the March Hare said to Alice, very earnestly.

"I've had nothing yet," Alice replied in an offended tone, "so I can't take more."

"You mean, you can't take *less*," said the Hatter: "It's very easy to take *more* than nothing."

"Nobody asked *your* opinion," said Alice.

"Who's making personal remarks now?" the Hatter asked triumphantly.

Alice did not quite know what to say to this: so she helped herself to some tea and bread-and-butter, and then turned to the Dormouse, and repeated her question.

"Why did they live at the bottom of a well?"

The Dormouse again took a minute or two to think about it, and then said, "It was a treacle-well."

"There's no such thing!" Alice was beginning very angrily, but the Hatter and the March Hare went "Sh! sh!" and the Dormouse sulkily remarked, "If you can't be civil, you'd better finish the story for yourself."

"No, please go on!" Alice said very humbly: "I won't interrupt you again. I dare say there may be *one*."

"One, indeed!" said the Dormouse indignantly. However, he consented to go on. "And so these three little sisters—they were learning to draw, you know—"

"What did they draw?" said Alice, quite forgetting her promise.

"Treacle," said the Dormouse, without considering at all this time.

"I want a clean cup," interrupted the Hatter: "let's all move one place on."

He moved on as he spoke, and the Dormouse followed him: the March Hare moved into the Dormouse's place, and Alice rather unwillingly took the place of the March

---

3. **Elsie, Lacie, and Tillie,** a reference to the Liddell sisters. *Elsie* stands for L. C. or Lorina C.; *Lacie* is an anagram for Alice; *Tillie* is a form of Matilda, Edith's nickname.
4. **treacle** (trē′kəl), *n.* molasses.

Hare. The Hatter was the only one who got any advantage from the change: and Alice was a good deal worse off than before, as the March Hare had just upset the milk-jug into his plate.

Alice did not wish to offend the Dormouse again, so she began very cautiously: "But I don't understand. Where did they draw the treacle from?"

"You can draw water out of a water-well," said the Hatter: "so I should think you could draw treacle out of a treacle-well—eh, stupid?"

"But they were *in* the well," Alice said to the Dormouse, not choosing to notice this last remark.

"Of course they were," said the Dormouse, "—well in." This answer so confused poor Alice, that she let the Dormouse go on for some time without interrupting it.

"They were learning to draw," the Dormouse went on, yawning and rubbing its eyes, for it was getting very sleepy; "and they drew all manner of things—everything that begins with an M—"

"Why with an M?" said Alice.

"Why not?" said the March Hare.

Alice was silent.

The Dormouse had closed its eyes by this time, and was going off into a doze, but on being pinched by the Hatter, it woke up again with a little shriek, and went on: "—that begins with an M, such as mousetraps, and the moon, and memory, and muchness—you know you say things are 'much of a muchness'[5]—did you ever see such a thing as a drawing of a muchness?"

"Really, now you ask me," said Alice, very much confused, "I don't think—"

"Then you shouldn't talk," said the Hatter.

This piece of rudeness was more than Alice could bear: she got up in great disgust, and walked off: the Dormouse fell asleep instantly, and neither of the others took the least notice of her going, though she looked back once or twice, half hoping that they would call after her: the last time she saw them, they were trying to put the Dormouse into the teapot.

"At any rate I'll never go *there* again!" said Alice as she picked her way through the wood. "It's the stupidest tea-party I ever was at in all my life!"

Just as she said this, she noticed that one of the trees had a door leading right into it. "That's very curious!" she thought. "But everything's curious today. I think I may as well go in at once." And in she went.

Once more she found herself in the long hall, and close to the little glass table. "Now, I'll manage better this time," she said to herself, and began by taking the little golden key, and unlocking the door that led into the garden. Then she set to work nibbling at the mushroom (she had kept a piece of it in her pocket) till she was about a foot high: then she walked down the little passage: and *then* she found herself at last in the beautiful garden, among the bright flowerbeds and the cool fountains.

"IT'S THE STUPIDEST TEA-PARTY I EVER WAS AT IN ALL MY LIFE!"

---

5. **much of a muchness.** This British phrase means "things are pretty much the same."

After Reading

Making Connections

Shaping Your
Response

1. How mad is the tea-party? Devise a mad scale to measure its madness. Go mad with it.

2. Who is the craziest character? the wittiest character?

Analyzing
the Novel Excerpt

3. Why isn't "I like what I get" the same as "I get what I like" when both sentences have the same words?

4. Alice is puzzled by the fact that she doesn't understand a remark by the Hatter even though it is spoken in English. What might account for her failure to understand?

5. What can you conclude about the **author's purpose** in including all the passages having to do with language, such as Alice's confusion about "drawing treacle"?

Extending the Ideas

6. Have you ever listened to or taken part in a conversation during which you felt as confused as Alice? Explain.

7. ☺ Dreams are often characterized by strange **changes** in characters, settings—even cultural conditions. What are some possible explanations for the fact that people so often dream about change?

Literary Focus: Pun

A **pun** is the humorous use of a word that can have different meanings, or of two or more words with the same or nearly the same sound but different meanings.

1. Alice says she has to "beat time" when she learns music. What does the Hatter think she means?

2. What is the pun on the word *draw*?

Vocabulary Study

Puns are based on **homophones** like *eight* and *ate,* which sound the same but are spelled differently, and **homonyms** like *mail* meaning "letters" and *mail* meaning "armor." Each item below contains two definitions. One of the words defined is shown. You are to provide the other word, which will sometimes have the same spelling and sometimes a different spelling as the word shown.

1. "a long cry of grief or pain" and "a ridge in the weave of corduroy": _____/wale

2. "the first whole number" and "the past tense of *win*": one/_____

3. "a short sleep" and "the short woolly threads on the surface of cloth": _____/nap

4. "the sweet fruit of a palm" and "a particular day, month, or year": date/_____

5. "a female sheep" and "a singular or plural pronoun": ewe/_____

6. "things arranged in a straight line" and "use oars to move a boat": _____/row

7. "vein of metal ore" and "a burden": lode/_____

8. "what we breathe" and "a person who inherits property": _____/heir

9. "time between evening and morning" and "a medieval man pledged to do good deeds": night/_____

10. "from a higher to a lower place" and "soft feathers": _____/down

The first letters in each pair combine to spell a place. What is it?

Expressing Your Ideas

Writing Choices

Writer's Notebook Update Use your notes on unreal characters and situations to write a brief scene that might take place in Wonderland or some other fantastic setting.

Riddle Me This Try your hand at writing a few **riddles** based on words in the Vocabulary Study or on other homographs or homophones. Here is an example:

Q. Why did Queen Victoria want to move to sunny Italy?
A. She was tired of the reign.

Alice's Illustrator John Tenniel was the first artist to illustrate Alice's adventures, and his illustrations became so widely known that it is almost impossible to think of Carroll's characters without recalling Tenniel's artwork. Research Tenniel's life and his troubles with Carroll and write a **feature story** that could be printed on the anniversary of Carroll's or Tenniel's birth.

Other Options

More Curious Adventures How are you at storytelling? Read at least one other chapter from *Alice's Adventures in Wonderland* or *Through the Looking Glass* and **tell the story** for the rest of the class.

Act Out With a group, prepare a **reader's theater performance** of "A Mad Tea-Party." Reader's theater requires no costumes or props, and the actors work with scripts. Actors may stand or be seated, and they act with a minimum of physical movement. If you wish, use a narrator to read descriptions; for example, the first sentences of paragraphs 1 and 2 on pages 547–548.

Before Reading

Dover Beach

by Matthew Arnold

Matthew Arnold
1822–1888

Matthew Arnold felt intensely the confusion of the modern world. "Everything is against one," he wrote in 1849. He tried to write poetry that would "not only . . . interest, but also . . . inspirit and rejoice the reader." His first volume, *The Strayed Reveller,* was published in 1849. To support himself and his family he worked as an inspector of private schools for poor children—an exhausting job, which required extensive travel—for thirty-five years. The job did permit Arnold direct involvement in some of the social problems of his day, however, and more and more he turned to writing prose. His range expanded from essays on literature to books on theology, education, and political issues.

Building Background

Channel Watch The town of Dover, sheltered by the towering chalk cliffs of the English south coast, lies within sight of France. For centuries it has served as a port for travelers bound across the English Channel for the continent. Arnold and his wife Fanny Lucy visited Dover twice in 1851: in June just after their wedding and in October on their way to a continental vacation. He almost certainly wrote "Dover Beach" during this period, and he clearly poured into this relatively short poem, which seems to be addressed to his wife, the ideas and feelings of the moment.

Literary Focus

Connotation/Denotation Connotation refers to the emotional associations surrounding a word, as opposed to the word's literal meaning, or **denotation.** A connotation may be personal, or it may have universal associations. The denotation of *sea,* for example, is "a great body of salt water." The connotations, however, may well depend on one's experience with the sea. Copy this chart and complete it with words and phrases you think each person might associate with the sea. Add other people to the chart if you can think of some. Look for the speaker's connotations of various key words in "Dover Beach," which help to enrich the meaning of the poem.

sea	
Denotation	**Connotations**
a great body of salt water	1. sailor
	2. fisherman
	3. surfer

Writer's Notebook

What is your impression of the Victorian era so far? Jot down a few comments based on your reading in this part.

554 UNIT SIX: THE VICTORIANS

DOVER BEACH

MATTHEW ARNOLD

Fingall's Cave, Island of Staffa, Scotland (Thomas Moran, 1884–5) captures conditions of weather and light. What elements give it an almost cinematic quality?

The sea is calm tonight,
The tide is full, the moon lies fair
Upon the straits; on the French coast the light
Gleams and is gone; the cliffs of England stand,
5 Glimmering and vast, out in the tranquil bay,
Come to the window, sweet is the night air!

Only, from the long line of spray
Where the sea meets the moon-blanched land,
Listen! you hear the grating roar
10 Of pebbles which the waves draw back, and fling,
At their return, up the high strand,
Begin, and cease, and then again begin,
With tremulous cadence slow, and bring
The eternal note of sadness in.

15 Sophocles long ago
Heard it on the Aegean, and it brought
Into his mind the turbid ebb and flow
Of human misery; we
Find also in the sound a thought,
20 Hearing it by this distant northern sea.

The Sea of Faith
Was once, too, at the full, and round earth's shore
Lay like the folds of a bright girdle furled.
But now I only hear
25 Its melancholy, long, withdrawing roar,
Retreating, to the breath
Of the night wind, down the vast edges drear
And naked shingles of the world.

Ah, love, let us be true
30 To one another! for the world, which seems
To lie before us like a land of dreams,
So various, so beautiful, so new,
Hath really neither joy, nor love, nor light,
Nor certitude, nor peace, nor help for pain;
35 And we are here as on a darkling plain
Swept with confused alarms of struggle and flight,
Where ignorant armies clash by night.

13 tremulous (trem′yə ləs), *adj.* quivering.
13 cadence (kād′ns), *n.* rhythm.
15 Sophocles (sof′ə klēz′), a Greek dramatist (495?–406? B.C.)
16 Aegean (i jē′ən), a sea between Greece and Turkey.
17 turbid (tėr′bid), *adj.* confused; disordered.

23 girdle (gėr′dl), *n.* a garment that encircles, or girds, the body.

27 drear (drir), *adj.* gloomy; sad; sorrowful.
28 shingle, pebble beach.

34 certitude (sėr′tə tyüd), *n.* certainty; sureness.

After Reading

Making Connections

Shaping Your Response

1. Do you think the speaker's solution (in lines 29–30) to life in a world that only *seems* beautiful and new is a good one?

Analyzing the Poem

2. Trace the way in which Arnold develops his **imagery** of the sea to lead finally to a philosophical conclusion.

3. Explain the ways in which both Sophocles and the modern speaker find **symbolism** in the ocean's roar. Does it mean the same to both or something different?

4. Summarize the speaker's vision of the human condition.

5. ☝️ What major **change** has occurred in the speaker's world? How does he feel about it?

Extending the Ideas

6. Does Arnold's use of the word *ignorant* to describe armies seem appropriate in the 1900s? Why or why not?

Literary Focus: Connotation/Denotation

Connotation is the personal or emotional association surrounding a word, as opposed to a word's literal meaning or **denotation.**

1. What connotation does the "grating roar of pebbles" have for the speaker?

2. What does the "ebb and flow" of the tide connote in the third stanza?

3. Choose another word from the poem and explain its denotation and connotation.

Vocabulary Study

Write the letter of the situation that best demonstrates the meaning of the numbered word.

1. tremulous
   a. a math teacher explaining an algebra problem
   b. a small child explaining that she is lost
   c. a coach explaining how to hold a golf club

2. cadence
   a. a band marching briskly down the street
   b. clouds drifting overhead
   c. the flight of a butterfly

3. drear
   a. an unexpected present
   b. a dark, gloomy day
   c. a get-well card from a friend

4. certitude

    a. the rising of the sun

    b. a phone call from your boyfriend or girlfriend

    c. rain on graduation day

5. turbid

    a. gate crashers at a rock concert

    b. actors on-stage taking a bow

    c. a person operating a construction crane

Expressing Your Ideas

Writing Choices

Writer's Notebook Update Look back at the impressions of the Victorian era that you wrote in your notebook. Have your impressions changed or grown after reading "Dover Beach"? If so, jot down some different or additional impressions.

Probing Symbolism The "Sea of Faith" (line 21) in Arnold's poem can have several meanings. In a **paragraph,** explain what you think it means to Arnold as expressed in this poem and what it means to you.

Let Us Be True Arnold apparently addressed "Dover Beach" to his new wife, Fanny Lucy. Write a **personal letter** to your love or to someone who means a great deal to you. In your letter describe a scene from nature or a scene from your everyday surroundings and then explain what that scene suggests to you about how you should live your life.

Other Options

The Way We Are The struggle to understand can affect anyone at any age, but it may show most strongly when people try to communicate across generations. Choose an aspect of teenage life, such as dating, hanging out, after school jobs, and so on. Write and illustrate a **picture book** appropriate for first-grade children about how teenagers behave and why, focusing on the aspect you have chosen. Share your book with some children.

Welcome to My World Arnold chose a beach at night as a point of departure for his thoughts about society and the world of his time. Which images would best express the world of your time? Prepare a **videotape** showing scenes from your school, your neighborhood, your community, or the surrounding countryside that you feel are typical examples of your world and that express the way you feel about it.

The Struggle to Understand

The Crystal Palace

A Visit to

THE GREAT EXHIBITION

History Connection

Promptly at noon on May 1, 1851, Queen Victoria and her husband Prince Albert arrived at the mammoth Crystal Palace in London's Hyde Park to open the "Great Exhibition of the Works of Industry of All Nations"—the first world's fair. In this section are her account of the opening day as well as images of the Crystal Palace and its contents.

QUEEN VICTORIA'S JOURNAL

May 1, 1851 This day is one of the greatest and most glorious days of our lives, with which to my pride and joy, the name of my dearly beloved Alfred is for ever associated! It is a day which makes my heart swell with thankfulness. We began the day with tenderest greetings and congratulations on the birth of our dear little Arthur. He was brought in at breakfast and looked beautiful with blue ribbon on his frock. Mama and Victor were there, as well as all the children and our dear guests. Our little gifts of toys were added to by ones from the P[rin]ce and P[rin]cess [of Prussia].

The Park presented a wonderful spectacle, crowds streaming through it,—carriages and troops passing, quite like the Coronation, and for *me*, the same anxiety. The day was bright and all bustle and excitement. At 1/2 p. 11 the whole procession in 9 State carriages was set in motion. Vicky and Bertie were in our carriage (the other children and Vivi did not go).

Vicky was dressed in lace over white satin, with small wreath of pink wild roses in her hair, and looked very nice. Bertie was in full Highland dress. The Green Park and Hyde Park were one mass of densely crowded human beings, in the highest good humor and most enthusiastic. I never saw Hyde Park look as it did, being filled with crowds as far as the eye could reach. A little rain fell, just as we started, but before we neared the Crystal Palace, the sun shone and gleamed upon the gigantic edifice, upon which the flags of every nation were flying. We drove up Rotten Row and got out of our carriages at the entrance on that side. The glimpse, through the iron gates of the Transept, the waving palms and flowers, the myriads of people filling the galleries and seats around, together with the flourish of trumpets as we entered the building, gave a sensation I shall never forget, and I felt much moved. We went for a moment into a little room where we left our cloaks and found Mama and Mary. Outside, all the princes were standing. In a few seconds we proceeded, Albert leading me, having Vicky at his hand and Bertie holding mine. The sight as we came to the

LIVING TREES AND A 27-FOOT CUT-GLASS FOUNTAIN DECORATED THE ENTRANCE TO THE CRYSTAL PALACE.

center where the steps and chair (on which I did *not* sit) was placed, facing the beautiful crystal fountain was magic and impressive. The tremendous cheering, the joy expressed in every face, the vastness of the building, with all its decoration and exhibits, the sound of the organ (with 200 instruments and 600 voices, which seemed nothing) and my beloved husband, the creator of this peace festival "uniting the industry and art of all nations of the earth," all this was indeed moving, and a day to live forever. God bless my dearest Albert, and my dear country, which has shown itself so great to-day. One felt so grateful to the great God, whose blessing seemed to pervade the whole undertaking. After the National Anthem had been sung, Albert left my side and at the head of the Commissioners,—a curious assemblage of political and distinguished men—read the report to me, which is a long one, and I read a short answer. After this the Archbishop of Canterbury offered up a short and appropriate prayer, followed by the singing of Handel's "Hallelujah Chorus," during which time the Chinese Mandarin came forward and made his

obeisance. This concluded, the Procession of great length began, which was beautifully arranged, the prescribed order being exactly adhered to. The Nave was full of people, which had not been intended, and deafening cheers and waving of handkerchiefs continued the whole time of our long walk from one end of the long building to the other. Every face was bright and smiling, and many had tears in their eyes. Many Frenchmen called out "Vive la Reine." One could, of course, see nothing but what was high up in the Nave, and nothing in the Courts. The organs were but little heard, but the Military Band at one end had a very fine effect, playing the march from *Athalie* as we passed along. The old Duke of Wellington and L[or]d. Anglesey walked arm in arm, which was a touching sight. I saw many acquaintances amongst those present. We returned to our place and Albert told L[or]d. Breadalbane to declare the Exhibition to be opened, which he did in a loud voice saying "Her Majesty commands me to declare this Exhibition open," when there was a flourish of trumpets, followed by immense cheering. We then made our bow and left.

THIS VIEW OF THE MAIN AVENUE OF THE CRYSTAL PALACE SHOWS HOW THE EXHIBITS WERE ORGANIZED.

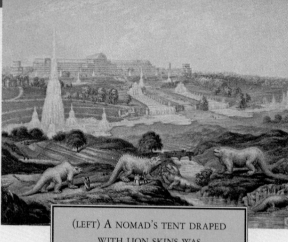

(LEFT) A NOMAD'S TENT DRAPED WITH LION SKINS WAS SURROUNDED BY A TUNISIAN BAZAAR. ALTHOUGH THE EXOTIC GOODS DISPLAYED THERE WERE NOT SUPPOSED TO BE SOLD, VISITORS OFTEN BOUGHT THEM ILLEGALLY.

(ABOVE) AFTER THE GREAT EXHIBITION CLOSED IN 1852, THE CRYSTAL PALACE AND ITS CONTENTS WERE MOVED TO A PARK AT SYDENHAM IN SOUTHEAST LONDON (WHERE IT REMAINED UNTIL DESTROYED BY A FIRE IN 1936). AMONG THE EXHIBITS ON ITS GROUNDS WERE THE FIRST MODELS OF DINOSAURS.

(BELOW) AMONG THE EXHIBITS OF BRITISH WORKMAN-SHIP WERE AN ELABORATE GAS CHANDELIER AND A SPORTSMAN'S KNIFE WITH 80 BLADES. FROM CANADA CAME INTRICATELY CARVED FURNITURE LIKE THIS DOUBLE ARMCHAIR.

Responding

1. What kind of person does Victoria's account of her visit to the Great Exhibition reveal her to be?

2. Which of these exhibits do you think you would have most enjoyed visiting?

3. The official goal of the Great Exhibition was to promote industry and world peace. What other purposes would such an event serve?

THE GREAT EXHIBITION

A STUFFED INDIAN ELEPHANT WAS BORROWED FROM A MUSEUM TO DISPLAY AN ELABORATE GOLD AND SILVER HOWDAH WITH A FRINGED AWNING.

Writing Workshop

What's Your Attitude?

Assignment In Tennyson's "The Lady of Shalott" and "Ulysses," the title characters live in two very different worlds—one of magic, one of legend; and they live their lives in very different ways. Compare and contrast what their actions and words tell you of their attitudes toward how life ought to be lived, and decide which comes closer to your own attitude.

WRITER'S BLUEPRINT

Product	A comparison/contrast essay
Purpose	To explore attitudes about how to live
Audience	People who are not familiar with the literature
Specs	As the writer of a successful essay, you should:

❑ Begin by introducing your readers to the two characters and the settings for the poems. Give your readers enough background to enable them to follow your train of thought.

❑ Go on to discuss what both characters' actions and words tell you about their attitudes on how to live life. Are the characters outgoing and adventurous, or repressed and cautious?

❑ Include a discussion of how the unique worlds the characters inhabit influence those attitudes. Do they feel comfortable in their worlds? Are they free to reach out and meet new challenges?

❑ Present your conclusions in a clear compare-and-contrast format. Use specific details and quotes from the poems to support your conclusions.

❑ End by explaining which character's attitude comes closer to your own attitude about how to live life, and why.

❑ Follow the rules of grammar, usage, spelling, and mechanics. Avoid run-on sentences.

Revisit the poems. Study each character and the world he or she inhabits. What can you find out about the characters' attitudes toward living life? Make notes in a chart like the one shown.

Ulysses

Things Character Does and Says	What This Reveals About the Character's Attitude	Setting: What His World Is Like	How This Might Influence the Character's Attitude
"I cannot rest from travel"		islands, stormy seas	

LITERARY SOURCE
"I cannot rest from travel: I will drink
Life to the lees: all times I have enjoyed
Greatly, have suffered greatly, both with those
That loved me, and alone; on shore, and when
Through scudding drifts the rainy Hyades
Vexed the dim sea: . . . ."
from "Ulysses" by Alfred, Lord Tennyson

Try a quickwrite. Based on your charts, imagine the kind of advice Ulysses and the Lady of Shalott would offer students today about how to live life. Quickwrite two brief monologues in which each character gives advice. Use modern American speech if you wish.

Discuss your ideas. With a partner, discuss the characters' views on how life should be lived. Which character's viewpoint comes closer to your own? Jot down some notes about your discussion to use when you make your writing plan.

OR . . .
Work with a partner to improvise a dialogue between the two characters in which they argue about how one should approach life. Tape-record your dialogue.

Make a writing plan. Use an outline like this one.

- **Introduction** (Introduce characters and settings)
  First character and setting
  Second character and setting
- **Body** (Compare and contrast attitudes of characters and influence of settings, including details and quotes from the poems)
  First character
  —words and actions
  —influence of setting
  Second character
  —words and actions
  —influence of setting
- **Conclusion** (Compare and contrast attitudes)
  Similarities
  Differences
  Which attitude is closer to mine and why

OR . . .
Do a point-by-point comparison of the subjects and their attitudes about how life should be lived.

2 DRAFTING

As you draft, remember that your primary objective is to show the similarities and differences between the characters' attitudes. The following tips may help you get started:

- Begin your essay with a dramatic firsthand description of the two characters in their worlds, as if you, the writer, were there watching them. You might even imagine the two characters side by side in their settings, like a split-screen shot in a movie, and move back and forth between the two characters as you introduce them.

- Use ideas from the monologue or dialogue material you created in "Try a quickwrite" when you write your conclusion.

3 REVISING

Ask a partner for comments on your draft before you revise it.

✔ Have I given readers unfamiliar with the poems enough information to be able to follow my train of thought?

✔ Have I used specific details and quotes from the poems to support my conclusions?

✔ Do I state comparisons and contrasts clearly?

Revising Strategy

Guiding the Reader

Words or phrases that set up compare-and-contrast statements act as signals, guiding the reader through the argument. Consider using some of these signal words and phrases as you revise.

To signal similarities: similarly, in much the same way, just as, like, alike, likewise, same, along the same lines, by comparison

To signal differences: however, as opposed to, in contrast, inversely, but, instead of, on the other hand, unlike, while, by contrast

Notice how comparison-contrast signals were added to the student model that follows.

In contrast to the Lady of Shalott,   *,not by walls.*

My view on life is like Ulysses'. He is held in by a duty.

He does not give into his restrictions, though. He takes steps to break

free of his duty by giving the kingdom to his son.

STUDENT
MODEL

Ask a partner to review your revised draft before you edit. When you edit, look for mistakes in grammar, usage, spelling, and mechanics. Look closely for errors with run-on sentences.

Editing Strategy

Avoiding Run-on Sentences

Proofread your essay for any run-on sentences. Run-on sentences are two or more independent clauses strung together with little or no punctuation. If the clauses are loosely related, separate them into different sentences:

FOR REFERENCE
You'll find more guidelines for avoiding run-on sentences in the Language and Grammar Handbook in the back of this book.

Run-on   Ulysses is an adventurous man Ithaca is his true home, the place he loves more than all the others.

Corrected   Ulysses is an adventurous man. Ithaca is his true home, the place he loves more than all the others.

If the clauses are closely related, join them with a comma and coordinating conjunction:

Run-on   Everything for which she had lived before—her weaving, her mirror—was gone she could have begun anew.

Corrected   Everything for which she had lived before—her weaving, her mirror—was gone, but she could have begun anew.

5 PRESENTING

Consider these ideas for presenting your essay:

- Read each other's essays in a small groups. Then pick the essay that most closely matches your attitude and explain why.

- Work with a group of classmates to write and perform monologues and dialogues based on your essays.

- Save this essay. Years from now you can look back to see how your attitudes about living life have developed over time.

6 LOOKING BACK

Self-evaluate. What grade would *you* give your paper? Look back at the Writer's Blueprint and give your paper a score for each separate item, from 6 (superior) to 1 (inadequate).

Reflect. Think about what you have learned from doing this comparison/contrast essay as you write answers to these questions.

✔ What thoughts prompted by this assignment will help you plan the next few years of your life?

✔ Based on comments from peers and your own assessment, which do you think was your greatest area of strength in this paper: being clear, being insightful, or being technically correct? Which area were you weakest in? How could you improve in your next paper?

For Your Working Portfolio Add your essay and your reflection responses to your working portfolio.

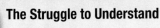

Beyond Print

Multimedia Presentations

Step up to the Information Age: an age in which you can use modern technology—computers, VCRs, CD-ROMs, and programs such as HyperCard—to energize traditional speeches and transform them into exciting media events. Whenever you use a combination of media to communicate to an audience, you are making a multimedia presentation. This includes speeches, posters, slides, video, projected images, graphs, computers, recordings, or even skits.

The computer is a powerful tool in producing any multimedia presentation. You can hook up the computer to a projection unit in order to use the program during an oral presentation and provide animation, special effects, sound, and video. You might engage your audience with an interactive program in which viewers manipulate the type and order of information they receive by clicking a button.

Since each piece of media you add makes the presentation more complex, be thoughtful and organized in preparing your materials. Save only the most important information for posters or computer screens. Make sure the type size is legible for your audience. Avoid materials that are cluttered or confusing.

Here are some hints for using multimedia in oral presentations.

- Use pictures and music that will supplement the information, not distract the audience.

- Use large type (for readability) and important heads (for emphasis) in projections. Present additional details orally or in handouts.

- Apply your writing skills to ensure concise, clear, and correctly spelled text.

- Plan, organize, and practice presenting your material.

- Project your voice so that everyone can hear.

Activity Option

Prepare a multimedia presentation based on a selection, an author, or a theme related to the selections in this part. Prepare a speech; then add a simple graphic, such as a poster, graph, transparency, or computer image, along with music or special sound effects.

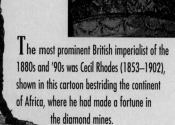

In his painting *The Old Bedford* (1897–98), British painter Walter Sickert depicts an audience at a music-hall. Both his subject matter and technique show the influence of French Impressionism.

HISTORICAL OVERVIEW

By 1880 opinion was strongly divided between imperialists, who advocated expanding the British empire, and those who saw this as dangerous. There was also conflict over England's domestic politics. The British working class was still overworked, underpaid, poorly fed, clothed, housed, and educated. Radical intellectuals such Bernard Shaw saw socialism as a cure for these ills. At the same time, British suffragettes were waging a campaign to gain women the vote. English culture expressed a less confident outlook than it had at the height of the Victorian era. Thomas Hardy's pessimistic rural novels and H. G. Wells's scientific fantasies disturbed many readers. There were also disturbing trends in the visual arts, such as impressionism, with its experimental approach to rendering the effects of light.

The most prominent British imperialist of the 1880s and '90s was Cecil Rhodes (1853–1902), shown in this cartoon bestriding the continent of Africa, where he had made a fortune in the diamond mines.

The most famous literary periodical of the 1890s was *The Yellow Book,* which was notorious for the decadent art and literature that appeared in it.

Mrs. Emmeline Pankhurst (1858–1928), leader of the British women's suffrage movement, appears third from the left in this photograph of a rally during an election campaign in 1907.

The End of an Era

Bearing a variety of socialist slogans, *Garland for May Day 1895—Dedicated to the Workers* was created by British artist Walter Crane (1845–1915).

Part Two

Hope and Despair

Some Victorians hoped that every problem had a solution; others despaired that their religious or cultural beliefs might not be valid after all.

Multicultural Connection Culture has a great influence on the **perspective** that a person brings to viewing the basic and universal aspects of life.

Before Reading

The Darkling Thrush
The Man He Killed
"Ah, Are You Digging on My Grave?" by Thomas Hardy

Thomas Hardy
1840–1928

After beginning a career in church architecture, Thomas Hardy tried writing poetry. When he could not get his poems published, he switched to the more profitable writing of fiction. After his first major success, *Far From the Madding Crowd* (1874), came *The Return of the Native* (1878), *The Mayor of Casterbridge* (1885), and *Tess of the D'Urbervilles* (1891) — all about the farmers and working-class people of his boyhood area, the Dorset countryside. Often criticized for rejecting middle-class moral values, Hardy nonetheless gained popularity. However, in 1895 *Jude the Obscure* was attacked so harshly that Hardy decided to give up writing novels and return to poetry. In 1898, at age 58, he published his first volume of poetry. Over the next 29 years Hardy completed over 900 lyrics.

Building Background

"A Poet's Power to Feel . . ." Poet and critic Mark Van Doren explains the special essence of Hardy's poetry: "A poet's power to feel is best proved in the stories he tells, provided he can tell stories. Hardy could; that was where his genius lay . . . Hardy's stories are little melodramas, sensational, unrelenting, and if need be mournful beyond bearing, as the great ballads are." Doubtless it was Hardy's many years of melodramatic storytelling in his novels that influenced the stories of his poetry. In both novels and poetry Hardy was able to take the small, almost insignificant, events of ordinary daily life, infuse them with details and emotion, and thereby relate them not only to the individual experience but to the whole of human experience.

Literary Focus

Assonance The repetition of similar vowel sounds followed by different consonant sounds in stressed words or syllables is called **assonance.** It is often used instead of rhyme. *Hate / great* is an example of rhyme; *hate / grade* is an example of assonance. In ". . . that hoard, and sleep, and feed, and know not me," from Tennyson's "Ulysses," the words *sleep, feed,* and *me* are assonant. As you read Hardy's poems, look for examples of assonance.

Writer's Notebook

War Words When you think of war, what descriptive words come to your mind? Jot down a list of five to ten words and phrases to describe war.

The Darkling Thrush

Thomas Hardy

I leaned upon a coppice[1] gate
    When Frost was specter[2]-gray,
And winter's dregs made desolate
    The weakening eye of day.
5 The tangled bine-stems[3] scored the sky
    Like strings of broken lyres,
And all mankind that haunted nigh
    Had sought their household fires.

The land's sharp features seemed to be
10   The Century's corpse outleant,[4]
His crypt[5] the cloudy canopy,[6]
    The wind his death-lament.
The ancient pulse of germ and birth
    Was shrunken hard and dry,
15 And every spirit upon earth
    Seemed fervorless[7] as I.

At once a voice arose among
    The bleak twigs overhead
In a full-hearted evensong
20   Of joy illimited;
An agèd thrush, frail, gaunt, and small,

In blast-beruffled plume,
Had chosen thus to fling his soul
    Upon the growing gloom.

25 So little cause for carolings
    Of such ecstatic[8] sound
Was written on terrestrial[9] things
    Afar or nigh around,
That I could think there trembled through
30   His happy good-night air
Some blessèd Hope, whereof he knew
    And I was unaware.

---

darkling (därk′ling), *adj.* dim; obscure.
1. **coppice** (kop′is), *n.* a thicket of small trees or shrubs.
2. **specter** (spek′tər) **-gray,** ghost-gray.
3. **bine-stems,** climbing vines.
4. **outleant** (out′lent′), *adj.* laid out.
5. **crypt** (kript), *n.* burial vault.
6. **canopy** (kan′ə pē), *n.* rooflike covering.
7. **fervorless** (fĕr′vər lis), *adj.* emotionless.
8. **ecstatic** (ek stat′ik), *adj.* full of joy.
9. **terrestrial** (tə res′trē əl), *adj.* earthly.

This work by Samuel Palmer, entitled *A Hilly Scene*, dates to about 1826. What is the mood of this work? How does the artist's choice of detail help to create that mood? ➤

The Man He Killed

Thomas Hardy

"Had he and I but met
   By some old ancient inn,
We should have sat us down to wet
   Right many a nipperkin![1]

5   "But ranged as infantry
   And staring face to face,
I shot at him as he at me,
   And killed him in his place.

"I shot him dead because—
10   Because he was my foe,
Just so: my foe of course he was;
   That's clear enough; although

"He thought he'd 'list,[2] perhaps,
   Off-hand like—just as I—
15 Was out of work—had sold his traps[3]—
   No other reason why.

"Yes; quaint and curious war is!
   You shoot a fellow down
You'd treat if met where any bar is,
20   Or help to half-a-crown."[4]

---

1. **to wet . . . nipperkin,** to drink many half-pints of ale.
2. **'list,** enlist, as in the army.
3. **traps,** personal belongings.
4. **half-a-crown,** an English coin worth about sixty
   cents at the time of the poem, though far more in
   purchasing power.

"Ah, Are You Digging on My Grave?"

Thomas Hardy

"Ah, are you digging on my grave
    My loved one?—planting rue?"[1]
"No: yesterday he went to wed
One of the brightest wealth has bred.
5 'It cannot hurt her now,' he said,
    'That I should not be true.' "

"Then who is digging on my grave?
    My nearest dearest kin?"
"Ah, no: they sit and think, 'What use!
10 What good will planting flowers produce?
No tendance[2] of her mound can loose
    Her spirit from Death's gin.' "[3]

"But some one digs upon my grave?
    My enemy?—prodding sly?"
15 "Nay: when she heard you had passed the
      Gate
That shuts on all flesh soon or late,
She thought you no more worth her hate,
    And cares not where you lie."

"Then, who is digging on my grave?
20   Say—since I have not guessed!"

"O it is I, my mistress dear,
Your little dog, who still lives near,
And much I hope my movements here
    Have not disturbed your rest?"

25 "Ah, yes! *You* dig upon my grave . . .
    Why flashed it not on me
That one true heart was left behind!
What feeling do we ever find
To equal among human kind
30   A dog's fidelity!"[4]

"Mistress, I dug upon your grave
    To bury a bone, in case
I should be hungry near this spot
When passing on my daily trot.
35 I am sorry, but I quite forgot
    It was your resting-place."

---

1. **rue** (rü), *n.* a woody herb, often used as a symbol of sorrow or regret.
2. **tendance** (ten′dəns), *n.* attention; care.
3. **gin** (jin), *n.* snare or trap.
4. **fidelity** (fə del′ə tē), *n.* faithfulness.

After Reading

Making Connections

Shaping Your Response

1. In which of the three poems do you believe Hardy tells the most touching story? Explain your response.

Analyzing the Poems

2. How would you describe the **mood** in "The Darkling Thrush"? Cite some phrases that contribute to that mood.

3. What **metaphor** dominates the second stanza?

4. What influence does the thrush seem to have on the speaker? Why?

5. ☙ In "The Man He Killed" what influence does the speaker's occupation and social class seem to have on his **perspective?**

6. What does the punctuation of stanzas 3 and 4 suggest about the speaker's thoughts?

7. In "Ah, Are You Digging on My Grave?" how do you interpret the guesses the speaker makes about who is digging on her grave and the order in which she makes them?

8. What **main idea** is suggested by the answers the speaker gets?

9. Explain what you find **ironic** about the last stanza?

Extending the Ideas

10. Compare Hardy's natural **settings** with those in the poems of Wordsworth and Coleridge.

Literary Focus: Assonance

Assonance, a kind of near rhyme, is the repetition of similar vowel sounds followed by different consonant sounds in stressed words or syllables. Hardy uses both rhyme and assonance in these poems to achieve strong, emphatic sounds. Find at least five examples of assonance in "A Darkling Thrush."

Vocabulary Study

Write the letter of the best answer for each question.

1. Who would display *ecstatic* behavior?

   a. a losing team   **b.** a crying baby
   c. an engaged couple   **d.** a comforting doctor

2. If you had just seen a *specter,* what would you have been looking at?

   a. a bird   **b.** a ghost
   c. a teacher   **d.** a soldier

3. *Fidelity* is a characteristic that might describe which of these?

   a. a late employee   **b.** a jilted lover
   c. a long-time pet   **d.** a maid who has just been fired

4. The animal was described as a *terrestrial* being. Where would it live?

   a. on the land   **b.** in the sea
   c. in the heavens   **d.** in trees

5. Where would you be most likely to find a *crypt*?

   a. on a beach   **b.** in an apartment building
   c. in a restaurant   **d.** in a church

Expressing Your Ideas

Writing Choices

Writer's Notebook Update Compare your list of adjectives with Hardy's choice of "quaint and curious" in "The Man He Killed." In a brief paragraph compare and contrast the attitudes implied by your words and Hardy's words.

A Century Ends Hardy's "The Darkling Thrush" is an *elegy,* a solemn, reflective poem, usually about death. In this poem he laments the end of the nineteenth century, the 1800s. Write an **analytic essay** in which you compare and contrast the reactions of the speaker and the thrush to the century's end.

A Different View of the World W. H. Auden said that Thomas Hardy wrote with a "hawk's vision, his way of looking at life from a very great height." If you could choose to look at life from a **perspective** different from your own, what perspective would you choose and why? Defend your choice in a **personal journal entry.**

Other Options

A Dialogue Between Living and Dead Working with a classmate, prepare a **dialogue** between two characters—both alive, both dead, or one alive and one dead. In your dialogue one speaker should reveal an insight or "truth" to the other speaker. That revelation could be ironic (as in "Ah, Are You Digging on My Grave?") or humorous, or serious, or whatever you like. Perform your dialogue for your class.

War Everywhere In "The Man He Killed" Hardy presents a touching picture which takes war from the general to the specific, to two human beings confronting each other. Create an **artistic treatment of confrontation** involving two soldiers, a soldier and a civilian, two civilians, a protester and a politician, and so on. War is an especially effective background for confrontation, but, of course, confrontation is not confined to wartime.

Fling Your Soul to the World Hardy's aged thrush, although frail, gaunt, and small, "flings his soul" to the world in ecstatic sound. Create a **musical composition** in which you fling your soul to the world. Your composition can be just music, or it can be words and music both. Perform your composition for your class, perhaps as part of a musical program with other similar compositions.

Before Reading

Pied Beauty
Spring and Fall: To a Young Child by Gerard Manley Hopkins

Gerard Manley Hopkins
1844–1889

Eldest of nine children in a family devoted to the Church of England, Gerard Manley Hopkins joined the Roman Catholic Church at age 22. When he began to train for the priesthood in the Jesuit order, he dramatically and symbolically burned all of his youthful poems. After his ordination in 1877 Hopkins served as a parish priest and as a teacher of Classical languages. In the last years of his life Hopkins became haunted by the suicides of several Oxford friends and overwhelmed by a "constant, crippling" melancholy which, he confessed, "is much like madness." He died in an outbreak of typhoid fever in 1889. A friend and fellow writer, the poet laureate Robert Bridges, saved Hopkins's poems and published them 29 years later, in 1918.

Building Background

"On the Side of Oddness" In a letter to Robert Bridges, who was often highly critical of his friend's poetry, Hopkins tried to explain his poetic technique: "No doubt my poetry errs on the side of oddness. I hope in time to have a more balanced and Miltonic style. But as air, melody, is what strikes me most of all in music, and design in painting, so design, pattern, or what I am in the habit of calling **inscape** is what I above all aim at in poetry." Hopkins created his inscape by experimenting with language, by adding new life to ordinary words, by combining words in unusual ways to suggest new possibilities of meaning, by choosing only concrete words of vigor and action. He also sought to re-create the natural rhythms of speech by using what he called **sprung rhythm.** Although he wrote in the Victorian age, his poetic works reflect little of the Victorian tradition; rather they are forerunners of twentieth-century verse.

Literary Focus

Alliteration The easiest way to remember **alliteration** is to memorize this definition, itself an example of alliteration: a succession of similar sounds. Look for Hopkins's skillful use of alliteration as you read his poems.

Writer's Notebook

A Lovely, Languid Lagoon Try your hand at the use of alliteration. For each of the following words write one example of a very alliterative phrase: shore, field, mountain, cottage, river.

Pied Beauty

Gerard Manley Hopkins

Glory be to God for dappled[1] things—
  For skies of couple-color as a brinded[2] cow;
    For rose-moles all in stipple[3] upon trout that swim;
Fresh-firecoal chestnut-falls;[4] finches' wings;
5   Landscape plotted and pieced[5]—fold, fallow, and plow;
    And all trades, their gear and tackle and trim.[6]

All things counter,[7] original, spare, strange;
  Whatever is fickle, freckled (who knows how?)
    With swift, slow; sweet, sour; adazzle, dim;
10 He fathers-forth whose beauty is past change:
                    Praise him.

---

pied (pīd), *adj.* variegated; streaked with many colors.
  1. **dappled** (dap'əld), *adj.* spotted.
  2. **brinded** (brin'did), *adj.* streaked with different colors.
  3. **stipple** (stip'əl), *n.* In art, areas of color or shade are sometimes represented by masses of tiny dots, called *stipples.*
  4. **fresh-firecoal chestnut-falls.** Newly fallen nuts stripped of their husks look like glowing coals.
  5. **plotted and pieced,** laid off into plots and fields.
  6. **trim,** equipment.
  7. **counter,** contrary to expectation.

"Pure color over pure color" is the way William Henry Hunt described the method he used to create paintings such as this one, entitled *Primroses and Bird's Nest.* What objects in this painting might be considered as examples of "Pied Beauty"? ▼

Spring and Fall: to a Young Child

Gerard Manley Hopkins

Márgarét, are you gríeving
Over Goldengrove unleaving?
Leáves, líke the things of man, you
With your fresh thoughts care for, can you?
5 Áh! ás the heart grows older
It will come to such sights colder
By and by, nor spare a sigh
Though worlds of wanwood leafmeal[1] lie;
And yet you will weep and know why.
10 Now no matter, child, the name:
Sórrow's spríngs áre the same.
Nor mouth had, no nor mind, expressed
What heart heard of, ghost guessed:
It ís the blight[2] man was born for,
15 It is Margaret you mourn for.

---

1. **wanwood leafmeal,** pale ("wan") colored autumn
   leaves have fallen to the ground where they lie matted and disintegrating ("leafmeal").
2. **blight** (blīt), *n.* decay; deterioration.

After Reading

Making Connections

1. In which of Hopkins's poems are you more conscious of the **rhythm** and the **rhyme?**

2. What do you think is the **main idea** of "Pied Beauty"? Why do you select that idea?

3. Why do you think Hopkins concludes his list of dappled things with the phrase "all trades"?

4. In stanza 2 Hopkins speeds up the rhythm of the poem by moving to a string of contrasting adjectives. What do you think he accomplishes with these contrasts?

5. Which of your senses are stimulated by Hopkins's word choices in "Pied Beauty"? Supply specific examples.

6. Why do you think Hopkins entitled the poem about falling leaves "Spring and Fall"? Is the title an integral part of the poem?

7. Why do you think Hopkins capitalized the combination-word *Goldengrove?*

8. What comment do you think Hopkins is making by using the **hyperbole** "worlds of wanwood leafmeal"?

9. How does the speaker relate Margaret's present grief to the sorrow she will feel in the future?

10. Which of these poems seems closer in spirit to the nature poetry of the Romantics? Explain your answer.

11. How does knowing that Hopkins is writing from the **perspective** of the priesthood help you understand his attitude toward the subject matter?

Literary Focus: Alliteration

Alliteration is a succession of similar sounds. Point out several instances of alliteration in Hopkins's poems. Why do you think Hopkins uses alliteration in addition to rhyme?

Expressing Your Ideas

Writing Choices

Writer's Notebook Update Look back at the alliterative phrases you created. Are your alliterations unique or commonplace? To answer that question, compare your alliterations with those of your classmates. Did several of you come up with the same or similar phrases? Try, this time, to use ordinary words in uncommon ways or to think of unusual word associations. Maybe you can even invent some new words.

Strange Things . . . In the first stanza of "Pied Beauty" Hopkins lists the dappled things for which he praises God. Following Hopkins's style, write a **poetic stanza** in which you list strange things or sweet / sour things or swift / slow things. Be very specific with the images you create. Try to use unusual word combinations, like *couple-color,* and alliteration, like *fresh-firecoal chestnut falls.*

Spring, Summer, Fall, Winter Select a season, perhaps your favorite season, and write a **short story** in which a character gains an understanding about himself or mankind from his observations of the season.

Other Options

Captured Images Critic John Wain says that Hopkins's imagination is "performing one of the chief functions for which we now use the cinema and television—that of presenting an image which moves and takes form while it is focused." Create a **video** or a series of slides in which you try to capture the feeling created by the images Hopkins presents in "Pied Beauty." You might even use the poem in your sound track.

Loss of Innocence In "Spring and Fall" Margaret is experiencing a loss of innocence as she comes to accept the inevitability of death. Recall a situation in your life in which you lost your innocence about the harsh realities of life. Perhaps a pet died or a family member or personal hero you admired turned out to be less than perfect. Tell about your loss of innocence in an **illustrated story** suitable for students in the fourth or fifth grade.

Unity in Variety A possible theme for Hopkins's "Pied Beauty" is unity in variety or changelessness in change. Select a topic other than nature, and develop this theme in a **musical piece** or a **dance.** Your notes or your movements should be concrete and powerful, just as Hopkins's words are.

The Lagoon

by Joseph Conrad

Joseph Conrad
1857–1924

Teodor Józef Konrad Korzeniowski was born in the Polish Ukraine. Because of the political activities of his father, a Polish noble, the family was exiled to Russia. At age 11 Józef was orphaned and was placed in the guardianship of his uncle. At 17 he joined the French merchant marine and later the British merchant navy. He worked his way up to the rank of ship's captain, changed his name to Joseph Conrad, and became a naturalized British subject. When his first novel was published in 1894, Conrad shifted his energies to literature. In the next 29 years he wrote 31 volumes of fiction and reminiscence, tales of the sea, such as *Lord Jim* (1900); of adventure, such as *Heart of Darkness* (1902); and of politics, such as *Nostromo* (1904).

Building Background

True to Himself As a sailor in the British merchant navy, Joseph Conrad traveled to the African Congo, the Indian Ocean, the China seas, and the Malay Peninsula. The peninsular states of Malaysia, the setting of Conrad's "The Lagoon," had become part of the British Empire in the mid 1800s. The British, seeking to protect their trade interests in the region and to control disputes between the Malay rulers and the Chinese immigrants who labored in the tin mines, had sent in resident advisers who dictated policy. Thus, there were a few white men who moved with ease among the Malaysian natives. Conrad was one who quickly gained the confidence of the natives, thereby also gaining the opportunity to share in their culture and their experiences. Those experiences he later examined with the eye of an older, more thoughtful man. Conrad says: ". . . I need not point out that I had to make material from my own life's incidents arranged, combined, colored for artistic purposes. . . . What I claim as true are my mental and emotional reactions to life, to men, to their affairs and passions as I have seen them. I have in that sense kept always true to myself."

Literary Focus

Setting The time and place in which the action of a narrative takes place is its **setting.** Setting can contribute strongly to the mood or atmosphere of a work as well as to its believability. Sometimes a setting plays a role in influencing events of the plot; at other times it is unimportant, merely a background. As you read this story, consider how important the setting is. How does the setting influence the plot?

Writer's Notebook

Out of Your Element Recall a situation in which you were out of your "natural element," among people (or even with just one person) very different from yourself. Jot down a few words to describe the differences you were aware of; then list some words that describe your feelings about those differences.

Does this 19th-century engraving of a chief's house on New Guinea convey the same mood as Conrad's description of Arsat's dwelling? Why or why not?

The Lagoon

Joseph Conrad

The white man, leaning with both arms over the roof of the little house in the stern of the boat, said to the steersman—

"We will pass the night in Arsat's clearing. It is late."

The Malay only grunted, and went on looking fixedly at the river. The white man rested his chin on his crossed arms and gazed at the wake of the boat. At the end of the straight avenue of forests cut by the intense glitter of the river, the sun appeared unclouded and dazzling, poised low over the water that shone smoothly like a band of metal. The forests, sombre and dull, stood motionless and silent on each side of the broad stream. At the foot of big, towering trees, trunkless nipa palms rose from the mud of the bank, in bunches of leaves enormous and heavy, that hung unstirring over the brown swirl of eddies. In the stillness of the air every tree, every leaf, every bough, every tendril of creeper and every petal of minute blossoms seemed to have been bewitched into an immobility perfect and final. Nothing moved on the river but the eight paddles that rose flashing regularly, dipped together with a single splash; while the steersman swept right and left with a periodic and sudden flourish of his blade describing a glinting semicircle above his head. The churned-up water frothed alongside with a confused murmur. And the white man's canoe, advancing upstream in the short-lived disturbance of its own making, seemed to enter the portals of a land from which the very memory of motion had forever departed.

> **PREDICT: The white man is entering "a land from which the very memory of motion had forever departed." What kind of a land might that be?**

The white man, turning his back upon the setting sun, looked along the empty and broad expanse of the sea-reach. For the last three miles of its course the wandering, hesitating river, as if enticed[1] irresistibly by the freedom of an open horizon, flows straight into the sea, flows straight to the east—to the east that harbors both light and darkness. Astern of the boat the repeated call of some bird, a cry discordant[2] and feeble, skipped along over the smooth water and lost itself, before it could reach the other shore, in the breathless silence of the world.

The steersman dug his paddle into the stream, and held hard with stiffened arms, his body thrown forward. The water gurgled aloud; and suddenly the long straight reach seemed to pivot on its center, the forests swung in a semicircle, and the slanting beams of sunset touched the broadside of the canoe with a fiery glow, throwing the slender and distorted shadows of its crew upon the streaked glitter of the river. The white man turned to look ahead. The course of the boat had been altered at right-angles to the stream, and the carved dragon-head of its prow was pointing now at a gap in the fringing bushes of the bank. It glided through, brushing the overhanging twigs, and disappeared from the river like some slim and amphibious[3] creature leaving the water for its lair[4] in the forests.

The narrow creek was like a ditch: torturous,

fabulously deep; filled with gloom under the thin strip of pure and shining blue of the heaven. Immense trees soared up, invisible behind the festooned draperies of creepers. Here and there, near the glistening blackness of the water, a twisted root of some tall tree showed amongst the tracery of small ferns, black and dull, writhing and motionless, like an arrested snake. The short words of the paddlers reverberated loudly between the thick and somber walls of vegetation. Darkness oozed out from between the trees, through the tangled maze of the creepers, from behind the great fantastic and unstirring leaves; the darkness, mysterious and invincible; the darkness scented and poisonous of impenetrable[5] forests.

The men poled in the shoaling[6] water. The creek broadened, opening out into a wide sweep of a stagnant[7] lagoon. The forests receded from the marshy bank, leaving a level strip of bright green, reedy grass to frame the reflected blueness of the sky. A fleecy pink cloud drifted high above, trailing the delicate coloring of its image under the floating leaves and the silvery blossoms of the lotus. A little house, perched on high piles, appeared black in the distance. Near it, two tall nibong palms, that seemed to have come out of the forests in the background, leaned slightly over the ragged roof, with a suggestion of sad tenderness and care in the droop of their leafy and soaring heads.

The steersman, pointing with his paddle, said, "Arsat is there. I see his canoe fast between the piles."

The polers ran along the sides of the boat glancing over their shoulders at the end of the day's journey. They would have preferred to

---

1. entice (en tīs′), *v.* tempt.
2. **discordant** (dis kôrd′nt), *adj.* harsh; clashing.
3. **amphibious** (am fib′ē əs), *adj.* of land and water.
4. **lair** (ler), *n.* hideaway.
5. impenetrable (im pen′ə trə bəl), *adj.* unable to be passed through.
6. **shoaling** (shō′ling), *adj.* shallow.
7. stagnant (stag′nənt), *adj.* still; not flowing.

spend the night somewhere else than on this lagoon of weird aspect and ghostly reputation. Moreover, they disliked Arsat, first as a stranger, and also because he who repairs a ruined house, and dwells in it, proclaims that he is not afraid to live amongst the spirits that haunt the places abandoned by mankind. Such a man can disturb the course of fate by glances or words; while his familiar ghosts are not easy to propitiate[8] by casual wayfarers upon whom they long to wreak[9] the malice of their human master. White men care not for such things, being unbelievers and in league with the Father of Evil, who leads them unharmed through the invisible dangers of this world. To the warnings of the righteous they oppose an offensive pretence of disbelief. What is there to be done?

> ☙ **CLARIFY: From what perspective do the boatsmen view Arsat? the white man?**

So they thought, throwing their weight on the end of their long poles. The big canoe glided on swiftly, noiselessly, and smoothly, towards Arsat's clearing, till, in a great rattling of poles thrown down, and the loud murmurs of "Allah be praised!" it came with a gentle knock against the crooked piles below the house.

The boatmen with uplifted faces shouted discordantly, "Arsat! O Arsat!" Nobody came. The white man began to climb the rude ladder giving access to the bamboo platform before the house. The juragan[10] of the boat said sulkily, "We will cook in the sampan,[11] and sleep on the water."

"Pass my blankets and the basket," said the white man, curtly.

He knelt on the edge of the platform to receive the bundle. Then the boat shoved off, and the white man, standing up, confronted Arsat, who had come out through the low door of his hut. He was a man young, powerful, with broad chest and muscular arms. He had nothing on but his sarong.[12] His head was bare. His big, soft eyes stared eagerly at the white man,

but his voice and demeanor[13] were composed as he asked, without any words of greeting—

"Have you medicine, Tuan?"[14]

"No," said the visitor in a startled tone. "No. Why? Is there sickness in the house?"

"Enter and see," replied Arsat, in the same calm manner, and turning short round, passed again through the small doorway. The white man, dropping his bundles, followed.

In the dim light of the dwelling he made out on a couch of bamboos a woman stretched on her back under a broad sheet of red cotton cloth. She lay still, as if dead; but her big eyes, wide open, glittered in the gloom, staring upwards at the slender rafters, motionless and unseeing. She was in a high fever, and evidently unconscious. Her cheeks were sunk slightly, her lips were partly open, and on the young face there was the ominous[15] and fixed expression— the absorbed, contemplating expression of the unconscious who are going to die. The two men stood looking down at her in silence.

"Has she been long ill?" asked the traveler.

"I have not slept for five nights," answered the Malay, in a deliberate tone. "At first she heard voices calling her from the water and struggled against me who held her. But since the sun of today rose she hears nothing—she hears not me. She sees nothing. She sees not me—me!"

He remained silent for a minute, then asked softly—

"Tuan, will she die?"

"I fear so," said the white man, sorrowfully. He had known Arsat years ago, in a far country

---

8. **propitiate** (prə pish′ē āt), *v.* win the favor of.
9. **wreak** (rēk), *v.* inflict.
10. **juragan** (ju′rä gän), *n.* the rower responsible for steering the boat.
11. **sampan** (sam′pan), *n.* small boat.
12. **sarong** (sə rông′) *n.* a brightly colored cloth, wrapped around the waist and worn as a skirt by both men and women in the Malay Archipelago and the Pacific Islands.
13. **demeanor** (di mē′nər), *n.* behavior.
14. **Tuan** (tü än′), *n.* "Lord," a Malay term of respect.
15. **ominous** (om′ə nəs), *adj.* unfavorable, threatening.

in times of trouble and danger, when no friendship is to be despised. And since his Malay friend had come unexpectedly to dwell in the hut on the lagoon with a strange woman, he had slept many times there, in his journeys up and down the river. He liked the man who knew how to keep faith in council and how to fight without fear by the side of his white friend. He liked him—not so much perhaps as a man likes his favorite dog—but still he liked him well enough to help and ask no questions, to think sometimes vaguely and hazily in the midst of his own pursuits, about the lonely man and the long-haired woman with audacious[16] face and triumphant eyes, who lived together hidden by the forests—alone and feared.

The white man came out of the hut in time to see the enormous conflagration[17] of sunset put out by the swift and stealthy shadows that, rising like a black and impalpable[18] vapor above the treetops, spread over the heaven, extinguishing the crimson glow of floating clouds and the red brilliance of departing daylight. In a few moments all the stars came out above the intense blackness of the earth and the great lagoon gleaming suddenly with reflected lights resembled an oval patch of night sky flung down into the hopeless and abysmal[19] night of the wilderness. The white man had some supper out of the basket, then collecting a few sticks that lay about the platform, made up a small fire, not for warmth, but for the sake of the smoke, which would keep off the mosquitos. He wrapped himself in the blankets and sat with his back against the reed wall of the house, smoking thoughtfully.

Arsat came through the doorway with noiseless steps and squatted down by the fire. The white man moved his outstretched legs a little.

"She breathes," said Arsat in a low voice, anticipating the expected question. "She breathes and burns as if with a great fire. She speaks not; she hears not—and burns!"

He paused for a moment, then asked in a quiet, incurious[20] tone—

"Tuan . . . will she die?"

The white man moved his shoulders uneasily and muttered in a hesitating manner—

"If such is her fate."

"No, Tuan," said Arsat, calmly. "If such is my fate. I hear, I see, I wait. I remember . . . Tuan, do you remember the old days? Do you remember my brother?"

"Yes," said the white man. The Malay rose suddenly and went in. The other, sitting still outside, could hear the voice in the hut. Arsat said: "Hear me! Speak!" His words were succeeded by a complete silence. "O Diamelen!" he cried, suddenly. After that cry there was deep sigh. Arsat came out and sank down again in his old place.

They sat in silence before the fire. There was no sound within the house, there was no sound near them; but far away on the lagoon they could hear the voices of the boatmen ringing fitful and distinct on the calm water. The fire in the bows of the sampan shone faintly in the distance with a hazy red glow. Then it died out. The voices ceased. The land and the water slept invisible, unstirring and mute. It was as though there had been nothing left in the world but the glitter of stars streaming, ceaseless and vain, through the black stillness of the night.

The white man gazed straight before him into the darkness with wide-open eyes. The fear and fascination, the inspiration and the wonder of death—of death near, unavoidable, and unseen, soothed the unrest of his race and stirred the most indistinct, the most intimate of his thoughts. The ever-ready suspicion of evil, the gnawing suspicion that lurks in our hearts, flowed out into the stillness round him—into the stillness profound and dumb, and made it appear untrustworthy

---

16. audacious (ô dā′shəs), *adj.* bold.
17. **conflagration** (kon′flə grā′shən), *n.* fire.
18. **impalpable** (im pal′pə bəl), *adj.* not capable of being touched.
19. abysmal (ə biz′məl), *adj.* bottomless.
20. **incurious** (in kyůr′ē əs), *adj.* unquestioning.

and infamous,[21] like the placid and impenetrable mask of an unjustifiable violence. In that fleeting and powerful disturbance of his being the earth enfolded in the starlight peace became a shadowy country of inhuman strife, a battlefield of phantoms terrible and charming, august or ignoble,[22] struggling ardently[23] for the possession of our helpless hearts. An unquiet and mysterious country of inextinguishable desires and fears.

A plaintive[24] murmur rose in the night; a murmur saddening and startling, as if the great solitudes of surrounding woods had tried to whisper into his ear the wisdom of their immense and lofty indifference. Sounds hesitating and vague floated in the air round him, shaped themselves slowly into words; and at last flowed on gently in a murmuring stream of soft and monotonous sentences. He stirred like a man waking up and changed his position slightly. Arsat, motionless and shadowy, sitting with bowed head under the stars, was speaking in a low and dreamy tone—

"... for where can we lay down the heaviness of our trouble but in a friend's heart? A man must speak of war and of love. You, Tuan, know what war is, and you have seen me in time of danger seek death as other men seek life! A writing may be lost; a lie may be written; but what the eye has seen is truth and remains in the mind!"

"I remember," said the white man, quietly. Arsat went on with mournful composure—

"Therefore I shall speak to you of love. Speak in the night. Speak before both night and love are gone—and the eye of day looks upon my sorrow and my shame; upon my blackened face; upon my burnt-up heart."

A sigh, short and faint, marked an almost imperceptible[25] pause, and then his words flowed on, without a stir, without a gesture.

"After the time of trouble and war was over and you went away from my country in the pur-

> ... what the eye has seen is truth and remains in the mind!

suit of your desires which we, men of the islands, cannot understand, I and my brother became again, as we had been before, the sword-bearers of the Ruler. You know we were men of family, belonging to a ruling race, and more fit than any to carry on our right shoulder the emblem of power. And in the time of prosperity Si Dendring showed us favor, as we, in time of sorrow, had showed to him the faithfulness of our courage. It was a time of peace. A time of deer-hunts and cock-fights; of idle talks and foolish squabbles between men whose bellies are full and weapons are rusty. But the sower watched the young rice-shoots grow up without fear, and the traders came and went, departed lean and returned fat into the river of peace. They brought news, too. Brought lies and truth mixed together, so that no man knew when to rejoice and when to be sorry. We heard from them about you also. They had seen you here and had seen you there. And I was glad to hear, for I remembered the stirring times, and I always remembered you, Tuan, till the time came when my eyes could see nothing in the past, because they had looked upon the one who is dying there—in the house."

He stopped to exclaim in an intense whisper, "O Mara bahia! O Calamity!" then went on speaking a little louder:

"There's no worse enemy and no better friend than a brother, Tuan, for one brother knows another, and in perfect knowledge is

21. infamous (in′fə məs), *adj.* disgraceful.
22. **august** (ô gust′), *adj.* **or ignoble** (ig nō′bəl), *adj.* majestic or humble.
23. **ardently** (ärd′nt lē), *adv.* eagerly.
24. plaintive (plān′tiv), *adj.* mournful.
25. **imperceptible** (im′pər sep′tə bəl), *adj.* that cannot be noticed; slight.

strength for good or evil. I loved my brother. I went to him and told him that I could see nothing but one face, hear nothing but one voice. He told me: 'Open your heart so that she can see what is in it—and wait. Patience is wisdom. Inchi Midah may die or our Ruler may throw off his fear of a woman!' . . . I waited! . . . You remember the lady with the veiled face, Tuan, and the fear of our Ruler before her cunning and temper. And if she wanted her servant, what could I do? But I fed the hunger of my heart on short glances and stealthy[26] words. I loitered on the path to the bath-houses in the daytime, and when the sun had fallen behind the forest I crept along the jasmine hedges of the women's courtyard. Unseeing, we spoke to one another through the scent of flowers, through the veil of leaves, through the blades of long grass that stood still before our lips; so great was our prudence, so faint was the murmur of our great longing. The time passed swiftly . . . and there were whispers amongst women—and our enemies watched—my brother was gloomy, and I began to think of killing and of a fierce death . . . . We are of a people who take what they want—like you whites. There is a time when a man should forget loyalty and respect. Might and authority are given to rulers, but to all men is given love and strength and courage. My brother said, 'You shall take her from the midst. We are two who are like one.' And I answered, 'Let it be soon, for I find no warmth in sunlight that does not shine upon her.' Our time came when the Ruler and all the great people went to the mouth of the river to fish by torchlight. There were hundreds of boats, and on the white sand, between the water and the forests, dwellings of leaves were built for the households of the Rajahs. The smoke of cooking-fires was like a blue mist of the evening, and many voices rang in it joyfully. While they were making the boats ready to beat up the fish, my brother came to me and said, 'To-night!' I looked to my weapons, and when the time came our canoe took its place in the circle of boats carrying the torches. The lights blazed on the water, but behind the boats there was darkness. When the shouting began and the excitement made them like mad we dropped out. The water swallowed our fire, and we floated back to the shore that was dark with only here and there the glimmer of embers. We could hear the talk of slavegirls amongst the sheds. Then we found a place deserted and silent. We waited there. She came. She came running along the shore, rapid and leaving no trace, like a leaf driven by the wind into the sea. My brother said gloomily, 'Go and take her; carry her into our boat.' I lifted her in my arms. She panted. Her heart was beating against my breast. I said, 'I take you from those people. You come to the cry of my heart, but my arms take you into my boat against the will of the great!' 'It is right,' said my brother. 'We are men who take what we want and can hold it against many. We should have taken her in daylight.' I said, 'Let us be off'; for since she was in my boat I began to think of our Ruler's many men. 'Yes. Let us be off,' said my brother. 'We are cast out and this boat is our country now—and the sea is our refuge.' He lingered with his foot on the shore, and I entreated[27] him to hasten, for I remembered the strokes of her heart against my breast and thought that two men cannot withstand a hundred. We left, paddling downstream close to the bank; and as we passed by the creek where they were fishing, the great shouting had ceased, but the murmur of voices was loud like the humming of insects flying at noonday. The boats floated, clustered together, in the red light of torches, under a black roof of smoke; and men talked of their sport. Men that boasted, and praised, and jeered—men that would have been our friends in the morning, but on that night were already our enemies. We paddled swiftly past. We had no more friends in the country of our birth. She sat in the middle of the canoe with covered face; silent as she is now; unseeing

---

26. **stealthy** (stel′thē), *adj.* secret.
27. **entreat** (en trēt′), *v.* beg.

as she is now—and I had no regret at what I was leaving because I could hear her breathing close to me—as I can hear her now."

He paused, listened with his ear turned to the doorway, then shook his head and went on:

"My brother wanted to shout the cry of challenge—one cry only—to let the people know we were freeborn robbers who trusted our arms and the great sea. And again I begged him in the name of our love to be silent. Could I not hear her breathing close to me? I knew the pursuit would come quick enough. My brother loved me. He dipped his paddle without a splash. He only said, 'There is half a man in you now—the other half is in that woman. I can wait. When you are a whole man again, you will come back with me here to shout defiance. We are sons of the same mother.' I made no answer. All my strength and all my spirit were in my hands that held the paddle—for I longed to be with her in a safe place beyond the reach of men's anger and of women's spite. My love was so great, that I thought it could guide me to a country where death was unknown, if I could only escape from Inchi Midah's fury and from our Ruler's sword. We paddled with haste, breathing through our teeth. The blades bit deep into the smooth water. We passed out of the river; we flew in clear channels amongst the shallows. We skirted the black coast; we skirted the sand beaches where the sea speaks in whispers to the land; and the gleam of white sand flashed back past our boat, so swiftly she ran upon the water. We spoke not. Only once I said, 'Sleep, Diamelen, for soon you may want all your strength.' I heard the sweetness of her voice, but I never turned my head. The sun rose and still we went on. Water fell from my face like rain from a cloud. We flew in the light and heat. I never looked back, but I knew that my brother's eyes, behind me, were looking steadily ahead, for the boat went as straight as a bushman's dart, when it leaves the end of the sumpitan.[28] There was no better paddler, no better steersman than my brother. Many times, together, we had won races in that canoe. But we never had put out our strength as we did then—then, when for the last time we paddled together! There was no braver or stronger man in our country than my brother. I could not spare the strength to turn my head and look at him, but every moment I heard the hiss of his breath getting louder behind me. Still he did not speak. The sun was high. The heat clung to my back like a flame of fire. My ribs were ready to burst, but I could no longer get enough air into my chest. And then I felt I must cry out with my last breath, 'Let us rest!' . . . 'Good!' he answered; and his voice was firm. He was strong. He was brave. He knew not fear and no fatigue . . . My brother!"

A murmur powerful and gentle, a murmur vast and faint; the murmur of trembling leaves, of stirring boughs, ran through the tangled depths of the forests, ran over the starry smoothness of the lagoon, and the water between the piles lapped the slimy timber once with a sudden splash. A breath of warm air touched the two men's faces and passed on with a mournful sound—a breath loud and short like an uneasy sigh of the dreaming earth.

Arsat went on in an even, low voice.

"We ran our canoe on the white beach of a little bay close to a long tongue of land that seemed to bar our road; a long wooded cape going far into the sea. My brother knew that place. Beyond the cape a river has its entrance, and through the jungle of that land there is a narrow path. We made a fire and cooked rice. Then we lay down to sleep on the soft sand in the shade of our canoe, while she watched. No sooner had I closed my eyes than I heard her cry of alarm. We leaped up. The sun was halfway down the sky already, and coming in sight in the opening of the bay we saw a prau[29] manned by many pad-

---

28. **sumpitan** (sum′pi tan), *n.* a type of blowgun used by the natives of Borneo and nearby islands to propel a poisoned dart.

29. **prau** (prou), *n.* a swift Malay sailing boat.

This engraving shows a lakatoi (lä′kä tō′ē), a double-hulled dugout canoe used by the islanders of Indonesia. What is the first impression you get from the image of this boat?

dlers. We knew it at once; it was one of our Rajah's praus. They were watching the shore, and saw us. They beat the gong, and turned the head of the prau into the bay. I felt my heart become weak within my breast. Diamelen sat on the sand and covered her face. There was no escape by sea. My brother laughed. He had the gun you had given him, Tuan, before you went away, but there was only a handful of powder. He spoke to me quickly: 'Run with her along the path. I shall keep them back, for they have no firearms, and landing in the face of a man with a gun is certain death for some. Run with her. On the other side of that wood there is a fisherman's house—and a canoe. When I have fired all the shots I will follow. I am a great runner, and before they can come up we shall be gone. I will hold out as long as I can, for she is but a woman—that can neither run nor fight, but she has your heart in her weak hands.' He dropped behind the canoe. The prau was coming. She and I ran, and as we rushed along the path I heard shots. My brother fired— once—twice—and the booming of the gong ceased. There was silence behind us. That neck of land is narrow. Before I heard my brother fire the third shot I saw the shelving[30] shore, and I saw the water again; the mouth of a broad river. We crossed a grassy glade. We ran down to the water. I saw a low hut above the black mud, and a small canoe hauled up. I heard another shot behind me. I thought, 'That is his last charge.' We rushed down to the canoe; a man came running from the hut, but I leaped on him, and we rolled together in the mud. Then I got up, and he lay still at my feet. I don't know whether I had killed him or not. I and Diamelen pushed the canoe

───────────

30. **shelving** (shel′ving), *adj.* sloping.

afloat. I heard yells behind me, and I saw my brother run across the glade. Many men were bounding after him. I took her in my arms and threw her into the boat, then leaped in myself. When I looked back I saw that my brother had fallen. He fell and was up again, but the men were closing round him. He shouted, 'I am coming!' The men were close to him. I looked. Many men. Then I looked at her. Tuan, I pushed the canoe! I pushed it into deep water. She was kneeling forward looking at me, and I said, 'Take your paddle,' while I struck the water with mine. Tuan, I heard him cry. I heard him cry my name twice; and I heard voices shouting, 'Kill! Strike!' I never turned back. I heard him calling my name again with a great shriek, as when life is going out together with the voice—and I never turned my head. My own name! . . . My brother! Three times he called—but I was not afraid of life. Was she not there in that canoe? And could I not with her find a country where death is forgotten—where death is unknown!"

SUMMARIZE: Summarize the events of the stealing of Diamelen.

The white man sat up. Arsat rose and stood, an indistinct and silent figure above the dying embers of the fire. Over the lagoon a mist drifting and low had crept, erasing slowly the glittering images of the stars. And now a great expanse of white vapor covered the land; it flowed cold and gray in the darkness, eddied in noiseless whirls round the tree-trunks and about the platform of the house, which seemed to float upon a restless and impalpable illusion of a sea. Only far away the tops of the trees stood outlined on the twinkle of heaven, like a somber and forbidding shore—a coast deceptive, pitiless and black.

What did I care who died? I wanted peace in my own heart.

Arsat's voice vibrated loudly in the profound peace.

"I had her there! I had her! To get her I would have faced all mankind. But I had her—and——"

His words went out ringing into the empty distances. He paused, and seemed to listen to them dying away very far—beyond help and beyond recall. Then he said quietly—

"Tuan, I loved my brother."

A breath of wind made him shiver. High above his head, high above the silent sea of mist the drooping leaves of the palms rattled together with a mournful and expiring sound. The white man stretched his legs. His chin rested on his chest, and he murmured sadly without lifting his head—

"We all love our brothers."

Arsat burst out with an intense whispering violence—

"What did I care who died? I wanted peace in my own heart."

He seemed to hear a stir in the house—listened—then stepped in noiselessly. The white man stood up. A breeze was coming in fitful puffs. The stars shone paler as if they had retreated into the frozen depths of immense space. After a chill gust of wind there were a few seconds of perfect calm and absolute silence. Then from behind the black and wavy line of the forests a column of golden light shot up into the heavens and spread over the semicircle of the eastern horizon. The sun had risen. The mist lifted, broke into drifting patches, vanished into thin flying wreaths; and the unveiled lagoon lay, polished and black, in the heavy shadows at the foot of the wall of trees.

A white eagle rose over it with a slanting and ponderous flight, reached the clear sunshine and appeared dazzlingly brilliant for a moment, then soaring higher, became a dark and motionless speck before it vanished into the blue as if it had left the earth forever. The white man, standing gazing upwards before the doorway, heard in the hut a confused broken murmur of distracted words ending with a loud groan. Suddenly Arsat stumbled out with outstretched hands, shivered, and stood still for some time with fixed eyes. Then he said—

"She burns no more."

Before his face the sun showed its edge above the tree-tops rising steadily. The breeze freshened; a great brilliance burst upon the lagoon, sparkled on the rippling water. The forests came out of the clear shadows of the morning, became distinct, as if they had rushed nearer—to stop short in a great stir of leaves, of nodding boughs, of swaying branches. In the merciless sunshine the whisper of unconscious life grew louder, speaking in an incomprehensible[31] voice round the dumb darkness of that human sorrow. Arsat's eyes wandered slowly, then stared at the rising sun.

"I can see nothing," he said half aloud to himself.

"There is nothing," said the white man, moving to the edge of the platform and waving his hand to his boat. A shout came faintly over the lagoon and the sampan began to glide towards the abode of the friend of ghosts.

"If you want to come with me, I will wait all the morning," said the white man, looking away upon the water.

EVALUATE: Judge the way the white man responds to Arsat's story and to the death of Diamelen.

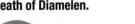

"No, Tuan," said Arsat, softly. "I shall not eat or sleep in this house, but I must first see my road. Now I can see nothing—see nothing! There is no light and no peace in the world; but there is death—death for many. We are sons of the same mother—and I left him in the midst of enemies; but I am going back now."

He drew a long breath and went on in a dreamy tone:

"In a little while I shall see clear enough to strike—to strike. But she has died, and . . . now . . . darkness."

He flung his arms wide open, let them fall along his body, then stood still with unmoved face and stony eyes, staring at the sun. The white man got down into his canoe. The polers ran smartly along the sides of the boat, looking over their shoulders at the beginning of a weary journey. High in the stern, his head muffled up in white rags, the juragan sat moody, letting his paddle trail in the water. The white man, leaning with both arms over the grass roof of the little cabin, looked back at the shining ripple of the boat's wake. Before the sampan passed out of the lagoon into the creek he lifted his eyes. Arsat had not moved. He stood lonely in the searching sunshine; and he looked beyond the great light of a cloudless day into the darkness of a world of illusions.

31. **incomprehensible** (in′kom pri hen′sə bəl), *adj.* impossible to understand.

After Reading

Making Connections

Shaping Your Response

1. For which character in the story do you feel the greatest sympathy? Why?

2. Do you feel that Conrad's general **tone** in this story is optimistic or pessimistic? Explain your response.

Analyzing the Story

3. Why do you think the author includes a white man in this story of Malay natives?

4. How close are the white man and Arsat, and how does their relationship affect Arsat's situation?

5. 👣 What is Arsat's **perspective** of the culture of the white man?

6. Arsat speaks repeatedly of "love." What is the nature of love in this story? What forces arise in opposition to it?

7. In your opinion, what is the connection between Arsat's crime and his punishment?

8. Why do you think Arsat decides to return to the kingdom from which he has escaped?

9. Trace the **images** of darkness and light throughout the story. Discuss the symbolism of each image.

Extending the Ideas

10. In the story of Arsat, what comment does Conrad seem to make about the way words and actions influence a person's life? Do you agree with him?

11. If you were writing the movie script for this story, where would you begin the story and where would you end it? Is the whole interest in the movie contained in the long **flashback?**

Literary Focus: Setting

Setting is the time (both time of day and period in history) and place in which the action of a story takes place. Could this story have taken place in England? in America? What is important about this particular setting? How does the setting influence the plot?

Vocabulary Study

Write the word from the list that best completes the meaning of each sentence. You will not use all the words.

1. The dark and mysterious forests along the river loomed so thick and imposing that they appeared to be _____ .

2. The black waters of the hidden lagoon were still and _____ .

abysmal
audacious
demeanor
enticed
impenetrable
incomprehensible
infamous
ominous
plaintive
propitiate
stagnant
stealthy

3. The night was so black and dark that it seemed like an _____ pit.

4. Arsat had been so _____ by the beauty and charm of Diamelen that he had to have her for his own.

5. The _____ meetings between Arsat and Diamelen were held at night in remote places.

6. The stealing of Diamelen by Arsat and his brother was an _____ move since they were just two against more than one hundred.

7. Arsat knew that stealing Diamelen had made him _____ among his people.

8. As soon as the white man saw how ill Diamelen was, he knew that the situation was _____.

9. As Arsat realized that Diamelen was indeed going to die, his cries became more _____.

10. Although at times Arsat found Diamelen's death _____, at other times he felt her death was a result of his treatment of his brother.

Expressing Your Ideas

Writing Choices

Writer's Notebook Update Look back at your notes about being out of your element. Think about what you learned or how you changed as a result of your encounter. Write a paragraph or so about your experience.

Analyze Conrad's Style The American writer H. L. Mencken once said, "Conrad may not have been the greatest novelist, but he was the greatest artist who wrote novels." Write an **essay** in which you analyze the artistic style of Joseph Conrad's writing. You might consider his use of simile, metaphor, repetition, imagery, and parallel structure.

Home Again Write the story of Arsat's return to the kingdom from which he stole Diamelen and where he abandoned his brother. First consider what characters to include. (Is there any way to work in the white man?) Then

decide what the main actions will be. Be sure you know the ending before you start to write.

Other Options

Debate Arsat's Dilemma Work with a partner to prepare an informal **debate** on the following question: Should Arsat have left his brother behind or should he have gone back to rescue him? Among the factors you may want to consider are the depth of Arsat's love, the importance of family, the time frame in which Arsat had to make his decision, the power of the men chasing his brother, and Arsat's current situation.

Diamelen Remembered Imagine how Arsat would want to remember Diamelen. Create a **marker and its inscription** for Diamelen's grave. Accompany your creation with a description of the memorial service you think Arsat would hold.

Before Reading

When I Was One-and-Twenty

Loveliest of Trees

To an Athlete Dying Young by A. E. Housman

A. E. Housman
1859–1936

A. E. Housman was a promising scholar of classical languages, but he failed his Oxford comprehensive examination through inadequate preparation. For ten years, while he held a dreary civil service job in London, he spent his free time studying the classics and publishing scholarly essays. In 1893 his stature as a scholar helped him earn the post of Professor of Latin at the University of London. That success seemed to inspire his poetic spirit and within two years he had assembled a collection of 58 poems. At his own expense he published *A Shropshire Lad,* also called *Poems by Terence Hearsay.* Although he published another collection, *Last Poems,* in 1922, most of those lyrics were from the time of his first book.

Building Background

The Bubbling Spring A. E. Housman describes how his poems often began: "Having drunk a pint of beer at luncheon—beer is a sedative to the brain, and my afternoons are the least intellectual portion of my life—I would go out for a walk of two or three hours. As I went along, thinking of nothing in particular, only looking at things around me and following the progress of the seasons, there would flow into my mind, with sudden and unaccountable emotion, sometimes a line or two of verse, sometimes a whole stanza at once, accompanied, not preceded, by a vague notion of the poem which they were destined to form a part of. Then there would usually be a lull of an hour or so, then perhaps the spring would bubble up again. . . When I got home I wrote them down, leaving gaps, and hoping that further inspiration might be forthcoming another day."

Literary Focus

Anastrophe The technique of inverting the normal, customary, or logical sequence of words in a sentence to achieve greater dramatic emphasis or to create particular rhythms or rhymes is called **anastrophe** (ə nas′trə fē). For example, Tennyson's "The Lady of Shalott" begins, "On either side the river lie / Long fields of barley and of rye. . . ." in which *fields* and *lie* are inverted from normal subject-verb order. Look for anastrophe in each of Housman's poems.

Writer's Notebook

Good Advice Think about all of the people who have given you advice—your parents, your teachers, your friends, your coaches, your pastor. Jot down the best piece of advice you have received in your life so far.

To an Athlete Dying Young

A. E. HOUSMAN

The time you won your town the race
We chaired you through the market place;
Man and boy stood cheering by,
And home we brought you shoulder-high.

5 Today, the road all runners come,
Shoulder-high we bring you home,
And set you at your threshold down,
Townsman of a stiller town.

Smart lad, to slip betimes[1] away
10 From fields where glory does not stay,
And early though the laurel[2] grows
It withers quicker than the rose.

Eyes the shady night has shut
Cannot see the record cut,[3]
15 And silence sounds no worse than cheers
After earth has stopped the ears.

Now you will not swell the rout[4]
Of lads that wore their honors out,
Runners whom renown[5] outran
20 And the name died before the man.

So set, before its echoes fade,
The fleet foot on the sill of shade,
And hold to the low lintel up
The still-defended challenge cup.

25 And round that early-laureled head
Will flock to gaze the strengthless dead,
And find unwithered on its curls
The garland briefer than a girl's.

---

1. **betimes** (bi tīmz′), *adv.* early.
2. **laurel.** In Greek and Roman times victorious athletes and celebrated poets would be crowned with a wreath of laurel leaves.
3. **cut,** improved upon; broken.
4. **swell the rout,** increase the crowd.
5. **renown** (ri noun′), *n.* fame.

When I Was One-and-Twenty

A. E. HOUSMAN

When I was one-and-twenty
  I heard a wise man say,
"Give crowns and pounds and guineas
  But not your heart away;
5 Give pearls away and rubies
  But keep your fancy free."
But I was one-and-twenty,
  No use to talk to me.

When I was one-and-twenty
10   I heard him say again,
"The heart out of the bosom
  Was never given in vain;
'Tis paid with sighs a plenty
  And sold for endless rue."[1]
15 And I am two-and-twenty,
  And oh, 'tis true, 'tis true.

1. **rue** (rü), *n.* sorrow.

Loveliest of Trees

A. E. HOUSMAN

Loveliest of trees, the cherry now
Is hung with bloom along the bough,
And stands about the woodland ride,
Wearing white for Eastertide.

5 Now, of my threescore years and ten,
Twenty will not come again,
And take from seventy springs a score,
It only leaves me fifty more.

And since to look at things in bloom
10 Fifty springs are little room,
About the woodlands I will go
To see the cherry hung with snow.

Trees in Bloom, Souvenir of Mauve (1888), is an oil painting created by Vincent van Gogh (1853–1890). Why does the speaker in "Loveliest of Trees" take the time now "to look at things in bloom"?

After Reading

Making Connections

Shaping Your Response

1. Reread Housman's description of how his poems began in Building Background on page 598. Select two or three lines from Housman's poetry that you think might have flown into his mind as inspiration.

Analyzing the Poems

2. In "To an Athlete Dying Young" why does the speaker consider the athlete a "smart lad" (line 9)?

3. Explain the various **images** Housman uses to suggest death and the final resting place.

4. In "When I Was One-and-Twenty" what do you think is suggested by the verbs the wise man uses: *give, keep, paid,* and *sold?*

5. ☙ What do you infer has happened to the speaker to cause him to change his **perspective** and finally to agree (in line 16) with the wise man?

6. Do you think that the speaker will live his life differently now that he is twenty-two?

7. In "Loveliest of Trees" compare and contrast the tree as described in stanza 1 and in stanza 3.

8. Why do you think the speaker is doing arithmetic in stanza 2?

Extending the Ideas

9. Why do you think boys and girls—indeed men and women—so often do not follow the advice they receive from others?

Literary Focus: Anastrophe

Anastrophe, the inversion of the usual order of the parts of a sentence, is used to emphasize a word or idea or to achieve a certain rhythm or rhyme. Find at least one example of anastrophe in each of Housman's poems. For each example explain why you think he chose to use this inversion.

Vocabulary Study

Create a word map of synonyms for *renown*. Then create a word map of adjectives that might describe someone who has achieved renown.

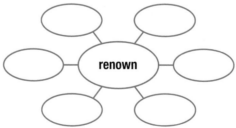

Expressing Your Ideas

Writing Choices

Writer's Notebook Update You've thought about advice given to you. Now write down two or three important "words of wisdom" you would like to share with a younger brother or sister or cousin.

Thanks to You Write a **thank-you letter** to someone who has given you some wise advice. Tell how you reacted to the advice initially, how you incorporated that advice into your life, and how following that advice has changed you. If you don't have such a person in your life, invent a wise character to write to.

Carpe Diem Revisited The speaker in "Loveliest of Trees" decides to "seize the day" and spend time looking at the cherry trees in full bloom. Write a **poem** in which you describe a scene or situation which would cause you to alter your schedule and *carpe diem.*

Carried Shoulder-high Write an **analytic essay** in which you compare and contrast the athlete at the height of his glory with the athlete in death. Use specific images from the poem.

Other Options

Join the Team! In his poem "To an Athlete Dying Young," Housman seems to suggest that the goal of competitive athletics is victory, the laurel wreath. Prepare a **speech** in which you talk about the importance of winning but put it in perspective with other values that can be gained from participating in sports activities. Your audience for your speech will be incoming freshmen and their parents.

Advice from an Upperclassman As an upperclass student you have a wealth of wisdom to share with the underclass students in your school. Prepare a **radio show** in which you answer questions you know are on the minds of many younger students. Your answers can be serious, or maybe you would prefer to write something humorously "tongue in cheek." If you can, record your talk show to play for your class or over the school's public-address system.

How to Decide Some of Housman's poems confront the choices that we must often make in life. Think about a major choice which you will have to make within the next year; for example: Will you attend college, work, or travel? Which college will you choose? What will you select as your major? First identify each of your alternatives; then, draw a **chart** like the following on which you list the pros and cons for each choice. What decision will you make, based on this analysis?

The Question		
Alternative 1	Pros	Cons
Alternative 2	Pros	Cons
Alternative 3	Pros	Cons
My Decision		

Before Reading

When You Are Old   The Second Coming

The Wild Swans at Coole   Sailing to Byzantium   by William Butler Yeats

William Butler Yeats
1865–1939

As a child W. B. Yeats (yāts) lived part-time in Dublin and London with his father, a portrait painter, and part-time in County Sligo, Ireland, where he lived with his mother's family. Yeats attended art school, but then he turned his energies to writing romantic lyrics and studying Irish myth and folklore. In 1905 Yeats and his friend Lady Augusta Gregory cofounded the Abbey Theatre in Dublin. Writing for the stage impressed Yeats with the importance of precise, lean language. His later poems show his evolution into a leader in modernist, experimental poetry. In 1923 Yeats received the Nobel Prize for literature. From 1922 to 1928 he served as a senator in the newly founded Irish Free State. He lived his remaining years in Italy and France.

Building Background

Metaphors from the Spirits Dissatisfied both with his father's atheism and with orthodox religion, yet wanting to believe in something, Yeats searched continuously for a hidden supernatural dimension in life. As a young man he became interested in the mystical occult philosophy of Helena Blavatsky and the Theosophical Society. He joined secret groups, attended seances, and studied alchemy. In 1917 he married Georgie Hyde-Lees, a woman half his age, who had the medium's gift for automatic writing, receiving written messages from spirits called Instructors. After several sessions Yeats offered to devote his life to interpreting the Instructors' communications. They responded, "No, we have come to give you metaphors for poetry." Shortly thereafter, Yeats began to develop a body of symbolic images that gave coherence to his beliefs and power to his writings. In *A Vision,* first published in 1925, Yeats tried to explain his understanding of the relationship between the occult and the imagination.

Literary Focus

Consonance Consonance is the use of words in which the final consonant sounds in stressed syllables are the same, but the vowel sounds that precede them differ; for example, *sad* and *reed* or *born* and *burn.* Keats used consonance along with rhyme to achieve a melancholy feeling in "Ode to a Nightingale":

> Forlorn! the very word is like a *bell*
> To *toll* me back from thee to my *sole self.*

Look for examples of consonance in Yeats's poetry.

Writer's Notebook

The Older Generation When you think of older people, what pictures come to your mind? What kinds of problems or issues are peculiar to the older generation? Jot down a few ideas.

When You Are Old

William Butler Yeats

When you are old and gray and full of sleep
And nodding by the fire, take down this book,
And slowly read, and dream of the soft look
Your eyes had once, and of their shadows deep;

5 How many loved your moments of glad grace,
And loved your beauty with love false or true,
But one man loved the pilgrim soul in you,
And loved the sorrows of your changing face;

And bending down beside the glowing bars,
10 Murmur, a little sadly, how Love fled
And paced upon the mountains overhead
And hid his face amid a crowd of stars.

The Wild Swans at Coole

William Butler Yeats

The trees are in their autumn beauty,
The woodland paths are dry,
Under the October twilight the water
Mirrors a still sky;
5 Upon the brimming water among the stones
Are nine-and-fifty swans.

The nineteenth autumn has come upon me
Since I first made my count;
I saw before I had well finished,
10 All suddenly mount

Coole (kül). Coole Park was the country estate of Yeats's
wealthy friend Lady Augusta Gregory
(1852–1932), the Irish playwright and folklorist.

◄ Walter Crane created this wallpaper design, called "Swan, Rush, and Iris," in 1877. What details in the design help to convey the grace and beauty of these majestic creatures?

And scatter wheeling in great broken rings
Upon their clamorous wings.

I have looked upon those brilliant creatures,
And now my heart is sore.
15 All's changed since I, hearing at twilight,
The first time on this shore,
The bell-beat of their wings above my head,
Trod with a lighter tread.

Unwearied still, lover by lover,
20 They paddle in the cold
Companionable streams or climb the air;
Their hearts have not grown old;
Passion or conquest, wander where they will,
Attend upon them still.
25 But now they drift on the still water,
Mysterious, beautiful;
Among what rushes will they build,
By what lake's edge or pool
Delight men's eyes when I awake some day
30 To find they have flown away?

The Second Coming

William Butler Yeats

Turning and turning in the widening gyre[1]
The falcon cannot hear the falconer;[2]
Things fall apart; the center cannot hold;
Mere anarchy[3] is loosed upon the world,
5 The blood-dimmed tide is loosed, and everywhere
The ceremony of innocence is drowned;
The best lack all conviction,[4] while the worst
Are full of passionate intensity.

Surely some revelation[5] is at hand;
10 Surely the Second Coming is at hand.
The Second Coming! Hardly are those words out
When a vast image out of *Spiritus Mundi*[6]
Troubles my sight: somewhere in sands of the desert
A shape with lion body and the head of a man,
15 A gaze blank and pitiless as the sun,
Is moving its slow thighs, while all about it
Reel shadows of the indignant[7] desert birds.
The darkness drops again; but now I know
That twenty centuries of stony sleep
20 Were vexed[8] to nightmare by a rocking cradle,
And what rough beast, its hour come round at last,
Slouches towards Bethlehem to be born?

---

1. **gyre** (jīr), *n.* a spiral motion.
2. **falcon cannot . . . . falconer,** hawk trained to hunt other birds and small animals cannot hear his trainer's instructions.
3. anarchy (an′ər kē), *n.* absence of a system of government and law.
4. conviction (kən vik′shən), *n.* firm belief.
5. revelation (rev′ə lā′shən), *n.* disclosure of divine truth.
6. *Spiritus Mundi,* "soul of the world." *[Latin]* Yeats believed in the existence of a "Great Memory," a collective unconscious that connects individuals with the Spiritus Mundi and serves as a reservoir of symbolic images from the past.
7. indignant (in dig′nənt), *adj.* angry at something unjust.
8. **vex** (veks), *v.* provoke.

Sailing to Byzantium

William Butler Yeats

That is no country for old men. The young
In one another's arms, birds in the trees,
—Those dying generations—at their song,
The salmon-falls, the mackerel-crowded
    seas,
5 Fish, flesh, or fowl, commend[1] all summer
    long
Whatever is begotten, born, and dies.
Caught in that sensual music all neglect
Monuments of unaging intellect.

An aged man is but a paltry[2] thing,
10 A tattered coat upon a stick, unless
Soul clap its hands and sing, and louder
    sing
For every tatter in its mortal dress,
Nor is there singing school but studying
Monuments of its own magnificence;
15 And therefore I have sailed the seas and
    come
To the holy city of Byzantium.

O sages[3] standing in God's holy fire
As in the gold mosaic[4] of a wall
Come from the holy fire, perne in a gyre,[5]
20 And be the singing-masters of my soul.
Consume my heart away; sick with desire
And fastened to a dying animal
It knows not what it is; and gather me
Into the artifice[6] of eternity.

25 Once out of nature I shall never take
My bodily form from any natural thing,
But such a form as Grecian goldsmiths
    make[7]
Of hammered gold and gold enameling
To keep a drowsy Emperor awake;
30 Or set upon a golden bough to sing
To lords and ladies of Byzantium
Of what is past, or passing, or to come.

Byzantium (bi zan′shē əm), an ancient name for the city that became Constantinople and later Istanbul, Turkey. For Yeats it was a symbol for the timeless world of art and intellect as opposed to the natural world of biological change. It was a "holy city"—literally, because it was the center of Eastern Christendom; symbolically, because it fostered the development of intellect and imagination that produces artistic perfection.

1. **commend** (kə mend′), v. praise.
2. paltry (pôl′trē), adj. almost worthless.
3. **sage** (sāj), n. wise person.
4. **mosaic** (mō zā′ik), n. picture made of small pieces of different colored stone, glass, or wood inlaid in a design.
5. **perne in a gyre.** A perne (or pirn) is a spool or bobbin; a gyre is a spiraling motion. The image seems to be of a long file of sages, spiraling down like the thread flying off a spinning bobbin, forming ever tighter circles that narrow to a single point.
6. artifice (är′tə fis), n. skillful construction.
7. **such a form . . . make,** an artificial singing bird. Yeats commented, "I use it as a symbol of the intellectual joy of eternity, as contrasted with the instinctive joy of human life."

After Reading

Making Connections

Shaping Your Response

1. What question would you most like to ask Yeats about his metaphors or about his poetry in general?

Analyzing the Poems

2. In "When You Are Old" what kind of a person do you think the speaker is describing when he says she has a "pilgrim soul" and a "changing face"?

3. Contrast the speaker and his beloved. Which one may really have the "pilgrim soul" after all?

4. In "The Wild Swans at Coole" compare the changes in the speaker's life with the changes in the lives of the swans.

5. Although he asks where the swans will alight, what question do you think the speaker is really asking in the last stanza?

6. In "The Second Coming" what do you think the **images** of the falcon and the falconer and the half-man/half-lion beast reveal about Yeats's view of civilization?

7. Describe the lives of those who dwell in the speaker's homeland in "Sailing to Byzantium." What qualities seem to be missing from their lives?

8. What do you think the speaker hopes to accomplish by going on a journey to Byzantium?

9. Why do you think the speaker chooses to take the form of a golden bird?

Extending the Ideas

10. Yeats wrote "The Second Coming" right after World War I. Do you think he would have cause to write from a similar **perspective** today?

Literary Focus: Consonance

Consonance, sometimes called half rhyme or near rhyme, is the repetition of consonant sounds that are preceded by different vowel sounds.

1. Find at least one example of consonance in each of Yeats's poems.

2. What other sound devices can you find in his poems?

3. Why do you think poets spend so much time searching for the exact words in order to achieve rhyme or assonance or consonance?

Vocabulary Study

Write the word from the list that best completes the meaning of the sentence. You will not use all the words.

anarchy
artifice
conviction
indignant
paltry
revelation

1. Yeats trusted in mystical sources to provide him with _____ and inspiration for his poetry.

2. Yeats believed that a nation without a strong sense of values was destined to end in _____.

3. Yeats held the strong _____ that the Irish people needed to become more aware of their national culture.

4. Yeats was _____ about the way the Irish were treated by the English.

5. Yeats's poetry suggests that he was worried that as an old man he would be considered _____.

Expressing Your Ideas

Writing Choices

Writer's Notebook Update Select one of the problems of older people you identified and write a brief paragraph about how effectively you think the younger generation is dealing with this issue.

Traveling to . . . In "Sailing to Byzantium" an aging man wishes to sail to Byzantium, maybe the real place, maybe the spiritual ideal, maybe both. Select a place, real, imaginary, or spiritual, to which you would like to travel. Write a **description** of your chosen destination, telling what hopes and dreams you believe this place will help you to realize.

Slouching Towards Bethlehem Select one of the images of the world in "The Second Coming" and develop that image into a commentary on some aspect of modern day society. Prepare your commentary as an **editorial** for your school or community newspaper. Use a quotation from the poem as the title of your editorial.

Other Options

Not At All Tattered Yeats describes the aged man as "A tattered coat upon a stick." Think of an older person who is quite the opposite of a "tattered coat." You might choose someone whom you know in your personal life or who has been prominent in the world of politics or sports or entertainment. Research that person's life to determine what has prevented him or her from becoming a "tattered coat" with age. Present your results as an **oral report** to your class.

What Rough Beast Make a composite **collage** of a beast that represents your vision of today's world. Include parts of as many animals as you wish, but use them for their symbolic, not their literal, attributes. For example, usually an owl represents wisdom and doves represent peace or love. Give your modern beast a symbolic name and write a descriptive caption.

Before Reading

The Star

by H. G. Wells

H. G. Wells
1866–1946

In his youth Herbert George Wells drifted from one dreary job to another. Eventually he became a science teacher, but after four years, when he had to stay in bed because of tuberculosis, he turned to writing short essays on science for popular magazines. In 1895 he became a full-time writer. Over the next fifty years Wells wrote 114 books, among them science fantasies, novels about contemporary society, satires, and philosophic commentaries. After World War I, stating that the future would be "a race between education and catastrophe," Wells wrote a very popular and influential historical work, *The Outline of History.* Said fellow writer George Orwell, "The minds of all of us, and therefore the physical world, would be perceptibly different if Wells had never existed."

Building Background

"Exercises of the Imagination" Building upon a base of scientific knowledge, H. G. Wells let his imagination carry science to unusual yet logical, terrifying yet hopeful, conclusions. In the preface to a collection of his scientific fantasies Wells said that his stories "do not pretend to deal with possible things; they are exercises of the imagination." He imagined traveling into the past and future (*The Time Machine,* 1895). He imagined a sinister doctor transforming beasts into men (*The Island of Dr. Moreau,* 1896). He imagined an ambitious scientist discovering how to make himself invisible (*The Invisible Man,* 1897). He imagined the earth being invaded by Martians (*The War of the Worlds,* 1898). He imagined men from earth landing on the moon (*The First Men in the Moon,* 1901). Through all of his tales, Wells mixed science and technology with adventure and social commentary. He predicted the hopes and the dangers of the technological revolution of the twentieth century. Although he became more pessimistic near the end of his life, in most of his books Wells retained a belief in the positive aspects of human nature. Wells was an immensely popular writer; his popularity was enhanced because many of his novels were made into movies.

Literary Focus

Point of View The vantage point from which an author presents the actions and characters in a story is called **point of view.** The story may be told by a character (**first-person** point of view) or by a narrator who does not participate in the action (**third-person** point of view). Further, the third-person narrator may be **omniscient**—able to see into the minds of all characters; **limited**—confined to a single character's perceptions; or **objective**—describing only what can be seen. Determine what point of view Wells uses in "The Star."

Writer's Notebook

Science Fact or Fiction? Wells was one of the first writers of science fiction. What characteristics come to your mind when you think of a science-fiction story? What expectations do you have when you pick up a science-fiction tale? Look at the picture on page 617. Jot down your expectations for "The Star."

THE STAR

H.G. WELLS

1 t was on the first day of the new year that the announcement was made, almost simultaneously[1] from three observatories, that the motion of the planet Neptune, the outermost[2] of all the planets that wheel about the sun, had become very erratic.[3] Ogilvy had already called attention to a suspected retardation in its velocity in December. Such a piece of news was scarcely calculated to interest a world the greater portion of whose inhabitants were unaware of the existence of the planet Neptune, nor outside the astronomical profession did the subsequent discovery of a faint remote speck of light in the region of the perturbed[4] planet cause any very great excitement. Scientific people, however, found the intelligence remarkable enough, even before it became known that the new body was rapidly growing larger and brighter, that its motion was quite different from the orderly progress of the planets, and that the deflection[5] of Neptune and its satellite was becoming now of an unprecedented[6] kind.

Few people without a training in science can realize the huge isolation of the solar system. The sun with its specks of planets, its dust of planetoids, and its impalpable comets, swims in a vacant immensity that almost defeats the imagination. Beyond the orbit of Neptune there is space, vacant so far as human observation has penetrated, without warmth or light or sound, blank emptiness, for twenty million times a million miles. That is the smallest estimate of the distance to be traversed before the very nearest of the stars is attained. And, saving a few comets more unsubstantial than the thinnest flame, no matter had ever to human knowledge crossed this gulf of space, until early in the twentieth century this strange wanderer appeared. A vast mass of matter it was, bulky, heavy, rushing with-

out warning out of the black mystery of the sky into the radiance of the sun. By the second day it was clearly visible to any decent instrument, as a speck with a barely sensible diameter, in the constellation Leo near Regulus. In a little while an opera glass could attain it.

On the third day of the new year the newspaper readers of two hemispheres were made aware for the first time of the real importance of this unusual apparition[7] in the heavens. "A Planetary Collision," one London paper headed the news, and proclaimed Duchaine's opinion that this strange new planet would probably collide with Neptune. The leader writers enlarged upon the topic. So that in most of the capitals of the world, on January 3rd, there was an expectation, however vague, of some imminent[8] phenomenon in the sky; and as the night followed the sunset round the globe, thousands of men turned their eyes skyward to see—the old familiar stars just as they had always been.

Until it was dawn in London and Pollux setting and the stars overhead grown pale. The winter's dawn it was, a sickly filtering accumulation of daylight, and the light of gas and candles shone yellow in the windows to show where people were astir. But the yawning policeman saw the thing, the busy crowds in the markets stopped agape,[9] workmen going to their work betimes,[10] milkmen,

1. **simultaneously** (sī′məl tā′nē əs lē), *adv.* at the same time.
2. **outermost.** When Wells wrote "The Star," Neptune was the outermost known planet. The planet Pluto was not discovered until 1930.
3. **erratic** (ə rat′ik), *adj.* irregular.
4. **perturbed** (pər tėrbd), *adj.* caused to be irregular in movement by the gravitational attraction of another body.
5. **deflection** (di flek′shən), *n.* changing of direction.
6. **unprecedented** (un pres′ə den′tid), *adj.* never done before; never known before.
7. **apparition** (ap′ə rish′ən), *n.* something strange, remarkable, or unexpected.
8. **imminent** (im′ə nənt), *adj.* about to happen.
9. **agape** (ə gāp′), *adj.* open-mouthed with wonder.
10. **betimes** (bi tīmz′), *adv.* early. *[archaic]*

the drivers of news-carts, dissipation[11] going home jaded and pale, homeless wanderers, sentinels on their beats, and in the country, laborers trudging afield, poachers slinking home, all over the dusky quickening country it could be seen—and out at sea by seamen watching for the day—a great white star, come suddenly into the westward sky!

Brighter it was than any star in our skies; brighter than the evening star at its brightest. It still glowed out white and large, no mere twinkling spot of light, but a small round clear shining disc, an hour after the day had come. And where science has not reached, men stared and feared, telling one another of the wars and pestilences that are foreshadowed by these fiery signs in the Heavens. Sturdy Boers, dusky Hottentots, Gold Coast Negroes, Frenchmen, Spaniards, Portuguese, stood in the warmth of the sunrise watching the setting of this strange new star.

And in a hundred observatories there had been suppressed excitement, rising almost to shouting pitch, as the two remote bodies had rushed together, and a hurrying to and fro to gather photographic apparatus and spectroscope, and this appliance and that, to record this novel astonishing sight, the destruction of a world. For it was a world, a sister planet of our earth, far greater than our earth indeed, that had so suddenly flashed into flaming death. Neptune it was, had been struck, fairly and squarely, by the strange planet from outer space and the heat of the concussion had incontinently turned two solid globes into one vast mass of incandescence.[12] Round the world that day, two hours before the dawn, went the pallid great white star, fading only as it sank westward and the sun mounted above it. Everywhere men marveled at it, but of all those who saw it none could have marveled more than those sailors, habitual watchers of the stars, who far way at sea had heard nothing of its advent and saw it now rise like a pigmy moon and climb zenithward and hang overhead and sink westward with the passing of the night.

And when next it rose over Europe everywhere were crowds of watchers on hilly slopes, on house-roofs, in open spaces, staring eastward for the rising of the great new star. It rose with a white glow in front of it, like the glare of a white fire, and those who had seen it come into existence the night before cried out at the sight of it. "It is larger," they cried. "It is brighter!" And, indeed the moon a quarter full and sinking in the west was in its apparent size beyond comparison, but scarcely in all its breadth had it as much brightness now as the little circle of the strange new star.

"It is brighter!" cried the people clustering in the streets. But in the dim observatories the watchers held their breath and peered at one another. *"It is nearer,"* they said. *"Nearer!"*

And voice after voice repeated, "It is nearer," and the clicking telegraph took that up, and it trembled along telephone wires, and in a thousand cities grimy compositors fingered the type. "It is nearer." Men writing in offices, struck with a strange realization, flung down their pens; men talking in a thousand places suddenly came upon a grotesque possibility in those words, "It is nearer." It hurried along awakening streets, it was shouted down the frost-stilled ways of quiet villages, men who had read these things from the throbbing tape stood in yellow-lit doorways shouting the news to the passers-by.

PREDICT: What is the "grotesque possibility" in the words "It is nearer"?

"It is nearer." Pretty women, flushed and glittering, heard the news told jestingly between the dances, and feigned[13] an intelligent interest they did not feel. "Nearer! Indeed. How curious! How very, very clever people must be to find out things like that!"

Lonely tramps faring through the wintry night murmured those words to comfort themselves—

---

11. **dissipation** (dis′ə pā′shən), *n.* people who indulge excessively in foolish pleasures.
12. **incandescence** (in′kən des′ns), *n.* shining brilliance.
13. **feign** (fān), *v.* pretend.

looking skyward. "It has need to be nearer, for the night's as cold as charity. Don't seem much warmth from it if it *is* nearer, all the same."

"What is a new star to me?" cried the weeping woman kneeling beside her dead.

The schoolboy, rising early for his examination work, puzzled it out for himself—with the great white star, shining broad and bright through the frost-flowers of his window. "Centrifugal, centripetal,"[14] he said, with his chin on his fist. "Stop a planet in its flight, rob it of its centrifugal force, what then? Centripetal has it, and down it falls into the sun! And this—!"

"Do *we* come in the way? I wonder—"

It is larger . . . It is brighter . . . It is nearer!

The light of that day went the way of its brethren, and with the later watches of the frosty darkness rose the strange star again. And it was now so bright that the waxing moon seemed but a pale yellow ghost of itself, hanging huge in the sunset. In a South African city a great man had married, and the streets were alight to welcome his return with his bride. "Even the skies have illuminated," said the flatterer. Under Capricorn, two Negro lovers daring the wild beasts and evil spirits, for love of one another, crouched together in a cane brake where the fire-flies hovered. "That is our star," they whispered, and felt strangely comforted by the sweet brilliance of its light.

The master mathematician sat in his private room and pushed the papers from him. His calculations were already finished. In a small white phial there still remained a little of the drug that had kept him awake and active for four long nights. Each day, serene, explicit, patient as ever, he had given his lecture to his students, and then had come back at once to this momentous calculation. His face was grave, a little drawn and hectic from his drugged activity. For some time

he seemed lost in thought. Then he went to the window, and the blind went up with a click. Half way up the sky, over the clustering roofs, chimneys and steeples of the city, hung the star.

He looked at it as one might look into the eyes of a brave enemy. "You may kill me," he said after a silence. "But I can hold you—and all the universe for that matter—in the grip of this little brain. I would not change. Even now."

He looked at the little phial. "There will be no need of sleep again," he said. The next day at noon, punctual to the minute, he entered his lecture theater, put his hat on the end of the table as his habit was, and carefully selected a large piece of chalk. It was a joke among his students that he could not lecture without that piece of chalk to fumble in his fingers, and once he had been stricken to impotence[15] by their hiding his supply. He came and looked under his gray eyebrows at the rising tiers of young fresh faces, and spoke with his accustomed studied commonness of phrasing. "Circumstances have arisen—circumstances beyond my control," he said and paused, "which will debar[16] me from completing the course I had designed. It would seem, gentlemen, if I may put the thing clearly and briefly, that—Man has lived in vain."

CLARIFY: What do you think the mathematician means when he tells his students, "Man has lived in vain"?

The students glanced at one another. Had they heard aright? Mad? Raised eyebrows and grinning lips there were, but one or two faces remained intent upon his calm gray-fringed face. "It will be interesting," he was saying, "to devote

---

14. centrifugal (sen trif′yə gəl), *adj.* . . .centripetal (sen-trip′ə təl), *adj.* Centrifugal means moving away from a center; centripetal means moving toward a center.
15. impotence (im′pə təns), *n.* condition of helplessness.
16. **debar** (di bär′), *v.* prevent.

this morning to an exposition, so far as I can make it clear to you, of the calculations that have led me to this conclusion. Let us assume—"

He turned towards the blackboard, meditating a diagram in the way that was usual to him. "What was that about 'lived in vain'?" whispered one student to another. "Listen," said the other, nodding towards the lecturer.

And presently they began to understand.

> **PREDICT: At this point in the story what do you predict will happen to the star?**

That night the star rose later, for its proper eastward motion had carried it some way across Leo towards Virgo, and its brightness was so great that the sky became a luminous[17] blue as it rose, and every star was hidden in its turn, save only Jupiter near the zenith, Capella, Aldebaran, Sirius and the pointers of the Bear. It was very white and beautiful. In many parts of the world that night a pallid halo encircled it about. It was perceptibly larger; in the clear refractive sky of the tropics it seemed as if it were nearly a quarter the size of the moon. The frost was still on the ground in England, but the world was as brightly lit as if it were midsummer moonlight. One could see to read quite ordinary print by that cold clear light, and in the cities the lamps burned yellow and wan.

And everywhere the world was awake that night, and throughout Christendom a somber murmur hung in the keen air over the countryside like the belling of bees in the heather, and this murmurous tumult grew to a clangor in the cities. It was the tolling of the bells in a million belfry towers and steeples, summoning the people to sleep no more, to sin no more, but to gather in their churches and pray. And overhead, growing larger and brighter as the earth rolled on its way and the night passed, rose the dazzling star.

And the streets and houses were alight in all the cities, the shipyards glared, and whatever roads led to high country were lit and crowded all night long. And in all the seas about the civilized lands, ships with throbbing engines, and ships with bellying sails, crowded with men and living creatures, were standing out to ocean and the north. For already the warning of the master mathematician had been telegraphed all over the world, and translated into a hundred tongues. The new planet and Neptune, locked in a fiery embrace, were whirling headlong, ever faster and faster towards the sun. Already every second this blazing mass flew a hundred miles, and every second its terrific velocity increased. As it flew now, indeed, it must pass a hundred million of miles wide of the earth and scarcely affect it. But near its destined path, as yet only slightly perturbed, spun the mighty planet Jupiter and his moons sweeping splendid round the sun. Every moment now the attraction between the fiery star and the greatest of planets grew stronger. And the result of that attraction? Inevitably Jupiter would be deflected from his orbit into an elliptical path, and the burning star, swung by his attraction wide of its sunward rush, would "describe a curved path" and perhaps collide with, and certainly pass very close to, our earth. "Earthquakes, volcanic outbreaks, cyclones, sea waves, floods, and a steady rise in temperature to I know not what limit"—so prophesied the master mathematician.

And overhead, to carry out his words, lonely and cold and livid, blazed the star of the coming doom.

To many who stared at it that night until their eyes ached, it seemed that it was visibly approaching. And that night, too, the weather changed, and the frost that had gripped all Central Europe and France and England softened towards a thaw.

But you must not imagine because I have spoken of people praying through the night and people going aboard ships and people fleeing towards mountainous country that the whole world was already in a terror because of the star. As a matter of fact, use and wont[18] still ruled the

---

17. luminous (lü′mə nəs), *adj.* shining; bright.
18. **wont** (wunt), *n.* custom.

This picture, which appeared in a magazine in 1908, shows the supposed destruction that would occur if a comet passed too close to the earth. "Buildings and human beings would be scorched to cinders in a second," said the caption that accompanied the picture. Compare the scene depicted here with the descriptions of destruction and death in "The Star." Why do you suppose their details are so similar?

world, and save for the talk of idle moments and the splendor of the night, nine human beings out of ten were still busy at their common occupations. In all the cities the shops, save one here and there, opened and closed at their proper hours, the doctor and the undertaker plied their trades, the workers gathered in the factories, soldiers drilled, scholars studied, lovers sought one another, thieves lurked and fled, politicians planned their schemes. The presses of the newspapers roared through the nights, and many a priest of this church and that would not open his holy building to further what he considered a foolish panic. The newspapers insisted on the lesson of the year 1000—for then, too, people had anticipated the end. The star was no star—mere gas—a comet; and were it a star it could not possibly strike the earth. There was no precedent for such a thing. Common sense was sturdy everywhere, scornful, jesting, a little inclined to persecute the obdurate[19] fearful. That night, at seven-fifteen by Greenwich time, the star would be at its nearest to Jupiter. Then the world would see the turn things would take. The master mathematician's grim warnings were treated by many as so much mere elaborate self-advertisement. Common sense at last, a little heated by argument, signified its unalterable convictions by going to bed. So, too, barbarism and savagery, already tired of the novelty, went about their mighty business, and save for a howling dog here and there, the beast world left the star unheeded.

. . . it grew with a terrible steadiness hour after hour. . . .

And yet, when at last the watchers in the European States saw the star rise, an hour later it is true, but no larger than it had been the night before, there were still plenty awake to laugh at the master mathematician—to take the danger as if it had passed.

But hereafter the laughter ceased. The star grew—it grew with a terrible steadiness hour after hour, a little larger each hour, a little nearer the midnight zenith, and brighter and brighter, until it had turned night into a second day. Had it come straight to the earth instead of in a curved path, had it lost no velocity to Jupiter, it must have leapt the intervening gulf in a day, but as it was it took five days altogether to come by our planet. The next night it had become a third the size of the moon before it set to English eyes,

and the thaw was assured. It rose over America near the size of the moon, but blinding white to look at, and *hot;* and a breath of hot wind blew now with its rising and gathering strength, and in Virginia, and Brazil, and down the St. Lawrence valley, it shone intermittently through a driving reek of thunder-clouds, flickering violet lightning, and hail unprecedented. In Manitoba was a thaw and devastating[20] floods. And upon all the mountains of the earth the snow and ice began to melt that night, and all the rivers coming out of high country flowed thick and turbid,[21] and soon—in their upper reaches—with swirling trees and the bodies of beasts and men. They rose steadily, steadily in the ghostly brilliance, and came trickling over their banks at last, behind the flying population of their valleys.

And along the coast of Argentina and up the South Atlantic the tides were higher than had ever been in the memory of man, and the storms drove the waters in many cases scores of miles inland, drowning whole cities. And so great grew the heat during the night that the rising of the sun was like the coming of a shadow. The earthquakes began and grew until all down America from the Arctic Circle to Cape Horn, hillsides were sliding, fissures were opening, and houses and walls crumbling to destruction. The whole side of Cotopaxi[22] slipped out in one vast convulsion, and a tumult of lava poured out so high and broad and swift and liquid that in one day it reached the sea.

So the star, with the wan moon in its wake, marched across the Pacific, trailed the thunderstorms like the hem of a robe, and the growing tidal wave that toiled behind it, frothing and eager, poured over island and island and swept them clear of men. Until that wave came at last—in a blinding light and with the breath of a fur-

---

19. **obdurate** (ob′dər it), *adj.* stubborn.
20. **devastating** (dev′ə stā′ting), *adj.* very destructive.
21. **turbid** (tèr′bid), *adj.* muddy.
22. **Cotopaxi,** the highest active volcano in the world, in the Andes of northern Ecuador.

nace, swift and terrible it came—a wall of water, fifty feet high, roaring hungrily, upon the long coasts of Asia, and swept inland across the plains of China. For a space the star, hotter now and larger and brighter than the sun in its strength, showed with pitiless brilliance the wide and populous country; towns and villages with their pagodas and trees, roads, wide cultivated fields, millions of sleepless people staring in helpless terror at the incandescent sky; and then, low and growing, came the murmur of the flood. And thus it was with millions of men that night—a flight nowhither, with limbs heavy with heat and breath fierce and scant, and the flood like a wall swift and white behind. And then death.

China was lit glowing white, but over Japan and Java and all the islands of Eastern Asia the great star was a ball of dull red fire because of the steam and smoke and ashes the volcanoes were spouting forth to salute its coming. Above was the lava, hot gases and ash, and below the seething floods, and the whole earth swayed and rumbled with the earthquake shocks. Soon the immemorial snows of Tibet and the Himalaya were melting and pouring down by ten million deepening converging channels upon the plains of Burma and Hindustan. The tangled summits of the Indian jungles were aflame in a thousand places, and below the hurrying waters around the stems were dark objects that still struggled feebly and reflected the blood-red tongues of fire. And in a rudderless confusion a multitude of men and women fled down the broad river-ways to that one last hope of men— the open sea.

Larger grew the star, and larger, hotter and brighter with a terrible swiftness now. The tropical ocean had lost its phosphorescence, and the whirling steam rose in ghostly wreaths from the black waves that plunged incessantly, speckled with storm-tossed ships.

And then came a wonder. It seemed to those who in Europe watched for the rising of the star

that the world must have ceased its rotation. In a thousand open spaces of down and upland the people who had fled thither from the floods and the falling houses and sliding slopes of hill watched for that rising in vain. Hour followed hour through a terrible suspense, and the star rose not. Once again men set their eyes upon the old constellations they had counted lost to them forever. In England it was hot and clear overhead, though the ground quivered perpetually, but in the tropics, Sirius and Capella and Aldebaran showed through a veil of steam. And when at last the great star rose near ten hours late, the sun rose close upon it, and in the center of its white heart was a disc of black.

Over Asia it was the star had begun to fall behind the movement of the sky, and then suddenly, as it hung over India, its light had been veiled. All the plain of India from the mouth of the Indus to the mouths of the Ganges was a shallow waste of shining water that night, out of which rose temples and palaces, mounds and hills, black with people. Every minaret was a clustering mass of people, who fell one by one into the turbid waters, as heat and terror overcame them. The whole land seemed a-wailing, and suddenly there swept a shadow across that furnace of despair, and a breath of cold wind, and a gathering of clouds, out of the cooling air. Men looking up, near blinded, at the star, saw that a black disc was creeping across the light. It was the moon, coming between the star and the earth. And even as man cried to God at this respite, out of the East with a strange inexplicable[23] swiftness sprang the sun. And then star, sun, and moon rushed together across the heavens.

So it was that presently, to the European watchers, star and sun rose close upon each other, drove headlong for a space and then slower, and at last came to rest, star and sun merged into one glare of flame at the zenith of the sky. The moon

---

23. inexplicable (in′ik splik′ə bəl), *adj.* mysterious; unable to be explained.

no longer eclipsed the star but was lost to sight in the brilliance of the sky. And though those who were still alive regarded it for the most part with that dull stupidity that hunger, fatigue, heat and despair engender, there were still men who could perceive the meaning of these signs. Star and earth had been at their nearest, had swung about one another, and the star had passed. Already it was receding, swifter and swifter, in the last stage of its headlong journey downward into the sun.

And then the clouds gathered, blotting out the vision of the sky, the thunder and lightning wove a garment round the world; all over the earth was such a downpour of rain as men had never before seen, and where the volcanoes flared red against the cloud canopy there descended torrents of mud. Everywhere the waters were pouring off the land, leaving mud-silted ruins, and the earth littered like a storm-worn beach with all that had floated, and the dead bodies of the men and brutes, its children. For days the water streamed off the land, sweeping away soil and trees and houses in the way, and piling huge dykes and scooping out titanic gullies over the country side. Those were the days of darkness that followed the star and the heat. All through them, and for many weeks and months, the earthquakes continued.

But the star had passed, and men, hunger-driven and gathering courage only slowly, might creep back to their ruined cities, buried granaries, and sodden fields. Such few ships as had escaped the storms of that time came stunned and shattered and sounding their way cautiously through the new marks and shoals of once familiar ports. And as the storms subsided men perceived that everywhere the days were hotter than of yore, and the sun larger, and the moon, shrunk to a third of its former size, took now fourscore days between its new and new.

But of the new brotherhood that grew presently among men, of the saving of laws and books and machines, of the strange change that had come over Iceland and Greenland and the shores of Baffin's Bay, so that the sailors coming there presently found them green and gracious, and could scarce believe their eyes, this story does not tell. Nor of the movement of mankind now that the earth was hotter, northward and southward towards the poles of the earth. It concerns itself only with the coming and the passing of the Star.

The Martian astronomers—for there are astronomers on Mars, although they are very different beings from men—were naturally profoundly interested by these things. They saw them from their own standpoint of course. "Considering the mass and temperature of the missile that was flung through our solar system into the sun," one wrote, "it is astonishing what a little damage the earth, which it missed so narrowly, has sustained. All the familiar continental markings and the masses of the seas remain intact, and indeed the only difference seems to be a shrinkage of the white discoloration (supposed to be frozen water) round either pole." Which only shows how small the vastest of human catastrophes may seem, at a distance of a few million miles.

CLARIFY: What do you think the conclusion the Martian astronomers draw from their different perspective indicates about their knowledge of the earth?

After Reading

Making Connections

Shaping Your Response

1. What emotions do you feel as the star grows larger and brighter? What emotions do you feel when the earth is spared?

2. With what tone of voice do you imagine the mathematician would deliver his final lecture? Choose a passage and read it in this tone.

Analyzing the Short Story

3. Why do you think Wells chooses to begin his story on the first day of the new year?

4. Trace the progress of the star from a "faint remote speck of light" (paragraph 1) to a "great white star" (paragraph 4). What do you think Wells achieves by describing the star in so many different ways throughout?

5. In presenting the different ways people react to the star, Wells is commenting on various elements of society. Draw a chart like the one shown. List several types of people, their reactions, and the commentary you think Wells is making about them.

Type of Person	Reaction to Star	Commentary

6. Why do you think Wells chooses a mathematician to be the one **character** he develops fully in this story?

7. Why do you think the mathematician looks at the star "as one might look into the eyes of a brave enemy"?

8. What do you think the prediction of a "new brotherhood" indicates about Wells's attitude toward mankind?

9. How does the last paragraph about the Martian astronomers cast an entirely different light on the events?

Extending the Ideas

10. Wells writes his tale from the **perspective** of a scientist. How do you think the story would be different if it had been written from the perspective of a politician or a clergyman?

Literary Focus: Point of View

Point of view is the vantage point from which an author presents the actions and characters in a story. What point of view does Wells use in "The Star"? What advantage does Wells gain by selecting this point of view? How might the story change if he were to select a different point of view?

Vocabulary Study

Select the word from the list that best completes the meaning of each sentence. You will not use all the words.

agape
apparition
centrifugal
devastating
erratic
imminent
impotence
inexplicable
luminous
obdurate
unprecedented

1. All the world is stunned by the _____ in the sky of a new star.

2. Because the strange star veers off its expected course, its movements are called _____.

3. Scientists think the star's behavior _____ because the star moves in a way they have never seen before.

4. When the mathematician predicts that the star will collide with the earth, the students believe that the end of the world is _____.

5. Some call the mathematician a fool for being _____ in his belief.

6. Fascinated by the brightness of the star, the people stand _____.

7. The star is so _____ that at night people are able to read without using lamplight.

8. People feel their complete _____ at not being able to do anything whatsoever about the approaching star.

9. Given the closeness of the star to the earth, it is amazing that the damage is not more _____.

10. Why the star collides with the sun rather than with the earth remains a(n) _____ mystery.

Expressing Your Ideas _____

Writing Choices

Writer's Notebook Update Look back at your expectations for this story. How many of the characteristics that you mentioned did you actually find in the story? What characteristics did you notice that you had not thought of?

It's Headline News Write the **headlines,** beginning with January 3, the day the story of the star first breaks in the newspapers. Continue with daily headlines until the star has passed. Conclude with headlines for a special edition summarizing the destruction.

Other Options

The Survival Lecture Assume that the mathematician and his class are among those who survive the star. Prepare the first five minutes of his opening **lecture** on the first day of class. Deliver the lecture in character as you imagine the mathematician might do it.

The War of the Worlds On October 30, 1938, the actor Orson Welles caused near panic with a radio broadcast of Wells's *The War of the Worlds* (see page 629). Many listeners believed that Martians were actually invading the earth. Research the event in books and old newspapers and prepare an **oral report** for your class.

Before Reading

Tommy

If— by Rudyard Kipling

Rudyard Kipling
1865–1936

Rudyard Kipling was born in Bombay, when England ruled the entire subcontinent of India. From age 6 on his parents sent him to school in England. At 17 he returned to India where he worked as an editorial assistant for a newspaper and began to write stories and poems, some of which served as newspaper fillers. In his first book of poetry, *Departmental Ditties* (1886), he described colonial society. Gaining great popularity as a writer, he moved to England where he published the two *Jungle Books* (1894, 1895) and the sea tale *Captains Courageous* (1897). In 1901 appeared his finest novel, *Kim,* the adventures of an orphan living in the streets of India. Kipling became the respected confidant of heads of state and military leaders, and he was the first English writer to win the Nobel Prize for literature (1907).

Building Background

Kipling's India During Kipling's lifetime India was part of the massive British Empire. In fact, in 1876 Queen Victoria was declared Empress of India. The masses in India, however, were living in poverty, and famines contributed to a general spirit of unrest. In 1885 the Indian National Congress raised the political consciousness of many Indians and called for national unification. Throughout many uprisings Kipling remained a solid supporter of British rule and the use of force. He believed that it was the duty of every Englishman to bring European culture to the uncivilized world; he once called that duty "the white man's burden." Even though his enthusiasm for war and power and imperialistic control made him controversial and isolated, Kipling retained his popularity as a writer.

Literary Focus

Synecdoche A figure of speech in which a part stands for the whole is called **synecdoche** (si nek′də kē). For example, in "hired hands" *hands* (the part) stands for the workers (the whole), those who labor with their hands. Synecdoche also refers to an expression in which the whole stands for a part, as in "call the law." Here, *law* (the whole) represents the police (a part of the whole system of law). Try to find examples of synecdoche in Kipling's poems.

Writer's Notebook

Adult Virtues As a typical Victorian, Kipling believed in a number of "manly virtues" that a successful, responsible man ought to possess. (Women would have been considered separately.) Make a list of ten or twelve virtues or characteristics that you think are important for a responsible adult to possess.

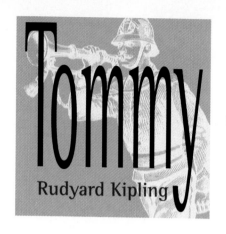

Tommy

Rudyard Kipling

I went into a public-'ouse to get a pint o' beer,
The publican[1] 'e up an' sez, "We serve no red-coats[2] here."
The girls be'ind the bar they laughed an' giggled fit to die,
I outs into the street again an' to myself sez I:
5   O it's Tommy this, an' Tommy that, an' "Tommy, go away";
      But it's "Thank you, Mister Atkins," when the band begins
        to play—
      The band begins to play, my boys, the band begins to play,
      O it's "Thank you, Mister Atkins," when the band begins to
        play.

I went into a theater as sober as could be,
10 They gave a drunk civilian room, but 'adn't none for me;
They sent me to the gallery or round the music-'alls,
But when it comes to fightin', Lord! they'll shove me in the stalls![3]
      For it's Tommy this, an' Tommy that, an' "Tommy, wait
        outside";
      But it's "Special train for Atkins" when the trooper's on the
        tide—
15   The troopship's on the tide, my boys, the troopship's on the
        tide,
      O it's "Special train for Atkins" when the trooper's on the
        tide.

Yes, makin' mock o' uniforms that guard you while you sleep
Is cheaper than them uniforms, an' they're starvation cheap;
An' hustlin' drunken soldiers when they're goin' large a bit
20 Is five times better business than paradin' in full kit.
      Then it's Tommy this, an' Tommy that, an' "Tommy, 'ow's
        yer soul?"
      But it's "Thin red line of 'eroes" when the drums begin to
        roll—
      The drums begin to roll, my boys, the drums begin to roll,
      O it's "Thin red line of 'eroes" when the drums begin to
        roll.

25 We aren't no thin red 'eroes, nor we aren't no blackguards[4] too,
But single men in barricks, most remarkable like you;
An' if sometimes our conduck isn't all your fancy paints,[5]
Why, single men in barricks don't grow into plaster saints;
      While it's Tommy this, an' Tommy that, an' "Tommy, fall
        be'ind,"
30   But it's "Please to walk in front, sir," when there's trouble
        in the wind—
      There's trouble in the wind, my boys, there's trouble in
        the wind,
      O it's "Please to walk in front, sir," when there's trouble in
        the wind.

You talk o' better food for us, an' schools, an' fires, an' all:
We'll wait for extry rations if you treat us rational.[6]
35 Don't mess about the cook-room slops, but prove it to our face
The Widow's[7] uniform is not the soldier-man's disgrace.
        For it's Tommy this, an' Tommy that, an' "Chuck him out, the brute!"
        But it's "Saviour of 'is country" when the guns begin to shoot;
        An' it's Tommy this, an' Tommy that, an' anything you please;
40   An' Tommy ain't a bloomin' fool—you bet that Tommy sees!

---

1. **publican** (pub′lə kən), *n.* keeper of the pub, or tavern.
2. **red-coats,** British soldiers.
3. **stalls,** seats in the front part of the theater; here, referring to the front lines on a battlefield.
4. **blackguard** (blag′ärd), *n.* scoundrel.
5. **fancy paints,** imagination pictures.
6. **rational** (rash′ə nəl), *adv.* rationally; reasonably.
7. **Widow,** Queen Victoria.

This illustration appeared on the cover of the sheet music for the song "The Queen's Own Little Box of Soldiers." In depicting real-life English soldiers as toys that spring out of a box, what attitude toward those soldiers does this illustration imply? How is this attitude similar to the one the speaker finds so offensive in the poem "Tommy"? ▼

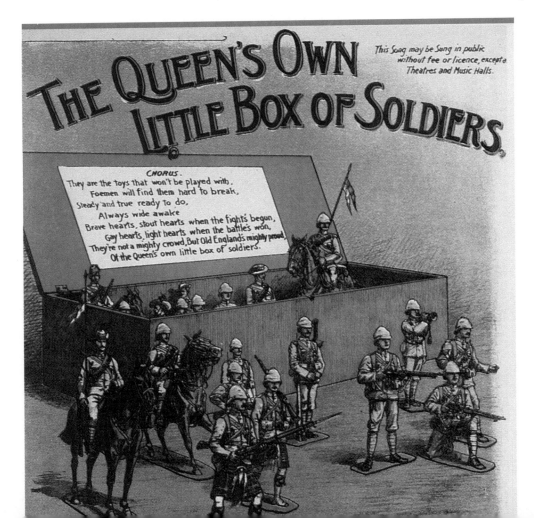

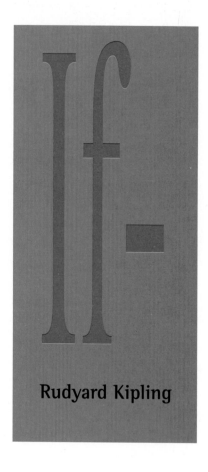

Rudyard Kipling

If you can keep your head when all about you
    Are losing theirs and blaming it on you,
If you can trust yourself when all men doubt you,
    But make allowance for their doubting too;
5 If you can wait and not be tired by waiting,
    Or being lied about, don't deal in lies,
Or being hated, don't give way to hating,
    And yet don't look too good, nor talk too wise:

If you can dream—and not make dreams your master;
10   If you can think—and not make thoughts your aim;
If you can meet with Triumph and Disaster
    And treat those two impostors[1] just the same;
If you can bear to hear the truth you've spoken
    Twisted by knaves[2] to make a trap for fools,
15 Or watch things you gave your life to, broken,
    And stoop and build 'em up with worn-out tools:

If you can make one heap of all your winnings
    And risk it on one turn of pitch-and-toss,
And lose, and start again at your beginnings
20   And never breathe a word about your loss;
If you can force your heart and nerve and sinew[3]
    To serve your turn long after they are gone,
And so hold on when there is nothing in you
    Except the Will which says to them: "Hold on!"

25 If you can talk with crowds and keep your virtue,
    Or walk with Kings—nor lose the common touch,
If neither foes nor loving friends can hurt you,
    If all men count with you, but none too much;
If you can fill the unforgiving minute
30   With sixty seconds' worth of distance run,
Yours is the Earth and everything that's in it,
    And—which is more—you'll be a Man, my son!

---

1. **impostor** (im pos′tər), *n.* pretender; deceiver.
2. **knave** (nāv), *n.* dishonest man; rascal.
3. **sinew** (sin′yū), *n.* tendon; here, body.

After Reading

Making Connections

Shaping Your Response

1. Do you think the virtues extolled in "If—" can be realistically attained? Explain your response.

Analyzing the Poems

2. Why do you think Kipling chose to write "Tommy" in **dialect?**

3. Whom or what do you think Tommy represents?

4. ☞ How does the **perspective** of the narrator help to convey a message about the contrasting treatment of soldiers on the battlefront and the home front? What is that message?

5. Explain the last line of the poem "Tommy."

6. Why do you think the speaker in "If—" pictures other people as he does?

7. In times of trouble what does the speaker seem to think is the most important characteristic to possess?

8. What importance do you think the speaker sees in the Will?

9. What skill is suggested by lines 29 and 30?

Extending the Ideas

10. Think back over those authors you have read who have used dialect—Burns, Hardy, Kipling. Why do you suppose these authors used dialect to represent speakers of the lower class?

Literary Focus: Synecdoche

In the figure of speech **synecdoche,** a part can stand for a whole, or a whole can stand for a part. For each sample word that is a part, tell what whole the words could represent. For each sample word that is a whole, tell what part the word could represent.

Sample Words		Sample Words	
Parts	**Wholes**	**Parts**	**Wholes**
wave			school
sail			government
stars			music
petal			forest
roof			church

What do you think the following Kipling synecdoches stand for? From "If—": *head* (line 1); *heart and nerve and sinew* (line 21); from "Tommy": *red-coats* (line 2); *uniforms* (line 16); *fires* (line 31).

Vocabulary Study

Redcoats were British soldiers; *blackguards* are scoundrels. There are many other instances of color adjectives being added to nouns to help define a particular kind of person. Look up one or more of the following words and explain its meaning and its etymology to your class: *black belt, black sheep, bluebeard, bluecollar, bluestocking, graybeard, greengrocer, greenhorn, Orangeman, redcap, redneck, white knight, Yellow Belly.*

Expressing Your Ideas

Writing Choices

Writer's Notebook Update Reread "If —" and make a list of the virtues or characteristics that Kipling suggests are important to possess in order to be a Man (with a capital letter). Compare Kipling's list with the list you wrote in your notebook.

I Recommend You may have observed someone—a friend, a relative, a public figure— who has exhibited one or more of the moral characteristics described by Kipling in "If—." Write a personal **letter of recommendation** for this person, discussing in depth a situation in which moral characteristics were displayed and why these virtues are important to explaining this person's approach to life.

Little Words That Count Kipling uses the repetition of a little but powerful word, *If,* to provide the structure for his poem of advice to the young. Find a little word of your own— such as *but* or *then* or *when*—and write a short **poem** using that word to give both structure and meaning to your ideas.

Other Options

Story Time Most of Kipling's books will be found in the children's section of your local library. Look through the many collections of Kipling's tales and select one you would like to prepare for reading to a class of second graders. Prepare an **oral reading** of the story complete with illustrations.

Perfect—and Then Some Create a **collage** of a character that embodies several of the virtues you consider important to be a Man or a Woman. You might combine features from magazine photos of various people in the news who display one virtue or another, along with other pictures that symbolize the virtues you have chosen. Label your collage with the people and qualities you have combined.

Kipling's India Select one of the following topics for research about Kipling's India: British colonial rule, India's struggle for independence, the culture of India. Prepare an **oral report** for your class. If possible, illustrate your report with pictures or with charts.

Popular Culture Connection

Like more serious literature, the popular fiction of the 1890s reflected the era's attitudes and anxieties. In his 1898 novel *The War of the Worlds*, H. G. Wells explored the possibility of a devastating invasion by ruthless, super-intelligent Martians. In the following excerpt from chapter 1, the narrator discusses how the end of the Martians' own planet forces them to look toward earth as a colony.

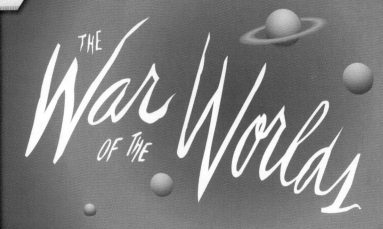

THE War OF THE Worlds

BY H. G. WELLS

No one would have believed in the last years of the nineteenth century that this world was being watched keenly and closely by intelligences greater than man's and yet as mortal as his own; that as men busied themselves about their various concerns they were scrutinized and studied, perhaps almost as narrowly as a man with a microscope might scrutinize the transient creatures that swarm and multiply in a drop of water. With infinite complacency men went to and fro over this globe about their little affairs, serene in their assurance of their empire over matter. It is possible that the infusoria under the microscope do the same. No one gave a thought to the older worlds of space as sources of human danger, or thought of them only to dismiss the idea of life upon them as impossible or improbable. It is curious to recall some of the mental habits of those departed days. At most, terrestial men fancied that there might be other men upon Mars, perhaps inferior to themselves and ready to welcome a missionary enterprise. Yet across the gulf of space, minds that are to our minds as ours are to those of the beasts that perish, intellects vast and cool and unsympathetic, regarded this earth with envious eyes, and slowly and surely drew their plans against us. And early in the twentieth century came the great disillusionment.

The planet Mars, I scarcely need remind the reader, revolves around the sun at a mean distance of 140,000,000 miles, and the light and heat it receives from the sun is barely half of that received by this world. It must be, if the nebular hypothesis has any truth, older than our world; and long before this earth ceased to be molten, life upon its surface must have begun its course. The fact that it is scarcely one-seventh of the volume of the earth must have accelerated its cooling to the temperature at which life could begin. It has air and water and all that is necessary for the support of animated existence.

Yet so vain is man and so blinded by his vanity, that no writer, up to the very end of the nineteenth century, expressed any idea that

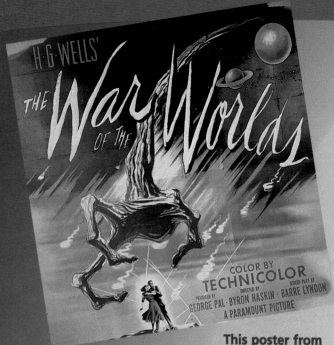

This poster from the 1953 film version of Wells's novel does not attempt to depict the invaders from Mars, but symbolizes them by a clutching hand poised over tiny, defenseless Earthlings. Do you think picturing the Martians would have been more effective? Why or why not?

intelligent life might have developed there far, or indeed at all, beyond its earthly level. Nor was it generally understood that since Mars is older than our earth, with scarcely a quarter of the superficial area and remoter from the sun, it necessarily follows that it is not only more distant from life's beginning but nearer its end.

The secular cooling that must some day overtake our planet has already gone far indeed with our neighbor. Its physical condition is still largely a mystery, but we know now that even in its equatorial region the mid-day temperature barely approaches that of our coldest winter. Its air is much more attenuated than ours, its oceans have shrunk until they cover but a third of its surface, and as its slow seasons change huge snow-caps gather and melt about either pole and periodically inundate its temperate zones. That last stage of exhaustion, which to us is still incredibly remote, has become a present-day problem for the inhabitants of Mars. The immediate pressure of necessity has brightened their intellects,

enlarged their powers, and hardened their hearts. And looking across space with instruments, and intelligences such as we have scarcely dreamed of, they see, at its nearest distance only 35,000,000 of miles sunward of them, a morning star of hope, our own warmer planet, green with vegetation and gray with water, with a cloudy atmosphere eloquent of fertility, with glimpses through its drifting cloud-wisps of broad stretches of populous country and narrow, navy-crowded seas.

And we men, the creatures who inhabit this earth, must be to them at least as alien and lowly as are the monkeys and lemurs to us. The intellectual side of man already admits that life is an incessant struggle for existence, and it would seem that this too is the belief of the minds upon Mars. Their world is far gone in its cooling and this world is still crowded with life, but crowded only with what they regard as inferior animals. To carry warfare sunward is, indeed, their only escape from the destruction that generation after generation creeps upon them.

And before we judge of them too harshly we must remember what ruthless and utter destruction our own species has wrought, not only upon animals, such as the vanished bison and the dodo, but upon its own inferior races. The Tasmanians, in spite of their human likeness, were entirely swept out of existence in a war of extermination waged by European immigrants, in the space of fifty years. Are we such apostles of mercy as to complain if the Martians warred in the same spirit?

Responding

1. How does Darwinism, with its belief in the "survival of the fittest," affect the narrator's attitude toward the Martian invasion?

2. Judging by the narrator's comment on the extermination of the Tasmanians, what is his attitude toward European imperialism?

Mathematics Connection

Regardless of whether we believe the new century actually begins on January 1, 2000, or January 1, 2001, it is sure to bring with it changes that turn today's dreams into tomorrow's reality. It is a reality that will be created by the people who live it, for better or worse. Will we be able to make it better?

COUNTING THE YEARS

BY LANCE MORROW

Purists like to point out that, technically speaking, the beginning of the new millenium does not really occur on January 1, 2000, but on January 1, 2001. This is because there is no year zero in the Christian era, on which historical calendars are calculated. The first year of the era is called A.D. 1, and the one immediately preceding is 1 B.C. Therefore, by the time the calendar reaches January 1, 2000, only 1,999 years will have elapsed since A.D.'s starting point. The same phenomenon occurs as each new century is recorded. In popular observance, however, the simultaneous turning of the zeros marks the beginning of each new century, and very few of the world's citizens will wait for January 1, 2001, to mark the millenium's beginning. In fact, numerous other systems have been devised to keep track of the passage of the years. The oldest in continuous use, China's lunisolar cycle, assigns an animal to each year based on the Chinese zodiac: the Year of the Tiger, Horse and so on. One of the longest counts is Judaism's reckoning of time from the creation of the world, by which the year 2000 will begin during 5760. For the world's Muslims, it will be the year 1420, counted from the Prophet Muhammad's Hegira (migration) to Medina.

All countries will join in using the year 2000 on their civil calendars, despite the number's Christian basis. Paradoxically, although Jesus' actual birth date is unknown, it is almost certain that he was born several years "before Christ." This anomaly occurred because of an error in the calculations of Denis the Little, the 6th century monk who decided that history should be split into B.C. and A.D.

The Future Poll

1. If you had to predict, which of the following do you think are likely to occur in the 21st century? (Percentages indicate which portion of those responding thought which events were likely to occur.)

Scientists will find a cure for AIDS	75%
Scientists will find a cure for cancer	80%
Scientists will find a cure for the common cold	39%
The average American will live to be a hundred	57%
A woman will be president of the U. S.	76%
A black will be president of the U. S.	76%
Automobiles will no longer run on gasoline	75%
Computers will be as smart as humans and have personalities like humans	44%
Humans will make regular trips to other planets	43%
Beings who live on other planets will come in contact with us	32%

© 1992 Roz Chast

2. Do you think the world will be in better shape at the end of the 21st century than it is today?

Better	41%
Worse	32%
About the same	15%

3. Compared with the 20th century, do you think the 21st century will have more:

Wars	32%
Environmental Disasters	59%
Poverty	61%
Disease	53%
Hope for the Future	62%

From a telephone poll of 800 adult Americans taken for *Time/CNN* on July 22-23, 1995 by Yankelovich Inc. Sampling error ± 3.5%

Responding

Run the Future Poll in your class. Determine the percentages for each response. Calculate the difference in the percentages listed in the chart to those in your class. How might you account for any great ranges in responses?

Language History

The Language of the Victorians

 . . . a man who labors under the pressure of pecuniary embarrassments, is, with the generality of people, at a disadvantage.
Charles Dickens, *David Copperfield* (1850)

Polite English of the Victorian period—especially the early years—was extremely formal. Men addressed their wives as "Mrs." and husbands were treated with equal courtesy. The utmost formality was extended to strangers, thereby implying they were solemn and important people. Certain classes of people—the ambitious businessman, the newly rich, the aspiring student—carried this formality to absurd lengths, as does Mr. Micawber in the example above, explaining that he is broke. They spoke an exaggerated English of their own called *genteelism*.

The first and most important rule of genteelism was to avoid the common word and use instead a learned, bookish synonym. The advocates of genteelism did not begin a meal—they commenced a collation; they did not use a toothpowder—they employed a dentifrice; and they never used *before, except,* or *about*—it was *ere, save,* and *anent*.

Other Victorians had more serious concerns with regard to the English language. One such group was the Philological Society, which in 1858 resolved to prepare a new dictionary that would display the entire history of every word that was or had been in the English language. The Society's monumental dictionary project produced the *Oxford English Dictionary*, published in ten volumes from 1884 to 1928.

As American English grew, it often used different words from British English for the same things. For example, Britishers were *ill, clever,* and *homely*; Americans were *sick, smart,* and *friendly*. Compare the following American and British words pertaining to the railroad industry: *railroad, railway; conductor, guard; fireman, stoker; car, carriage; track, line; freight, goods; trunk, box;* and *check, register*.

The rapid advance of invention and mechanization all during the Victorian Age created a need for many new words. Grammarians protested the forming of such words as *telegraph* and *typewriter* by scientists, inventors, and manufacturers, and felt that the making of words should be left to the etymologists. Nevertheless, people used or invented words as needed, with little regard for "correctness."

Writing Workshop

Found Images

Assignment A found poem is created by collecting favorite lines and phrases from other writers' works and knitting them together with words of your own. Using the literature in this part of the unit, create a found poem and then explain what your poem has to say about the themes of hope and despair.

WRITER'S BLUEPRINT

Product	A found poem and an explanation
Purpose	To explore the themes of hope and despair
Audience	Other people who have read the literature
Specs	To write a successful poem and explanation, you should:

❏ Collect ten lines or phrases from the literature that you think best illustrate the theme of hope. Look for strong images. Do the same for despair.

❏ Create a found poem, using some or all of the images you've collected and knitting them together with words of your own. Your goal is to make a powerful statement about hope and despair.

❏ Write a short, informal essay that contains:
  —an opening statement summing up what your poem has to say about the themes of hope and despair
  —comments on how some of the individual images in the poem illustrate this statement
  —a closing statement that leaves the reader with your single, most important message about hope and despair

❏ Follow the rules of grammar, usage, spelling, and mechanics. Take care to spell homophones correctly.

Review the literature for lines and phrases about hope and despair that create strong images for you. Record these images in two charts, one for hope and one for despair. Include your reactions to these images. For example:

Despair

Images from the Literature	Reactions
"a cry discordant and feeble" (from "The Lagoon")	This could be a sound that Despair would make if it could speak.
"anarchy is loosed upon the world" (from "The Second Coming")	I see Despair as a raging beast. Despair can lead a person to anger, to violence.

Then circle the ten images in each chart that seem strongest to you.

Compose your poem. Begin by writing each of the circled images from your charts onto a separate note card. Then start grouping and arranging them, deleting some, if you wish. You might end up using all the images, or just a few. Experiment with different arrangements until you find the order that works best. As you proceed, jot down words and phrases on the cards that will help you knit these images together into a poem.

OR...
Try a quickdraw. Draw the images you circled to create a rich mental picture. Use this drawing for inspiration when you write your poem.

Then write your final draft. Here are parts of two writers' poems. (The lines from the literature have been underlined so that you can more easily see the different ways these writers have knitted them together.)

I close my eyes and hear
a cry discordant and feeble.
I look up and see a star,
the sweet brilliance of its light.
I look out to see that
anarchy is loosed upon the world,
and I tell myself:
If you can keep your head
when all about you
are losing theirs . . .

STUDENT MODEL

A cry discordant and feeble
announces that
anarchy is loosed upon the
world.
If you can keep your head
when all about you
are losing theirs . . .

STUDENT MODEL

Try a quickwrite. For five minutes, write about your poem. Jot down whatever comes to mind as you ask yourself: *What do these images seem to say about the nature of hope and despair?*

Exchange poems with a partner and react to your partner's poem with a quickwrite like the one you wrote in reaction to your own poem. Then return quickwrites and poems. Use your partner's reactions to help you write your essay of explanation.

Plan your explanation. Review your poem, quickwrites, and charts as you plan your essay of explanation. Make notes on these points:

- An opening statement about hope and despair

- How specific images illustrate the general statement

- A closing statement of your most important message about hope and despair

STEP  DRAFTING

Start writing. Here are some drafting tips to consider:

- Choose the strongest three or four images of hope and of despair and deal with them one at a time.

- For your closing statement, return to your single strongest image and focus on its significance.

- Take care that you develop your general ideas with specific details. See the Revising Strategy in Step 3 of this lesson.

OR . . .
Group similar images and deal with one group at a time.

STEP **3** REVISING

Ask a partner to react to your draft before you revise it. Make sure your partner has a copy of your poem to refer to. Use this checklist as a guide.

✔ Does the essay address the poem?

✔ Does the essay develop the opening statement with specific details?

Revising Strategy

Development by Detail

Good explanatory writing demands that each general idea be developed by specific details. The reader can't be expected to know specifically what the writer means by such a general term as *hope* or *despair*. The reader needs to see specific details that clearly illustrate what this particular writer is getting at. If the reader can't see the connection, the writing loses focus.

Notice how the student model was revised to make it clearer how the details relate to the general statement they are meant to illustrate.

> My poem shows hope and despair as opposites but as existing simultaneously. Each opposite is seen in terms of the other. They are two sides of the same coin. One leads directly to the other. I see hope in terms of clarity and despair as confusion. Before looking up at the star I hear a "cry discordant and feeble." The ~~star~~ *star's clear, brilliant light* represents hope, while the *confusing, discordant* cry stands for despair.

Ask a partner to review your revised draft before you edit. When you edit, look for errors in grammar, usage, spelling, and mechanics. Pay special attention to the spellings of short, simple words that you may otherwise overlook. Look over each sentence to make sure you have used homophones correctly.

Editing Strategy

COMPUTER TIP
If your computer has a spell checker, use it—but don't rely on it to give your perfect spelling. A spell checker won't catch a homophone mistake or a mistake like the one with *your* in the preceding sentence.

Spelling Homophones Correctly

Homophones sound alike but have different spellings and meanings. The key to spelling homophones correctly is paying close attention to their meaning within the context of a passage. For example:

There are three key images in the first stanza. **They're** the strongest images in the poem. I hope readers feel **their** strength. **It's** a difficult task to bring abstract concepts like these to life. A concept like *hope* has **its** own special meaning for each of us, and **it's** the poet's task to narrow all those meanings down to one. As a poet, you know that **your** personal meaning is what **you're** out to communicate.

When you edit for spelling, don't overlook short, simple words like these.

STEP 5 PRESENTING

- Form groups of three and read your poems to each other. As a group, choose what you feel are the four best lines in each poem and combine them to create a new, group poem.

- Make a collage to accompany your poem.

STEP 6 LOOKING BACK

Self-evaluate. Look back at the Writer's Blueprint and give yourself a score on each point, from 6 (superior) to 1 (inadequate).

Reflect. Respond to these items in writing:

✔ Think back to the literature in this part of the unit. Of all the writers you read, which one most closely reflects the ideas about hope and despair in your poem and why?

✔ Give an example of how the general statement in your explanation applies to an experience from your own life.

For Your Working Portfolio Add your poem, essay, and reflection responses to your working portfolio.

Beyond Print

Images of the Future

Every generation tries to predict the future. H. G. Wells, whose story "The Star" appears in this part, was one of the best futurists ever. A surprising number of the technological innovations he created for his stories and novels have actually been developed in this century. Polls, like the Future Poll on page 632, show that everyone has opinions about the future. But how can we tell what is true?

We can't. The future hasn't happened yet. That hasn't stopped innumerable writers, movie and television designers and technicians, and science-fiction illustrators from making the attempt. The interesting thing is that you can often tell more about the artists and the times in which they live than you can tell about the future. For example, the movie *2001* presented a finely detailed picture of space flight (one famous detail: the instructions posted on a spaceship wall on how to use a zero-gravity toilet), but the movie ended with a light show and surrealistic images that strongly hinted at the movie maker's optimism. The movie *Blade Runner* presented a future society that is corrupt and disintegrating, and the sets and costumes supported that viewpoint.

Look closely at the illustration, a comic book cover by Frank R. Paul, created in 1928. Consider these points.

The Technology Much science fiction is dependent upon believable future technology. How is this man flying?

Can you imagine the technology that enables him to do so? To your knowledge, has a device for individual flight ever been invented in this century? If so, can you describe the technology involved?

The Costumes Is the man's outfit believable as a costume for flying? Are the costumes of the other characters believable as futuristic at-home wear? How do they differ from costumes you might actually see people wearing today?

The Setting What do the houses and the countryside tell you about the climate? Do the houses seem appropriately futuristic? Why or why not?

The Relationships Consider who is doing the flying and who is waving good-bye. Do you think this 1928 artist could have imagined the relative equality of the sexes that has evolved through the later part of the twentieth century?

The Artistic Style Consider the poses of the characters, the lines and colors employed, and the overall composition. What vision of the future do you think this comic book cover was apparently intended to convey?

Activity Options

1. Choose an area of technology, such as transportation, entertainment, or household upkeep, and create a picture that shows what you think one item will look like at a specific time in the future. You might choose 10 years, 100 years, or 1000 years—and your technological innovation is limited only by your imagination.

2. Write a short science-fiction story in which your main character makes use of some futuristic technology. Describe in detail what it looks like and what it does. (You don't, however, have to explain *how* it works.)

Multicultural Connections

Change

Part One: The Struggle to Understand Understanding the world can be difficult enough to start with, but changes can make such understanding even more difficult. The characters in these selections see their world changing in bewildering ways—as Alice does in Wonderland—or in sad, frightening ways—as the speaker does in "Dover Beach." Depending on their perspectives, they respond with action, with violence, or with love.

■ Do you think that simply knowing that change is coming is enough to help a person cope with it? Are there other, more specific methods that can help a person deal with change?

Perspective

Part Two: Hope and Despair The particular viewpoint, or perspective, that a person applies to his or her life and the changes that occur in it can influence to a large extent whether that person will respond with positive or negative emotions, with hope or despair. Falling in love, growing old, dying—all such life experiences can be looked upon as either obstacles or challenges.

■ Which of the fictional characters in this part seems to be regarding life with most hope? with most despair? Is that character's response an appropriate one, in your opinion?

Activities

1. Work in a small group to list the major changes in technology, economy, world politics, and so on that have happened during your lifetime. Poll your group members for their opinions on whether each of these changes is good or bad, a challenge or an obstacle. Then devise some sort of graphic organizer to display the results of your poll.

2. Attempt to summarize your perspective—your view of the world— in no more than three sentences. Compare your summary with those of one or more classmates. To what extent can your personal experiences account for any differences among them?

Independent and Group Projects

Art

"To Make You See" Joseph Conrad described his task as a writer: "By the power of the written word, to make you hear, to make you feel—it is, before all, to make you see." Which of the writers in this unit created a literary work that made you hear, feel, and see? Create an **artistic work**—a painting, a sculpture, a collage, a photograph— that depicts what your chosen writer made you hear, feel, and see.

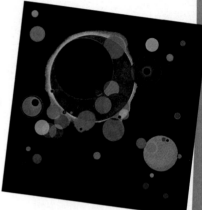

History

Victorian Time Line Queen Victoria was a remarkable ruler, and a remarkable period of history is named after her. With a group, create a **time line** of the Victorian Age (1837–1901) in which you put what was happening in Great Britain into context with what was happening in the United States and around the world. In your time line include the following: political leaders; historical events; figures in literature, art, and music; advances in science and medicine; inventions.

Literature

The English Novel During the nineteenth century the English novel developed into an important source of entertainment as well as a commentary on the social conditions and the cultural and moral values of the English people. Read one of the following novels of this period: *Pride and Prejudice* by Jane Austen, *David Copperfield* by Charles Dickens, *Wuthering Heights* by Emily Brontë, *Jane Eyre* by Charlotte Brontë, *The Mill on the Floss* by George Eliot, or *Tess of the D'Urbervilles* by Thomas Hardy. Prepare an **oral report** for your class in which you introduce the important characters, summarize the main plot, and comment on the picture of English life that is presented. You might include several quotations from the novel.

Music

Sing Out in Praise What can you find to celebrate about the last century or this century? Write an **anthem**—a song of praise—for the centennial, the movement from the 1800s (nineteenth century) to the 1900s (twentieth century). Or, if you prefer, write an anthem for the millennium, the movement to the year 2000. Your anthem can include praise for past achievements and perhaps a vision of the future.

RULE
BRITANNIA

THEMES *in*
ENGLISH
LITERATURE

The British empire lasted for several centuries and at its greatest extent covered one-fourth of the world. How this came about is a complex story of politics and economics, but English people managed to convince themselves that it was a moral duty on the part of England to guide the destinies of less "civilized" nations—a duty that Rudyard Kipling once called the "white man's burden." Needless to say, this position had its detractors as well as its adherents.

*

The sun never sets on the British Empire.

popular saying

*

BRITANNIA!

British possessions appear in pink on this 1886 map of the world.

*

Oh, England.
Sick in head and sick in heart,
Sick in whole and every part,
And yet sicker thou art still
For thinking, that thou art not ill.

Anonymous (1600s)

*

RULE, BRITANNIA

When Britain first, at Heaven's command,
Arose from out the azure main,[1]
This was the charter of the land,
And guardian angels sung the strain:
Rule Britannia, rule the waves,
Britons never will be slaves.

The nations not so blessed as thee
Must, in their turns, to tyrants fall,
Whilst thou shalt flourish, great and free,
The dread and envy of them all.

Still more majestic shalt thou rise,
More dreadful from each foreign stroke;
As the loud blast that tears the skies
Serves but to root thy native oak.

Thee haughty tyrants ne'er shall tame;
All their attempts to bend thee down
Will but arouse thy generous flame,
But work their woe, and thy renown. . . .
Rule, Britannia, rule the waves,
Britons never will be slaves.

James Thomson (1740)

from

THE TRAGEDY OF
KING RICHARD II

This royal throne of kings, this sceptered isle,
This earth of majesty, this seat of Mars,[1]
This other Eden, demi-paradise,
This fortress built by Nature for herself
Against infection and the hand of war,
This happy breed of men, this little world,
This precious stone set in the silver sea,
Which serves it in the office of a wall
Or as a moat defensive to a house,
Against the envy of less happier lands,
This blessed plot, this earth, this realm, this
England. . . .

William Shakespeare (1597)

---

1. **main,** sea; ocean.   1. **Mars,** Roman god of war.

A 1900 Dutch cartoon presents a hostile view of
British imperialism in the Boer War, showing
Queen Victoria, like Pilate in the New Testament,
attempting to cleanse herself of guilt.

IMPERIALISM

*The following excerpt advocating coloniza-
tion is from a speech given to the House of
Commons by Charles Buller, a member of
Parliament.*

I think, sir, that we cannot contemplate the conditions of this country without coming to the conclusion that there is a permanent cause of suffering in the constant accumulation of capital[1] and the constant increase of population within the same restricted field of employment. Every year adds its profits to the amount of capital previously accumulated; and certainly leaves the population considerably larger at its close than at its commencement. This fresh amount both of capital and population have to be employed, they must compete for a share of the previous amount of profits and wages. . . .

I propose that you should investigate the efficacy[2] of colonization as a remedy against the distress of the country. . . . I propose colonization as subsidiary[3] to free trade; as an additional mode of carrying out the same principles and attaining the same object. You advocates of free trade wish to bring food to the people. I suggest to you at the same time to take your people to the food. You wish to get the fresh markets by removing the barriers which now keep you from those that exist throughout the world. . . .

But the whole, nay the main advantage of colonization, is not secured by that mere removal of the laborer from the crowded mother country. . . His absence is only the first relief which he affords you. You take him hence to place him on a fertile soil, from which a very small amount of labor will suffice to raise the food which he wants. He soon finds that by applying his spare time and energies to raising additional food, or some article of trade or material of manufacture, he can obtain that which he can exchange for luxuries of which he never dreamed at home. He raises some article of export and appears in your market as a customer. He who a few years ago added nothing to the wealth of the country, but received all from charity . . . comes, after providing his own food, to purchase from you a better quality and a larger quantity of the clothing, and other manufactures which he used to take as a dole,[4] and to give employment and offer food to those on whose energies he was a burden before. . . .

It seems a paradox to assert that removing a portion of your population enables a country to support more inhabitants than it could before; and that the place of every man who quits his country because he cannot get a subsistence[5] may speedily be filled up by another whom that very removal will enable to subsist there in comfort. But the assertion is as true as it is strange.

Charles Buller (1843)

---

1. **capital,** wealth; money invested.
2. **efficacy** (ef′ə kə sē), *n.* effectiveness.
3. **subsidiary** (səb sid′ē er′ē), *n.* supplement.
4. **dole** (dōl), *n.* money, food, etc. given in charity.
5. **subsistence** (səb sis′təns), *n.* means of keeping alive.

STANLEY MEETS MUTESA

Welsh-born Henry Morton Stanley (1841–1904) explored Africa over the course of many years. He found the explorer David Livingstone, who was presumed lost; traced the course of the Congo River, helped establish the Congo Free State; and aided colonial ruler Emin Pasha.

Such a time of it they had;
The heat of the day
The chill of the night
And the mosquitoes that followed.
Such was the time and
They bound for a kingdom.

The thin weary line of carriers
With tattered dirty rags to cover their backs;
The battered bulky chests
That kept on falling off their shaven heads.
Their tempers high and hot
The sun fierce and scorching
With it rose their spirits
With its fall their hopes
As each day sweated their bodies dry and
Flies clung in clumps on their sweat-scented
    backs.
Such was the march
And the hot season just breaking.

Each day a weary pony dropped,
Left for the vultures on the plains;
Each afternoon a human skeleton collapsed,
Left for the Masai[1] on the plains;
But the march trudged on
Its Khaki[2] leader in front
He the spirit that inspired.
He the light of hope.

Then came the afternoon of a hungry march,
A hot and hungry march it was;
The Nile and the Nyanza[3]
Lay like two twins
Azure across the green countryside.
The match leapt on chanting
Like young gazelles to a water hole.
Hearts beat faster
Loads felt lighter
As the cool water lapped their sore soft feet.
No more the dread of hungry hyenas
But only tales of valor when
At Mutesa's court fires are lit.
No more the burning heat of the day
But song, laughter and dance.

The village looks on behind banana groves,
Children peer behind reed fences.
Such was the welcome
No singing women to chant a welcome
Or drums to greet the white ambassador;
Only a few silent nods from aged faces
And one rumbling drum roll
To summon Mutesa's court to parley[4]
For the country was not sure.

The gate of reeds is flung open,
There is silence
But only a moment's silence—
A silence of assessment.
The tall black king steps forward,
He towers over the thin bearded white man
Then grabbing his lean white hand
Manages to whisper
"Mtu mweupe karibu"
White man you are welcome.
The gate of polished reed closes behind them
And the West is let in.

James D. Rubadiri

Mutesa (1838?–1884), king of the African kingdom of Buganda (now in Uganda), who welcomed Christian missionaries in 1877.
1. **Masai** (mä sī′), *n.* member of a tribe of tall people of East Africa, noted as hunters and as cattle raisers.
2. **Khaki** (kak′ē), *n.* a heavy twilled cloth of yellowish brown; here, a uniformed officer.
3. **Nile . . . Nyanza.** Uganda lies between the Nile River and Lake Nyanza.
4. **parley** (pär′lē), *v.* speak; talk.

To tear treasure out of the bowels of the land was their desire, with no more moral purpose at the back of it than burglars breaking into a safe.

Joseph Conrad (1902)

A Treaty Between Queen Victoria and the King of Mellella
River Congo, March 19, 1877

1. The export of slaves to foreign countries is forever abolished in my territory.

2. No European or other person whatever shall be permitted to reside in my territories or those of my heirs or successors for the purpose of carrying on in any way the traffic in slaves; and no houses, stores, or buildings of any kind whatsoever shall be erected for the purpose of the slave trade.

3. If at any time it shall appear that the slave trade is being carried on through or from any part of my territories, the slave trade may be put down by force.

4. The subjects of Her Britannic Majesty and all white foreigners may always trade freely with my people. I, for myself, my heirs or successors, pledge myself to show no favor and to give no privilege to the ships and trade of other countries which I do not show to those of Great Britain. . . .

ENGLAND, MY ENGLAND

What have I done for you,
    England, my England?
What is there I would not do,
    England, my own?
With your glorious eyes austere,[1]
As the Lord were walking near,
Whispering terrible things and dear
    As the Song on your bugles blown,
        England—
    Round the world on your bugles blown!

Where shall the watchful sun,
    England, my England,
Match the master-work you've done,
    England, my own?
When shall he rejoice again
Such a breed of mighty men
As come forward, one to ten,
    To the Song on your bugles blown,
        England—
    Down the years on your bugles blown?. . .

They call you proud and hard,
    England, my England:
You with worlds to watch and ward,
    England, my own!
You whose mailed hand keeps the keys
Of such teeming[2] destinies
You could know nor dread nor ease
    Were the Song on your bugles blown,
        England—
    Round the Pit on your bugles blown!

William Ernest Henley (1889-92)

---

1. **austere** (ô stir′), *adj.* severe in self-discipline.
2. **teeming** (tē′ming), *adj.* full; alive.

England Your England

Yes, there is something distinctive and recognisable in English civilisation. It is a culture as individual as that of Spain. It is somehow bound up with solid breakfasts and gloomy Sundays, smoky towns and winding roads, green fields and red pillar-boxes.[1] It has a flavor of its own. Moreover it is continuous, it stretches into the future and the past, there is something in it that persists, as in a living creature. What can the England of 1940 have in common with the England of 1840? But then, what have you in common with the child of five whose photograph your mother keeps on the mantelpiece? Nothing, except that you happen to be the same person.

And above all, it is your civilisation, it is you. However much you hate it or laugh at it, you will never be happy away from it for any length of time. The suet puddings and the red pillar-boxes have entered into your soul. Good or evil, it is yours, you belong to it, and this side the grave you will never get away from the marks that it has given you.

Meanwhile England, together with the rest of the world, is changing. And like everything else it can change only in certain directions, which up to a point can be foreseen. That is not to say that the future is fixed, merely that certain alternatives are possible and others not. A seed may grow or not grow, but at any rate a turnip seed never grows into a parsnip. It is therefore of the deepest importance to try and determine what England is, before guessing what part England can play in the huge events that are happening. . . .

National characteristics are not easy to pin down, and when pinned down they often turn out to be trivialities[2] or seem to have no connection with one another. Spaniards are cruel to animals, Italians can do nothing without making a deafening noise, the Chinese are addicted to gambling. Obviously such things don't matter in themselves. Nevertheless, nothing is causeless, and even the fact that Englishmen have bad teeth can tell one something about the realities of English life. . . .

The gentleness of the English civilisation is perhaps its most marked characteristic. You notice it the instant you set foot on English soil. It is

a land where the bus conductors are good-tempered and the policemen carry no revolvers. In no country inhabited by whitemen is it easier to shove people off the pavement. And with this goes something that is always written off by European observers as "decadence"[3]

---

1. **pillar-boxes,** mailboxes.
2. **triviality** (triv/ē al/ə tē), *n.* small, unimportant thing.

3. **decadence** (dek/ədəns), *n.* decline; decay.

4. **hypocrisy** (hi pok/rə sē), *n.* a pretending to be what one is not.
5. **redcoat,** British soldier.

or hypocrisy,[4] the English hatred of war and militarism. It is rooted deep in history, and it is strong in the lower-middle class as well as the working class. Successive wars have shaken it but not

A British family in India shown in front of their bungalow with their servants.

destroyed it. Well within living memory it was common for "the redcoats"[5] to be booed at in the street and for the landlords of respectable public-houses[6] to refuse to allow soldiers on the premises.

In peace-time, even when there are two million unemployed, it is difficult to fill the ranks of the tiny standing army, which is officered by the county gentry[7] and a specialized stratum[8] of the middle class, and manned by farm laborers and slum proletarians[9]. The mass of the people are without military knowledge or tradition, and their attitude towards war is invariably defensive. No politician could rise to power by promising them conquest of military "glory," no Hymn of Hate has ever made any appeal to them. In the 1914-18 war the songs which the soldiers made up and sang of their own accord were not vengeful but humorous and mock-defeatist. The only enemy they ever named was the sergeant-major.

In England all the boasting and flag-wagging, the "Rule Britannia" stuff, is done by small minorities. . . .

The reason why the English anti-militarism disgusts foreign observers is that it ignores the existence of the British Empire. It looks like sheer hypocrisy. After all, the English absorbed a quarter of the earth and held on to it by means of a huge navy. How dare they then turn round and say that war is wicked?

It is quite true that the English are hypocritical about their Empire. In the working class this hypocrisy takes the form of not knowing that the Empire exists. But their dislike of standing armies is a perfectly sound instinct. A navy employs comparatively few people, and it is an external weapon which cannot affect home politics directly. Military dictatorships exist everywhere, but there is no such thing as a naval dictatorship. What English people of nearly all classes loathe from the bottom of their hearts is the swaggering officer type, the jingle of spurs and the crash of boots. Decades before Hitler was ever heard of, the word "Prussian" had much the same significance in England as "Nazi" has today. So deep does this feeling go that for a hundred years past the officers of the British Army, in peace-time, have always worn civilian clothes when off duty. . . .

George Orwell (1953)

6. **public house,** tavern.
7. **gentry** (jen′trē), *n.* the upper class.
8. **stratum** (strā′təm), *n.* layer.
9. **proletarian** (prō′lə ter′ē ən), *n.* lower-class worker.

from PLAIN TALES FROM THE RAJ

If pomp[1] and ceremony dominated the native court it was no less in evidence in the higher circles of the British Raj. The Prince of Wales[2] was reported to have said that he had never realized what royalty really was until he stayed at Government House, Bombay, during his tour of India in 1920–1: "If the Governor was entertaining, all the guests would be arranged in a circle and he and his lady would be led round the circle and each would be introduced. The ladies would bob to him and the men would bow their heads, and the Governor and his lady would then lead the way into the meal." Here, too, hierarchy was clearly displayed. "At any formal dinner at Government House the precedence[3] was of the utmost importance," explains Christopher Masterman. "I once attended three dinners running at Government House and got the same lady beside me each time, strictly according to precedence. I was in the secretariat, he was a fellow secretary, so his wife was always invited to the same dinner as myself and I always got her as a partner. I really got very knowledgeable about her family."

To assist in the proper ordering of official society the Government published a warrant of precedence which was added to from time to time as new posts were created. This Civil List, variously known as the Blue, Green or even the Red Book, was to be found on every civil official's desk. "The Warrant of Precedence," declares David Symington, "was a very humorous document if read in the right spirit. It occupied about ten closely printed pages and showed the relative precedence of various jobs. If you

The Englishman in India has no home and leaves no memory.

Sir William Hunter (1895)

wanted to know whether an Inspector of Smoke Nuisances was a bit higher than a Junior Settlement Officer you had only to look it up and you'd find out what their relative position was." Armed with his book the junior official or the ADC[4] could plan the seating for a burra-khana[5] in full confidence. Only those outside the system created problems, Christopher Masterman once discovered: "A Mr. Abrahams had written his name in the Governor's book and the police reported to me that he was a very important international financier who was making a tour of India. So Mr. and Mrs. Abrahams were invited to a state dinner. As Collector I was also invited and when I arrived I was greeted by a member of the staff who said, "You must go and see your Mr. and Mrs. Abrahams." So I went to see them and I found they were very black, and he was improperly dressed in a blue serge suit. So I had the rather difficult job of telling them we were very sorry but they couldn't come into dinner, but they could be invited to the garden party. They took it very well."

Charles Allen (1975)

Raj, British rule in India.
1. **pomp** (pomp), *n.* a stately display.
2. **Prince of Wales,** the heir to the British throne.

3. **precedence** (presʹə dəns), *n.* a putting in order by rank.
4. **ADC,** aide-de-camp; secretary to a superior officer.

5. **burra-khana** (bėrʹə käʹnə), *n.* meeting of native leaders.

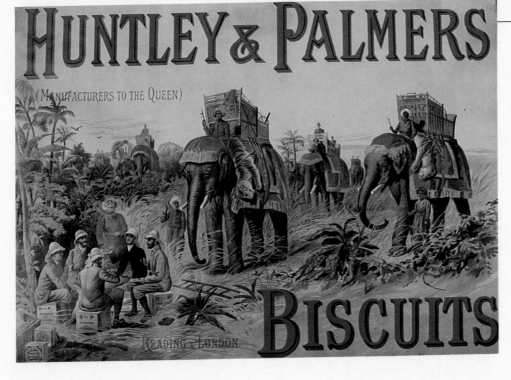

HUNTLEY & PALMERS

(MANUFACTURERS TO THE QUEEN)

BISCUITS

READING & LONDON.

An 1884 advertising poster shows a British hunting party in India.

RECESSIONAL

God of our fathers, known of old,
Lord of our far-flung battle line,
Beneath whose awful hand we hold
Dominion[1] over palm and pine
Lord God of Hosts, be with us yet,
Lest we forget—lest we forget!

The tumult[2] and the shouting dies;
The captains and the kings depart:
Still stands Thine ancient sacrifice,
A humble and a contrite[3] heart.
Lord God of Hosts, be with us yet,
Lest we forget—lest we forget!

Far-called, our navies melt away;
On dune and headland sinks the fire:
Lo, all our pomp of yesterday
Is one with Nineveh and Tyre![4]

Judge of the Nations, spare us yet,
Lest we forget—lest we forget!

If, drunk with sight of power, we loose
Wild tongues that have not Thee in awe,
Such boastings as the Gentiles[5] use,
Or lesser breeds without the Law—
Lord God of Hosts, be with us yet,
Lest we forget—lest we forget!

For heathen[6] heart that puts her trust
In reeking tube and iron shard,
All valiant dust that builds on dust,
And guarding, calls not Thee to guard,
For frantic boast and foolish word—
Thy Mercy on Thy People, Lord!

Rudyard Kipling (1897)

---

recessional (ri sesh′ə nəl), *n.* a hymn sung as the clergy and the choir leave the church at the end of a service.
1. **dominion** (də min′yən), *n.* rule; control.

2. **tumult** (tū′mult), *n.* noise; commotion.
3. **contrite** (kən trīt′), *adj.* showing deep regret and sorrow.
4. **Nineveh** (nin′ə və) . . . **Tyre** (tīr), two ancient cities, capitals of empires that no longer exist.

5. **Gentile** (jen′tīl), n. heathen; pagan; here, anyone not English.
6. **heathen** (hē′FHən), *adj.* referring to someone who does not believe in God or the Bible.

653

from THE CRACK IN THE TEACUP

The transition from a great empire to a commonwealth was achieved with remarkable ease and some harmony, but British citizens from commonwealth countries have experienced prejudice and tension here, which political parties of the right, notably the National Front and even some irresponsible members of the Conservatives, have exploited for their own ends. The popularity of the monarchy, and of the Queen herself, seems to have little power to alleviate[1] these problems though she visits commonwealth countries regularly, and recognizes, by bestowing official honors on individual leaders, their contribution to the position of Britain in the world. Mahatma Gandhi, for instance, the pacifist[2] leader of Indian nationalism, was first treated disgracefully by the British, harassed, and even imprisoned. But his wisdom, integrity and justice were at last recognized, and he is now honored by a statue in Russell Square, Bloomsbury. . . .

One of the worst prevalent contemporary attitudes is the ignorance shown, even by people who are not prejudiced, about the benefits Britain draws from the heterogeneousness[3] of its society. Citizens who came originally from former colonies or dominions, from India, Pakistan, the West Indies, Africa, or from Hong Kong, which is still under British rule, have enriched the country, not only by their invaluable labor, but also by the different cultural and religious and philosophical and social attitudes with which they broaden and enliven English life. Insularity[4] has been a British curse, xenophobia[5] a national illness, and it is time for this to pass, and for it to be understood that a nation withers at its roots if it does not receive continual stimulus from outside influences. The Press, in race questions, is usually excitable.

An abiding problem, which makes such changes in attitudes difficult to achieve, is the quality of the country's leadership. . . . But the chief source of disillusion has been the ever-fugitive vision of the successful and just society. Taxes rise, wages lose value, crime increases, poverty refuses to disappear. On the other hand, some causes, the rights of workers and the equality of women, have made progress.

Progress has also been made, most significantly, in the attitudes to social inequality, not in the inequality itself. It is no longer acceptable behavior to flaunt social divisions of class or wealth. But England remains a divided nation. The top 10 percent who owned 92 percent of the national capital in 1911–13 still own 83 percent today. It is an astonishing figure.

Marina Warner (1979)

> THE CONQUEST OF THE EARTH, WHICH MOSTLY MEANS THE TAKING IT AWAY FROM THOSE WHO HAVE A DIFFERENT COMPLEXION OR SLIGHTLY FLATTER NOSES THAN OURSELVES, IS NOT A PRETTY THING WHEN YOU LOOK INTO IT TOO MUCH.
>
> *Joseph Conrad (1902)*

1. **alleviate** (ə lē′vē āt), *v.* relieve.
2. **pacifist** (pas′ə fist), *adj.* peaceful; opposed to violence.
3. **heterogeneousness** (het′ər ə jē′nē əs-nis), *n.* mixture of unlike parts.
4. **insularity** (in′sə lar′ə tē), *n.* condition of living on an island
5. **xenophobia** (zen′ə fō′bē ə), *n.* hatred or fear of foreigners or strangers.

Alfonse de Neuville's painting shows a famous episode from the Zulu War. On January 22, 1879, a British regiment was overwhelmed by a Zulu force at the Battle of Isandhlwana. Two officers, Lieutenants Melvill and Coghill, were killed attempting to save the regimental flag.

GOD SAVE THE QUEEN

God save our gracious Queen,
Long live our noble Queen,
God save the Queen!
Send her victorious,
Happy and glorious,
Long to reign over us
God save the Queen!

O Lord our God, arise,
Scatter her enemies
And make them fall!
Confound their politics,
Frustrate their knavish tricks,
On thee our hopes we fix,
God save the Queen!

Thy choicest gifts in store,
On her be pleased to pour,
Long may she reign!
May she defend our laws,
And ever give us cause,
To sing with heart and voice,
God save the Queen!

attributed to Henry Carey (about 1692)

RESPONDING

1. Summarize the viewpoint expressed in "Rule, Britannia" and the other pro-colonialist writing in this section.
2. In your opinion, what is the harshest criticism expressed?
3. Compare the rise and decline of the British empire with what you know of other colonizing countries.

The Early Twentieth Century

Upward Mobility
Part One, pages 658–729

War and Aftermath
Part Two, pages 730–785

The Search for Identity
Part Three, pages 786–853

657

HISTORICAL OVERVIEW

As one Victorian observed, England was "two nations . . . as ignorant of each other's habits, thoughts, and feelings, as if they were of different planets; who are . . . fed by different food, are ordered by different manners, and are not governed by the same laws." These "two nations"—the rich and the poor—also differed in speech. As Bernard Shaw observes in the preface to *Pygmalion*, "It is impossible for an Englishman to open his mouth without making some other Englishman despise him." Although the early 1900s saw the passage of legislation designed to ease the effects of poverty, including the first old-age pensions, the "two nations" still inhabited their separate worlds when *Pygmalion* opened in 1912. On the right are a few famous individuals and social types from early 20th-century England.

THE ENGLISH

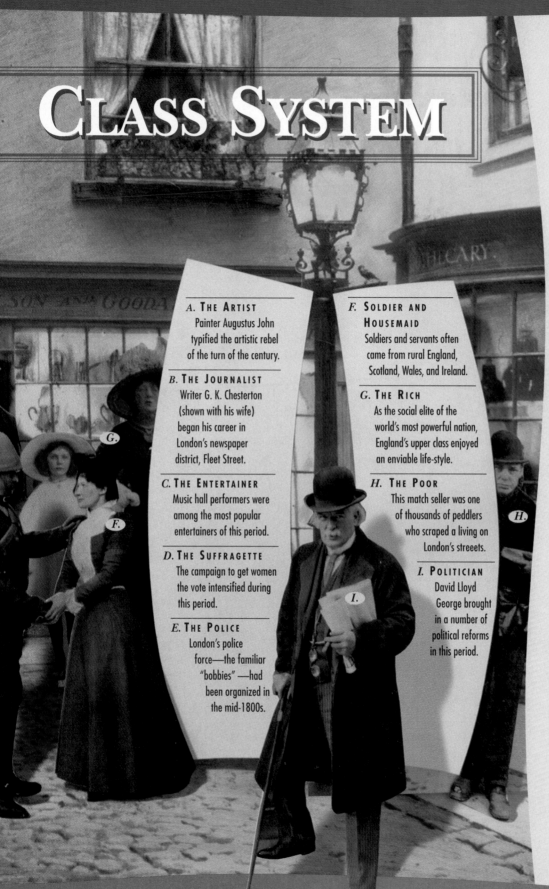

CLASS SYSTEM

A. THE ARTIST
Painter Augustus John typified the artistic rebel of the turn of the century.

B. THE JOURNALIST
Writer G. K. Chesterton (shown with his wife) began his career in London's newspaper district, Fleet Street.

C. THE ENTERTAINER
Music hall performers were among the most popular entertainers of this period.

D. THE SUFFRAGETTE
The campaign to get women the vote intensified during this period.

E. THE POLICE
London's police force—the familiar "bobbies" —had been organized in the mid-1800s.

F. SOLDIER AND HOUSEMAID
Soldiers and servants often came from rural England, Scotland, Wales, and Ireland.

G. THE RICH
As the social elite of the world's most powerful nation, England's upper class enjoyed an enviable life-style.

H. THE POOR
This match seller was one of thousands of peddlers who scraped a living on London's streeets.

I. POLITICIAN
David Lloyd George brought in a number of political reforms in this period.

Key Dates

1883
The first volume of the Oxford English Dictionary appears.

1884
The Fabian Society is founded.

1897
Queen Victoria's Diamond Jubilee is celebrated.

1900
The British Labour party is formed.

1901
Queen Victoria dies.

1909
Old-Age Pension Law passed.

1912
Shaw's Pygmalion *first produced.*

1913
Suffragettes demonstrate in London.

1914
World War I begins.

Part One

Upward Mobility

Everyone wants to get ahead, to rise in the world, to become better off, to *arrive*. Not everyone has the opportunity, however, to move up. Some people must make great efforts, it seems, just to maintain their lifestyle and not actually decline. For those people, upward mobility may seem like a cruel and unattainable dream.

Most everyone who does achieve success knows one secret: **communication.** The more adept a person is at communicating with people on a certain level of society, the more likely that person is to be accepted by those people. It is a secret that is intuitively grasped by the main character of the play *Pygmalion,* and it is a secret that changes her life.

Before Reading

Pygmalion

by Bernard Shaw

Bernard Shaw
1856–1950

Bernard Shaw was born in Dublin. His father drank and, seeking a way to help support the family, his mother and older sister took vocal lessons from a local musician, George Vandaleur Lee. In 1872 Lee went to London, and Mrs. Shaw and her daughter followed. Shaw joined them in 1876 and wrote music criticism, sold telephones, and wrote five novels that no one would publish. In 1884, along with friends, he helped found the Fabian Society, Socialists committed to the peaceful redistribution of wealth. Shaw came to think he might make the theater a vehicle for his ideas, and he eventually wrote over fifty plays, including *Major Barbara* (1905), *Pygmalion* (1912), *Heartbreak House* (1919), and *Saint Joan* (1923). He received a Nobel Prize in 1925.

Building Background

An Old Story Updated In the original story of Pygmalion (pig mā′lē ən) told by the Roman poet Ovid (43 B.C.–A.D. 17?), Pygmalion is a sculptor who carves a statue of a woman so beautiful and so irresistible that he falls in love with her. Venus, the goddess of love, takes pity on him and brings the statue to life. Pygmalion names his love Galatea (gal′ə tē′ə), and Venus is present at their marriage. Many authors have written works on this theme, but one, Tobias Smollett (1721–1777), altered the story in an incident in his novel *Peregrine Pickle.* An early critic of Shaw's play, which opened in Vienna in 1913 and in London in 1914, recognized the similarity between this incident and Shaw's *Pygmalion.* When Shaw was questioned about this, he irritably admitted having read Smollett's work in his Dublin boyhood but not since and said he had not realized that "Smollett had got hold of my plot." Regardless of Shaw's source, his play contains some reversals of the original story. Since no character in the play is named Pygmalion, readers and playgoers must understand the **allusion** for themselves. The person who seems to be a Pygmalion expects far different things from his creation, who in turn expects much from him. And whether or not Shaw's comedy, set in London in the early twentieth century, has a happy ending, which a comedy is supposed to have, depends on your viewpoint.

Literary Focus

Inference An **inference** is a reasonable conclusion based on hints and clues. The characters in *Pygmalion* make inferences about each other, their backgrounds, their feelings, and their intentions. In turn, readers and playgoers must make inferences about characters, relationships, and motivations when they are not expressly mentioned.

Writer's Notebook

Dressing the Actors Costumes tell a great deal about characters in a play, and they are especially important in *Pygmalion.* As you read the play, make notes on any mention of clothing or accessories, either by the characters themselves or in the stage directions.

PYGMALION

BERHARD SHAW

Audrey Hepburn as Eliza Dooliittle—before and after—
in the film My Fair Lady.

All subsequent illustrations for *Pygmalion* (except the
ones on pages 696–697 are photographs of a 1987 New
York production starring Peter O'Toole as Henry Higgins,
Amanda Plummer as Eliza Doolittle, Lionel Jeffries as
Colonel Pickering, and John Mills as Alfred Doolittle.

ACT ONE

Covent Garden[1] at 11:15 P.M. Torrents of heavy summer rain. Cab whistles blowing frantically in all directions. Pedestrians running for shelter into the market and under the portico of St. Paul's Church, where there are already several people, among them a LADY *and her* DAUGHTER *in evening dress. They are all peering out gloomily at the rain, except one man with his back turned to the rest, who seems wholly preoccupied with a notebook in which he is writing busily.*

The church clock strikes the first quarter.

THE DAUGHTER (*in the space between the central pillars, close to the one on her left*). I'm getting chilled to the bone. What can Freddy be doing all this time? He's been gone twenty minutes.

THE MOTHER (*on her* DAUGHTER'S *right*). Not so long. But he ought to have got us a cab by this.

A BYSTANDER (*on the* LADY'S *right*). He won't get no cab not until half-past eleven, missus, when they come back after dropping their theater fares.

THE MOTHER. But we must have a cab. We can't stand here until half-past eleven. It's too bad.

THE BYSTANDER. Well, it ain't my fault, missus.

THE DAUGHTER. If Freddy had a bit of gumption, he would have got one at the theater door.

THE MOTHER. What could he have done, poor boy?

THE DAUGHTER. Other people got cabs. Why couldn't he?

(FREDDY *rushes in out of the rain from the Southampton Street side, and comes between them closing a dripping umbrella. He is a young man of twenty, in evening dress, very wet round the ankles.*)

THE DAUGHTER. Well, haven't you got a cab?

FREDDY. There's not one to be had for love or money.

THE MOTHER. Oh, Freddy, there must be one. You can't have tried.

THE DAUGHTER. It's too tiresome. Do you expect us to go and get one ourselves?

FREDDY. I tell you they're all engaged. The rain was so sudden: nobody was prepared; and everybody had to take a cab. I've been to Charing Cross one way and nearly to Ludgate Circus the other; and they were all engaged.

THE MOTHER. Did you try Trafalgar Square?

FREDDY. There wasn't one at Trafalgar Square.

THE DAUGHTER. Did you try?

FREDDY. I tried as far as Charing Cross Station. Did you expect me to walk to Hammersmith?

THE DAUGHTER. You haven't tried at all.

THE MOTHER. You really are very helpless, Freddy. Go again; and don't come back until you have found a cab.

FREDDY. I shall simply get soaked for nothing.

THE DAUGHTER. And what about us? Are we to stay here all night in this draft, with next to nothing on? You selfish pig—

FREDDY. Oh, very well: I'll go, I'll go. (*He opens his umbrella and dashes off Strandwards,[2] but comes into collision with a* FLOWER GIRL, *who is hurrying for shelter, knocking her basket out of her hands. A blinding flash of lightning, followed instantly by a rattling peal of thunder, orchestrates the incident.*)

THE FLOWER GIRL. Nah then, Freddy: look wh' y' gowin, deah.

FREDDY. Sorry. (*He rushes off.*)

THE FLOWER GIRL (*picking up her scattered flowers and replacing them in the basket*). There's menners f' yer! Te-oo banches o voylets trod into the mad. (*She sits down on the plinth[3] of the column, sorting her flowers, on the* LADY'S *right. She is not at all an attractive person. She is perhaps eighteen, perhaps twenty, hardly older. She wears a little sailor hat of black straw that has long been exposed to the dust and soot of London and has seldom if ever been brushed. Her hair needs wash-*

---

1. **Covent Garden.** At the time of the play, the chief fruit, vegetable, and flower market district of London. The area also contains the Covent Garden Opera House and St. Paul's Church, designed by architect Inigo Jones (1573–1652).
2. **Strandwards,** toward the Strand, the main thoroughfare between the West End—the fashionable residential area—and the business and commercial center of London.
3. **plinth** (plinth), *n.* the lower, square part of the base of a column.

ing rather badly: its mousy color can hardly be natural. She wears a shoddy black coat that reaches nearly to her knees and is shaped to her waist. She has a brown skirt with a coarse apron. Her boots are much the worse for wear. She is no doubt as clean as she can afford to be; but compared to the ladies she is very dirty. Her features are no worse than theirs; but their condition leaves something to be desired; and she needs the services of a dentist.)

THE MOTHER. How do you know that my son's name is Freddy, pray?

THE FLOWER GIRL. Ow, eez ye-ooa san, is e? Wal, fewd dan y' de-ooty bawms a mather should, eed now bettern to spawl a pore gel's flahrzn than ran awy athat pyin. Will ye-oo py me f'them? *(Here, with apologies, this desperate attempt to represent her dialect without a phonetic alphabet must be abandoned as unintelligible outside London.)*

THE DAUGHTER. Do nothing of the sort, mother. The idea!

THE MOTHER. Please allow me, Clara. Have you any pennies?

THE DAUGHTER. No. I've nothing smaller than a sixpence.

THE FLOWER GIRL *(hopefully)*. I can give you change for a tanner,[4] kind lady.

THE MOTHER *(to* CLARA*)*. Give it to me. (CLARA *parts reluctantly.)* Now *(to the* GIRL*)* this is for your flowers.

THE FLOWER GIRL. Thank you kindly, lady.

THE DAUGHTER. Make her give you the change. These things are only a penny a bunch.

THE MOTHER. Do hold your tongue, Clara. *(To the* GIRL.*)* You can keep the change.

THE FLOWER GIRL. Oh, thank you, lady.

THE MOTHER. Now tell me how you know that young gentleman's name.

THE FLOWER GIRL. I didn't.

THE MOTHER. I heard you call him by it. Don't try to deceive me.

THE FLOWER GIRL *(protesting)*. Who's trying to deceive you? I called him Freddy or Charlie same as you might yourself if you was talking to a stranger and wished to be pleasant. *(She sits down beside her basket.)*

THE DAUGHTER. Sixpence thrown away! Really, mamma, you might have spared Freddy that. *(She retreats in disgust behind the pillar.)*

(An elderly GENTLEMAN *of the amiable military type rushes into the shelter, and closes a dripping umbrella. He is in the same plight as* FREDDY, *very wet about the ankles. He is in evening dress, with a light overcoat. He takes the place left vacant by the* DAUGHTER'S *retirement.)*

THE GENTLEMAN. Phew!

THE MOTHER *(to the* GENTLEMAN*)*. Oh, sir, is there any sign of its stopping?

THE GENTLEMAN. I'm afraid not. It started worse than ever about two minutes ago. *(He goes to the plinth beside the* FLOWER GIRL; *puts up his foot on it; and stoops to turn down his trouser ends.)*

THE MOTHER. Oh dear! *(She retires sadly and joins her* DAUGHTER.*)*

THE FLOWER GIRL *(taking advantage of the military* GENTLEMAN'S *proximity to establish friendly relations with him)*. If it's worse, it's a sign it's nearly over. So cheer up, Captain; and buy a flower off a poor girl.

THE GENTLEMAN. I'm sorry. I haven't any change.

THE FLOWER GIRL. I can give you change, Captain.

THE GENTLEMAN. For a sovereign?[5] I've nothing less.

THE FLOWER GIRL. Garn! Oh do buy a flower off me, Captain. I can change half-a-crown. Take this for tuppence.

THE GENTLEMAN. Now don't be troublesome: there's a good girl. *(Trying his pockets.)* I really haven't any change—Stop: here's three hapence, if that's any use to you. *(He retreats to the other pillar.)*

THE FLOWER GIRL *(disappointed, but thinking three half-pence better than nothing)*. Thank you, sir.

---

4. **tanner** (tan′ər), *n.* sixpence (six pennies). *[Slang]*
5. **sovereign** (sov′rən), *n.* former British gold coin; the crown, worth much less, is also a former British coin.

THE BYSTANDER (to the girl). You be careful: give him a flower for it. There's a bloke here behind taking down every blessed word you're saying. (All turn to the man who is taking notes.)

THE FLOWER GIRL (springing up terrified). I ain't done nothing wrong by speaking to the gentleman. I've a right to sell flowers if I keep off the curb. (Hysterically.) I'm a respectable girl: so help me, I never spoke to him except to ask him to buy a flower off me. (General hubbub, mostly sympathetic to the FLOWER GIRL, but deprecating[6] her excessive sensibility.[7] Cries of Don't start hollerin. Who's hurting you? Nobody's going to touch you. What's the good of fussing? Steady on. Easy easy, etc., come from the elderly staid[8] spectators, who pat her comfortingly. Less patient ones bid her shut her head, or ask her roughly what is wrong with her. A remoter group, not knowing what the matter is, crowd in and increase the noise with question and answer: What's the row? What she do? Where is he? A tec[9] taking her down. What! Him? Yes, him over there. Took money off the gentleman, etc. The FLOWER GIRL, distraught and mobbed, breaks through them to the GENTLEMAN, crying wildly.) Oh, sir, don't let him charge me. You dunno what it means to me. They'll take away my character and drive me on the streets for speaking to gentlemen. They—

THE NOTE TAKER (coming forward on her right, the rest crowding after him). There, there, there, there! Who's hurting you, you silly girl? What do you take me for?

THE BYSTANDER. It's all right: he's a gentleman: look at his boots. (Explaining to the NOTE TAKER.) She thought you was a copper's nark, sir.

THE NOTE TAKER (with quick interest). What's a copper's nark?

THE BYSTANDER (inapt at definition). It's a—well, it's a copper's nark, as you might say. What else would you call it? A sort of informer.

THE FLOWER GIRL (still hysterical). I take my Bible oath I never said a word—

THE NOTE TAKER (overbearing but good-humored). Oh, shut up, shut up. Do I look like a policeman?

THE FLOWER GIRL (far from reassured). Then what did you take down my words for? How do I know whether you took me down right? You just show me what you've wrote about me. (The NOTE TAKER opens his book and holds it steadily under her nose, though the pressure of the mob trying to read it over his shoulders would upset a weaker man.) What's that? That ain't proper writing. I can't read that.

THE NOTE TAKER. I can. (Reads, reproducing her pronunciation exactly.) "Cheer ap, Keptin; n' baw ya flahr orf a pore gel."

THE FLOWER GIRL (much distressed). It's because I called him Captain. I meant no harm. (To the GENTLEMAN.) Oh, sir, don't let him lay a charge agen me for a word like that. You—

THE GENTLEMAN. Charge! I make no charge. (To the NOTE TAKER.) Really, sir, if you are a detective, you need not begin protecting me against molestation by young women until I ask you. Anybody could see that the girl meant no harm.

THE BYSTANDERS GENERALLY (demonstrating against police espionage). Course they could. What business is it of yours? You mind your own affairs. He wants promotion, he does. Taking down people's words! Girl never said a word to him. What harm if she did? Nice thing a girl can't shelter from the rain without being insulted, etc., etc., etc. (She is conducted by the more sympathetic demonstrators back to her plinth, where she resumes her seat and struggles with her emotion.)

THE BYSTANDER. He ain't a tec. He's a blooming busybody: that's what he is. I tell you, look at his boots.

---

6. **deprecate** (dep′rə kāt), v. express strong disapproval of; belittle.
7. **sensibility** (sen′sə bil′ə tē), n. tendency to be hurt or offended too easily.
8. **staid** (stād), adj. having a settled, quiet character; sober; sedate.
9. **tec** (tek), n. short for "detective." [Slang]

THE NOTE TAKER (*turning on him genially*). And how are all your people down at Selsey?

THE BYSTANDER (*suspiciously*). Who told you my people come from Selsey?

THE NOTE TAKER. Never you mind. They did. (*To the* GIRL.) How do you come to be up so far east? You were born in Lisson Grove.

THE FLOWER GIRL (*appalled*). Oh, what harm is there in my leaving Lisson Grove? It wasn't fit for a pig to live in; and I had to pay four-and-six[10] a week. (*In tears.*) Oh, boo—hoo—oo—

THE NOTE TAKER. Live where you like; but stop that noise.

THE GENTLEMAN (*to the girl*). Come, come! He can't touch you: you have a right to live where you please.

A SARCASTIC BYSTANDER (*thrusting himself between the* NOTE TAKER *and the* GENTLEMAN). Park Lane, for instance. I'd like to go into the Housing Question with you, I would.

THE FLOWER GIRL (*subsiding into a brooding melancholy over her basket, and talking very low-spiritedly to herself*). I'm a good girl, I am.

THE SARCASTIC BYSTANDER (*not attending to her*). Do you know where *I* come from?

THE NOTE TAKER (*promptly*). Hoxton.

(*Titterings. Popular interest in the* NOTE TAKER'S *performance increases.*)

THE SARCASTIC ONE (*amazed*). Well, who said I didn't? Bly me! You know everything, you do.

THE FLOWER GIRL (*still nursing her sense of injury*). Ain't no call to meddle with me, he ain't.

THE BYSTANDER (*to her*). Of course he ain't. Don't you stand it from him. (*To the* NOTE TAKER.) See here: what call have you to know about people what never offered to meddle with you? Where's your warrant?

SEVERAL BYSTANDERS (*encouraged by this seeming point of law*). Yes, where's your warrant?

THE FLOWER GIRL. Let him say what he likes. I don't want to have no truck with him.

THE BYSTANDER. You take us for dirt under your feet, don't you? Catch you taking liberties with a gentleman!

THE SARCASTIC BYSTANDER. Yes: tell him where he come from if you want to go fortune-telling.

THE NOTE TAKER. Cheltenham, Harrow,[11] Cambridge, and India.

THE GENTLEMAN. Quite right. (*Great laughter. Reaction in the* NOTE TAKER'S *favor. Exclamations of* He knows all about it. Told him proper. Hear him tell the toff[12] where he come from? *etc.*) May I ask, sir, do you do this for your living at a music hall?

THE NOTE TAKER. I've thought of that. Perhaps I shall some day.

(*The rain has stopped, and the persons on the outside of the crowd begin to drop off.*)

THE FLOWER GIRL (*resenting the reaction*). He's no gentleman, he ain't, to interfere with a poor girl.

THE DAUGHTER (*out of patience, pushing her way rudely to the front and displacing the* GENTLEMAN, *who politely retires to the other side of the pillar*). What on earth is Freddy doing? I shall get pneumonia if I stay in this draft any longer.

THE NOTE TAKER (*to himself, hastily making a note of her pronunciation of "monia"*). Earlscourt.

THE DAUGHTER (*violently*). Will you please keep your impertinent remarks to yourself?

THE NOTE TAKER. Did I say that out loud? I didn't mean to. I beg your pardon. Your mother's Epsom; unmistakeably.

THE MOTHER (*advancing between her* DAUGHTER *and the* NOTE TAKER). How very curious! I was brought up in Largelady Park, near Epsom.

THE NOTE TAKER (*uproariously amused*). Ha! ha! What a devil of a name! Excuse me. (*To the* DAUGHTER.) You want a cab, do you?

THE DAUGHTER. Don't dare speak to me.

THE MOTHER. Oh, please, please, Clara. (*Her* DAUGHTER *repudiates her with an angry shrug and retires haughtily.*) We should be so grateful to you, sir, if you found us a cab. (*The* NOTE

---

10. **four-and-six,** British money: four pounds and six shillings.
11. **Cheltenham, Harrow,** exclusive preparatory schools.
12. **toff** (tôf), *n.* dandy; well-to-do person. [*Slang*]

TAKER *produces a whistle.*) Oh, thank you. (*She joins her* DAUGHTER.)

(*The* NOTE TAKER *blows a piercing blast.*)

THE SARCASTIC BYSTANDER. There! I knowed he was a plain-clothes copper.

THE BYSTANDER. That ain't a police whistle: that's a sporting whistle.

THE FLOWER GIRL (*still preoccupied with her wounded feelings*). He's no right to take away my character. My character is the same to me as any lady's.

THE NOTE TAKER. I don't know whether you've noticed it, but the rain stopped about two minutes ago.

THE BYSTANDER. So it has. Why didn't you say so before? And us losing our time listening to your silliness! (*He walks off towards the Strand.*)

THE SARCASTIC BYSTANDER. I can tell where you come from. You come from Anwell.[13] Go back there.

THE NOTE TAKER (*helpfully*). *H*anwell.

THE SARCASTIC BYSTANDER (*affecting great distinction of speech*). Thenk you, teacher. Haw haw! So long! (*He touches his hat with mock respect and strolls off.*)

THE FLOWER GIRL. Frightening people like that! How would he like it himself?

THE MOTHER. It's quite fine now, Clara. We can walk to a motor bus. Come. (*She gathers her skirts above her ankles and hurries off towards the Strand.*)

THE DAUGHTER. But the cab— (*Her* MOTHER *is out of hearing.*) Oh, how tiresome! (*She follows angrily.*)

(*All the rest have gone except the* NOTE TAKER, *the* GENTLEMAN, *and the* FLOWER GIRL, *who sits arranging her basket and still pitying herself in murmurs.*)

THE FLOWER GIRL. Poor girl! Hard enough for her to live without being worried and chivied.

THE GENTLEMAN (*returning to his former place on the* NOTE TAKER'*s left*). How do you do it, if I may ask?

THE NOTE TAKER. Simply phonetics. The science of speech. That's my profession: also my hobby. Happy is the man who can make

a living by his hobby! You can spot an Irishman or a Yorkshireman by his brogue. *I* can place any man within six miles. I can place him within two miles in London. Sometimes within two streets.

THE FLOWER GIRL. Ought to be ashamed of himself, unmanly coward!

THE GENTLEMAN. But is there a living in that?

THE NOTE TAKER. Oh yes. Quite a fat one. This is an age of upstarts. Men begin in Kentish Town with £80 a year, and end in Park Lane with a hundred thousand. They want to drop Kentish Town, but they give themselves away every time they open their mouths. Now I can teach them—

THE FLOWER GIRL. Let him mind his own business and leave a poor girl—

THE NOTE TAKER (*explosively*). Woman: cease this detestable boohooing instantly; or else seek the shelter of some other place of worship.

THE FLOWER GIRL (*with feeble defiance*). I've a right to be here if I like, same as you.

THE NOTE TAKER. A woman who utters such depressing and disgusting sounds has no right to be anywhere—no right to live. Remember that you are a human being with a soul and the divine gift of articulate speech: that your native language is the language of Shakespeare and Milton and The Bible: and

---

13. **Anwell,** Hanwell, an insane asylum.

don't sit there crooning like a bilious pigeon.

THE FLOWER GIRL (*quite overwhelmed, looking up at him in mingled wonder and deprecation without daring to raise her head*). Ah-ah-ah-ow-ow-ow-oo!

THE NOTE TAKER (*whipping out his book*). Heavens! What a sound! (*He writes; then holds out the book and reads, reproducing her vowels exactly.*) Ah-ah-ah-ow-ow-ow-oo!

THE FLOWER GIRL (*tickled by the performance, and laughing in spite of herself*). Garn!

THE NOTE TAKER. You see this creature with her curbstone English: the English that will keep her in the gutter to the end of her days. Well, sir, in three months I could pass that girl off as a duchess at an ambassador's garden party. I could even get her a place as lady's maid or shop assistant, which requires better English. That's the sort of thing I do for commercial millionaires. And on the profits of it I do genuine scientific work in phonetics, and a little as a poet on Miltonic lines.

THE GENTLEMAN. I am myself a student of Indian dialects; and—

THE NOTE TAKER (*eagerly*). Are you? Do you know Colonel Pickering, the author of *Spoken Sanskrit?*

THE GENTLEMAN. I am Colonel Pickering. Who are you?

THE NOTE TAKER. Henry Higgins, author of *Higgins's Universal Alphabet.*

PICKERING (*with enthusiasm*). I came from India to meet you.

HIGGINS. I was going to India to meet you.

PICKERING. Where do you live?

HIGGINS. 27A Wimpole Street. Come and see me tomorrow.

PICKERING. I'm at the Carlton. Come with me now and let's have a jaw over some supper.

HIGGINS. Right you are.

THE FLOWER GIRL (*to* PICKERING, *as he passes her*). Buy a flower, kind gentleman. I'm short for my lodging.

PICKERING. I really haven't any change. I'm sorry. (*He goes away.*)

HIGGINS (*shocked at the girl's mendacity*).[14] Liar. You said you could change half-a-crown.

THE FLOWER GIRL (*rising in desperation*). You ought to be stuffed with nails, you ought. (*Flinging the basket at his feet.*) Take the whole blooming basket for sixpence.

(*The church clock strikes the second quarter.*)

HIGGINS (*hearing in it the voice of God, rebuking him for his Pharisaic[15] want of charity to the poor girl*). A reminder. (*He raises his hat solemnly, then throws a handful of money into the basket and follows* PICKERING.)

THE FLOWER GIRL (*picking up a half-crown*). Ah-ow-ooh! (*Picking up a couple of florins.*) Aah-ow-ooh! (*Picking up several coins.*) Aaaaah-ow-ooh! (*Picking up a half-sovereign.*) Aaaaaaaaaaaaah-ow-ooh!!!

FREDDY (*springing out of a taxicab*). Got one at last. Hallo! (*To the* GIRL.) Where are the two ladies that were here?

THE FLOWER GIRL. They walked to the bus when the rain stopped.

FREDDY. And left me with a cab on my hands! Damnation!

THE FLOWER GIRL (*with grandeur*). Never mind, young man. *I'm* going home in a taxi. (*She sails off to the cab. The* DRIVER *puts his hand behind him and holds the door firmly shut against her. Quite understanding his mistrust, she shows him her handful of money.*) Eightpence ain't no object to me, Charlie. (*He grins and opens the door.*) Angel Court, Drury Lane, round the corner of Micklejohn's oil shop. Let's see how fast you can make her hop it. (*She gets in and pulls the door to with a slam as the taxicab starts.*)

FREDDY. Well, I'm dashed!

---

14. mendacity (men das′ə tē), *n.* untruthfulness; lie.
15. **Pharisaic** (far′ə sā′ik), *adj.* self-righteous. The Pharisees were a strict Jewish sect at the time of Jesus.

Act 1

After Reading

Shaping Your Response

Analyzing the Play

Extending the Ideas

Making Connections

1. A playwright must capture and hold an audience's attention just as soon as the curtain goes up. How effective is the opening scene in your opinion?

2. **Dialect** is a variety of language characteristic of a particular region or class. It is different from the standard language in pronunciation, usage, and vocabulary. What seems to be Shaw's purpose in emphasizing dialect here?

3. 🐾 What—if anything—proves a hindrance to **communication** in this act? Explain.

4. Rank the characters according to how the Note Taker treats them, starting with the character he treats best. (You might list the bystanders as one character.) What can you conclude from this ranking?

5. How important is the **setting** to act 1? Explain.

6. If such a varied gathering of people took place in your community, where would it be?

Literary Focus: Inference

An **inference** is a reasonable conclusion about the behavior of a character or the meaning of events drawn from limited information. Characters in a play, as well as readers and playgoers, must continually make inferences.

1. What do the Bystanders and then the Flower Girl infer about the Note Taker?

2. What can you infer about the Flower Girl from her speech to the Mother, her persistence in not moving on after the rain ends, and her reaction to Higgins's coins?

3. What can you infer about Freddy's character?

Vocabulary Study

deprecate
mendacity
plinth
sensibility
staid

Use the listed words in sentences that show you understand the meaning of the words.

ACT TWO

Next day at 11 A.M. HIGGINS'S *laboratory in Wimpole Street. It is a room on the first floor, looking on the street, and was meant for the drawing room. The double doors are in the middle of the back wall, and persons entering find in the corner to their right two tall file cabinets at right angles to one another against the walls. In this corner stands a flat writing table, on which are a phonograph, a laryngoscope,[1] a row of tiny organ pipes with bellows, a set of lamp chimneys for singing flames with burners attached to a gas plug in the wall by an india-rubber tube, several tuning forks[2] of different sizes, a life-size image of half a human head, showing in section the vocal organs,*

---

1. **laryngoscope** (lə ring'gə skōp), *n.* instrument with a mirror for examining the larynx, including the vocal cords.
2. **tuning fork,** a small two-pronged steel instrument used for finding the standard pitch and for tuning musical instruments.

and a box containing a supply of wax cylinders for the phonograph.

Further down the room, on the same side, is a fireplace, with a comfortable leather-covered easy chair at the side of the hearth nearest the door, and a coal scuttle. There is a clock on the mantelpiece. Between the fireplace and the phonograph table is a stand for newspapers.

On the other side of the central door, to the left of the visitor, is a cabinet of shallow drawers. On it is a telephone and the telephone directory. The corner beyond, and most of the side wall, is occupied by a grand piano, with the keyboard at the end furthest from the door, and a bench for the player extending the full length of the keyboard. On the piano is a dessert dish heaped with fruit and sweets, mostly chocolates.

The middle of the room is clear. Besides the easy chair, the piano bench, and two chairs at the phonograph table, there is one stray chair. It stands near the fireplace. On the walls, engravings: mostly Piranesi and mezzotint portraits.[3] No paintings.

PICKERING is seated at the table, putting down some cards and a tuning fork which he has been using. HIGGINS is standing up near him, closing two or three file drawers which are hanging out. He appears in the morning light as a robust,[4] vital, appetizing sort of man of forty or thereabouts, dressed in a professional-looking black frock coat with a white linen collar and black silk tie. He is of the energetic, scientific type, heartily, even violently interested in everything that can be studied as a scientific subject, and careless about himself and other people, including their feelings. He is, in fact, but for his years and size, rather like a very impetuous baby "taking notice" eagerly and loudly, and requiring almost as much watching to keep him out of unintended mischief. His manner varies from genial[5] bullying when he is in a good humor to stormy petulance when anything goes wrong; but he is so entirely frank and void of malice that he remains likeable even in his least reasonable moments.

HIGGINS (as he shuts the last drawer). Well, I think that's the whole show.

PICKERING. It's really amazing. I haven't taken half of it in, you know.

HIGGINS. Would you like to go over any of it again?

PICKERING (rising and coming to the fireplace, where he plants himself with his back to the fire). No, thank you; not now. I'm quite done up for this morning.

HIGGINS (following him, and standing beside him on his left). Tired of listening to sounds?

PICKERING. Yes. It's a fearful strain. I rather fancied myself because I can pronounce twenty-four distinct vowel sounds; but your hundred and thirty beat me. I can't hear a bit of difference between most of them.

HIGGINS (chuckling, and going over to the piano to eat sweets). Oh, that comes with practice. You hear no difference at first, but you keep on listening, and presently you find they're all as different as A from B. (MRS. PEARCE looks in: she is HIGGINS'S housekeeper.) What's the matter?

MRS. PEARCE (hesitating, evidently perplexed). A young woman wants to see you, sir.

HIGGINS. A young woman! What does she want?

MRS. PEARCE. Well, sir, she says you'll be glad to see her when you know what she's come about. She's quite a common girl, sir. Very common indeed. I should have sent her away, only I thought perhaps you wanted her to talk into your machines. I hope I've not done wrong; but really you see such queer people sometimes—you'll excuse me, I'm sure, sir—

HIGGINS. Oh, that's all right, Mrs. Pearce. Has she an interesting accent?

MRS. PEARCE. Oh, something dreadful, sir, really. I don't know how you can take an interest in it.

---

3. **Piranesis and mezzotint portraits.** Giovanni Battista Piranesi (1720–1778) was an Italian graphic artist known for his large prints of buildings of classical and post-classical Rome. A mezzotint is a picture engraved on a roughened copper or steel plate.
4. robust (rō bust′), adj. strong and healthy; sturdy.
5. genial (jē′nyəl), adj. cheerful and friendly; kindly.

HIGGINS (*to* PICKERING). Let's have her up. Show her up, Mrs. Pearce. (*He rushes across to his working table and picks out a cylinder to use on the phonograph.*)

MRS. PEARCE (*only half resigned to it*). Very well, sir. It's for you to say. (*She goes downstairs.*)

HIGGINS. This is rather a bit of luck. I'll show you how I make records. We'll set her talking; and I'll take it down first in Bell's Visible Speech; then in broad Romic; and then we'll get her on the phonograph so that you can turn her on as often as you like with the written transcript before you.

MRS. PEARCE (*returning*). This is the young woman, sir.

(*The* FLOWER GIRL *enters in state. She has a hat with three ostrich feathers, orange, sky-blue, and red. She has a nearly clean apron, and the shoddy coat has been tidied a little. The pathos of this deplorable figure, with its innocent vanity and consequential air, touches* PICKERING, *who has already straightened himself in the presence of* MRS. PEARCE. *But as to* HIGGINS, *the only distinction he makes between men and women is that when he is neither bullying nor exclaiming to the heavens against some feather-weight cross, he coaxes women as a child coaxes its nurse when it wants to get anything out of her.*)

HIGGINS (*brusquely, recognizing her with unconcealed disappointment, and at once, babylike, making an intolerable grievance of it*). Why, this is the girl I jotted down last night. She's no use. I've got all the records I want of the Lisson Grove lingo; and I'm not going to waste another cylinder on it. (*To the* GIRL.) Be off with you: I don't want you.

THE FLOWER GIRL. Don't you be so saucy. You ain't heard what I come for yet. (*To* MRS. PEARCE, *who is waiting at the door for further instructions.*) Did you tell him I come in a taxi?

MRS. PEARCE. Nonsense, girl! What do you think a gentleman like Mr. Higgins cares what you came in?

THE FLOWER GIRL. Oh, we are proud! He ain't above giving lessons, not him: I heard him say so. Well, I ain't come here to ask for any compliment; and if my money's not good enough I can go elsewhere.

HIGGINS. Good enough for what?

THE FLOWER GIRL. Good enough for ye-oo. Now you know, don't you? I'm come to have lessons, I am. And to pay for em too: make no mistake.

HIGGINS (*stupent*⁶). Well!!! (*Recovering his breath with a gasp.*) What do you expect me to say to you?

THE FLOWER GIRL. Well, if you was a gentleman, you might ask me to sit down, I think. Don't I tell you I'm bringing you business?

HIGGINS. Pickering: shall we ask this baggage to sit down, or shall we throw her out of the window?

THE FLOWER GIRL (*running away in terror to the piano, where she turns at bay*). Ah-ah-oh-ow-ow-ow-oo! (*Wounded and whimpering.*) I won't be called a baggage when I've offered to pay like any lady.

(*Motionless, the two men stare at her from the other side of the room, amazed.*)

PICKERING (*gently*). What is it you want, my girl?

THE FLOWER GIRL. I want to be a lady in a flower shop stead of selling at the corner of Tottenham Court Road. But they won't take me unless I can talk more genteel.⁷ He said he could teach me. Well, here I am ready to pay him—not asking any favor—and he treats me as if I was dirt.

MRS. PEARCE. How can you be such a foolish ignorant girl as to think you could afford to pay Mr. Higgins?

THE FLOWER GIRL. Why shouldn't I? I know what lessons cost as well as you do; and I'm ready to pay.

HIGGINS. How much?

THE FLOWER GIRL (*coming back to him, triumphant*). Now you're talking! I thought you'd come off it when you saw a chance of getting back a bit of what you chucked at me

---

6. **stupent** (stŭp′nt), *adj.* dumfounded; amazed.
7. **genteel** (jen tēl′), *adj.* polite; well-bred.

last night. *(Confidentially.)* You'd had a drop in,[8] hadn't you?

HIGGINS *(peremptorily).* Sit down.

THE FLOWER GIRL. Oh, if you're going to make a compliment of it—

HIGGINS *(thundering at her).* Sit down.

MRS. PEARCE *(severely).* Sit down, girl. Do as you're told.

(She places the stray chair near the hearthrug between HIGGINS *and* PICKERING, *and stands behind it waiting for the* GIRL *to sit down.)*

THE FLOWER GIRL. Ah-ah-ah-ow-ow-ee! *(She stands, half rebellious, half bewildered.)*

PICKERING *(very courteous).* Won't you sit down?

THE FLOWER GIRL *(coyly).* Don't mind if I do. *(She sits down.* PICKERING *returns to the hearthrug.)*

HIGGINS. What's your name?

THE FLOWER GIRL. Liza Doolittle.

HIGGINS *(declaiming gravely).*

Eliza, Elizabeth, Betsy, and Bess,
They went to the woods to get a bird's nes':

PICKERING. They found a nest with four eggs in it:

HIGGINS. They took one apiece, and left three in it.

(They laugh heartily at their own wit.)

LIZA. Oh, don't be silly.

MRS. PEARCE. You mustn't speak to the gentleman like that.

LIZA. Well, why won't he speak sensible to me?

HIGGINS. Come back to business. How much do you propose to pay me for the lessons?

LIZA. Oh, I know what's right. A lady friend of mine gets French lessons for eighteenpence an hour from a real French gentleman. Well, you wouldn't have the face to ask me the same for teaching me my own language as you would for French; so I won't give more than a shilling. Take it or leave it.

HIGGINS *(walking up and down the room, rattling his keys and his cash in his pockets).* You know, Pickering, if you consider a shilling, not as a simple shilling, but as a percentage of this girl's income, it works out as fully equivalent to sixty or seventy guineas[9] from a millionaire.

PICKERING. How so?

HIGGINS. Figure it out. A millionaire has about £150[10] a day. She earns about half-a-crown.

LIZA *(haughtily).* Who told you I only—

HIGGINS *(continuing).* She offers me two-fifths of her day's income for a lesson. Two-fifths of a millionaire's income for a day would be somewhere about £60. It's handsome. By George, it's enormous! It's the biggest offer I ever had.

LIZA *(rising, terrified).* Sixty pounds! What are you talking about? I never offered you sixty pounds. Where would I get—

HIGGINS. Hold your tongue.

LIZA *(weeping).* But I ain't got sixty pounds. Oh—

MRS. PEARCE. Don't cry, you silly girl. Sit down. Nobody is going to touch your money.

HIGGINS. Somebody is going to touch you, with a broomstick, if you don't stop snivelling. Sit down.

LIZA *(obeying slowly).* Ah-ah-ah-ow-oo-o! One would think you was my father.

HIGGINS. If I decide to teach you, I'll be worse than two fathers to you. Here! *(He offers her his silk handkerchief.)*

LIZA. What's this for?

HIGGINS. To wipe your eyes. To wipe any part of your face that feels moist. Remember: that's your handkerchief; and that's your sleeve. Don't mistake the one for the other if you wish to become a lady in a shop.

*(*LIZA, *utterly bewildered, stares helplessly at him.)*

MRS. PEARCE. It's no use talking to her like that, Mr. Higgins: she doesn't understand you. Besides, you're quite wrong: she doesn't do it that way at all. *(She takes the handkerchief.)*

LIZA *(snatching it).* Here! You give that handkerchief. He give it to me, not to you.

---

8. **had a drop in,** had been drinking.

9. **guinea** (gin′ē), *n.* a British gold coin. It was discontinued in 1813, but the word continued in use for stating prices and fees.

10. **£150.** £ is the symbol for *pound,* a unit of British money.

PICKERING (*laughing*). He did. I think it must be regarded as her property, Mrs. Pearce.

MRS. PEARCE (*resigning herself*). Serve you right, Mr. Higgins.

PICKERING. Higgins: I'm interested. What about the ambassador's garden party? I'll say you're the greatest teacher alive if you make that good. I'll bet you all the expenses of the experiment you can't do it. And I'll pay for the lessons.

LIZA. Oh, you are real good. Thank you, Captain.

HIGGINS (*tempted, looking at her*). It's almost irresistible. She's so deliciously low—so horribly dirty—

LIZA (*protesting extremely*). Ah-ah-ah-ah-ow-ow-oo-oo!!! I ain't dirty: I washed my face and hands afore I come, I did.

PICKERING. You're certainly not going to turn her head with flattery, Higgins.

MRS. PEARCE (*uneasy*). Oh, don't say that, sir: there's more ways than one of turning a girl's head; and nobody can do it better than Mr. Higgins, though he may not always mean it. I do hope, sir, you won't encourage him to do anything foolish.

HIGGINS (*becoming excited as the idea grows on him*). What is life but a series of inspired follies? The difficulty is to find them to do. Never lose a chance: it doesn't come every day. I shall make a duchess of this draggletailed guttersnipe.

LIZA (*strongly deprecating this view of her*). Ah-ah-ah-ow-ow-oo!

HIGGINS (*carried away*). Yes: in six months—in three if she has a good ear and a quick tongue—I'll take her anywhere and pass her off as anything. We'll start today: now! This moment! Take her away and clean her, Mrs. Pearce. Monkey Brand, if it won't come off any other way. Is there a good fire in the kitchen?

MRS. PEARCE (*protesting*). Yes; but—

HIGGINS (*storming on*). Take all her clothes off and burn them. Ring up Whiteley or some-body for new ones. Wrap her up in brown paper till they come.

LIZA. You're no gentleman, you're not, to talk of such things. I'm a good girl, I am; and I know what the like of you are, I do.

HIGGINS. We want none of your Lisson Grove prudery here, young woman. You've got to learn to behave like a duchess. Take her away, Mrs. Pearce. If she gives you any trouble, wallop her.

LIZA (*springing up and running between* PICKERING *and* MRS. PEARCE *for protection*). No! I'll call the police, I will.

MRS. PEARCE. But I've no place to put her.

HIGGINS. Put her in the dustbin.

LIZA. Ah-ah-ah-ow-ow-oo!

PICKERING. Oh come, Higgins! Be reasonable.

MRS. PEARCE (*resolutely*). You must be reasonable, Mr. Higgins: really you must. You can't walk over everybody like this.

(HIGGINS, *thus scolded, subsides. The hurricane is succeeded by a zephyr*[11] *of amiable surprise.*)

HIGGINS (*with professional exquisiteness of modulation*). *I* walk over everybody! My dear Mrs. Pearce, my dear Pickering, I never had the slightest intention of walking over anyone. All I propose is that we should be kind to this poor girl. We must help her to prepare and fit herself for her new station in life. If I did not express myself clearly it was because I did not wish to hurt her delicacy, or yours.

(LIZA, *reassured, steals back to her chair.*)

MRS. PEARCE (*to* PICKERING). Well, did you ever hear anything like that, sir?

PICKERING (*laughing heartily*). Never, Mrs. Pearce: never.

HIGGINS (*patiently*). What's the matter?

MRS. PEARCE. Well, the matter is, sir, that you can't take a girl up like that as if you were picking up a pebble on the beach.

HIGGINS. Why not?

MRS. PEARCE. Why not! But you don't know any-

---

11. **zephyr** (zef′ər), *n.* mild breeze; gentle wind.

thing about her. What about her parents? She may be married.

LIZA. Garn!

HIGGINS. There! As the girl very properly says, Garn! Married indeed! Don't you know that a woman of that class looks a worn out drudge of fifty a year after she's married!

LIZA. Who'd marry me?

HIGGINS *(suddenly resorting to the most thrillingly beautiful low tones in his best elocutionary style).* By George, Eliza, the streets will be strewn[12] with the bodies of men shooting themselves for your sake before I've done with you.

MRS. PEARCE. Nonsense, sir. You mustn't talk like that to her.

LIZA *(rising and squaring herself determinedly).* I'm going away. He's off his chump, he is. I don't want no balmies teaching me.

HIGGINS *(wounded in his tenderest point by her insensibility to his elocution).* Oh, indeed! I'm mad, am I? Very well, Mrs. Pearce: you needn't order the new clothes for her. Throw her out.

LIZA *(whimpering).* Nah-ow. You got no right to touch me.

MRS. PEARCE. You see now what comes of being saucy. *(Indicating the door.)* This way, please.

LIZA *(almost in tears).* I didn't want no clothes. I wouldn't have taken them. *(She throws away the handkerchief.)* I can buy my own clothes.

HIGGINS *(deftly retrieving the handkerchief and intercepting her on her reluctant way to the door).* You're an ungrateful wicked girl. This is my return for offering to take you out of the gutter and dress you beautifully and make a lady of you.

MRS. PEARCE. Stop, Mr. Higgins. I won't allow it. It's you that are wicked. Go home to your parents, girl; and tell them to take better care of you.

LIZA. I ain't got no mother. Her that turned me out was my sixth stepmother. But I done without them. And I'm a good girl, I am.

HIGGINS. Very well, then, what on earth is all this fuss about? The girl doesn't belong to anybody— is no use to anybody but me. *(He goes to* MRS. PEARCE *and begins coaxing.)* You can adopt her, Mrs. Pearce: I'm sure a daughter would be a great amusement to you. Now don't make any more fuss. Take her downstairs; and—

MRS. PEARCE. But what's to become of her? Is she to be paid anything? Do be sensible, sir.

HIGGINS. Oh, pay her whatever is necessary: put it down in the housekeeping book. *(Impatiently.)* What on earth will she want with money? She'll have her food and her clothes. She'll only drink if you give her money.

LIZA *(turning on him).* Oh you are a brute. It's a lie: nobody ever saw the sign of liquor on me. *(She goes back to her chair and plants herself there defiantly.)*

PICKERING *(in good-humored remonstrance).*[13] Does it occur to you, Higgins, that the girl has some feelings?

HIGGINS *(looking critically at her).* Oh no, I don't think so. Not any feelings that we need bother about. *(Cheerily.)* Have you, Eliza?

LIZA. I got my feelings same as anyone else.

HIGGINS *(to* PICKERING, *reflectively).* You see the difficulty?

PICKERING. Eh? What difficulty?

HIGGINS. To get her to talk grammar. The mere pronunciation is easy enough.

LIZA. I don't want to talk grammar. I want to talk like a lady.

MRS. PEARCE. Will you please keep to the point, Mr. Higgins? I want to know on what terms the girl is to be here. Is she to have any wages? And what is to become of her when you've finished your teaching? You must look ahead a little.

HIGGINS *(impatiently).* What's to become of her if I leave her in the gutter? Tell me that, Mrs. Pearce.

MRS. PEARCE. That's her own business, not yours, Mr. Higgins.

HIGGINS. Well, when I've done with her, we can throw her back into the gutter; and then it

---

12. **strew** (strü), *v.* scatter or sprinkle.
13. **remonstrance** (ri mon′strəns), *n.* protest; complaint.

will be her own business again; so that's all right.

LIZA. Oh, you've no feeling heart in you: you don't care for nothing but yourself. *(She rises and takes the floor resolutely.)* Here! I've had enough of this. I'm going. *(Making for the door.)* You ought to be ashamed of yourself, you ought.

HIGGINS *(snatching a chocolate cream from the piano, his eyes suddenly beginning to twinkle with mischief).* Have some chocolates, Eliza.

LIZA *(halting, tempted).* How do I know what might be in them? I've heard of girls being drugged by the like of you.

(HIGGINS whips out his penknife; cuts a chocolate in two; puts one half into his mouth and bolts it; and offers her the other half.)

HIGGINS. Pledge of good faith, Eliza. I eat one half: you eat the other. *(LIZA opens her mouth to retort: he pops the half chocolate into it.)* You shall have boxes of them, barrels of them, every day. You shall live on them. Eh?

LIZA *(who has disposed of the chocolate after being nearly choked by it).* I wouldn't have ate it, only I'm too ladylike to take it out of my mouth.

HIGGINS. Listen, Eliza. I think you said you came in a taxi.

LIZA. Well, what if I did? I've as good a right to take a taxi as anyone else.

HIGGINS. You have, Eliza; and in future you shall have as many taxis as you want. You shall go up and down and round the town in a taxi every day. Think of that, Eliza.

MRS. PEARCE. Mr. Higgins: you're tempting the girl. It's not right. She should think of the future.

HIGGINS. At her age! Nonsense! Time enough to think of the future when you haven't any future to think of. No, Eliza: do as this lady does: think of other people's futures; but never think of your own. Think of chocolates, and taxis, and gold, and diamonds.

LIZA. No: I don't want no gold and no diamonds. I'm a good girl, I am. *(She sits down again, with an attempt at dignity.)*

HIGGINS. You shall remain so, Eliza, under the care of Mrs. Pearce. And you shall marry an officer in the Guards, with a beautiful mustache: the son of a marquis, who will disinherit him for marrying you, but will relent when he sees your beauty and goodness—

PICKERING. Excuse me, Higgins; but I really must interfere. Mrs. Pearce is quite right. If this girl is to put herself in your hands for six months for an experiment in teaching, she must understand thoroughly what she's doing.

HIGGINS. How can she? She's incapable of understanding anything. Besides, do any of us understand what we are doing? If we did, would we ever do it?

PICKERING. Very clever, Higgins; but not sound sense. *(To ELIZA.)* Miss Doolittle—

LIZA *(overwhelmed).* Ah-ah-ow-oo!

HIGGINS. There! That's all you'll get out of Eliza. Ah-ah-ow-oo! No use explaining. As a military man you ought to know that. Give her orders: that's what she wants. Eliza: you are to live here for the next six months, learning how to speak beautifully, like a lady in a florist's shop. If you're good and do whatever you're told, you shall sleep in a proper bedroom, and have lots to eat, and money to buy chocolates and take rides in taxis. If you're naughty and idle you will sleep in the back kitchen among the black beetles, and be walloped by Mrs. Pearce with a broomstick. At the end of six months you shall go to Buckingham Palace in a carriage, beautifully dressed. If the King finds out you're not a lady, you will be taken by the police to the Tower of London, where your head will be cut off as a warning to other presumptuous flower girls. If you are not found out, you shall have a present of seven-and-sixpence to start life with as a lady in a shop. If you refuse this offer you will be a most ungrateful and wicked girl; and the angels will weep for you. *(To PICKERING.)* Now are you satisfied, Pickering? *(To MRS. PEARCE.)* Can I put it more plainly and fairly, Mrs. Pearce?

MRS. PEARCE *(patiently)*. I think you'd better let me speak to the girl properly in private. I don't know that I can take charge of her or consent to the arrangement at all. Of course I know you don't mean her any harm; but when you get what you call interested in people's accents, you never think or care what may happen to them or you. Come with me, Eliza.

HIGGINS. That's all right. Thank you, Mrs. Pearce. Bundle her off to the bathroom.

LIZA *(rising reluctantly and suspiciously)*. You're a great bully, you are. I won't stay here if I don't like. I won't let nobody wallop me. I never asked to go to Bucknam Palace, I didn't. I was never in trouble with the police, not me. I'm a good girl—

MRS. PEARCE. Don't answer back, girl. You don't understand the gentleman. Come with me. *(She leads the way to the door, and holds it open for* ELIZA.*)*

LIZA *(as she goes out)*. Well, what I say is right. I won't go near the King, not if I'm going to have my head cut off. If I'd known what I was letting myself in for, I wouldn't have come here. I always been a good girl; and I never offered to say a word to him; and I don't owe him nothing; and I don't care; and I won't be put upon; and I have my feelings the same as anyone else—

*(*MRS. PEARCE *shuts the door; and* ELIZA'S *plaints are no longer audible.* PICKERING *comes from the hearth to the chair and sits astride it with his arms on the back.)*

PICKERING. Excuse the straight question, Higgins. Are you a man of good character where women are concerned?

HIGGINS *(moodily)*. Have you ever met a man of good character where women are concerned?

PICKERING. Yes: very frequently.

HIGGINS *(dogmatically, lifting himself on his hands to the level of the piano, and sitting on it with a bounce)*. Well, I haven't. I find that the moment I let a woman make friends with me, she becomes jealous, exacting, suspi-cious, and a damned nuisance. I find that the moment I let myself make friends with a woman, I become selfish and tyrannical. Women upset everything. When you let them into your life, you find that the woman is driving at one thing and you're driving at another.

PICKERING. At what, for example?

HIGGINS *(coming off the piano restlessly)*. Oh, Lord knows! I suppose the woman wants to live her own life; and the man wants to live his; and each tries to drag the other on to the wrong track. One wants to go north and the other south; and the result is that both have to go east, though they both hate the east wind. *(He sits down on the bench at the keyboard.)* So here I am, a confirmed old bachelor, and likely to remain so.

PICKERING *(rising and standing over him gravely)*. Come, Higgins! You know what I mean. If I'm to be in this business I shall feel responsible for that girl. I hope it's understood that no advantage is to be taken of her position.

HIGGINS. What! That thing! Sacred, I assure you. *(Rising to explain.)* You see, she'll be a pupil; and teaching would be impossible unless the pupils were sacred. I've taught scores of American millionairesses how to speak English: the best looking women in the world. I'm seasoned. They might as well be blocks of wood. *I* might as well be a block of wood. It's—

*(*MRS. PEARCE *opens the door. She has* ELIZA'S *hat in her hand.* PICKERING *retires to the easy chair at the hearth and sits down.)*

HIGGINS *(eagerly)*. Well, Mrs. Pearce: is it all right?

MRS. PEARCE *(at the door)*. I just wish to trouble you with a word, if I may, Mr. Higgins.

HIGGINS. Yes, certainly. Come in. *(She comes forward.)* Don't burn that, Mrs. Pearce. I'll keep it as a curiosity. *(He takes the hat.)*

MRS. PEARCE. Handle it carefully, sir, please. I had to promise her not to burn it; but I had better put it in the oven for a while.

HIGGINS (*putting it down hastily on the piano*). Oh! Thank you. Well, what have you to say to me?

PICKERING. Am I in the way?

MRS. PEARCE. Not at all, sir. Mr. Higgins: will you please be very particular what you say before the girl?

HIGGINS (*sternly*). Of course. I'm always particular about what I say. Why do you say this to me?

MRS. PEARCE (*unmoved*). No, sir; you're not at all particular when you've mislaid anything or when you get a little impatient. Now it doesn't matter before me: I'm used to it. But you really must not swear before the girl.

HIGGINS (*indignantly*). I swear! (*Most emphatically.*) I never swear. I detest the habit. What the devil do you mean?

MRS. PEARCE (*stolidly*). That's what I mean, sir. You swear a great deal too much. I don't mind your damning and blasting, and what the devil and where the devil and who the devil—

HIGGINS. Mrs. Pearce: this language from your lips! Really!

MRS. PEARCE (*not to be put off*).—but there is a certain word I must ask you not to use. The girl has just used it herself because the bath was too hot. It begins with the same letter as bath. She knows no better: she learned it at her mother's knee. But she must not hear it from your lips.

HIGGINS (*loftily*). I cannot charge myself with having ever uttered it, Mrs. Pearce. (*She looks at him steadfastly. He adds, hiding an uneasy conscience with a judicial air.*) Except perhaps in a moment of extreme and justifiable excitement.

MRS. PEARCE. Only this morning, sir, you applied it to your boots, to the butter, and to the brown bread.

HIGGINS. Oh, that! Mere alliteration, Mrs. Pearce, natural to a poet.

MRS. PEARCE. Well, sir, whatever you choose to call it, I beg you not to let the girl hear you repeat it.

HIGGINS. Oh, very well, very well. Is that all?

MRS. PEARCE. No, sir. We shall have to be very particular with this girl as to personal cleanliness.

HIGGINS. Certainly. Quite right. Most important.

MRS. PEARCE. I mean not to be slovenly about her dress or untidy in leaving things about.

HIGGINS (*going to her solemnly*). Just so. I intended to call your attention to that. (*He passes on to* PICKERING, *who is enjoying the conversation immensely.*) It is these little things that matter, Pickering. Take care of the pence and the pounds will take care of themselves is as true of personal habits as of money. (*He comes to anchor on the hearthrug, with the air of a man in an unassailable[14] position.*)

MRS. PEARCE. Yes, sir. Then might I ask you not to come down to breakfast in your dressing-gown, or at any rate not to use it as a napkin to the extent you do, sir. And if you

---

14. **unassailable** (un ə sāl′ə bəl), *adj.* untroubled by doubt; unconquerable.

would be so good as not to eat everything off the same plate, and to remember not to put the porridge saucepan out of your hand on the clean tablecloth, it would be a better example to the girl. You know you nearly choked yourself with a fishbone in the jam only last week.

HIGGINS (*routed from the hearthrug and drifting back to the piano*). I may do these things sometimes in absence of mind; but surely I don't do them habitually. (*Angrily.*) By the way: my dressing-gown smells most damnably of benzine.

MRS. PEARCE. No doubt it does, Mr. Higgins. But if you will wipe your fingers—

HIGGINS (*yelling*). Oh very well, very well: I'll wipe them in my hair in the future.

MRS. PEARCE. I hope you're not offended, Mr. Higgins.

HIGGINS (*shocked at finding himself thought capable of an unamiable*[15] *sentiment*). Not at all, not at all. You're quite right, Mrs. Pearce: I shall be particularly careful before the girl. Is that all?

MRS. PEARCE. No, sir. Might she use some of those Japanese dresses you brought from abroad? I really can't put her back into her old things.

HIGGINS. Certainly. Anything you like. Is that all?

MRS. PEARCE. Thank you, sir. That's all. (*She goes out.*)

HIGGINS. You know, Pickering, that woman has the most extraordinary ideas about me. Here I am, a shy, diffident[16] sort of man. I've never been able to feel really grown-up and tremendous, like other chaps. And yet she's firmly persuaded that I'm an arbitrary over-bearing bossing kind of person. I can't account for it.

(MRS. PEARCE *returns.*)

MRS. PEARCE. If you please, sir, the trouble's beginning already. There's a dustman[17] downstairs, Alfred Doolittle, wants to see you. He says you have his daughter here.

PICKERING (*rising*). Phew! I say! (*He retreats to the hearthrug.*)

HIGGINS (*promptly*). Send the blackguard[18] up.

MRS. PEARCE. Oh, very well, sir. (*She goes out.*)

PICKERING. He may not be a blackguard, Higgins.

HIGGINS. Nonsense. Of course he's a blackguard.

PICKERING. Whether he is or not, I'm afraid we shall have some trouble with him.

HIGGINS (*confidently*). Oh no: I think not. If there's any trouble he shall have it with me, not I with him. And we are sure to get something interesting out of him.

PICKERING. About the girl?

HIGGINS. No. I mean his dialect.

PICKERING. Oh!

MRS. PEARCE (*at the door*). Doolittle, sir. (*She admits* DOOLITTLE *and retires.*)

(ALFRED DOOLITTLE *is an elderly but vigorous dustman, clad in the costume of his profession, including a hat with a back brim covering his neck and shoulders. He has well marked and rather interesting features, and seems equally free from fear and conscience. He has a remarkably expressive voice, the result of a habit of giving vent to his feelings without reserve. His present pose is that of wounded honor and stern resolution.*)

DOOLITTLE (*at the door, uncertain which of the two gentlemen is his man*). Professor Higgins?

HIGGINS. Here. Good morning. Sit down.

DOOLITTLE. Morning, Governor. (*He sits down magisterially.*) I come about a very serious matter, Governor.

HIGGINS (*to* PICKERING). Brought up in Hounslow. Mother Welsh, I should think. (DOOLITTLE *opens his mouth, amazed.* HIGGINS *continues.*) What do you want, Doolittle?

DOOLITTLE (*menacingly*). I want my daughter: that's what I want. See?

---

15. **unamiable** (un ā′mē ə bəl), *adj.* unpleasant; disagreeable.
16. **diffident** (dif′ə dənt), *adj.* lacking in self-confidence; shy.
17. **dustman,** a trash or garbage collector.
18. **blackguard** (blag′ärd), *n.* low, contemptible person; scoundrel.

HIGGINS. Of course you do. You're her father, aren't you? You don't suppose anyone else wants her, do you? I'm glad to see you have some spark of family feeling left. She's upstairs. Take her away at once.

DOOLITTLE (*rising, fearfully taken aback*). What!

HIGGINS. Take her away. Do you suppose I'm going to keep your daughter for you?

DOOLITTLE (*remonstrating*). Now, now, look here, Governor. Is this reasonable? Is it fairity to take advantage of a man like this? The girl belongs to me. You got her. Where do I come in? (*He sits down again.*)

HIGGINS. Your daughter had the audacity to come to my house and ask me to teach her how to speak properly so that she could get a place in a flower-shop. This gentleman and my housekeeper have been here all the time. (*Bullying him.*) How dare you come here and attempt to blackmail me? You sent her here on purpose.

DOOLITTLE (*protesting*). No, Governor.

HIGGINS. You must have. How else could you possibly know that she is here?

DOOLITTLE. Don't take a man up like that, Governor.

HIGGINS. The police shall take you up. This is a plant—a plot to extort money by threats. I shall telephone for the police. (*He goes resolutely to the telephone and opens the directory.*)

DOOLITTLE. Have I asked you for a brass farthing? I leave it to the gentleman here: have I said a word about money?

HIGGINS (*throwing the book aside and marching down on* DOOLITTLE *with a poser*). What else did you come for?

DOOLITTLE (*sweetly*). Well, what would a man come for? Be human, Governor.

HIGGINS (*disarmed*). Alfred: did you put her up to it?

DOOLITTLE. So help me, Governor, I never did. I take my Bible oath. I ain't seen the girl these two months past.

HIGGINS. Then how did you know she was here?

DOOLITTLE (*"most musical, most melancholy"*). I'll tell you, Governor, if you'll only let me get a word in. I'm willing to tell you. I'm wanting to tell you. I'm waiting to tell you.

HIGGINS. Pickering: this chap has a certain natural gift of rhetoric. Observe the rhythm of his native woodnotes wild. "I'm willing to tell you: I'm wanting to tell you: I'm waiting to tell you." Sentimental rhetoric! That's the Welsh strain in him. It also accounts for his mendacity and dishonesty.

PICKERING. Oh, please, Higgins: I'm west country[19] myself. (*To* DOOLITTLE.) How did you know the girl was here if you didn't send her?

DOOLITTLE. It was like this, Governor. The girl took a boy in the taxi to give him a jaunt. Son of her landlady, he is. He hung about on the chance of her giving him another ride home. Well, she sent him back for her luggage when she heard you was willing for her to stop here. I met the boy at the corner of Long Acre and Endell Street.

HIGGINS. Public house. Yes?

DOOLITTLE. The poor man's club, Governor: why shouldn't I?

PICKERING. Do let him tell his story, Higgins.

DOOLITTLE. He told me what was up. And I ask you, what was my feelings and my duty as a father? I says to the boy, "You bring me the luggage," I says—

PICKERING. Why didn't you go for it yourself?

DOOLITTLE. Landlady wouldn't have trusted me with it, Governor. She's that kind of woman: you know. I had to give the boy a penny afore he trusted me with it, the little swine. I brought it to her just to oblige you like, and make myself agreeable. That's all.

HIGGINS. How much luggage?

DOOLITTLE. Musical instrument, Governor. A few pictures, a trifle of jewelry, and a bird-cage. She said she didn't want no clothes.

---

19. **west country,** the counties in the southwest of England, especially Devon and Cornwall, which are near Wales.

What was I to think from that, Governor? I ask you as a parent what was I to think?

HIGGINS. So you came to rescue her from worse than death, eh?

DOOLITTLE (*appreciatively, relieved at being so well understood*). Just so, Governor. That's right.

PICKERING. But why did you bring her luggage if you intended to take her away?

DOOLITTLE. Have I said a word about taking her away? Have I now?

HIGGINS (*determinedly*). You're going to take her away, double quick. (*He crosses to the hearth and rings the bell.*)

DOOLITTLE (*rising*). No, Governor. Don't say that. I'm not the man to stand in my girl's light. Here's a career opening for her, as you might say; and—

(MRS. PEARCE *opens the door and awaits orders.*)

HIGGINS. Mrs. Pearce: this is Eliza's father. He has come to take her away. Give her to him. (*He goes back to the piano, with an air of washing his hands of the whole affair.*)

DOOLITTLE. No. This is a misunderstanding. Listen here—

MRS. PEARCE. He can't take her away, Mr. Higgins: how can he? You told me to burn her clothes.

DOOLITTLE. That's right. I can't carry the girl through the streets like a blooming monkey, can I? I put it to you.

HIGGINS. You have put it to me that you want your daughter. Take your daughter. If she has no clothes go out and buy her some.

DOOLITTLE (*desperate*). Where's the clothes she come in? Did I burn them or did your missus here?

MRS. PEARCE. I am the housekeeper, if you please. I have sent for some clothes for your girl. When they come you can take her away. You can wait in the kitchen. This way, please.

(DOOLITTLE, *much troubled, accompanies her to the door; then hesitates; finally turns confidentially to* HIGGINS.)

DOOLITTLE. Listen here, Governor. You and me is men of the world, ain't we?

HIGGINS. Oh! Men of the world, are we? You'd better go, Mrs. Pearce.

MRS. PEARCE. I think so, indeed, sir. (*She goes, with dignity.*)

PICKERING. The floor is yours, Mr. Doolittle.

DOOLITTLE (*to* PICKERING). I thank you, Governor. (*To* HIGGINS, *who takes refuge on the piano bench, a little overwhelmed by the proximity of his visitor; for* DOOLITTLE *has a professional flavor of dust about him.*) Well, the truth is, I've taken a sort of fancy to you, Governor; and if you want the girl, I'm not so set on having her back home again but what I might be open to an arrangement. Regarded in the light of a young woman, she's a fine handsome girl. As a daughter she's not worth her keep and so I tell you straight. All I ask is my rights as a father; and you're the last man alive to expect me to let her go for nothing; for I can see you're one of the straight sort, Governor. Well, what's a five-pound note to you? And what's Eliza to me? (*He returns to his chair and sits down judicially.*)

PICKERING. I think you ought to know, Doolittle, that Mr. Higgins's intentions are entirely honorable.

DOOLITTLE. Course they are, Governor. If I thought they wasn't, I'd ask fifty.

HIGGINS (*revolted*). Do you mean to say, you callous rascal, that you would sell your daughter for £50?

DOOLITTLE. Not in a general way I wouldn't; but to oblige a gentleman like you I'd do a good deal, I do assure you.

PICKERING. Have you no morals, man?

DOOLITTLE (*unabashed*).[20] Can't afford them, Governor. Neither could you if you was as poor as me. Not that I mean any harm, you know. But if Liza is going to have a bit out of this, why not me too?

HIGGINS (*troubled*). I don't know what to do, Pickering. There can be no question that as

---

20. **unabashed** (un′ə basht′), *adj.* not ashamed or embarrassed.

a matter of morals it's a positive crime to give this chap a farthing. And yet I feel a sort of rough justice in his claim.

DOOLITTLE. That's it, Governor. That's all I say. A father's heart, as it were.

PICKERING. Well, I know the feeling; but really it seems hardly right—

DOOLITTLE. Don't say that, Governor. Don't look at it that way. What am I, Governors both? I ask you, what am I? I'm one of the undeserving poor: that's what I am. Think of what that means to a man. It means that he's up agen middle class morality all the time. If there's anything going, and I put in for a bit of it, it's always the same story: "You're undeserving; so you can't have it." But my needs is as great as the most deserving widow that ever got money out of six different charities in one week for the death of the same husband. I don't need less than a deserving man: I need more. I don't eat less hearty than him; and I drink a lot more. I want a bit of amusement, cause I'm a thinking man. I want cheerfulness and a song and a band when I feel low. Well, they charge me just the same for everything as they charge the deserving. What is middle class morality? Just an excuse for never giving me anything. Therefore, I ask you, as two gentlemen, not to play that game on me. I'm playing straight with you. I ain't pretending to be deserving. I'm undeserving; and I mean to go on being undeserving. I like it; and that's the truth. Will you take advantage of a man's nature to do him out of the price of his own daughter what he's brought up and fed and clothed by the sweat of his brow until she's growed big enough to be interesting to you two gentlemen? Is five pounds unreasonable? I put it to you; and I leave it to you.

HIGGINS (*rising, and going over to* PICKERING). Pickering: if we were to take this man in hand for three months, he could choose between a seat in the Cabinet and a popular pulpit in Wales.

PICKERING. What do you say to that, Doolittle?

DOOLITTLE. Not me, Governor, thank you kindly. I've heard all the preachers and all the prime ministers—for I'm a thinking man and game for politics or religion or social reform same as all the other amusements—and I tell you it's a dog's life any way you look at it. Undeserving poverty is my line. Taking one station in society with another, it's—it's—well, it's the only one that has any ginger in it, to my taste.

HIGGINS. I suppose we must give him a fiver.

PICKERING. He'll make a bad use of it, I'm afraid.

DOOLITTLE. Not me, Governor, so help me I won't. Don't you be afraid that I'll save it and spare it and live idle on it. There won't be a penny of it left by Monday: I'll have to go to work same as if I'd never had it. It won't pauperize me, you bet. Just one good spree for myself and the missus, giving pleasure to ourselves and employment to others, and satisfaction to you to think it's not been throwed away. You couldn't spend it better.

HIGGINS (*taking out his pocket book and coming between* DOOLITTLE *and the piano*). This is irresistible. Let's give him ten. (*He offers two notes to the dustman.*)

DOOLITTLE. No, Governor. She wouldn't have the heart to spend ten; and perhaps I shouldn't neither. Ten pounds is a lot of money: it makes a man feel prudent[21] like; and then goodbye to happiness. You give me what I ask you, Governor: not a penny more, and not a penny less.

PICKERING. Why don't you marry that missus of yours? I rather draw the line at encouraging that sort of immorality.

DOOLITTLE. Tell her so, Governor: tell her so. *I'm* willing. It's me that suffers by it. I've no hold on her. I got to be agreeable to her. I got to give her presents. I got to buy her clothes something sinful. I'm a slave to that

---

21. **prudent** (prüd′nt), *adj.* sensible; discreet.

woman, Governor, just because I'm not her lawful husband. And she knows it too. Catch her marrying me! Take my advice, Governor: marry Eliza while she's young and don't know no better. If you don't you'll be sorry for it after. If you do, she'll be sorry for it after; but better her than you, because you're a man, and she's only a woman and don't know how to be happy anyhow.

HIGGINS. Pickering: if we listen to this man another minute, we shall have no convictions left. (*To* DOOLITTLE.) Five pounds I think you said.

DOOLITTLE. Thank you kindly, Governor.

HIGGINS. You're sure you won't take ten?

DOOLITTLE. Not now. Another time, Governor.

HIGGINS (*handing him a five-pound note*). Here you are.

DOOLITTLE. Thank you, Governor. Good morning. (*He hurries to the door, anxious to get away with his booty.*[22] *When he opens it he is confronted with a dainty and exquisitely clean young* JAPANESE LADY *in a simple blue cotton kimono printed cunningly with small white jasmine blossoms.* MRS. PEARCE *is with her. He gets out of her way deferentially and apologizes.*) Beg pardon, miss.

THE JAPANESE LADY. Garn! Don't you know your own daughter?

DOOLITTLE.   (*exclaiming*   Bly me! It's Eliza!
HIGGINS.   *simul-*   What's that! This!
PICKERING.   *taneously*)   By Jove!

LIZA. Don't I look silly?

HIGGINS. Silly?

MRS. PEARCE (*at the door*). Now, Mr. Higgins, please don't say anything to make the girl conceited about herself.

HIGGINS (*conscientiously*). Oh! Quite right, Mrs. Pearce. (*To* LIZA.) Yes: damned silly.

MRS. PEARCE. Please, sir.

HIGGINS (*correcting himself*). I mean extremely silly.

LIZA. I should look all right with my hat on. (*She takes up her hat; puts it on; and walks across the room to the fireplace with a fashionable air.*)

HIGGINS. A new fashion, by George! And it ought to look horrible!

DOOLITTLE (*with fatherly pride*). Well, I never thought she'd clean up as good looking as that, Governor. She's a credit to me, ain't she?

LIZA. I tell you, it's easy to clean up here. Hot and cold water on tap, just as much as you like, there is. Woolly towels, there is; and a towel horse so hot, it burns your fingers. Soft brushes to scrub yourself, and a wooden bowl of soap smelling like primroses. Now I know why ladies is so clean. Washing's a treat for them. Wish they saw what it is for the like of me!

HIGGINS. I'm glad the bathroom met with your approval.

LIZA. It didn't: not all of it; and I don't care who hears me say it. Mrs. Pearce knows.

HIGGINS. What was wrong, Mrs. Pearce?

MRS. PEARCE (*blandly*). Oh, nothing, sir. It doesn't matter.

LIZA. I had a good mind to break it. I didn't know which way to look. But I hung a towel over it, I did.

HIGGINS. Over what?

MRS. PEARCE. Over the looking-glass, sir.

HIGGINS. Doolittle: you have brought your daughter up too strictly.

DOOLITTLE. Me! I never brought her up at all, except to give her a lick of a strap now and again. She ain't accustomed to it, you see: that's all. But she'll soon pick up your free-and-easy ways.

LIZA. I'm a good girl, I am; and I won't pick up no free-and-easy ways.

HIGGINS. Eliza: if you say again that you're a good girl, your father shall take you home.

LIZA. Not him. You don't know my father. All he come here for was to touch you for some money to get drunk on.

DOOLITTLE. Well, what else would I want money for? To put into the plate in church, I suppose. (*She puts out her tongue at him. He is so incensed by this that* PICKERING *presently finds it*

---

22. **booty** (bü′tē), *n.* money, especially seized illegally; gains; winnings.

necessary to step between them.) Don't you give me none of your lip; and don't let me hear you giving this gentleman any of it neither, or you'll hear from me about it. See?

HIGGINS. Have you any further advice to give her before you go, Doolittle? Your blessing, for instance.

DOOLITTLE. No, Governor: I ain't such a mug as to put up my children to all I know myself. Hard enough to hold them in without that. If you want Eliza's mind improved, Governor, you do it yourself with a strap. So long, gentlemen. *(He turns to go.)*

HIGGINS *(impressively).* Stop. You'll come regularly to see your daughter. It's your duty, you know. My brother is a clergyman; and he could help you in your talks with her.

DOOLITTLE *(evasively).* Certainly. I'll come, Governor. Not just this week, because I have a job at a distance. But later on you may depend on me. Afternoon, gentlemen. Afternoon, ma'am. *(He takes off his hat to* MRS. PEARCE, *who disdains the salutation and goes out. He winks at* HIGGINS, *thinking him probably a fellow-sufferer from* MRS. PEARCE'S *difficult disposition, and follows her.)*

LIZA. Don't you believe the old liar. He'd as soon you set a bull-dog on him as a clergyman. You won't see him again in a hurry.

HIGGINS. I don't want to, Eliza. Do you?

LIZA. Not me. I don't want never to see him again, I don't.

PICKERING. What is his trade, Eliza?

LIZA. Taking money out of other people's pockets into his own. His proper trade's a navvy;[23] and he works at it sometimes too—for exercise—and earns good money at it. Ain't you going to call me Miss Doolittle any more?

PICKERING. I beg your pardon, Miss Doolittle. It was a slip of the tongue.

LIZA. Oh, I don't mind; only it sounded so genteel. I should just like to take a taxi to the corner of Tottenham Court Road and get out there and tell it to wait for me, just to put the girls in their place a bit. I wouldn't speak to them, you know.

PICKERING. Better wait till we get you something really fashionable.

HIGGINS. Besides, you shouldn't cut[24] your old friends now that you have risen in the world. That's what we call snobbery.

LIZA. You don't call the like of them my friends now, I should hope. They've took it out of me often enough with their ridicule when they had the chance; and now I mean to get a bit of my own back. But if I'm to have fashionable clothes, I'll wait. I should like to have some. Mrs. Pearce says you're going to give me some to wear in bed at night different to what I wear in the daytime; but it do seem a waste of money when you could get something to show. Besides, I never could fancy changing into cold things on a winter night.

MRS. PEARCE *(coming back).* Now, Eliza. The new things have come for you to try on.

LIZA. Ah-ow-oo-oooh! *(She rushes out.)*

MRS. PEARCE *(following her).* Oh, don't rush about like that, girl. *(She shuts the door behind her.)*

HIGGINS. Pickering: we have taken on a stiff job.

PICKERING *(with conviction).* Higgins: we have.

---

23. **navvy** (nav′ē), *n.* unskilled laborer, especially one doing excavation or construction work.
24. **cut,** snub; refuse to recognize socially.

After Reading

Act 2

Making Connections

Shaping Your Response

1. Do you agree more with Doolittle's characterization of himself as one of the "undeserving poor" or with Liza's description of him as a liar and a disgrace? Explain.

Analyzing the Play

2. What can you **infer** about the way Higgins lives from Mrs. Pearce's instructions to him?

3. In your opinion, is Higgins a gentleman? Explain.

4. Both Doolittle and Higgins threaten Liza with violence. Why do you think they feel free to make these threats?

5. 👣 Explain how the inferences Higgins and Pickering make about Doolittle and the inferences he makes about them get in the way of their **communication.**

6. Explain how Doolittle redefines conventional ideas about a father's rights, morals, and the life of the undeserving poor.

Extending the Ideas

7. In turning Liza's plans into a bet, Higgins and Pickering assume their right to take over her life. Does this assumption of the rights of one class or gender over another occur in the U.S. today? Explain.

8. If you wanted to improve your life, what would you change about yourself?

Vocabulary Study

For each phrase in the first column, choose the phrase in the second column that is closest in meaning.

1. astounded and dumfounded		a. *unabashed* celebrity
2. sturdy birdie		b. *stupent* and overwhelmed
3. faint complaint		c. *genteel* argument
4. battered and scattered		d. quiet *remonstrance*
5. famed, not ashamed		e. *diffident* male
6. polite fight		f. *genial* announcement
7. seize a breeze		g. beaten and *strewn*
8. cheerful earful		h. gets *booty*
9. shy guy		i. *robust* canary
10. obtains gains		j. catch a *zephyr*

ACT THREE

It is MRS. HIGGINS'S *at-home day.[1] Nobody has yet arrived. Her drawing room, in a flat on Chelsea Embankment,[2] has three windows looking on the river; and the ceiling is not so lofty as it would be in an older house of the same pretension. The windows are open, giving access to a balcony with flowers in pots. If you stand with your face to the windows, you have the fireplace on your left and the door in the right-hand wall close to the corner nearest the windows.*

MRS. HIGGINS *was brought up on Morris and Burne Jones;[3] and her room, which is very unlike her son's room in Wimpole Street, is not crowded with furniture and little tables and nick-nacks. In the middle of the room there is a big ottoman; and this, with the carpet, the Morris wallpapers, and the Morris chintz window curtains and brocade covers of the ottoman and its cushions, supply all the ornament, and are much too handsome to be hidden by odds and ends of useless things. A few good oil-paintings from the exhibitions in the Grosvenor Gallery thirty years ago (the Burne Jones, not the Whistler side of them) are on the walls. The only landscape is a Cecil Lawson on the scale of a Rubens.[4] There is a portrait of* MRS. HIGGINS *as she was when she defied fashion in her youth in one of the beautiful Rossettian[5] costumes which, when caricatured by people who did not understand, led to the absurdities of popular estheticism in the eighteen-seventies.*

In the corner diagonally opposite the door MRS. HIGGINS, *now over sixty and long past taking the trouble to dress out of the fashion, sits writing at an elegantly simple writing table with a bell button within reach of her hand. There is a Chippendale chair further back in the room between her and the window nearest her side. At the other side of the room, further forward, is an Elizabethan chair roughly carved in the taste of Inigo Jones. On the same side a piano in a decorated case. The corner between the fireplace and the window is occupied by a divan cushioned in Morris chintz.*

It is between four and five in the afternoon.

The door is opened violently; and HIGGINS *enters with his hat on.*

MRS. HIGGINS (*dismayed*). Henry! (*Scolding him.*) What are you doing here today? It is my at-home day: you promised not to come. (*As he bends to kiss her, she takes his hat off, and presents it to him.*)

HIGGINS. Oh bother! (*He throws the hat down on the table.*)

MRS. HIGGINS. Go home at once.

HIGGINS (*kissing her*). I know, Mother. I came on purpose.

MRS. HIGGINS. But you mustn't. I'm serious, Henry. You offend all my friends: they stop coming whenever they meet you.

HIGGINS. Nonsense! I know I have no small talk; but people don't mind. (*He sits on the settee.*)

MRS. HIGGINS. Oh! Don't they? Small talk indeed! What about your large talk? Really, dear, you mustn't stay.

HIGGINS. I must. I've a job for you. A phonetic job.

MRS. HIGGINS. No use, dear. I'm sorry; but I can't get round your vowels; and though I like to get pretty postcards in your patent shorthand, I always have to read the copies in ordinary writing you so thoughtfully send me.

HIGGINS. Well, this isn't a phonetic job.

---

1. **at-home day,** the day a person in society receives callers.
2. **drawing room . . . Chelsea Embankment.** A drawing room is used mostly for entertaining guests. Chelsea is a pleasant residential district along the bank of the Thames.
3. **Morris and Burne-Jones.** William Morris (1834–1896) and Edward Burne-Jones (1833–1898) were members of a decorating firm noted for fine carvings, stained glass, metalwork, wallpapers, chintzes, tiles, and carpets. (See page 1 for a painting by Burne-Jones. The theme portfolio covers on pages 207, 383, 643, and 955 are designs by Morris.)
4. **Cecil Lawson . . . Rubens.** Cecil Lawson (1851–1882) was an English landscape painter. Peter Paul Rubens (1577–1640) was a Flemish painter known for his large canvases.
5. **Rossettian,** inspired by the paintings of Dante Gabriel Rosetti (1828–1882), whose work often pictures women in flowing robes. (See pages 90–91.)

MRS. HIGGINS. You said it was.

HIGGINS. Not your part of it. I've picked up a girl.

MRS. HIGGINS. Does that mean some girl has picked you up?

HIGGINS. Not at all. I don't mean a love affair.

MRS. HIGGINS. What a pity!

HIGGINS. Why?

MRS. HIGGINS. Well, you never fall in love with anyone under forty-five. When will you discover that there are some rather nice-looking young women about?

HIGGINS. Oh, I can't be bothered with young women. My idea of a lovable woman is something as like you as possible. I shall never get into the way of seriously liking young women: some habits lie too deep to be changed. (*Rising abruptly and walking about, jingling his money and his keys in his trouser pocket.*) Besides, they're all idiots.

MRS. HIGGINS. Do you know what you would do if you really loved me, Henry?

HIGGINS. Oh bother! What? Marry, I suppose?

MRS. HIGGINS. No. Stop fidgeting and take your hands out of your pockets. (*With a gesture of despair, he obeys and sits down again.*) That's a good boy. Now tell me about the girl.

HIGGINS. She's coming to see you.

MRS. HIGGINS. I don't remember asking her.

HIGGINS. You didn't. *I* asked her. If you'd known her you wouldn't have asked her.

MRS. HIGGINS. Indeed! Why?

HIGGINS. Well, it's like this. She's a common flower girl. I picked her off the curbstone.

MRS. HIGGINS. And invited her to my at-home!

HIGGINS (*rising and coming to her to coax her*). Oh, that'll be all right. I've taught her to speak properly; and she has strict orders as to her behavior. She's to keep to two subjects: the weather and everybody's health—Fine day and How do you do, you know—and not to let herself go on things in general. That will be safe.

MRS. HIGGINS. Safe! To talk about our health! About our insides! Perhaps about our outsides! How could you be so silly, Henry?

HIGGINS (*impatiently*). Well, she must talk about something. (*He controls himself and sits down again.*) Oh, she'll be all right; don't you fuss. Pickering is in it with me. I've a sort of bet on that I'll pass her off as a duchess in six months. I started on her some months ago; and she's getting on like a house on fire. I shall win my bet. She has a quick ear; and she's been easier to teach than my middle-class pupils because she's had to learn a complete new language. She talks English almost as you talk French.

MRS. HIGGINS. That's satisfactory, at all events.

HIGGINS. Well, it is and it isn't.

MRS. HIGGINS. What does that mean?

HIGGINS. You see, I've got her pronunciation all right; but you have to consider not only how a girl pronounces, but what she pronounces; and that's where—

(*They are interrupted by the* PARLOR MAID, *announcing guests.*)

THE PARLOR MAID. Mrs. and Miss Eynsford Hill. (*She withdraws.*)

HIGGINS. Oh Lord! (*He rises; snatches his hat from the table; and makes for the door; but before he reaches it his mother introduces him.*)

(MRS. *and* MISS EYNSFORD HILL *are the mother and daughter who sheltered from the rain in Covent Garden. The mother is well bred, quiet, and has the habitual anxiety of straitened means.*[6] *The daughter has acquired a gay air of being very much at home in society; the bravado of genteel poverty.*)

MRS. EYNSFORD HILL (*to* MRS. HIGGINS). How do you do? (*They shake hands.*)

MISS EYNSFORD HILL. How d'you do? (*She shakes.*)

MRS. HIGGINS (*introducing*). My son Henry.

MRS. EYNSFORD HILL. Your celebrated son! I have so longed to meet you, Professor Higgins.

HIGGINS (*glumly, making no movement in her direction*). Delighted. (*He backs against the piano and bows brusquely.*)

---

6. **straitened means,** limited financial resources.

MISS EYNSFORD HILL (*going to him with confident familiarity*). How do you do?

HIGGINS (*staring at her*). I've seen you before somewhere. I haven't the ghost of a notion where; but I've heard your voice. (*Drearily.*) It doesn't matter. You'd better sit down.

MRS. HIGGINS. I'm sorry to say that my celebrated son has no manners. You mustn't mind him.

MISS EYNSFORD HILL (*gaily*). I don't. (*She sits in the Elizabethan chair.*)

MRS. EYNSFORD HILL (*a little bewildered*). Not at all. (*She sits on the ottoman between her daughter and* MRS. HIGGINS, *who has turned her chair away from the writing-table.*)

HIGGINS. Oh, have I been rude? I didn't mean to be.

(*He goes to the central window, through which, with his back to the company, he contemplates the river and the flowers in Battersea Park on the opposite bank as if they were a frozen desert. The* PARLOR MAID *returns, ushering in* PICKERING.)

THE PARLOR MAID. Colonel Pickering. (*She withdraws.*)

PICKERING. How do you do, Mrs. Higgins?

MRS. HIGGINS. So glad you've come. Do you know Mrs. Eynsford Hill—Miss Eynsford Hill? (*Exchange of bows. The* COLONEL *brings the Chippendale chair a little forward between* MRS. HILL *and* MRS. HIGGINS, *and sits down.*)

PICKERING. Has Henry told you what we've come for?

HIGGINS (*over his shoulder*). We were interrupted: damn it!

MRS. HIGGINS. Oh Henry, Henry, really!

MRS. EYNSFORD HILL (*half rising*). Are we in the way?

MRS. HIGGINS (*rising and making her sit down again*). No, no. You couldn't have come more fortunately: we want you to meet a friend of ours.

HIGGINS (*turning hopefully*). Yes, by George! We want two or three people. You'll do as well as anybody else.

(*The* PARLOR MAID *returns, ushering* FREDDY.)

THE PARLOR MAID. Mr. Eynsford Hill.

HIGGINS (*almost audibly, past endurance*). God of Heaven! Another of them.

FREDDY (*shaking hands with* MRS. HIGGINS). Ahdedo?

MRS. HIGGINS. Very good of you to come. (*Introducing.*) Colonel Pickering.

FREDDY (*bowing*). Ahdedo?

MRS. HIGGINS. I don't think you know my son, Professor Higgins.

FREDDY (*going to* HIGGINS). Ahdedo?

HIGGINS (*looking at him much as if he were a pickpocket*). I'll take my oath I've met you before somewhere. Where was it?

FREDDY. I don't think so.

HIGGINS (*resignedly*). It don't matter, anyhow. Sit down.

(*He shakes* FREDDY'S *hand, and almost slings him on to the ottoman with his face to the windows; then comes round to the other side of it.*)

HIGGINS. Well, here we are, anyhow! (*He sits down on the ottoman next* MRS. EYNSFORD HILL, *on her left.*) And now, what the devil are we going to talk about until Eliza comes?

MRS. HIGGINS. Henry: you are the life and soul of the Royal Society's soirées;[7] but really you're rather trying on more commonplace occasions.

HIGGINS. Am I? Very sorry. (*Beaming suddenly.*) I suppose I am, you know. (*Uproariously.*) Ha, ha!

MISS EYNSFORD HILL (*who considers* HIGGINS *quite eligible matrimonially*). I sympathize. *I* haven't any small talk. If people would only be frank and say what they really think!

HIGGINS (*relapsing into gloom*). Lord forbid!

MRS. EYNSFORD HILL (*taking up her daughter's cue*). But why?

HIGGINS. What they think they ought to think is bad enough, Lord knows; but what they really think would break up the whole show.

---

7. **Royal Society . . . soirée** (swä rā′), *n.* The Royal Society is a well-known scientific society in England. A soirée is an evening social gathering.

Do you suppose it would be really agreeable if I were to come out now with what *I* really think?

MISS EYNSFORD HILL *(gaily)*. Is it so very cynical?

HIGGINS. Cynical! Who the dickens said it was cynical? I mean it wouldn't be decent.

MRS. EYNSFORD HILL *(seriously)*. Oh! I'm sure you don't mean that, Mr. Higgins.

HIGGINS. You see, we're all savages, more or less. We're supposed to be civilized and cultured—to know all about poetry and philosophy and art and science, and so on; but how many of us know even the meanings of these names? *(To MISS HILL.)* What do you know of poetry? *(To MRS. HILL.)* What do you know of science? *(Indicating FREDDY.)* What does he know of art or science or anything else? What the devil do you imagine I know of philosophy?

MRS. HIGGINS *(warningly)*. Or of manners, Henry?

THE PARLOR MAID *(opening the door)*. Miss Doolittle. *(She withdraws.)*

HIGGINS *(rising hastily and running to MRS. HIGGINS)*. Here she is, Mother. *(He stands on tiptoe and makes signs over his mother's head to ELIZA to indicate to her which lady is her hostess.)*

(ELIZA, who is exquisitely dressed, produces an impression of such remarkable distinction and beauty as she enters that they all rise, quite fluttered. Guided by HIGGINS's signals, she comes to MRS. HIGGINS with studied grace.)

LIZA *(speaking with pedantic correctness of pronunciation and great beauty of tone)*. How do you do, Mrs. Higgins? *(She gasps slightly in making sure of the H in Higgins, but is quite successful.)* Mr. Higgins told me I might come.

MRS. HIGGINS *(cordially)*. Quite right: I'm very glad indeed to see you.

PICKERING. How do you do, Miss Doolittle?

LIZA *(shaking hands with him)*. Colonel Pickering, is it not?

MRS. EYNSFORD HILL. I feel sure we have met before, Miss Doolittle. I remember your eyes.

LIZA. How do you do? *(She sits down on the ottoman gracefully in the place just left vacant by HIGGINS.)*

MRS. EYNSFORD HILL *(introducing)*. My daughter Clara.

LIZA. How do you do?

CLARA *(impulsively)*. How do you do? *(She sits down on the ottoman beside ELIZA, devouring her with her eyes.)*

FREDDY *(coming to their side of the ottoman)*. I've certainly had the pleasure.

MRS. EYNSFORD HILL *(introducing)*. My son Freddy.

LIZA. How do you do?

(FREDDY bows and sits down in the Elizabethan chair, infatuated.)

HIGGINS *(suddenly)*. By George, yes: it all comes back to me! *(They stare at him.)* Covent Garden! *(Lamentably.)* What a damned thing!

MRS. HIGGINS. Henry, please! *(He is about to sit on the edge of the table.)* Don't sit on my writing table: you'll break it.

HIGGINS *(sulkily)*. Sorry.

(He goes to the divan, stumbling into the fender and over the fire-irons on his way; extricating himself with muttered imprecations; and finishing his disastrous journey by throwing himself so impatiently on the divan that he almost breaks it. MRS. HIGGINS looks at him, but controls herself and says nothing. A long and painful pause ensues.)

MRS. HIGGINS *(at last, conversationally)*. Will it rain, do you think?

LIZA. The shallow depression in the west of these islands is likely to move slowly in an easterly direction. There are no indications of any great change in the barometrical situation.

FREDDY. Ha! ha! How awfully funny!

LIZA. What is wrong with that, young man? I bet I got it right.

FREDDY. Killing!

MRS. EYNSFORD HILL. I'm sure I hope it won't turn cold. There's so much influenza about. It runs right through our whole family regularly every spring.

LIZA *(darkly)*. My aunt died of influenza: so they said.

MRS. EYNSFORD HILL *(clicks her tongue sympathetically)*. !!!

LIZA *(in the same tragic tone)*. But it's my belief they done the old woman in.

MRS. HIGGINS *(puzzled)*. Done her in?

LIZA. Y-e-e-e-es, Lord love you! Why should she die of influenza? She come through diphtheria right enough the year before. I saw her with my own eyes. Fairly blue with it, she was. They all thought she was dead; but my father he kept ladling gin down her throat till she came to so sudden that she bit the bowl off the spoon.

MRS. EYNSFORD HILL *(startled)*. Dear me!

LIZA *(piling up the indictment)*. What call would a woman with that strength in her have to die of influenza? What become of her new straw hat that should have come to me? Somebody pinched it; and what I say is, them as pinched it done her in.

MRS. EYSNFORD HILL. What does doing her in mean?

HIGGINS *(hastily)*. Oh, that's the new small talk. To do a person in means to kill them.

MRS. EYNSFORD HILL *(to ELIZA, horrified)*. You surely don't believe that your aunt was killed?

LIZA. Do I not! Them she lived with would have killed her for a hatpin, let alone a hat.

MRS. EYNSFORD HILL. But it can't have been right for your father to pour spirits down her throat like that. It might have killed her.

LIZA. Not her. Gin was mother's milk to her. Besides, he'd poured so much down his own throat that he knew the good of it.

MRS. EYNSFORD HILL. Do you mean that he drank?

LIZA. Drank! My word! Something chronic.

MRS. EYNSFORD HILL. How dreadful for you!

LIZA. Not a bit. It never did him no harm what I could see. But then he did not keep it up regular. *(Cheerfully.)* On the burst, as you might say, from time to time. And always more agreeable when he had a drop in. When he was out of work, my mother used to give him fourpence and tell him to go out and not come back until he'd drunk himself cheerful and loving-like. There's lots of women has to make their husbands drunk to make them fit to live with. *(Now quite at her ease.)* You see, it's like this. If a man has a bit of a conscience, it always takes him when he's sober; and then it makes him low-spirited. A drop of booze just takes that off and makes him happy. *(To* FREDDY, *who is in convulsions of suppressed laughter.)* Here! What are you sniggering at?

FREDDY *(opening the door for her).* Are you walking across the Park, Miss Doolittle? If so—

LIZA. Walk! Not bloody[8] likely. *(Sensation.)* I am going in a taxi. *(She goes out.)*

*(*PICKERING *gasps and sits down.* FREDDY *goes out on the balcony to catch another glimpse of* ELIZA.*)*

MRS. EYNSFORD HILL *(suffering from shock).* Well, I really can't get used to the new ways.

CLARA *(throwing herself discontentedly into the Elizabethan chair).* Oh, it's all right, Mamma, quite right. People will think we never go anywhere or see anybody if you are so old-fashioned.

MRS. EYNSFORD HILL. I daresay I am very old-fashioned; but I do hope you won't begin using that expression, Clara. I have got accustomed to hear you talking about men as rotters, and calling everything filthy and beastly; though I do think it horrible and unladylike. But this last is really too much. Don't you think so, Colonel Pickering?

PICKERING. Don't ask me. I've been away in India for several years; and manners have changed so much that I sometimes don't know whether I'm at a respectable dinnertable or in a ship's forecastle.

CLARA. It's all a matter of habit. There's no right or wrong in it. Nobody means anything by it. And it's so quaint, and gives such a smart emphasis to things that are not in themselves very witty. I find the new small talk delightful and quite innocent.

FREDDY. The new small talk. You do it so awfully well.

LIZA. If I was doing it proper, what was you laughing at? *(To* HIGGINS.*)* Have I said anything I oughtn't?

MRS. HIGGINS *(interposing).* Not at all, Miss Doolittle.

LIZA. Well, that's a mercy, anyhow. *(Expansively.)* What I always say is—

HIGGINS *(rising and looking at his watch).* Ahem!

LIZA *(looking round at him; taking the hint; and rising).* Well: I must go. *(They all rise.* FREDDY *goes to the door.)* So pleased to have met you. Goodbye. *(She shakes hands with* MRS. HIGGINS.*)*

MRS. HIGGINS. Goodbye.

LIZA. Goodbye, Colonel Pickering.

PICKERING. Goodbye, Miss Doolittle. *(They shake hands.)*

LIZA *(nodding to the others).* Goodbye, all.

---

8. **bloody,** British slang for "cursed" or "confounded" but considered so improper in Shaw's day that he was urged to remove the word from the play. Audiences gasped and then laughed uproariously when they heard it.

MRS. EYNSFORD HILL (*rising*). Well, after that, I think it's time for us to go.

(PICKERING *and* HIGGINS *rise.*)

CLARA (*rising*). Oh yes: we have three at-homes to go to still. Goodbye, Mrs. Higgins. Goodbye, Colonel Pickering. Goodbye, Professor Higgins.

HIGGINS (*coming grimly at her from the divan, and accompanying her to the door*). Goodbye. Be sure you try on that small talk at the three at-homes. Don't be nervous about it. Pitch it in strong.

CLARA (*all smiles*). I will. Goodbye. Such nonsense, all this early Victorian prudery!

HIGGINS (*tempting her*). Such damned nonsense!

CLARA. Such bloody nonsense!

MRS. EYNSFORD HILL (*convulsively*). Clara!

CLARA. Ha! ha! (*She goes out radiant, conscious of being thoroughly up to date, and is heard descending the stairs in a stream of silvery laughter.*)

FREDDY (*to the heavens at large*). Well, I ask you— (*He gives it up, and comes to* MRS. HIGGINS.) Goodbye.

MRS. HIGGINS (*shaking hands*). Goodbye. Would you like to meet Miss Doolittle again?

FREDDY (*eagerly*). Yes, I should, most awfully.

MRS. HIGGINS. Well, you know my days.

FREDDY. Yes. Thanks awfully. Goodbye. (*He goes out.*)

MRS. EYNSFORD HILL. Goodbye, Mr. Higgins.

HIGGINS. Goodbye. Goodbye.

MRS. EYNSFORD HILL (*to* PICKERING). It's no use. I shall never be able to bring myself to use that word.

PICKERING. Don't. It's not compulsory, you know. You'll get on quite well without it.

MRS. EYNSFORD HILL. Only, Clara is so down on me if I am not positively reeking with the latest slang. Goodbye.

PICKERING. Goodbye (*They shake hands.*)

MRS. EYNSFORD HILL (*to* MRS. HIGGINS). You mustn't mind Clara. (PICKERING, *catching from her lowered tone that this is not meant for him to hear, discreetly joins* HIGGINS *at the window.*) We're so poor! And she gets so few par-

ties, poor child! She doesn't quite know. (MRS. HIGGINS, *seeing that her eyes are moist, takes her hand sympathetically and goes with her to the door.*) But the boy is nice. Don't you think so?

MRS. HIGGINS. Oh, quite nice. I shall always be delighted to see him.

MRS. EYNSFORD HILL. Thank you, dear. Goodbye. (*She goes out.*)

HIGGINS (*eagerly*). Well? Is Eliza presentable? (*He swoops on his mother and drags her to the ottoman, where she sits down in* ELIZA'S *place with her son on her left.* PICKERING *returns to his chair on her right.*)

MRS. HIGGINS. You silly boy, of course she's not presentable. She's a triumph of your art and of her dressmaker's; but if you suppose for a moment that she doesn't give herself away in every sentence she utters, you must be perfectly cracked about her.

PICKERING. But don't you think something might be done? I mean something to eliminate the sanguinary[9] element from her conversation.

MRS. HIGGINS. Not as long as she is in Henry's hands.

HIGGINS (*aggrieved*). Do you mean that my language is improper?

MRS. HIGGINS. No, dearest: it would be quite proper—say on a canal barge; but it would not be proper for her at a garden party.

HIGGINS (*deeply injured*). Well I must say—

PICKERING (*interrupting him*). Come, Higgins: you must learn to know yourself. I haven't heard such language as yours since we used to review the volunteers in Hyde Park twenty years ago.

HIGGINS (*sulkily*). Oh, well, if you say so, I suppose I don't always talk like a bishop.

MRS. HIGGINS (*quieting* HENRY *with a touch*). Colonel Pickering: will you tell me what is the exact state of things in Wimpole Street?

PICKERING (*cheerfully: as if this completely changed the subject*). Well, I have come to live there

---

9. **sanguinary** (sang′gwə ner′ē), *adj.* with much blood, a reference to Liza's use of the word *bloody*.

with Henry. We work together at my Indian Dialects; and we think it more convenient—

MRS. HIGGINS. Quite so. I know all about that: it's an excellent arrangement. But where does this girl live?

HIGGINS. With us, of course. Where should she live?

MRS. HIGGINS. But on what terms? Is she a servant? If not, what is she?

PICKERING (slowly). I think I know what you mean, Mrs. Higgins.

HIGGINS. Well, dash me if *I* do! I've had to work at the girl every day for months to get her to the present pitch. Besides, she's useful. She knows where my things are, and remembers my appointments and so forth.

MRS. HIGGINS. How does your housekeeper get on with her?

HIGGINS. Mrs. Pearce? Oh, she's jolly glad to get so much taken off her hands; for before Eliza came, she used to have to find things and remind me of my appointments. But she's got some silly bee in her bonnet about Eliza. She keeps saying "You don't think, sir": doesn't she, Pick?

PICKERING. Yes: that's the formula. "You don't think, sir." That's the end of every conversation about Eliza.

HIGGINS. As if I ever stop thinking about the girl and her confounded vowels and consonants. I'm worn out, thinking about her, and watching her lips and her teeth and her tongue, not to mention her soul, which is the quaintest of the lot.

MRS. HIGGINS. You certainly are a pretty pair of babies, playing with your live doll.

HIGGINS. Playing! The hardest job I ever tackled: make no mistake about that, Mother. But you have no idea how frightfully interesting it is to take a human being and change her into a quite different human being by creating a new speech for her. It's filling up the deepest gulf that separates class from class and soul from soul.

PICKERING (drawing his chair closer to MRS. HIGGINS *and bending over to her eagerly*). Yes: it's enormously interesting. I assure you, Mrs. Higgins, we take Eliza very seriously. Every week—every day almost—there is some new change. (*Closer again.*) We keep records of every stage—dozens of gramophone disks and photographs—

HIGGINS (*assailing her at the other ear*). Yes, by George: it's the most absorbing experiment I ever tackled. She regularly fills our lives up: doesn't she, Pick?

PICKERING. We're always talking Eliza.

HIGGINS. Teaching Eliza.

PICKERING. Dressing Eliza.

MRS. HIGGINS. What!

HIGGINS. Inventing new Elizas.

	(speaking together)	
HIGGINS.		You know, she has the most extraordinary quickness of ear.
PICKERING.		I assure you, my dear Mrs. Higgins, that girl
HIGGINS.		Just like a parrot. I've tried her with every
PICKERING.		is a genius. She can play the piano quite beautifully.
HIGGINS.		possible sort of sound that a human being can make—
PICKERING.		We have taken her to classical concerts and to music
HIGGINS.		Continental dialects, African dialects, Hottentot
PICKERING.		halls; and it's all the same to her: she plays everything
HIGGINS.		clicks, things it took me years to get hold of; and
PICKERING.		she hears right off when she comes home, whether it's

HIGGINS.			she picks them up like a shot, right away, as if she had Beethoven and Brahms or Lehar and Lionel Monckton:[10]
PICKERING.	*(speaking together)*		
HIGGINS.			been at it all her life. though six months ago, she'd never as much as touched a piano—
PICKERING.			

MRS. HIGGINS (*putting her fingers in her ears, as they are by this time shouting one another down with an intolerable noise*). Sh-sh-sh—sh! (*They stop.*)

PICKERING. I beg your pardon. (*He draws his chair back apologetically.*)

HIGGINS. Sorry. When Pickering starts shouting nobody can get a word in edgeways.

MRS. HIGGINS. Be quiet, Henry. Colonel Pickering: don't you realize that when Eliza walked into Wimpole Street, something walked in with her?

PICKERING. Her father did. But Henry soon got rid of him.

MRS. HIGGINS. It would have been more to the point if her mother had. But as her mother didn't something else did.

PICKERING. But what?

MRS. HIGGINS (*unconsciously dating herself by the word*). A problem.

PICKERING. Oh, I see. The problem of how to pass her off as a lady.

HIGGINS. I'll solve that problem. I've half solved it already.

MRS. HIGGINS. No, you two infinitely stupid male creatures: the problem of what is to be done with her afterwards.

HIGGINS. I don't see anything in that. She can go her own way, with all the advantages I have given her.

MRS. HIGGINS. The advantages of that poor woman who was here just now! The manners and habits that disqualify a fine lady from earning her own living without giving her a fine lady's income! Is that what you mean?

PICKERING (*indulgently, being rather bored*). Oh, that will be all right, Mrs. Higgins. (*He rises to go.*)

HIGGINS (*rising also*). We'll find her some light employment.

PICKERING. She's happy enough. Don't you worry about her. Goodbye. (*He shakes hands as if he were consoling a frightened child, and makes for the door.*)

HIGGINS. Anyhow, there's no good bothering now. The thing's done. Goodbye, Mother. (*He kisses her, and follows* PICKERING.)

PICKERING (*turning for a final consolation*). There are plenty of openings. We'll do what's right. Goodbye.

HIGGINS (*to* PICKERING *as they go out together*). Let's take her to the Shakespeare exhibition at Earls Court.

PICKERING. Yes: let's. Her remarks will be delicious.

HIGGINS. She'll mimic all the people for us when we get home.

PICKERING. Ripping. (*Both are heard laughing as they go downstairs.*)

MRS. HIGGINS (*rises with an impatient bounce, and returns to her work at the writing table. She sweeps a litter of disarranged papers out of her way; snatches a sheet of paper from her stationery case; and tries resolutely to write. At the third line she gives it up; flings down her pen; grips the table angrily and exclaims*). Oh, men! Men!!! Men!!!

---

10. **Beethoven . . . Monckton,** all composers, the last two of light music.

Act 3

After Reading

Making Connections

Shaping Your Response

1. What do you think of Liza's "performance" in Mrs. Higgins's drawing room?

2. What advice could you give her to help improve her conversation?

Analyzing the Play

3. During Mrs. Higgins's at-home, who has better manners, Higgins or Liza? What is the point of this contrast?

4. Why do you think Clara chooses to say "bloody nonsense!" at the end of her visit?

5. 👣 Higgins and Pickering praise Liza's ability to imitate sounds "just like a parrot" and to play the piano by ear. What might such abilities have to do with **communication** using language?

6. What insights have you gained so far into possible reasons why Higgins is a bachelor?

Extending the Ideas

7. In your opinion, how important are good manners today, and who defines good or bad manners?

Literary Focus: Inference

An **inference** is a reasonable conclusion based on hints and clues. The characters in *Pygmalion* make many inferences about each other, and we, in turn, make inferences about them.

1. What inference does Mrs. Higgins make when Higgins tells her he has picked up a girl?

2. What inferences do Mrs. Eynsford Hill, Clara, and Freddy make about Liza? Upon what clues do they base their inferences?

3. What inference does Mrs. Higgins make about possible problems inherent in the situation?

4. From Mrs. Eynsford Hill's admission to Mrs. Higgins about how poor they are and how few parties Clara gets, what do you infer about the Eynsford Hills' position in society?

ACT FOUR

The Wimpole Street laboratory. Midnight. Nobody in the room. The clock on the mantelpiece strikes twelve. The fire is not alight: it is a summer night. Presently HIGGINS *and* PICKERING *are heard on the stairs.*

HIGGINS (*calling down to* PICKERING). I say, Pick: lock up, will you? I shan't be going out again.

PICKERING. Right. Can Mrs. Pearce go to bed? We don't want anything more, do we?

HIGGINS. Lord, no!

(ELIZA *opens the door and is seen on the lighted landing in opera cloak, brilliant evening dress, and diamonds, with fan, flowers, and all accessories. She comes to the hearth, and switches on the electric lights there. She is tired: her pallor contrasts strongly with her dark eyes and hair; and her expression is almost tragic. She takes off her cloak; puts her fan and flowers on the piano; and sits down on the bench, brooding and silent.* HIGGINS, *in evening dress, with overcoat and hat, comes in, carrying a smoking jacket which he has picked up downstairs. He takes off the hat and overcoat; throws them carelessly on the newspaper stand; disposes of his coat in the same way; puts on the smoking jacket; and throws himself wearily into the easy chair at the hearth.* PICKERING, *similarly attired, comes in. He also takes off his hat and overcoat, and is about to throw them on* HIGGINS'S *when he hesitates.*)

PICKERING. I say: Mrs. Pearce will row if we leave these things lying about in the drawing room.

HIGGINS. Oh, chuck them over the bannisters into the hall. She'll find them there in the morning and put them away all right. She'll think we were drunk.

PICKERING. We are, slightly. Are there any letters?

HIGGINS. I didn't look. (PICKERING *takes the overcoats and hats and goes downstairs.* HIGGINS *begins half singing half yawning an air from* La Fanciulla del Golden West.[1] *Suddenly he stops and exclaims.*) I wonder where the devil my slippers are!

(ELIZA *looks at him darkly; then rises suddenly and leaves the room.* HIGGINS *yawns again, and resumes his song.* PICKERING *returns, with the contents of the letterbox in his hand.*)

PICKERING. Only circulars, and this coroneted billet-doux[2] for you. (*He throws the circulars into the fender, and posts himself on the hearthrug, with his back to the grate.*)

HIGGINS (*glancing at the billet-doux*). Money-

---

1. **La Fanciulla del Golden West,** a combination of two titles. *La Fanciulla del West* is an opera by Giacomo Puccini that opened in New York in 1910 and is based on *The Girl of the Golden West,* a play by David Belasco.

2. **coroneted billet-doux.** *Billet-doux* (bil′ē dü′) is French for "love letter," but Pickering is using the word ironically. This one bears a coronet, or crown, indicating that it is from someone of noble birth, but Higgins's response seems to indicate he feels the writer is an upstart.

◄ Other actresses who have portrayed Liza on stage or screen are shown in their formal gowns. The actresses are (from the left): Diana Wynard, Diana Rigg, Cathy Tyson, and Audrey Hepburn. What special qualities do you imagine each of these actresses brought to the role of Eliza?

lender. *(He throws the letter after the circulars.)* *(ELIZA returns with a pair of large-down-at-heel slippers. She places them on the carpet before HIGGINS, and sits as before without a word.)*

HIGGINS *(yawning again).* Oh Lord! What an evening! What a crew! What a silly tomfoolery! *(He raises his shoe to unlace it, and catches sight of the slippers. He stops unlacing and looks at them as if they had appeared there of their own accord.)* Oh! They're here, are they?

PICKERING *(stretching himself).* Well, I feel a bit tired. It's been a long day. The garden party, a dinner party, and the opera! Rather too much of a good thing. But you've won your bet, Higgins. Eliza did the trick, and something to spare, eh?

HIGGINS *(fervently).* Thank God it's over!

(ELIZA flinches violently; but they take no notice of her; and she recovers herself and sits stonily as before.)

PICKERING. Were you nervous at the garden party? *I* was. Eliza didn't seem a bit nervous.

HIGGINS. Oh, she wasn't nervous. I knew she'd be all right. No: it's the strain of putting the job through all these months that has told on me. It was interesting enough at first, while we were at the phonetics; but after that

I got deadly sick of it. If I hadn't backed myself to do it I should have chucked the whole thing up two months ago. It was a silly notion: the whole thing has been a bore.

PICKERING. Oh come! The garden party was frightfully exciting. My heart began beating like anything.

HIGGINS. Yes, for the first three minutes. But when I saw we were going to win hands down, I felt like a bear in a cage, hanging about doing nothing. The dinner was worse: sitting gorging there for over an hour, with nobody but a damned fool of a fashionable woman to talk to! I tell you, Pickering, never again for me. No more artificial duchesses. The whole thing has been simple purgatory.[3]

PICKERING. You've never been broken in properly to the social routine. *(Strolling over to the piano.)* I rather enjoy dipping into it occasionally myself: it makes me feel young again. Anyhow, it was a great success: an immense success. I was quite frightened

---

3. **purgatory** (pėr′gə tôr′ē), *n.* any condition of temporary suffering.

once or twice because Eliza was doing it so well. You see, lots of the real people can't do it at all: they're such fools that they think style comes by nature to people in their position; and so they never learn. There's always something professional about doing a thing superlatively well.

HIGGINS. Yes: that's what drives me mad: the silly people don't know their own silly business. *(Rising.)* However, it's over and done with; and now I can go to bed at last without dreading tomorrow.

(ELIZA'S *beauty becomes murderous.*)

PICKERING. I think I shall turn in too. Still, it's been a great occasion: a triumph for you. Goodnight. *(He goes.)*

HIGGINS *(following him).* Goodnight. *(Over his shoulder, at the door.)* Put out the lights, Eliza; and tell Mrs. Pearce not to make coffee for me in the morning: I'll take tea. *(He goes out.)*

(ELIZA *tries to control herself and feel indifferent as she rises and walks across to the hearth to switch off the light. By the time she gets there she is on the point of screaming. She sits down in* HIGGINS'S *chair and holds on hard to the arms. Finally she gives way and flings herself furiously on the floor, raging.)*

HIGGINS *(in despairing wrath outside).* What the devil have I done with my slippers? *(He appears at the door.)*

LIZA *(snatching up the slippers, and hurling them at him one after the other with all her force).* There are your slippers. And there. Take your slippers; and may you never have a day's luck with them!

HIGGINS *(astounded).* What on earth—? *(He comes to her.)* What's the matter? Get up. *(He pulls her up.)* Anything wrong?

LIZA *(breathless).* Nothing wrong—with you. I've won your bet for you, haven't I? That's enough for you. *I* don't matter, I suppose.

HIGGINS. You won my bet! You! Presumptuous[4] insect! *I* won it. What did you throw those slippers at for me for?

LIZA. Because I wanted to smash your face. I'd like to kill you, you selfish brute. Why didn't you leave me where you picked me out of—in the gutter? You thank God it's all over, and that now you can throw me back again there, do you? *(She crisps her fingers[5] frantically.)*

HIGGINS *(looking at her in cool wonder).* The creature is nervous, after all.

LIZA *(gives a suffocated scream of fury, and instinctively darts her nails at his face).* !!

HIGGINS *(catching her wrists).* Ah! Would you? Claws in, you cat. How dare you show your temper to me? Sit down and be quiet. *(He throws her roughly into the easy chair.)*

LIZA *(crushed by superior strength and weight).* What's to become of me? What's to become of me?

HIGGINS. How the devil do I know what's to become of you? What does it matter what becomes of you?

LIZA. You don't care. I know you don't care. You wouldn't care if I was dead. I'm nothing to you—not so much as them slippers.

HIGGINS *(thundering).* Those slippers.

LIZA *(with bitter submission).* Those slippers. I didn't think it made any difference now.

(*A pause.* ELIZA *hopeless and crushed.* HIGGINS *a little uneasy.)*

HIGGINS *(in his loftiest manner).* Why have you begun going on like this? May I ask whether you complain of your treatment here?

LIZA. No.

HIGGINS. Has anybody behaved badly to you? Colonel Pickering? Mrs. Pearce? Any of the servants?

LIZA. No.

HIGGINS. I presume you don't pretend that *I* have treated you badly?

LIZA. No.

HIGGINS. I am glad to hear it. *(He moderates his tone.)* Perhaps you're tired after the strain of the day. Will you have a glass of champagne? *(He moves towards the door.)*

---

4. **presumptuous** (pri zump′chŭ əs), *adj.* too bold; forward.

5. **crisps her fingers,** clenches and relaxes her fists.

LIZA. No. *(Recollecting her manners.)* Thank you.

HIGGINS *(good-humored again).* This has been coming on for some days. I suppose it was natural for you to be anxious about the garden party. But that's all over now. *(He pats her kindly on the shoulder. She writhes.⁶)* There's nothing more to worry about.

LIZA. No. Nothing for you to worry about. *(She suddenly rises and gets away from him by going to the piano bench, where she sits and hides her face.)* Oh God! I wish I was dead.

HIGGINS *(staring after her in sincere surprise).* Why? In heaven's name, why? *(Reasonably, going to her.)* Listen to me, Eliza. All this irritation is purely subjective.⁷

LIZA. I don't understand. I'm too ignorant.

HIGGINS. It's only imagination. Low spirits and nothing else. Nobody's hurting you. Nothing's wrong. You go to bed like a good girl and sleep it off. Have a little cry and say your prayers: that will make you comfortable.

LIZA. I heard your prayers, "Thank God it's all over!"

HIGGINS *(impatiently).* Well, don't you thank God it's all over? Now you are free and can do what you like.

LIZA *(pulling herself together in desperation).* What am I fit for? What have you left me fit for? Where am I to go? What am I to do? What's to become of me?

HIGGINS *(enlightened, but not at all impressed).* Oh that's what's worrying you, is it? *(He thrusts his hands into his pockets, and walks about in his usual manner, rattling the contents of his pockets, as if condescending to a trivial subject out of pure kindness.)* I shouldn't bother about it if I were you. I should imagine you won't have much difficulty in settling yourself somewhere or other, though I hadn't quite realized that you were going away. *(She looks quickly at him: he does not look at her, but examines the dessert stand on the piano and decides that he will eat an apple.)* You might marry, you know. *(He bites a large piece out of the apple and munches it noisily.)* You see, Eliza, all men are not confirmed old bachelors like me and the Colonel. Most men are the marrying sort (poor devils!); and you're not bad-looking: it's quite a pleasure to look at you sometimes—not now, of course, because you're crying and looking as ugly as the very devil; but when you're all right and quite yourself, you're what I should call attractive. That is, to the people in the marrying line, you understand. You go to bed and have a good nice rest; and then get up and look at yourself in the glass; and you won't feel so cheap.

(ELIZA again looks at him, speechless, and does not stir. The look is quite lost on him: he eats his apple with a dreamy expression of happiness, as it is quite a good one.)

HIGGINS *(a genial afterthought occurring to him).* I daresay my mother could find some chap or other who would do very well.

LIZA. We were above that at the corner of Tottenham Court Road.

HIGGINS *(waking up).* What do you mean?

LIZA. I sold flowers. I didn't sell myself. Now you've made a lady of me I'm not fit to sell anything else. I wish you'd left me where you found me.

HIGGINS *(slinging the core of the apple decisively into the grate).* Tosh, Eliza. Don't you insult human relations by dragging all this cant⁸ about buying and selling into it. You needn't marry the fellow if you don't like him.

LIZA. What else am I to do?

HIGGINS. Oh, lots of things. What about your old idea of a florist's shop? Pickering could set you up in one: he's lots of money. *(Chuckling.)* He'll have to pay for all those togs you have been wearing today; and that, with the hire of the jewelry, will make a big hole in two hundred pounds. Why, six months ago you would have thought it the millennium to have a flower shop of your own. Come! You'll be all

---

6. **writhe** (rīᴛʜ), *v.* twist and turn; suffer mentally.

7. **subjective** (səb jek′tiv), *adj.* existing in the mind.

8. **cant** (kant), *n.* insincere talk.

right. I must clear off to bed: I'm devilish sleepy. By the way, I came down for something: I forget what it was.

LIZA. Your slippers.

HIGGINS. Oh yes, of course. You shied them at me. *(He picks them up, and is going out when she rises and speaks to him.)*

LIZA. Before you go, Sir—

HIGGINS *(dropping the slippers in his surprise at her calling him Sir).* Eh?

LIZA. Do my clothes belong to me or to Colonel Pickering?

HIGGINS *(coming back into the room as if her question were the very climax of unreason).* What the devil use would they be to Pickering?

LIZA. He might want them for the next girl you pick up to experiment on.

HIGGINS *(shocked and hurt).* Is that the way you feel towards us?

LIZA. I don't want to hear anything more about that. All I want to know is whether anything belongs to me. My own clothes were burned.

HIGGINS. But what does it matter? Why need you start bothering about that in the middle of the night?

LIZA. I want to know what I may take away with me. I don't want to be accused of stealing.

HIGGINS *(now deeply wounded).* Stealing! You shouldn't have said that, Eliza. That shows a want of feeling.

LIZA. I'm sorry. I'm only a common ignorant girl; and in my station[9] I have to be careful. There can't be any feelings between the like of you and the like of me. Please will you tell me what belongs to me and what doesn't?

HIGGINS *(very sulkily).* You may take the whole damned houseful if you like. Except the jewels. They're hired. Will that satisfy you? *(He turns on his heel and is about to go in extreme dudgeon.)*[10]

LIZA *(drinking in his emotion like nectar, and nagging him to provoke a further supply).* Stop, please. *(She takes off her jewels.)* Will you take these to your room and keep them safe? I don't want to run the risk of their being missing.

HIGGINS *(furious).* Hand them over. *(She puts them into his hands.)* If these belonged to me instead of to the jeweler, I'd ram them down your ungrateful throat. *(He perfunctorily[11] thrusts them into his pockets, unconsciously decorating himself with the protruding ends of the chains.)*

LIZA *(taking a ring off).* This ring isn't the jeweler's: it's the one you bought me in Brighton. I don't want it now. *(*HIGGINS *dashes the ring violently into the fireplace, and turns on her so threateningly that she crouches over the piano with her hands over her face, and exclaims.)* Don't you hit me.

HIGGINS. Hit you! You infamous[12] creature, how dare you accuse me of such a thing? It is you who have hit me. You have wounded me to the heart.

LIZA *(thrilling with hidden joy).* I'm glad. I've got a little of my own back, anyhow.

HIGGINS *(with dignity, in his finest professional style).* You have caused me to lose my temper: a thing that has hardly ever happened to me before. I prefer to say nothing more tonight. I am going to bed.

LIZA *(pertly).* You'd better leave a note for Mrs. Pearce about the coffee; for she won't be told by me.

HIGGINS *(formally).* Damn Mrs. Pearce; and damn the coffee; and damn you; and damn my own folly in having lavished[13] hard-earned knowledge and the treasure of my regard and intimacy on a heartless guttersnipe. *(He goes out with impressive decorum,[14] and spoils it by slamming the door savagely.* ELIZA *smiles for the first time; expresses her feelings by a wild pantomime in which an imitation of* HIGGINS'S *exit is confused with her own triumph; and finally goes down on her knees on the hearthrug to look for the ring.)*

---

9. **station,** social position.
10. dudgeon (duj′ən), *n.* feeling of anger or resentment.
11. perfunctorily (pər fungk′tər i lē), *adv.* mechanically; indifferently.
12. **infamous** (in′fə məs), *adj.* shamefully bad; disgraceful.
13. lavish (lav′ish), *v.* give or spend freely.
14. decorum (di kôr′əm), *n.* proper behavior.

After Reading

Act 4

Making Connections

Shaping Your Response

1. Have your expectations about Higgins and Liza changed or remained about the same? Explain.

Analyzing the Play

2. Mrs. Patrick Campbell, the first actress to play Liza in London, complained about not having any lines in the first part of act 4 and said that the audience would think she had gone to sleep. In your opinion, whose instincts were right, hers or Shaw's? Explain.

3. When Higgins suggests that his mother could find a husband for Liza, her response is, "We were above that at the corner of Tottenham Court Road." What does she mean?

4. Liza insists that "in my station I have to be careful. There can't be any feelings between the like of you and the like of me." Why not?

5. Do you think the gap between social classes has been bridged in any way in this act? If so, what has achieved this bridge? If not, what has prevented it?

6. The 1938 film of *Pygmalion* includes a scene at the party although Shaw never intended it to be part of the play. Why do you think Shaw did not include the scene of Liza's triumph? Why might a film maker insist on inserting this scene?

Extending the Ideas

7. 🐾 Do differences in language separate people today? How much do they affect **communication** between people? Are there other factors that divide people? Explain.

Vocabulary Study

cant
decorum
dudgeon
lavish
perfunctorily
presumptuous
purgatory
subjective
writhe

Create a dialogue between Liza and Freddy or some other character in which you use at least five of the listed words in such a way that you demonstrate your understanding of their meanings.

ACT FIVE

MRS. HIGGINS's *drawing room. She is at her writing-table as before. The* PARLOR MAID *comes in.*

THE PARLOR MAID *(at the door).* Mr. Henry, ma'am, is downstairs with Colonel Pickering.

MRS. HIGGINS. Well, show them up.

THE PARLOR MAID. They're using the telephone, ma'am. Telephoning to the police, I think.

MRS. HIGGINS. What?

THE PARLOR MAID *(coming further in and lowering her voice).* Mr. Henry is in a state, ma'am. I thought I'd better tell you.

MRS. HIGGINS. If you had told me that Mr. Henry was not in a state it would have been more surprising. Tell them to come up when they've finished with the police. I suppose he's lost something.

THE PARLOR MAID. Yes, ma'am. *(Going.)*

MRS. HIGGINS. Go upstairs and tell Miss Doolittle that Mr. Henry and the Colonel are here. Ask her not to come down till I send for her.

THE PARLOR MAID. Yes, ma'am.

*(*HIGGINS *bursts in. He is, as the* PARLOR MAID *has said, in a state.)*

HIGGINS. Look here, Mother: here's a confounded thing!

MRS. HIGGINS. Yes, dear. Good morning. *(He checks his impatience and kisses her, whilst the* PARLOR MAID *goes out.)* What is it?

HIGGINS. Eliza's bolted.

MRS. HIGGINS *(calmly continuing her writing).* You must have frightened her.

HIGGINS. Frightened her! Nonsense! She was left last night, as usual, to turn out the lights and all that: and instead of going to bed she changed her clothes and went right off: her bed wasn't slept in. She came in a cab for her things before seven this morning; and that fool Mrs. Pearce let her have them without telling me a word about it. What am I to do?

MRS. HIGGINS. Do without, I'm afraid, Henry. The girl has a perfect right to leave if she chooses.

HIGGINS *(wandering distractedly across the room).* But I can't find anything. I don't know what appointments I've got. I'm— *(*PICKERING *comes in.* MRS. HIGGINS *puts down her pen and turns away from the writing-table.)*

PICKERING *(shaking hands).* Good morning, Mrs. Higgins. Has Henry told you? *(He sits down on the ottoman.)*

HIGGINS. What does that ass of an inspector say? Have you offered a reward?

MRS. HIGGINS *(rising in indignant amazement).* You don't mean to say you have set the police after Eliza.

HIGGINS. Of course. What are the police for? What else could we do? *(He sits in the Elizabethan chair.)*

PICKERING. The inspector made a lot of difficulties. I really think he suspected us of some improper purpose.

MRS. HIGGINS. Well, of course he did. What right have you to go to the police and give the girl's name as if she were a thief, or a lost umbrella, or something? Really! *(She sits down again, deeply vexed.)*

HIGGINS. But we want to find her.

PICKERING. We can't let her go like this, you know, Mrs. Higgins. What were we to do?

MRS. HIGGINS. You have no more sense, either of you, than two children. Why—

(The PARLOR MAID *comes in and breaks off the conversation.)*

THE PARLOR MAID. Mr. Henry: a gentleman wants to see you very particular. He's been sent on from Wimpole Street.

HIGGINS. Oh, bother! I can't see anyone now. Who is it?

THE PARLOR MAID. A Mr. Doolittle, sir.

PICKERING. Doolittle. Do you mean the dustman?

THE PARLOR MAID. Dustman! Oh no, sir: a gentleman.

HIGGINS *(springing up excitedly).* By George, Pick, it's some relative of hers that she's gone to. Somebody we know nothing about. *(To the* PARLOR MAID.*)* Send him up, quick.

THE PARLOR MAID. Yes, sir. *(She goes.)*

HIGGINS *(eagerly, going to his mother)*. Genteel relatives! Now we shall hear something. *(He sits down in the Chippendale chair.)*

MRS. HIGGINS. Do you know any of her people?

PICKERING. Only her father: the fellow we told you about.

THE PARLOR MAID *(announcing)*. Mr. Doolittle. *(She withdraws.)*

(DOOLITTLE enters. He is brilliantly dressed in a new fashionable frock coat, with white waistcoat and gray trousers. A flower in his buttonhole, a dazzling silk hat, and patent leather shoes complete the effect. He is too concerned with the business he has come on to notice MRS. HIGGINS. He walks straight to HIGGINS, and accosts him with vehement reproach.)

DOOLITTLE *(indicating his own person)*. See here! Do you see this? You done this.

HIGGINS. Done what, man?

DOOLITTLE. This, I tell you. Look at it. Look at this hat. Look at this coat.

PICKERING. Has Eliza been buying you clothes?

DOOLITTLE. Eliza! Not she. Not half. Why would she buy me clothes?

MRS. HIGGINS. Good morning, Mr. Doolittle. Won't you sit down?

DOOLITTLE *(taken aback as he becomes conscious that he has forgotten his hostess)*. Asking your pardon, ma'am. *(He approaches her and shakes her proffered hand.)* Thank you. *(He sits down on the ottoman, on PICKERING's right.)* I am that full of what has happened to me that I can't think of anything else.

HIGGINS. What the dickens has happened to you?

DOOLITTLE. I shouldn't mind if it had only happened to me: anything might happen to anybody and nobody to blame but Providence, as you might say. But this is something that you done to me: yes, you, Henry Higgins.

HIGGINS. Have you found Eliza? That's the point.

DOOLITTLE. Have you lost her?

HIGGINS. Yes.

DOOLITTLE. You have all the luck, you have. I ain't found her; but she'll find me quick enough now after what you done to me.

MRS. HIGGINS. But what has my son done to you, Mr. Doolittle?

DOOLITTLE. Done to me! Ruined me. Destroyed my happiness. Tied me up and delivered me into the hands of middle class morality.

HIGGINS *(rising intolerantly and standing over DOOLITTLE)*. You're raving. You're drunk. You're mad. I gave you five pounds. After that I had two conversations with you, at half a crown an hour. I've never seen you since.

DOOLITTLE. Oh! Drunk! am I? Mad! am I? Tell me this. Did you or did you not write a letter to an old blighter in America that was giving five millions to found Moral Reform Societies all over the world, and that wanted you to invent a universal language for him?

HIGGINS. What! Ezra D. Wannafeller! He's dead. *(He sits down again carelessly.)*

DOOLITTLE. Yes: he's dead; and I'm done for. Now did you or did you not write a letter to him to say that the most original moralist at present in England, to the best of your knowledge, was Alfred Doolittle, a common dustman.

HIGGINS. Oh, after your last visit I remember making some silly joke of the kind.

DOOLITTLE. Ah! You may well call it a silly joke. It put the lid on me right enough. Just give him the chance he wanted to show that Americans is not like us: that they recognize and respect merit in every class of life, however humble. Them words is in his blooming will, in which, Henry Higgins, thanks to your silly joking, he leaves me a share in his Pre-digested Cheese Trust worth three thousand a year on condition that I lecture for his Wannafeller Moral Reform World League as often as they ask me up to six times a year.

HIGGINS. The devil he does! Whew! *(Brightening suddenly.)* What a lark!

PICKERING. A safe thing for you, Doolittle. They won't ask you twice.

DOOLITTLE. It ain't the lecturing I mind. I'll lecture them blue in the face, I will, and not turn a hair. It's making a gentleman of me that I object to. Who asked him to make a gentleman of me? I was happy. I was free. I touched pretty nigh everybody for money when I wanted it, same as I touched you, Henry Higgins. Now I am worrited; tied neck and heels; and everybody touches me for money. It's a fine thing for you, says my solicitor.[1] Is it? says I. You mean it's a good thing for you, I says. When I was a poor man and had a solicitor once when they found a pram in the dust cart, he got me off, and got shut of me and got me shut of him as quick as he could. Same with the doctors: used to shove me out of the hospital before I could hardly stand on my legs, and nothing to pay. Now they finds out that I'm not a healthy man and can't live unless they looks after me twice a day. In the house I'm not let do a hand's turn for myself: somebody else must do it and touch me for it. A year ago I hadn't a relative in the world except two or three that wouldn't speak to me. Now I've fifty, and not a decent week's wages among the lot of them. I have to live for others and not for myself: that's middle class morality. You talk of losing Eliza. Don't you be anxious: I bet she's on my doorstep by this: she that could support herself easy by selling flowers if I wasn't respectable. And the next one to touch me will be you, Henry Higgins. I'll have to learn to speak middle class language from you, instead of speaking proper English. That's where you'll come in; and I daresay that's what you done it for.

MRS. HIGGINS. But, my dear Mr. Doolittle, you need not suffer all this if you are really in earnest. Nobody can force you to accept this bequest. You can repudiate[2] it. Isn't that so, Colonel Pickering?

PICKERING. I believe so.

DOOLITTLE *(softening his manner in deference to her sex)*. That's the tragedy of it, ma'am. It's easy to say chuck it; but I haven't the nerve. Which of us has? We're all intimidated. Intimidated, ma'am: that's what we are. What is there for me if I chuck it but the workhouse in my old age? I have to dye my hair already to keep my job as a dustman. If I was one of the deserving poor, and had put by a bit, I could chuck it; but then why should I, acause the deserving poor might as well be millionaires for all the happiness they ever has. They don't know what happiness is. But I, as one of the undeserving poor, have nothing between me and the pauper's uniform but this here blasted three thousand a year that shoves me into the middle class. (Excuse the expression, ma'am: you'd use it yourself if you had my provocation.[3]) They've got you every way you turn: it's a choice between the Skilly of the workhouse and the Char Bydis[4] of the middle class; and I haven't the nerve for the workhouse. Intimidated: that's what I am. Broke. Bought up. Happier men than me will call for my dust, and touch me for their tip; and I'll look on helpless, and envy them. And that's what your son has brought me to. *(He is overcome by emotion.)*

MRS. HIGGINS. Well, I'm very glad you're not going to do anything foolish, Mr. Doolittle. For this solves the problem of Eliza's future. You can provide for her now.

DOOLITTLE *(with melancholy resignation)*. Yes, ma'am: I'm expected to provide for everyone now, out of three thousand a year.

HIGGINS *(jumping up)*. Nonsense! He can't provide for her. He shan't provide for her. She doesn't belong to him. I paid him five pounds for her. Doolittle: either you're an honest man or a rogue.

---

1. **solicitor** (sə lis′ə tər), *n.* in Britain, a lawyer.
2. **repudiate** (ri pyü′dē āt), *v.* reject.
3. **provocation** (prov′ə kā′shən), *n.* something that stirs up or irritates.
4. **Skilly . . . Char Bydis.** Doolittle is referring to Scylla (sil′ə) and Charybdis (kə rib′dis). In the narrow strait that separates Italy and Sicily there is a dangerous rock and a whirlpool, which the ancient Greeks named Scylla and Charybdis. The expression "to be between Scylla and Charybdis" means to be between two evils, either one of which can be safely avoided only by risking the other.

DOOLITTLE *(tolerantly).* A little of both, Henry, like the rest of us: a little of both.

HIGGINS. Well, you took that money for the girl; and you have no right to take her as well.

MRS. HIGGINS. Henry: don't be absurd. If you want to know where Eliza is, she is upstairs.

HIGGINS *(amazed).* Upstairs!!! Then I shall jolly soon fetch her downstairs. *(He makes resolutely for the door.)*

MRS. HIGGINS *(rising and following him).* Be quiet, Henry. Sit down.

HIGGINS. I—

MRS. HIGGINS. Sit down, dear; and listen to me.

HIGGINS. Oh very well, very well, very well. *(He throws himself ungraciously on the ottoman, with his face towards the windows.)* But I think you might have told us this half an hour ago.

MRS. HIGGINS. Eliza came to me this morning. She passed the night partly walking about in a rage, partly trying to throw herself into the river and being afraid to, and partly in the Carlton Hotel. She told me of the brutal way you two treated her.

HIGGINS *(bounding up again).* What!

PICKERING (*rising also*). My dear Mrs. Higgins, she's been telling you stories. We didn't treat her brutally. We hardly said a word to her; and we parted on particularly good terms. (*Turning on* HIGGINS.) Higgins: did you bully her after I went to bed?

HIGGINS. Just the other way about. She threw my slippers in my face. She behaved in the most outrageous way. I never gave her the slightest provocation. The slippers came bang into my face the moment I entered the room—before I had uttered a word. And used perfectly awful language.

PICKERING (*astonished*). But why? What did we do to her?

MRS. HIGGINS. I think I know pretty well what you did. The girl is naturally rather affectionate, I think. Isn't she, Mr. Doolittle?

DOOLITTLE. Very tender-hearted, ma'am. Takes after me.

MRS. HIGGINS. Just so. She had become attached to you both. She worked very hard for you, Henry. I don't think you quite realize what anything in the nature of brain work means to a girl like that. Well, it seems that when the great day of trial came, and she did this wonderful thing for you without making a single mistake, you two sat there and never said a word to her, but talked together of how glad you were that it was all over and how you had been bored with the whole thing. And then you were surprised because she threw your slippers at you! *I* should have thrown the fire-irons at you.

HIGGINS. We said nothing except that we were tired and wanted to go to bed. Did we, Pick?

PICKERING (*shrugging his shoulders*). That was all.

MRS. HIGGINS (*ironically*). Quite sure?

PICKERING. Absolutely. Really, that was all.

MRS. HIGGINS. You didn't thank her, or pet her, or admire her, or tell her how splendid she'd been.

HIGGINS (*impatiently*). But she knew all about that. We didn't make speeches to her, if that's what you mean.

PICKERING (*conscience stricken*). Perhaps we were a little inconsiderate. Is she very angry?

MRS. HIGGINS (*returning to her place at the writing-table*). Well, I'm afraid she won't go back to Wimpole Street, especially now that Mr. Doolittle is able to keep up the position you have thrust on her; but she says she is quite willing to meet you on friendly terms and to let bygones be bygones.

HIGGINS (*furious*). Is she, by George? Ho!

MRS. HIGGINS. If you promise to behave yourself, Henry, I'll ask her to come down. If not, go home; for you have taken up quite enough of my time.

HIGGINS. Oh, all right. Very well. Pick: you behave yourself. Let us put on our best Sunday manners for this creature that we picked out of the mud. (*He flings himself sulkily into the Elizabethan chair.*)

DOOLITTLE (*remonstrating*). Now, now, Henry Higgins! Have some consideration for my feelings as a middle class man.

MRS. HIGGINS. Remember your promise, Henry. (*She presses the bell-button on the writing-table.*) Mr. Doolittle: will you be so good as to step out on the balcony for a moment. I don't want Eliza to have the shock of your news until she has made it up with these two gentlemen. Would you mind?

DOOLITTLE. As you wish, lady. Anything to help Henry to keep her off my hands. (*He disappears through the window.*)

(*The* PARLOR MAID *answers the bell.* PICKERING *sits down in* DOOLITTLE'S *place.*)

MRS. HIGGINS. Ask Miss Doolittle to come down, please.

THE PARLOR MAID. Yes, ma'am. (*She goes out.*)

MRS. HIGGINS. Now, Henry: be good.

HIGGINS. I am behaving myself perfectly.

PICKERING. He is doing his best, Mrs. Higgins.

(*A pause.* HIGGINS *throws back his head; stretches out his legs; and begins to whistle.*)

MRS. HIGGINS. Henry, dearest, you don't look at all nice in that attitude.

HIGGINS (*pulling himself together*). I was not trying to look nice, Mother.

MRS. HIGGINS. It doesn't matter, dear. I only wanted to make you speak.

HIGGINS. Why?

MRS. HIGGINS. Because you can't speak and whistle at the same time.

(HIGGINS *groans. Another very trying pause.*)

HIGGINS (*springing up, out of patience*). Where the devil is that girl? Are we to wait here all day?

(ELIZA *enters, sunny, self-possessed, and giving a staggeringly convincing exhibition of ease of manner. She carries a little workbasket, and is very much at home.* PICKERING *is too much taken aback to rise.*)

LIZA. How do you do, Professor Higgins? Are you quite well?

HIGGINS (*choking*). Am I—(*He can say no more.*)

LIZA. But of course you are: you are never ill. So glad to see you again, Colonel Pickering. (*He rises hastily; and they shake hands.*) Quite chilly this morning, isn't it? (*She sits down on his left. He sits beside her.*)

HIGGINS. Don't you dare try this game on me. I taught it to you; and it doesn't take me in. Get up and come home; and don't be a fool.

(ELIZA *takes a piece of needlework from her basket, and begins to stitch at it, without taking the least notice of this outburst.*)

MRS. HIGGINS. Very nicely put, indeed, Henry. No woman could resist such an invitation.

HIGGINS. You let her alone, Mother. Let her speak for herself. You will jolly soon see whether she has an idea that I haven't put into her head or a word that I haven't put into her mouth. I tell you I have created this thing out of the squashed cabbage leaves of Covent Garden; and now she pretends to play the fine lady with me.

MRS. HIGGINS (*placidly*). Yes, dear; but you'll sit down, won't you?

(HIGGINS *sits down again, savagely.*)

LIZA (*to* PICKERING, *taking no apparent notice of* HIGGINS, *and working away deftly*). Will you drop me altogether now that the experiment is over, Colonel Pickering?

PICKERING. Oh don't. You mustn't think of it as an experiment. It shocks me, somehow.

LIZA. Oh, I'm only a squashed cabbage leaf—

PICKERING (*impulsively*). No.

LIZA (*continuing quietly*). —but I owe so much to you that I should be very unhappy if you forgot me.

PICKERING. It's very kind of you to say so, Miss Doolittle.

LIZA. It's not because you paid for my dresses. I know you are generous to everybody with money. But it was from you that I learned really nice manners; and that is what makes one a lady, isn't it? You see it was so very difficult for me with the example of Professor Higgins always before me. I was brought up to be just like him, unable to control myself, and using bad language on the slightest provocation. And I should never have known that ladies and gentlemen didn't behave like that if you hadn't been there.

HIGGINS. Well!!

PICKERING. Oh, that's only his way, you know. He doesn't mean it.

LIZA. Oh, *I* didn't mean it either, when I was a flower girl. It was only my way. But you see I did it; and that's what makes the difference after all.

PICKERING. No doubt. Still, he taught you to speak; and I couldn't have done that, you know.

LIZA (*trivially*). Of course: that is his profession.

HIGGINS. Damnation!

LIZA (*continuing*). It was just like learning to dance in the fashionable way: there was nothing more than that in it. But do you know what began my real education?

PICKERING. What?

LIZA (*stopping her work for a moment*). Your calling me Miss Doolittle that day when I first came to Wimpole Street. That was the beginning of self-respect for me. (*She resumes her stitching.*) And there were a hundred little things you never noticed, because they came naturally to you. Things about standing up and taking off your hat and opening doors—

PICKERING. Oh, that was nothing.

LIZA. Yes: things that showed you thought and felt about me as if I were something better than a scullery maid; though of course I know you would have been just the same to a scullery maid if she had been let into the drawing room. You never took off your boots in the dining room when I was there.

PICKERING. You mustn't mind that. Higgins takes off his boots all over the place.

LIZA. I know. I am not blaming him. It is his way, isn't it? But it made such a difference to me that you didn't do it. You see, really and truly, apart from the things anyone can pick up (the dressing and the proper way of speaking, and so on), the difference between a lady and a flower girl is not how she behaves, but how she's treated. I shall always be a flower girl to Professor Higgins, because he always treats me as a flower girl, and always will; but I know I can be a lady to you, because you always treat me as a lady, and always will.

MRS. HIGGINS. Please don't grind your teeth, Henry.

PICKERING. Well, this is really very nice of you, Miss Doolittle.

LIZA. I should like you to call me Eliza, now, if you would.

PICKERING. Thank you. Eliza, of course.

LIZA. And I should like Professor Higgins to call me Miss Doolittle.

HIGGINS. I'll see you damned first.

MRS. HIGGINS. Henry! Henry!

PICKERING (*laughing*). Why don't you slang back at him? Don't stand it. It would do him a lot of good.

LIZA. I can't. I could have done it once; but now I can't go back to it. Last night, when I was wandering about, a girl spoke to me; and I tried to get back into the old way with her; but it was no use. You told me, you know, that when a child is brought to a foreign country, it picks up the language in a few weeks, and forgets its own. Well, I am a child in your country. I have forgotten my own language, and can speak nothing but yours. That's the real break-off with the corner of Tottenham Court Road. Leaving Wimpole Street finishes it.

PICKERING (*much alarmed*). Oh! But you're coming back to Wimpole Street, aren't you? You'll forgive Higgins?

HIGGINS (*rising*). Forgive! Will she, by George! Let her go. Let her find out how she can get on without us. She will relapse into the gutter in three weeks without me at her elbow.

(DOOLITTLE *appears at the center window. With a look of dignified reproach at* HIGGINS, *he comes slowly and silently to his daughter, who, with her back to the window, is unconscious of his approach.*)

PICKERING. He's incorrigible,[5] Eliza. You won't relapse, will you?

LIZA. No: not now. Never again. I have learned my lesson. I don't believe I could utter one of the old sounds if I tried. (DOOLITTLE *touches her on her left shoulder. She drops her work, losing her self-possession utterly at the spectacle of her father's splendor.*) A-a-a-a-ah-ow-oh!

HIGGINS (*with a crow of triumph*). Aha! Just so. A-a-a-a-ahowooh! A-a-a-a-ahowooh! A-a-a-ahowooh! Victory! Victory! (*He throws himself on the divan, folding his arms, and spraddling arrogantly.*)

DOOLITTLE. Can you blame the girl? Don't look at me like that, Eliza. It ain't my fault. I've come into some money.

LIZA. You must have touched a millionaire this time, Dad.

DOOLITTLE. I have. But I'm dressed something special today. I'm going to St. George's, Hanover Square.[6] Your stepmother is going to marry me.

LIZA (*angrily*). You're going to let yourself down to marry that low common woman!

---

5. **incorrigible** (in kôr′ə jə bəl), *adj.* too firmly fixed in bad ways to be changed.

6. **St. George's, Hanover Square,** a church where many fashionable weddings took place.

PICKERING (*quietly*). He ought to, Eliza. (*To* DOOLITTLE.) Why has she changed her mind?

DOOLITTLE (*sadly*). Intimidated, Governor. Intimidated. Middle class morality claims its victim. Won't you put on your hat, Liza, and come and see me turned off?

LIZA. If the Colonel says I must, I—I'll (*almost sobbing*) I'll demean[7] myself. And get insulted for my pains, like enough.

DOOLITTLE. Don't be afraid: she never comes to words with anyone now, poor woman! Respectability has broke all the spirit out of her.

PICKERING (*squeezing* ELIZA'S *elbow gently*). Be kind to them, Eliza. Make the best of it.

LIZA (*forcing a little smile for him through her vexation*). Oh well, just to show there's no ill feeling. I'll be back in a moment. (*She goes out.*)

DOOLITTLE (*sitting down beside* PICKERING). I feel uncommon nervous about the ceremony, Colonel. I wish you'd come and see me through it.

PICKERING. But you've been through it before, man. You were married to Eliza's mother.

DOOLITTLE. Who told you that, Colonel?

PICKERING. Well, nobody told me. But I concluded—naturally—

DOOLITTLE. No: that ain't the natural way, Colonel: it's only the middle class way. My way was always the undeserving way. But don't say nothing to Eliza. She don't know: I always had a delicacy about telling her.

PICKERING. Quite right. We'll leave it so, if you don't mind.

DOOLITTLE. And you'll come to the church, Colonel, and put me through straight?

PICKERING. With pleasure. As far as a bachelor can.

MRS. HIGGINS. May I come, Mr. Doolittle? I should be very sorry to miss your wedding.

DOOLITTLE. I should indeed be honored by your condescension, ma'am; and my poor old woman would take it as a tremenjous compliment. She's been very low, thinking of the happy days that are no more.

MRS. HIGGINS (*rising*). I'll order the carriage and get ready. (*The men rise, except* HIGGINS.) I shan't be more than fifteen minutes. (*As she goes to the door* ELIZA *comes in, hatted and buttoning her gloves.*) I'm going to the church to see your father married, Eliza. You had better come in the brougham[8] with me. Colonel Pickering can go on with the bridegroom.

(MRS. HIGGINS *goes out.* ELIZA *comes to the middle of the room between the center window and the ottoman.* PICKERING *joins her.*)

DOOLITTLE. Bridegroom! What a word! It makes a man realize his position, somehow. (*He takes up his hat and goes towards the door.*)

PICKERING. Before I go, Eliza, do forgive him and come back to us.

LIZA. I don't think Papa would allow me. Would you, Dad?

DOOLITTLE (*sad but magnanimous*).[9] They played you off very cunning, Eliza, them two sportsmen. If it had been only one of them, you could have nailed him. But you see, there was two; and one of them chaperoned the other, as you might say. (*To* PICKERING.) It was artful of you, Colonel; but I bear no malice: I should have done the same myself. I been the victim of one woman after another all my life; and I don't grudge you two getting the better of Eliza. I shan't interfere. It's time for us to go, Colonel. So long, Henry. See you in St. George's, Eliza. (*He goes out.*)

PICKERING (*coaxing*). Do stay with us, Eliza. (*He follows* DOOLITTLE.)

(ELIZA *goes out on the balcony to avoid being alone with* HIGGINS. *He rises and joins her there. She immediately comes back into the room and makes for the door; but he goes along the balcony quickly and gets his back to the door before she reaches it.*)

---

7. **demean** (di mēn′), *v.* lower in dignity; degrade.
8. **brougham** (brüm), *n.* a closed carriage or automobile, having an outside seat for the driver.
9. **magnanimous** (mag nan′ə məs), *adj.* generous in forgiving.

HIGGINS. Well, Eliza, you've had a bit of your own back, as you call it. Have you had enough? And are you going to be reasonable? Or do you want any more?

LIZA. You want me back only to pick up your slippers and put up with your tempers and fetch and carry for you.

HIGGINS. I haven't said I wanted you back at all.

LIZA. Oh, indeed. Then what are we talking about?

HIGGINS. About you, not about me. If you come back I shall treat you just as I have always treated you. I can't change my nature; and I don't intend to change my manners. My manners are exactly the same as Colonel Pickering's.

LIZA. That's not true. He treats a flower girl as if she was a duchess.

HIGGINS. And I treat a duchess as if she was a flower girl.

LIZA. I see. (*She turns away composedly, and sits on the ottoman, facing the window.*) The same to everybody.

HIGGINS. Just so.

LIZA. Like Father.

HIGGINS (*grinning, a little taken down*). Without accepting the comparison at all points, Eliza, it's quite true that your father is not a snob, and that he will be quite at home in any station of life to which his eccentric destiny may call him. (*Seriously.*) The great secret, Eliza, is not having bad manners or good manners or any other particular sort of manners, but having the same manner for all human souls: in short, behaving as if you were in Heaven, where there are no third-class carriages, and one soul is as good as another.

LIZA. Amen. You are a born preacher.

HIGGINS (*irritated*). The question is not whether I treat you rudely, but whether you ever heard me treat anyone else better.

LIZA (*with sudden sincerity*). I don't care how you treat me. I don't mind your swearing at me. I don't mind a black eye: I've had one before

this. But (*standing up and facing him*) I won't be passed over.

HIGGINS. Then get out of my way; for I won't stop for you. You talk about me as if I were a motor bus.

LIZA. So you are a motor bus: all bounce and go, and no consideration for anyone. But I can do without you: don't think I can't.

HIGGINS. I know you can. I told you you could.

LIZA (*wounded, getting away from him to the other side of the ottoman with her face to the hearth*). I know you did, you brute. You wanted to get rid of me.

HIGGINS. Liar.

LIZA. Thank you. (*She sits down with dignity.*)

HIGGINS. You never asked yourself, I suppose, whether *I* could do without you.

LIZA (*earnestly*). Don't you try to get round me. You'll have to do without me.

HIGGINS (*arrogant*). I can do without anybody. I have my own soul: my own spark of divine fire. But (*with sudden humility*) I shall miss you, Eliza. (*He sits down near her on the ottoman.*) I have learned something from your idiotic notions: I confess that humbly and gratefully. And I have grown accustomed to your voice and appearance. I like them, rather.

LIZA. Well, you have both of them on your gramophone and in your book of photographs. When you feel lonely without me, you can turn the machine on. It's got no feelings to hurt.

HIGGINS. I can't turn your soul on. Leave me those feelings; and you can take away the voice and the face. They are not you.

LIZA. Oh, you are a devil. You can twist the heart in a girl as easy as some could twist her arms to hurt her. Mrs. Pearce warned me. Time and again she has wanted to leave you; and you always got round her at the last minute. And you don't care a bit for her. And you don't care a bit for me.

HIGGINS. I care for life, for humanity; and you are a part of it that has come my way and been built into my house. What more can you or anybody ask?

LIZA. I won't care for anybody that doesn't care for me.

HIGGINS. Commercial principles, Eliza. Like *(reproducing her Covent Garden pronunciation with professional exactness)* s'yollin voylets [selling violets], isn't it?

LIZA. Don't sneer at me. It's mean to sneer at me.

HIGGINS. I have never sneered in my life. Sneering doesn't become either the human face or the human soul. I am expressing my righteous contempt for Commercialism. I don't and won't trade in affection. You call me a brute because you couldn't buy a claim on me by fetching my slippers and finding my spectacles. You were a fool: I think a woman fetching a man's slippers is a disgusting sight: did I ever fetch your slippers? I think a good deal more of you for throwing them in my face. No use slaving for me and then saying you want to be cared for: who cares for a slave? If you come back, come back for the sake of good fellowship; for you'll get nothing else. You've had a thousand times as much out of me as I have out of you; and if you dare to set up your little dog's tricks of fetching and carrying slippers against my creation of a Duchess Eliza, I'll slam the door in your silly face.

LIZA. What did you do it for if you didn't care for me?

HIGGINS *(heartily)*. Why, because it was my job.

LIZA. You never thought of the trouble it would make for me.

HIGGINS. Would the world ever have been made if its maker had been afraid of making trouble? Making life means making trouble. There's only one way of escaping trouble; and that's killing things. Cowards, you notice, are always shrieking to have troublesome people killed.

LIZA. I'm no preacher: I don't notice things like that. I notice that you don't notice me.

HIGGINS *(jumping up and walking about intolerantly)*. Eliza: you're an idiot. I waste the trea-sures of my Miltonic mind by spreading them before you. Once for all, understand that I go my way and do my work without caring twopence what happens to either of us. I am not intimidated, like your father and your stepmother. So you can come back or go to the devil: which you please.

LIZA. What am I to come back for?

HIGGINS *(bouncing up on his knees on the ottoman and leaning over it to her)*. For the fun of it. That's why I took you on.

LIZA *(with averted face)*. And you may throw me out tomorrow if I don't do everything you want me to?

HIGGINS. Yes; and you may walk out tomorrow if I don't do everything you want me to.

LIZA. And live with my stepmother?

HIGGINS. Yes, or sell flowers.

LIZA. Oh! If I only could go back to my flower basket! I should be independent of both you and Father and all the world! Why did you take my independence from me? Why did I give it up? I'm a slave now, for all my fine clothes.

HIGGINS. Not a bit. I'll adopt you as my daughter and settle money on you if you like. Or would you rather marry Pickering?

LIZA *(looking fiercely round at him)*. I wouldn't marry you if you asked me; and you're nearer my age than what he is.

HIGGINS *(gently)*. Than he is: not "than what he is."

LIZA *(losing her temper and rising)*. I'll talk as I like. You're not my teacher now.

HIGGINS *(reflectively)*. I don't suppose Pickering would, though. He's as confirmed an old bachelor as I am.

LIZA. That's not what I want; and don't you think it. I've always had chaps enough wanting me that way. Freddy Hill writes to me twice and three times a day, sheets and sheets.

HIGGINS *(disagreeably surprised)*. Damn his impudence! *(He recoils and finds himself sitting on his heels.)*

LIZA. He has a right to if he likes, poor lad. And he does love me.

HIGGINS (*getting off the ottoman*). You have no right to encourage him.

LIZA. Every girl has a right to be loved.

HIGGINS. What! By fools like that?

LIZA. Freddy's not a fool. And if he's weak and poor and wants me, maybe he'd make me happier than my betters that bully me and don't want me.

HIGGINS. Can he make anything of you? That's the point.

LIZA. Perhaps I could make something of him. But I never thought of us making anything of one another; and you never think of anything else. I only want to be natural.

HIGGINS. In short, you want me to be as infatuated about you as Freddy? Is that it?

LIZA. No I don't. That's not the sort of feeling I want from you. And don't you be too sure of yourself or of me. I could have been a bad girl if I'd liked. I've seen more of some things than you, for all your learning. Girls like me can drag gentlemen down to make love to them easy enough. And they wish each other dead the next minute.

HIGGINS. Of course they do. Then what in thunder are we quarrelling about?

LIZA (*much troubled*). I want a little kindness. I know I'm a common ignorant girl, and you a book-learned gentleman; but I'm not dirt under your feet. What I done (*correcting herself*) what I did was not for the dresses and the taxis: I did it because we were pleasant together and I come—came—to care for you; not to want you to make love to me, and not forgetting the difference between us, but more friendly like.

HIGGINS. Well, of course. That's just how I feel. And how Pickering feels. Eliza: you're a fool.

LIZA. That's not a proper answer to give me. (*She sinks on the chair at the writing-table in tears.*)

HIGGINS. It's all you'll get until you stop being a common idiot. If you're going to be a lady, you'll have to give up feeling neglected if the men you know don't spend half their time snivelling over you and the other half giving you black eyes. If you can't stand the coldness of my sort of life, and the strain of it, go back to the gutter. Work till you are more a brute than a human being; and then cuddle and squabble and drink till you fall asleep. Oh, it's a fine life, the life of the gutter. It's real: it's warm: it's violent: you can feel it through the thickest skin: you can taste it and smell it without any training or any work. Not like Science and Literature and Classical Music and Philosophy and Art. You find me cold, unfeeling, selfish, don't you? Very well: be off with you to the sort of people you like. Marry some sentimental hog or other with lots of money, and a thick pair of lips to kiss you with and a thick pair of boots to kick you with. If you can't appreciate what you've got, you'd better get what you can appreciate.

LIZA (*desperate*). Oh, you are a cruel tyrant. I can't talk to you: you turn everything against me: I'm always in the wrong. But you know very well all the time that you're nothing but a bully. You know I can't go back to the gutter, as you call it, and that I have no real friends in the world but you and the Colonel. You know well I couldn't bear to live with a low common man after you two: and it's wicked and cruel of you to insult me by pretending I could. You think I must go back to Wimpole Street because I have nowhere else to go but Father's. But don't you be too sure that you have me under your feet to be trampled on and talked down. I'll marry Freddy, I will, as soon as he's able to support me.

HIGGINS (*sitting down beside her*). Rubbish! You shall marry an ambassador. You shall marry the Governor-General of India or the Lord-Lieutenant of Ireland, or somebody who wants a deputy-queen. I'm not going to have my masterpiece thrown away on Freddy.

LIZA. You think I like you to say that. But I haven't forgot what you said a minute ago; and I won't be coaxed round as if I was a baby or a puppy. If I can't have kindness, I'll have independence.

HIGGINS. Independence? That's middle class blasphemy. We are all dependent on one another, every soul of us on earth.

LIZA *(rising determinedly)*. I'll let you see whether I'm dependent on you. If you can preach, I can teach. I'll go and be a teacher.

HIGGINS. What'll you teach, in heaven's name?

LIZA. What you taught me. I'll teach phonetics.

HIGGINS. Ha! ha! ha!

LIZA. I'll offer myself as an assistant to Professor Nepean.

HIGGINS *(rising in a fury)*. What! That impostor! That humbug! That toadying ignoramus! Teach him my methods! My discoveries! You take one step in his direction and I'll wring your neck. *(He lays hands on her.)* Do you hear?

LIZA *(defiantly non-resistant)*. Wring away. What do I care? I knew you'd strike me some day. *(He lets her go, stamping with rage at having forgotten himself, and recoils so hastily that he stumbles back into his seat on the ottoman.)* Aha! Now I know how to deal with you. What a fool I was not to think of it before! You can't take away the knowledge you gave me. You said I had a finer ear than you. And I can be civil and kind to people, which is more than you can. Aha! That's done you, Henry Higgins, it has. Now I don't care that *(snapping her fingers)* for your bullying and your big talk. I'll advertize it in the papers that your duchess is only a flower girl that you taught, and that she'll teach anybody to be a duchess just the same in six months for a thousand guineas. Oh, when I think of myself crawling under your feet and being trampled on and called names, when all the time I had only to lift up my finger to be as good as you, I could just kick myself.

HIGGINS *(wondering at her)*. You damned impudent slut, you! But it's better than snivelling;

better than fetching slippers and finding spectacles, isn't it? *(Rising.)* By George, Eliza, I said I'd make a woman of you; and I have. I like you like this.

LIZA. Yes: you turn round and make up to me now that I'm not afraid of you, and can do without you.

HIGGINS. Of course I do, you little fool. Five minutes ago you were like a millstone round my neck. Now you're a tower of strength: a consort battleship. You and I and Pickering will be three old bachelors together instead of only two men and a silly girl.

(MRS. HIGGINS returns, dressed for the wedding. ELIZA instantly becomes cool and elegant.)

MRS. HIGGINS. The carriage is waiting, Eliza. Are you ready?

LIZA. Quite. Is the Professor coming?

MRS. HIGGINS. Certainly not. He can't behave himself in church. He makes remarks out loud all the time on the clergyman's pronunciation.

LIZA. Then I shall not see you again, Professor. Goodbye. *(She goes to the door.)*

MRS. HIGGINS *(coming to HIGGINS)*. Goodbye, dear.

HIGGINS. Goodbye, Mother. *(He is about to kiss her, when he recollects something.)* Oh, by the way, Eliza, order a ham and a Stilton cheese, will you? And buy me a pair of reindeer gloves, number eights, and a tie to match that new suit of mine, at Eale & Binman's. You can choose the color. *(His cheerful, careless, vigorous voice shows that he is incorrigible.)*

LIZA *(disdainfully)*. Buy them yourself. *(She sweeps out.)*

MRS. HIGGINS. I'm afraid you've spoiled that girl, Henry. But never mind, dear: I'll buy you the tie and gloves.

HIGGINS *(sunnily)*. Oh, don't bother. She'll buy em all right enough. Goodbye.

(They kiss. MRS. HIGGINS runs out. HIGGINS, left alone, rattles his cash in his pocket; chuckles; and disports himself in a highly self-satisfied manner.)

After Reading

Making Connections

1. Are you satisfied with the ending of the play? Why or why not?

2. Many comedies end with a wedding or, at the least, a happy reunion of lovers. How has Shaw both followed this tradition and turned it upside down?

3. Compare Liza's entrance in act 5 to her appearance after a bath in act 2 and her introduction to Mrs. Higgins's at-home. What levels of development are apparent in each case?

4. What is the central **conflict** in Pygmalion? Is it resolved?

5. What are the differences in the causes and results of both Liza's and her father's transformations?

6. What details support Liza's claim that "the difference between a lady and a flower girl is not how she behaves, but how she's treated"?

7. Throughout the play, almost everyone has been trying to instruct the teacher, Henry Higgins. Do you think he learns anything? Explain.

8. 👂 Do you think there is genuine **communication** between Higgins and Liza in act 5? Does communication imply agreement between people? Explain.

9. In your opinion, is there anything in the play that serves as convincing evidence about what Liza will do next? Explain.

10. What **main idea** do you think Shaw wanted the audience to carry home from *Pygmalion?*

11. Americans have always boasted that there is no class system in the United States. Is this true in your opinion? Explain.

Literary Focus: Inference

An **inference** is a reasonable conclusion about the behavior of a character or the meaning of events. Characters in a play as well as readers and playgoers must make inferences.

1. What inference might the audience make when Doolittle first appears in act 5, and what might that inference be based on?

2. Does Liza make any incorrect inferences in the play? Does Higgins? Explain.

3. What inferences do you make about Shaw's views in general about a class system?

Vocabulary Study

Match each example with the most appropriate word from the list. You will not use all the words.

demean
brougham
incorrigible
magnamimous
provocation
repudiate

1. refusing to accept someone's opinion
2. making fun of someone's appearance
3. writing a kind letter to someone who insulted you
4. being convicted of a crime for the third time
5. throwing stones to tease a dog

Expressing Your Ideas

Writing Choices

Writer's Notebook Update Review your notes on costumes throughout the play. Write a paragraph or so in which you discuss the importance of clothes and accessories in *Pygmalion* and the relation of clothes to themes in the play.

Protagonist / Antagonist Write an **essay** in which you analyze the characterization of Liza. Skim the play to find examples of what she says about herself, what others say about her, how she treats others and is treated by others, and her emotional reactions as suggested in the stage directions. You might devote one paragraph to the best examples you can find of each of these, concluding with a summary of what kind of person she seems to be. As an alternative, write about Higgins, following the same pattern, and attempting to answer some of these questions: Is he truly a confirmed bachelor? What does he want from Liza? Why does he seem to despise the Eynsford Hills?

Classtime? Expand your answer to question 11 into a community or school newspaper **editorial.** Be sure to include supporting examples for your opinions and to anticipate and rebut the arguments for the other side.

You might conclude with a plan of action for people in the U. S.

Other Options

Spinoffs Obtain copies of the 1938 film of *Pygmalion,* starring Wendy Hiller and Leslie Howard, and the film of the musical *My Fair Lady,* based on *Pygmalion* and starring Audrey Hepburn and Rex Harrison. In small groups **analyze these different versions** and compare them with Shaw's play. Have Shaw's chief ideas been retained?

Shaw Revival! Suppose that a new movie or stage production of *Pygmalion* is going to open. Design a full-page **newspaper ad** for the production. Decide what modern actors would best fit these roles, and also choose a producer and director if you wish. Include artwork as well as type in your ad.

Dressing Eliza You are the costume designer for a new production of *Pygmalion.* **Design and sketch costumes** for at least two of the characters throughout the play. Use clues from the text, but when Shaw says nothing, rely on your imagination. If possible, consult some library books on clothing of the period.

History Connection

In the following passages, two social historians describe how England's "two nations"—the rich and the poor—lived their very different lives during the Edwardian period (1901–1910, the reign of Victoria's son, King Edward VII) that forms the background of Bernard Shaw's *Pygmalion*.

The rich man in his castle, the poor man at his gate . . .

At the top of the class structure were people like this upper-class couple shown on their way to the King's garden party at Windsor Castle in 1912.

At the bottom of the social pyramid were slum-dwellers like this mother and her child.

The Upper Class

by Marina Warner

Britain was a narrow world, with its own hard and fast rules. The most important code of all concerned class. The chief ingredient in any man's personality, when assessed by anyone else at that time, was his social position—his class. Society was stratified very clearly and it was an expected form of behavior for everyone, at each level, to lord it over anyone beneath. This hierarchical instinct sometimes took subtler forms—a gentleman would not for instance be rude to a servant—but it was deeply ingrained, so ingrained in fact that the inequity was considered inevitable, natural, insurmountable.

The class in power was the rich, often synonymous with the old landed aristocracy. When a man of humbler birth became rich through business and industry—not uncommon then and earlier—he usually copied the behavior of the aristocracy, followed its traditions, and did not seek to change the customs of the upper classes. A successful factory-owner for instance would often bring up his son to pursue one of the "gentlemanly" professions—the Empire, Politics, the Church—rather than let him remain in trade like his own father. So although Edwardian society was mobile, in the sense that some individuals did move up the social ladder, it was at the same time stagnant, because their advancement did not cause any ripple in the calm lake of Edwardian self-assurance.

The wealth was fabulous. There was hardly any tax, and no death duties. Estates passed intact from father to son. From the evidence of wills, it has been estimated that 1 percent of the population over 25 owned 67 percent of the wealth of the country. . . . The gap between rich and poor was wider than it had been since the days of serfs.

The life of the wealthy was pure pleasure, and was enjoyed openly, with conspicuous display. The King himself, Edward VII, personified the age: jolly,

The Lower Classes

by Mary Cathcart Borer

All sections of the community, from the lowest of the middle classes upward, strove to copy, to the best of their ability, the manners and customs, the dress and household furnishings of the class immediately above them, for "keeping up with the Joneses" was a national pastime. At the bottom of this social structure, however, well below any real human contact and understanding, existed the bulk of England's population. They were the untouchables, the unconsidered poor, whose numbers were so vast that some foretold that, if they were not kept in their place, they might one day threaten the financial security of the entire country.

These lower classes were the artisans, the factory workers, the miners and industrial workers, the fishermen, the farm hands, the dockers, the seamstresses and domestic servants, the shop assistants and a large and murky residue of casual laborers and vagrants.

They worked incredibly long hours for starvation wages, they had little or no education and were appallingly badly housed. When they fell out of work there was no unemployment pay. They had little money for medical attention and there were no pensions for old age.

The consciences of many Victorians had been roused by the terrible inequalities in the distribution of wealth, and throughout the nineteenth century reforms had been made, not only by philanthropic individuals and societies, but also by succeeding governments, both Conservative and Liberal, which were to lead in time to the establishment of the Welfare State of today. Nevertheless, there were many from all walks of life, from the rich to the working classes themselves, who accepted the state of the poor unquestioningly, believing that the position in life to which one was born was part of the plan of an all-wise God, whose ways should not be questioned. Wealth was regarded as almost a divine right and poverty and misfortune a burden to be borne without demur, tempered by the debatable solace that things might be better in the next world. There had been a strong

sensual, rough and ready when it came to anything like the appreciation of music and poetry. His aristocratic subjects were idle, fun-loving, hearty as himself; there was a wide distrust of the arts, as if they were somehow unrespectable, and a corresponding confidence in the "manly" pursuits: huntin', shootin', fishin'. The families of substance followed the racing season around Britain. . . .

Edwardian hedonism was only made possible by the work of others, less advantaged. Everything a rich man required was provided by servants. A country house, visited only once a year for a month at the right time of the shooting season, might need fifty servants to keep it up. For these enormous establishments were without gas, electricity or running water. Servants carried coal down long corridors, up long flights of stairs to each bedroom at dawn so that the room might be warm when the gentleman or lady rose; later they brought hot water up from the kitchen hob—so that they could wash in comfort. For a bath, several journeys with kettles and buckets had to be made. Edwardians of the upper class also ate prodigiously: sideboards at breakfast would be laden with hams, porridge, poached eggs, muffins, sausages, boiled plovers' eggs, tea, milk, coffee. They also dressed themselves elaborately, so that every lady needed a maid to help pull her stays tighter and button her up, and more servants behind the green baize door to wash, iron, crimp and goffer the starched and lacy undergarments she wore. She needed help to wash her long hair—never cut from birth—and dress it in the high voluptuous styles of the period. The daughter of a woman who had been "in service" remembered that one of her mother's employers, at the age of 30, had still never washed herself. Children too were waited upon: taught by governesses or sometimes private tutors, washed and walked and fed by maids. Forty-six percent of the population—most of them women—worked in domestic situations in 1911. For this they were poorly rewarded financially, and, at a broader level, emotionally. It was a life of complete poverty of spirit for most people.

religious revival in the mid-nineteenth century and people were still singing with fervent conviction:

> The rich man in his castle,
> The poor man at his gate,
> God made them high and lowly,
> And ordered their estate.

In his book *The Condition of England*, published in 1909, C. F. G. Mastermen wrote of Britain's laboring population: "They work in unventilated rooms. They are stinted of holidays. They are compelled to work overtime. They endure accident and disease. They are fined and cheated in innumerable ways. Their life is often confined to a mere routine of work and sleep. Yet they endure; and even at the heart of foul and impossible conditions retain always some rags of decency and honor."

In the pottery towns people were still suffering as they had from the beginning. A Medical Officer of Health found forty little girls "licking adhesive labels by the mouth at the rate of thirty gross a day. Their tongues had the polished tip characteristic of label lickers, and the rest of the tongue coated with brown gum." In the Nottingham lace trade children were still being blinded by the double work of school and the terrible eye-strain of their employment in the lace industry.

The long monotonous hours, the drudgery and hopelessness of it all dulled them into apathy. "Can you suggest anything that anybody could do for you which would induce your master or perhaps compel him to give you a fairer or a larger wage?" one woman was asked. "If he would only time an article," she replied, "and state how long the article would take to make, and give you a certain rate of so much an hour, it would be fair, if it was only a living wage. We only want to live."

They only wanted to live! That is what so many people forgot. They did not want charity. Large, organized charities certainly existed. They were a feature of Victorian and Edwardian times. But charities are . . . little more than a sign of indifference to the fundamental problem, an effortless palliative to quieten the stirrings of conscience. The brief moment of compassion passes and is usually forgotten as quickly as the cause which aroused it.

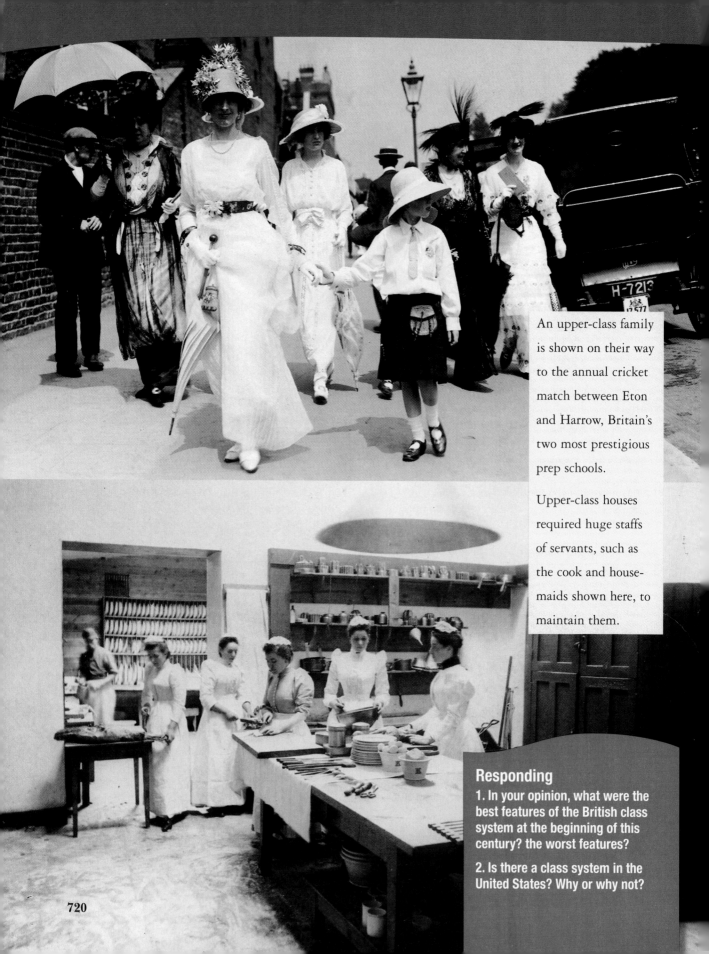

An upper-class family is shown on their way to the annual cricket match between Eton and Harrow, Britain's two most prestigious prep schools.

Upper-class houses required huge staffs of servants, such as the cook and housemaids shown here, to maintain them.

Responding
1. In your opinion, what were the best features of the British class system at the beginning of this century? the worst features?

2. Is there a class system in the United States? Why or why not?

Here, Julie Andrews plays Bertie in Star!, *a movie about the life of entertainer Gertrude Lawrence. First sung in 1918, this comic song about a hobo was popular in music halls, which featured vaudeville or variety acts that appealed to the middle- and working-class audiences.*

Burlington Bertie from Bow

by William Hargreaves

I'm Bert, p'raps you've heard of me,
Bert, you've had word of me,
Jogging along,
hearty and strong,
living on plates of fresh air.
I dress up in fashion,
and, when I am feeling depress'd,
I shave from my cuff
all the whiskers and fluff,
Stick my hat on and toddle up West.[1]

I'm Burlington Bertie, I rise at
  ten thirty
and saunter along like a toff,[2]
I walk down the Strand[3]
with my gloves on my hand,
then I walk down again with
  them off,
I'm all airs and graces,
correct easy paces,
without food so long I've forgot
      where my face is—
I'm Bert, Bert, I haven't a shirt,
but my people are well off,
  you know!
Nearly ev'ryone knows me,
from Smith to Lord Roseb'ry[4]

I'm Burlington Bertie from
  Bow! . . .

My pose, tho' ironical—
shows that my monocle[5]
  holds up my face,
  keeps it in place,
stops it from slipping away.
Cigars—I smoke thousands,
  I usually deal in the Strand,
   But you've got to take care,
   when you're getting them there
or some idiot might stand on
     your hand.

I'm Burlington Bertie, I rise at
   ten thirty
 Then Buckingham Palace, I view;
I stand in the yard
 while they're changing the guard,
  and the King shouts across "Toodle-oo";
  The Prince of Wales' brother,
  along with some other,
slaps me on the back, and says, "Come and
  see Mother."
I'm Bert, Bert, and Royalty's hurt;
When they ask me to dine I say, "No!
I've just had a banana
 with Lady Diana,
  I'm Burlington Bertie from Bow!"

Bow, a lower-class district in the East End of London
1. **West**, the fashionable West End of London.
2. **toff**, a fashionably dressed upper-class male. [*slang*]
3. **Strand**, a famous street in London.
4. **Lord Rosebr'y**, the Earl of Rosebery (1847–1929), British prime minister in the 1890s.

---

5. **monocle** (mon′ə kəl), *n.* an eyeglass for one eye, once considered very fashionable.

The popular, melodramatic television series *Upstairs / Downstairs* focused on the lives of the servants as well as their aristocratic employers.

Responding

1. What attitude toward the British class system is reflected in "Burlington Bertie from Bow"?

2. Could a comic song like this be popular in the contemporary United States? Why or why not?

3. Why do you think an audience would enjoy watching a drama about the lives of the poor as well as the lives of the rich?

Writing Workshop

Moving Up in the World

Assignment In the time of *Pygmalion*, most people could only wonder how the upper classes really lived. Today, mass media advertising gives us a barrage of images that show what supposedly makes up an upwardly-mobile lifestyle. Analyze these images in a magazine article.

WRITER'S BLUEPRINT

Product	An article for a consumer magazine
Purpose	To educate consumers
Audience	People interested in understanding advertising
Specs	To write a successful article, you should:

❑ Imagine that you have been asked to write an article about upward mobility for a consumer magazine. Examine advertising in TV, radio, magazines, and newspapers. Try to determine what advertisers are telling us about these questions: *What should an upwardly mobile person be striving for? What defines an upwardly mobile person?* Consider things this person is urged to have, such as cars and clothing, and things this person is urged to be, such as slim and sophisticated.

❑ Begin your article with an intriguing opening that will grab your readers' interest and make them want to go on reading.

❑ Present your findings. Focus on the five most significant attributes of upward mobility promoted in the advertising you examined. Describe the messages that advertising sends to consumers about these attributes. Illustrate your conclusions with quotations and, where possible, visuals.

❑ Conclude by summarizing your findings.

❑ Write with confidence, but be reasonable and don't overstate your case.

❑ Follow the rules of grammar for correct usage, spelling, and mechanics. Use apostrophes correctly.

1 PREWRITING

Review the literature with a group of classmates. Look for attributes that Higgins and other characters define as essential for Eliza to become upwardly mobile. Take turns reading aloud excerpts from the play that reveal these details. Use these attributes as a jumping-off point when you move on to the next activity.

Examine advertising in television, radio, magazines, billboards, and newspapers. Record your findings in a chart like the one shown. In the second column, note both direct messages and implied messages (suggested through words or pictures) about how these attributes contribute to upward mobility. Along the way, collect illustrations to include with your article.

Attribute of Upward Mobility	Messages
luxury car	—"deep reserves of passing power" (you need to be faster) —"space-age design" (you want only the latest and the best) —picture of admiring crowds watching car drive by (you'll be moving on up, leaving the others behind)

Discuss your findings in a small group. Share the attributes and messages you charted. As you do, put things in perspective by discussing how these attributes compare and contrast with the attributes you noted in "Review the literature." Then move on to the next activity.

Identify the five attributes you'll focus on. Choose attributes that show up again and again, and that give a variety of messages about what an upwardly mobile person ought to strive for.

Develop an intriguing opening. Decide on how you'll grab your readers' attention at the beginning. Here are some ideas:

• Start with an advertisement for an upwardly-mobile lifestyle that incorporates some of your five attributes. Write as if you were trying to sell this lifestyle to your readers: "Picture yourself behind the wheel of a . . . ."

• Pose a question to the reader: "What five ingredients would you say . . . .?"

• Start as if you were telling a fairy tale: "Once upon a time there was a man who wanted all the good things in life . . . ."

Plan your essay, using your prewriting materials as a guide. Make notes on these categories from the Writer's Blueprint:

- An intriguing opening

- First attribute
  —messages
  —supporting quotations, visuals

- Second attribute
  —messages
  —supporting quotations, visuals

and so on . . .

- Summary of findings

  DRAFTING

As you draft, use your ideas from "Develop an intriguing opening" to get started. Here are more drafting tips to keep in mind.

- Lay the visuals you've collected from your research out in front of you. Use them for reference and inspiration as you draft.

- If you're writing by hand, use a separate piece of paper for each attribute and write on every other line. This should give you plenty of room to revise.

- Write with confidence, but take care not to overstate your case. See the Revising Strategy in Step 3 of this lesson.

STEP **3** REVISING

Ask a partner for comments on your draft before you revise it.

✔ Have I begun with an intriguing opening?

✔ Have I dealt with five different attributes?

✔ Have I described how these attributes contribute to an upwardly mobile lifestyle?

✔ Have I been careful to avoid overstating my case?

Revising Strategy

Avoiding Overstatement

Overstating your case can work against you when you're trying to reason with readers. Avoid overstatement by choosing words that accurately reflect the facts behind your claims. For example:

> Every single magazine ad has some Amazon supermodel shoving some product in your face.

The writer has a point but goes too far with it. *Every single*, *Amazon,* and *shoving some product in your face* all say that this writer is not reasoning with the reader. Here is the revised version:

> Advertisers tend to use beautiful female models to sell everything from new cars to soap.

The revised version still makes a broad claim, but this claim will ring true with many readers and can be backed up with factual examples. The use of *tend to* and *beautiful female models* give the statement a more reasonable tone than the original version.

Notice how this student has revised for overstatement.

> The mass media are ~~by far~~ *among* the most influential forces in our
> lives. We are ~~constantly~~ exposed to them, ~~day in and day out~~. *every day.* They
> *take a part in shaping*
> ~~shape everything about~~ how we look, think, feel, and act. ~~They shape~~ *For example, some*
> ~~our bodies.~~ People who have anorexia and other weight-related
> *been influenced by* *that says that you have to be thin*
> diseases have ~~them because~~ advertising ~~has convinced them that~~
> *to be happy.*
> ~~they must be thin or they have no hope of ever living a happy day in~~
> ~~their whole lives.~~

STEP 4 EDITING

Ask a partner to review your revised draft before you edit. When you edit, pay special attention to using apostrophes correctly.

Editing Strategy

Using Apostrophes Correctly

- Use apostrophes to form the possessives of nouns:

1. Add **'s** to form the possessive of most singular nouns: Eliza**'s** hat, the upper class**'s** manners.

2. Add only an apostrophe to form the possessive of plural nouns ending in **s:** all the girls**'** possessions, the middle and upper classes**'** lifestyles.

3. Add **'s** to form the possessive of plural nouns that do not end in **s:** the men**'s** tuxedos, the women**'s** gowns.

- Use apostrophes to form contractions, showing where letters have been omitted: can not = can**'t**, we are = we**'re**, that is = that**'s**.

FOR REFERENCE
More information on using apostrophes correctly can be found in the Language and Grammar Handbook at the back of this text.

STEP 5 PRESENTING

- Work the visuals you collected into the final copy. (See the Computer Tip.)

- Work with some classmates and prepare a multimedia presentation about the images and attributes you have examined.

COMPUTER TIP
If you have access to a scanner, try scanning your captioned pictures into your final copy to give it a true magazine-article look.

STEP 6 LOOKING BACK

Self-evaluate. Look back at the Writer's Blueprint and give yourself a score on each point, from 6 (superior) to 1 (inadequate).

Reflect. Write responses to these questions.

✔ How would you change your essay if your audience were advertisers instead of consumers?

✔ How do you think the attributes of an upwardly mobile lifestyle have changed since the time of Eliza Doolittle?

For Your Working Portfolio Add your essay and your reflection responses to your working portfolio.

Beyond Print

Looking at Advertising

In *Pygmalion,* a classic story of a makeover, Professor Higgins takes a lower-class cockney woman and turns her into a high-society lady by changing the way she speaks, the way she dresses, and the way she comports herself. It's a very old story—and a very new one. In our modern world the packaging often outshines the goods. People who aspire to positions in politics and other areas hire experts to teach them how to speak in public, how to dress, and how to project a certain kind of image.

Advertising was not born in the twentieth century, but it has been developed in this century until it has reached the status of a science. Today advertisers know their target audiences down to surprisingly specific details, and they know how to reach those audiences. Earlier advertising was designed for a more general audience, but it was based on some general assumptions that still hold true today. Look at these two advertisements, a showcard (display card) from about 1900 for Pink's jams, and a display card from about 1930 for Theobroma candies. Think about the appeals that are being made.

Living the High Life Everyone wants to get ahead. That's the basic idea behind upward mobility. And it must follow—or so the advertisers would have you believe—that if you look and act rich, you will feel rich (even if you don't actually have the money to qualify otherwise). Looking rich may mean wearing the clothes that are shown in ads, wearing your hair in certain styles, using certain cosmetics. Acting rich may mean driving a certain make of car, consuming certain brands of food and drink—and treating yourself with certain luxurious goodies.

Snob Appeal No one wants to be thought a snob these days, but snobbery still has a certain

amount of appeal. People like the idea of hobnobbing with the rich and famous, and using the products they are seen (in the paid advertisements) to be using is one way to feel a little closer. In fact, testimonials by celebrities are a basic device of advertising.

Activity Options

1. Comb newspaper and magazine ads, mail-order catalogs, and other kinds of advertising to find images and descriptions of various "high-life" products. Assemble them in a scrapbook, sorted according to categories of clothing, foods, and so on. Devise your own rating system and label those items that seem to have acquired a reputation as the "best" of a large number of similar items.

2. Imagine that money's no problem, and you want to be up there among the best. Plan your own upward move. What sort of wardrobe will you need to move in high society? What sort of physical appearance do you want to present? What would you need to do in order to achieve that physical appearance? Does your general behavior need some polishing? Last, but not least—could your vocabulary and speech patterns use some improvement?

HISTORICAL OVERVIEW

World War I was an ugly and futile blood bath fought between the Allies (Britain, France, Russia, and later, the United States) and the Central Powers (Germany, Austria-Hungary, and Turkey). The war decimated a generation of young men, caused massive social and political changes, and shattered romantic conceptions of war, heroism, and patriotism. Six months after the fighting began in 1914, the war had become a murderous stalemate conducted from trenches stretching from the North Sea to the Alps. The soldiers of the two sides faced each other across a hideous wilderness of shell craters and barbed wire called "No Man's Land." New weapons—including submarines, airplanes, heavy artillery, machine guns, poison gas, and tanks—added to the horror.

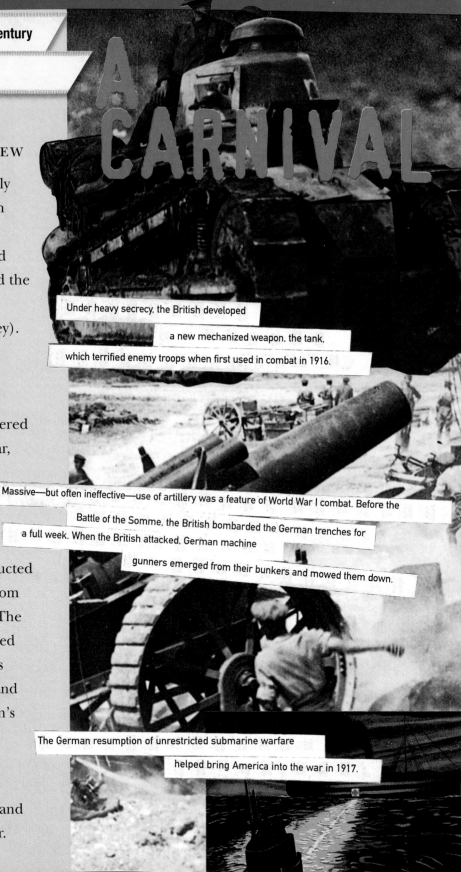

A CARNIVAL

Under heavy secrecy, the British developed a new mechanized weapon, the tank, which terrified enemy troops when first used in combat in 1916.

Massive—but often ineffective—use of artillery was a feature of World War I combat. Before the Battle of the Somme, the British bombarded the German trenches for a full week. When the British attacked, German machine gunners emerged from their bunkers and mowed them down.

The German resumption of unrestricted submarine warfare helped bring America into the war in 1917.

OF DEATH

During the Battle of the Somme, British soldiers wearing gas masks fire a machine gun. Both sides used poison gas, a fearful but unpredictable weapon: a shift in the wind might send it back on those using it.

The most revolutionary weapon introduced during the war was the airplane, but its full military potential would not be realized until World War II.

WAR WEAPONS WEEK APRIL 8th TO 13th

HELP TO PROVIDE THIS WAR WEAPON

BUY NATIONAL WAR BONDS (£5 TO £5000) AND WAR SAVINGS CERTIFICATES 15/6

Key Dates

1914
World War I begins.

1916
Battle of the Somme; 60,000 British casualties the first day.

1917
Russian Revolution begins; United States enters the war.

1918
World War I ends.

1919
Treaty of Versailles negotiated.

1921
Irish Free State established.

1922
Joyce's Ulysses *and Eliot's* The Waste Land *are published.*

1928
British women get the vote.

1929
Great Depression begins.

Part Two

War and Aftermath

War never involves just opposing armies. It also involves civilians, whether they are people who live where a war is being fought, whose lives may be in equal danger, or people who live back home, who may not be in personal danger but whose lives may nevertheless be forever changed.

Individuals may fight a duel; a war is fought by **groups.** As a member of a military group, it is your duty to go where you're told and do what you're ordered to do, even though you might not agree with—or even understand—what you're fighting for.

Before Reading

The Soldier by Rupert Brooke

Dulce et Decorum Est by Wilfred Owen

Suicide in the Trenches by Siegfried Sassoon

Disabled by Wilfred Owen

Building Background

"True Poets Must Be Truthful" In the unfinished preface to the collection of war poems he hoped to publish, Wilfred Owen wrote:

"This book is not about heroes. English Poetry is not yet fit to speak of them.

"Nor is it about deeds, or lands, nor anything about glory, honor, might, majesty, dominion, or power, except War.

"Above all I am not concerned with Poetry.

"My subject is War, and the pity of War.

"The Poetry is in the pity.

"Yet these elegies are to this generation in no sense consolatory. They may be to the next. All a poet can do today is warn. That is why the true Poets must be truthful. . . ."

Throughout the course of World War I the poetry of war changed from romanticism and glory to harsh realism and bitter truth.

Literary Focus

Tone An author's attitude toward his or her subject matter or toward the audience is the **tone** of a work. Tone in writing is like tone of voice—it can alter the meaning of words. By recognizing a writer's tone, a reader can determine whether the writer views the subject with sympathy, sarcasm, affection, bitterness, or optimism. As you read these poems of war, look for clues to their tone.

Writer's Notebook

Idealism and Realism Write your definitions for the following two words: *idealism* and *realism.* What do you think are the positive characteristics of an idealist? of a realist? What are the negative characteristics of each?

Rupert Brooke
1887–1915

For the English, handsome and gifted Rupert Brooke represented the glamor and patriotism of war. At King's College, Cambridge, he became the acknowledged leader of the literary community, and his publication of *Poems 1911* was well received. At the outbreak of World War I, Brooke hurried to enlist, urging a friend, "Come and die. It'll be great fun!" He received a commission in the Royal Navy Division. His five "War Sonnets" (1915), which included "The Soldier," contributed to his immense national popularity, which was enhanced by the posthumous publication of *1914 and Other Poems.* Ironically, Brooke attained his legendary status as a war poet without ever having engaged in actual combat. In the early stages of the war, enroute to the Dardanelles campaign, he contracted blood poisoning and died on a hospital ship anchored off the Greek island of Skyros.

Siegfried Sassoon
1886–1967

Before the war Siegfried Sassoon's life consisted of hunting, book-collecting, and writing exquisite verses. His life changed dramatically when, as "Mad Jack," he fought with exceptional bravery in France. His personal experiences also dramatically changed his attitudes toward war and toward those ignorant of the hell that soldiers were going through. By the summer of 1917, convinced that the war was being unnecessarily prolonged, he issued a statement calling for an immediate negotiated peace. Instead of being court-martialed as he had hoped, he was judged temporarily insane and hospitalized. While in the hospital he met Wilfred Owen, whom he encouraged in his writing. Sassoon was the most widely read poet of World War I.

Wilfred Owen
1893–1918

Wilfred Owen participated in some of the hardest fighting in France during the cold winter of 1917. Following a nervous collapse, Owen was hospitalized from June 1917 until September 1918 when he volunteered to return to the front. One week before the Armistice of 1918 and two weeks after being decorated for gallantry, Owen was killed by machine-gun fire. During his lifetime he had published only four poems. Through the efforts of his mother and friends, eight more poems were published in 1919. Owen's collected poems, edited by Siegfried Sassoon, appeared in 1920. Today Owen is regarded by many as the finest poet of World War I.

THE SOLDIER

Rupert Brooke

If I should die, think only this of me:
That there's some corner of a foreign field
That is forever England. There shall be
In that rich earth a richer dust concealed;
5 A dust whom England bore, shaped, made aware;
Gave, once, her flowers to love, her ways to roam,
A body of England's breathing English air,
Washed by the rivers, blest by suns of home.

And think, this heart, all evil shed away,
10 A pulse in the eternal mind, no less
Gives somewhere back the thoughts by England given;
Her sights and sounds; dreams happy as her day;
And laughter, learned of friends; and gentleness,
In hearts at peace, under an English heaven.

SUICIDE IN THE TRENCHES

Siegfried Sassoon

I knew a simple soldier boy
Who grinned at life in empty joy,
Slept soundly through the lonesome dark,
And whistled early with the lark.

5 In winter trenches, cowed[1] and glum,
With crumps[2] and lice and lack of rum,
He put a bullet through his brain.
No one spoke of him again.

You smug-faced crowds with kindling[3] eye
10 Who cheer when soldier lads march by,
Sneak home and pray you'll never know
The hell where youth and laughter go.

---

1. **cowed** (koud), *adj.* frightened.
2. **crumps,** soldiers' slang for exploding shells, from the sound made by them.
3. **kindling** (kind'ling), *adj.* brightening.

John Nash's painting *Over the Top* (1918) shows a group of British soldiers moving up to repel a German attack on December 30, 1917. Does this image reflect a romantic view of heroism in war? Why or why not? ▼

DULCE ET DECORUM EST

Wilfred Owen

Bent double, like old beggars under sacks,
Knock-kneed, coughing like hags, we cursed through sludge,[1]
Till on the haunting flares we turned our backs
And towards our distant rest began to trudge.
5 Men marched asleep. Many had lost their boots
But limped on, blood-shod.[2] All went lame; all blind;
Drunk with fatigue; deaf even to the hoots
Of tired, outstripped Five-Nines[3] that dropped behind.

Gas! GAS! Quick, boys! An ecstasy of fumbling,
10 Fitting the clumsy helmets just in time;
But someone still was yelling out and stumbling
And flound'ring like a man in fire or lime . . .
Dim, through the misty panes and thick green light,
As under a green sea, I saw him drowning.

15 In all my dreams, before my helpless sight,
He plunges at me, guttering, choking, drowning.
If in some smothering dreams you too could pace
Behind the wagon that we flung him in,
And watch the white eyes writhing[4] in his face,
20 His hanging face, like a devil's sick of sin;
If you could hear, at every jolt, the blood
Come gargling from the froth-corrupted lungs,
Obscene as cancer, bitter as the cud
Of vile, incurable sores on innocent tongues—
25 My friend, you would not tell with such high zest
To children ardent[5] for some desperate glory,
The old Lie: Dulce et decorum est
Pro patria mori.[6]

---

1. **sludge** (sluj), *n.* soft mud.
2. **blood-shod,** with only blood for shoes.
3. **Five-Nines,** shells containing poison gas. The use of poison gas by both sides on
   the Western Front was widely viewed as immoral. (See page 773.)
4. **writhe** (rīᴛн), *v.* twist and turn.
5. **ardent** (ärd′nt), *adj.* enthusiastic; passionate.
6. **Dulce . . . mori** (dùl′chä et də kôr′əm est prō pä′trē ə môr′ē). "It is sweet
   and honorable to die for one's country," a quotation from one of Horace's *Odes*
   well known to British schoolboys. *[Latin]*

DISABLED

Wilfred Owen

He sat in a wheeled chair, waiting for dark,
And shivered in his ghastly suit of gray,
Legless, sewn short at elbow. Through the park
Voices of boys rang saddening like a hymn,
5 Voices of play and pleasure after day,
Till gathering sleep had mothered them from him.

About this time Town used to swing so gay
When glow-lamps budded in the light blue trees,
And girls glanced lovelier as the air grew dim—
10 In the old times, before he threw away his knees.
Now he will never feel again how slim
Girls' waists are, or how warm their subtle hands;
All of them touch him like some queer disease.

There was an artist silly for his face,
15 For it was younger than his youth, last year.
Now, he is old; his back will never brace;
He's lost his color very far from here,
Poured it down shell-holes till the veins ran dry,
And half his lifetime lapsed in the hot race,
20 And leap of purple spurted from his thigh.

One time he liked a blood-smear down his leg,
After the matches, carried shoulder-high.
It was after football, when he'd drunk a peg,[1]
He thought he'd better join—He wonders why.
25 Someone had said he'd look a god in kilts,[2]
That's why; and may be, too, to please his Meg;
Aye, that was it, to please the giddy jilts[3]
He asked to join. He didn't have to beg;
Smiling they wrote his lie; aged nineteen years.

---

1. **peg,** an alcoholic drink.
2. **kilt** (kilt), *n.* a plaid pleated skirt, worn especially by
   Scottish soldiers or men in the Scottish Highlands.
3. **jilts,** girls.

30 Germans he scarcely thought of; all their guilt,
And Austria's, did not move him. And no fears
Of Fear came yet. He thought of jewelled hilts
For daggers in plaid socks; of smart salutes;
And care of arms; and leave; and pay arrears;[4]
35 *Esprit de corps*;[5] and hints for young recruits.
And soon, he was drafted out with drums and cheers.

Some cheered him home, but not as crowds cheer Goal.
Only a solemn man who brought him fruits
Thanked him; and then inquired about his soul.
40 Now, he will spend a few sick years in Institutes,
And do what things the rules consider wise,
And take whatever pity they may dole.[6]
Tonight he noticed how the women's eyes
Passed from him to the strong men that were whole.
45 How cold and late it is! Why don't they come
And put him into bed? Why don't they come?

---

4. **arrears** (ə rirz′), *n. pl.* money due but not yet paid.
5. ***Esprit de corps*** (e sprē′ də kôr′), group spirit;
morale. *[French]*
6. **dole** (dōl), *v.* give in charity.

After Reading

Making Connections

1. Which of the four war poems most closely reflects your personal attitude toward war? Explain your response.

2. In "The Soldier" why do you think the speaker is able to anticipate and accept the possibility of his death with such a positive and peaceful attitude?

3. Compare what England has given the speaker (in the first eight lines of this **sonnet**) with what the speaker's spirit will return in death (in the last six lines).

4. What words in the first stanza of "Suicide in the Trenches" indicate to you that the boy is innocent and naive?

5. Judging from the few details given, why do you think the boy kills himself?

6. In "Dulce et Decorum Est" what about the physical and mental conditions of the soldiers make them easy prey for a gas attack?

7. How does Owen's use of **figurative language** emphasize the horror of the situation surrounding the gas attack?

8. What do you think is the purpose of the quotation that ends the poem?

9. In "Disabled" contrast the young man's life before the war with his life after serving his country.

10. In what different ways might you interpret the last two lines of the poem?

11. 👁 What similarities in thought do you think may be caused by the **group** membership of these three soldier / poets? What differences do you find?

12. What makes these poems, written by Englishmen reflecting on England at war, universally applicable?

Literary Focus: Tone

An author's attitude toward his or her subject matter or toward the audience is the **tone** of a work. The ways an author manipulates words, chooses images, and describes characters and events are clues to a work's tone. For each of the poems in this group identify the tone and discuss which words, phrases, and images contribute to that tone.

Vocabulary

What other adjectives come to mind when you think of *ardent*? Create a word map of at least five adjectives that could be used as synonyms for *ardent*.

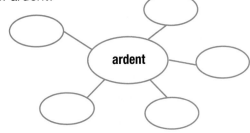

Expressing Your Ideas

Writing Choices

Writer's Notebook Update Label each poet in this group as an idealist or a realist. Would you prefer to be called an idealist or a realist? Explain your choice in a sentence or two.

The "Glory" of War Write an **essay** of comparison and contrast in which you discuss the treatment of death in war as presented by Brooke, Sassoon, and Owen. Consider especially the differences in tone, word choice, and patriotic feeling. In your conclusion try to account for the differences you have found.

Join My Cause At the beginning of World War I, when love of country was at its height in England, young men expressed their patriotism by enlisting to fight in "the Great War." If you wanted to express your patriotism and love for your country today, what method of expression would you choose? Write an **editorial** for your school newspaper urging other students to join you in your patriotic endeavor.

Other Options

Tones of War Select one of the four war poems and choose a musical composition that you think reflects the tone of the poem. Prepare an **oral reading** of the poem using the musical piece as background.

Types of Therapy Imagine that a wounded soldier such as the speaker in "Disabled" is taking therapy to deal with his feelings about the war. Draw a **picture** or create a **sculpture** that you think the soldier might work on as part of his therapy for confronting what happened to him in the war. Or, if the soldier you imagine is too disabled to draw or sculpt, demonstrate some **physical exercises** that he might undergo to maintain his health.

War on Display Prepare a **bulletin board display** on an aspect of World War I. Include pictures, charts, and maps. Choose from one of the following topics or select your own subject: Causes of World War I, Allied Powers and Central Powers, The Western Front, Types of Warfare, Great Battles, U. S. Involvement, British Losses, The Treaty of Versailles.

Before Reading

from Testament of Youth

by Vera Brittain

Vera Brittain
1893–1970

The daughter of middle-class parents, Vera Brittain spent her youth sheltered and chaperoned. Her parents believed that only boys should seek higher education, but Brittain persuaded them to allow her to prepare for the rigorous entrance examinations for Oxford. When war broke out, she had just received her acceptance to Oxford. With her fiancé, Roland Leighton; her brother, Edward; and various of their friends at war, Brittain joined the war effort herself by serving for four years as a Red Cross nurse. After the Armistice she completed her studies at Oxford and became a writer and social activist. In 1933 Brittain completed *Testament of Youth,* an autobiography set against the larger background of war and social change.

Building Background

To Enlighten the Old; to Console the Young These words from Vera Brittain's foreword to her personal diary explain why she valued her diary and wanted it and her later reflections on it to be widely read:

"I belong to the few who believe in all sincerity that their own lives provide the answers to some of the many problems which puzzle humanity. I should like to help the experienced, who think they understand youth, to realize how easy it is to mistake illusion for conviction, bewilderment for weakness, enthusiasm for indiscretion or self-will. It is in the hope that these records of my own ardors, absurdities, weaknesses, and failures will enlighten the old who are puzzled about the young, and console the young who are confused about themselves, that I venture to expose them to the searchlight of public criticism."

Literary Focus

Mood The **mood** of a literary work is the prevailing emotion or overall atmosphere. An author creates mood partly through the description of the setting and partly through the people and events being described. In the following selection, look for changes in mood and the reasons for these changes.

Writer's Notebook

Women in War What role or roles do you think women should assume if their country is involved in a war? Should women serve in the same ways as men? Jot down a few thoughts on these questions.

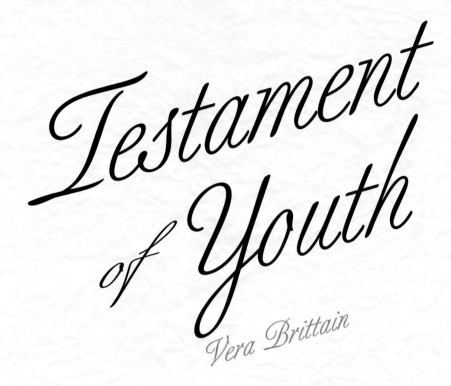

Testament of Youth

Vera Brittain

When the Great War broke out, it came to me not as a superlative tragedy, but as an interruption of the most exasperating kind to my personal plans. . . .

It would not, I think, be possible for any present-day girl of the same age even to imagine how abysmally ignorant, how romantically idealistic, and how utterly unsophisticated my more sensitive contemporaries and I were at that time. The naiveties of the diary which I began to write consistently soon after leaving school, and kept up until more than half way through the War, must be read in order to be believed. My "Reflective Record, 1913," is endorsed on its title page with the following comprehensive aspirations:

"To extend love, to promote thought, to lighten suffering, to combat indifference, to inspire activity."

"To know everything of something and something of everything."

My diary for August 3rd, 1914, contains a most incongruous[1] mixture of war and tennis.

The day was Bank Holiday,[2] and a tennis tournament had been arranged at the Buxton[3] Club. I had promised to play with my discouraged but still faithful suitor, and did not in the least want to forgo the amusement that I knew this partnership would afford me—particularly as the events reported in the newspapers seemed too incredible to be taken quite seriously. "I do not know," I wrote in my diary, "how we all managed to play tennis so calmly and take quite an interest in the result. I suppose it is because we all know so little of the real meaning of war that we are so indifferent. B. and I had to owe 30. It was good handicapping as we had a very close game with everybody." . . .

---

1. **incongruous** (in kong′grü əs), *adj.* out of place; inconsistent.
2. **Bank Holiday,** any weekday on which banks are legally closed. August 3, 1914, was a Monday.
3. **Buxton,** Brittain's home town, an attractive tourist town in Derbyshire, England.

After that[4] events moved, even in Buxton, very quickly. The German cousins of some local acquaintances left the town in a panic. My parents rushed over in the car to familiar shops in Macclesfield and Leek, where they laid in stores of cheese, bacon, and butter under the generally shared impression that by next week we might all be besieged by the Germans. Wild rumors circulated from mouth to mouth; they were more plentiful than the newspapers, over which a free fight broke out on the station platform every time a batch came by train from London or Manchester. Our elderly cook, who had three Reservist sons, dissolved into continuous tears and was too much upset to prepare the meals with her usual competence; her young daughter-in-law, who had had a baby only the previous Friday, became hysterical and had to be forcibly restrained from getting up and following her husband to the station. One or two Buxton girls were hurriedly married to officers summoned to unknown destinations. Pandemonium[5] swept over the town. Holiday trippers wrestled with one another for the *Daily Mail;* habitually quiet and respectable citizens struggled like wolves for the provisions in the food-shops, and vented upon the distracted assistants their dismay at learning that all prices had suddenly gone up. . . .

My father vehemently[6] forbade Edward, who was still under military age, to join anything whatsoever. Having himself escaped immersion in the public-school tradition, which stood for militaristic heroism unimpaired by the damping exercise of reason, he withheld his permission for any kind of military training, and ended by taking Edward daily to the mills to divert his mind from the War. Needless to say, these uncongenial expeditions entirely failed of their desired effect, and constant explosions—to which, having inherited so many of my father's characteristics, I seemed only to add by my presence—made our house quite intolerable. A new one boiled up after each of Edward's tentative efforts at defiance, and these were numerous, for his enforced subservience[7] seemed to him synonymous with ever-

lasting disgrace. One vague application for a commission which he sent to a Notts and Derby regiment actually was forwarded to the War Office—"from which," I related with ingenuous optimism, "we are expecting to hear every post."

When my father discovered this exercise of initiative, his wrath and anxiety reached the point of effervescence.[8] Work of any kind was quite impossible in the midst of so much chaos and apprehension, and letters to Edward from Roland, describing his endeavors to get a commission in a Norfolk regiment, did nothing to ease the perpetual tension. Even after the result of my Oxford Senior[9] came through, I abandoned in despair the Greek textbooks that Roland had lent me. I even took to knitting for the soldiers, though only for a very short time; utterly incompetent at all forms of needlework, I found the simplest bed-socks and sleeping-helmets altogether beyond me. "Oh, how I wish I could wake up in the morning," concludes one typical day's entry describing these commotions, "to find this terrible war the dream it seems to me to be!"

At the beginning of 1915 I was more deeply and ardently in love than I have ever been or am ever likely to be, yet at that time Roland and I had hardly been alone together, and never at all without the constant possibility of observation and interruption. In Buxton our occasional walks had always been taken either through the town in full view of my family's inquisitive[10]

---

4. **that,** August 4, when at midnight, since the Germans had not responded to an English ultimatum that they withdraw from Belgium, the English entered the war.
5. pandemonium (pan′də mō′nē əm), *n.* wild uproar; lawlessness.
6. **vehemently** (vē′ə mənt lē), *adv.* forcefully.
7. **subservience** (səb sėr′vē əns), *n.* slavish obedience.
8. **effervescence** (ef′ər ves′ns), *n.* boiling over.
9. **Oxford Senior,** an entrance exam.
10. inquisitive (in kwiz′ə tiv), *adj.* curious; prying.

acquaintances, or as one half of a quartet whose other members kept us continually in sight. At Uppingham[11] every conversation that we had was exposed to inspection and facetious[12] remark by schoolmasters or relatives. In London we could only meet under the benevolent but embarrassingly interested eyes of an aunt. Consequently, by the middle of January, our desire to see one another alone had passed beyond the bounds of toleration.

In my closely supervised life, a secret visit to London was impossible even en route for Oxford; I knew that I should be seen off by a train which had been discussed for days and, as usual, have my ticket taken for me. But Leicester was a conceivable rendezvous,[13] for I had been that way before, even though from Buxton the obvious route was via Birmingham. So for my family's benefit, I invented some objectionable students, likely to travel by Birmingham, whom I wanted to avoid. Roland, in similar mood, wrote that if he could not get leave he would come without it.

When the morning arrived, my mother decided that I seemed what she called "nervy," and insisted upon accompanying me to Miller's Dale, the junction at which travelers from Buxton change to the main line. I began in despair to wonder whether she would elect to come with me all the way to Oxford, but I finally escaped without her suspecting that I had any intention other than that of catching the first available train from Leicester. The usual telegram was demanded, but I protested that at Oxford station there was always such a rush for a cab that I couldn't possibly find time to telegraph until after tea.

At Leicester, Roland, who had started from Peterborough soon after dawn, was waiting for me with another sheaf of pale pink roses. He looked tired, and said he had had a cold; actually, it was incipient influenza and he ought to have been in bed, but I did not discover this till afterwards.

To be alone with one another after so much observation was quite overwhelming, and for a time conversation in the Grand Hotel lounge moved somewhat spasmodically. But constraint disappeared when he told me with obvious pride that he had asked his own colonel for permission to interview the colonel of the 5th Norfolks, who were stationed some distance away and were shortly going to the front, with a view to getting a transfer.

"Next time I see the C. O.,"[14] he announced, "I shall tell him the colonel of the 5th was away. I shall say I spent the whole day looking for him—so after lunch I'm coming with you to Oxford."

I tried to subdue my leaping joy by a protest about his cold, but as we both knew this to be insincere it was quite ineffective. I only stipulated that when we arrived he must lose me at the station; "chap. rules,"[15] even more Victorian than the social code of Buxton, made it inexpedient[16] for a woman student to be seen in Oxford with a young man who was not her brother.

CONNECT: Compare and contrast the rules of courtship that Vera and Roland had to observe with those followed in today's society.

So we found an empty first-class carriage and traveled together from Leicester to Oxford. It was a queer journey; the memory of its profound unsatisfactoriness remains with me still. I had not realized before that to be alone together would bring, all too quickly, the knowledge that being alone together was not enough.

11. **Uppingham,** the private school attended by Edward Brittain and his friends. In 1913 there were about 400 boys in the school. The school's First World War Memorial lists 449 names.
12. **facetious** (fə sē′shəs), *adj.* slyly humorous.
13. rendezvous (rän′də vü), *n.* secret meeting place.
14. **C. O.,** commanding officer.
15. **"chap. rules,"** chaperone rules. A chaperone (shap′ə-rōn′) is an older person appointed to make sure that proper behavior is observed.
16. inexpedient (in′ik spē′dē ənt), *adj.* unwise.

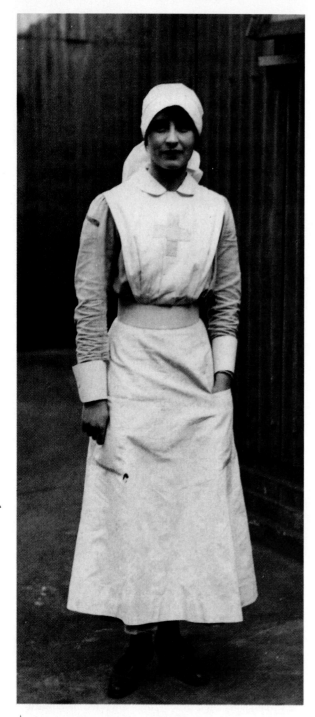

Compare this image of Vera Brittain as a wartime nurse with the picture she gives of herself at the beginning of the war (page 743).

he had only his pay, and we were both so distressingly young.

Thus a new constraint arose between us which again made it difficult to talk. We tried to discuss impersonally the places that we wanted to see when it was possible to travel once more; we'd go to Florence together, he said, directly the War was over.

"But," I objected—my age-perspective being somewhat different from that of today—"it wouldn't be proper until I'm at least thirty."

"Don't worry," he replied persuasively. "I'm sure I can arrange for it to be 'proper' before you get to that age!"

And then, somehow, we found ourselves suddenly admitting that each had kept the other's letters right from the beginning. We were now only a few miles from Oxford, and it was the first real thing that we had said. As we sat together silently watching the crimson sun set over the flooded land, some quality in his nearness became so unbearable that, all unsophisticated as I was, I felt afraid. I tried to explain it to myself afterwards by a familiar quotation: "There is no beauty that hath not some strangeness in the proportion...."

Like so many of the idealistic but naive young men of his generation, Roland Leighton regarded going to war as a duty, a test of heroism, and a potentially glamorous adventure. In a letter to Brittain describing his determination to secure a commission, he wrote: "I feel that I am meant to take an active part in this War. It is to me a very fascinating thing— something, if very horrible, yet very ennobling and very beautiful, something whose elemental reality raises it above the reach of all cold theorizing." On Wednesday, March 31, 1915, Vera saw Roland off to the front and returned home to the dreary realization that the war was beginning to overshadow everything in her life—school, personal relationships, ambitions, and dreams.

It was an intolerable realization, for I knew too that death might so easily overtake us before there could be anything more. I was dependent,

The next day I saw him off, although he had said that he would rather I didn't come. In the early morning we walked to the station beneath a dazzling sun, but the platform from which his train went out was dark and very cold. In the railway carriage we sat hand in hand until the whistle blew. We never kissed and never said a word. I got down from the carriage still clasping his hand, and held it until the gathering speed of the train made me let go. He leaned through the window looking at me with sad, heavy eyes, and I watched the train wind out of the station and swing round the curve until there was nothing left but the snowy distance, and the sun shining harshly on the bright, empty rails.

*W*hen I got back to the house, where everyone mercifully left me to myself, I realized that my hands were nearly frozen. Vaguely resenting the physical discomfort, I crouched beside the morning-room fire for almost an hour, unable to believe that I could ever again suffer such acute and conscious agony of mind. On every side there seemed to be cause for despair and no way out of it. I tried not to think because thought was intolerable, yet every effort to stop my mind from working only led to a fresh outburst of miserable speculation. I tried to read; I tried to look at the gaunt white hills across the valley, but nothing was any good, so in the end I just stayed huddled by the fire, immersed in a mood of blank hopelessness in which years seemed to have passed since the morning.

At last I fell asleep for some moments, and awoke feeling better; I was, I suppose, too young for hope to be extinguished for very long. Perhaps, I thought, Wordsworth or Browning or Shelley would have some consolation to offer; all through the War poetry was the only form of literature that I could read for comfort, and the only kind that I ever attempted to write. So I turned at once to Shelley's "Adonais,"[17] only to be provoked to new anguish by the words:

> O gentle child, beautiful as thou wert,
> Why didst thou leave the trodden paths of men

> Too soon, and with weak hands though mighty heart
> Dare the unpastured dragon in his den?

But the lovely cadences[18] stirred me at last to articulateness; there was no one to whom I wanted to talk, but at least I could tell my diary a good deal of the sorrow that seemed so fathomless. . . .

With that Easter vacation began the wearing anxiety of waiting for letters which for me was to last, with only brief intervals, for more than three years, and which, I think, made all non-combatants feel more distracted than anything else in the War. Even when the letters came they were four days old, and the writer since sending them had had time to die over and over again. My diary, with its long-drawn-out record of days upon days of miserable speculation, still gives a melancholy impression of that nerve-racking suspense.

"Morning," it observes, "creeps on into afternoon, and afternoon passes into evening, while I go from one occupation to another, in apparent unconcern—but all the time this gnawing anxiety beneath it all."

Ordinary household sounds became a torment. The clock, marking off each hour of dread, struck into the immobility of tension with the shattering effect of a thunderclap. Every ring at the door suggested a telegram, every telephone call a long-distance message giving bad news. With some of us the effect of this prolonged apprehension still lingers on; even now I cannot work comfortably in a room from which it is possible to hear the front-door bell.

Having successfully competed her first-year exams at Oxford, Vera dropped all studies to commence training as a Red Cross nurse in Devonshire Hospital. In August, Roland returned home on leave, a strained reunion for the young lovers, despite their becoming officially engaged. Frustrated and depressed by lack of

---

17. **Shelley's "Adonais,"** the pastoral elegy composed in 1821 by Percy Shelley in honor of John Keats.
18. **cadence** (kād′ns), *n.* rising and falling sound.

privacy and the brevity of their time together, they parted in a mood of despair and foreboding that was to persist in the grim weeks that followed.

As September wore on and the Battle of Loos came nearer, an anxious stillness seemed to settle upon the country, making everyone taut[19] and breathless. The Press and personal letters from France were alike full of anticipation and suspense. Roland wrote vaguely but significantly of movements of troops, of great changes impending, and seemed more obsessed with the idea of death than ever before. One letter, describing how he had superintended the reconstruction of some old trenches, was grim with a disgust and bitterness that I had never known him put into words:

"The dugouts have been nearly all blown in, the wire entanglements are a wreck, and in among the chaos of twisted iron and splintered timber and shapeless earth are the fleshless, blackened bones of simple men who poured out their red, sweet wine of youth[20] unknowing, for nothing more tangible than Honor or their Country's Glory or another's Lust of Power. Let him who thinks War is a glorious, golden thing, who loves to roll forth stirring words of exhortation,[21] invoking Honor and Praise and Valor and Love of Country with as thoughtless and fervid[22] a faith as inspired the priests of Baal[23] to call on their own slumbering deity, let him but look at a little pile of sodden gray rags that cover half a skull and a shinbone and what might have been Its ribs, or at this skeleton lying on its side, resting half crouching as it fell, perfect but that it is headless, and with the tattered clothing still draped round it; and let him realize how grand and glorious a thing it is to have distilled all Youth and Joy and Life into a fetid[24] heap of hideous putrescence![25] Who is there who has known and seen who can say that Victory is worth the death of even one of these?"

Had there really been a time, I wondered, when I believed that it was?

"When I think of these things," I told him in reply, "I feel that awful Abstraction, the Unknown God, must be some dread and wrathful deity before whom I can only kneel and plead for mercy, perhaps in the words of a quaint hymn of George Herbert's[26] that we used to sing at Oxford:

Throw away Thy wrath!
Throw away Thy rod!
O my God
Take the gentle path!"

In October, Vera received orders to report to First London General Hospital, Camberwell, an army hospital to which she had applied, lying about her age. Here she experienced miserable living conditions, twelve-hour workdays, and daily exposure to grisly wounds in the surgical wards, in addition to incessant anxiety over Roland's safety and the possible weakening of their love by separation and war. The last week of 1915 she spent in nervous, yet ecstatic anticipation of Roland's leave on December 25, Christmas Day.

Certainly the stage seemed perfectly set for his leave. Now that my parents had at last migrated temporarily to the Grand Hotel at Brighton, our two families were so near; the Matron had promised yet again that my own week's holiday should coincide with his, and even Edward wrote cheerfully for once to say that as soon as the actual date was known, he and Victor[27] would both be able to get leave at the same time.

---

19. **taut** (tôt), *adj.* tense.
20. **red, sweet wine of youth.** Here Leighton quotes a famous line from Rupert Brooke's poem, "The Dead." See The Language of Heroism, page 777.
21. **exhortation** (eg/zôr tā/shən), *n.* earnest advice.
22. **fervid** (fėr/vid), *adj.* spirited.
23. **priests of Baal,** those who worshipped a false god.
24. **fetid** (fet/id), *adj.* stinking.
25. **putrescence** (pyü tres/ns), *n.* rottenness.
26. **hymn of George Herbert's,** "Discipline," by the religious poet George Herbert (1593–1633).
27. **Victor,** another school friend of Edward Brittain's.

"Very wet and muddy and many of the communication trenches are quite impassable," ran a letter from Roland written on December 9th. "Three men were killed the other day by a dugout falling in on top of them and one man was drowned in a sump hole. The whole of one's world, at least of one's visible and palpable world, is mud in various stages of solidity or stickiness. . . . I can be perfectly certain about the date of my leave by tomorrow morning and will let you know."

And, when the final information did come, hurriedly written in pencil on a thin slip of paper torn from his Field Service notebook, it brought the enchanted day still nearer than I had dared to hope.

"Shall be home on leave from 24th Dec.— 31st. Land Christmas Day. R."

Even to the unusual concession of a leave which began on Christmas morning after night-duty the Matron proved amenable,[28] and in the encouraging quietness of the winter's war, with no Loos in prospect, no great push in the west even possible, I dared to glorify my days—or rather my nights—by looking forward. In the pleasant peace of Ward 25, where all the patients, now well on the road to health, slept soundly, the sympathetic Scottish Sister teased me a little for my irrepressible[29] excitement. . . .

Directly after breakfast, sent on my way by exuberant good wishes from Betty and Marjorie and many of the others, I went down to Brighton. All day I waited there for a telephone message or a telegram, sitting drowsily in the lounge of the Grand Hotel, or walking up and down the promenade, watching the gray sea tossing rough with white surf-crested waves, and wondering still what kind of crossing he had had or was having.

When, by ten o'clock at night, no news had come, I concluded that the complications of telegraph and telephone on a combined Sunday and Christmas Day had made communication impossible. So, unable to fight sleep any longer after a night and a day of wakefulness, I went to bed a little disappointed, but still unperturbed. Roland's family, at their Keymer cottage, kept an even longer vigil; they sat up till nearly midnight over their Christmas dinner in the hope that he would join them, and, in their dramatic, impulsive fashion, they drank a toast to the Dead.

The next morning I had just finished dressing, and was putting the final touches to the pastel-blue crêpe-de-Chine blouse, when the expected message came to say that I was wanted on the telephone. Believing that I was at last to hear the voice for which I had waited for twenty-four hours, I dashed joyously into the corridor. But the message was not from Roland but from Clare;[30] it was not to say that he had arrived home that morning, but to tell me that he had died of wounds at a Casualty Clearing Station on December 23rd. . . .

Plunged into anguish and nightmarish confusion by the death of Roland, Brittain suffered through months of loneliness, strained communication with family and friends, and unresolved perplexity about the meaning of Roland's death.

Whenever I think of the weeks that followed the news of Roland's death, a series of pictures, disconnected but crystal clear, unroll themselves like a kaleidoscope through my mind.

A solitary cup of coffee stands before me on a hotel breakfast-table; I try to drink it, but fail ignominiously. . . .

It is Sunday, and I am out for a solitary walk through the dreary streets of Camberwell before going to bed after the night's work. In front of me on the frozen pavement a long red worm wriggles slimily. I remember that, after our death, worms destroy this body—however lovely, however beloved—and I run from the obscene thing in horror.

It is Wednesday, and I am walking up the Brixton Road on a mild, fresh morning of early

---

28. amenable (ə mē′nə bəl), *adj.* responsive; agreeable.
29. irrepressible (ir′i pres′ə bəl), *adj.* uncontrollable.
30. **Clare,** Roland Leighton's sister.

spring. Half-consciously I am repeating a line from Rupert Brooke: "The deep night, and birds singing, and clouds flying . . ." For a moment I have become conscious of the old joy in rain-washed skies and scuttling, fleecy clouds, when suddenly I remember—Roland is dead and I am not keeping faith with him; it is mean and cruel, even for a second, to feel glad to be alive.

In Sussex, by the end of January, the season was already on its upward grade; catkins hung bronze from the bare, black branches, and in the damp lanes between Hassocks and Keymer the birds sang loudly. How I hated them as I walked back to the station one late afternoon, when a red sunset turned the puddles on the road into gleaming pools of blood, and a new horror of mud and death darkened my mind with its dreadful obsession. Roland, I reflected bitterly, was now part of the corrupt clay into which war had transformed the fertile soil of France; he would never again know the smell of a wet evening in early spring.

I had arrived at the cottage that morning to find his mother and sister standing in helpless distress in the midst of his returned kit, which was lying, just opened, all over the floor. The garments sent back included the outfit that he had been wearing when he was hit. I wondered, and I wonder still, why it was thought necessary to return such relics—the tunic torn back and front by the bullet, a khaki vest dark and stiff with blood, and a pair of blood-stained breeches slit open at the top by someone obviously in a violent hurry. Those gruesome rags made me realize, as I had never realized before, all that France really meant. Eighteen months afterwards the smell of Etaples village, though fainter and more diffused, brought back to me the memory of those poor remnants of patriotism.

CLARIFY: Why do you think Vera calls Roland's blood-stained garments "poor remnants of patriotism"?

"Everything," I wrote later to Edward, "was damp and worn and simply caked with mud. And I was glad that neither you nor Victor nor anyone who may some day go to the front was there to see. If you had been, you would have been overwhelmed by the horror of war without its glory. For though he had only worn the things when living, the smell of those clothes was the smell of graveyards and the Dead. The mud of France which covered them was not ordinary mud; it had not the usual clean pure smell of earth, but it was as though it were saturated with dead bodies—dead that had been dead a long, long time. . . . There was his cap, bent in and shapeless out of recognition—the soft cap he wore rakishly on the back of his head—with the badge thickly coated with mud. He must have fallen on top of it, or perhaps one of the people who fetched him in trampled on it."

What actually happened to the clothes I never knew, but, incongruously enough, it was amid this heap of horror and decay that we found, surrounded by torn bills and letters, the black manuscript notebook containing his poems. On the flyleaf he had copied a few lines written by John Masefield[31] on the subject of patriotism:

"It is not a song in the street and a wreath on a column and a flag flying from a window and a pro-Boer under a pump.[32] It is a thing very holy and very terrible, like life itself. It is a burden to be borne, a thing to labor for and to suffer for and to die for, a thing which gives no happiness and no pleasantness—but a hard life, an unknown grave, and the respect and bowed heads of those who follow."

31. **John Masefield** (1878–1967), English poet.
32. **a pro-Boer . . . pump.** Public opinion had been strongly divided on the subject of the Boer War (1899–1902), with a number of the British sympathetic to the Boer cause. Here Masefield alludes to the false patriotism of a mob punishing someone opposed to English imperialism by dousing them with water.

(Left to right) Edward Brittain, Roland Leighton, and Victor Richardson pose together at Uppingham School O.T.C. camp in July 1915. Do any of these faces suggest Wilfred Owen's schoolboys "ardent for some desperate glory" (page 737, line 26)?

The months of unrelieved pain and hopelessness following the death of Roland were further darkened by the departure of Vera's brother Edward for the front in February of 1916 and his later wounding in action, for which he earned the Military Cross. In September, Vera was assigned to eight months of duty on the island of Malta, where the remoteness of the war and exposure to daily sunshine effected a resurgence of hopefulness and personal vitality. After the death of two more of their friends, Edward wrote: ". . . we have lost almost all there was to lose and what have we gained? Truly as you say has patriotism worn very threadbare. . . ." In August of 1917 Vera went to France to begin work at No. 24 General Hospital, Etaples, caring for the wounded on both sides and exposing herself to considerable personal danger.

"Never in my life have I been so absolutely filthy as I get on duty here," I wrote to my mother on December 5th in answer to her request for a description of my work.

"Sister A. has six wards and there is no V.A.D.[33] in the next-door one, only an orderly, so neither she nor he spend very much time in here. Consequently I am Sister, V.A.D. and orderly all in one (somebody said the other day that no one less than God Almighty could give a correct definition of the job of a V.A.D.!) and after, quite apart from the nursing, I have stoked the stove all night, done two or three rounds of bed-pans and kept the kettles going and prepared feeds on exceedingly black Beatrice oil-stoves and refilled them from the steam kettles, literally wallowing in paraffin all the time, I feel as if I had been dragged through the gutter! Possibly acute surgical is the heaviest kind of work there is, but acute medical is, I think, more wearing than anything else on earth. You are kept on the go the whole time and in the end there seems nothing definite to show for it—except that one or two people are still alive who might otherwise have been dead."

The rest of my letter referred to the effect, upon ourselves, of the new offensive at Cambrai.[34]

"The hospital is very heavy now—as heavy as when I came; the fighting is continuing very long this year, and the convoys keep coming down, two or three a night. . . . Sometimes in the middle of the night we have to turn people out of bed and make them sleep on the floor to make room for more seriously ill ones that have come down from the line. We have heaps of gassed cases at present who came in a day or two ago; there are ten in this ward alone. I wish those people who write so glibly about this being a holy War, and the orators who talk so much about going on no matter how long the War lasts and what it may mean, could see a case—to say nothing of ten cases—of mustard gas in its early stages—could see the poor things burned and blistered all over with great mustard-colored suppurating[35] blisters, with blind eyes—

---

33. **V. A. D.,** a nurse of the Voluntary Aid Detachment. "Sister" is the title of a head nurse in a hospital ward.
34. **Cambrai,** a town in France. The offensive, beginning November 20, 1917, was the first battle in which a notable use was made of tanks.
35. suppurating (sup′yə rā′ting), *adj.* oozing.

sometimes temporarily, sometimes permanently—all sticky and stuck together, and always fighting for breath, with voices a mere whisper, saying that their throats are closing and they know they will choke. The only thing one can say is that such severe cases don't last long; either they die soon or else improve—usually the former; they certainly never reach England in the state we have them here, and yet people persist in saying that God made the War, when there are such inventions of the Devil about. . . .

While enduring the front-line hardship in an understaffed and besieged camp hospital, Vera was simultaneously forced to deal with the complaints and crises of her parents, who were becoming increasingly incapable of coping with wartime stress and her extended absence.

*T*he despondency[36] at home was certainly making many of us in France quite alarmed: because we were women we feared perpetually that, just as our work was reaching its climax, our families would need our youth and vitality for their own support. One of my cousins, the daughter of an aunt, had already been summoned home from her canteen work in Boulogne; she was only one of many, for as the War continued to wear out strength and spirits, the middle-aged generation, having irrevocably yielded up its sons, began to lean with increasing weight upon its daughters. Thus the desperate choice between incompatible claims—by which the women of my generation, with their carefully trained consciences, have always been tormented—showed signs of afflicting us with new pertinacity. . . .[37]

Early in April a letter arrived from my father to say that my mother had "crocked up" and had been obliged, owing to the inefficiency of the domestic help then available, to go into a nursing-home. What exactly was wrong remained unspecified, though phrases referred to "toxic heart" and "complete general breakdown." My father had temporarily closed the flat and moved into an hotel, but he did not, he told me, wish to remain there. "As your mother and I can no longer manage without you," he concluded, "it is now your duty to leave France immediately and return to Kensington."

I read these words with real dismay, for my father's interpretation of my duty was not, I knew only too well, in the least likely to agree with that of the Army, which had always been singularly unmoved by the worries of relatives. What was I to do? I wondered desperately. There was my family, confidently demanding my presence, and here was the offensive, which made every pair of experienced hands worth ten pairs under normal conditions. I remembered how the hastily imported V.A.D.s had gone sick at the 1st London during the rush after the Somme; a great push was no time in which to teach a tyro[38] her job. How much of my mother's breakdown was physical and how much psychological—the cumulative result of pessimism at home? It did not then occur to me that my father's sense of emergency was probably heightened by a subconscious determination to get me back to London before the Germans reached the Channel ports, as everyone in England felt certain they would. I only knew that no one in France would believe a domestic difficulty to be so insoluble; if I were dead, or a male, it would have to be settled without me. I should merely be thought to have "wind-up," to be using my mother's health as an excuse to escape the advancing enemy or the threatening air raids.

Half-frantic with the misery of conflicting obligations, I envied Edward his complete powerlessness to leave the Army whatever happened at home. Today, remembering the violent clash

---

36. **despondency** (di spon′dən sē), *n.* discouragement.
37. **pertinacity** (pèrt′n as′ə tē), *n.* persistence.
38. **tyro** (tī′rō), *n.* beginner.

between family and profession, between "duty" and ambition, between conscience and achievement, which has always harassed the women now in their thirties and forties, I find myself still hoping that if the efforts of various interested parties succeed in destroying the fragile international structure built up since the Armistice, and war breaks out on a scale comparable to that of 1914, the organizers of the machine will not hesitate to conscript all women under fifty for service at home or abroad. In the long run, an irrevocable allegiance in a time of emergency makes the decision easier for the older as well as for the younger generation. What exhausts women in wartime is not the strenuous and unfamiliar tasks that fall upon them, nor even the hourly dread of death for husbands or lovers or brothers or sons; it is the incessant conflict between personal and national claims which wears out their energy and breaks their spirit. . . .

It seemed to me then, with my crude judgments and black-and-white values, quite inexplicable that the older generation, which had merely looked on at the War, should break under the strain so much more quickly than those of us who had faced death or horror at first hand for months on end. Today, with middle-age just round the corner, and children who tug my anxious thoughts relentlessly back to them whenever I have to leave them for a week, I realize how completely I underestimated the effect upon the civilian population of year upon year of diminishing hope, diminishing food, diminishing light, diminishing heat, of waiting and waiting for news which was nearly always bad when it came. . . .

SUMMARIZE: How do the different groups that Brittain belongs to throughout influence her attitudes and behaviors?

Nevertheless, in April 1918 Vera reluctantly returned to England to take charge of her parents' household and settle into weeks of dreary domesticity and heightened anxiety over the safety of Edward, now stationed in Italy.

For some time now, my apprehensions for Edward's safety had been lulled by the long quiescence[39] of the Italian front, which had seemed a haven of peace in contrast to our own raging vortex.[40] Repeatedly, during the German offensive, I had thanked God and the Italians who fled at Caporetto[41] that Edward was out of it, and rejoiced that the worst I had to fear from this particular push was the comparatively trivial danger that threatened myself. But now I felt the familiar stirrings of the old tense fear which had been such a persistent companion throughout the War, and my alarm was increased when Edward asked me a week or two later to send him "a funny cat from Liberty's[42] . . . to alleviate tragedy with comedy."

On Sunday morning, June 16th, I opened the *Observer*, which appeared to be chiefly concerned with the new offensive—for the moment at a standstill—in the Noyon-Montdidier sector of the Western Front, and instantly saw at the head of a column the paragraph for which I had looked so long and so fearfully:

ITALIAN FRONT ABLAZE
GUN DUELS FROM MOUNTAIN TO SEA
BAD OPENING OF AN OFFENSIVE. . . .

A day or two later, more details were published of the fighting in Italy, and I learned that the Sherwood Foresters[43] had been involved in

---

39. **quiescence** (kwī es′ns), *n.* stillness.
40. **vortex** (vôr′teks), *n.* whirlwind.
41. **Caporetto,** a town in Austria, the site of the defeat of the Italian Second Army by a combined Austrian-German attack, October 24, 1917.
42. **Liberty's,** a London department store.
43. **Sherwood Foresters,** Edward Brittain's regiment.

the "show" on the Plateau. After that I made no pretense at doing anything but wander restlessly round Kensington or up and down the flat, and, though my father retired glumly to bed every evening at nine o'clock, I gave up writing the semi-fictitious record which I had begun of my life in France. Somehow I couldn't bring myself even to wrap up the *Spectator* and *Saturday Review* that I sent every week to Italy, and they remained in my bedroom, silent yet eloquent witnesses to the dread which my father and I, determinedly conversing on commonplace topics, each refused to put into words.

By the following Saturday we had still heard nothing of Edward. The interval usually allowed for news of casualties after a battle was seldom so long as this, and I began, with an artificial sense of lightness unaccompanied by real conviction, to think that there was perhaps, after all, no news to come. I had just announced to my father, as we sat over tea in the dining-room, that I really must do up Edward's papers and take them to the post office before it closed for the week-end, when there came the sudden loud clattering at the front-door knocker that always meant a telegram.

For a moment I thought that my legs would not carry me, but they behaved quite normally as I got up and went to the door. I knew what was in the telegram—I had known for a week—but because the persistent hopefulness of the human heart refuses to allow intuitive certainty to persuade the reason of that which it knows, I opened and read it in a tearing anguish of suspense.

"Regret to inform you Captain E. H. Brittain M.C. killed in action Italy June 15th."

"No answer," I told the boy mechanically, and handed the telegram to my father, who had followed me into the hall. As we went back into the dining-room I saw, as though I had never seen them before, the bowl of blue delphiniums on the table; their intense color, vivid, ethereal,[44] seemed too radiant for earthly flowers.

Then I remembered that we should have to go down to Purley and tell the news to my mother. . . .

Long after [Father] had gone to bed and the world had grown silent, I crept into the dining-room to be alone with Edward's portrait. Carefully closing the door, I turned on the light and looked at the pale, pictured face, so dignified, so steadfast, so tragically mature. He had been through so much—far, far more than those beloved friends who had died at an earlier stage of the interminable War, leaving him alone to mourn their loss. Fate might have allowed him the little, sorry compensation of survival, the chance to make his lovely music in honor of their memory. It seemed indeed the last irony that he should have been killed by the countrymen of Fritz Kreisler,[45] the violinist whom of all others he had most greatly admired.

And suddenly, as I remembered all the dear afternoons and evenings when I had followed him on the piano as he played his violin, the sad, searching eyes of the portrait were more than I could bear, and falling on my knees before it I began to cry "Edward! Oh, Edward!" in dazed repetition, as though my persistent crying and calling would somehow bring him back. . . .

---

44. **ethereal** (i thir′ē əl), *adj.* heavenly.
45. **Fritz Kreisler** (1875–1962), Austrian violinist.

After Reading

Making Connections

Shaping Your
Response

1. Which death do you think was more devastating to Brittain—Roland's or Edward's? Explain your answer.

Analyzing the
Memoir

2. ☝ How does Brittain characterize herself and her entire **group** of peers at the outbreak of the war?

3. What does the **imagery** she uses suggest about her feelings on the day she saw Roland off to war?

4. What contradictory feelings following Roland's death do you think contribute to Brittain's personal torment?

5. Brittain expresses the hope that, in any future war, women will be able to serve in the same ways as men. What do you think causes her to feel this way?

6. In what ways do you see Brittain in conflict with her parents? Do you think her complaints are justified? How do her views of the "older generation" change when she herself reaches middle age?

7. Brittain wrote this memoir fifteen years after the end of the war. What effect on her writing might this delay have had?

Extending the Ideas

8. Compare Roland's description of the suffering of the men at the front and his attack on idealistic attitudes toward war with Wilfred Owen's "Dulce et Decorum Est" (page 737). What similarities do you find?

Literary Focus: Mood

Mood is the prevailing atmosphere of a literary work.

1. What do you believe is the overall emotional mood of the excerpts from *Testament of Youth*?

2. Contrast the mood in the periods immediately before and after Christmas, 1915.

3. What is the mood of Brittain's description of learning of Edward's death?

Vocabulary Study

Write the word from the list that is most clearly related to the situation being described.

amenable
despondency
incongruous
inexpedient
inquisitive
irrepressible
pandemonium
rendezvous
suppurating
taut

1. the unlikely mixture of war and tennis
2. the wild reactions of the people after war is declared
3. the unwise decision of a girl to travel unchaperoned in 1914
4. her mother's prying questions about Vera's trip to Oxford
5. Vera and Roland's secret meeting
6. Edward's uncontrollable attempts to join the war effort
7. Vera's tense feelings after she sees Roland off to the front
8. the oozing blisters that soldiers suffer because of poison gas
9. the agreeable attitude of the Sister who gives Vera leave
10. Vera's discouraged emotional state as she waits for Roland's arrival

Expressing Your Ideas

Writing Choices

Writer's Notebook Update Jot down a few ideas about how Brittain's opinion about women and war compares with your own.

It's Pandemonium Brittain describes the uproar that sweeps over the town when war is declared. Write a **description** of another kind of pandemonium: a victory celebration for a winning team, a bombing of a public building in a major city, the crash of the stock market, for example.

For Comfort's Sake Brittain says that "all through the War poetry was the only form of literature that I could read for comfort." What kind of literature do you read—or what other activity do you do—for comfort? Write a personal **journal entry** in which you explain what gives you comfort and consolation when you are tense or worried or unhappy.

Other Options

In Memoriam Compose and perform a **musical piece** that you think Edward, if he had survived, might have written in honor of the friends he lost in the war. You might want to use some words or phrases from Brooke, Sassoon, Owen, or one of the poems quoted in Brittain's memoir as inspiration for your composition.

A Conversation About Women Imagine a conversation among Mary Wollstonecroft, Elizabeth Browning, Vera Brittain, and a modern woman of your choice about women in society: their education, their relationships with men, their contributions to the world. With three of your classmates write a **script** of this conversation and present it as a dramatic reading.

Before Reading

Tickets, Please

by D. H. Lawrence

D. H. Lawrence
1885–1930

David Herbert Lawrence was born in an English coal-mining town, the son of an uneducated miner and an ambitious mother. Lawrence taught school for a few years before establishing himself as a writer. In 1912 he eloped with the aristocratic wife of one of his professors. In 1913 Lawrence's reputation began to spread with the publication of a volume of poems and the novel *Sons and Lovers,* a fictional portrait of Lawrence as an artist struggling to break free from his mother. Since most of his work is an exploration of the primitive and sexual in human nature, Lawrence was constantly in trouble with the censors, most notably for his novel, *Lady Chatterley's Lover* (1928), which was not published in Great Britain until 1960.

Building Background

Love and Power

"I told you there were two urges—two great life-urges, didn't I? There may be more. But it comes on me so strongly, now, that there are two: love and power."

In these lines from his novel *Aaron's Rod* Lawrence sets up the tension between men and women that was to form the thematic basis of almost all of his prose and poetry: power relationships in love. Smothered by an overly possessive mother, Lawrence craved the attention of women, yet often rejected them when they demanded too much of him or became too personal. He was critical of women for wanting to be loved, for being too intelligent, for desiring to conquer men. The critic Lionel Trilling suggests that it is Lawrence's "equal recognition of both the antagonism [between the sexes] and the reciprocal need, and of the interplay between the two, that gives his writing about love its unique air of discovery and truth."

Literary Focus

Idiom An **idiom** is an expression whose meaning cannot be understood from the ordinary, literal meanings of the words within the expression. For example, the idiomatic phrase "hold your tongue" means "be quiet" and the expression "get the lead out" means "start moving." Look for Lawrence's use of idiomatic expressions, particularly in the dialogue of the characters.

Writer's Notebook

Getting Even—Again Think of a situation in your life when you were so hurt by someone's actions that you wanted to do something to strike back, to get revenge. Jot down a few sentences to describe the situation that made you feel so terrible.

TICKETS, PLEASE

D. H. Lawrence

There is here in the Midlands[1] a single-line tramway system[2] which boldly leaves the county town and plunges off into the black, industrial countryside, up hill and down dale, through the long ugly villages of workmen's houses, over canals and railways, past churches perched high and nobly over the smoke and shadows, through stark, grimy cold little marketplaces, tilting away in a rush past cinemas and shops down to the hollow where the collieries[3] are, then up again, past a little rural church, under the ash trees, on in a rush to the terminus,[4] the last little ugly place of industry, the cold little town that shivers on the edge of the wild, gloomy country beyond. There the green and creamy colored tram-car seems to pause and purr with curious satisfaction. But in a few minutes—the clock on the turret of the Cooperative Wholesale Society's shops gives the time—away it starts once more on the adventure. Again there are the reckless swoops downhill, bouncing the loops: again the chilly wait in the hilltop marketplace: again the breathless slithering round the precipitous[5] drop under the church: again the patient halts at the loops, waiting for the outcoming car: so on and on, for two long hours, till at last the city looms beyond the fat gasworks, the narrow factories draw near, we are in the sordid[6] streets of the great town, once more we sidle to a standstill at our terminus, abashed[7] by the great crimson and cream-colored city cars, but still perky, jaunty, somewhat dare-devil, green as a jaunty sprig of parsley out of a black colliery garden.

To ride on these cars is always an adventure. Since we are in war-time, the drivers are men unfit for active service: cripples and hunchbacks. So they have the spirit of the devil in them. The ride becomes a steeplechase.[8] Hurray! we have leapt in a clear jump over the canal bridges—now for the four-lane corner. With a shriek and a trail of sparks we are clear again. To be sure, a tram often leaps the rails—but what matter! It sits in a ditch till other trams come to haul it out. It is quite common for a car, packed with one solid mass of living people, to come to a dead halt in the midst of unbroken blackness, the heart of nowhere on a dark night, and for the driver and the girl conductor to call: "All get off—car's on fire!" Instead, however, of rushing out in a panic, the passengers stolidly[9] reply: "Get on—get on! We're not coming out. We're stopping where we are. Push on, George." So till flames actually appear.

---

1. **Midlands,** the central part of England.
2. **tramway system,** streetcar tracks.
3. **colliery** (kol′yər ē), *n.* coal mine.
4. **terminus** (tėr′mə nəs), *n.* the end of the line.
5. precipitous (pri sip′ə təs), *adj.* very steep.
6. sordid (sôr′did), *adj.* filthy.
7. abashed (ə basht′), *adj.* ashamed.
8. **steeplechase** (stē′pəl chās′), *n.* a horse race over an obstacle course.
9. **stolidly** (stol′id lē), *adv.* unemotionally; dully.

The reason for this reluctance to dismount is that the nights are howlingly cold, black, and windswept, and a car is a haven of refuge. From village to village the miners travel, for a change of cinema, of girl, of pub. The trams are desperately packed. Who is going to risk himself in the black gulf outside, to wait perhaps an hour for another tram, then to see the forlorn notice "Depot Only," because there is something wrong! Or to greet a unit of three bright cars all so tight with people that they sail past with a howl of derision.[10] Trams that pass in the night.

This, the most dangerous tram-service in England, as the authorities themselves declare, with pride, is entirely conducted by girls, and driven by rash young men, a little crippled, or by delicate young men, who creep forward in terror. The girls are fearless young hussies.[11] In their ugly blue uniform, skirts up to their knees, shapeless old peaked caps on their heads, they have all the *sang-froid*[12] of an old non-commissioned officer. With a tram packed with howling colliers, roaring hymns downstairs and a sort of antiphony[13] of obscenities upstairs, the lasses are perfectly at their ease. They pounce on the youths who try to evade their ticket-machine. They push off the men at the end of their distance. They are not going to be done in the eye—not they. They fear nobody—and everybody fears them.

"Hello, Annie!"

"Hello, Ted!"

"Oh, mind my corn, Miss Stone. It's my belief you've got a heart of stone, for you've trod on it again."

"You should keep it in your pocket," replies Miss Stone, and she goes sturdily upstairs in her high boots.

"Tickets, please."

She is peremptory,[14] suspicious, and ready to hit first. She can hold her own against ten thousand. The step of that tram-car is her Thermopylae.[15]

Therefore, there is a certain wild romance aboard these cars—and in the sturdy bosom of Annie herself. The time for soft romance is in the morning, between ten o'clock and one, when things are rather slack: that is, except marketday and Saturday. Thus Annie has time to look about her. Then she often hops off her car and into a shop where she has spied something, while the driver chats in the main road. There is very good feeling between the girls and the drivers. Are they not companions in peril, shipmates aboard this careering vessel of a tram-car, forever rocking on the waves of a stormy land.

Then, also, during the early hours, the inspectors are most in evidence. For some reason, everybody employed in this tram-service is young: there are no grey heads. It would not do. Therefore the inspectors are of the right age, and one, the chief, is also good-looking. See him stand on a wet, gloomy morning, in his long oilskin, his peaked cap well down over his eyes, waiting to board a car. His face ruddy, his small brown moustache is weathered, he has a faint impudent[16] smile. Fairly tall and agile, even in his waterproof, he springs aboard a car and greets Annie.

"Hello, Annie! Keeping the wet out?"

"Trying to."

There are only two people in the car. Inspecting is soon over. Then for a long and impudent chat on the foot-board, a good, easy, twelve-mile chat.

The inspector's name is John Thomas Raynor—always called John Thomas, except sometimes, in malice,[17] Coddy. His face sets in fury when he is addressed, from a distance, with this abbreviation. There is considerable scandal

---

10. **derision** (di rizh′ən), *n.* ridicule.
11. **hussy** (huz′ē), *n.* bad-mannered girl.
12. *sang-froid* (sang frwä′), *n.* calmness; composure; literally "cold blood." *[French]*
13. **antiphony** (an tif′ə nē), *n.* hymn sung or chanted in alternate parts.
14. peremptory (pə remp′tər ē), *adj.* decisive; dictatorial.
15. **Thermopylae** (thər mop′ə lē), a narrow mountain pass in Greece where in 480 B. C. a small force of Greeks held off a huge army of Persians.
16. **impudent** (im′pyə dənt), *adj.* bold; rude.
17. **malice** (mal′is), *n.* spite; ill will.

about John Thomas in half a dozen villages. He flirts with the girl conductors in the morning, and walks out with them in the dark night, when they leave their tram-car at the depot. Of course, the girls quit the service frequently. Then he flirts and walks out with the newcomer: always providing she is sufficiently attractive, and that she will consent to walk. It is remarkable, however, that most of the girls are quite comely,[18] they are all young, and this roving life aboard the car gives them a sailor's dash and recklessness. What matter how they behave when the ship is in port? Tomorrow they will be aboard again.

CONNECT: Why do you think girls quit the service frequently?

Annie, however, was something of a Tartar,[19] and her sharp tongue had kept John Thomas at arm's length for many months. Perhaps, therefore, she liked him all the more: for he always came up smiling, with impudence. She watched him vanquish[20] one girl, then another. She could tell by the movement of his mouth and eyes, when he flirted with her in the morning, that he had been walking out with this lass, or the other, the night before. A fine cock-of-the-walk he was. She could sum him up pretty well.

In this subtle antagonism[21] they knew each other like old friends, they were as shrewd with one another almost as man and wife. But Annie had always kept him sufficiently at arm's length. Besides, she had a boy of her own.

The Statutes fair, however, came in November, at Bestwood. It happened that Annie had the Monday night off. It was a drizzling ugly night, yet she dressed herself up and went to the fairground. She was alone, but she expected soon to find a pal of some sort.

The roundabouts[22] were veering round and grinding out their music, the side-shows were making as much commotion as possible. In the coconut shies[23] there were no coconuts, but artificial wartime substitutes, which the lads declared

were fastened into the irons. There was a sad decline in brilliance and luxury. None the less, the ground was muddy as ever, there was the same crush, the press of faces lighted up by the flares and the electric lights, the same smell of naphtha[24] and a few fried potatoes, and of electricity.

Who should be the first to greet Miss Annie on the showground but John Thomas. He had a black overcoat buttoned up to his chin, and a tweed cap pulled down over his brows, his face between was ruddy and smiling and handy as ever. She knew so well the way his mouth moved.

She was very glad to have a "boy." To be at the Statutes without a fellow was no fun. Instantly, like the gallant he was, he took her on the Dragons, grim-toothed, roundabout switchbacks. It was not nearly so exciting as a tram-car actually. But, then, to be seated in a shaking, green dragon, uplifted above the sea of bubble faces, careering in a rickety fashion in the lower heavens, whilst John Thomas leaned over her, his cigarette in his mouth, was after all the right style. She was a plump, quick, alive little creature. So she was quite excited and happy.

John Thomas made her stay on for the next round. And therefore she could hardly for shame repulse[25] him when he put his arm round her and drew her a little nearer to him, in a very warm and cuddly manner. Besides, he was fairly discreet, he kept his movement as hidden as possible. She looked down, and saw that his red, clean hand was out of sight of the crowd. And they knew each other so well. So they warmed up to the fair.

After the dragons they went on the horses. John Thomas paid each time, so she could but

---

18. comely (kum′lē), *adj.* attractive.
19. **Tartar** (tär′tər), *n.* bad-tempered person, from *Tartar,* a fierce Mongolian warrior.
20. **vanquish** (vang′kwish), *v.* conquer.
21. **antagonism** (an tag′ə niz′əm), *n.* hostility.
22. **roundabout,** merry-go-round.
23. **coconut shy,** a carnival game in which one throws coconuts at a target.
24. **naphtha** (naf′thə), *n.* liquid fuel.
25. **repulse** (ri puls′), *v.* reject.

be complaisant.[26] He, of course, sat astride on the outer horse—named "Black Bess"—and she sat sideways towards him, on the inner horse—named "Wildfire." But of course John Thomas was not going to sit discreetly on "Black Bess," holding the brass bar. Round they spun and heaved, in the light. And round he swung on his wooden steed, flipping one leg across her mount, and perilously tipping up and down, across the space, half lying back, laughing at her. He was perfectly happy; she was afraid her hat was on one side, but she was excited.

He threw quoits[27] on a table, and won for her two large, pale blue hat-pins. And then, hearing the noise of the cinemas, announcing another performance, they climbed the boards and went in.

Of course, during these performances pitch darkness falls from time to time, when the machine goes wrong. Then there is a wild whooping, and a loud smacking of simulated kisses. In these moments John Thomas drew Annie towards him. After all, he had a wonderfully warm, cozy way of holding a girl with his arm, he seemed to make such a nice fit. And, after all, it was pleasant to be so held: so very comforting and cozy and nice. He leaned over her and she felt his breath on her hair; she knew he wanted to kiss her on the lips. And, after all, he was so warm and she fitted into him so softly. After all, she wanted him to touch her lips.

But the light sprang up; she also started electrically, and put her hat straight. He left his arm lying nonchalantly[28] behind her. Well, it was fun, it was exciting to be at the Statutes with John Thomas.

When the cinema was over they went for a walk across the dark, damp fields. He had all the arts of love-making. He was especially good at holding a girl, when he sat with her on a stile[29] in the black, drizzling darkness. He seemed to be holding her in space, against his own warmth and gratification. And his kisses were soft and slow and searching.

So Annie walked out with John Thomas, though she kept her own boy dangling in the distance. Some of the tram-girls chose to be huffy. But there, you must take things as you find them in this life.

There was no mistake about it, Annie liked John Thomas a good deal. She felt so rich and warm in herself whenever he was near. And John Thomas really liked Annie, more than usual. The soft, melting way in which she could flow into a fellow, as if she melted into his very bones, was something rare and good. He fully appreciated this.

But with a developing acquaintance there began a developing intimacy. Annie wanted to consider him a person, a man: she wanted to take an intelligent interest in him, and to have an intelligent response. She did not want a mere nocturnal[30] presence, which was what he was so far. And she prided herself that he could not leave her.

Here she made a mistake. John Thomas intended to remain a nocturnal presence; he had no idea of becoming an all-round individual to her. When she started to take an intelligent interest in him and his life and his character, he sheered off. He hated intelligent interest. And he knew that the only way to stop it was to avoid it. The possessive female was aroused in Annie. So he left her.

It is no use saying she was not surprised. She was at first startled, thrown out of her count. For she had been so *very* sure of holding him. For a while she was staggered, and everything became uncertain to her. Then she wept with fury, indignation, desolation, and misery. Then she had a spasm of despair. And then, when he came, still impudently, on to her car, still familiar, but letting her see by the movement of his head that he had gone away to somebody else for the time being, and was enjoying pastures new, then she determined to have her own back.

---

26. complaisant (kəm plā′snt), *adj.* gracious; courteous.
27. quoits (kwoits), *n. pl.* a game in which a ring is tossed over a peg.
28. nonchalantly (non′shə lənt lē), *adv.* indifferently; casually.
29. stile (stīl), *n.* step for getting over a fence or wall.
30. nocturnal (nok tėr′nl), *adj.* nighttime.

She had a very shrewd idea what girls John Thomas had taken out. She went to Nora Purdy. Nora was a tall, rather pale, but well-built girl, with beautiful yellow hair. She was rather secretive.

"Hey!" said Annie, accosting[31] her; then softly: "Who's John Thomas on with now?"

"I don't know," said Nora.

"Why, tha does," said Annie, ironically lapsing into dialect. "Tha knows as well as I do."

"Well, I do, then," said Nora. "It isn't me, so don't bother."

"It's Cissy Meakin, isn't it?"

"It is, for all I know."

"Hasn't he got a face on him!" said Annie. "I don't half like his cheek. I could knock him off the foot-board when he comes round at me."

"He'll get dropped on one of these days," said Nora.

"Ay, he will, when somebody makes up their mind to drop it on him. I should like to see him taken down a peg or two, shouldn't you?"

"I shouldn't mind," said Nora.

"You've got quite as much cause to as I have," said Annie. "But we'll drop on him one of these days, my girl. What? Don't you want to?"

"I don't mind," said Nora.

But as a matter of fact, Nora was much more vindictive[32] than Annie.

One by one Annie went the round of the old flames. It so happened that Cissy Meakin left the tramway service in quite a short time. Her mother made her leave. Then John Thomas was on the *qui vive.*[33] He cast his eyes over his old flock. And his eyes lighted on Annie. He thought she would be safe now. Besides, he liked her.

She arranged to walk home with him on Sunday night. It so happened that her car would be in the depot at half-past nine: the last car would come in at 10:15. So John Thomas was to wait for her there.

At the depot the girls had a little waiting-room of their own. It was quite rough, but cozy, with a fire and an oven and a mirror, and table and wooden chairs. The half-dozen girls who knew John Thomas only too well had arranged to take service this Sunday afternoon. So, as the cars began to come in, early, the girls dropped into the waiting-room. And instead of hurrying off home, they sat around the fire and had a cup of tea. Outside was the darkness and lawlessness of wartime.

John Thomas came on the car after Annie, at about a quarter to ten. He poked his head easily into the girls' waiting-room.

"Prayer-meeting?" he asked.

"Ay," said Laura Sharp. "Ladies only."

"That's me!" said John Thomas. It was one of his favorite exclamations.

"Shut the door, boy," said Muriel Baggaley.

"Oh, which side of me?" said John Thomas.

"Which tha likes," said Polly Birkin.

He had come in and closed the door behind him. The girls moved in their circle, to make a place for him near the fire. He took off his greatcoat and pushed back his hat.

"Who handles the teapot?" he said.

Nora Purdy silently poured him out a cup of tea.

"Want a bit o' my bread and drippin'?" said Muriel Baggaley to him.

"Ay, give us a bit."

And he began to eat his piece of bread.

"There's no place like home, girls," he said.

They all looked at him as he uttered this piece of impudence. He seemed to be sunning himself in the presence of so many damsels.

"Especially if you're not afraid to go home in the dark," said Laura Sharp.

"Me! By myself I am."

They sat till they heard the last tram come in. In a few minutes Emma Houselay entered.

"Come on, my old duck!" cried Polly Birkin.

"It *is* perishing," said Emma, holding her fingers to the fire.

---

31. **accost** (ə kôst′), *v.* approach and speak to.
32. vindictive (vin dik′tiv), *adj.* bearing a grudge; wanting revenge.
33. **on the** *qui vive* (kē vēv′), on the alert. *[French]*

"But—I'm afraid to, go home in, the dark," sang Laura Sharp, the tune having got into her mind.

"Who're you going with to-night, John Thomas?" asked Muriel Baggaley coolly.

"To-night?" said John Thomas. "Oh, I'm going home by myself to-night—all on my lonely-o."

"That's me!" said Nora Purdy, using his own ejaculation.[34]

The girls laughed shrilly.

"Me as well, Nora," said John Thomas.

"Don't know what you mean," said Laura.

"Yes, I'm toddling," said he, rising and reaching for his overcoat.

"Nay," said Polly, "We're all here waiting for you."

"We've got to be up in good time in the morning," he said, in the benevolent official manner.

They all laughed.

"Nay," said Muriel, "Don't leave us all lonely, John Thomas. Take one!"

"I'll take the lot, if you like," he responded gallantly.

"That you won't, either," said Muriel. "Two's company; seven's too much of a good thing."

"Nay—take one," said Laura. "Fair and square, all above board and say which."

"Ay," cried Annie, speaking for the first time. "Pick, John Thomas; let's hear thee."

"Nay," he said. "I'm going home quiet tonight. Feeling good, for once."

"Whereabouts?" said Annie. "Take a good 'un, then. But tha's got to take one of us!"

"Nay, how can I take one," he said, laughing uneasily. "I don't want to make enemies."

"You'd only make *one*," said Annie.

"The chosen *one*," added Laura.

"Oh, my! Who said girls!" exclaimed John Thomas, again turning, as if to escape. "Well—goodnight."

"Nay, you've got to make your pick," said Muriel. "Turn your face to the wall, and say which one touches you. Go on—we shall only just touch your back—one of us. Go on—turn your face to the wall, and don't look, and say which one touches you."

He was uneasy, mistrusting them. Yet he had not the courage to break away. They pushed him to a wall and stood him there with his face to it. Behind his back they all grimaced, tittering. He looked so comical. He looked around uneasily.

"Go on!" he cried.

"You're looking—you're looking!" they shouted.

He turned his head away. And suddenly, with a movement like a swift cat, Annie went forward and fetched him a box in the side of the head that sent his cap flying and himself staggering. He started round.

But at Annie's signal they all flew at him, slapping him, pinching him, pulling his hair, though more in fun than in spite or anger. He, however, saw red. His blue eyes flamed with strange fear as well as fury, and he butted through the girls to the door. It was locked. He wrenched at it. Roused, alert, the girls stood round and looked at him. He faced them, at bay. At that moment they were rather horrifying to him, as they stood in their short uniforms. He was distinctly afraid.

"Come on, John Thomas! Come on! Choose!" said Annie.

"What are you after? Open the door," he said.

"We shan't—not till you've chosen!" said Muriel.

"Chosen what?" he said.

"Chosen the one you're going to marry," she replied.

He hesitated a moment.

"Open the blasted door," he said, "and get back to your senses." He spoke with official authority.

"You've got to choose!" cried the girls.

---

34. **ejaculation** (i jak′yə lā′shən), *n.* exclamation.

"Come on!" cried Annie, looking him in the eye. "Come on! Come on!"

He went forward, rather vaguely. She had taken off her belt, and swinging it, she fetched him a sharp blow over the head with the buckle end. He sprang and seized her. But immediately the other girls rushed upon him, pulling and tearing and beating him. Their blood was now thoroughly up. He was their sport now. They were going to have their own back, out of him. Strange, wild creatures, they hung on him and rushed at him to bear him down. His tunic was torn right up the back. Nora had hold at the back of his collar, and was actually strangling him. Luckily the button burst. He struggled in a wild frenzy of fury and terror, almost mad terror. His tunic was simply torn off his back, his shirtsleeves were torn away, his arms were naked. The girls rushed at him, clenched their hands on him, and pulled at him: or they rushed at him and pushed him, butted him with all their might: or they struck him wild blows. He ducked and cringed and struck sideways. They became more intense.

🐾 EVALUATE: What effect does being together in a group seem to have on the girls' behavior?

At last he was down. They rushed on him, kneeling on him. He had neither breath nor strength to move. His face was bleeding with a long scratch, his brow was bruised.

Annie knelt on him, the other girls knelt and hung on to him. Their faces were flushed, their hair wild, their eyes were all glittering strangely. He lay at last quite still, with face averted,[35] as an animal lies when it is defeated and at the mercy of the captor. Sometimes his eye glanced back at the wild faces of the girls. His breast rose heavily, his wrists were torn.

"Now, then, my fellow!" gasped Annie at length. "Now then—now—"

At the sound of her terrifying, cold triumph, he suddenly started to struggle as an animal might, but the girls threw themselves upon him with unnatural strength and power, forcing him down.

"Yes—now, then!" gasped Annie at length.

And there was a dead silence, in which the thud of heart-beating was to be heard. It was a suspense of pure silence in every soul.

"Now you know where you are," said Annie.

The sight of his white, bare arm maddened the girls. He lay in a kind of trance of fear and antagonism. They felt themselves with supernatural strength.

Suddenly Polly started to laugh—to giggle wildly—helplessly—and Emma and Muriel joined in. But Annie and Nora and Laura remained the same, tense, watchful, with gleaming eyes. He winced away from these eyes.

"Yes," said Annie, in a curious low tone, secret and deadly. "Yes! You've got it now. You know what you've done, don't you? You know what you've done."

He made no sound nor sign, but lay with bright, averted eyes, and averted, bleeding face.

"You ought to be *killed*, that's what you ought," said Annie, tensely. "You ought to be *killed*." And there was a terrifying lust in her voice.

Polly was ceasing to laugh, and giving long-drawn Oh-h-hs and sighs as she came to herself.

"He's got to choose," she said vaguely.

"Oh, yes, he has," said Laura, with vindictive decision.

"Do you hear—do you hear?" said Annie. And with a sharp movement, that made him wince, she turned his face to her.

"Do you hear?" she repeated, shaking him.

But he was quite dumb. She fetched him a sharp slap on the face. He started, and his eyes widened. Then his face darkened with defiance after all.

"Do you hear?" she repeated.

He only looked at her with hostile eyes.

---

35. averted (ə vėr′tid), *adj.* turned away.

"Speak!" she said, putting her face devilishly near his.

"What?" he said, almost overcome.

"You've got to *choose!*" she cried, as if it were some terrible menace, and as if it hurt her that she could not exact more.

"What?" he said, in fear.

"Choose your girl, Coddy. You've got to choose her now. And you'll get your neck broken if you play any more of your tricks, my boy. You're settled now."

There was a pause. Again he averted his face. He was cunning in his overthrow. He did not give in to them really—no, not if they tore him to bits.

"All right, then," he said. "I choose Annie." His voice was strange and full of malice. Annie let go of him as if he had been a hot coal.

"He's chosen Annie!" said the girls in chorus.

"Me!" cried Annie. She was still kneeling, but away from him. He was still lying prostrate,[36] with averted face. The girls grouped uneasily around.

"Me!" repeated Annie, with a terrible bitter accent.

Then she got up, drawing away from him with strange disgust and bitterness.

"I wouldn't touch him," she said.

But her face quivered with a kind of agony, she seemed as if she would fall. The other girls turned aside. He remained lying on the floor, with his torn clothes and bleeding, averted face.

"Oh, if he's chosen—" said Polly.

"I don't want him—he can choose again," said Annie, with the same rather bitter hopelessness.

"Get up," said Polly, lifting his shoulder. "Get up."

He rose slowly, a strange, ragged, dazed creature. The girls eyed him from a distance, curiously, furtively,[37] dangerously.

"Who wants him?" cried Laura, roughly.

"Nobody," they answered, with contempt.

Yet each one of them waited for him to look at her, hoped he would look at her. All except Annie, and something was broken in her.

He, however, kept his face closed and averted from them all. There was a silence of the end. He picked up the torn pieces of his tunic, without knowing what to do with them. The girls stood about uneasily, flushed, panting, tidying their hair and their dress unconsciously, and watching. He looked at none of them. He espied his cap in a corner, and went and picked it up. He put it on his head, and one of the girls burst into a shrill, hysterical laugh at the sight he presented. He, however, took no heed, but went straight to where his overcoat hung on a peg. The girls moved away from contact with him as if he had been an electric wire. He put on his coat and buttoned it down. Then he rolled his tunic-rags into a bundle, and stood before the locked door, dumbly.

"Open the door, somebody," said Laura.

"Annie's got the key," said one.

Annie silently offered the key to the girls. Nora unlocked the door.

"Tit for tat, old man," she said. "Show yourself a man, and don't bear a grudge."

ut without a word or sign he had opened the door and gone, his face closed, his head dropped.

"That'll learn him," said Laura.

"Coddy!" said Nora.

"Shut up, for God's sake!" cried Annie fiercely, as if in torture.

"Well, I'm about ready to go, Polly. Look sharp!" said Muriel.

The girls were all anxious to be off. They were tidying themselves hurriedly, with mute, stupefied faces.

---

36. **prostrate** (pros′trāt), *adj.* overcome; helpless.
37. **furtively** (fèr′tiv lē), *adv.* secretly; slyly.

After Reading

Making Connections

Shaping Your
Response

1. For which character—Annie or John Thomas—do you feel the greater sympathy? Why?

Analyzing the Story

2. What indications are given that, in each other, John Thomas and Annie have met their match?

3. In what ways do you think the wartime **setting** influences the events of the story?

4. Do you think John Thomas deserves the harsh treatment he endures at the hands of his former girlfriends? Is he ever in real danger?

5. At the end of the story why do you think the girls behave so strangely after they have succeeded in humiliating John Thomas?

6. Why do you think Annie refuses John Thomas after he selects her?

7. Contrast the **mood** of the opening paragraphs with the mood of the closing episode.

Extending the Ideas

8. Do you think revenge is ever justified? Explain your answer.

9. 👆 How do the characters and events of the story reflect the changing status of women in twentieth-century life? What, in your opinion, do Annie, Nora Purdy, and the other girls have in common with militant feminist **groups** today?

Literary Focus: Idiom

A phrase or expression whose meaning cannot be understood from the ordinary, literal meanings of the words is called an **idiom.** Look back at the following idioms in Lawrence's story and translate what you think each idiom means. Add other idioms that you find in the story.

- "a fine cock-of-the-walk" (page 760)
- "thrown out of her count" (page 761)
- "enjoying pastures new" (page 761)
- "to have her own back" (page 761)
- "taken down a peg or two" (page 762)
- "old flames" (page 762)
- "fair and square, all above board" (page 763)
- "he . . . saw red" (page 763)
- "their blood was . . . up" (page 764)

Vocabulary Study

Select the word that best completes each sentence. Use your Glossary, if necessary.

1. Riding on the tramway system could be dangerous because there were many dangerous curves and (peremptory, precipitous) hills.

2. At first, Annie feels (averted, complaisant) at the thought of having a "boy."

3. Annie's (vindictive, nocturnal) nature is evident in her plan for revenge on John Thomas.

4. For a time John Thomas is so defeated by the girls' attack that he can do nothing but lie (prostrate, sordid) on the ground.

5. After they have time to think about their savage attack on John Thomas, several of the girls may be (abashed, comely) by their actions.

Expressing Your Ideas

Writing Choices

Writer's Notebook Update Look back at the situation that made you want to get revenge. Write a few sentences about how you felt either about taking revenge or about not being able to strike back.

What Makes Annie Tick Write an **expository essay** explaining what you think is Annie's strongest motive—love, revenge, self-interest, hate, or a combination of these. Defend your explanation with quotations from the story.

The Verb's the Word D. H. Lawrence uses strong verbs in portraying action. Write several **descriptive paragraphs** in which you portray a scene of intense action, such as a sporting event, a rock concert, a street brawl. First describe the setting of the action. Then describe the event itself, using strong, active verbs.

Other Options

The Morning After Prepare a **dramatic monologue** that Annie might have with herself or that John Thomas might have with himself the morning after the attack. What would be the emotional state of this character? Would Annie be embarrassed? frightened? ashamed? Would John Thomas be angry? humbled? revengeful? In your monologue, review the events of the previous night and think about the future. How will the past evening's events affect the relationship between Annie and John Thomas?

Mob Psychology The scene in which the girls take revenge on John Thomas shows how a **group** can get out of control and become a mob. Research an historical situation—for example, the Haymarket Riot of 1886 or the disorder at the Democratic Convention in Chicago in 1968—in which a group became a mob and prepare an **oral report**. Include the events leading up to the action, what seemed to trigger it, and what the final outcome was.

The Hollow Men

by T. S. Eliot

T. S. Eliot
1888–1965

Born in St. Louis, Missouri, and educated at Harvard, Thomas Stearns Eliot attended Oxford and settled in London in 1914, becoming a naturalized British subject in 1917. Beginning with "The Love Song of J. Alfred Prufrock," Eliot's works attracted considerable critical attention. From *The Waste Land* (1922), in which he expresses the despair of life without faith, to *Ash Wednesday* (1930), in which he professes an acquired Christianity, Eliot's work reflects disillusionment with contemporary values and hunger for spiritual rebirth. His collection *Old Possum's Book of Practical Cats* (1939) reached a wide audience in 1981 through the success of Andrew Lloyd Webber's musical *Cats.* Eliot was awarded the Nobel Prize in 1948.

Building Background

Defining the "Lost Generation" T. S. Eliot called his eight years at Smith Academy in St. Louis the most important of his education. There he studied classical and modern languages, classical literature and history, English and American history. Eliot turned to this classical education again and again in his roles as critic, editor, publisher, and, most importantly, poet. Many of his themes and images are references to classical works. Eliot's poetry often presents difficulties to readers who frequently must consult footnotes in order to grasp his many **metaphors, symbols,** and **allusions** to Shakespeare and other writers. His dominant influence was Dante's *Divine Comedy,* which provided a metaphor for the hell that Eliot saw in the lives of the "lost generation" following World War I. He viewed the 1920s as a time in which traditional beliefs and values were abandoned in the search for immediate pleasure and personal enjoyment.

Literary Focus

Free Verse The form known as **free verse** differs from conventional verse forms because it is free from a fixed pattern of rhythm and rhyme. Yet free verse may be highly rhythmic and may utilize a wide variety of sound devices and poetic techniques. As you read "The Hollow Men," look for the devices that indicate you are reading poetry, not prose.

Writer's Notebook

Structured Verse Choose one of the following subjects—or a subject of your own choice—and write an eight-line poem that has a definite rhyme and rhythmic pattern.

- my hero
- a pitiful sight
- holiday memories
- a painful experience
- a beautiful day

The Hollow Men

T. S. Eliot

Mistah Kurtz—he dead.[1]
A penny for the Old Guy[2]

1

We are the hollow men
We are the stuffed men
Leaning together
Headpiece filled with straw. Alas!
5 Our dried voices, when
We whisper together
Are quiet and meaningless
As wind in dry grass
Or rats' feet over broken glass
10 In our dry cellar

Shape without form, shade without color,
Paralyzed force, gesture without motion;

Those who have crossed
With direct eyes,[3] to death's other
      Kingdom[4]
15 Remember us—if at all—not as lost
Violent souls, but only
As the hollow men
The stuffed men.

2

Eyes[5] I dare not meet in dreams
20 In death's dream kingdom
These do not appear:
There, the eyes are
Sunlight on a broken column
There, is a tree swinging
25 And voices are
In the wind's singing
More distant and more solemn
Than a fading star.

Let me be no nearer
30 In death's dream kingdom
Let me also wear
Such deliberate disguises
Rat's coat, crowskin, crossed staves
In a field[6]
35 Behaving as the wind behaves
No nearer—

Not that final meeting
In the twilight kingdom

---

1. **Mistah Kurtz—he dead.** In Joseph Conrad's novella *Heart of Darkness,* Kurtz, a European trader, goes into "the heart of darkness"—the central African jungle. He brings with him European standards of conduct but no moral or spiritual strength, and he soon turns into a barbarian. However, he is not paralyzed, as Eliot's "hollow men" are; he commits acts of overwhelming evil. He is not blind as they are, but at his death glimpses the nature of his actions when he exclaims, "The horror! The horror!" Kurtz is thus one of the "lost / Violent souls" mentioned in lines 15–16.
2. **A penny . . . Guy,** traditional cry of English children begging money for fireworks to celebrate Guy Fawkes Day, November 5. This commemorates the prevention of the Gunpowder Plot of 1605 in which Guy Fawkes and other conspirators planned to blow up both Houses of Parliament. On this day straw-stuffed images of Fawkes called *guys* are burned.
3. **those . . . direct eyes,** those who have represented something positive (direct), either for good or evil.
4. **death's other Kingdom,** the afterlife; eternity.
5. **eyes,** the eyes of those in the afterworld who had confident faith; those who represent positive spiritual force as opposed to the spiritual stagnation or paralysis of the "hollow men."
6. **rat's coat . . . field,** a scarecrow decorated with dead rats and crows.

3

This is the dead land
40 This is cactus land
Here the stone images
Are raised, here they receive
The supplications[7] of a dead man's hand
Under the twinkle of a fading star.
45 Is it like this
In death's other kingdom
Waking alone
At the hour when we are
Trembling with tenderness
50 Lips that would kiss
Form prayers to broken stone.

4

The eyes are not here
There are no eyes here
In this valley of dying stars
55 In this hollow valley
This broken jaw of our lost kingdoms

In this last of meeting places
We grope[8] together
And avoid speech
60 Gathered on this beach of the tumid[9] river

Sightless, unless
The eyes reappear
As the perpetual star
Multifoliate rose[10]
65 Of death's twilight kingdom
The hope only
Of empty men.

5

Here we go round the prickly pear
Prickly pear prickly pear
70 *Here we go round the prickly pear*
At five o'clock in the morning.[11]

Between the idea
And the reality
Between the motion
75 And the act
Falls the Shadow
        For Thine is the Kingdom[12]

Between the conception
And the creation
80 Between the emotion
And the response
Falls the Shadow
        Life is very long

Between the desire
85 And the spasm
Between the potency
And the existence
Between the essence
And the descent
90 Falls the Shadow
        For Thine is the Kingdom

For Thine is
Life is
For Thine is the
95 *This is the way the world ends*
This is the way the world ends
This is the way the world ends
Not with a bang but a whimper.

---

7. **supplication** (sup′lə kā′shən), *n.* humble prayer.
8. grope (grōp), *v.* search blindly.
9. **tumid** (tü′mid), *adj.* swollen.
10. **Multifoliate rose,** in Dante's *Divine Comedy* a symbol of Paradise, in which the saints are the many petals of the rose.
11. **Here we go . . . morning,** a parody of the children's rhyme "Here we go round the mulberry bush."
12. **For Thine . . . Kingdom,** a phrase from the Lord's Prayer (Matthew 6:9–13).

After Reading

Making Connections

Shaping Your Response

1. What about Eliot's poem presented the most difficulty for you?

Analyzing the Poem

2. What conclusion can you draw from the many comparisons of the hollow men to scarecrows?

3. In section 1, what do you see as the difference between those who have crossed to eternity "With direct eyes" and "the hollow men"?

4. What indication is there in section 2 that the speaker, like the other hollow men, has given up the struggle to give new meaning to his life?

5. In sections 3 and 4, what elements of the **setting** do you think reflect the emotional and spiritual emptiness of the hollow men?

6. What effect do you think the "Shadow" has on such human actions as thinking, creating, and feeling?

7. What do you think the fragments of the Lord's Prayer and the **parody** of "Here we go round the mulberry bush" suggest about the spiritual condition of the hollow men?

8. How are the hollow men shown to be unlike Mistah Kurtz and the Old Guy?

9. Why do you think the speaker suggests that the world will end "Not with a bang but a whimper"?

Extending the Ideas

10. Eliot portrayed people of the post-World War I era as "hollow men." Do you think that Eliot, if he were writing today, would hold a similar view of society or of any **group** of people in today's society?

Literary Focus: Free Verse

Free verse contains no standard rhyme and no fixed rhythmic pattern, but it does contain other sound devices, as well as figurative language. Give an example of each of the following poetic devices that contribute to the poetic quality of this verse.

- alliteration
- consonance
- simile
- imagery
- parallel structure

Vocabulary Study

examine
explore
inspect
investigate
probe
rummage
seek

The verb *grope* means "to search blindly and uncertainly." Each of the listed words also means "to search," but each carries a slightly different **connotation.** Choose five of these words and use each in a sentence that shows that you understand the subtle difference in meaning. Use a dictionary if you need help.

Expressing Your Ideas

Writing Choices

Writer's Notebook Update Using the same subject you chose for your rhyming poem, write an eight-line poem in free verse. Which poem do you like better? Why?

A Sense of Loss A recurrent theme in Eliot's poetry is the sense of loss; in the words of one critic, "the lost vision, the lost purpose, the lost meaning, the lost sense of fellowship, the lost sense of self." Do you see any similar sense of loss, any similar hollowness in today's society? In an **informal essay** discuss the particular sense of loss you see. Try to account for the cause and try to suggest a resolution to that loss.

Better Violent Than Hollow? The French poet Charles Baudelaire, a favorite author of Eliot's, wrote: "So far as we are human, what we do must be either evil or good; . . . and it is better, in a paradoxical way, to do evil than to do nothing: at least we exist." Do you agree with Baudelaire and Eliot that it is better to be evil than to be "hollow men"? Write your response in the form of a **letter** to Eliot in which you reinforce your position with examples from modern day society.

Other Options

"Our Dried Voices . . ." T. S. Eliot's poems lend themselves especially well to reading aloud. As a group, prepare a **choral reading** of "The Hollow Men." Start by determining which lines should be read by solo voices and which by combined voices or the entire chorus. Work to capture the multiple rhythms of the poem and vary tempos and vocal tones to match the shifting moods. After rehearsal, make a tape recording to play for other classes.

Thoroughly Modernist After World War I, many poets moved away from traditional forms and techniques and developed new forms of poetry. Likewise, painters and composers experimented with techniques that led some critics to say, "That's not art" or "That's not music." Select one of these *modernist* artists like Pablo Picasso, Joan Miro, or Paul Klee, or composers like Igor Stravinsky, Arnold Schoenberg, or Bela Bartok. Prepare an **illustrated oral report** for your class in which you show how this artist or composer is representative of the modernist movement.

War and Aftermath

The Wasteland

History Connection

With the use of modern weapons on a mammoth scale, World War I achieved levels of horror and destructiveness unparalled in human history. The following passages explore two aspects of the frightful man-made wasteland of the Western Front.

At 5:00 on the afternoon of April 22, 1915, shelling at Langemarck near the Belgian village of Ypres had stopped. The front was quiet.

The World War I Allied soldiers were tired after the daylong shelling bout with the Germans, and they lay heavily in their trenches during the respite.

Suddenly the Germans began another deafening round of shelling from their position in the south. Seconds later the Allied soldiers noticed two greenish yellow clouds a few hundred yards in front of them. Hanging low on the horizon, the clouds were rapidly approaching them from the German line, and within one minute the clouds had reached the first Allied troops. The men quickly fell into a state of confusion; they were completely unprepared and unprotected for what was to be a devastating poison gas attack.

The gas instantly caused severe burning in their throats and lungs. The men clutched at their chests, coughed, and gasped for breath. Attempts to shield themselves from the gas were largely futile. Many tried to burrow their noses and mouths, or to cover them with cloth, but the moist, dense poison penetrated everything. Others tried to outrun the clouds, inevitably receiving lethal doses as running made them inhale even more deeply. Most fell, choking, their panic turning to agony.

The gas causing these profound, immediate effects upon the Allied troops was chlorine. The Germans, having waited for the appropriate change in wind direction, had released 160 tons of liquid chlorine from nearly 6,000 pressurized cylinders. On release the chlorine formed a thick, odorous gas cloud. Because of its form, it was impossible to control the direction of the weapon. The Germans had waited for days to release the chlorine, but at 5:00 on April 22, the breeze began to blow toward the Allied lines.

Chlorine, a poison, begins by irritating the eyes, nose, and throat. It quickly scorches the lining of the windpipe and the lungs, resulting in severe—often fatal—coughing bouts. In an extreme dose, such as was used that horrific day at Ypres, chlorine causes massive amounts of a yellowish fluid to develop in the lungs. Many of the men who died during or soon after the April 22 attack actually choked to death from the heavy liquid in their chests and throats.

After the Allied front had fallen silent, the Germans, wearing crude gas masks, advanced to survey the effects of the day's battle and of their new weapon. Even they were amazed at what they found. In all, more than 5,000 had died as a result of the poisonings. Over 10,000 were injured. Four miles of the Allied line had collapsed, and the gap was several miles deep. Yet the Germans, lacking sufficient reserves in that sector, were unable to capitalize on the Allies' fallen defenses. Indeed, they were not prepared for such a significant victory with their fledgling weapon, or they might have marched through to the English Channel and soon attempted the capture of the French city of Calais. Had that occurred, the course of World War I might have been drastically altered.

THE HORROR AT YPRES

by L. B. Taylor, Jr. and C. L. Taylor

GUIDING THEMSELVES BY HOLDING ONTO THE MAN IN FRONT OF THEM, SOLDIERS BLINDED BY POISON GAS WAIT FOR TREATMENT IN APRIL 1918.

The Germans did, however, follow up with a second chlorine attack two days later. Again at Ypres, they were battling Canadian regiments called in to seal the gap caused by the initial gas attack. The Canadians, still without sufficient protection against the chlorine, held fabric soaked with urine to their faces in an attempt to escape the effects of the gas. The ensuing panic was similar to that of two days before, and over 5,000 Allied men died from the combination artillery/gas attack. Still, the Germans lacked the aggressiveness to follow up on their attack, allowing the Canadian soldiers eventually to force them to retreat. These initial German poison gas attacks, however, marked the onset of modern chemical warfare—a method that was to play a significant and devastating role during the rest of World War I.

THE BONEYARD

by Paul Fussell

Writing his sister in August, 1916, one soldier marvels at the fantastic holes and ditches which scar the whole landscape and wonders, "How ever will they get it smoothed out again is more than I can imagine." The work of smoothing it out continues to this day. At first, some thought restoration of the area impossible and advised that it simply be abandoned. In 1919 the battlefields were still much as 1918 had left them, but a tourist could visit them, assisted by a series of *Illustrated Michelin Guides to the Battlefields* (1914-1918) written in English and printed in England. Gradually the road network was re-established; craters and trenches were filled in; duds were collected and exploded; nasty things were collected and buried; and villagers began returning and rebuilding, often exactly reproducing a leveled town on its original site.

Today the Somme[1] is a peaceful but sullen place, unforgetting and unforgiving. The people, who work largely at raising vegetables and grains, are "correct" but not friendly. To wander now over the fields destined to extrude their rusty metal fragments for centuries is to appreciate in the most intimate way the permanent rever-berations of July 1916. When the air is damp you can smell rusted iron everywhere, even though you see only wheat and barley. The farmers work the fields without joy. They collect the duds, shell-casings, fuses, and shards of old barbed wire as the plow unearths them and stack them in the corners of their fields. Some of the old barbed wire, both British and German, is used for fencing. Many of the shell craters are still there, though smoothed out and grown over. The mine craters are too deep to be filled and remain much as they were. When the sun is low in the afternoon, on the gradual slopes of the low hills you see the traces of the zig-zag of trenches. Many farmhouses have out in back one of the little British wooden huts that used to house soldiers well behind the lines; they make handy toolsheds. Lurking in every spot of undergrowth just off the beaten track are eloquent little things: rusted buckles, rounds of corroded small-arms ammunition, metal tabs from ammunition boxes, bits of Bully tin[2], buttons.

Albert[3] today is one of the saddest places in France. It has all been restored to its original ugliness. The red-brick Basilica is as it was before the war, with the gilded virgin back up on top of the tower, quite erect. But despite an appearance of adequacy, everything human in Albert seems to have been permanently defeated. The inhabitants are dour. Everywhere there

---

1. **Somme** (sôm), area in northern France that was the scene of a series of massive battles in late 1916.
2. **Bully tin**, container for canned meat used as rations.
3. **Albert**, town in northern France almost completely destroyed by shelling in 1918.

is an air of bitterness about being passed over by the modernity, sophistication, and affluence of modern France. Everywhere one senses a quiet fury at being condemned to live in this boneyard and backwater, where even the crops contend with soil once ruined by gas.

And a boneyard it is. Every week bones come to light. Depending on one's mood one either quietly buries them again, or flings them into the nearby brush, or saves them to turn over to the employees of the Commonwealth (formerly "Imperial") War Graves Commission, which supervises the 2,500 British military cemeteries from offices in the main cities. The cemeteries are both pretty and bizarre, fertile with roses, projecting an almost unendurably ironic peacefulness. They memorialize not just the men buried in them, but the talents for weighty public rhetoric of Rudyard Kipling. He was called on to devise almost all the verbal formulas employed by the Imperial War Graves Commission, from "Their Name Liveth For Evermore," carved on the large "Stone of Remembrance" in each cemetery, to the words incised on headstones over the bodies of the unidentified: "A Soldier of the Great War/Known unto God." The unforgettable, infinitely pathetic inscriptions are not Kipling's but those which the families of the dead were allowed—after long debate within the Commission about "uniformity"—to place on their stones. In addition to the still hopeful ones about dawn and fleeing shadows we find some which are more "modern," that is, more personal, particular, and hopeless:

> *Our dear Ted.*
> *He died for us.*
>
> *. . .*
>
> *Our Dick*
>
> *. . .*
>
> *If love could have*
> *saved him*
> *he would*
> *not have died.*

And some read as if refusing to play the game of memorial language at all:

> *A sorrow too deep*
> *for words.*

The notorious Butte of Warlencourt, a fifty-foot knoll on the road to Bapaume from which the Germans strenuously held the British advance in the autumn and winter of 1916, is overgrown and silent. Crops grow right to its foot, dipping here and there to betray the persistent shapes of shell holes and mine craters. Tens of thousands of men simply disappeared here. The sticky Somme mud makes large unwieldy spheres of your shoes as you climb to the top through the thick undergrowth. At the top you can picnic, if you have the heart for it, and inspect the large weathered wooden cross erected by the Germans at the summit and apparently renewed at the end of the Second World War. On it is carved the word *Friede*.[4]

4. **Friede** (frē′də), peace. *[German]*

IN HIS PAINTING *Oppy Wood* (1917), BRITISH ARTIST JOHN NASH CAPTURES THE FRIGHTFUL DEVASTATION OF THE WESTERN FRONT IN WORLD WAR I.

Responding

1. After World War I, an attempt was made to outlaw chemical weapons. Do you think to try to legislate "rules of warfare" makes sense? Why or why not?

2. Do you think battlefields should be turned into memorials? Why or why not?

Language History

The Language of Heroism

 These laid the world away; poured out the red
Sweet wine of youth; gave up the years to be
Of work and joy . . . .
Rupert Brooke, "The Dead" (1914)

In his book *The Great War and Modern Memory,* literary historian Paul Fussell observes that one of the casualties of World War I was the system of "high" diction relating to warfare to which several generations of readers had become accustomed. "The tutors in this special diction had been the boys' books of George Alfred Henty; the male romances of Rider Haggard; the poems of Robert Bridges; and especially the Arthurian poems of Tennyson and the pseudo-medieval romances of William Morris." As examples of this "high" diction, Fussell offers a series of equivalents:

friend / *comrade*
horse / *steed* or *charger*
enemy / *foe* or *host*
danger / *peril*
conquer / *vanquish*
earnestly brave / *gallant*
cheerfully brave / *plucky*
stolidly brave / *staunch*
front / *field*
dead / *the fallen*

obedient soldiers / *the brave*
warfare / *strife*
die / *perish*
draft notice / *the summons*
enlist / *join the colors*
death / *fate*
sky / *heavens*
contemptible / *base*
legs and arms of young men / *limbs*
bodies / *ashes* or *dust*

How different from the elevated diction of Rupert Brooke's "red / Sweet wine of youth" was Wilfred Owen's forthright "the blood / Come gargling from the froth-corrupted lungs, / Obscene as cancer . . . ." Rejecting high-sounding abstractions that no longer held any meaning for them, Owen and other soldier poets adopted a colloquial, concrete, realistic style, bitter and deeply ironic in tone. It was a transformation that would have a profound effect on the language used by the common people for the rest of the century.

Writing Workshop

Selling an Idea

Assignment You have read about war and its aftermath from different perspectives. Now the producer of a TV series about World War I titled *Homefront / Battlefront* has asked you and a partner to submit a proposal for an hour-long episode. See the Writer's Blueprint for details.

WRITER'S BLUEPRINT

Product   A proposal for an episode of a TV series

Purpose   To sell an idea

Audience   A TV producer

Specs   As the creator of a persuasive proposal, you and your partner should:

❏ Develop an intriguing plot, appealing main characters, and vivid settings, using the literature in this part of the unit for inspiration.

❏ Begin your proposal by briefly summarizing the plot.

❏ Describe the main characters and settings in your episode and provide a scene-by-scene outline of the plot. Make sure that at least one scene takes place on each front and that the characters on the two fronts are connected in some significant way.

❏ Present two of the scenes—one set on each front—in teleplay form.

❏ End by urging the producer to accept your proposal by giving persuasive reasons why. Address your audience in a tone enthusiastic and assured but not overly informal: one professional to another.

❏ Follow the rules of grammar, usage, spelling, and mechanics. Use a consistent teleplay format for your scenes.

Review the literature to get ideas for your episode. For example, what ideas for plot or setting does the Literary Source suggest? Record the details you find in a chart like this.

LITERARY SOURCE
"In the early morning we walked to the station beneath a dazzling sun, but the platform from which his train went out was dark and very cold. In the railway carriage we sat hand in hand until the whistle blew."
from *Testament of Youth* by Vera Brittain

Main Characters	Setting	Plot
boy lying about his age to join army ("Disabled")	recruiting office	wants to impress his girlfriend/romanticizes going to war
Vera Brittain and Roland *(Testament of Youth)*	train station	saying goodbye as he goes off to war

Brainstorm ideas for plots, characters, and settings. Refer to your literature review chart for inspiration. Characters and settings could be directly from the literature, completely new, or a combination. After you've finished, decide with your partner which ideas to use in your episode.

Outline the plot of your episode with your partner. You might draw a time line for the entire episode and fill it in with notes about each scene. Refer to your character and setting notes as you plan. Make sure that you set some scenes on the homefront and some on the battlefront.

OR . . .
Instead of outlining the plot, create a storyboard for each scene. Sketch a key moment in the scene and add notes about narration, dialogue, and stage directions.

Try a quickwrite. With your partner, review your plot outline and choose two scenes—one from the homefront and one from the battlefront—to develop in detail. Discuss the action in each scene. Then, take one scene each and write for five minutes about it. Consider how your scene advances the plot. What has happened before this scene? What will happen after? How is the scene linked to the one your partner is writing? How do the characters know each other?

OR . . .
Instead of quickwriting, you and your partner could improvise the two scenes, acting them out loud together. After each scene, quickly jot down notes about the parts that worked well.

List persuasive reasons. With your partner, brainstorm a list of reasons why a producer should accept your proposal. Consider all the strengths of the episode you've planned. Find reasons that persuasively answer the questions on the next page.

- Why will viewers want to watch your episode instead of, say, a situation comedy or a crime drama?

- What is appealing about the characters? What is it about them that viewers will identify with?

- What basic human emotions will your episode appeal to, and how?

- What will it show viewers about the nature of war that they may not have realized before?

- What makes it different from other dramas they've seen about war?

Review your list and circle the three strongest reasons. Try to sell your proposal by emphasizing these points.

Plan your proposal, using your prewriting materials for inspiration. You might use a plan like this one, which takes into account the points in the Writer's Blueprint.

- Cover page (series title, episode title, writer's names)

- Brief plot summary

- Major issues plot will address

- Characters

- Settings

- Scene-by-scene plot outline

- Homefront scene (setting, characters, action)

- Battlefront scene (setting, characters, action)

- Persuasive reasons

 STEP **2** DRAFTING

Before you write, review the Writer's Blueprint and plan. Then decide how to divide the drafting responsibilities with your partner.

As you draft, keep in mind that the two scenes you've chosen will be written as teleplays. On the next page are some guidelines and a model to help you.

Guidelines for Teleplay Format

- Names of characters and technical directions, such as camera moves and sound effects, are in SMALL CAPITAL LETTERS.

- Other stage directions are in *italic type,* which you can create on a computer. If you're writing by hand, you can underline the stage directions to set them off from the dialogue. (Stage directions within dialogue passages should also be enclosed in parentheses.)

INTERIOR. THE PARLOR. CAMERA FOLLOWS MOM AS SHE ENTERS AND CROSSES TO UNCLE ALBERT.

MOM *(running across the room waving a letter in her hand).* Albert, it's here. Thomas has written. Oh, I've been waiting for an eternity!

UNCLE ALBERT *(lying on a cot, buried under wool blankets and an intricate homemade quilt).* Oh, yes, that's wonderful, Please read it to me, Anna.

CLOSEUP ON UNCLE ALBERT, WHO MAKES A WEAK ATTEMPT TO SIT UP IN BED, THEN LIES BACK WITH A SIGH.

STUDENT MODEL

STEP 3 REVISING

Ask another pair of writers for comments on your draft before you revise it. Use this checklist as a guide.

✔ Have we described the main characters, settings, and plot of our episode?

✔ Have we written two scenes, one set at the homefront and one at the battlefront?

✔ Have we given three persuasive reasons why our proposal should be accepted?

✔ Have we addressed our audience, the producer, in an appropriate tone?

Revising Strategy

Using an Appropriate Tone

Since you're communicating with another professional, you'll want to establish a confident, businesslike tone. You can accomplish this through your choice of words, details, and sentence structure. What changes in the revised model that follows make it more appropriate than the first version?

FIRST DRAFT

Check out this idea. It's all about a family's money problems while the dad's away at war. We could show how Mom's knocking herself out on the homefront to keep the family going while Dad's knocking himself out to stay alive on the battlefront. Get the contrast? We'd show how bummed he is that he can't help his family and how bummed she is that she can't help him.

REVISED

Our episode contrasts the problems one family faces on the homefront and battlefront. On both fronts they struggle to survive. On the homefront, the mother struggles to provide for her family, while on the battlefront, the father struggles just to survive each day. Our episode focuses on the helpless anguish that the father and mother feel because they can't help one another.

 STEP **4** EDITING

Ask another pair of writers to review your revised draft before you edit. When you edit, watch for errors in grammar, usage, spelling, and mechanics. Pay special attention to errors in using the correct form for a teleplay.

Editing Strategy

Using a Consistent Teleplay Format

Check your scenes for consistency when you edit. Notice how the writer of the student model made changes to clear up confusion between screen directions and dialogue.

○   MOM (with great relief). Teddy! Where have you been? I've

       been worried sick!

○   TEDDY. I was delivering groceries and I lost track of the

       time. (Holding out a coin.) But look! (Brightening.) Look

○   how much I earned!

STEP 5 PRESENTING

- Make a videotape or audiotape of your scenes, using classmates as cast members.

- With your partner, do a live presentation of your proposal. Have classmates comment on how persuasive they find it.

COMPUTER TIP
If your school has a computer with multimedia capabilities, you could create a short presentation that includes the text of your screenplay and a video of parts of your scenes, using student actors.

STEP 6 LOOKING BACK

Self-evaluate. Look back at the Writer's Blueprint and give your paper a score on each point, from 6 (superior) to 1 (inadequate).

Reflect. Write your responses to these questions.

✔ Which part did you enjoy writing more: the teleplay or the persuasive appeal to the producer? Why?

✔ What did you learn about the changes that war brings in the daily lives of people involved on the homefront and battlefront?

For Your Working Portfolio Add your proposal and reflection responses to your working portfolio.

Beyond Print

Looking at Television News

One of the reasons World War I made people change their minds about the glory of war is that, before the war, people in general had no way to experience—or even imagine—its horrors. In World War I the technology made news impossibly slow; people in the United States were even more removed from the events. By the time of World War II, radio was able to carry live accounts of many of the most important moments, and movie newsreels could give people an unprecedented visual impression of events.

The most dramatic change in war coverage came with Vietnam. Now the technology allowed nightly battlefield coverage on the national news programs. This unending stream of death and destruction brought in living color to the homes of the United States helped make Vietnam the

This ABC News photo shows a film crew at work in the combat area of Vietnam. ▼

most unpopular war in history. Wars can no longer be fought without considering the power of the media. The ability to understand television news is arguably the most important media knowledge you can develop. Here are some criteria to consider.

The Anchor An anchorperson introduces and concludes a newscast and reads much of the news. Anchors are very carefully chosen because they must be able to relay bad news yet still give a sense of confidence; they must appear intelligent without being threateningly intelligent; they must be good-looking without being removed from everyday people.

Production Features Although news is not considered entertainment, it is still produced like a show. Notice how the anchor is dressed, and what impression the set conveys. Notice how news boxes are used to focus attention on images and how graphics help understanding. Notice how music is used to set a tone.

The Story Lineup The stories at the beginning are the most important of the day, while those at the end are "softer." Notice how anchors introduce the stories and how later stories are "teased" through promos at the beginning of the newscast.

Editing All television requires editing. This means that speeches are cut, shots are carefully selected and spliced together, and reporters' words are thoughtfully chosen. Only CSPAN shows uninterrupted feed. Notice how the news is put together, as crafted as a movie.

Commercials News programs need to attract advertising just as other shows do, and newspeople have to consider their audience. Notice the type of ads that are shown on a news program and think about what they tell you about the business side of the news.

Activity Options

1. Work with a partner to tape-record at least two early evening national news programs. Watch them both and compare them in terms of the above criteria.

2. Imagine that you are the producer of a network newscast. The United States is about to send troops to another country to help the government protect itself from rebels. Develop a plan to cover this action, including how many reporters you will send, rules for them to follow, how you will report on the enemy, which U. S. politicians to interview, and what you will or won't show on your news program.

HISTORICAL OVERVIEW

In 1900 the pioneering psychologist Sigmund Freud asserted, "The interpretation of dreams is the royal road to a knowledge of the unconscious activities of the mind." Though the focus of Freud's work was clinical, his interest in dreams was shared by many modern artists and writers and reflected the new creative emphasis on the less rational sides of the human personality. In their search for identity, writers and artists looked again—as the Romantics had—to dreams and feelings for their deepest truths. An example of this is *Landscape from a Dream,* painted in 1936 by artist Paul Nash. Influenced by the Surrealists, Nash was trying to wed their emphasis on dream symbolism with the English Romantic tradition of the quest for truth in nature. The face mirrored in the sphere in the foreground is that of Sigmund Freud.

Mirror

# of Dreams

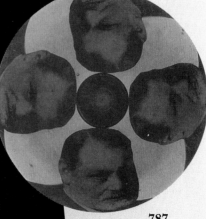

Part Three

The Search for Identity

Who am I? Through much of history, that question for most people was answered by others—family, community, church, monarch. You didn't think to question your identity because you were told who you were and what your duties were. The freedom and the ability to ask that question, to search for your identity, may be seen by some as a blessing, by others as a curse.

Multicultural Connection **Individuality** may arise either from accepting or rejecting different cultural norms or group standards. It can sometimes be a fragile thing, paradoxically needing confirmation by various groups in order to flourish.

Before Reading

Eveline

by James Joyce

James Joyce
1881–1941

In form and content, most of James Joyce's work was controversial, and during his lifetime some of his works were banned, burned, and confiscated. Born in Dublin, the eldest of ten children, Joyce attended a Jesuit boarding school until increasing family poverty forced him to leave. He later attended University College in Dublin. He and Nora Barnacle then lived together in various places— Italy, Switzerland, and, after World War I, in France. His semi-autobiographical work, *A Portrait of the Artist as a Young Man* appeared in 1916. His novels *Ulysses* (1922) and *Finnegans Wake* (1940) greatly influenced the development of the stream-of-consciousness technique, the re-creation of a character's flow of thought.

Building Background

The Center of Paralysis Joyce said that his purpose in writing the short stories collected in *Dubliners* (1914), which includes "Eveline," was to produce "a chapter of the moral history of my country, and I chose Dublin for the scenes because the city seemed to me the center of paralysis." The style of *Dubliners* marks a sharp break with nineteenth-century fiction. Joyce locates the center of the action in the minds of the characters, and plot is not as important as psychological revelation. He also said that he wanted to give "the Irish people . . . one good look at themselves in my nicely polished looking glass."

Literary Focus

Epiphany An **epiphany** (i pifʹə nē) is a moment of enlightenment in which the underlying truth, essential nature, or meaning of something is suddenly made clear. In a mystery story, for example, an epiphany occurs when the detective discovers the identity of a murderer. In other types of stories an epiphany may occur when a character achieves insight into the reasons for his or her feelings or becomes aware of another character's motivations. In a short work, an epiphany may occur at the moment of climax or turning point in the plot. The climax does not always involve an epiphany, however. As you read "Eveline," look for the epiphany.

Writer's Notebook

Setting a Mood Details of **setting** strongly influence the mood of "Eveline." Jot down some words or phrases that describe the setting of your home and that, taken together, would help to describe the general mood or atmosphere of your surroundings. For example, consider what mood the following details would convey when taken together: polished furniture, sagging sofa, thriving plants, old television set, whir of a sewing machine, catcher's mitt on chair, pair of shoes under kitchen table, large dog asleep in the hallway.

Eveline

JAMES JOYCE

She sat at the window watching the evening invade the avenue. Her head was leaned against the window curtains and in her nostrils was the odor of dusty cretonne.[1] She was tired.

Few people passed. The man out of the last house passed on his way home; she heard his footsteps clacking along the concrete pavement and afterwards crunching on the cinder path before the new red houses. One time there used to be a field there in which they used to play every evening with other people's children. Then a man from Belfast bought the field and built houses in it—not like their little brown houses but bright brick houses with shining roofs. The children of the avenue used to play together in that field—the Devines, the Waters, the Dunns, little Keogh the cripple, she and her brothers and sisters. Ernest, however, never played: he was too grown up. Her father used often to hunt them in out of the field with his blackthorn stick; but usually little Keogh used to keep nix[2] and call out when he saw her father coming. Still they seemed to have been rather happy then. Her father was not so bad then; and besides, her mother was alive. That was a long time ago; she and her brothers and sisters were all grown up; her mother was dead. Tizzie Dunn was dead, too, and the Waters had gone back to England. Everything changes. Now she was going to go away like the others, to leave her home.

Home! She looked round the room, reviewing all its familiar objects which she had dusted once a week for so many years, wondering where on earth all the dust came from. Perhaps she would never see again those familiar objects from which she had never dreamed of being divided. And yet during all those years she had never found out the name of the priest whose yellowing photograph hung on the wall above the broken harmonium beside the colored print of the promises made to Blessed Margaret Mary Alacoque.[3] He had been a school friend of her father. Whenever he showed the photograph to a visitor her father used to pass it with a casual word: "He is in Melbourne now."

SUMMARIZE: What details so far suggest the condition of the home?

She had consented to go away, to leave her home. Was that wise? She tried to weigh each side of the question. In her home anyway she had shelter and food; she had those whom she had known all her life about her. Of course she had to work hard, both in the house and at business. What would they say of her in the Stores when they found out that she had run away with a fellow? Say she was a fool, perhaps; and her place would be filled up by advertisement. Miss Gavan would be glad. She had always had an edge on her, especially whenever there were people listening.

"Miss Hill, don't you see these ladies are waiting?"

"Look lively, Miss Hill, please."

---

1. **cretonne** (kri ton′), *n.* a strong cotton, linen, or rayon cloth with designs printed in colors.
2. **nix** (niks), *n.* watch. *[slang]*
3. **Blessed . . . Alacoque** (1647–1690), a French nun who experienced visions of Jesus.

Does the use of color in Spencer Gore's painting *Woman in a Flowered Hat* (about 1907) convey an impression of warmth or coolness? ➤

She would not cry many tears at leaving the Stores.

But in her new home, in a distant unknown country, it would not be like that. Then she would be married—she, Eveline. People would treat her with respect then. She would not be treated as her mother had been. Even now, though she was over nineteen, she sometimes felt herself in danger of her father's violence. She knew it was that that had given her the palpitations.[4] When they were growing up he had never gone for her, like he used to go for Harry and Ernest, because she was a girl; but latterly he had begun to threaten her and say what he would do to her only for her dead mother's sake. And now she had nobody to protect her. Ernest was dead and Harry, who was in the church decorating business, was nearly always down somewhere in the country. Besides, the invariable squabble for money on Saturday nights had begun to weary her unspeakably. She always gave her entire wages—seven shillings—and Harry always sent up what he could but the trouble was to get any money from her father. He said she used to squander the money, that she had no head, that he wasn't going to give her his hard-earned money to throw about the streets, and much more, for he was usually fairly bad on Saturday night. In the end he would give her the money and ask her had she any intention of buying Sunday's dinner. Then she had to rush out as quickly as she could and do her marketing, holding her black leather purse tightly in her hand as she elbowed her way through the crowds and returning home late under her load of provisions. She had hard work to keep the house together and to see that the two young children

She was about to explore another life with Frank.

who had been left to her charge went to school regularly and got their meals regularly. It was hard work—a hard life—but now that she was about to leave it she did not find it a wholly undesirable life.

She was about to explore another life with Frank. Frank was very kind, manly, open-hearted. She was to go away with him by the night boat to be his wife and to live with him in Buenos Aires where he had a home waiting for her. How well she remembered the first time she had seen him; he was lodging in a house on the main road where she used to visit. It seemed a few weeks ago. He was standing at the gate, his peaked cap pushed back on his head and his hair tumbled forward over a face of bronze. Then they had come to know each other. He used to meet her outside the Stores every evening and see her home. He took her to see *The Bohemian Girl*[5] and she felt elated as she sat in an unaccustomed part of the theater with him. He was awfully fond of music and sang a little. People knew that they were courting and, when he sang about the lass that loves a sailor, she always felt pleasantly confused. He used to call her Poppens out of fun. First of all it had been an excitement for her to have a fellow and then she had begun to like him. He had tales of distant countries. He had started as a deck boy at a pound a month on a ship of the Allan Line going out to Canada. He told her the names of the ships he had been on and the names of the different services. He had sailed through the Straits of Magellan and he told her stories of the terrible Patagonians.[6] He had fallen on his feet in Buenos Aires, he said, and had come over to the old country just for a holiday. Of course, her father had found out the affair and had forbidden her to have anything to say to him.

---

4. **palpitation** (pal/pə tā/shən), *n.* a very rapid beating of the heart.
5. ***The Bohemian Girl,*** an opera by the Irish-born composer Michael Balfe (1808–1870).
6. **Patagonians,** people living in Patagonia in the extreme south of South America.

CLARIFY: Why might Eveline have been attracted to Frank?

"I know these sailor chaps," he said.

One day he had quarreled with Frank and after that she had to meet her lover secretly.

The evening deepened in the avenue. The white of two letters in her lap grew indistinct. One was to Harry; the other was to her father. Ernest had been her favorite but she liked Harry too. Her father was becoming old lately, she noticed; he would miss her. Sometimes he could be very nice. Not long before, when she had been laid up for a day, he had read her out a ghost story and made toast for her at the fire. Another day, when their mother was alive, they had all gone for a picnic to the Hill of Howth. She remembered her father putting on her mother's bonnet to make the children laugh.

Her time was running out but she continued to sit by the window, leaning her head against the window curtain, inhaling the odor of dusty cretonne. Down far in the avenue she could hear a street organ playing. She knew the air. Strange that it should come that very night to remind her of the promise to her mother, her promise to keep the home together as long as she could. She remembered the last night of her mother's illness; she was again in the close dark room at the other side of the hall and outside she heard a melancholy air of Italy. The organ player had been ordered to go away and given sixpence. She remembered her father strutting back into the sickroom saying: "Damned Italians! coming over here!"

As she mused the pitiful vision of her mother's life laid its spell on the very quick of her being—that life of commonplace sacrifices closing in final craziness. She trembled as she heard again her mother's voice saying constantly with foolish insistence: "Derevaun Seraun! Derevaun Seraun!"[7]

She stood up in a sudden impulse of terror.

Escape! She must escape! Frank would save her. He would give her life, perhaps love, too. But she wanted to live. Why should she be unhappy? She had a right to happiness. Frank would take her in his arms, fold her in his arms. He would save her.

She stood among the swaying crowd in the station at the North Wall. He held her hand and she knew that he was speaking to her, saying something about the passage over and over again. The station was full of soldiers with brown baggages. Through the wide doors of the sheds she caught a glimpse of the black mass of the boat, lying in beside the quay wall, with illumined portholes. She answered nothing. She felt her cheek pale and cold and, out of a maze of distress, she prayed to God to direct her, to show her what was her duty. The boat blew a long mournful whistle into the mist. If she went, tomorrow she would be on the sea with Frank, steaming toward Buenos Aires. Their passage had been booked. Could she still draw back after all he had done for her? Her distress awoke a nausea in her body and she kept moving her lips in silent fervent prayer.

A bell clanged upon her heart. She felt him seize her hand:

"Come!"

All the seas of the world tumbled about her heart. He was drawing her into them: he would drown her. She gripped with both hands at the iron railing.

"Come!"

No! No! No! It was impossible. Her hand clutched the iron in frenzy. Amid the seas she sent a cry of anguish.

"Eveline! Evvy!"

He rushed beyond the barrier and called to her to follow. He was shouted at to go on but he still called to her. She set her white face to him, passive, like a helpless animal. Her eyes gave him no sign of love or farewell or recognition.

---

7. **"Derevaun Seraun,"** possibly, corrupt Gaelic (the original language of the Irish) for "the end of pleasure is pain."

After Reading

Shaping Your Response

1. Were you surprised at the ending?

2. Are you sympathetic to Eveline? Explain.

Analyzing the Story

3. What **mood** is established in the first three paragraphs? What is the mood in the paragraph beginning "She stood among the swaying crowd . . ."?

4. How might this story have changed if it had been told from an omniscient rather than a limited **point of view?**

5. What do you suppose causes Eveline to send Frank away without a "sign of love or farewell or recognition"?

Extending the Ideas

6. American author Ralph Waldo Emerson wrote, "Trust thyself: every heart vibrates to that iron string." Does Eveline trust herself? What do you think are some things that have to happen before a person can trust herself or himself?

7. ⚆ What does this story tell you about how much the culture Joyce writes about prizes **individuality?**

Literary Focus: Epiphany

When the underlying truth, essential nature, or meaning of something is suddenly made clear in a literary work, this moment is called an **epiphany.**

1. Where does the epiphany occur in "Eveline"?

2. Who or what is responsible for Eveline's final decision?

Expressing Your Ideas

Writing Choices

Writer's Notebook Update Combine some of the words or phrases that describe the setting of your home into a single paragraph. Ask a partner to identify the mood you have created.

Eveline's Role How much do expectations about women and women's roles in Eveline's culture influence her life and her actions? Write an **essay** analyzing this question. Consider her relationships with her mother, father, and brothers, and her childhood and work.

On the Aisle "The Dead," a long story by Joyce from *Dubliners,* was made into a 1987 move directed by John Huston and starring Anjelica Houston, Rachel Dowling, and Dan O'Herlihy. View and write a **review** of the film.

Other Options

No Sign of Love Create an **illustration** for this story. Since there is little action, how will you depict the mood or atmosphere or Eveline's psychological state? Will you illustrate the setting? Will you show other characters mentioned in the story? Think about what technique or colors might be suitable before beginning your work.

Research Nations as well as individuals seek identity, and Ireland is no exception. Joyce's story, which tells in part about a search for identity, was published in 1914, just two years before the Easter uprising in Dublin in 1916. Research this historic event, including reasons for the uprising and the results, and give an **oral report** to the class.

In Performance John Millington Synge (1871–1909), an Irish playwright, was one of the founders of the famous Abbey Theatre, which opened in Dublin in 1904. His one-act play "Riders to the Sea" takes place on an island off the west coast of Ireland. Read this short play for another glimpse of Irish life and, with one or more partners, choose and **perform a section** from it for the class.

Before Reading

A Cup of Tea

by Katherine Mansfield

Katherine Mansfield
1888–1923

Katherine Mansfield was born in New Zealand and educated, along with her sisters, in London. Although she studied at the Royal Academy of Music, she soon realized that writing was her true calling. Her life was somewhat unconventional for the times in which she lived, and her several affairs embarrassed her family and resulted in her mother cutting Mansfield from her will. Soon after her marriage in 1918 to John Middleton Murry, a literary critic and editor, she became a virtual invalid from tuberculosis, and she died in France in 1923. Her stories depend more on atmosphere, character, and effects of language than on plot and can be found in *Collected Stories of Katherine Mansfield*.

Building Background

"Ah! but to write better!" Katherine Mansfield's journals include accounts of her daily life, the weather, and her feelings. They also show how she longed to be better at her craft:

"Jan. 2, 1922. I have not done the work I should have done. I shirk the lunch party [a part of the story 'The Dove's Nest']. This is very bad. In fact I am disgusted with myself. There must be a change from now on.

"Jan. 7. It ceased snowing, and a deep, almost gentian blue sky showed. The snow lay heaped on the trees, big blobs of snow like whipped cream . . . I wrote at my story, but did not finish the lunch party as I ought have to [sic] done. How very bad this is!

"Jan. 10. Dreamed I was back in New Zealand . . .

"Jan. 11. In bed again. Heard from Pinker *The Dial* had taken "The Doll's House." Wrote and finished "A Cup of Tea." It took about 4–5 hours . . . There is no feeling to be compared with the feeling of having written and finished a story.

"Jan. 12. I don't feel so sinful this day as I did, because I have written something and the tide is still high . . . Ah! but to write better! Let me write better, more deeply, more largely. Baleful icicles hang in a frieze outside our window pane. . . ."

Literary Focus

Stereotype A **stereotype** is a conventional character, plot, or setting that has little or no individuality. Stereotypical characters are based on fixed, generalized ideas about people or groups of people. An author may use a stereotype as background for a main character or as a contrast to that character. As you read "A Cup of Tea," decide which character if any seems to be a stereotype.

Writer's Notebook

Making It Up As You Go Think of someone you don't know but have seen—perhaps on a bus, at a mall, or at a sporting event. Jot down some ideas for a story involving that person.

A Cup of Tea

BY KATHERINE MANSFIELD

◄ In what ways does the young woman in William McGregor Paxson's painting *Pretty Girl* (1926) resemble Rosemary Fell?

ROSEMARY FELL was not exactly beautiful. No, you couldn't have called her beautiful. Pretty? Well, if you took her to pieces . . . But why be so cruel as to take anyone to pieces? She was young, brilliant, extremely modern, exquisitely[1] well dressed, amazingly well read in the newest of the new books, and her parties were the most delicious mixture of the really important people and . . . artists—quaint creatures, discoveries of hers, some of them too terrifying for words, but others quite presentable and amusing.

Rosemary had been married two years. She had a duck[2] of a boy. No, not Peter—Michael.

---

1. **exquisitely** (ek′skwi zit lē), *adv.* beautifully; admirably.
2. **duck,** a term of endearment. *[slang]*

And her husband absolutely adored her. They were rich, really rich, not just comfortably well off, which is odious[3] and stuffy and sounds like one's grandparents. But if Rosemary wanted to shop she would go to Paris as you and I would go to Bond Street.[4] If she wanted to buy flowers, the car pulled up at that perfect shop in Regent Street, and Rosemary inside the shop just gazed in her dazzled rather exotic way, and said: "I want those and those and those. Give me four bunches of those. And that jar of roses. Yes, I'll have all the roses in the jar. No, no lilac. I hate lilac. It's got no shape." The attendant bowed and put the lilac out of sight, as though this was only too true; lilac was dreadfully shapeless. "Give me those stumpy little tulips. Those red and white ones." And she was followed to the car by a thin shopgirl staggering under an immense white paper armful that looked like a baby in long clothes. . . .

One winter afternoon she had been buying something in a little antique shop in Curzon Street. It was a shop she liked. For one thing, one usually had it to oneself. And then the man who kept it was ridiculously fond of serving her. He beamed whenever she came in. He clasped his hands; he was so gratified he could scarcely speak. Flattery, of course. All the same, there was something . . .

"You see, madam," he would explain in his low respectful tones, "I love my things. I would rather not part with them than sell them to someone who does not appreciate them, who has not that fine feeling which is so rare. . . ." And, breathing deeply, he unrolled a tiny square of blue velvet and pressed it on the glass counter with his pale finger-tips.

Today it was a little box. He had been keeping it for her. He had shown it to nobody as yet. An exquisite little enamel box with a glaze[5] so fine it looked as though it had been baked in cream. On the lid a minute creature stood under a flowery tree, and a more minute creature still had her arms around his neck. Her hat, really no bigger than a geranium petal, hung

from a branch; it had green ribbons. And there was a pink cloud like a watchful cherub[6] floating above their heads. Rosemary took her hands out of her long gloves. She always took off her gloves to examine such things. Yes, she liked it very much. She loved it; it was a great duck. She must have it. And, turning the creamy box, opening and shutting it, she couldn't help noticing how charming her hands were against the blue velvet. The shopman, in some dim cavern of his mind, may have dared to think so too. For he took a pencil, leaned over the counter, and his pale bloodless fingers crept timidly towards those rosy, flashing ones, as he murmured gently: "If I may venture to point out to madam, the flowers on the little lady's bodice."

"Charming!" Rosemary admired the flowers. But what was the price? For a moment the shopman did not seem to hear. Then a murmur reached her.

"Twenty-eight guineas, madame."

"Twenty-eight guineas." Rosemary gave no sign. She laid the little box down: she buttoned her gloves again. Twenty-eight guineas. Even if one is rich . . . She looked vague. She stared at a plump tea-kettle like a plump hen above the shopman's head, and her voice was dreamy as she answered: "Well, keep it for me—will you? I'll . . ."

But the shopman had already bowed as though keeping it for her was all any human being could ask. He would be willing, of course, to keep it for her for ever.

The discreet[7] door shut with a click. She was outside on the step, gazing at the winter afternoon. Rain was falling, and with the rain it

---

3. **odious** (ō′dē əs), *adj.* hateful; offensive.
4. **Bond Street.** Like Regent Street (mentioned later), Bond Street is in an elegant shopping area in London.
5. glaze (glāz), *n.* smooth, glossy coating.
6. cherub (cher′əb), *n.* here, an angel in the form of a child with wings.
7. discreet (dis krēt′), *adj.* careful and sensible; proper.

seemed the dark came too, spinning down like ashes. There was a cold bitter taste in the air, and the new-lighted lamps looked sad. Sad were the lights in the houses opposite. Dimly they burned as if regretting something. And people hurried by, hidden under their hateful umbrellas. Rosemary felt a strange pang. She pressed her muff to her breast; she wished she had the little box, too, to cling to. Of course, the car was there. She'd only to cross the pavement. But still she waited. There are moments, horrible moments in life, when one emerges from shelter and looks out, and it's awful. One oughtn't to give way to them. One ought to go home and have an extra-special tea. But at the very instant of thinking that, a young girl, thin, dark, shadowy—where had she come from?—was standing at Rosemary's elbow and a voice like a sigh, almost like a sob, breathed: "Madame, may I speak to you a moment?"

"Speak to me?" Rosemary turned. She saw a little battered creature with enormous eyes, someone quite young, no older than herself, who clutched at her coat-collar with reddened hands, and shivered as though she had just come out of the water.

"M-madam," stammered the voice. "Would you let me have the price of a cup of tea?"

"A cup of tea?" There was something simple, sincere in that voice; it wasn't in the least the voice of a beggar. "Then have you no money at all?" asked Rosemary.

"None, madam," came the answer.

"How extraordinary!" Rosemary peered through the dusk, and the girl gazed back at her. How more than ordinary! And suddenly it seemed to Rosemary such an adventure. It was like something out of a novel by Dostoevski,[8] this meeting in the dusk. Supposing she took the girl home? Supposing she did do one of

Supposing she did do one of those things she was always reading about or seeing on the stage . . . ?

those things she was always reading about or seeing on the stage, what would happen? It would be thrilling. And she heard herself saying afterwards to the amazement of her friends: "I simply took her home with me," as she stepped forward and said to that dim person beside her: "Come home to tea with me."

The girl drew back startled. She even stopped shivering for a moment. Rosemary put out a hand and touched her arm. "I mean it," she said, smiling. And she felt how simple and kind her smile was. "Why won't you? Do. Come home with me now in my car and have tea."

"You—you don't mean it, madam," said the girl, and there was pain in her voice.

"But I do," cried Rosemary. "I want you to. To please me. Come along."

The girl put her fingers to her lips and her eyes devoured Rosemary. "You're—you're not taking me to the police station?" she stammered.

"The police station!" Rosemary laughed out. "Why should I be so cruel? No, I only want to make you warm and to hear—anything you care to tell me."

Hungry people are easily led. The footman held the door of the car open, and a moment later they were skimming through the dusk.

"There!" said Rosemary. She had a feeling of triumph as she slipped her hand through the velvet strap. She could have said, "Now I've got you," as she gazed at the little captive she had netted. But of course she meant it kindly. Oh, more than kindly. She was going to prove to this

---

8. **Dostoevski** (dos′tə yef′skē), Feodor (1821–1881), Russian novelist. (See from *Crime and Punishment* on page 194.)

girl that—wonderful things did happen in life, that—fairy godmothers were real, that—rich people had hearts, and that women *were* sisters. She turned impulsively, saying: "Don't be frightened. After all, why shouldn't you come back with me? We're both women. If I'm the more fortunate, you ought to expect . . ."

But happily at that moment, for she didn't know how the sentence was going to end, the car stopped. The bell was rung, the door opened, and with a charming, protecting, almost embracing movement, Rosemary drew the other into the hall. Warmth, softness, light, a sweet scent, all those things so familiar to her she never even thought about them, she watched that other receive. It was fascinating. She was like the little rich girl in her nursery with all the cupboards to open, all the boxes to unpack.

"Come, come upstairs," said Rosemary, longing to begin to be generous. "Come up to my room." And, besides, she wanted to spare this poor little thing from being stared at by the servants; she decided as they mounted the stairs she would not even ring for Jeanne, but take off her things by herself. The great thing was to be natural!

And "There!" cried Rosemary again, as they reached her beautiful big bedroom with the curtains drawn, the fire leaping on her wonderful lacquer furniture, her gold cushions and the primrose and blue rugs.

The girl stood just inside the door; she seemed dazed. But Rosemary didn't mind that.

"Come and sit down," she cried, dragging her big chair up to the fire, "in this comfy chair. Come and get warm. You look so dreadfully cold."

"I daren't, madam," said the girl, and she edged backwards.

"Oh, please,"—Rosemary ran forward—"you mustn't be frightened, you mustn't, really. Sit

To be quite sincere, she looked rather stupid. But Rosemary wouldn't acknowledge it.

down, and when I've taken off my things we shall go into the next room and have tea and be cosy. Why are you afraid?" And gently she half pushed the thin figure into its deep cradle.

But there was no answer. The girl stayed just as she had been put, with her hands by her sides and her mouth slightly open. To be quite sincere, she looked rather stupid. But Rosemary wouldn't acknowledge it. She leaned over her, saying: "Won't you take off your hat? Your pretty hair is all wet. And one is so much more comfortable without a hat, isn't one?"

There was a whisper that sounded like "Very good, madam," and the crushed hat was taken off.

"Let me help you off with your coat, too," said Rosemary.

The girl stood up. But she held on to the chair with one hand and let Rosemary pull. It was quite an effort. The other scarcely helped her at all. She seemed to stagger like a child, and the thought came and went through Rosemary's mind, that if people wanted helping they must respond a little, just a little, otherwise it became very difficult indeed. And what was she to do with the coat now? She left it on the floor, and the hat too. She was just going to take a cigarette off the mantelpiece when the girl said quickly, but so lightly and strangely: "I'm very sorry, madam, but I'm going to faint. I shall go off, madam, if I don't have something."

EVALUATE: What do you learn about Rosemary from her response to the fact that the girl doesn't help remove her own coat?

"Good heavens, how thoughtless I am!" Rosemary rushed to the bell.

"Tea! Tea at once! And some brandy immediately!"

The maid was gone again, but the girl almost cried out. "No, I don't want no brandy. I never drink brandy. It's a cup of tea I want, madam." And she burst into tears.

It was a terrible and fascinating moment. Rosemary knelt beside her chair.

"Don't cry, poor little thing," she said. "Don't cry." And she gave the other her lace handkerchief. She really was touched beyond words. She put her arm round those thin, birdlike shoulders.

*n*ow at last the other forgot to be shy, forgot everything except that they were both women, and gasped out: "I can't go on no longer like this. I can't bear it. I shall do away with myself. I can't bear no more."

"You shan't have to. I'll look after you. Don't cry any more. Don't you see what a good thing it was that you met me? We'll have tea and you'll tell me everything. And I shall arrange something. I promise. *Do* stop crying. It's so exhausting. Please!"

The other did stop just in time for Rosemary to get up before the tea came. She had the table placed between them. She plied[9] the poor little creature with everything, all the sandwiches, all the bread and butter, and every time her cup was empty she filled it with tea, cream and sugar. People always said sugar was so nourishing. As for herself she didn't eat; she smoked and looked away tactfully so that the other should not be shy.

And really the effect of that slight meal was marvelous. When the tea-table was carried away a new being, a light, frail creature with tangled hair, dark lips, deep, lighted eyes, lay back in the big chair in a kind of sweet languor,[10] looking at the blaze. Rosemary lit a fresh cigarette; it was time to begin.

"And when did you have your last meal?" she asked softly.

But at the moment the door-handle turned.

"Rosemary, may I come in?" It was Philip.

"Of course."

He came in. "Oh, I'm so sorry," he said, and stopped and stared.

"It's quite all right," said Rosemary smiling. "This is my friend, Miss—"

"Smith, madam," said the languid figure, who was strangely still and unafraid.

"Smith," said Rosemary. "We are going to have a little talk."

"Oh, yes," said Philip. "Quite." and his eye caught sight of the coat and hat on the floor. He came over to the fire and turned his back to it. "It's a beastly afternoon," he said curiously, still looking at that listless[11] figure, looking at its hands and boots, and then at Rosemary again.

"Yes, isn't it?" said Rosemary enthusiastically. "Vile."[12]

Philip smiled his charming smile. "As a matter of fact," said he, "I wanted you to come into the library for a moment. Would you? Will Miss Smith excuse us?"

The big eyes were raised to him, but Rosemary answered for her. "Of course she will." And they went out of the room together.

"I say," said Philip, when they were alone. "Explain. Who is she? What does it all mean?"

Rosemary, laughing, leaned against the door and said: "I picked her up in Curzon Street. Really. She's a real pick-up. She asked me for the price of a cup of tea, and I brought her home with me."

"But what on earth are you going to do with her?" cried Philip.

"Be nice to her," said Rosemary quickly. "Be frightfully nice to her. Look after her. I don't know how. We haven't talked yet. But show her—treat her—make her feel—"

---

9. ply (plī), *v.* supply with in a pressing manner.
10. languor (lang′gər), *n.* lack of energy; weariness.
11. listless (list′lis), *adj.* seeming too tired to care about anything.
12. vile (vīl), *adj.* very bad.

"My darling girl," said Philip, "you're quite mad, you know. It simply can't be done."

"I knew you'd say that," retorted Rosemary. "Why not? I want to. Isn't that a reason? And besides, one's always reading about these things. I decided—"

"But," said Philip slowly, and he cut the end of a cigar, "she's so astonishingly pretty."

"Pretty?" Rosemary was so surprised that she blushed. "Do you think so? I—I hadn't thought about it."

CLARIFY: Why is Rosemary surprised?

"Good Lord!" Philip struck a match. "She's absolutely lovely. Look again, my child. I was bowled over when I came into your room just now. However . . . I think you're making a ghastly[13] mistake. Sorry, darling, if I'm crude and all that. But let me know if Miss Smith is going to dine with us in time for me to look up *The Milliner's Gazette.*"

"You absurd creature!" said Rosemary, and she went out of the library, but not back to her bedroom. She went to her writing-room and sat down at her desk. Pretty! Absolutely lovely! Bowled over! Her heart beat like a heavy bell. Pretty! Lovely! She drew her check book towards her. But no, checks would be no use, of course. She opened a drawer and took out five pound notes, looked at them, put two back, and holding the three squeezed in her hand, she went back to her bedroom.

Half an hour later Philip was still in the library, when Rosemary came in.

"I only wanted to tell you," said she, and she leaned against the door again and looked at him with her dazzled exotic[14] gaze, "Miss Smith won't dine with us tonight."

Philip put down the paper. "Oh, what's happened? Previous engagement?"

Rosemary came over and sat down on his knee. "She insisted on going," said she, "so I gave the poor little thing a present of money. I couldn't keep her against her will, could I?" she added softly.

Rosemary had just done her hair, darkened her eyes a little, and put on her pearls. She put up her hands and touched Philip's cheeks.

"Do you like me?" said she, and her tone, sweet, husky, troubled him.

"I like you awfully," he said, and he held her tighter. "Kiss me."

There was a pause.

Then Rosemary said dreamily, "I saw a fascinating little box today. It cost twenty-eight guineas. May I have it?"

Philip jumped her on his knee. "You may, little wasteful one," said he.

But that was not really what Rosemary wanted to say.

"Philip," she whispered, and she pressed his head against her bosom, "am I *pretty?*"

---

13. ghastly (gast′lē), *adj.* very bad. *[informal]*
14. exotic (eg zot′ik), *adj.* from a foreign country; strange or different.

After Reading

Making Connections

Shaping Your Response

1. If invited, would you attend one of Rosemary's parties, with its "most delicious mixture of the really important people"? Why or why not?

Analyzing the Story

2. Part of the **characterization** of Rosemary is the description of her feelings immediately after leaving the antique shop. What does this description tell about her?

3. How do we learn Rosemary's true motives in inviting the girl home?

4. Where does the **climax** come in the story?

5. In your opinion, what is Rosemary's chief purpose in life? Support your answer with evidence from the story.

Extending the Ideas

6. If you had asked for the price of a cup of tea and received several times more than you asked for, would you feel grateful? embarrassed? demeaned? ashamed? something else? Discuss.

7. Do you think Mansfield is criticizing the values of the society in which Rosemary and her husband live, or is she merely representing it?

Literary Focus: Stereotype

A **stereotype** is based on a conventional idea, and stereotypical characters are based on fixed, generalized notions about people or groups of people. Stereotypical characters often serve as foils; that is they point up the strengths or weaknesses of another character.

1. Does Rosemary seem to consider Miss Smith a type or an individual?

2. Do you think the author intended the character of Rosemary to help portray Miss Smith, or is Miss Smith created to help portray Rosemary?

3. Miss Smith is allowed one mark of **individuality.** What is it?

Vocabulary Study

Decide whether the italicized words are used correctly in the sentences. On your paper write *Correct* or *Incorrect* for each one.

1. Stephanie liked to shop on Plum Drive, where the shops were full of *exotic* imported merchandise.

2. Yesterday she found a beautiful and *listless* pearl ring.

3. Alex found a *langour* in a shop nearby.

4. Later the two of them *plied* onto a bus and went to an art gallery.

5. There, Stephanie saw an *exquisitely* painted bowl.

6. Alex, however, was more interested in an antique painting of a *cherub.*

7. He made a *discreet* inquiry about the price.

8. Stephanie thought the painting was *ghastly.*

9. She explained that she was in a *vile* mood.

10. Perhaps the *glaze* she was wearing affected her judgment.

Expressing Your Ideas

Writing Choices

Writer's Notebook Update Review the ideas you jotted down for a character based on someone you have seen but do not know. Now write a character sketch or a short short story based on that character.

A Weird Experience Assume that you are Miss Smith, and write a **letter** to a friend describing your experience with Rosemary and her husband Philip, including what happened just before you left their home.

Two Fictional Women In an **essay** compare and contrast Rosemary and Eveline in James Joyce's story. Consider their relationships with others, their economic situations, and their personalities. Does Rosemary have an epiphany too?

Other Options

The Rattle of Teacups With a small group, adapt "A Cup of Tea" into a one-act **radio play.** Use dialogue from the story, and make up the rest. You will need lines for Rosemary, Philip, the clerk, Miss Smith, the maid, and perhaps a narrator. If you can, include some sound effects—such as the sound of rain and of Rosemary's car, the crackling of a fire, the sound of teacups rattling, and the closing of a door. Record your production and play it for the class.

Artistic Values Look carefully at the painting that accompanies this story on page 797. With a partner, plan an **interview** with questions and answers about the artist's decisions regarding the subject, the pose, colors, shapes, and artistic style of the work. You might include some comments about the young woman who posed for the picture. With you playing the interviewer and your partner playing the artist, practice the interview and present it to the class.

Before Reading

The Unknown Citizen
Musée des Beaux Arts
Who's Who by W. H. Auden

W. H. Auden
1907–1973

W. H. Auden, the youngest of three brothers, was born in York and lived in Birmingham until he attended boarding school. He graduated from Oxford in 1928, spent a year in Germany, and taught school in England and Scotland in the early 1920s. In 1939 Auden settled in the U. S., becoming an American citizen in 1946. Later he spent his summers abroad, first in Italy and then in Austria, where he lived with American poet Chester Kallman. Auden became a poetry professor at Oxford in 1956 and died suddenly in Vienna in 1973. His works include the libretto for Igor Stravinsky's opera, *The Rake's Progress* (1949, 1951) with Kallman; criticism in *The Dyer's Hand* (1962), and *Collected Poems* (1976).

Building Background

Poetry's Role For more than four decades Auden's poetry succeeded in capturing the horrors, hopes, and anxieties of the time. He characterized the 1930s as a "low, dishonest decade," and the title of one of his works, *The Age of Anxiety* (1948), a long dramatic poem, came to characterize the post-World War II period for many. Auden delighted in playing with words, in employing a variety of rhythms, and in creating striking literary effects. But he was also insistent that poetry must fulfill a moral function, principally that of dispelling hate and promoting love. "Poetry is not concerned with telling people what to do," he once wrote, "but with extending our knowledge of good and evil . . . leading us to the point where it is possible for us to make a rational moral choice."

Literary Focus

Satire The technique that uses wit to ridicule a subject is called **satire.** Its focus is usually some social institution or human foible, and the intention is to inspire reform. What aspects of twentieth-century society does Auden satirize in "The Unknown Citizen"?

Writer's Notebook

Who's Who Today? Who are the most widely known people in the world today? Make a list of at least ten of these people. Where did you learn about them in the first place?

THE *Unknown Citizen*

W. H. Auden

He was found by the Bureau of Statistics to be
One against whom there was no official complaint,
And all the reports on his conduct agree
That, in the modern sense of an old-fashioned word, he
    was a saint,
5 For in everything he did he served the Greater Community.
Except for the War till the day he retired
He worked in a factory and never got fired,
But satisfied his employers, Fudge Motors Inc.
Yet he wasn't a scab[1] or odd in his views,
10 For his Union reports that he paid his dues,
(Our report on his Union shows it was sound)
And our Social Psychology workers found
That he was popular with his mates and liked a drink.
The Press are convinced that he bought a paper every day
15 And that his reactions to advertisements were normal in every way.
Policies taken out in his name prove that he was fully insured,
And his Health-card shows he was once in hospital but
    left it cured.
Both Producers Research and High-Grade Living declare
He was fully sensible to the advantages of the Installment Plan
20 And had everything necessary to the Modern Man,
A phonograph, a radio, a car and a frigidaire.
Our researchers into Public Opinion are content
That he held the proper opinions for the time of year;
When there was peace, he was for peace; when there was war,
    he went.
25 He was married and added five children to the population,
Which our Eugenist[2] says was the right number for a parent of
    his generation.
And our teachers report that he never interfered with
    their education.
Was he free? Was he happy? The question is absurd:
Had anything been wrong, we should certainly have heard.

---

1. **scab,** worker who will not join a labor union or who takes a striker's job.
2. **Eugenist,** eugenicist, an expert in eugenics, the science of improving the human race by a careful selection of parents in order to breed healthier and more intelligent children.

Is the **tone** of W. H. Auden's poem "The Unknown Citizen" similar to that of René Magritte's painting *Reproduction Prohibited* (1937)? Why or why not? ➤

MUSÉE DES
Beaux Arts

W. H. Auden

About suffering they were never wrong,
The Old Masters;[1] how well they understood
Its human position; how it takes place
While someone else is eating or opening a
    window or just walking dully along;
5 How, when the aged are reverently,
    passionately waiting
For the miraculous birth, there always must be
Children who did not specially want it to
    happen, skating
On a pond at the edge of the wood:
They never forgot
10 That even the dreadful martyrdom must run
    its course
Anyhow in a corner, some untidy spot
Where the dogs go on with their doggy life
    and the torturer's horse
Scratches its innocent behind on a tree.

In Bruegel's *Icarus*,[2] for instance: how
    everything turns away
15 Quite leisurely from the disaster; the
    ploughman may
Have heard the splash, the forsaken cry,
But for him it was not an important failure;
    the sun shone
As it had to on the white legs disappearing
    into the green
Water; and the expensive delicate ship that
    must have seen
20 Something amazing, a boy falling out of the sky,
Had somewhere to get to and sailed calmly on.

Musée des Beaux Arts (mü zā′ dā bō
zär′), the Royal Museum of Fine Arts in
Brussels, Belgium.
1. **Old Masters,** any great painters before 1700.
2. **Bruegel's *Icarus*** (ik′ər əs). The painting
The Fall of Icarus by Pieter Bruegel (pē′tər
broi′gəl) was inspired by the Greek myth
that relates how Daedalus made wings of
feathers and wax for his son Icarus and
himself in order to escape imprisonment.
Despite his father's warnings, Icarus flew
too near the sun; the wax holding together
the feathers of his wings melted, and he fell
into the sea and drowned.

The *Fall of Icarus* seems a minor detail in this painting by Pieter Bruegel the Elder (1525–1569). If you were renaming this picture, what title would you give it?

WHO'S *Who*

W. H. Auden

A shilling life[1] will give you all the facts:
How Father beat him, how he ran away,
What were the struggles of his youth, what acts
Made him the greatest figure of his day:
5 Of how he fought, fished, hunted, worked all night,
Though giddy, climbed new mountains; named a sea;
Some of the last researchers even write
Love made him weep his pints like you and me.

With all his honors on, he sighed for one
10 Who, say astonished critics, lived at home;
Did little jobs about the house with skill
And nothing else; could whistle; would sit still
Or potter round the garden; answered some
Of his long marvellous letters but kept none.

---

1. **shilling life,** an inexpensive biography, one costing a
   shilling, a former British coin worth about 25 cents
   when Auden wrote this poem.

After Reading

Making Connections

Shaping Your Response

1. From these three poems, what can you **infer** was Auden's view of life?

Analyzing the Poems

2. Explain the double meaning of *unknown* in the title of the poem

3. The **rhyme scheme** of "The Unknown Citizen" is not quite regular. Chart it. Why do you think Auden didn't choose to make it completely regular?

4. The title "The Unknown Citizen" may be an **allusion** to the unknown soldier honored in several graveyards around the world. What might such a connection add to the overall effect of the poem?

5. In "Musée des Beaux Arts," what truth about human suffering does the speaker feel the Old Masters understood, and how does Bruegel's painting illustrate this truth?

6. Explain why the critics mentioned in "Who's Who" are astonished (line 10).

Extending the Ideas

7. If you had a choice, would you rather be an unknown or a known citizen? Explain.

8. Auden thought poetry should extend our knowledge of good and evil (see page 805). Explain whether or not "Musée des Beaux Arts" achieves this aim.

Literary Focus: Satire

Satire uses wit to ridicule a subject, usually a human trait such as envy, greed, or stupidity, or a social institution such as government, business, religion, or the family. Usually the intent is to inspire reform.

1. For what kinds of behavior is the Unknown Citizen praised?

2. What kind of world did the Unknown Citizen inhabit?

3. In the next-to-last line of "The Unknown Citizen" the speaker asks two questions. Judging by the tone of the speaker's answer, do you think the poet endorses the speaker's views?

4. What human traits and what social institutions are satirized in "The Unknown Citizen"?

Expressing Your Ideas

Writing Choices

Writer's Notebook Update Look over the list you made of well-known people today. Now add their occupations or claims to fame.

Who're You? Study an entry from a biographical work such as *Who's Who*, and following this model write your own **biographical entry** as you would wish it to be ten years from now.

Auden's Use of Satire Develop your answers to the questions under Literary Focus: Satire into an **analytical essay** in which you discuss how Auden uses satire in "The Unknown Citizen." Quote lines from the poem to support your statements. If Auden's intent was to inspire reform, what sort of reform do you think he had in mind?

Wealth and Fame	
Rock Musicians	𝄞𝄞𝄞𝄞𝄞𝄞𝄞 𝄞𝄞𝄞𝄞𝄞
Movie Stars	𝄞𝄞𝄞𝄞 𝄞𝄞𝄞𝄞𝄞
Politicians	𝄞𝄞

Other Options

Private Lives Many people are concerned about the amount of personal information stored on computers and the resulting decrease in privacy. With a partner, develop an argument for each side of this issue: People have less privacy than they once had. Consider some of these questions and any others you think of: Does lack of privacy matter? Can stored computer information about private matters be put to illegal or immoral use? Is the matter serious enough to warrant some kind of action—either personal or legal? Present your **debate** to the class.

Rich and Famous? Take another look at the list you made of well-known people and each person's claim to fame. Compare your list with others in the class, and prepare a **statistical report** showing the number of times individuals are listed, the types of occupations shown, the number of women versus men, and any other statistics the lists bring to mind. Create one or more graphic organizers to illustrate your report. What if anything can you conclude about famous people and reasons for fame?

Before Reading

Shakespeare's Sister from A Room of One's Own

by Virginia Woolf

Virginia Woolf
1882–1941

Virginia Woolf was born into a literary and artistic family and educated at home by her father Leslie Stephen. After his death in 1904 she, with her brothers and her sister Vanessa, a painter, formed what came to be known as the Bloomsbury Group, an informal association of writers and artists. One member was Leonard Woolf, whom Virginia married in 1912. Her novels, which include *Mrs. Dalloway* (1925), *To the Lighthouse* (1927), and *The Waves* (1931), were increasingly experimental. She also wrote literary criticism and short stories, and her now-published letters and diaries contain fascinating insights. Frequently troubled by periods of mental illness, she drowned herself near her Sussex home.

Building Background

Critical Reception *A Room of One's Own,* from which the following excerpt is taken, has become in the words of one critic "a classic of the feminist movement." It is a book-length essay based on two lectures given by Woolf in 1928. Asked to speak about women and fiction to women at Cambridge University, Woolf began by expressing the view that "a woman must have money and a room of her own if she is to write fiction." When the essay was published, critic Arnold Bennett commented on Woolf's main theme:

"... I beg to state that I have myself written long and formidable novels in bedrooms whose doors certainly had no locks, and in the full dreadful knowledge that I had not five hundred a year of my own—nor fifty. And I beg to state further that from the moment when I obtained possession of both money and a lockable door all the high-brows in London conspired together to assert that I could no longer write."

Before this excerpt, Woolf tells of visiting the British Museum library to research the lives of some men and women in history.

Literary Focus

Paradox A **paradox** is a statement that seems to say two opposite things, such as this Robert Browning line often quoted: "Less is more." A paradox can also be a person, thing, or situation that is full of contradictions. In her essay, Woolf writes of a paradox.

Writer's Notebook

Distinguishing the Sexes At one time, many English nouns had "feminine" suffixes to distinguish males from females. Although many of these have almost disappeared from the language, some are still in use. Place the following words into two lists: (1) words that have virtually disappeared; (2) words still in use: actress, aviatrix, countess, executrix, giantess, huntress, laundress, lioness, majorette, mistress, princess, seamstress, shepherdess, songstress, sorceress, suffragette, temptress, tigress, usherette, waitress.

SHAKESPEARE'S SISTER

Virginia Woolf

It was disappointing not to have brought back in the evening some important statement, some authentic fact. Women are poorer than men because— this or that. Perhaps now it would be better to give up seeking for the truth, and receiving on one's head an avalanche of opinion hot as lava, discolored as dishwater. It would be better to draw the curtains; to shut out distractions; to light the lamp; to narrow the inquiry and to ask the historian, who records not opinions but facts, to describe under what conditions women lived, not throughout the ages, but in England, say in the time of Elizabeth.

For it is a perennial[1] puzzle why no woman wrote a word of that extraordinary literature when every other man, it seemed, was capable of song or sonnet. What were the conditions in which women lived, I asked myself; for fiction, imaginative work that is, is not dropped like a pebble upon the ground, as science may be; fiction is like a spider's web, attached ever so lightly perhaps, but still attached to life at all four corners. Often the attachment is scarcely perceptible; Shakespeare's plays, for instance, seem to hang there complete by themselves. But

◄ Does Hans Holbein's portrait of *Mrs. Pemberton* (1556) suggest that she was a confident, outgoing person or a thoughtful, introspective one?

when the web is pulled askew, hooked up at the edge, torn in the middle, one remembers that these webs are not spun in midair by incorporeal[2] creatures, but are the work of suffering human beings, and are attached to grossly material things, like health and money and the houses we live in.

CLARIFY: Explain Woolf's simile comparing fiction and a spider's web.

I went, therefore, to the shelf where the histories stand and took down one of the latest, Professor Trevelyan's *History of England*.[3] Once more I looked up Women, found "position of," and turned to the pages indicated. "Wife-beating,"

---

1. perennial (pə ren′ē əl), *adj.* lasting for a very long time; enduring.
2. incorporeal (in′kôr pôr′ē əl), *adj.* not made of any material substance; spiritual.
3. **Professor . . . England.** British historian G. M. Trevelyan published a one-volume history in 1926.

I read, "was a recognized right of man, and was practiced without shame by high as well as low. . . . Similarly," the historian goes on, "the daughter who refused to marry the gentleman of her parents' choice was liable to be locked up, beaten, and flung about the room, without any shock being inflicted on public opinion. Marriage was not an affair of personal affection, but of family avarice,[4] particularly in the 'chivalrous' upper classes. . . . Betrothal often took place while one or both of the parties was in the cradle, and marriage when they were scarcely out of the nurses' charge." That was about 1470, soon after Chaucer's time. The next reference to the position of women is some two hundred years later, in the time of the Stuarts. "It was still the exception for women of the upper and middle class to choose their own husbands, and when the husband had been assigned, he was lord and master, so far at least as law and custom could make him. Yet even so," Professor Trevelyan concludes, "neither Shakespeare's women nor those of authentic seventeenth-century memoirs, like the Verneys and the Hutchinsons,[5] seem wanting in personality and character." Certainly, if we consider it, Cleopatra must have had a way with her; Lady Macbeth, one would suppose, had a will of her own; Rosalind,[6] one might conclude, was an attractive girl. Professor Trevelyan is speaking no more than the truth when he remarks that Shakespeare's women do not seem wanting in personality and character. Not being a historian, one might go even further and say that women have burned like beacons in all the works of all the poets from the beginning of time—Clytemnestra, Antigone, Cleopatra, Lady Macbeth, Phedre, Cressida, Rosalind, Desdemona, the Duchess of Malfi, among the dramatists; then among the prose writers: Millamant, Clarissa, Becky Sharp, Anna Karenina, Emma Bovary, Madame de Guermantes[7]—the names flock to mind, nor do they recall women "lacking in personality and character." Indeed, if woman had no existence save

in the fiction written by men, one would imagine her a person of the utmost importance; very various; heroic and mean; splendid and sordid; infinitely beautiful and hideous in the extreme; as great as a man, some think even greater. But this is woman in fiction. In fact, as Professor Trevelyan points out, she was locked up, beaten, flung about the room.

A very queer, composite being thus emerges. Imaginatively she is of the highest importance; practically she is completely insignificant. She pervades poetry from cover to cover; she is all but absent from history. She dominates the lives of kings and conquerors in fiction; in fact she was the slave of any boy whose parents forced a ring upon her finger. Some of the most inspired words, some of the most profound thoughts in literature fall from her lips; in real life she could hardly read, could scarcely spell, and was the property of her husband.

It was certainly an odd monster that one made up by reading the historians first and the poets afterwards—a worm winged like an eagle; the spirit of life and beauty in a kitchen chopping up suet. But these monsters, however amusing to the imagination, have no existence in fact. What one must do to bring her to life

---

4. **avarice** (avʹər is), *n.* greed for wealth.

5. **Verneys . . . Hutchinsons,** two families of the 1600s. Lucy Hutchinson wrote a biography of her husband after his death.

6. **Cleopatra . . . Rosalind,** leading characters in Shakespeare's *Antony and Cleopatra, Macbeth,* and *As You Like It.*

7. **Clytemnestra . . . Madame de Guermantes.** Clytemnestra is in Aeschylus' *Agamemnon;* Antigone is in Sophocles' *Antigone;* Phedre is in Racine's *Phedre;* Cressida is in Shakespeare's *Troilus and Cressida;* Desdemona is in his *Othello; The Duchess of Malfi* is a play by Webster; Millamant is in Congreve's *The Way of the World;* Clarissa Harlowe is a novel by Richardson; Becky Sharp is the heroine in Thackeray's *Vanity Fair; Anna Karenina* is a novel by Tolstoy; Emma Bovary is in Flaubert's *Madame Bovary;* and Madame de Guermantes is in Proust's *Remembrance of Things Past.*

was to think poetically and prosaically[8] at one and the same moment, thus keeping in touch with fact—that she is Mrs. Martin, aged thirty-six, dressed in blue, wearing a black hat and brown shoes; but not losing sight of fiction either—that she is a vessel in which all sorts of spirits and forces are coursing and flashing perpetually. The moment, however, that one tries this method with the Elizabethan woman, one branch of illumination fails; one is held up by the scarcity of facts. One knows nothing detailed, nothing perfectly true and substantial about her. History scarcely mentions her. And I turned to Professor Trevelyan again to see what history meant to him. I found by looking at his chapter headings that it meant—

"The Manor Court and the Methods of Open-Field Agriculture . . . The Cistercians and Sheep-Farming . . . The Crusades . . . The University . . . The House of Commons . . . The Hundred Years' War . . . The Wars of the Roses . . . The Renaissance Scholars . . . The Dissolution of the Monasteries . . . Agrarian and Religious Strife . . . The Origin of English Sea-Power . . . The Armada . . ." and so on. Occasionally an individual woman is mentioned, an Elizabeth, or a Mary; a queen or a great lady. But by no possible means could middle-class women with nothing but brains and character at their command have taken part in any one of the great movements which, brought together, constitute the historian's view of the past. Nor shall we find her in any collection of anecdotes. Aubrey[9] hardly mentions her. She never writes her own life and scarcely keeps a diary; there are only a handful of her letters in existence. She left no plays or poems by which we can judge her. What one wants, I thought—and why does not some brilliant student at Newnham or Girton[10] supply it?—is a mass of information; at what age did she marry; how many children had she as a rule; what was her house like; had she a room to herself; did she do the cooking; would she be likely to have a servant? All these facts lie somewhere, presumably, in parish registers and account books; the life of the average Elizabethan woman must be scattered about somewhere, could one collect it and make a book of it. It would be ambitious beyond my daring. I thought, looking about the shelves for books that were not there, to suggest to the students of those famous colleges that they should rewrite history, though I own that it often seems a little queer as it is, unreal, lopsided; but why should they not add a supplement to history? calling it, of course, by some inconspicuous name so that women might figure there without impropriety?[11] For one often catches a glimpse of them in the lives of the great, whisking away into the background, concealing, I sometimes think, a wink, a laugh, perhaps a tear. And, after all, we have lives enough of Jane Austen; it scarcely seems necessary to consider again the influence of the tragedies of Joanna Baillie[12] upon the poetry of Edgar Allen Poe; as for myself, I should not mind if the homes and haunts of Mary Russell Mitford[13] were closed to the public for a century at least. But what I find deplorable, I continued, looking about the bookshelves again, is that nothing is known about women before the eighteenth century. I have no model in my mind to turn about this way and that. Here am I asking why women did not write poetry in the Elizabethan age, and I am not sure how they were educated; whether they were taught to write; whether they had sitting rooms to themselves; how many women had children before they were twenty-one; what, in short, they did from eight in the morning till

---

8. prosaically (prō zā′ik lē), *adv.* in an ordinary way.
9. **Aubrey,** John Aubrey (1626–1697), English biographer chiefly known for his *Brief Lives* of eminent people.
10. **Newnham or Girton,** two women's colleges at Cambridge University.
11. impropriety (im′prə prī′ə tē), *n.* improper conduct.
12. **Joanna Baillie** (1762–1851), Scottish dramatist and poet.
13. **Mary Russell Mitford** (1787–1855), English poet and dramatist. She is chiefly remembered for *Our Village: sketches of rural life, character, and scenery.*

eight at night. They had no money evidently; according to Professor Trevelyan they were married whether they liked it or not before they were out of the nursery, at fifteen or sixteen very likely. It would have been extremely odd, even upon this showing, had one of them suddenly written the plays of Shakespeare, I concluded, and I thought of that old gentleman, who is dead now, but was a bishop, I think, who declared that it was impossible for any woman, past, present, or to come, to have the genius of Shakespeare. He wrote to the papers about it. He also told a lady who applied to him for information that cats do not as a matter of fact go to heaven, thought they have, he added, souls of a sort. How much thinking those old gentlemen used to save one! How the borders of ignorance shrank back at their approach! Cats do not go to heaven. Women cannot write the plays of Shakespeare.

Be that as it may, I could not help thinking, as I looked at the works of Shakespeare on the shelf, that the bishop was right at least in this; it would have been impossible, completely and entirely, for any woman to have written the plays of Shakespeare in the age of Shakespeare. Let me imagine, since facts are so hard to come by, what would have happened had Shakespeare had a wonderfully gifted sister, called Judith, let us say. Shakespeare himself went, very probably—his mother was an heiress—to grammar school, where he may have learned Latin—Ovid, Virgil, and Horace[14]—and the elements of grammar and logic. He was, it is well known, a wild boy who poached rabbits, perhaps shot a deer, and had, rather sooner than he should have done, to marry a woman in the neighborhood, who bore him a child rather quicker than was right. That escapade sent him to seek his fortune in London. He had, it seemed, a taste for the theater; he began by holding horses at the stage door. Very soon he got work in the theater, became a successful actor, and lived at the hub of the universe, meeting everybody, knowing everybody, practicing his art on the boards, exercising his wits in the streets, and even getting access to the palace of the queen. Meanwhile his extraordinarily gifted sister, let us suppose, remained at home. She was as adventurous, as imaginative, as agog[15] to see the world as he was. But she was not sent to school. She had no chance of learning grammar and logic, let alone of reading Horace and Virgil. She picked up a book now and then, one of her brother's perhaps, and read a few pages. But then her parents came in and told her to mend the stockings or mind the stew and not moon about with books and papers. They would have spoken sharply but kindly, for they were substantial people who knew the conditions of life for a woman and loved their daughter—indeed, more likely than not she was the apple of her father's eye. Perhaps she scribbled some pages up in an apple loft on the sly, but was careful to hide them or set fire to them. Soon, however, before she was out of her teens, she was to be betrothed to the son of a neighboring wool-stapler.[16] She cried out that marriage was hateful to her, and for that she was severely beaten by her father. Then he ceased to scold her. He begged her instead not to hurt him, not to shame him in this matter of her marriage. He would give her a chain of beads or a fine petticoat, he said; and there were tears in his eyes. How could she disobey him? How could she break his heart? The force of her own gift alone drove her to it. She made up a small parcel of her belongings, let herself down by a rope one summer's night, and took the road to London. She was not seventeen. The birds that sang in the hedge were not more musical than she was. She had the quickest fancy, a gift like her brother's, for the tune of words. Like him, she had a taste for the

---

14. **Ovid, Virgil, and Horace,** Latin poets.
15. agog (ə gog′), *adj.* full of expectation or excitement; eager.
16. **wool-stapler,** a dealer who buys, grades, and sells wool.

theater. She stood at the stage door: she wanted to act, she said. Men laughed in her face. The manager—a fat, loose-lipped man—guffawed. He bellowed something about poodles dancing and women acting—no woman, he said, could possibly be an actress. He hinted—you can imagine what. She could get no training in her craft. Could she even seek her dinner in a tavern or roam the streets at midnight? Yet her genius was for fiction and lusted to feed abundantly upon the lives of men and women and the study of their ways. At last—for she was very young, oddly like Shakespeare the poet in her face, with the same gray eyes and rounded brows—at last Nick Greene the actor-manager took pity on her; she found herself with child by that gentleman and so—who shall measure the heat and violence of the poet's heart when caught and tangled in a woman's body?—killed herself one winter's night and lies buried at some crossroads where the omnibuses now stop outside the Elephant and Castle![17]

SUMMARIZE: What would have prevented Shakespeare's sister from writing?

That, more or less, is how the story would run, I think, if a woman in Shakespeare's day had had Shakespeare's genius. But for my part, I agree with the deceased bishop, if such he was—it is unthinkable that any woman in Shakespeare's day should have had Shakespeare's genius. For genius like Shakespeare's is not born among laboring, uneducated servile[18] people. It was not born in England among the Saxons and the Britons. It is not born today among the working classes. How, then, could it have been born among women whose work began, according to Professor Trevelyan, almost before they were out of the nursery, who were forced to it by their parents and held to it by all the power of law and custom? Yet genius of a sort must have existed among women as it must have existed among the working classes. Now and again an Emily Brontë

or a Robert Burns blazes out and proves its presence. But certainly it never got itself on to paper. When, however, one reads of a witch being ducked, of a woman possessed by devils, of a wise woman selling herbs, or even of a very remarkable man who had a mother, then I think we are on the track of a lost novelist, a suppressed poet, of some mute and inglorious[19] Jane Austen, some Emily Brontë who dashed her brains out on the moor or mopped and mowed about the highways crazed with the torture that her gift had put her to. Indeed, I would venture to guess that Anon, who wrote so many poems without signing them, was often a woman. It was a woman Edward FitzGerald, I think, suggested who made the ballads and the folk songs, crooning them to her children, beguiling her spinning with them, or the length of the winter's night.

This may be true or it may be false—who can say?—but what is true in it, so it seemed to me, reviewing the story of Shakespeare's sister as I had made it, is that any woman born with a great gift in the sixteenth century would certainly have gone crazed, shot herself, or ended her days in some lonely cottage outside the village, half witch, half wizard, feared and mocked at. For it needs little skill in psychology to be sure that a highly gifted girl who had tried to use her gift for poetry would have been so thwarted[20] and hindered by other people, so tortured and pulled asunder[21] by her own contrary instincts, that she must have lost her health and sanity to a certainty. No girl could have walked to London and stood at a stage door and forced her way into the presence of actor-managers without doing herself a violence and suffering an anguish which may have been irrational—for chastity may

---

17. **crossroads . . . Elephant and Castle.** Suicides were often buried at crossroads; the Elephant and Castle is a common name for a tavern.
18. servile (sėr′vəl), *adj.* slavelike.
19. inglorious (in glôr′ē əs), *adj.* shameful; disgraceful.
20. thwart (thwôrt), *v.* prevent from doing something.
21. asunder (ə sun′dər), *adv.* in pieces or separate parts.

be a fetish invented by certain societies for unknown reasons—but were none the less inevitable. Chastity had then, it has even now, a religious importance in a woman's life, and has so wrapped itself round with nerves and instincts that to cut it free and bring it to the light of day demands courage of the rarest. To have lived a free life in London in the sixteenth century would have meant for a woman who was poet and playwright a nervous stress and dilemma which might well have killed her. Had she survived, whatever she had written would have been twisted and deformed, issuing from a strained and morbid imagination. And undoubtedly, I thought, looking at the shelf where there are no plays by women, her work would have gone unsigned. That refuge she would have sought certainly. It was the relic of the sense of chastity that dictated anonymity[22] to women even so late as the nineteenth century. Currer Bell, George Eliot, George Sand,[23] all the victims of inner strife as their writings prove, sought ineffectively to veil themselves by using the name of a man. Thus they did homage to the convention, which if not implanted by the other sex was liberally encouraged by them (the chief glory of a woman is not to be talked of, said Pericles,[24] himself a much-talked-of man), that publicity in women is detestable. Anonymity runs in their blood. The desire to be veiled still possesses them. . . .

🐾 **CLARIFY: Why did these women deny their individuality to choose anonymity?**

I told you in the course of this paper that Shakespeare had a sister; but do not look for her in Sir Sidney Lee's life of the poet. She died young—alas, she never wrote a word. She lies buried where the omnibuses now stop, opposite the Elephant and Castle. Now my belief is that this poet who never wrote a word and was buried at the crossroads still lives. She lives in you and in me, and in many other women who are not here tonight, for they are washing up the dishes and putting the children to bed. But she lives; for great poets do not die; they are continuing presences; they need only the opportunity to walk among us in the flesh. This opportunity, as I think, it is now coming within your power to give her. For my belief is that if we live another century or so—I am talking of the common life which is the real life and not of the little separate lives which we live as individuals—and have five hundred a year each of us and rooms of our own; if we have the habit of freedom and the courage to write exactly what we think; if we escape a little from the common sitting room and see human beings not always in their relation to each other but in relation to reality; and the sky, too, and the trees or whatever it may be in themselves; if we look past Milton's bogey,[25] for no human being should shut out the view; if we face the fact, for it is a fact, that there is no arm to cling to, but that we go alone and that our relation is to the world of reality and not only to the world of men and women, then the opportunity will come and the dead poet who was Shakespeare's sister will put on the body which she has so often laid down. Drawing her life from the lives of the unknown who were her forerunners, as her brother did before her, she will be born. As for her coming without that preparation, without that effort on our part, without that determination that when she is born again she shall find it possible to live and write her poetry, that we cannot expect, for that would be impossible. But I maintain that she would come if we worked for her, and that so to work, even in poverty and obscurity, is worth while.

---

22. anonymity (an′ə nim′ə tē), *n.* condition of being unknown.
23. **Currer Bell, George Eliot, George Sand,** male pen names of the English novelists Charlotte Brontë and Mary Ann Evans, and the French novelist Amandine-Aurore Dupin.
24. **Pericles** (per′ə klēz′), Greek statesman and orator (495–429 B.C.)
25. **Milton's bogey.** In *Paradise Lost*, Milton portrays Eve as inferior to Adam. A bogey is a person or thing feared without reason.

After Reading

Making Connections

Shaping Your
Response

1. Do you find this essay relevant to your life? Why or
why not?

Analyzing the Essay

2. Why do you suppose Woolf mentions so many fictional female
characters? Is this technique effective, in your opinion?

3. What does Woolf achieve through her invention of a character she
calls Shakespeare's sister?

4. Woolf says that it is necessary for women to "have five hundred a
year . . . and rooms of our own" to succeed artistically. Why does she
say this? Do you agree?

5. 👆 The struggle for **individuality** often means that a person cannot
be a conformist. What aspects of this essay mark Woolf as a noncon-
formist?

Extending the Ideas

6. Some people seem to feel threatened by changing roles for women,
by women's achievements outside the home, and by women who
achieve. Why do you think they have these feelings?

Literary Focus: Paradox

A statement that may be valid but that seems to say two different and
contradictory things is a **paradox.** A paradox can also be a person,
thing, or situation that is full of contradictions.

1. Woolf says that a "composite being . . . emerges" when one considers
women in the 1500s and 1600s. What makes this "being" a paradox?

2. What does Professor Trevelyan have to do with this paradox?

Vocabulary Study

Choose the word from the list that most closely describes each idea
or event.

agog
anonymity
asunder
impropriety
incorporeal
inglorious
perennial
prosaically
servile
thwart

1. Stories about that crumbling pile of stonework known as Hoxley Hall
were enduring in our small town.

2. Over the years the previous owner had acquired a reputation that was
shameful.

3. Had he become rich through some kind of improper conduct?

4. It was known that he had treated his servants in a way to make them
feel like slaves.

5. Whatever the truth, it seemed that he had not lived his life in a plain,
unexciting fashion.

6 Hoxley Hall, too, had hardly become an unknown and forgotten building.

7. Now Brian, Rosemary, and I approached the mansion, all extremely eager to learn its secrets.

8. At first we were prevented from entering because of an iron chain through the handles of the front double doors.

9. Brian had thoughtfully brought a tool to snap the chain, however, and soon the links fell to the porch.

10. Imagine our surprise when, as we opened the front door, we witnessed a ghostly, translucent figure gliding down the stairway.

Expressing Your Ideas

Writing Choices

Reader's Log Update Review your lists of feminine endings, and in a paragraph explain whether you think such endings are useful and why or why not.

I Want to Be Me Finding your identity or striving to become an individual is part of growing up. Have you ever felt that people or circumstances were working to prevent you from finding your identity? In an **informal essay** describe one such episode in your life and what the outcome was.

Dear Ms. Woolf Write a **letter** to Virginia Woolf describing major events in women's rights today. You may want to do some research on the status of women's rights and on events of the last few years before starting your letter.

Other Options

Uncovering the Past Woolf has some insights into the writing of history that ignores women, but how *is* history written? In a small group, review the school year or the last semester, and discuss how you will decide which events in your school would be suitable for a history of that time. Who or what defines a "major" event? Is a major happening one that affects a few people or many? Should a controversial matter be included? Should you consider the relevance of an event to the community as a whole? Will you include more than one viewpoint in your history? Summarize the **discussion** and present the **summary** to the rest of the class.

Picture the Past Design a **mural** showing major events in the history of women's rights. If you want to include words or quotations in your mural, you might review Daniel Defoe's essay "The Education of Women" (page 306) and the excerpt from Mary Wollstonecraft's *A Vindication of the Rights of Woman* (page 456).

Before Reading

Do Not Go Gentle into That Good Night
A Child's Christmas in Wales by Dylan Thomas

Dylan Thomas
1914–1953

Dylan Thomas's fame—based in part on his exuberant lifestyle and popular public readings—threatened to over-shadow his poetry. He was born in Swansea, Wales, left school at sixteen to work as a newspaper reporter, and pub-lished his first volume of poetry at nineteen. *Portrait of the Artist as a Young Dog,* a collection of stories about his childhood and youth, appeared in 1940. He married Caitlin Macnamara in 1937, and they and their children were often partly supported by friends. *Deaths and Entrances* (1946) is his most famous poetry collection. *Quite Early One Morning* (1954), another book of boyhood reminiscences, and a verse play, *Under Milk Wood* (1954) were published after his death in New York during his fourth lecture tour.

Building Background

Galloping Words Dylan Thomas's father was a schoolteacher who read to Dylan when the boy was young. Thomas described "the colors the words cast on my eyes . . . and though what the words meant was, in its own way, often deliciously funny enough, so much funnier seemed to me, at that almost forgotten time, the shape and shade and size and noise of words as they hummed, strummed, jigged, and galloped along." Thomas wrote "Do Not Go Gentle into That Good Night" just before the death of his father. "A Child's Christmas in Wales" is an expanded version of a talk Thomas gave on the BBC radio station. It was first published in *Harper's Bazaar* and then recorded, becoming one of the most famous works Thomas ever read for the public.

Literary Focus

Imagery Details that appeal to the senses and provide vividness in a literary work or tend to arouse emotions or feelings in a reader are called **imagery.** Effective imagery often appeals to more than one sense at a time, as in this passage from Dylan Thomas's *Portrait of the Artist as a Young Dog.*

"On windy October nights, dry leaves scraped across the sidewalk, and the dust of them caught in our throats. Already the air nipped at our noses, and our breath hung for an instant in the icy air and vanished. Always, the shadow of a cat crossed the alley behind Mrs. Wiley's house, and the bushes were full of strange and fearful shapes."

Notice the imagery in these selections by Thomas.

Writer's Notebook

Remember When? Think of your favorite holiday, and under headings for the five senses (sight, hearing, taste, smell, and touch) jot down several words or phrases that appeal to these senses and help to describe the holiday. For example, under *hearing,* you might write "murmur of voices"; under *sight,* you might describe a burning candle.

Do Not Go Gentle into That Good Night

Dylan Thomas

Do not go gentle into that good night,
Old age should burn and rave at close of day;
Rage, rage against the dying of the light.

Though wise men at their end know dark is right,
5 Because their words had forked no lightning they
Do not go gentle into that good night.

Good men, the last wave by, crying how bright
Their frail deeds might have danced in a green bay,
Rage, rage against the dying of the light.

10 Wild men who caught and sang the sun in flight,
And learn, too late, they grieved it on its way,
Do not go gentle into that good night.

Grave men, near death, who see with blinding sight
Blind eyes could blaze like meteors and be gay,
15 Rage, rage against the dying of the light.

And you, my father, there on the sad height,
Curse, bless, me now with your fierce tears, I pray.
Do not go gentle into that good night.
Rage, rage against the dying of the light.

A Child's Christmas in Wales

DYLAN THOMAS

▲ *Snow Scene* was painted in 1879 by an amateur artist identified as W. Park. In its depiction of childhood, what qualities does it share with Dylan Thomas's memoir?

One Christmas was so much like another, in those years around the sea-town corner now and out of all sound except the distant speaking of the voices I sometimes hear a moment before sleep, that I can never remember whether it snowed for six days and six nights when I was twelve or whether it snowed for twelve days and twelve nights when I was six. All the Christmases roll down toward the two-tongued sea, like a cold and headlong moon bundling down the sky that was our street; and they stop at the rim of the ice-edged, fish-freezing waves, and I plunge my hands in the snow and bring out whatever I can find. In goes my hand into that wool-white bell-tongued ball of holidays resting at the rim of the carol-singing sea, and out come Mrs. Prothero and the firemen.

It was on the afternoon of the day of Christmas Eve, and I was in Mrs. Prothero's garden, waiting for cats, with her son Jim. It was snowing. It was always snowing at Christmas. December, in my memory, is white as Lapland, though there were no reindeers. But there were cats. Patient, cold and callous, our hands wrapped in socks, we waited to snowball the cats. Sleek and long as jaguars and horrible-whiskered, spitting and snarling, they would slink and sidle[1] over the white back-garden walls, and the lynx-eyed hunters, Jim and I, fur-capped and moccasined trappers from Hudson Bay, off Mumbles Road, would hurl our deadly snowballs at the green of their eyes. The wise cats never appeared. We were so still, Eskimo-footed arctic marksmen in the muffling silence of the eternal snows—eternal, ever since Wednesday—that we never heard Mrs. Prothero's first cry from her igloo at the bottom of the garden. Or, if we heard it at all, it was, to us, like the far-off challenge of our enemy and prey, the neighbour's polar cat. But soon the voice grew louder.

"Fire!" cried Mrs. Prothero, and she beat the dinner-gong.

And we ran down the garden, with the snowballs in our arms, toward the house; and smoke, indeed, was pouring out of the dining-room, and the bong was bombilating,[2] and Mrs. Prothero was announcing ruin like a town crier in Pompeii.[3] This was better than all the cats in Wales standing on the wall in a row. We bounded into the house, laden with snowballs, and stopped at the open door of the smoke-filled room. Something was burning all right; perhaps it was Mr. Prothero, who always slept there after midday dinner with a new paper over his face. But he was standing in the middle of the room, saying, "A fine Christmas!" and smacking at the smoke with a slipper.

"Call the fire brigade," cried Mrs. Prothero as she beat the gong.

"They won't be there," said Mr. Prothero, "It's Christmas."

There was no fire to be seen, only clouds of smoke and Mr. Prothero standing in the middle of them, waving his slipper as though he were conducting.

"Do something," he said.

And we threw all our snowballs into the smoke—I think we missed Mr. Prothero—and ran out of the house to the telephone box.

"Let's call the police as well," Jim said.

"And the ambulance."

"And Ernie Jenkins, he likes fires."

But we only called the fire brigade, and soon

. . . Mrs. Prothero was announcing ruin like a town crier in Pompeii.

---

1. sidle (sī′dl), v. move sideways.
2. bombilate (bom′bə lāt), v. hum; boom.
3. Pompeii (pom pā′), city in ancient Italy buried by an eruption of the volcano Mount Vesuvius in A.D. 79.

the fire engine came and three tall men in helmets brought a hose into the house and Mr. Prothero got out just in time before they turned it on. Nobody could have had a noisier Christmas Eve. And when the firemen turned off the hose and were standing in the wet, smoky room, Jim's aunt, Miss Prothero, came downstairs and peered in at them. Jim and I waited, very quietly, to hear what she would say to them. She said the right thing, always. She looked at the three tall firemen in their shining helmets, standing among the smoke and cinders and dissolving snowballs, and she said: "Would you like anything to read?"

Years and years and years ago, when I was a boy, when there were wolves in Wales, and birds the color of red-flannel petticoats whisked past the harp-shaped hills, when we sang and wallowed all night and day in caves that smelt like Sunday afternoons in damp front farmhouse parlors, and we chased, with the jawbones of deacons, the English and the bears, before the motor car, before the wheel, before the duchess-faced horse when we rode the daft[4] and happy hills bareback, it snowed and it snowed. But here a small boy says: "It snowed last year, too. I made a snowman and my brother knocked it down and I knocked my brother down and then we had tea."

"But that was not the same snow," I say. "Our snow was not only shaken from whitewash buckets down the sky, it came shawling out of the ground and swam and drifted out of the arms and hands and bodies of the trees; snow grew overnight on the roofs of the houses like a pure and grandfather moss, minutely white-ivied the walls and settled on the postman, opening the gate, like a dumb, numb thunderstorm of white, torn Christmas cards."

"Were there postmen then, too?"

"With sprinkling eyes and wind-cherried noses, on spread, frozen feet they crunched up to the doors and mittened on them manfully. But all that the children could hear was a ringing of bells."

"You mean that the postman went rat-a-tat-tat and the doors rang?"

"I mean that the bells that the children could hear were inside them."

"I only hear thunder sometimes, never bells."

"There were church bells, too."

"Inside them?"

"No, no, no, in the bat-black, snow-white belfries, tugged by bishops and storks. And they rang their tidings over the bandaged town, over the frozen foam of the powder and ice-cream hills, over the crackling sea. It seemed that all the churches boomed for joy under my window; and the weathercocks[5] crew for Christmas, on our fence."

CLARIFY: Why might Thomas use the word *bandaged* to describe the town?

"Get back to the postmen."

"They were just ordinary postmen, fond of walking and dogs and Christmas and the snow. They knocked on the doors with blue knuckles. . . ."

"Ours has got a black knocker. . . ."

"And then they stood on the white Welcome mat in the little, drifted porches and huffed and puffed, making ghosts with their breath, and jogged from foot to foot like small boys wanting to go out."

"And then the Presents?"

"And then the Presents, after the Christmas box.[6] And the cold postman, with a rose on his button-nose, tingled down the tea-tray-slithered run of the chilly glinting hill. He went in his ice-bound boots like a man on fishmonger's slabs. He wagged his bag like a frozen camel's hump, dizzily turned the corner on one foot, and, by God, he was gone."

---

4. **daft** (daft), *adj.* without sense or reason; silly.
5. **weathercock,** vane to show which way the wind is blowing, especially one in the shape of a rooster.
6. **Christmas box,** Christmas gift given to the postman.

"Get back to the Presents."

"There were the Useful Presents: engulfing mufflers of the old coach days, and mittens made for giant sloths; zebra scarfs of a substance like silky gum that could be tug-o'-warred down to the galoshes, blinding tam-o'-shanters like patchwork tea cozies and bunny-suited busbies and balaclavas[7] for victims of head-shrinking tribes; from aunts who always wore wool next to the skin there were mustached and rasping vests that made you wonder why the aunts had any skin left at all; and once I had a little crocheted nose bag from an aunt now, alas, no longer whinnying with us. And pictureless books in which small boys, though warned with quotations not to, *would* skate on Farmer Giles' pond and did and drowned; and books that told me everything about the wasp, except why."

"Go on to the Useless Presents."

"Bags of moist and many-colored jelly babies and a folded flag and a false nose and a tram-conductor's cap and a machine that punched tickets and rang a bell; never a catapult;[8] once, by mistake that no one could explain, a little hatchet; and a celluloid duck that made, when you pressed it, a most unducklike sound, a mewing moo that an ambitious cat might make who wished to be a cow; and a painting book in which I could make the grass, the trees, the sea and the animals any color I pleased, and still the dazzling sky-blue sheep are grazing in the red field under the rainbow-billed and pea-green birds. Hard-boileds, toffee, fudge and allsorts, crunches, cracknels, humbugs, glaciers, marzipan, and butterwelsh for the Welsh. And troops of bright tin soldiers who, if they could not fight, could always run. And Snakes-and-Families and Happy Ladders. And Easy Hobbi-Games for Little Engineers, complete with instructions. Oh, easy for Leonardo![9] And a whistle to make the dogs bark to wake up the old man next door to make him beat on the wall with his stick to shake our picture off the wall. And a packet of cigarettes: you put one in your mouth and you stood at the corner of the street and you waited for hours, in vain, for an old lady to scold you for smoking a cig-arette, and then with a smirk you ate it. And then it was breakfast under the balloons."

"Were there Uncles, like in our house?"

"There are always Uncles at Christmas. The same Uncles. And on Christmas mornings, with dog-disturbing whistle and sugar fags, I would scour the swatched town for the news of the little world, and find always a dead bird by the white Post Office or by the deserted swings; perhaps a robin, all but one of his fires out. Men and women wading or scooping back from chapel, with taproom noses and wind-bussed cheeks, all albinos, huddled their stiff black jarring feathers against the irreligious snow. Mistletoe hung from the gas brackets in all the front parlors; there was sherry and walnuts and bottled beer and crackers[10] by the dessertspoons; and cats in their furabouts watched the fires; and the high-heaped fire spat, all ready for the chestnuts and the mulling pokers.[11] Some few large men sat in the front parlors, without their collars, Uncles almost certainly, trying their new cigars, holding them out judiciously[12] at arms' length, returning them to their mouths, coughing, then holding them out again as though waiting for the explosion; and some few small aunts, not wanted in the kitchen, nor anywhere else for that matter, sat on the very edges of their chairs, poised and brittle, afraid to break, like faded cups and saucers."

CLARIFY: The Uncles are given no individual identity. Why?

---

7. **busby** (buz′bē) *n.* . . . **balaclava** (bal′ə klä′və), *n.* two kinds of hats.
8. **catapult** (kat′ə pult), *n.* slingshot.
9. **Leonardo,** Leonardo da Vinci (1452–1519), Italian painter, architect, engineer, and scientist.
10. **cracker,** party favor containing jokes or gifts that pops when the ends are pulled.
11. **mulling pokers,** fireplace pokers used to heat and stir a mulled drink. To *mull* is to heat, sweeten, and spice ale, wine, cider, and so on.
12. **judiciously** (jü dish′əs lē), *adv.* wisely; sensibly.

Not many those mornings trod[13] the piling streets: an old man always, fawn-bowlered,[14] yellow-gloved and, at this time of year, with spats[15] of snow, would take his constitutional[16] to the white bowling green and back, as he would take it wet or fine on Christmas Day or Doomsday; sometimes two hale young men, with big pipes blazing, no overcoats and wind-blown scarfs, would trudge, unspeaking, down to the forlorn sea, to work up an appetite, to blow away the fumes, who knows, to walk into the waves until nothing of them was left but the two curling smoke clouds of their inextinguishable briars. Then I would be slapdashing home, the gravy smell of the dinners of others, the bird smell, the brandy, the pudding and mince, coiling up to my nostrils, when out of a snow-clogged side lane would come a boy the spit of myself, with a pink-tipped cigarette and the violet past of a black eye, cocky as a bullfinch, leering all to himself. I hated him on sight and sound, and would be about to put my dog whistle to my lips and blow him off the face of Christmas when suddenly he, with a violet wink, put *his* whistle to *his* lips and blew so stridently, so high, so exquisitely loud, that gobbling faces, their cheeks bulged with goose, would press against their tinseled windows, the whole length of the white echoing street. For dinner we had turkey and blazing pudding, and after dinner the Uncles sat in front of the fire, loosened all buttons, put their large moist hands over their watch chains, groaned a little and slept. Mothers, aunts and sisters scuttled to and fro, bearing tureens.[17] Auntie Bessie, who had already been frightened, twice, by a clock-work mouse, whimpered at the sideboard and had some elderberry wine. The dog was sick. Auntie Dosie had to have three aspirins, but Auntie Hannah, who liked port, stood in the middle of the snow-bound back yard, singing like a big-bosomed thrush. I would blow up balloons to see how big they would blow up to; and when they burst, which they all did, the Uncles jumped and rumbled. In the rich and heavy afternoon, the Uncles breathing like dolphins and the snow descending, I would sit

among festoons and Chinese lanterns and nibble dates and try to make a model man-o'-war,[18] following the Instructions for Little Engineers, and produce what might be mistaken for a sea-going tramcar. Or I would go out, my bright new boots squeaking, into the white world, on to the seaward hill, to call on Jim and Dan and Jack and to pad through the still streets, leaving huge deep footprints on the hidden pavements.

CLARIFY: Who is speaking here?

"I bet people will think there's been hippos."

"What would you do if you saw a hippo coming down our street?"

"I'd go like this, bang! I'd throw him over the railings and roll him down the hill and then I'd tickle him under the ear and he'd wag his tail."

"What would you do if you saw *two* hippos?"

Iron-flanked and bellowing he-hippos clanked and battered through the scudding snow toward us as we passed Mr. Daniel's house.

"Let's post Mr. Daniel a snowball through his letter box."

"Let's write things in the snow."

"Let's write, 'Mr. Daniel looks like a spaniel' all over his lawn."

Or we walked on the white shore. "Can the fishes see it's snowing?"

The silent one-clouded heavens drifted on to the sea. Now we were snow-blind travelers lost on the north hills, and vast dewlapped dogs, with

---

13. tread (tred), *v.* trod, trodden or trod, treading, set the foot down; walk; step.
14. **bowlered,** wearing a bowler, a stiff felt hat with a narrow brim.
15. **spats** (spats), *n. pl.* short gaiters, outer coverings for the lower leg or ankle made of cloth or leather and worn over the instep, reaching just above the ankle.
16. constitutional (kon′stə tü′shə nəl), *n.* walk or other exercise taken for one's health.
17. **tureen** (tə rēn′), *n.* deep, covered dish for serving soup.
18. **man-o'-war,** warship used in past wars.

flasks round their necks, ambled and shambled up to us, baying "Excelsior."[19] We returned him through the poor streets where only a few children fumbled with bare red fingers in the wheel-rutted snow and catcalled after us, their voices fading away, as we trudged uphill, into the cries of the dock birds and the hooting of ships out in the whirling bay. And then, at tea the recovered Uncles would be jolly; and the ice cake loomed in the center of the table like a marble grave. Auntie Hannah laced her tea with rum, because it was only once a year.

Bring out the tall tales now that we told by the fire as the gaslight bubbled like a diver. Ghosts whooed like owls in the long nights when I dared not look over my shoulder; animals lurked in the cubbyhole under the stairs where the gas meter ticked. And I remember that we went singing carols once, when there wasn't the shaving of a moon to light the flying street. At the end of a long road was a drive that led to a large house, and we stumbled up the darkness of the drive that night, each one of us afraid, each one holding a stone in his hand in case, and all of us too brave to say a word. The wind through the trees made noises as of old and unpleasant and maybe webfooted men wheezing in caves. We reached the black bulk of the house.

"What shall we give them? Hark, the Herald?"

"No," Jack said, "Good King Wenceslas. I'll count three."

One, two, three, and we began to sing, our voices high and seemingly distant in the snow-felted darkness round the house that was occupied by nobody we knew. We stood close together, near the dark door.

The wind through the trees made noises as of old and unpleasant and maybe webfooted men wheezing in caves.

Good King Wenceslas looked out
On the Feast of Stephen . . .

And then a small, dry voice, like the voice of someone who has not spoken for a long time, joined our singing: a small, dry, eggshell voice from the other side of the door: a small dry voice through the keyhole. And when we stopped running we were outside *our* house; the front room was lovely; balloons floated under the hot-water-bottle-gulping gas; everything was good again and shone over the town.

"Perhaps it was a ghost," Jim said.

"Perhaps it was trolls,"[20] Dan said, who was always reading.

"Let's go in and see if there's any jelly left," Jack said. And we did that.

Always on Christmas night there was music. An uncle played the fiddle, a cousin sang "Cherry Ripe," and another uncle sang "Drake's Drum." It was very warm in the little house. Auntie Hannah, who had got on to the parsnip wine, sang about Bleeding Hearts and Death, and then another in which she said her heart was like a Bird's Nest; and then everybody laughed again; and then I went to bed. Looking through my bedroom window, out into the moonlight and the unending smoke-colored snow, I could see the lights in the windows of all the other houses on our hill and hear the music rising from them up the long, steadily falling night. I turned the gas down, I got into bed. I said some words to the close and holy darkness, and then I slept.

---

19. **excelsior** (ek sel′sē ôr), *adj.* ever upward; higher. [*Latin*]
20. **troll** (trōl), *n.* in Scandinavian folklore, an ugly dwarf or giant with supernatural powers living underground or in a cave.

After Reading

Making Connections

Shaping Your
Response

1. In "Do Not Go Gentle . . ." why do you think the speaker urges resistance to instead of acceptance of death?

2. Is there anything in "A Child's Christmas in Wales" with which you can identify, or is the reminiscence too foreign or too dated? Explain.

Analyzing the
Selections

3. Does line 17 of the poem contain a **paradox?** Why, or why not?

4. Explain how Thomas combines many Christmases into this one essay. How does he signal the reader what he is doing?

5. For what purpose do you think Thomas introduces the small boy who speaks in the essay?

6. How would you describe the **mood** of this essay?

Extending the Ideas

7. Name some presents that you have received or given that would fit into either of the two categories of presents Thomas mentions in "A Child's Christmas in Wales."

Literary Focus: Imagery

Details that tend to arouse emotions or feelings in a reader or that appeal to the senses and provide vividness in a literary work are called **imagery.**

1. In "Do Not Go Gentle . . ." what contrasting and repeated images appeal to the sense of sight?

2. Why are images appealing to the sense of sight particularly appropriate in this poem?

3. What images in "A Child's Christmas in Wales" seem most vivid to you?

Vocabulary Study

catapult
constitutional
daft
sidle
tread

Using context clues, fill in each blank with the most appropriate word from the list.

After an enormous Thanksgiving dinner, Grandfather decided to take his usual ____. He stepped across an icy street, making an effort to ____ carefully. He was just reaching the curb when he felt a small object, evidently shot from a ____, strike him lightly between his shoulder blades. He turned around just in time to see a small boy ____ between two buildings. "Are you ____?" shouted Grandfather after the disappearing shape. "You might have hurt someone!"

Expressing Your Ideas

Writing Choices

Writer's Notebook Update Describe your favorite holiday, and include some of the images you jotted down before reading Dylan Thomas. Try to create a particular mood such as reverence, joy, nostalgia, contentment, humor, or excitement.

Brain-Stretching Lists Thomas makes use of compound words like "fish-freezing waves," which are similar to the kennings used in *Beowulf.* Point out several examples of these compounds and then devise your own **list of compounds** to describe waves, sand, sky, clouds, or people in a warm climate.

Relatively Speaking When Thomas describes uncles and aunts in his reminiscence they often, but not always, tend to be types, not individuals. Write a **description** of a relative, such as an uncle or an aunt, in a few paragraphs. Make an effort to demonstrate the **individuality** of this person by exactly describing physical characteristics and by detailing this person's actions.

Write a Villanelle "Do Not Go Gentle . . ." is a **villanelle** (vil′ə nel′), a verse form consisting of five three-line stanzas and a final quatrain. The rhyme scheme is *aba* in every stanza except the last, which is *abaa.* Lines 1 and 3 repeat alternatively as refrains. Although this is a challenging verse form, many poets have used it successfully. Work with a partner, if you wish, to write a poem in this verse form.

Other Options

Season's Greetings Design and illustrate a **greeting card** based on "A Child's Christmas in Wales," perhaps using a short quotation from the essay.

And the Winner Is . . . Hold a **photo competition** for black-and-white or color photographs of holiday celebrations. Work with a group to set a deadline for entries, assign judges, decide how many and what prizes you will award, and where winning photos will be displayed.

Before Reading

Studies in the Park

by Anita Desai

Anita Desai
born 1937

Anita Desai was born in Mussorie, India. She was educated at Queen Mary's School in Delhi and received her B. A. degree from the University of Delhi. She married Ashvin Desai in 1952; they have two sons and two daughters. In the United States she has taught writing at Smith College and at Mount Holyoke, and in 1993 became a professor of writing at the Massachusetts Institute of Technology. Desai's works include short stories, children's books, and several novels for adults, including *In Custody* (1984), recently made into a film by Merchant Ivory Productions, *Baumgartner's Bombay* (1989), which one critic called "a wonder of exquisitely crafted prose," and *Journey to Ithaca* (1995).

Building Background

India India is a complex country containing several religions and over 1,600 languages and dialects. Fifteen of these are recognized in India's Constitution, but Hindi is the official language, spoken by a little over thirty percent of the population. English is spoken by more than fifteen million people in India, however. In fact, all students are required to be bilingual, and many are trilingual, speaking Hindi, English, and their mother tongue.

The English language is a legacy from the days of British dominance over India, a legacy that also extended to banking, the judicial system, a network of railroads and roads, and education. In general, students who attend school have six years of primary school, three years of secondary school, and three years of upper secondary school. The narrator in the following story is in secondary school, but he soon finds other avenues of interest—to the dismay of his father.

Literary Focus

Simile A **simile** is a kind of figurative language, usually signaled by the words *like* or *as.* It is a comparison between two unlike things that have something in common. For example, the narrator says his father's voice "came out of his nose like the whistle of a punctual train," a comparison of two sounds. Similes help to make writing more vivid. Watch for them in the following story.

Writer's Notebook

Devising Similes Try your hand at creating some similes by completing the following phrases. Be as original as you can.

car engine sounded like . . .

eyes as bright as . . .

sweater as red as . . .

breeze smelled like . . .

weather as hot as . . .

STUDIES IN THE PARK

Anita Desai

Turn it off, turn it off, turn it off! First he listens to the news in Hindi. Directly after, in English. Broom—brroom—brrroom—the voice of doom roars. Next, in Tamil. Then in Punjabi. In Gujarati.[1] What next, my god, what next? Turn it off before I smash it onto his head, fling it out of the window, do nothing of the sort of course, nothing of the sort.

—And my mother. She cuts and fries, cuts and fries. All day I hear her chopping and slicing and the pan of oil hissing. What all does she find to fry and feed us on, for God's sake? Eggplants, potatoes, spinach, shoe soles, newspapers, finally she'll slice me and feed me to my brothers and sisters. Ah, now she's turned on the tap. It's roaring and pouring, pouring and roaring into a bucket without a bottom.

—The bell rings. Voices clash, clatter and break. The tin-and-bottle man? The neighbors? The police? The Help-the-Blind man? Thieves and burglars? All of them, all of them, ten or twenty or a hundred of them, marching up the stairs, hammering at the door, breaking in and climbing over me—ten, twenty or a hundred of them.

—Then, worst of all, the milk arrives. In the tallest glass in the house. "Suno, drink your milk. Good for you, Suno. You need it. Now, before the exams. Must have it, Suno. Drink." The voice wheedles its way into my ear like a worm. I shudder. The table tips over. The milk runs. The tumbler clangs on the floor. "Suno, Suno, how will you do your exams?"

—That is precisely what I ask myself. All very well to give me a room—Uncle's been pushed off on a pilgrimage to Hardwar to clear a room for me—and to bring me milk and say, "Study, Suno, study for your exam." What about the uproar around me? These people don't know the meaning of the word Quiet. When my mother fills buckets, sloshes the kitchen floor, fries and sizzles things in the pan, she thinks she is being Quiet. The children have never even heard the word, it amazes and puzzles them. On their way back from school they fling their satchels in at my door, then tear in to snatch them back before I tear them to bits. Bawl when I pull their ears, screech when mother whacks them. Stuff themselves with her fries and then smear the grease on my books.

So I raced out of my room, with my fingers in my ears, to scream till the roof fell down about their ears. But the radio suddenly went off, the door to my parents' room suddenly opened and my father appeared, bathed and shaven, stuffed and set up with the news of the world in six different languages—his white *dhoti*[2] blazing, his white shirt crackling, his patent leather pumps glittering. He stopped in the doorway and I stopped on the balls of my feet and wavered. My fingers came out of my ears, my hair came down over my eyes. Then he looked away from me, took his watch out of his pocket and inquired, "Is the food ready?" in a voice that came out of his nose like the whistle of a punctual train. He skated off towards his meal, I turned and slouched back to my room. On his way to work, he looked in to say, "Remember, Suno, I expect good results from you. Study hard, Suno." Just behind him, I saw all the rest of them standing,

---

1. **Hindi** (hin′dē) . . . **Tamil** (tam′əl) . . . **Punjabi** (punjä′bē) . . . **Gujarati** (gŭj′ə rät′ē). Four of the languages spoken in India.
2. *dhoti* (dō′tē), *n.* a loincloth worn by Hindu men in India.

peering in, silently. All of them stared at me, at the exam I was to take. At the degree I was to get. Or not get. Horrifying thought. Oh study, study, study, they all breathed at me while my father's footsteps went down the stairs, crushing each underfoot in turn. I felt their eyes on me, goggling, and their breath on me, hot with earnestness. I looked back at them, into their open mouths and staring eyes.

I snarled at him but he only smiled, determined to be friendly

"Study," I said, and found I croaked. "I know I ought to study. And how do you expect me to study—in this madhouse? You run wild, *wild*. I'm getting out," I screamed, leaping up and grabbing my books, "I'm going to study outside. Even the street is quieter," I screeched and threw myself past them and down the stairs that my father had just cowed and subjugated[3] so that they still lay quivering, and paid no attention to the howls that broke out behind me of "Suno, Suno, listen. Your milk—your studies—your exams, Suno!"

At first I tried the tea shop at the corner. In my reading I had often come across men who wrote at cafe tables—letters, verse, whole novels—over a cup of coffee or a glass of absinthe.[4] I thought it would be simple to read a chapter of history over a cup of tea. There was no crowd in the mornings, none of my friends would be there. But the proprietor would not leave me alone. Bored, picking his nose, he wandered down from behind the counter to my table by the weighing machine and tried to pass the time of day by complaining about his piles, the new waiter and the high prices. "And sugar," he whined. "How can I give you anything to put in

your tea with sugar at four rupees[5] a kilo? There's rationed sugar, I know, at two rupees, but that's not enough to feed even an ant. And the way you all sugar your tea—*hai, hai*," he sighed, worse than my mother. I didn't answer. I frowned at my book and looked stubborn. But when I got rid of him, the waiter arrived. "Have a biscuit?" he murmured, flicking at my table and chair with his filthy duster. "A bun? Fritters? Make you some hot fritters?" I snarled at him but he only smiled, determined to be friendly. Just a boy, really, in a pink shirt with purple circles stamped all over it—he thought he looked so smart. He was growing sideburns, he kept fingering them. "I'm a student, too," he said, "sixth class, fail. My mother wanted me to go back and try again, but I didn't like the teacher—he beat me. So I came here to look for a job. Lala-*ji* had just thrown out a boy called Hari for selling lottery tickets to the clients so he took me on. I can make out a bill . . ." He would have babbled on if Lala-*ji* had not come and shoved him into the kitchen with an oath. So it went on. I didn't read more than half a chapter that whole morning. I didn't want to go home either. I walked along the street, staring at my shoes, with my shoulders slumped in the way that makes my father scream, "What's the matter? Haven't you bones? A spine?" I kicked some rubble along the pavement, down the drain, then stopped at the iron gates of King Edward's Park.

"Exam troubles?" asked a *gram*[6] vendor who sat outside it, in a friendly voice. Not insinuating,[7] but low, pleasant. "The park's full of boys like you," he continued in that sympathetic voice. "I see them walk up and down, up and down with their books, like mad poets. Then I'm glad I was

---

3. subjugate (sub′jə gāt), *v.* subdue; conquer.
4. **absinthe** (ab′sinth), *n.* a bitter, green alcoholic drink flavored with anise, or other herbs.
5. **rupee** (rü pē′), *n.* monetary unit of India and some other countries.
6. *gram* (gram), *n.* any of various beans grown for food in India and often served roasted.
7. insinuate (in sin′yü āt), *v.* act or speak to gain favor in an indirect way.

never sent to school," and he began to whistle, not impertinently but so cheerfully that I stopped and stared at him. He had a crippled arm that hung out of his shirt sleeve like a leg of mutton dangling on a hook. His face was scarred as though he had been dragged out of some terrible accident. But he was shuffling hot *gram* into paper cones with his one hand and whistling like a bird, whistling the tune of, "We are the *bul-buls*[8] of our land, our land is Paradise." Nodding at the greenery beyond the gates, he said, "The park's a good place to study in," and, taking his hint, I went in.

I wonder how it is I never thought of the park before. It isn't far from our house and I sometimes went there as a boy, if I managed to run away from school, to lie on a bench, eat peanuts, shy stones at the chipmunks that came for the shells, and drink from the fountain. But then it was not as exciting as playing marbles in the street or stoning rats with my school friends in the vacant lot behind the cinema. It had straight paths, beds of flapping red flowers—cannas, I think—rows of palm trees like limp flags, a dry fountain and some green benches. Old men sat on them with their legs far apart, heads dropping over the tops of sticks, mumbling through their dentures or cackling with that mad, ripping laughter that makes children think of old men as wizards and bogey-men. Bag-like women in gray and fawn *saris* or black *borkhas*[9] screamed, just as gray and fawn and black birds do, at children falling into the fountain or racing on rickety legs after the chipmunks and pigeons. A madman or two, prancing around in paper caps and bits of rags, munching banana peels and scratching like monkeys. Corners behind hibiscus bushes stinking of piss. Iron rails with rows of beggars contentedly dozing, scratching, gambling, with their sackcloth backs to the rails. A city park.

What I hadn't noticed, or thought of, were all the students who escaped from their city flats and families like mine to come and study here. Now, walking down a path with my history book

tucked under my arm, I felt like a gatecrasher at a party or a visitor to a public library trying to control a sneeze. They all seemed to belong here, to be at home here. Dressed in loose pajamas, they strolled up and down under the palms, books open in their hands, heads lowered into them. Or they sat in twos and threes on the grass, reading aloud in turns. Or lay full length under the trees, books spread out across their faces—sleeping, or else imbibing[10] information through the subconscious. Opening out my book, I too strolled up and down, reading to myself in a low murmur.

CLARIFY: Why does Suno feel like a gatecrasher?

In the beginning, when I first started studying in the park, I couldn't concentrate on my studies. I'd keep looking up at the boy strolling in front of me, reciting poetry in a kind of thundering whisper, waving his arms about and running his bony fingers through his hair till it stood up like a thorn bush. Or at the chipmunks that fought and played and chased each other all over the park, now and then joining forces against the sparrows over a nest or a paper cone of *gram*. Or at the madman going through the rubble at the bottom of the dry fountain and coming up with a rubber shoe, a banana peel or a piece of glittering tin that he appreciated so much that he put it in his mouth and chewed it till blood ran in strings from his mouth.

It took me time to get accustomed to the ways of the park. I went there daily, for the

---

8. *bul-bul* (bŭl′bŭl), *n.* song bird of southern Asia and Africa, of the same family as the thrush.
9. *sari . . . borkha.* A sari (sär′ē) is the outer garment of Hindu women, a long piece of cotton or silk wrapped around the body, with one end falling nearly to the feet and the other end thrown over the head or shoulder. A borkha (bŭr′kə) is a garment worn by Muslim women that covers the head and face.
10. imbibe (im bīb′), *v.* drink in; absorb.

whole day, and soon I got to know it as well as my own room at home and found I could study there, or sleep, or daydream, as I chose. Then I fell into its routine, its rhythm, and my time moved in accordance with its time. We were like a house-owner and his house, or a turtle and its shell, or a river and its bank—so close. I resented everyone else who came to the park—I thought they couldn't possibly share my feeling for it. Except, perhaps, the students.

The park was like a hotel, or a hospital, belonging to the city but with its own order and routine, enclosed by iron rails, laid out according to prescription in rows of palms, benches and paths. If I went there very early in the morning, I'd come upon a yoga class. It consisted of young bodybuilders rippling their muscles like snakes as well as old crack-pots determined to keep up with the youngest and fittest, all sitting cross-legged on the grass and displaying *hus-mukh*[11] to the sun just rising over the palms; the Laughing Face pose it was called, but they looked like gargoyles[12] with their mouths torn open and their thick, discolored tongues sticking out. If I were the sun, I'd feel so disgusted by such a reception I'd just turn around and go back. And that was the simplest of their poses—after that they'd go into contortions that would embarrass an ape. Once their leader, a black and hirsute[13] man like an aborigine, saw me watching and called me to join them. I shook my head and ducked behind an oleander. . . . I despise all that body-beautiful worship anyway. What's the body compared to the soul, the mind?

I'd stroll under the palms, breathing in the cool of the early morning, feeling it drive out, or wash clean, the stifling dark of the night, and try to avoid bumping into all the other early morning visitors to the park—mostly aged men sent by their wives to fetch the milk from the Government dairy booth just outside the gates. Their bottles clinking in green cloth bags and newspapers rolled up and tucked under their arms, they strutted along like stiff puppets and mostly they would be discussing philosophy. "Ah but in Vedanta[14] it

is a different matter," one would say, his eyes gleaming fanatically, and another would announce, "The sage Shanakaracharya showed the way," and some would refer to the Upanishads or the Bhagavad Puranas,[15] but in such argumentative, hacking tones that you could see they were quite capable of coming to blows over some theological argument. Certainly it was the mind above the body for these old coots but I found nothing to admire in them either. I particularly resented it when one of them disengaged himself from the discussion long enough to notice me and throw me a gentle look of commiseration.[16] As if he'd been through exams, too, long long ago, and knew all about them. So what?

Worst of all were the athletes, wrestlers, Mr. Indias and others who lay on their backs and were massaged with oil till every muscle shone and glittered. The men who massaged them huffed and puffed and cursed as they climbed up and down the supine[17] bodies, pounding and pummeling the men who lay there wearing nothing but little greasy clouts, groaning and panting in a way I found obscene and disgusting. They never looked up at me or at anyone. They lived in a meaty, sweating world of their own—massages, oils, the body, a match to be fought and won—I kicked up dust in their direction but never went too close.

The afternoons would be quiet, almost empty. I would sit under a tree and read, stroll and study, doze too. Then, in the evening, as the sky softened from its blank white glare and took

---

11. **hus-mukh** (hus′mŭk), *n.* a cheerful or laughing face. [*Hindi*]
12. **gargoyle** (gär′goil), *n.* figure in the shape of a grotesque animal or human being, often draining water from the gutter of a building.
13. **hirsute** (hėr′sūt), *adj.* hairy.
14. **Vedanta** (vi dan′tə), *n.* a system of philosophy founded on the Vedas, sacred writings of the ancient Hindus.
15. **Upanishads** (ü pan′ə shadz) . . . **Bhagavad Puranas** (bug′ə vəd pù rä′nəz), *n. pl.* ancient commentaries and Hindu epics, myths, and other literature.
16. **commiseration** (kə miz′ə rā′shən), *n.* feeling of sympathy for another's trouble.
17. **supine** (sŭ pīn′), *adj.* lazily inactive; listless.

▲ *Head of a Woman* (1937) was painted by the Nobel Prize-winning Indian poet and dramatist Rabindranath Tagore (1861–1941). What is the chief feeling conveyed by this image?

on shades of pink and orange and the palm trees rustled a little in an invisible breeze, the crowds would begin to pour out of Darya Ganji, Mori Gate, Chandni Chowk and the Jama Masjid bazaars and slums. Large families would come to sit about on the grass, eating peanuts and listening to a transistor radio placed in the center of the circle. Mothers would sit together in flocks like screeching birds while children jumped into the dry fountains, broke flowers and terrorized each other. There would be a few young men moaning at the corners, waiting for a girl to roll her hips and dart her fish eyes in their direction, and then start the exciting adventure of pursuit. The children's cries would grow more piercing with the dark; frightened, shrill and exalted with mystery and farewell. I would wander back to the flat.

The exams drew nearer. Not three, not two, but only one month to go. I had to stop daydreaming and set myself tasks for every day and remind myself constantly to complete them. It grew so hot I had to give up strolling on the paths and staked out a private place for myself under a tree. I noticed the tension tightening the eyes and mouths of other students—they applied themselves more diligently to their books, talked less, slept less. Everyone looked a little demented from lack of sleep. Our books seemed attached to our hands as though by roots, they were a part of us, they lived because we fed them. They were parasites[18] and, like parasites, were sucking us dry. We mumbled to ourselves, not always consciously. Chipmunks jumped over our feet, mocking us. The *gram* seller down at the gate whistled softly "I'm glad I never went to school, I am a *bul-bul*, I live in Paradise . . ."

My brains began to jam up. I could feel it happening, slowly. As if the oil were all used up. As if everything was getting locked together, rusted. The white cells, the gray matter, the springs and nuts and bolts. I yelled at my mother—I think it was my mother—"What do you think I am? What do you want of me?" and crushed a glass of milk between my hands. It was

sticky. She had put sugar in my milk. As if I were a baby. I wanted to cry. They wouldn't let me sleep, they wanted to see my light on all night, they made sure I never stopped studying. Then they brought me milk and sugar and made clicking sounds with their tongues. I raced out to the park. I think I sobbed as I paced up and down, up and down, in the corner that stank of piss. My head ached worse than ever. I slept all day under the tree and had to work all night.

My father laid his hand on my shoulder. I knew I was not to fling it off. So I sat still, slouching, ready to spring aside if he lifted it only slightly. "You must get a first,[19] Suno," he said through his nose, "must get a first, or else you won't get a job. Must get a job, Suno," he sighed and wiped his nose and went off, his patent leather pumps squealing like mice. I flung myself back in my chair and howled. Get a first, get a first, get a first—like a railway engine, it went charging over me, grinding me down, and left me dead and mangled on the tracks.

Everything hung still and yellow in the park. I lay sluggishly on a heap of waste paper under my tree and read without seeing, slept without sleeping. Sometimes I went to the water tap that leaked and drank the leak. It tasted of brass. I spat out a mouthful. It nearly went over the feet of the student waiting for his turn at that dripping tap. I stepped aside for him. He swilled the water around his mouth and spat, too, carefully missing my feet. Wiping his mouth, he asked, "B.A.?"

"No, Inter."[20]

"Hu," he burped. "Wait till you do your B.A. Then you'll get to know." His face was like a gray bone. It was not unkind, it simply had no expression. "Another two weeks," he sighed and slouched off to his own lair.

I touched my face. I thought it would be all

---

18. parasite (par′ə sīt), *n.* person who lives on others without making any useful or fitting returns.
19. **first,** the highest grade.
20. **Inter,** intermediate degree, taken during high school and before the B. A. (Bachelor of Arts) or college degree.

bone, like his. I was surprised to find a bit of skin still covering it. I felt as if we were all dying in the park, that when we entered the examination hall it would be to be declared officially dead. That's what the degree was about. What else was it all about? Why were we creeping around here, hiding from the city, from teachers and parents, pretending to study and prepare? Prepare for what? We hadn't been told. Inter, they said, or B.A. or M.A. These were like official stamps—they would declare us dead. Ready for a dead world. A world in which ghosts went about, squeaking or whining, rattling or rustling. Slowly, slowly we were killing ourselves in order to join them. The ball-point pen in my pocket was the only thing that still lived, that still worked. I didn't work myself any more—I mean physically, my body no longer functioned. I was constipated, I was dying. I was lying under a yellow tree, feeling the dust sift through the leaves to cover me. It was filling my eyes, my throat. I could barely walk. I never strolled. Only on the way out of the park, late in the evening, I crept down the path under the palms, past the benches.

PREDICT: Do you think Suno will pass the exam?

Then I saw the scene that stopped it all, stopped me just before I died.

Hidden behind an oleander was a bench. A woman lay on it, stretched out. She was a Muslim, wrapped in a black *borkha*. I hesitated when I saw this straight, still figure in black on the bench. Just then she lifted a pale, thin hand and lifted her veil. I saw her face. It lay bared, in the black folds of her *borkha*, like a flower, wax-white and composed, like a Persian lily or a tobacco flower at night. She was young. Very young, very pale, beautiful with a beauty I had never come across even in a dream. It caught me and held me tight, tight till I couldn't breathe and couldn't move. She was so white, so still, I saw she was very ill—with anemia, perhaps, or T.B.[21] Too pale, too white—I could see she was dying. Her head—so still and

white it might have been carved if it weren't for this softness, this softness of a flower at night—lay in the lap of a very old man. Very much older than her. With spectacles and a long gray beard like a goat's, or a scholar's. He was looking down at her and caressing her face—so tenderly, so tenderly, I had never seen a hand move so gently and tenderly. Beside them, on the ground, two little girls were playing. Round little girls, rather dirty, drawing lines in the gravel. They stared at me but the man and the woman did not notice me. They never looked at anyone else, only at each other, with an expression that halted me. It was tender, loving, yes, but in an inhuman way, so intense. Divine, I felt, or insane. I stood, half-hidden by the bush, holding my book, and wondered at them. She was ill, I could see, dying. Perhaps she had only a short time to live. Why didn't he take her to the Victoria Zenana Hospital, so close to the park? Who was this man—her husband, her father, a lover? I couldn't make out although I watched them without moving, without breathing. I felt not as if I were staring rudely at strangers, but as if I were gazing at a painting or a sculpture, some work of art. Or seeing a vision. They were still and I stood still and the children stared. Then she lifted her arms above her head and laughed. Very quietly.

I broke away and hurried down the path, in order to leave them alone, in privacy. They

Then I saw the scene that stopped it all, stopped me just before I died.

21. **anemia** (ə nē′mē ə) . . . **TB.** Anemia is a condition resulting from an insufficiency of red blood cells and characterized by weakness and pallor. *TB* is short for *tuberculosis,* an infectious disease most often of the lungs.

Studies in the Park **839**

weren't a work of art, or a vision, but real, human and alive as no one else in my life had been real and alive. I had only that glimpse of them. But I felt I could never open my books and study or take degrees after that. They belonged to the dead, and now I had seen what being alive meant. The vision burned the surfaces of my eyes so that they watered as I groped my way up the stairs to the flat. I could hardly find my way to the bed.

It was not just the examination but everything else had suddenly withered and died, gone lifeless and purposeless when compared with this vision. My studies, my family, my life—they all belonged to the dead and only what I had seen in the park had any meaning.

Since I did not know how to span the distance between that beautiful ideal and my stupid, dull existence, I simply lay still and shut my eyes. I kept them shut so as not to see all the puzzled, pleading, indignant faces of my family around me, but I could not shut out their voices.

"Suno, Suno," I heard them croon and coax and mourn.

"Suno, drink milk."

"Suno, study."

"Suno, take the exam."

And when they tired of being so patient with me and I still would not get up, they began to crackle and spit and storm.

"Get up, Suno."

"Study, Suno."

"At once, Suno."

Only my mother became resigned and gentle. She must have seen something quite out of the ordinary on my face to make her so. I felt her hand on my forehead and heard her say, "Leave him alone. Let him sleep tonight. He is tired out, that is what it is—he has driven himself too much and now he must sleep."

Then I heard all of them leave the room. Her hand stayed on my forehead, wet and smelling of onions, and after a bit my tears began to flow from under my lids.

"Poor Suno, sleep," she murmured.

I went back to the park of course. But now I was changed. I had stopped being a student—I was a "professional." My life was dictated by the rules and routine of the park. I still had my book open on the palms of my hands as I strolled but now my eyes strayed without guilt, darting at the young girls walking in pairs, their arms linked, giggling and bumping into each other. Sometimes I stopped to rest on a bench and conversed with one of the old men, told him who my father was and what examination I was preparing for, and allowing him to tell me about his youth, his politics, his philosophy, his youth and again his youth. Or I joked with the other students, sitting on the grass and throwing peanut shells at the chipmunks, and shocking them, I could see, with my irreverence and cynicism about the school, the exam, the system. Once I even nodded at the yoga teacher and exchanged a few words with him. He suggested I join his class and I nodded vaguely and said I would think it over. It might help. My father says I need help. He says I am hopeless but that I need help. I just laugh but I know that he knows I will never appear for the examination, I will never come up to that hurdle or cross it—life has taken a different path for me, in the form of a search, not a race as it is for him, for them.

Yes, it is a search, a kind of perpetual search for me and now that I have accepted it and don't struggle, I find it satisfies me entirely, and I wander about the park as freely as a prince in his palace garden. I look over the benches, I glance behind the bushes, and wonder if I shall ever get another glimpse of that strange vision that set me free. I never have but I keep hoping, wishing.

After Reading

Making Connections

Shaping Your Response

1. Are you sympathetic to Suno? Why or Why not?

Analyzing the Story

2. What are the **conflicts** in this story?

3. If Suno is the **protagonist** in this story, does he have an **antogonist?** If so, who—or what?

4. Trace the changes in Suno's feelings about himself throughout the story.

5. Why do you think Suno is so affected by the man and woman he sees in the park?

6. Discuss whether or not Suno undergoes an **epiphany.** Do you think he will be permanently changed?

7. In a different time and place, Suno might be called a dropout. Yet he now refers to himself as a "professional." What do you think he means?

Extending the Ideas

8. 🐾 People have their own personal ways of responding to group pressures to achieve, such as getting a first in an exam. Do you think that such pressures are harmful to **individuality,** or do they test it and improve it?

Literary Focus: Simile

A **simile** is a figurative comparison between two unlike things that have something in common. It is usually signaled by the words *like* or *as.*

1. The narrator says that he and the park "were like a house-owner and his house, or a turtle and its shell, or a river and its bank—so close." Later he compares the park to a hotel or a hospital. What is the effect of these similes?

2. The body builders ripple their muscles "like snakes" and Suno's father's shoes squeal "like mice." How do these similes reveal the narrator's state of mind?

Vocabulary Study

Write the letter of the word that is not related in meaning to the other words in the set.

imbibe
insinuate
parasite
subjugate
supine

1. **a.** sleep   **b.** imbibe   **c.** drink   **d.** absorb
2. **a.** subjugate   **b.** subtract   **c.** defeat   **d.** enslave
3. **a.** supine   **b.** active   **c.** lively   **d.** energetic
4. **a.** hanger-on   **b.** partner   **c.** parasite   **d.** dependent
5. **a.** insinuate   **b.** hint   **c.** ask   **d.** imply

Expressing Your Ideas

Writing Choices

Writer's Log Update Compare the similes you wrote before reading "Studies in the Park" with those of others in your class, and have someone put them on the chalkboard. How many red things were suggested to compare with a red sweater, for example? (an apple? blood? a rose? a sunset?) Which seem most appropriate?

Great Expectations "Remember, Suno, I expect good results from you," Suno's father says. What are some expectations other people have for you? What are your expectations for yourself? In a short **essay** write about them, how you feel about them, and how you think you will achieve them.

Urban Space If you live near a city park or often visit one, describe the people, animals, and plants you see there in a **column** suitable for a daily newspaper. Include your feelings about the place. Does it seem hospitable? safe? clean? Or is it just the opposite?

Other Options

On the Aisle View one of the films described here and give an **oral review** for the class. The 1984 movie *A Passage to India* is based on E. M. Forster's novel of the same name and depicts India under British rule and the consequences of racial prejudice. *Gandhi* (1982), an Academy-Award winning film starring Ben Kingsley as Mohandas K. Gandhi (1869–1948), is the story of the work and the death of this Hindu political, social, and religious leader.

Good Listening Find and **play a recording** of the music of Ravi Shankar (pictured here) for the class. Shankar plays the sitar (si tär⁄), an Indian instrument with a long neck and two sets of strings, one beneath the other. What else can you learn about this unique instrument and the music it produces?

The Search For Identity

Modern Faces

Fine Art Connection

In a famous observation, Virginia Woolf stated, "In or about December, 1910, human character changed." The portraits in this section were created by artists who were contemporaries of Woolf's.

MODERN FACES

MODERN

FACES

(top left) Gwen John, *Self-Portrait* (1900)
Gwen John spent most of her artistic career in Paris,
living as a recluse, often in great poverty. Does this
self–portrait reflect a timid nature?

(above) Meredith Frampton
Portrait of a Young Woman (1935)
A painstaking craftsman, Frampton worked very slowly
at his portraits. Why do you think he grouped these
objects around his subject?

(left) Henry Lamb, *Portrait of Lytton Strachey* (1914)
Lytton Strachey was famous for the satiric biographical
sketches in his book *Eminent Victorians*. Do you think
Henry Lamb was attempting satire in his portrait of
Strachey?

(top left) Simon Bussy, *Lady Ottoline Morrell* (1920)
Lady Ottoline Morrell was an upper-class hostess
famous for her gatherings of artists, writers, and other
cultural figures. Does her portrait suggest a self-confi-
dent person?

(above) Ann Rice, *Portrait of Katherine Mansfield*
Mansfield's fiction ranged from sympathetic studies of
the victimized to sharp social satire. Which quality –
sympathy or satire – seems to be most reflected in Ann
Rice's portrait?

(left) Percy Wyndham Lewis
Portrait of Stephen Spender (1938)
Lewis's paintings show the influence of cubism, with
its attempt to interpret the world in terms of geometric
forms. What shapes can you see in his portrait of poet
Stephen Spender?

Responding

1. Which of these painters would
you commission to do a portrait
of you?

2. Are there qualities shared by all
these faces? If so, what are they?

Writing Workshop

Turning Points

Assignment In James Joyce's "Eveline" and Anita Desai's "Studies in the Park," the main characters seem to change in some significant way, but the authors never directly define the change. Try to get into the mind of one of these characters and identify this change.

WRITER'S BLUEPRINT

Product   An interpretive essay
Purpose   To interpret how a character changes
Audience   Readers who are familiar with these stories
Specs   As the writer of a successful essay, you should:

☐ Choose either Joyce's Eveline or Desai's Suno as your subject.

☐ Begin your essay with a thesis statement that summarizes your views on how this character has changed and why. The rest of your essay will amplify and explain this thesis. Then give a brief profile of your character.

☐ Identify the point in the story when the character changes by experiencing an epiphany—a moment of heightened awareness that signals a turning point in her or his life—and explain how you think this turning point comes about.

☐ End by describing how the character's life will be different as a result of this heightened awareness, how the character's behavior will change.

☐ Use quotations from the story to support your conclusions.

☐ Follow the rules of grammar, usage, spelling, and mechanics. Avoid sentence fragments.

STEP **1** PREWRITING

Choose a character. Joyce's Eveline or Desai's Suno—which character intrigues you more? Does either character's situation remind you of an experience in your own life? Which character do you find more sympathetic? The answers to these questions should help you decide which character you'll write about.

Define the epiphany—the moment that you think the author means to signal a turning point in the character's life, after which the character's behavior will change. Reread this part of the story carefully and make notes on the character's reactions.

Profile your character to find out how this epiphany comes about. Look over the character traits listed below. Which ones strike you as particularly fitting for your character? Note these, as well as any other traits that come to mind:

> independent, dependent, passive, aggressive, logical, illogical, happy, unhappy, hard-working, lazy, self-confident, uncertain, kind, cruel, decisive, indecisive, strong, weak, brave, cowardly, patient, impatient, lively, dull

OR . . .
Plot your character's progression on a time line. Indicate and illustrate with brief quotations the moment at which your character experiences an epiphany.

Compose your thesis statement—your argument, which the rest of your essay will prove. For this essay, your thesis statement will focus on how your character has changed. It should:

- consist of a sentence or two

- state the claim you intend to prove (how your character has changed)

- raise questions that your essay must answer

Look ahead to the Revising Strategy in Step 3 of this lesson for more detailed information on what goes into an effective thesis statement. Look closely at the examples you'll find there. Then look back at your character profile notes and fill in a chart like the one that follows:

Before: Character at Start of Story	After: Character at End of Story	Differences Between Before and After	Insights Character Has Gained

From your chart, compose your thesis statement: a sentence or two that states your claim.

Plan your essay. Consider using a writing plan like this one:

Introduction
- Thesis statement
- Questions it raises
- A brief profile of your character

Body
- Your character's epiphany
  —supporting quotations
- Analysis of how character's change occurs
  —supporting quotations

Conclusion
- Summary of argument: how you have answered questions raised by the thesis statement

- How you think the character's life will be different in the future

STEP 2 DRAFTING

Start writing. Here are some drafting tips.

- Drafting is a process of discovery. Be prepared to refine and restate your thesis as your argument develops.

- Remember that your audience is familiar with the literature. Avoid a long, detailed plot summary. Concentrate on your character.

STEP 3 REVISING

Ask a partner for comments on your draft before you revise it.

✔ Have I identified the point in the story when the character has an epiphany?

✔ Have I analyzed how this turning point comes about?

✔ Does my conclusion describe how I think the character's life will be different as a result of this heightened awareness?

✔ Does my thesis raise questions?

Revising Strategy

Writing an Effective Thesis Statement

A thesis statement in an essay like this one must make a claim that raises questions—questions that demand answers. If the thesis statement raises no questions, the essay has nowhere to go.

> Eveline lives a sad and depressing life.

This claim raises no questions for the essay to answer. It gives us nothing to disagree with or wonder about. Here is a revised example:

> Eveline's life is joyless, but at the end of the story she realizes that she actually prefers it that way.

How could someone *prefer* a joyless life, and why? This is an effective thesis statement because it makes a claim that raises questions. Make sure your thesis statement raises questions that your essay goes on to answer.

STEP 4 EDITING

Ask a partner to review your revised draft before you edit. Look closely for errors with sentence fragments.

Editing Strategy

Avoiding Sentence Fragments

A sentence fragment is a group of words that is punctuated as a sentence but is not a complete thought. It leaves the reader wondering.

> Because Eveline lacked the courage to take a chance. (*Because she lacked the courage—who?*)

> At the station while the boat pulled away. (*What happened at the station while the boat pulled away?*)

You can correct a sentence fragment either by pulling it into an adjacent sentence or by adding words. See the model on the next page.

She remembers
A promise she made to her mother years before. She

promised to keep the home together, As long as she could. However,

she fears that she will become like her mother.

STEP 5 PRESENTING

Here are a few suggestions for sharing your essay.

- Read your essay to a small group of classmates who chose the same character. Have them comment on whether your views agree or disagree with theirs.

- To illustrate your essay, create a piece of visual art that depicts your character at the moment of insight. Place him or her in the setting as you imagine it and with an expression that you imagine he or she might have at that moment.

STEP 6 LOOKING BACK

Self-evaluate. How would you evaluate your work? Look back at the Writer's Blueprint and give yourself a score for each item, from 6 (superior) to 1 (inadequate).

Reflect. Write responses to these questions.

- In what ways did your ideas about your thesis change during drafting and revising?

- Have you ever experienced an epiphany? If so, what was it? If not, try to imagine a moment like this occurring in your life, and describe what it might be like.

For Your Working Portfolio Add your essay and your reflection responses to your working portfolio.

Beyond Print

Looking at a Portrait

Portrait pointers can capture the complexities of a person at the same time that they convey their own impressions and feelings about their subject. Explain which of the portraits on pages 844–845 you consider flattering. Which do you find unflattering? Why? What insights do these portraits give you about each subject? Use the following guidelines to analyze a portrait, or any work of art.

Try to determine the artist's purpose. Does the painter seem more concerned with artistic style and composition than with the subject? Is the artist conveying a message? What, for example, might Henry Lamb's portrait of Lytton Strachey on page 844 suggest about its subject?

Remember that every artist has a point of view. Does the painter appear to be sympathetic? appreciative? critical? How might culture shape the artist's attitudes? Does the artist espouse a special idea or philosophy? From whose vantage point are subjects seen?

Note details that lead to the big picture. Look for patterns in shapes, colors, lines, and textures. Is there a focal point that draws your attention? Do things such as color, facial expressions, shadows, surroundings, and print provide clues to what's going on? Look at the background. Note, for example, the objects surrounding the woman in Frampton's portrait on page 844. What impressions do they convey about his subject? What do her hands and body language suggest?

Be an active viewer. Think about what appeals to you and why. How do these modern portraits differ from older ones such as the *Mona Lisa?* Viewing art is a personal experience, and individuals react differently to a piece of art. If you view art actively, knowledgeably, and with an open mind, you can enrich your experience.

Activity Option

You have commissioned someone to paint your portrait. Decide the following: What will you wear? What setting and details will you choose? How will you wear your hair? What features do you want highlighted? What impression about yourself do you wish to convey?

Multicultural Connections

Communication

Part One: Upward Mobility Eliza Doolittle is sure that improving her communication skills will enable her to improve her life. Not only does her ability to speak like a lady change the way different groups of people react to her, it changes the way she thinks about herself as an individual, and it changes the choices that are open to her.

■ Do you think changing a person's communication skills could possibly have such drastic results in today's world?

Groups

Part Two: War and Aftermath The individuality of each of these authors was changed profoundly and forever by their identities as group members in time of war. A saving grace—perhaps—lay in their abilities to communicate their experiences.

■ How would you hold on to your individuality if you were being pressured to join a group such as an army or an excited mob?

Individuality

Part Three: The Search for Identity The question "Who am I?" is one that no other individual or member of your group can answer for you, as these fictional characters all learn. And if you do find an answer, you can never be sure of communicating it clearly to anyone else.

■ In your opinion, what is the greatest obstacle to any individual's learning his or her true identity? What is the greatest obstacle to communicating that knowledge, once found?

Activities

1. Discuss specific ways you might improve your communication skills—with members of your own group or other groups.

2. Write a letter either applying for membership in a group or resigning membership in a group. The group may be real, such as a student activity club or a business association, or it may be abstract, such as adults or curly-haired people. Be sure to explain your reasons for wanting in or out.

3. Create a graphic image or a symbol that in your own mind represents the individual that is *you*.

Independent and Group Projects

Research

Women United In the early twentieth century, women intensified their already longstanding campaigns in England and the United States to obtain the right to vote. Their efforts included meetings, marches, vandalism, and hunger strikes. Research the views for and against the women's suffrage movement and the actions that women were taking. Give an **oral presentation**—illustrated, if possible—of the women's suffrage movement during this time.

Art

Plans for Peace Prepare an advertising campaign for a world without war. Develop an eye-catching logo and a forceful slogan (keep it simple). Adapt your design to posters, key chains, greeting cards, calendars, mugs, tee shirts, or anything else you can think of that will help you spread the word of world peace. Display your work for the class.

Language

Many Accents Research several languages to find out their ways of saying everyday expressions such as *hello, good-bye, please, thank you, happy birthday,* and the designations for family members such as *mother, father, sister, brother, aunt,* and *uncle.* Or, if you have access to a variety of language speakers, write a brief message for them all to translate. Create a bulletin board, using a large world map as a centerpiece, of languages around the world. If possible, include photos of people from the different countries who are saying these things.

Media

You Are There Work with a group to prepare a **multimedia overview** of the early twentieth century. Use bits of dialogue, lines of poetry, excerpts from the prose in this unit, and any other bits of writing you can cull from old magazines, newspapers, letters, and so on. Add popular World War I songs; photographs of people, objects, and events; and cartoons or paintings. Figure out how best to organize these various things for easy accessibility, and link them with a voice-over narration.

The Late
Twentieth Century

The Passing of Empire
Part One, pages 856–901

The Slant View
Part Two, pages 902–954

The Absurd Person
Theme Portfolio, pages 955–965

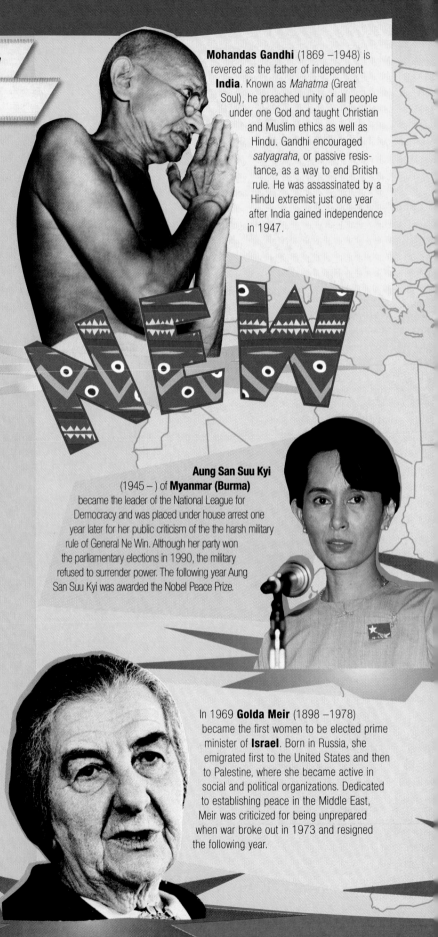

Mohandas Gandhi (1869 –1948) is revered as the father of independent **India**. Known as *Mahatma* (Great Soul), he preached unity of all people under one God and taught Christian and Muslim ethics as well as Hindu. Gandhi encouraged *satyagraha*, or passive resistance, as a way to end British rule. He was assassinated by a Hindu extremist just one year after India gained independence in 1947.

HISTORICAL OVERVIEW

After World War II new nations were created from former European colonies in Africa and Asia. The partition of British India into Hindu India and Muslim Pakistan sparked massive sectarian violence that continues today. British Palestine was divided into Jewish Israel and Arab Jordan, but the Arabs did not accept this, and there have frequent wars between Israel and its Arab neighbors. Before World War II, most of Africa was European colonies; by 1980 there were over 50 independent states, but many of the new nations continue to face hunger, disease, illiteracy, lack of industry, and violence. A hopeful exception has been the peaceful transfer of power in South Africa from all-white rule to govern-ment by the black majority. The individuals profiled here had major roles in the history of some of these new nations.

Aung San Suu Kyi (1945 –) of **Myanmar (Burma)** became the leader of the National League for Democracy and was placed under house arrest one year later for her public criticism of the the harsh military rule of General Ne Win. Although her party won the parliamentary elections in 1990, the military refused to surrender power. The following year Aung San Suu Kyi was awarded the Nobel Peace Prize.

In 1969 **Golda Meir** (1898 –1978) became the first women to be elected prime minister of **Israel**. Born in Russia, she emigrated first to the United States and then to Palestine, where she became active in social and political organizations. Dedicated to establishing peace in the Middle East, Meir was criticized for being unprepared when war broke out in 1973 and resigned the following year.

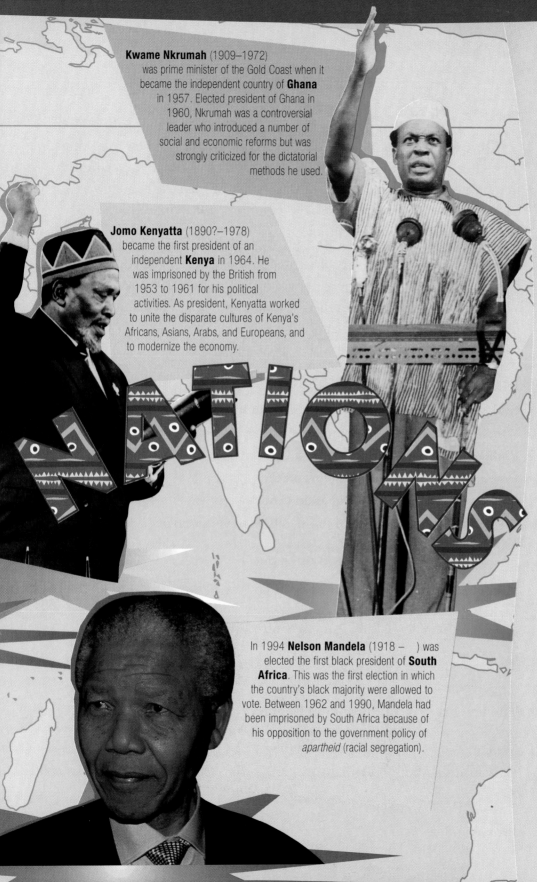

Kwame Nkrumah (1909–1972) was prime minister of the Gold Coast when it became the independent country of **Ghana** in 1957. Elected president of Ghana in 1960, Nkrumah was a controversial leader who introduced a number of social and economic reforms but was strongly criticized for the dictatorial methods he used.

Jomo Kenyatta (1890?–1978) became the first president of an independent **Kenya** in 1964. He was imprisoned by the British from 1953 to 1961 for his political activities. As president, Kenyatta worked to unite the disparate cultures of Kenya's Africans, Asians, Arabs, and Europeans, and to modernize the economy.

In 1994 **Nelson Mandela** (1918 –   ) was elected the first black president of **South Africa**. This was the first election in which the country's black majority were allowed to vote. Between 1962 and 1990, Mandela had been imprisoned by South Africa because of his opposition to the government policy of *apartheid* (racial segregation).

Key Dates

1945
World War II ends; United Nations established.

1947
British India partitioned; Palestine partitioned.

1948
Gandhi assassinated; Israel becomes independent.

1949
South African policy of apartheid goes into effect.

1952
Mau Mau uprising begins in Kenya.

1957
Ghana becomes independent.

1963
Kenya becomes independent.

1964
Mandela imprisoned in South Africa.

1991
Aung San Suu Kyi wins Nobel Peace Prize.

1994
Mandela elected president of South Africa.

Part One

The Passing of Empire

The British Empire at its peak had been widespread and powerful, but now, after World War II, the empire was fast diminishing. For a country that had largely defined itself by its influence abroad the change was not an easy one. The people who had been in control for so many years now found control slipping from their grasp.

Multicultural Focus **Interactions** Encounters between people of diverse cultural backgrounds are heightened under conditions of colonialism. Who gains, and who loses in these encounters? George Orwell observed that when one person rules another, he "wears a mask, and his face grows to fit it." What might that face look like once the mask comes off?

Before Reading

Shooting an Elephant

by George Orwell

George Orwell
1903–1950

George Orwell was born Eric Arthur Blair in Bengal, India. He won a scholarship to Eton, but instead of continuing on to a university, he joined the Imperial Police in Burma, an English colony. After five years (1922–1927) he returned to England determined to become a writer. Experiences as a dishwasher, a farm worker, and a tramp helped him understand the effects of poverty on the working class, which he chronicled in his first book, *Down and Out in Paris and London* (1933). Orwell is best known for *Animal Farm* (1945), a satire on Stalinist Russia in the form of a beast fable, and *Nineteen Eighty-Four* (1949), a picture of a future society in which everyone is under the constant watch of "Big Brother." Orwell died of tuberculosis at the age of forty-six.

Building Background

With Hostility and Contempt From the 1500s to the early 1900s, the nation of Great Britain acquired possessions on every continent, ruling large parts of Africa, Asia, and North America. In a series of three wars in the 1800s Britain conquered Burma and ruled the country as a part of India, its neighbor to the west. Under British rule the production of rice and timber flourished, and Burma became one of the wealthiest countries in Southeast Asia. Still, the British presence became progressively less popular. After World War I agitation and unrest in many colonies, including India and Burma, increased as the native peoples felt oppressed rather than cared for by the British government. Consequently the natives often treated the English people working in their country with hostility and contempt. Burma, now officially known as the Union of Myanmar, became a self-governing country in 1937.

Literary Focus

Irony A contrast between what is expected and what actually happens, or between what appears to be and what actually is, is called **irony.** In *verbal irony* the intended meaning of a statement is different from, or opposite to, what the statement literally says. Look for examples of irony in "Shooting an Elephant."

Writer's Notebook

Saving Face Have you ever done something not because you wanted to do it but because someone else expected you to do it? Maybe you did it because you would disappoint someone. Maybe you did it to maintain your image or to "save face." Jot down a few sentences to describe the situation.

SHOOTING AN

ELEPHANT

GEORGE ORWELL

In Moulmein, in Lower Burma, I was hated by large numbers of people—the only time in my life that I have been important enough for this to happen to me. I was subdivisional police officer of the town, and in an aimless, petty kind of way anti-European feeling was very bitter. No one had the guts to raise a riot, but if a European woman went through the bazaars alone somebody would probably spit betel juice[1] over her dress. As a police officer I was an obvious target and was baited whenever it seemed safe to do so. When a nimble Burman tripped me up on the football field and the referee (another Burman) looked the other way, the crowd yelled with hideous laughter. This happened more than once. In the end the sneering yellow faces of young men that met me everywhere, the insults hooted after me when I was at a safe distance, got badly on my nerves. The young Buddhist priests were the worst of all. There were several thousands of them in the town and none of them seemed to have anything to do except stand on street corners and jeer at Europeans.

All this was perplexing and upsetting. For at that time I had already made up my mind that imperialism[2] was an evil thing and the sooner I chucked up my job and got out of it the better. Theoretically—and secretly, of course—I was all for the Burmese and all against their oppressors,[3]

◄ Does this photograph showing a group of Burmese catching wild elephants suggest that these animals are dangerous? Why or why not?

the British. As for the job I was doing, I hated it more bitterly than I can perhaps make clear. In a job like that you see the dirty work of Empire at close quarters. The wretched prisoners huddling in the stinking cages of the lock-ups, the gray, cowed faces of the long-term convicts, the scarred buttocks of the men who had been flogged with bamboos—all these oppressed me with an intolerable sense of guilt. But I could get nothing into perspective. I was young and ill-educated and I had to think out my problems in the utter silence that is imposed on every Englishman in the East. I did not even know that the British Empire is dying, still less did I know that it is a great deal better than the younger empires that are going to supplant[4] it. All I knew was that I was stuck between my hatred of the empire I served and my rage against the evil-spirited little beasts who tried to make my job impossible. With one part of my mind I thought of the British Raj[5] as an unbreakable tyranny,[6] as something clamped down, *in saecula saeculorum*,[7] upon the will of prostrate[8] peoples; with another part I thought that the greatest joy in the world would be to drive a bayonet into a Buddhist priest's guts. Feelings like these are the normal by-products of imperialism; ask any Anglo-Indian official, if you can catch him off duty.

---

1. **betel juice,** juice from chewing the nut of a palm tree.
2. imperialism (im pir′ē ə liz′əm), *n.* policy of extending the rule or authority of one country over other countries and colonies.
3. oppressor (ə pres′ər), *n.* person who is cruel or unjust.
4. **supplant** (sə plant′), *v.* take the place of.
5. **British Raj,** the British Empire in the East, including what is now India, Pakistan, Bangladesh, and Burma. *Raj* (räj) is a Hindu word meaning "rule."
6. tyranny (tir′ə nē) *n.* cruel or unjust use of power.
7. *in saecula saeculorum* (in sā′kü lä sā′kü lôr′əm), forever. *[Latin]*
8. **prostrate** (pros′trāt), *adj.* helpless; overcome.

🐾 CLARIFY: What do you think "the utter silence that is imposed on every Englishman in the East" implies about the interactions between Englishmen and people of Eastern countries?

One day something happened which in a roundabout way was enlightening. It was a tiny incident in itself, but it gave me a better glimpse than I had had before of the real nature of imperialism—the real motives for which despotic[9] governments act. Early one morning the sub-inspector at a police station the other end of the town rang me up on the phone and said that an elephant was ravaging the bazaar. Would I please come and do something about it? I did not know what I could do, but I wanted to see what was happening and I got on to a pony and started out. I took my rifle, an old .44 Winchester and much too small to kill an elephant, but I thought the noise might be useful *in terrorem*. Various Burmans stopped me on the way and told me about the elephant's doings. It was not, of course, a wild elephant, but a tame one which had gone "must."[10] It had been chained up as tame elephants always are when their attack of "must" is due, but on the previous night it had broken its chain and escaped. Its mahout,[11] the only person who could manage it when it was in that state, had set out in pursuit, but he had taken the wrong direction and was now twelve hours' journey away, and in the morning the elephant had suddenly reappeared in the town. The Burmese population had no weapons and were quite helpless against it. It had already destroyed somebody's bamboo hut, killed a cow and raided some fruit-stalls and devoured the stock; also it had met the municipal rubbish van, and, when the driver jumped out and took to his heels, had turned the van over and inflicted violence upon it.

The Burmese sub-inspector and some Indian constables were waiting for me in the quarter where the elephant had been seen. It was a very poor quarter, a labyrinth of squalid[12] bamboo huts, thatched with palm-leaf, winding all over a steep hillside. I remember that it was a cloudy stuffy morning at the beginning of the rains. We began questioning the people as to where the elephant had gone, and, as usual, failed to get any definite information. That is invariably the case in the East; a story always sounds clear enough at a distance, but the nearer you get to the scene of events the vaguer it becomes. Some of the people said that the elephant had gone in one direction, some said that he had gone in another, some professed not even to have heard of any elephant. I had almost made up my mind that the whole story was a pack of lies, when we heard yells a little distance away. There was a loud, scandalized cry of "Go away, child! Go away this instant!" and an old woman with a switch in her hand came round a corner of a hut, violently shooing away a crowd of naked children. Some more women followed, clicking their tongues and exclaiming; evidently there was something there that the children ought not to have seen. I rounded the hut and saw a man's dead body sprawling in the mud. He was an Indian, a black Dravidian coolie,[13] almost naked, and he could not have been dead many minutes. The people said that the elephant had come suddenly upon him round the corner of the hut, caught him with its trunk, put its foot on his back and ground him into the earth. This was the rainy season and the ground was soft, and his face had scored a trench a foot deep and a couple of yards long. He was lying on his belly with arms crucified and head sharply twisted to one side. His face was coated

---

9. despotic (des pot′ik), *adj.* having unlimited power.
10. **must,** a frenzied state occurring periodically in male elephants.
11. **mahout** (mə hout′), *n.* an elephant-driver.
12. **squalid** (skwol′id), *adj.* dirty; filthy.
13. **Dravidian** (drə vid′ē ən) **coolie,** an unskilled laborer of mixed race.

with mud, the eyes wide open, the teeth bared and grinning with an expression of unendurable agony. (Never tell me, by the way, that the dead look peaceful. Most of the corpses I have seen looked devilish.) The friction of the great beast's foot had stripped the skin from his back as neatly as one skins a rabbit. As soon as I saw the dead man I sent an orderly to a friend's house nearby to borrow an elephant rifle. I had already sent back the pony, not wanting it to go mad with fright and throw me if it smelled the elephant.

The orderly came back in a few minutes with a rifle and five cartridges, and meanwhile some Burmans had arrived and told us that the elephant was in the paddy fields below, only a few hundred yards away. As I started forward practically the whole population of the quarter flocked out of their houses and followed me. They had seen the rifle and were all shouting excitedly that I was going to shoot the elephant. They had not shown much interest in the elephant when he was merely ravaging their homes, but it was different now that he was going to be shot. It was a bit of fun to them, as it would be to an English crowd; besides, they wanted the meat. It made me vaguely uneasy. I had no intention of shooting the elephant—I had merely sent for the rifle to defend myself if necessary—and it is always unnerving to have a crowd following you. I marched down the hill, looking and feeling a fool, with the rifle over my shoulder and an ever-growing army of people jostling at my heels. At the bottom, when you got away from the huts, there was a metalled road and beyond that a miry waste of paddy fields a thousand yards across, not yet ploughed but soggy from the first rains and dotted with coarse grass. The elephant was standing eighty yards from the road, his left side towards us. He took not the slightest notice of the crowd's approach. He was tearing up bunches of grass, beating them against his knees to clean them and stuffing them into his mouth.

I had halted on the road. As soon as I saw the elephant I knew with perfect certainty that I ought not to shoot him. It is a serious matter to shoot a working elephant—it is comparable to destroying a huge and costly piece of machinery—and obviously one ought not to do it if it can possibly be avoided. And at that distance, peacefully eating, the elephant looked no more dangerous than a cow. I thought then and I think now that his attack of "must" was already passing off; in which case he would merely wander harmlessly about until the mahout came back and caught him. Moreover, I did not in the least want to shoot him. I decided that I would watch him for a little while to make sure that he did not turn savage again, and then go home.

SUMMARIZE: What are the reasons Orwell gives for not wanting to kill the elephant?

But at that moment I glanced round at the crowd that had followed me. It was an immense crowd, two thousand at the least and growing every minute. It blocked the road for a long distance on either side. I looked at the sea of yellow faces above the garish clothes—faces all happy and excited over this bit of fun, all certain that the elephant was going to be shot. They were watching me as they would watch a conjuror[14] about to perform a trick. They did not like me, but with the magical rifle in my hands I was momentarily worth watching. And suddenly I realized that I should have to shoot the elephant after all. The people expected it of me and I had got to do it; I could feel their two thousand wills pressing me forward, irresistibly. And it was at this moment, as I stood there with the rifle in my hands, that I first grasped the hollowness, the futility of the white man's dominion in the East. Here was I, the

---

14. **conjuror** (kon′jər ər), *n.* magician.

white man with his gun, standing in front of the unarmed native crowd—seemingly the leading actor of the piece; but in reality I was only an absurd puppet pushed to and fro by the will of those yellow faces behind. I perceived in this moment that when the white man turns tyrant it is his own freedom that he destroys. He becomes a sort of hollow, posing dummy, the conventionalized figure of a sahib.[15] For it is the condition of his rule that he shall spend his life in trying to impress the "natives" and so in every crisis he has got to do what the "natives" expect of him. He wears a mask, and his face grows to fit it. I had got to shoot the elephant. I had committed myself to doing it when I sent for the rifle. A sahib has got to act like a sahib; he has got to appear resolute,[16] to know his own mind and do definite things. To come all that way, rifle in hand, with two thousand people marching at my heels, and then to trail feebly away, having done nothing—no, that was impossible. The crowd would laugh at me. And my whole life, every white man's life in the East, was one long struggle not to be laughed at.

But I did not want to shoot the elephant. I watched him beating his bunch of grass against his knees, with that preoccupied grandmotherly air that elephants have. It seemed to me that it would be murder to shoot him. At that age I was not squeamish[17] about killing animals, but I had never shot an elephant and never wanted to. (Somehow it always seems worse to kill a *large* animal.) Besides, there was the beast's owner to be considered. Alive, the elephant was worth at least a hundred pounds; dead, he would only be worth the value of his tusks—five pounds, possibly. But I had to act quickly. I turned to some experienced-looking Burmans who had been there when we arrived, and asked them how the elephant had been behaving. They all said the same thing: he took no notice of you if you left him alone, but he might charge if you went too close to him.

It was perfectly clear to me what I ought to do. I ought to walk up to within, say, twenty-five yards of the elephant and test his behavior. If he charged I could shoot, if he took no notice of me it would be safe to leave him until the mahout came back. But also I knew that I was going to do no such thing. I was a poor shot with a rifle and the ground was soft mud into which one would sink at every step. If the elephant charged and I missed him, I should have about as much chance as a toad under a steam-roller. But even then I was not thinking particularly of my own skin, only the watchful yellow faces behind. For at that moment, with the crowd watching me, I was not afraid in the ordinary sense, as I would have been if I had been alone. A white man mustn't be frightened of "natives"; and so, in general, he isn't frightened. The sole thought in my mind was that if anything went wrong those two thousand Burmans would see me pursued, caught, trampled on and reduced to a grinning corpse like that Indian up the hill. And if that happened it was quite probable that some of them would laugh. That would never do. There was only one alternative. I shoved the cartridges into the magazine and lay down on the road to get a better aim.

EVALUATE: What do you think is the real reason Orwell decides to shoot the elephant?

The crowd grew very still, and a deep, low, happy sigh, as of people who see the theater curtain go up at last, breathed from innumerable throats. They were going to have their bit of fun after all. The rifle was a beautiful German thing with cross-hair sights. I did not then know that in shooting an elephant one should shoot to cut an imaginary bar running from ear-hole to ear-hole. I ought therefore, as the elephant was side-

---

15. **sahib** (sä′ib), *n.* in British India, a European.
16. **resolute** (rez′ə lüt), *adj.* determined.
17. **squeamish** (skwē′mish), *adj.* easily shocked; nauseated.

ways on, to have aimed straight at his ear-hole; actually I aimed several inches in front of this, thinking the brain would be further forward.

When I pulled the trigger I did not hear the bang or feel the kick—one never does when a shot goes home—but I heard the devilish roar of glee that went up from the crowd. In that instant, in too short a time, one would have thought, even for the bullet to get there, a mysterious, terrible change had come over the elephant. He neither stirred nor fell, but every line of his body had altered. He looked suddenly stricken, shrunken, immensely old, as though the frightful impact of the bullet had paralyzed him without knocking him down. At last, after what seemed a long time—it might have been five seconds, I dare say—he sagged flabbily to his knees. His mouth slobbered. An enormous senility[18] seemed to have settled upon him. One could have imagined him thousands of years old. I fired again into the same spot. At the second shot he did not collapse but climbed with desperate slowness to his feet and stood weakly upright, with legs sagging and head dropping. I fired a third time. That was the shot that did for him. You could see the agony of it jolt his whole body and knock the last remnant of strength from his legs. But in falling he seemed for a moment to rise, for as his hind legs collapsed beneath him he seemed to tower upwards like a huge rock toppling, his trunk reaching skyward like a tree. He trumpeted, for the first and only time. And then down he came, his belly towards me, with a crash that seemed to shake the ground even where I lay.

I got up. The Burmans were already racing past me across the mud. It was obvious that the elephant would never rise again, but he was not dead. He was breathing very rhythmically with long rattling gasps, his great mound of a side painfully rising and falling. His mouth was wide open—I could see far down into caverns of pale pink throat. I waited a long time for him to die, but his breathing did not weaken. Finally I fired my two remaining

HE WAS DYING, VERY SLOWLY AND IN GREAT AGONY . . .

shots into the spot where I thought his heart must be. The thick blood welled out of him like red velvet, but still he did not die. His body did not even jerk when the shots hit him, the tortured breathing continued without a pause. He was dying, very slowly and in great agony, but in some world remote from me where not even a bullet could damage him further. I felt that I had got to put an end to that dreadful noise. It seemed dreadful to see the great beast lying there, powerless to move and yet powerless to die, and not even to be able to finish him. I sent back for my small rifle and poured shot after shot into his heart and down his throat. They seemed to make no impression. The tortured gasps continued as steadily as the ticking of a clock.

In the end I could not stand it any longer and went away. I heard later that it took him half an hour to die. Burmans were arriving with dahs[19] and baskets even before I left, and I was told they had stripped his body almost to the bones by the afternoon.

Afterwards, of course, there were endless discussions about the shooting of the elephant. The owner was furious, but he was only an Indian and could do nothing. Besides, legally I had done the right thing, for a mad elephant has to be killed, like a mad dog, if its owner fails to control it. Among the Europeans opinion was divided. The older men said I was right, the younger men said it was a damn shame to shoot an elephant for killing a coolie, because an elephant was worth more than any damn Coringhee coolie. And afterwards I was very glad that the coolie had been killed; it put me legally in the right and it gave me a sufficient pretext for shooting the elephant. I often wondered whether any of the others grasped that I had done it solely to avoid looking a fool.

---

18. **senility** (sə nil′ə tē), *n.* mental and physical deterioration associated with old age.
19. **dah** (dä), *n.* a heavy Burmese knife.

After Reading

Making Connections

Shaping Your Response

1. Do you think Orwell should have shot the elephant? Explain your response.

Analyzing the Essay

2. 🐾 Why do you think the **interactions** between the Burmese people and the Europeans are so hostile?

3. As a member of the Imperial Police in Burma, Orwell found himself hating both the empire he served and the Burmese. What do you think accounts for the mixed feelings he describes?

4. Orwell's better judgment tells him not to kill the elephant. Why, then, do you think he decides to kill it after all?

5. What lesson does Orwell feel this episode offers into the "real nature of imperialism—the real motives for which despotic governments act"?

6. How do the reactions of the younger Europeans to the incident support Orwell's criticism of British imperialism?

Extending the Ideas

7. Judging from this selection, what abuses of power in the modern world would Orwell be likely to attack if he were living today?

Literary Focus: Irony

Irony is a term used to describe the contrast between what appears to be and what really is. What do you find ironic about the following situations?

1. Orwell is an important police officer.

2. Orwell secretly favors the Burmese people.

3. Orwell decides to kill the elephant.

4. When he is shot, the elephant is calmly grazing in a field.

5. The white man is dominant in the East.

Vocabulary Study

despotic
imperialism
oppressor
resolute
tyranny

Each of the listed words can be used to discuss the actions of a government that has extended its authority over another country. Using these five words, write a paragraph describing the actions of an agent of the government taking control of a group of people. Your paragraph should demonstrate that you understand the meaning of each word.

Expressing Your Ideas

Writing Choices

Writer's Notebook Update Look back at the situation you described in your writer's notebook. As you think about that situation now, jot down several words to describe your feelings about the event.

The Dirty Work of Empire In "Shooting an Elephant," Orwell states that, in a job like that he held in Burma, "you see the dirty work of Empire at close quarters." Write a **letter** such as Orwell might have written home to a close friend or relative about the evils of imperialism as he has come to know them first hand.

(S)he Was Only . . . Orwell tells us that the owner of the elephant could do nothing because "he was only an Indian." Write a **short story** of a modern injustice which can be explained in part because "he or she was only . . . ." You might choose, for example, "he was only a child," or "she was only a woman," or "he was only a freshman."

Obvious Targets Orwell states, "As a police officer I was an obvious target and was baited whenever it seemed safe to do so." Why do you think officers of the law are so often the targets of people's antagonism? Write an **editorial** for your school newspaper in which you discuss this predicament and offer solutions for correcting the situation.

Other Options

Tyranny Destroys Freedom The theme of Orwell's essay can best be described in his own words: "When the white man turns tyrant it is his own freedom that he destroys." Use that quotation as the theme of an **artistic creation**—a painting, a sculpture, a collage, or whatever art form you are best at.

Should Have / Shouldn't Have Join with two classmates and prepare a script of the **discussion and debate** that might have taken place among Europeans in the town square after the shooting of the elephant. One classmate can present the position of the older Europeans, one can speak for the younger men, and one can be Orwell himself. Perform your script for the class.

Guilt, Shame, and Outrage Orwell felt a strong sense of guilt, shame, and outrage at the effects of imperialism on the Burmese people. Is there something in American society today that makes you feel guilty or ashamed or outraged? Prepare a **photo essay,** using photographs that you have taken yourself and/or that you have clipped from newspapers and magazines, to explain why you feel as you do.

Before Reading

Wartime Speeches

by Winston Churchill

Winston Churchill
1874–1965

Eldest son of Lord Randolph Churchill and American heiress Jennie Jerome, Winston Churchill first served with the cavalry. A correspondent during the Boer War, he was first elected to Parliament in 1900. When Great Britain declared war on Germany in 1939, he returned to the Admiralty. In 1940 Churchill became Prime Minister. Throughout World War II he coordinated military strategies to defeat Hitler. His conferences with U. S. President Franklin Delano Roosevelt and Soviet leader Josef Stalin helped shape postwar Europe. He served again as Prime Minister from 1951 to 1955. Churchill wrote many outstanding historical works, most notably *The Second World War* and *A History of the English-Speaking Peoples*. He was knighted in 1953, the same year he received the Nobel Prize for literature.

Building Background

"Their Finest Hour" In the early months of his prime ministry Winston Churchill inspired the English people with words of hope and undying spirit. His opening speech, delivered in the House of Commons on May 13, 1940, just three days after receiving his appointment from King George VI, set an optimistic tone. Just three weeks later, on June 4, 1940, an ever-confident Churchill told of the great military feat at Dunkirk in which 335,000 Allied soldiers were evacuated by naval vessels and small civilian craft that were under continual German attack. The frightened people of Britain, fully aware that a German invasion of their island was possible, rejoiced with Churchill as he praised the strong young airmen who would defend their country. How their attitude might have been different had they heard Churchill's remark made with his hand covering the microphone: "And we will hit them over the head with beer bottles, which is all we have really got." Two weeks later, when France had fallen, Churchill again bolstered English morale by calling for full attention to the duty ahead, for the people's "finest hour." Churchill's memorable phrases kept the English people hopeful through the bitter summer weeks of 1940.

Literary Focus

Theme A **theme** is a main idea or an underlying meaning of a literary work. A theme may be stated directly or it may be implied. As you read these excerpts from Churchill's speeches, look for common themes that run through all the speeches.

Writer's Notebook

A Great Speech What do you think makes a great speech? What makes a great speaker? Write down characteristics of each.

Richard Eurich's *Evacuation of Duinkirk* depicts a British flotilla of small boats rescuing Allied troops trapped by German forces at Dunkirk in May 1940. What qualities of this famous episode does the painting emphasize?

WARTIME SPEECHES

WINSTON CHURCHILL

BLOOD, TOIL, TEARS, AND SWEAT

. . . In this crisis[1] I hope I may be pardoned if I do not address the House[2] at any length today. I hope that any of my friends and colleagues, or former colleagues, who are affected by the political reconstruction,[3] will make all allowance for any lack of ceremony with which it has been necessary to act. I would say to the House, as I said to those who have joined this Government: "I have nothing to offer but blood, toil, tears, and sweat."

We have before us an ordeal of the most grievous[4] kind. We have before us many, many long months of struggle and of suffering. You ask what is our policy? I will say: It is to wage war, by sea, land, and air, with all our might and with all the strength that God can give us: to wage war

---

1. **this crisis.** Great Britain was fully engaged in World War II with fighting going on in several different countries and with threats of invasion at home.
2. **the House,** the House of Commons, a part of the British Parliament.
3. **political reconstruction.** Three days before this speech King George VI had asked Churchill to form a new administration.
4. **grievous** (grē′vəs), *adj.* severe; causing great pain and suffering.

against a monstrous tyranny, never surpassed in the dark, lamentable[5] catalog of human crime. That is our policy. You ask, What is our aim? I can answer in one word: Victory—victory at all costs, victory in spite of all terror, victory, however long and hard the road may be; for without victory, there is no survival. Let that be realized; no survival for the British Empire; no survival for all that the British Empire has stood for, no survival for the urge and impulse of the ages, that mankind will move forward towards its goal. But I take up my task with buoyancy[6] and hope. I feel sure that our cause will not be suffered to fail among men. At this time I feel entitled to claim the aid of all, and I say, "Come, then, let us go forward together with our united strength."

CLARIFY: What tone do you think Churchill is trying to set for the English people?

A MIRACLE OF DELIVERANCE

. . . The German eruption swept like a sharp scythe around the right and rear of the armies of the north. Eight or nine armored divisions, each of about four hundred armored vehicles of different kinds, but carefully assorted to be complementary[1] and divisible into small self-contained units, cut off all communications between us and the main French armies. It severed our own communications for food and ammunition, which ran first to Amiens and afterward through Abbeville, and it shored its way up the coast to Boulogne and Calais, and almost to Dunkirk.[2] Behind this armored and mechanized onslaught came a number of German divisions in lorries,[3] and behind them again there plodded comparatively slowly the dull brute mass of the ordinary Germany Army and German people, always so ready to be led to the trampling down in other lands of liberties and comforts which they have never know in their own. . . .

Meanwhile, the Royal Air Force, which had

already been intervening in the battle, so far as its range would allow, from home bases, now used part of its main metropolitan fighter strength, and struck at the German bombers and at the fighters which in large numbers protected them. This struggle was protracted[4] and fierce. Suddenly the scene has cleared, the crash and thunder has for the moment—but only for the moment—died away. A miracle of deliverance, achieved by valor, by perseverance, by perfect discipline, by faultless service, by resource, by skill, by unconquerable fidelity, is manifest[5] to us all. The enemy was hurled back by the retreating British and French troops. He was so roughly handled that he did not hurry their departure seriously. The Royal Air Force engaged the main strength of the German Air Force, and inflicted upon them losses of at least four to one; and the navy, using nearly one thousand ships of all kinds, carried over 335,000 men, French and British, out of the jaws of death and shame, to their native land and to the tasks which lie immediately ahead. We must be very careful not to assign to this deliverance the attributes of a victory. Wars are not won by evacuations. But there was a victory inside this deliverance, which should be noted. It was gained by the air force. Many of our soldiers coming back have not seen the air force at work; they saw only the bombers which escaped its protective attack. They underrate its achievements. I have heard much talk of this; that is

---

5. **lamentable** (lam′ən tə bəl), *adj.* deplorable; to be regretted or pitied.
6. buoyancy (boi′ən sē), *n.* tendency to be hopeful and cheerful.

1. **complementary** (kom′plə men′tər ē), *adj.* formed together as a complete unit.
2. **Amiens . . . Dunkirk.** Towns in northern France under attack by German forces.
3. **lorry** (lôr′ē), *n.* truck.
4. protracted (prō trak′tid), *adj.* drawn out; prolonged.
5. **manifest** (man′ə fest), *adj.* clear.

why I go out of my way to say this. I will tell you about it.

This was a great trial of strength between the British and German air forces. Can you conceive a greater objective for the Germans in the air than to make evacuation from these beaches impossible, and to sink all these ships which were displayed, almost to the extent of thousands? Could there have been an objective of greater military importance and significance for the whole purpose of the war than this? They tried hard, and they were beaten back; they were frustrated in their task. We got the army away; and they have paid fourfold for any loses which they have inflicted. Very large formations of German airplanes—and we know that they are a very brave race—have turned on several occasions from the attack of one quarter of their number of the Royal Air Force, and have dispersed in different directions. Twelve airplanes have been hunted by two. One airplane was driven into the water and cast away by the mere charge of a British airplane, which had no more ammunition. All of our types—the Hurricane, the Spitfire, and the new Defiant—and all our pilots have been vindicated[6] as superior to what they have at present to face.

When we consider how much greater would be our advantage in defending the air above this island against an overseas attack, I must say that I find in these facts a sure basis upon which practical and reassuring thoughts may rest. I will pay my tribute to these young airmen. The great French Army was very largely, for the time being, cast back and disturbed by the onrush of a few thousands of armored vehicles. May it not also be that the cause of civilization itself will be defended by the skill and devotion of a few thousand airmen? There never has been, I suppose, in all the world, in all the history of war, such an opportunity for youth. The Knights of the Round Table, the Crusaders, all fall back into the past—not only distant but prosaic;[7] these young men, going forth every morn to guard their native land and all that we stand for, holding in their hands these instruments of colossal and shattering power, of whom it may be said that

Every morn brought forth a noble chance,
And every chance brought forth a noble knight,[8]

deserve our gratitude, as do all of the brave men who, in so many ways and on so many occasions, are ready, and continue ready, to give life and all for their native land. . . .

Turning once again, and this time more generally, to the question of invasion, I would observe that there has never been a period in all these long centuries of which we boast when an absolute guarantee against invasion, still less against serious raids, could have been given to our people. In the days of Napoleon the same wind which would have carried his transports across the Channel might have driven away the blockading fleet. There was always the chance, and it is that chance which has excited and befooled[9] the imaginations of many Continental tyrants. Many are the tales that are told. We are assured that novel methods will be adopted, and when we see the originality of malice, the ingenuity of aggression, which our enemy displays, we may certainly prepare ourselves for every kind of novel stratagem and every kind of brutal and treacherous maneuver. I think that no idea is so outlandish that it should not be considered and viewed with a searching, but at the same time, I hope, with a steady eye. We must never forget the solid assurances of sea power and those which belong to air power if it can be locally exercised.

I have, myself, full confidence that if all do their duty, if nothing is neglected, and if the best arrangements are made, as they are being made, we shall prove ourselves once again able to defend our island home, to ride out the storm of

---

6. **vindicate** (vin′də kāt), *v.* uphold; justify.
7. **prosaic** (prō zā′ik), *adj.* ordinary; not exciting.
8. **Every . . . knight.** These lines, slightly misquoted, are from "The Passing of Arthur" in Tennyson's *Idylls of the King.*
9. **befool** (bi fül′), *v.* deceive.

war, and to outlive the menace of tyranny, if necessary for years, if necessary alone. At any rate, that is what we are going to try to do. That is the resolve of His Majesty's Government—every man of them. That is the will of Parliament and the nation. The British Empire and the French Republic, linked together in their cause and in their need, will defend to the death their native soil, aiding each other like good comrades to the utmost of their strength. Even though large tracts of Europe and many old and famous states have fallen or may fall into the grip of the Gestapo[10] and all the odious[11] apparatus of Nazi rule, we shall not flag or fail. We shall go on to the end, we shall fight in France, we shall fight on the seas and oceans, we shall fight with growing confidence and growing strength in the air, we shall defend our island, whatever the cost may be, we shall fight on the beaches, we shall fight on the landing grounds, we shall fight in the fields and in the streets, we shall fight in the hills; we shall never surrender, and even if, which I do not for a moment believe, this island or a large part of it were subjugated[12] and starving, then our Empire beyond the seas, armed and guarded by the British fleet, would carry on the struggle, until, in God's good time, the New World,[13] with all its power and might, steps forth to the rescue and the liberation of the old.

THEIR FINEST HOUR

During the first four years of the last war the Allies experienced nothing but disaster and disappointment. . . . We repeatedly asked ourselves the question, "How are we going to win?" and no one was ever able to answer it with much precision, until at the end, quite suddenly, quite unexpectedly, our terrible foe collapsed before us, and we were so glutted with victory that in our folly we threw it away.

However matters may go in France or with the French government or other French governments, we in this island and in the British

Empire will never lose our sense of comradeship with the French people. . . . If final victory rewards our toils they shall share the gains—aye, and freedom shall be restored to all. We abate[1] nothing of our just demands; not one jot or tittle do we recede. . . . Czechs, Poles, Norwegians, Dutch, Belgians, have joined their causes to our own. All these shall be restored.

What General Weygand[2] called the Battle of France is over. I expect that the Battle of Britain is about to begin. Upon this battle depends the survival of Christian civilization. Upon it depends our own British life, and the long continuity of our institutions and our Empire. The whole fury and might of the enemy must very soon be turned on us. Hitler knows that he will have to break us in this island or lose the war. If we can stand up to him, all Europe may be free and the life of the world may move forward into broad, sunlit uplands. But if we fail, then the whole world, including the United States, including all that we have known and cared for, will sink into the abyss[3] of a new Dark Age, made more sinister,[4] and perhaps more protracted, by the lights of perverted[5] science. Let us therefore brace ourselves to our duties, and so bear ourselves that, if the British Empire and its Commonwealth last for a thousand years, men will say, "This was their finest hour."

CLARIFY: What do you think Churchill means by "perverted science"?

---

10. **Gestapo** (gə stä′pō), the secret police in Nazi Germany.
11. **odious** (ō′dē əs), *adj.* hateful; offensive.
12. **subjugate** (sub′jə gāt), *v.* conquer.
13. **New World,** the United States.

1. abate (ə bāt′), *v.* decrease; reduce.
2. **General Weygand,** commander in chief of the French army.
3. **abyss** (ə bis′), *n.* lowest depth.
4. sinister (sin′ə stər), *adj.* threatening.
5. **perverted** (pər vėr′tid), *adj.* used for wrong purposes.

After Reading

Making Connections

Shaping Your Response

1. What characteristic of Churchill's speeches impresses you the most?

2. Do you think Churchill wrote his own speeches? Why or why not?

Analyzing the Speeches

3. When he says he has "nothing to offer but blood, toil, tears, and sweat," what message do you think Churchill is sending to the English people?

4. What distinction, if any, do you draw between the *policy* and the *aim* Churchill defines for his administration?

5. What do Churchill's comments about the German Army indicate about his opinions of the German people?

6. Why do you think Churchill spends so much time talking about the air war?

7. Why do you think Churchill mentions the New World at the end of his speech "A Miracle of Deliverance"?

8. 👣 What does Churchill conclude about Britain's **interactions** with the nations of the world?

Extending the Ideas

9. If Churchill were alive today, what advice do you think he might give to the President of the United States?

Literary Focus: Theme

A **theme** is a main idea or an underlying meaning of a literary work. In a few words tell what you think is the theme of each speech excerpt. What do you think is the common theme that runs through all three speeches?

Vocabulary Study

Use your understanding of the italicized word to write the letter of the word or phrase that best completes each sentence. Use your Glossary if necessary.

1. If you were looking at *sinister* clouds, you might predict ___.

   a. a warm, balmy day **b.** a light drizzle **c.** a heavy thunderstorm

2. The man with a *protracted* illness would ___.

   a. return to work the next day **b.** face a lengthy hospital stay
   c. die in the near future

3. The test grade that would most likely lead to a feeling of *bouyancy* is ___.

   a. an *A* **b.** a *C* **c.** an *F*

4. When the flood waters *abated* ___.

   a. more of the land was covered with water
   b. trees and houses were knocked down with its force
   c. more of the land was left exposed

5. The defendant felt *vindicated* when the jury ___.

   a. could not reach a verdict   **b.** declared him guilty
   c. declared him innocent

Expressing Your Ideas

Writing Choices

Writer's Notebook Update Which of the characteristics of a great speech do you find in the Churchill excerpts? Are there additional characteristics you would add after reading Churchill?

A Lamentable Catalog Churchill says that Hitler's tyranny is the darkest in the "lamentable catalog of human crime." Make a **list of crimes** that you would place in the catalog of human crime. Then write a brief summary of the common elements you find among the crimes on your list.

Prepare for Invasion The people of the United States have never experienced invasion of their own country. Imagine how you would need to prepare yourself if you received word that your town was going to be invaded by a hostile force. (You can decide what that force will be.) Write a **short story** in which you describe your preparations for invasion.

Other Options

Inspirational Speakers Study the speeches of another great inspirational speaker. (You can find such speeches in anthologies; ask your teacher or librarian for help.) Select several excerpts from your chosen speaker's famous speeches and study his or her style of expression. If you can, listen to a recording of the speeches to get a sense of his or her style of delivery. Present your **speech excerpts** to your class.

A Pictorial Time Line Work with a small group to prepare a **pictorial time line** of what you have researched to be the key events of World War II. Remember to consider not only the war itself but also the events that led up to the war and the events that followed the end of the war. Be sure to include pictures of the people who influenced and were influenced by the events.

I Remember It Well Find someone who has vivid memories of World War II. You might, for example, find a soldier who served in the war, a mother who was left alone to raise small children, a victim of the Holocaust, a citizen who recalls F. D. Roosevelt's fireside chats. Videotape an interview of remembrances. If your school has a media lab, edit your interview to the best ten minutes or so. Play your **videotaped interview** for your class.

Before Reading

Homage to a Government by Philip Larkin
Two Poems on the Passing of an Empire by Derek Walcott

Philip Larkin
1922–1985

Born in Coventry and educated at Oxford, Larkin became a university librarian in 1943. His first collection of poetry was *The North Ship* (1945); his last was *High Windows* (1974). From 1961 to 1971 Larkin was jazz critic for the London *Daily Telegraph*.

Derek Walcott
Born 1930

Born on the Caribbean island of St. Lucia, Walcott attended University College of West Indies. He taught at schools and colleges in several countries and in 1959 founded the Trinidad Theatre Workshop. Poet, playwright, reviewer, art critic, Walcott received the Nobel Prize for literature in 1992.

Building Background

Reflections on Colonialism As the British government gradually relinquished its power throughout the world, it met with diverse reactions. Many people at home demanded that British dominance continue; most of the people in dominated countries struggled with how to gain their freedom or how to handle their new-found independence. Derek Walcott reflects on attitudes in the West Indies: "The whole idea of America, and the whole idea of everything on this side of the world . . . is imported; we're all imported, black, Spanish. When one says one is American, that's the experience of being American—that transference of whatever color, or name, or place. The difficult part is the realization that one is part of the whole idea of colonization. Because the easiest thing to do about colonialism is to refer to history in terms of guilt or punishment or revenge, or whatever. Whereas the rare thing is the resolution of being where one is and doing something positive about that reality."

Literary Focus

Repetition The use of the same word or phrase in two or more places to achieve a particular effect is **repetition.** Sometimes the words repeated are exactly the same; at other times the author may vary a word or phrase slightly. Look for Larkin's use of repetition in "Homage to a Government."

Writer's Notebook

Advantages and Disadvantages Fill in a chart like the one below with what you think might be the advantages and the disadvantages of colonialism, both for the country in power and for the colony.

	The Country in Power	The Colony
Advantages		
Disadvantages		

HOMAGE TO A GOVERNMENT

PHILIP LARKIN

Next year we are to bring the soldiers home
For lack of money, and it is all right.
Places they guarded, or kept orderly,
Must guard themselves, and keep themselves orderly.
5 We want the money for ourselves at home
Instead of working. And this is all right.

It's hard to say who wanted it to happen,
But now it's been decided nobody minds.
The places are a long way off, not here,
10 Which is all right, and from what we hear
The soldiers there only made trouble happen.
Next year we shall be easier in our minds.

Next year we shall be living in a country
That brought its soldiers home for lack of money.
15 The statues will be standing in the same
Tree-muffled squares, and look nearly the same.
Our children will not know it's a different country.
All we can hope to leave them now is money.

---

homage (hom′ij), *n.* dutiful respect.

Their jackets draped with medals, World War II veterans attend a British celebration of the anniversary of VE (Victory in Europe) Day, May 8, 1945. Do you think that, years from now, veterans of recent American military actions like the Persian Gulf War will gather in this way? Why or why not? ▼

TWO POEMS ON THE PASSING OF AN EMPIRE

DEREK WALCOTT

1

A heron flies across the morning marsh and brakes
its teetering wings to decorate a stump
                                    (thank God
that from this act the landscape is complete
and time and motion at a period
as such an emblem[1] led Rome's trampling feet,
pursued by late proconsuls[2] bearing law)
and underline this quiet with a caw.

2

In the small coffin of his house, the pensioner,[3]
A veteran of the African campaign,
Bends, as if threading an eternal needle;
One-eyed as any grave, his skull, cropped wool,
Or lifts his desert squint to hear
The children singing, "Rule, Britannia, rule,"
As if they needed practise to play dead.
Boys will still pour their blood out for a sieve[4]
Despite his balsam[5] eye and doddering[6] jaw;
And if one eye should weep, would they believe
In such a poor flag as an empty sleeve?

---

1. **such an emblem,** the Roman eagle on a standard—a
   flag or a symbol—carried before Roman armies.
2. **proconsul** (prō kon′səl), *n.* governor of an ancient
   Roman province; governor of a colony or other
   dependent territory during British colonial expansion.
3. **pensioner** (pen′shə nər), *n.* retired or disabled person who receives a regular payment.
4. **sieve** (siv), *n.* utensil with holes that let liquids, but
   not large pieces, pass through.
5. **balsam** (bôl′səm), *adj.* running, as sap from a tree.
6. **doddering** (dod′ər ing), *adj.* trembling.

After Reading

Making Connections

Shaping Your Response

1. Which of these poems expressing attitudes toward imperialism do you prefer? Why?

Analyzing the Poems

2. What kinds of places do you think the soldiers are leaving in "Homage to a Government"?

3. What seems to be the reaction of the speaker in the poem to the evacuation process?

4. What is the **tone** of the poem? Does the speaker really intend an "homage"?

5. What do you **infer** is the speaker's attitude toward imperialism?

6. In "Two Poems on the Passing of an Empire" how does the heron on the stump differ from the eagle carried before advancing Roman armies?

7. If the heron is a **symbol,** what do you think the heron represents?

8. What seems to be suggested by comparing the pensioner's house to a coffin?

9. What is the **tone** of "Two Poems . . ."? What **images** contribute to that tone?

Extending the Ideas

10. ☝ What is your attitude toward the **interactions** of people that characterize colonialism? Is it appropriate for one country to have power and control over another country—even if both countries benefit from it in some way?

Literary Focus: Repetition

Repetition is the use of the same word or phrase in exactly the same way or with a slight variation. Identify the three repetitive word sets that Larkin uses in "Homage to a Government." What effect do you think this repetition has?

Vocabulary Study

Study the dictionary entry shown here for *homage*.

1. Why are two pronunciations given? Which is the preferred pronunciation? How do you know?

> **hom age** (hom′ij, om′ij), *n.* **1** dutiful respect; reverence: *Everyone paid homage to the great leader.* See **honor** for synonym study. **2** (in the Middle Ages) a pledge of loyalty and service by a vassal to a lord. **3** thing done or given to show such acknowledgement. [< Old French < Medieval Latin *hominaticum* < Latin *hominem* human being, man]

2. What special meaning did the word have during the Middle Ages that it doesn't have now?

3. Explain the derivation of the word.

4. *Honor* is named as a synonym for *homage*. List at least three other words that could be used as synonyms for *homage.*

5. If you needed to hyphenate *homage* in a paper, where should you break it?

Expressing Your Ideas

Writing Choices

Writer's Notebook Update In your chart you listed advantages and disadvantages of colonialism for the countries. Add to your consideration the individual people in those countries. What are the advantages and disadvantages for the common man or woman?

Repeat for Emphasis In "Homage to a Government" Philip Larkin repeats variations of "and it is all right" to emphasize his attitude that it *wasn't* all right. Write a **poem** on a subject of your choice. Repeat a phrase—or a variation of that phrase—several times so that its use becomes ironic.

Feature the Poet These Larkin and Walcott poems express their individual attitudes toward British colonialism and imperialism. The complete collections of each poet deal with many other subjects as well. Select either Larkin or Walcott and read at least five other poems by that author. Write a **feature story** for a literary magazine in which you introduce a range of your chosen author's poetry.

Other Options

Honoring the Winners Derek Walcott is the most recent writer featured in this book to receive the Nobel Prize for literature (1992). Work with other class members to prepare a **bulletin board display** that features the Nobel Prize for literature in general and concentrates on several of the specific Nobel winners you have studied this year.

Caribbean Color Walcott has been called the poet of the Caribbean people. In his verse he attempts to capture the color, the culture, the music, the spirit of the islands. Create a **fabric design** that captures your impression of the Caribbean islands and people. (You might want to do some research in books on art or design before you create your own design.)

Speak Your Mind Larkin and Walcott used poetry to express their attitudes toward the British government's imperialism. Select one of the following United States governmental policy issues—national educational goals, continued space exploration, a balanced national budget, foreign policy—or a governmental issue of your choice, and prepare a **persuasive speech** in which you support your personal feelings with documented facts.

Before Reading

from In the Ditch

by Buchi Emecheta

Buchi Emecheta
born 1945

Born in Lagos, Nigeria, Buchi Emecheta (bü′chē em′ə-chē′ta) was married at age 16 and had five children by age 22. In England she supported the family while her husband studied. When they divorced—because her husband objected to her personal educational and writing ambitions—she became a single parent struggling to raise children and earn a college degree. Her first novel, *In the Ditch,* originally appeared as a series of magazine columns, and later it served as her master's thesis in sociology. In addition to novels drawn from her own life, Emecheta has written several novels about life in Nigeria. Today Emecheta continues to lecture, teach, and write. Her works are published by her own publishing company, Ogugwu Afor.

Building Background

Struggling for Position With over one hundred million people, including more than fifty ethnic groups, Nigeria is the most populous country in Africa. A British colony since 1906, Nigeria became an independent country in 1960, just two years before Emecheta and her husband moved to England. Emecheta had lived in the southeastern part of Nigeria where the Ibo people are the dominant culture. Most prominent in the Ibo society is a respect for personal achievement and a strong sense of community spirit. However, Ibo women are clearly subordinate to Ibo men. In her personal struggle for position, Emecheta was dealing not only with her Ibo background, but also with her status as a black woman in white society.

Literary Focus

Dialogue A conversation between two or more people in a literary work is called **dialogue.** Dialogue can serve many purposes; among them are characterization, creation of mood, advancement of the plot, and development of a theme. As you read this selection, look for Emecheta's purpose in using dialogue.

Writer's Notebook

Pick Up and Pack Out Imagine a move you might make to a foreign country. Make a list of the obstacles you think you and your family might have to overcome in order to feel comfortable in a different land. What obstacles would you add to your list if you were very poor?

IN THE DITCH

BUCHI EMECHETA

1

QUALIFYING FOR THE MANSIONS

Consuelo Kanaga's 1950 photograph of a black woman and her children is titled *She Is a Tree of Life to Them.* Does this seem an appropriate title? Why or why not?

There was a crik, and a crack, then another crik, then crack, crack, cra. . . . Adah pulled herself up with a start and sat in the hollow of the large double bed. It had a gradual valley-like hollow, which gave it a sort of *U* look. On both sides of her the mattress rose gently, just like two table-lands sheltering her in a hollow valley. The crik and the crack sounds came once more and she grabbed her four-month-old baby from its carry-cot. The cot was lying on one of the table-lands.

The sleepy baby was cross, her little face twisted in anger. Adah held the wet bundle to her breast and stared at her roommate, the Great Rat. The rat was by now used to Adah's fright, he had long sensed that Adah was terrified of his sharp piercing eyes, long mouth, and his big brown body. He stood

In the Ditch **881**

there, relaxed but watchful, wondering what trick Adah was up to now.

She was always too scared to shout. Her mouth was dry and she was too frightened even to move. The rat got bored with watching her, started to hop from one table to another, happily enjoying its night play. Adah's eyes followed its movements in the dim candlelight, then carefully and noiselessly she stretched out to reach the small reading-table by the big bed, picked up one of the library books she had piled on the table, aimed carefully at the hopping rat, and flung. The rat, for once, was scared. It ran right into the broken wardrobe at the end of the room, disturbing a group of sleeping cockroaches. One of the frightened cockroaches ran into Adah's hollow for maternal protection.

She had been told the week before that the Council[1] would soon have them rehoused.

She put the baby back in her cot, but did not dare go to sleep again. She was happy in her victory over the rat; at least she might now get some peace for a few nights. Another crashing noise jarred into her happy thoughts from the outside. "Oh, not *again!*" she moaned to herself, nearly in tears.

This time it was her landlord. He had long given her notice to quit the premises with her five young children. But unfortunately for Adah, she was black, separated from her husband, and, with five kids all under six, there were few landlords who would dream of taking the like of her into their houses.

Her landlord, a Nigerian, like herself, being aware of Adah's predicament, was, of course, taking the best advantage of the situation. The rent he charged was double what was normally asked for rooms in such houses. He now wanted her to leave because she had had the effrontery[2] to ask him to do something about the rats, the cockroaches, and the filth. When he had failed to do anything about them, she had been to the Town Hall and, because there was no other place for her to live just then, the Council had stepped in.

They had asked the landlord to do some repairs, and even asked him to give Adah a rent-book.

To give Adah a rent-book would have put him in trouble because, being a council tenant, he had pretended to the authorities that Adah was a relative and only a guest. He had begged Adah to withdraw her application for a flat from the Council but it was too late. There were, however, still lots of things he could do to make her life miserable. He would thunder at her kids for any of the slightest childish noises; this happened so frequently that one of her boys would run at the sight of any black man, and she dared not leave them alone in the flat for fear of what might happen to them. She could not leave any piece of food or drink in the filthy shared kitchen for fear of it being poisoned. All their food had to be kept under her bed, so it was hardly surprising that the number of rats had increased. The man was desperate and would stop at nothing. He had switched off the electricity so that she had to keep a candle burning all night, conscious of the terrible fire risk to the children, but even more afraid of what accidents could happen in utter darkness. But now there was something new: he was trying magic.

CLARIFY: Why would her landlord get in trouble for giving Adah a rent-book?

The poor man, instead of sleeping like everybody else, would wake up very early in the morning, round three or four, drape himself in colorful African material, just like juju masqueraders in Lagos,[3] and start moving to and fro to the music of his low-toned mournful songs. When Adah had first seen this figure she could

---

1. **the Council,** in Britain, a local government that provides low-rent housing for low-income families.
2. **effrontery** (ə frun′tər ē), *n.* shameless boldness.
3. **juju masqueraders in Lagos.** In Adah's hometown of Lagos, the capital of Nigeria, medicine men used fetishes or charms (jujus) to cast magic spells.

not believe her eyes. She was on the verge of screaming, but when she looked closer and saw it was only her landlord, she could feel only pity and contempt for him. Adah was more afraid of the rat than the juju landlord.

This morning she simply stared at him, not knowing what to do next; then, amused, she decided to join in his songs which, of course, she had known from childhood. Why was it that she was not afraid? she wondered. Was it because here in England one's mind was always taken up with worrying about the things that really matter? But juju mattered to her at home in Nigeria all right; there, such a scene in the middle of the night could even mean death for some. Probably, she thought, it was because there it was the custom, the norm, and what everybody believed in. The people not only believed in juju but such beliefs had become internalised[4] and it would not occur to anyone to think otherwise. But here, in north-west London, how could she think of the little man who was so familiar to her by day in his greasy second-hand lounge suit as a medicine man? She had heard rumors, and read in the papers of other Africans in London being "terrorised" by juju. *But I am tough and free,* she thought, *free,* she repeated to herself. In England she was free to keep her job, keep her kids, do her studies; she felt safe to ignore the juju man and his pranks. No, the juju trick would not work in England, it was out of place, on alien ground. God dammit, juju, in England, where you're surrounded by walls of unbelief!

On that particular morning, the landlord had either slept late or was very tired, or both, for Adah soon heard the rattling of the milkman's van; it must be six A.M. Mrs. Devlin, the Irish woman living in the top flat, padded down with her empty bottles rattling, the milkman came up the road with his merry whistle, and the landlord stood on the pavement, just outside Adah's ground-floor window, like a statue, apprehensive[5] of the rattle and whistle. Adah watched from the window, fascinated. What would happen now? she wondered.

Mrs. Devlin gave such a scream that the poor milkman had to lean against his van for support. The landlord could not push the old lady away, for she blocked the only doorway leading into the house. He simply did not know how to begin to explain what he had been doing, and stared at them all, his eyes looking ridiculously white in his black face. Adah did not want to miss the show so, tying a *lappa*[6] over her nightdress, went out. The landlord's wife also came out, and so did the other Nigerians living down the road. How could the landlord explain to this group of Londoners why at such an early hour he had tied a red cloth round his naked body and arranged an ostrich feather sticking up at the back of his head, looking to them like a television Red Indian who had had a shot too many?

The milkman fixed his gaze on him, silently demanding an explanation. The face of the landlady was another picture. It was still unmade-up and she still had her hair threaded (like many African women, she "threaded" her hair before going to bed, in small pleats, so that when the thread was taken out, the hair would lie on the head in attractive coils and not stick out), and in her haste she had not remembered to cover it with her wig. Mrs. Devlin, who was on good speaking terms and neighborly with Adah, looked appealingly to her to explain. Just then the landlady's face turned to her, saying without words, "Please don't say anything, please don't."

Adah started to stare at the ceiling by the doorway to avoid looking at any more faces. Then she thought of the picture they, the Nigerians, must present to their neighbors. The plaits[7] on the landlady's head would definitely

---

4. **internalised** (in tėr′nl īzd), *adj.* incorporated into one's own personality.
5. **apprehensive** (ap′ri hen′siv), *adj.* fearful; anxious about the future.
6. *lappa* (lap′ə), *n.* dressing gown.
7. **plait** (plāt), *n.* braid.

remind any foreign person of the pictures of black devils they knew from their childhoods, for her plaits stood out straight, just like four horns. The landlord with the feather looked like the Devil's servant. Adah too was part of the picture. Her *lappa* with yellow and red splashes provided a good background.

Blast these illustrators! Who told them that the Devil was black? Who told them that angels are always white? Had it never occurred to them that there might be black angels and a white devil?

The milkman recovered first from the shock. "Were you going to *her* room?" he asked, deliberately, with accusation in every word, pointing at Adah's room.

Adah did nothing to help the landlord's dilemma but was quite regretting coming out in the first place. She did not know why she was so keen on keeping her landlord's secret. Patriotism? After all, one did not like to have one's dirty linen washed in public. Whatever happened, they were all originally from the same country, the same color, both caught in the entangled web of an industrial society. He wanted to make money from his house to pay for his studies. Adah wanted the proper value for the rent she paid. In their own country, the situation would never have occurred in the first place. Ibo people seldom separate from their husbands after the birth of five children. But in England, anything could be tried, and even done. It's a free country.

The landlady started scolding her husband in Yoruba.[8] The other Nigerians agreed with her. Why should he take it upon himself to frighten a lonely woman? Did he not fear God? The whole race of men were beasts. She had always said that, in fact her mother told her so at home when she was little. He had made a fool of himself. God only knew what these whites were going to do.

EVALUATE: What do you think the landlord's wife means when she says that God only knew what these whites were going to do?

To Adah she said nothing, but her frank speech was meant as an apology. It was very funny really, because everybody knew that everything the landlord had done had been planned by the two of them.

When the landlady started her speech in the Yoruba language, which Adah understood perfectly, the white people started to move away. The milkman swore, so did Mr. Devlin and his two sons, who by now had joined the party. Mrs. Devlin would go to the "Town 'all, Monday."

2

DRIFTING TO THE MANSIONS

After a cold and rainy night, the day was warm. It was early spring. Adah found a space on a bench beside two women who were talking about death, and sat down. It seemed very odd to be talking about death on such a beautiful afternoon, and in such a beautiful park. She looked at the two women momentarily and decided that the day was too fresh, too pure and too lovely to listen to death-talk.

The blue sky was liberally dotted with white clouds. The flats opposite had window-boxes displaying the first flowering shrubs. There were daffodils everywhere. Daffodils in the park, daffodils in the front and back gardens of houses, daffodils edging the park's footpaths, all planted with the type of carelessness that has a touch of calculation.

She inhaled the pure fresh air around her and said under her breath, "I feel so happy I could burst." A group of pigeons wobbled towards her as she unpacked her fish sandwich. She broke one slice of bread into pieces and threw it at them. They pecked at the crumbs agitatedly. Why was it that pigeons were always hun-

---

8. **Yoruba** (yor′ù bə), people from the southwest of Nigeria and the language they speak.

gry? Eating as quickly as they did must give them stomach ache.

It was a Friday, and her half-day. She would have her sandwich and spend a couple of hours in the library, then she would cook, then what, she would clean the flat, then bed. Q.E.D.![9]

But the warmth of the sun was caressing and, after the sort of nights she had been having lately, the lure to doze off was too much of a temptation. The last bit of resistance to sleep was removed when the two women talking about death decided to leave. So she could snore if she liked.

Africans say that it is possible to have four seasons in one day in England, and indeed when Adah woke it might have been any winter day. The park was empty, even the pigeons had taken shelter from the icy cold rain. She got up quickly, looked at the clock on the tower and realised that she had slept the two hours she had saved for reading. Not to worry . . . she had enough fresh air in her lungs to face her choky[10] flat. She hurried home.

Mrs. Devlin was at the door of their house when she got home. She was excitedly talking to her friend Mrs. Marshall, who was, as usual, holding the lead of her black dog. The two women turned to look in Adah's direction when they saw her coming. She was sure they were still talking of the juju episode which had been so spiced to flavor that she was already the heroine of a rather dramatic story. But heroines, being human like everybody else, do get bored of being praised. Not being in the mood to listen to any more new versions of the juju episode, she decided to dash past them, without greeting, to the nursery.

"Hey, what do you think *you're* doing? Come 'ere, we've good news for yer."

Adah wondered what good news there could be for her. She seldom got any news, but good news—well, she might as well listen.

"They've got a flat for yer. The manager was 'ere a minute ago, he said he would come back in thirty minutes to see if you were back."

"Me? A council flat for me? Are you sure he was asking for me? I can't believe it. Are you quite sure? I mean . . ." Adah was becoming incoherent[11] in her excitement. Her voice was loud and panicky.

"Yes, of course, dear, he came for you. Aahr, dear, don't cry, it's going to be all right now. He's coming soon," Mrs. Devlin assured her.

Adah did not realise that her eyes were watering. She wiped her face, peered at the thin face of Mrs. Marshall to make sure she was not dreaming, and in response Mrs. Marshall pulled her dog to herself, nodding intermittently. "It is true, it is true."

Yes, it must be true, but she still had to fetch her babies from the nursery. The day was too good to be ruined by Matron's anger. The matron of her kids' nursery had become a friend, but was very keen on punctuality. She never hid the fact that she too had children of her own who would be waiting for her at home. So mothers were usually begged to come for their babies on time. Though she was so happy about Mrs. Devlin's announcement, though she was dying to see the manager himself and get all the particulars, she would rather have taken the risk of missing all these than face an angry matron. She had a frightening anger, that matron had.

Aloud she said, "I must get the children first, otherwise I'll get told off by the matron."

"That's all right, you run along and get them; we'll wait for him when he comes. I am so happy for yer."

She thanked Mrs. Devlin and ran excitedly to the nursery. She picked up the baby from the pram[12] where she had been left in the clean hospital-like room. The babies' room was painted

---

9. **Q.E.D.,** "which was to be proved" [for Latin *quod erat demonstrandum*].

10. **choky** (chō′kē), *adj.* suffocating.

11. **incoherent** (in′kō hir′ənt), *adj.* confused; having no logical connection of ideas.

12. **pram** (pram), *n.* baby carriage.

blue with blue and pink teddies painted all over the blue furniture. Even the drinking mugs had teddies drawn on them. Did babies, when only four months old, really take notice of all those teddies, or were the teddies for the delight of the plump nurses with merry faces and fixed smiles? Her baby was gurgling at nothing in the pram. She even gave a smile of recognition when she saw her mother. Adah did not have much time to talk to her as she was supposed to be doing. It took her a long time to learn this ritual of talking to a baby who either did not understand or in most cases did not know what to make of it. In England they said it was very good to chatter to your child, even when it was a few hours old, so she too started doing it, but would make sure that none of her people were around. They might well think her a witch, talking to something that did not answer back.

In the toddlers' room there was always noise and clatter. Shrill repetitive and nerve-racking voices piped in the air. The nurses clad in their shapeless flowered overalls moved about in the confusion, soothing, separating, yelling and laughing alternately. The floor was cluttered with children's litter. Toys of all shapes—kangaroos, lizards, ducks—all sorts. Some were very good, soft and cuddly, though in most cases the little devils would rather throw them at one another than play with them.

One of the nurses, on seeing Adah, made several attempts to call her children away from the confusion, but the kids found it funny to pretend not to hear her. Adah, annoyed, marched into the confusion, pulled Bubu, one of her two boys, by the collar, but he jerked away and she had to let him go for fear of dropping the baby. Triumphant, Bubu laughed and invited his mother to "chase me, Mummy, you can't catch me, you can't catch me." Luckily for Adah, a nurse saw her predicament and, marching in like a sergeant-major, took Bubu and his younger sister Dada by the hand to the cloakroom for their coats. The kids protested fiercely, "I don't want to go home, I want to play."

"You'll come back tomorrow, then if the weather is nice we'll go to the park, we'll go by bus, we'll . . ." The nurse went on and on, telling them what they were going to do "tomorrow." To kids tomorrow is always a long time away and they would scarcely remember what it was the nurse had said the day before. She went on cooing to them in that sugary tone some people reserve for kids. They eventually came out of the nursery.

The next argument was who was to be on the right or the left of the baby's pram. Bubu said he had been on the right of the pram in the morning, and would now stay on the left. Dada said she took the left first, and was not going to give it up. She looked determined, clutching the coveted[13] side with her little hands, and leaning her head against it. Bubu tried to pull her away, and Adah commanded him to stop. "Tomorrow you'll be on the left." Bubu was pacified,[14] especially as Adah agreed with him that Dada was a naughty girl and would not have sweets tomorrow.

She hurried them home as fast as she could in the circumstances. Coming into her street, she could see that the man was already waiting for her. She quickened her pace and the children on either side of her started to trot, just like horses, their unworn gloves dangling lifelessly from the sleeves of their coats.

The man who was waiting for her was in his mid-thirties, with his belly slightly protruding. With a belly like that he must watch his diet, his beer . . . "Hello," she said breathless.

The man seemed unsure of what he should do next. He had glasses, his gray top coat was unbuttoned, revealing a very clean shirt. The glasses he had on gave him a highly intelligent look, but he ruined the effect by keeping his mouth open most of the time. With his mouth

---

13. **coveted** (kuv′ə tid), *adj.* strongly desired.
14. **pacify** (pas′ə fī), *v.* quiet down.

opened like that he looked both intelligent and stupid simultaneously.[15]

He decided to come to the point. "Are you Mrs. Obi?"

"Of course."

She wondered why professionals ask this sort of question. What exactly was she supposed to do, wear a label? Of course she was Mrs. Obi. She was beginning to hate the suspense. "Have you a flat for me?" She might as well know the worst. This man now managed to look like both a sharp plain-clothes detective and a mere clerk.

He cleared his throat. There was nothing to clear—he was just embarrassed or something. "Yes, we've got temporary accommodation for you at the Pussy Mansions, not very far, just around the corner."

"Come now, that's unfair," Mrs. Devlin cried. "Why do you put a girl like her in such a Godforsaken place? Her children are very young, and she's very hard working. It's not fair at all. Why, she might as well stay where she is now!"

"Huh?" cried Adah wondering whether Mrs. Devlin had gone mad. "Stay here? You must be joking. Any hole is better than this filth."

This pleased the man in the gray coat, and he gave Mrs. Devlin a why-don't-you-shut-your-mouth sort of look. Mrs. Devlin went on protesting.

"It's a rough place to put a girl like that."

The gray-coated man felt that he had to volunteer an explanation as Adah was beginning to look at him dubiously.[16] "You see, we have to rehouse you rather quickly because we were told about the kind of bitter experiences you are being subjected to and gather that this place is not very safe for your children. You are going to stay at the Mansions for a short while—just a temporary arrangement, nothing permanent at all. Of course you can reject the offer if you don't particularly like it."

He started to dangle two keys in front of Adah's face as if tantalising her. "Take it or leave it!" his attitude seemed to be saying.

His cuff links were real gold, and his wristwatch was golden too. He probably was the manager after all. The keys kept on dangling in front of her. Should she refuse the offer to save Mrs. Devlin the humiliation of being slighted? Should she accept the offer just to move away from the oppressive situation she was in? *Poor Mrs. Devlin, you don't know the gripping fears I go through every time I leave my children indoors to do some shopping, you don't know what it is like to realise that all your letters are being opened and read before you lay your hands on them, and you cannot dream what independence it is to have your own front door, your own toilet and bath, just for you and your family.*

Her feelings were transparent,[17] and Mrs. Devlin started to shuffle her way inside. Adah took the keys from the man very quickly. The man's mouth opened wider, surprised. He collected himself with a jerk, and said, "You'll let us know tomorrow if you are going to accept it, won't you, so that the flat could be redecorated for you?"

It had taken Adah nine months of court-going, letter-writing and tribunal-visiting to get her this much. Now this man wanted her to approve first of all, then wait for redecoration before moving in; he must be out of his mind.

"I'm moving in tonight!"

"What?" The man jumped to attention as if giving a military salute. "Are you quite sure, madam? We don't want to rush you, and we always want our tenants to move into clean flats, you know, we could have it done over for you."

"Is there any law preventing me from moving in today? Is there any law preventing you and your people from decorating when we've already moved in?"

"Of course not, madam." The man began to look over his shoulder as if he was about to sell Adah some stolen goods. "In that case, er, I do

---

15. simultaneously (sī′məl tā′nē əs lē), *adv.* at the same time.
16. dubiously (dü′bē əs lē), *adv.* doubtfully.
17. transparent (tran sper′ənt), *adj.* easily seen through.

wish you a happy stay at the Mansions. Er . . . if you want anything, we will do the best we can. Goodbye."

He turned around, walked quickly round the corner and disappeared, leaving Adah with the keys, and a hollow in her stomach, as if she had not eaten for days. She was going to take the flat and move out of this horrible place. She couldn't care less if in doing so she was offending a friend like Mrs. Devlin—it was her own life. Why couldn't people leave her to make her own mistakes? She was going to take the flat. She must move, and move that very night.

Having collected her two older youngsters from school, Adah avoided Mrs. Devlin for the rest of the evening. She did not wish to sing her joy aloud in case the landlord and landlady should guess that she was up to something. With suppressed[18] excitement she told her children, the ones who were old enough to understand. "We can't believe it," they had chorused. She sped to the news-agent round the corner, and the man agreed to move her few possessions to the Mansions for her for thirty shillings. It was then the thought occurred to her that she had not even seen the flat. She sped down the road to the block. So this was the block of flats.

The outside looked like a prison, red bricks with tiny yellow windows. The shape of the whole block was square, with those tiny windows peeping into the streets. The block looked dependable, solid. The outside look was not too encouraging, but she must not despair. She went round in circles looking for an opening into the block, found one eventually, but it was so dark that she was not at first sure that she was not walking into a cave. She emerged into an open space, with a crowd of children playing.

She looked on both sides of her, feeling lost. She saw a little boy with a friendly face and asked him where flat number *X* was.

The boy looked at her and said, "They moved yesterday, they've moved to Hampstead."

Adah thanked him, and told him that she was going to be the new tenant, and asked him could he please show her where the flat was. The boy did not look too happy at this question. He seemed to consider it for a while, shrugged his little shoulders as if to say, "After all, what must be, must be." He got up reluctantly[19] and took her up what seemed to Adah to be ten flights of stone steps. She had never climbed such steep steps in her life, and at that speed too.

When they got to the top, the boy pointed to a door by a gaping shute. "There it is." He waited for Adah to open the door. She did, and the boy peeped inside just once and ran away, his mind already preoccupied with something else.

Adah went in, gingerly at first, inspecting one room after the other. It was not bad at all compared to what she had. She was very pleased with the bath in particular. All these rooms, just for her—well, God was wonderful. He had heard her prayers. Oh, yes, they were going to spend the night there. She went down the stairs quickly, ran down to her old house, calling on the news agent on her way, picked up her odds and ends, and two hours later she was a tenant of the Mansions.

On that first night they had no beds, no curtains and no floor coverings, but Adah made do with an oil heater and piles of old blankets and bed sheets. There were three important things she knew she had acquired that night, her independence, her freedom, and peace of mind.

PREDICT: What kind of a life do you think Adah will make for the children and herself in the Mansions?

---

18. **suppressed** (sə prest′), *adj.* held back; subdued.
19. reluctantly (ri luk′tənt lē), *adv.* slowly and unwillingly.

After Reading

Making Connections

Shaping Your Response

1. Why do you think Emecheta might have chosen *In the Ditch* as the title of her book?

2. What actress would you choose to play Adah in a film version of *In the Ditch?*

Analyzing the Novel Excerpt

3. Why do you think the landlord wants to make Adah's life miserable?

4. Why might Adah agree to protect her landlord by keeping quiet in front of the Londoners?

5. What commentary on cultural differences is suggested by Adah's thoughts about the colors of the devil and angels?

6. 👣 Compare and contrast Adah's **interactions** with the Nigerians with her interactions with the Londoners.

7. Why do you think Adah feels freer in London than she had in Nigeria?

8. What beliefs and values seem to govern Adah's life?

Extending the Ideas

9. Do you think that a woman today in circumstances similar to Adah's would have the same experiences that Adah does?

Literary Focus: Dialogue

With two classmates read aloud the two dialogue scenes from "Drifting to the Mansions" on pages 885 and 887. For each scene determine what purpose or purposes the dialogue serves:

Dialogue Purposes	Adah and Mrs. Devlin (page 885)	Adah, Mrs. Devlin, and the manager (page 887)
Characterization		
Creation of Mood		
Plot Advancement		
Theme Development		

Vocabulary Study

coveted
effrontery
incoherent
pacify
reluctantly
simultaneously

Select the vocabulary word that is most clearly related to the situation conveyed in the sentence. You will not use all the words.

1. So excited was she—far beyond being tense—
   That her words sounded crazy: they didn't make sense.

2. How she envies big diamonds (say, set in a ring);
   Her wish list is quite long; she just wants everything!

3. With an attitude bold—no, I'll even say brash—
   Their behavior is shocking and shameless and rash.
4. He was very unwilling, did not want to go;
   When at last he consented, his movements were slow.
5. He was true to his form, he was reckless and wild,
   But a cookie from Grandma becalmed the small child.

Expressing Your Ideas

Writing Choices

Writer's Notebook Update Review the obstacles you listed in your notebook. Put a check by each obstacle that matches Adah's problems in England. List additional obstacles that Adah confronts.

You Won't Believe What I Saw Write the **dialogue** that you imagine might take place between the milkman and his wife when he returns from his workday to tell her about the strange scene he observed early in the morning. Remember that he is unfamiliar with the landlord's Ibo culture and may well be suspicious of anyone who looks different and acts in a strange manner.

Advice from Adah Write a **letter of advice** that Adah might send to a young woman from her country who wishes to move to London. Include both warnings and encouragements. Emphasize also how important it is to understand and cope with cultural differences.

Other Options

Cooking with Adah Research the food of Nigeria and prepare an **illustrated recipe book** containing recipes for several dishes that Adah might serve to her children to celebrate their new life in the Mansions. If you can, prepare one or more of the recipes for your class.

Imagine the Ritual Imagine the music, the dance, and the ritual that might surround the masquerader wearing this traditional African mask that comes from the country of Liberia. Select appropriate music and choreograph a ritualistic **dance.** Perform your dance for your class. Or, if you wish, you might design a colorful **costume** that you think a juju masquerader might wear. You may design it on paper or, if you can sew, you might want to stitch it up and model it for your class.

The Passing of Empire

Effects of Empire

SOUTH AFRICA
LOSS OF FREEDOM

History Connection

The story of South Africa for over three hundred years has been a story of European domination. Not until the 1980s did the black majority of the country begin to win the rights that had been denied them for centuries.

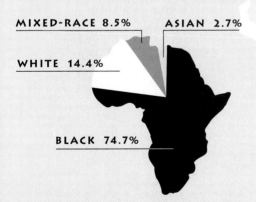

1652 THE FIRST EUROPEANS TO SETTLE IN SOUTHERNMOST AFRICA ARRIVE. WORKERS OF THE DUTCH EAST INDIA COMPANY, HEADED BY JAN VAN RIEBEECK, ESTABLISH A COMPANY OUTPOST NEAR THE CAPE OF GOOD HOPE. PEOPLE WHO LEAVE THE COMPANY START FARMS IN THE AREA. THEY CALL THEMSELVES AFRIKANERS (af′rə kä′nərz), AND OVER TIME THEY SPEAK A FORM OF DUTCH CALLED AFRIKAANS, WHICH IS INFLUENCED BY AFRICAN LANGUAGES.

1795 BRITAIN SEIZES THE CAPE COLONY. BRITISH SETTLERS AND OFFICIALS LOOK DOWN ON THE AFRIKANERS, WHO ALSO ARE CALLED BOERS (bôrz), A DUTCH WORD FOR FARMERS.

1873 AFRIKANERS MOVE HUNDREDS OF MILES INLAND TO ESCAPE BRITISH DOMINATION. DURING THIS MIGRATION, CALLED THE GREAT TREK, HOSTILITIES INCREASE BETWEEN THE AFRIKANERS AND BLACK AFRICANS, WHOSE LANDS THE DUTCH DESCENDANTS ENTER. THE BOERS SETTLE IN AREAS THAT THEY TAKE FROM ZULUS, XHOSAS, AND OTHER AFRICAN PEOPLES.

1879 THE ZULU WAR BEGINS WITH BRITISH INVASION OF ZULULAND. AFTER AN INITIAL DISASTER AT ISANDHLWANA, THE BRITISH ARMY DEFEATS ZULU FORCES, FINALLY CAPTURING ZULU KING CETEWAYO.

PERCENT OF POPULATION BY RACE

MIXED-RACE 8.5%   ASIAN 2.7%

WHITE 14.4%

BLACK 74.7%

1899 BRITAIN ATTEMPTS TO ADD INLAND REGIONS, INCLUDING GOLD-PRODUCING LANDS, TO ITS EMPIRE. THE BOER WAR BEGINS. THE BOERS SURRENDER IN 1902. BRITAIN TURNS OVER AUTHORITY FOR COLONIES— NATAL, THE CAPE COLONY, THE TRANSVAAL, AND THE ORANGE FREE STATE—TO THEIR EUROPEAN SETTLERS. MOST OF THE POPULATION, WHO ARE BLACK PEOPLE, HOLD NO POLITICAL POWER.

1910 THE UNION OF SOUTH AFRICA IS FORMED. AS IN THE COLONIES, BLACK AFRICANS ARE NOT ALLOWED TO VOTE, CONTROL ANY APPRECIABLE WEALTH, OR SHARE THE RIGHTS HELD BY WHITE SOUTH AFRICANS.

Even though blacks have always been in the majority in South Africa, whites have controlled the political system for most of the last 350 years.

(Source: Countries of the World and Their Leaders Yearbook 1994)

1912 THE AFRICAN NATIVE NATIONAL CONGRESS IS FORMED TO FIGHT AGAINST RACIAL INEQUALITY. THE GROUP LATER IS KNOWN AS THE AFRICAN NATIONAL CONGRESS, OR ANC.

STRUGGLE FOR FREEDOM

1948 THE NATIONAL PARTY, DOMINATED BY AFRIKANERS, COMES TO POWER. THE TRADITIONAL PRACTICES OF APARTHEID (ə pärt´hāt), A SYSTEM OF RACIAL SEPARATION AND WHITE SUPREMACY, BECOMES LAW. BLACK AFRICANS IN SOUTH AFRICA ARE FORCED TO LIVE IN CROWDED, UNPRODUCTIVE "HOMELANDS," WHILE WHITE PEOPLE ARE GIVEN ADDITIONAL PRODUCTIVE LANDS. THREE QUARTERS OF THE POPULATION ARE FORCED TO MOVE ONTO THIRTEEN PERCENT OF THE LAND.

1962 NELSON MANDELA, A LEADER OF THE AFRICAN NATIONAL CONGRESS, IS IMPRISONED. THE GOVERNMENT CONTINUALLY ACTS TO WEAKEN ATTEMPTS TO ORGANIZE OR UNIFY BLACK SOUTH AFRICANS.

1976 AFTER THE GOVERNMENT MANDATES THE TEACHING OF AFRICAN CHILDREN IN AFRIKAANS, BLACK STUDENTS IN THE TOWNSHIP OF SOWETO PROTEST, AND DISTURBANCES ARISE IN VARIOUS COMMUNITIES. THE GOVERNMENT BRUTALLY SUPPRESSES THE "SOWETO UPRISING," KILLING MORE THAN 600 PEOPLE.

1977 CHARISMATIC BLACK ACTIVIST STEVEN BIKO IS TORTURED WHILE IN POLICE CUSTODY. HE DIES, AND THE MOVEMENT FOR FREEDOM AMONG BLACK SOUTH AFRICANS GAINS SUPPORT. INTERNATIONAL REACTIONS AGAINST SOUTH AFRICAN GOVERNMENT POLICIES GROW. INVESTMENT IN SOUTH AFRICA DECLINES.

IN DETENTION

He fell from the ninth floor
He hanged himself
He slipped on a piece of
    soap while washing
He hanged himself
He slipped on a piece of soap
    while washing
He fell from the ninth floor
He hanged himself while washing
He slipped from the ninth floor
He hung from the ninth floor
He slipped on the ninth floor
    while washing
He fell from a piece of soap
    while slipping
He hung from the ninth floor
He washed from the ninth
    floor while slipping
He hung from a piece of
    soap while washing

This poem by South African Christopher van Wyk gives a cynical view of official explanations for deaths in detention.

Hector Peterson, 13, was the first child killed in the Soweto uprising of 1976. Students were protesting a mandate that required classes to be taught in Afrikaans when police opened fire.

ACHIEVEMENT OF FREEDOM

1986 SOUTH AFRICA BEGINS TO REPEAL APARTHEID LAWS, A PROCESS THAT CONTINUES UNTIL 1991.

1990 NELSON MANDELA IS RELEASED FROM PRISON. HIS LEADERSHIP IS HAILED AROUND THE WORLD.

1994 THE FIRST NATIONAL ELECTIONS IN WHICH PEOPLE OF ALL RACES CAN VOTE ARE HELD. NELSON MANDELA IS ELECTED PRESIDENT.

During my lifetime I have dedicated myself to this struggle of the African people. I have fought against white domination and I have fought against black domination. I have cherished the idea of a democratic and free society in which all persons live together in harmony and with equal opportunities. It is an ideal which I hope to live for and achieve. But if needs be, it is an ideal for which I am prepared to die.
--Nelson Mandela

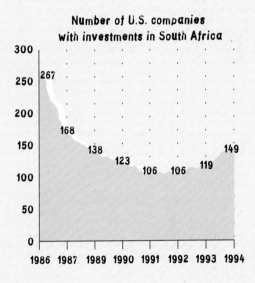

Number of U.S. companies with investments in South Africa

Year	Number
1986	267
1987	168
1989	138
1990	123
1991	106
1992	106
1993	119
1994	149

Responding
What parallels do you see between the struggle of blacks in South Africa during the 1970s and '80s and that of blacks in the U.S. during the 1960s? what differences?

During the late 1980s public disapproval of apartheid among people throughout the world caused many businesses to limit their investments in South Africa. The number of U.S. companies with investments in South Africa declined until reforms took effect in the 1990s. (No data is available for 1988.)

Career Connection

Achieving independence, a glorious development to many nations and peoples, to others seems a mixed blessing. An American diplomat encountered uneasy feelings and economic distress in a west African country granted independence by the British.

THE PULSE OF VILLAGE LIFE

INTERVIEW WITH DR. EDWARD BRYNN

When Dr. Edward Brynn arrived in The Gambia, in western Africa, in April 1984 to start a short tour as Chief of Mission for the United States, most African states had been independent for twenty years. However, in the British Empire, not every colony was equally eager for that independence. The Gambia, an approximately 200-mile-long sliver of a country that cuts into Senegal, was one of the reluctant ones. Foreign Service officer Dr. Brynn wrote, "Britain forced independence on to this mini-colony more than the Gambians demanded it. In 1984 nostalgia for olden times remained very lively. Judges sweltered under wigs as they heard cases and issued judgments. Photos of the Queen graced the walls of villagers throughout the country. All news emanated from the BBC. . . .

"My days were not so pressed with work to preclude travel. Despite the heat I found a bike and pedaled down dozens of dusty roads through villages little changed over the centuries. My ambition was to seek our Peace Corps Volunteers and to hear their thoughts on development and the role of Americans. . . .

"In Sub-Saharan Africa per capita income levels are on average about 50 percent of what they were at independence. In The Gambia all the indexes are down: people are less healthy, hungrier, more crowded, less content with their lives. Independence was sold to them as a panacea, a way to escape a heritage of poverty, inequality, even slavery. The reality was quite different: the firm, unfeeling, distant hand of colonial administrators was supplanted by an indigenous elite which tended toward corruption or, at least, favoritism of kith and kin. Sitting in a small village, my bike leaning heavily against a frail tree, I found myself feeling keenly the pulse of village life on the banks of one of Africa's grand rivers. Drama in the pounding of the drums, sorrow in the soft crying of a mother seeing her malnourished baby at death's door, a ubiquitous silence induced by intense, enervating heat—all of these made up a rural African evening.

"Back in the capital, I entertained the elite at a fancy table. I engaged senior ministers, whose own ties to the village down the road had almost disappeared, as they sought to do good and often did well—for themselves and their families. They were amused, and sometimes embarrassed, to see that I spent so much time with their poorest cousins. Their hearts and minds were in London and New York. Another generation would have to pass before real independence came to The Gambia."

Responding

1. Is independence always a good thing for a country? Why or why not?

2. The U.S. and The Gambia are both former colonies of Britain. From what you have read in this article, what similarities and differences do you see in their achievement of independence?

Language History

The Language of the Twentieth Century

 War is peace. Freedom is slavery. Ignorance is strength.
George Orwell, *Nineteen Eighty-four* (1948)

The English language has continued to grow and change during the twentieth century, as it has throughout its long and rich history. Two world wars have provided such terms as *zeppelin, U-boat, blitzkrieg, jeep, concentration camp,* and *A-bomb;* from science and technology came *neurosis, antibiotic, radio, television, videotape,* and *megabyte;* from the arts came *montage, surrealism,* and *absurdist.* As the language continued to change, words took on new meanings. *Scan* once meant to study with great care; now it means to glance at hastily. *Sophistication,* once a term of condemnation, now signifies approval.

The widespread use of manipulative language by propagandists and advertisers has disturbed many people. Probably the best-known analyst of the corruption of English by politicians and salespeople in the recent past was George Orwell (see page 859). In essays like "Politics and the English Language," he protested against bad language habits that corrupt thinking: "Modern writing at its worst does not consist in picking out words for the sake of their meaning and inventing images in order to make the meaning clearer. It consists in gumming together long strips of words which have already been set in order by someone else, and making the results presentable by sheer humbug."

Orwell's novel *Nineteen Eighty-four* depicts a slave society ruled by a self-perpetuating elite. The official language is called *Newspeak.* Each year words are eliminated from its vocabulary. The purpose of impoverishing the language is to narrow the range of thought of the citizens, so that it will become increasingly difficult for them to express, or even to form, an unorthodox concept. Ultimately, they will cease to think altogether. In order to create more mental confusion in the citizens, the elite promote the practice of *doublethink,* the ability to hold two contradictory beliefs simultaneously. Perhaps Orwell's bleak fantasy should be seen more as a warning than a prediction. But in a world full of official euphemism, in which murder is referred to as "termination with extreme prejudice," Orwell's admonition to rid ourselves of bad language habits seems more relevant than ever before.

Writing Workshop

Conclusions About Colonialism

Assignment Authors from former colonies of the British Empire have expressed their attitudes toward colonialism in their works. Analyze one of these author's attitudes.

WRITER'S BLUEPRINT

Product   A literary analysis
Purpose   To explore an author's attitudes toward colonialism
Audience   A British literary magazine
Specs   As the writer of a successful analysis, you should:

❏ Imagine that you are writing for a British literary magazine on the theme Attitudes Toward Colonialism. Focus on one of the six writers from "Choose an author," on the next page.

❏ Read at least two of this author's stories, poems, articles, or essays. Draw conclusions about the author's attitudes toward the influence of British colonial rule on the life of the colony. Also, look for biographical information that might help.

❏ Begin with a thesis statement that sums up the author's attitudes toward colonialism. It will serve as the guiding force in your paper. Go on to explain how you arrived at this statement. Support your conclusions with examples from the author's works, including quotations.

❏ End by summing up your personal reactions to these attitudes.

❏ Be concise. Avoid empty words and phrases.

❏ Follow the rules of grammar, usage, spelling, and mechanics. Use commas correctly.

STEP  **1** PREWRITING

Look for clues about attitudes toward colonialism. Before you look at your chosen author, practice finding clues in another author's work. Review George Orwell's "Shooting an Elephant" on pages 860–865 with a small group. Add entries to the first column of the chart shown and fill in the second column with your own conclusions and questions.

Orwell's "Shooting an Elephant"	Conclusions and Questions
When a Burman tripped him on the football field, "the crowd yelled with hideous laughter."	Orwell sees that the Burmese hate the British. But how does he, himself, feel about the situation?
"I perceived in this moment that when the white man turns tyrant it is his own freedom that he destroys."	

Choose an author to focus on from the six shown in the author web. Read about your author in encyclopedias or other sources such as the *Contemporary Author* series before making your choice.

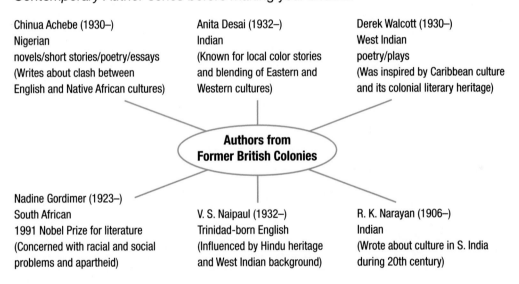

Chinua Achebe (1930–)
Nigerian
novels/short stories/poetry/essays
(Writes about clash between
English and Native African cultures)

Anita Desai (1932–)
Indian
(Known for local color stories
and blending of Eastern and
Western cultures)

Derek Walcott (1930–)
West Indian
poetry/plays
(Was inspired by Caribbean culture
and its colonial literary heritage)

**Authors from
Former British Colonies**

Nadine Gordimer (1923–)
South African
1991 Nobel Prize for literature
(Concerned with racial and social
problems and apartheid)

V. S. Naipaul (1932–)
Trinidad-born English
(Influenced by Hindu heritage
and West Indian background)

R. K. Narayan (1906–)
Indian
(Wrote about culture in S. India
during 20th century)

Read at least two stories, poems, or essays by the author you've chosen. Make notes on the author's attitudes, using a chart like the one you made in "Look for clues about attitudes." As you proceed, search for answers to any questions you posed in the second column.

Don't be surprised if your conclusions reveal mixed feelings on the author's part toward both the British and native peoples. These authors are dealing with complex political and social issues.

Compose a thesis statement to serve as the guiding force for your essay. It should consist of a sentence or two that sums up your author's attitudes toward colonialism and should be specific and limited enough to provide well-defined boundaries for your essay. Use your chart as a

OR . . .
Read something by several other authors on the list as well to get an idea of their attitudes toward colonialism. This will give you insight on the attitudes of the author you chose.

guide. Here are two examples of thesis statements. Notice how vague and ill-defined the first version is when compared with the second, revised version:

> In "Shooting an Elephant," Orwell shows that he does not approve of what goes on between the British and the native peoples in Burma.

> In "Shooting an Elephant," Orwell sees the colonial process as a mutual loss of freedom. Each side, in its own way, enslaves the other.

Plan your essay. Here is one way to organize your ideas. Make notes on each category.

- **Introduction**
  Author and works to be discussed
  Thesis statement (author's attitudes toward colonialism)

- **Body**
  First conclusion
  —examples from text
  Second conclusion
  —examples from text
  and so on . . .

- **Conclusion**
  Personal reaction to author's attitudes
  —agree or disagree
  —reasons why

STEP 2 DRAFTING

Start writing. Consider these suggestions:

- Write your thesis statement on an index card and keep it in front of you while you draft to help you stay focused.

- Begin with a quotation or a provocative question that leads into your thesis statement. For example: *When does the slave become the master and the master the slave?*

- When you finish the introduction and body, reread them and make a fresh set of notes on your reactions before you write the ending.

3 REVISING

Ask a partner for comments on your draft before you revise it.

✔ Have I begun with a thesis statement about the author's attitudes toward colonialism?

✔ Does the rest of my essay relate to this thesis?

✔ Have I supported my conclusions with evidence from the literature?

✔ Have I given my personal reactions to the author's attitudes?

✔ Is my writing concise?

Revising Strategy

Being Concise

One goal in revising is to eliminate unnecessary words and phrases that slow the reader down, such as the ones in italics.

WORDY   *The reason that* this author is critical of colonialism is because it supports apartheid.

REVISED   This author is critical of colonialism because it supports apartheid.

WORDY   *In my opinion, it seems to me that* Desai is highly critical of the British.

REVISED   Desai seems highly critical of the British.

When you revise, make every word count.

4 EDITING

Ask a partner to review your revised draft before you edit. When you edit, watch for errors in grammar, usage, spelling, and mechanics. Pay special attention to errors with commas. See the Editing Strategy and student model on the next page.

Editing Strategy

Using Commas Correctly

Without commas, elements of sentences may run together, causing confusion. Notice how this writer paid close attention to commas during editing.

> The authors of these works, all from former colonies of the British Empire, have expressed their attitudes toward colonialism in their stories, poems, articles, and essays. One of these authors, Derek Walcott, conveys his attitudes through poetry.

STUDENT MODEL

FOR REFERENCE
You'll find more rules for using commas in the Language and Grammar Handbook at the back of this text.

STEP 5 PRESENTING

- Read your analysis to a world history class that's studying colonialism.

- Locate and share with your classmates art, film, and music that represents the period and culture your author writes about.

STEP 6 LOOKING BACK

Self-evaluate. What grade would you give your paper? Look back at the Writer's Blueprint and give yourself a score on each point, from 6 (superior) to 1 (inadequate).

Reflect. Write answers to these questions.

✔ Put yourself in the place of the colonized people you read about. How would you have felt in their situation?

✔ Compare your writing plan and your final draft. What kinds of changes did you make? What do they tell you about how to use a writing plan?

For Your Working Portfolio Add your analysis and your reflection responses to your working portfolio.

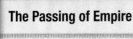

Beyond Print

Propaganda

Propaganda is a systematic effort to spread opinions or beliefs. Advertising uses propaganda techniques to convince us that we need, or want, a product or service. Propaganda can also be used for the public good, such as the nationwide effort to ban smoking in public places. In his wartime speeches, Winston Churchill was a master at convincing people of his viewpoint. Equally adept was his adversary, Adolph Hitler, who used propaganda to incite the Germans to action. Use the following criteria to evaluate ads, articles, and speeches.

Fact and Opinion Examine words and phrases like *clearly, everybody knows,* and *without question.* Look at the rest of the statement. Is it a fact that expansion of an airport will improve a community or that building low-income housing will ruin the area?

Authoritative Sources Are speakers qualified to offer an opinion on a given subject? Educational background, professional experience, and personal knowledge are just a few of the factors that make sources reliable. An experienced statesman such as Winston Churchill, for example, would have informed opinions about how to conduct World War II.

Loaded Words Be on the lookout for words designed to appeal to your emotions. In "Shooting an Elephant," George Orwell uses words like *oppressors* and *tyranny* to convey his strong feelings about imperialism and to sway the emotions of his readers.

Testimonial Authority figures or celebrities are often used to support or oppose something. Watch out! A man in a white coat is not necessarily a doctor. An NBA player may not be the best judge of orange juice.

Bandwagon An ad that urges us to buy a book because it is a best seller, or campaign literature urging us to vote for a candidate who is leading in the polls is an example of the bandwagon technique.

Activity Option

Examine these selections, listing words and phrases designed to sway your emotions—for or against the British Empire. Based on biographical information, which authors do you consider authoritative?

A PUZZLING FUTURE

HISTORICAL OVERVIEW

England was once a country where most people, however dissatisfied with their place in society, at least knew what that place was. The future of England presents a puzzle—a society where many elements no longer seem to fit. After World War II, the British Empire was dismantled, but many former colonials immigrated to their onetime Mother Country, creating the stresses of a multi-racial society. How closely England should be united to the rest of Europe continues to be an issue. The end of the Welfare State has contributed to old problems like unemployment and home-lessness. The Royal Family, once a symbol of national unity, now seems as fragmented as the rest of Britain. Whether the English will be able to fit their complex political, social, and cultural puzzle together remains a question for the 21st century.

A. The marital problems of the Prince and Princess of Wales damaged the Royal Family as a national symbol.

B. Persistent unemployment, particularly among the young, increased the number of England's homeless.

C. Youthful rebellion took the form of exaggerated punk styles in hair, clothing, and music.

E

D

F

G

H

Key Dates

1972
British troops kill 13 in Northern Ireland on "Bloody Sunday."

1973
England joins the Common Market.

1976
Punk rock becomes popular with British working class youth.

1978
Margaret Thatcher becomes Prime Minister.

1980
Unemployment reaches highest level since 1930s Depression.

1982
England defeats Argentina in the Falklands War.

1984
Widespread strike begins by British miners.

1985
Racial violence breaks out in Brixton.

1994
Channel Tunnel completed.

D. The Channel Tunnel between England and France physically linked the island nation to the European mainland.

E. England's victory over Argentina in the brief Falklands War marked a brief return of British imperialism.

F. Miners were no longer central to a British economy moving away from heavy industry.

G. The erection of Europe's largest Hindu temple indicated England's growing multiculturalism.

H. A hopeful sign was movement in the negotiations to end decades of violence in Northern Ireland.

903

Part Two

The Slant View

How are we supposed to regard a world that—as we are told more and more—is not what it appears to be? Modern physics and mathematics have created new dimensions to aid in thinking about the world, and modern philosophy and psychology have their counterparts.

Multicultural Connection **Perspective** It may be that the best way to view an increasingly confusing world is from new **perspectives.** Perspective involves seeing people and events from diverse viewpoints; yet a person's culture has a great influence on the ways that person views such basic and universal aspects of life as youth, time, love, and death.

Before Reading

Eve to Her Daughters by Judith Wright

The Frog Prince by Stevie Smith

Not Waving but Drowning by Stevie Smith

The Explorers by Margaret Atwood

Building Background

Poetry's Sources In "Eve to Her Daughters," Judith Wright's inspiration comes from the Genesis account of the first humans to be created. In her poetry, Stevie Smith made use of nursery rhymes, fairy tales, history, and popular songs, employing clever twists and witty verbal maneuvers to create verse that is fresh and engaging. Margaret Atwood says that when she was in high school and college she was writing "borderline literary material" and that she "even wrote an opera about synthetic fabrics for . . . Home Economics class. It was about that time," she says, "I realized I didn't want to be a home economist." The work of these poets proves that the wellsprings of literature are deep and varied, and that artists always bring their own special slant to their work.

Literary Focus

Allusion A brief reference to a person, event, or place, real or fictitious, or to a piece of music or work of art is called an **allusion.** An allusion can concisely convey much information. In the title of his novel, *For Whom the Bell Tolls,* Ernest Hemingway alludes to John Donne's essay (page 228), for example. Edward Albee's play, *Who's Afraid of Virginia Woolf?,* is obviously an allusion, though an obscure one, to the author. Two of the four poems that follow contain allusions.

Writer's Notebook

Yesterdays Writers often recall events from their childhood in their work. In fact, Dylan Thomas based "A Child's Christmas in Wales" (page 824) on such memories. Can you recall a story read to you as a child? childhood games? childhood superstitions? Make a list of some of these memories in your notebook for possible use in a poem, paragraph, or essay.

Judith Wright
born 1915

Born in Armidale, New South Wales, Australia, Wright was educated at New England Girls' School in Armidale and the University of Sydney. She has written poetry, children's stories, literary criticism, and works based on the life of her grandfather, who first settled in Australia. Her books of poetry include *Fourth Quarter and Other Poems* (1976) and *The Double Tree: Selected Poems* (1978). She is active in the conservation movement in Australia.

Stevie Smith
1902–1971

Stevie Smith lived most of her life in a London suburb, although she was born in the Yorkshire city of Hull. Christened Florence Margaret, she acquired her nickname when she was horseback riding with a friend, and some boys called to her, "Come on Steve," after a famous jockey. After attending the North London Collegiate School for Girls, she went to work for a magazine publishing company, for whom she worked for thirty years. Her first book of poetry was *A Good Time Was Had by All* (1937). She published three novels and seven more books of poetry, including *Not Waving, but Drowning* (1957) and *The Frog Prince and Other Poems* (1966). *Me Again* (1981) is a collection of some of her short stories, essays, reviews, and letters.

Margaret Atwood
born 1939

Margaret Atwood writes poems, novels, and short stories. She has also written children's books and plays. Born in Ottawa, Canada, she moved to Toronto with her family in 1946 and spent many summers with her parents in the north woods of Canada, resulting in experiences that, according to critic Jerome H. Rosenberg, "have contributed to both the imagery and the vision of her works." Atwood graduated from the University of Toronto and received a master's degree in English from Harvard. She has taught literture and creative writing. Her works include *Lady Oracle* (1976); *Bluebeard's Egg* (1982), a collection of stories; *The Handmaid's Tale* (1985), a novel that won a Governor General's Award; and *Wilderness Trips* (1991), a book of poetry.

Eve to Her Daughters

Judith Wright

It was not I who began it.
Turned out into draughty caves,
hungry so often, having to work for our bread,
hearing the children whining,
5 I was nevertheless not unhappy.
Where Adam went I was fairly contented to go.
I adapted myself to the punishment: it was my life.

But Adam, you know . . . !
He kept on brooding over the insult,
10 over the trick They had played on us, over the scolding.
He had discovered a flaw in himself
and he had to make up for it.
Outside Eden the earth was imperfect,
the seasons changed, the game was fleet-footed,
15 he had to work for our living, and he didn't like it.
He even complained of my cooking
(it was hard to compete with Heaven).

So, he set to work.
The earth must be made a new Eden
20 with central heating, domesticated animals,
mechanical harvesters, combustion engines,
escalators, refrigerators,
and modern means of communication
and multiplied opportunities for safe investment
25 and higher education for Abel and Cain
and the rest of the family.
You can see how his pride has been hurt.

In the process he had to unravel everything,
because he believed that mechanism
30 was the whole secret—he was always mechanical-minded.
He got to the very inside of the whole machine
exclaiming as he went, So this is how it works!
And now that I know how it works, why, I must have
       invented it.
As for God and the Other, they cannot be demonstrated,
35 and what cannot be demonstrated
doesn't exist.
You see, he had always been jealous.

Yes, he got to the center
where nothing at all can be demonstrated.
40 And clearly he doesn't exist; but he refuses
to accept the conclusion.
You see, he was always an egotist.

It was warmer than this in the cave;
there was none of this fallout.
45 I would suggest, for the sake of the children,
that it's time you took over.

But you are my daughters, you inherit my own faults
       of character;
you are submissive, following Adam
even beyond existence.
50 Faults of character have their own logic
and it always works out.
I observed this with Abel and Cain.

Perhaps the whole elaborate fable
right from the beginning
55 is meant to demonstrate this; perhaps it's the whole secret.
Perhaps nothing exists but our faults?

But it's useless to make
such a suggestion to Adam.
He has turned himself into God,
60 who is faultless and doesn't exist.

Does this illustration by Ken Joudry have a humorous or serious **tone**? Explain. ➤

The FROG PRINCE

Stevie Smith

I am a frog
I live under a spell
I live at the bottom
Of a green well

5 And here I must wait
Until a maiden places me
On her royal pillow
And kisses me
In her father's palace.

10 The story is familiar
Everybody knows it well
But do other enchanted people feel as
    nervous
As I do? The stories do not tell,

Ask if they will be happier
15 When the changes come,
As already they are fairly happy
In a frog's doom?

I have been a frog now
For a hundred years
20 And in all this time
I have not shed many tears.

I am happy, I like the life,
Can swim for many a mile
(When I have hopped to the river)
25 And am for ever agile.

And the quietness,
Yes, I like to be quiet
I am habituated

To a quiet life,

30 But always when I think these thoughts
As I sit in my well
Another thought comes to me and says:
It is part of the spell

To be happy
35 To work up contentment
To make much of being a frog
To fear disenchantment

Says, It will be *heavenly*
To be set free
40 Cries, *Heavenly* the girl who disenchants
And the royal times, *heavenly,*
And I think it will be.

Come then, royal girl and royal times,
Come quickly,
45 I can be happy until you come
But I cannot be heavenly,
Only disenchanted people
Can be heavenly.

NOT WAVING BUT DROWNING

Stevie Smith

Nobody heard him, the dead man,
But still he lay moaning:
I was much farther out than you thought
And not waving but drowning.

5 Poor chap, he always loved larking
And now he's dead
It must have been too cold for him his heart gave way,
They said.

O no no no, it was cold always
10 (Still the dead one lay moaning)
I was much too far out all my life
And not waving but drowning.

◄ The Frog Prince in Stevie Smith's poem says he feels
both nervous and contented. Does her drawing of him
suggest either feeling?

The Explorers

Margaret Atwood

The explorers will come
in several minutes
and find this island.

    (It is a stunted island,
5 rocky, with room
for only a few trees, a thin
layer of soil; hardly
bigger than a bed.
That is how they've missed it
10 until now)

Already their boats draw near,
their flags flutter,
their oars push at the water.

They will be jubilant
15 and shout, at finding
that there was something
they had not found before,

although this island will afford
not much more than a foothold:
20 little to explore;

but they will be surprised

    (we can't see them yet;
we know they must be
coming, because they always come
25 several minutes too late)

    (they won't be able
to tell how long
we were cast away, or why,
or, from these
30 gnawed bones,
which was the survivor)

at the two skeletons

After Reading

Making Connections

Shaping Your Response

1. Which one of these poems seems most modern to you?

2. What things do you associate with being "cast away"?

Analyzing the Poems

3. What can you **infer** is the "secret" Adam was trying to discover in "Eve to Her Daughters"?

4. If Adam has "turned himself into God, / Who . . . doesn't exist," where does this leave Adam?

5. How do the last four lines of "The Frog Prince" explain why he is eager for the "royal girl" to arrive?

6. What can you infer is the social criticism implied in the title and the **repetition** of the line "not waving but drowning"?

7. What is **ironic** about the fact that the explorers of Atwood's poem will find two skeletons?

8. Do you think the speaker in "The Explorers" is the survivor? Discuss.

Extending the Ideas

9. In Wright's poem, Adam thought that "what cannot be demonstrated doesn't exist." Do you think that everything in this world can be demonstrated? Explain.

Literary Focus: Allusion

An **allusion** is a brief reference to a person, event, or place, real or fictitious, or to a piece of music or work of art. Much information can be conveyed concisely in an allusion.

1. Wright refers to a "new Eden." What do you have to know to understand this allusion?

2. Is there a connection between Wright's reference to Adam's character and modern people? Explain.

3. To what traditional literary form does Smith allude in "The Frog Prince"?

Expressing Your Ideas

Writing Choices

Writer's Notebook Update Compare your lists of childhood memories with a partner and collaborate on a poem using some of these remembrances.

The *Real* Story Think of a character in a fairy tale, fable, or old story that you know well, and give that character a new point of view. Maybe Cinderella didn't want to marry the prince? Maybe Dorothy's dog, Toto, didn't really like being carried all over Oz? Write your version as a **journal entry** made by the character you choose.

Dear Mom Assume that you are one of the daughters to whom Eve has addressed her remarks in Judith Wright's poem. In a **letter** to Eve, react to your mother's analysis and criticism of your father, Adam.

Other Options

Composing Set "Not Waving but Drowning" to music. Think about the tempo, whether it will be in a major or minor key, and whether it will have a refrain. You may have to rewrite the poem slightly to make it into a lyric. Perform your **song** for the class.

A Perfect Place Using any medium you wish, create an **artwork** depicting a "new Eden." Consider whether it will contain people (if so, who?), where it will be situated, and whether it will contain buildings, animals, and /or natural surroundings. You may wish to review the description in Genesis (pages 268–271), and then decide what would make your new place "perfect."

You Won't Believe What I Tell You Take on the character of an explorer and tell the story of how you discovered an island or other surprising place—but tell it as a **tall tale.** Imagine that your audience is gathered for a luncheon at a natural history museum and that you're their entertaining speaker. Exaggerate as wildly as you please, but remember that a tall tale is always told with a completely straight face. If you like, illustrate your talk with some "snapshots" or "slides" that you have taken.

Before Reading

The Truly Married Woman

by Abioseh Nicol

Abioseh Nicol
1924–1994

Dr. Davidson Sylvester Hector Willoughby Nicol—Abioseh (ab ē ō′sə) was a pen name—was born in Freetown, Sierra Leone. He earned B.A., M.A., M.D., and Ph.D degrees and was ambassador from Sierra Leone to the United Nations from 1968 to 1971. He was also Under Secretary General of the United Nations and the executive director of the United Nations Institute for Training and Research until his retirement in 1982. He taught at the University of South Carolina and the Center of International Studies at Cambridge University in England, published many articles on medicine, education, and politics, and wrote poetry and short stories. His story collections include *The Truly Married Woman and Other Stories* and *Two African Tales,* both published in 1965.

Building Background

The Lure of Tradition Tradition plays an important part in this story, and though the beliefs, customs, and opinions may not be quite the same as those in your family, you may find many similarities. While it is true that the couple in the story at first have a somewhat unconventional lifestyle, they are fully aware that their arrangement is not acceptable in their church or their families, though it seems acceptable to many of their neighbors. The author explores the effect of tradition on the lives of his characters, and in an ironic twist shows how, finally, adherence to tradition results in a nontraditional outcome, illustrating once again that there is no one **perspective** on how to live one's life.

Literary Focus

Point of View The vantage point from which an author presents the actions and characters in a story is called **point of view.** The story may be related by a character (*first-person* point of view), or by a narrator who does not participate in the actions (*third-person* point of view). The third-person narrator may be *omniscient*—able to see into the minds of all characters; *limited*—confined to a single character's perception; or *objective*—describing only what can be seen. Decide the point of view as you read the following story.

Writer's Notebook

Crime and Punishment Have you ever been punished unjustly, either for something you didn't know was wrong or for something you didn't do? Write about the situation in your notebook, telling about the incident and how you feel about it now.

The Truly Married Woman

Abioseh Nicol

AJAYI stirred for a while and then sat up. He looked at the cheap alarm clock on the chair by his bedside. It was six-fifteen, and light outside already; the African town was slowly waking to life. The night-watchmen roused from sleep by the angry crowing of cockerels were officiously[1] banging the locks of stores and houses to assure themselves and their employers, if near, of their efficiency. Village women were tramping through the streets to the market place with their wares, arguing and gossiping.

Ajayi sipped his cup of morning tea. It was as he liked it, weak and sugary, without milk. With an effort of will, he got up and walked to the window, and standing there he took six deep breaths. This done daily, he firmly believed, would prevent tuberculosis. He walked through his ramshackle compound to an outhouse and took a quick bath, pouring the water over his head from a tin cup with which he scooped water from a bucket.

By then Ayo had laid out his breakfast. Ayo was his wife. Not really one, he would explain to close friends, but a mistress. A good one. She had borne him three children and was now three months gone with another. They had been together for twelve years. She was a patient, handsome woman. Very dark with very

white teeth and open sincere eyes. Her hair was always carefully plaited. When she first came to him—to the exasperation of her parents—he had fully intended marrying her as soon as she had shown satisfactory evidence of fertility, but he had never quite got round to it. In the first year or so she would report to him in great detail the splendor of the marriage celebrations of her friends, looking at him with hopeful eyes. He would close the matter with a tirade[2] on the sinfulness of ostentation.[3] She gave up after some

---

1. officiously (ə fish′əs lē), *adv.* too readily offering services or advice; meddling.
2. tirade (tī′rād), *n.* long, scolding speech.
3. ostentation (os′ten tā′shən), *n.* showing off.

▲ 🎨 The group of painted wooden figures that form *The Wedding* were done by South African artist Johannes Mashego Segogela in 1993. What different cultural **perspectives** are reflected in this work of art?

After such occasions, their friends would sympathize with them and other couples in similar positions. There would be a little grumbling and the male members of the congregation would say that the trouble with the Church was that it did not stick to its business of preaching the Gospel, but meddled in people's private lives. Ajayi would indignantly absent himself from Church for a few weeks but would go back eventually because he liked singing hymns and because he knew secretly that the pastor was right.

Ayo was a good mistress. Her father was convinced she could have married a high-school teacher at least, or a pharmacist, but instead, she had attached herself to a junior Government clerk. But Ayo loved Ajayi, and was happy in her own slow, private way. She cooked his meals and bore him children. In what spare time she had she either did a little petty trading, visited friends, or gossiped with Omo, the woman next door.

With his towel round his waist, Ajayi strode back to the bedroom, dried himself and dressed quickly but carefully in his pink tussore[5] suit. He got down the new bottle of patent medicine which one of his friends who worked in a drug store had recommended to him. Ajayi believed that to keep healthy, a man must regularly take a dose of some medicine. He read the label of this one. It listed about twenty diseased conditions of widely differing pathology[6] which the contents of the bottle were reputed to cure if the patient persevered in its daily intake. Ajayi underlined in his own mind at least six from which he believed he either suffered or was on the threshold of suffering: dizziness, muscle pain, impotence, fever, jaundice, and paralytic tremors. Intelligence and courage caused him to skip the obviously female maladies and others

time. Her father never spoke to her again after she had left home. Her mother visited her secretly and attended the baptismal ceremonies of all her children. The Church charged extra for illegitimate children as a deterrent;[4] two dollars instead of fifty cents. Apart from this, there was no other great objection. Occasionally, two or three times a year, the pastor would preach violently against adultery, polygamy, and unmarried couples living together. Ajayi and Ayo were good church-people and attended regularly, but sat in different pews.

---

4. **deterrent** (di tėr′ənt), *n.* something that discourages or hinders.
5. **tussore** (tus′ōr), *adj.* made from *tussah,* a coarse, Asian silk.
6. **pathology** (pa thol′ə jē), *n.* unhealthy conditions and processes caused by a disease.

such as nervous debility or bladder pains. It said on the label too that a teaspoonful should be taken three times a day. But since he only remembered to take it in the morning and in any case believed in shock treatment, he took a swig and two large gulps. The medicine was bitter and astringent. He grimaced but was satisfied. It was obviously a good and strong medicine or else it would not have been so bitter.

He went in to breakfast. He soon finished his maize porridge, fried beans, and cocoa. He then severely flogged his eldest son, a ten-year-old boy, for wetting his sleeping-mat last night. Ayo came in after the boy had fled screaming to the backyard.

"Ajayi, you flog that boy too much," she said. "He should stop wetting the floor, he is a big boy," he replied. "In any case, no one is going to instruct me on how to bring up my son." "He is mine too," Ayo said. She seldom opposed him unless she felt strongly about something. "He has not stopped wetting, although you beat him every time he does. In fact, he is doing it more and more now. Perhaps if you stopped whipping him he might get better." "Did I whip him to begin doing it?" Ajayi asked. "No." "Well, how will stopping whipping him stop him doing it?" Ajayi asked triumphantly. "Nevertheless," Ayo said, "our own countrywoman Bimbola, who has just come back from England and America studying nursing, told us in a women's group meeting that it was wrong to punish children for such things." "All right, I'll see," he said, reaching for his sun-helmet.

All that day at the office he thought about this and other matters. So Ayo had been attending women's meetings. Well, what do you know. She would be running for the Town Council next. The sly woman. Always looking so quiet and meek and then quoting modern theories from overseas doctors at him. He smiled with pride. Indeed Ayo was an asset. Perhaps it was wrong to beat the boy. He decided he would not do so again.

Towards closing-time the chief clerk sent for him. Wondering what mistake he had made that day, or on what mission he was to be sent, he hurried along to the forward office. There were three white men sitting on chairs by the chief clerk, who was an aging African dressed with severe respectability. On seeing them, Ajayi's heart started thudding. The police, he thought; heavens, what have I done?

"Mr. Ajayi, these gentlemen have inquired for you," the chief clerk said formally. "Pleased to meet you, Mr. Ajayi," the tallest said, with a smile. "We represent the World Gospel Crusading Alliance from Minnesota. My name is Jonathan Olsen." Ajayi shook hands and the other two were introduced.

"You expressed an interest in our work a year ago and we have not forgotten. We are on our way to India and we thought we would look you up personally."

It transpired that the three Crusaders were *en route* and that their ship had stopped for refueling off the African port for a few hours. The chief clerk looked at Ajayi with new respect. Ajayi tried desperately to remember any connection with W.G.C.A. (as Olsen by then had proceeded to call it) whilst he made conversation with them a little haltingly. Then suddenly he remembered. Some time ago he had got hold of a magazine from his sub-tenant who worked at the United States Information Service. He had cut a coupon from it and posted it to W.G.C.A. asking for information, but really hoping that they would send illustrated Bibles free which he might give away or sell. He hoped for at least large reproductions of religious paintings which, suitably framed, would decorate his parlor or which he might paste up on his bedroom wall. But nothing had come of it and he had forgotten. Now here was W.G.C.A. as large as life. Three lives. Instantly and recklessly he invited all three and the chief clerk to come to his house for a cold drink. They all agreed.

"Mine is a humble <u>abode</u>,"[7] he warned them.

---

7. **abode** (ə bōd′), *n.* place of residence; house or home.

"No abode is humble that is illumined[8] by Christian love," Olsen replied. "His is illumined all right, I can assure you," the chief clerk remarked dryly.

Olsen suggested a taxi, but Ajayi neatly blocked that by saying the roads were bad. He had hurriedly whispered to a fellow clerk to rush home on a bicycle and tell Ayo he was coming in half an hour with white men and that she should clean up and get fruit drinks. Ayo was puzzled by the message as she firmly imagined all white men drank only whisky and iced beer. But the messenger had said that there was a mixture of friendliness and piety in the visitors' mien,[9] which made him suspect that they might be missionaries. Another confirmatory point was that they were walking instead of being in a car. That cleared up the anomaly[10] in Ayo's mind and she set to work at once. Oju, now recovered from his morning disgrace, was dispatched with a basket on his head to buy soft drinks. Ayo whisked off the wall all their commercial calendars with suggestive pictures. She propped up family photographs which had fallen face downwards on the table. She removed the Wild West novels and romance magazines from the parlor and put instead an old copy of Bunyan's *Pilgrim's Progress* [11] and a prayer-book which she believed would add culture and religious force to the decorations. She remembered the wine glasses and the beer-advertising table-mats in time and put those under the sofa. She just had time to change to her Sunday frock and borrow a wedding ring from her neighbor when Ajayi and the guests arrived. The chief clerk was rather surprised at the changes in the room—which he had visited before—and in Ayo's dress and ring. But he concealed his feelings. Ayo was introduced and made a little conversation in English. This pleased Ajayi a great deal. The children had been changed too into Sunday suits, faces washed and hair brushed. Olsen was delighted and insisted on taking photographs for the Crusade journal. Ayo served drinks and then

modestly retired, leaving the men to discuss serious matters. Olsen by then was talking earnestly on the imminence[12] of Christ's Second Coming and offering Ajayi ordination[13] into deaconship.

EVALUATE: What is Ayo assuming by making all the changes in her house?

The visit passed off well and soon the missionaries left to catch their boat. Ajayi had been saved from holy orders by the chief clerk's timely explanation that it was strictly against Government regulations for civil servants to indulge in non-official organisations. To help Ajayi out of his quandary, he had even gone further and said that contravention[14] might result in a fine or imprisonment. "Talk about colonial oppression," the youngest of the missionaries had said, gloomily.

The next day Ajayi called at the chief clerk's office with a carefully wrapped bottle of beer as a present for his help generally on the occasion. They discussed happily the friendliness and interest the white men had shown.

This incident and Ayo's protest against flagellation[15] as a specific against enuresis[16] made Ajayi very thoughtful for a week. He decided to marry Ayo. Another consideration which added weight to the thought was the snapshot Olsen took for

---

8. **illumine** (i lü′mən), *v.* make bright.
9. mien (mēn), *n.* manner of holding the head and body; way of acting and looking.
10. anomaly (ə nom′ə lē), *n.* something deviating from the rule; something abnormal.
11. **Bunyan's *Pilgrim's Progress*,** a long, prose allegory by John Bunyan, published in 1678 and 1684, that tells of a Christian's progress from this world to Heaven.
12. **imminence** (im′ə nəns), *n.* likeliness; probability of happening soon.
13. **ordination** (ôrd′n ā′shən), *n.* act or ceremony of making a person a member of the clergy.
14. contravention (kon′trə ven′shən), *n.* conflict; opposition.
15. **flagellation** (flaj′ə lā′shən), *n.* a whipping.
16. **enuresis** (en′yù rē′sis), *n.* bed-wetting.

his magazine. In some peculiar way Ajayi felt he and Ayo should marry, as millions of Americans would see their picture—Olsen had assured him of this—as "one saved and happy African family." He announced his intention of marrying her to Ayo one evening, after a particularly good meal and a satisfactory bout of belching. Ayo at once became extremely solicitous and got up looking at him with some anxiety. Was he ill? she asked. Was there anything wrong at the office? Had anyone insulted him? No, he answered, there was nothing wrong with his wanting to get married, was there? Or had she anyone else in mind? Ayo laughed, "As you will," she said; "let us get married, but do not say I forced you into it."

They discussed the wedding that night. Ajayi wanted to have a white wedding with veil and orange blossom. But Ayo with regret decided it would not be quite right. They agreed on gray. Ayo particularly wanted a corset to strap down her obvious bulge; Ajayi gave way gallantly to this feminine whim, chucking her under the chin and saying, "You women with your vanity!" But he was firm about no honeymoon. He said he could not afford the expense and that one bed was as good as another. Ayo gave way on that. They agreed, however, on a church wedding and that their children could act as bridal pages to keep the cost of clothes within the family.

That evening Ajayi, inflamed by the idea and arrangements for the wedding, pulled Ayo excitedly to him as they lay in bed. "No," said Ayo, shyly, pushing him back gently, "you mustn't. Wait until after the marriage." "Why?" said Ajayi, rather surprised, but obedient. "Because it will not somehow be right," Ayo replied seriously and determinedly.

Ayo's father unbent somewhat when he heard of the proposed marriage. He insisted, however, that Ayo move herself and all her possessions back home to his house. The children were sent to Ayo's married sister. Most of Ajayi's family were in favor of the union, except his sister, who, moved by the threat implicit in Ayo's improved social position, had advised Ajayi to

see a soothsayer first. As Ayo had got wind of this through friends met at market on Saturday, she saw the soothsayer first and fixed things. When Ajayi and his sister called at night to see him, he had, after consulting the oracles, pronounced future happiness, avoiding the sister's eye. The latter had restrained herself from scratching the old man's face and had accepted defeat.

The only other flaw in a felicitous situation had been Ayo's neighbor Omo, who had always on urgent occasions at short notice loaned Ayo her wedding ring. She had suddenly turned cold. Especially after Ayo had shown her the wedding presents Ajayi intended to give her. The neighbor had handled the flimsy nylon articles with a mixture of envy and rage.

"Do you mean you are going to wear these?" she had asked. "Yes," Ayo had replied simply. "But, my sister," she had protested, "you will catch cold with these. Suppose you had an accident and all those doctors lifted your clothes in hospital. They will see everything through these." "I never have accidents," Ayo answered, and added, "Ajayi says all the Hollywood cinema women wear these. It says so there. Look—'Trademark Hollywood.'" "These are disgraceful; they hide nothing, it is extremely fast of you to wear them," the jealous girl said, pushing them back furiously over the fence to Ayo.

"Why should I want to hide anything from my husband when we are married?" Ayo said triumphantly, moving back to her own kitchen and feeling safe in future from the patronizing way the wedding ring had always been lent her.

The arrangements had to be made swiftly, since time and the corset ribs were both against them; Ajayi's domestic routine was also sorely tried, especially his morning cup of tea which he badly missed. He borrowed heavily from a moneylender to pay the dowry and for the music, dancing, and feasting, and for dresses of the same pattern which Ayo and her female relations would wear after the ceremony on the wedding day.

The engagement took place quietly, Ajayi's

uncle and other relations taking a Bible and a ring to Ayo's father and asking for her hand in marriage, the day before the wedding. They took with them two small girls carrying on their heads large hollow gourds. These contained articles like pins, farthings, fruit, kola nuts, and cloth. The articles were symbolic gifts to the bride from the bridegroom, so that she might be precluded in future marital disputes from saying, "Not a pin or a farthing has the blackguard given me since we got married."

On arrival at Ayo's father's house, the small procession passed it first as if uncertain, then returned to it. This gave warning to the occupants. Ajayi's uncle then knocked several times. Voices from within shouted back and ordered him to name himself, his ancestry, and his mission. He did this. Argument and some abuse followed on either side. After his family credentials had been seriously examined, questioned, doubted, and disparaged,[17] Ajayi's uncle started wheedling and cajoling. This went on for about half an hour to the enjoyment and mock trepidation[18] of Ajayi's relations. He himself had remained at home, waiting. Finally, Ayo's father opened the door. Honor was satisfied and it was now supposed to be clearly evident to Ajayi's relations, in case it had not been before, that they were entering a family and a household which was distinguished, difficult, and jealous of their distinction.

"What is your mission here?" Ayo's father then asked sternly.

Ajayi's uncle answered humbly:

"We have come to pluck a red, red rose
That in your beautiful garden grows.
Which never has been plucked before,
So lovelier than any other."

"Will you be able to nurture our lovely rose well?" another of Ayo's male relations asked.

Ajayi's family party replied:

"So well shall we nurture your rose
"Twill bring forth many others."

They were finally admitted; drinks were served and prayers offered. The gifts were accepted and other given in exchange. Conversation went on for about thirty minutes on every conceivable subject but the one at hand. All through this, Ayo and her sisters and some young female relations were kept hidden in an adjoining bedroom. Finally with some delicacy, Ajayi's uncle broached the subject after Ayo's father had given him an opening by asking what, apart from the honor of being entertained by himself and his family, did Ajayi's relations seek. They had heard, the latter replied, that in this very household there was a maiden chaste, beautiful, and obedient, known to all by the name of Ayo. This maiden they sought as wife for their kinsman Ajayi. Ayo's father opened the bedroom door and brought forth Ayo's sister. Was this the one? he asked, testing them. They examined her. No it was not this one they replied, this one was too short to be Ayo. Then a cousin was brought out. Was this she? No, this one is too fat, the applicants said. About ten women in all were brought out. But none was the correct one. Each was too short or too fat or too fair, as the case was, to suit the description of the maiden they sought. At this point, Ajayi's uncle slapped his thigh, as if to show that his doubts were confirmed; turning to his party, he stated that it was a good thing they had insisted on seeing for themselves the bride demanded, or else the wrong woman would have been foisted on them. They agreed, nodding. All right, all right, Ayo's father had replied, there was no cause for impatience. He wanted to be sure they knew whom they wanted. Standing on guard at the bedroom door, he turned his back to the assembly, and with tears in his eyes beckoned to Ayo sitting on the bed inside. He kissed her lightly on the forehead to forgive the past years. Then he led her forth and turned fiercely to the audience. Was this then the girl they wanted, he asked them sternly.

---

17. disparage (dis par′ij), v. speak slightingly of; belittle.
18. trepidation (trep′ə dā′shən), n. fear; fright.

🐾 **CLARIFY: In your opinion, what is the author's perspective on all this ceremony?**

"This *is* the very one," Ajayi's uncle replied with joy. "Hip, hip, hip, hooray," everybody shouted, encircling Ayo and waving white handkerchiefs over her head. The musicians smote their guitars instantly; someone beat an empty wine bottle rhythmically with a corkscrew; after a few preliminary trills the flutes rose high in melody; all danced round Ayo. And as she stood in the center, a woman in her mid-thirties, her hair slightly streaked gray, undergoing a ceremony of honor she had often witnessed and long put outside her fate, remembering the classic description of chastity, obedience, and beauty, she wept with joy and the unborn child stirred within her for the first time.

The next morning she was bathed by an old and respected female member of her family, and her mother helped her to dress. Her father gave her away at the marriage service at church. It was a quiet wedding with only sixty guests or so. Ajayi looked stiff in dinner jacket with buttonhole, an ensemble which he wore only on special occasions. Afterwards they went to Ayo's family home for the wedding luncheon. At the door they were met by another of Ayo's numerous elderly aunts, who held a glass of water to their lips for them to sip in turn, Ajayi being first. The guests were all gathered outside behind the couple. The aunt made a conveniently long speech until all the guests had foregathered. She warned Ayo not to be too friendly with other women as they would inevitably steal her husband; that they should live peaceably and not let the sun go down on a quarrel between them. Turning to Ajayi, she told him with a twinkle in her eye that a wife could be quite as exciting as a mistress, and also not to use physical violence against their daughter, his wife.

After this they entered and the western part of the ceremony took place. The wedding cake (which Ayo had made) was cut and speeches made. Then Ajayi departed to his own family home where other celebrations went on. Later he changed into a lounge suit and called for Ayo. There was weeping in Ayo's household as if she was setting off on a long journey. Her mother in saying goodbye, remarked between tears, that although she would not have the honor next morning of showing the world evidence of Ayo's virginity, yet in the true feminine powers of procreation none except the blind and deaf could say Ayo had lacked zeal.

They called on various relations on both sides of the family and at last they were home. Ayo seemed different in Ajayi's eyes. He had never really looked at her carefully before. Now he observed her head held erectly and gracefully through years of balancing loads on it in childhood; her statuesque neck with its three natural horizontal ridges—to him, signs of beauty; her handsome shoulders. He clasped her with a new tenderness.

The next morning, as his alarm clock went off, he stirred and reached for his morning cup of tea. It was not there. He sprang up and looked. Nothing. He listened for Ayo's footsteps outside in the kitchen. Nothing. He turned to look beside him. Ayo was there and her bare ebony back was heaving gently. She must be ill, he thought; all that excitement yesterday.

"Ayo, Ayo," he cried, "are you ill?" She turned round slowly still lying down and faced him. She tweaked her toes luxuriously under the cotton coverlet and patted her breast slowly. There was a terrible calm about her. "No, Ajayi," she replied, "are you?" she asked him. "Are your legs paralysed?" she continued. "No," he said. He was puzzled and alarmed, thinking that her mind had become unhinged under the strain.

"Ajayi, my husband," she said, "for twelve years I have got up every morning at five to make tea for you and breakfast. Now I am a truly married woman you must treat me with a little more respect. You are now a husband and not a lover. Get up and make yourself a cup of tea."

After Reading

Making Connections

Shaping Your Response

1. Do you think Ajayi will regret having married Ayo? Will she regret having married him?

Analyzing the Story

2. What methods does the author use to **characterize** Ajayi and Ayo?

3. Who is the **protagonist** in the story, in your opinion?

4. What is the **climax** or turning point in the story?

5. 👁 Do you find the author's **perspective** sympathetic? ironic? humorous? something else?

6. Why, in your opinion, has marriage changed Ayo's morning routine?

7. Do Ajayi and Ayo have an equal partnership before they are married? Explain.

Extending the Ideas

8. Are marriage partners usually equal, in your opinion? Should they be, or is it better if one partner makes most of the decisions?

Literary Focus: Point of View

Point of view is the vantage point from which an author presents the actions and characters in a story. "The Truly Married Woman" is told from the third-person point of view.

1. Is the third-person narrator *omniscient*—able to see into the minds of all the characters?

2. Is the narrator *objective*—describing only what can be seen?

3. Is the point of view *limited*—confined to a single character's perception? If so, who is that character?

Vocabulary Study

Use your understanding of the meaning of the italicized word to choose the word or phrase that best completes each sentence.

1. You would expect a *tirade* to be ___.
   a. whispered   **b.** sung   **c.** shouted

2. The person most likely to act *officiously* would be a ___.
   a. guitar player   **b.** government clerk   **c.** television weatherperson

3. The best example of an *anomaly* is a ___.
   a. billionaire wearing rags   **b.** dog wearing a collar
   c. cyclist wearing a helmet

4. A common *deterrent* to overweight is ___.
   a. having clothes that are too tight   **b.** watching chefs on television
   c. eating junk food

The Truly Married Woman   **923**

5. Many people feel *trepidation* at the sound of ___.
   a. a police siren   **b.** rain on a roof   **c.** a robin's song

6. If you described someone's *mien*, you would include his ___.
   a. singing voice   **b.** terrible temper   **c.** way of holding his body

7. If you wanted help in designing your *abode,* you might consult ___.
   a. a rabbi   **b.** an architect   **c.** a gardener

8. If you found yourself involved in a *contravention,* you might try___.
   a. to avoid the conflict
   b. to vote for the best candidate
   c. to be considerate to your loved one

9. If someone were to *disparage* your athletic ability, you would probably feel ___.
   a. proud   **b.** flattered   **c.** dejected

10. To many people, an example of *ostentation* would be ___.
    a. bragging about your parents' income
    b. collecting money for the homeless
    c. hitchhiking on an expressway

Expressing Your Ideas

Writing Choices

Writer's Notebook Update In the story, Ajayi beats his eldest son. Write a paragraph telling how you feel about physical punishment for a child. Does it help a child to learn the right way to live, or does it make the child resentful?

Can This Marriage Work? Will the marriage of Ajayi and Ayo be a success? If you were a marriage counselor, how would you rate their chances? In an **article** that might appear in a popular magazine, analyze their past life together, their personalities, their community of friends and relatives, and propose any changes you feel will be necessary for success.

Your Ideal Many people have a type of person in mind with whom they would like to spend their lives. What is your ideal? In a

character sketch, describe that person. Consider the factors most important to you— looks? education? kindliness? something else?—and tell why they are important.

Other Options

Cartoon Art Create a **cartoon strip** showing the main events in the story. How many panels will it take to tell the whole story? Make the cartoons black and white or in color (for Sunday editions). Display them in the classroom or submit them to your school newspaper.

Congratulations! Assume that you must buy a **wedding gift** for the newly married couple. What will you buy? Find or draw a picture of the gift you think will be most appropriate.

Before Reading

A Shocking Accident

by Graham Greene

Graham Greene
1904–1991

Graham Greene classified his fiction into "entertainments" and "novels." The former are thrillers and detective stories, including *The Ministry of Fear* (1943); *The Third Man* (1950), originally written as a screen-play; and *Our Man in Havana* (1958), filmed in 1959. Greene was educated at Berkhamsted School, where his father was headmaster, and then at Balliol College. He married in 1927, and after four years at *The Times* in London, he left to try to earn his living as a writer. He converted to Catholicism, and his religious convictions often influenced his writing, especially in such works as *The Quiet American* (1955), set in Vietnam; and *A Burnt Out Case* (1961), set in a leper colony. He also wrote plays, essays, short stories, and many travel books.

Building Background

The Role of the Subconscious In the Foreword to his book titled *A World of My Own,* published after Greene's death, editor Yvonne Cloetta wrote about his method of working: "It is well known that Graham was always very interested in dreams, and that he relied a great deal on the role played by the subconscious in writing. He would sit down to work straightway after breakfast, writing until he had five hundred words (which in the last while he reduced to approximately two hundred). He was in the habit of then rereading, every evening before going to bed, the section of the novel or story he had written in the morning, leaving his subconscious to work during the night. Some dreams enabled him to overcome a 'blockage'; others provided him on occasion with material for short stories or even an idea for a new novel. . . ."

Literary Focus

Tone An author's attitude toward his or her subject matter is called **tone.** By recognizing tone a reader can determine whether a writer views the subject with sympathy, humor, affection, or disapproval. Any of the following might provide a clue to the tone of a work: word choice, style, choice of images, treatment of events and characters. How does tone play an important part in "A Shocking Accident"?

Writer's Notebook

Jot down some words to describe the feelings you would have on discovering that you have taken the wrong bus, train, or plane and are headed in the direction opposite to the one you had planned.

A Shocking Accident

GRAHAM GREENE

Jerome was called into his house master's room in the break between the second and third class on a Thursday morning. He had no fear of trouble, for he was a warden—the name that the proprietor and headmaster of a rather expensive preparatory school had chosen to give to approved, reliable boys in the lower forms[1] (from a warden one became a guardian and finally before leaving, it was hoped for Marlborough or Rugby,[2] a crusader). The house master, Mr. Wordsworth, sat behind his desk with an appearance of perplexity and apprehension.[3] Jerome had the odd impression when he entered that he was a cause of fear.

"Sit down, Jerome," Mr. Wordsworth said. "All going well with the trigonometry?"

"Yes, sir."

"I've had a telephone call, Jerome. From your aunt. I'm afraid I have bad news for you."

"Yes, sir?"

"Your father has had an accident."

"Oh."

Mr. Wordsworth looked at him with some surprise. "A serious accident."

"Yes, sir?"

Jerome worshipped his father: the verb is exact. As man re-creates God, so Jerome re-created his father—from a restless widowed author into a mysterious adventurer who traveled in far places—Nice, Beirut, Majorca, even the Canaries. The time had arrived about his eighth birthday when Jerome believed that his father either "ran guns" or was a member of the British Secret Service. Now it occurred to him that his father might have been wounded in "a hail of machine-gun bullets."

Mr. Wordsworth played with the ruler on his desk. He seemed at a loss how to continue. He said, "You know your father was in Naples?"

"Yes, sir."

"Your aunt heard from the hospital today."

"Oh."

Mr. Wordsworth said with desperation, "It was a street accident."

"Yes sir?" It seemed quite likely to Jerome that they would call it a street accident. The police of course had fired first; his father would not take human life except as a last resort.

"I'm afraid your father was very seriously hurt indeed."

"Oh."

"In fact, Jerome, he died yesterday. Quite without pain."

"Did they shoot him through the heart?"

"I beg your pardon. What did you say, Jerome?"

"Did they shoot him through the heart?"

"Nobody shot him, Jerome. A pig fell on him." An inexplicable[4] convulsion took place in the nerves of Mr. Wordsworth's face; it really looked for a moment as though he were going to laugh. He closed his eyes, composed his features and said rapidly as though it were necessary to expel the story as quickly as possible, "Your father was walking along a street in Naples when a pig fell on him. A shocking accident. Apparently in the poorer quarters of Naples they keep pigs on their balconies. This one was on the fifth floor. It had grown too fat. The balcony broke. The pig fell on your father."

Mr. Wordsworth left his desk rapidly and

---

1. **lower forms,** lower grades.
2. **Marlborough or Rugby,** two well-known boarding schools.
3. apprehension (ap/ri hen/shən), *n.* expectation of misfortune; dread of impending danger.
4. **inexplicable** (in/ik splik/ə bəl), *adj.* mysterious.

went to the window, turning his back on Jerome. He shook a little with emotion.

Jerome said, "What happened to the pig?"

CLARIFY: What "emotion" do you imagine Mr Wordsworth is shaking with?

This was not callousness on the part of Jerome, as it was interpreted by Mr. Wordsworth to his colleagues (he even discussed with them whether, perhaps, Jerome was yet fitted to be a warden). Jerome was only attempting to visualize the strange scene to get the details right. Nor was Jerome a boy who cried; he was a boy who brooded, and it never occurred to him at his preparatory school that the circumstances of his father's death were comic—they were still part of the mystery of life. It was later, in his first term at his public school, when he told the story to his best friend, that he began to realize how it affected others. Naturally after that disclosure he was known, rather unreasonably, as Pig.

Unfortunately his aunt had no sense of humor. There was an enlarged snapshot of his father on the piano; a large sad man in an unsuitable dark suit posed in Capri with an umbrella (to guard him against sunstroke), the Faraglione rocks forming the background. By the age of sixteen Jerome was well aware that the portrait looked more like the author of *Sunshine and Shade* and *Rambles in the Balearics* than an agent of the Secret Service. All the same he loved the memory of his father:

he still possessed an album filled with picture-postcards (the stamps had been soaked off long ago for his other collection), and it pained him when his aunt embarked[5] with strangers on the story of his father's death.

"A shocking accident," she would begin, and the stranger would compose his or her features into the correct shape for interest and commiseration. Both reactions, of course, were false, but it was terrible for Jerome to see how suddenly, midway in her rambling discourse, the interest would become genuine. "I can't think how such things can be allowed in a civilized country," his aunt would say. "I suppose one has to regard Italy as civilized. One is prepared for all kinds of things abroad, of course, and my brother was a great traveler. He always carried a water-filter with him. It was far less expensive,

5. embark (em bärk′), v. begin an undertaking.

British artist Fred Aris chose a famous example of Georgian architecture, the Royal Crescent at Bath, as the background for his painting *Pigs in Bath* (1981). How does the setting affect the **perspective** of this work of fantasy?

you know, than buying all those bottles of mineral water. My brother always said that his filter paid for his dinner wine. You can see from that what a careful man he was, but who could possibly have expected when he was walking along the Via Dottore Manuele Panucci on his way to the Hydrographic Museum that a pig would fall on him?" That was the moment when the interest became genuine.

Jerome's father had not been a very distinguished writer, but the time always seems to come, after an author's death, when somebody thinks it worth his while to write a letter to the *Times Literary Supplement* announcing the preparation of a biography and asking to see any letters or documents or receive any anecdotes from the friends of the dead man. Most of the biographies, of course, never appear—one wonders whether the whole thing may not be an obscure form of blackmail and whether many a potential writer of a biography or thesis finds the means in this way to finish his education at Kansas or Nottingham. Jerome, however, as a chartered accountant, lived far from the literary world. He did not realize how small the menace really was, or that the danger period for someone of his father's obscurity had long passed. Sometimes he rehearsed the method of recounting his father's death so as to reduce the comic element to its smallest dimensions—it would be of no use to refuse information, for in that case the biographer would undoubtedly visit his aunt who was living to a great old age with no sign of flagging.

It seemed to Jerome that there were two possible methods—the first led gently up to the accident, so that by the time it was described the listener was so well prepared that the death came really as an anti-climax. The chief danger of laughter in such a story was always surprise. When he rehearsed this method Jerome began boringly enough.

"You know Naples and those high tenement buildings? Somebody once told me that the Neapolitan always feels at home in New York just as the man from Turin feels at home in London because the river runs in much the same way in both cities. Where was I? Oh, yes. Naples, of course. You'd be surprised in the poorer quarters what things they keep on the balconies of those sky-scraping tenements—not washing, you know, or bedding, but things like livestock, chickens or even pigs. Of course the pigs get no exercise whatever and fatten all the quicker." He could imagine how his hearer's eyes would have glazed by this time. "I've no idea, have you, how heavy a pig can be, but these old buildings are all badly in need of repair. A balcony on the fifth floor gave way under one of those pigs. It struck the third floor balcony on its way down and sort of ricocheted[6] into the street. My father was on the way to the Hydrographic Museum when the pig hit him. Coming from that height and that angle it broke his neck." This was really a masterly attempt to make an intrinsically[7] interesting subject boring.

The other method Jerome rehearsed had the virtue of brevity.[8]

"My father was killed by a pig."

"Really? In India?"

"No, in Italy."

"How interesting. I never realized there was pig-sticking[9] in Italy. Was your father keen on polo?"

In course of time, neither too early nor too late, rather as though, in his capacity as a chartered accountant, Jerome had studied the statistics and taken the average, he became engaged to be married: to a pleasant fresh-faced girl of twenty-five whose father was a doctor in Pinner. Her name was Sally, her favorite author

---

6. ricochet (rik′ə shā′), *v.* move with a bounce or jump.
7. intrinsically (in trin′sik lē), *adv.* essentially; belonging to a thing by its very nature.
8. brevity (brev′ə tē), *n.* shortness in time.
9. **pig-sticking,** the hunting of wild boars with a spear, especially in India.

was still Hugh Walpole,[10] and she had adored babies ever since she had been given a doll at the age of five which moved its eyes and made water. Their relationship was contented rather than exciting, as became the love-affair of a chartered accountant; it would never have done if it had interfered with the figures.

CLARIFY: Why wouldn't an accountant have an exciting relationship?

One thought worried Jerome, however. Now that within a year he might himself become a father, his love for the dead man increased; he realized what affection had gone into the picture-postcards. He felt a longing to protect his memory, and uncertain whether this quiet love of his would survive if Sally were so insensitive as to laugh when she heard the story of his father's death. Inevitably she would hear it when Jerome brought her to dinner with his aunt. Several times he tried to tell her himself, as she was naturally anxious to know all she could that concerned him.

"You were very small when your father died?"

"Just nine."

"Poor little boy," she said.

"I was at school. They broke the news to me."

"Did you take it very hard?"

"I can't remember."

"You never told me how it happened."

"It was very sudden. A street accident."

"You'll never drive fast, will you, Jemmy?" (She had begun to call him "Jemmy.") It was too late then to try the second method—the one he thought of as the pig-sticking one.

They were going to marry quietly in a registry-office and have their honeymoon at Torquay. He avoided taking her to see his aunt until a week before the wedding, but then the night came, and he could not have told himself whether his apprehension was more for his father's memory or the security of his own love.

The moment came all to soon. "Is that Jemmy's father?" Sally asked, picking up the portrait of the man with the umbrella.

"Yes dear. How did you guess?"

"He has Jemmy's eyes and brow, hasn't he?"

"Has Jerome lent you his books?"

"No."

"I will give you a set for your wedding. He wrote so tenderly about his travels. My own favorite is *Nooks and Crannies*. He would have had a great future. It made that shocking accident all the worse."

"Yes?"

Jerome longed to leave the room and not see that loved face crinkle with irresistible amusement.

"I had so many letters from his readers after the pig fell on him." She had never been so abrupt before.

And then the miracle happened. Sally did not laugh. Sally sat with open eyes of horror while his aunt told her the story, and at the end, "How horrible," Sally said. "It makes you think, doesn't it? Happening like that. Out of a clear sky."

Jerome's heart sang with joy. It was as though she had appeased[11] his fear for ever. In the taxi going home he kissed her with more passion than he had ever shown and she returned it. There were babies in her pale blue pupils, babies that rolled their eyes and made water.

"A week today," Jerome said, and she squeezed his hand. "Penny for your thoughts, my darling."

"I was wondering," Sally said, "what happened to the poor pig?"

"They almost certainly had it for dinner," Jerome said happily and kissed the dear child again.

---

10. **Hugh Walpole** (1884–1941), popular English novelist of the 1920s and 1930s. Greene is suggesting that Sally is a person of conventional taste.

11. appease (ə pēz′), *v.* put an end to.

After Reading

Making Connections

Shaping Your
Response

1. Does Jerome's response to the report of his father's death—"What happened to the pig?"—seem insensitive or logical to you?

Analyzing the Story

2. 👆 How is Jerome's **perspective** on his father different from a true one? Why?

3. From what **point of view** is the story told?

4. Which of Jerome's two versions of his father's death, the brief or the boring, seems more likely to achieve Jerome's desired result in your opinion?

5. In what ways is Sally an ideal mate for Jerome?

Extending the Ideas

6. Graham Greene was himself a travel writer. What do you think his **purpose** may have been in portraying Jerome's father the way he did?

Literary Focus: Tone

An author's attitude toward his or her subject matter is called **tone.**

1. Do you think the author thought he was writing a humorous story? How can you tell?

2. How would you express the tone of the story?

3. Is the title of the story appropriate in your opinion? Explain.

Vocabulary Study

Choose the word from the list that is most clearly related to the situation conveyed in each sentence. You will not use all of the words.

**appease
apprehension
brevity
embark
intrinscally
ricochet**

1. You might feel this when alone at night;
It's akin to terror and close to fright.

2. The shot had gone wild, for the bullet, they found,
Had bounced off of a car and gone into the ground.

3. When an answer machine tells you, "Wait for the beep,"
Keep it short, to the point—don't put someone to sleep.

4. The bus is too slow, and you're sure to be late;
You will have to do this to a friend who's irate.

5. Now it's time to set out on our cross-country tour;
Let's be sure that the doors are all locked and secure.

Expressing Your Ideas

Writing Choices

Writer's Notebook Update Look back at the words you wrote to express the emotions you would feel on taking the wrong bus, train, or plane. Then write a dialogue between you and a fellow passenger who seems uninterested in your plight. Try to convey by the words you choose and by sentence length or stucture the feelings of both yourself and the other passenger.

Beginnings The opening paragraph of any short story is extremely important. Often it indicates the point of view, introduces an important character, establishes the setting, and may suggest the direction of the plot. Recall some episode from your own life that might be expanded into a short story. Then write the **opening paragraph.** (Review the first paragraph of Greene's story and of some of the other short stories in units 7 and 8.)

Adding Details Greene provides no details about Jerome's appearance. Imagine how he looks and dresses, and write a **description** that could be inserted into the story at some point.

Other Options

On the Aisle *The Third Man* is probably the best film of Graham Greene's works which were made into films, although many other of his works, including *Our Man in Havana,* deserve viewing. With a partner, view one of his films and **review** it as if the two of you were on your own television show. Briefly describe the plot, without giving away too much; then analyze the acting and photography, and conclude with your rating. How many stars will you give it?

It's Already Happened? American author Willa Cather once wrote, "Most of the basic material a writer works with is acquired before the age of fifteen." Prefacing your remarks with the title, "Everything I Need to Know I Learned Before I Was Fifteen," tell a partner **five important things** that you have learned.

It Happened Like This . . . What other bizarre and—let's face it—funny ways can you think of for a person to die? Make up a **tall tale** to share with the class or a group of storytellers about someone's death in another "shocking accident." Remember, a tall tale is funnier if it's told with a straight face. Who can tell the tallest, most outlandish tale?

Before Reading

The Courtship of Mr. Lyon

by Angela Carter

Angela Carter
1940–1992

A novelist, short-story writer, teacher, and critic, Angela Carter lived in England, the United States, and Australia. She was born in London and received her B. A. degree from Bristol University. She taught at Sheffield University from 1976 to 1978. Her first novel, *Shadow Dance,* was published in 1965 and her last, *Wise Children,* in 1992. She also wrote screenplays based on her works for *The Magic Toyshop* (1968), and *The Company of Wolves* (1984). She published three collections of short stories, including *The Bloody Chamber* (1979), a collection of adult fairy tales which contains "The Courtship of Mr. Lyon." Her work has elements of fantasy and sensuality, and Joyce Carol Oates, writing in the *New York Times,* called Carter "gifted and inventive."

Building Background

A Tale Retold The story of Beauty and the Beast has fascinated children, artists, musicians, moviemakers, and writers for decades. Probably of French origin, the tale tells of Beauty, the daughter of a merchant who has suffered financial misfortune. On his return from an unsuccessful journey to try to recover his losses, he discovers a rose in a deserted garden and plucks it for Beauty. The Beast, who owns the garden and the adjoining palace, threatens him with death unless he gives him his daughter. To save her father, Beauty agrees to live with the Beast. If you know the story, or similar ones (which appear in many of the world's languages), you know the ending—an ending that Angela Carter preserves in her story. However, she introduces new plot elements, expands the characterizations, and devises an unexpected setting, so that her story is as mysterious and satisfying as the original.

Literary Focus

Magic Realism Stories and novels that combine elements of dreams, magic, myths, and fairy tales, along with realistic elements are often labeled **magic realism**. In magic realist works, inexplicable events and dreamlike settings may exist with everyday happenings and ordinary characters. Or fantastic characters who do the unexpected may exist in quite realistic settings. The themes of magic realism are related to everyday life as most people know it, however.

Writer's Notebook

Up, Up, And Away! Recall some of the fantastic events or settings or characters you have read about, seen in films, or dreamed about, such as people (you?) who can fly. On your paper make a web like the one that follows.

One of the most famous treatments of the story of Beauty and the Beast is the 1946 movie version by French film maker Jean Cocteau. What aspects of the Beast does Cocteau's make-up and costuming emphasize?

The Courtship of Mr. Lyon

ANGELA CARTER

Outside her kitchen window, the hedgerow glistened as if the snow possessed a light of its own; when the sky darkened towards evening, an unearthly, reflected pallor remained behind upon the winter's landscape, while still the soft flakes floated down. This lovely girl, whose skin possesses that same inner light so you would have thought she, too, was made all of snow, pauses in her chores in the mean kitchen to look out at the country road. Nothing has passed that way all day; the road is white and unmarked as a spilled bolt of bridal satin.

Father said he would be home before nightfall.

The snow brought down all the telephone wires; he couldn't have called, even with the best of news.

The roads are bad. I hope he'll be safe.

But the old car stuck fast in a rut, wouldn't budge an inch; the engine whirred, coughed and died and he was far from home. Ruined once; then ruined again, as he had learned from his lawyers that very morning; at the conclusion of the lengthy, slow attempt to restore his fortunes, he had turned out his pockets to find the cash for petrol[1] to take him home. And not even enough money left over to buy his Beauty, his girl child, his pet, the one white rose she said she wanted; the only gift she wanted, no matter how the case went, how rich he might once again be. She had asked for so little and he had not been able to give it to her. He cursed the useless car, the last straw that broke his spirit; then, nothing for it but to fasten his old sheepskin coat around him, abandon the heap of metal and set off down the snow-filled lane to look for help.

Behind wrought-iron gates, a short, snowy drive performed a reticent[2] flourish before a miniature, perfect, Palladian[3] house that seemed to hide itself shyly behind snow-laden skirts of an antique cypress. It was almost night; that house, with its sweet, retiring, melancholy grace, would have seemed deserted but for a light that flickered in an upstairs window, so vague it might have been the reflection of a star, if any stars could have penetrated the snow that whirled yet more thickly. Chilled through, he pressed the latch of the gate and saw, with a pang, how, on the withered ghost of a tangle of thorns, there clung, still, the faded rag of a white rose.

The gate clanged loudly shut behind him; too loudly. For an instant, that reverberating clang seemed final, emphatic, ominous, as if the gate, now closed, barred all within it from the world outside the walled, wintry garden. And,

from a distance, though from what distance he could not tell, he heard the most singular sound in the world: a great roaring, as of a beast of prey.

In too much need to allow himself to be intimidated, he squared up to the mahogany door. This door was equipped with a knocker in the shape of a lion's head, with a ring through the nose; as he raised his hand towards it, it came to him this lion's head was not, as he had thought at first, made of brass, but, instead, of solid gold. Before, however, he could announce his presence, the door swung silently inward on well-oiled hinges and he saw a white hall where the candles of a great chandelier cast their benign[4] light upon so many, many flowers in great, free-standing jars of crystal that it seemed the whole of spring drew him into its warmth with a profound intake of perfumed breath. Yet there was no living person in the hall.

The door behind him closed as silently as it had opened, yet, this time, he felt no fear although he knew by the pervasive atmosphere of a suspension of reality that he had entered a place of privilege where all the laws of the world he knew need not necessarily apply, for the very rich are often very eccentric and the house was plainly that of an exceedingly wealthy man. As it was, when nobody came to help him with his coat, he took it off himself. At that, the crystals of the chandelier tinkled a little, as if emitting a pleased chuckle, and the door of a cloakroom opened of its own accord. There were, however, no clothes at all in this cloakroom, not even the statutory[5] country-house garden mackintosh to greet his own squirearchal sheepskin, but when he emerged again into the hall, he found a greeting waiting for him at last—there was, of all things, a liver-and-white King Charles spaniel

---

1. **petrol** (pet'rəl), *n.* gasoline. *[British]*
2. **reticent** (ret'ə sənt), *adj.* reserved; quiet.
3. **Palladian,** in the style of Andrea Palladio, an Italian architect who lived in the 1500s.
4. **benign** (bi nīn'), *adj.* gracious; gentle.
5. **statutory** (stach'ù tôr'ē), *adj.* required by a statute or law; here, so common as to seem required.

crouched, with head intelligently cocked, on the Kelim[6] runner. It gave him further, comforting proof of his unseen host's wealth and eccentricity to see the dog wore, in place of a collar, a diamond necklace.

The dog sprang to its feet in welcome and busily shepherded him (how amusing!) to a snug little leather-paneled study on the first floor, where a low table was drawn up to a roaring log fire. On the table, a silver tray; round the neck of the whisky decanter, a silver tag with the legend *Drink me*, while the cover of the silver dish was engraved with the exhortation *Eat me*, in a flowing hand. This dish contained sandwiches of thick-cut roast beef, still bloody. He drank the one with soda and ate the other with some excellent mustard thoughtfully provided in a stoneware pot, and when the spaniel saw to it he had served himself, she trotted off about her own business.

All that remained to make Beauty's father entirely comfortable was to find, in a curtained recess, not only a telephone, but the card of a garage that advertised a twenty-four-hour rescue service; a couple of calls later and he had confirmed, thank God, there was no serious trouble, only the car's age and the cold weather. . . . Could he pick it up from the village in an hour? And directions to the village, but half a mile away, were supplied, in a new tone of deference,[7] as soon as he described the house from where he was calling.

And he was disconcerted but, in his impecunious[8] circumstances, relieved to hear the bill would go on his hospitable if absent host's account; no question, assured the mechanic. It was the master's custom.

Time for another whisky as he tried, unsuccessfully, to call Beauty and tell her he would be late; but the lines were still down, although, miraculously, the storm had cleared as the moon rose and now a glance between the velvet curtains revealed a landscape as of ivory with an inlay of silver. Then the spaniel appeared again, with his hat in her careful mouth, prettily wagging her tail, as if to tell him it was time to be gone, that this magical hospitality was over.

As the door swung to behind him, he saw the lion's eyes were made of agate.[9]

Great wreaths of snow now precariously curded the rose trees, and when he brushed against a stem on his way to the gate, a chill armful softly thudded to the ground to reveal, as if miraculously preserved beneath it, one last, single, perfect rose that might have been the last rose left living in all the white winter, and of so intense and yet delicate a fragrance it seemed to ring like a dulcimer[10] on the frozen air.

How could his host, so mysterious, so kind, deny Beauty her present?

Not now distant but close at hand, close as that mahogany front door, rose a mighty, furious roaring; the garden seemed to hold its breath in apprehension. But still, because he loved his daughter, Beauty's father stole the rose.

At that, every window of the house blazed with furious light and a fugal[11] baying, as of a pride of lions, introduced his host.

There is always a dignity about great bulk, an assertiveness, a quality of being more *there* than most of us are. The being who now confronted Beauty's father seemed to him, in his confusion, vaster than the house he owned, ponderous yet swift, and the moonlight glittered on his great, mazy head of hair, on the eyes green as agate, on the golden hairs of the great paws that grasped his shoulders so that their claws pierced the sheepskin as he shook him like an angry child shakes a doll.

This leonine[12] apparition[13] shook Beauty's

---

6. **Kelim** (kə lēm′), also spelled Kilim, a woven carpet, without pile, made in Turkey, Kurdistan, and elsewhere.
7. **deference** (def′ər əns), *n.* great respect.
8. impecunious (im′pi kyü′nē əs), *adj.* having little or no money.
9. **agate** (ag′it), *n.* a variety of quartz, a very hard mineral.
10. **dulcimer** (dul′sə mər), *n.* musical instrument with metal strings.
11. **fugal** (fyü′gəl), *adj.* in the style of a fugue, a musical composition based on one or more short themes.
12. leonine (lē′ə nīn), *adj.* of or like a lion.
13. **apparition** (ap′ə rish′ən), *n.* the appearance of something strange, remarkable, or unexpected.

The Courtship of Mr. Lyon   **935**

father until his teeth rattled and then dropped him sprawling on his knees while the spaniel, darting from the open door, danced round them, yapping distractedly, like a lady at whose dinner party blows have been exchanged.

"My good fellow—" stammered Beauty's father; but the only response was a renewed roar.

"Good fellow? I am no good fellow! I am the Beast, and you must call me Beast, while I call you Thief!"

"Forgive me for robbing your garden, Beast!"

Head of a lion; mane and mighty paws of a lion; he reared on his hind legs like an angry lion yet wore a smoking jacket of dull red brocade and was the owner of that lovely house and the low hills that cupped it.

"It was for my daughter," said Beauty's father. "All she wanted, in the whole world, was one white, perfect rose."

The Beast rudely snatched the photograph her father drew from his wallet and inspected it, first brusquely, then with a strange kind of wonder, almost the dawning of surmise. The camera had captured a certain look she had, sometimes, of absolute sweetness and absolute gravity,[14] as if her eyes might pierce appearances and see your soul. When he handed the picture back, the Beast took good care not to scratch the surface with his claws.

"Take her the rose, then, but bring her to dinner," he growled; and what else was there to be done?

Although her father had told her of the nature of the one who waited for her, she could not control an instinctual shudder of fear when she saw him, for a lion is a lion and a man is a man, and though lions are more beautiful by far than we are, yet they belong to a different order of beauty and, besides, they have no respect for us; why should they? Yet wild things have a far more rational fear of us than is ours of them, and some kind of sadness in his agate eyes, that looked almost blind, as if sick of sight, moved her heart.

He sat, impassive as a figurehead, at the top of the table; the dining room was Queen Anne,[15] tapestried, a gem. Apart from an aromatic soup kept hot over a spirit lamp, the food, though exquisite, was cold—a cold bird, a cold soufflé, cheese. He asked her father to serve them from a buffet and, himself, ate nothing. He grudgingly admitted what she had already guessed, that he disliked the presence of servants because, she thought, a constant human presence would remind him too bitterly of his otherness, but the spaniel sat at his feet throughout the meal, jumping up from time to time to see that everything was in order.

How strange he was. She found his bewildering difference from herself almost intolerable; its presence choked her. There seemed a heavy, soundless pressure upon her in his house, as if it lay under water, and when she saw the great paws lying on the arm of his chair, she thought: They are the death of any tender herbivore.[16] And such a one she felt herself to be, Miss Lamb, spotless, sacrificial.

Yet she stayed, and smiled, because her father wanted her to do so; and when the Beast told her how he would aid her father's appeal against the judgment, she smiled with both her mouth and her eyes. But when, as they sipped their brandy, the Beast, in the diffuse, rumbling purr with which he conversed, suggested, with a hint of shyness, of fear of refusal, that she should stay here, with him, in comfort, while her father returned to London to take up the legal cudgels again, she forced a smile. For she knew with a pang of dread, as soon as he spoke, that it would be so and her visit to the Beast must be, on some magically reciprocal scale, the price of her father's good fortune.

Do not think she had no will of her own; only, she was possessed by a sense of obligation

---

14. **gravity** (grav′ə tē), *n.* seriousness.
15. **Queen Anne**, of or having to do with a style of English architecture and furniture first popular in the early 1700s, during the reign of Queen Anne.
16. **herbivore** (hèr′bə vôr), *n.* any of a large group of animals that feed chiefly on plants.

to an unusual degree and, besides, she would gladly have gone to the ends of the earth for her father, whom she loved dearly.

Her bedroom contained a marvelous glass bed; she had a bathroom, with towels thick as fleece and vials of suave unguents;[17] and a little parlor of her own, the walls of which were covered with an antique paper of birds of paradise and Chinamen, where there were precious books and pictures and the flowers grown by invisible gardeners in the Beast's hot-houses. Next morning, her father kissed her and drove away with a renewed hope about him that made her glad, but all the same, she longed for the shabby home of their poverty. The unaccustomed luxury about her she found poignant, because it gave no pleasure to its possessor, and himself she did not see all day as if, curious reversal, she frightened him, although the spaniel came and sat with her, to keep her company. Today the spaniel wore a neat choker of turquoises.

Who prepared her meals? Loneliness of the Beast; all the time she stayed there, she saw no evidence of another human presence but the trays of food that arrived on a dumbwaiter inside a mahogany cupboard in her parlor. Dinner was eggs Benedict and grilled veal; she ate it as she browsed in a book she had found in the rosewood revolving bookcase, a collection of courtly and elegant French fairy tales about white cats who were transformed princesses and fairies who were birds. Then she pulled a sprig of muscat grapes from a fat bunch for her dessert and found herself yawning; she discovered she was bored. At that, the spaniel took hold of her skirt with its velvet mouth and gave it a firm but gentle tug. She allowed the dog to trot before her to the study in which her father had been entertained and there, to her well-disguised dismay, she found her host, seated beside the fire with a tray of coffee at his elbow from which she must pour.

The voice that seemed to issue from a cave full of echoes, his dark, soft rumbling growl— after her day of pastel-colored idleness, how could she converse with the possessor of a voice that seemed an instrument created to inspire the terror that the chords of great organs bring? Fascinated, almost awed, she watched the fire-light play on the gold fringes of his mane; he was irradiated, as if with a kind of halo, and she thought of the first great beast of the Apocalypse, the winged lion with his paw upon the Gospel, Saint Mark.[18] Small talk turned to dust in her mouth; small talk had never, at the best of times, been Beauty's forte, and she had little practice at it.

But he, hesitantly, as if he himself were in awe of a young girl who looked as though she had been carved out of a single pearl, asked after her father's law case; and her dead mother; and how they, who had been so rich, had come to be so poor. He forced himself to master his shyness, which was that of a wild creature, and so she contrived to master her own—to such effect that soon she was chattering away to him as if she had known him all her life. When the little cupid in the gilt clock on the mantelpiece struck its miniature tambourine, she was astonished to discover it did so twelve times.

"So late! You will want to sleep," he said.

At that, they both fell silent, as if these strange companions were suddenly overcome with embarrassment to find themselves together, alone, in that room in the depths of the winter's night. As she was about to rise, he flung himself at her feet and buried his head in her lap. She stayed stock-still, transfixed; she felt his hot breath on her fingers, the stiff bristles of his muzzle grazing her skin, the rough lapping of his tongue, and then, with a flood of compassion, understood: All he is doing is kissing my hands.

He drew back his head and gazed at her with his green, inscrutable eyes, in which she saw her

---

17. **unguent** (ung′gwənt), *n.* ointment; cream.
18. **Apocalypse . . . Saint Mark.** Revelation, the last book of the New Testament in the Bible, is sometimes called The Apocalypse. The symbol of St. Mark, author of one of the four Gospels, is a winged lion.

face repeated twice, as small as if it were in bud. Then, without another word, he sprang from the room and she saw, with an indescribable shock, he went on all fours.

Next day, all day, the hills on which the snow still settled echoed with the Beast's rumbling roar. Has master gone a-hunting? Beauty asked the spaniel. But the spaniel growled, almost bad-temperedly, as if to say that she would not have answered, even if she could have.

Beauty would pass the day in her suite reading or, perhaps, doing a little embroidery; a box of colored silks and a frame had been provided for her. Or, well wrapped up, she wandered in the walled garden, among the leafless roses, with the spaniel at her heels, and did a little raking and rearranging. An idle, restful time; a holiday. The enchantment of that bright, sad, pretty place enveloped her and she found that, against all her expectations, she was happy there. She no longer felt the slightest apprehension at her nightly interviews with the Beast. All the natural laws of the world were held in suspension here, where an army of invisibles tenderly waited on her, and she would talk with the lion, under the patient chaperonage of the brown-eyed dog, on the nature of the moon and its borrowed light, about the stars and the substances of which they were made, about the variable transformations of the weather. Yet still his strangeness made her shiver; and when he helplessly fell before her to kiss her hands, as he did every night when they parted, she would retreat nervously into her skin, flinching at his touch.

The telephone shrilled; for her. Her father. Such news!

The Beast sunk his great head on his paws. You will come back to me? It will be lonely here, without you.

She was moved almost to tears that he should care for her so. It was in her heart to drop a kiss upon his shaggy mane, but though she stretched out her hand towards him, she could not bring herself to touch him of her own free will, he was so different from herself. But, yes, she said; I will come back. Soon, before the winter is over. Then the taxi came and took her away.

You are never at the mercy of the elements in London, where the huddled warmth of humanity melts the snow before it has time to settle; and her father was as good as rich again, since his hirsute[19] friend's lawyers had the business so well in hand that his credit brought them nothing but the best. A resplendent hotel; the opera, theaters; a whole new wardrobe for his darling, so she could step out on his arm to parties, to receptions, to restaurants, and life was as she had never known it, for her father had ruined himself before her birth killed her mother.

Although the Beast was the source of the new-found prosperity and they talked of him often, now that they were so far away from the timeless spell of his house it seemed to possess the radiant and finite quality of dream and the Beast himself, so monstrous, so benign, some kind of spirit of good fortune who had smiled on them and let them go. She sent him flowers, white roses in return for the ones he had given her; and when she left the florist, she experienced a sudden sense of perfect freedom, as if she had just escaped from an unknown danger, had been grazed by the possibility of some change but, finally, left intact. Yet, with this exhilaration, a desolating emptiness. But her father was waiting for her at the hotel; they had planned a delicious expedition to buy her furs and she was as eager for the treat as any girl might be.

Since the flowers in the shop were the same all year round, nothing in the window could tell her that winter had almost gone.

Returning late from supper after the theater, she took off her earrings in front of the mirror: Beauty. She smiled at herself with satisfaction. She was learning, at the end of her adolescence,

---

19. **hirsute** (hėr′sūt), *adj.* hairy.

how to be a spoiled child and that pearly skin of hers was plumping out, a little, with high living and compliments, a certain inwardness was beginning to transform the lines around her mouth, those signatures of the personality, and her sweetness and her gravity could sometimes turn a mite petulant[20] when things went not quite as she wanted them to go. You could not have said that her freshness was fading, but she smiled at herself in mirrors a little too often these days, and the face that smiled back was not quite the one she had seen contained in the Beast's agate eyes. Her face was acquiring, instead of beauty, a lacquer of the invincible prettiness that characterizes certain pampered, exquisite, expensive cats.

The soft wind of spring breathed in from the nearby park through the open windows; she did not know why it made her want to cry.

There was a sudden, urgent, scrabbling sound, as of claws, at her door.

Her trance before the mirror broke; all at once, she remembered everything perfectly. Spring was here and she had broken her promise. Now the Beast himself had come in pursuit of her! First, she was frightened of his anger; then, mysteriously joyful, she ran to open the door. But it was his liver-and-white spotted spaniel who hurled herself into the girl's arms in a flurry of little barks and gruff murmuring, of whimpering and relief.

Yet where was the well-brushed, jeweled dog who had sat beside her embroidery frame in the parlor with birds of paradise nodding on the walls? This one's fringed ears were matted with mud, her coat was dusty and snarled, she was thin as a dog that has walked a long way, and if she had not been a dog, she would have been in tears.

After that first, rapturous greeting, she did not wait for Beauty to order her food and water; she seized the chiffon hem of her evening dress, whimpered and tugged. Threw back her head, howled, then tugged and whimpered again.

There was a slow, late train that would take her to the station where she had left for London three months ago. Beauty scribbled a note for her father, threw a coat round her shoulders. Quickly, quickly, urged the spaniel soundlessly; and Beauty knew the Beast was dying.

In the thick dark before dawn, the station-master roused a sleepy driver for her. Fast as you can.

It seemed December still possessed his garden. The ground was hard as iron, the skirts of the dark cypress moved on the chill wind with a mournful rustle and there were no green shoots on the roses, as if, this year, they would not bloom. And not one light in any of the windows, only, in the topmost attic, the faintest smear of radiance on a pane, the thin ghost of a light on the verge of extinction.

The spaniel had slept a little, in her arms, for the poor thing was exhausted. But now her grieving agitation fed Beauty's urgency, and as the girl pushed open the front door, she saw, with a thrust of conscience, how the golden door knocker was thickly muffled in black crepe.

The door did not open silently, as before, but with a doleful groaning of the hinges and, this time, onto perfect darkness. Beauty clicked her gold cigarette lighter; the tapers in the chandelier had drowned in their own wax and the prisms were wreathed with drifting arabesques of cobwebs. The flowers in the glass jars were dead, as if nobody had had the heart to replace them after she was gone. Dust, everywhere; and it was cold. There was an air of exhaustion, of despair, in the house and, worse, a kind of physical disillusion, as if its glamor had been sustained by a cheap conjuring trick and now the conjurer, having failed to pull the crowds, had departed to try his luck elsewhere.

Beauty found a candle to light her way and followed the faithful spaniel up the staircase, past the study, past her suite, through a house

---

20. **petulant** (pech′ə lənt), *adj.* likely to have little fits of bad temper.

echoing with desertion up a little back staircase dedicated to mice and spiders, stumbling, ripping the hem of her dress in her haste.

This wood engraving of Beauty discovering the dying Beast was based on a watercolor drawing done in 1874 by British artist Walter Crane. How does Crane 's image of the Beast differ from Cocteau's?

What a modest bedroom! An attic, with a sloping roof, they might have given the chambermaid if the Beast had employed staff. A night light on the mantelpiece, no curtains at the windows, no carpet on the floor and a narrow, iron bedstead on which he lay, sadly diminished, his bulk scarcely disturbing the faded patchwork quilt, his mane a grayish rat's nest and his eyes closed. On the stick-backed chair where his clothes had been thrown, the roses she had sent him were thrust into the jug from the washstand, but they were all dead.

The spaniel jumped up on the bed and burrowed her way under the scanty covers, softly keening.

"Oh, Beast," said Beauty. "I have come home."

His eyelids flickered. How was it she had never noticed before that his agate eyes were equipped with lids, like those of a man? Was it because she had only looked at her own face, reflected there?

"I'm dying, Beauty," he said in a cracked whisper of his former purr. "Since you left me, I have been sick. I could not go hunting, I found I had not the stomach to kill the gentle beasts, I could not eat. I am sick and I must die; but I shall die happy because you have come to say goodbye to me."

She flung herself upon him, so that the iron bedstead groaned, and covered his poor paws with her kisses.

"Don't die, Beast! If you'll have me, I'll never leave you."

When her lips touched the meat-hook claws, they drew back into their pads and she saw how he had always kept his fists clenched but now, painfully, tentatively, at last began to stretch his fingers. Her tears fell on his face like snow and, under their soft transformation, the bones showed through the pelt, the flesh through the wide, tawny brow. And then it was no longer a lion in her arms but a man, a man with an unkempt mane of hair and, how strange, a broken nose, such as the noses of retired boxers, that gave him a distant, heroic resemblance to the handsomest of all the beasts.

"Do you know," said Mr. Lyon, "I think I might be able to manage a little breakfast today, Beauty, if you would eat something with me."

Mr. and Mrs. Lyon walk in the garden; the old spaniel drowses on the grass, in a drift of fallen petals.

After Reading

Making Connections

Shaping Your Response

1. Why do you think the author chose the title she did, instead of calling the story "Beauty and the Beast"?

Analyzing the Story

2. The Beast wears a brocade smoking jacket, a somewhat strange article of clothing for a lion. What are some other examples of the combination of realism with unreality?

3. What do we learn of the Beast from the **setting?**

4. How does the author elicit sympathy for the Beast?

5. Where does the **climax** of the story occur, in your opinion?

Extending the Ideas

6. ☺ How might this story have changed if it had been told from the Beast's **perspective**?

7. What truths about life do you think are evident in this story, fantasy though it may be?

Literary Focus: Magic Realism

Stories and novels that combine elements of dreams, magic, myths, and fairy tales, along with realistic elements, are often labeled **magic realism.**

1. What kinds of magic do you find in "The Courtship of Mr. Lyon"?

2. Carter often places a realistic detail, such as the Beast's Queen Anne dining room, alongside the mystery of how the food gets prepared. Yet Beauty never asks the Beast about this mystery, though she wonders about it. What does this reveal about Beauty?

3. Many old myths and tales tell of women who marry and thus transform animals (think also of "The Frog Prince" on page 909), but almost none tell about men who do so. Why do you think this might be true?

Vocabulary Study

benign
gravity
herbivore
hirsute
impecunious
leonine
petrol
petulant
reticent
unguent

Choose the word that best answers each question. Use a dictionary if you need help.

1. What is the first word that describes how the Beast looks?

2. Which word can mean both "seriousness" and "a natural force that causes objects to move toward the center of the earth"?

3. *Pecunia* is the Latin word for money. Which word means "having no money"?

4. Which word means the opposite of "loud and effusive"?

5. Which word is related to *petroleum?*

6. Which word describes Beauty, when she can't get her way?

7. A *carnivore* eats meat. What word names an animal that eats plants?

8. Which word has the same root as *benefit?*

9. Which word names something to put on a burn?

10. What is the second word that describes how the Beast looks?

Expressing Your Ideas

Writing Choices

Writer's Notebook Update Review the web you made, and make additions to it, if you wish, based on your reading of "The Courtship of Mr. Lyon." In a paragraph, tell your feelings about this type of story. Do you find yourself accepting the many unexplainable details, or do you want more explanation for some of the happenings?

Goldilocks And the Chicago Bears? Read a fairy tale and outline what you might do to update the characters, the setting, and the plot. Then write a **modern fairy story** that is at least recognizable as coming from its source.

The Mane Problem How did the Beast get to be a beast? Was he under an evil spell, and if so, who cast the spell and why? Write **the Beast's story** in the first person from his **perspective,** explaining how you as the Beast were originally transformed from a man into an animal and why.

Other Options

Illustration The illustrations on page 933 and 940 show how two different artists have interpreted the Beast; many others have done so over the years. Try your hand at creating an **illustration** for one or two scenes of Angela Carter's story: perhaps the Beast's Palladian house (you may need to do some research on architectural history), the door knocker, the King Charles spaniel, Beauty, or Mr. Lyon.

Other Versions After doing the necessary research, prepare a **bibliography** of other works (picture books, operas, films, musicals, television programs, and so on) based on Beauty and the Beast, and distribute it to the class.

Roar Like a Lion With a small group, write a script based on the original story of Beauty and the Beast and, using hand puppets which you and your partners have made, present a **puppet play** of the story for a group of young children.

The Slant View

Myth Under a Microscope

Science Connection
In the following essay, biologist Lewis Thomas examines several mythological creatures from the perspective of science.

GRiffon

SOME BIOMYTHOLOGY

by Lewis Thomas

The mythical animals cataloged in the bestiaries[1] of the world seem, at a casual glance, nothing but exotic nonsense. The thought comes that Western civilized, scientific, technologic society is a standing proof of human progress, in having risen above such imaginings. They are as obsolete as the old anecdotes in which they played their puzzling, ambiguous roles, and we have no more need for the beasts than for the stories. The Griffon, Phoenix, Centaur, Sphinx, Manticore, Ganesha, Ch'i-lin, and all the rest are like recurrent bad dreams, and we are well rid of them. So we say.

The trouble is that they are in fact like dreams, and not necessarily bad ones, and we may have a hard time doing without them. They may be as essential for society as mythology itself, as loaded with symbols, and as necessary for the architecture of our collective unconscious. If Levi-Strauss[2] is right, myths are constructed by a universal logic that, like language itself, is as characteristic for human beings as nest-building is for birds.

The stories seem to be different stories, but the underlying structure is always the same, in any part of the world, at any time. They are like engrams,[3] built into our genes. In this sense, bestiaries are part of our inheritance.

There is something basically similar about most of these crazy animals. They are all unbiologic, but unbiologic in the same way. Bestiaries do not contain, as a rule, totally novel creatures of the imagination made up of parts that we have never seen before. On the contrary, they are made up of parts that are entirely familiar. What is novel, and startling, is that they are mixtures of species.

It is perhaps this characteristic that makes the usual bestiary so outlandish to the twentieth-century mind. Our most powerful story, equivalent in its way to a universal myth, is evolution. Never mind that it is true whereas myths are not; it is filled with symbolism, and this is the way it has influenced the mind of society. In our latest enlightenment, the fabulous beasts are worse than improbable—

---

1. bestiary (besʹtē er ē), *n.* collection of natural history and animal tales popular in the Middle Ages.

2. Lévi-Strauss, Claude Lévi-Strauss (born 1908), French anthropologist who has written extensively on mythology.

3. engram (enʹgram), *n.* whatever happens to the brain when a memory is formed, thought by scientists to be some change in brain cells.

PHOENIX

they are impossible, because they violate evolution. They are not species, and they deny the existence of species.

The Phoenix comes the closest to being a conventional animal, all bird for all of its adult life. It is, in fact, the most exuberant, elaborate, and ornamented of all plumed birds. It exists in the mythology of Egypt, Greece, the Middle East, and Europe, and is the same as the vermilion bird of ancient China. It lives for five hundred triumphant years, and when it dies it constructs a sort of egg-shaped cocoon around itself. Inside, it disintegrates and gives rise to a wormlike creature, which then develops into the new Phoenix, ready for the next five hundred years. In other versions the dead bird bursts into flames, and the new one arises from the ashes, but the worm story is very old, told no doubt by an early biologist.

There are so many examples of hybrid beings in bestiaries that you could say that an ardent belief in mixed forms of life is an ancient human idea, or that something else, deeply believed in, is symbolized by these consortia.[4] They are disturbing to look at, nightmarish, but most of them, oddly enough, are intended as lucky benignities. The Ch'i-lin, for instance, out of ancient China, has the body of a deer covered with gleaming scales, a marvelous bushy tail, cloven hooves, and small horns. Whoever saw a Ch'i-lin was in luck, and if you got to ride one, you had it made.

The Ganesha is one of the oldest and most familiar Hindu deities, possessing a fat human body, four human arms, and the head of a cheerful-looking elephant. Prayers to Ganesha are regarded as the quickest way around obstacles.

Not all mythical beasts are friendly, of course, but even the hostile ones have certain amiable redeeming aspects. The Manticore has a lion's body, a

man's face, and a tail with a venomous snake's head at the end of it. It bounds around seeking prey with huge claws and three rows of teeth, but it makes the sounds of a beautiful silver flute.

Some of the animal myths have the ring of contemporary biologic theory, if you allow for differences in jargon. An ancient idea in India postulates an initial Being, the first form of life on the earth, analogous to our version of the earliest procaryotic[5] arrangement of membrane-limited nucleic acid, the initial cell, born of lightning and methane. The Indian Being, undefined and indefinable, finding itself alone, fearing death, yearning for company, began to swell in size, rearranged itself inside, and then split into two identical halves. One of these changed into a cow, the other a bull, and they mated, then changed again to a mare and stallion, and so on, down to the ants, and thus the earth was populated. There is a lot of oversimplification here, and too much short-hand for modern purposes, but the essential myth is recognizable.

The serpent keeps recurring through the earliest cycles of mythology, always as a central symbol for the life of the universe and the continuity of creation. There are two great identical snakes on a Levantine libation vase of around 2000 B.C., coiled around each other in a double helix, representing the original generation of life. They are the replicated parts of the first source of living, and they are wonderfully homologous.[6]

There is a Peruvian deity, painted on a clay pot dating from around A.D. 300, believed

---

4. **consortia** (kən sôr′shē ə), *n. pl.* of **consortium** (kən sôr′shē əm), partnership; association.

5. **procaryotic** (prō kar′ē ot′ik), *adj.* referring to a type of single-celled organism.

6. **homologous** (hō mol′ə gəs), *adj.* corresponding in structure and origin but not in function, like the wing of a bird and the foreleg of a horse.

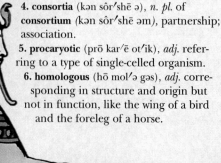

SPHINX

to be responsible for guarding farms. His hair is made of snakes, entwined in braids, with wings for his headdress. Plants of various kinds are growing out of his sides and back, and a vegetable of some sort seems to be growing from his mouth. The whole effect is wild and disheveled but essentially friendly. He is, in fact, an imaginary version of a genuine animal, symbiopholus, described in *Nature* several years back, a species of weevil in the mountains of northern New Guinea that lives symbiotically[7] with dozens of plants, growing in the niches and clefts in its carapace,[8] rooted all the way down to its flesh, plus a whole ecosystem of mites, rotifers, nematodes, and bacteria attached to the garden. The weevil could be taken for a good-luck omen on its own evidence; it is not attacked by predators, it lives a long, untroubled life, and nothing else will eat it, either because of something distasteful in the system or simply because of the ambiguity. The weevil is only about thirty millimeters long, easily overlooked; but it has the makings of a myth.

MANTICORE

Perhaps we should be looking around for other candidates. I suggest the need for a new bestiary, to take the place of the old ones. I can think of several creatures that seem designed for this function, if you will accept a microbestiary, and if you are looking for metaphors.

First of all, there is Myxotricha paradoxa. This is the protozoan,[9] not yet as famous as he should be, who seems to be telling us everything about everything, all at once. His cilia[10]

are not cilia at all, but individual spirochetes,[11] and at the base of attachment of each spirochete is an oval organelle,[12] embedded in the myxotricha membrane, which is a bacterium. It is not an animal after all—it is a company, an assemblage.

The story told by myxotricha is as deep as any myth, as profoundly allusive. This creature has lagged behind the rest of us, and is still going through the process of being assembled. Our cilia gave up any independent existence long ago, and our organelles are now truly ours, but the genomes[13] controlling separate parts of our cells are still different genomes, lodged in separate compartments; doctrinally, we are still assemblages.

There is another protozoan, called blepharisma, telling a long story about the chanciness and fallibility of complex life. Blepharisma is called that because of a conspicuous fringe of ciliated membranes around the oral cavity, which evidently reminded someone of eyelashes (blepharidos). The whole mythlike tale has been related in a book by Giese. Blepharisma has come much further along than myxotricha, but not far enough to be free of slip-ups. There are three different sets of self-duplicating nuclei,

CH'I-LIN

7. **symbiotically** (sim′bē ot′i kal lē), *adj.* referring to the relationship of two unlike organisms that live together for mutual benefit.
8. **carapace** (kar′ə pās), *n.* shell or bony covering on the back of an animal.
9. **protozoan** (prō′tə zō′ən), *n.* a microscopic animal that reproduces by dividing itself.
10. **cilia** (sil′ē ə), *n. pl.* of **cilium** (sil′ē əm), in microorganisms, very small, hairlike projections used to propel them through water.
11. **spirochete** (spī′rə kēt′), *n.* a kind of bacterium.
12. **organelle** (ôr′gə nel′), *n.* in microorganisms, a minute, specialized part of a cell.
13. **genome** (jē′nōm), *n.* the total genetic structure of a cell or organism.

with the DNA in each set serving different purposes: a large macronucleus, governing the events in regeneration after injury, a set of eight or more micronuclei containing the parts of the genome needed for reproduction, and great numbers of tiny nuclei from which the cilia arise.

One part of the organism produces a pinkish pigment, now called blepharismin, which is similar to hypericin and certain other photosensitizing plant pigments. Blepharismin causes no trouble unless the animal swims into sunlight, but then the pigment kills it outright. Under certain circumstances, the membrane surrounding blepharisma disintegrates and comes independently loose, like a cast-off shell, leaving the creature a transient albino. At times of famine, a single blepharisma will begin eating its neighbors; it then enlarges to an immense size and turns into a cannibalistic giant, straight out of any Norse fable. Evidently, this creature still has trouble getting along with the several parts of itself, and with the collective parts of other blepharismae.

There are innumerable plant-animal combinations, mostly in the sea, where the green plant cells provide carbohydrate and oxygen for the animal and receive a share of energy in return. It is the fairest of arrangements. When the paramecium bursaria runs out of food, all he needs to do is stay in the sun and his green endosymbionts will keep him supplied as though he were a grain.

Bacteria are the greatest of all at setting up joint enterprises, on which the lives of their hosts are totally dependent. The nitrogen-fixing rhizobia in root nodules, the mycetomes of insects, and the enzyme-producing colonies in the digestive tracts of many animals are variations of this meticulously symmetrical symbiosis.

The meaning of these stories may be basically the same as the meaning of a medieval bestiary. There is a tendency for living things to join up, establish linkages, live inside each other, return to earlier arrangements, get along, whenever possible. This is the way of the world.

The new phenomenon of cell fusion, a laboratory trick on which much of today's science of molecular genetics relies for its data, is the simplest and most spectacular symbol of the tendency. In a way, it is the most unbiologic of all phenomena, violating the most fundamental myth of the last century, for it denies the importance of specificity, integrity, and separateness in living things. Any cell—man, animal, fish, fowl, or insect—given the chance and under the right conditions, brought into contact with any other cell, however foreign, will fuse with it. Cytoplasm will flow easily from one to the other, the nuclei will combine, and it will become, for a time anyway, a single cell with two complete, alien genomes, ready to dance, ready to multiply. It is a Chimera, a Griffon, a Sphinx, a Ganesha, a Peruvian god, a Ch'i-lin, an omen of good fortune, a wish for the world.

Responding

1. Thomas seems to feel that the ability to create genetic mutations in the laboratory is a good thing. Do you agree? Why or why not?

2. Using any medium you like, create a composite fantasy creature of your own that combines different features from two or more real animals.

Writing Workshop

Life from Odd Angles

Assignment You have read several selections in which the characters see things from unique viewpoints. Now tell a story of your own from a unique viewpoint.

WRITER'S BLUEPRINT

Product A monologue

Purpose To get into the mind of a character who sees things from a unique viewpoint

Audience Readers whom your character is addressing directly

Specs As the writer of a successful monologue, you should:

❑ Choose a narrator, living or nonliving, who sees things from a unique viewpoint and an appropriate event for this narrator to describe. For example:

—a picnic as seen by an ant

—a rush-hour ride across a big city as seen by a taxicab

—the arrival home of a new baby as seen by the baby

—a morning in the life of a bathroom mirror

❑ Present your monologue as a series of incidents in time order, from first to last.

❑ Use the first-person ("I") point of view, with the narrator telling readers what's going through his or her (or its) mind as the event unfolds. Don't reveal your narrator's identify directly but hint at it along the way, so that your audience can discover it for themselves.

❑ Begin with a mysterious or startling detail to grab your reader's attention. Include information about sensory details, feelings, and thoughts that run through the narrator's mind as the event unfolds.

❑ End with a humorous touch.

❑ Follow the rules of grammar, usage, spelling, and mechanics—with one exception. Use sentence fragments if they realistically portray the way your narrator thinks and speaks.

Review the literature in this part of the unit. Meet with a group to discuss the main characters. Make notes in charts like the one shown. Think of each category as contributing to the character's unique viewpoint.

LITERARY SOURCE
"But you are my daughters, you inherit my own faults/of character;/you are submissive, following Adam/even beyond existence."
    from "Eve to Her Daughters" by Judith Wright

Eve in "Eve to Her Daughters"

Location	Desires, Goals	Problems, Fears, Complaints	Limitations, Restrictions
outside Eden	to have her daughters take over for her	Adam's discontent and egotism	submissive, subject to Adam's will and God's punishment

Brainstorm ideas for characters and events. List characters who experience life from a unique viewpoint. These characters may be living or nonliving (see the examples in the Writer's Blueprint). Choose the character and event that you feel would interest readers most.

Define your narrator's viewpoint in a chart like the one you made in "Review the literature." For example:

a morning in the life of a bathroom mirror

Location	Desires, Goals	Problems, Fears, Complaints	Limitations, Restrictions
bathroom of a house, on wall above sink	—to be able to give grooming tips to sloppy family members —to be able to see more of world	—afraid they'll break me —They never look at _me_, only themselves!	—can't move, can't look around —full of ideas but can't communicate, can't express myself

Brainstorm sensory details in a quickwrite. Visualize yourself in the position of your narrator. How do things look and sound and feel and smell? Write for a few minutes about everything your senses pick up. When you finish, underline the sensory details you've come up with.

OR . . .
Take on your character's voice and improvise a monologue about what you see, feel, and smell. Audiotape it and make notes on sensory details as you play it back.

Plan your opening. You'll want to grab your readers' attention by hinting at your narrator's identity. Jot down some ideas. For example:

> In a moment the door will open and the first of them will stagger in, rub the sleep from her eyes, and stare at me as if I held the answer to the riddle of life itself.

Not you again. I've seen your face so many times I'd know it like the back of my hand—if I had a hand.

Break down your event into a series of incidents in time order, from first to last. List them or arrange them in a time line.

Plan your monologue by making notes in a plan like the one shown. Use your prewriting materials to guide you.

Narrator
Event
Mysterious or startling detail to begin

Incident #1
—Sights
—Sounds
—Smells
—Feelings
—Thoughts

Incident #2
and so on . . .

Humorous touch to close (see the Revising Strategy in Step 3)

OR . . .
Make your plan in the form of a storyboard. On a separate piece of paper, sketch a key moment from each incident and on the back make notes on sights, sounds, smells, feelings, and thoughts.

STEP 2 DRAFTING

Start writing. Use your prewriting materials as a guide, but be flexible. Here are some tips that may help you as you draft.

- Close your eyes and visualize the setting as your monologue begins. Then begin writing.

- As you write, keep in mind that you'll be hinting at your narrator's identity all along without ever stating it directly.

- End with a humorous touch. See the Revising Strategy in Step 3.

STEP 3 REVISING

Ask a partner for comments on your draft before you revise it. Use the checklist on the next page to guide your comments.

✔ Did I begin with a startling or mysterious detail to hook the reader?

✔ Have I effectively hinted at the narrator's identity without directly revealing it?

✔ Have I ended with a humorous touch?

Revising Strategy

Ending with a Humorous Touch

One way is to end a monologue like this one is with a humorous touch, a little joke or anecdote. Here are two examples of humorous closings (a pun and a reference to a popular fairy tale), using the idea of a morning in the life of a bathroom mirror:

> No! Don't walk out, don't leave me again! Oh well, I guess I'll do what I do every day after they leave for work, sit here on the wall and reflect on the morning's events.

> If only you could hear me, my sweet Angela, I would tell you, and you would know, that you and you alone are the fairest of them all. Perhaps someday, somehow, I will find a way to tell you.

Notice how this writer, who wrote from the point of view of a television set, adds a line to bring his monologue to a clever close.

> ○   What I need is a change of scenery. I've been sitting in this
>
> same spot for what seems like years now. My view isn't so bad,
>
> ○   though. I can look out the window and watch cars go by. That's a
>
> good thing. But I feel like I have no control over my life. ^ *If only I could reach the remote control.*

STUDENT MODEL

Ask a partner to review your revised draft before you edit. When you edit, watch for errors in grammar, and leave them in your monologue if they help show how your character thinks and speaks.

Editing Strategy

FOR REFERENCE
More information about sentence fragments can be found in the Language and Grammar Handbook at the back of this text.

Using Sentence Fragments

Sentence fragments are to be avoided in most writing. But since people often think and speak in fragments, they're acceptable when they appear in a monologue. Notice how this writer uses fragments to give his narrator's thoughts a realistic structure.

> He stares at me. Really stares. Bores a hole right through me. I can't look him in the eye. I bet it gives him great pleasure to watch me squirm.

STUDENT MODEL

STEP 5 PRESENTING

- Create a unique *voice* for your narrator before reading your monologue to classmates.

- Share your monologue with a small group and have them talk about when they figured out the narrator's identity and how.

STEP 6 LOOKING BACK

Self-evaluate. Look back at the Writer's Blueprint and give yourself a score on each point, from 6 (superior) to 1 (inadequate).

Reflect. Write answers to these questions.

✔ Was this particular assignment fun to write? Why or why not?

✔ If you were to make this monologue part of a longer story, what are some other events that might happen in the story?

For Your Working Portfolio Add your monologue and reflection responses to your working portfolio.

Beyond Print

Cause and Effect

Any person, thing, or event that produces an effect is a *cause*. It is the reason something happens. The result of an event, idea, or action is an *effect*. It is whatever is produced or made to happen by a cause. In simple cause-effect relationships, one cause has one effect; for example, you turn on the TV set, and a picture appears.

Cause-effect relationships, however, are usually more complex than those in which a single cause produces a single effect. One type of complex cause-effect relationship occurs when a single cause produces a chain of effects. For example, in Graham Greene's story "A Shocking Accident," a pig falls from a balcony and kills Jerome's father. Classmates who hear the story laugh and call Jerome "Pig," making him self-conscious and fearful that others will learn about the mishap and laugh. Later, when his fiancée hears the story, however, she delights him with her serious, thoughtful reaction.

Drawing a diagram can help you understand this kind of chain of causation:

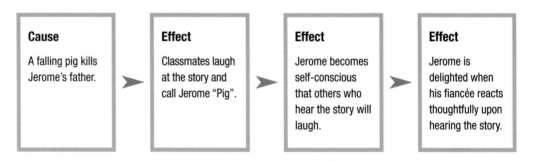

Cause	Effect	Effect	Effect
A falling pig kills Jerome's father.	Classmates laugh at the story and call Jerome "Pig".	Jerome becomes self-conscious that others who hear the story will laugh.	Jerome is delighted when his fiancée reacts thoughtfully upon hearing the story.

Activity Options

1. Diagram cause-effect relationships in either "The Truly Married Woman" or "The Courtship of Mr. Lyon."

2. Create a cause-effect diagram in the form of a storyboard illustrating key events in one of the other stories in this book.

3. With a group of students, select a movie that exhibits complex cause-effect relationships and discuss how they contribute to the film's theme.

Multicultural Connections

Interactions

Part One: The Passing of Empire George Orwell acquires a unique perspective on imperialism when his job forces him to interact with hostile Burmese. Winston Churchill oversees the interactions of civilians and military personnel as England battles for its existence. Philip Larkin and Derek Walcott comment from their own perspectives on colonial interactions, and Buchi Emecheta's character, Adah, struggles to survive in a world she has inherited from others.

■ Do you think that rulers and their subjects can ever interact with understanding, or are their perspectives so influenced by their positions that they cannot?

Perspective

Part Two: The Slant View The perspective from which a story is told may drastically alter the participants' views of each other and of their interactions. Each of the characters in these selections responds to a situation in a way that is not quite expected.

■ What advantages are there in being able to look at life from different perspectives?

Activities

1. Choose a selection from this unit and stage the interactions—the conflicts and the resolutions—as a series of "frozen moments" in pantomime. Use as many students as there are main characters and plan in advance exactly what poses (and how many) are needed to tell the story. Practice your pantomime before staging it for the class.

2. Choose a selection and retell it briefly from the perspective of another character; for example, recount the events in "Eveline" from Frank's point of view or the soldier in "Disabled" from the point of view of a nurse.

Independent and Group Projects

Media

The British Monarchy The British monarchy has always been a dominant force in the lives of the British people. Working with several other members of your class, prepare a **television documentary** about British rulers. Using appropriate time lines and illustrations, briefly trace the history of the monarchy. Place your greatest emphasis on the roles of British rulers in the twentieth century. Conclude your show with a panel discussion in which you and your colleagues attempt to predict the future of the monarchy.

Graphic Arts

The Commonwealth of Nations The Commonwealth of Nations is an association of forty-nine nations and dependencies that give allegiance, real and symbolic, to the British crown. It is what the British Empire has evolved into in the later twentieth century. Prepare a **map of the world** that identifies all the members of the Commonwealth of Nations. Include a caption for each nation telling briefly its history and its present relationship to England.

Music

Monkeeing with Beatlemania Beginning with the release of the Beatles' first album in 1963, British rock groups invaded the musical world with new sounds and styles. Select one of the following British groups—the Beatles, the Rolling Stones, the Monkees, Herman's Hermits, the Animals—or a group of your choice, and prepare an **interactive museum exhibit** (select from audio, video, graphics, and computer "hands-on" activities) designed to explain the influence of your chosen rock group to a teenage audience in the year 2025.

Popular Culture

Boundless British Humor British humor abounds on American television. With a group of classmates, view several British comedy shows. You might choose from *Monty Python's Flying Circus* (see pages 961–962), *Dr. Who, Fawlty Towers, Are You Being Served?,* or *Absolutely Fabulous,* for example. Try to determine what special qualities of humor are present in these shows. Working together, write a **humorous script** that attempts to capture some elements of British humor. Perform your script for your class.

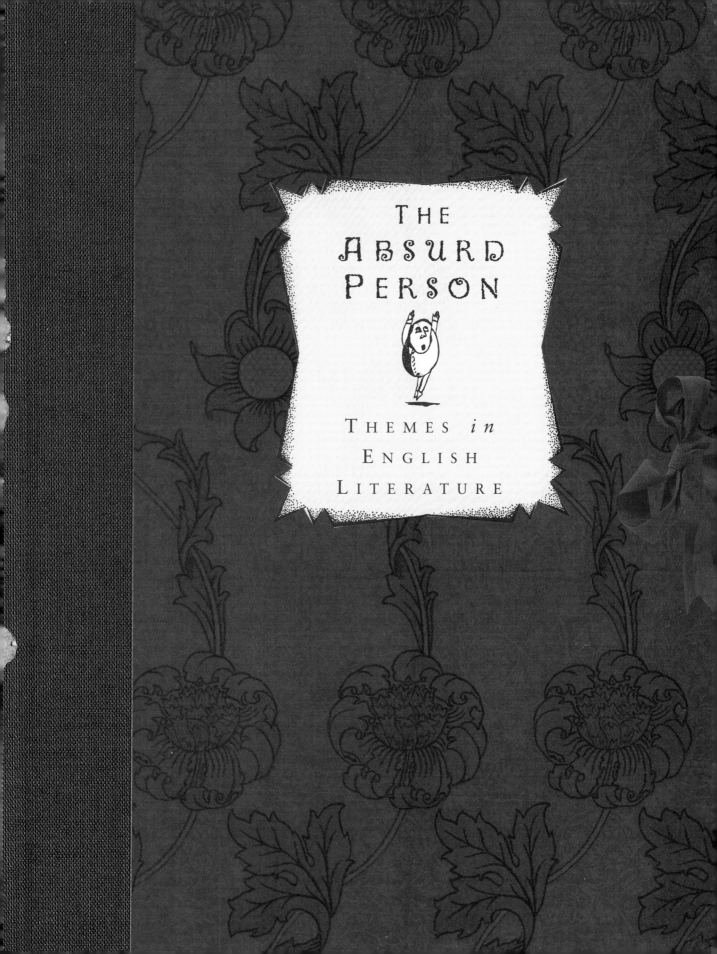

THE ABSURD PERSON

THEMES *in* ENGLISH LITERATURE

THE

ABSURD PERSON

Edward Lear, caricature of himself (1870s)

Absurd means "ridiculous," but in the later twentieth century it has come to be used also for a philosophy and an artistic movement. Theater of the Absurd, as it has come to be called, relies in part on theatrical effects, such as are seen in the work of jugglers, acrobats, bullfighters, or mimes; clowning, fooling, and mad scenes; verbal nonsense; and elements of dream and fantasy. None of these is new, of course—they go back untold centuries. What *is* new is the term (coined by theater critic Martin Esslin) and its application to a philosophy of life, to a sense that life in the late 1900s doesn't have the same kind of meaning—or doesn't have meaning in the same way—as life seemed to have in earlier, simpler times.

from The Theater of the Absurd

The hallmark of this attitude is its sense that the certitudes and unshakable basic assumptions of former ages have been swept away, that they have been tested and found wanting, that they have been discredited as cheap and somewhat childish illusions. The decline of religious faith was masked until the end of the Second World War by the substitute religions of faith in progress, nationalism, and various totalitarian fallacies. All this was shattered by the war. By 1942, Albert Camus[1] . . . tried to diagnose the human situation in a world of shattered beliefs:

"A world that can be explained by reasoning, however faulty, is a familiar world. But in a universe that is suddenly deprived of illusions and of light, man feels a stranger. His is an irremediable[2] exile, because he is deprived of memories of a lost homeland as much as he lacks the hope of a promised land to come. This divorce between man and his life, the actor and his setting, truly constitutes the feeling of Absurdity."

Nicely Nicely Clive

Absurd originally means "out of harmony," in a musical context. Hence its dictionary definition: "out of harmony with reason or propriety; incongruous, unreasonable, illogical." In common usage, *absurd* may simply mean "ridiculous," but this is not the sense in which Camus uses the word, . . . [Eugène] Ionesco[3] defined his understanding of the term as follows: "Absurd is that which is devoid of purpose. . . . Cut off from his religious, metaphysical, and transcendental roots, man is lost; all his actions become senseless, absurd, useless."

Martin Esslin (1961)

To Clive Barrow it was just an ordinary day nothing unusual or strange about it, everything quite novel, nothing outstanley just another day but to Roger it was something special, a day amongst days . . . a red lettuce day . . . because Roger was getting married and as he dressed that morning he thought about the gay batchelor soups he'd had with all his pals. And Clive said nothing. To Roger everything was different, wasn't this the day his Mother had told him about, in his best suit and all that, grimming and shakeing hands, people tying boots and ricebudda on his car.

To have and to harm . . . till death duty part . . . he knew it all off by hertz. Clive Barrow seemed oblivious. Roger could visualise Anne in her flowing weddy drag, being wheeled up the aisle, smiling a blessing. He had butterfield in his stomarce as he fastened his bough tie and brushed his hairs. "I hope I'm doing the right thing" he thought looking in the mirror, "Am I good enough for her?" Roger need not have worried because he was. "Should I have flowers all round the spokes?" said Anne polishing her foot rest. "Or should I keep it syble?" she continued looking down on her grain haired Mother.

"Does it really matter?" repaid her Mother wearily wiping her sign. "He won't be looking at your spokes anyway." Anne smiled the smile of someone who's seen a few laughs.

Then luckily Anne's father came home from sea and cancelled the husband.

John Lennon (1964)

Life's But a Walking Shadow

LIFE'S BUT A WALKING SHADOW, A POOR PLAYER
THAT STRUTS AND FRETS HIS HOUR UPON THE STAGE
AND THEN IS HEARD NO MORE; IT IS A TALE
TOLD BY AN IDIOT, FULL OF SOUND AND FURY,
SIGNIFYING NOTHING.

William Shakespeare (about 1606)

---

1. **Albert Camus** (àl ber′ kȧ mY′) (1913–1960), French novelist and essayist.
2. **irremediable** (ir′i mē′dē ə bəl), *adj.* incurable.

3. **Eugène Ionesco** (œ zhen′ yo nes′kō), born 1912, French playright, born in Romania.

Incidents in the Life
of My Uncle Arly

O my agèd Uncle Arly!
Sitting on a heap of Barley
    Through the silent hours of night,
Close beside a leafy thicket:
In his hat a Railway-Ticket.
      (But his shoes were far too tight.)

Long ago, in youth, he squandered
All his goods away, and wandered
    To the Tiniskoop-hills afar.
There on golden sunsets blazing,
Every evening found him gazing,
Singing, "Orb! you're quite amazing!
      How I wonder what you are!"

Like the ancient Medes and Persians,
Always by his own exertions
    He subsisted on those hills;
Whiles—by teaching children spelling—
Or at times by merely yelling—
Or at intervals by selling
      "Propter's Nicodemus Pills."

Later in his morning rambles
He perceived the moving brambles
    Something square and white disclose.
'Twas a First-Class Railway-Ticket;
But, on stooping down to pick it
Off the ground, a pea-green Cricket
      Settled on my uncle's Nose.

Never—never more—oh! never,
Did that Cricket leave him ever,
    Dawn or evening, day or night;
Clinging as a constant treasure,
Chirping with a cheerious measure,
Wholly to my uncle's pleasure.
      (Though his shoes were far too tight.)

So for three-and-forty winters,
Till his shoes were worn to splinters,
    All those hills he wandered o'er—
Sometimes silent; sometimes yelling;
Till he came to Borley-Melling,
Near his old ancestral dwelling.
      (But his shoes were far too tight.)

On a little heap of Barley
Died my agèd uncle Arly,
    And they buried him one night
Close beside the leafy thicket;
There—his hat and Railway-Ticket;
There—his ever faithful Cricket.
      (But his shoes were far too tight.)

Edward Lear (1895)

TO
NOBODADDY

Why art thou silent & invisible,
Father of Jealousy?
Why dost thou hide thyself in clouds
From every searching Eye?

Why darkness & obscurity
In all thy words & laws,
That none dare eat the fruit but from
The wily serpent's jaws?
Or is it because Secrecy
Gains female's loud applause?

William Blake (1863)

nobodaddy. The speaker is suggesting that God the Father is actually nobody's daddy.

from
The Crack
in the Teacup

There is no doubt the post-war period has seen the intensification of the gloom that characterizes influential twentieth-century art. This is the time of the bomb, of the spread of dictatorships and torture, of forces of destruction unleashed against innocent people, of the collapse of the rich societies of the west. Such ideas are not cheerful, they are painful to hear, and impossible to solve. Therefore, the larger audiences gravitate to escapist culture, and in spite of huge resources deployed[1] to foster it, art is still the domain[2] of a small élite, and its predominant theme is despair. Man's immense powers for self-destruction are contrasted to the littleness of his spiritual capacities; the accessibility of riches and power is compared to the emotional emptiness of the individual; the vast organized fabric of society is shown to engulf the people within it. But futility and the sense of meaninglessness have penetrated all modern European literature so deeply that the case cannot be said to be peculiarly British. It certainly belongs to Britain, too, though, for some of the most articulate[3] voices of contemporary goallessness have come from Britain.

Marina Warner (1979)

S O L O M O N
G R U N D Y

Solomon Grundy,
Born on a Monday,
Christened on Tuesday,
Married on Wednesday,
Took ill on Thursday,
Worse on Friday,
Died on Saturday,
Buried on Sunday,
This is the end
Of Solomon Grundy.

Mother Goose rhyme (1700s)

Ronald Searle,
The Greedy Carpet *(1972)*

---

1. **deploy** (di ploi′), *v.* use.
2. **domain** (dō mān′), *n.* area of activity or control.

3. **articulate** (är tik′yə lit), *adj.* able to put into words easily and clearly.

James Grainger, Clergy Tossing *(1981)*

THE DEAD PARROT SKETCH

Mr. Praline walks into a pet shop carrying a dead parrot in a cage. He walks to counter where shopkeeper tries to hide below cash register.

PRALINE. Hello, I wish to register a complaint . . . Hello? Miss?

SHOPKEEPER. What do you mean, miss?

PRALINE. Oh, I'm sorry, I have a cold. I wish to make a complaint.

SHOPKEEPER. Sorry, we're closing for lunch.

PRALINE. Never mind that, my lad, I wish to complain about this parrot what I purchased not half an hour ago from this very boutique.

SHOPKEEPER. Oh yes, the Norwegian Blue. What's wrong with it?

PRALINE. I'll tell you what's wrong with it. It's dead, that's what's wrong with it.

SHOPKEEPER. No, no, it's resting. Look!

PRALINE. Look my lad, I know a dead parrot when I see one, and I'm looking at one right now.

SHOPKEEPER. No, no sir, it's not dead. It's resting.

PRALINE. Resting?

SHOPKEEPER. Yeah, remarkable bird the Norwegian Blue, beautiful plumage, innit?

PRALINE. The plumage don't enter into it—it's stone dead.

SHOPKEEPER. No, no—it's just resting.

PRALINE. All right then, if it's resting I'll wake it up. *(Shouts into cage.)* Hello Polly! I've got a nice cuttlefish for you when you wake up, Polly Parrot!

SHOPKEEPER *(jogging cage)*. There, it moved.

PRALINE. No he didn't. That was you pushing the cage.

SHOPKEEPER. I did not.

PRALINE. Yes, you did. *(Takes parrot out of cage, shouts.)* Hello Polly, Polly! *(Bangs it against counter.)* Polly Parrot, wake up. Polly. *(Throws it in the air and lets it fall to the floor.)* Now that's what I call a dead parrot.

SHOPKEEPER. No, no—it's stunned.

PRALINE. Look my lad, I've had just about enough of this. That parrot is definitely deceased. And when I bought it not half an hour ago, you assured me that its lack of movements was due to it being tired and shagged out after a long squawk.

SHOPKEEPER. It's probably pining for the fiords.[1]

PRALINE. Pining for the fiords, what kind of talk is that? Look, why did it fall flat on its back the moment I got it home?

SHOPKEEPER. The Norwegian Blue prefers kipping[2] on its back. Beautiful bird, lovely plumage.

PRALINE. Look, I took the liberty of examining that parrot, and I discovered that the only reason that it had been sitting on its perch in the first place was that it had been nailed there.

SHOPKEEPER. Well of course it was nailed there. Otherwise it would muscle up to those bars and voom.

PRALINE. Look matey *(picks up parrot)*, this parrot wouldn't voom if I put four thousand volts through it. It's bleeding demised.

SHOPKEEPER. It's not, it's pining.

PRALINE. It's not pining, it's passed on. This

---

1. **fiord** (fyôrd), *n.* a long, narrow bay of the sea bordered by steep cliffs, such as found in Norway.
2. **kip,** sleep.

parrot is no more. It has ceased to be. It's expired and gone to meet its maker. This is a late parrot. It's a stiff. Bereft of life, it rests in peace. If you hadn't nailed it to the perch, it would be pushing up the daisies. It's rung down the curtain and joined the choir invisible. This is an ex-parrot.

SHOPKEEPER. Well, I'd better replace it then.

PRALINE *(to camera)*. If you want to get any thing done in this country you've got to complain till you're blue in the mouth.

SHOPKEEPER. Sorry guv, we're right out of parrots.

PRALINE. I see. I see. I get the picture.

SHOPKEEPER. I've got a slug.

PRALINE. Does it talk?

SHOPKEEPER. Not really, no.

PRALINE. Well, it's scarcely a replacement then, is it?

SHOPKEEPER. Listen, I'll tell you what *(handing over a card)*, tell you what, if you go to my brother's pet shop in Bolton he'll replace your parrot for you.

PRALINE. Bolton, eh?

SHOPKEEPER. Yeah.

PRALINE. All right.

(He leaves, holding the parrot.
Caption: A similar pet shop in Bolton, Lancs.
Closeup of sign on door reading: "Similar Pet Shops Ltd." Pull back from sign to see same pet shop. Shopkeeper now has mustache. Praline walks into shop. He looks around with interest, noticing the empty parrot cage still on the floor.)

PRALINE. Er, excuse me. This is Bolton, is it?

SHOPKEEPER. No, no it's, er, Ipswich.

PRALINE *(to camera)*. That's Inter-City Rail for you. *(Leaves.)*

Monty Python's Flying Circus (1989)

Epilogus Incerti Authoris

Like to the mowing tones of unspoke speeches

Or like two lobsters clad in logic breeches;

Or like the gray fleece of a crimson cat,

Or like the mooncalf[1] in a slipshod hat;

Or like the shadow when the sun is gone,

Or like a thought that never was thought upon:

Even such is man who never was begotten

Until his children were both dead and rotten. . . .

Richard Corbet (1600s)

Delight in nonsense has its root in the feeling of freedom we enjoy when we are able to abandon the straitjacket of logic.

Sigmund Freud (1905)

Epilogus . . . Authoris (ep/i lō/gəs in ker/tē ow thôr/əs), Epilogue of a Doubtful Author. *[Latin]*

1. **mooncalf** (mŭn/kaf/), *n.* a foolish person; dolt.

from THE PERILS OF INVISIBILITY

W. S. Gilbert, drawing from
The Bab Ballads *(1869)*

Old PETER led a wretched life—
Old PETER had a furious wife;
Old PETER, too, was truly stout,
He measured several yards about.

The little fairy PICKLEKIN
One summer afternoon looked in,
And said, "Old PETER, how-de-do?
Can I do anything for you?

"I have three gifts—the first will give
Unbounded riches while you live;
The second, health where'er you be;
The third, invisibility."

"O, little fairy PICKLEKIN,"
Old PETER answered, with a grin,
"To hesitate would be absurd—
Undoubtedly I choose the third."

"'Tis yours," the fairy said; "be quite
Invisible to mortal sight
Whene'er you please. Remember me
Most kindly, pray, to MRS. P."

Old MRS. PETER overheard
Wee PICKLEKIN'S concluding word,
And, jealous of her girlhood's choice,
Said, "That was some young woman's voice!"

Old PETER let her scold and swear—
Old PETER, bless him, didn't care.

"My dear, your rage is wasted quite—
Observe, I disappear from sight!"

A well-bred fairy (so I've heard)
Is always faithful to her word:
Old PETER vanished like a shot,
But then—*his suit of clothes did not.*

For when conferred[1] the fairy slim
Invisibility on him,
She popped away on fairy wings,
Without referring to his "things."

So there remained a coat of blue,
A vest and double eyeglass too,
His tail, his shoes, his socks as well,
His pair of—no, I must not tell.

---

1. **confer** (kən fėr′), *v.* award; bestow.

Old MRS. PETER soon began
To see the failure of his plan,
And then resolved (I quote the bard)
To "hoist him with his own petard."[2]

Old PETER woke next day and dressed,
Put on his coat and shoes and vest,
His shirt and stock —*but could not find
His only pair of* —never mind!

Old PETER was a decent man,
And though he twigged[3] his lady's plan,
Yet, hearing her approaching, he
Resumed invisibility.

"Dear Mrs. P., my only joy,"
Exclaimed the horrified old boy;
"Now give them up, I beg of you—
You know what I'm referring to!"

But no; the cross old lady swore
She'd keep his—what I said before—
To make him publicly absurd;
And MRS. PETER kept her word. . . .

W. S. Gilbert (1870)

G L O R Y

"There's glory for you!" [said Humpty Dumpty.]

"I don't know what you mean by 'glory,'" Alice said.

Humpty Dumpty smiled contemptuously. "Of course you don't—till I tell you. I meant there's a 'nice knock-down argument for you!'"

"But 'glory' doesn't mean 'a nice knock-down argument,'" Alice objected.

"When I use a word," Humpty Dumpty said, in rather a scornful tone, "it means just what I choose it to mean—neither more nor less."

"The question is," said Alice, "whether you can make words mean so many different things."

"The question is," said Humpty Dumpty, "which is to be master—that's all."

Lewis Carroll (1872)

John Tenniel, drawing of Alice and Humpty Dumpty, from Through the Looking Glass *(1872)*

2. **"hoist . . . petard,"** destroy him with his own weapon, as an artilleryman blown up with his own explosives. From Shakespeare's *Hamlet* (act 3, scene 4, line 207).

3. **twig,** understand. *[slang]*

Terry Clark, Sergeant Pilot *(1990)*

from **Tom o' Bedlam**

From the hag and hungry goblin
    That into rags would rend ye,
    The spirit that stands by the naked man
    In the Book of Moons[1] defend ye,
That of your five sound senses
You never be forsaken,
Nor wander from yourselves with Tom
Abroad to beg your bacon,
        While I do sing, Any food, any feeding,
        Feeding, drink, or clothing;
        Come dame or maid, be not afraid,
        Poor Tom will injure nothing. . . .

Anonymous (about 1620)

RESPONDING

1. Which of these selections contain theatrical effects? Which contain clowning and verbal nonsense? Which contain elements of dream and fantasy?
2. Which selections seem to support the notion that life is meaningless? Did they convince you?
3. Which selection did you find the most humorous? Why?
4. List other works you are familiar with that contain similar elements. (You might find them in stories, poems, songs, movies, television, videos, comic strips, and elsewhere.) Discuss just how widespread are elements of the absurd in today's art and popular culture.

Bedlam (bed′ləm), old name for the Hospital of St. Mary of Bethlehem, an insane asylum in London. By custom, certain patients were turned out to become wandering beggars.
1. **Book of Moons,** an astrological treatise for fortune-telling.

Glossaries, Handbooks, and Indexes

Glossary of Literary Terms

Words within entries in SMALL CAPITAL LETTERS refer to other entries in the Glossary of Literary Terms.

allegory (al′ə gôr′ē), a NARRATIVE either in VERSE or prose, in which characters, action, and sometimes SETTING represent abstract concepts apart from the literal meaning of the story. The underlying meaning may have moral, social, religious, or political significance, and the characters are often PERSONIFICATIONS of abstract ideas such as charity, hope, greed, or envy. Edmund Spenser used allegory in his long poem, *The Faerie Queene,* which was dedicated to Queen Elizabeth I.

alliteration (ə lit′ə rā′ shən), the REPETITION of consonant sounds at the beginnings of words or within words, particularly in accented syllables. It can be used to reinforce meaning, to unify thought, or simply to produce a musical effect. "Grim and greedy the gruesome monster . . ." *(Beowulf,* page 8) is an example.

allusion (ə lü′zhən), a brief reference to a person, event, or place, real or fictitious, or to a work of art. Auden's "Musée des Beaux Arts" (page 808) alludes to *The Fall of Icarus,* a painting by Bruegel, and to the Greek MYTH that inspired the painting.

analogy (ə nal′ə jē), a comparison made between two objects, situations, or ideas that are somewhat alike but unlike in most respects. Frequently an unfamiliar or complex object or idea will be explained through comparison to a familiar or simpler one. For example, Blake refers to Jesus as the meek and mild "Lamb of God" (page 404).

anapest (an′ə pest), a three-syllable metrical FOOT consisting of two unaccented syllables followed by an accented syllable (‿ ‿ ′), as in *interfere.* In the following lines, anapestic feet combine with iambic feet.

> It was in/and about/the Mar-/tinmas time,/
> When the green/leaves were/a falling. . . .
> from "Bonny Barbara Allan"

anastrophe (ə nas′trə fē)
See INVERSION.

antagonist (an tag′ə nist), a character in a story or play who opposes the chief character or PROTAGONIST. In *Beowulf* (page 8) Grendel is an antagonist, as is Satan in Milton's *Paradise Lost* (page 255).

aphorism (af′ə riz′əm), a brief saying embodying a moral, such as Pope's "Know then thyself, presume not God to scan; / The proper study of mankind is Man."

apostrophe (ə pos′trə fē), a figure of speech in which an absent person, an abstract concept, or an inanimate object is directly addressed. "Milton! thou shouldst be living at this hour . . ." from Wordsworth's "London, 1802" is an example of the first; "Death, be not proud . . ." from Donne's Holy Sonnet 10 is an example of the second; and "O sylvan Wye! thou wanderer through the woods . . ." from Wordsworth's "Tintern Abbey" (page 409) is an example of the third.

archetype (är′kə tīp), an image, story pattern, or character type that recurs frequently in literature and evokes strong, often unconscious, associations in the reader. For example, the wicked witch and the enchanted prince are character types widely dispersed throughout folk tales and literature. The story of a hero who undertakes a dangerous quest, as in *Beowulf* (page 8) or *Sir Gawain and the Green Knight* (page 61), is a recurrent story pattern.

assonance (as′n əns), the REPETITION of similar vowel sounds followed by different consonant sounds in stressed syllables or words. It is often used instead of RHYME. In this line from Tennyson's "Ulysses" (page 531), the words *sleep, feed,* and *me* are assonant.

> . . . That hoard, and sleep, and feed, and know
> not me.

autobiography *See* BIOGRAPHY.

ballad, a NARRATIVE song or poem passed on in the oral tradition. It often makes use of REPETITION and DIALOGUE. An example is "Edward" (page 26). If the author of a ballad is unknown, it is called a *folk ballad;* if the author is known, it is called a *literary ballad.*

ballad stanza, a STANZA usually consisting of four alternating lines of iambic TETRAMETER and TRIMETER and rhyming the second and fourth lines.

> The wind sae cauld blew south and north,
> And blew into the floor;
> Quoth our goodman to our goodwife,
> "Gae out and bar the door."
> from "Get Up and Bar the Door" (page 28)

See IAMB.

biography, an account of a person's life. An example is Boswell's *The Life of Samuel Johnson, L L. D.* (page 361). AUTOBIOGRAPHY is the story of all or part of a person's life written by the person who lived it. Brittain's *Testament of Youth* (page 743) is an autobiography.

blank verse, unrhymed iambic PENTAMETER.

> I may/assert/Eter-/nal Prov/idence,
> And jus/tify/the ways/of God/to men.
> Milton, from Paradise Lost (page 255)

Macbeth (page 118) and "Ulysses" (page 531) are also written in blank verse.

See IAMB.

cacophony (kə kof′ə nē), a succession of harsh, discordant sounds in either poetry or prose, used to achieve a specific effect. Note the harshness of sound and difficulty of articulation in these lines:

> Light thickens, and the crow
> Makes wing to the rooky wood. . . .
> Shakespeare, from Macbeth (page 118)

caesura (si zhùr′ə), a pause in a line of VERSE, usually near the middle. It most often reflects the sense of the line and is frequently greater than a normal pause. It is used to add variety to regular METER and therefore to add emphasis to certain words. A caesura can be indicated by punctuation, the grammatical construction of a sentence, or the placement of lines on a page. For purposes of study, the mark indicating a caesura is two short, vertical lines.

> Born but to die, ‖ and reasoning but to err:
> Alike in ignorance, ‖ his reason such,
> Whether he thinks too little, ‖ or too much . . .
> Pope, from An Essay on Man

The caesura is a particularly important device in Anglo-Saxon poetry.

caricature (kar′ə kə chùr), exaggeration of prominent features of appearance or character.

carpe diem (kär′pe dē′əm), Latin for "seize the day," or enjoy life's pleasures while you are able. The term is applied to a THEME frequently found in LYRIC poetry, as in Herrick's "To the Virgins, to Make Much of Time" (page 233).

Cavalier poetry, a type of LYRIC poetry of the late Renaissance period, influenced by poet Ben Jonson and the Elizabethan court poets, and consisting mostly of love poems. Supporters of Charles I (1625–1649) were called Cavaliers and included Robert Herrick (page 233).

characterization, the methods an author uses to develop a character in a literary work. A character's physical traits and personality may be described, as are those of John Thomas in Lawrence's "Tickets, Please" (page 758). A character's speech and behavior may be described, as are those of the Beast in "The Courting of Mr. Lyon" (page 933). The thoughts and feelings of a character or the reactions of other characters to an individual may be shown, as in Greene's "A Shocking Accident" (page 926). Any or all of these methods may be used in the same work.

classicism (klas′ə siz′əm), a style of literature characterized by attention to form and influenced by the classical writers of Greece and Rome. Many authors have been influenced by classicism, and it flourished especially during the Age of Reason.

climax, the decisive point in a story or play when the action changes course and begins to resolve itself. In *Macbeth,* the banquet scene in act 3 (page 148) when the ghost of Banquo appears to Macbeth is often regarded as the climax. Not every story or play has this kind of dramatic climax. Sometimes a character may simply resolve a problem in his or her mind. At times there is no resolution of the PLOT; the climax then comes when a character realizes that a resolution is impossible.

See also PLOT.

comedy, a play written primarily to amuse. In addition to arousing laughter, comic writing often appeals to the intellect. Thus the comic mode has often been used to "instruct" the audience about the follies of certain social conventions and human foibles, as in Shaw's *Pygmalion* (page 662). When used in this way, the comedy tends toward SATIRE.

comic relief, an amusing episode in a serious or tragic literary work, especially a drama, that is introduced to relieve tension. The drunken porter's scene in *Macbeth,* act 2, scene 3 is an example of comic relief.

conceit, an elaborate and surprising figure of speech comparing two very dissimilar things. It usually involves intellectual cleverness and ingenuity. In the last three STANZAS of "A Valediction: Forbidding Mourning" (page 227), Donne compares his soul and that of his love to the two legs or branches of a draftsman's compass used to make a circle. The previously unseen likeness as developed by the poet helps us to understand the subject described (the relationship of the lovers' souls) more clearly.

conflict, the struggle between two opposing forces. The four basic kinds of conflict are these: 1. a person against another person or ANTAGONIST, as in *Beowulf* (page 8); 2. a person against nature; 3. a person against society, as in Desai's "Studies in the Park" (page 833); and 4. two elements within a person struggling for mastery, as in Joyce's "Eveline" (page 790).

connotation, the emotional associations surrounding a word, as opposed to the word's literal meaning or DENOTATION. Some connotations are fairly universal, others quite personal. Many of the words in Shakespeare's "Sonnet 18" (page 111) suggest associations that cluster around the idea of summer.

consonance (kon′sə nəns), the repetition of consonant sounds that are preceded by different vowel sounds:

> For*l*orn! the very word is like a be*ll*
> To to*ll* me back from thee to my so*l*e se*l*f!
>> Keats, from "Ode to a Nightingale" (page 426)

Consonance (also called SLANT RHYME) is an effective device for linking sound, MOOD, and meaning. In the lines above, the *l* sounds reinforce the melancholy mood.

couplet, a pair of rhyming lines with identical METER:

> True wit is Nature to advantage dressed,
> What oft was thought, but ne'er so well expressed.
>> Pope, from *An Essay on Criticism* (page 325)

dactyl (dak′tl), a three-syllable metrical FOOT consisting of an accented syllable followed by two unaccented syllables (′‿‿) as in *settlement.* The following line is basically in dactylic HEXAMETER:

> Loosing his/arms from her/waist he flew/upward, a-/waiting the/sea beast.
>> Charles Kingsley, from *Andromeda*

denotation the strict, literal meaning of a word.

> *See also* CONNOTATION.

denouement (dā′nü mäN′), the resolution of the PLOT. The word is derived from a French word meaning "to untie."

dialect, a form of speech characteristic of a particular region or class, differing from the standard language in pronunciation, vocabulary, and grammatical form. Burns's poems (pages 450–452) are written in Scottish dialect. In Shaw's *Pygmalion* (page 662), Eliza Doolittle, as a flower girl, speaks in the cockney dialect characteristic of a certain part of London.

dialogue, conversation between two or more people in a literary work. Dialogue can help develop CHARACTERIZATION of those speaking and those spoken about, create MOOD, advance PLOT, and develop THEME.

diary, a record of daily happenings written by a person for his or her own use. The diarist is moved by a need to record daily routine and confess innermost thoughts. The diary makes up in immediacy and frankness what it lacks in artistic shape and coherence. An example is *The Diary* of Pepys (page 340).

> *See also* JOURNAL.

diction, the author's choice of words and phrases in a literary work. This choice involves both the CONNOTATION and DENOTATION of a word as well as levels of usage. For example, the diction of the characters in Shaw's *Pygmalion* (page 662) indicates their education, background, and social standing.

drama, a literary work in verse or prose, written to be acted, that tells a story through the speech and actions of the characters. A drama may be a TRAGEDY, such as *Macbeth* (page 118), or a COMEDY, such as *Pygmalion* (page 662).

dramatic convention, any of several devices that the audience accepts as reality in a dramatic work. For instance, the audience accepts that an interval between acts may represent hours, days, weeks, months, or years; that a bare stage may be a meadow or an inner room; or that audible dialogue is supposed to represent whispered conversation.

dramatic monologue (mon′l ôg), a LYRIC poem in which the speaker addresses someone whose replies are not recorded. Sometimes the one addressed seems to be present, sometimes not. Examples are Robert Browning's "Porphyria's Lover" (page 539) and "My Last Duchess" (page 542).

elegy (el′ə gē), a solemn, reflective poem, usually about death, or about someone who has died, written in a formal style.

end rhyme, the rhyming of words at the ends of lines of poetry, as in Housman's "Loveliest of Trees" (page 601).

end-stopped line, a line of poetry that contains a complete thought, thus necessitating the use of a semicolon, colon, or period at the end:

> Great lord of all things, yet a prey to all;

Sole judge of truth, in endless error hurled:
The glory, jest, and riddle of the world!
                    Pope, from *An Essay on Man*

See also RUN-ON LINE.

epic, a long NARRATIVE poem (originally handed down in oral tradition—later a literary form) dealing with great heroes and adventures; having a national, world-wide, or cosmic setting; involving supernatural forces; and written in a deliberately ceremonial STYLE. Examples are *Beowulf* (page 8) and Milton's *Paradise Lost* (page 255).

epigram, any short, witty VERSE or saying, often ending with a wry twist:
       'Tis with our judgments as our watches; none
       Go just alike, yet each believes his own.
                    Pope, from *An Essay on Criticism* (page 325)
Compare with MAXIM *and* PROVERB.

epigraph, a motto or quotation at the beginning of a book, poem, or chapter, often indicating the THEME. An example is found at the beginning of Eliot's "The Hollow Men" (page 769).

epiphany (i pif′ə nē), a moment of enlightenment in which the underlying truth, essential nature, or meaning of something is suddenly made clear. Each of James Joyce's stories builds to an epiphany. In "Eveline" (page 790), it is the moment when she realizes she cannot go away with Frank.

epitaph (ep′ə taf), a brief statement commemorating a dead person, often inscribed on a tombstone. Malory's "Day of Destiny" (page 79) concludes with King Arthur's epitaph.

epithet (ep′ə thet), a descriptive expression, usually mentioning a quality or attribute of the person or thing being described. In *Beowulf* (page 8) the epithet *Spear-Danes* is used for the Danes. Often the epithet *Lion-Hearted* is applied to King Richard I (1157–1199).

essay, a brief composition that presents a personal viewpoint. An essay may present a viewpoint through formal analysis and argument, as in Defoe's "The Education of Women" (page 306), or it may be more informal in style, as in Orwell's "Shooting an Elephant" (page 860).

exposition, the beginning of a work of fiction, particularly a play, in which the author sets the amosphere and TONE, explains the SETTING, introduces the characters, and provides the reader with any other information needed in order to understand the PLOT.

extended metaphor, a comparison that is developed at great length, often through a whole work or a great part of it. It is common in poetry but is used in prose as well. Sir Walter Raleigh develops an extended metaphor comparing life to a play in his poem "What Is Our Life?" the first four lines of which appear here:
       What is our life? a play of passion;
       Our mirth, the music of division,
       Our mothers' wombs the tiring-houses be
       Where we are dressed for this short comedy.
See also METAPHOR.

fable, a brief TALE in which the characters are often animals, told to point out a moral truth.

falling action, the RESOLUTION of a dramatic PLOT, which takes place after the CLIMAX.

fantasy, a work that takes place in an unreal world, concerns incredible characters, or employs fictional scientific principles, as in "A Mad Tea Party" (page 547).
See also SCIENCE FICTION.

fiction, a type of literature drawn from the imagination of the author that tells about imaginary people and happenings. NOVELS and SHORT STORIES are fiction.

figurative language, language used in a nonliteral way to express a suitable relationship between essentially unlike things in order to furnish new effects or fresh insights. The more common figures of speech are SIMILE, METAPHOR, PERSONIFICATION, HYPERBOLE, and SYNECDOCHE.

flashback, interruption of a NARRATIVE to show an episode that happened before that particular point in the story.

foil, a character whose traits are the opposite of those of another character, and who thus points up the strengths or weaknesses of the other character. Henry Higgins and Liza Doolittle are foils in Shaw's *Pygmalion* (page 662).

folk literature, a type of early literature that was passed orally from generation to generation, and only written down after centuries. The authorship of folk literature is unknown. Folk literature includes MYTHS, FABLES, fairy tales, EPICS, and LEGENDS. Examples are *Beowulf* (page 8) and the Folk Ballads (pages 25–28).

foot, a group of syllables in VERSE usually consisting of one accented syllable and one or more unaccented syllables. A foot may occasionally, for variety, have two accented syllables (a SPONDEE) or two unaccented syllables. In the following lines the feet are separated by slanted lines.

> Come live/with me/and be/my Love,
> And we/will all/the plea-/sures prove. . . .
>
> > Marlowe, from "The Passionate
> > Shepherd to His Love"

The most common line lengths are five feet (PENTAMETER), four feet (TETRAMETER), and three feet (TRIMETER). The lines quoted above are iambic tetrameter.

See also ANAPEST, DACTYL, IAMB *and* TROCHEE.

foreshadowing, a hint given to the reader of what is to come.

frame, a NARRATIVE device presenting a story or group of stories within the frame of a larger narrative. In Chaucer's *The Canterbury Tales* (page 47), the pilgrimage is the frame unifying and providing continuity for the stories told by the pilgrims.

free verse, a type of poetry that differs from conventional VERSE forms in being "free" from a fixed pattern of METER and RHYME, but using RHYTHM and other poetic devices. An example is Eliot's "The Hollow Men" (page 769).

gothic novel, a NOVEL written in a STYLE characterized by mystery, horror, and the supernatural, and usually having a medieval or other period SETTING. An example is Mary Shelly's *Frankenstein* (page 492).

heroic couplet, a pair of rhymed VERSE lines in iambic PENTAMETER:

> All human things are subject to decay,
> And when fate summons, monarchs must obey.
>
> > Dryden, from *Mac Flecknoe*

hexameter (hek sam′ə tər), a metrical line of six feet.

> How man-/y weep-/ing eyes/I made/to pine/with woe . . .
>
> > Elizabeth I, "When I was Fair and Young"

humor, in literature, writing whose purpose is to amuse or to evoke laughter. Humorous writing can be sympathetic to human nature or satirical. Some forms of humor are IRONY, SATIRE, PARODY, and CARICATURE.

hyperbole (hī pėr′bə lē) a figure of speech involving great exaggeration. The effect may be serious or comic.

> If thou be'st born to strange sights,
> Things invisible to see,
> Ride ten thousand days and nights,
> Till age snow white hairs on thee. . . .
>
> > Donne, from "Song" (page 226)

iamb (ī′amb), a two-syllable metrical FOOT consisting of an unaccented syllable followed by an accented syllable (‿ ′), as in *until.* The following line is in iambic PENTAMETER:

> For God's/sake, hold/your tongue,/and let/me love. . . .
>
> > Donne, from "The Canonization"

idiom, an expression whose meaning cannot be understood from the ordinary meanings of the words in it. For example, "to give a leg up," is to provide someone assistance or encouragement; "to knuckle down" means to apply oneself or work hard.

imagery, the sensory details that provide vividness in a literary work and tend to arouse emotions or feelings in a reader that abstract language does not. Carter's "The Courtship of Mr. Lyon" (page 933) contains many sensory details.

incremental repetition, a form of REPETITION in which successive STANZAS advance the story or reveal a situation by changes in a single phrase or line. Often a question and answer form is used. An example is the ballad "Edward" (page 26).

inference, a reasonable conclusion about the behavior of a character or the meaning of an event, drawn from the limited information presented by the author. In Browning's "My Last Duchess" (page 542), the reader can infer a great deal about the character of the speaker, the Duke, from what he says.

in medias res (in mä′dē äs räs′), Latin for "in the middle of things." In a traditional EPIC the opening scene often begins in the middle of the action. Milton's *Paradise Lost* (page 255) opens with Satan and his angels already defeated and in Hell; later in the poem the story of the battle between Satan and the forces of Heaven, which led to this defeat, is told. This device may be used in any NARRATIVE form.

interior monologue, a technique used by writers to present the STREAM OF CONSCIOUSNESS of a fictional character, either directly by presenting what is passing through the character's mind or indirectly by the author's selection of and comments upon the character's thoughts. Joyce's

"Eveline" (page 790) consists largely of interior monologue.

internal rhyme, the rhyming of words or accented syllables within a line that may or may not have a RHYME at the end as well.

inversion, reversal of the usual order of the parts of a sentence, primarily for emphasis or to achieve a certain RHYTHM or RHYME. In the example that follows, lines 1, 4, and 5 contain inverted order.

> In Seville was he born, a pleasant city,
>> Famous for oranges and women—he
> Who has not seen it will be much to pity,
>> So says the proverb—and I quite agree;
> Of all the Spanish towns is none more pretty.
>> Byron, from *Don Juan*

invocation the call on a deity or muse (classical goddess who inspired a poet) for help and inspiration. It is found at the beginning of traditional EPIC poems. In *Paradise Lost* (page 255) Milton invokes the "Heavenly Muse" instead of one of the traditional muses of poetry.

irony, the term used to describe a contrast between what appears to be and what really is. In *verbal irony,* the intended meaning of a statement or work is different from (often the opposite of) what the statement or work literally says, as in Swift's "A Modest Proposal" (page 296). *Understatement,* in which an idea is expressed less emphatically than it might be, is a form of verbal irony often used for humorous or cutting effect. For example, Johnson's remark in his "Letter to Chesterfield" (page 357): "To be so distinguished is an honor which, being very little accustomed to favors from the great, I know not well how to receive." *Irony of situation* refers to an occurrence that is contrary to what is expected or intended, as in Hardy's "Ah, Are You Digging on My Grave?" (page 577). *Dramatic irony* refers to a situation in which events or facts not known to a character on stage or in a fictional work are known to another character and the audience or reader. In Pope's *The Rape of the Lock* (page 314), events known to the sylph Ariel and to the reader are unknown to Belinda.

journal, a formal record of a person's daily experiences. It is less intimate or personal than a DIARY and more chronological than an AUTOBIOGRAPHY.

kenning, a metaphorical compound word used as a poetic device. In *Beowulf* (page 8) there are many examples of kennings: the king is the "ring-giver," the rough sea is the "whale-road," and the calm sea is the "swan-road."

legend, a story handed down from the past, often associated with some period in the history of a people. A legend differs from a MYTH in having some historical truth and often less of the supernatural. Malory's *Morte Darthur* (page 79) is based on legends of King Arthur and the Knights of the Round Table.

literary ballad *See* BALLAD.

lyric, a poem, usually short, that expresses some basic emotion or state of mind. It usually creates a single impression and is highly personal. It may be rhymed or unrhymed. A SONNET is a lyric poem. Other examples of lyrics are Burns's "A Red, Red Rose" (page 452) and most of the shorter poems of the Romantics.

magic realism, a fictional literary work that combines elements of dreams, magic, myths, and fairy tales, along with realistic elements. Carter's "The Courtship of Mr. Lyon" (page 933) can be described as magic realism.

maxim, a brief saying embodying a moral, such as "Look before you leap."

memoir (mem′wär), a form of AUTOBIOGRAPHY that is more concerned with personalities, events, and actions of public importance than with the private life of the writer. Orwell's "Shooting an Elephant" (page 860) is an example of memoir in the form of an essay.

metaphor, a figure of speech that makes a comparison, without *like* or *as,* between two basically unlike things that have something in common. This comparison may be stated (She was a stone) or implied (Her stony silence filled the room). In "Meditation 17" (page 228) Donne compares the individual to a chapter in a book and, later, to a piece of a continent.
See also SIMILE *and* FIGURATIVE LANGUAGE.

metaphysical poetry, poetry exhibiting a highly intellectual style that is witty, subtle, and sometimes fantastic, particularly in the use of CONCEITS. See especially the poems of Donne (pages 226–227).

meter, the pattern of stressed and unstressed syllables in POETRY. *See also* RHYTHM and FOOT.

metonymy a figure of speech in which a specific word naming an object is substituted for another word with which it is closely associated. An example is in Genesis: "In the sweat of thy face shalt thou eat bread." Here, *sweat* is used to represent hard physical labor.

mock epic, a SATIRE using the form and style of an EPIC poem to treat a trivial incident. Pope's *The Rape of the Lock* (page 314) is a mock epic.

monologue *See* SOLILOQUY *and* DRAMATIC MONOLOGUE.

mood, the overall atmosphere or prevailing emotional aura of a work. Coleridge's "Kubla Khan" (page 417) might be described as having a hypnotic, dreamlike mood or atmosphere. *See* TONE for a comparison.

moral, the lesson or inner meaning to be learned from a FABLE, TALE, or other story. The moral of "The Pardoner's Tale" in *The Canterbury Tales* (page 48), as stated by the Pardoner, is "Avarice is the root of all evil."

motif a character, incident, idea, or object that appears over and over in various works or in various parts of the same work. In Shakespeare's SONNETS (pages 111–112) the effect of time is a recurrent motif.

motivation, the process of presenting a convincing cause for the actions of a character in a dramatic or fictional work in order to justify those actions. Motivation usually involves a combination of external events and the character's psychological traits.

myth, a traditional story connected with the religion of a people, usually attempting to account for something in nature. A myth has less historical background than a LEGEND. Milton's *Paradise Lost* (page 255) has mythic elements in its attempts to interpret aspects of the universe.

narrative, a story or account of an event or a series of events. It may be told either in POETRY or in prose, and it may be either fictional or true.

narrative poetry, a poem that tells a story or recounts a series of events. It may be either long or short. EPICS and BALLADS are types of narrative poetry.

narrator, the teller of a story. The teller may be a character in the story, as in Mary Shelley's *Frankenstein* (page 492); an anonymous voice outside the story, as in Greene's "A Shocking Accident" (page 926); or the author, as in Brittain's *Testament of Youth* (page 776). A narrator's attitude toward his or her subject is capable of much variation; it can range from one of indifference to one of extreme conviction and feeling.

See also PERSONA *and* POINT OF VIEW.

naturalism, a literary movement in the late nineteenth and early twentieth century characterized by writing that depicts events as rigidly determined by the forces of heredity and environment. The world described tends to be bleak. There are elements of naturalism in the work of Thomas Hardy.

neoclassicism, writing of a later period that shows the influence of the Greek and Roman classics. The term is often applied to English literature of the eighteenth century.

See also CLASSICISM.

nonfiction, any writing that is not FICTION; any type of prose that deals with real people and happenings. BIOGRAPHY and history are types of nonfiction. An example is the excerpt from Boswell's *The Life of Samuel Johnson, LL. D.* (page 401).

novel, a long work of NARRATIVE prose fiction dealing with characters, situations, and SETTINGS that imitate those of real life. Among the authors in this text who have written novels are Thomas Hardy, Joseph Conrad, James Joyce, Virginia Woolf, H. G. Wells, Anita Desai, Graham Greene, and Angela Carter.

ode, a long LYRIC poem, formal in STYLE and complex in form, often written in commemoration or celebration of a special quality, object, or occasion. Examples are Shelley's "Ode to the West Wind" (page 469) and Keats's "Ode to a Nightingale" (page 426).

onomatopoeia (on/ə mat/ə pē/ə), a word or words used in such a way that the sound imitates the thing spoken of. Some single words in which sound suggests meaning are *hiss, smack, buzz, and hum.* An example in which sound echoes sense throughout the whole phrase is "The murmurous haunt of flies on summer eves," from Keats's "Ode to a Nightingale"(page 426).

parable, a brief fictional work that concretely illustrates an abstract idea or teaches some lesson or truth. It differs from a FABLE in that its characters are generally people rather than animals, and it differs from an ALLEGORY in that its characters do not necessarily represent abstract qualities.

paradox, a statement, often metaphorical, that seems to be self-contradictory but that has valid meaning, as in "The child is father of the Man" from Wordsworth's poem "My Heart Leaps Up" (page 413). Woolf describes a paradoxical woman in "Shakespeare's Sister" (page 814).

parallelism, the use of phrases or sentences that are similar in structure. Churchill's words in his Blood, Toil, Tears, and Sweat speech (page 869) are an example of parallelism: "You ask, What is our aim? I can answer in one word: Victory—victory at all costs, victory in spite of all terror, victory, however long and hard the road may be. . . ."

parody, a humorous imitation of serious writing. It follows the form of the original, but often changes the sense to ridicule the writer's STYLE. Eliot's "The Hollow Men" (page 769) has a parody of the children's rhyme "Here we go round the mulberry bush."

See also SATIRE.

pastoral, a conventional form of LYRIC poetry presenting an idealized picture of rural life.

pentameter (pen tam′ə ter), a metrical line of five feet.

> Shall I/compare/thee to/a sum-/mer's day?
> Thou art/more love-/ly and/more tem-/perate.
> Shakespeare, from Sonnet 18 (page 111)

persona (pər sō′nə), the mask or voice of the author or the author's creation in a particular work. Tennyson is the author of "Ulysses" (page 531), but the persona, in this case the SPEAKER, is Ulysses, through whom Tennyson speaks. In "A Shocking Accident" (page 926), Graham Greene has assumed a voice or persona—detached, witty, ironic—in telling the story.

See also NARRATOR.

personification (pər son′ə fə kā′shən), the representation of abstractions, ideas, animals, or inanimate objects as human beings by endowing them with human qualities. In Shelley's "Ode to the West Wind" (page 469), the Mediterranean is personified:

> Thou who didst waken from his summer dreams
> The blue Mediterranean, where he lay,
> Lulled by the coil of his crystàlline streams. . . .

Personification is one kind of FIGURATIVE LANGUAGE.

play See DRAMA.

plot, a series of happenings in a literary work. The term is used to refer to the action as it is organized around a CONFLICT and builds through complication to a CLIMAX followed by a DENOUEMENT or RESOLUTION. (See the plot diagram on page 116.)

poetry, a type of literature that creates an emotional response by the imaginative use of words patterned to produce a desired effect through RHYTHM, sound, and meaning. Poetry may be RHYMED or unrhymed. Among the many forms of poetry are the EPIC, ODE, LYRIC, SONNET, BALLAD, and ELEGY.

point of view, the vantage point from which an author presents the actions and characters of a story. The story may be related by a character (the *first-person* point of view), or the story may be told by a NARRATOR who does not participate in the action (the *third-person* point of view). Further, the third-person narrator may be *omniscient* (om nish′ənt)—able to see into the minds of all characters, as in Lawrence's "Tickets, Please" (page 758). Or the third-person narrator may be *limited*—confined to a single character's perceptions, as in Joyce's "Eveline" (page 790). An author who describes only what can be seen, like a newspaper reporter, is said to use an *objective* or *dramatic* point of view.

prologue, a section preceding the main body of a work and serving as an introduction. An example is the *Prologue to The Canterbury Tales* (page 47).

protagonist (prō tag′ənist), the leading character in a literary work.

See also ANTAGONIST.

proverb, a short, wise saying, often handed down from the past, that expresses a truth or shrewd observation about life. "Haste makes waste" is an example. There are many proverbs in the Bible.

psalm, a song or poem in praise of God. The term is most often applied to the songs or hymns in the Book of Psalms in the Bible. An example is the Twenty-third Psalm on page 272.

pun, a play on words; a humorous use of a word where it can have two different meanings (*pitcher / pitcher*) or two or more words with the same or nearly the same sound but with different meanings (*night / knight*).

quatrain, a verse STANZA of four lines. This stanza may take many forms, according to line lengths and RHYME patterns. Herrick's poem "To the Virgins, to Make Much of Time" (page 233) contains quatrains.

rationalism, a philosophy that emphasizes the role of reason rather than of sensory experience and faith in answering basic questions of human existence. It was most influential during the Age of Reason (1660–1780) and influenced such writers of that period as Swift and Pope.

realism, a way of representing life that emphasizes ordinary people in everyday experiences. The excerpt from Emecheta's *In the Ditch* (page 881) is an example of realism.

refrain, the REPETITION of one or more lines in each STANZA of a poem. The ballad "Edward" (page 26) makes use of refrain.

repetition, a poetic device in which a sound, word, or phrase is repeated for style and emphasis, as in Thomas's "Do Not Go Gentle into That Good Night" (page 823).

resolution, events that follow the climax of a PLOT in which the complications of the plot are resolved.

rhyme, the exact repetition of sounds in at least the final accented syllables of two or more words:

Hither the heroes and the nymphs *resort*,
To taste awhile the pleasures of a *court*.
Pope, from *The Rape of the Lock* (page 314)

rhyme scheme, any pattern of end rhyme in a STANZA. For purposes of study, the pattern is labeled as shown below, with the first rhyme and all the words rhyming with it labeled *a*, the second rhyme and all the words rhyming with it labeled *b*, and so on.

Queen and huntress, chaste and fair,   *a*
Now the sun is laid to sleep,   *b*
Seated in thy silver chair,   *a*
State in wonted manner keep;   *b*
Hesperus entreats thy light,   *c*
Goddess excellently bright.   *c*
Jonson, from "To Cynthia"

rhythm, the arrangement of stressed and unstressed sounds into patterns in speech or writing. Rhythm, or METER, may be regular, or it may vary within a line or work. The four most common meters are IAMB ($\smile$ ′), TROCHEE (′ $\smile$), ANAPEST ($\smile\smile$ ′), and DACTYL (′ $\smile\smile$).

rising action, the part of a dramatic PLOT that leads up to the CLIMAX. In rising action, the complication caused by the CONFLICT of opposing forces is developed.

romance, a long NARRATIVE in poetry or prose that originated in the medieval period. Its main elements are adventure, love, and magic. There are elements of the romance in the excerpts from *Morte Darthur* (page 79) and *Sir Gawain and the Green Knight* (page 61).

romanticism, a type of literature that, unlike REALISM, tends to portray the uncommon. The material selected tends to deal with extraordinary people in unusual settings having unusual experiences. In romantic literature there is often a stress on the past and an emphasis on nature. Examples are Coleridge's "Kubla Khan" (page 417) and Mary Shelley's *Frankenstein* (page 492). There are many other examples in Unit 5.

run-on line, a line in which the thought continues beyond the end of the poetic line. For example, there should be no pause after *thine* in the first line that follows:

For sure our souls were near allied, and thine
Cast in the same poetic mold with mine.
Dryden, from "To the Memory of Mr. Oldham"

satire, the technique that employs wit to ridicule a subject, usually some social institution or human foible, with the intention of inspiring reform. IRONY and sarcasm are often used in writing satire, and PARODY is closely related. Swift's "A Modest Proposal" (page 296), and Shaw's *Pygmalion* (page 662) provide examples of satire.

scansion (skan′shən), the result of *scanning*, or marking off lines of POETRY into feet and indicating the stressed and unstressed syllables.

See RHYTHM *and* FOOT.

science fiction, a fictional literary work that uses scientific and technological facts and hypotheses as a basis for stories about such subjects as extraterrestrial beings, adventures in the future or on other planets, and travel through time. Wells's "The Star" (page 612) is science fiction.

sermon, a written version of a speech on some aspect of religion, morality, conduct, or the like, meant to be delivered in a church. Donne wrote many sermons.

setting, the time (both time of day and period in history) and place in which the action of a NARRA-

TIVE occurs. The setting may be suggested through DIALOGUE and action, or it may be described by the NARRATOR or one of the characters. Setting contributes strongly to the MOOD, atmosphere, and plausibility of a work. For example, the setting of Conrad's "The Lagoon" (page 586) contributes greatly to the atmosphere of the story.

short story, a short prose NARRATIVE that is carefully crafted and usually tightly constructed. The short story form developed in the 1800s.

simile (sim′ə lē), a figure of speech involving a direct comparison, using *like* or *as,* between two basically unlike things that have something in common.

> And so I dare to hope,
> Though changed, no doubt, from what I was when first
> I came among these hills, when like a roe
> I bounded o'er the mountains. . . .
>> Wordsworth, from "Lines Composed a Few Miles Above Tintern Abbey" (page 409)

In this example the narrator compares himself when a young man to a small, agile deer.

slant rhyme (also called CONSONANCE), rhyme in which the vowel sounds are not quite identical, as in the first and third lines that follow:

> And I untightened next the *tress*
> About her neck; her cheek once more
> Blushed bright beneath my burning *kiss* . . .
>> Browning, from "Porphyria's Lover" (page 539)

soliloquy (sə lil′ə kwē), a DRAMATIC CONVENTION that allows a character alone on stage to speak his or her thoughts aloud. If someone else is on stage but cannot hear the character's words, the soliloquy becomes an *aside.*

> *Compare with* DRAMATIC MONOLOGUE.

sonnet, a LYRIC poem with a traditional form of fourteen iambic PENTAMETER lines. Sonnets fall into two groups, according to their RHYME SCHEMES. The *Italian* or *Petrarchan* sonnet, named after the Italian poet Petrarch, is usually rhymed *abbaabba cdecde* (with variations permitted in the *cdecde* rhyme scheme). It forms basically a two-part poem of eight lines *(octave)* and six lines *(sestet)* respectively. These two parts are played off against each other in a great variety of ways. The *English* or *Shakespearean* sonnet is usually rhymed *abab cdcd efef gg,* presenting a four-part structure in which an idea or theme is developed in three QUATRAINS and then brought to a conclusion in the COUPLET.

sound devices, the choice and arrangement of words to please the ear and suit meaning. RHYME, RHYTHM, ASSONANCE, CONSONANCE, ONOMATOPOEIA, and ALLITERATION are examples of sound devices.

speaker, the person or PERSONA who is speaking in a poem, as in Elizabeth Barrett Browning's "Sonnet 43" (page 539).

spondee, a metrical FOOT of two accented syllables (′′), as in *pipe dream.* It serves occasionally as a substitute to vary the meter, as in the last foot of the second line that follows:

> The sedge/has with-/ered from/the lake
> And no/birds sing!
>> Keats, from "La Belle Dame Sans Merci" (page 423)

sprung rhythm, a metrical form in which the accented or stressed syllables are *scanned* without regard to the number of unstressed syllables in a FOOT. A foot may have from one to four syllables, with the accent always on the first syllable. The term was invented and the technique developed by Gerard Manley Hopkins. The following line is scanned according to Hopkins's theory:

> And for all/this,/nature is/never/spent. . . .
>> Hopkins, from "God's Grandeur"

The first foot has three syllables, the second foot one, the third foot three, the fourth foot two, and the fifth foot one, with the accent on the first syllable of each foot.

stage directions, directions given by the author of a play to indicate the action, costumes, SETTING, arrangement of the stage, and so on. For examples of stage directions, see Shaw's *Pygmalion* (page 662), where they are printed in italic type.

stanza, a group of lines that are set off and form a division in a poem, sometimes linked with other stanzas by RHYME.

stereotype (ster′ē ə tīp′), a conventional character, PLOT, or SETTING that possesses little or no individuality but that may be used for a purpose. Such situations, characters, or settings are usually predictable. Orwell, in "Shooting an Elephant" (page 860), depicts the Burmese somewhat stereotypically.

stream of consciousness, the recording or re-creation of a character's flow of thought. Raw images, perceptions, and memories come and go in seemingly random, but actually controlled, fashion, much as they do in people's minds. James Joyce and Virginia Woolf often depicted stream of consciousness in their writings.

style, the distinctive handling of language by an author. It involves the specific choices made with regard to DICTION, syntax, FIGURATIVE LANGUAGE, and so on. For a comparison of two different styles, see Coleridge's "Kubla Khan" (page 417) and Pope's *The Rape of the Lock* (page 314).

symbol, something relatively concrete, such as an object, action, character, or scene, that signifies something relatively abstract, such as a concept or idea. In Yeats's "Sailing to Byzantium" (page 608), the city of Byzantium is a symbol for the unity of all aspects of life—religious, aesthetic, practical, and intellectual.

synecdoche (si nek′də kē), a figure of speech in which a part stands for the whole, as in "hired *hands.*" *Hands* (the part) stands for the whole (those who do manual labor; those who work with their hands). The term also refers to a figurative expression in which the whole stands for a part, as in "call the *law.*" *Law* (the whole) represents the police (a part of the whole system of law).

tale, a simple prose or verse NARRATIVE, either true or fictitious, such as those told by Chaucer's pilgrims in *The Canterbury Tales* (page 47).

terza rima (ter′tsä rē′mä), a VERSE form with a three-line STANZA rhyming *aba bcb cdc,* and so on.

> O wild West Wind, thou breath of Autumn's being,
> Thou, from whose unseen presence the leaves
>   dead
> Are driven, like ghosts from an enchanter fleeing,
>
> Yellow, and black, and pale, and hectic red,
> Pestilence-stricken multitudes: O thou,
> Who chariotest to their dark wintry bed. . . .
> > Shelley, from "Ode to the West Wind" (page 469)

tetrameter (te tram′ə ter), a metrical line of four feet.

> Had we/but world/enough/and time . . . .
> > Marvell, "To His Coy Mistress" (page 234)

theme, the underlying meaning of a literary work. A theme may be directly stated but more often is implied. The topic of Wilfred Owen's poem "Disabled" (page 739) is stated in the title. The theme concerns the poignant thoughts of a veteran and the bitter waste of a life once full of promise.

tone, the author's attitude, either stated or implied, toward his or her subject matter and toward the audience. Swift's tone in "A Modest Proposal" (page 296) is ironic. He pretends to be setting forth serious suggestions for alleviating the poverty of the Irish, all the while knowing that his proposal will shock even the most hardened politician or clergyman.

tragedy, dramatic or NARRATIVE writing in which the main character suffers disaster after a serious and significant struggle, but faces his or her downfall in such a way as to attain heroic stature. Shakespeare's *Macbeth* (page 118) is a tragedy.

trimeter (trim′ə ter), a metrical line of three feet.

> Down to/a sun-/less sea.
> > Coleridge, from "Kubla Khan" (page 417)

trochee (trō′kē) (′‿), a metrical FOOT made up of one accented syllable followed by an unaccented syllable, as in *answer:*

> Double,/double,/toil and/trouble;
> Fire/burn and/caldron/bubble.
> > Shakespeare, from *Macbeth* (page 118)

verse, in its most general sense, a synonym for POETRY. *Verse* may also be used to refer to poetry carefully composed as to RHYTHM and RHYME XSCHEME, but of inferior literary value.

villanelle (vil′ə nel′), a poetic form normally consisting of five three-line STANZAS and a final QUATRAIN, rhyming *aba aba aba aba aba abaa,* and with lines 1 and 3 repeating alternately as REFRAINS throughout. An example is Thomas's "Do Not Go Gentle into That Good Night" (page 823).

Glossary of Vocabulary Words

a	hat	ī	ice	ü	rule
ā	age	o	hot	ch	child
ä	far	ō	open	ng	long
â	care	ô	order, all	sh	she
e	let	oi	oil	th	thin
ē	equal	ou	out	ᴛʜ	then
ė	term	u	cup	zh	measure
i	it	u̇	put		

ə { a in about / e in taken / i in pencil / o in lemon / u in circus

A

abashed (ə basht′), *adj.* ashamed.

abate (ə bāt′), *v.* decrease; reduce.

abject (ab′jekt), *adj.* miserable.

abjure (ab jùr′), *v.* take back.

abode (ə bōd′), *n.* place of residence; house or home.

absolution (ab′sə lü′shən), *n.* a declaration that frees a person from guilt or punishment for sin.

abstemious (ab stē′mē əs), *adj.* moderate.

abysmal (ə biz′məl), *adj.* bottomless.

adversary (ad′vər ser′ē), *n.* opponent; enemy.

affliction (ə flik′shən), *n.* pain; misery.

agape (ə gāp′), *adj.* openmouthed with wonder.

agog (ə gog′), *adj.* full of expectation or excitement; eager.

amenable (ə mē′nə bəl), *adj.* responsive; agreeable.

anarchy (an′ər kē), *n.* absence of a system of government and law.

anomaly (ə nom′ə lē), *n.* something deviating from the rule; something abnormal.

anonymity (an′ə nim′ə tē), *n.* condition of being unknown.

apparition (ap′ə rish′ən), *n.* something strange, remarkable, or unexpected.

appease (ə pēz′), *v.* put an end to.

apprehension (ap′ri hen′shən), *n.* expectation of misfortune; dread of impending danger.

arbitrate (är′bə trāt), *v.* decide a dispute.

ardent (ärd′nt), *adj.* enthusiastic; passionate.

arduous (är′jü əs), *adj.* difficult.

artifice (är′tə fis), *n.* skillful construction.

asperity (a sper′ə tē), *n.* harshness.

aspire (ə spīr′), *v.* rise high.

asunder (ə sun′dər), *adv.* in pieces or separate parts.

audacious (ô dā′shəs), *adj.* bold.

augment (ôg ment′), *v.* increase.

avarice (av′ər is), *n.* greed for wealth.

avenge (ə venj′), *v.* revenge.

averted (ə vėr′tid), *adj.* turned away.

avouch (ə vouch′), *v.* affirm.

B

baldric (bôl′drik), *n.* a belt hung from one shoulder to the opposite side of the body, to support the wearer's sword.

baleful (bāl′fəl), *adj.* destructive.

bane (bān), *n.* destruction.

beguile (bi gīl′), *v.* trick.

benign (bi nīn′), *adj.* gracious; gentle.

bewitch (bi wich′), *v.* charm; fascinate.

blackguard (blag′ärd), *n.* scoundrel.

boon (bün), *n.* favor.

booty (bü′tē), *n.* money, especially seized illegally; gains; winnings.

bower (bou′ər), *n.* shelter.

brandish (bran′dish), *v.* wave or shake threateningly.

breach (brēch), *n.* break or gap.

brevity (brev′ə tē), *n.* shortness in time, speech, or writing; conciseness.

brougham (brüm), *n.* a closed carriage or automobile, having an outside seat for the driver.

bruit (brüt), *v.* announce by a great noise.

buoyancy (boi′ən sē), *n.* tendency to be hopeful and cheerful.

C

cadence (kād′ns), *n.* rhythm.

calumnious (kə lum′nē əs), *adj.* slanderous.

cant (kant), *n.* insincere talk.

casement (kās′mənt), *n.* window.

catapult (kat′ə pult), *n.* slingshot.

cataract (kat′ə rakt′), *n.* waterfall.

cauldron (kôl′drən), *n.* large kettle.

censure (sen′shər), *v.* criticize.

centrifugal (sen trif′yə gəl), *adj.* moving away from a center.

certitude (sėr′tə tyüd), *n.* certainty; sureness.

chasten (chā′sn), *v.* discipline.

cherub (cher′əb), *n.* an angel in the form of a child with wings.

chid (chid), past tense of **chide** (chīd), *v.* scold.

cistern (sis′tərn), *n.* reservoir for holding water.

clad (klad), *adj.* clothed.

clamorous (klam′ər əs), *adj.* noisy.

clemency (klem′ən sē), *n.* mercy or leniency.

combustible (kəm bus′tə bəl), *adj.* easily burned.

comely (kum′lē), *adj.* attractive.

commendation (kom′ən dā′shən), *n.* praise.

commiserate (kə miz′ə rāt), *v.* pity; sympathize with.

compass (kum′pəs), *v.* plot; scheme.

complaisant (kəm plā′snt), *adj.* gracious; courteous.

constitutional (kon′stə tü′shə nəl), *n.* walk or other exercise taken for one's health.

contend (kən tend′), *v.* fight; struggle.

contravention (kon′trə ven′shən), *n.* conflict; opposition.

conviction (kən vik′shən), *n.* firm belief.

copse (kops), *n.* thicket of small bushes or shrubs.

corporeal (kôr pôr′ē əl), *adj.* of or for the body.

coveted (kuv′ə tid), *adj.* strongly desired.

crypt (kript), *n.* burial vault.

D

daft (daft), *adj.* without sense or reason; silly.

darkling (därk′ling), *adv.* in the dark.

dauntless (dônt′lis), *adj.* brave.

decorum (di kôr′əm), *n.* proper behavior.

delineate (di lin′ē āt), *v.* describe in words; portray.

deluge (del′yüj), *n.* downpour; a heavy fall, as of rain.

demean (di mēn′), *v.* lower in dignity; degrade.

demeanor (di mē′nər), *n.* behavior.

deprecate (dep′rə kāt), *v.* express strong disapproval of; belittle.

desolation (des′ə lā′shən), *n.* sad loneliness.

despondency (di spon′dən sē), *n.* discouragement.

despotic (des pot′ik), *adj.* having unlimited power.

deterrent (di tėr′ənt), *n.* something that discourages or hinders.

devastating (dev′ə stā′ting), *adj.* very destructive.

diffident (dif′ə dənt), *adj.* lacking in self-confidence; shy.

diminutive (də min′yə tiv), *adj.* very small.

dire (dīr), *adj.* dreadful.

dirge (dėrj), *n.* funeral song.

disburse (dis pėrs′), *v.* pay out.

discreet (dis krēt′), *adj.* careful and sensible; proper.

disdain (dis dān′), *v.* scorn.

disparage (dis par′ij), *v.* speak slightingly of; belittle.

dissipate (dis′ə pāt), *v.* spread in different directions; scatter.

dissuade (di swād′), *v.* persuade not to do something.

dolorous (dol′ər əs), *adj.* sorrowful.

doughty (dou′tē), *adj.* brave.

drear (drir), *adj.* gloomy; sad; sorrowful.

dudgeon (duj′ən), *n.* feeling of anger or resentment.

E

ecstatic (ek stat′ik), *adj.* full of joy.

effrontery (ə frun′tər ē), *n.* shameless boldness.

embark (em bärk′), *v.* begin an undertaking; set out; start.

enmity (en′mə tē), *n.* hatred.

enthrall (en thrôl′), *v.* hold captive.

entice (en tīs′), *v.* tempt.

entreat (en trēt′), *v.* beg.

epicure (ep′ə kyu̇r), *n.* lover of luxury.

epithet (ep′ə thet), *n.* descriptive expression.

erratic (ə rat′ik), *adj.* irregular.

erring (ėr′ing), *adj.* wandering; straying.

essay (es′ā), *n.* trial.

esteem (e stēm′), *n.* high regard.

exhortation (eg′zôr tā′shən), *n.* strong urging to do something.

exotic (eg zot′ik), *adj.* from a foreign country; not native; fascinating or interesting because strange or different.

expedient (ek spē′dē ənt), *n.* method of bringing about desired results.

exquisitely (ek′skwi zit lē), *adv.* beautifully; admirably.

extrinsic (ek strin′sik), *adj.* external.

F

factitious (fak tish′əs), *adj.* artificial.

fallacy (fal′ə sē), *n.* false idea.

fidelity (fə del′ə tē), *n.* faithfulness.

flout (flout), *v.* treat with scorn or contempt.

folly (fol′ē), *n.* a being foolish; lack of sense.

forlorn (fôr lôrn′), *adj.* abandoned; desolate.

G

gallant (gal′ənt), *adj.* noble in spirit or in conduct.

genial (jē′nyəl), *adj.* cheerful and friendly; kindly.

genteel (jen tēl′), *adj.* polite; well-bred.

ghastly (gast′lē), *adj.* very bad. *[informal]*

gibbet (jib′it), *n.* gallows, a structure for hanging criminals.

glaze (glāz), *n.* smooth, glossy coating.

gloam (glōm), *n.* gloaming; twilight.

gravity (grav′ə tē), *n.* seriousness.

grievous (grē′vəs), *adj.* causing great pain or suffering; severe.

grope (grōp), *v.* search blindly.

grot (grot), *n.* grotto; a cave or cavern. *[archaic]*

grovel (gruv′əl), *v.* crawl humbly on the ground.

guile (gīl), *n.* deceit.

H

harbinger (här′bən jər), *n.* forerunner.

hauberk (hô′bərk), *n.* a flexible coat of armor made of small loops of chain linked together.

hemlock (hem′lok), *n.* a poison.

herbivore (hėr′bə vôr), *n.* any of a large group of animals that feed chiefly on plants.

hirsute (hėr′süt), *adj.* hairy.

homage (hom′ij), *n.* dutiful respect.

I

imbibe (im bīb′), *v.* drink in; absorb.

imminent (im′ə nənt), *adj.* about to happen.

immortal (i môr′tl), *adj.* living forever.

impartiality (im′pär shē al′ə tē), *n.* fairness.

impecunious (im′pi kyü′nē əs), *adj.* having little or no money.

impenetrable (im pen′ə trə bəl), *adj.* unable to be passed through.

imperialism (im pir′ē ə liz′əm), *n.* policy of extending the rule or authority of one country over other countries and colonies.

impertinent (im pėrt′n ənt), *adj.* rudely bold.

impetuous (im pech′ü əs), *adj.* rash; hasty.

impotence (im′pə təns), *n.* condition of helplessness.

impropriety (im′prə prī′ə tē), *n.* improper conduct.

impudent (im′pyə dənt), *adj.* very rude.

incipient (in sip′ē ənt), *adj.* just beginning; in an early stage.

incoherent (in′kō hir′ənt), *adj.* confused; having no logical connection of ideas.

incomprehensible (in′kom pri hen′sə bəl), *adj.* impossible to understand.

incongruous (in kong′grü əs), *adj.* out of place; inconsistent.

incorporeal (in′kôr pôr′ē əl), *adj.* not made of any material substance; spiritual.

incorrigible (in kôr′ə jə bəl), *adj.* too firmly fixed in bad ways to be changed.

indignant (in dig′nənt), *adj.* angry at something unjust.

indolent (in′dl ənt), *adj.* lazy.

inexpedient (in′ik spē′dē ənt), *adj.* unwise.

inexplicable (in′ik splik′ə bəl), *adj.* mysterious; unable to be explained.

infamous (in′fə məs), *adj.* disgraceful.

infinite (in′fə nit), *adj.* endless.

ingenious (in jē′nyəs), *adj.* cleverly planned.

inglorious (in glôr′ē əs), *adj.* shameful; disgraceful.

inquisitive (in kwiz′ə tiv), *adj.* curious; prying.

insinuate (in sin′yü āt), *v.* act or speak to gain favor in an indirect way.

insolence (in′sə ləns), *n.* bold rudeness.

interfuse (in′tər fyüz′), *v.* blend; mix.

intrinsically (in trin′sik lē), *adv.* essentially; belonging to a thing by its very nature.

irrepressible (ir′i pres′ə bəl), *adj.* uncontrollable.

J

jovial (jō′vē əl), *adj.* cheerful.

judicious (jü dish′əs), *adj.* wise.

L

lamentable (lam′ən tə bəl), *adj.* sorrowful.

languish (lang′guish), *v.* become weak or worn out.

languor (lang′gər), *n.* lack of energy; weariness.

lassitude (las′ə tüd), *n.* lack of energy; weariness.

laudable (lô′də bəl), *adj.* praiseworthy.

lavish (lav′ish), *v.* give or spend freely.

leonine (lē′ə nīn), *adj.* of or like a lion.

liege (lēj), *adj.* honorable; having a right to respect and service.

lissomely (lis′əm lē), *adv.* limberly; supplely.

listless (list′lis), *adj.* seeming too tired to care about anything.

loath (lōth), *adj.* reluctant.

luminous (lü′mə nəs), *adj.* shining; bright.

M

magnanimous (mag nan′ə məs), *adj.* generous in forgiving.

malevolence (mə lev′ə ləns), *n.* ill will.

malicious (mə lish′əs), *adj.* evil.

manifest (man′ə fest), *adj.* plain; clear.

mead (mēd), *n.* meadow.

mendacity (men das′ə tē), *n.* untruthfulness; lie.

mettle (met′l), *n.* courage.

mien (mēn), *n.* manner of holding the head and body; way of acting and looking.

minion (min′yən), *n.* favorite; darling.

N

negligent (neg′lə jənt), *adj.* careless.

nocturnal (nok tėr′nl), *adj.* nighttime.

O

obdurate (ob′dər it), *adj.* stubborn.

oblivious (ə bliv′ē əs), *adj.* unmindful; forgetful.

odious (ō′dē əs), *adj.* hateful; offensive.

officiously (ə fish′əs lē), *adv.* too readily offering services or advice; meddling.

ominous (om′ə nəs), *adj.* unfavorable; threatening.

oppressor (ə pres′ər), *n.* person who is cruel or unjust.

ostentation (os′ten tā′shən), *n.* showing off.

P

pacify (pas′ə fī), *v.* quiet down.

palpable (pal′pə bəl), *adj.* definite.

paltry (pôl′trē), *adj.* worthless.

pandemonium (pan′də mō′nē əm), *n.* wild uproar; lawlessness.

parasite (par′ə sīt), *n.* person who lives on others without making any useful or fitting returns.

parsimony (pär′sə mō′nē), *n.* stinginess.

peerless (pir′lis), *adj.* without equal; matchless.

peremptory (pə remp′tər ē), *adj.* decisive; dictatorial.

perennial (pə ren′ē əl), *adj.* lasting for a very long time; enduring.

perfunctorily (pər fungk′tər i lē), *adv.* mechanically; indifferently.

pernicious (pər nish′əs), *adj.* harmful.

perplexity (pər plek′sə tē), *n.* confusion.

pestilence (pes′tl əns), *n.* epidemic disease.

petrol (pet′rəl), *n.* gasoline. *[British]*

petulant (pech′ə lənt), *adj.* likely to have little fits of bad temper.

piety (pī′ə tē), *n.* reverence for God.

pique (pēk), *n.* anger; wounded pride.

plaintive (plān′tiv), *adj.* mournful.

plinth (plinth), *n.* the lower, square part of the base of a column.

plunder (plun′dər), *v.* steal by force, especially during war.

ply (plī), *v.* supply with in a pressing manner.

precipitous (pri sip′ə təs), *adj.* very steep.

prerogative (pri rog′ə tiv), *n.* right or privilege that nobody else has.

presumptuous (pri zump′chü əs), *adj.* too bold; forward.

pristine (pris′tēn′), *adj.* original.

procrastinate (prō kras′tə nāt), *v.* put things off until later; delay.

prodigious (prə dij′əs), *adj.* huge.

promontory (prom′ən tôr′ē), *n.* a high point of land extending from the coast into the water.

propitiate (prə pish′ē āt), *v.* win the favor of.

propriety (prə prī′ə tē), *n.* proper behavior.

prosaically (prō zā′ik lē), *adv.* in an ordinary way.

prostrate (pros′trāt), *adj.* overcome; helpless.

protracted (prō trak′tid), *adj.* drawn out; prolonged.

provocation (prov′ə kā′shən), *n.* something that stirs up or irritates.

prowess (prou′is), *n.* bravery; daring.

prudent (prüd′nt), *adj.* sensible; discreet.

publican (pub′lə kən), *n.* tavern keeper.

purgatory (pėr′gə tôr′ē), *n.* any condition of temporary suffering.

R

ragout (ra gü′), *n.* a highly seasoned meat stew.

raiment (rā′mənt), *n.* clothing.

recompense (rek′əm pens), *n.* reward.

recourse (rē′kôrs), *n.* appeal for help or protection.

recreant (rek′rē ənt), *n.* coward.

redcoat (red′kōt′), *n.* a British soldier.

reluctantly (ri luk′tənt lē), *adv.* slowly and unwillingly.

remonstrance (ri mon′strəns), *n.* protest; complaint.

rendezvous (rän′də vü), *n.* secret meeting place.

renown (ri noun′), *n.* fame.

replenish (ri plen′ish), *v.* refill.

repudiate (ri pyü′dē āt), *v.* reject.

requiem (rek′wē əm), *n.* musical service or hymn for the dead.

requite (ri kwīt′), *v.* repay.

resolute (rez′ə lüt), *adj.* determined.

restraint (ri strānt′), *n.* limit; restriction.

reticent (ret′ə sənt), *adj.* reserved; quiet.

revelation (rev′ə lā′shən), *n.* disclosure of divine truth.

revelry (rev′əl rē), *n.* noisy partying.

ricochet (rik′ə shā′), *v.* move with a bounce or jump.

robust (rōbust′), *adj.* strong and healthy; sturdy.

S

salutary (sal′yə ter′ē), *adj.* beneficial.

sanctify (sangk′tə fī), *v.* make holy.

scruple (skrü′pəl), *n.* doubt.

sensibility (sen′sə bil′ə tē), *n.* tendency to be hurt or offended too easily.

sepulcher (sep′əl kər), *n.* tomb.

servile (sėr′vəl), *adj.* slavelike.

sidle (sī′dl), *v.* move sideways.

simultaneously (sī′məl tā′nē əs lē), *adv.* at the same time.

sinister (sin′ə stər), *adj.* threatening.

slay (slā), *v.* **slew, slain, slaying.** kill with violence.

slovenly (sluv′ən lē), *adj.* untidy.

smite (smīt), *v.* **smote, smitten** or **smote, smiting.** hit; give a hard blow to.

sordid (sôr′did), *adj.* filthy.

spate (spāt), *n.* a sudden flood.

specious (spē′shəs), *adj.* apparently good, but not really so.

specter (spek′tər), *n.* ghost.

stagnant (stag′nənt), *adj.* still; not flowing.

staid (stād), *adj.* having a settled, quiet character; sober; sedate.

stealthy (stel′thē), *adj.* secret.

steed (stēd), *n.* horse.

strew (strü), *v.* scatter or sprinkle.

stupent (stüp′nt), *adj.* dumfounded; amazed.

subdue (səb dü′), *v.* conquer.

subjective (səb jek′tiv), *adj.* existing in the mind.

subjugate (sub′jə gāt), *v.* subdue; conquer.

suborn (sə bôrn′), *v.* hire or bribe.

superfluous (su pėr′flü əs), *adj.* needless; unnecessary.

supine (sü pīn′), *adj.* lazily inactive; listless.

suppurating (sup′yə rā′ting), *adj.* oozing.

surmise (sər mīz′), *n.* guesswork.

swoon (swün), *n., v.* faint.

sylvan (sil′vən), *adj.* of or flowing through woods.

symmetry (sim′ə trē), *n.* pleasing proportions between the parts of a whole; harmony.

T

tarry (tar′ē), *v.* delay.

taut (tôt), *adj.* tense.

tempestuous (tem pes′chü əs), *adj.* stormy; violent.

terrestrial (tə res′trē əl), *adj.* earthly.

thrall (thrôl), *n.* bondage; condition of being under some power or influence.

thwart (thwôrt), *v.* prevent from doing something.

tirade (tī′rād), *n.* long, scolding speech.

toll (tōl), *v.* ring.

tranquillity (trang kwil′ə tē), *n.* peacefulness.

transgress (trans gres′), *v.* sin against.

transitory (tran′sə tôr′ē), *adj.* passing soon or quickly.

transpire (tran spīr′), *v.* breathe out.

tread (tred), *v.* **trod, trodden** or **trod, treading.** set the foot down; walk; step.

tremulous (trem′yə ləs), *adj.* quivering.

trepidation (trep′ə dā′shən), *n.* fear; fright.

tumult (tü′mult), *n.* commotion.

turbid (tėr′bid), *adj.* confused; disordered.

tyranny (tir′ə nē), *n.* cruel or unjust use of power.

U

unabashed (un′ə basht′), *adj.* not ashamed or embarrassed.

unguent (ung′gwənt), *n.* ointment; salve; cream.

unprecedented (un pres′ə den′tid), *adj.* never done before; never known before.

upbraid (up brād′), *v.* find fault with.

V

vagrant (vā′grənt), *adj.* wandering.

valiant (val′yənt), *adj.* courageous.

vanquish (vang′kwish), *v.* defeat.

vehement (vē′ə mənt), *adj.* forceful.

verdurous (vėr′jər əs), *adj.* green and fresh.

verity (ver′ə tē), *n.* truth.

vie (vī), *v.* compete.

vile (vīl), *adj.* very bad.

vindicate (vin′də kāt), *v.* uphold; justify.

vindictive (vin dik′tiv), *adj.* bearing a grudge; wanting revenge.

vintner (vint′nər), *n.* wine merchant.

W

wantonness (won′tən nis), *n.* lack of restraint.

wrath (rath), *n.* great anger.

writhe (rīᵺ), *v.* twist and turn; suffer mentally.

wrought (rôt), *v.* a past tense and a past participle of **work.** *[archaic]*

Z

zealous (zel′əs), *adj.* enthusiastic.

zephyr (zef′ər), *n.* mild breeze; gentle wind.

Language and Grammar Handbook

When your teacher returns papers, are you sometimes confused by comments such as "Incorrect subject-verb agreement" or "Unclear antecedent"? This Handbook will help you respond to such comments as you edit your writing and also provide answers to questions that arise about language during peer- and self-evaluation.

The Handbook is alphabetically arranged, with each entry explaining a certain term or concept. For example, if you can't remember when to use *good* or *well* look up the entry **good, well** and you'll find an explanation of when to use each word and a sentence using each word.

active and passive voice A verb is said to be in the active voice when its subject is the doer of the action, and in the passive voice when its subject is the receiver of the action. A passive verb is a form of the verb *be* plus the past participle of the verb: *is* prepared, *had been* prepared, *will be* prepared, and so on.

> **active:** The coach *prepared* the team for the playoffs.
> **passive:** The team *was prepared* for the playoffs by the coach.

Active verbs are more natural, direct, and forceful than passive verbs. Passive verbs are useful and effective, however, when the doer of the action is unknown or unimportant, or to emphasize the receiver of the action:

> ◆ The soul *is placed* in the body like a rough diamond. . . .
> from "The Education of Women" by Daniel Defoe

> ◆ In Moulmein, in Lower Burma, I *was hated* by large numbers of people
> . . . .
> from "Shooting an Elephant" by George Orwell

adjective Adjectives are modifiers that describe nouns and pronouns and make their meaning more exact. Adjectives tell *what kind, which one,* or *how many.*

What kind:	*red* car	*denim* jacket	*fast* food
Which one:	*that* video	*this* computer	*those* families
How many:	*six* weeks	*several* papers	*many* years

adverb Adverbs modify verbs, adjectives, or other adverbs. They tell *how, when,* or *where* about verbs.

How:	quickly	fearfully	courageously
When:	soon	now	tomorrow
Where:	there	near	here

See also **comparative forms of adjectives and adverbs.**

agreement

1. **Subject-verb agreement.** When the subject and verb of a sentence are both singular or both plural, they agree in number. This is called subject-verb agreement.

	Singular	Plural
1st person	I drive	we drive
2nd person	you drive	you drive
3rd person	he/she/it/drives	they drive

Some verbs, like *to be,* have irregular forms.

Present tense Singular	Present tense Plural	Past tense Singular	Past tense Plural
I am	we are	I was	we were
you are	you are	you were	you were
he/she/it is	they are	he/she/it was	they were

a. Most compound subjects joined by *and* or *both . . . and* are plural and are followed by plural verbs.

        S   S   V

Both Tomas and Matt were standing in the cafeteria line.

b. A compound subject joined by *or, either. . . or,* or *neither . . . nor* is followed by a verb that agrees in number with the closer subject.

            S   S   V

Neither Margarita nor her sisters attend that school.

           S   S   V

Neither her sisters nor Margarita attends that school.

Problems arise when it isn't obvious what the subject is. The following rules should help you with some of the most troublesome situations:

c. Phrases or clauses coming between the subject and the verb do not affect the subject-verb agreement.

◆ The appointment of the other Ministers usually takes a little longer. . .
    from "Wartime Speeches" by Winston Churchill

◆ Some persons of a desponding spirit are in great concern about that vast number of poor people who are aged, diseased, or maimed. . . .
    from *A Modest Proposal* by Jonathan Swift

d. Singular verbs are used with singular indefinite pronouns—*each, every, either, neither, anyone, anybody, one, everyone, everybody, someone, somebody, nobody, no one.*

S   V
Neither of us was on time.

S   V
Everyone attends the free film on Monday.

e. Plural indefinite pronouns take plural verbs. They are *both, few, many,* and *several.*

S   V
Both of the bands travel frequently.

f. The indefinite pronouns *all, any, more, most, none,* and *some* may take a singular or plural verb, depending on their meaning in a sentence.

Singular	Plural
Most of the van *is* filled.	*Most* of the buses *were* full.
All of the snow *has* melted	*All* of the clouds *have* vanished.

g. The verb agrees with the subject regardless of the number of the predicate complement (after a form of a linking verb).

S   V
Her greatest delight was her flowers.

S   V
Flowers were her greatest delight.

h. Unusual word order does not affect agreement; the verb generally agrees with the subject, whether the subject follows or precedes it.

◆ . . . between the layers of cotton-wool were little brass figures . . . .
  from "The Lumber-Room" by Saki

i. Be especially careful of sentences beginning with *There;* be sure the verb agrees with the subject.

◆ There are only two people in the car.
  from "Tickets, Please" by D. H. Lawrence

2. Pronoun-antecedent agreement. An antecedent is a word, clause, or phrase to which a pronoun refers. The pronoun agrees with its antecedent in person, number, and gender.

antec.   pron.
José must let me know when he is free.

antec.   pron.
My cousins didn't know it, but their car was in the shop.

b. Singular pronouns are generally used to refer to the indefinite pronouns *one, anyone, each, either, neither, everybody, everyone, somebody, someone, nobody,* and *no one.*

antec.   pron.
Did anyone misplace her notes?

antec.   pron.
Everybody was told to bring his lunch.

The second sentence poses problems. It is clearly plural in meaning, and *everybody* may not refer to men only. To avoid the latter problem, you could write "Everybody was told to bring his or her lunch." This solution is clumsy and wordy, though. Sometimes it is best to revise: "*Students* were told to bring *their* lunches."

all right *All right* is used both as an adjective and as an adverb. The spelling *alright* is not accepted in either formal or informal writing.

ambiguity An ambiguous sentence is one that has two or more possible meanings. The most common causes of ambiguity are these:

1. Unclear pronoun reference

> Ambiguous: He told his Dad that *he* missed the plane.

Since it is not clear who missed the plane, the sentence should be revised.

> Clear: "I missed the plane, Dad," he said.
> Clear: "You missed the plane, Dad," he said.

2. Misplaced modifiers. Misplaced modifiers, because of their position in a sentence, do not clearly modify the word they are intended to modify. They are also often a source of humor that the writer does not intend.

> Ambiguous: The queen left the palace leaning on her husband.
> Clear: Leaning on her husband, the queen left the palace.
> Clear: The queen, leaning on her husband, left the palace.

3. Incomplete comparisons

> Ambiguous: Maria likes pizza as much as Kim.
> Clear: Maria likes pizza as much as Kim does.

amount, number *Amount* is used to refer to nouns which name things that can be measured or weighed: large amount of sand, small amount of gold. *Number* is used in referring to nouns which name things that can be counted: large number of rocks, small number of coins.

NOTE: An apostrophe is not used in forming other plurals or in the possessive form of personal pronouns: "The tickets are theirs."

apostrophe (') An apostrophe is used in possessive words, both singular and plural, and in contractions. It is also used to form the plurals of letters and numbers.

women's hockey	Marta's boots	won't
P's and Q's	11's and 12's	weren't

It may be used to indicate places in words in which the speaker does not pronounce certain sounds.

> ◆ I went into a public-'ouse to get a pint o' beer,
> The publican 'e up an' sez, "We serve no red-coats here."
> from "Tommy" by Rudyard Kipling

appositive Apposition means, literally, a "putting beside." An appositive is a noun or phrase that follows a noun and identifies or explains it more fully. It is usually set off by commas or dashes.

> ◆ The glorious lamp of heaven, the sun, / The higher he's a-getting. . . .
> from "To the Virgins, to Make Much of Time" by Robert Herrick

If, however, the appositive is used to specify a particular person or thing, it is not set off.

> ◆ . . . I was in Mrs. Prothero's garden . . . with her son Jim.
> from *A Child's Christmas in Wales* by Dylan Thomas

awkward writing A general term (abbreviated *awk*) sometimes used in theme correcting to indicate such faults as inappropriate word choice, unnecessary repetition, clumsy phrasing, confusing word order, or any other weakness or expression that makes reading difficult and obscures meaning.

Many writers have found that reading their first drafts aloud helps them detect clumsy or unclear phrasing in their work. Once identified, awkward construction can almost always be improved by rethinking and rewording.

B

bad, badly In formal English and in writing, *bad* (the adjective) is used to modify a noun or pronoun and is used after a linking verb. *Badly* (the adverb) modifies a verb.

> She felt *bad* about forgetting to write to her dad. [adjective used with linking verb *felt*]

> He limped *badly* after his fall. [adverb modifying the verb *limped*]

HINT: To check yourself, mentally eliminate the first term. You would never say "between *we*," you would say "between *us*," *us* being the objective form of the pronoun *we*.

between you and me After prepositions such as *between,* use the objective form of the personal pronouns: between you and *me*, between you and *her*, between you and *him*, between you and us, between you and *them*.

> The contest will be between you and *us*.

> ◆ . . . those were the terms of the covenant made between *us* in Arthur's hall. . . .
> from "Sir Gawain and the Green Knight"

capitalization
1. Capitalize all proper nouns and adjectives.

Britain	Wales	Edward
British	Welsh	Edwardian

NOTE: If an article or possessive pronoun comes before a family title, the title is not capitalized: "My dad took us to Wrigley Field." "An aunt arrived from Sioux City."

2. Capitalize people's names and titles.

Mister Fell	Dr. Johnson	Bishop Carr
Ms. Anita Patel	Mother	Uncle John
Senator Rodriguez	Prince Henry	Justice O'Connor

3. Capitalize the names of races, languages, religions, revered persons, deities, and religious bodies, buildings, and writings. Also capitalize any adjectives made from these names.

Indo-European	Islam	Beth Emet Synagogue
Hindu	God	Church of England
Buddha	French	the Bible

NOTE: Do not capitalize directions of the compass or adjectives that indicate direction: "Is Trafalgar Square north or south of here?" "There is a mild wind from the southwest."

4. Capitalize geographical names (except for articles and prepositions) and any adjectives made from these names.

Canterbury	the Lake District	Stratford-on-Avon
the Thames River	North Sea	Irish stew
Loch Lomond	Yorkshire	Sherwood Forest

NOTE: Such terms as *avenue, bridge, square, street* are capitalized when part of a specific name: *Shaftesbury Avenue, Golden Gate Bridge, Times Square, Sutter Street.*

5. Capitalize the names of structures, public places, organizations, and bodies in the universe.

Windsor Castle	the Senate	Scotland Yard
Parliament	the Capitol	the Milky Way
Saturn	Stonehenge	Labour Party

6. Capitalize the names of historical events, times, and documents.

Battle of Hastings	Wars of the Roses	Domesday Book
Magna Carta	the Age of Reason	Gun Powder Plot

7. Capitalize the names of months, days, holidays, and time abbreviations. The seasons are not capitalized.

November	Tuesday	B.C.
Thanksgiving	A. M.	summer

8. Capitalize the first words in sentences, lines of poetry, and direct quotations.

NOTE: Some modern poets do not begin each line with a capital letter.

◆ On either side the river lie
   Long fields of barley and of rye. . . .
      from "The Lady of Shalott" by Alfred, Lord Tennyson

9. Capitalize certain parts of letters, outlines, and the first, last, and all other important words in titles.

Dear Mr. O'Brien,   I. Mary Queen of Scots
Sincerely yours,   A. Early Life
                                      1. Parents
                                      2. Cousin
                                 B. Adult Life

Language and Grammar Handbook   **991**

Our Mutual Friend (book)
The Times (newspaper)
Macbeth (play)
Masterpiece Theatre (TV series)
"A Shocking Accident" (short story)
The Gondoliers (operetta)
"Born in America" (song)
Time (magazine)
"Ode to a Nightingale" (poem)
The Return of the Jedi (movie)

See also **Italics.**

clause A clause is a group of words that has a subject and a verb. A clause is independent when it can stand alone and make sense. A dependent clause has a subject and a verb, but when it stands alone it is incomplete, and the reader is left wondering about the meaning.

Independent Clause	**Dependent Clause**
s v	s v
Jane Austen wrote *Pride and Prejudice.*	Because Jane Austen wrote *Pride and Prejudice.*

collective nouns A collective noun is one that though singular in form names a group of people or things: *committee, mob, team, class.* When a collective noun means the group taken as a whole, use a singular verb and pronoun. When individual members of a group are meant, use a plural verb and pronoun.

The class should bring *its* petition to the study hall at noon.

The committee *were* still in disgreement about *their* purpose.

colon (:) A colon is often used to explain or clarify what has preceded it.

◆ Ernest, however, never played: he was too grown up.
   from "Eveline" by James Joyce

A colon is also used after phrases that introduce a list or quotation.

◆ "There were the Useful Presents: engulfing mufflers of the old coach days, and mittens made for giant sloths; zebra scarfs of a substance like silky gum. . . .
   from *A Child's Christmas in Wales* by Dylan Thomas

comma (,) Commas are used to show a pause or separation between words and word groups in sentences and to avoid confusion in sentences.

1. Use a comma between items in a series. Words, phrases, and clauses in a series are separated by commas:

NOTE: If the items in a series are all separated by a word like *and,* no comma is necessary: Dolphins and whales and seals were the main attractions.

◆ The sun with its specks of planets, its dust of planetoids, and its impalpable comets, swims in a vacant immensity that almost defeats the imagination.
from "The Star" by H. G. Wells

2. Use a comma after certain introductory words and groups of words such as clauses and prepositional phrases of five words or more.

◆ With his towel round his waist, Ajayi strode back to the bedroom, ...
from "The Truly Married Woman" by Abioseh Nicol

3. Use a comma to set off nouns in direct address. The name or title by which persons (or animals) are addressed is called a noun of direct address.

◆ "Mr. Ajayi, these gentlemen have enquired for you," the chief clark said formally.
from "The Truly Married Woman" by Abioseh Nicol

4. Use commas to set off interrupting elements and appositives. Any phrase or clause that interrupts the flow of a sentence is often set off by commas. Parenthetical expressions like *of course, after all, to be sure, on the other hand, I suppose,* and *as you know;* and words like *yes, no, oh,* and *well* are all set off by commas.

◆ The white man, turning his back upon the setting sun, looked along the empty and broad expanse of the sea-reach.
from "The Lagoon" by Joseph Conrad

◆ "After all, why shouldn't you come back with me?"
from "A Cup of Tea" by Katherine Mansfield

NOTE: No comma is used when the connecting words are *so that:*

5. Use a comma before a coordinating conjunction *(and, but, for, or, nor, yet, so)* in a compound sentence.

◆ They were all amazed at his color, for they saw that he was bright green all over. . . . The hood of the mantle was the same . . . and he had thrown it back off his hair so that it lay on his shoulders.
from "Sir Gawain and the Green Knight"

6. Use a comma after a dependent clause that begins a sentence. Do not use a comma before a dependent clause that follows the independent clause.

◆ Though his imagination might incline him to a belief of the marvelous and mysterious, his vigorous reason examined the evidence with jealousy.
from *The Life of Samuel Johnson, LL.D* by James Boswell

◆ Those were the days of darkness that followed the star and the heat.
from "The Star" by H. G. Wells

comma splice *See* **run-on.**

comparative forms of adjectives and adverbs To show a greater degree of the quality or characteristic named by an adjective or adverb, *-er* or *-est* is added to the word or *more* or *most* is put before it.

> **Positive:** Ramon is *tall.*

> **Comparative:** Ramon is *taller* than Bill.

> **Superlative:** Ramon is the *tallest* person in the class.

More and *most* are generally used with longer adjectives and adverbs, and with all adverbs ending in *-ly.*

> **Positive:** The video was *disturbing.*

> **Comparative:** The second video was *more disturbing* than the first.

> **Superlative:** That video was the *most disturbing* one I have seen.

See also **modifiers.**

conjunction A conjunction is a word that links one part of a sentence to another. It can join words, phrases, or entire sentences. Coordinating conjunctions *(and, but, for, yet, or, nor, so)* connect words, phrases, and clauses of equal value. Subordinating conjunctions *(after, because, so that, unless, while,* and so on) connect dependent, or subordinate, clauses with main clauses.

> **Coordinating:** He arrived early, *yet* he left late.

> **Subordinating:** Marta spoke first *because* she had to leave.

D

dangling modifiers A modifier that has no word in a sentence which it can logically modify is said to be dangling.

> **Dangling:** *Born in Ireland in 1950,* Ian Murphy's books have been translated into many languages. [The books weren't born in 1950.]

> **Revised:** The books of Ian Murphy, who was born in Ireland in 1950, have been translated into many languages.

> **Dangling:** *Having driven the same route for several years,* the landscape was familiar. [Who was familiar with the landscape?]

> **Revised:** *Having driven the same route for several years,* I was familiar with the landscape.

dash (—) A dash is used to indicate a sudden break or change of thought in a sentence:

> ◆ For brave Macbeth—well he deserves that name— . . .
> Like valor's minion carved out his passage . . . .
> from *Macbeth* by William Shakespeare

dialogue Dialogue is often used to enliven many types of writing. Notice the punctuation, capitalization, and paragraphing of the following passage.

◆ But he was standing in the middle of the room, saying, "A fine Christmas!" and smacking at the smoke with a slipper.

"Call the fire brigade," cried Mrs. Prothero as she beat the gong.

"They won't be there," said Mr. Prothero, "it's Christmas."

from *A Child's Christmas in Wales* by Dylan Thomas

See also **quotation marks.**

direct address *See* **comma 3.**

E

ellipsis (. . .) An ellipsis is used to indicate that words (or sentences or paragraphs) have been omitted. An ellipsis consists of three dots, but if the omitted portion would have completed the sentence, a fourth dot is added for the period.

◆ . . . Our labor must be to pervert that end,
And out of good still to find means of evil. . . .

from *Paradise Lost* by John Milton

etc. Etc. is the abbreviation for the Latin *et cetera,* meaning "and others." It is usually read *and so forth* or pronounced (et set′ər ə). It is acceptable in reference and business usage but out of place in most other writing.

exclamation point (!) An exclamation mark is used at the end of an exclamatory sentence——one that shows excitement or strong emotion. Exclamation points can also be used with strong interjections.

F

fragment *See* **sentence fragment.**

G

gerund A verb form ending in *-ing* that is used as a noun.

◆ By the pricking of my thumbs,
Something wicked this way comes.

from *Macbeth* by William Shakespeare

HINT: When you are referring to health, use *well* if the meaning is "not ill." "I am quite well, thank you." If the meaning is "pleasant" or "in good spirits," use *good.* "I feel good today."

good, well *Good* is used as an adjective to modify a noun or pronoun. Do not use it to modify a verb. *Well* is usually used as an adverb to modify a verb.

◆ "Don't you see what a *good* thing it was that you met me?"

from "A Cup of Tea" by Katherine Mansfield

◆ "Sit down, Jerome," Mr. Wordsworth said. "All going *well* with the trigonometry?"

from "A Shocking Accident" by Graham Greene

H

hopefully This is often used to mean "it is hoped" or "I hope," as in the following sentence, "*Hopefully,* I may be pardoned." However, in formal writing, avoid this usage.

however Words like *however, moreover, nevertheless, therefore, consequently,* etc. (known as conjunctive adverbs) require special punctuation. If the word comes within a clause, it is generally set off by commas:

> ◆ He, however, kept his face closed and averted from them all.
> from "Tickets, Please" by D. H. Lawrence

If the conjunctive adverb separates two independent clauses, a semicolon is used preceding the word. If it begins a sentence, a comma is used after it:

> ◆ Therefore, I repeat, let no man talk to me of these . . . .
> from "A Modest Proposal" by Jonathan Swift

infinitive The infinitive is the simple form of the verb, usually preceded by *to.* Infinitives are used as nouns, adjectives, or adverbs. In the following lines, each infinitive acts as a noun phrase:

> ◆ Good nature and good sense must ever join;
> *To error* is human, *to forgive* divine.
> from *An Essay on Criticism* by Alexander Pope

interjection An interjection is a word or phrase used to express strong emotion.

> ◆ Ring the alarum-bell. Murder and treason!
> Banquo and Donalbain! Malcolm! awake!
> from *Macbeth* by William Shakespeare

italics Italic type is used to indicate titles of whole works such as books, magazines, newspapers, plays, films, and so on. It is also used to indicate foreign words and phrases or to emphasize a word.

> ◆ And pictureless books in which small boys, though warned with quotations not to, *would* skate on Farmer Giles' pond. . . .
> from *A Child's Christmas in Wales* by Dylan Thomas

See also **Capitalization 9** for titles that are italicized.

its, it's *Its* is the possessive form of the personal pronoun *it; it's* is the contraction meaning "it is."

NOTE: In formal English the correct way to respond to a question such as, "Who's there?" is "It is I." This sounds too formal in some situations, however. While it is not correct to say, "It's them," "It's him," "it's us," or "it's her"— "It's me" is generally accepted as standard usage.

lay, lie This verb pair presents problems because, in addition to the similarity between the words, the past tense of *lie* is *lay.* The verb to *lay* means "to put or place something somewhere." The verb *to lie* means "to rest" or "to be at rest."

Present	Past	Past Participle	Present Participle
lay	laid	(has) laid	(is) laying
lie	lay	(has) lain	(is) lying

Notice how the verbs are used in the following sentences:

NOTE: *Lied* refers only to not telling the truth: "The jury was convinced that the defendent lied."

◆ Hark! *I laid* [placed] their daggers ready; He could not miss 'em.
   from *Macbeth* by William Shakespeare

◆ Here let them *lie* [rest] / Till famine and the ague eat them up.
   from *Macbeth* by William Shakespeare

M

media *Media* is the plural of *medium.* Many people use a singular verb when referring to the mass media. In formal writing it is best to use a plural verb.

All the media *are* focused on the national election.

misplaced modifier *See* **ambiguity.**

modifier A modifier is a word or group of words that restrict, limit, or make more exact the meaning of other words. The modifiers of nouns and pronouns are usually adjectives, participles, adjective phrases, and adjective clauses. The modifiers of verbs, adjectives, and adverbs are adverbs, adverb phrases, and adverb clauses. In the following example, the italicized words modify the words in boldface type.

Besides, the *invariable* **squabble** for money on *Saturday* **nights** had begun **to weary** her *unspeakably.*
   from "Eveline" by James Joyce

HINT: When trying to decide which pronoun to use, remember that you would not say, "Myself is going to the game." You would use *I.* Use *I* with a compound subject, too.

myself (and **himself, herself,** and so on) A reflexive pronoun reflects the action of the verb back to the subject. An intensive pronoun adds emphasis to the noun or pronoun just named.

◆ "I'm going to study outside. Even the street is quieter," I screeched and threw *myself* past them. . . .[reflexive]
   from "Studies in the Park" by Anita Desai

◆ THE DAUGHTER. It's too tiresome. Do you expect us to go and get one *ourselves?* [intensive]
   from *Pygmalion* by Bernard Shaw

Be careful not to use *myself* and the other reflexive and intensive pronouns when you simply need to use the personal pronoun *I* or its objective form *me.*

Incorrect: Ismail told Stephanie and *myself* a good story.

Correct: Ismail told Stephanie and *me* a good story.

N

noun A noun is a word that names a person, place, thing, or idea. Most nouns are made plural by adding *-s* or *-es* to the singular. When you are unsure about a plural form, check a dictionary.

P

parallel construction Items in a sentence that are of equal importance should be expressed in parallel (or similar) forms. These can take the form of noun phrases, verb phrases, infinitive phrases, and prepositional phrases:

◆ . . . it has been delayed till I am indifferent, and cannot enjoy it; till I am solitary, and cannot impart it; till I am known, and do not want it.
from "Letter to Chesterfield" by Samuel Johnson

◆ . . . we shall fight in France, we shall fight on the seas, we shall fight with growing confidence and growing strength in the air, . . . we shall fight in the fields and in the streets, we shall fight in the hills. . . .
from "Wartime Speeches" by Winston Churchill

parentheses ( ) Parentheses are used to enclose words that interrupt or add explanation to a sentence. They are also used to enclose references to page numbers, chapters, or dates. Punctuation marks that belong to the sentence come after the parentheses, not before.

◆ Those who are more thrifty (as I must confess the times require) may flay the carcass . . . .
from *A Modest Proposal* by Jonathan Swift

participle A participle is a verb form used in forming various tenses of verbs. The present participle ends in -*ing: growing.* The past participle usually ends in -*ed, -t, -d, -en,* or -*n: scared, wept, said, risen, grown.* Participles are also used as adjectives, modifying nouns and pronouns.

◆ . . . when the sky darkened towards evening, an unearthly, *reflected* pallor remained. . . . [*Reflected* modifies the noun *pallor.*]
from "The Courtship of Mr. Lyon" by Angela Carter

plagiarism Using the words, ideas, or expressions of others as if they were your own is called plagiarism. Plagiarism problems usually grow from the following circumstances: 1. copying a passage from a source without giving credit; 2. paraphrasing a source so closely that only a few words or phrases are changed; 3. using someone else's ideas without giving credit. In a short paper credit is usually given directly in the text. In a longer piece of writing, you will need to footnote your sources.

possessive case The possessive case is formed in various ways. For singular nouns and indefinite pronouns, add an apostrophe and -*s:*

my *brother's* car   *no one's* notebook   *everybody's* children

For plural nouns ending in an -*s,* add only an apostrophe:

the *doctors'* offices   the *babies'* shoes   the *teachers'* rooms

NOTE: Apostrophes are not used with personal pronouns such as *his, hers,* or *ours* to show possession.

If the plural is irregular and does not end in -*s,* add an apostrophe and then an -*s: women's* clothing.

prepositions Prepositions are words such as *about, between, during, from, in, of, over, under, until,* and *with* that show the relationship between a noun or pronoun and some other word in a sentence.

prepositional phrase Prepositional phrases are groups of words that begin with a preposition and end with a noun or pronoun (the object of the preposition). These phrases act as modifiers.

◆ There was a table set out under a tree in front of the house. . . .

from "A Mad Tea Party" by Lewis Carroll

pronoun A pronoun is a word used instead of a noun to designate a person or object. Subject pronouns are used as subjects of sentences. Object pronouns can be used as direct objects, indirect objects, or objects of prepositions.

HINT: When you are uncertain about whether to use a subject pronoun or an object pronoun, take out the first pronoun to test the sentence. (You wouldn't say "Me played yesterday" or "Tom asked I to stay.")

When a pronoun is used as the subject, it is in the nominative case. When a pronoun is used as an object, it is in the objective case.

Subject Pronouns	**Object Pronouns**
Singular: I; you; he, she, it	me; you; him, her, it
Plural: we; you; they	us; you; them
He and *I* played yesterday	Tom asked *her* and *me* to stay.

See also **ambiguity.**

quotation marks (" ") Quotation marks enclose a speaker's words. They are also used to enclose some titles. When you use someone's words in your writing, use the following rules:

1. Enclose all quoted words within quotation marks.

   Matthew Arnold wrote, "And we are here as on a darkling plain."

2. Introductory and explanatory expressions *(he said, I replied)* are set off by a comma, or if they interrupt a sentence, by two commas.

3. Periods and commas are always put inside quotation marks. Semicolons are put outside quotation marks.

   "I've read several of his poems," he said, "and liked them."

4. A question mark or exclamation point is put inside the quotation mark if it applies only to the quoted matter, outside if it applies to the complete sentence that contains the quotation.

   Didn't Matthew Arnold write "Dover Beach"?

5. When both the sentence and the quotation ending the sentence are questions or exclamations, only one mark is used—inside the quotation marks.

   Who wrote "Ah, Are You Digging On My Grave?"

6. A long quoted passage is often presented without quotation marks and indented instead, sometimes in smaller type.

See also **dialogue.**

R **real, really** *Real* is used as an adjective, and *really* is used as an adverb.

We couldn't tell the *real* picture from the fake one.

The concert was *really* great. [not "real great"]

run-on sentence A run-on sentence occurs when there is only a comma (known as a comma splice) or no punctuation between two independent clauses. Separate the clauses into two complete sentences, join them with a semicolon, or use a comma and a coordinating conjunction.

Run on: The student received her schedule, then she went home.
Correct: The student received her schedule. Then she went home.
Correct: The student received her schedule; then she went home.
Correct: The student received her schedule, and then she went home.

Often, in narrative writing, authors purposely choose to use run-ons for effect, such as in the following passage:

◆ There was no mistake about it, Annie liked John Thomas a good deal.
    from "Tickets, Please" by D. H. Lawrence

See also **stringy sentences.**

S **semicolon (;)** Use this punctuation mark to separate the two parts of a compound sentence when they are not joined by a comma and a conjunction.

◆ No man is an island, entire of itself; every man is a piece of the continent, a part of the main.
    from Meditation 17 by John Donne

NOTE: While some words or word groups are not complete sentences with a subject and a verb, they are complete in thought and are known as "minor-type sentences." Notice their use in the quoted passage.

sentence fragment A fragment often occurs when one sentence is finished, but another thought occurs to the writer and that thought is written and punctuated as a complete sentence.

Fragment: I loved the movie. Especially when Hamlet stages the play.
Correct: I loved the movie, especially when Hamlet stages the play.

◆ The bell rings. Voices clash, clatter, and break. The tin-and-bottle man? The neighbors? The police? The Help-the-Blind Man? Thieves and burglars?
    from "Studies in the Park" by Anita Desai

stringy sentences A stringy sentence is one in which several independent clauses are strung together with *and.* Correct a stringy sentence by breaking it into individual sentences or changing some of the independent clauses into subordinate clauses or phrases.

Stringy: Saturday morning I have to take my brother to his music lesson and pick up some dry cleaning and then I'm supposed to let Mom have the car so she can shop and I guess I'll have to walk or hitch a ride to football practice.

Correct: Saturday morning I have to take my brother to his music lesson and pick up some dry cleaning. Since I'm supposed to let Mom have the car so she can shop, I guess I'll have to walk or hitch a ride to football practice.

T

titles *See* **capitalization 2** and **9**.

V

verb A verb is a word that tells about an action or a state of being. The form or tense of the verb tells whether the action occurred in the past, the present, or the future.

verb tense Verb tenses indicate action in the past, present, future, and so on. Use the same tense to show two or more actions that occur at the same time.

Incorrect: She *brought* [past] two videos and some popcorn. Then she *talks* [present] all through the movies.

Correct: She *brought* [past] two videos and some popcorn. Then she *talked* [past] all through the movies.

When the verb in the main clause is in the present tense, the verb in the subordinate clause is in whatever tense expresses the meaning intended.

Mr. Washington *thinks* that the dinner *was* a success.

voice *See* **active and passive voice.**

W

who, whom Use *who* as the subject of a sentence or clause:

Who is the author of this short story?

Use *whom* as a direct object or as the object of a preposition:

◆ So, thanks to all at once and to each one,
  Whom we invite to see us crowned at Scone.
     from *Macbeth* by William Shakespeare

◆ Any man's death diminishes me, because I am involved in mankind; and therefore never send to know for *whom* the bell tolls . . . .
     from Meditation 17 by John Donne

who's, whose *Who's* is a contraction meaning "who is"; *whose* is a possessive.

After talking to everyone, decide *who's* planning to go.

◆ A knave *whose* practice it is to invite the unwary to game . . . .
    from *Dictionary of the English Language* by Samuel Johnson

NOTE: In the example from "Shooting an Elephant," notice the last clause, "if I had been alone." In *if-*clauses and wishes pertaining to the past, the verb to use is *had,* not *would have.*

would of This expression is often used mistakenly because it sounds like *would've,* the contraction for *would have.* In formal writing, write out *would have,* and you won't be confused:

◆ For at that moment, with the crowd watching me, I was not afraid in the ordinary sense, as I *would have* been if I *had* been alone.
    from "Shooting an Elephant" by George Orwell

your, you're *Your* is the possessive form of the personal pronoun *you; you're* is a contraction meaning "you are."

◆ Commend to me *your* fair and gracious lady. . . .
    from "Sir Gawain and the Green Knight"

Even though it's late, I hope *you're* going with me.

Index of Skills

Titles
   capitalization in, 991
   italics in, 996
Transitions, 333
Usage and spelling problems. *See*
      also specific terms
Verbs, 1001
   active, 767
   consistent tense, 516, 1001
   tense, 1001
   voice of, 986
Voice
   active, 986
   passive, 986
Well/good, 995
Who/whom, 1001
Who's/whose, 1001
Words, eliminating unnecessary, 900
Would of, 1002
Writing, awkward, 990
Your/you're, 1002

■
Interdisciplinary Connections
Archeology, 23, 78, 103
Art, 8, 31, 46, 642, 853
Career, 196, 330, 480, 894
Fine art, 372–373, 436, 843–845
Graphic art, 954
History, 2–3, 6, 7, 23, 24, 42–43,
      45, 60, 75, 78, 106–107, 109,
      117, 147–148, 222–223, 225,
      232, 250–251, 253, 267, 272,
      292–293, 295, 305, 313, 314,
      336–337, 339, 340, 350, 360,
      369–371, 398–399, 400, 401,
      408, 416, 422, 446–447, 448,
      449, 455, 462, 468, 488–489,
      490, 524–525, 526, 527, 536,
      538, 546, 559–563, 568–569,
      570–571, 572, 573, 580, 585,
      598, 604, 611, 623, 642,
      644–645, 656–657, 658–659,
      661, 717–720, 730–731, 732,
      773–776, 786–787, 788, 789,
      796, 805, 822, 832, 856–857,
      858, 859, 868, 875, 880,
      891–893, 902–903
Humanities, 88, 192–195, 241,
      276–280

Interdisciplinary Studies
   The Bubble Boy, 239–241
   The Burden of Guilt, 192–195
   Century's End, 629–632
   Creating Life, 507–512
   The Crystal Palace, 559–563
   Effects of Empire, 891–894
   English Class System, 717–722
   Faces of Evil, 32–34
   Our Glorious Leaders, 328–329
   Heaven, Hell and Paradise,
      276–280
   Legends of Arthur, 88–89
   Modern Faces, 843–845
   Other People's Lives, 369–373
   Rebels with Causes, 475–480
   Romantic Visionaries, 431–436
   Myth under a Microscope,
      943–946
   The Wasteland, 773–776
Language, 633, 777, 832, 853, 895
   Scottish English, 449
Literature, 642
Mathematics, 631–632
Media, 853, 954
Multicultural, 32, 431–433, 448,
      475–479, 510–511. *See also*
      Multicultural Awareness and
      Appreciation
Music, 31, 642, 954
Popular culture, 328–329, 512,
      629–630, 721–722, 954
Science, 239–240, 434–435,
      507–509, 942–946

■
Literary, Genres, Terms, and Techniques
Allegory, 968
Alliteration, 5, 7, 22, 32, 407, 580,
      583, 585, 771, 968
Allusion, 455, 460, 768, 811, 905,
      913, 968
Analogy, 401, 406, 968
Anapest, 968
Anastrophe, 598, 602, 968
Antagonist, 78, 86, 716, 841, 968
Aphorism, 968
Apostrophe, 468, 473, 598, 602,
      968
Archetype, 968

Aside. *See* Soliloquy
Assonance, 573, 578, 968
Author's purpose, 552, 930
Autobiography, 368, 968
Ballad, 31, 968
   folk, 24, 30
   literary, 968
   stanza, 968
Biography, 350, 351–354,
      360–366, 368, 969
Cacophony, 969
Caesura, 5, 414, 969
Caricature, 969
Central conflict, 715
Characterization, 265, 348, 360,
      365, 367, 467, 621, 669, 803,
      849, 923, 932, 969
Classicism, 969
Climax, 24, 162, 803, 923, 941, 969
Comedy, 969
Comic relief, 145, 969
Conceit, 225, 230, 969
Conflict, 715, 841, 970
Connotation, 350, 358, 406, 407,
      462, 554, 557, 970
Consonance, 604, 609, 771, 970
Couplet, 970
Dactyl, 970
Denotation, 350, 358, 462, 554,
      557, 970
Denouement, 970
Dialect, 449, 453, 627, 669, 970
Dialogue, 30, 880, 889, 970
Diary, 970
Diction, 462, 466, 970
Drama, 970
Dramatic convention, 970
Dramatic monologue, 970
Echoic words, 422, 430
Elegy, 579, 970
End-stopped line, 970
Epigrams, 313, 324, 326, 327, 971
Epigraph, 971
Epiphany, 789, 794, 841, 849, 852,
      971
Epitaph, 971
Epithets, 6, 13, 971
Essay, 971
Exposition, 117, 971
Extended metaphor, 536, 971
Fable, 971

Media and Technology

Multicultural Awareness and Appreciation

Reading/Thinking Strategies

■
Speaking, Listening, and Viewing

■

Vocabulary and Study Skills

Writing Forms, Modes, and Processes

Index of Fine Arts & Artists

Index of Authors and Titles

Acknowledgments

continued from page iv

599–601 "Loveliest of Trees," "When I Was One-and-Twenty," and "To An Athlete Dying Young" from *The Collected Poems Of A. E. Housman.* Copyright 1939, 1940 by Henry Holt and Co., Inc. Copyright © 1967 by Robert F. Symons. Reprinted by permission of Henry Holt and Co., Inc. and The Society of Authors as the literary representative of the Estate of A. E. Housman. **607** "The Second Coming" by W.B. Yeats from *The Poems Of W.B. Yeats: A New Edition,* edited by Richard J. Finneran. Copyright 1924 by Macmillan Publishing Company, renewed 1952 by Bertha Georgie Yeats. Reprinted with permission of Simon & Schuster, Inc. **608** "Sailing to Byzantium" by W.B. Yeats from *The Poems Of W.B. Yeats: A New Edition,* edited by Richard J. Finneran. Copyright 1928 by Macmillan Publishing Company, renewed © 1956 by Georgie Yeats. Reprinted with permission of Simon & Schuster, Inc. **612** "The Star" by H. G. Wells. Reprinted by permission of A. P. Watt on behalf of the Literary Executors of the Estate of H. G. Wells. **631** "Counting the Years" from *Time,* Fall 1992. Copyright © 1992 by Time Inc. Reprinted by permission. **648** "Stanley Meets Mutesa" by James D. Rubadiri. Reprinted by permission. **649** "England, My England" by William Ernest Henley. Reprinted by permission. **650** "England Your England" by George Orwell. Reprinted by permission. **654** From *The Crack in the Teacup* by Marina Warner. Reprinted by permission. **718** The Upper Class by Marina Warner. **718** Excerpts from *Britain—Twentieth Century: The Story of Social Conditions* by Mary Cathcart Borer. Reprinted by permission. **721** "Burlington Bertie from Bow" by William Hargreaves. Reprinted by permission. **743** From *Testament Of Youth* by Vera Brittain. Copyright 1933 by Vera Brittain. Reprinted by permission of Virago Press and Victor Gollancz Limited. **758** "Tickets, Please" from *Complete Short Stories Of D.H. Lawrence* by D. H. Lawrence. Copyright 1922 by Thomas Seltzer, Inc., renewal copyright 1950 by Frieda Lawrence. Used by permission of Viking Penguin, a division of Penguin Books USA Inc. **769** "The Hollow Men" by T.S. Eliot from *Collected Poems 1909-1962.* Copyright © 1936 by Harcourt Brace & Company; copyright © 1964, 1963 by T.S. Eliot. Reprinted by permission of the publisher and Faber and Faber Limited. **773** "The Horror at Ypres" from *Chemical And Biological Warfare* by L. B. Taylor, Jr. and C. L. Taylor. Copyright © 1985 by L. B. Taylor, Jr. and C. L. Taylor. Reprinted by permission of Franklin Watts. **775** "The Boneyard" from *The Great War And Modern Memory* by Paul Fussell, pp. 69-71. Reprinted by permission. **790** "Eveline" from *Dubliners* by James Joyce. Copyright 1916 by B.W. Heubsch. Definitive text copyright © 1967 by the Estate of James Joyce. Used by permission of Viking Penguin, a division of Penguin Books USA Inc. **797** "A Cup of Tea" from *The Short Stories Of Katherine Mansfield* by Katherine Mansfield.

Copyright 1923 by Alfred A. Knopf Inc. and renewed 1951 by John Middleton Murry. Reprinted by permission of Alfred A. Knopf Inc. **806–808** "The Unknown Citizen" and "Musée des Beaux Arts" by W.H. Auden from *W.H. Auden: Collected Poems.* Copyright 1940 and renewed © 1968 by W.H. Auden. Reprinted by permission of Random House, Inc. and Faber and Faber Limited. **810** "Who's Who" by W.H. Auden from *W.H. Auden: Collected Poems.* Copyright 1937 and renewed © 1965 by W.H. Auden. Reprinted by permission of Random House, Inc. and Faber and Faber Limited. **814** "Shakespeare's Sister" from *A Room Of One's Own* by Virginia Woolf. Copyright 1929 by Harcourt Brace & Company and renewed 1957 by Leonard Woolf. Reprinted by permission of Harcourt Brace & Company and The Society of Authors as the literary representative of the Estate of Virginia Woolf. **823** Dylan Thomas, "Do Not Go Gentle into That Good Night." Reprinted by permission. **824** Dylan Thomas, *A Child's Christmas In Wales.* Copyright 1954 by New Directions Publishing Corporation and David Higham Associates Limited. **833** "Studies in the Park" from *Games At Twilight* by Anita Desai. Copyright © 1978 by Anita Desai. Reproduced by permission of the author c/o Rogers, Coleridge & White Ltd., 20 Powis Mews, London W11 1JN. **860** "Shooting an Elephant" by George Orwell from *Shooting an Elephant and Other Essays.* Copyright 1950 by Sonia Brownell Orwell; renewed © 1978 by Sonia Pitt-Rivers. Reprinted by permission of Harcourt Brace & Company, the estate of the late Sonia Brownell Orwell and Martin Secker & Warburg Ltd **876** "Homage To a Government" from *High Windows* by Philip Larkin. Reprinted by permission. **877** "Two Poems on the Passing of an Empire" from *Collected Poems 1948-1984* by Derek Walcott. Reprinted by permission. **881** "Qualifying for the Mansions" and "Drifting to the Mansions" from *In The Ditch* by Buchi Emecheta. Copyright © 1972 by Buchi Emecheta. Reprinted by permission of the author. **907** "Eve To Her Daughters" from *Collected Poems* by Judith Wright. Reprinted by permission. **910–911** "The Frog Prince" and "Not Waving but Drowning" by Stevie Smith from *The Collected Poems of Stevie Smith.* Copyright © 1972 by Stevie Smith. Reprinted by permission of New Directions Publishing Corporation and James MacGibbon. **912** "The Explorers" by Margaret Atwood. Reprinted by permission. **916** "The Truly Married Woman" from *The Truly Married Woman And Other Stories* by Abioseh Nicol. Copyright ©1965 by Oxford University Press. Reprinted by permission of David Higham Associates Limited. **926** Graham Greene, "A Shocking Accident." Reprinted by permission. **933** Angela Carter, "The Courtship of Mr. Lyon." Reprinted by permission. **943** "Some Biomythology" from *The Lives of a Cell* by Lewis Thomas. Reprinted by permission. **956** From *The Theater of the Absurd* by Martin Esslin. Reprinted by permission. **957** "Nicely Nicely Clive" from *In His Own Write* by John Lennon. Reprinted by permission. **959**

From *The Crack In The Teacup* by Marina Warner. Reprinted by permission. **961** "The Dead Parrot Sketch" from *Monty Python's Flying Circus.* Reprinted by permission. **963** From *The Perils of Invisibility* by W.S. Gilbert. Reprinted by permission. **964** "Glory" by Lewis Carroll. Reprinted by permision.

Illustrations

Unless otherwise acknowledged, all photographs are the property of Scott, Foresman and Company. Page abbreviations are as follows: (t)top, (c)center, (b)bottom, (l)left, (r)right.

Front cover & frontispiece page ii Dante Gabriel Rossetti, "The Beloved"/Tate Gallery, London/Bridgeman Art Library, London/Superstock, Inc. **vii** William Morris and Edward Burne-Jones, "The Arming of the Knights," Birmingham Museums and Art Gallery **x** Private Collection **xii** Gerard ter Borch II, "The Suitor's Visit," (detail), c. 1658, Andrew W. Mellon Collection, © 1995 Board of Trustees, National Gallery of Art, Washington **xiv** "View of Broad Quay, Bristol," anonymous, British School, c.1735, City of Bristol Museum and Art Gallery **xxi** David Hockney, "Mr. and Mrs. Clark and Percy," 1970-1971. Acrylic, 84" x 120". © David Hockney/Tate Gallery, London/Art Resource **xxviii** "The Terrible Twins" by P. J. Crook, 1989. Courtesy Montpelier Sandelson, London **xxxvi–1** William Morris and Edward Burne-Jones, "The Arming of the Knights," (detail)/Birmingham Museums and Art Gallery **1, 42, 44, 88, 95,100(icon)** M805fol.48/The Pierpont Morgan Library/ Art Resource **2(t)** Copyright British Museum **2(bl)** Superstock, Inc. **2(br)** Erich Lessing/Art Resource **3(t)** Colchester and Essex Museum **3(bl)** Universitetets Oldsaksamling, Oslo **3(br)** Copyright British Museum **8, 13, 16–17, 21** Werner Forman/Art Resource, NY **27** Bibliothèque Nationale, Paris **31** Scala/Art Resource **32** Michael Holford **33(t)** Copyright British Museum **33(bl)** Koninklijk Instituut voor de Tropen, Amsterdam **33(br)** Hirmer Fotoarchiv, Munich **34(t)** Sonia Halliday **34(cl,cr,br)** Photofest **34(bl)** Foto Marburg/Art Resource **42(l)** Giraudon/Art Resource **42(r), 43(l)** British Library **43(c)** Reverend K. Wilkinson Riddle **43(r)** Erich Lessing/Art Resource **45** Bodleian Library, Oxford **46** British Library **51** Museum of London **53** M630fol.12/The Pierpont Morgan Library/Art Resource **54** Copyright British Museum **56** The Huntington Library, San Marino, California **61** Bridgeman/Art Resource **69** British Library **74** M805fol.48/The Pierpont Morgan Library/ Art Resource **77** E. Hugo **80** Lambeth Palace Library **84** Museo de Arte de Ponce **88** P. Kent **89** The Metropolitan Museum of Art, The Cloisters Collection, Munsey Fund, 1932 (32.130.3a) **90(t)** Bridgeman/Art Resource **90–91** Birmingham Museums and Art Gallery **90(b)** New York Public Library **91(t)** Art Resource **91(b)** Kobal Collection **92** New York Public Library **93** Illustrations by N. C. Wyeth, from *The Boy's King Arthur* by Sidney Lanier are used with the permission of Charles Scribner's Sons,

copyright renewed 1945 N. C. Wyeth **101** Richard C. Allen/The Carson Collection **102** Bridgeman/Art Resource **103(t)** Bibliothèque Nationale, Paris **103(b)** M630fol.12, The Pierpont Morgan Library/Art Resource **104–105** Private Collection **106–107** title art, Janice Clark **106(t)** Scala/Art Resource **106(b)** National Portrait Gallery, London **107(t)** Armillary sphere & telescope, Ancient Art & Architecture Collection/Ronald Sheridan Photo-Library; Books, Erich Lessing/Art Resource; da Vinci Self-Portrait, Scala/Art Resource; Sheet music, Folger Shakespeare Library; Lute, The Granger Collection **109** National Portrait Gallery, London **110, 119** Victoria & Albert Museum, London/Art Resource **128** Tate Gallery, London/Art Resource **146(t)** Copyright British Museum **147** Scale drawing by Irwin Smith from *Shakespeare's Globe Playhouse: A Modern Reconstruction in Text and Scale Drawings* by Irwin Smith. Charles Scribner's Sons, New York, 1956. Hand colored by Cheryl Kucharzak **155** Kunsthaus Zurich, © 1995, Copyright by Kunsthaus Zurich. All rights reserved. **165, 179** From the Art Collection of the Folger Shakespeare Library **192–193, 194–195** bloody backrounds, Diane Cole **192, 193** Copyright British Museum **194** Photofest **195** UPI/Corbis-Bettmann **196** Courtesy Diane Bray **205(t)** Victoria & Albert Museum, London/Art Resource **205(b)** Tate Gallery, London/Art Resource **209** Art Resource **210** Laing Art Gallery, Newcastle upon Tyne (Tyne and Wear Museums) **215(tl)** Bridgeman/Art Resource **215(tr)** Courtesy Anthony Green. R. A. c/o The Piccadilly Gallery, London, W1X 1PF **215(b)** © National Trust Photographic Library **217** Kenwood House, Hampstead/Bridgeman Art Library, London/Superstock, Inc. **220–221** Gerard ter Borch II, "The Suitor's Visit" (detail), c. 1658, Andrew W. Mellon Collection, © 1995 Board of Trustees, National Gallery of Art, Washington **222–223** ARXIU MAS **225** National Portrait Gallery, London **228** Staatliche Kunstsammlungen, Dresden. Photo: Sachische Landesbibliothek, Dresden **232(t)** Copyright British Museum **232(b)** Granger Collection **235** Courtesy Lord Sackville, Photo: Lime Tree Studios **239** UPI/Corbis-Bettmann **240(t)** Gamma-Liaison **240(b)** Gamma-Liaison **242–243** UPI/Corbis-Bettmann **244** Diltz/Gamma-Liaison **250–251(t&b)** Scala/Art Resource **250–251(c)** Bridgeman/Art Resource **253** National Portrait Gallery, London **257** Courtesy of the Fogg Art Museum, Harvard University Art Museums, Gift of W. A. White **263** Copyright British Museum **263(background)** Superstock, Inc. **268** Scala/Art Resource **276** Worcester Art Museum, Worcester, MA/Superstock, Inc. **276–277(background)** Superstock, Inc. **277** Everett Collection, Inc. **278(t)** M945fol.168v/The Pierpont Morgan Library/Art Resource **278(b)** Victoria & Albert Museum, London/Art Resource **279(tl)** Tate Gallery, London/E. T. Archives, London/Superstock, Inc. **279(b)** Museo del Prado, Madrid, Spain/A. K. G., Berlin/Superstock, Inc. **288(t)** Courtesy Lord Sackville, Photo: Lime Tree Studios **288(b)** Copyright British Museum **289** Scala/Art Resource **290–291** "View of Broad Quay, Bristol" (detail), anonymous, British School, c.1735, City of Bristol Museum and Art Gallery

291, 292, 294, 328, 331, 335(icon) T. H. Shepherd, "Arthur's Club House, St. James's Street," (detail)/Superstock, Inc. **295** National Portrait Gallery, London **297** Tate Gallery, London/Art Resource **304** Copyright British Museum **305** National Portrait Gallery, London **307** Winslow Homer, "Blackboard," Gift (Partial and Promised) of Jo Ann and Julian Ganz, Jr., in Honor of the 50th Anniversary of the National Gallery of Art, © 1995 Board of Trustees, National Gallery of Art, Washington **313** Bodleian Library, University of Oxford **328(b)** Central Broadcasting **329(tr&b)** Tribune Media Services **330** Jack Higgins **336(t)** National Portrait Gallery, London/Superstock, Inc. **336(c)** Granger Collection **336(b), 337(all)** National Portrait Gallery, London/Superstock, Inc. **339** Corbis-Bettmann Archive **341** Yale Center for British Art, Paul Mellon Collection **343, 349** Pepys Library, by permission of the Master and Fellows, Magdalene College, Cambridge **350, 352–353** National Portrait Gallery, London **360** Scottish National Portrait Gallery, photo by Tom Scott **362, 370(t)** Copyright British Museum **370(b)** Bibliothèque Nationale, Paris **371** Scala/Art Resource **372(t)** Giraudon/Art Resource **372(c)** Erich Lessing/Art Resource **372–373(background)** FPG International Corp. **373(t)** © 1997 Andy Warhol Foundation for the Visual Arts/ARS, New York **373(l)** Library of Congress **381(t)** Tate Gallery, London/Art Resource **381(b)** National Portrait Gallery, London **386–387(t), 390** Museum of London **386–387(b)** Bridgeman/Art Resource **391(t)** The Minneapolis Institute of Arts **391(b)** Associated Newspapers Limited **397, 398, 400, 431, 438, 444(icon)** Dante Gabriel Rossetti, "Reverie" (detail), Christie's, London/Superstock, Inc. **397, 446, 448, 475, 481, 487(icon)** Edvard Munch, "Self-Portrait in Weimar," (detail)/Munch Museum, Oslo, Norway/Lerner Fine Art/Superstock, Inc. **397, 488, 490, 507, 513, 518(icon)** Giovanni Stradano, "Alchemist Laboratory" (detail), Palazzo Vecchio, Florence, Italy/E. T. Archives, London/Superstock, Inc. **396–397** John Constable, "The Hay Wain," 1821 (detail) Reproduced by courtesy of the Trustees, The National Gallery, London **398(t)** Victoria & Albert Museum, London/Art Resource **398–399** Superstock, Inc. **399(tl&tr)** Copyright British Museum **399(b)** Tate Gallery, London/Art Resource **401** National Portrait Gallery, London **403** The Metropolitan Museum of Art, The Elisha Whittelsey Collection, The Elisha Whittelsey Fund, 1967 (67.809.16) **407** Copyright British Museum **408** National Portrait Gallery, London **411** National Railway Museum/Science & Society Picture Library **416** National Portrait Gallery, London **419** Courtesy of the Arthur M. Sackler Museum, Harvard University Art Museums, Loan from Private Collection **422** National Portrait Gallery, London **424** Bridgeman/Art Resource **431** Honolulu Academy of Arts **432** Staatliche Museen Preussischer Kulturbesitz, Antikenmuseum, Berlin **433** National Museum of American History/Smithsonian Institution **434 & 435(all)** Allan Hobson/SS/Photo Researchers **436** Detroit Institute of Arts, Michigan/A.K.G., Berlin/Superstock, Inc. **445** Yale Center for British Art, Paul Mellon Collection **446–447(t)** Copyright British Museum **446(c)** Mansell Collection **446(b)** Bulloz **447(c)** Trustees of the Wedgwood Museum, Barlaston, Staffordshire, England **447(b)** Library of Congress **449** National Portrait Gallery, London **451** Bridgeman/Art Resource **455** Corbis-Bettmann Archive **456** Plate 66 from *Mrs. Hurst Dancing*, text by Gordon Mingay, Watercolors by Diana Sperling. © Victor Gollancz Ltd. 1981 **462** Granger Collection **465** Tate Gallery, London/Art Resource **468** Corbis-Bettmann Archive **472** Bequest of Mrs. Martin Brimmer, Courtesy, Museum of Fine Arts, Boston **475, 476(l)** Corbis-Bettmann Archive **476(r), 478(l)** Granger Collection **477(l)** National Portrait Gallery, London **477(r)** UPI/Corbis-Bettmann **478(r), 479(r)** Sophia Smith Collection, Smith College **479(l)** League of Women Voters of Japan **480** Courtesy Tanya Wallace **488–489(E)(b)** Mansell Collection **489(B)(t)** Museo del Prado, Madrid, Spain/Jack Novak/Superstock, Inc. **489(C)(tc)** Walker Art Gallery, Liverpool **489(F)(cl)** Smithsonian Institution **491** Bodleian Library, University of Oxford **492–493** diorama, Diane Cole **493** Bridgeman/Art Resource **499** Everett Collection, Inc. Hand-colored by Cheryl Kucharzak **503** Scala/Art Resource **507(background)** FPG International Corp. **507** British Library **508–509(background)** FPG International Corp. **508** Museum of Modern Art, Film Stills Archive **510(t)** Alinari/Art Resource **510(bl)** Boltin Picture Library **510(br)** Everett Collection, Inc. **511(bl)** Copyright British Museum **511(br)** Everett Collection, Inc. **512(background)** Michael Orton/Tony Stone Images **512** From *A Pictorial History Of Science Fiction* by David Kyle. Copyright © The Hamlyn Publishing Group Limited, 1976 **519** Museum of Modern Art, Film Stills Archive **520(t)** Bridgeman/Art Resource **520(b)** Everett Collection, Inc. Hand-colored by Cheryl Kucharzak **521** Bridgeman/Art Resource **523, 524, 526, 559, 564, 569(icon)** Illustration by John Tenniel for *Alice's Adventures in Wonderland* **523, 570, 572, 629, 634, 639(icon)** Ernst Ludwig Kirchner, "Bildnis des Dichters Frank" (detail), Christie's London/Superstock, Inc. **523–524** George Williams Joy, "The Bayswater Omnibus," 1895 (detail)/Museum of London **524(t), 524(b), 525(b)** Hulton Deutsch Collection Ltd. **524(c)** International Museum of Photography/George Eastman House **525(t)** Mansell Collection **527** National Portrait Gallery, London **528** Bridgeman/Art Resource **533** The Saint Louis Art Museum, Bequest of Morton D. May **538(t&b)** National Portrait Gallery, London **541** Erich Lessing/Art Resource **546** Library of Congress **547** Everett Collection, Inc. **554** Corbis-Bettmann Archive **555** High Museum of Art, Atlanta, Georgia; purchase with funds from the Friends of Art 36.20 **560** Brown Brothers **562(tl)** Hulton Deutsch Collection Ltd. **562(tr)** Edwin H. Colbert **562(cr,cl,b)** Mansell Collection **563** Hulton Deutsch Collection Ltd. **570(t)** National Gallery of Canada, Ottawa. Gift of the Massey Collection of English Painting, 1946 **570(tc)** From *Punch*, December 10, 1892, Hand-colored by Cheryl Kucharzak **570(bc)** Newberry Library, Chicago **570(b)** Museum of London **571** Mansell Collection. Hand-colored by Cheryl Kucharzak **573** National Portrait Gallery, London **575**

Tate Gallery, London/Art Resource **580** National Portrait Gallery, London **581** Tate Gallery, London/Art Resource **585** Drawing by Walter Tiffle **586, 593** North Wind Picture Archives **600** Granger Collection **602** National Portrait Gallery, London **606** By courtesy of the Victoria & Albert Museum, London **611** UPI/Corbis-Bettmann **612** Vasily Kandinsky, "Several Circles No. 323," 1926. The Solomon R. Guggenheim Museum, New York, Photograph by David Heald, © The Solomon R.Guggenheim Foundation, New York (FN41.283) **623** National Portrait Gallery, London **628** Richard C. Allen/Carson Collection **639** From *A Pictorial History Of Science Fiction* by David Kyle. Copyright © The Hamlyn Publishing Group Limited, 1976 **641(t)**, Everett Collection **641(b)** Erich Lessing/Art Resource **642** Vasily Kandinsky, "Several Circles No. 323," 1926. The Solomon R. Guggenheim Museum, New York, Photograph by David Heald, © The Solomon R.Guggenheim Foundation, New York (FN41.283) **644–645** Mansell Collection **646** Hand-colored by Cheryl Kucharzak **650–651** Oriental and India Office Collections/British Library, Photo 154 f.31d neg. B6140 **653** Robert Opie Collection **655** National Army Museum, London, **657, 658, 660, 717, 723, 728(icon)** Courtesy Bassano Studios, London **657, 730, 732, 773, 778, 784(icon)** Imperial War Museum, London **657, 786, 788, 843, 846, 851(icon)** Amedeo Modigliani, "Jeanne Hebuterne au Foulard" (detail), Christie's, London/Superstock, Inc. **656–657** Charles Ginner, "Piccadilly Circus," 1912 (detail), Tate Gallery, London/Art Resource **658–659** diorama, Diane Cole **658 & 659 (A,B,C,F,G,I & 658–659(background)** Hulton Deutsch Collection Ltd. **658(D)** Museum of London **658(E)** Mary Evans Picture Library **659(H)** Copyright British Museum **661** National Portrait Gallery, London **662(r)** Kobal Collection **662(l)** Museum of Modern Art, Film Stills Archive **667, 670, 678, 690–691** Martha Swope/© Time, Inc. **696(l)** Angus McBean **696(r)** Zoe Dominic **697(l)** Mark Douet **697(r)** Photofest **705, 713** Martha Swope/Time, Inc. **717(t), 720(t&b)** Hulton Deutsch Collection Ltd. **717(b)** International Museum of Photography/George Eastman House **721** Everett Collection, Inc. **722** Photofest **728, 729** Robert Opie Collection **730(t)** National Archives **730(c)** Imperial War Museum, London **730(b) & 731(inset)** From the copy in the Bowman Gray Collection, University of North Carolina at Chapel Hill **731(t)** Imperial War Museum, London **734(t)** Culver Pictures Inc. **734(c)** Fitzwilliam Museum, University of Cambridge **734(b)** Culver Pictures Inc. **736** Imperial War Museum, London **742, 746, 751** Vera Brittain Archive/Mills Memorial Library/McMaster University, Hamilton, Ontario, Canada **757** Corbis-Bettmann Archive **758** From the copy in the Bowman Gray Collection, University of North Carolina at Chapel Hill **768** AP/Wide World **774, 776** Imperial War Museum, London **784** ABC News photo **786–787** Tate Gallery, London/Art Resource **787(br)** Corbis-Bettmann Archive **789** National Portrait Gallery, London **791** Plymouth City Museums & Art Gallery **796** Courtesy of Alfred Knopf **797** Collection of Dr. John Boreske/Vose Galleries of Boston **805** UPI/Corbis-Bettmann **807** ©1996 C. Hercovici, Brussels/Artists Rights Society (ARS), New York/Giraudon/Art Resource **808–809** Musee Royaux des Beaux-Arts de Belgique, Brussels **813** Courtesy of Harcourt, Brace **814** Victoria & Albert Museum, London/Art Resource **822** National Portrait Gallery, London **824** Bridgeman/Art Resource **837** Gallery, Vishva-Bharati University, Santiniketan, India **842** UPI/Corbis-Bettmann **843(l&r), 844(tl,tr,b), 845(tl)** Tate Gallery, London/Art Resource **845(tr)** National Art Gallery of New Zealand **845(b)** Bridgeman/Art Resource **852(t)** Martha Swope, © Time, Inc. **852(b)** Plymouth City Museums & Art Gallery **853** Imperial War Museum, London **854–855** David Hockney, "Mr. and Mrs. Clark and Percy" (detail), 1970-1971. Acrylic, 84" x 120". © David Hockney. Tate Gallery, London/Art Resource **855, 856, 858, 891, 896, 901(icon)** Superstock, Inc. **855, 902, 904, 943, 947, 952(icon)** Pablo Picasso, "Buste D'Homme au Chapeau," (detail) ©1997 Succession Picasso/Artists Rights Society (ARS), New York/Superstock, Inc. **856(t&b)** UPI/Corbis-Bettmann **856(c)** AFP/Corbis-Bettmann **857(tl&tr)** UPI/Corbis-Bettmann **857(b)** S. Ferry/Gamma-Liaison **859** AP/Wide World **860** Popperfoto **868** Brian Seed/Life Magazine, Time, Inc. **869** National Maritime Museum, London **875(t)** Rogers RBO/Camera Press/Globe Photos, Inc. **875(b)** Evan Richman/Reuters/Corbis-Bettmann **876** Diana Walker/Gamma-Liaison **880** George Braziller **881** The Brooklyn Museum, 82.65.2250, Collection of Charles and Lucille Plotz **890** The Seattle Art Museum, Gift of Katherine White and the Boeing Company, Photo: Paul Macapia **891** Corbis-Bettmann Archive **892** AP/Wide World **893(t)** Ian Berry/Magnum Photos **893(b)** Dick Arthur/*Honolulu Advertiser*, HI/Rothco **894** Courtesy Dr. Edward Brynn **902(A)** Spooner/ Gamma-Liaison **902(B)** Joe Taver/Gamma-Liaison **902(D)** Alistair Berg/Spooner/Gamma-Liaison **902(E)** Karim Daher/Gamma-Liaison **902(icon)** Superstock, Inc. **903(C)** Reuters/Corbis-Bettmann **903(F)** Katie Arkell/Gamma-Liaison **903(G)** Alistair Berg/Spooner/Gamma-Liaison **903(H)** Jacob Sutton/Gamma-Liaison **906(c)** National Portrait Gallery, London **906(b)** Laurence Acland **909** Ken Joudrey **915** New York Times/NYT Pictures **916–917** The Jean Pigozzi Collection, C. A. A. C., Ltd. **925** Corbis-Bettmann Archive **927** Portal Gallery, London **932** © Tara Heinemann 1984 **933** Everett Collection, Inc. **953** The Brooklyn Museum, 82.65.2250, Collection of Charles and Lucille Plotz **954(t)** Diana Walker/Gamma-Liaison **954(b)** Portal Gallery, London **959** Bibliothèque Nationale, Paris **960, 965** Portal Gallery, London **964** Granger Collection

Handlettering by Eliza Schulte.

Electronic Illustrations by Bruce Burdick, Steven Kiecker, Nikki Limper, and Gwen Plogman.